C000179026

The Oxford Colour Portuguese Dictionary

The Oxford Colour Portuguese Dictionary

PORTUGUESE–ENGLISH
Compiled by John Whitlam

ENGLISH–PORTUGUESE
Compiled by Lia Correia Raitt

OXFORD
UNIVERSITY PRESS

Great Clarendon Street, Oxford OX2 6DP

Oxford University Press is a department of the University of Oxford.
It furthers the University's objective of excellence in research, scholarship,
and education by publishing worldwide in

Oxford New York

Athens Auckland Bangkok Bogotá Buenos Aires Calcutta
Cape Town Chennai Dar es Salaam Delhi Florence Hong Kong Istanbul
Karachi Kuala Lumpur Madrid Melbourne Mexico City Mumbai
Nairobi Paris São Paulo Singapore Taipei Tokyo Toronto Warsaw

with associated companies in Berlin Ibadan

Published in the United States
by Oxford University Press Inc., New York

First published as the Oxford Portuguese Minidictionary, 1996
First published under the title The Oxford Paperback Portuguese Dictionary, 1996
First published under the title The Oxford Colour Portuguese Dictionary, 1999

British Library Cataloguing in Publication Data
Data available

Library of Congress Cataloging in Publication Data
Data available

ISBN 0-19-860272-3

10 9 8 7 6 5 4 3 2 1

Typeset in Nimrod and Arial
by PureTech India Ltd
Printed in Great Britain by
The Bath Press

Contents/Indice

Preface

The Oxford Colour Portuguese Dictionary has been written for speakers of both Portuguese and English and contains the most useful words and expressions in use today.

The dictionary provides a handy and comprehensive reference work for tourists, students, and business people who require quick and reliable answers to their translation needs.

Thanks are due to: Dr John Sykes, Prof. A. W. Raitt, Commander Virgílio Correia, Marcelo Affonso, Eng. Pedro Carvalho, Eng. Vasco Carvalho, Dr Iva Correia, Dr Ida Reis de Carvalho, Eng. J. Reis de Carvalho, Prof. A. Falcão, Bishop Manuel Falcão, Dr M. Luísa Falcão, Prof. J. Ferraz, Prof. M. de Lourdes Ferraz, Drs Ana and Jorge Fonseca, Mr Robert Howes, Irene Lakhani, Eng. Hugo Pires, Prof. M. Kaura Pires, Dr M. Alexandre Pires, Ambassador L. Pazos Alonso, Dr Teresa Pinto Pereira, Dr Isabel Tully, Carlos Wallenstein, Ligia Xavier, and Dr H. Martins and the members of his Mesa Lusófona at St Antony's College, Oxford.

Prefácio

O *Oxford Colour Portuguese Dictionary* foi escrito por pessoas de língua portuguesa e inglesa, e contém as palavras e expressões mais úteis em uso atualmente.

O dicionário constitui uma obra de referência prática e abrangente para turistas, estudantes e pessoas de negócios que necessitam de respostas rápidas e confiáveis para as suas traduções.

Agradecimentos a: Dr John Sykes, Prof. A. W. Raitt, Comandante Virgílio Correia, Marcelo Affonso, Eng. Pedro Carvalho, Eng. Vasco Carvalho, Dr Iva Correia, Dr Ida Reis de Carvalho, Eng. J. Reis de Carvalho, Prof. A. Falcão, Bispo Manuel Falcão, Dr M. Luísa Falcão, Prof. J. Ferraz, Prof. M. de Lourdes Ferraz, Drs Ana e Jorge Fonseca, Mr Robert Howes, Eng. Hugo Pires, Prof. M. Laura Pires, Dr M. Alexandre Pires, Embaixador L. Pazos Alonso, Dr Teresa Pinto Pereira, Dr Isabel Tully, Carlos Wallenstein, e Dr H. Martins e os membros de sua Mesa Lusófona do St Antony's College, em Oxford.

Introduction

The swung dash (~) is used to replace a headword, or that part of a headword preceding the vertical bar (|).

In both English and Portuguese, only irregular plural forms are given. Plural forms of Portuguese nouns and adjectives ending in a single vowel are formed by adding an *s* (e.g. *livro, livros*). Those ending in *n, r, s* where the stress falls on the final syllable, and *z*, add *es* (e.g. *mulher, mulheres, falaz, falazes*). Nouns and adjectives ending in *m* change the final *m* to *ns* (e.g. *homem, homens, bom, bons*). Most of those ending in *ão* change their ending to *ões* (e.g. *estação, estações*).

Portuguese nouns and adjectives ending in an unstressed *o* form the feminine by changing the *o* to *a* (e.g. *belo, bela*). Those ending in *or* become *ora* (e.g. *trabalhador, trabalhadora*). All other masculine–feminine changes are shown at the main headword.

English and Portuguese pronunciation is given by means of the International Phonetic Alphabet. It is shown for all headwords, and for those derived words whose pronunciation is not easily deduced from that of a headword.

Portuguese verb tables will be found in the appendix.

Introdução

O sinal (~) é usado para substituir o verbete, ou parte deste precedendo a barra vertical (|).

Tanto em inglês como em português, somente as formas irregulares do plural são dadas. As formas regulares do plural dos substantivos ingleses recebem um *s* (ex. *teacher, teachers*), ou *es* quando terminarem em *ch, sh, s, ss, us, x* ou *z* (ex. *sash, sashes*). Os substantivos terminados em *y* e precedidos por uma consoante, mudam no plural para *ies* (ex. *baby, babies*).

O passado e o particípio passado dos verbos regulares ingleses são formados pelo acréscimo de *ed* á forma infinitiva (ex. *last, lasted*). Os verbos terminados em *e* recebem *d* (ex. *move, moved*). Aqueles terminados em *y* têm o *y* substituído por *ied* (*carry, carried*). As formas irregulares dos verbos aparecem no dicionário em ordem alfabética, remetidas à forma infinitiva, e também, na lista de verbos no apêndice.

As pronúncias inglesa e portuguesa são dadas em acordo com o Alfabeto Fonético Internacional. A pronúncia é dada para todos os verbetes, assim como para aquelas palavras derivadas cuja pronúncia não seja facilmente deduzida a partir do verbete.

Proprietary terms

This dictionary includes some words which are, or are asserted to be, proprietary names or trade marks. Their inclusion does not imply that they have acquired for legal purposes a non-proprietary or general significance, nor is any other judgement implied concerning their legal status. In cases where the editor has some evidence that a word is used as a proprietary name or trade mark this is indicated by the label *propr*, but no judgement concerning the legal status of such words is made or implied thereby.

Nomes comerciais

Este dicionário inclui algumas palavras que são, ou acreditase ser, nomes comerciais ou marcas registradas. A sua inclusão no dicionário não implica que elas tenham adquirido para fins legais um significado geral ou não-comercial, assim como não afeta em nenhum dos conceitos implícitos o seu status legal.

Nos casos em que o editor tenha prova suficiente de que uma palavra seja usada como um nome comercial ou marca registrada, este emprego é indicado pela etiqueta *propr*, mas nenhuma apreciação relativa ao status legal de tais palavras é feita ou sugerida por esta indicação.

Portuguese pronunciation

Vowels and Diphthongs

a, à, á, â	/ã/	cham*am*, *a*mbos, *a*ntes	1) before *m* at the end of a word, or before *m* or *n* and another consonant, is nasalized
	/a/	*a*b*a*, *à*, *a*col*á*, des*â*nimo	2) in other positions is like *a* in English r*a*ther
ã	/ã/	irm*ã*	is nasalized
e	/ẽ/	s*e*m, v*e*nda	1) before *m* at the end of a word, or before *m* or *n* and another consonant, is nasalized
	/i/	art*e*	2) at the end of a word is like *y* in English happ*y*
	/e/	m*e*nas	3) in other positions is like *e* in English th*ey*
é	/ɛ/	art*é*ria	is like *e* in English g*e*t
ê	/e/	f*ê*mur	is like *e* in English th*ey*
i	/ĩ/	s*i*m, v*i*ndo	1) before *m* at the end of a word, or before *m* or *n* and another consonant, is nasalized
	/i/	f*i*la	2) in other positions is like *ee* in English s*ee*
o	/õ/	c*o*m, s*o*mbra, *o*nda	1) before *m* at the end of a word, or before *m* or *n* and another consonant, is nasalized
	/u/	muit*o*	2) at the end of a word, unstressed, is like *u* in English r*u*le

	/o/	c*o*m*o*ver	3) in other positions, unstressed, is like *o* in English p*o*le
	/o/ /ɔ/	bob*o* l*o*ja	4) stressed, is like *o* in English p*o*le or *o* in sh*o*p
ó	/ɔ/	*ó*pera	is like *o* in English p*o*le
ô	/o/	tônica	is like *o* in English p*o*le
u, ú		g*u*erra, g*u*isado, q*u*e, q*u*ilo	1) is silent in *gue*, and *gui*, *que*, *qui*
	/u/	m*u*la, p*ú*rp*u*ra	2) in other positions is like *u* in English r*u*le
ü gü	/gw/	un*gü*ento	in the combinations *güe* and *güi* is like *g* in English *g*ot, followed by English *w*
	/kw/	tranq*üi*lo	in the combinations *qüe* and *qüi* is like *qu* in English *qu*een
ãe	/ãj/	m*ãe*, p*ãe*s, alem*ãe*s	is like *y* in English b*y*, but nasalized
ai	/aj/	v*ai*, p*ai*, s*ai*, c*ai*ta	is like *y* in English b*y*
ao, au	/aw/	*ao*s, *au*todefesa	is like *ow* in English h*ow*
ão	/ãw/	n*ão*	is like *ow* in English h*ow*, but nasalized
ei	/ej/	l*ei*	is like *ey* in English th*ey*
eu	/ew/	d*eu*s, fl*eu*gma	both vowels pronounced separately
oẽ	/õj/	eleiç*õe*s	is like *oi* in English c*oi*n, but nasalized
oi	/oj/	n*oi*te	is like *oi* in English c*oi*n
ou	/o/	p*ou*co	is like *o* in English p*o*le

Consonants

b	/b/	*b*anho	is like *b* in English *b*all
c	/s/	*c*inza, *c*em	1) before *e* or *i* is like *s* in English *s*it
	/k/	*c*asa	2) in other positions is like *c* in English *c*at
ç	/s/	esta*ç*ão	is like *s* in English *s*it
ch	/ʃ/	*ch*á	is like *sh* in English *sh*out
d	/dʒ/	*d*izer, don*d*e	1) before *i* or final unstressed *e* is like *j* in English *j*oin
	/d/	*d*ar	2) in other positions is like *d* in English *d*og
f	/f/	*f*alar	is like *f* in English *f*all
g	/ʒ/	a*g*ente, *g*iro	1) before *e* or *i* is like *s* in English vi*s*ion
	/g/	*g*ato	2) in other positions is like *g* in English *g*et
h		haver	is silent in Portuguese, but see *ch*, *lh*, *nh*
j	/ʒ/	*j*unta	is like *s* in English vi*s*ion
k	/k/	*k*it	is like English *k* in *k*ey
l	/w/	fa*l*ta	1) between a vowel and a consonant, or following a vowel at the end of a word, is like *w* in English *w*ater
	/l/	*l*ata	2) in other positions is like *l* in English *l*ike
l	/ʎ/	ca*lh*ar	is like *lli* in English mi*ll*ion
m		a*m*bas/ãbuʃ/ co*m* /kõ/	1) between a vowel and a consonant, or after a vowel at the end of a word, *m* nasalizes the preceding vowel

	/m/	*m*ato, *m*ão	2) in other positions is like *m* in English *m*other
n		ci*n*ʒa /'sĩza/	1) between a vowel and a consonant, *n* nasalizes the preceding vowel
	/n/	be*n*ig*n*o	2) in other positions is like *n* in English *n*ear
nh	/ɲ/	ba*nh*o	is like *ni* in English opi*ni*on
p	/p/	*p*az	is like *p* in English *p*oor
q	/k/	*q*ue, in*q*uieto	1) *qu* before *e* or *i* is like English *k*
	/kw/	*q*uase, *q*uórum	2) *qu* before *a* or *o*, or *qü* before *e* or *i*, is like *qu* in English *qu*een
r	/r/	apa*r*ato, go*r*do	1) between two vowels, or between a vowel and a consonant, is trilled
	/x/	*r*ato, ga*rr*a, mel*r*o, gen*r*o, Is*r*ael	2) at the beginning of a word, or in *rr*, or after *l*, *n*, or *s*, is like *ch* in Scottish lo*ch*
s	/ʃ/	depoi*s*	at the end of a word is like *sh* in English *sh*oot
	/z/	a*s*a, de*s*de, abi*s*mo, I*s*rael	2) between two vowels, or before *b*, *d*, *g*, *l*, *m*, *n*, *r*, *v*, is like *z* in English *z*ebra
	/s/	*s*uave	3) in other positions is like *s* in English *s*it
t	/tʃ/	*t*io, an*t*es	1) before *i* or final unstressed *e* is like *ch* in English *ch*eese
	/tʃi/	ki*t*	2) at the end of a word is like *chy* in English it*chy*

	/t/	a*t*ar	3) in other positions is like *t* in English *t*ap
v	/v/	lu*v*a	is like *v* in English *v*ain
w	/u/	*w*att	is shorter than English *w*
x	/z/	e*x*ato, e*x*emplo	1) in the prefix *ex* before a vowel, is pronounced like *z* in *z*ero
	/ʃ/	*x*ícara, bai*x*o, pei*x*e, frou*x*o	2) at the beginning of a word or after *ai*, *ei* or *ou*, is pronounced like *sh* in *sh*ow
	/s/	e*x*plodir,	3) is like *s* in English au*x*iliar*s*it
	/ks/	a*x*ila, fi*x*o	4) is like *x* in English e*x*it
			5) in the combination *xce*, *xci*, *x* is not pronounced in Portuguese e.g. e*x*celente, e*x*citar
z	/s/	fala*z*	1) at the end of a word, is like *s* in English *s*it
	/z/	di*z*er	2) in other positions, is like English *z*

Pronuncia Inglesa

Vogals e Ditongos

/iː/	s*ee*, t*ea*	como *i* em g*i*ro
/ɪ/	s*i*t, happ*y*	é um som mais breve do que *i* em l*i*
/e/	s*e*t	como *e* em t*é*pido
/æ/	h*a*t	é um som mais breve do que *a* em *a*mor
/ɑː/	*a*rm, c*a*lm	como *a* em c*a*rtaz
/ɒ/	g*o*t	como *o* em ex*ó*tico
/ɔː/	s*a*w, m*o*re	como *o* em c*o*rte
/ʊ/	p*u*t, l*oo*k	como *u* em m*u*rro
/uː/	t*oo*, d*ue*	como *u* em d*u*ro
/ʌ/	c*u*p, s*o*me	como *a* em p*a*no
/ɜː/	f*i*rm, f*u*r	como *e* em enx*e*rto
/ə/	*a*go, weath*e*r	como *e* no português europeu part*e*
/eɪ/	p*a*ge, p*ai*n, p*ay*	como *ei* em l*ei*te
/əʊ/	h*o*me, r*oa*m	é um som mais longo do que *o* em c*o*ma
/aɪ/	f*i*ne, b*y*, g*uy*	como *ai* em s*ai*
/aɪə/	f*i*re, t*y*re	como *ai* em s*ai* seguido por /ə/
/aʊ/	n*ow*, sh*ou*t	como *au* em *au*la
/aʊə/	h*ou*r, fl*ow*er	como *au* em *au*la seguido por /ə/
/ɔɪ/	j*oi*n, b*oy*	como *oi* em d*ói*
/ɪə/	d*ea*r, h*e*re, b*ee*r	como *ia* em d*ia*
/eə/	h*ai*r, c*a*re, b*ea*r, th*e*re	como *e* em et*é*reo
/ʊə/	p*oo*r, d*u*ring	como *ua* em s*ua*

Consoantes

/p/	sna*p*	como *p* em *p*ato
/b/	*b*ath	como *b* em *b*ala
/t/	*t*ap	como *t* em *t*ela
/d/	*d*ip	como *d* em *d*ar
/k/	*c*at, *k*ite, stoma*ch*, pi*qu*e	como *c* em *c*asa
/ks/	e*x*ercise	como *x* em a*x*ila
/g/	*g*ot	como *g* em *g*ato
/tʃ/	*ch*in	como *t* em *t*io
/dʒ/	*J*une, *g*eneral, *j*u*dg*e	como *d* em *d*izer
/f/	*f*all	como *f* em *f*aca
/v/	*v*ine, o*f*	como *v* em *v*aca
/θ/	*th*in, mo*th*	não tem equivalente, soa como um *s* entre os dentes
/ð/	*th*is	não tem equivalente, soa como um *z* entre os dentes
/s/	*s*o, voi*c*e	como *s* em *s*uave
/z/	*z*oo, ro*s*e	como *z* em fa*z*er
/ʃ/	*sh*e, lun*ch*	como *ch* em *ch*egar
/ʒ/	mea*s*ure, vi*s*ion	como *j* em *j*amais
/h/	*h*ow	*h* aspirado
/m/	*m*an	como *m* em *m*ala
/n/	*n*o*n*e	como *n* em *n*ada
/ŋ/	si*ng*	como *n* em ci*n*to
/l/	*l*eg	como *l* em *l*uva
/r/	*r*ed, *wr*ite	como *r* em ca*r*a
/j/	*y*es, *y*oke	como *i* em *i*oga
/w/	*w*eather, s*w*itch	como *u* ág*u*a

European Portuguese

Brazilian Portuguese, which is used in this dictionary, differs in a number of respects from that used in Portugal and the rest of the Portuguese-speaking world. These differences affect both spelling and pronunciation. Spelling variations appear on the Portuguese–English side. In so far as they affect pronunciation, the main variants are:

Brazilian Portuguese often omits the letters *b*, *c*, *m*, and *p*, which are retained by European Portuguese:

	Brazilian	**European**
b	sutil	su*b*til
c	ação	a*c*ção
	ato	a*c*to
	elétrico	elé*c*trico
m	indenizar	inde*m*nizar
p	batismo	ba*p*tismo
	exceção	exce*p*ção

Letters *c* and *p* in such variant forms are usually silent, hence acto /'atu/,ba'ptismo /batiʒmu/. However, *c* is pronounced in the combination *ect*, hence eléctrico /i'lektriku/.

The combinations *gü* and *qü* become *gu* and *qu*:

Brazilian	**European**
un*gü*ento	un*gu*ento
tran*qü*ilo	tran*qu*ilo

However, they are still pronounced /gw/ and /kw/ respectively.

The other main differences in pronunciation are:

d	/d/	*d*ar, *d*izer, bal*d*e, *d*on*d*e	1) at the beginning of a word, or after *l*, or *n*, is like *d* in English *d*og

	/ð/	ci*d*a*d*e, me*d*roso	2) in other positions is a sound between *d* in English *d*og and *th* in English *th*is
e	/ə/	arte	at the end of a word, is like *e* in English quarr*e*l
r	/rr/	*r*ato, ga*rr*a, mel*r*o, gen*r*o, Is*r*ael, guel*r*a, ten*r*o, is*r*aelense	at the beginning of a word, or in *rr*, or after *l*, *n*, or *s*, is strongly trilled
s	/ʃ/	depoi*s*, a*s*co, ra*s*par, co*s*tura	1) at the end of a word, or before *c*, *f*, *p*, *qu*, or *t*, is like English *sh*
	/ʒ/	de*s*de, I*s*lã abi*s*mo, I*s*rael	2) before *b*, *d*, *g*, *l*, *m*, *n*, *r*, or *v* is like *s* in English vi*s*ion
t	/t/	a*t*ar, an*t*es, *t*io	is like *t* in English *t*ap
z	/ʃ/	fala*z*	at the end of a word, is like *sh* in English *sh*ake

Abbreviations/Abreviaturas

adjective	a	adjetivo
abbreviation	abbr/abr	abreviatura
something	aco	alguma coisa
adverb	adv	advérbio
somebody, someone	alg	algúem
article	art	artigo
American (English)	Amer	(inglês) americano
anatomy	anat	anatomia
architecture	arquit	arquitetura
astrology	astr/astrol	astrologia
motoring	auto	automobilismo
aviation	aviat	aviação
Brazilian Portuguese	B	português do Brasil
biology	biol	biologia
botany	bot	botânica
Brazilian Portuguese	Bras	português do Brasil
cinema	cine	cinema
colloquial	colloq	coloquial
commerce	comm/com	comércio
computing	comput	computação
conjunction	conj	conjunção
cookery	culin	cozinha
electricity	electr/eletr	eletricidade
feminine	f	feminina
familiar	fam	familiar
figurative	fig	figurativo
geography	geog	geografia

grammar	gramm/gram	gramática
infinitive	inf	infinitivo
interjection	int	interjeição
interrogative	interr	interrogativo
invariable	invar	invariável
legal, law	jur/jurid	jurídico
language	lang	linguagem
literal	lit	literal
masculine	m	masculino
mathematics	mat	matemática
mechanics	mech	mecânica
medicine	med	medicina
military	mil	militar
music	mus	música
noun	n	substantivo
nautical	naut	náutico
negative	neg	negativo
oneself	o.s.	se, si mesmo
European Portuguese	P	português de Portugal
pejorative	pej	pejorativo
philosophy	phil	filosofia
plural	pl	plural
politics	pol	política
European Portuguese	Port	português de Portugal
past participle	pp	particípio passado
prefix	pref	prefixo
preposition	prep	preposição
present	pres	presente
present participle	pres p	particípio presente
pronoun	pron	pronome

psychology	psych/psic	psicologia
past tense	pt	pretérito
relative	rel	relativo
religion	relig	religião
somebody	sb	alguém
singular	sing	singular
slang	sl	gíria
someone	s.o.	alguém
something	sth	alguma coisa
subjunctive	subj	subjuntivo
technology	techn/tecn	tecnologia
theatre	theat/teat	teatro
television	TV	televisão
university	univ	universidade
auxiliary verb	v aux	verbo auxiliar
intransitive verb	vi	verbo intransitivo
pronominal verb	vpr	verbo pronominal
transitive verb	vt	verbo transitivo
transitive & intransitive verb	vt/i	verbo transitivo e intransitivo

PORTUGUÊS-INGLÊS
PORTUGUESE-ENGLISH

A

a[1] /a/ *artigo* the □ *pron* (*mulher*) her; (*coisa*) it; (*você*) you

a[2] /a/ *prep* (*para*) to; (*em*) at; **às 3 horas** at 3 o'clock; **à noite** at night; **a lápis** in pencil; **a mão** by hand

à /a/ = a[2] + a[1]

aba /'aba/ *f* (*de chapéu*) brim; (*de camisa*) tail; (*de mesa*) flap

abacate /aba'katʃi/ *m* avocado (pear)

abacaxi /abaka'ʃi/ *m* pineapple; (*fam: problema*) pain, headache

aba|de /a'badʒi/ *m* abbot; **~dia** *f* abbey

aba|fado /aba'fadu/ *a* (*tempo*) humid, close; (*quarto*) stuffy; **~far** *vt* (*asfixiar*) stifle; muffle <*som*>; smother <*fogo*>; suppress <*informação*>; cover up <*escândalo, assunto*>

abagunçar /abagu'sar/ *vt* mess up

abaixar /aba'ʃar/ *vt* lower; turn down <*som, rádio*> □ *vi* **~-se** *vpr* bend down

abaixo /a'baʃu/ *adv* down; **~ de** below; **mais ~** further down; **~-assinado** *m* petition

abajur /aba'ʒur/ *m* (*quebra-luz*) lampshade; (*lâmpada*) (table) lamp

aba|lar /aba'lar/ *vt* shake; (*fig*) shock; **~lar-se** *vpr* be shocked, be shaken; **~lo** *m* shock

abanar /aba'nar/ *vt* shake, wave; wag <*rabo*>; (*com leque*) fan

abando|nar /abãdo'nar/ *vt* abandon; (*deixar*) leave; **~no** /o/ *m* abandonment; (*estado*) neglect

abarcar /abar'kar/ *vt* comprise, cover

abarro|tado /abaxo'tadu/ *a* crammed full; (*lotado*) crowded, packed; **~tar** *vt* cram full, stuff

abastado /abas'tadu/ *a* wealthy

abaste|cer /abaste'ser/ *vt* supply; fuel <*motor*>; fill up (with petrol) <*carro*>; refuel <*avião*>; **~cimento** *m* supply; (*de carro, avião*) refuelling

aba|ter /aba'ter/ *vt* knock down; cut down, fell <*árvore*>; shoot down <*avião, ave*>; slaughter <*gado*>; knock down, cut <*preço*>; **~ter alg** <*trabalho*> get s.o. down, wear s.o. out; <*má notícia*> sadden s.o.; <*doença*> lay s.o. low, knock the stuffing out of s.o.; **~tido** *a* dispirited, dejected; <*cara*> haggard, worn; **~timento** *m* dejection; (*de preço*) reduction

abaulado /abaw'ladu/ *a* convex; <*estrada*> cambered

abcesso /ab'sɛsu/ *m* (*Port*) *veja* abscesso

abdi|cação /abidʒika'sãw/ *f* abdication; **~car** *vt/i* abdicate

abdômen /abi'domẽ/ *m* abdomen

abecedário /abese'dariu/ *m* alphabet, ABC

abeirar-se /abe'rarsi/ *vr* draw near

abe|lha /a'beʎa/ *f* bee; **~lhudo** *a* inquisitive, nosy

abençoar /abẽso'ar/ *vt* bless

aber|to /a'bɛrtu/ *pp de* **abrir** □ *a* open; <*céu*> clear; <*gás, torneira*> on; <*sinal*> green; **~tura** *f* opening; (*foto*) aperture; (*pol*) liberalization

abeto /a'betu/ *m* fir (tree)

abis|mado /abiz'madu/ *a* astonished; **~mo** *m* abyss

abjeto /abi'ʒɛtu/ *a* abject

abóbada /a'bɔbada/ *f* vault

abobalhado /aboba'ʎadu/ *a* silly

abóbora /a'bɔbora/ *f* pumpkin

abobrinha /abo'briɲa/ *f* courgette, (*Amer*) zucchini

abo|lição /aboli'sãw/ *f* abolition; **~lir** *vt* abolish

abomi|nação /abomina'sãw/ *f* abomination; **~nável** (*pl* **~náveis**) *a* abominable

abo|nar /abo'nar/ *vt* guarantee <*dívida*>; give a bonus to <*empregado*>; **~no** /o/ *m* guarantee; (*no salário*) bonus; (*subsídio*) allowance, benefit; (*reforço*) endorsement

abordar /abor'dar/ *vt* approach <*pessoa*>; broach, tackle <*assunto*>; (*naut*) board

aborre|cer /aboxe'ser/ *vt* (*irritar*) annoy; (*entediar*) bore; **~cer-se** *vpr* get annoyed; get bored; **~cido** *a* annoyed; bored; **~cimento** *m* annoyance; boredom

abor|tar /abor'tar/ *vi* miscarry, have a miscarriage □ *vt* abort; **~to** /o/ *m* abortion; (*natural*) miscarriage

aboto|adura /abotoa'dura/ *f* cufflink; **~ar** *vt* button (up) □ *vi* bud

abra|çar /abra'sar/ *vt* hug, embrace;

embrace <*causa*>; **~ço** *m* hug, embrace

abrandar /abrã'dar/ *vt* ease <*dor*>; temper <*calor, frio*>; mollify, appease, placate <*povo*>; tone down, smooth over <*escândalo*> □ *vi* <*dor*> ease; <*calor, frio*> become less extreme; <*tempestade*> die down

abranger /abrã'ʒer/ *vt* cover; (*entender*) take in, grasp; **~ a** extend to

abrasileirar /abrazile'rar/ *vt* Brazilianize

abre-|garrafas /abriga'xafas/ *m invar* (*Port*) bottle-opener; **~latas** *m invar* (*Port*) can-opener

abreugrafia /abrewgra'fia/ *f* X-ray

abrevi|ar /abrevi'ar/ *vt* abbreviate <*palavra*>; abridge <*livro*>; **~atura** *f* abbreviation

abridor /abri'dor/ *m* **~ (de lata)** can-opener; **~ de garrafa** bottle-opener

abri|gar /abri'gar/ *vt* shelter; house <*sem-teto*>; **~gar-se** *vpr* (take) shelter; **~go** *m* shelter

abril /a'briw/ *m* April

abrir /a'brir/ *vt* open; (*a chave*) unlock; turn on <*gás, torneira*>; make <*buraco, exceção*> □ *vi* open; <*céu, tempo*> clear (up); <*sinal*> turn green; **~-se** *vpr* open; (*desabafar*) open up

abrupto /a'bruptu/ *a* abrupt

abrutalhado /abruta'ʎadu/ *a* <*sapato*> heavy; <*pessoa*> coarse

abscesso /abi'sɛsu/ *m* abscess

absolu|tamente /abisoluta'mẽtʃi/ *adv* absolutely; (*não*) not at all; **~to** *a* absolute; **em ~to** not at all, absolutely not

absol|ver /abisow'ver/ *vt* absolve; (*jurid*) acquit; **~vição** *f* absolution; (*jurid*) acquittal

absor|ção /abisor'sãw/ *f* absorption; **~to** *a* absorbed; **~vente** *a* <*tecido*> absorbent; <*livro*> absorbing; **~ver** *vt* absorb; **~ver-se** *vpr* get absorbed

abs|têmio /abis'temiu/ *a* abstemious; (*de álcool*) teetotal □ *m* teetotaller; **~tenção** *f* abstention; **~tencionista** *a* abstaining □ *m/f* abstainer; **~ter-se** *vpr* abstain; **~ter-se de** refrain from; **~tinência** *f* abstinence

abstra|ção /abistra'sãw/ *f* abstraction; (*mental*) distraction; **~ir** *vt* separate; **~to** *a* abstract

absurdo /abi'surdu/ *a* absurd □ *m* nonsense

abun|dância /abũ'dãsia/ *f* abundance; **~dante** *a* abundant; **~dar** *vi* abound

abu|sar /abu'zar/ *vi* go too far; **~sar de** abuse; (*aproveitar-se*) take advantage of; **~so** *m* abuse

abutre /a'butri/ *m* vulture

aca|bado /aka'badu/ *a* finished; (*exausto*) exhausted; (*velho*) decrepit; **~bamento** *m* finish; **~bar** *vt* finish □ *vi* finish, end; (*esgotar-se*) run out; **~bar-se** *vpr* end, be over; (*esgotar-se*) run out; **~bar com** put an end to, end; (*abolir, matar*) do away with; split up with <*namorado*>; wipe out <*adversário*>; **~bou de chegar** he has just arrived; **~bar fazendo** *or* **por fazer** end up doing

acabrunhado /akabru'ɲadu/ *a* dejected

aca|demia /akade'mia/ *f* academy; (*de ginástica etc*) gym; **~dêmico** *a & m* academic

açafrão /asa'frãw/ *m* saffron

acalentar /akalẽ'tar/ *vt* lull to sleep <*bebê*>; cherish <*esperanças*>; have in mind <*planos*>

acalmar /akaw'mar/ *vt* calm (down) □ *vi* <*vento*> drop; <*mar*> grow calm; **~-se** *vpr* calm down

acam|pamento /akãpa'mẽtu/ *m* camp; (*ato*) camping; **~par** *vi* camp

aca|nhado /aka'ɲadu/ *a* shy; **~nhamento** *m* shyness; **~nhar-se** *vpr* be shy

ação /a'sãw/ *f* action; (*jurid*) lawsuit; (*com*) share

acariciar /akarisi'ar/ *vt* (*com a mão*) caress, stroke; (*adular*) make a fuss of; cherish <*esperanças*>

acarretar /akaxe'tar/ *vt* bring, cause

acasalar /akaza'lar/ *vt* mate; **~-se** *vpr* mate

acaso /a'kazu/ *m* chance; **ao ~** at random; **por ~** by chance

aca|tamento /akata'mẽtu/ *m* respect, deference; **~tar** *vt* respect, defer to <*pessoa, opinião*>; obey, abide by <*leis, ordens*>; take in <*criança*>

acc-, acç- (*Port*) *veja* **ac-, aç-**

acautelar-se /akawte'larsi/ *vpr* be cautious

acei|tação /asejta'sãw/ *f* acceptance; **~tar** *vt* accept; **~tável** (*pl* **~táveis**) *a* acceptable

acele|ração /aselera'sãw/ *f* acceleration; **~rador** *m* accelerator; **~rar** *vi* accelerate □ *vt* speed up

acenar /ase'nar/ *vi* signal; (*saudando*) wave; **~ com** promise, offer

acender /asẽ'der/ *vt* light <*cigarro, fogo, vela*>; switch on <*luz*>; heat up <*debate*>

aceno /a'senu/ *m* signal; (*de saudação*) wave

acen|to /a'sẽtu/ *m* accent; **~tuar** *vt* accentuate; accent <*letra*>

acepção /asep'sãw/ *f* sense

acepipes /ase'pipʃ/ *m pl* (*Port*) cocktail snacks

acerca /a'serka/ **~ de** *prep* about, concerning

acercar-se /aser'karsi/ *vpr* ~ de approach

acertar /aser'tar/ *vt* find <(*com o*) *caminho*, (*a*) *casa*>; put right, set <*relógio*>; get right <*pergunta*>; guess (correctly) <*solução*>; hit <*alvo*>; make <*acordo, negócio*>; fix, arrange <*encontro*> □ *vi* (*ter razão*) be right; (*atingir o alvo*) hit the mark; ~ com find, happen upon; ~ em hit

acervo /a'servu/ *m* collection; (*jurid*) estate

aceso /a'sezu/ *pp de* acender □ *a* <*luz*> on; <*fogo*> alight

aces|sar /ase'sar/ *vt* access; ~sível (*pl* ~síveis) *a* accessible; affordable <*preço*>; ~so /ɛ/ *m* access; (*de raiva, tosse*) fit; (*de febre*) attack; ~sório *a* & *m* accessory

acetona /ase'tona/ *f* (*para unhas*) nail varnish remover

achado /a'ʃadu/ *m* find

achaque /a'ʃaki/ *m* ailment

achar /a'ʃar/ *vt* find; (*pensar*) think; ~-se *vpr* (*estar*) be; (*considerar-se*) think that one is; acho que sim/não I think so/I don't think so

achatar /aʃa'tar/ *vt* flatten; cut <*salário*>

aciden|tado /asidẽ'tadu/ *a* rough <*terreno*>; bumpy <*estrada*>; eventful <*viagem, vida*>; injured <*pessoa*>; ~tal (*pl* ~tais) *a* accidental; ~te *m* accident

acidez /asi'des/ *f* acidity

ácido /'asidu/ *a* & *m* acid

acima /a'sima/ *adv* above; ~ de above; mais ~ higher up

acio|nar /asio'nar/ *vt* operate; (*jurid*) sue; ~nista *m/f* shareholder

acirrado /asi'xadu/ *a* stiff, tough

acla|mação /aklama'sãw/ *f* acclaim; (*de rei*) acclamation; ~mar *vt* acclaim

aclarar /akla'rar/ *vt* clarify, clear up □ *vi* clear up; ~-se *vpr* become clear

aclimatar /aklima'tar/ *vt* acclimatize, (*Amer*) acclimate; ~-se *vpr* get acclimatized, (*Amer*) get acclimated

aço /'asu/ *m* steel; ~ inoxidável stainless steel

acocorar-se /akoko'rarsi/ *vpr* squat (down)

acolá /ako'la/ *adv* over there

acolcho|ado /akowʃo'adu/ *m* quilt; ~ar *vt* quilt; upholster <*móveis*>

aco|lhedor /akoʎe'dor/ *a* welcoming; ~lher *vt* welcome <*hóspede*>; take in <*criança, refugiado*>; accept <*decisão, convite*>; respond to <*pedido*>; ~lhida *f*, ~lhimento *m* welcome; (*abrigo*) refuge

acomodar /akomo'dar/ *vt* accommodate; (*ordenar*) arrange; (*tornar cômodo*) make comfortable; ~-se *vpr* make o.s. comfortable

acompa|nhamento /akõpaɲa'mẽtu/ *m* (*mus*) accompaniment; (*prato*) side dish; (*comitiva*) escort; ~nhante *m/f* companion; (*mus*) accompanist; ~nhar *vt* accompany, go with; watch <*jogo, progresso*>; keep up with <*eventos, caso*>; keep up with, follow <*aula, conversa*>; share <*política, opinião*>; (*mus*) accompany; a estrada ~nha o rio the road runs alongside the river

aconche|gante /akõʃe'gãtʃi/ *a* cosy, (*Amer*) cozy; ~gar *vt* (*chegar a si*) cuddle; (*agasalhar*) wrap up; (*na cama*) tuck up; (*tornar cômodo*) make comfortable; ~gar-se *vpr* ensconce o.s.; ~gar-se com snuggle up to; ~go /e/ *m* cosiness, (*Amer*) coziness; (*abraço*) cuddle

acondicionar /akõdʒisio'nar/ *vt* condition; pack, package <*mercadoria*>

aconse|lhar /akõse'ʎar/ *vt* advise; ~lhar-se *vpr* consult; ~lhar alg a advise s.o. to; ~lhar aco a alg recommend sth to s.o.; ~lhável (*pl* ~lháveis) *a* advisable

aconte|cer /akõte'ser/ *vi* happen; ~cimento *m* event

acordar /akor'dar/ *vt/i* wake up

acorde /a'kɔrdʒi/ *m* chord

acordeão /akordʒi'ãw/ *m* accordion

acordo /a'kordu/ *m* agreement; de ~ com in agreement with <*pessoa*>; in accordance with <*lei etc*>; estar de ~ agree

Açores /a'soris/ *m pl* Azores

açoriano /asori'ano/ *a* & *m* Azorean

acorrentar /akoxẽ'tar/ *vt* chain (up)

acossar /ako'sar/ *vt* hound, badger

acos|tamento /akosta'mẽtu/ *m* hard shoulder, (*Amer*) berm; ~tar-se *vpr* lean back

acostu|mado /akostu'madu/ *a* usual, customary; estar ~mado a be used to; ~mar *vt* accustom; ~mar-se a get used to

acotovelar /akotove'lar/ *vt* (*empurrar*) jostle; (*para avisar*) nudge

açou|gue /a'sogi/ *m* butcher's (shop); ~gueiro *m* butcher

acovardar /akovar'dar/ *vt* cow, intimidate

acre /'akri/ *a* <*gosto*> bitter; <*aroma*> acrid, pungent; <*tom*> harsh

acredi|tar /akredʒi'tar/ *vt* believe; accredit <*representante*>; ~tar em believe <*pessoa, história*>; believe in <*Deus, fantasmas*>; (*ter confiança*) have faith in; ~tável (*pl* ~táveis) *a* believable

acre-doce /akri'dosi/ *a* sweet and sour

acrescentar /akresẽ'tar/ *vt* add

acres|cer /akre'ser/ *vt* (*juntar*) add; (*aumentar*) increase □ *vi* increase; **~cido de** with the addition of; **~ce que** add to that the fact that

acréscimo /a'krɛsimu/ *m* addition; (*aumento*) increase

acriançado /akriã'sadu/ *a* childish

acrílico /a'kriliku/ *a* acrylic

acroba|cia /akroba'sia/ *f* acrobatics; **~ta** *m/f* acrobat

act- (*Port*) *veja* **at-**

acuar /aku'ar/ *vt* corner

açúcar /a'sukar/ *m* sugar

açuca|rar /asuka'rar/ *vt* sweeten; sugar <*café, chá*>; **~reiro** *m* sugar bowl

açude /a'sudʒi/ *m* dam

acudir /aku'dʒir/ *vt/i* ~ (a) come to the rescue (of)

acumular /akumu'lar/ *vt* accumulate; combine <*cargos*>

acupuntura /akupũ'tura/ *f* acupuncture

acu|sação /akuza'sãw/ *f* accusation; **~sar** *vt* accuse; (*jurid*) charge; (*revelar*) reveal, show up; acknowledge <*recebimento*>

acústi|ca /a'kustʃika/ *f* acoustics; **~co** *a* acoustic

adap|tação /adapta'sãw/ *f* adaptation; **~tado** *a* <*criança*> well-adjusted; **~tar** *vt* adapt; (*para encaixar*) tailor; **~tar-se** *vpr* adapt; **~tável** (*pl* **~táveis**) *a* adaptable

adega /a'dɛga/ *f* wine cellar

adentro /a'dẽtru/ *adv* inside; **selva ~** into the jungle

adepto /a'dɛptu/ *m* follower; (*Port: de equipa*) supporter

ade|quado /ade'kwadu/ *a* appropriate, suitable; **~quar** *vt* adapt, tailor

adereços /ade'resus/ *m pl* props

ade|rente /ade'rẽtʃi/ *m/f* follower; **~rir** *vi* (*colar*) stick; join <*a partido, causa*>; follow <*a moda*>; **~são** *f* adhesion; (*apoio*) support; **~sivo** *a* sticky, adhesive □ *m* sticker

ades|trado /ades'tradu/ *a* skilled; **~trador** *m* trainer; **~trar** *vt* train; break in <*cavalo*>

adeus /a'dews/ *int* goodbye □ *m* goodbye, farewell

adian|tado /adʒiã'tadu/ *a* advanced; <*relógio*> fast; **chegar ~tado** be early; **~tamento** *m* progress; (*pagamento*) advance; **~tar** *vt* advance <*dinheiro*>; put forward <*relógio*>; bring forward <*data, reunião*>; get ahead with <*trabalho*> □ *vi* <*relógio*> gain; (*ter efeito*) be of use; **~tar-se** *vpr* progress, get ahead; **não ~ta (fazer)** it's no use (doing); **~te** *adv* ahead

adia|r /adʒi'ar/ *vt* postpone; adjourn <*sessão*>; **~mento** *m* postponement, adjournment

adi|ção /adʒi'sãw/ *f* addition; **~cionar** *vt* add; **~do** *m* attaché

adivi|nhação /adʒiviɲa'sãw/ *f* guesswork; (*por adivinho*) fortune-telling; **~nhar** *vt* guess; tell <*futuro, sorte*>; read <*pensamento*>; **~nho** *m* fortuneteller

adjetivo /adʒe'tʃivu/ *m* adjective

adminis|tração /adʒiministra'sãw/ *f* administration; (*de empresas*) management; **~trador** *m* administrator; manager; **~trar** *vt* administer; manage <*empresa*>

admi|ração /adʒimira'sãw/ *f* admiration; (*assombro*) wonder(ment); **~rado** *a* admired; (*surpreso*) amazed, surprised; **~rador** *m* admirer □ *a* admiring; **~rar** *vt* admire; (*assombrar*) amaze; **~rar-se** *vpr* be amazed; **~rável** (*pl* **~ráveis**) *a* admirable; (*assombroso*) amazing

admis|são /adʒimi'sãw/ *f* admission; (*de escola*) intake; **~sível** (*pl* **~síveis**) *a* admissible

admitir /adʒimi'tʃir/ *vt* admit; (*permitir*) permit, allow; (*contratar*) take on

adoção /ado'sãw/ *f* adoption

ado|çar /ado'sar/ *vt* sweeten; **~cicado** *a* slightly sweet

adoecer /adoe'ser/ *vi* fall ill □ *vt* make ill

adoles|cência /adole'sẽsia/ *f* adolescence; **~cente** *a & m* adolescent

adopt- (*Port*) *veja* **adot-**

adorar /ado'rar/ *vt* (*amar*) adore; worship <*deus*>; (*fam: gostar de*) love

adorme|cer /adorme'ser/ *vi* fall asleep; <*perna*> go to sleep, go numb; **~cido** *a* sleeping; <*perna*> numb

ador|nar /ador'nar/ *vt* adorn; **~no** /o/ *m* adornment

ado|tar /ado'tar/ *vt* adopt; **~tivo** *a* adopted

adquirir /adʒiki'rir/ *vt* acquire

adu|bar /adu'bar/ *vt* fertilize; **~bo** *m* fertilizer

adu|lação /adula'sãw/ *f* flattery; (*do público*) adulation; **~lar** *vt* make a fuss of; (*com palavras*) flatter

adulterar /aduwte'rar/ *vt* adulterate; cook, doctor <*contas*> □ *vi* commit adultery

adúltero /a'duwteru/ *m* adulterer (*f* -ess) □ *a* adulterous

adul|tério /aduw'tɛriu/ *m* adultery; **~to** *a & m* adult

advento /adʒi'vẽtu/ *m* advent

advérbio /adʒi'vɛrbiu/ *m* adverb

adver|sário /adʒiver'sariu/ *m* opponent; (*inimigo*) adversary; **~sidade** *f* adversity; **~so** *a* adverse; (*adversário*) opposed

adver|tência /adʒiver'tẽsia/ *f* warning; **~tir** *vt* warn

advo|cacia /adʒivoka'sia/ *f* legal practice; **~gado** *m* lawyer; **~gar** *vt* advocate; (*jurid*) plead □ *vi* practise law

aéreo /a'ɛriu/ *a* air

aero|dinâmica /aerodʒi'namika/ *f* aerodynamics; **~dinâmico** *a* aerodynamic; **~dromo** *m* airfield; **~moça** /o/ *f* air hostess; **~nauta** *m* airman (*f* -woman); **~náutica** *f* (*força*) air force; (*ciência*) aeronautics; **~nave** *f* aircraft; **~porto** /o/ *m* airport

aeros|sol /aero'sɔw/ (*pl* **~sóis**) *m* aerosol

afabilidade /afabili'dadʒi/ *f* friendliness, kindness

afagar /afa'gar/ *vt* stroke

afamado /afa'madu/ *a* renowned, famed

afas|tado /afas'tadu/ *a* remote; <*parente*> distant; **~tado de** (far) away from; **~tamento** *m* removal; (*distância*) distance; (*de candidato*) rejection; **~tar** *vt* move away; (*tirar*) remove; ward off <*perigo, ameaça*>; put out of one's mind <*idéia*>; **~tar-se** *vpr* move away; (*distanciar-se*) distance o.s.; (*de cargo*) step down

afá|vel /a'favew/ (*pl* **~veis**) *a* friendly, genial

afazeres /afa'zeris/ *m pl* business; **~ domésticos** (household) chores

afect- (*Port*) *veja* **afet-**

Afeganistão /afeganis'tãw/ *m* Afghanistan

afe|gão /afe'gãw/ *a* & *m* (*f* **~gã**) Afghan

afeição /afej'sãw/ *f* affection, fondness

afeiçoado /afejsu'adu/ *a* (*devoto*) devoted; (*amoroso*) fond

afeminado /afemi'nadu/ *a* effeminate

aferir /afe'rir/ *vt* check, inspect <*pesos, medidas*>; (*avaliar*) assess; (*cotejar*) compare

aferrar /afe'xar/ *vt* grasp; **~-se a** cling to

afe|tação /afeta'sãw/ *f* affectation; **~tado** *a* affected; **~tar** *vt* affect; **~tivo** *a* (*carinhoso*) affectionate; (*sentimental*) emotional; **~to** /ɛ/ *m* affection; **~tuoso** /o/ *a* affectionate

afi|ado /afi'adu/ *a* sharp; skilled <*pessoa*>; **~ar** *vt* sharpen

aficionado /afisio'nadu/ *m* enthusiast

afilhado /afi'ʎadu/ *m* godson (*f* -daughter)

afili|ação /afilia'sãw/ *f* affiliation; **~ada** *f* affiliate; **~ar** *vt* affiliate

afim /a'fĩ/ *a* related, similar

afinado /afi'nadu/ *a* in tune

afinal /afi'naw/ *adv* **~ (de contas)** (*por fim*) in the end; (*pensando bem*) after all

afinar /afi'nar/ *vt* tune □ *vi* taper

afinco /a'fĩku/ *m* perseverance, determination

afinidade /afini'dadʒi/ *f* affinity

afir|mação /afirma'sãw/ *f* assertion; **~mar** *vt* claim, assert; **~mativo** *a* affirmative

afivelar /afive'lar/ *vt* buckle

afixar /afik'sar/ *vt* stick, post

afli|ção /afli'sãw/ *f* (*física*) affliction; (*cuidado*) anxiety; **~gir** *vt* <*doença*> afflict; (*inquietar*) trouble; **~gir-se** *vpr* worry; **~to** *a* troubled, worried

afluente /aflu'ẽtʃi/ *m* tributary

afo|bação /afoba'sãw/ *f* fluster, flap; **~bado** *a* in a flap, flustered; **~bar** *vt* fluster; **~bar-se** *vpr* get flustered, get in a flap

afo|gado /afo'gadu/ *a* drowned; **morrer ~gado** drown; **~gador** *m* choke; **~gar** *vt/i* drown; (*auto*) flood; **~gar-se** *vpr* (*matar-se*) drown o.s.

afoito /a'fojtu/ *a* bold, daring

afora /a'fɔra/ *adv* **pelo mundo ~** throughout the world

afortunado /afortu'nadu/ *a* fortunate

afresco /a'fresku/ *m* fresco

África /'afrika/ *f* Africa; **~ do Sul** South Africa

africano /afri'kanu/ *a* & *m* African

afrodisíaco /afrodʒi'ziaku/ *a* & *m* aphrodisiac

afron|ta /a'frõta/ *f* affront, insult; **~tar** *vt* affront, insult

afrouxar /afro'ʃar/ *vt/i* loosen; (*de rapidez*) slow down; (*de disciplina*) relax

afta /'afta/ *f* (mouth) ulcer

afugentar /afuʒẽ'tar/ *vt* drive away; rout <*inimigo*>

afundar /afũ'dar/ *vt* sink; **~-se** *vpr* sink

agachar /aga'ʃar/ *vi* **~-se** *vpr* bend down

agarrar /aga'xar/ *vt* grab, snatch; **~-se** *vpr* **~-se a** cling to, hold on to

agasa|lhar /agaza'ʎar/ *vt* **~lhar-se** *vpr* wrap up (warmly); **~lho** *m* (*casaco*) coat; (*suéter*) sweater

agência /a'ʒẽsia/ *f* agency; **~ de correio** post office; **~ de viagens** travel agency

agenda /a'ʒẽda/ *f* diary

agente /a'ʒẽtʃi/ *m/f* agent

ágil /'aʒiw/ (*pl* **ágeis**) *a* <*pessoa*> agile; <*serviço*> quick, efficient

agili|dade /aʒili'dadʒi/ *f* agility; (*rapidez*) speed; **~zar** *vt* speed up, streamline

ágio /'aʒiu/ *m* premium

agiota /aʒi'ɔta/ *m/f* loan shark
agir /a'ʒir/ *vi* act
agi|tado /aʒi'tadu/ *a* agitated; <*mar*> rough; ~**tar** *vt* wave <*braços*>; wag <*rabo*>; shake <*garrafa*>; (*perturbar*) agitate; ~**tar-se** *vpr* get agitated; <*mar*> get rough
aglome|ração /aglomera'sãw/ *f* collection; (*de pessoas*) crowd; ~**rar** collect; ~**rar-se** *vpr* gather
agonia /ago'nia/ *f* anguish; (*da morte*) death throes
agora /a'gɔra/ *adv* now; (*há pouco*) just now; ~ **mesmo** right now; **de** ~ **em diante** from now on; **até** ~ so far, up till now
agosto /a'gostu/ *m* August
agouro /a'goru/ *m* omen
agraciar /agrasi'ar/ *vt* decorate
agra|dar /agra'dar/ *vt* please; (*fazer agrados*) be nice to, fuss over □ *vi* be pleasing, please; (*cair no gosto*) go down well; ~**dável** (*pl* ~**dáveis**) *a* pleasant
agrade|cer /agrade'ser/ *vt* ~**cer aco a alg,** ~**cer a alg por aco** thank s.o. for sth □ *vi* say thank you; ~**cido** *a* grateful; ~**cimento** *m* gratitude; *pl* thanks
agrado /a'gradu/ *m* **fazer** ~**s a** be nice to, make a fuss of
agrafa|r /agra'far/ *vt* (*Port*) staple; ~**dor** *m* stapler
agrário /a'grariu/ *a* land, agrarian
agra|vante /agra'vãtʃi/ *a* aggravating □ *f* aggravating circumstance; ~**var** *vt* aggravate, make worse; ~**var-se** *vpr* get worse
agredir /agre'dʒir/ *vt* attack
agregado /agre'gadu/ *m* (*em casa*) lodger
agres|são /agre'sãw/ *f* aggression; (*ataque*) assault; ~**sivo** *a* aggressive; ~**sor** *m* aggressor
agreste /a'grɛstʃi/ *a* rural
agrião /agri'ãw/ *m* watercress
agrícola /a'grikola/ *a* agricultural
agricul|tor /agrikuw'tor/ *m* farmer; ~**tura** *f* agriculture, farming
agridoce /agri'dosi/ *a* bittersweet
agropecuá|ria /agropeku'aria/ *f* farming; ~**rio** *a* agricultural
agru|pamento /agrupa'mẽtu/ *m* grouping; ~**par** *vt* group; ~**par-se** *vpr* group (together)
água /'agwa/ *f* water; **dar** ~ **na boca** be mouthwatering; **ir por** ~ **abaixo** go down the drain; ~ **benta** holy water; ~ **doce** fresh water; ~ **mineral** mineral water; ~ **salgada** salt water; ~ **sanitária** household bleach
aguaceiro /agwa'seru/ *m* downpour
água-de|-coco /agwadʒi'koku/ *f* coconut water; ~**-colônia** *f* eau de cologne
aguado /a'gwadu/ *a* watery
aguardar /agwar'dar/ *vt* wait for, await □ *vi* wait
aguardente /agwar'dẽtʃi/ *f* spirit
aguarrás /agwa'xas/ *m* turpentine
água-viva /agwa'viva/ *f* jellyfish
agu|çado /agu'sadu/ *a* pointed; <*sentidos*> acute; ~**çar** *vt* sharpen; ~**deza** *f* sharpness; (*mental*) perceptiveness; ~**do** *a* sharp; <*som*> shrill; (*fig*) acute
agüentar /agwẽ'tar/ *vt* stand, put up with; hold <*peso*> □ *vi* <*pessoa*> hold out; <*suporte*> hold
águia /'agia/ *f* eagle
agulha /a'guʎa/ *f* needle
ai /aj/ *m* sigh; (*de dor*) groan □ *int* ah!; (*de dor*) ouch!
aí /a'i/ *adv* there; (*então*) then
aidético /aj'dɛtʃiku/ *a* suffering from Aids □ *m* Aids sufferer
AIDS /'ajdʒis/ *f* Aids
ainda /a'ĩda/ *adv* still; **melhor** ~ even better; **não ...** ~ not ... yet; ~ **assim** even so; ~ **bem** just as well; ~ **por cima** moreover, in addition; ~ **que** even if
aipim /aj'pĩ/ *m* cassava
aipo /'ajpu/ *m* celery
ajeitar /aʒej'tar/ *vt* (*arrumar*) sort out; (*arranjar*) arrange; (*ajustar*) adjust; ~**-se** *vpr* adapt; (*dar certo*) turn out right, sort o.s. out
ajoe|lhado /aʒoe'ʎadu/ *a* kneeling (down); ~**lhar** *vi,* ~**lhar-se** *vpr* kneel (down)
aju|da /a'ʒuda/ *f* help; ~**dante** *m/f* helper; ~**dar** *vt* help
ajuizado /aʒui'zadu/ *a* sensible
ajus|tar /aʒus'tar/ *vt* adjust; settle <*disputa*>; take in <*roupa*>; ~**tar-se** *vpr* conform; ~**tável** (*pl* ~**táveis**) *a* adjustable; ~**te** *m* adjustment; (*acordo*) settlement
ala /'ala/ *f* wing
ala|gação /alaga'sãw/ *f* flooding; ~**gadiço** *a* marshy □ *m* marsh; ~**gar** *vt* flood
alameda /ala'meda/ *f* avenue
álamo /'alamu/ *m* poplar (tree)
alarde /a'lardʒi/ *m* **fazer** ~ **de** flaunt; make a big thing of <*notícia*>; ~**ar** *vt/i* flaunt
alargar /alar'gar/ *vt* widen; (*fig*) broaden; let out <*roupa*>
alarido /ala'ridu/ *m* outcry
alar|ma /a'larma/ *m* alarm; ~**mante** *a* alarming; ~**mar** *vt* alarm; ~**me** *m* alarm; ~**mista** *a & m* alarmist
alastrar /alas'trar/ *vt* scatter; (*disseminar*) spread □ *vi* spread

alavanca /ala'vãka/ *f* lever; ~ **de mudanças** gear lever
alban|ês /awba'nes/ *a & m* (*f* ~**esa**) Albanian
Albânia /aw'bania/ *f* Albania
albergue /aw'bɛrgi/ *m* hostel
álbum /'awbũ/ *m* album
alça /'awsa/ *f* handle; (*de roupa*) strap; (*de fusil*) sight
alcachofra /awka'ʃofra/ *f* artichoke
alçada /aw'sada/ *f* competence, power
álcali /'awkali/ *m* alkali
alcan|çar /awkã'sar/ *vt* reach; (*conseguir*) attain; (*compreender*) understand □ *vi* reach; ~**çável** (*pl* ~**çáveis**) *a* reachable; attainable; ~**ce** *m* reach; (*de tiro*) range; (*importância*) consequence; (*compreensão*) understanding
alcaparra /awka'paxa/ *f* caper
alcatra /aw'katra/ *f* rump steak
alcatrão /awka'trãw/ *m* tar
álcool /'awkɔw/ *m* alcohol
alcoó|latra /awko'ɔlatra/ *m/f* alcoholic; ~**lico** *a & m* alcoholic
alcunha /aw'kuɲa/ *f* nickname
aldeia /aw'deja/ *f* village
aleatório /alia'tɔriu/ *a* random, arbitrary
alecrim /ale'krĩ/ *m* rosemary
ale|gação /alega'sãw/ *f* allegation; ~**gar** *vt* allege
ale|goria /alego'ria/ *f* allegory; ~**górico** *a* allegorical
ale|grar /ale'grar/ *vt* cheer up; brighten up <*casa*>; ~**grar-se** *vpr* cheer up; ~**gre** /ɛ/ *a* cheerful; <*cores*> bright; ~**gria** *f* joy
alei|jado /ale'ʒadu/ *a* crippled □ *m* cripple; ~**jar** *vt* cripple
alei|tamento /alejta'mẽtu/ *m* breast-feeding; ~**tar** *vt* breast-feed
além /a'lẽj/ *adv* beyond; ~ **de** (*ao lado de lá de*) beyond; (*mais de*) over; (*ademais de*) apart from
Alemanha /ale'maɲa/ *f* Germany
alemão /ale'mãw/ (*pl* ~**mães**) *a & m* (*f* ~**mã**) German
alen|tador /alẽta'dor/ *a* encouraging; ~**tar** *vt* encourage; ~**tar-se** *vpr* cheer up; ~**to** *m* courage; (*fôlego*) breath
alergia /aler'ʒia/ *f* allergy
alérgico /a'lɛrʒiku/ *a* allergic (a to)
aler|ta /a'lɛrta/ *a & m* alert □ *adv* on the alert; ~**tar** *vt* alert
alfa|bético /awfa'bɛtʃiku/ *a* alphabetical; ~**betização** *f* literacy; ~**betizar** *vt* teach to read and write; ~**beto** *m* alphabet
alface /aw'fasi/ *f* lettuce
alfaiate /awfaj'atʃi/ *m* tailor
al|fândega /aw'fãdʒiga/ *f* customs; ~**fandegário** *a* customs □ *m* customs officer
alfine|tada /awfine'tada/ *f* prick; (*dor*) stabbing pain; (*fig*) dig; ~**te** /e/ *m* pin; ~**te de segurança** safety pin
alforreca /alfo'xeka/ *f* (*Port*) jellyfish
alga /'awga/ *f* seaweed
algarismo /awga'rizmu/ *m* numeral
algazarra /awga'zaxa/ *f* uproar, racket
alge|mar /awʒe'mar/ *vt* handcuff; ~**mas** /e/ *f pl* handcuffs
algibeira /alʒi'bejra/ *f* (*Port*) pocket
algo /'awgu/ *pron* something; (*numa pergunta*) anything □ *adv* somewhat
algodão /awgo'dãw/ *m* cotton; ~(-**doce**) candy floss, (*Amer*) cotton candy; ~ (**hidrófilo**) cotton wool, (*Amer*) absorbent cotton
alguém /aw'gẽj/ *pron* somebody, someone; (*numa pergunta*) anybody, anyone
al|gum /aw'gũ/ (*f* ~**guma**) *a* some; (*numa pergunta*) any; (*nenhum*) no, not one □ *pron pl* some; ~**guma coisa** something
algures /aw'guris/ *adv* somewhere
alheio /a'ʎeju/ *a* (*de outra pessoa*) someone else's; (*de outras pessoas*) other people's; ~ **a** foreign to; (*impróprio*) irrelevant to; (*desatento*) unaware of; ~ **de** removed from
alho /'aʎu/ *m* garlic; ~**-poró** *m* leek
ali /a'li/ *adv* (over) there
ali|ado /ali'adu/ *a* allied □ *m* ally; ~**ança** *f* alliance; (*anel*) wedding ring; ~**ar** *vt*, ~**ar-se** *vpr* ally
aliás /a'ljaʃ/ *adv* (*além disso*) what's more, furthermore; (*no entanto*) however; (*diga-se de passagem*) by the way, incidentally; (*senão*) otherwise
álibi /'alibi/ *m* alibi
alicate /ali'katʃi/ *m* pliers; ~ **de unhas** nail clippers
alicerce /ali'sɛrsi/ *m* foundation; (*fig*) basis
alie|nado /alie'nadu/ *a* alienated; (*demente*) insane; ~**nar** *vt* alienate; transfer <*bens*>; ~**nígena** *a & m/f* alien
alimen|tação /alimẽta'sãw/ *f* (*ato*) feeding; (*comida*) food; (*tecn*) supply; ~**tar** *a* food; <*hábitos*> eating □ *vt* feed; (*fig*) nurture; ~**tar-se de** live on; ~**tício** *a* **gêneros** ~**tícios** foodstuffs; ~**to** *m* food
ali|nhado /ali'ɲadu/ *a* aligned; <*pessoa*> smart, (*Amer*) sharp; ~**nhar** *vt* align
alíquota /a'likwota/ *f* (*de imposto*) bracket
alisar /ali'zar/ *vt* smooth (out); straighten <*cabelo*>

alistar /alis'tar/ *vt* recruit; **~-se** *vpr* enlist

aliviar /alivi'ar/ *vt* relieve

alívio /a'liviu/ *m* relief

alma /'awma/ *f* soul

almanaque /awma'naki/ *m* yearbook

almejar /awme'ʒar/ *vt* long for

almirante /awmi'rãtʃi/ *m* admiral

almo|çar /awmo'sar/ *vi* have lunch □ *vt* have for lunch; **~ço** /o/ *m* lunch

almofada /awmo'fada/ *f* cushion; (*Port: de cama*) pillow

almôndega /aw'mõdʒiga/ *f* meatball

almoxarifado /awmoʃari'fadu/ *m* storeroom

alô /a'lo/ *int* hallo

alocar /alo'kar/ *vt* allocate

alo|jamento /aloʒa'mẽtu/ *m* accommodation, (*Amer*) accommodations; (*habitação*) housing; **~jar** *vt* accommodate; house <*sem-teto*>; **~jar-se** *vpr* stay

alongar /alõ'gar/ *vt* lengthen; extend, stretch out <*braço*>

alpendre /aw'pẽdri/ *m* shed; (*pórtico*) porch

Alpes /'awpis/ *m pl* Alps

alpinis|mo /awpi'nizmu/ *m* mountaineering; **~ta** *m/f* mountaineer

alqueire /aw'keri/ *m* = *4.84 hectares,* (*in São Paulo = 2.42 hectares*)

alquimi|a /awki'mia/ *f* alchemy; **~sta** *mf* alchemist

alta /'awta/ *f* rise; **dar ~ a** discharge; **ter ~** be discharged

altar /aw'tar/ *m* altar

alterar /awte'rar/ *vt* alter; (*falsificar*) falsify; **~-se** *vpr* change; (*zangar-se*) get angry

alter|nado /awter'nadu/ *a* alternate; **~nar** *vt/i*, **~nar-se** *vpr* alternate; **~nativa** *f* alternative; **~nativo** *a* alternative; <*corrente*> alternating

al|teza /aw'teza/ *f* highness; **~titude** *f* altitude

alti|vez /awtʃi'ves/ *f* arrogance; **~vo** *a* arrogant; (*elevado*) majestic

alto /'awtu/ *a* high; <*pessoa*> tall; <*barulho*> loud □ *adv* high; <*falar*> loud(ly); <*ler*> aloud □ *m* top; **os ~s e baixos** the ups and downs □ *int* halt!; **~-falante** *m* loudspeaker

altura /aw'tura/ *f* height; (*momento*) moment; **ser à ~ de** be up to

aluci|nação /alusina'sãw/ *f* hallucination; **~nante** *a* mind-boggling, crazy

aludir /alu'dʒir/ *vi* allude (**a** to)

alu|gar /alu'gar/ *vt* rent <*casa*>; hire, rent <*carro*>; <*locador*> let, rent out, hire out; **~guel** (*Port*), **~guer** /ɛ/ *m* rent; (*ato*) renting

alumiar /alumi'ar/ *vt* light (up)

alumínio /alu'miniu/ *m* aluminium, (*Amer*) aluminum

aluno /a'lunu/ *m* pupil

alusão /alu'zãw/ *f* allusion (**a** to)

alvará /awva'ra/ *m* permit, licence

alve|jante /awve'ʒãtʃi/ *m* bleach; **~jar** *vt* bleach; (*visar*) aim at

alvenaria /awvena'ria/ *f* masonry

alvo /'awvu/ *m* target

alvorada /awvo'rada/ *f* dawn

alvoro|çar /awvoro'sar/ *vt* stir up, agitate; (*entusiasmar*) excite; **~ço** /o/ *m* (*tumulto*) uproar; (*entusiasmo*) excitement

amabilidade /amabili'dadʒi/ *f* kindness

amaci|ante /amasi'ãtʃi/ *m* (*de roupa*) (fabric) conditioner; **~ar** *vt* soften; run in <*carro*>

amador /ama'dor/ *a & m* amateur; **~ismo** *m* amateurism; **~ístico** *a* amateurish

amadurecer /amadure'ser/ *vt/i* <*fruta*> ripen; (*fig*) mature

âmago /'amagu/ *m* heart, core; (*da questão*) crux

amaldiçoar /amawdʒiso'ar/ *vt* curse

amamentar /amamẽ'tar/ *vt* breastfeed

amanhã /ama'ɲã/ *m & adv* tomorrow; **depois de ~** the day after tomorrow

amanhecer /amaɲe'ser/ *vi & m* dawn

amansar /amã'sar/ *vt* tame; (*fig*) placate <*pessoa*>

a|mante /a'mãtʃi/ *m/f* lover; **~mar** *vt/i* love

amarelo /ama'rɛlu/ *a & m* yellow

amar|go /a'margu/ *a* bitter; **~gura** *f* bitterness; **~gurar** *vt* embitter; (*sofrer*) endure

amarrar /ama'xar/ *vt* tie (up); (*naut*) moor; **~ a cara** frown, scowl

amarrotar /amaxo'tar/ *vt* crease

amassar /ama'sar/ *vt* crush, squash; screw up <*papel*>; crease <*roupa*>; dent <*carro*>; knead <*pão*>; mash <*batatas*>

amá|vel /a'mavew/ (*pl* **~veis**) *a* kind

Ama|zonas /ama'zonas/ *m* Amazon; **~zônia** *f* Amazonia

âmbar /'ãbar/ *m* amber

ambi|ção /ãbi'sãw/ *f* ambition; **~cionar** *vt* aspire to; **~cioso** /o/ *a* ambitious

ambien|tal /ãbiẽ'taw/ (*pl* **~tais**) *a* environmental; **~tar** *vt* set <*filme, livro*>; set up <*casa*>; **~tar-se** *vpr* settle in; **~te** *m* environment; (*atmosfera*) atmosphere

am|bigüidade /ãbigwi'dadʒi/ *f* ambiguity; **~bíguo** *a* ambiguous

âmbito /'ãbitu/ *m* scope, range

ambos /'ãbus/ *a & pron* both

ambu|lância /ãbu'lãsia/ *f* ambulance; **~lante** *a* (*que anda*) walking; <*músico*> wandering; <*venda*> mobile; **~latório** *m* out-patient clinic

amea|ça /ami'asa/ *f* threat; **~çador** *a* threatening; **~çar** *vt* threaten

ameba /a'mɛba/ *f* amoeba

amedrontar /amedrõ'tar/ *vt* scare; **~-se** *vpr* get scared

ameixa /a'meʃa/ *f* plum; (*passa*) prune

amém /a'mẽj/ *int* amen □ *m* agreement; **dizer ~ a** go along with

amêndoa /a'mẽdoa/ *f* almond

amendoim /amẽdo'ĩ/ *m* peanut

ame|nidade /ameni'dadʒi/ *f* pleasantness; *pl* pleasantries, small talk; **~nizar** *vt* ease; calm <*ânimos*>; settle <*disputa*>; tone down <*repreensão*>; **~no** /e/ *a* pleasant; mild <*clima*>

América /a'mɛrika/ *f* America; **~ do Norte/Sul** North/South America

america|nizar /amerikani'zar/ *vt* Americanize; **~no** *a* & *m* American

amestrar /ames'trar/ *vt* train

ametista /ame'tʃista/ *f* amethyst

amianto /ami'ãtu/ *m* asbestos

ami|gar-se /ami'garsi/ *vpr* make friends; **~gável** (*pl* **~gáveis**) *a* amicable

amígdala /a'migdala/ *f* tonsil

amigdalite /amigda'litʃi/ *f* tonsillitis

amigo /a'migu/ *a* friendly □ *m* friend; **~ da onça** false friend

amistoso /amis'tozu/ *a* & *m* friendly

amiúde /ami'udʒi/ *adv* often

amizade /ami'zadʒi/ *f* friendship

amnésia /ami'nɛzia/ *f* amnesia

amnistia /amnis'tia/ *f* (*Port*) *veja* anistia

amo|lação /amola'sãw/ *f* annoyance; **~lante** *a* annoying; **~lar** *vt* annoy, bother; sharpen <*faca*>; **~lar-se** *vpr* get annoyed

amolecer /amole'ser/ *vt/i* soften

amol|gadura /amowga'dura/ *f* dent; **~gar** *vt* dent

amoníaco /amo'niaku/ *m* ammonia

amontoar /amõto'ar/ *vt* pile up; amass <*riquezas*>; **~-se** *vpr* pile up

amor /a'mor/ *m* love; **~ próprio** self-esteem

amora /a'mɔra/ *f* **~ preta**, (*Port*) **~ silvestre** blackberry

amordaçar /amorda'sar/ *vt* gag

amoroso /amo'rozu/ *adj* loving

amor-perfeito /amorper'fejtu/ *m* pansy

amorte|cedor /amortese'dor/ *m* shock absorber; **~cer** *vt* deaden; absorb <*impacto*>; break <*queda*> □ *vi* fade

amostra /a'mɔstra/ *f* sample

ampa|rar /ãpa'rar/ *vt* support; (*fig*) protect; **~rar-se** *vpr* lean; **~ro** *m* (*apoio*) support; (*proteção*) protection; (*ajuda*) aid

ampère /ã'pɛri/ *m* amp(ere)

ampli|ação /ãplia'sãw/ *f* (*de foto*) enlargement; (*de casa*) extension; **~ar** *vt* enlarge <*foto*>; extend <*casa*>; broaden <*conhecimentos*>

amplifi|cador /ãplifika'dor/ *m* amplifier; **~car** *vt* amplify

amplo /'ãplu/ *a* <*sala*> spacious; <*roupa*> full; <*sentido, conhecimento*> broad

ampola /ã'pola/ *f* ampoule

amputar /ãpu'tar/ *vt* amputate

Amsterdã /amister'dã/, (*Port*) **Amsterdão** /amiʃter'dãw/ *f* Amsterdam

amu|ado /amu'adu/ *a* in a sulk, sulky; **~ar** *vi* sulk

amuleto /amu'leto/ *m* charm

amuo /a'muu/ *m* sulk

ana|crônico /ana'kroniku/ *a* anachronistic; **~cronismo** *m* anachronism

anais /a'najs/ *m pl* annals

analfabeto /anawfa'bɛtu/ *a* & *m* illiterate

analisar /anali'zar/ *vt* analyse

análise /a'nalizi/ *f* analysis

ana|lista /ana'lista/ *m/f* analyst; **~lítico** *a* analytical

analogia /analo'ʒia/ *f* analogy

análogo /a'nalogu/ *a* analogous

ananás /ana'naʃ/ *m invar* (*Port*) pineapple

anão /a'nãw/ *a* & *m* (*f* **anã**) dwarf

anarquia /anar'kia/ *f* anarchy; (*fig*) chaos

anárquico /a'narkiku/ *a* anarchic

anarquista /anar'kista/ *m/f* anarchist

ana|tomia /anato'mia/ *f* anatomy; **~tômico** *a* anatomical

anca /'ãka/ *f* (*de pessoa*) hip; (*de animal*) rump

anchova /ã'ʃova/ *f* anchovy

ancinho /ã'siɲu/ *m* rake

âncora /'ãkora/ *f* anchor

anco|radouro /ãkora'doru/ *m* anchorage; **~rar** *vt/i* anchor

andaime /ã'dajmi/ *m* scaffolding

an|damento /ãda'mẽtu/ *m* (*progresso*) progress; (*rumo*) course; **dar ~damento a** set in motion; **~dar** *m* (*jeito de andar*) gait, walk; (*de prédio*) floor; (*Port: apartamento*) flat, (*Amer*) apartment □ *vi* (*ir a pé*) walk; (*de trem, ônibus*) travel; (*a cavalo, de bicicleta*) ride; (*funcionar, progredir*) go; **ele anda deprimido** he's been depressed lately

Andes /'ãdʒis/ *m pl* Andes

andorinha /ãdo'riɲa/ *f* swallow

anedota /ane'dæta/ *f* anecdote

anel /a'nɛw/ (*pl* **anéis**) *m* ring; (*no cabelo*) curl; ~ **viário** ringroad

anelado /ane'ladu/ *a* curly

anemia /ane'mia/ *f* anaemia

anêmico /a'nemiku/ *a* anaemic

anes|tesia /aneste'zia/ *f* anaesthesia; (*droga*) anaesthetic; ~**tesiar** *vt* anaesthetize; ~**tésico** *a* & *m* anaesthetic; ~**tesista** *m/f* anaesthetist

ane|xar /anek'sar/ *vt* annex <*terras*>; (*em carta*) enclose; (*juntar*) attach; ~**xo** /ɛ/ *a* attached; (*em carta*) enclosed □ *m* annexe; (*em carta*) enclosure

anfíbio /ã'fibiu/ *a* amphibious □ *m* amphibian

anfiteatro /ãfitʃi'atru/ *m* amphitheatre; (*no teatro*) dress circle

anfi|trião /ãfitri'ãw/ *m* (*f* ~**triã**) host (*f* -ess)

angariar /ãgari'ar/ *vt* raise <*fundos*>; canvass for <*votos*>; win <*adeptos, simpatia*>

angli|cano /ãgli'kanu/ *a* & *m* Anglican; ~**cismo** *m* Anglicism

anglo-saxônico /ãglusak'soniku/ *a* Anglo-Saxon

Angola /ã'gɔla/ *f* Angola

angolano /ãgo'lanu/ *a* & *m* Angolan

angra /'ãgra/ *f* inlet, cove

angular /ãgu'lar/ *a* angular

ângulo /'ãgulu/ *m* angle

angústia /ã'gustʃia/ *f* anguish, anxiety

angustiante /ãgustʃi'ãtʃi/ *a* distressing; <*momento*> anxious

ani|mado /ani'madu/ *a* (*vivo*) lively; (*alegre*) cheerful; (*entusiasmado*) enthusiastic; ~**mador** *a* encouraging □ *m* presenter; ~**mal** (*pl* ~**mais**) *a* & *m* animal; ~**mar** *vt* encourage; liven up <*festa*>; ~**mar-se** *vpr* cheer up; <*festa*> liven up

ânimo /'animu/ *m* courage, spirit; *pl* tempers

animosidade /animozi'dadʒi/ *f* animosity

aniquilar /aniki'lar/ *vt* destroy; (*prostrar*) shatter

anis /a'nis/ *m* aniseed

anistia /anis'tʃia/ *f* amnesty

aniver|sariante /aniversari'ãtʃi/ *m/f* birthday boy (*f* girl); ~**sário** *m* birthday; (*de casamento etc*) anniversary

anjo /'ãʒu/ *m* angel

ano /'anu/ *m* year; **fazer** ~**s** have a birthday; ~ **bissexto** leap year; ~ **letivo** academic year; ~**-bom** *m* New Year

anoite|cer /anojte'ser/ *m* nightfall □ *vi* ~**ceu** night fell

anomalia /anoma'lia/ *f* anomaly

anonimato /anoni'matu/ *m* anonymity

anônimo /a'nonimu/ *a* anonymous

anor|mal /anor'maw/ (*pl* ~**mais**) *a* abnormal

ano|tação /anota'sãw/ *f* note; ~**tar** *vt* note down, write down

ânsia /'ãsia/ *f* anxiety; (*desejo*) longing; ~**s de vômito** nausea

ansi|ar /ãsi'ar/ *vi* ~ **por** long for; ~**edade** *f* anxiety; (*desejo*) eagerness; ~**oso** /o/ *a* anxious

antártico /ã'tartʃiku/ *a* & *m* Antarctic

antebraço /ãtʃi'brasu/ *m* forearm

antece|dência /ãtese'dẽsia/ *f* **com** ~**dência** in advance; ~**dente** *a* preceding; ~**dentes** *m pl* record, past

antecessor /ãtese'sor/ *m* (*f* ~**a**) predecessor

anteci|pação /ãtʃisipa'sãw/ *f* anticipation; **com** ~**pação** in advance; ~**padamente** *adv* in advance; ~**pado** *a* advance; ~**par** *vt* anticipate, forestall; (*adiantar*) bring forward; ~**par-se** *vpr* be previous

antena /ã'tena/ *f* aerial, (*Amer*) antenna; (*de inseto*) feeler

anteontem /ãtʃi'õtẽ/ *adv* the day before yesterday

antepassado /ãtʃipa'sadu/ *m* ancestor

anterior /ãteri'or/ *a* previous; (*dianteiro*) front

antes /'ãtʃis/ *adv* before; (*ao contrário*) rather; ~ **de/que** before

ante-sala /ãtʃi'sala/ *f* ante-room

anti|biótico /ãtʃibi'ɔtʃiku/ *a* & *m* antibiotic; ~**caspa** *a* anti-dandruff; ~**concepcional** (*pl* ~**concepcionais**) *a* & *m* contraceptive; ~**congelante** *m* antifreeze; ~**corpo** *m* antibody

antídoto /ã'tʃidotu/ *m* antidote

antiético /ãtʃi'ɛtʃiku/ *a* unethical

antigamente /ãtʃiga'mẽtʃi/ *adv* formerly

anti|go /ã'tʃigu/ *a* old; (*da antiguidade*) ancient; <*móveis etc*> antique; (*anterior*) former; ~**guidade** *f* antiquity; (*numa firma*) seniority; *pl* (*monumentos*) antiquities; (*móveis etc*) antiques

anti-|higiênico /ãtʃiʒi'eniku/ *a* unhygienic; ~**histamínico** *a* & *m* antihistamine; ~**horário** *a* anticlockwise

antilhano /ãtʃi'ʎanu/ *a* & *m* West Indian

Antilhas /ã'tʃiʎas/ *f pl* West Indies

anti|patia /ãtʃipa'tʃia/ *f* dislike; ~**pático** *a* unpleasant, unfriendly

antiquado /ãtʃi'kwadu/ *a* antiquated, out-dated

anti-|semitismo /ãtʃisemi'tʃizmu/ *m* anti-Semitism; **~séptico** *a & m* antiseptic; **~social** (*pl* **~sociais**) *a* antisocial

antítese /ã'tʃitezi/ *f* antithesis

antologia /ãtolo'ʒia/ *f* anthology

antônimo /ã'tonimu/ *m* antonym

antro /'ãtru/ *m* cavern; (*de animal*) lair; (*de ladrões*) den

antro|pófago /ãtro'pɔfagu/ *a* maneating; **~pologia** *f* anthropology; **~pólogo** *m* anthropologist

anu|al /anu'aw/ (*pl* **~ais**) *a* annual, yearly

anu|lação /anula'sãw/ *f* cancellation; **~lar** *vt* cancel; annul <*casamento*>; (*compensar*) cancel out □ *m* ring finger

anunciar /anũsi'ar/ *vt* announce; advertise <*produto*>

anúncio /a'nũsiu/ *m* announcement; (*propaganda, classificado*) advert(isement); (*cartaz*) notice

ânus /'anus/ *m invar* anus

an|zol /ã'zɔw/ (*pl* **~zóis**) *m* fish-hook

aonde /a'õdʒi/ *adv* where

apadrinhar /apadri'ɲar/ *vt* be godfather to <*afilhado*>; be best man for <*noivo*>; (*proteger*) protect; (*patrocinar*) support

apa|gado /apa'gadu/ *a* <*fogo*> out; <*luz, TV*> off; (*indistinto*) faint; <*pessoa*> dull; **~gar** *vt* put out <*cigarro, fogo*>; blow out <*vela*>; switch off <*luz, TV*>; rub out <*erro*>; clean <*quadro-negro*>; **~gar-se** *vpr* <*fogo, luz*> go out; <*lembrança*> fade; (*desmaiar*) pass out; (*fam: dormir*) nod off

apaixo|nado /apaʃo'nadu/ *a* in love (por with); **~nante** *a* captivating; **~nar-se** *vpr* fall in love (por with)

apalpar /apaw'par/ *vt* touch, feel; <*médico*> examine

apanhar /apa'ɲar/ *vt* catch; (*do chão*) pick up; pick <*flores, frutas*>; (*ir buscar*) pick up; (*alcançar*) catch up □ *vi* be beaten

aparafusar /aparafu'zar/ *vt* screw

apa|ra-lápis /apara'lapiʃ/ *m invar* (*Port*) pencil sharpener; **~rar** *vt* catch <*bola*>; parry <*golpe*>; trim <*cabelo*>; sharpen <*lápis*>

aparato /apa'ratu/ *m* pomp, ceremony

apare|cer /apare'ser/ *vi* appear; **~ça!** do drop in!; **~cimento** *m* appearance

apare|lhagem /apare'ʎaʒẽ/ *f* equipment; **~lhar** *vt* equip; **~lho** /e/ *m* apparatus; (*máquina*) machine; (*de chá*) set, service; (*fone*) phone

aparência /apa'rẽsia/ *f* appearance; **na ~** apparently

aparen|tado /aparẽ'tadu/ *a* related; **~tar** *vt* show; (*fingir*) feign; **~te** *a* apparent

apar|tamento /aparta'mẽtu/ *m* flat, (*Amer*) apartment; **~tar** *vt*, **~tar-se** *vpr* separate; **~te** *m* aside

apatia /apa'tʃia/ *f* apathy

apático /a'patʃiku/ *a* apathetic

apavo|rante /apavo'rãtʃi/ *a* terrifying; **~rar** *vt* terrify; **~rar-se** *vpr* be terrified

apaziguar /apazi'gwar/ *vt* appease

apear-se /api'arsi/ *vpr* (*de cavalo*) dismount; (*de ônibus*) alight

ape|gar-se /ape'garsi/ *vpr* become attached (a to); **~go** /e/ *m* attachment

ape|lação /apela'sãw/ *f* appeal; (*fig*) exhibitionism; **~lar** *vi* appeal (de against); **~lar para** appeal to; (*fig*) resort to

apeli|dar /apeli'dar/ *vt* nickname; **~do** *m* nickname

apelo /a'pelu/ *m* appeal

apenas /a'penas/ *adv* only

apêndice /a'pẽdʒisi/ *m* appendix

apendicite /apẽdʒi'sitʃi/ *f* appendicitis

aperceber-se /aperse'bersi/ *vpr* ~ (de) notice, realize

aperfeiçoar /aperfejso'ar/ *vt* perfect

aperitivo /aperi'tʃivu/ *m* aperitif

aper|tado /aper'tadu/ *a* tight; (*sem dinheiro*) hard-up; **~tar** *vt* (*segurar*) hold tight; tighten <*cinto*>; press <*botão*>; squeeze <*esponja*>; take in <*vestido*>; fasten <*cinto de segurança*>; step up <*vigilância*>; cut down on <*despesas*>; break <*coração*>; (*fig*) pressurize <*pessoa*> □ *vi* <*sapato*> pinch; <*chuva, frio*> get worse; <*estrada*> narrow; **~tar-se** *vpr* (*gastar menos*) tighten one's belt; (*não ter dinheiro*) feel the pinch; **~tar a mão de alg** shake hands with s.o.; **~to** /e/ *m* pressure; (*de botão*) press; (*dificuldade*) tight spot, jam; **~to de mãos** handshake

apesar /ape'zar/ ~ **de** *prep* in spite of

apeti|te /ape'tʃitʃi/ *m* appetite; **~toso** /o/ *a* appetizing

apetrechos /ape'treʃus/ *m pl* gear; (*de pesca*) tackle

apimentado /apimẽ'tadu/ *a* spicy, hot

apinhar /api'ɲar/ *vt* crowd, pack; **~-se** *vpr* crowd

api|tar /api'tar/ *vi* whistle □ *vt* referee <*jogo*>; **~to** *m* whistle

aplanar /apla'nar/ *vt* level <*terreno*>; (*fig*) smooth <*caminho*>; smooth over <*problema*>

aplau|dir /aplaw'dʒir/ *vt* applaud; **~so(s)** *m* (*pl*) applause

apli|cação /aplika'sãw/ *f* application; (*de dinheiro*) investment; (*de lei*) enforcement; ~**car** *vt* apply; invest <*dinheiro*>; enforce <*lei*>; ~**car-se** *vpr* apply (a to); (*ao estudo etc*) apply o.s. (a to); ~**que** *m* hairpiece

apoderar-se /apode'rarsi/ *vpr* ~ **de** take possession of; <*raiva*> take hold of

apodrecer /apodre'ser/ *vt/i* rot

apoi|ar /apoj'ar/ *vt* lean; (*fig*) support; (*basear*) base; ~**ar-se** *vpr* ~**ar-se em** lean on; (*fig*) be based on, rest on; ~**o** *m* support

apólice /a'pɔlisi/ *f* policy; (*ação*) bond

apon|tador /apõta'dor/ *m* pencil sharpener; ~**tar** *vt* (*com o dedo*) point at, point to; point out <*erro, caso interessante*>; aim <*arma*>; name <*nomes*>; put forward <*razão*> □ *vi* <*sol, planta*> come up; (*com o dedo*) point (para to)

apoquentar /apokẽ'tar/ *vt* annoy

aporrinhar /apoxi'ɲar/ *vt* annoy

após /a'pɔs/ *adv* after; **loção** ~**-barba** after-shave (lotion)

aposen|tado /apozẽ'tadu/ *a* retired □ *m* pensioner; ~**tadoria** *f* retirement; (*pensão*) pension; ~**tar** *vt*, ~**tar-se** *vpr* retire; ~**to** *m* room

após-guerra /apɔz'gɛxa/ *m* post-war period

apos|ta /a'pɔsta/ *f* bet; ~**tar** *vt* bet (em on); (*fig*) have faith (em in)

apostila /apos'tʃila/ *f* revision aid, book of key facts

apóstolo /a'pɔstolu/ *m* apostle

apóstrofo /a'pɔstrofu/ *m* apostrophe

apre|ciação /apresia'sãw/ *f* appreciation; ~**ciar** *vt* appreciate; think highly of <*pessoa*>; ~**ciativo** *a* appreciative; ~**ciável** (*pl* ~**ciáveis**) *a* appreciable; ~**ço** /e/ *m* regard

apreen|der /apriẽ'der/ *vt* seize <*contrabando*>; apprehend <*criminoso*>; grasp <*sentido*>; ~**são** *f* apprehension; (*de contrabando*) seizure; ~**sivo** *a* apprehensive

apregoar /aprego'ar/ *vt* proclaim; cry <*mercadoria*>

apren|der /aprẽ'der/ *vt/i* learn; ~**diz** *m/f* (*de ofício*) apprentice; (*de direção*) learner; ~**dizado** *m*, ~**dizagem** *f* (*de ofício*) apprenticeship; (*de profissão*) training; (*escolar*) learning

apresen|tação /aprezẽta'sãw/ *f* presentation; (*teatral etc*) performance; (*de pessoas*) introduction; ~**tador** *m* presenter; ~**tar** *vt* present; introduce <*pessoa*>; ~**tar-se** *vpr* (*identificar-se*) introduce o.s.; <*ocasião, problema*> present o.s., arise; ~**tar-se a** report to <*polícia etc*>; go in for <*exame*>; stand for <*eleição*>; ~**tável** (*pl* ~**táveis**) *a* presentable

apres|sado /apre'sadu/ *a* hurried; ~**sar** *vt* hurry; ~**sar-se** *vpr* hurry (up)

aprimorar /aprimo'rar/ *vt* perfect, refine

aprofundar /aprofũ'dar/ *vt* deepen; study carefully <*questão*>; ~**-se** *vpr* get deeper; ~**-se em** go deeper into

aprontar /aprõ'tar/ *vt* get ready; pick <*briga*> □ *vi* act up; ~**-se** *vpr* get ready

apropriado /apropri'adu/ *a* appropriate, suitable

apro|vação /aprova'sãw/ *f* approval; (*num exame*) pass; ~**var** *vt* approve of; approve <*lei*> □ *vi* make the grade; **ser** ~**vado** (*num exame*) pass

aprovei|tador /aprovejta'dor/ *m* opportunist; ~**tamento** *m* utilization; ~**tar** *vt* take advantage of; take <*ocasião*>; (*utilizar*) use □ *vi* make the most of it; (*Port: adiantar*) be of use; ~**tar-se** *vpr* take advantage (de of); ~**te!** (*divirta-se*) have a good time!

aproxi|mação /aprosima'sãw/ *f* (*chegada*) approach; (*estimativa*) approximation; ~**mado** *a* <*valor*> approximate; ~**mar** *vt* move nearer; (*aliar*) bring together; ~**mar-se** *vpr* approach, get nearer (de to)

ap|tidão /aptʃi'dãw/ *f* aptitude, suitability; ~**to** *a* suitable

apunhalar /apuɲa'lar/ *vt* stab

apu|rado /apu'radu/ *a* refined; ~**rar** *vt* (*aprimorar*) refine; (*descobrir*) ascertain; investigate <*caso*>; collect <*dinheiro*>; count <*votos*>; ~**rar-se** *vpr* (*com a roupa*) dress smartly; ~**ro** *m* refinement; (*no vestir*) elegance; (*dificuldade*) difficulty; *pl* trouble

aquarela /akwa'rɛla/ *f* watercolour

aquariano /akwari'anu/ *a* & *m* Aquarian

aquário /a'kwariu/ *m* aquarium; **Aquário** Aquarius

aquartelar /akwarte'lar/ *vt* billet

aquático /a'kwatʃiku/ *a* aquatic, water

aque|cedor /akese'dor/ *m* heater; ~**cer** *vt* heat □ *vi*, ~**cer-se** *vpr* heat up; ~**cimento** *m* heating

aqueduto /ake'dutu/ *m* aqueduct

aquele /a'keli/ *a* that; *pl* those □ *pron* that one; *pl* those; ~ **que** the one that

àquele = a^2 + **aquele**

aqui /a'ki/ *adv* here

aquilo /a'kilu/ *pron* that

àquilo = a^2 + **aquilo**

aquisi|ção /akizi'sãw/ *f* acquisition; ~**tivo** *a* **poder** ~**tivo** purchasing power

ar /ar/ *m* air; (*aspecto*) look, air; (*Port: no carro*) choke; **ao** ~ **livre** in the open air; **no ~** (*fig*) up in the air; (*TV*) on air; **~ condicionado** air conditioning

árabe /'arabi/ *a & m* Arab; (*ling*) Arabic

Arábia /a'rabia/ *f* Arabia; **~ Saudita** Saudi Arabia

arado /a'radu/ *m* plough, (*Amer*) plow

aragem /a'raʒẽ/ *f* breeze

arame /a'rami/ *m* wire; **~ farpado** barbed wire

aranha /a'raɲa/ *f* spider

arar /a'rar/ *vt* plough, (*Amer*) plow

arara /a'rara/ *f* parrot

arbi|trar /arbi'trar/ *vt/i* referee <*jogo*>; arbitrate <*disputa*>; **~trário** *a* arbitrary

arbítrio /ar'bitriu/ *m* judgement; **livre ~** free will

árbitro /'arbitru/ *m* arbiter <*da moda etc*>; (*jurid*) arbitrator; (*de futebol*) referee; (*de tênis*) umpire

arborizado /arbori'zadu/ *a* wooded, green; <*rua*> tree-lined

arbusto /ar'bustu/ *m* shrub

ar|ca /'arka/ *f* **~ca de Noé** Noah's Ark; **~cada** *f* (*galeria*) arcade; (*arco*) arch

arcaico /ar'kajku/ *a* archaic

arcar /ar'kar/ *vt* **~ com** deal with

arcebispo /arse'bispu/ *m* archbishop

arco /'arku/ *m* (*arquit*) arch; (*arma, mus*) bow; (*eletr, mat*) arc; **~-da-velha** *m* **coisa do ~-da-velha** amazing thing; **~-íris** *m invar* rainbow

ar|dente /ar'dẽtʃi/ *a* burning; (*fig*) ardent; **~der** *vi* burn; <*olhos, ferida*> sting

ar|dil /ar'dʒiw/ (*pl* **~dis**) *m* trick, ruse

ardor /ar'dor/ *m* heat; (*fig*) ardour; **com ~** ardently

árduo /'arduu/ *a* strenuous, arduous

área /'aria/ *f* area; **(grande) ~** penalty area; **~ (de serviço)** yard

arear /ari'ar/ *vt* scour <*panela*>

areia /a'reja/ *f* sand

arejar /are'ʒar/ *vt* air □ *vi*, **~-se** *vpr* get some air; (*descansar*) have a breather

are|na /a'rena/ *f* arena; **~noso** /o/ *a* sandy

arenque /a'rẽki/ *m* herring

argamassa /arga'masa/ *f* mortar

Argélia /ar'ʒɛlia/ *f* Algeria

argelino /arʒe'linu/ *a & m* Algerian

Argentina /arʒẽ'tʃina/ *f* Argentina

argentino /arʒẽ'tʃinu/ *a & m* Argentinian

argila /ar'ʒila/ *f* clay

argola /ar'gɔla/ *f* ring

argumen|tar /argumẽ'tar/ *vt/i* argue; **~to** *m* argument; (*de filme etc*) subject-matter

ariano /ari'anu/ *a & m* (*do signo Aries*) Arian

árido /'aridu/ *a* arid; barren <*deserto*>; (*fig*) dull, dry

Aries /'aris/ *f* Aries

arisco /a'risku/ *a* timid

aristo|cracia /aristokra'sia/ *f* aristocracy; **~crata** *m/f* aristocrat; **~crático** *a* aristocratic

aritmética /aritʃ'mɛtʃika/ *f* arithmetic

arma /'arma/ *f* weapon; *pl* arms; **~ de fogo** firearm

ar|mação /arma'sãw/ *f* frame; (*de óculos*) frames; (*naut*) rigging; **~madilha** *f* trap; **~madura** *f* suit of armour; (*armação*) framework; **~mar** *vt* (*dar armas a*) arm; (*montar*) put up, assemble; set up <*máquina*>; set, lay <*armadilha*>; fit out <*navio*>;hatch <*plano, complô*>; cause <*briga*>; **~mar-se** *vpr* arm o.s.

armarinho /arma'riɲu/ *m* haberdashery, (*Amer*) notions

armário /ar'mariu/ *m* cupboard; (*de roupa*) wardrobe

arma|zém /arma'zẽj/ *m* warehouse; (*loja*) general store; (*depósito*) storeroom; **~zenagem** *f*, **~zenamento** *m* storage; **~zenar** *vt* store

Armênia /ar'menia/ *f* Armenia

armênio /ar'meniu/ *a & m* Armenian

aro /'aru/ *m* (*de roda, óculos*) rim; (*de porta*) frame

aro|ma /a'roma/ *f* aroma; (*perfume*) fragrance; **~mático** *a* aromatic; fragrant

ar|pão /ar'pãw/ *m* harpoon; **~poar** *vt* harpoon

arquear /arki'ar/ *vt* arch; **~-se** *vpr* bend, bow

arque|ologia /arkiolo'ʒia/ *f* archaeology; **~ológico** *a* archaeological; **~ólogo** *m* archaeologist

arquétipo /ar'kɛtʃipu/ *m* archetype

arquibancada /arkibã'kada/ *f* terraces, (*Amer*) bleachers

arquipélago /arki'pɛlagu/ *m* archipelago

arquite|tar /arkite'tar/ *vt* think up; **~to** /ɛ/ *m* architect; **~tônico** *a* architectural; **~tura** *f* architecture

arqui|var /arki'var/ *vt* file <*papéis*>; shelve <*plano, processo*>; **~vista** *m/f* archivist; **~vo** *m* file; (*conjunto*) files; (*móvel*) filing cabinet; *pl* (*do Estado etc*) archives

arran|cada /axã'kada/ *f* lurch; (*de atleta, fig*) spurt; **~car** *vt* pull out <*cabelo etc*>; pull off <*botão etc*>; pull up <*erva daninha etc*>; take out <*dente*>; (*das mãos de alg*) wrench, snatch; extract <*confissão, dinheiro*> □ *vi* <*carro*> roar off; <*pessoa*> take off; (*dar solavanco*) lurch forward; **~car-se** *vpr* take off; **~co** *m* pull, tug; *veja* **~cada**

arranha-céu /axaɲa'sɛw/ *m* skyscraper

arra|nhadura /axaɲa'dura/ *f* scratch; **~nhão** *m* scratch; **~nhar** *vt* scratch; have a smattering of <*língua*>

arran|jar /axã'ʒar/ *vt* arrange; (*achar*) get, find; (*resolver*) settle, sort out; **~jar-se** *vpr* manage; **~jo** *m* arrangement

arrasar /axa'zar/ *vt* devastate; raze, flatten <*casa, cidade*>; **~-se** *vpr* be devastated

arrastar /axas'tar/ *vt* drag; <*corrente, avalancha*> sweep away; (*atrair*) draw □ *vi* trail; **~-se** *vpr* crawl; <*tempo*> drag; <*processo*> drag out

arreba|tador /axebata'dor/ *a* entrancing; shocking <*notícia*>; **~tar** *vt* (*enlevar*) entrance, send; (*chocar*) shock

arreben|tação /axebẽta'sãw/ *f* surf; **~tar** *vi* <*bomba*> explode; <*corda*> snap, break; <*balão, pessoa*> burst; <*onda*> break; <*guerra, incêndio*> break out □ *vt* snap, break <*corda*>; burst <*balão*>; break down <*porta*>

arrebitar /axebi'tar/ *vt* turn up <*nariz*>; prick up <*orelhas*>

arreca|dação /axekada'sãw/ *f* (*dinheiro*) tax revenue; **~dar** *vt* collect

arredar /axe'dar/ *vt* **não ~ pé** stand one's ground

arredio /axe'dʒiu/ *a* withdrawn

arredondar /axedõ'dar/ *vt* round up <*quantia*>; round off <*ângulo*>

arredores /axe'dɔris/ *m pl* surroundings; (*de cidade*) outskirts

arrefecer /axefe'ser/ *vt/i* cool

arregaçar /axega'sar/ *vt* roll up

arrega|lado /axega'ladu/ *a* <*olhos*> wide; **~lar** *vt* **~lar os olhos** be wide-eyed with amazement

arreganhar /axega'ɲar/ *vt* bare <*dentes*>; **~-se** *vpr* grin

arrema|tar /axema'tar/ *vt* finish off; (*no tricô*) cast off; **~te** *m* conclusion; (*na costura*) finishing off; (*no futebol*) finishing

arremes|sar /axeme'sar/ *vt* hurl; **~so** /e/ *m* throw

arrepen|der-se /axepẽ'dersi/ *vpr* be sorry; <*pecador*> repent; **~der-se de** regret; **~dido** *a* sorry; <*pecador*> repentant; **~dimento** *m* regret; (*de pecado, crime*) repentance

arrepi|ado /axepi'adu/ *a* <*cabelo*> standing on end; <*pele, pessoa*> covered in goose pimples; **~ar** *vt* (*dar calafrios*) make shudder; make stand on end <*cabelo*>; **me ~a (a pele)** it gives me goose pimples; **~ar-se** *vpr* (*estremecer*) shudder; <*cabelo*> stand on end; (*na pele*) get goose pimples; **~o** *m* shudder; **me dá ~os** it makes me shudder

arris|cado /axis'kadu/ *a* risky; **~car** *vt* risk; **~car-se** *vpr* take a risk, risk it; **~car-se a fazer** risk doing

arro|char /axo'ʃar/ *vt* tighten up □ *vi* be tough; **~cho** /o/ *m* squeeze

arro|gância /axo'gãsia/ *f* arrogance; **~gante** *a* arrogant

arro|jado /axo'ʒadu/ *a* bold; **~jar** *vt* throw

arrombar /axõ'bar/ *vt* break down <*porta*>; break into <*casa*>; crack <*cofre*>

arro|tar /axo'tar/ *vi* burp, belch; **~to** /o/ *m* burp

arroz /a'xoz/ *m* rice; **~ doce** rice pudding; **~al** (*pl* **~ais**) *m* rice field

arrua|ça /axu'asa/ *f* riot; **~ceiro** *m* rioter

arruela /axu'ɛla/ *f* washer

arruinar /axui'nar/ *vt* ruin; **~-se** *vpr* be ruined

arru|madeira /axuma'dera/ *f* (*de hotel*) chambermaid; **~mar** *vt* tidy (up) <*casa*>; sort out <*papéis, vida*>; pack <*mala*>; (*achar*) find, get; make up <*desculpa*>; (*vestir*) dress up; **~mar-se** *vpr* (*aprontar-se*) get ready; (*na vida*) sort o.s. out

arse|nal /arse'naw/ (*pl* **~nais**) *m* arsenal

arsênio /ar'seniu/ *m* arsenic

arte /'artʃi/ *f* art; **fazer ~** <*criança*> get up to mischief; **~fato** *m* product, article

arteiro /ar'teru/ *a* mischievous

artéria /ar'tɛria/ *f* artery

artesa|nal /arteza'naw/ (*pl* **~nais**) *a* craft; **~nato** *m* craftwork

arte|são /arte'zãw/ (*pl* **~s**) *m* (*f* **~sã**) artisan, craftsman (*f* -woman)

ártico /'artʃiku/ *a* & *m* arctic

articu|lação /artʃikula'sãw/ *f* articulation; (*anat, tecn*) joint; **~lar** *vt* articulate

arti|ficial /artʃifisi'aw/ (*pl* **~ficiais**) *a* artificial; **~fício** *m* trick

artigo /ar'tʃigu/ *m* article; (*com*) item

arti|lharia /artʃiʎa'ria/ *f* artillery; **~lheiro** *m* (*mil*) gunner; (*no futebol*) striker

artimanha /artʃi'maɲa/ *f* trick; (*método*) clever way

ar|tista /ar'tʃista/ *m/f* artist; **~tístico** *a* artistic

artrite /ar'tritʃi/ *f* arthritis

árvore /'arvori/ *f* tree

arvoredo /arvo'redu/ *m* grove

as /as/ *artigo & pron veja* **a**[1]

ás /as/ *m* ace

às = a² + as

asa /'aza/ *f* wing; (*de xícara*) handle; **~-delta** *f* hang-glider

ascen|dência /asẽ'dẽsia/ *f* ancestry; (*superioridade*) ascendancy; **~dente** *a* rising; **~der** *vi* rise; ascend <*ao trono*>; **~são** *f* rise; (*relig*) Ascension; em **~são** rising; (*fig*) up and coming; **~sor** *m* lift, (*Amer*) elevator; **~sorista** *m/f* lift operator

asco /'asku/ *m* revulsion, disgust; dar **~** be revolting

asfalto /as'fawtu/ *m* asphalt

asfixiar /asfiksi'ar/ *vt/i* asphyxiate

Asia /'azia/ *f* Asia

asiático /azi'atʃiku/ *a & m* Asian

asilo /a'zilu/ *m* (*refúgio*) asylum; (*de velhos, crianças*) home

as|ma /'azma/ *f* asthma; **~mático** *a & m* asthmatic

asneira /az'nera/ *f* stupidity; (*uma*) stupid thing

aspas /'aspas/ *f pl* inverted commas

aspargo /as'pargu/ *m* asparagus

aspecto /as'pɛktu/ *m* appearance, look; (*de um problema*) aspect

aspereza /aspe'reza/ *f* roughness; (*do clima, de um som*) harshness; (*fig*) rudeness

áspero /'asperu/ *a* rough; <*clima, som*> harsh; (*fig*) rude

aspi|ração /aspira'sãw/ *f* aspiration; (*med*) inhalation; **~rador** *m* vacuum cleaner; **~rar** *vt* inhale, breathe in <*ar, fumaça*>; suck up <*líquido*>; **~rar a** aspire to

aspirina /aspi'rina/ *f* aspirin

asqueroso /aske'rozu/ *a* revolting, disgusting

assa|do /a'sadu/ *a & m* roast; **~dura** *f* (*na pele*) sore patch

assalariado /asalari'adu/ *a* salaried □ *m* salaried worker

assal|tante /asaw'tãtʃi/ *m* robber; (*na rua*) mugger; (*de casa*) burglar; **~tar** *vt* rob; burgle, (*Amer*) burglarize <*casa*>; **~to** *m* (*roubo*) robbery; (*a uma casa*) burglary; (*ataque*) assault; (*no boxe*) round

assanhado /asa'ɲadu/ *a* worked up; <*criança*> excitable; (*erótico*) amorous

assar /a'sar/ *vt* roast

assassi|nar /asasi'nar/ *vt* murder; (*pol*) assassinate; **~nato** *m* murder; (*pol*) assassination; **~no** *m* murderer; (*pol*) assassin

asseado /asi'adu/ *a* well-groomed

as|sediar /asedʒi'ar/ *vt* besiege <*cidade*>; (*fig*) pester; **~sédio** *m* siege; (*fig*) pestering

assegurar /asegu'rar/ *vt* (*tornar seguro*) secure; (*afirmar*) guarantee; **~ a alg aco/que** assure s.o. of sth/that; **~-se de/que** make sure of/that

assembléia /asẽ'blɛja/ *f* (*pol*) assembly; (*com*) meeting

assemelhar /aseme'ʎar/ *vt* liken; **~-se** *vpr* be alike; **~-se a** resemble, be like

assen|tar /asẽ'tar/ *vt* (*estabelecer*) establish, define; settle <*povo*>; lay <*tijolo*> □ *vi* <*pó*> settle; **~tar-se** *vpr* settle down; **~tar com** go with; **~tar a** <*roupa*> suit; **~to** *m* seat; (*fig*) basis; **tomar ~to** take a seat; <*pó*> settle

assen|tir /asẽ'tʃir/ *vi* agree; **~timento** *m* agreement

assessor /ase'sor/ *m* adviser; **~ar** *vt* advise

assexuado /aseksu'adu/ *a* asexual

assiduidade /asidui'dadʒi/ *f* (*à escola*) regular attendance; (*diligência*) diligence

assíduo /a'siduu/ *a* (*que freqüenta*) regular; (*diligente*) assiduous

assim /a'sĩ/ *adv* like this, like that; (*portanto*) therefore; **e ~ por diante** and so on; **~ como** as well as; **~ que** as soon as

assimétrico /asi'mɛtriku/ *a* asymmetrical

assimilar /asimi'lar/ *vt* assimilate; **~-se** *vpr* be assimilated

assinalar /asina'lar/ *vt* (*marcar*) mark; (*distinguir*) distinguish; (*apontar*) point out

assi|nante /asi'nãtʃi/ *m/f* subscriber; **~nar** *vt/i* sign; **~natura** *f* (*nome*) signature; (*de revista*) subscription

assis|tência /asis'tẽsia/ *f* assistance; (*presença*) attendance; (*público*) audience; **~tente** *a* assistant □ *m/f* assistant; **~tente social** social worker; **~tir (a)** *vt/i* (*ver*) watch; (*presenciar*) attend; assist <*doente*>

assoalho /aso'aʎu/ *m* floor

assoar /aso'ar/ *vt* **~ o nariz**, (*Port*) **~-se** blow one's nose

assobi|ar /asobi'ar/ *vt/i* whistle; **~o** *m* whistle

associ|ação /asosia'sãw/ *f* association; **~ado** *a & m* associate; **~ar** *vt* associate (**a** with); **~ar-se** *vpr* associate; (*com*) go into partnership (**a** with)

assolar /aso'lar/ *vt* devastate

assom|bração /asõbra'sãw/ *f* ghost; **~brar** *vt* astonish, amaze; **~brar-se** *vpr* be amazed; **~bro** *m* amazement, astonishment; (*coisa*) marvel; **~broso** /o/ *a* astonishing, amazing

assoprar /aso'prar/ *vi* blow □ *vt* blow; blow out <*vela*>

assovi- *veja* **assobi-**

assu|mido /asu'midu/ *a* (*confesso*) confirmed, self-confessed; **~mir** *vt* assume, take on; accept, admit <*defeito*> □ *vi* take office

assunto /a'sũtu/ *m* subject; (*negócio*) matter

assus|tador /asusta'dor/ *a* frightening; **~tar** *vt* frighten, scare; **~tar-se** *vpr* get frightened, get scared

asterisco /aste'risku/ *m* asterisk

as|tral /as'traw/ (*pl* **~trais**) *m* (*fam*) state of mind; **~tro** *m* star; **~trologia** *f* astrology; **~trólogo** *m* astrologer; **~tronauta** *m/f* astronaut; **~tronave** *f* spaceship; **~tronomia** *f* astronomy; **~tronômico** *a* astronomical; **~trônomo** *m* astronomer

as|túcia /as'tusia/ *f* cunning; **~tuto** *a* cunning; <*comerciante*> astute

ata /'ata/ *f* minutes

ataca|dista /ataka'dʒista/ *m/f* wholesaler; **~do** *m* **por ~do** wholesale

ata|cante /ata'kãtʃi/ *a* attacking □ *m/f* attacker; **~car** *vt* attack; tackle <*problema*>

atadura /ata'dura/ *f* bandage

ata|lhar /ata'ʎar/ *vi* take a shortcut; **~lho** *m* shortcut

ataque /a'taki/ *m* attack; (*de raiva, riso*) fit

atar /a'tar/ *vt* tie

atarantado /atarã'tadu/ *a* flustered, in a flap

atarefado /atare'fadu/ *a* busy

atarracado /ataxa'kadu/ *a* stocky

atarraxar /ataxa'ʃar/ *vt* screw

até /a'tɛ/ *prep* (up) to, as far as; (*tempo*) until □ *adv* even; **~ logo** goodbye; **~ que** until

atéia /a'tɛja/ *a & f veja* **ateu**

ateliê /ateli'e/ *m* studio

atemorizar /atemori'zar/ *vt* frighten

Atenas /a'tenas/ *f* Athens

aten|ção /atẽ'sãw/ *f* attention; *pl* (*bondade*) thoughtfulness; **com ~ção** attentively; **~cioso** *a* thoughtful, considerate

aten|der /atẽ'der/ **~der (a)** *vt/i* answer <*telefone, porta*>; answer to <*nome*>; serve <*freguês*>; see <*paciente, visitante*>; grant, meet <*pedido*>; heed <*conselho*>; **~dimento** *m* service; (*de médico etc*) consultation

aten|tado /atẽ'tadu/ *m* murder attempt; (*pol*) assassination attempt; (*ataque*) attack (**contra** on); **~tar** *vi* **~tar contra** make an attempt on

atento /a'tẽtu/ *a* attentive; **~ a** mindful of

aterrador /atexa'dor/ *a* terrifying

ater|ragem /ate'xaʒẽ/ *f* (*Port*) landing; **~rar** *vi* (*Port*) land

aterris|sagem /atexi'saʒẽ/ *f* landing; **~sar** *vi* land

ater-se /a'tersi/ *vpr* **~ a** keep to, go by

ates|tado /ates'tadu/ *m* certificate; **~tar** *vt* attest (to)

ateu /a'tew/ *a & m* (*f* **atéia**) atheist

atiçar /atʃi'sar/ *vt* poke <*fogo*>; stir up <*ódio, discórdia*>; arouse <*pessoa*>

atinar /atʃi'nar/ *vt* work out, guess; **~ com** find; **~ em** notice

atingir /atʃĩ'ʒir/ *vt* reach; hit <*alvo*>; (*conseguir*) attain; (*afetar*) affect

atirar /atʃi'rar/ *vt* throw □ *vi* shoot; **~ em** fire at

atitude /atʃi'tudʒi/ *f* attitude; **tomar uma ~** take action

ati|va /a'tʃiva/ *f* active service; **~var** *vt* activate; **~vidade** *f* activity; **~vo** *a* active □ *m* (*com*) assets

Atlântico /at'lãtʃiku/ *m* Atlantic

atlas /'atlas/ *m* atlas

at|leta /at'lɛta/ *m/f* athlete; **~lético** *a* athletic; **~letismo** *m* athletics

atmosfera /atʃimos'fɛra/ *f* atmosphere

ato /'atu/ *m* act; (*ação*) action; **no ~** on the spot

ato|lar /ato'lar/ *vt* bog down; **~lar-se** *vpr* get bogged down; **~leiro** *m* bog; (*fig*) fix, spot of trouble

atômico /a'tomiku/ *a* atomic

atomizador /atomiza'dor/ *m* atomizer spray

átomo /'atomu/ *m* atom

atônito /a'tonitu/ *a* astonished, stunned

ator /a'tor/ *m* actor

atordoar /atordo'ar/ *vt* <*golpe, notícia*> stun; <*som*> deafen; (*alucinar*) bewilder

atormentar /atormẽ'tar/ *vt* plague, torment

atração /atra'sãw/ *f* attraction

atracar /atra'kar/ *vt/i* (*naut*) moor; **~-se** *vpr* grapple; (*fam*) neck

atractivo (*Port*) *veja* **atrativo**

atraente /atra'ẽtʃi/ *a* attractive

atraiçoar /atrajso'ar/ *vt* betray

atrair /atra'ir/ *vt* attract

atrapalhar /atrapa'ʎar/ *vt/i* (*confundir*) confuse; (*estorvar*) hinder; (*perturbar*) disturb; **~-se** *vpr* get mixed up

atrás /a'traʃ/ *adv* behind; (*no fundo*) at the back; **~ de** behind; (*depois de, no encalço de*) after; **um mês ~** a month ago; **ficar ~** be left behind

atra|sado /atra'zadu/ *a* late; <*país, criança*> backward; <*relógio*> slow; <*pagamento*> overdue; <*idéias*> old-fashioned; **~sar** *vt* delay; put back <*relógio*> □ *vi* be late; <*relógio*> lose; **~sar-se** *vpr* be late; (*num trabalho*) get behind; (*no pagar*) get into arrears; **~so** *m* delay; (*de país etc*) backwardness; *pl* (*com*) arrears; **com ~so** late

atrativo /atra'tʃivu/ *m* attraction

através /atra'vɛs/ ~ **de** *prep* through; (*de um lado ao outro*) across

atravessado /atrave'sadu/ *a* <*espinha*> stuck; **estar com alg ~ na garganta** be fed up with s.o.

atravessar /atrave'sar/ *vt* go through; cross <*rua, rio*>

atre|ver-se /atre'versi/ *vpr* dare; **~ver-se a** dare to; **~vido** *a* daring; (*insolente*) impudent; **~vimento** *m* daring, boldness; (*insolência*) impudence

atribu|ir /atribu'ir/ *vt* attribute (a to); confer <*prêmio, poderes*> (a on); attach <*importância*> (a to); **~to** *m* attribute

atrito /a'tritu/ *m* friction; (*desavença*) disagreement

atriz /a'tris/ *f* actress

atrocidade /atrosi'dadʒi/ *f* atrocity

atrope|lar /atrope'lar/ *vt* run over, knock down <*pedestre*>; (*empurrar*) jostle; mix up <*palavras*>; **~lamento** *m* (*de pedestre*) running over; **~lo** /e/ *m* scramble

atroz /a'tros/ *a* awful, terrible; heinous <*crime*>; cruel <*pessoa*>

atuação /atua'sãw/ *f* (*ação*) action; (*desempenho*) performance

atu|al /atu'aw/ (*pl* **~ais**) *a* current, present; <*assunto, interesse*> topical; <*pessoa, carro*> up-to-date; **~alidade** *f* (*presente*) present (time); (*de um livro*) topicality; *pl* current affairs; **~alizado** *a* up-to-date; **~alizar** *vt* update; **~alizar-se** *vpr* bring o.s. up to date; **~almente** *adv* at present, currently

atum /a'tũ/ *m* tuna

aturdir /atur'dʒir/ *vt veja* atordoar

audácia /aw'dasia/ *f* boldness; (*insolência*) audacity

audi|ção /awdʒi'sãw/ *f* hearing; (*concerto*) recital; **~ência** *f* audience; (*jurid*) hearing

audiovisu|al /awdʒiovizu'aw/ (*pl* **~ais**) *a* audiovisual

auditório /awdʒi'tɔriu/ *m* auditorium; **programa de ~** variety show

auge /'awʒi/ *m* peak, height

aula /'awla/ *f* class, lesson; **dar ~** teach

aumen|tar /awmẽ'tar/ *vt* increase; raise <*preço, salário*>; extend <*casa*>; (*com lente*) magnify; (*acrescentar*) add □ *vi* increase; <*preço, salário*> go up; **~to** *m* increase; (*de salário*) rise, (*Amer*) raise

au|sência /aw'zẽsia/ *f* absence; **~sente** *a* absent □ *m/f* absentee

aus|pícios /aws'pisius/ *m pl* auspices; **~picioso** /o/ *a* auspicious

auste|ridade /awsteri'dadʒi/ *f* austerity; **~ro** /ɛ/ *a* austere

Austrália /aw'stralia/ *f* Australia

australiano /awstrali'anu/ *a & m* Australian

Austria /'awstria/ *f* Austria

austríaco /aws'triaku/ *a & m* Austrian

autarquia /awtar'kia/ *f* public authority

autêntico /aw'tẽtʃiku/ *a* authentic; genuine <*pessoa*>; true <*fato*>

autobio|grafia /awtobiogra'fia/ *f* autobiography; **~gráfico** *a* autobiographical

autocarro /awto'kaxu/ *m* (*Port*) bus

autocrata /awto'krata/ *a* autocratic

autodefesa /awtode'feza/ *f* self-defence

autodidata /awtodʒi'data/ *a & m/f* self-taught (person)

autódromo /aw'tɔdromu/ *m* race track

auto-escola /awtois'kɔla/ *f* driving school

auto-estrada /awtois'trada/ *f* motorway, (*Amer*) expressway

autógrafo /aw'tɔgrafu/ *m* autograph

auto|mação /awtoma'sãw/ *f* automation; **~mático** *a* automatic; **~matizar** *vt* automate

auto|mobilismo /awtomobi'lizmu/ *m* motoring; (*esporte*) motor racing; **~móvel** (*pl* **~móveis**) *m* motor car, (*Amer*) automobile

au|tonomia /awtono'mia/ *f* autonomy; **~tônomo** *a* autonomous; <*trabalhador*> selfemployed

autopeça /awto'pɛsa/ *f* car spare

autópsia /aw'tɔpsia/ *f* autopsy

autor /aw'tor/ *m* (*f* **~a**) author; (*de crime*) perpetrator; (*jurid*) plaintiff

auto-retrato /awtoxe'tratu/ *m* self-portrait

autoria /awto'ria/ *f* authorship; (*de crime*) responsibility (de for)

autori|dade /awtori'dadʒi/ *f* authority; **~zação** *f* authorization; **~zar** *vt* authorize

autuar /awtu'ar/ *vt* sue

au|xiliar /awsili'ar/ *a* auxiliary □ *m/f* assistant □ *vt* assist; **~xílio** *m* assistance, aid

aval /a'vaw/ (*pl* **avais**) *m* endorsement; (*com*) guarantee

avali|ação /avalia'sãw/ *f* (*de preço*) valuation; (*fig*) evaluation; **~ar** *vt* value <*quadro etc*> (em at); assess <*danos, riscos*>; (*fig*) evaluate

avan|çar /avã'sar/ *vt* move forward □ *vi* move forward; (*mil, fig*) advance; **~çar a** (*montar*) amount to; **~ço** *m* advance

avar|eza /ava'reza/ *f* meanness; **~ento** *a* mean

ava|ria /ava'ria/ *f* damage; (*de máquina*) breakdown; **~riado** *a* damaged; <*máquina*> out of order; <*carro*> broken down; **~riar** *vt* damage □ *vi* be damaged; <*máquina*> break down

ave /'avi/ *f* bird; **~ de rapina** bird of prey

aveia /a'veja/ *f* oats

avelã /ave'lã/ *f* hazelnut

avenida /ave'nida/ *f* avenue

aven|tal /avẽ'taw/ (*pl* **~tais**) *m* apron

aventu|ra /avẽ'tura/ *f* adventure; (*amorosa*) fling; **~rar** *vt* venture; **~rar-se** *vpr* venture (a to); **~reiro** *a* adventurous □ *m* adventurer

averiguar /averi'gwar/ *vt* check (out)

avermelhado /averme'ʎadu/ *a* reddish

aver|são /aver'sãw/ *f* aversion; **~so** *a* averse (a to)

aves|sas /a'vɛsas/ **às ~sas** the wrong way round; (*de cabeça para baixo*) upside down; **~so** /e/ *m* **ao ~so** inside out

avestruz /aves'trus/ *m* ostrich

avi|ação /avia'sãw/ *f* aviation; **~ão** *m* (aero)plane, (*Amer*) (air)plane; **~ão a jato** jet

avi|dez /avi'des/ *f* (*cobiça*) greediness; **~do** *a* greedy

avi|sar /avi'zar/ *vt* (*informar*) tell, let know; (*advertir*) warn; **~so** *m* notice; (*advertência*) warning

avistar /avis'tar/ *vt* catch sight of

avo /'avu/ *m* **um doze ~s** one twelfth

avó /a'vɔ/ *f* grandmother; **~s** *m pl* grandparents

avô /a'vo/ *m* grandfather

avoado /avo'adu/ *a* dizzy, scatterbrained

avulso /a'vuwsu/ *a* loose, odd

avultado /avuw'tadu/ *a* bulky

axila /ak'sila/ *f* armpit

azaléia /aza'lɛja/ *f* azalea

azar /a'zar/ *m* bad luck; **ter ~** be unlucky; **~ado**, **~ento** *a* unlucky

aze|dar /aze'dar/ *vt* sour □ *vi* go sour; **~do** /e/ *a* sour

azei|te /a'zejtʃi/ *m* oil; **~tona** /o/ *f* olive

azevinho /aze'viɲu/ *m* holly

azia /a'zia/ *f* heartburn

azucrinar /azukri'nar/ *vt* annoy

azul /a'zuw/ (*pl* **azuis**) *a* blue

azulejo /azu'leʒu/ *m* (ceramic) tile

azul-marinho /azuwma'riɲu/ *a invar* navy blue

B

babá /ba'ba/ *f* nanny; **~ eletrônica** baby alarm

ba|bado /ba'badu/ *m* frill; **~bador** *m* bib; **~bar** *vt/i*, **~bar-se** *vpr* drool (por over); <*bebê*> dribble; **~beiro** (*Port*) *m* bib

baby-sitter /bejbi'siter/ (*pl* **~s**) *m/f* babysitter

bacalhau /baka'ʎaw/ *m* cod

bacana /ba'kana/ (*fam*) *a* great

bacha|rel /baʃa'rɛw/ (*pl* **~réis**) bachelor; **~relado** *m* bachelor's degree; **~relar-se** *vpr* graduate

bacia /ba'sia/ *f* basin; (*da privada*) bowl; (*anat*) pelvis

baço /'basu/ *m* spleen

bacon /'bejkõ/ *m* bacon

bactéria /bak'tɛria/ *f* bacterium; *pl* bacteria

bada|lado /bada'ladu/ *a* (*fam*) talked about; **~lar** *vt* ring <*sino*> □ *vi* ring; (*fam*) go out and about; **~lativo** (*fam*) *a* fun-loving, gadabout

badejo /ba'dɛʒu/ *m* sea bass

baderna /ba'dɛrna/ *f* (*tumulto*) commotion; (*desordem*) mess

badulaque /badu'laki/ *m* trinket

bafafá /bafa'fa/ (*fam*) *m* to-do, kerfuffle

ba|fo /'bafu/ *m* bad breath; **~fômetro** *m* Breathalyser; **~forada** *f* puff

bagaço /ba'gasu/ *m* pulp; (*Port: aguardente*) brandy

baga|geiro /baga'ʒeru/ *m* (*de carro*) roofrack; (*Port: homem*) porter; **~gem** *f* luggage; (*cultural etc*) baggage

bagatela /baga'tɛla/ *f* trifle

Bagdá /bagi'da/ *f* Baghdad

bago /'bagu/ *m* berry; (*de chumbo*) pellet

bagulho /ba'guʎu/ *m* piece of junk; *pl* junk; **ele é um ~** he's as ugly as sin

bagun|ça /ba'gũsa/ *f* mess; **~çar** *vt* mess up; **~ceiro** *a* messy □ *m* messer

baía /ba'ia/ *f* bay

baiano /ba'janu/ *a & m* Bahian

baila /'bajla/ *f* **trazer/vir à ~** bring/come up

bai|lar /baj'lar/ *vt/i* dance; **~larino** *m* ballet dancer; **~le** *m* dance; (*de gala*) ball

bainha /ba'iɲa/ *f* (*de vestido*) hem; (*de arma*) sheath

baioneta /bajo'neta/ *f* bayonet

bairro /'bajxu/ *m* neighbourhood, area

baixa /'baʃa/ *f* drop, fall; (*de guerra*) casualty; (*dispensa*) discharge; **~-mar** *f* low tide

baixar /ba'ʃar/ *vt* lower; issue <*ordem*>; pass <*lei*> □ *vi* drop, fall; (*fam: pintar*) turn up

baixaria /baʃa'ria/ *f* sordidness; (*uma*) sordid thing

baixela /ba'ʃɛla/ *f* set of cutlery

baixeza /ba'ʃeza/ *f* baseness

baixo /'baʃu/ *a* low; <*pessoa*> short; <*som, voz*> quiet, soft; <*cabeça, olhos*> lowered; (*vil*) sordid □ *adv* low; <*falar*> softly, quietly □ *m* bass; **em ~** underneath; (*em casa*) downstairs; **em ~ de** under; **para ~** down; (*em casa*) downstairs; **por ~ de** under(neath)

baju|lador /baʒula'dor/ *a* obsequious □ *m* sycophant; **~lar** *vt* fawn on

bala /'bala/ *f* (*de revólver*) bullet; (*doce*) sweet

balada /ba'lada/ *f* ballad

balaio /ba'laju/ *m* linen basket

balan|ça /ba'lãsa/ *f* scales; **Balança** (*signo*) Libra; **~ça de pagamentos** balance of payments; **~çar** *vt/i* (*no ar*) swing; (*numa cadeira etc*) rock; <*carro, avião*> shake; <*navio*> roll; **~çar-se** *vpr* swing; **~cete** /e/ *m* trial balance; **~ço** *m* (*com*) balance sheet; (*brinquedo*) swing; (*movimento no ar*) swinging; (*de carro, avião*) shaking; (*de navio*) rolling; (*de cadeira*) rocking; **fazer um ~ço de** (*fig*) take stock of

balangandã /balãgã'dã/ *m* bauble

balão /ba'lãw/ *m* balloon; **soltar um ~-de-ensaio** (*fig*) put out feelers

balar /ba'lar/ *vi* bleat

balbu|ciar /bawbusi'ar/ *vt/i* babble; **~cio** *m* babble, babbling

balbúrdia /baw'burdʒia/ *f* hubbub

bal|cão /baw'kãw/ *m* (*em loja*) counter; (*de informações, bilhetes*) desk; (*de cozinha*) worktop, (*Amer*) counter; (*no teatro*) circle; **~conista** *m/f* shop assistant

balde /'bawdʒi/ *m* bucket

baldeação /bawdʒia'sãw/ *f* **fazer ~** change (trains)

baldio /baw'dʒiu/ *a* fallow; **terreno ~** (piece of) waste ground

balé /ba'lɛ/ *m* ballet

balear /bali'ar/ *vt* shoot

baleia /ba'leja/ *f* whale

balido /ba'lidu/ *m* bleat, bleating

balísti|ca /ba'listʃika/ *f* ballistics; **~co** *a* ballistic

bali|za /ba'liza/ *f* marker; (*luminosa*) beacon; **~zar** *vt* mark out

balneário /bawni'ariu/ *m* seaside resort

balofo /ba'lofu/ *a* fat, tubby

baloiço, balouço /ba'lojsu, ba'losu/ (*Port*) *m* (*de criança*) swing

balsa /'bawsa/ *f* (*de madeira etc*) raft; (*que vai e vem*) ferry

bálsamo /'bawsamu/ *m* balm

báltico /'bawtʃiku/ *a* & *m* Baltic

baluarte /balu'artʃi/ *m* bulwark

bambo /'bãbu/ *a* loose, slack; <*pernas*> limp; <*mesa*> wobbly

bambo|lê /bãbo'le/ *m* hula hoop; **~lear** *vi* <*pessoa*> sway, totter; <*coisa*> wobble

bambu /bã'bu/ *m* bamboo

ba|nal /ba'naw/ (*pl* **~nais**) *a* banal; **~nalidade** *f* banality

bana|na /ba'nana/ *f* banana □ (*fam*) *m/f* wimp; **~nada** *f* banana fudge; **~neira** *f* banana tree; **plantar ~neira** do a handstand

banca /'bãka/ *f* (*de trabalho*) bench; (*de jornais*) newsstand; **~ examinadora** examining board; **~da** *f* (*pol*) bench

bancar /bã'kar/ *vt* (*custear*) finance; (*fazer papel de*) play; (*fingir*) pretend

bancário /bã'kariu/ *a* bank □ *m* bank employee

bancarrota /bãka'xota/ *f* bankruptcy; **ir à ~** go bankrupt

banco /'bãku/ *m* (*com*) bank; (*no parque*) bench; (*na cozinha, num bar*) stool; (*de bicicleta*) saddle; (*de carro*) seat; **~ de areia** sandbank; **~ de dados** database

banda /'bãda/ *f* band; (*lado*) side; **de ~** sideways on; **nestas ~s** in these parts; **~ desenhada** (*Port*) cartoon

bandei|ra /bã'dera/ *f* flag; (*divisa*) banner; **dar ~ra** (*fam*) give o.s. away; **~rante** *m/f* pioneer □ *f* girl guide; **~rinha** *m* linesman

bandeja /bã'deʒa/ *f* tray

bandido /bã'dʒidu/ *m* bandit

bando /'bãdu/ *m* (*de pessoas*) band; (*de pássaros*) flock

bandolim /bãdo'lĩ/ *m* mandolin

bangalô /bãga'lo/ *m* bungalow

Bangcoc /bã'koki/ *f* Bangkok

bangue-bangue /bãgi'bãgi/ (*fam*) *m* western

banguela /bã'gɛla/ *a* toothless

banha /'baɲa/ *f* lard; *pl* (*no corpo*) flab

banhar /ba'ɲar/ *vt* (*molhar*) bathe; (*lavar*) bath; **~-se** *vpr* bathe

banhei|ra /ba'ɲera/ *f* bath, (*Amer*) bathtub; **~ro** *m* bathroom; (*Port*) lifeguard

banhista /ba'ɲista/ *m/f* bather

banho /'baɲu/ *m* bath; (*no mar*) bathe, dip; **tomar ~** have a bath; (*no chuveiro*) have a shower; **tomar um ~ de loja/cultura** go on a shopping/cultural spree; **~ de espuma** bubble bath; **~ de sol** sunbathing; **~-maria** (*pl* **~s-maria**) *m* bain marie

ba|nimento /bani'mẽtu/ *m* banishment; **~nir** *vt* banish

banjo /'bãʒu/ *m* banjo

banqueiro /bã'keru/ *m* banker

banqueta /bã'keta/ *f* foot-stool

banque|te /bã'ketʃi/ *m* banquet; **~teiro** *m* caterer

banzé /bã'zɛ/ (*fam*) *m* commotion, uproar

bapt- (*Port*) *veja* **bat-**

baque /'baki/ *m* thud, crash; (*revés*) blow; **~ar** *vi* topple over □ *vt* hit hard, knock for six

bar /bar/ *m* bar

barafunda /bara'fũda/ *f* jumble; (*barulho*) racket

bara|lhada /bara'ʎada/ *f* jumble; **~lho** *m* pack of cards, (*Amer*) deck of cards

barão /ba'rãw/ *m* baron

barata /ba'rata/ *f* cockroach

bara|tear /baratʃi'ar/ *vt* cheapen; **~teiro** *a* cheap

baratinar /baratʃi'nar/ *vt* fluster; (*transtornar*) rattle, shake up

barato /ba'ratu/ *a* cheap □ *adv* cheaply □ (*fam*) *m* **um ~** great; **que ~!** that's brilliant!

barba /'barba/ *f* beard; *pl* (*de gato etc*) whiskers; **fazer a ~** shave; **~da** *f* walkover; (*cavalo*) favourite; **~do** *a* bearded

barbante /bar'bãtʃi/ *m* string

bar|baridade /barbari'dadʒi/ *f* barbarity; (*fam: muito dinheiro*) fortune; **~bárie** *f*, **~barismo** *m* barbarism

bárbaro /'barbaru/ *m* barbarian □ *a* barbaric; (*fam: forte, bom*) terrific

barbatana /barba'tana/ *f* fin

bar|beador /barbia'dor/ *m* shaver; **~bear** *vt* shave; **~bear-se** *vpr* shave; **~bearia** *f* barber's shop; **~beiragem** (*fam*) *f* bit of bad driving; **~beiro** *m* barber; (*fam: motorista*) bad driver

bar|ca /'barka/ *f* barge; (*balsa*) ferry; **~caça** *f* barge; **~co** *m* boat; **~co a motor** motorboat; **~co a remo/vela** rowing/sailing boat, (*Amer*) rowboat/sailboat

barga|nha /bar'gaɲa/ *f* bargain; **~nhar** *vt/i* bargain

barítono /ba'ritonu/ *m* baritone

barômetro /ba'rometru/ *m* barometer

baronesa /baro'neza/ *f* baroness

barra /'baxa/ *f* bar; (*sinal gráfico*) slash, stroke; (*fam: situação*) situation; **segurar a ~** hold out; **forçar a ~** force the issue

barra|ca /ba'xaka/ *f* (*de acampar*) tent; (*na feira*) stall; (*casinha*) hut; (*guarda-sol*) sunshade; **~cão** *m* shed; **~co** *m* shack, shanty

barragem /ba'xaʒẽ/ *f* (*represa*) dam

barra-pesada /baxape'zada/ (*fam*) *a invar* <*bairro*> rough; <*pessoa*> shady; (*difícil*) tough

bar|rar /ba'xar/ *vt* bar; **~reira** *f* barrier; (*em corrida*) hurdle; (*em futebol*) wall

barrento /ba'xẽtu/ *a* muddy

barricada /baxi'kada/ *f* barricade

barri|ga /ba'xiga/ *f* stomach, (*Amer*) belly; **~ga da perna** calf; **~gudo** *a* pot-bellied

bar|ril /ba'xiw/ (*pl* **~ris**) *m* barrel

barro /'baxu/ *m* (*argila*) clay; (*lama*) mud

barroco /ba'xoku/ *a* & *m* baroque

barrote /ba'xɔtʃi/ *m* beam, joist

baru|lheira /baru'ʎera/ *f* racket, din; **~lhento** *a* noisy; **~lho** *m* noise

base /'bazi/ *f* base; (*fig: fundamento*) basis; **com ~ em** on the basis of; **na ~ de** based on; **~ado** *a* based; (*firme*) well-founded □ (*fam*) *m* joint; **~ar** *vt* base; **~ar-se em** be based on

básico /'baziku/ *a* basic

basquete /bas'kɛtʃi/ *m*, **basquetebol** /basketʃi'bɔw/ *m* basketball

bas|ta /'basta/ *m* **dar um ~ta em** call a halt to; **~tante** *a* (*muito*) quite a lot of; (*suficiente*) enough □ *adv* (*com adjetivo, advérbio*) quite; (*com verbo*) quite a lot; (*suficientemente*) enough

bastão /bas'tãw/ *m* stick; (*num revezamento, de comando*) baton

bastar /bas'tar/ *vi* be enough

bastidores /bastʃi'doris/ *m pl* (*no teatro*) wings; **nos ~** (*fig*) behind the scenes

bata /'bata/ *f* (*de mulher*) smock; (*de médico etc*) overall

bata|lha /ba'taʎa/ *f* battle; **~lhador** *a* plucky, feisty □ *m* fighter; **~lhão** *m* battalion; **~lhar** *vi* battle; (*esforçar-se*) fight hard □ *vt* fight hard to get

batata /ba'tata/ *f* potato; **~ doce** sweet potato; **~ frita** chips, (*Amer*) French fries; (*salgadinhos*) crisps, (*Amer*) potato chips

bate-boca /batʃi'boka/ *m* row, argument

bate|deira /bate'dera/ *f* whisk; (*de manteiga*) churn; **~dor** *m* (*policial etc*) outrider; (*no criquete*) batsman; (*no beisebol*) batter; (*de caça*) beater; **~dor de carteiras** pickpocket

batelada /bate'lada/ *f* batch; **~s de** heaps of

batente /ba'tẽtʃi/ *m* (*de porta*) doorway; **para o/no ~** (*fam: ao trabalho*) to/at work

bate-papo /batʃi'papu/ *m* chat.

bater /ba'ter/ *vt* beat; stamp <*pé*>; slam <*porta*>; strike <*horas*>; take <*foto*>; flap <*asas*>; (*datilografar*) type; (*lavar*) wash; (*usar muito*) wear a lot <*roupa*>; (*fam*) pinch <*carteira*> □ *vi* <*coração*> beat; <*porta*> slam; <*janela*> bang; <*horas*> strike; <*sino*> ring; (*à porta*) knock; (*com o carro*) crash; **~-se** *vpr* (*lutar*) fight; **~ à máquina** type; **~ à**

ou na porta knock at the door; ~ em hit; harp on <*assunto*>; <*luz, sol*> shine on; ~ com o carro crash one's car, have a crash; ~ com a cabeça bang one's head; ele batia os dentes de frio his teeth were chattering with cold; ele não bate bem (*fam*) he's not all there

bate|ria /bate'ria/ *f* (*eletr*) battery; (*mus*) drums; ~ria de cozinha kitchen utensils; ~rista *m/f* drummer

bati|da /ba'tʃida/ *f* beat; (*à porta*) knock; (*no carro*) crash; (*policial*) raid; (*bebida*) cocktail of rum, sugar and fruit juice; ~do *a* beaten; <*roupa*> well worn; <*assunto*> hackneyed □ *m* ~do de leite (*Port*) milkshake

batina /ba'tʃina/ *f* cassock

ba|tismo /ba'tʃizmu/ *m* baptism; ~tizado *m* christening; ~tizar *vt* baptize; (*pôr nome*) christen

batom /ba'tõ/ *m* lipstick

batu|cada /batu'kada/ *f* samba percussion group; ~car *vt/i* drum in a samba rhythm; ~que *m* samba rhythm

batuta /ba'tuta/ *f* baton; sob a ~ de under the direction of

baú /ba'u/ *m* trunk

baunilha /baw'niʎa/ *f* vanilla

bazar /ba'zar/ *m* bazaar; (*loja*) stationery and haberdashery shop

bê-a-bá /bea'ba/ *m* ABC

bea|titude /beatʃi'tudʒi/ *f* (*felicidade*) bliss; (*devoção*) piety, devoutness; ~to *a* (*devoto*) pious, devout; (*feliz*) blissful

bêbado /'bebadu/ *a & m* drunk

bebê /be'be/ *m* baby; ~ de proveta test-tube baby

bebe|deira /bebe'dera/ *f* (*estado*) drunkenness; (*ato*) drinking bout; ~dor *m* drinker; ~douro *m* drinking fountain

beber /be'ber/ *vt/i* drink

bebericar /beberi'kar/ *vt/i* sip

bebida /be'bida/ *f* drink

beca /'bɛka/ *f* gown

beça /'bɛsa/ *f* à ~ (*fam*) (*com substantivo*) loads of; (*com adjetivo*) really; (*com verbo*) a lot

beco /'beku/ *m* alley; ~ sem saída dead end

bedelho /be'deʎu/ *m* meter o ~ (em) stick one's oar in(to)

bege /'bɛʒi/ *a invar* beige

bei|cinho /bej'siɲu/ *m* fazer ~cinho pout; ~ço *m* lip; ~çudo *a* thick-lipped

beija-flor /bejʒa'flor/ *m* hummingbird

bei|jar /be'ʒar/ *vt* kiss; ~jo *m* kiss; ~joca /ɔ/ *f* peck

bei|ra /'bera/ *f* edge; (*fig: do desastre etc*) verge, brink; à ~ra de at the edge of; (*fig*) on the verge of; ~rada *f* edge; ~ra-mar *f* seaside; ~rar *vt* (*ficar*) border (on); (*andar*) skirt; (*fig*) border on, verge on; ele está ~rando os 30 anos he's nearing thirty

beisebol /beijsi'bɔw/ *m* baseball

belas-artes /bɛlaʃ'artʃiʃ/ *f pl* fine arts

beldade /bew'dadʒi/ *f*, **beleza** /be'leza/ *f* beauty

belga /'bɛwga/ *a & m* Belgian

Bélgica /'bɛwʒika/ *f* Belgium

beliche /be'liʃi/ *m* bunk

bélico /'bɛliku/ *a* war

belicoso /beli'kozu/ *a* warlike

belis|cão /belis'kãw/ *m* pinch; ~car *vt* pinch; nibble <*comida*>

Belize /be'lizi/ *m* Belize

belo /'bɛlu/ *a* beautiful

beltrano /bew'tranu/ *m* such-and-such

bem /bẽj/ *adv* well; (*bastante*) quite; (*muito*) very □ *m* good; *pl* goods, property; está ~ (it's) fine, OK; fazer ~ a be good for; tudo ~? (*fam*) how's things?; se ~ que even though; ~ feito (por você) (*fam*) it serves you right; muito ~! well done!; de ~ com alg on good terms with s.o.; ~ como as well as

bem|-apessoado /bẽjapeso'adu/ *a* nice-looking; ~-comportado *a* well-behaved; ~-disposto *a* keen, willing; ~-estar *m* well-being; ~-humorado *a* good-humoured; ~-intencionado *a* well-intentioned; ~-passado *a* <*carne*> well-done; ~-sucedido *a* successful; ~-vindo *a* welcome; ~-visto *a* well thought of

bênção /'bẽsãw/ (*pl* ~s) *f* blessing

bendito /bẽ'dʒitu/ *a* blessed

benefi|cência /benefi'sẽsia/ *f* (*bondade*) goodness, kindness; (*caridade*) charity; ~cente *a* <*associação*> charitable; <*concerto, feira*> charity; ~ciado *m* beneficiary; ~ciar *vt* benefit; ~ciar-se *vpr* benefit (de from)

benefício /bene'fisiu/ *m* benefit; em ~ de in aid of

benéfico /be'nɛfiku/ *a* beneficial (a to)

benevolência /benevo'lẽsia/ *f* benevolence

benévolo /be'nɛvolu/ *a* benevolent

benfeitor /bẽfej'tor/ *m* benefactor

bengala /bẽ'gala/ *f* walking stick; (*pão*) French stick

benigno /be'niginu/ *a* benign

ben|to /'bẽtu/ *a* blessed; <*água*> holy; ~zer *vt* bless; ~zer-se *vpr* cross o.s.

berço /'bersu/ *m* (*de embalar*) cradle; (*caminha*) cot; (*fig*) birthplace; ter ~ be from a good family

berimbau /berĩ'baw/ *m Brazilian percussion instrument shaped like a bow*

berinjela /berĩ'ʒɛla/ *f* aubergine, (*Amer*) eggplant

Berlim /ber'lĩ/ *f* Berlin

berma /'bɛrma/ (*Port*) *f* hard shoulder, (*Amer*) berm

bermuda /ber'muda/ *f* Bermuda shorts

Berna /'bɛrna/ *f* Berne

ber|rante /be'xãtʃi/ *a* loud, flashy; **~rar** *vi* <*pessoa*> shout; <*criança*> bawl; <*boi*> bellow; **~reiro** *m* (*gritaria*) yelling, shouting; (*choro*) crying, bawling; **~ro** /ɛ/ *m* yell, shout; (*de boi*) bellow; **aos ~ros** shouting

besouro /be'zoru/ *m* beetle

bes|ta /'besta/ *a* (*idiota*) stupid; (*cheio de si*) full of o.s.; (*pedante*) pretentious □ *f* (*pessoa*) dimwit, numbskull; **ficar ~ta** (*fam*) be taken aback; **~teira** *f* stupidity; (*uma*) stupid thing; **falar ~teira** talk rubbish; **~tial** (*pl* **~tiais**) *a* bestial; **~tificar** *vt* astound, dumbfound

besuntar /bezũ'tar/ *vt* coat; (*sujar*) smear

betão /be'tãw/ (*Port*) *m* concrete

beterraba /bete'xaba/ *f* beetroot

betoneira /beto'nera/ *f* cement mixer

bexiga /be'ʃiga/ *f* bladder

bezerro /be'zeru/ *m* calf

bibelô /bibe'lo/ *m* ornament

Bíblia /'biblia/ *f* Bible

bíblico /'bibliku/ *a* biblical

biblio|grafia /bibliogra'fia/ *f* bibliography; **~teca** /ɛ/ *f* library; **~tecário** *m* librarian □ *a* library

bica /'bika/ *f* tap; (*Port: cafezinho*) espresso; **suar em ~s** drip with sweat

bicama /bi'kama/ *f* truckle bed

bicar /bi'kar/ *vt* peck

bíceps /'bisɛps/ *m invar* biceps

bicha /'biʃa/ *f* (*Port: fila*) queue; (*Bras: fam*) queer, fairy

bicheiro /bi'ʃeru/ *m* organizer of illegal numbers game, racketeer

bicho /'biʃu/ *m* animal; (*inseto*) insect, (*Amer*) bug; **que ~ te mordeu?** what's got into you?; **~-da-seda** (*pl* **~s-da-seda**) *m* silkworm; **~-de-sete-cabeças** (*fam*) *m* big deal, big thing; **~-do-mato** (*pl* **~s-do-mato**) *m* very shy person

bicicleta /bisi'klɛta/ *f* bicycle, bike

bico /'biku/ *m* (*de ave*) beak; (*de faca*) point; (*de sapato*) toe; (*de bule*) spout; (*de caneta*) nib; (*do seio*) nipple; (*de gás*) jet; (*fam*) (*emprego*) odd job, sideline; (*boca*) mouth

bidê /bi'de/ *m* bidet

bidimensio|nal /bidʒimẽsio'naw/ (*pl* **~nais**) *a* two-dimensional

biela /bi'ɛla/ *f* connecting rod

Bielo-Rússia /bielo'xusia/ *f* Byelorussia

bielo-russo /bielo'xusu/ *a & m* Byelorussian

bie|nal /bie'naw/ (*pl* **~nais**) *a* biennial □ *f* biennial art exhibition

bife /'bifi/ *m* steak

bifo|cal /bifo'kaw/ (*pl* **~cais**) *a* bifocal

bifur|cação /bifurka'sãw/ *f* fork; **~car-se** *vpr* fork

bigamia /biga'mia/ *f* bigamy

bígamo /'bigamu/ *a* bigamous □ *m* bigamist

bigo|de /bi'gɔdʒi/ *m* moustache; **~dudo** *a* with a big moustache

bigorna /bi'gɔrna/ *f* anvil

bijuteria /biʒute'ria/ *f* costume jewellery

bilate|ral /bilate'raw/ (*pl* **~rais**) *a* bilateral

bilhão /bi'ʎãw/ *m* thousand million, (*Amer*) billion

bilhar /bi'ʎar/ *m* pool, billiards

bilhe|te /bi'ʎetʃi/ *m* ticket; (*recado*) note; **~te de ida e volta** return ticket, (*Amer*) round-trip ticket; **o ~te azul** (*fam*) the sack; **~teria** *f*, (*Port*) **~teira** *f* (*no cinema, teatro*) box office; (*na estação*) ticket office

bilíngüe /bi'lĩgwi/ *a* bilingual

bilionário /bilio'nariu/ *a & m* billionaire

bílis /'bilis/ *f* bile

binário /bi'nariu/ *a* binary

bingo /'bĩgu/ *m* bingo

binóculo /bi'nɔkulu/ *m* binoculars

biodegradá|vel /biodegra'davew/ (*pl* **~veis**) *a* biodegradable

bio|grafia /biogra'fia/ *f* biography; **~gráfico** *a* biographical

biógrafo /bi'ɔgrafu/ *m* biographer

bio|logia /biolo'ʒia/ *f* biology; **~lógico** *a* biological

biólogo /bi'ɔlogu/ *m* biologist

biombo /bi'õbu/ *m* screen

biônico /bi'oniku/ *a* bionic; (*pol*) unelected

biópsia /bi'ɔpsia/ *f* biopsy

bioquími|ca /bio'kimika/ *f* biochemistry; **~co** *a* biochemical □ *m* biochemist

biquíni /bi'kini/ *m* bikini

birma|nês /birma'nes/ *a & m* (*f* **~nesa**) Burmese

Birmânia /bir'mania/ *f* Burma

birô /bi'ro/ *m* bureau

bir|ra /'bixa/ *f* wilfulness; **fazer ~ra** have a tantrum; **~rento** *a* wilful

biruta /bi'ruta/ (*fam*) *a* crazy □ *f* windsock

bis /bis/ *int* encore!, more! □ *m invar* encore

bisa|vó /biza'vɔ/ *f* great-grandmother; **~vós** *m pl* great-grandparents; **~vô** *m* great-grandfather

bisbilho|tar /bizbiʎo'tar/ *vt* pry into □ *vi* pry; **~teiro** *a* prying □ *m* busybody; **~tice** *f* prying

bisca|te /bis'katʃi/ *m* odd job; **~teiro** *m* odd-job man

biscoito /bis'kojtu/ *m* biscuit, (*Amer*) cookie

bisnaga /biz'naga/ *f* (*pão*) bridge roll; (*tubo*) tube

bisne|ta /biz'nɛta/ *f* great-granddaughter; **~to** /ɛ/ *m* great-grandson; *pl* great-grandchildren

bis|pado /bis'padu/ *m* bishopric; **~po** *m* bishop

bissexto /bi'sestu/ *a* occasional; ano **~** leap year

bissexu|al /biseksu'aw/ (*pl* **~ais**) *a* & *m/f* bisexual

bisturi /bistu'ri/ *m* scalpel

bito|la /bi'tɔla/ *f* gauge; **~lado** *a* narrow-minded

bizarro /bi'zaxu/ *a* bizarre

blablablá /blabla'bla/ (*fam*) *m* chit-chat

black /'blɛki/ *m* black market; **~-tie** *m* evening dress

blas|femar /blasfe'mar/ *vi* blaspheme; **~fêmia** *f* blasphemy; **~femo** /e/ *a* blasphemous □ *m* blasphemer

blecaute /ble'kawtʃi/ *m* power cut

ble|far /ble'far/ *vi* bluff; **~fe** /ɛ/ *m* bluff

blin|dado /blĩ'dadu/ *a* armoured; **~dagem** *f* armour-plating

blitz /blits/ *f invar* police spot-check (on vehicles)

blo|co /'blɔku/ *m* block; (*pol*) bloc; (*de papel*) pad; (*no carnaval*) section; **~quear** *vt* block; (*mil*) blockade; **~queio** *m* blockage; (*psic*) mental block; (*mil*) blockade

blusa /'bluza/ *f* shirt; (*de mulher*) blouse; (*de lã*) sweater

boa /'boa/ *f de* **bom**; **numa ~** (*fam*) well; (*sem problemas*) easily; **estar numa ~** (*fam*) be doing fine; **~-gente** (*fam*) *a invar* nice; **~-pinta** (*pl* **~s-pintas**) (*fam*) *a* nice-looking; **~-praça** (*pl* **~s-praças**) (*fam*) *a* friendly, sociable

boate /bo'atʃi/ *f* nightclub

boato /bo'atu/ *m* rumour

boa|-nova /boa'nɔva/ (*pl* **~s-novas**) *f* good news; **~-vida** (*pl* **~s-vidas**) *m/f* good-for-nothing, waster; **~zinha** *a* sweet, kind

bo|bagem /bo'baʒẽ/ *f* silliness; (*uma*) silly thing; **~beada** *f* slip-up; **~bear** *vi* slip up; **~beira** *f veja* **bobagem**

bobe /'bɔbi/ *m* curler, roller

bobina /bo'bina/ *f* reel; (*eletr*) coil

bobo /'bobu/ *a* silly □ *m* fool; (*da corte*) jester; **~ca** /ɔ/ (*fam*) *a* stupid □ *m/f* twit

bo|ca /'boka/ *f* mouth; (*no fogão*) ring; **~ca da noite** nightfall; **~cado** *m* (*na boca*) mouthful; (*pedaço*) piece, bit; **~cal** (*pl* **~cais**) *m* mouthpiece

boce|jar /bose'ʒar/ *vi* yawn; **~jo** /e/ *m* yawn

boche|cha /bo'ʃeʃa/ *f* cheek; **~char** *vi* rinse one's mouth; **~cho** /e/ *m* mouthwash; **~chudo** *a* with puffy cheeks

bodas /'bodas/ *f pl* wedding anniversary; **~ de prata/ouro** silver/golden wedding

bode /'bɔdʒi/ *m* (billy) goat; **~ expiatório** scapegoat

bodega /bo'dɛga/ *f* (*de bebidas*) off-licence, (*Amer*) liquor store; (*de secos e molhados*) grocer's shop, corner shop

boêmio /bo'emiu/ *a* & *m* Bohemian

bofe|tada /bofe'tada/ *f*, **bofe|tão** /bofe'tãw/ *m* slap; **~tear** *vt* slap

boi /boj/ *m* bullock, (*Amer*) steer

bói /bɔj/ *m* office boy

bóia /'bɔja/ *f* (*de balizamento*) buoy; (*de cortiça, isopor etc*) float; (*câmara de borracha*) rubber ring; (*de braço*) armband, water wing; (*na caixa-d'água*) ballcock; (*fam: comida*) grub; **~ salva-vidas** lifebelt; **~-fria** (*pl* **~s-frias**) *m/f* itinerant farm labourer

boiar /bo'jar/ *vt/i* float; (*fam*) be lost

boico|tar /bojko'tar/ *vt* boycott; **~te** /ɔ/ *m* boycott

boiler /'bojler/ (*pl* **~s**) *m* boiler

boina /'bojna/ *f* beret

bo|jo /'boʒu/ *m* bulge; **~judo** *a* (*cheio*) bulging; (*arredondado*) bulbous

bola /'bɔla/ *f* ball; **dar ~ para** (*fam*) give attention to <*pessoa*>; care about <*coisa*>; **~ de gude** marble; **~ de neve** snowball

bolacha /bo'laʃa/ *f* (*biscoito*) biscuit, (*Amer*) cookie; (*descanso*) beermat; (*fam: tapa*) slap

bo|lada /bo'lada/ *f* large sum of money; **~lar** *vt* think up, devise

boléia /bo'lɛja/ *f* cab; (*Port: carona*) lift

boletim /bole'tʃĩ/ *m* bulletin; (*escolar*) report

bolha /'boʎa/ *f* bubble; (*na pele*) blister □ (*fam*) *m/f* pain

boliche /bo'liʃi/ *m* skittles

Bolívia /bo'livia/ *f* Bolivia

boliviano /bolivi'anu/ *a* & *m* Bolivian

bolo /'bolu/ *m* cake

bo|lor /bo'lor/ *m* mould, mildew; **~lorento** *a* mouldy

bolota /bo'lɔta/ *f* (*glande*) acorn; (*bolinha*) little ball

bol|sa /'bowsa/ *f* bag; **~sa (de estudo)** scholarship; **~sa (de valores)** stock exchange; **~sista** *m/f*, (*Port*) **~seiro** *m* scholarship student; **~so** /o/ *m* pocket

bom /bõ/ *a* (*f* **boa**) good; (*de saúde*) well; <*comida*> nice; **está ~** that's fine

bomba[1] /'bõba/ *f* (*explosiva*) bomb; (*doce*) eclair; (*fig*) bombshell; **levar ~** (*fam*) fail

bomba[2] /'bõba/ *f* (*de bombear*) pump

Bombaim /bõba'ĩ/ *f* Bombay

bombar|dear /bõbardʒi'ar/ *vt* bombard; (*do ar*) bomb; **~deio** *m* bombardment; (*do ar*) bombing

bomba|-relógio /bõbaxe'lɔʒiu/ (*pl* **~s-relógio**) *f* time bomb

bom|bear /bõbi'ar/ *vt* pump; **~beiro** *m* fireman; (*encanador*) plumber

bombom /bõ'bõ/ *m* chocolate

bombordo /bõ'bɔrdu/ *m* port

bondade /bõ'dadʒi/ *f* goodness

bonde /'bõdʒi/ *m* tram; (*teleférico*) cable car

bondoso /bõ'dozu/ *a* good(-hearted)

boné /bo'nɛ/ *m* cap

bone|ca /bo'nɛka/ *f* doll; **~co** /ɛ/ *m* dummy

bonificação /bonifika'sãw/ *f* bonus

bonito /bo'nitu/ *a* <*mulher*> pretty; <*homem*> handsome; <*tempo, casa etc*> lovely

bônus /'bonus/ *m invar* bonus

boqui|aberto /bokia'bɛrtu/ *a* open-mouthed, flabbergasted; **~nha** *f* snack

borboleta /borbo'leta/ *f* butterfly; (*roleta*) turnstile

borbotão /borbo'tãw/ *m* spurt

borbu|lha /bor'buʎa/ *f* bubble; **~lhar** *vi* bubble

borda /'bɔrda/ *f* edge; **~do** *a* edged; (*à linha*) embroidered □ *m* embroidery

bordão /bor'dãw/ *m* (*frase*) catch-phrase

bordar /bor'dar/ *vt* (*à linha*) embroider

bor|del /bor'dɛw/ (*pl* **~déis**) *m* brothel

bordo /'bɔrdu/ *m* **a ~** aboard

borra /'boxa/ *f* dregs; (*de café*) grounds

borra|cha /bo'xaʃa/ *f* rubber; **~cheiro** *m* tyre fitter

bor|rão /bo'xãw/ *m* (*de tinta*) blot; (*rascunho*) rough draft; **~rar** *vt* (*sujar*) blot; (*riscar*) cross out; (*pintar*) daub

borrasca /bo'xaska/ *f* squall

borri|far /boxi'far/ *vt* sprinkle; **~fo** *m* sprinkling

bosque /'bɔski/ *m* wood

bosta /'bɔsta/ *f* (*de animal*) dung; (*chulo*) crap

bota /'bɔta/ *f* boot

botâni|ca /bo'tanika/ *f* botany; **~co** *a* botanical □ *m* botanist

bo|tão /bo'tãw/ *m* button; (*de flor*) bud; **falar com os seus ~tões** say to o.s.

botar /bo'tar/ *vt* put; put on <*roupa*>; set <*mesa, despertador*>; lay <*ovo*>; find <*defeito*>

bote[1] /'bɔtʃi/ *m* (*barco*) dinghy; **~ salva-vidas** lifeboat; (*de borracha*) life-raft

bote[2] /'bɔtʃi/ *m* (*de animal etc*) lunge

botequim /butʃi'kĩ/ *m* bar

botoeira /boto'era/ *f* buttonhole

boxe /'bɔksi/ *m* boxing; **~ador** *m* boxer

brabo /'brabu/ *a* <*animal*> ferocious; <*calor, sol*> fierce; <*doença*> bad; <*prova, experiência*> tough; (*zangado*) angry

bra|çada /bra'sada/ *f* armful; (*em natação*) stroke; **~çadeira** (*faixa*) armband; (*ferragem*) bracket; (*de atleta*) sweatband; **~çal** (*pl* **~çais**) *a* manual; **~celete** /e/ *m* bracelet; **~ço** *m* arm; **~ço direito** (*fig: pessoa*) right-hand man

bra|dar /bra'dar/ *vt/i* shout; **~do** *m* shout

braguilha /bra'giʎa/ *f* fly, flies

braile /'brajli/ *m* Braille

bra|mido /bra'midu/ *m* roar; **~mir** *vi* roar

branco /'brãku/ *a* white □ *m* (*homem*) white man; (*espaço*) blank; **em ~** <*cheque etc*> blank; **noite em ~** sleepless night

bran|do /'brãdu/ *a* gentle; <*doença*> mild; (*indulgente*) lenient, soft; **~dura** *f* gentleness; (*indulgência*) softness, leniency

brasa /'braza/ *f* **em ~** red-hot; **mandar ~** (*fam*) go to town

brasão /bra'zãw/ *m* coat of arms

braseiro /bra'zeru/ *m* brasier

Brasil /bra'ziw/ *m* Brazil

brasi|leiro /brazi'leru/ *a & m* Brazilian; **~liense** *a & m/f* (person) from Brasilia

bra|vata /bra'vata/ *f* bravado; **~vio** *a* wild; <*mar*> rough; **~vo** *a* (*corajoso*) brave; (*zangado*) angry; <*mar*> rough; **~vura** *f* bravery

breca /'brɛka/ *f* **levado da ~** very naughty

brecar /bre'kar/ *vt* stop <*carro*>; (*fig*) curb □ *vi* brake

brecha /'brɛʃa/ *f* gap; (*na lei*) loophole

bre|ga /'brɛga/ (*fam*) *a* tacky, naff; **~guice** (*fam*) *f* tack, tackiness

brejo /'brɛʒu/ *m* marsh; **ir para o ~** (*fig*) go down the drain
brenha /'brɛɲa/ *f* thicket
breque /'brɛki/ *m* brake
breu /brew/ *m* tar, pitch
bre|ve /'brɛvi/ *a* short, brief; **em ~ve** soon, shortly; **~vidade** *f* shortness, brevity
briga /'briga/ *f* fight; (*bate-boca*) argument
briga|da /bri'gada/ *f* brigade; **~deiro** *m* brigadier; (*doce*) chocolate truffle
bri|gão /bri'gãw/ *a* (*f* **~gona**) belligerent; (*na fala*) argumentative □ *m* (*f* **~gona**) troublemaker; **~gar** *vi* fight; (*com palavras*) argue; <*cores*> clash
bri|lhante /bri'ʎãtʃi/ *a* (*reluzente*) shiny; (*fig*) brilliant; **~lhar** *vi* shine; **~lho** *m* (*de sapatos etc*) shine; (*dos olhos, de metais*) gleam; (*das estrelas*) brightness; (*de uma cor*) brilliance; (*fig: esplendor*) splendour
brin|cadeira /brĩka'dera/ *f* (*piada*) joke; (*brinquedo, jogo*) game; **de ~cadeira** for fun; **~calhão** (*f* **~calhona**) *a* playful □ *m* joker; **~car** *vi* (*divertir-se*) play; (*gracejar*) joke
brinco /'brĩku/ *m* earring
brin|dar /brĩ'dar/ *vt* (*saudar*) toast, drink to; (*presentear*) give a gift to; **~dar alg com aco** afford s.o. sth; (*de presente*) give s.o. sth as a gift; **~de** *m* (*saudação*) toast; (*presente*) free gift
brinquedo /brĩ'kedu/ *m* toy
brio /'briu/ *m* self-esteem, character; **~so** /o/ *a* self-confident
brisa /'briza/ *f* breeze
britadeira /brita'dera/ *f* pneumatic drill
britânico /bri'taniku/ *a* British □ *m* Briton; **os ~s** the British
broca /'brɔka/ *f* drill
broche /'brɔʃi/ *m* brooch
brochura /bro'ʃura/ *f* **livro de ~** paperback
brócolis /'brɔkulis/ *m pl*, (*Port*) **brócolos** /'brɔkuluʃ/ *m pl* broccoli
bron|ca /'brõka/ (*fam*) *f* telling-off; **dar uma ~ca em alg** tell s.o. off; **~co** *a* coarse, rough
bronquite /brõ'kitʃi/ *f* bronchitis
bronze /'brõzi/ *m* bronze; **~ado** *a* tanned, brown □ *m* (sun)tan; **~ador** *a* tanning □ *m* suntan lotion; **~amento** *m* tanning; **~ar** *vt* tan; **~ar-se** *vpr* go brown, tan
bro|tar /bro'tar/ *vt* sprout <*folhas, flores*>; spout <*lágrimas, palavras*> □ *vi* <*planta*> sprout; <*água*> spout; <*idéias*> pop up; **~tinho** (*fam*) *m* youngster; **~to** /o/ *m* shoot; (*fam*) youngster
broxa /'brɔʃa/ *f* (large) paint brush □ (*fam*) *a* impotent
bruços /'brusus/ **de ~** face down
bru|ma /'bruma/ *f* mist; **~moso** /o/ *a* misty
brusco /'brusku/ *a* brusque, abrupt
bru|tal /bru'taw/ (*pl* **~tais**) *a* brutal; **~talidade** *f* brutality; **~to** *a* <*feições*> coarse; <*homem*> brutish; <*tom, comentário*> aggressive; <*petróleo*> crude; <*peso, lucro, salário*> gross □ *m* brute
bruxa /'bruʃa/ *f* witch; (*feia*) hag; **~ria** *f* witchcraft
Bruxelas /bru'ʃɛlas/ *f* Brussels
bruxo /'bruʃu/ *m* wizard
bruxulear /bruʃuli'ar/ *vi* flicker
bucha /'buʃa/ *f* (*tampão*) bung; (*para paredes*) rawlplug (R); **acertar na ~** (*fam*) hit the nail on the head
bucho /'buʃu/ *m* gut; **~ de boi** tripe
budis|mo /bu'dʒizmu/ *m* Buddhism; **~ta** *a* & *m/f* Buddhist
bueiro /bu'eru/ *m* storm drain
búfalo /'bufalu/ *m* buffalo
bu|fante /bu'fãtʃi/ *a* full, puffed; **~far** *vi* snort; (*reclamar*) grumble, moan
bufê /bu'fe/ *m* (*refeição*) buffet; (*serviço*) catering service; (*móvel*) sideboard
bugiganga /buʒi'gãga/ *f* knickknack
bujão /bu'ʒãw/ *m* **~ de gás** gas cylinder
bula /'bula/ *f* (*de remédio*) directions; (*do Papa*) bull
bulbo /'buwbu/ *m* bulb
bule /'buli/ *m* (*de chá*) teapot; (*de café etc*) pot
Bulgária /buw'garia/ *f* Bulgaria
búlgaro /'buwgaru/ *a* & *m* Bulgarian
bulhufas /bu'ʎufas/ (*fam*) *pron* nothing
bulício /bu'lisiu/ *m* bustle
bumbum /bũ'bũ/ (*fam*) *m* bottom, bum
bunda /'bũda/ *f* bottom
buquê /bu'ke/ *m* bouquet
buraco /bu'raku/ *m* hole; (*de agulha*) eye; (*jogo de cartas*) rummy; **~ da fechadura** keyhole
burburinho /burbu'riɲu/ *m* (*de vozes*) hubbub
bur|guês /bur'ges/ *a* & *m* (*f* **~guesa**) bourgeois; **~guesia** *f* bourgeoisie
burlar /bur'lar/ *vt* get round <*lei*>; get past <*defesas, vigilância*>
buro|cracia /burokra'sia/ *f* bureaucracy; **~crata** *m/f* bureaucrat; **~crático** *a* bureaucratic; **~cratizar** *vt* make bureaucratic
bur|rice /bu'xisi/ *f* stupidity; (*uma*) stupid thing; **~ro** *a* stupid; (*ignorante*) dim □ *m* (*animal*) donkey; (*pessoa*) halfwit, dunce; **~ro de carga** (*fig*) workhorse

bus|ca /'buska/ *f* search; **dar ~ca em** search; **~ca-pé** *m* banger; **~car** *vt* fetch; (*de carro*) pick up; **mandar ~car** send for
bússola /'busola/ *f* compass; (*fig*) guide
busto /'bustu/ *m* bust
butique /bu'tʃiki/ *f* boutique
buzi|na /bu'zina/ *f* horn; **~nada** *f* toot (of the horn); **~nar** *vi* sound the horn, toot the horn

C

cá /ka/ *adv* here; **o lado de ~** this side; **para ~** here; **de ~ para lá** back and forth; **de lá para ~** since then; **~ entre nós** between you and me
ca|bal /ka'baw/ (*pl* **~bais**) *a* complete, full; <*prova*> conclusive
cabana /ka'bana/ *f* hut; (*casinha no campo*) cottage
cabeça /ka'besa/ *f* head; (*de lista*) top; (*pessoa inteligente*) mind □ *m/f* (*chefe*) ringleader; (*integrante mais inteligente*) brains; **de ~** <*saber*> off the top of one's head; <*calcular*> in one's head; **de ~ para baixo** upside down; **deu-lhe na ~ de** he took it into his head to; **esquentar a ~** (*fam*) get worked up; **fazer a ~ de alg** convince s.o.; **quebrar a ~** rack one's brains; **subir à ~** go to s.o.'s head; **ter a ~ no lugar** have one's head screwed on; **~da** *f* (*no futebol*) header; (*pancada*) head butt; **dar uma ~da no teto** bang one's head on the ceiling; **~-de-porco** (*pl* **~s-de-porco**) *f* tenement; **~-de-vento** (*pl* **~s-de-vento**) *m/f* scatterbrain, airhead; **~lho** *m* heading
cabe|cear /kabesi'ar/ *vt* head <*bola*>; **~ceira** *f* head; **~çudo** *a* pigheaded
cabe|dal /kabe'daw/ (*pl* **~dais**) *m* wealth
cabelei|ra /kabe'lera/ *f* head of hair; (*peruca*) wig; **~reiro** *m* hairdresser
cabe|lo /ka'belu/ *m* hair; **cortar o ~lo** have one's hair cut; **~ludo** *a* hairy; (*difícil*) complicated; <*palavra, piada*> dirty
caber /ka'ber/ *vi* fit; (*ter cabimento*) be fitting; **~ a** <*mérito, parte*> be due to; <*tarefa*> fall to; **cabe a você ir** it is up to you to go; **~ em alg** <*roupa*> fit s.o.
cabide /ka'bidʒi/ *m* (*peça de madeira, arame etc*) hanger; (*móvel*) hat stand; (*na parede*) coat rack
cabimento /kabi'mẽtu/ *m* **ter ~** be fitting, be appropriate; **não ter ~** be out of the question
cabine /ka'bini/ *f* cabin; (*de avião*) cockpit; (*de loja*) changing room; **~ telefônica** phone box, (*Amer*) phone booth
cabisbaixo /kabiz'baʃu/ *a* crestfallen
cabí|vel /ka'bivew/ (*pl* **~veis**) *a* appropriate, fitting
cabo[1] /'kabu/ *m* (*militar*) corporal; **ao ~ de** after; **levar a ~** carry out; **~ eleitoral** campaign worker
cabo[2] /'kabu/ *m* (*fio*) cable; (*de panela etc*) handle; **TV por ~** cable TV; **~ de extensão** extension lead; **~ de força** tug of war
caboclo /ka'boklu/ *a & m* mestizo
ca|bra /'kabra/ *f* goat; **~brito** *m* kid
ca|ça /'kasa/ *f* (*atividade*) hunting; (*caçada*) hunt; (*animais*) game □ *m* (*avião*) fighter; **à ~ça de** in pursuit of; **~ça das bruxas** (*fig*) witch hunt; **~çador** *m* hunter; **~ça-minas** *m invar* minesweeper; **~ça-níqueis** *m invar* slot machine; **~çar** *vt* hunt <*animais, criminoso etc*>; (*procurar*) hunt for □ *vi* hunt
cacareco /kaka'rɛku/ *m* piece of junk; *pl* junk
cacare|jar /kakare'ʒar/ *vi* cluck; **~jo** /e/ *m* clucking
caçarola /kasa'rɔla/ *f* saucepan
cacau /ka'kaw/ *m* cocoa
cace|tada /kase'tada/ *f* blow with a club; (*fig*) annoyance; **~te** /e/ *m* club □ (*fam*) *int* damn
cachaça /ka'ʃasa/ *f* white rum
cachê /ka'ʃe/ *m* fee
cache|col /kaʃe'kɔw/ (*pl* **~cóis**) *m* scarf
cachimbo /ka'ʃĩbu/ *m* pipe
cacho /'kaʃu/ *m* (*de banana, uva*) bunch; (*de cabelo*) lock; (*fam: caso*) affair
cachoeira /kaʃo'era/ *f* waterfall
cachor|rinho /kaʃo'xiɲu/ *m* (*nado*) doggy paddle; **~ro** /o/ *m* dog; (*Port*) puppy; (*pessoa*) scoundrel; **~ro-quente** (*pl* **~ros-quentes**) *m* hot dog
cacife /ka'sifi/ *m* (*fig*) pull
caci|que /ka'siki/ *m* (*índio*) chief; (*político*) boss; **~quia** *f* leadership
caco /'kaku/ *m* shard; (*pessoa*) old crock
cacto /'kaktu/ *m* cactus
caçula /ka'sula/ *m/f* youngest child □ *a* youngest
cada /'kada/ *a* each; **~ duas horas** every two hours; **custam £5 ~ (um)** they cost £5 each; **~ vez mais** more and more; **~ vez mais fácil** easier and easier; **ele fala ~ coisa** (*fam*) he says the most amazing things
cadafalso /kada'fawsu/ *m* gallows
cadarço /ka'darsu/ *m* shoelace
cadas|trar /kadas'trar/ *vt* register; **~tro** *m* register; (*ato*) registration;

(*policial, bancário*) records, files; (*imobiliário*) land register

ca|dáver /ka'daver/ *m* (dead) body, corpse; **~daverico** *a* cadaverous, corpse-like; <*exame*> post-mortem

cadê /ka'de/ (*fam*) *adv* where is/ are...?

cadeado /kadʒi'adu/ *m* padlock

cadeia /ka'deja/ *f* (*de eventos, lojas etc*) chain; (*prisão*) prison; (*rádio, TV*) network

cadeira /ka'dera/ *f* (*móvel*) chair; (*no teatro*) stall; (*de político*) seat; (*função de professor*) chair; (*matéria*) subject; *pl* (*anat*) hips; **~ de balanço** rocking chair; **~ de rodas** wheelchair; **~ elétrica** electric chair

ca|dência /ka'dẽsia/ *f* (*mus, da voz*) cadence; (*compasso*) rhythm; **~denciado** *a* rhythmic; <*passos*> measured

cader|neta /kader'neta/ *f* notebook; (*de professor*) register; (*de banco*) passbook; **~neta de poupança** savings account; **~no** /ɛ/ *m* exercise book; (*pequeno*) notebook; (*no jornal*) section

cadete /ka'detʃi/ *m* cadet

cadu|car /kadu'kar/ *vi* <*pessoa*> become senile; <*contrato*> lapse; **~co** *a* <*pessoa*> senile; <*contrato*> lapsed; **~quice** *f* senility

cafajeste /kafa'ʒɛstʃi/ *m* swine

ca|fé /ka'fɛ/ *m* coffee; (*botequim*) café; **~fé da manhã** breakfast; **tomar ~fé** have breakfast; **~fé-com-leite** *a invar* coffee-coloured, light brown □ *m* white coffee; **~feeiro** *a* coffee □ *m* coffee plant; **~feicultura** *f* coffee-growing; **~feína** *f* caffein(e)

cafetã /kafe'tã/ *m* caftan

cafetão /kafe'tãw/ *m* pimp

cafe|teira /kafe'tera/ *f* coffee pot; **~zal** (*pl* **~zais**) *m* coffee plantation; **~zinho** *m* small black coffee

cafo|na /ka'fɔna/ (*fam*) *a* naff, tacky; **~nice** *f* tackiness; (*coisa*) tacky thing

cágado /'kagadu/ *m* turtle

caiar /kaj'ar/ *vt* whitewash

cãibra /'kãjbra/ *f* cramp

caí|da /ka'ida/ *f* fall; *veja* **queda**; **~do** *a* <*árvore etc*> fallen; <*beiços etc*> drooping; (*deprimido*) dejected; (*apaixonado*) smitten

caimento /kaj'mẽtu/ *m* fall

caipi|ra /kaj'pira/ *a* <*pessoa*> countrified; <*festa, música*> country; <*sotaque*> rural □ *m/f* country person; (*depreciativo*) country bumpkin; **~rinha** *f* cachaça with limes, sugar and ice

cair /ka'ir/ *vi* fall; <*dente, cabelo*> fall out; <*botão etc*> fall off; <*comércio, trânsito etc*> fall off; <*tecido, cortina*> hang; **~ bem/mal** <*roupa*> go well/ badly; <*ato, dito*> go down well, badly; **estou caindo de sono** I'm really sleepy

cais /kajs/ *m* quay; (*Port: na estação*) platform

caixa /'kaʃa/ *f* box; (*de loja etc*) cash-desk □ *m/f* cashier; **~ de correio** letter box; **~ de mudanças**, (*Port*) **~ de velocidades** gear box; **~ postal** post office box, PO Box; **~-d'água** (*pl* **~s-d'água**) *f* water tank; **~-forte** (*pl* **~s-fortes**) *f* vault

cai|xão /ka'ʃãw/ *m* coffin; **~xeiro** *m* (*em loja*) assistant; salesman; **~xilho** *m* frame; **~xote** /ɔ/ *m* crate

caju /ka'ʒu/ *m* cashew fruit; **~eiro** *m* cashew tree

cal /kaw/ *f* lime

calado /ka'ladu/ *a* quiet

calafrio /kala'friu/ *m* shudder, shiver

calami|dade /kalami'dadʒi/ *f* calamity; **~toso** /o/ *a* calamitous

calar /ka'lar/ *vi* be quiet □ *vt* keep quiet about <*segredo, sentimento*>; silence <*pessoa*>; **~-se** *vpr* go quiet

calça /'kawsa/ *f* trousers, (*Amer*) pants

calça|da /kaw'sada/ *f* pavement, (*Amer*) sidewalk; (*Port: rua*) roadway; **~dão** *m* pedestrian precinct; **~deira** *f* shoe-horn; **~do** *a* paved □ *m* shoe; *pl* footwear

calcanhar /kawka'ɲar/ *m* heel

calção /kaw'sãw/ *m* shorts; **~ de banho** swimming trunks

calcar /kaw'kar/ *vt* (*pisar*) trample; (*comprimir*) press; **~ aco em** (*fig*) base sth on, model sth on

calçar /kaw'sar/ *vt* put on <*sapatos, luvas*>; take <*número*>; pave <*rua*>; (*com calço*) wedge □ *vi* <*sapato*> fit; **~-se** *vpr* put one's shoes on

calcário /kaw'kariu/ *m* limestone □ *a* <*água*> hard

calças /'kawsas/ *f pl veja* **calça**

calcinha /kaw'siɲa/ *f* knickers, (*Amer*) panties

cálcio /'kawsiu/ *m* calcium

calço /'kawsu/ *m* wedge

calcu|ladora /kawkula'dora/ *f* calculator; **~lar** *vt/i* calculate; **~lista** *a* calculating □ *m/f* opportunist

cálculo /'kawkulu/ *m* calculation; (*diferencial*) calculus; (*med*) stone

cal|da /'kawda/ *f* syrup; *pl* hot springs; **~deira** *f* boiler; **~deirão** *m* cauldron; **~do** *m* (*sopa*) broth; (*suco*) juice; **~do de carne/galinha** beef/ chicken stock

calefação /kalefa'sãw/ *f* heating

caleidoscópio /kalejdos'kɔpiu/ *m* kaleidoscope

calejado /kale'ʒadu/ *a* <*mãos*> calloused; <*pessoa*> experienced
calendário /kalẽ'dariu/ *m* calendar
calha /'kaʎa/ *f* (*no telhado*) gutter; (*sulco*) gulley
calhamaço /kaʎa'masu/ *m* tome
calhambeque /kaʎã'bɛki/ (*fam*) *m* banger
calhar /ka'ʎar/ *vi* **calhou que** it so happened that; **calhou pegar em o mesmo trem** they happened to get the same train; **~ de** happen to; **vir a ~** come at the right time
cali|brado /kali'bradu/ *a* (*bêbado*) tipsy; **~brar** *vt* calibrate; check (the pressure of) <*pneu*>; **~bre** *m* calibre; **coisas desse ~bre** things of this order
cálice /'kalisi/ *m* (*copo*) liqueur glass; (*na missa*) chalice
caligrafia /kaligra'fia/ *f* (*letra*) handwriting; (*arte*) calligraphy
calista /ka'lista/ *m/f* chiropodist, (*Amer*) podiatrist
cal|ma /'kawma/ *f* calm; **com ~ma** calmly □ *int* calm down; **~mante** *m* tranquilizer; **~mo** *a* calm
calo /'kalu/ *m* (*na mão*) callus; (*no pé*) corn
calombo /ka'lõbu/ *m* bump
calor /ka'lor/ *m* heat; (*agradável, fig*) warmth; **estar com ~** be hot
calo|rento /kalo'rẽtu/ *a* <*pessoa*> sensitive to heat; <*lugar*> hot; **~ria** *f* calorie; **~roso** /o/ *a* warm; <*protesto*> lively
calota /ka'lɔta/ *f* hubcap
calo|te /ka'lɔtʃi/ *m* bad debt; **~teiro** *m* bad risk
calouro /ka'loru/ *m* (*na faculdade*) freshman; (*em outros ramos*) novice
ca|lúnia /ka'lunia/ *f* slander; **~luniar** *vt* slander; **~lunioso** /o/ *a* slanderous
cal|vície /kaw'visi/ *f* baldness; **~vo** *a* bald
cama /'kama/ *f* bed; **~ de casal/solteiro** double/single bed; **~-beliche** (*pl* **~s-beliches**) *f* bunk bed
camada /ka'mada/ *f* layer; (*de tinta*) coat
câmara /'kamara/ *f* chamber; (*fotográfica*) camera; **em ~ lenta** in slow motion; **~ municipal** town council; (*Port*) town hall
camarada /kama'rada/ *a* friendly □ *m/f* comrade; **~gem** *f* comradeship; (*convivência agradável*) camaraderie
câmara-de-ar /kamaradʒi'ar/ (*pl* **câmaras-de-ar**) *f* inner tube
camarão /kama'rãw/ *m* shrimp; (*maior*) prawn
cama|reira /kama'rera/ *f* chambermaid; **~rim** *m* dressing room; **~rote** /ɔ/ *m* (*no teatro*) box; (*num navio*) cabin
cambada /kã'bada/ *f* gang, horde
cambalacho /kãba'laʃu/ *m* scam
camba|lear /kãbali'ar/ *vi* stagger; **~lhota** *f* somersault
cambi|al /kãbi'aw/ (*pl* **~ais**) *a* exchange; **~ante** *m* shade; **~ar** *vt* change
câmbio /'kãbiu/ *m* exchange; (*taxa*) rate of exchange; **~ oficial/paralelo** official/black market exchange rate
cambista /kã'bista/ *m/f* (*de entradas*) ticket-tout, (*Amer*) scalper; (*de dinheiro*) money changer
Camboja /kã'bɔʒa/ *m* Cambodia
cambojano /kãbo'ʒanu/ *a & m* Cambodian
camburão /kãbu'rãw/ *m* police van
camélia /ka'mɛlia/ *f* camelia
camelo /ka'melu/ *m* camel
camelô /kame'lo/ *m* street vendor
camião /kami'ãw/ (*Port*) *m veja* **caminhão**
caminhada /kami'ɲada/ *f* walk
caminhão /kami'ɲãw/ *m* lorry, (*Amer*) truck
cami|nhar /kami'ɲar/ *vi* walk; (*fig*) advance, progress; **~nho** *m* way; (*estrada*) road; (*trilho*) path; **a ~nho** on the way; **a meio ~nho** halfway; **~nho de ferro** (*Port*) railway, (*Amer*) railroad
caminho|neiro /kamiɲo'neru/ *m* lorry driver, (*Amer*) truck driver; **~nete** /ɛ/ *m* van
camio|neta /kamio'neta/ *f* van; **~nista** (*Port*) *m/f veja* **caminhoneiro**
cami|sa /ka'miza/ *f* shirt; **~sa-de-força** (*pl* **~sas-de-força**) *f* straitjacket; **~sa-de-vênus** (*pl* **~sas-de-vênus**) *f* condom; **~seta** /e/ *f* T-shirt; (*de baixo*) vest; **~sinha** (*fam*) *f* condom; **~sola** /ɔ/ *f* nightdress; (*Port*) sweater
camomila /kamo'mila/ *f* camomile
campainha /kãpa'iɲa/ *f* bell; (*da porta*) doorbell
campanário /kãpa'nariu/ *m* belfry
campanha /kã'paɲa/ *f* campaign
campe|ão /kãpi'ãw/ *m* (*f* **~ã**) champion; **~onato** *m* championship
cam|pestre /kã'pɛstri/ *a* rural; **~pina** *f* grassland
cam|ping /'kãpĩ/ *m* camping; (*lugar*) campsite; **~pismo** (*Port*) *m* camping
campo /'kãpu/ *m* field; (*interior*) country; (*de futebol*) pitch; (*de golfe*) course; **~ de concentração** concentration camp; **~nês** *m* (*f* **~nesa**) peasant
camu|flagem /kamu'flaʒẽ/ *f* camouflage; **~flar** *vt* camouflage
camundongo /kamũ'dõgu/ *m* mouse

cana /'kana/ *f* cane; ~ **de açúcar** sugar cane
Canadá /kana'da/ *m* Canada
canadense /kana'dẽsi/ *a & m* Canadian
ca|nal /ka'naw/ (*pl* ~**nais**) *m* channel; (*hidrovia*) canal
canalha /ka'naʎa/ *m/f* scoundrel
canali|zação /kanaliza'sãw/ *f* piping; ~**zador** (*Port*) *m* plumber; ~**zar** *vt* channel <*líquido, esforço, recursos*>; canalize <*rio*>; pipe for water and drainage <*cidade*>
canário /ka'nariu/ *m* canary
canastrão /kanas'trãw/ *m* (*f* ~**trona**) ham actor (*f* actress)
canavi|al /kanavi'aw/ (*pl* ~**ais**) *m* cane field; ~**eiro** *a* sugar cane
canção /kã'sãw/ *f* song
cance|lamento /kãsela'mẽtu/ *m* cancellation; ~**lar** *vt* cancel; (*riscar*) cross out
câncer /'kãser/ *m* cancer; **Câncer** (*signo*) Cancer
cance|riano /kãseri'anu/ *a & m* Cancerian; ~**rígeno** *a* carcinogenic; ~**roso** /o/ *a* cancerous □ *m* person with cancer
cancro /'kãkru/ *m* (*Port: câncer*) cancer; (*fig*) canker
candango /kã'dãgu/ *m* person from Brasilia
cande|eiro /kãdʒi'eru/ *m* (oil-)lamp; ~**labro** *m* candelabra
candida|tar-se /kãdʒida'tarsi/ *vpr* (*a vaga*) apply (a for); (*à presidência etc*) stand, (*Amer*) run (a for); ~**to** *m* candidate (a for); (*a vaga*) applicant (a for); ~**tura** *f* candidature; (*a vaga*) application (a for)
cândido /'kãdʒidu/ *a* innocent
candomblê /kãdõ'blɛ/ *m* Afro-Brazilian cult; (*reunião*) candomble meeting
candura /kã'dura/ *f* innocence
cane|ca /ka'nɛka/ *f* mug; ~**co** /ɛ/ *m* tankard
canela[1] /ka'nɛla/ *f* (*condimento*) cinnamon
canela[2] /ka'nɛla/ *f* (*da perna*) shin; ~**da** *f* **dar uma** ~**da em alg** kick s.o. in the shins; **dar uma** ~**da em aco** hit one's shins on sth
cane|ta /ka'neta/ *f* pen; ~ **esferográfica** ball-point pen; ~**ta-tinteiro** (*pl* ~**tas-tinteiro**) *f* fountain pen
cangote /kã'gɔtʃi/ *m* nape of the neck
canguru /kãgu'ru/ *m* kangaroo
canhão /ka'ɲãw/ *m* (*arma*) cannon; (*vale*) canyon
canhoto /ka'ɲotu/ *a* left-handed □ *m* (*talão*) stub
cani|bal /kani'baw/ (*pl* ~**bais**) *m/f* cannibal; ~**balismo** *m* cannibalism
caniço /ka'nisu/ *m* reed; (*pessoa*) skinny person
canícula /ka'nikula/ *f* heat wave
ca|nil /ka'niw/ (*pl* ~**nis**) *m* kennel
canivete /kani'vɛtʃi/ *m* penknife
canja /'kãʒa/ *f* chicken soup; (*fam*) piece of cake
canjica /kã'ʒika/ *f* corn porridge
cano /'kanu/ *m* pipe; (*de bota*) top; (*de arma de fogo*) barrel
cano|a /ka'noa/ *f* canoe; ~**agem** *f* canoeing; ~**ista** *m/f* canoeist
canonizar /kanoni'zar/ *vt* canonize
can|saço /kã'sasu/ *m* tiredness; ~**sado** *a* tired; ~**sar** *vt* tire; (*aborrecer*) bore □ *vi*, ~**sar-se** *vpr* get tired; ~**sativo** *a* tiring; (*aborrecido*) boring; ~**seira** *f* tiredness; (*lida*) toil
can|tada /kã'tada/ *f* (*fam*) chat-up; ~**tar** *vt/i* sing; (*fam*) chat up
cântaro /'kãtaru/ *m* **chover a** ~**s** pour down, bucket down
cantarolar /kãtaro'lar/ *vt/i* hum
cantei|ra /kã'tera/ *f* quarry; ~**ro** *m* (*de flores*) flowerbed; (*artífice*) stonemason; ~**ro de obras** site office
cantiga /kã'tʃiga/ *f* ballad
can|til /kã'tʃiw/ (*pl* ~**tis**) *m* canteen; ~**tina** *f* canteen
canto[1] /'kãtu/ *m* (*ângulo*) corner
can|to[2] /'kãtu/ *m* (*cantar*) singing; ~**tor** *m* singer; ~**toria** *f* singing
canudo /ka'nudu/ *m* (*de beber*) straw; (*tubo*) tube; (*fam: diploma*) diploma
cão /kãw/ (*pl* **cães**) *m* dog
caolho /ka'oʎu/ *a* one-eyed
ca|os /kaws/ *m* chaos; ~**ótico** *a* chaotic
capa /'kapa/ *f* (*de livro, revista*) cover; (*roupa sem mangas*) cape; ~ **de chuva** raincoat
capacete /kapa'setʃi/ *m* helmet
capacho /ka'paʃu/ *m* doormat
capaci|dade /kapasi'dadʒi/ *f* capacity; (*aptidão*) ability; ~**tar** *vt* enable; (*convencer*) convince
capataz /kapa'tas/ *m* foreman
capaz /ka'pas/ *a* capable (de of); **ser** ~ **de** (*poder*) be able to; (*ser provável*) be likely to
cape|la /ka'pɛla/ *f* chapel; ~**lão** (*pl* ~**lães**) *m* chaplain
capen|ga /ka'pẽga/ *a* doddery; ~**gar** *vi* dodder
capeta /ka'peta/ *m* (*diabo*) devil; (*criança*) little devil
capilar /kapi'lar/ *a* hair
ca|pim /ka'pĩ/ *m* grass; ~**pinar** *vt/i* weed
capi|tal /kapi'taw/ (*pl* ~**tais**) *a & m/f* capital; ~**talismo** *m* capitalism; ~**talista** *a & m/f* capitalist; ~**talizar** *vt* (*com*) capitalize; (*aproveitar*) capitalize on

capi|tanear /kapitani'ar/ *vt* captain <*navio*>; (*fig*) lead; **~tania** *f* captaincy; **~tania do porto** port authority; **~tão** (*pl* **~tães**) *m* captain
capitulação /kapitula'sãw/ *f* capitulation, surrender
capítulo /ka'pitulu/ *m* chapter; (*de telenovela*) episode
capô /ka'po/ *m* bonnet, (*Amer*) hood
capoeira /kapo'era/ *f* Brazilian kick-boxing
capo|ta /ka'pɔta/ *f* roof; **~tar** *vi* overturn
capote /ka'pɔtʃi/ *m* overcoat
capri|char /kapri'ʃar/ *vi* excel o.s.; **~cho** *m* (*esmero*) care; (*desejo*) whim; (*teimosia*) contrariness; **~choso** /o/ *a* (*cheio de caprichos*) capricious; (*com esmero*) painstaking, meticulous
Capricórnio /kapri'kɔrniu/ *m* Capricorn
capricorniano /kaprikorni'anu/ *a* & *m* Capricorn
cápsula /'kapsula/ *f* capsule
cap|tar /kap'tar/ *vt* pick up <*emissão, sinais*>; tap <*água*>; catch, grasp <*sentido*>; win <*simpatia, admiração*>; **~tura** *f* capture; **~turar** *vt* capture
capuz /ka'pus/ *m* hood
caquético /ka'kɛtʃiku/ *a* broken-down, on one's last legs
caqui /ka'ki/ *m* persimmon
cáqui /'kaki/ *a invar* & *m* khaki
cara /'kara/ *f* face; (*aparência*) look; (*ousadia*) cheek □ (*fam*) *m* guy; **~ a ~** face to face; **de ~** straightaway; **dar de ~ com** run into; **está na ~** it's obvious; **fechar a ~** frown; **~ de pau** cheek; **~ de tacho** (*fam*) sheepish look
cara|col /kara'kɔw/ (*pl* **~cóis**) *m* snail
caracte|re /karak'tɛri/ *m* character; **~rística** *f* characteristic, feature; **~rístico** *a* characteristic; **~rizar** *vt* characterize; **~rizar-se** *vpr* be characterized
cara-de-pau /karadʒi'paw/ (*pl* **caras-de-pau**) *a* cheeky, brazen
caramba /ka'rãba/ *int* (*de espanto*) wow; (*de desagrado*) damn
caramelo /kara'mɛlu/ *m* caramel; (*bala*) toffee
caramujo /kara'muʒu/ *m* water snail
caranguejo /karã'geʒu/ *m* crab
caratê /kara'te/ *m* karate
caráter /ka'rater/ *m* character
caravana /kara'vana/ *f* caravan
car|boidrato /karboi'dratu/ *m* carbohydrate; **~bono** /o/ *m* carbon
carbu|rador /karbura'dor/ *m* carburettor, (*Amer*) carburator; **~rante** *m* fuel
carcaça /kar'kasa/ *f* carcass; (*de navio etc*) frame
cárcere /'karseri/ *m* jail
carcereiro /karse'reru/ *m* jailer, warder
carcomido /karko'midu/ *a* worm-eaten; <*rosto*> pock-marked
cardápio /kar'dapiu/ *m* menu
carde|al /kardʒi'aw/ (*pl* **~ais**) *a* cardinal
cardíaco /kar'dʒiaku/ *a* cardiac; **ataque ~** heart attack
cardio|lógico /kardʒio'lɔʒiku/ *a* heart; **~logista** *m/f* heart specialist, cardiologist
cardume /kar'dumi/ *m* shoal
careca /ka'rɛka/ *a* bald □ *f* bald patch
ca|recer /kare'ser/ **~recer de** *vt* lack; **~rência** *f* lack; (*social*) deprivation; (*afetiva*) lack of affection; **~rente** *a* lacking; (*socialmente*) deprived; (*afetivamente*) in need of affection
carestia /kares'tʃia/ *f* high cost; (*geral*) high cost of living; (*escassez*) shortage
careta /ka'reta/ *f* grimace □ *a* (*fam*) straight, square
car|ga /'karga/ *f* load; (*mercadorias*) cargo; (*elétrica*) charge; (*de cavalaria*) charge; (*de caneta*) refill; (*fig*) burden; **~ga horária** workload; **~go** *m* (*função*) post, job; **a ~go de** in the charge of; **~gueiro** *m* (*navio*) cargo ship, freighter
cariar /kari'ar/ *vi* decay
Caribe /ka'ribi/ *m* Caribbean
caricatu|ra /karika'tura/ *f* caricature; **~rar** *vt* caricature; **~rista** *m/f* caricaturist
carícia /ka'risia/ *f* (*com a mão*) stroke, caress; (*carinho*) affection
cari|dade /kari'dadʒi/ *f* charity; **obra de ~dade** charity; **~doso** /o/ *a* charitable
cárie /'kari/ *f* tooth decay
carim|bar /karĩ'bar/ *vt* stamp; postmark <*carta*>; **~bo** *m* stamp; (*do correio*) postmark
cari|nho /ka'riɲu/ *m* affection; (*um*) caress; **~nhoso** /o/ *a* affectionate
carioca /kari'ɔka/ *a* from Rio de Janeiro □ *m/f* person from Rio de Janeiro □ (*Port*) *m* weak coffee
caris|ma /ka'rizma/ *m* charisma; **~mático** *a* charismatic
carna|val /karna'vaw/ (*pl* **~vais**) *m* carnival; **~valesco** /e/ *a* carnival; <*roupa*> over the top, overdone □ *m* carnival organizer
car|ne /'karni/ *f* (*humana etc*) flesh; (*comida*) meat; **~neiro** *m* sheep; (*macho*) ram; (*como comida*) mutton; **~niça** *f* carrion; **~nificina** *f*

slaughter; ~**nívoro** *a* carnivorous □ *m* carnivore; ~**nudo** *a* fleshy

caro /'karu/ *a* expensive; (*querido*) dear □ *adv* <*custar, cobrar*> a lot; <*comprar, vender*> at a high price; **pagar** ~ pay a high price (for)

caroço /ka'rosu/ *m* (*de pêssego etc*) stone; (*de maçã*) core; (*em sopa, molho etc*) lump

carona /ka'rɔna/ *f* lift

carpete /kar'pɛtʃi/ *m* fitted carpet

carpin|taria /karpĩta'ria/ *f* carpentry; ~**teiro** *m* carpenter

carran|ca /ka'xãka/ *f* scowl; ~**cudo** *a* <*cara*> scowling; <*pessoa*> sullen

carrapato /kaxa'patu/ *m* (*animal*) tick; (*fig*) hanger-on

carrasco /ka'xasku/ *m* executioner; (*fig*) butcher

carre|gado /kaxe'gadu/ *a* <*céu*> dark, black; <*cor*> dark; <*ambiente*> tense; ~**gador** *m* porter; ~**gamento** *m* loading; (*carga*) load; ~**gar** *vt* load <*navio, arma, máquina fotográfica*>; (*levar*) carry; charge <*bateria, pilha*>; ~**gar em** overdo; pronounce strongly <*letra*>; (*Port*) press

carreira /ka'xera/ *f* career

carre|tel /kaxe'tɛw/ (*pl* ~**téis**) *m* reel

car|ril /ka'xiw/ (*pl* ~**ris**) (*Port*) *m* rail

carrinho /ka'xiɲu/ *m* (*para bagagem, compras*) trolley; (*de criança*) pram; ~ **de mão** wheel-barrow

carro /'kaxu/ *m* car; (*de bois*) cart; ~ **alegórico** float; ~ **esporte** sports car; ~ **fúnebre** hearse; ~**ça** /ɔ/ *f* cart; ~**ceria** *f* bodywork; ~**-chefe** (*pl* ~**s-chefes**) *m* (*no carnaval*) main float; (*fig*) centrepiece; ~**-forte** (*pl* ~**s-fortes**) *m* security van

carros|sel /kaxo'sɛw/ (*pl* ~**séis**) *m* merry-go-round

carruagem /kaxu'aʒẽ/ *f* carriage, coach

carta /'karta/ *f* letter; (*mapa*) chart; (*do baralho*) card; ~ **branca** (*fig*) carte blanche; ~ **de condução** (*Port*) driving licence, (*Amer*) driver's license; ~**-bomba** (*pl* ~**s-bomba**) *f* letter bomb; ~**da** *f* (*fig*) move

cartão /kar'tãw/ *m* card; (*Port: papelão*) cardboard; ~ **de crédito** credit card; ~ **de visita** visiting card; ~**-postal** (*pl* **cartões-postais**) *m* postcard

car|taz /kar'tas/ *m* poster, (*Amer*) bill; **em** ~ showing, (*Amer*) playing; ~**teira** *f* (*para dinheiro*) wallet; (*cartão*) card; (*mesa*) desk; ~**teira de identidade** identity card; ~**teira de motorista** driving licence, (*Amer*) driver's license; ~**teiro** *m* postman

car|tel /kar'tɛw/ (*pl* ~**téis**) *m* cartel

cárter /'karter/ *m* sump

carto|la /kar'tɔla/ *f* top hat □ *m* director; ~**lina** *f* card; ~**mante** *m/f* tarot reader, fortune-teller

cartório /kar'tɔriu/ *m* registry office

cartucho /kar'tuʃu/ *m* cartridge; (*de dinamite*) stick; (*de amendoim etc*) bag

car|tum /kar'tũ/ *m* cartoon; ~**tunista** *m/f* cartoonist

caruncho /ka'rũʃu/ *m* woodcorm

carvalho /kar'vaʎu/ *m* oak

car|vão /kar'vãw/ *m* coal; (*de desenho*) charcoal; ~**voeiro** *a* coal

casa /'kaza/ *f* house; (*comercial*) firm; (*de tabuleiro*) square; (*de botão*) hole; **em** ~ at home; **para** ~ home; **na** ~ **dos 30 anos** in one's thirties; ~ **da moeda** mint; ~ **de banho** (*Port*) bathroom; ~ **de campo** country house; ~ **de saúde** private hospital; ~ **decimal** decimal place; ~ **popular** council house

casaco /ka'zaku/ *m* (*sobretudo*) coat; (*paletó*) jacket; (*de lã*) pullover

ca|sal /ka'zaw/ (*pl* ~**sais**) *m* couple; ~**samento** *m* marriage; (*cerimônia*) wedding; ~**sar** *vt* marry; (*fig*) combine □ *vi* get married; (*fig*) go together; ~**sar-se** *vpr* get married; (*fig*) combine; ~**sar-se com** marry

casarão /kaza'rãw/ *m* mansion

casca /'kaska/ *f* (*de árvore*) bark; (*de laranja, limão*) peel; (*de banana*) skin; (*de noz, ovo*) shell; (*de milho*) husk; (*de pão*) crust; (*de ferida*) scab

cascalho /kas'kaʎu/ *m* gravel

cascata /kas'kata/ *f* waterfall; (*fam*) fib

casca|vel /kaska'vɛw/ (*pl* ~**véis**) *m* (*cobra*) rattlesnake □ *f* (*mulher*) shrew

casco /'kasku/ *m* (*de cavalo etc*) hoof; (*de navio*) hull; (*garrafa vazia*) empty

ca|sebre /ka'zɛbri/ *m* hovel, shack; ~**seiro** *a* <*comida*> home-made; <*pessoa*> home-loving; <*vida*> home □ *m* housekeeper

caserna /ka'zɛrna/ *f* barracks

casmurro /kaz'muxu/ *a* sullen

caso /'kazu/ *m* case; (*amoroso*) affair; (*conto*) story □ *conj* in case; **em todo ou qualquer** ~ in any case; **fazer** ~ **de** take notice of; **vir ao** ~ be relevant; ~ **contrário** otherwise

casório /ka'zɔriu/ (*fam*) *m* wedding

caspa /'kaspa/ *f* dandruff

casquinha /kas'kiɲa/ *f* (*de sorvete*) cone, cornet

cassar /ka'sar/ *vt* revoke, withdraw <*direitos, autorização*>; ban <*político*>

cassete /ka'sɛtʃi/ *m* cassette

cassetete /kase'tɛtʃi/ *m* truncheon, (*Amer*) nightstick

cassino /ka'sinu/ *m* casino; ~ **de oficiais** officers' mess

casta|nha /kas'taɲa/ *f* chestnut; **~nha de caju** cashew nut; **~nha-do-pará** (*pl* **~nhas-do-pará**) *f* Brazil nut; **~nheiro** *m* chestnut tree; **~nho** *a* chestnut(-coloured); **~nholas** /ɔ/ *f pl* castanets

castelhano /kaste'ʎanu/ *a & m* Castilian

castelo /kas'tɛlu/ *m* castle

casti|çal /kastʃi'saw/ (*pl* **~çais**) *m* candlestick

cas|tidade /kastʃi'dadʒi/ *f* chastity; **~tigar** *vt* punish; **~tigo** *m* punishment; **~to** *a* chaste

castor /kas'tor/ *m* beaver

castrar /kas'trar/ *vt* castrate

casu|al /kazu'aw/ (*pl* **~ais**) *a* chance; (*fortuito*) fortuitous; **~alidade** *f* chance

casulo /ka'zulu/ *m* (*de larva*) cocoon

cata /'kata/ *f* **à ~ de** in search of

cata|lão /kata'lãw/ (*pl* **~lães**) *a & m* (*f* **~lã**) Catalan

catalisador /kataliza'dor/ *m* catalyst; (*de carro*) catalytic convertor

catalogar /katalo'gar/ *vt* catalogue

catálogo /ka'talogu/ *m* catalogue; (*de telefones*) phone book

Catalunha /kata'luɲa/ *f* Catalonia

catapora /kata'pɔra/ *f* chicken pox

catar /ka'tar/ *vt* (*procurar*) search for; (*recolher*) gather; (*do chão*) pick up; sort <*arroz, café*>

catarata /kata'rata/ *f* waterfall; (*no olho*) cataract

catarro /ka'taxu/ *m* catarrh

catástrofe /ka'tastrofi/ *f* catastrophe

catastrófico /katas'trɔfiku/ *a* catastrophic

catecismo /kate'sizmu/ *m* catechism

cátedra /'katedra/ *f* chair

cate|dral /kate'draw/ (*pl* **~drais**) *f* cathedral; **~drático** *m* professor

cate|goria /katego'ria/ *f* category; (*social*) class; (*qualidade*) quality; **~górico** *a* categorical; **~gorizar** *vt* categorize

catinga /ka'tʃĩga/ *f* body odour, stink

cati|vante /katʃi'vãtʃi/ *a* captivating; **~var** *vt* captivate; **~veiro** *m* captivity; **~vo** *a & m* captive

catolicismo /katoli'sizmu/ *m* Catholicism

católico /ka'tɔliku/ *a & m* Catholic

catorze /ka'torzi/ *a & m* fourteen

cau|da /'kawda/ *f* tail; **~dal** (*pl* **~dais**) *m* torrent

caule /'kawli/ *m* stem

cau|sa /'kawza/ *f* cause; (*jurid*) case; **por ~sa de** because of; **~sar** *vt* cause

caute|la /kaw'tɛla/ *f* caution; (*documento*) ticket; **~loso** /o/ *a* cautious, careful

cava /'kava/ *f* armhole

cava|do /ka'vadu/ *a* <*vestido*> low-cut; <*olhos*> deep-set; **~dor** *a* hard-working □ *m* hard worker

cava|laria /kavala'ria/ *f* cavalry; **~lariça** *f* stable; **~leiro** *m* horseman; (*na Idade Média*) knight

cavalete /kava'letʃi/ *m* easel

caval|gadura /kavawga'dura/ *f* mount; **~gar** *vt/i* ride; sit astride <*muro, banco*>; (*saltar*) jump

cavalhei|resco /kavaʎe'resku/ *a* gallant, gentlemanly; **~ro** *m* gentleman □ *a* gallant, gentlemanly

cavalo /ka'valu/ *m* horse; **a ~** on horseback; **~-vapor** (*pl* **~s-vapor**) horsepower

cavanhaque /kava'ɲaki/ *m* goatee

cavaquinho /kava'kiɲu/ *m* ukulele

cavar /ka'var/ *vt* dig; (*fig*) go all out for □ *vi* dig; (*fig*) go all out; **~ em** (*vasculhar*) delve into; **~ a vida** make a living

caveira /ka'vera/ *f* skull

caverna /ka'vɛrna/ *f* cavern

caviar /kavi'ar/ *m* caviar

cavidade /kavi'dadʒi/ *f* cavity

cavilha /ka'viʎa/ *f* peg

cavo /'kavu/ *a* hollow

cavoucar /kavo'kar/ *vt* excavate

caxemira /kaʃe'mira/ *f* cashmere

caxumba /ka'ʃũba/ *f* mumps

cear /si'ar/ *vt* have for supper □ *vi* have supper

cebo|la /se'bola/ *f* onion; **~linha** *f* spring onion

ceder /se'der/ *vt* give up; (*dar*) give; (*emprestar*) lend □ *vi* (*não resistir*) give way; **~ a** yield to

cedilha /se'dʒiʎa/ *f* cedilla

cedo /'sedu/ *adv* early; **mais ~ ou mais tarde** sooner or later

cedro /'sɛdru/ *m* cedar

cédula /'sɛdula/ *f* (*de banco*) note, (*Amer*) bill; (*eleitoral*) ballot paper

ce|gar /se'gar/ *vt* blind; blunt <*faca*>; **~go** /ɛ/ *a* blind; <*faca*> blunt □ *m* blind man; **às ~gas** blindly

cegonha /se'goɲa/ *f* stork

cegueira /se'gera/ *f* blindness

ceia /'seja/ *f* supper

cei|fa /'sejfa/ *f* harvest; (*massacre*) slaughter; **~far** *vt* reap; claim <*vidas*>; (*matar*) mow down

cela /'sɛla/ *f* cell

cele|bração /selebra'sãw/ *f* celebration; **~brar** *vt* celebrate

célebre /'sɛlebri/ *a* celebrated

celebridade /selebri'dadʒi/ *f* celebrity

celeiro /se'leru/ *m* granary

célere /'sɛleri/ *a* swift, fast

celeste /se'lɛstʃi/ *a* celestial

celeuma /se'lewma/ *f* pandemonium

celibato /seli'batu/ *m* celibacy

celofane /selo'fani/ *m* cellophane

celta /'sɛwta/ *a* Celtic □ *m/f* Celt □ *m* (*língua*) Celtic

célula /'sɛlula/ *f* cell

celu|lar /selu'lar/ *a* cellular; **~lite** *f* cellulite; **~lose** /ɔ/ *f* cellulose

cem /sẽj/ *a & m* hundred

cemitério /semi'tɛriu/ *m* cemetery; (*fig*) graveyard

cena /'sena/ *f* scene; (*palco*) stage; **em ~** on stage

cenário /se'nariu/ *m* scenery; (*de crime etc*) scene

cênico /'seniku/ *a* stage

cenoura /se'nora/ *f* carrot

cen|so /'sẽsu/ *m* census; **~sor** *m* censor; **~sura** *f* (*de jornais etc*) censorship; (*órgão*) censor(s); (*condenação*) censure; **~surar** *vt* censor <*jornal, filme etc*>; (*condenar*) censure

centavo /sẽ'tavu/ *m* cent

centeio /sẽ'teju/ *m* rye

centelha /sẽ'teʎa/ *f* spark; (*fig: de gênio etc*) flash

cente|na /sẽ'tena/ *f* hundred; **uma ~na de** about a hundred; **às ~nas** in their hundreds; **~nário** *m* centenary

centésimo /sẽ'tɛzimu/ *a* hundredth

centí|grado /sẽ'tʃigradu/ *m* centigrade; **~litro** *m* centilitre; **~metro** *m* centimetre

cento /'sẽtu/ *a & m* hundred; **por ~** per cent

cen|tral /sẽ'traw/ (*pl* **~trais**) *a* central; **~tralizar** *vt* centralize; **~trar** *vt* centre; **~tro** *m* centre

cepti- (*Port*) *veja* **ceti-**

cera /'sera/ *f* wax; **fazer ~** waste time, faff about

cerâmi|ca /se'ramika/ *f* ceramics, pottery; **~co** *a* ceramic

cer|ca /'serka/ *f* fence; **~ca viva** hedge □ *adv* **~ca de** around, about; **~cado** *m* enclosure; (*para criança*) playpen; **~car** *vt* surround; (*com muro, cerca*) enclose; (*assediar*) besiege

cercear /sersi'ar/ *vt* (*fig*) curtail, restrict

cerco /'serku/ *m* (*mil*) siege; (*policial*) dragnet

cere|al /seri'aw/ (*pl* **~ais**) *m* cereal

cere|bral /sere'braw/ (*pl* **~brais**) *a* cerebral

cérebro /'sɛrebru/ *m* brain; (*inteligência*) intellect

cere|ja /se'reʒa/ *f* cherry; **~jeira** *f* cherry tree

cerimônia /seri'monia/ *f* ceremony; **sem ~** unceremoniously; **fazer ~** stand on ceremony

cerimoni|al /serimoni'aw/ (*pl* **~ais**) *a & m* ceremonial; **~oso** /o/ *a* ceremonious

cer|rado /se'xadu/ *a* <*barba, mata*> thick; <*punho, dentes*> clenched □ *m* scrubland; **~rar** *vt* close; **~rar-se** *vpr* close; <*noites, trevas*> close in

certeiro /ser'teru/ *a* well-aimed, accurate

certeza /ser'teza/ *f* certainty; **com ~** certainly; **ter ~** be sure (**de** of; **de que** that)

certidão /sertʃi'dãw/ *f* certificate; **~ de nascimento** birth certificate

certifi|cado /sertʃifi'kadu/ *m* certificate; **~car** *vt* certify; **~car-se de** make sure of

certo /'sɛrtu/ *a* (*correto*) right; (*seguro*) certain; (*algum*) a certain □ *adv* right; **dar ~** work

cerveja /ser'veʒa/ *f* beer; **~ria** *f* brewery; (*bar*) pub

cervo /'sɛrvu/ *m* deer

cer|zidura /serzi'dura/ *f* darning; **~zir** *vt* darn

cesariana /sezari'ana/ *f* Caesarian

césio /'sɛziu/ *m* caesium

cessar /se'sar/ *vt/i* cease

ces|ta /'sesta/ *f* basket; (*de comida*) hamper; **~to** /e/ *m* basket; **~to de lixo** wastepaper basket

ceticismo /setʃi'sizmu/ *m* scepticism

cético /'sɛtʃiku/ *a* sceptical □ *m* sceptic

cetim /se'tʃĩ/ *m* satin

céu /sɛw/ *m* sky; (*na religião*) heaven; **~ da boca** roof of the mouth

cevada /se'vada/ *f* barley

chá /ʃa/ *m* tea

chacal /ʃa'kaw/ (*pl* **~cais**) *m* jackal

chácara /'ʃakara/ *f* smallholding; (*casa*) country cottage

chaci|na /ʃa'sina/ *f* slaughter; **~nar** *vt* slaughter

chá|-de-bar /ʃadʒi'bar/ (*pl* **~s-de-bar**) *m* bachelor party; **~-de-panela** (*pl* **~s-de-panela**) *m* hen night, (*Amer*) wedding shower

chafariz /ʃafa'ris/ *m* fountain

chaga /'ʃaga/ *f* sore

chaleira /ʃa'lera/ *f* kettle

chama /'ʃama/ *f* flame

cha|mada /ʃa'mada/ *f* call; (*dos presentes*) roll call; (*dos alunos*) register; **~mado** *m* call □ *a* (*depois do substantivo*) called; (*antes do substantivo*) so-called; **~mar** *vt* call; (*para sair etc*) ask, invite; attract <*atenção*> □ *vi* call; <*telefone*> ring; **~mar-se** *vpr* be called; **~mariz** *m* decoy; **~mativo** *a* showy, flashy

chamejar /ʃame'ʒar/ *vi* flare

chaminé /ʃami'nɛ/ *f* (*de casa, fábrica*) chimney; (*de navio, trem*) funnel

champanhe /ʃã'paɲi/ *m* champagne

champu /ʃã'pu/ (*Port*) *m* shampoo

chamuscar /ʃamus'kar/ *vt* singe, scorch

chance /'ʃãsi/ *f* chance

chanceler /ʃãse'ler/ *m* chancellor

chanchada /ʃã'ʃada/ *f* (*peça*) second-rate play; (*filme*) B movie

chanta|gear /ʃãtaʒi'ar/ *vt* blackmail; **~gem** *f* blackmail; **~gista** *m/f* blackmailer

chão /ʃãw/ (*pl* **~s**) *m* ground; (*dentro de casa etc*) floor

chapa /'ʃapa/ *f* sheet; (*foto*) plate; **~ eleitoral** electoral list; **~ de matrícula** (*Port*) number plate, (*Amer*) license plate □ (*fam*) *m* mate

chapéu /ʃa'pɛw/ *m* hat

charada /ʃa'rada/ *f* riddle

char|ge /'ʃarʒi/ *f* (political) cartoon; **~gista** *m/f* cartoonist

charla|tanismo /ʃarlata'nizmu/ *m* charlatanism; **~tão** (*pl* **~tães**) *m* (*f* **~tona**) charlatan

char|me /'ʃarmi/ *m* charm; **fazer ~me** turn on the charm; **~moso** /o/ *a* charming

charneca /ʃar'nɛka/ *f* moor

charuto /ʃa'rutu/ *m* cigar

chassi /ʃa'si/ *m* chassis

chata /'ʃata/ *f* (*barca*) barge

chate|ação /ʃatʃia'sãw/ *f* annoyance; **~ar** *vt* annoy; **~ar-se** *vpr* get annoyed

cha|tice /ʃa'tʃisi/ *f* nuisance; **~to** *a* (*tedioso*) boring; (*irritante*) annoying; (*mal-educado*) rude; (*plano*) flat

chauvinis|mo /ʃovi'nizmu/ *m* chauvinism; **~ta** *m/f* chauvinist □ *a* chauvinistic

cha|vão /ʃa'vãw/ *m* cliché; **~ve** *f* key; (*ferramenta*) spanner; **~ve de fenda** screwdriver; **~ve inglesa** wrench; **~veiro** *m* (*aro*) keyring; (*pessoa*) locksmith

chávena /'ʃavena/ *f* soup bowl; (*Port: xícara*) cup

checar /ʃe'kar/ *vt* check

che|fe /'ʃɛfi/ *m/f* (*patrão*) boss; (*gerente*) manager; (*dirigente*) leader; **~fia** *f* leadership; (*de empresa*) management; (*sede*) headquarters; **~fiar** *vt* lead; be in charge of <*trabalho*>

che|gada /ʃe'gada/ *f* arrival; **~gado** *a* <*amigo, relação*> close; **~gar** *vi* arrive; (*deslocar-se*) move up; (*ser suficiente*) be enough □ *vt* bring up <*prato, cadeira*>; **~gar a fazer** go as far as doing; **aonde você quer ~gar?** what are you driving at?; **~gar lá** (*fig*) make it

cheia /'ʃeja/ *f* flood

cheio /'ʃeju/ *a* full; (*fam: farto*) fed up

chei|rar /ʃe'rar/ *vt/i* smell (a of); **~roso** /o/ *a* scented

cheque /'ʃɛki/ *m* cheque, (*Amer*) check; **~ de viagem** traveller's cheque; **~ em branco** blank cheque

chi|ado /ʃi'adu/ *m* (*de pneus, freios*) screech; (*de porta*) squeak; (*de vapor, numa fita*) hiss; **~ar** *vi* <*porta*> squeak; <*pneus, freios*> screech; <*vapor, fita*> hiss; <*fritura*> sizzle; (*fam: reclamar*) grumble, moan

chiclete /ʃi'klɛtʃi/ *m* chewing gum; **~ de bola** bubble gum

chico|tada /ʃiko'tada/ *f* lash; **~te** /ɔ/ *m* whip; **~tear** *vt* whip

chi|frar /ʃi'frar/ (*fam*) *vt* cheat on <*marido, esposa*>; two-time <*namorado, namorada*>; **~fre** *m* horn; **~frudo** *a* horned; (*fam*) cuckolded □ *m* cuckold

Chile /'ʃili/ *m* Chile

chileno /ʃi'lenu/ *a & m* Chilean

chilique /ʃi'liki/ (*fam*) *m* funny turn

chil|rear /ʃiwxi'ar/ *vi* chirp, twitter; **~reio** *m* chirping, twittering

chimarrão /ʃima'xãw/ *m* unsweetened maté tea

chimpanzé /ʃĩpã'zɛ/ *m* chimpanzee

China /'ʃina/ *f* China

chinelo /ʃi'nɛlu/ *m* slipper

chi|nês /ʃi'nes/ *a & m* (*f* **~nesa**) Chinese

chinfrim /ʃĩ'frĩ/ *a* tatty, shoddy

chio /'ʃiu/ *m* squeak; (*de pneus*) screech; (*de vapor*) hiss

chique /'ʃiki/ *a* <*pessoa, aparência, roupa*> smart, (*Amer*) sharp; <*hotel, bairro, loja etc*> smart, up-market, posh

chiqueiro /ʃi'keru/ *m* pigsty

chis|pa /'ʃispa/ *f* flash; **~pada** *f* dash; **~par** *vi* (*soltar chispas*) flash; (*correr*) dash

choca|lhar /ʃoka'ʎar/ *vt/i* rattle; **~lho** *m* rattle

cho|cante /ʃo'kãtʃi/ *a* shocking; (*fam*) incredible; **~car** *vt/i* hatch <*ovos*>; (*ultrajar*) shock; **~car-se** *vpr* <*carros etc*> crash; <*teorias etc*> clash

chocho /'ʃoʃu/ *a* dull, insipid

chocolate /ʃoko'latʃi/ *m* chocolate

chofer /ʃo'fɛr/ *m* chauffeur

chope /'ʃopi/ *m* draught lager

choque /'ʃɔki/ *m* shock; (*colisão*) collision; (*conflito*) clash

cho|radeira /ʃora'dera/ *f* fit of crying; **~ramingar** *vi* whine; **~ramingas** *m/f invar* whiner; **~rão** *m* (*salgueiro*) weeping willow □ *a* (**~rona**) tearful; **~rar** *vi* cry; **~ro** /o/ *m* crying; **~roso** /o/ *a* tearful

chouriço /ʃo'risu/ *m* black pudding; (*Port*) sausage

chover /ʃo'ver/ *vi* rain
chuchu /ʃu'ʃu/ *m* chayote
chucrute /ʃu'krutʃi/ *m* sauerkraut
chumaço /ʃu'masu/ *m* wad
chum|bado /ʃũ'badu/ (*fam*) *a* knocked out; **~bar** (*Port*) *vt* fill <*dente*>; fail <*aluno*> □ *vi* <*aluno*> fail; **~bo** *m* lead; (*Port: obturação*) filling
chu|par /ʃu'par/ *vt* suck; <*esponja*> suck up; **~peta** /e/ *f* dummy, (*Amer*) pacifier
churras|caria /ʃuxaska'ria/ *f* barbecue restaurant; **~co** *m* barbecue; **~queira** *f* barbecue; **~quinho** *m* kebab
chu|tar /ʃu'tar/ *vt/i* kick; (*fam: adivinhar*) guess; **~te** *m* kick; **~teira** *f* football boot
chu|va /'ʃuva/ *f* rain; **~va de pedra** hail; **~varada** *f* torrential rainstorm; **~veiro** *m* shower; **~viscar** *vi* drizzle; **~visco** *m* drizzle; **~voso** /o/ *a* rainy
cica|triz /sika'tris/ *f* scar; **~trizar** *vt* scar □ *vi* <*ferida*> heal
cic|lismo /si'klizmu/ *m* cycling; **~lista** *m/f* cyclist; **~lo** *m* cycle; **~lone** /o/ *m* cyclone; **~lovia** *f* cycle lane
cida|dania /sidada'nia/ *f* citizenship; **~dão** (*pl* **~dãos**) *m* (*f* **~dã**) citizen; **~de** *f* town; (*grande*) city; **~dela** /ɛ/ *f* citadel
ciência /si'ẽsia/ *f* science
cien|te /si'ẽtʃi/ *a* aware; **~tífico** *a* scientific; **~tista** *m/f* scientist
ci|fra /'sifra/ *f* figure; (*código*) cipher; **~frão** *m* dollar sign; **~frar** *vt* encode
cigano /si'ganu/ *a* & *m* gypsy
cigarra /si'gaxa/ *f* cicada; (*dispositivo*) buzzer
cigar|reira /siga'xera/ *f* cigarette case; **~ro** *m* cigarette
cilada /si'lada/ *f* trap; (*estratagema*) trick
cilindrada /silĩ'drada/ *f* (engine) capacity
cilíndrico /si'lĩdriku/ *a* cylindrical
cilindro /si'lĩdru/ *m* cylinder; (*rolo*) roller
cílio /'siliu/ *m* eyelash
cima /'sima/ *f* **em ~** on top; (*na casa*) upstairs; **em ~ de** on, on top of; **para ~** up; (*na casa*) upstairs; **por ~** over the top; **por ~ de** over; **de ~** from above; **ainda por ~** moreover
címbalo /'sĩbalu/ *m* cymbal
cimeira /si'mera/ *f* crest; (*Port: cúpula*) summit
cimen|tar /simẽ'tar/ *vt* cement; **~to** *m* cement
cinco /'sĩku/ *a* & *m* five
cine|asta /sini'asta/ *m/f* film-maker; **~ma** /e/ *m* cinema
Cingapura /sĩga'pura/ *f* Singapore
cínico /'siniku/ *a* cynical □ *m* cynic
cinismo /si'nizmu/ *m* cynicism
cinqüen|ta /sĩ'kwẽta/ *a* & *m* fifty; **~tão** *a* & *m* (*f* **~tona**) fifty-year-old
cinti|lante /sĩtʃi'lãtʃi/ *a* glittering; **~lar** *vi* glitter
cin|to /'sĩtu/ *m* belt; **~to de segurança** seatbelt; **~tura** *f* waist; **~turão** *m* belt
cin|za /'sĩza/ *f* ash □ *a invar* grey; **~zeiro** *m* ashtray
cin|zel /sĩ'zɛw/ (*pl* **~zéis**) *m* chisel; **~zelar** *vt* carve
cinzento /sĩ'zẽtu/ *a* grey
cipó /si'pɔ/ *m* vine, liana; **~poal** (*pl* **~poais**) *m* jungle
cipreste /si'prɛstʃi/ *m* cypress
cipriota /sipri'ɔta/ *a* & *m* Cypriot
ciranda /si'rãda/ *f* (*fig*) merry-go-round
cir|cense /sir'sẽsi/ *a* circus; **~co** *m* circus
circu|ito /sir'kuitu/ *m* circuit; **~lação** *f* circulation; **~lar** *a* & *f* circular □ *vt* circulate □ *vi* <*dinheiro, sangue*> circulate; <*carro*> drive; <*ônibus*> run; <*trânsito*> move; <*pessoa*> go round
círculo /'sirkulu/ *m* circle
circunci|dar /sirkũsi'dar/ *vt* circumcise; **~ção** *f* circumcision
circun|dar /sirkũ'dar/ *vt* surround; **~ferência** *f* circumference; **~flexo** /ɛks/ *a* & *m* circumflex; **~scrição** *f* district; **~scrição eleitoral** constituency; **~specto** /ɛ/ *a* circumspect; **~stância** *f* circumstance; **~stanciado** *a* detailed; **~stancial** (*pl* **~stanciais**) *a* circumstantial; **~stante** *m/f* bystander
cirrose /si'xɔzi/ *f* cirrhosis
cirur|gia /sirur'ʒia/ *f* surgery; **~gião** *m* (*f* **~giã**) surgeon
cirúrgico /si'rurʒiku/ *a* surgical
cisão /si'zãw/ *f* split, division
cisco /'sisku/ *m* speck
cisma[1] /'sizma/ *m* schism
cis|ma[2] /'sizma/ *f* (*mania*) fixation; (*devaneio*) imagining, daydream; (*prevenção*) irrational dislike; (*de criança*) whim; **~mar** *vt/i* be lost in thought; <*criança*> be insistent; **~mar em** brood over; **~mar de** *ou* **em fazer** insist on doing; **~mar que** insist on thinking that; **~mar com alg** take a dislike to s.o.
cisne /'sizni/ *m* swan
cistite /sis'tʃitʃi/ *f* cystitis
ci|tação /sita'sãw/ *f* quotation; (*jurid*) summons; **~tar** *vt* quote; (*jurid*) summon

ciúme /si'umi/ *m* jealousy; ter ~s de be jealous of

ciu|meira /siu'mera/ *f* fit of jealousy; ~**mento** *a* jealous

cívico /'siviku/ *a* civic

ci|vil /si'viw/ (*pl* ~vis) *a* civil □ *m* civilian; ~**vilidade** *f* civility

civili|zação /siviliza'sãw/ *f* civilization; ~**zado** *a* civilized; ~**zar** *vt* civilize

civismo /si'vizmu/ *m* public spirit

cla|mar /kla'mar/ *vt/i* cry out, clamour (por for); ~**mor** *m* outcry; ~**moroso** /o/ *a* <*protesto*> loud, noisy; <*erro, injustiça*> blatant

clandestino /klãdes'tʃinu/ *a* clandestine

cla|ra /'klara/ *f* egg white; ~**rabóia** *f* skylight; ~**rão** *m* flash; ~**rear** *vt* brighten; clarify <*questão*> □ *vi* brighten up; (*fazer-se dia*) become light; ~**reira** *f* clearing; ~**reza** /e/ *f* clarity; ~**ridade** *f* brightness; (*do dia*) daylight

cla|rim /kla'rĩ/ *m* bugle; ~**rinete** /e/ *m* clarinet

clarividente /klarivi'dẽtʃi/ *m/f* clairvoyant

claro /'klaru/ *a* clear; <*luz*> bright; <*cor*> light □ *adv* clearly □ *int* of course; ~ **que sim/não** of course/of course not; **às claras** openly; **noite em** ~ sleepless night; **já é dia** ~ it's already daylight

classe /'klasi/ *f* class; ~ **média** middle class

clássico /'klasiku/ *a* classical; (*famoso, exemplar*) classic □ *m* classic

classifi|cação /klasifika'sãw/ *f* classification; (*numa competição esportiva*) placing, place; ~**cado** *a* classified; <*candidato*> successful; <*esportista, time*> qualified; ~**car** *vt* classify; (*considerar*) describe (de as); ~**car-se** *vpr* <*candidato, esportista*> qualify; (*chamar-se*) describe o.s. (de as); ~**catório** *a* qualifying

classudo /kla'sudu/ (*fam*) *a* classy

claustro|fobia /klawstrofo'bia/ *f* claustrophobia; ~**fóbico** *a* claustrophobic

cláusula /'klawzula/ *f* clause

cla|ve /'klavi/ *f* clef; ~**vícula** *f* collar bone

cle|mência /kle'mẽsia/ *f* clemency; ~**mente** *a* <*pessoa*> lenient; <*tempo*> clement

cleptomaníaco /kleptoma'niaku/ *m* kleptomaniac

clérigo /'klɛrigu/ *m* cleric, clergyman

clero /'klɛru/ *m* clergy

clien|te /kli'ẽtʃi/ *m/f* (*de loja*) customer; (*de advogado, empresa*) client; ~**tela** /ɛ/ *f* (*de loja*) customers; (*de restaurante, empresa*) clientele

cli|ma /'klima/ *m* climate; ~**mático** *a* climatic

clímax /'klimaks/ *m invar* climax

clíni|ca /'klinika/ *f* clinic; ~**ca geral** general practice; ~**co** *a* clinical □ *m* ~**co geral** general practitioner, GP

clipe /'klipi/ *m* clip; (*para papéis*) paper clip

clone /'kloni/ *m* clone

cloro /'klɔru/ *m* chlorine

close /'klozi/ *m* close-up

clube /'klubi/ *m* club

coação /koa'sãw/ *f* coercion

coadjuvante /koadʒu'vãtʃi/ *a* <*ator*> supporting □ *m/f* (*em peça, filme*) co-star; (*em crime*) accomplice

coador /koa'dor/ *m* strainer; (*de legumes*) colander; (*de café*) filter bag

coadunar /koadu'nar/ *vt* combine

coagir /koa'ʒir/ *vt* compel

coagular /koagu'lar/ *vt/i* clot; ~**-se** *vpr* clot

coágulo /ko'agulu/ *m* clot

coalhar /koa'ʎar/ *vt/i* curdle; ~**-se** *vpr* curdle

coalizão /koali'zãw/ *f* coalition

coar /ko'ar/ *vt* strain

coaxar /koa'ʃar/ *vi* croak □ *m* croaking

cobaia /ko'baja/ *f* guinea pig

cober|ta /ko'bɛrta/ *f* (*de cama*) bedcover; (*de navio*) deck; ~**to** /ɛ/ *a* covered □ *pp de* **cobrir**; ~**tor** *m* blanket; ~**tura** *f* (*revestimento*) covering; (*reportagem*) coverage; (*seguro*) cover; (*apartamento*) penthouse

cobi|ça /ko'bisa/ *f* greed, covetousness; ~**çar** *vt* covet; ~**çoso** /o/ *a* covetous

cobra /'kɔbra/ *f* snake

co|brador /kobra'dor/ *m* (*no ônibus*) conductor; ~**brança** *f* (*de dívida*) collection; (*de preço*) charging; (*de atitudes*) asking for something in return (de for); ~**brança de pênalti/falta** penalty (kick)/free kick; ~**brar** *vt* collect <*dívida*>; ask for <*coisa prometida*>; take <*pênalti*>; ~**brar aco a alg** (*em dinheiro*) charge s.o. for sth; (*fig*) make s.o. pay for sth; ~**brar uma falta** (*no futebol*) take a free kick

cobre /'kɔbri/ *m* copper

cobrir /ko'brir/ *vt* cover; ~**-se** *vpr* <*pessoa*> cover o.s. up; <*coisa*> be covered

cocaína /koka'ina/ *f* cocaine

coçar /ko'sar/ *vt* scratch □ *vi* (*esfregar-se*) scratch; (*comichar*) itch; ~**-se** *vpr* scratch o.s.

cócegas /'kɔsegas/ *f pl* **fazer** ~ **em** tickle; **sentir** ~ be ticklish

coceira /ko'sera/ *f* itch
cochi|char /koʃi'ʃar/ *vt/i* whisper; **~cho** *m* whisper
cochi|lada /koʃi'lada/ *f* doze; **~lar** *vi* doze; **~lo** *m* snooze
coco /'koku/ *m* coconut
cócoras /'kɔkoras/ *f pl* **de ~** squatting; **ficar de ~** squat
côdea /'kodʒia/ *f* crust
codificar /kodʒifi'kar/ *vt* encode <*mensagem*>; codify <*leis*>
código /'kɔdʒigu/ *m* code; **~ de barras** bar code
codinome /kodʒi'nomi/ *m* codename
coeficiente /koefisi'ẽtʃi/ *m* coefficient; (*fig: fator*) factor
coelho /ko'eʎu/ *m* rabbit
coentro /ko'ẽtru/ *m* coriander
coerção /koer'sãw/ *f* coercion
coe|rência /koe'rẽsia/ *f* (*lógica*) coherence; (*conseqüência*) consistency; **~rente** *a* (*lógico*) coherent; (*conseqüente*) consistent
coexis|tência /koezis'tẽsia/ *f* coexistence; **~tir** *vi* coexist
cofre /'kɔfri/ *m* safe; (*de dinheiro público*) coffer
cogi|tação /koʒita'sãw/ *f* contemplation; **fora de ~tação** out of the question; **~tar** *vt/i* contemplate
cogumelo /kogu'mɛlu/ *m* mushroom
coibir /koi'bir/ *vt* restrict; **~-se de** keep o.s. from
coice /'kojsi/ *m* kick
coinci|dência /koĩsi'dẽsia/ *f* coincidence; **~dir** *vi* coincide
coisa /'kojza/ *f* thing
coitado /koj'tadu/ *m* poor thing; **~ do pai** poor father
cola /'kɔla/ *f* glue; (*cópia*) crib
colabo|ração /kolabora'sãw/ *f* collaboration; (*de escritor etc*) contribution; **~rador** *m* collaborator; (*em jornal, livro*) contributor; **~rar** *vi* collaborate; (*em jornal, livro*) contribute (em to)
colagem /ko'laʒẽ/ *f* collage
colágeno /ko'laʒenu/ *m* collagen
colapso /ko'lapsu/ *m* collapse
colar[1] /ko'lar/ *m* necklace
colar[2] /ko'lar/ *vt* (*grudar*) stick; (*copiar*) crib □ *vi* stick; (*copiar*) crib; <*desculpa etc*> stand up, stick
colarinho /kola'riɲu/ *m* collar; (*de cerveja*) head
colate|ral /kolate'raw/ (*pl* **~rais**) *a* **efeito ~ral** side effect
col|cha /'kowʃa/ *f* bedspread; **~chão** *m* mattress
colchete /kow'ʃetʃi/ *m* fastener; (*sinal de pontuação*) square bracket; **~ de pressão** press stud, popper
colchonete /kowʃo'nɛtʃi/ *m* (foldaway) mattress
coldre /'kɔwdri/ *m* holster
cole|ção /kole'sãw/ *f* collection; **~cionador** *m* collector; **~cionar** *vt* collect
colega /ko'lɛga/ *m/f* (*amigo*) friend; (*de trabalho*) colleague
colegi|al /koleʒi'aw/ (*pl* **~ais**) *a* school □ *m/f* schoolboy (*f* -girl)
colégio /ko'lɛʒiu/ *m* secondary school, (*Amer*) high school
coleira /ko'lera/ *f* collar
cólera /'kɔlera/ *f* (*doença*) cholera; (*raiva*) fury
colérico /ko'lɛriku/ *a* (*furioso*) furious □ *m* (*doente*) cholera victim
colesterol /koleste'rɔw/ *m* cholesterol
cole|ta /ko'lɛta/ *f* collection; **~tânea** *f* collection; **~tar** *vt* collect
colete /ko'letʃi/ *m* waistcoat, (*Amer*) vest; **~ salva-vidas** life-jacket, (*Amer*) life-preserver
coletivo /kole'tʃivu/ *a* collective; <*transporte*> public □ *m* bus
colheita /ko'ʎejta/ *f* harvest; (*produtos colhidos*) crop
colher[1] /ko'ʎɛr/ *f* spoon
colher[2] /ko'ʎer/ *vt* pick <*flores, frutos*>; gather <*informações*>
colherada /koʎe'rada/ *f* spoonful
colibri /koli'bri/ *m* hummingbird
cólica /'kɔlika/ *f* colic
colidir /koli'dʒir/ *vi* collide
coli|gação /koliga'sãw/ *f* (*pol*) coalition; **~gado** *m* (*pol*) coalition partner; **~gar** *vt* bring together; **~gar-se** *vpr* join forces; (*pol*) form a coalition
colina /ko'lina/ *f* hill
colírio /ko'liriu/ *m* eyewash
colisão /koli'zãw/ *f* collision
collant /ko'lã/ (*pl* **~s**) *m* body; (*de ginástica*) leotard
colmeia /kow'meja/ *f* beehive
colo /'kɔlu/ *f* (*regaço*) lap; (*pescoço*) neck
colo|cação /koloka'sãw/ *f* placing; (*emprego*) position; (*exposição de fatos*) statement; (*de aparelho, pneus, carpete etc*) fitting; **~cado** *a* placed; **o primeiro ~cado** (*em ranking*) person in first place; **~cador** *m* fitter; **~car** put; fit <*aparelho, pneus, carpete etc*>; put forward, state <*opinião, idéias*>; (*empregar*) get a job for
Colômbia /ko'lõbia/ *f* Colombia
colombiano /kolõbi'anu/ *a & m* Colombian
cólon /'kɔlõ/ *m* colon
colônia[1] /ko'lonia/ *f* (*colonos*) colony
colônia[2] /ko'lonia/ *f* (*perfume*) cologne
coloni|al /koloni'aw/ (*pl* **~ais**) *a* colonial; **~alismo** *m* colonialism;

~alista *a & m/f* colonialist; **~zar** *vt* colonize

colono /ko'lonu/ *m* settler, colonist; (*lavrador*) tenant farmer

coloqui|al /koloki'aw/ (*pl* **~ais**) *a* colloquial

colóquio /ko'lɔkiu/ *m* (*conversa*) conversation; (*congresso*) conference

colo|rido /kolo'ridu/ *a* colourful □ *m* colouring; **~rir** *vt* colour

colu|na /ko'luna/ *f* column; (*vertebral*) spine; **~nável** (*pl* **~náveis**) *a* famous □ *m/f* celebrity; **~nista** *m/f* columnist

com /kõ/ *prep* with; **o comentário foi comigo** the comment was meant for me; **você está ~ a chave?** have you got the key?; **~ seis anos de idade** at six years of age

coma /'koma/ *f* coma

comadre /ko'madri/ *f* (*madrinha*) godmother of one's child; (*mãe do afilhado*) mother of one's godchild; (*urinol*) bedpan

coman|dante /komã'dãtʃi/ *m* commander; **~dar** *vt* lead; (*ordenar*) command; (*elevar-se acima de*) dominate; **~do** *m* command; (*grupo*) commando group

comba|te /kõ'batʃi/ *m* combat; (*a drogas, doença etc*) fight (a against); **~ter** *vt/i* fight; **~ter-se** *vpr* fight

combi|nação /kõbina'sãw/ *f* combination; (*acordo*) arrangement; (*plano*) scheme; (*roupa*) petticoat; **~nar** *vt* (*juntar*) combine; (*ajustar*) arrange □ *vi* go together, match; **~nar com** go with, match; **~nar de sair** arrange to go out; **~nar-se** *vpr* (*juntar-se*) combine; (*harmonizar-se*) go together, match

comboio /kõ'boju/ *m* convoy; (*Port: trem*) train

combustí|vel /kõbus'tʃivew/ (*pl* **~veis**) *m* fuel

come|çar /kome'sar/ *vt/i* start, begin; **~ço** /e/ *m* beginning, start

comédia /ko'mɛdʒia/ *f* comedy

comediante /komedʒi'ãtʃi/ *m/f* comedian (*f* comedienne)

comemo|ração /komemora'sãw/ *f* (*celebração*) celebration; (*lembrança*) commemoration; **~rar** *vt* (*festejar*) celebrate; (*lembrar*) commemorate; **~rativo** *a* commemorative

comen|tar /komẽ'tar/ *vt* comment on; (*falar mal de*) make comments about; **~tário** *m* comment; (*de texto, na TV etc*) commentary; **sem ~tários** no comment; **~tarista** *m/f* commentator

comer /ko'mer/ *vt* eat; <*ferrugem etc*> eat away; take <*peça de xadrez*> □ *vi* eat; **~-se** *vpr* (*de raiva etc*) be consumed (**de** with); **dar de ~ a** feed

comerci|al /komersi'aw/ (*pl* **~ais**) *a & m* commercial; **~alizar** *vt* market; **~ante** *m/f* trader; **~ar** *vi* do business, trade; **~ário** *m* shopworker

comércio /ko'mɛrsiu/ *m* (*atividade*) trade; (*loja etc*) business; (*lojas*) shops

comes /'komis/ *m pl* **~ e bebes** (*fam*) food and drink; **~tíveis** *m pl* foods, food; **~tível** (*pl* **~tíveis**) *a* edible

cometa /ko'meta/ *m* comet

cometer /kome'ter/ *vt* commit <*crime*>; make <*erro*>

comichão /komi'ʃãw/ *f* itch

comício /ko'misiu/ *m* rally

cômico /'komiku/ *a* (*de comédia*) comic; (*engraçado*) comical

comida /ko'mida/ *f* food; (*uma*) meal

comigo = **com** + **mim**

comi|lão /komi'lãw/ *a* (*f* **~lona**) greedy □ *m* (*f* **~lona**) glutton

cominho /ko'miɲu/ *m* cummin

comiserar-se /komize'rarsi/ *vpr* commiserate (**de** with)

comis|são /komi'sãw/ *f* commission; **~sário** *m* commissioner; **~sário de bordo** (*aéreo*) steward; (*de navio*) purser; **~sionar** *vt* commission

comi|tê /komi'te/ *m* committee; **~tiva** *f* group; (*de uma pessoa*) retinue

como /'komu/ *adv* (*na condição de*) as; (*da mesma forma que*) like; (*de que maneira*) how □ *conj* as; **~?** (*pedindo repetição*) pardon?; **~ se** as if; **assim ~** as well as

cômoda /'komoda/ *f* chest of drawers, (*Amer*) bureau

como|didade /komodʒi'dadʒi/ *f* comfort; (*conveniência*) convenience; **~dismo** *m* complacency; **~dista** *a* complacent

cômodo /'komodu/ *a* comfortable; (*conveniente*) convenient □ *m* (*aposento*) room

como|vente /komo'vẽtʃi/ *a* moving; **~ver** *vt* move □ *vi* be moving; **~ver-se** *vpr* be moved

compacto /kõ'paktu/ *a* compact □ *m* single

compadecer-se /kõpade'sersi/ *vpr* feel pity (**de** for)

compadre /kõ'padri/ *m* (*padrinho*) godfather of one's child; (*pai do afilhado*) father of one's godchild

compaixão /kõpa'ʃãw/ *f* compassion

companhei|rismo /kõpaɲe'rizmu/ *m* companionship; **~ro** *m* (*de viagem etc*) companion; (*amigo*) friend, mate

companhia /kõpa'ɲia/ *f* company; **fazer ~ a alg** keep s.o. company

compa|ração /kõpara'sãw/ *f* comparison; **~rar** *vt* compare; **~rativo**

a comparative; **~rável** (*pl* **~ráveis**) *a* comparable

compare|cer /kõpare'ser/ *vi* appear; **~cer a** attend; **~cimento** *m* attendance

comparsa /kõ'parsa/ *m/f* (*ator*) bit player; (*cúmplice*) sidekick

comparti|lhar /kõpartʃi'ʎar/ *vt/i* share (**de** in); **~mento** *m* compartment

compassado /kõpa'sadu/ *a* (*medido*) measured; (*ritmado*) regular

compassivo /kõpa'sivu/ *a* compassionate

compasso /kõ'pasu/ *m* (*mus*) beat, time; (*instrumento*) compass, pair of compasses

compatí|vel /kõpa'tʃivew/ (*pl* **~veis**) *a* compatible

compatriota /kõpatri'ɔta/ *m/f* compatriot, fellow countryman (*f* -woman)

compelir /kõpe'lir/ *vt* compel

compene|tração /kõpenetra'sãw/ *f* conviction; **~trar** *vt* convince; **~trar-se** *vpr* convince o.s.

compen|sação /kõpēsa'sãw/ *f* compensation; (*de cheques*) clearing; **~sar** *vt* make up for <*defeitos, danos*>; offset <*peso, gastos*>; clear <*cheques*> □ *vi* <*crime*> pay

compe|tência /kõpe'tēsia/ *f* competence; **~tente** *a* competent

compe|tição /kõpetʃi'sãw/ *f* competition; **~tidor** *m* competitor; **~tir** *vi* compete; **~tir a** be up to; **~tividade** *f* competitiveness; **~titivo** *a* competitive

compla|cência /kõpla'sēsia/ *f* complaisance; **~cente** *a* obliging

complemen|tar /kõplemẽ'tar/ *vt* complement □ *a* complementary; **~to** *m* complement

comple|tar /kõple'tar/ *vt* complete; top up <*copo, tanque etc*>; **~tar 20 anos** turn 20; **~to** /ɛ/ *a* complete; (*cheio*) full up; **por ~to** completely; **escrever por ~to** write out in full

comple|xado /kõplek'sadu/ *a* with a complex; **~xidade** *f* complexity; **~xo** /ɛ/ *a* & *m* complex

compli|cação /kõplika'sãw/ *f* complication; **~cado** *a* complicated; **~car** *vt* complicate; **~car-se** *vpr* get complicated

complô /kõ'plo/ *m* conspiracy, plot

com|ponente /kõpo'nẽtʃi/ *a* & *m* component; **~por** *vt/i* compose; **~por-se** *vpr* (*controlar-se*) compose o.s.; **~por-se de** be composed of

compor|tamento /kõporta'mẽtu/ *m* behaviour; **~tar** *vt* hold; bear <*dor, prejuízo*>; **~tar-se** *vpr* behave

composi|ção /kõpozi'sãw/ *f* composition; (*acordo*) conciliation; **~tor** *m* (*de música*) composer; (*gráfico*) compositor

compos|to /kõ'postu/ *pp de* **compor** □ *a* compound; <*pessoa*> level-headed □ *m* compound; **~to de** made up of; **~tura** *f* composure

compota /kõ'pɔta/ *f* fruit in syrup

com|pra /'kõpra/ *f* purchase; *pl* shopping; **fazer ~pras** go shopping; **~prador** *m* buyer; **~prar** *vt* buy; bribe <*oficial, juiz*>; pick <*briga*>

compreen|der /kõpriẽ'der/ *vt* (*conter em si*) contain; (*estender-se a*) cover, take in; (*entender*) understand; **~são** *f* understanding; **~sível** (*pl* **~síveis**) *a* understandable; **~sivo** *a* understanding

compres|sa /kõ'prɛsa/ *f* compress; **~são** *f* compression; **~sor** *m* compressor; **rolo ~sor** steamroller

compri|do /kõ'pridu/ *a* long; **~mento** *m* length

compri|mido /kõpri'midu/ *m* pill, tablet □ *a* <*ar*> compressed; **~mir** *vt* (*apertar*) press; (*reduzir o volume de*) compress

comprome|tedor /kõpromete'dor/ *a* compromising; **~ter** *vt* (*envolver*) involve; (*prejudicar*) compromise; **~ter alg a fazer** commit s.o. to doing; **~ter-se** *vpr* (*obrigar-se*) commit o.s.; (*prejudicar-se*) compromise o.s.; **~tido** *a* (*ocupado*) busy; (*noivo*) spoken for

compromisso /kõpro'misu/ *m* commitment; (*encontro marcado*) appointment; **sem ~** without obligation

compro|vação /kõprova'sãw/ *f* proof; **~vante** *m* receipt; **~var** *vt* prove

compul|são /kõpuw'sãw/ *f* compulsion; **~sivo** *a* compulsive; **~sório** *a* compulsory

compu|tação /kõputa'sãw/ *f* computation; (*matéria, ramo*) computing; **~tador** *m* computer; **~tadorizar** *vt* computerize; **~tar** *vt* compute

comum /ko'mũ/ *a* common; (*não especial*) ordinary; **fora do ~** out of the ordinary; **em ~** <*trabalho*> joint; <*atuar*> jointly; **ter muito em ~** have a lot in common

comungar /komũ'gar/ *vi* take communion

comunhão /komu'ɲãw/ *f* communion; (*relig*) (Holy) Communion

comuni|cação /komunika'sãw/ *f* communication; **~cação social/visual** media studies/ graphic design; **~cado** *m* notice; (*pol*) communiqué; **~car** *vt* communicate; (*unir*) connect □ *vi*, **~car-se** *vpr* communicate; **~cativo** *a* communicative

comu|nidade /komuni'dadʒi/ *f* community; **~nismo** *m* communism; **~nista** *a & m/f* communist; **~nitário** *a* (*da comunidade*) community; (*para todos juntos*) communal
côncavo /'kõkavu/ *a* concave
conce|ber /kõse'ber/ *vt* conceive; (*imaginar*) conceive of □ *vi* conceive; **~bível** (*pl* **~bíveis**) *a* conceivable
conceder /kõse'der/ *vt* grant; **~** em accede to
concei|to /kõ'sejtu/ *m* concept; (*opinião*) opinion; (*fama*) reputation; **~tuado** *a* highly thought of; **~tuar** *vt* (*imaginar*) conceptualize; (*avaliar*) assess
concen|tração /kõsẽtra'sãw/ *f* concentration; (*de jogadores*) training camp; **~trar** *vt* concentrate; **~trar-se** *vpr* concentrate
concepção /kõsep'sãw/ *f* conception; (*opinião*) view
concernir /kõser'nir/ *vt* **~** a concern
concerto /kõ'sertu/ *m* concert
conces|são /kõse'sãw/ *f* concession; **~sionária** *f* dealership; **~sionário** *m* dealer
concha /'kõʃa/ *f* (*de molusco*) shell; (*colher*) ladle
concili|ação /kõsilia'sãw/ *f* conciliation; **~ador** *a* conciliatory; **~ar** *vt* reconcile
concílio /kõ'siliu/ *m* council
conci|são /kõsi'zãw/ *f* conciseness; **~so** *a* concise
conclamar /kõkla'mar/ *vt* call <*eleição, greve*>; call upon <*pessoa*>
conclu|dente /kõklu'dẽtʃi/ *a* conclusive; **~ir** *vt/i* conclude; **~são** *f* conclusion; **~sivo** *a* concluding
concor|dância /kõkor'dãsia/ *f* agreement; **~dante** *a* consistent; **~dar** *vi* agree (em to) □ *vt* bring into line; **~data** *f* abrir **~data** go into liquidation
concórdia /kõ'kɔrdʒia/ *f* concord
concor|rência /kõko'xẽsia/ *f* competition (a for); **~rente** *a* competing; **~rer** *vi* compete (a for); **~rer** para contribute to; **~rido** *a* popular
concre|tizar /kõkretʃi'zar/ *vt* realize; **~tizar-se** *vpr* be realized; **~to** /ɛ/ *a & m* concrete
concurso /kõ'kursu/ *m* contest; (*prova*) competition
con|dado /kõ'dadu/ *m* county; **~de** *m* count
condeco|ração /kõdekora'sãw/ *f* decoration; **~rar** *vt* decorate
conde|nação /kõdena'sãw/ *f* condemnation; (*jurid*) conviction; **~nar** *vt* condemn; (*jurid*) convict
conden|sação /kõdẽsa'sãw/ *f* condensation; **~sar** *vt* condense; **~sar-se** *vpr* condense
condescen|dência /kõdesẽ'dẽsia/ *f* acquiescence; **~dente** *a* acquiescent; **~der** *vi* acquiesce; **~der** a comply with <*pedido, desejo*>; **~der** a ir condescend to go
condessa /kõ'desa/ *f* countess
condi|ção /kõdʒi'sãw/ *f* condition; (*qualidade*) capacity; ter **~ção** *ou* **~ções** para be able to; em boas **~ções** in good condition; **~cionado** *a* conditioned; **~cional** (*pl* **~cionais**) *a* conditional; **~cionamento** *m* conditioning
condimen|tar /kõdʒimẽ'tar/ *vt* season; **~to** *m* seasoning
condoer-se /kõdo'ersi/ *vpr* **~** de feel sorry for
condolência /kõdo'lẽsia/ *f* sympathy; *pl* condolences
condomínio /kõdo'miniu/ *m* (*taxa*) service charge
condu|ção /kõdu'sãw/ *f* (*de carro etc*) driving; (*transporte*) transport; **~cente** *a* conducive (a to); **~ta** *f* conduct; **~to** *m* conduit; **~tor** *m* (*de carro*) driver; (*eletr*) conductor; **~zir** *vt* lead; drive <*carro*>; (*eletr*) conduct □ *vi* (*de carro*) drive; (*levar*) lead (a to)
cone /'koni/ *m* cone
conectar /konek'tar/ *vt* connect
cone|xão /konek'sãw/ *f* connection; **~xo** /ɛ/ *a* connected
confec|ção /kõfek'sãw/ *f* (*roupa*) off-the-peg outfit; (*loja*) clothes shop, boutique; (*fábrica*) clothes manufacturer; **~cionar** *vt* make
confederação /kõfedera'sãw/ *f* confederation
confei|tar /kõfej'tar/ *vt* ice; **~taria** *f* cake shop; **~teiro** *m* confectioner
confe|rência /kõfe'rẽsia/ *f* conference; (*palestra*) lecture; **~rencista** *m/f* speaker
conferir /kõfe'rir/ *vt* check (com against); (*conceder*) confer (a on) □ *vi* (*controlar*) check; (*estar exato*) tally
confes|sar /kõfe'sar/ *vt/i* confess; **~sar-se** *vpr* confess; **~sionário** *m* confessional; **~sor** *m* confessor
confete /kõ'fɛtʃi/ *m* confetti
confi|ança /kõfi'ãsa/ *f* (*convicção*) confidence; (*fé*) trust; **~ante** *a* confident (em of); **~ar** (*dar*) entrust; **~ar** em trust; **~ável** (*pl* **~áveis**) *a* reliable; **~dência** *f* confidence; **~dencial** (*pl* **~denciais**) *a* confidential; **~denciar** *vt* tell in confidence; **~dente** *m/f* confidant (*f* confidante)
configu|ração /kõfigura'sãw/ *f* configuration; **~rar** *vt* (*representar*) represent; (*formar*) shape; (*comput*) configure

con|finar /kõfi'nar/ *vi* **~finar com** border on; **~fins** *m pl* borders

confir|mação /kõfirma'sãw/ *f* confirmation; **~mar** *vt* confirm; **~mar-se** *vpr* be confirmed

confis|car /kõfis'kar/ *vt* confiscate; **~co** *m* confiscation

confissão /kõfi'sãw/ *f* confession

confla|gração /kõflagra'sãw/ *f* conflagration; **~grar** *vt* set alight; (*fig*) throw into turmoil

confli|tante /kõfli'tãtʃi/ *a* conflicting; **~to** *m* conflict

confor|mação /kõforma'sãw/ *f* resignation; **~mado** *a* resigned (**com** to); **~mar** *vt* adapt (**a** to); **~mar-se com** conform to <*regra, política*>; resign o.s. to, come to terms with <*destino, evento*>; **~me** /ɔ/ *prep* according to □ *conj* depending on; **~me** it depends; **~midade** *f* conformity; **~mismo** *m* conformism; **~mista** *a* & *m/f* conformist

confor|tar /kõfor'tar/ *vt* comfort; **~tável** (*pl* **~táveis**) *a* comfortable; **~to** /o/ *m* comfort

confraternizar /kõfraterni'zar/ *vi* fraternize

confron|tação /kõfrõta'sãw/ *f* confrontation; **~tar** *vt* confront; (*comparar*) compare; **~to** *m* confrontation; (*comparação*) comparison

con|fundir /kõfũ'dʒir/ *vt* confuse; **~fundir-se** *vpr* get confused; **~fusão** *f* confusion; (*desordem*) mess; (*tumulto*) commotion; **~fuso** *a* (*confundido*) confused; (*que confunde*) confusing

conge|lador /kõʒela'dor/ *m* freezer; **~lamento** *m* (*de preços etc*) freeze; **~lar** *vt* freeze; **~lar-se** *vpr* freeze

congênito /kõ'ʒenitu/ *a* congenital

congestão /kõʒes'tãw/ *f* congestion

congestio|nado /kõʒestʃio'nadu/ *a* <*rua, cidade*> congested; <*pessoa, rosto*> flushed; <*olhos*> bloodshot; **~namento** *m* (*de trânsito*) traffic jam; **~nar** *vt* congest; **~nar-se** *vpr* <*rua*> get congested; <*rosto*> flush

conglomerado /kõglome'radu/ *m* conglomerate

congratular /kõgratu'lar/ *vt* congratulate (**por** on)

congre|gação /kõgrega'sãw/ *f* (*na igreja*) congregation; (*reunião*) gathering; **~gar** *vt* bring together; **~gar-se** *vpr* congregate

congresso /kõ'grɛsu/ *m* congress

conhaque /ko'ɲaki/ *m* brandy

conhe|cedor /koɲese'dor/ *a* knowing □ *m* connoisseur; **~cer** *vt* know; (*ser apresentado a*) get to know; (*visitar*) go to, visit; **~cido** *a* known; (*famoso*) well-known □ *m* acquaintance; **~cimento** *m* knowledge; **tomar ~cimento de** learn of; **travar ~cimento com alg** make s.o.'s acquaintance, become acquainted with s.o.

cônico /'koniku/ *a* conical

coni|vência /koni'vẽsia/ *f* connivance; **~vente** *a* conniving (**em** at)

conjetu|ra /kõʒe'tura/ *f* conjecture; **~rar** *vt/i* conjecture

conju|gação /kõʒuga'sãw/ *f* (*ling*) conjugation; **~gar** *vt* conjugate <*verbo*>

cônjuge /'kõʒuʒi/ *m/f* spouse

conjun|ção /kõʒũ'sãw/ *f* conjunction; **~tivo** *a* & *m* subjunctive; **~to** *a* joint □ *m* set; (*roupa*) outfit; (*musical*) group; **o ~to de** the body of; **em ~to** jointly; **~tura** *f* state of affairs; (*econômica*) state of the economy

conosco = **com** + **nós**

cono|tação /konota'sãw/ *f* connotation; **~tar** *vt* connote

conquanto /kõ'kwãtu/ *conj* although, even though

conquis|ta /kõ'kista/ *f* conquest; (*proeza*) achievement; **~tador** *m* conqueror □ *a* conquering; **~tar** *vt* conquer <*terra, país*>; win <*riqueza, independência*>; win over <*pessoa*>

consa|gração /kõsagra'sãw/ *f* (*de uma igreja*) consecration; (*dedicação*) dedication; **~grado** *a* <*artista, expressão*> established; **~grar** *vt* consecrate <*igreja*>; establish <*artista, estilo*>; (*dedicar*) dedicate (**a** to); **~grar-se a** dedicate o.s. to

consci|ência /kõsi'ẽsia/ *f* (*moralidade*) conscience; (*sentidos*) consciousness; (*no trabalho*) conscientiousness; (*de um fato etc*) awareness; **~encioso** /o/ *a* conscientious; **~ente** *a* conscious; **~entizar** *vt* make aware (**de** of); **~entizar-se** *vpr* become aware (**de** of)

consecutivo /kõseku'tʃivu/ *a* consecutive

conse|guinte /kõse'gĩtʃi/ *a* **por ~guinte** consequently; **~guir** *vt* get; **~guir fazer** manage to do □ *vi* succeed

conse|lheiro /kõse'ʎeru/ *m* counsellor, adviser; **~lho** /e/ *m* piece of advice; *pl* advice; (*órgão*) council

consen|so /kõ'sẽsu/ *m* consensus; **~timento** *m* consent; **~tir** *vt* allow □ *vi* consent (**em** to)

conse|qüência /kõse'kwẽsia/ *f* consequence; **por ~qüência** consequently; **~qüente** *a* consequent; (*coerente*) consistent

conser|tar /kõser'tar/ *vt* repair; **~to** /e/ *m* repair

conser|va /kõ'sɛrva/ *f* (*em vidro*) preserve; (*em lata*) tinned food; **~vação** *f* preservation; **~vador** *a* & *m* conservative; **~vadorismo** *m* conservatism; **~vante** *a* & *m* preservative; **~var** *vt* preserve; (*manter, guardar*) keep; **~var-se** *vpr* keep; **~vatório** *m* conservatory

conside|ração /kõsidera'sãw/ *f* consideration; (*estima*) esteem; **levar em ~ração** take into consideration; **~rar** *vt* consider; (*estimar*) think highly of □ *vi* consider; **~rar-se** *vpr* consider o.s.; **~rável** (*pl* **~ráveis**) *a* considerable

consig|nação /kõsigna'sãw/ *f* consignment; **~nar** *vt* consign

consigo = com + si

consis|tência /kõsis'tẽsia/ *f* consistency; **~tente** *a* firm; **~tir** *vi* consist (em in)

consoante /kõso'ãtʃi/ *f* consonant

conso|lação /kõsola'sãw/ *f* consolation; **~lador** *a* consoling; **~lar** *vt* console; **~lar-se** *vpr* console o.s.

consolidar /kõsoli'dar/ *vt* consolidate; mend <*fratura*>

consolo /kõ'solu/ *m* consolation

consórcio /kõ'sɔrsiu/ *m* consortium

consorte /kõ'sɔrtʃi/ *m/f* consort

conspícuo /kõs'pikuu/ *a* conspicuous

conspi|ração /kõspira'sãw/ *f* conspiracy; **~rador** *m* conspirator; **~rar** *vi* conspire

cons|tância /kõs'tãsia/ *f* constancy; **~tante** *a* & *f* constant; **~tar** *vi* (*em lista etc*) appear; **não me ~ta** I am not aware; **~ta que** it is said that; **~tar de** consist of

consta|tação /kõstata'sãw/ *f* observation; **~tar** *vt* note, notice; certify <*óbito*>

conste|lação /kõstela'sãw/ *f* constellation; **~lado** *a* star-studded

conster|nação /kõsterna'sãw/ *f* consternation; **~nar** *vt* dismay

consti|pação /kõstʃipa'sãw/ *f* (*Port: resfriado*) cold; **~pado** *a* (*resfriado*) with a cold; (*no intestino*) constipated; **~par-se** *vpr* (*Port: resfriar-se*) get a cold

constitu|cional /kõstʃitusio'naw/ (*pl* **~cionais**) *a* constitutional; **~ição** *f* constitution; **~inte** *a* constituent □ *f* **Constituinte** Constituent Assembly; **~ir** *vt* form <*governo, sociedade*>; (*representar*) constitute; (*nomear*) appoint

constran|gedor /kõstrãʒe'dor/ *a* embarrassing; **~ger** *vt* embarrass; (*coagir*) constrain; **~ger-se** *vpr* get embarrassed; **~gimento** *m* (*embaraço*) embarrassment; (*coação*) constraint

constru|ção /kõstru'sãw/ *f* construction; (*terreno*) building site; **~ir** *vt* build <*casa, prédio*>; (*fig*) construct; **~tivo** *a* constructive; **~tor** *m* builder; **~tora** *f* building firm

cônsul /'kõsuw/ (*pl* **~es**) *m* consul

consulado /kõsu'ladu/ *m* consulate

consul|ta /kõ'suwta/ *f* consultation; **~tar** *vt* consult; **~tor** *m* consultant; **~toria** *f* consultancy; **~tório** *m* (*médico*) surgery, (*Amer*) office

consu|mação /kõsuma'sãw/ *f* (*taxa*) minimum charge; **~mado** *a* **fato ~mado** fait accompli; **~mar** *vt* accomplish <*projeto*>; carry out <*crime, sacrifício*>; consummate <*casamento*>

consu|midor /kõsumi'dor/ *a* & *m* consumer; **~mir** *vt* consume; take up <*tempo*>; **~mismo** *m* consumerism; **~mista** *a* & *m/f* consumerist; **~mo** *m* consumption

conta /'kõta/ *f* (*a pagar*) bill; (*bancária*) account; (*contagem*) count; (*de vidro etc*) bead; *pl* (*com*) accounts; **em ~** economical; **por ~ de** on account of; **por ~ própria** on one's own account; **ajustar ~s** settle up; **dar ~ de** (*fig*) be up to; **dar ~ do recado** (*fam*) deliver the goods; **dar-se ~ de** realize; **fazer de ~** pretend; **ficar por ~ de** be left to; **levar** *ou* **ter em ~** take into account; **prestar ~s de** account for; **tomar ~ de** take care of; **~ bancária** bank account; **~ corrente** current account

contabi|lidade /kõtabili'dadʒi/ *f* accountancy; (*contas*) accounts; (*seção*) accounts department; **~lista** (*Port*) *m/f* accountant; **~lizar** *vt* write up <*quantia*>; (*fig*) notch up

contact- (*Port*) *veja* **contat-**

conta|dor /kõta'dor/ *m* (*pessoa*) accountant; (*de luz etc*) meter; **~gem** *f* counting; (*de pontos num jogo*) scoring; **~gem regressiva** countdown

contagi|ante /kõtaʒi'ãtʃi/ *a* infectious; **~ar** *vt* infect; **~ar-se** *vpr* become infected

contágio /kõ'taʒiu/ *m* infection

contagioso /kõtaʒi'ozu/ *a* contagious

contami|nação /kõtamina'sãw/ *f* contamination; **~nar** *vt* contaminate

contanto /kõ'tãtu/ *adv* **~ que** provided that

contar /kõ'tar/ *vt/i* count; (*narrar*) tell; **~ com** count on

conta|tar /kõta'tar/ *vt* contact; **~to** *m* contact; **entrar em ~to com** get in touch with; **tomar ~to com** come into contact with

contem|plação /kõtẽpla'sãw/ *f* contemplation; **~plar** *vt* (*considerar*) contemplate; (*dizer respeito a*) concern; ~**plar alg com** treat s.o. to □ *vi* ponder; ~**plativo** *a* contemplative

contemporâneo /kõtẽpo'raniu/ *a & m* contemporary

contenção /kõtẽ'sãw/ *f* containment

conten|cioso /kõtẽsi'ozu/ *a* contentious; ~**da** *f* dispute

conten|tamento /kõtẽta'mẽtu/ *m* contentment; ~**tar** *vt* satisfy; ~**tar-se** *vpr* be content; ~**te** *a* (*feliz*) happy; (*satisfeito*) content; ~**to** *m* **a** ~**to** satisfactorily

conter /kõ'ter/ *vt* contain; ~**-se** *vpr* contain o.s.

conterrâneo /kõte'xaniu/ *m* fellow countryman (*f* -woman)

contestar /kõtes'tar/ *vt* question; (*jurid*) contest

conteúdo /kõte'udu/ *m* (*de recipiente*) contents; (*fig: de carta etc*) content

contexto /kõ'testu/ *m* context

contigo = **com** + **ti**

continência /kõtʃi'nẽsia/ *f* (*mil*) salute

continen|tal /kõtʃinẽ'taw/ (*pl* ~**tais**) *a* continental; ~**te** *m* continent

contin|gência /kõtʃĩ'ʒẽsia/ *f* contingency; ~**gente** *a* (*eventual*) possible; (*incerto*) contingent □ *m* contingent

continu|ação /kõtʃinua'sãw/ *f* continuation; ~**ar** *vt/i* continue; eles ~**am** ricos they are still rich; ~**idade** *f* continuity

contínuo /kõ'tʃinuu/ *a* continuous □ *m* office junior

con|tista /kõ'tʃista/ *m/f* (short) story writer; ~**to** *m* (short) story; ~**to de fadas** fairy tale; ~**to-do-vigário** (*pl* ~**tos-do-vigário**) *m* confidence trick, swindle

contorcer /kõtor'ser/ *vt* twist; ~**-se** *vpr* (*de dor*) writhe

contor|nar /kõtor'nar/ *vt* go round; (*fig*) get round <*obstáculo, problema*>; (*cercar*) surround; (*delinear*) outline; ~**no** /o/ *m* outline; (*da paisagem*) contour

contra /'kõtra/ *prep* against

contra-|atacar /kõtrata'kar/ *vt* counterattack; ~**-ataque** *m* counterattack

contrabaixo /kõtra'baʃu/ *m* double bass

contrabalançar /kõtrabalã'sar/ *vt* counterbalance

contraban|dear /kõtrabãdʒi'ar/ *vt* smuggle; ~**dista** *m/f* smuggler; ~**do** *m* (*ato*) smuggling; (*artigos*) contraband

contração /kõtra'sãw/ *f* contraction

contracenar /kõtrase'nar/ *vi* ~ **com** play up to

contraceptivo /kõtrasep'tʃivu/ *a & m* contraceptive

contracheque /kõtra'ʃɛki/ *m* pay slip

contradi|ção /kõtradʒi'sãw/ *f* contradiction; ~**tório** *a* contradictory; ~**zer** *vt* contradict; ~**zer-se** *vpr* <*pessoa*> contradict o.s.; <*idéias etc*> be contradictory

contragosto /kõtra'gostu/ *m* **a** ~ reluctantly

contrair /kõtra'ir/ *vt* contract; pick up <*hábito, vício*>; ~**-se** *vpr* contract

contramão /kõtra'mãw/ *f* opposite direction □ *a invar* one way

contramestre /kõtra'mɛstri/ *m* supervisor; (*em navio*) bosun

contra-ofensiva /kõtraofẽ'siva/ *f* counter-offensive

contrapartida /kõtrapar'tʃida/ *f* (*fig*) compensation; **em** ~ on the other hand

contraproducente /kõtraprodu'sẽtʃi/ *a* counter-productive

contrari|ar /kõtrari'ar/ *vt* go against, run counter to; (*aborrecer*) annoy; ~**edade** *f* adversity; (*aborrecimento*) annoyance

contrário /kõ'trariu/ *a* opposite; (*desfavorável*) adverse; ~ **a** contrary to; <*pessoa*> opposed to □ *m* opposite; **pelo** *ou* **ao** ~ on the contrary; **ao** ~ **de** contrary to; **em** ~ to the contrary

contras|tante /kõtras'tãtʃi/ *a* contrasting; ~**tar** *vt/i* contrast; ~**te** *m* contrast

contra|tante /kõtra'tãtʃi/ *m/f* contractor; ~**tar** *vt* employ, take on <*operários*>

contra|tempo /kõtra'tẽpu/ *m* hitch

contra|to /kõ'tratu/ *m* contract; ~**tual** (*pl* ~**tuais**) *a* contractual

contraven|ção /kõtravẽ'sãw/ *f* contravention; ~**tor** *m* offender

contribu|ição /kõtribui'sãw/ *f* contribution; ~**inte** *m/f* contributor; (*pagador de impostos*) taxpayer; ~**ir** *vt* contribute □ *vi* contribute; (*pagar impostos*) pay tax

contrição /kõtri'sãw/ *f* contrition

contro|lar /kõtro'lar/ *vt* control; (*fiscalizar*) check; ~**le** /o/, (*Port*) ~**lo** /o/ *m* control; (*fiscalização*) check

contro|vérsia /kõtro'vɛrsia/ *f* controversy; ~**verso** /ɛ/ *a* controversial

contudo /kõ'tudu/ *conj* nevertheless

contundir /kõtũ'dʒir/ *vt* (*dar hematoma em*) bruise; injure <*jogador*>; ~**-se** *vpr* bruise o.s.; <*jogador*> get injured

conturbado /kõtur'badu/ *a* troubled

contu|são /kõtu'zãw/ *f* bruise; (*de jogador*) injury; ~**so** *a* bruised; <*jogador*> injured

convales|cença /kõvale'sẽsa/ *f* convalescence; ~**cer** *vi* convalesce

convenção /kõvẽ'sãw/ *f* convention

conven|cer /kõvẽ'ser/ *vt* convince; ~**cido** *a* (*convicto*) convinced; (*metido*) conceited; ~**cimento** *m* (*convicção*) conviction; (*imodéstia*) conceitedness

convencio|nal /kõvẽsio'naw/ (*pl* ~**nais**) *a* conventional

conveni|ência /kõveni'ẽsia/ *f* convenience; ~**ente** *a* convenient; (*cabível*) appropriate

convênio /kõ'veniu/ *m* agreement

convento /kõ'vẽtu/ *m* convent

convergir /kõver'ʒir/ *vi* converge

conver|sa /kõ'vɛrsa/ *f* conversation; **a** ~**sa dele** the things he says; ~**sa fiada** idle talk; ~**sação** *f* conversation; ~**sado** *a* <*pessoa*> talkative; <*assunto*> talked about; ~**sador** *a* talkative

conversão /kõver'sãw/ *f* conversion

conversar /kõver'sar/ *vi* talk

conver|sível /kõver'sivew/ (*pl* ~**síveis**) *a & m* convertible; ~**ter** *vt* convert; ~**ter-se** *vpr* be converted; ~**tido** *m* convert

con|vés /kõ'vɛs/ (*pl* ~**veses**) *m* deck

convexo /kõ'vɛksu/ *a* convex

convic|ção /kõvik'sãw/ *f* conviction; ~**to** *a* convinced; (*ferrenho*) confirmed; <*criminoso*> convicted

convi|dado /kõvi'dadu/ *m* guest; ~**dar** *vt* invite; ~**dativo** *a* inviting

convincente /kõvĩ'sẽtʃi/ *a* convincing

convir /kõ'vir/ *vi* (*ficar bem*) be appropriate; (*concordar*) agree (**em** on); ~ **a** suit, be convenient for; **convém notar que** one should note that

convite /kõ'vitʃi/ *m* invitation

convi|vência /kõvi'vẽsia/ *f* coexistence; (*relação*) close contact; ~**ver** *vi* coexist; (*ter relações*) associate (**com** with)

convívio /kõ'viviu/ *m* association (**com** with)

convocar /kõvo'kar/ *vt* call <*eleições, greve*>; call upon <*pessoa*> (**a** to); (*ao serviço militar*) call up

convosco = **com** + **vós**

convul|são /kõvuw'sãw/ *f* (*do corpo*) convulsion; (*da sociedade etc*) upheaval; ~**sionar** *vt* convulse <*corpo*>; (*fig*) churn up; ~**sivo** *a* convulsive

cooper /'kuper/ *m* jogging; **fazer** ~ go jogging

coope|ração /koopera'sãw/ *f* cooperation; ~**rar** *vi* cooperate; ~**rativa** *f* cooperative; ~**rativo** *a* cooperative

coorde|nação /koordena'sãw/ *f* coordination; ~**nada** *f* coordinate; ~**nar** *vt* coordinate

copa /'kɔpa/ *f* (*de árvore*) top; (*aposento*) breakfast room; (*torneio*) cup; *pl* (*naipe*) hearts; **a Copa (do Mundo)** the World Cup; ~**-cozinha** (*pl* ~**s-cozinhas**) *f* kitchen-diner

cópia /'kɔpia/ *f* copy

copiar /kopi'ar/ *vt* copy

co-piloto /kopi'lotu/ *m* co-pilot

copioso /kopi'ozu/ *a* ample; <*refeição*> substantial

copo /'kɔpu/ *m* glass

coque /'kɔki/ *m* (*penteado*) bun

coqueiro /ko'keru/ *m* coconut palm

coqueluche /koke'luʃi/ *f* (*doença*) whooping cough; (*mania*) fad

coque|tel /koke'tɛw/ (*pl* ~**téis**) *m* cocktail; (*reunião*) cocktail party

cor[1] /kɔr/ *m* **de** ~ by heart

cor[2] /kor/ *f* colour; **TV a** ~**es** colour TV; **pessoa de** ~ coloured person

coração /kora'sãw/ *m* heart

cora|gem /ko'raʒẽ/ *f* courage; ~**joso** /o/ *a* courageous

co|ral[1] /ko'raw/ (*pl* ~**rais**) *m* (*animal*) coral

co|ral[2] /ko'raw/ (*pl* ~**rais**) *m* (*de cantores*) choir □ *a* choral

co|rante /ko'rãtʃi/ *a & m* colouring; ~**rar** *vt* colour □ *vi* blush

cor|da /'kɔrda/ *f* rope; (*mus*) string; (*para roupa lavada*) clothes line; **dar** ~**da em** wind <*relógio*>; ~**da bamba** tightrope; ~**das vocais** vocal chords; ~**dão** *m* cord; (*de sapatos*) lace; (*policial*) cordon

cordeiro /kor'deru/ *m* lamb

cor|del /kor'dɛw/ (*pl* ~**déis**) (*Port*) *m* string; **literatura de** ~**del** trash

cor-de-rosa /kordʒi'rɔza/ *a invar* pink

cordi|al /kordʒi'aw/ (*pl* ~**ais**) *a & m* cordial; ~**alidade** *f* cordiality

cordilheira /kordʒi'ʎera/ *f* chain of mountains

coreano /kori'anu/ *a & m* Korean

Coréia /ko'rɛja/ *f* Korea

core|ografia /koriogra'fia/ *f* choreography; ~**ógrafo** *m* choreographer

coreto /ko'retu/ *m* bandstand

coriza /ko'riza/ *f* runny nose

corja /'kɔrʒa/ *f* pack; (*de pessoas*) rabble

córner /'kɔrner/ *m* corner

coro /'koru/ *m* chorus

coro|a /ko'roa/ *f* crown; (*de flores etc*) wreath □ (*fam*) *m/f* old man (*f* woman); ~**ação** *f* coronation; ~**ar** *vt* crown

coro|nel /koro'nɛw/ (*pl* ~**néis**) *m* colonel

coronha /ko'roɲa/ *f* butt

corpete /kor'petʃi/ *m* bodice

corpo /'korpu/ *m* body; (*físico de mulher*) figure; (*físico de homem*) physique; ~ **de bombeiros** fire brigade; ~ **diplomático** diplomatic corps; ~ **docente** teaching staff, (*Amer*) faculty; ~**-a-**~ *m invar* pitched battle; ~**ral** (*pl* ~**rais**) *a* physical; <*pena*> corporal

corpu|lência /korpu'lẽsia/ *f* stoutness; ~**lento** *a* stout

correção /koxe'sãw/ *f* correction

corre-corre /kɔxi'kɔxi/ *m* (*debandada*) stampede; (*correria*) rush

correct- (*Port*) *veja* **corret-**

corre|diço /koxe'dʒisu/ *a* <*porta*> sliding; ~**dor** *m* (*atleta*) runner; (*passagem*) corridor

correia /ko'xeja/ *f* strap; (*peça de máquina*) belt; (*para cachorro*) lead, (*Amer*) leash

correio /ko'xeju/ *m* post, mail; (*repartição*) post office; **pôr no** ~ post, (*Amer*) mail; ~ **aéreo** air mail

correlação /koxela'sãw/ *f* correlation

correligionário /koxeliʒio'nariu/ *m* party colleague

corrente /ko'xẽtʃi/ *a* <*água*> running; <*mês, conta*> current; <*estilo*> fluid; (*usual*) common □ *f* (*de água, eletricidade*) current; (*cadeia*) chain; ~ **de ar** draught; ~**za** /e/ *f* current; (*de ar*) draught

cor|rer /ko'xer/ *vi* (*à pé*) run; (*de carro*) drive fast, speed; (*fazer rápido*) rush; <*água, sangue*> flow; <*tempo*> elapse; <*boato*> go round □ *vt* draw <*cortina*>; run <*risco*>; ~**reria** *f* rush

correspon|dência /koxespõ'dẽsia/ *f* correspondence; ~**dente** *a* corresponding □ *m/f* correspondent; (*equivalente*) equivalent; ~**der** *vi* ~**der a** correspond to; (*retribuir*) return; ~**der-se** *vpr* correspond (**com** with)

corre|tivo /koxe'tʃivu/ *a* corrective □ *m* punishment; ~**to** /ɛ/ *a* correct

corretor /koxe'tor/ *m* broker; ~ **de imóveis** estate agent, (*Amer*) realtor

corrida /ko'xida/ *f* (*prova*) race; (*ação de correr*) run; (*de taxi*) ride

corrigir /koxi'ʒir/ *vt* correct

corrimão /koxi'mãw/ (*pl* ~**s**) *m* handrail; (*de escada*) banister

corriqueiro /koxi'keru/ *a* ordinary, run-of-the-mill

corroborar /koxobo'rar/ *vt* corroborate

corroer /koxo'er/ *vt* corrode <*metal*>; (*fig*) erode; ~**-se** *vpr* corrode; (*fig*) erode

corromper /koxõ'per/ *vt* corrupt; ~**-se** *vpr* be corrupted

corro|são /koxo'zãw/ *f* (*de metal*) corrosion; (*fig*) erosion; ~**sivo** *a* corrosive

corrup|ção /koxup'sãw/ *f* corruption; ~**to** *a* corrupt

cor|tada /kor'tada/ *f* (*em tênis*) smash; (*em pessoa*) put-down; ~**tante** *a* cutting; ~**tar** *vt* cut; cut off <*luz, telefone, perna etc*>; cut down <*árvore*>; cut out <*efeito, vício*>; take away <*prazer*>; (*com o carro*) cut up; (*desprezar*) cut dead □ *vi* cut; ~**tar o cabelo** (*no cabeleireiro*) get one's hair cut; ~**te**[1] /ɔ/ *m* cut; (*gume*) blade; (*desenho*) cross-section; **sem** ~**te** <*faca*> blunt; ~**te de cabelo** haircut

cor|te[2] /'kortʃi/ *f* court; ~**tejar** *vt* court; ~**tejo** /e/ *m* (*séquito*) retinue; (*fúnebre*) cortège; ~**tês** *a* (*f* ~**tesa**) courteous, polite; ~**tesão** (*pl* ~**tesãos**) *m* courtier; ~**tesia** *f* courtesy

corti|ça /kor'tʃisa/ *f* cork; ~**ço** *m* (*casa popular*) slum tenement

cortina /kor'tʃina/ *f* curtain

cortisona /kortʃi'zona/ *f* cortisone

coruja /ko'ruʒa/ *f* owl □ *a* <*pai, mãe*> proud, doting

coruscar /korus'kar/ *vi* flash

corvo /'korvu/ *m* crow

cós /kɔs/ *m invar* waistband

coser /ko'zer/ *vt/i* sew

cosmético /koz'mɛtʃiku/ *a* & *m* cosmetic

cósmico /'kɔzmiku/ *a* cosmic

cosmo /'kɔzmu/ *m* cosmos; ~**nauta** *m/f* cosmonaut; ~**polita** *a* cosmopolitan □ *m/f* globetrotter

costa /'kɔsta/ *f* coast; *pl* (*dorso*) back; **Costa do Marfim** Ivory Coast; **Costa Rica** Costa Rica

costarriquenho /kostaxi'keɲu/ *a* & *m* Costa Rican

cos|teiro /kos'teru/ *a* coastal; ~**tela** /ɛ/ *f* rib; ~**teleta** /e/ *f* chop; *pl* (*suíças*) sideburns; ~**telinha** *f* (*de porco*) spare rib

costu|mar /kostu'mar/ *vt* ~**ma fazer** he usually does; ~**mava fazer** he used to do; ~**me** *m* (*uso*) custom; (*traje*) costume; **de** ~**me** usually; **como de** ~**me** as usual; **ter o** ~**me de** have a habit of; ~**meiro** *a* customary

costu|ra /kos'tura/ *f* sewing; ~**rar** *vt/i* sew; ~**reira** *f* (*mulher*) dressmaker; (*caixa*) needlework box

co|ta /'kɔta/ *f* quota; ~**tação** *f* (*preço*) rate; (*apreço*) rating; ~**tado** *a* <*ação*> quoted; (*conceituado*) highly rated; ~**tar** *vt* rate; quote <*ações*>

cote|jar /kote'ʒar/ *vt* compare; ~**jo** /e/ *m* comparison

cotidiano /kotʃidʒi'anu/ *a* everyday □ *m* everyday life

cotonete /koto'nɛtʃi/ *m* cotton bud

cotove|lada /kotove'lada/ *f* (*para abrir caminho*) shove; (*para chamar atenção*) nudge; **~lo** /e/ *m* elbow
coura|ça /ko'rasa/ *f* (*armadura*) breastplate; (*de navio, animal*) armour; **~çado** (*Port*) *m* battleship
couro /'koru/ *m* leather; **~ cabeludo** scalp
couve /'kovi/ *f* spring greens; **~-de-bruxelas** (*pl* **~s-de-bruxelas**) *f* Brussels sprout; **~-flor** (*pl* **~s-flores**) *f* cauliflower
couvert /ku'vɛr/ (*pl* **~s**) *m* cover charge
cova /'kɔva/ *f* (*buraco*) pit; (*sepultura*) grave
covar|de /ko'vardʒi/ *m/f* coward □ *a* cowardly; **~dia** *f* cowardice
coveiro /ko'veru/ *m* gravedigger
covil /ko'viw/ (*pl* **~vis**) *m* den, lair
covinha /ko'viɲa/ *f* dimple
co|xa /'koʃa/ *f* thigh; **~xear** *vi* hobble
coxia /ko'ʃia/ *f* aisle
coxo /'koʃu/ *a* hobbling; **ser ~** hobble
co|zer /ko'zer/ *vt/i* cook; **~zido** *m* stew, casserole
cozi|nha /ko'ziɲa/ *f* (*aposento*) kitchen; (*comida, ação*) cooking; (*arte*) cookery; **~nhar** *vt/i* cook; **~nheiro** *m* cook
crachá /kra'ʃa/ *m* badge, (*Amer*) button
crânio /'kraniu/ *m* skull; (*pessoa*) genius
crápula /'krapula/ *m/f* scoundrel
craque /'kraki/ *m* (*de futebol*) soccer star; (*fam*) expert
crase /'krazi/ *f* contraction; **a com ~** a grave (à)
crasso /'krasu/ *a* crass
cratera /kra'tɛra/ *f* crater
cravar /kra'var/ *vt* drive in <*prego*>; dig <*unha*>; stick <*estaca*>; **~ com os olhos** stare at; **~-se** *vpr* stick
cravejar /krave'ʒar/ *vt* nail; (*com balas*) spray, riddle
cravo[1] /'kravu/ *m* (*flor*) carnation; (*condimento*) clove
cravo[2] /'kravu/ *m* (*na pele*) blackhead; (*prego*) nail
cravo[3] /'kravu/ *m* (*instrumento*) harpsichord
creche /'krɛʃi/ *f* crèche
credenci|ais /kredẽsi'ajs/ *f pl* credentials; **~ar** *vt* qualify
credi|ário /kredʒi'ariu/ *m* hire purchase agreement, credit plan; **~bilidade** *f* credibility; **~tar** *vt* credit
crédito /'krɛdʒitu/ *m* credit; **a ~** on credit
cre|do /'krɛdu/ *m* creed □ *int* heavens; **~dor** *m* creditor □ *a* <*saldo*> credit
crédulo /'krɛdulu/ *a* gullible
cre|mação /krema'sãw/ *f* cremation; **~mar** *vt* cremate; **~matório** *m* crematorium
cre|me /'kremi/ *a invar & m* cream; **~me Chantilly** whipped cream; **~me de leite** (sterilized) cream; **~moso** /o/ *a* creamy
cren|ça /'krẽsa/ *f* belief; **~dice** *f* superstition; **~te** *m* believer; (*protestante*) Protestant □ *a* religious; (*protestante*) Protestant; **estar ~te que** believe that
crepe /'krɛpi/ *m* crepe
crepitar /krepi'tar/ *vi* crackle
crepom /kre'põ/ *m* crepe; **papel ~** tissue paper
crepúsculo /kre'puskulu/ *m* twilight
crer /krer/ *vt/i* believe (**em** in); **creio que** I think (that); **~-se** *vpr* believe o.s. to be
cres|cendo /kre'sẽdu/ *m* crescendo; **~cente** *a* growing □ *m* crescent; **~cer** *vi* grow; <*bolo*> rise; **~cido** *a* grown; **~cimento** *m* growth
crespo /'krespu/ *a* <*cabelo*> frizzy; <*mar*> choppy
cretino /kre'tʃinu/ *m* cretin
cria /'kria/ *f* baby; *pl* young
criação /kria'sãw/ *f* creation; (*educação*) upbringing; (*de animais*) raising; (*gado*) livestock
criado /kri'adu/ *m* servant; **~-mudo** (*pl* **~s-mudos**) *m* bedside table
criador /kria'dor/ *m* creator; (*de animais*) farmer, breeder
crian|ça /kri'ãsa/ *f* child □ *a* childish; **~çada** *f* kids; **~cice** *f* childishness; (*uma*) childish thing
criar /kri'ar/ *vt* (*fazer*) create; bring up <*filhos*>; rear <*animais*>; grow <*planta*>; pluck up <*coragem*>; **~-se** *vpr* be brought up, grow up
criati|vidade /kriatʃivi'dadʒi/ *f* creativity; **~vo** *a* creative
criatura /kria'tura/ *f* creature
crime /'krimi/ *m* crime
crimi|nal /krimi'naw/ (*pl* **~nais**) *a* criminal; **~nalidade** *f* crime; **~noso** *m* criminal
crina /'krina/ *f* mane
crioulo /kri'olu/ *a & m* creole; (*negro*) black
cripta /'kripta/ *f* crypt
crisálida /kri'zalida/ *f* chrysalis
crisântemo /kri'zãtemu/ *m* chrysanthemum
crise /'krizi/ *f* crisis
cris|ma /'krizma/ *f* confirmation; **~mar** *vt* confirm; **~mar-se** *vpr* get confirmed
crista /'krista/ *f* crest
cris|tal /kris'taw/ (*pl* **~tais**) *m* crystal; (*vidro*) glass; **~talino** *a* crystal-clear; **~talizar** *vt/i* crystallize

cris|tandade /kristã'dadʒi/ *f* Christendom; ~**tão** (*pl* ~**tãos**) *a* & *m* (*f* ~**tã**) Christian; ~**tianismo** *m* Christianity

Cristo /'kristu/ *m* Christ

cri|tério /kri'tɛriu/ *m* discretion; (*norma*) criterion; ~**terioso** *a* perceptive, discerning

crítica /'kritʃika/ *f* criticism; (*análise*) critique; (*de filme, livro*) review; (*críticos*) critics

criticar /kritʃi'kar/ *vt* criticize; review <*filme, livro*>

crítico /'kritʃiku/ *a* critical □ *m* critic

crivar /kri'var/ *vt* (*furar*) riddle

crí|vel /'krivew/ (*pl* ~**veis**) *a* credible

crivo /'krivu/ *m* sieve; (*fig*) scrutiny

crocante /kro'kãtʃi/ *a* crunchy

crochê /kro'ʃe/ *m* crochet

crocodilo /kroko'dʒilu/ *m* crocodile

cromo /'kromu/ *m* chrome

cromossomo /kromo'somu/ *m* chromosome

crôni|ca /'kronika/ *f* (*histórica*) chronicle; (*no jornal*) feature; (*conto*) short story; ~**co** *a* chronic

cronista /kro'nista/ *m/f* (*de jornal*) feature writer; (*contista*) short story writer; (*historiador*) chronicler

crono|grama /krono'grama/ *m* schedule; ~**logia** *f* chronology; ~**lógico** *a* chronological; ~**metrar** *vt* time

cronômetro /kro'nometru/ *m* stopwatch

croquete /kro'kɛtʃi/ *m* savoury meatball in breadcrumbs

croqui /kro'ki/ *m* sketch

crosta /'krosta/ *f* crust; (*em ferida*) scab

cru /kru/ *a* (*f* ~**a**) raw; <*luz, tom, palavra*> harsh; crude; <*verdade*> unvarnished, plain

cruci|al /krusi'aw/ (*pl* ~**ais**) *a* crucial

crucifi|cação /krusifika'sãw/ *f* crucifixion; ~**car** *vt* crucify; ~**xo** /ks/ *m* crucifix

cru|el /kru'ɛw/ (*pl* ~**éis**) *a* cruel; ~**eldade** *f* cruelty; ~**ento** *a* bloody

crupe /'krupi/ *m* croup

crustáceos /krus'tasius/ *m pl* shellfish

cruz /krus/ *f* cross

cruza|da /kru'zada/ *f* crusade; ~**do**[1] *m* (*soldado*) crusader

cru|zado[2] /kru'zadu/ *m* (*moeda*) cruzado; ~**zador** *m* cruiser; ~**zamento** *m* (*de ruas*) crossroads, junction, (*Amer*) intersection; (*de raças*) cross; ~**zar** *vt* cross □ *vi* <*navio*> cruise; ~**zar com** pass; ~**zar-se** *vpr* cross; <*pessoas*> pass each other; ~**zeiro** *m* (*moeda*) cruzeiro; (*viagem*) cruise; (*cruz*) cross

cu /ku/ *m* (*chulo*) arse, (*Amer*) ass

Cuba /'kuba/ *f* Cuba

cubano /ku'banu/ *a* & *m* Cuban

cúbico /'kubiku/ *a* cubic

cubículo /ku'bikulu/ *m* cubicle

cubis|mo /ku'bizmu/ *m* cubism; ~**ta** *a* & *m/f* cubist

cubo /'kubu/ *m* cube; (*de roda*) hub

cuca /'kuka/ (*fam*) *f* head

cuco /'kuku/ *m* cuckoo; (*relógio*) cuckoo clock

cu|-de-ferro /kudʒi'fɛxu/ (*pl* ~**s-de-ferro**) (*fam*) *m* swot

cueca /ku'ɛka/ *f* underpants; *pl* (*Port: de mulher*) knickers

cueiro /ku'eru/ *m* baby wrap

cuia /'kuia/ *f* gourd

cuidado /kui'dadu/ *m* care; **com** ~ carefully; **ter** *ou* **tomar** ~ be careful; ~**so** /o/ *a* careful

cuidar /kui'dar/ *vi* ~ **de** take care of; ~**-se** *vpr* look after o.s.

cujo /'kuʒu/ *pron* whose

culatra /ku'latra/ *f* breech; **sair pela** ~ (*fig*) backfire

culiná|ria /kuli'naria/ *f* cookery; ~**rio** *a* culinary

culmi|nância /kuwmi'nãsia/ *f* culmination; ~**nante** *a* culminating; ~**nar** *vi* culminate (**em** in)

cul|pa /'kuwpa/ *f* guilt; **foi** ~**pa minha** it was my fault; **ter** ~**pa de** be to blame for; ~**pabilidade** *f* guilt; ~**pado** *a* guilty □ *m* culprit; ~**par** *vt* blame (**de** for); (*na justiça*) find guilty (**de** of); ~**par-se** *vpr* take the blame (**de** for); ~**pável** (*pl* ~**páveis**) *a* culpable, guilty

culti|var /kuwtʃi'var/ *vt* cultivate; grow <*plantas*>; ~**vo** *m* cultivation; (*de plantas*) growing

cul|to /'kuwtu/ *a* cultured □ *m* cult; ~**tura** *f* culture; (*de terra*) cultivation; ~**tural** (*pl* ~**turais**) *a* cultural

cumbuca /kũ'buka/ *f* bowl

cume /'kumi/ *m* peak

cúmplice /'kũplisi/ *m/f* accomplice

cumplicidade /kũplisi'dadʒi/ *f* complicity

cumprimen|tar /kũprimẽ'tar/ *vt/i* (*saudar*) greet; (*parabenizar*) compliment; ~**to** *m* (*saudação*) greeting; (*elogio*) compliment; (*de lei, ordem*) compliance (**de** with); (*de promessa, palavra*) fulfilment

cumprir /kũ'prir/ *vt* keep <*promessa, palavra*>; comply with <*lei, ordem*>; do <*dever*>; carry out <*obrigações*>; serve <*pena*>; ~ **com** keep to □ *vi* **cumpre-nos ir** we should go; ~**-se** *vpr* be fulfilled

cúmulo /'kumulu/ *m* height; é o ~! that's the limit!
cunha /'kuɲa/ *f* wedge
cunha|da /ku'ɲada/ *f* sister-in-law; ~**do** *m* brother-in-law
cunhar /'kuɲar/ *vt* coin <*palavra, expressão*>; mint <*moedas*>
cunho /'kuɲu/ *m* hallmark
cupim /ku'pĩ/ *m* termite
cupom /ku'põ/ *m* coupon
cúpula /'kupula/ *f* (*abóbada*) dome; (*de abajur*) shade; (*chefia*) leadership; (**reunião de**) ~ summit (meeting)
cura /'kura/ *f* cure □ *m* curate, priest
curandeiro /kurã'deru/ *m* (*religioso*) faith-healer; (*índio*) medicine man; (*charlatão*) quack
curar /ku'rar/ *vt* cure; dress <*ferida*>; ~-**se** *vpr* be cured
curativo /kura'tʃivu/ *m* dressing
curá|vel /ku'ravew/ (*pl* ~**veis**) *a* curable
curin|ga /ku'rĩga/ *m* wild card; ~**gão** *m* joker
curio|sidade /kuriozi'dadʒi/ *f* curiosity; ~**so** /o/ *a* curious □ *m* (*espectador*) onlooker
cur|ral /ku'xaw/ (*pl* ~**rais**) *m* pen
currículo /ku'xikulu/ *m* curriculum; (*resumo*) curriculum vitae, CV
cur|sar /kur'sar/ *vt* attend <*escola, aula*>; study <*matéria*>; ~**so** *m* course; ~**sor** *m* cursor
curta|-metragem /kurtame'traʒẽ/ (*pl* ~**s-metragens**) *m* short (film)
cur|tição /kurtʃi'sãw/ (*fam*) *f* enjoyment; ~**tir** *vt* (*fam*) enjoy; tan <*couro*>
curto /'kurtu/ *a* short; <*conhecimento, inteligência*> limited; ~-**circuito** (*pl* ~**s-circuitos**) *m* short circuit
cur|va /'kurva/ *f* curve; (*de estrada, rio*) bend; ~**va fechada** hairpin bend; ~**var** *vt* bend; ~**var-se** *vpr* bend; (*fig*) bow (a to); ~**vo** *a* curved; <*estrada*> winding
cus|parada /kuspa'rada/ *f* spit; ~**pe** *m* spit, spittle; ~**pir** *vt/i* spit
cus|ta /'kusta/ *f* à ~**ta de** at the expense of; ~**tar** *vt* cost □ *vi* (*ser difícil*) be hard; ~**tar a fazer** (*ter dificuldade*) find it hard to do; (*demorar*) take a long time to do; ~**tear** *vt* finance, fund; ~**teio** *m* funding; (*relação de despesas*) costing; ~**to** *m* cost; a ~**to** with difficulty
custódia /kus'tɔdʒia/ *f* custody
cutelo /ku'tɛlu/ *m* cleaver
cutícula /ku'tʃikula/ *f* cuticle
cútis /'kutʃis/ *f invar* complexion
cutucar /kutu'kar/ *vt* (*com o cotovelo, joelho*) nudge; (*com o dedo*) poke; (*com instrumento*) prod
czar /zar/ *m* tsar

D

da = de + a
dádiva /'dadʒiva/ *f* gift; (*donativo*) donation
dado /'dadu/ *m* (*de jogar*) die, dice; (*informação*) fact, piece of information; *pl* data
daí /da'i/ *adv* (*no espaço*) from there; (*no tempo*) then; ~ **por diante** from then on; e ~? (*fam*) so what?
dali /da'li/ *adv* from over there
dália /'dalia/ *f* dahlia
dal|tônico /daw'toniku/ *a* colour-blind; ~**tonismo** *m* colour-blindness
dama /'dama/ *f* lady; (*em jogos*) queen; *pl* (*jogo*) draughts, (*Amer*) checkers; ~ **de honra** bridesmaid
da|nado /da'nadu/ *a* damned; (*zangado*) angry; (*travesso*) naughty; ~**nar-se** *vpr* get angry; ~**ne-se!** (*fam*) who cares?
dan|ça /'dãsa/ *f* dance; ~**çar** *vt* dance □ *vi* dance; (*fam*) miss out; <*coisa*> go by the board; <*crimonoso*> get caught; ~**çarino** *m* dancer; ~**ceteria** *f* discotheque
da|nificar /danifi'kar/ *vt* damage; ~**ninho** *a* undesirable; ~**no** *m* (*pl*) damage; ~**noso** /o/ *a* damaging
dantes /'dãtʃiʃ/ *adv* formerly
daquela(s), daquele(s) = de + aquela(s), aquele(s)
daqui /da'ki/ *adv* from here; ~ **a 2 dias** in 2 days(' time); ~ **a pouco** in a minute; ~ **em diante** from now on
daquilo = de + aquilo
dar /dar/ *vt* give; have <*dormida, lida etc*>; do <*pulo, cambalhota etc*>; cause <*problemas*>; produce <*frutas, leite*>; deal <*cartas*>; (*lecionar*) teach □ *vi* (*ser possível*) be possible; (*ser suficiente*) be enough; ~ **com** come across; ~ **em** lead to; **ele dá para ator** he'd make a good actor; ~ **por** (*considerar como*) consider to be; (*reparar em*) notice; ~-**se** *vpr* <*coisa*> happen; <*pessoa*> get on
dardo /'dardu/ *m* dart; (*no atletismo*) javelin
das = de + as
da|ta /'data/ *f* date; **de longa** ~ long since; ~**tar** *vt/i* date
dati|lografar /datʃilogra'far/ *vt/i* type; ~**lografia** *f* typing; ~**lógrafo** *m* typist
de /dʒi/ *prep* of; (*procedência*) from; ~ **carro** by car; **trabalho** ~ **repórter** I work as a reporter

debaixo /dʒi'baʃu/ *adv* below; ~ **de** under
debalde /dʒi'bawdʒi/ *adv* in vain
debandada /debã'dada/ *f* stampede
deba|te /de'batʃi/ *m* debate; ~**ter** *vt* debate; ~**ter-se** *vpr* grapple
debelar /debe'lar/ *vt* overcome
dé|bil /'dɛbiw/ (*pl* ~**beis**) *a* feeble; ~**bil mental** retarded (person)
debili|dade /debili'dadʒi/ *f* debility; ~**tar** *vt* debilitate; ~**tar-se** *vpr* become debilitated
debitar /debi'tar/ *vt* debit
débito /'dɛbitu/ *m* debit
debo|chado /debo'ʃadu/ *a* sardonic; ~**char** *vt* mock; ~**che** /ɔ/ *m* jibe
debruar /debru'ar/ *vt/i* edge
debruçar-se /debru'sarsi/ *vpr* bend over; ~ **sobre** study
debrum /de'brũ/ *m* edging
debulhar /debu'ʎar/ *vt* thresh
debu|tante /debu'tãtʃi/ *f* debutante; ~**tar** *vi* debut, make one's debut
década /'dɛkada/ *f* decade; **a ~ dos 60** the sixties
deca|dência /deka'dẽsia/ *f* decadence; ~**dente** *a* decadent
decair /deka'ir/ *vi* decline; (*degringolar*) go downhill; <*planta*> wilt
decal|car /dekaw'kar/ *vt* trace; ~**que** *m* tracing
decapitar /dekapi'tar/ *vt* decapitate
decatlo /de'katlu/ *m* decathlon
de|cência /de'sẽsia/ *f* decency; ~**cente** *a* decent
decepar /dese'par/ *vt* cut off
decep|ção /desep'sãw/ *f* disappointment; ~**cionar** *vt* disappoint; ~**cionar-se** *vpr* be disappointed
decerto /dʒi'sɛrtu/ *adv* certainly
deci|dido /desi'dʒidu/ *a* <*pessoa*> determined; ~**dir** *vt/i* decide; ~**dir-se** *vpr* make up one's mind; ~**dir-se por** decide on
decíduo /de'siduu/ *a* deciduous
decifrar /desi'frar/ *vt* decipher
deci|mal /desi'maw/ (*pl* ~**mais**) *a & m* decimal
décimo /'dɛsimu/ *a & m* tenth; ~ **primeiro** eleventh; ~ **segundo** twelfth; ~ **terceiro** thirteenth; ~ **quarto** fourteenth; ~ **quinto** fifteenth; ~ **sexto** sixteenth; ~ **sétimo** seventeenth; ~ **oitavo** eighteenth; ~ **nono** nineteenth
deci|são /desi'zãw/ *f* decision; ~**sivo** *a* decisive
decla|ração /deklara'sãw/ *f* declaration; ~**rado** *a* <*inimigo*> sworn; <*crente*> avowed; <*ladrão*> self-confessed; ~**rar** *vt* declare
decli|nação /deklina'sãw/ *f* declension; ~**nar** *vt* ~**nar (de)** decline ▫ *vi* decline; <*sol*> go down; <*chão*> slope down
declínio /de'kliniu/ *m* decline
declive /de'klivi/ *m* (downward) slope, incline
decodificar /dekodʒifi'kar/ *vt* decode
deco|lagem /deko'laʒẽ/ *f* take-off; ~**lar** *vi* take off; (*fig*) get off the ground
decom|por /dekõ'por/ *vt* break down; contort <*feições*>; ~**por-se** *vpr* break down; <*cadáver*> decompose; ~**posição** *f* (*de cadáver*) decomposition
deco|ração /dekora'sãw/ *f* decoration; (*aprendizagem*) learning by heart; ~**rar** *vt* (*adornar*) decorate; (*aprender*) learn by heart, memorize; ~**rativo** *a* decorative; ~**reba** /ɛ/ (*fam*) *f* rote-learning; ~**ro** /o/ *m* decorum; ~**roso** /o/ *a* decorous
decor|rência /deko'xẽsia/ *f* consequence; ~**rente** *a* resulting (**de** from); ~**rer** *vi* <*tempo*> elapse; <*acontecimento*> pass off; (*resultar*) result (**de** from) ▫ *m* **no ~rer de** in the course of; **com o ~rer do tempo** in time, with the passing of time
deco|tado /deko'tadu/ *a* low-cut; ~**te** /ɔ/ *m* neckline
decrépito /de'krɛpitu/ *a* decrepit
decres|cente /dekre'sẽtʃi/ *a* decreasing; ~**cer** *vi* decrease
decre|tar /dekre'tar/ *vt* decree; declare <*estado de sítio*>; ~**to** /ɛ/ *m* decree; ~**to-lei** (*pl* ~**tos-leis**) *m* act
decurso /de'kursu/ *m* course
de|dal /de'daw/ (*pl* ~**dais**) *m* thimble; ~**dão** *m* (*da mão*) thumb; (*do pé*) big toe
dedetizar /dedetʃi'zar/ *vt* spray with insecticide
dedi|cação /dedʒika'sãw/ *f* dedication; ~**car** *vt* dedicate; devote <*tempo*>; ~**car-se** *vpr* dedicate o.s. (**a** to); ~**catória** *f* dedication
dedilhar /dedʒi'ʎar/ *vt* pluck
dedo /'dedu/ *m* finger; (*do pé*) toe; **cheio de ~s** all fingers and thumbs; (*sem graça*) awkward; ~**-duro** (*pl* ~**s-duros**) *m* sneak; (*político, criminoso*) informer
dedução /dedu'sãw/ *f* deduction
dedurar /dedu'rar/ *vt* sneak on; (*à polícia*) inform on
dedu|tivo /dedu'tʃivu/ *a* deductive; ~**zir** *vt* (*descontar*) deduct; (*concluir*) deduce
defa|sado /defa'zadu/ *a* out of step; ~**sagem** *f* gap, lag
defecar /defe'kar/ *vi* defecate
defei|to /de'fejtu/ *m* defect; **botar ~to em** find fault with; ~**tuoso** /o/ *a* defective

defen|der /defẽ'der/ *vt* defend; **~der-se** *vpr* (*virar-se*) fend for o.s.; (*contra-atacar*) defend o.s. (de against); **~siva** *f* na **~siva** on the defensive; **~sor** *m* defender; (*advogado*) defence counsel

defe|rência /defe'rẽsia/ *f* deference; **~rente** *a* deferential

defesa /de'feza/ *f* defence □ *m* defender

defici|ência /defisi'ẽsia/ *f* deficiency; **~ente** *a* deficient; (*física ou mentalmente*) handicapped □ *m/f* handicapped person

déficit /'dɛfisitʃi/ (*pl* **~s**) *m* deficit

deficitário /defisitʃi'ariu/ *a* in deficit; <*empresa*> loss-making

definhar /defi'ɲar/ *vi* waste away; <*planta*> wither

defi|nição /defini'sãw/ *f* definition; **~nir** *vt* define; **~nir-se** *vpr* (*descrever-se*) define o.s.; (*decidir-se*) come to a decision; (*explicar-se*) make one's position clear; **~nitivo** *a* definitive; **~nível** (*pl* **~níveis**) *a* definable

defla|ção /defla'sãw/ *f* deflation; **~cionário** *a* deflationary

deflagrar /defla'grar/ *vt* set off □ *vi* break out

defor|mar /defor'mar/ *vt* misshape; deform <*corpo*>; distort <*imagem*>; **~midade** *f* deformity

defraudar /defraw'dar/ *vt* defraud (de of)

defron|tar /defrõ'tar/ *vt* **~tar com** face; **~te** *adv* opposite; **~te de** opposite

defumar /defu'mar/ *vt* smoke

defunto /de'fũtu/ *a* & *m* deceased

dege|lar /deʒe'lar/ *vt/i* thaw; **~lo** /e/ *m* thaw

degeneração /deʒenera'sãw/ *f* degeneration

degenerar /deʒene'rar/ *vi* degenerate (em into)

degolar /dego'lar/ *vt* cut the throat of

degra|dação /degrada'sãw/ *f* degradation; **~dante** *a* degrading; **~dar** *vt* degrade

degrau /de'graw/ *m* step

degringolar /degrĩgo'lar/ *vi* deteriorate, go downhill

degustar /degus'tar/ *vt* taste

dei|tada /dej'tada/ *f* lie-down; **~tado** *a* lying down; (*dormindo*) in bed; (*fam: preguiçoso*) idle; **~tar** *vt* lay down; (*na cama*) put to bed; (*pôr*) put; (*Port: jogar*) throw □ *vi*, **~tar-se** *vpr* lie down; (*ir para cama*) go to bed

dei|xa /'deʃa/ *f* cue; **~xar** *vt* leave; (*permitir*) let; **~xar de** (*parar*) stop; (*omitir*) fail; **não pôde ~xar de rir** he couldn't help laughing; **~xar alg nervoso** make s.o. annoyed; **~xar cair** drop; **~xar a desejar** leave a lot to be desired; **~xa (para lá)** (*fam*) never mind, forget it

dela(s) = **de** + **ela(s)**

delatar /dela'tar/ *vt* report

délavé /dela've/ *a invar* faded

dele(s) = **de** + **ele(s)**

dele|gação /delega'sãw/ *f* delegation; **~gacia** *f* police station; **~gado** *m* delegate; **~gado de polícia** police chief; **~gar** *vt* delegate

delei|tar /delej'tar/ *vt* delight; **~tar-se** *vpr* delight (com in); **~te** *m* delight; **~toso** /o/ *a* delightful

delgado /dew'gadu/ *a* slender

delibe|ração /delibera'sãw/ *f* deliberation; **~rar** *vt/i* deliberate

delica|deza /delika'deza/ *f* delicacy; (*cortesia*) politeness; **~do** *a* delicate; (*cortês*) polite

delícia /de'lisia/ *f* delight; **ser uma ~** <*comida*> be delicious; <*sol etc*> be lovely

delici|ar /delisi'ar/ *vt* delight; **~ar-se** delight (com in); **~oso** /o/ *a* delightful, lovely; <*comida*> delicious

deline|ador /delinia'dor/ *m* eye-liner; **~ar** *vt* outline

delin|qüência /delĩ'kwẽsia/ *f* delinquency; **~qüente** *a* & *m* delinquent

deli|rante /deli'rãtʃi/ *a* rapturous; (*med*) delirious; **~rar** *vi* go into raptures; <*doente*> be delirious

delírio /de'liriu/ *m* (*febre*) delirium; (*excitação*) raptures

delito /de'litu/ *m* crime

delonga /de'lõga/ *f* delay

delta /'dɛwta/ *f* delta

dema|gogia /demago'ʒia/ *f* demagogy; **~gógico** *a* demagogic; **~gogo** /o/ *m* demagogue

demais /dʒi'majs/ *a* & *adv* (*muito*) very much; (*em demasia*) too much; **os ~** the rest, the others; **é ~!** (*fam*) it's great!

deman|da /de'mãda/ *f* demand; (*jurid*) action; **~dar** *vt* sue

demão /de'mãw/ *f* coat

demar|car /demar'kar/ *vt* demarcate; **~catório** *a* demarcation

demasia /dema'zia/ *f* excess; **em ~** too (much, many)

de|mência /de'mẽsia/ *f* insanity; (*med*) dementia; **~mente** *a* insane; (*med*) demented

demissão /demi'sãw/ *f* sacking, dismissal; **pedir ~** resign

demitir /demi'tʃir/ *vt* sack, dismiss; **~-se** *vpr* resign

demo|cracia /demokra'sia/ *f* democracy; **~crata** *m/f* democrat; **~crático** *a* democratic; **~cratizar**

vt democratize; ~grafia *f* demography; ~gráfico *a* demographic

demo|lição /demoli'sãw/ *f* demolition; ~lir *vt* demolish

demônio /de'moniu/ *m* demon

demons|tração /demõstra'sãw/ *f* demonstration; ~trar *vt* demonstrate; ~trativo *a* demonstrative

demo|ra /de'mɔra/ *f* delay; ~rado *a* lengthy; ~rar *vi* (*levar*) take; (*tardar a voltar, terminar etc*) be long; (*levar muito tempo*) take a long time □ *vt* delay

dendê /dẽ'de/ *m* (*óleo*) palm oil

denegrir /dene'grir/ *vt* denigrate

dengoso /dẽ'gozu/ *a* coy

dengue /'dẽgi/ *m* dengue

denomi|nação /denomina'sãw/ *f* denomination; ~nar *vt* name

denotar /deno'tar/ *vt* denote

den|sidade /dẽsi'dadʒi/ *f* density; ~so *a* dense

den|tado /dẽ'tadu/ *a* serrated; ~tadura *f* (set of) teeth; (*postiça*) dentures, false teeth; ~tal (*pl* ~tais) *a* dental; ~tário *a* dental; ~te *m* tooth; (*de alho*) clove; ~te do siso wisdom tooth; ~tição *f* teething; (*dentadura*) teeth; ~tífrico *m* toothpaste; ~tista *m/f* dentist

dentre = de + entre

dentro /'dẽtru/ *adv* inside; lá ~ in there; por ~ on the inside; ~ de inside; (*tempo*) within

dentu|ça /dẽ'tusa/ *f* buck teeth; ~ço *a* with buck teeth

denúncia /de'nũsia/ *f* (*à polícia etc*) report; (*na imprensa etc*) disclosure

denunciar /denũsi'ar/ *vt* (*à polícia etc*) report; (*na imprensa etc*) denounce

deparar /depa'rar/ *vi* ~ com come across

departamento /departa'mẽtu/ *m* department

depauperar /depawpe'rar/ *vt* impoverish

depenar /depe'nar/ *vt* pluck <*aves*>; (*roubar*) fleece

depen|dência /depẽ'dẽsia/ *f* dependence; *pl* premises; ~dente *a* dependent (de on) □ *m/f* dependant; ~der *vi* depend (de on)

depi|lação /depila'sãw/ *f* depilation; ~lar *vt* depilate; ~latório *m* depilatory cream

deplo|rar /deplo'rar/ *vt* deplore; ~rável (*pl* ~ráveis) *a* deplorable

de|poente /depo'ẽtʃi/ *m/f* witness; ~poimento *m* (*à polícia*) statement; (*na justiça, fig*) testimony

depois /de'pojs/ *adv* after(wards); ~ de after; ~ que after

depor /de'por/ *vi* (*na polícia*) make a statement; (*na justiça*) give evidence, testify □ *vt* lay down <*armas*>; depose <*rei, presidente*>

depor|tação /deporta'sãw/ *f* deportation; ~tar *vt* deport

deposi|tante /depozi'tãtʃi/ *m/f* depositor; ~tar *vt* deposit; cast <*voto*>; place <*confiança*>

depósito /de'pɔzitu/ *m* deposit; (*armazém*) warehouse

depra|vação /deprava'sãw/ *f* depravity; ~vado *a* depraved; ~var *vt* deprave

depre|ciação /depresia'sãw/ *f* (*perda de valor*) depreciation; (*menosprezo*) deprecation; ~ciar *vt* (*desvalorizar*) devalue; (*menosprezar*) deprecate; ~ciar-se *vpr* <*bens*> depreciate; <*pessoa*> deprecate o.s.; ~ciativo *a* deprecatory

depre|dação /depreda'sãw/ *f* depredation; ~dar *vt* wreck

depressa /dʒi'prɛsa/ *adv* fast, quickly

depres|são /depre'sãw/ *f* depression; ~sivo *a* depressive

depri|mente /depri'mẽtʃi/ *a* depressing; ~mido *a* depressed; ~mir *vt* depress; ~mir-se *vpr* get depressed

depurar /depu'rar/ *vt* purify

depu|tação /deputa'sãw/ *f* deputation; ~tado *m* deputy, MP, (*Amer*) congressman (*f* -woman); ~tar *vt* delegate

deque /'dɛki/ *m* (sun)deck

deri|va /de'riva/ *f* à ~va adrift; andar à ~va drift; ~vação *f* derivation; ~var *vt* derive; (*desviar*) divert □ *vi*, ~var-se *vpr* derive, be derived (de from); <*navio*> drift

dermatolo|gia /dermatolo'ʒia/ *f* dermatology; ~gista *m/f* dermatologist

derradeiro /dexa'deru/ *a* last, final

derra|mamento /dexama'mẽtu/ *m* spill, spillage; ~mamento de sangue bloodshed; ~mar *vt* spill; shed <*lágrimas*>; ~mar-se *vpr* spill; ~me *m* spill, spillage; ~me cerebral stroke

derra|pagem /dexa'paʒẽ/ *f* skidding; (*uma*) skid; ~par *vi* skid

derreter /dexe'ter/ *vt* melt; ~-se *vpr* melt

derro|ta /de'xɔta/ *f* defeat; ~tar *vt* defeat; ~tismo *m* defeatism; ~tista *a* & *m/f* defeatist

derrubar /dexu'bar/ *vt* knock down; bring down <*governo*>

desaba|far /dʒizaba'far/ *vi* speak one's mind; ~fo *m* outburst

desa|bamento /dʒizaba'mẽtu/ *m* collapse; ~bar *vi* collapse; <*chuva*> pour down

desabotoar /dʒiaboto'ar/ *vt* unbutton

desabri|gado /dʒizabri'gadu/ *a* homeless; **~gar** *vt* make homeless

desabrochar /dʒizabro'ʃar/ *vi* blossom, bloom

desaca|tar /dʒizaka'tar/ *vt* defy; **~to** *m* (*de pessoa*) disrespect; (*da lei etc*) disregard

desacerto /dʒiza'sertu/ *m* mistake

desacompanhado /dʒizakõpa'ɲadu/ *a* unaccompanied

desaconse|lhar /dʒizakõse'ʎar/ *vt* advise against; **~lhável** (*pl* **~lháveis**) *a* inadvisable

desacor|dado /dʒizakor'dadu/ *a* unconscious; **~do** /o/ *m* disagreement

desacostu|mado /dʒizakostu'madu/ *a* unaccustomed; **~mar** *vt* **~mar alg de** break s.o. of the habit of; **~mar-se de** get out of the habit of

desacreditar /dʒizakredʒi'tar/ *vt* discredit

desafeto /dʒiza'fɛtu/ *m* disaffection

desafi|ador /dʒizafia'dor/ *a* <*tarefa*> challenging; <*pessoa*> defiant; **~ar** *vt* challenge; (*fazer face a*) defy <*perigo, morte*>

desafi|nado /dʒizafi'nadu/ *a* out of tune; **~nar** *vi* (*cantando*) sing out of tune; (*tocando*) play out of tune □ *vt* put out of tune

desafio /dʒiza'fiu/ *m* challenge

desafivelar /dʒizafive'lar/ *vt* unbuckle

desafo|gar /dʒizafo'gar/ *vt* vent; (*desapertar*) relieve; **~gar-se** *vpr* give vent to one's feelings; **~go** /o/ *m* (*alívio*) relief

desafo|rado /dʒizafo'radu/ *a* cheeky; **~ro** /o/ *m* cheek; (*um*) liberty

desafortunado /dʒizafortu'nadu/ *a* unfortunate

desagra|dar /dʒizagra'dar/ *vt* displease; **~dável** (*pl* **~dáveis**) *a* unpleasant; **~do** *m* displeasure

desagravo *m* redress, amends

desagregar /dʒizagre'gar/ *vt* split up; **~-se** *vpr* split up

desaguar /dʒiza'gwar/ *vt* drain □ *vi* <*rio*> flow (**em** into)

desajeitado /dʒizaʒej'tadu/ *a* clumsy

desajuizado /dʒizaʒui'zadu/ *a* foolish

desajus|tado /dʒizaʒus'tadu/ *a* (*psic*) maladjusted; **~te** *m* (*psic*) maladjustment

desalen|tar /dʒizalẽ'tar/ *vt* dishearten; **~tar-se** *vpr* get disheartened; **~to** *m* discouragement

desali|nhado /dʒizali'ɲadu/ *a* untidy; **~nho** *m* untidiness

desalojar /dʒizalo'ʒar/ *vt* turn out <*inquilino*>; flush out <*inimigo, ladrões*>

desamarrar /dʒizama'xar/ *vt* untie □ *vi* cast off

desamarrotar /dʒizamaxo'tar/ *vt* smooth out

desamassar /dʒizama'sar/ *vt* smooth out

desambientado /dʒizãbiẽ'tadu/ *a* unsettled

desampa|rar /dʒizãpa'rar/ *vt* abandon; **~ro** *m* abandonment

desandar /dʒizã'dar/ *vi* <*molho*> separate; **~ a** start to

de|sanimar /dʒizani'mar/ *vt* discourage □ *vi* <*pessoa*> lose heart; <*fato*> be discouraging; **~sânimo** *m* discouragement

desapaixonado /dʒizapaʃo'nadu/ *a* dispassionate

desaparafusar /dʒizaparafu'zar/ *vt* unscrew

desapare|cer /dʒizapare'ser/ *vi* disappear; **~cimento** *m* disappearance

desapego /dʒiza'pegu/ *m* detachment; (*indiferença*) indifference

desapercebido /dʒizaperse'bidu/ *a* unnoticed

desapertar /dʒizaper'tar/ *vt* loosen

desapon|tamento /dʒizapõta'mẽtu/ *m* disapointment; **~tar** *vt* disappoint

desapropriar /dʒizapropri'ar/ *vt* expropriate

desapro|vação /dʒizaprova'sãw/ *f* disapproval; **~var** *vt* disapprove of

desaproveitado /dʒizaprovej'tadu/ *a* wasted

desar|mamento /dʒizarma'mẽtu/ *m* disarmament; **~mar** *vt* disarm; take down <*barraca*>

desarran|jar /dʒizaxã'ʒar/ *vt* mess up; upset <*estômago*>; **~jo** *m* mess; (*do estômago*) upset

desarregaçar /dʒizaxega'sar/ *vt* roll down

desarru|mado /dʒizaxu'madu/ *a* untidy; **~mar** *vt* untidy; unpack <*mala*>

desarticular /dʒizartʃiku'lar/ *vt* dislocate

desarvorado /dʒizarvo'radu/ *a* disoriented, at a loss

desassociar /dʒizasosi'ar/ *vt* disassociate; **~-se** *vpr* disassociate o.s.

desas|trado /dʒizas'tradu/ *a* accident-prone; **~tre** *m* disaster; **~troso** /o/ *a* disastrous

desatar /dʒiza'tar/ *vt* untie; **~ a chorar** dissolve in tears

desatarraxar /dʒizataxa'ʃar/ *vt* unscrew

desaten|cioso /dʒizatẽsi'ozu/ *a* inattentive; **~to** *a* oblivious (**a** to)

desati|nar /dʒizatʃi'nar/ *vt* bewilder □ *vi* not think straight; **~no** *m* mental aberration, bewilderment; (*um*) folly

desativar /dʒizatʃi'var/ *vt* deactivate; shut down <*fábrica*>
desatrelar /dʒizatre'lar/ *vt* unhitch
desatualizado /dʒizatuali'zadu/ *a* out-of-date
desavença /dʒiza'vẽsa/ *f* disagreement
desavergonhado /dʒizavergo'ɲadu/ *a* shameless
desbancar /dʒizbã'kar/ *vt* outdo
desbaratar /dʒizbara'tar/ *vt* (*desperdiçar*) waste
desbocado /dʒizbo'kadu/ *a* outspoken
desbotar /dʒizbo'tar/ *vt/i* fade
desbra|vador /dʒizbrava'dor/ *m* explorer; **~var** *vt* explore
desbun|dante /dʒizbũ'dãtʃi/ (*fam*) *a* mind-blowing; **~dar** (*fam*) *vt* blow the mind of □ *vi* flip, freak out; **~de** (*fam*) *m* knockout
descabido /dʒiska'bidu/ *a* inappropriate
descalabro /dʒiska'labru/ *m* débâcle
descalço /dʒis'kawsu/ *a* barefoot
descambar /dʒiskã'bar/ *vi* deteriorate, degenerate
descan|sar /dʒiskã'sar/ *vt/i* rest; **~so** *m* rest; (*de prato, copo*) mat
desca|rado /dʒiska'radu/ *a* blatant; **~ramento** *m* cheek
descarga /dʒis'karga/ *f* (*eletr*) discharge; (*da privada*) flush; **dar ~** flush (the toilet)
descarregar /dʒiskaxe'gar/ *vt* unload <*mercadorias*>; discharge <*poluentes*>; vent <*raiva*> □ *vi* <*bateria*> go flat; **~ em cima de alg** take it out on s.o.
descarrilhar /dʒiskaxi'ʎar/ *vt/i* derail
descar|tar /dʒiskar'tar/ *vt* discard; **~tável** (*pl* **~táveis**) *a* disposable
descascar /dʒiskas'kar/ *vt* peel <*frutas, batatas*>; shell <*nozes*> □ *vi* <*pessoa, pele*> peel
descaso /dʒis'kazu/ *m* indifference
descen|dência /desẽ'dẽsia/ *f* descent; **~dente** *a* descended □ *m/f* descendant; **~der** *vi* descend (**de** from)
descentralizar /dʒisẽtrali'zar/ *vt* decentralize
des|cer /de'ser/ *vi* go down; <*avião*> descend; (*do ônibus, trem*) get off; (*do carro*) get out □ *vt* go down <*escada, ladeira*>; **~cida** *f* descent
desclassificar /dʒisklasifi'kar/ *vt* disqualify
desco|berta /dʒisko'bɛrta/ *f* discovery; **~berto** /ɛ/ *a* uncovered; <*conta*> overdrawn; **a ~berto** overdrawn; **~bridor** *m* discoverer; **~brimento** *m* discovery; **~brir** *vt* discover; (*expor*) uncover
descolar /dʒisko'lar/ *vt* unstick; (*fam*) (*dar*) give; (*arranjar*) get hold of, rustle up; (*Port*) <*avião*> take off
descom|por /dʒiskõ'por/ *vt* (*censurar*) scold; **~-se** *vpr* <*pessoa*> lose one's composure; **~postura** *f* (*estado*) loss of composure; (*censura*) talking-to
descomprometido /dʒiskõprome'tʃidu/ *a* free
descomu|nal /dʒiskomu'naw/ (*pl* **~nais**) *a* extraordinary; (*grande*) huge
desconcentrar /dʒiskõsẽ'trar/ *vt* distract
desconcer|tante /dʒiskõser'tãtʃi/ *a* disconcerting; **~tar** *vt* disconcert
desconexo /dʒisko'nɛksu/ *a* incoherent
desconfi|ado /dʒiskõfi'adu/ *a* suspicious; **~ança** *f* mistrust; **~ar** *vi* suspect
desconfor|tável /dʒiskõfor'tavew/ (*pl* **~táveis**) *a* uncomfortable; **~to** /o/ *m* discomfort
descongelar /dʒiskõʒe'lar/ *vt* defrost <*geladeira*>; thaw <*comida*>
descongestio|nante /dʒiskõʒestʃio'nãtʃi/ *a & m* decongestant; **~nar** *vt* decongest
desconhe|cer /dʒiskoɲe'ser/ *vt* not know; **~cido** *a* unknown □ *m* stranger
desconsiderar /dʒiskõside'rar/ *vt* ignore
desconsolado /dʒiskõso'ladu/ *a* disconsolate
descontar /dʒiskõ'tar/ *vt* deduct; (*não levar em conta*) discount
desconten|tamento /dʒiskõtẽta'mẽtu/ *m* discontent; **~te** *a* discontent
desconto /dʒis'kõtu/ *m* discount; **dar um ~** (*fig*) make allowances
descontra|ção /dʒiskõtra'sãw/ *f* informality; **~ído** *a* informal, casual; **~ir** *vt* relax; **~ir-se** *vpr* relax
descontro|lar-se /dʒiskõtro'larsi/ *vpr* <*pessoa*> lose control; <*coisa*> go out of control; **~le** /o/ *m* lack of control
desconversar /dʒiskõver'sar/ *vi* change the subject
descortesia /dʒiskorte'zia/ *f* rudeness
descostu|rar /dʒiskostu'rar/ *vt* unrip; **~rar-se** *vpr* come undone
descrédito /dʒis'krɛdʒitu/ *m* discredit
descren|ça /dʒis'krẽsa/ *f* disbelief; **~te** *a* sceptical, disbelieving
des|crever /dʒiskre'ver/ *vt* describe; **~crição** *f* description; **~critivo** *a* descriptive
descui|dado /dʒiskui'dadu/ *a* careless; **~dar** *vt* neglect; **~do** *m* carelessness; (*um*) oversight

descul|pa /dʒis'kuwpa/ *f* excuse; pedir **~pas** apologize; **~par** *vt* excuse; **~pe!** sorry!; **~par-se** *vpr* apologize; **~pável** (*pl* **~páveis**) *a* excusable

desde /'dezdʒi/ *prep* since; **~ que** since

des|dém /dez'dẽj/ *m* disdain; **~denhar** *vt* disdain; **~nhoso** /o/ *a* disdainful

desdentado /dʒizdẽ'tadu/ *a* toothless

desdita /dʒiz'dʒita/ *f* unhappiness

desdizer /dʒizdʒi'zer/ *vt* take back, withdraw □ *vi* take back what one said

desdo|bramento /dʒizdobra'mẽtu/ *m* implication; **~brar** *vt* (*abrir*) unfold; break down <*dados, contas*>; **~brar-se** *vpr* unfold; (*empenhar-se*) go to a lot of trouble, bend over backwards

dese|jar /deze'ʒar/ *vt* want; (*apaixonadamente*) desire; **~jar aco a alg** wish s.o. sth; **~jável** (*pl* **~jáveis**) *a* desirable; **~jo** /e/ *m* wish; (*forte*) desire; **~joso** /o/ *a* desirous

deselegante /dʒizele'gãtʃi/ *a* inelegant

desemaranhar /dʒizemara'ɲar/ *vt* untangle

desembara|çado /dʒizĩbara'sadu/ *a* <*pessoa*> confident, nonchalant; **~çar-se** *vpr* rid o.s. (**de** of); **~ço** *m* confidence, ease

desembar|car /dʒizĩbar'kar/ *vt/i* disembark; **~que** *m* disembarkation; (*seção do aeroporto*) arrivals

desembocar /dʒizĩbo'kar/ *vi* flow

desembol|sar /dʒizĩbow'sar/ *vt* spend, pay out; **~so** /o/ *m* expenditure

desembrulhar /dʒizĩbru'ʎar/ *vt* unwrap

desembuchar /dʒizĩbu'ʃar/ (*fam*) *vi* (*desabafar*) get things off one's chest; (*falar logo*) spit it out

desempacotar /dʒizĩpako'tar/ *vt* unpack

desempatar /dʒizĩpa'tar/ *vt* decide <*jogo*>

desempe|nhar /dʒizĩpe'ɲar/ *vt* perform; play <*papel*>; **~nho** *m* performance

desempre|gado /dʒizĩpre'gadu/ *a* unemployed; **~go** /e/ *m* unemployment

desencadear /dʒizĩkadʒi'ar/ *vt* set off, trigger

desencaminhar /dʒizĩkami'ɲar/ *vt* lead astray; embezzle <*dinheiro*>

desencantar /dʒizĩkã'tar/ *vt* disenchant

desencon|trar-se /dʒizĩkõ'trarsi/ *vpr* miss each other, fail to meet; **~tro** *m* failure to meet

desencorajar /dʒizĩkora'ʒar/ *vt* discourage

desenferrujar /dʒizĩfexu'ʒar/ *vt* derust <*metal*>; stretch <*pernas*>; brush up <*língua*>

desenfreado /dʒizĩfri'adu/ *a* unbridled

desenganar /dʒizĩga'nar/ *vt* disabuse; declare incurable <*doente*>

desengonçado /dʒizĩgõ'sadu/ *a* <*pessoa*> ungainly

desengre|nado /dʒizĩgre'nadu/ *a* <*carro*> in neutral; **~nar** *vt* put in neutral <*carro*>; (*tec*) disengage

dese|nhar /deze'ɲar/ *vt* draw; **~nhista** *m/f* drawer; (*industrial*) designer; **~nho** /e/ *m* drawing

desenlace /dʒizĩ'lasi/ *m* dénouement, outcome

desenredar /dʒizĩxe'dar/ *vt* unravel

desenrolar /dʒizĩxo'lar/ *vt* unroll <*rolo*>

desenten|der /dʒizĩtẽ'der/ *vt* misunderstand; **~der-se** *vpr* (*não se dar bem*) not get on; **~dimento** *m* misunderstanding

desenterrar /dʒizĩte'xar/ *vt* dig up <*cadáver*>; unearth <*informação*>

desentortar /dʒizĩtor'tar/ *vt* straighten out

desentupir /dʒizĩtu'pir/ *vt* unblock

desenvol|to /dʒizĩ'vowtu/ *a* casual, nonchalant; **~tura** *f* casualness, nonchalance; **com ~tura** nonchalantly; **~ver** *vt* develop; **~ver-se** *vpr* develop; **~vimento** *m* development

desequi|librado *a* unbalanced; **~librar** *vt* unbalance; **~librar-se** *vpr* become unbalanced; **~líbrio** *m* imbalance

deser|ção /dezer'sãw/ *f* desertion; **~tar** *vt/i* desert; **~to** /ɛ/ *a* deserted; **ilha ~ta** desert island □ *m* desert; **~tor** *m* deserter

desespe|rado /dʒizispe'radu/ *a* desperate; **~rador** *a* hopeless; **~rar** *vt* (*desesperançar*) make despair □ *vi*, **~rar-se** *vpr* despair; **~ro** /e/ *m* despair

desestabilizar /dʒizistabili'zar/ *vt* destabilize

desestimular /dʒizistʃimu'lar/ *vt* discourage

desfal|car /dʒisfaw'kar/ *vt* embezzle; **~que** *m* embezzlement

desfal|ecer /dʒisfale'ser/ *vt* (*desmaiar*) faint; **~ecimento** *m* faint

desfavor /dʒisfa'vor/ *m* disfavour

desfavo|rável /dʒisfavo'ravew/ (*pl* **~ráveis**) *a* unfavourable; **~recer** *vt* be unfavourable to; treat less favourably <*minorias etc*>

desfazer /dʒisfa'zer/ *vt* undo; unpack <*mala*>; strip <*cama*>; break <*contrato*>; clear up <*mistério*>; **~-se**

vpr come undone; <*casamento*> break up; <*sonhos*> crumble; **~-se em lágrimas** dissolve into tears

desfe|char /dʒisfe'ʃar/ *vt* throw <*murro, olhar*>; **~cho** /e/ *m* outcome, dénouement

desfeita /dʒis'fejta/ *f* slight, insult

desferir /dʒisfe'rir/ *vt* give <*pontapé*>; launch <*ataque*>; fire <*flecha*>

desfiar /dʒisfi'ar/ *vt* pick the meat off <*frango*>; **~-se** *vpr* <*tecido*> fray

desfigurar /dʒisfigu'rar/ *vt* disfigure; (*fig*) distort

desfi|ladeiro /dʒisfila'deru/ *m* pass; **~lar** *vi* parade; **~le** *m* parade; **~le de modas** fashion show

desflorestamento /dʒisfloresta'mẽtu/ *m* deforestation

desforra /dʒis'fɔxa/ *f* revenge

desfraldar /dʒisfraw'dar/ *vt* unfurl

desfrutar /dʒisfru'tar/ *vt* enjoy

desgas|tante /dʒizgas'tãtʃi/ *a* wearing, stressful; **~tar** *vt* wear out; **~te** *m* (*de máquina etc*) wear and tear; (*de pessoa*) stress and strain

desgosto /dʒiz'gostu/ *m* sorrow

desgovernar-se /dʒizgover'narsi/ *vpr* go out of control

desgraça /dʒiz'grasa/ *f* misfortune; **~do** *a* wretched □ *m* wretch

desgravar /dʒizgra'var/ *vt* erase

desgrenhado /dʒizgre'ɲadu/ *a* unkempt

desgrudar /dʒizgru'dar/ *vt* unstick; **~-se** *vpr* <*pessoa*> tear o.s. away

desidra|tação /dʒizidrata'sãw/ *f* dehydration; **~tar** *vt* dehydrate

desig|nação /dezigna'sãw/ *f* designation; **~nar** *vt* designate

desi|gual /dʒizi'gwaw/ (*pl* **~guais**) *a* unequal; <*terreno*> uneven; **~gualdade** *f* inequality; (*de terreno*) unevenness

desilu|dir /dʒizilu'dʒir/ *vt* disillusion; **~são** *f* disillusionment

desinfe|tante /dʒizĩfe'tãtʃi/ *a & m* disinfectant; **~tar** *vt* disinfect

desinibido /dʒizini'bidu/ *a* uninhibited

desintegrar-se /dʒizĩte'grarsi/ *vpr* disintegrate

desinteres|sado /dʒizĩtere'sadu/ *a* uninterested; **~sante** *a* uninteresting; **~sar-se** *vpr* lose interest (**de** in); **~se** /e/ *m* disinterest

desis|tência /dezis'tẽsia/ *f* giving up; **~tir** *vt/i* **~tir (de)** give up

desle|al /dʒizle'aw/ (*pl* **~ais**) *a* disloyal; **~aldade** *f* disloyalty

deslei|xado /dʒizle'ʃadu/ *a* sloppy; (*no vestir*) scruffy; **~xo** *m* carelessness; (*no vestir*) scruffiness

desli|gado /dʒizli'gadu/ *a* <*luz, TV*> off; <*pessoa*> absent-minded; **~gar** *vt* turn off <*luz, TV, motor*>; hang up, put down <*telefone*> □ *vi* (*ao telefonar*) hang up, put the phone down

deslindar /dʒizlĩ'dar/ *vt* clear up, solve

desli|zante /dʒizli'zãtʃi/ *a* slippery; <*inflação*> creeping; **~zar** *vi* slip; **~zar-se** *vpr* creep; **~ze** *m* slip; (*fig: erro*) slip-up

deslo|cado *a* <*membro*> dislocated; (*fig*) out of place; **~car** *vt* move; (*med*) dislocate; **~car-se** *vpr* move

deslum|brado /dʒizlũ'bradu/ *a* (*fig*) starry-eyed; **~bramento** *m* (*fig*) wonderment; **~brante** *a* dazzling; **~brar** *vt* dazzle; **~brar-se** *vpr* (*fig*) be dazzled

desmai|ado /dʒizmaj'adu/ *a* unconscious; **~ar** *vi* faint; **~o** *m* faint

desman|cha-prazeres /dʒizmãʃapra'zeris/ *m/f invar* spoilsport; **~char** *vt* break up; break off <*noivado*>; shatter <*sonhos*>; **~char-se** *vpr* break up; (*no ar, na água, em lágrimas*) dissolve

desmantelar /dʒizmãte'lar/ *vt* dismantle

desmarcar /dʒizmar'kar/ *vt* cancel <*encontro*>

desmascarar /dʒizmaske'rar/ *vt* unmask

desma|tamento /dʒizmata'mẽtu/ *m* deforestation; **~tar** *vt* clear (of forest)

desmedido /dʒizme'didu/ *a* excessive

desmemoriado /dʒizmemori'adu/ *a* forgetful

desmen|tido /dʒizmẽ'tʃidu/ *m* denial; **~tir** *vt* deny

desmiolado /dʒizmio'ladu/ *a* brainless

desmontar /dʒizmõ'tar/ *vt* dismantle

desmorali|zante /dʒizmorali'zãtʃi/ *a* demoralizing; **~zar** *vt* demoralize

desmoro|namento /dʒizmorona'mẽtu/ *m* collapse; **~nar** *vt* destroy; **~nar-se** *vpr* collapse

desnatar /dʒizna'tar/ *vi* skim <*leite*>

desnecessário /dʒiznese'sariu/ *a* unnecessary

desní|vel /dʒiz'nivew/ (*pl* **~veis**) *m* difference in height

desnortear /dʒiznortʃi'ar/ *vt* disorientate, (*Amer*) disorient

desnutrição /dʒiznutri'sãw/ *f* malnutrition

desobe|decer /dʒizobede'ser/ *vt/i* **~decer (a)** disobey; **~diência** *f* disobedience; **~diente** *a* disobedient

desobrigar /dʒizobri'gar/ *vt* release (**de** from)

desobstruir /dʒizobistru'ir/ *vt* unblock; empty <*casa*>

desocupado /dʒizoku'padu/ *a* unoccupied

desodorante /dʒizodo'rãtʃi/ *m*, (*Port*) **desodorizante** /dʒizoduri'zãtʃi/ *m* deodorant

deso|lação /dezola'sãw/ *f* desolation; **~lado** *a* <*lugar*> desolate; <*pessoa*> desolated; **~lar** *vt* desolate

desones|tidade /dʒizonestʃi'dadʒi/ *f* dishonesty; **~to** /ɛ/ *a* dishonest

deson|ra /dʒi'zõxa/ *f* dishonour; **~rar** *vt* dishonour; **~roso** /o/ *a* dishonourable

desor|deiro /dʒizor'deru/ *a* troublemaking □ *m* troublemaker; **~dem** *f* disorder; **~denado** *a* disorganized; <*vida*> disordered; **~denar** *vt* disorganize

desorgani|zação /dʒizorganiza'sãw/ *f* disorganization; **~zar** *vt* disorganize; **~zar-se** *vpr* get disorganized

desorientar /dʒizoriẽ'tar/ *vt* disorientate, (*Amer*) disorient

desossar /dʒizo'sar/ *vt* bone

deso|va /dʒi'zɔva/ *f* roe; **~var** *vi* spawn

despa|chado /dʒispa'ʃadu/ *a* efficient; **~chante** *m/f* (*de mercadorias*) shipping agent; (*de documentos*) documentation agent; **~char** *vt* deal with; dispatch, forward <*mercadorias*>; **~cho** *m* dispatch

desparafusar /dʒisparafu'zar/ *vt* unscrew

despedaçar /dʒispeda'sar/ *vt* (*rasgar*) tear to pieces; (*quebrar*) smash; **~-se** *vpr* <*vidro, vaso*> smash; <*papel, tecido*> tear

despe|dida /dʒispe'dʒida/ *f* farewell; **~dida de solteiro** stag night, (*Amer*) bachelor party; **~dir** *vt* dismiss; sack <*empregado*>; **~dir-se** *vpr* say goodbye (de to)

despei|tado /dʒispej'tadu/ *a* spiteful; **~to** *m* spite; **a ~to de** despite, in spite of

despe|jar /dʒispe'ʒar/ *vt* pour out <*líquido*>; empty <*recipiente*>; evict <*inquilino*>; **~jo** /e/ *m* (*de inquilino*) eviction

despencar /dʒispẽ'kar/ *vi* plummet

despender /dʒispẽ'der/ *vt* spend <*dinheiro*>

despensa /dʒis'pẽsa/ *f* pantry, larder

despentear /dʒispẽtʃi'ar/ *vt* mess up <*cabelo*>; mess up the hair of <*pessoa*>

despercebido /dʒisperse'bidu/ *a* unnoticed

desper|diçar /dʒisperdʒi'sar/ *vt* waste; **~dício** *m* waste

desper|tador /dʒisperta'dor/ *m* alarm clock; **~tar** *vt* rouse <*pessoa*>; (*fig*) arouse <*interesse, suspeitas etc*> □ *vi* awake

despesa /dʒis'peza/ *f* expense

des|pido /des'pidu/ *a* bare, stripped (de of); **~pir** *vt* strip (de of); strip off <*roupa*>; **~pir-se** *vpr* strip (off), get undressed

despo|jar /dʒispo'ʒar/ *vt* strip (de of); **~jar-se** *vpr* divest o.s. (de of); **~jo** /o/ *m* spoils, booty; **~jos mortais** mortal remains

despontar /dʒispõ'tar/ *vi* emerge

despor|tista /diʃpur'tiʃta/ (*Port*) *m/f* sportsman (*f* -woman); **~tivo** (*Port*) *a* sporting; **~to** /o/ (*Port*) *m* sport; **carro de ~to** sports car

déspota /'dɛspota/ *m/f* despot

despótico /des'pɔtʃiku/ *a* despotic

despovoar /dʒispovo'ar/ *vt* depopulate

desprender /dʒisprẽ'der/ *vt* detach; (*da parede*) take down; **~-se** *vpr* come off; (*fig*) detach o.s.

despreocupado /dʒisprioku'padu/ *a* unconcerned

despreparado /dʒisprepa'radu/ *a* unprepared

despretensioso /dʒispretẽsi'ozu/ *a* unpretentious

desprestigiar /dʒisprestʃiʒi'ar/ *vt* discredit

desprevenido /dʒispreve'nidu/ *a* off one's guard, unprepared; **apanhar ~** catch unawares

despre|zar /dʒispre'zar/ *vt* despise; (*ignorar*) ignore; **~zível** (*pl* **~zíveis**) *a* despicable; **~zo** /e/ *m* contempt

desproporção /dʒispropor'sãw/ *f* disproportion

desproporcio|nado /dʒisproporsio'nadu/ *a* disproportionate; **~nal** (*pl* **~nais**) *a* disproportional

despropositado /dʒispropozi'tadu/ *a* (*absurdo*) preposterous

desprovido /dʒispro'vidu/ *a* **~ de** without

desqualificar /dʒiskwalifi'kar/ *vt* disqualify

desqui|tar-se /dʒiski'tarsi/ *vpr* (legally) separate; **~te** *m* (legal) separation

desrespei|tar /dʒizxespej'tar/ *vt* not respect; (*ignorar*) disregard; **~to** *m* disrespect; **~toso** /o/ *a* disrespectful

dessa(s), desse(s) = **de** + **essa(s), esse(s)**

desta = **de** + **esta**

desta|camento /dʒistaka'mẽtu/ *m* detachment; **~car** *vt* detach; (*ressaltar*) bring out, make stand out; **~car-se** *vpr* (*desprender-se*) come off; <*corredor*> break away; (*sobressair*) stand out (sobre against); **~cável** (*pl*

~**cáveis**) *a* detachable; <*caderno*> pull-out

destam|pado /dʒistã'padu/ *a* (*panela*) uncovered; ~**par** *vt* remove the lid of

destapar /dʒista'par/ *vt* uncover

destaque /dʒis'taki/ *m* prominence; (*coisa, pessoa*) highlight; (*do noticiário*) headline

destas, deste = de + estas, este

destemido /dʒiste'midu/ *a* intrepid, courageous

desterrar /dʒiste'xar/ *vt* (*exilar*) exile

destes = de + estes

destilar /desti'lar/ *vt* distil; ~**ia** *f* distillery

desti|nado /destʃi'nadu/ *a* (*fadado*) destined; ~**nar** *vt* intend, mean (para for); ~**natário** *m* addressee; ~**no** *m* (*de viagem*) destination; (*sorte*) fate

destituir /destʃitu'ir/ *vt* remove

desto|ante /dʒisto'ãtʃi/ *a* <*sons*> discordant; <*cores*> clashing; ~**ar** *vi* ~**ar de** clash with

destrancar /dʒistrã'kar/ *vt* unlock

destreza /des'treza/ *f* skill

destrinchar /dʒistrĩ'ʃar/ *vt* (*expor*) dissect; (*resolver*) sort out

destro /'destru/ *a* skilful

destro|çar /dʒistro'sar/ *vt* wreck; ~**ços** *m pl* wreckage

destronar /dʒistro'nar/ *vt* depose

destroncar /dʒistrõ'kar/ *vt* rick

destru|ição /dʒistrui'sãw/ *f* destruction; ~**idor** *a* destructive □ *m* destroyer; ~**ir** *vt* destroy

desumano /dʒizu'manu/ *a* inhuman; (*cruel*) inhumane

desunião /dʒizuni'ãw/ *f* disunity

desu|sado /dʒizu'zadu/ *a* disused; ~**so** *m* disuse

desvairado /dʒizvaj'radu/ *a* delirious, raving

desvalori|zação /dʒizvaloriza'sãw/ *f* devaluation; ~**zar** *vt* devalue

desvanta|gem /dʒizvã'taʒẽ/ *f* disadvantage; ~**joso** /o/ *a* disadvantageous

desve|lar /dʒizve'lar/ *vt* unveil; uncover <*segredo*>; ~**lar-se** *vpr* go to a lot of trouble; ~**lo** /e/ *m* great care

desvencilhar /dʒizvẽsi'ʎar/ *vt* extricate, free

desvendar /dʒizvẽ'dar/ *vt* reveal <*segredo*>; solve <*mistério*>

desventura /dʒizvẽ'tura/ *f* misfortune; (*infelicidade*) unhappiness

desviar /dʒizvi'ar/ *vt* divert <*trânsito, rio, atenção, dinheiro*>; avert <*golpe, suspeitas, olhos*>; ~**-se** *vpr* deviate; <*do tema*> digress

desvincular /dʒizvĩku'lar/ *vt* free

desvio /dʒiz'viu/ *m* diversion; (*do trânsito*) diversion, (*Amer*) detour; (*linha ferroviária*) siding

desvirtuar /dʒizvirtu'ar/ *vt* misrepresent <*verdade*>

deta|lhado /deta'ʎadu/ *a* detailed; ~**lhar** *vt* detail; ~**lhe** *m* detail

detec|tar /detek'tar/ *vt* detect; ~**tive** (*Port*) *m* **veja detetive**; ~**tor** *m* detector

de|tenção /detẽ'sãw/ *f* (*prisão*) detention; ~**tentor** *m* holder; ~**ter** *vt* (*ter*) hold; (*prender*) detain

detergente /deter'ʒẽtʃi/ *m* detergent

deterio|ração /deteriora'sãw/ *f* deterioration; ~**rar** *vt* damage; ~**rar-se** *vpr* deteriorate

determi|nação /determina'sãw/ *f* determination; ~**nado** *a* (*certo*) certain; (*resoluto*) determined; ~**nar** *vt* determine

detestar /detes'tar/ *vt* hate

detetive /dete'tʃivi/ *m* detective

detido /de'tʃidu/ *pp de* **deter** □ *a* thorough □ *m* detainee

detonar /deto'nar/ *vt* detonate; (*fam: criticar*) pull to pieces □ *vi* detonate

detrás /de'traʃ/ *adv* behind □ *prep* ~ **de** behind

detrito /de'tritu/ *m* detritus

deturpar /detur'par/ *vt* misrepresent, distort

deus /dews/ *m* (*f* **deusa**) god (*f* goddess); ~**-dará** *m* **ao** ~**-dará** at the mercy of chance

devagar /dʒiva'gar/ *adv* slowly

deva|near /devani'ar/ *vi* daydream; ~**neio** *m* daydream

devas|sar /deva'sar/ *vt* expose; ~**sidão** *f* debauchery; ~**so** *a* debauched

devastar /devas'tar/ *vt* devastate

de|vedor /deve'dor/ *a* debit □ *m* debtor; ~**ver** *vt* owe □ *v aux* ~**ve fazer** (*obrigação*) he has to do; ~**ve chegar** (*probabilidade*) he should arrive; ~**ve ser** (*suposição*) he must be; ~**ve ter ido** he must have gone; ~**v(er)ia fazer** he ought to do; ~**v(er)ia ter feito** he ought to have done; ~**vidamente** *adv* duly; ~**vido** *a* due (a to)

devoção /devo'sãw/ *f* devotion

de|volução /devolu'sãw/ *f* return; ~**volver** *vt* return

devorar /devo'rar/ *vt* devour

devo|tar /devo'tar/ *vt* devote; ~**tar-se** *vpr* devote o.s. (a to); ~**to** /ɔ/ *a* devout

dez /dɛs/ *a & m* ten

dezanove /dza'nɔv/ (*Port*) *a & m* nineteen

dezas|seis /dza'sejʃ/ (*Port*) *a & m* sixteen; ~**sete** /ɛ/ (*Port*) *a & m* seventeen

dezembro /de'zẽbru/ *m* December

deze|na /de'zena/ *f* ten; uma ~ (de) about ten; **~nove** /ɔ/ *a & m* nineteen
dezes|seis /dʒize'sejs/ *a & m* sixteen; **~sete** /ɛ/ *a & m* seventeen
dezoito /dʒi'zojtu/ *a & m* eighteen
dia /'dʒia/ *m* day; de ~ by day; (no) ~ 20 de julho (on) July 20th; ~ de folga day off; ~ útil working day; **~-a-~** *m* everyday life
dia|bete /dʒia'bɛtʃi/ *f* diabetes; **~bético** *a & m* diabetic
dia|bo /dʒi'abu/ *m* devil; **~bólico** *a* diabolical, devilish; **~brete** /e/ *m* little devil; **~brura** *f* (*de criança*) bit of mischief; *pl* mischief
diadema /dʒia'dema/ *m* tiara
diafragma /dʒia'fragima/ *m* diaphragm
dia|gnosticar /dʒiagnostʃi'kar/ *vt* diagnose; **~gnóstico** *m* diagnosis □ *a* diagnostic
diago|nal /dʒiago'naw/ (*pl* **~nais**) *a & f* diagonal
diagra|ma /dʒia'grama/ *m* diagram; **~mação** *f* design; **~mador** *m* designer; **~mar** *vt* design <*livro, revista*>
dialect- (*Port*) *veja* **dialet-**
dia|lética /dʒia'lɛtʃika/ *f* dialectics; **~leto** /ɛ/ *m* dialect
dialogar /dʒialo'gar/ *vi* talk; (*pol*) hold talks
diálogo /dʒi'alogu/ *m* dialogue
diamante /dʒia'mãtʃi/ *m* diamond
diâmetro /dʒi'ametru/ *m* diameter
dian|te /dʒi'ãtʃi/ *adv* de ... em ~te from ... on(wards); ~te de (*enfrentando*) faced with; (*perante*) before; **~teira** *f* lead; **~teiro** *a* front
diapasão /dʒiapa'zãw/ *m* tuning-fork
diapositivo /dʒiapozi'tʃivu/ *m* transparency
diá|ria /dʒi'aria/ *f* daily rate; **~rio** *a* daily
diarista /dʒia'rista/ *m/f* day labourer; (*faxineira*) daily (help)
diarréia /dʒia'xɛja/ *f* diarrhoea
dica /'dʒika/ *f* tip, hint
dicção /dʒik'sãw/ *f* diction
dicionário /dʒisio'nariu/ *m* dictionary
didáti|ca /dʒi'datʃika/ *f* teaching methodology; **~co** *a* teaching; <*livro*> educational; <*estilo*> didactic
die|ta /dʒi'ɛta/ *f* diet; de ~ta on a diet; **~tista** *m/f* dietician
difa|mação /dʒifama'sãw/ *f* defamation; **~mar** *vt* defame; **~matório** *a* defamatory
diferen|ça /dʒife'rẽsa/ *f* difference; **~cial** (*pl* **~ciais**) *a & f* differential; **~ciar** *vt* differentiate; **~ciar-se** *vpr* differ; **~te** *a* different
dife|rimento /dʒiferi'mẽtu/ *m* deferment; **~rir** *vt* defer □ *vi* differ
difí|cil /dʒi'fisiw/ (*pl* **~ceis**) *a* difficult; (*improvável*) unlikely
dificilmente /dʒifisiw'mẽtʃi/ *adv* ~ poderá fazê-lo he's unlikely to be able to do it
dificul|dade /dʒifikuw'dadʒi/ *f* difficulty; **~tar** *vt* make difficult
difteria /dʒifte'ria/ *f* diphtheria
difun|dir /dʒifũ'dʒir/ *vt* spread; (*pela rádio*) broadcast; diffuse <*luz, calor*>; **~dir-se** *vpr* spread
difu|são /dʒifu'zãw/ *f* diffusion; **~so** *a* diffuse
dige|rir /dʒiʒe'rir/ *vt* digest; **~rível** (*pl* **~ríveis**) *a* digestible
diges|tão /dʒiʒes'tãw/ *f* digestion; **~tivo** *a* digestive
digi|tal /dʒiʒi'taw/ (*pl* **~tais**) *a* digital; impressão ~tal fingerprint; **~tar** *vt* key
dígito /'dʒiʒitu/ *m* digit
digladiar /dʒigladʒi'ar/ *vi* do battle
dig|nar-se /dʒig'narsi/ *vpr* deign (de to); **~nidade** *f* dignity; **~nificar** *vt* dignify; **~no** *a* worthy (de of); (*decoroso*) dignified
dilace|rante /dʒilase'rãtʃi/ *a* <*dor*> excruciating; **~rar** *vt* tear to pieces
dilapidar /dʒilapi'dar/ *vt* squander
dilatar /dʒila'tar/ *vt* expand; (*med*) dilate; **~-se** *vpr* expand; (*med*) dilate
dilema /dʒi'lema/ *m* dilemma
diletante /dʒile'tãtʃi/ *a & m/f* dilettante
dili|gência /dʒili'ʒẽsia/ *f* diligence; (*carruagem*) stagecoach; **~gente** *a* diligent, hard-working
diluir /dʒilu'ir/ *vt* dilute
dilúvio /dʒi'luviu/ *m* deluge
dimen|são /dʒimẽ'sãw/ *f* dimension; **~sionar** *vt* size up
diminu|ição /dʒiminui'sãw/ *f* reduction; **~ir** *vt* reduce □ *vi* lessen; <*carro, motorista*> slow down; **~tivo** *a & m* diminutive; **~to** *a* minute
Dinamarca /dʒina'marka/ *f* Denmark
dinamar|quês /dʒinamar'kes/ (*f* **~quesa**) *a* Danish □ *m* Dane
dinâmi|ca /dʒi'namika/ *f* dynamics; **~co** *a* dynamic
dina|mismo /dʒina'mizmu/ *m* dynamism; **~mite** *f* dynamite
dínamo /'dʒinamu/ *m* dynamo
dinastia /dʒinas'tʃia/ *f* dynasty
dinda /'dʒĩda/ (*fam*) *f* godmother
dinheiro /dʒi'ɲeru/ *m* money
dinossauro /dʒino'sawru/ *m* dinosaur
diocese /dʒio'sɛzi/ *f* diocese
dióxido /dʒi'ɔksidu/ *m* dioxide; ~ de carbono carbon dioxide
diplo|ma /dʒi'ploma/ *m* diploma; **~macia** *f* diplomacy; **~mar-se** *vpr*

take one's diploma; ~**mata** *m/f* diplomat □ *a* diplomatic; ~**mático** *a* diplomatic

direção /dʒire'sãw/ *f* (*sentido*) direction; (*de empresa*) management; (*condução de carro*) driving; (*manuseio do volante*) steering

direct- (*Port*) *veja* **diret-**

direi|ta /dʒi'rejta/ *f* right; ~**tinho** *adv* exactly right; ~**tista** *a* rightwing □ *m/f* rightwinger, rightist; ~**to** *a* right; (*ereto*) straight □ *adv* properly □ *m* right

dire|tas /dʒi'rɛtas/ *f pl* direct (presidential) elections; ~**to** *a* direct □ *adv* directly; ~**tor** *m* director; (*de escola*) headteacher; (*de jornal*) editor; ~**tor-gerente** managing director; ~**toria** *f* (*diretores*) board of directors; (*sala*) boardroom; ~**tório** *m* directory; ~**triz** *f* directive

diri|gente /dʒiri'ʒẽtʃi/ *a* leading □ *m/f* leader; ~**gir** *vt* direct; manage <*empresa*>; drive <*carro*>; ~**gir-se** *vpr* (*ir*) make one's way; ~**gir-se a** (*falar com*) address

dis|cagem /dʒis'kaʒẽ/ *f* dialling; ~**car** *vt/i* dial

discente /dʒi'sẽtʃi/ *a* **corpo ~** student body

discer|nimento /dʒiserni'mẽtu/ *m* discernment; ~**nir** *vt* discern

discipli|na /dʒisi'plina/ *f* discipline; ~**nador** *a* disciplinary; ~**nar** *vt* discipline

discípulo /dʒi'sipulu/ *m* disciple

disc-jóquei /dʒisk'ʒɔkej/ *m* disc-jockey

disco /'dʒisku/ *m* disc; (*de música*) record; (*no atletismo*) discus □ (*fam*) *f* disco; **~ flexível/rígido** floppy/hard disk; **~ laser** CD, compact disc; **~ voador** flying saucer

discor|dante /dʒiskor'dãtʃi/ *a* conflicting; ~**dar** *vi* disagree (de with)

discote|ca /dʒisko'tɛka/ *f* discotheque; ~**cário** *m* DJ

discre|pância /dʒiskre'pãsia/ *f* discrepancy; ~**pante** *a* inconsistent; ~**par** *vi* diverge (de from)

dis|creto /dʒis'krɛtu/ *a* discreet; ~**crição** *f* discretion

discrimi|nação /dʒiskrimina'sãw/ *f* discrimination; (*descrição*) description; ~**nar** *vt* discriminate; ~**natório** *a* discriminatory

discur|sar /dʒiskur'sar/ *vi* speak; ~**so** *m* speech

discussão /dʒisku'sãw/ *f* discussion; (*briga*) argument

discu|tir /dʒisku'tʃir/ *vt/i* discuss; (*brigar*) argue; ~**tível** (*pl* ~**tíveis**) *a* debatable

disenteria /dʒizẽte'ria/ *f* dysentery

disfar|çar /dʒisfar'sar/ *vt* disguise; ~**çar-se** *vpr* disguise o.s.; ~**ce** *m* disguise

dis|lético /dʒiz'lɛtʃiku/ *a & m* dyslexic; ~**lexia** *f* dyslexia; ~**léxico** *a & m* dyslexic

dispa|rada /dʒispa'rada/ *f* bolt; ~**rado** *adv* **o melhor ~rado** the best by a long way; ~**rar** *vt* fire <*arma*> □ *vi* (*com arma*) fire; <*preços, inflação*> shoot up; <*corredor*> surge ahead

disparate /dʒispa'ratʃi/ *m* piece of nonsense; *pl* nonsense

dis|pêndio /dʒis'pẽdʒiu/ *m* expenditure; ~**pendioso** /o/ *a* costly

dispen|sa /dʒis'pẽsa/ *f* exemption; ~**sar** *vt* (*distribuir*) dispense; (*isentar*) exempt (de from); (*prescindir de*) dispense with; ~**sável** (*pl* ~**sáveis**) *a* dispensable

dispersar /dʒisper'sar/ *vt* disperse; waste <*energias*> □ *vi*, ~**-se** *vpr* disperse

disperso /dʒis'pɛrsu/ *adj* scattered

dispo|nibilidade /dʒisponibili'dadʒi/ *f* availability; ~**nível** (*pl* ~**níveis**) *a* available

dis|por /dʒis'por/ *vt* arrange □ *vi* ~**por de** have at one's disposal; ~**por-se** *vpr* form up □ *m* **ao seu ~por** at your disposal; ~**posição** *f* (*vontade*) willingness; (*arranjo*) arrangement; (*de espírito*) frame of mind; (*de testamento etc*) provision; **à ~posição de alg** at s.o.'s disposal; ~**positivo** *m* device; ~**posto** *a* prepared, willing (a to)

dispu|ta /dʒis'puta/ *f* dispute; ~**tar** *vt* dispute; (*tentar ganhar*) compete for

disquete /dʒis'ketʃi/ *m* diskette, floppy (disk)

dissabores /dʒisa'boris/ *m pl* troubles

disseminar /dʒisemi'nar/ *vt* disseminate

dissertação /dʒiserta'sãw/ *f* dissertation, lecture

dissi|dência /dʒisi'dẽsia/ *f* dissidence; ~**dente** *a & m* dissident

dissídio /dʒi'sidʒiu/ *m* dispute

dissimular /dʒisimu'lar/ *vt* hide □ *vi* dissimulate

disso = de + isso

dissipar /dʒisi'par/ *vt* clear <*nevoeiro*>; dispel <*dúvidas, suspeitas, ilusões*>; dissipate <*fortuna*>; ~**-se** *vpr* <*nevoeiro*> clear; <*dúvidas etc*> be dispelled

dissolu|ção /dʒisolu'sãw/ *f* dissolution; ~**to** *a* dissolute

dissolver /dʒisow'ver/ *vt* dissolve; ~**-se** *vpr* dissolve

dissuadir /dʒisua'dʒir/ *vt* dissuade (de from)

distância /dʒis'tãsia/ *f* distance

distan|ciar /dʒistãsi'ar/ *vt* distance; **~ciar-se** *vpr* distance o.s.; **~te** *a* distant

disten|der /dʒistẽ'der/ *vt* stretch <*pernas*>; relax <*músculo*>; **~der-se** *vpr* relax; **~são** *f* (*med*) pull; **~são muscular** pulled muscle

distin|ção /dʒistʃĩ'sãw/ *f* distinction; **~guir** *vt* distinguish (de from); **~guir-se** *vpr* distinguish o.s.; **~tivo** *a* distinctive □ *m* badge; **~to** *a* distinct; <*senhor*> distinguished

disto = de + isto

distor|ção /dʒistor'sãw/ *f* distortion; **~cer** *vt* distort

distra|ção /dʒistra'sãw/ *f* distraction; **~ído** *a* absent-minded; **~ir** *vt* distract; (*divertir*) amuse; **~ir-se** *vpr* be distracted; (*divertir-se*) amuse o.s.

distribu|ição /dʒistribui'sãw/ *f* distribution; **~idor** *m* distributor; **~idora** *f* distributor, distribution company; **~ir** *vt* distribute

distrito /dʒis'tritu/ *m* district

distúrbio /dʒis'turbiu/ *m* trouble

di|tado /dʒi'tadu/ *m* dictation; (*provérbio*) saying; **~tador** *m* dictator; **~tadura** *f* dictatorship; **~tame** *m* dictate; **~tar** *vt* dictate; **~tatorial** (*pl* **~tatoriais**) *a* dictatorial

dito /'dʒitu/ *a* **~ e feito** no sooner said than done □ *m* remark

ditongo /dʒi'tõgu/ *m* diphthong

DIU /'dʒiu/ *m* IUD, coil

diurno /dʒi'urnu/ *a* day

divã /dʒi'vã/ *m* couch

divagar /dʒiva'gar/ *vi* digress

diver|gência /dʒiver'ʒẽsia/ *a* divergence; **~gente** *a* divergent; **~gir** *vi* diverge (de from); **~são** *f* diversion; (*divertimento*) amusement; **~sidade** *f* diversity; **~sificar** *vt/i* diversify; **~so** /ɛ/ *a* (*diferente*) diverse; *pl* (*vários*) several; **~tido** *a* (*engraçado*) funny; (*que se curte*) enjoyable; **~timento** *m* enjoyment, fun; (*um*) amusement; **~tir** *vt* amuse; **~tir-se** *vpr* enjoy o.s., have fun

dívida /'dʒivida/ *f* debt; **~ externa** foreign debt

divi|dendo /dʒivi'dẽdu/ *m* dividend; **~dido** *a* <*pessoa*> torn; **~dir** *vt* divide; (*compartilhar*) share; **~dir-se** *vpr* be divided

divindade /dʒivĩ'dadʒi/ *f* divinity

divino /dʒi'vinu/ *a* divine

divi|sa /dʒi'viza/ *f* (*lema*) motto; (*galão*) stripes; (*fronteira*) border; *pl* foreign currency; **~são** *f* division; **~sória** *f* partition; **~sório** *a* dividing

divorci|ado /dʒivorsi'adu/ *a* divorced □ *m* divorcé (*f* divorcée); **~ar** *vt* divorce; **~ar-se** *vpr* get divorced; **~ar-se de** divorce

divórcio /dʒi'vɔrsiu/ *m* divorce

divul|gado /dʒivuw'gadu/ *a* widespread; **~gar** *vt* spread; publish <*notícia*>; divulge <*segredo*>; **~gar-se** *vpr* be spread

dizer /dʒi'zer/ *vt* say; **~ a alg que** tell sb that; **~ para alg fazer** tell s.o. to do □ *vi* **~ com** go with; **~-se** *vpr* claim to be □ *m* saying

dizimar /dʒizi'mar/ *vt* decimate

do = de +o

dó /dɔ/ *m* pity; **dar ~** be pitiful; **ter ~ de** feel sorry for

do|ação /doa'sãw/ *f* donation; **~ador** *m* donor; **~ar** *vt* donate

do|bra /'dɔbra/ *f* fold; (*de calça*) turn-up, (*Amer*) cuff; **~bradiça** *f* hinge; **~bradiço** *a* pliable; **~brado** *a* (*duplo*) double; **~brar** *vt* (*duplicar*) double; (*fazer dobra em*) fold; (*curvar*) bend; go round <*esquina*>; ring <*sinos*>; (*Port*) dub <*filme*> □ *vi* double; <*sinos*> ring; **~brar-se** *vpr* bend; **~bro** *m* double

doca /'dɔka/ *f* dock

doce /'dosi/ *a* sweet; <*água*> fresh □ *m* sweet; **~ de leite** fudge

docente /do'sẽtʃi/ *a* teaching; **corpo ~** teaching staff, (*Amer*) faculty

dó|cil /'dɔsiw/ (*pl* **~ceis**) *a* docile

documen|tação /dokumẽta'sãw/ *f* documentation; **~tar** *vt* document; **~tário** *a & m* documentary; **~to** *m* document

doçura /do'sura/ *f* sweetness

dodói /do'dɔj/ (*fam*) *m* **ter ~** have a pain □ *a* poorly, ill

doen|ça /do'ẽsa/ *f* illness; (*infecciosa, fig*) disease; **~te** *a* ill; **~tio** *a* <*criança, aspecto*> sickly; <*interesse, curiosidade*> morbid

doer /do'er/ *vi* hurt; <*cabeça, músculo*> ache

dog|ma /'dɔgima/ *m* dogma; **~mático** *a* dogmatic

doido /'dojdu/ *a* crazy

dois /dojs/ *a & m* (*f* **duas**) two

dólar /'dɔlar/ *m* dollar

dolo|rido /dolo'ridu/ *a* sore; **~roso** /o/ *a* painful

dom /dõ/ *m* gift

do|mador /doma'dor/ *m* tamer; **~mar** *vt* tame

doméstica /do'mɛstʃika/ *f* housemaid

domesticar /domestʃi'kar/ *vt* domesticate

doméstico /do'mɛstʃiku/ *a* domestic

domi|ciliar /domisili'ar/ *a* home; **~cílio** *m* home

domi|nação /domina'sãw/ *f* domination; **~nador** *a* domineering; **~nante** *a* dominant; **~nar** *vt* dom-

inate; have a command of <*língua*>; ~**nar-se** *vpr* control o.s.
domin|go /do'mĩgu/ *m* Sunday; ~**gueiro** *a* Sunday
domini|cal /domini'kaw/ (*pl* ~**cais**) *a* Sunday; ~**cano** *a & m* Dominican
domínio /do'miniu/ *m* command
dona /'dona/ *f* owner; **Dona** (*com nome*) Miss; ~ **de casa** *f* housewife
donativo /dona'tʃivu/ *m* donation
donde /'dõdʒi/ *adv* from where; (*motivo*) from whence
dono /'donu/ *m* owner
donzela /dõ'zɛla/ *f* maiden
dopar /do'par/ *vt* drug
dor /dor/ *f* pain; (*menos aguda*) ache; ~ **de cabeça** headache
dor|mente /dor'mẽtʃi/ *a* numb □ *m* sleeper; ~**mida** *f* sleep; ~**minhoco** /o/ *m* sleepyhead; ~**mir** *vi* sleep; ~**mitar** *vi* doze; ~**mitório** *m* bedroom; (*comunitário*) dormitory
dorso /'dorsu/ *m* back; (*de livro*) spine
dos = **de** + **os**
do|sagem /do'zaʒẽ/ *f* dosage; ~**sar** *vt* moderate; ~**se** /ɔ/ *f* dose; (*de uísque etc*) shot, measure
dossiê /dosi'e/ *m* file
do|tação /dota'sãw/ *f* endowment; ~**tado** *a* gifted; ~**tado de** endowed with; ~**tar** *vt* endow (**de** with); ~**te** /ɔ/ *m* (*de noiva*) dowry; (*dom*) endowment
dou|rado /do'radu/ *a* (*de cor*) golden; (*revestido de ouro*) gilded, gilt □ *m* gilt; ~**rar** *vt* gild
dou|to /'dotu/ *a* learned; ~**tor** *m* doctor; ~**torado** *m* doctorate, PhD; ~**trina** *f* doctrine; ~**trinar** *vt* indoctrinate
doze /'dozi/ *a & m* twelve
dragão /dra'gãw/ *m* dragon
dragar /dra'gar/ *vt* dredge
drágea /'draʒia/ *f* lozenge
dra|ma /'drama/ *m* drama; ~**malhão** *m* melodrama; ~**mático** *a* dramatic; ~**matizar** *vt* dramatize; ~**maturgo** *m* dramatist, playwright
drapeado /drapi'adu/ *a* draped
drástico /'drastʃiku/ *a* drastic
dre|nagem /dre'naʒẽ/ *f* drainage; ~**nar** *vt* drain; ~**no** /ɛ/ *m* drain
driblar /dri'blar/ *vt* (*em futebol*) dribble round, beat; (*fig*) get round
drinque /'drĩki/ *m* drink
drive /'drajvi/ *m* disk drive
dro|ga /'drɔga/ *f* drug; (*fam*) (*coisa sem valor*) dead loss; (*coisa chata*) drag □ *int* damn; ~**gado** *a* on drugs □ *m* drug addict; ~**gar** *vt* drug; ~**gar-se** *vpr* take drugs; ~**garia** *f* dispensing chemist's, pharmacy
duas /'duas/ *veja* **dois**
dúbio /'dubiu/ *a* dubious
dub|lagem /du'blaʒẽ/ *f* dubbing; ~**lar** *vt* dub <*filme*>; mime <*música*>; ~**lê** *m* double
ducentésimo /dusẽ'tɛzimu/ *a* two-hundredth
ducha /'duʃa/ *f* shower
ducto /'duktu/ *m* duct
duelo /du'ɛlu/ *m* duel
duende /du'ẽdʒi/ *m* elf
dueto /du'etu/ *m* duet
duna /'duna/ *f* dune
duodécimo /duo'dɛsimu/ *a* twelfth
duodeno /duo'dɛnu/ *m* duodenum
dupla /'dupla/ *f* pair, duo; <*no tênis*> doubles
duplex /du'plɛks/ *a invar* two-floor □ *m invar* two-floor apartment, (*Amer*) duplex
dupli|car /dupli'kar/ *vt/i* double; ~**cidade** *f* duplicity; ~**cata** *f* duplicate
duplo /'duplu/ *a* double
duque /'duki/ duke; ~**sa** /e/ *f* duchess
du|ração /dura'sãw/ *f* duration; ~**radouro** *a* lasting; ~**rante** *prep* during; ~**rar** *vi* last; ~**rável** (*pl* ~**ráveis**) *a* durable
durex /du'rɛks/ *m invar* sellotape
du|reza /du'reza/ *f* hardness; ~**ro** *a* hard; (*fam: sem dinheiro*) hard up, broke
dúvida /'duvida/ *f* doubt; (*pergunta*) query
duvi|dar /duvi'dar/ *vt/i* doubt; ~**doso** /o/ *a* doubtful
duzentos /du'zẽtus/ *a & m* two hundred
dúzia /'duzia/ *f* dozen

E

e /i/ *conj* and
ébano /'ɛbanu/ *m* ebony
ébrio /'ɛbriu/ *a* drunk □ *m* drunkard
ebulição /ebuli'sãw/ *f* boiling
eclesiástico /eklezi'astʃiku/ *a* ecclesiastical
eclético /e'klɛtʃiku/ *a* eclectic
eclip|sar /eklip'sar/ *vt* eclipse; ~**se** *m* eclipse
eclodir /eklo'dʒir/ *vi* emerge; (*estourar*) break out; open
eco /'ɛku/ *m* echo; **ter** ~ have repercussions; ~**ar** *vt/i* echo
eco|logia /ekolo'ʒia/ *f* ecology; ~**lógico** *a* ecological; ~**logista** *m/f* ecologist
eco|nomia /ekono'mia/ *f* economy; (*ciência*) economics; *pl* (*dinheiro poupado*) savings; ~**nômico** *a* economic; (*rentável, barato*) economical; ~**nomista** *m/f* economist; ~**nomizar** *vt* save □ *vi* economize

écran /ɛ'krã/ (*Port*) *m* screen

eczema /ek'zɛma/ *m* eczema

edição /edʒi'sãw/ *f* edition; (*de filmes*) editing

edificante /edʒifi'kãtʃi/ *a* edifying

edifício /edʒi'fisiu/ *m* building

Edimburgo /edʒĩ'burgu/ *f* Edinburgh

edi|tal /edʒi'taw/ (*pl* **~tais**) *m* announcement; **~tar** *vt* publish; (*comput*) edit; **~to** *m* edict; **~tor** *m* publisher; **~tora** *f* publishing company; **~torial** (*pl* **~toriais**) *a* publishing □ *m* editorial

edredom /edre'dõ/ *m*, (*Port*) **edredão** /edre'dãw/ *m* quilt

educa|ção /eduka'sãw/ *f* (*ensino*) education; (*polidez*) good manners; **é falta de ~ção** it's rude; **~cional** (*pl* **~cionais**) *a* education

edu|cado /edu'kadu/ *a* polite; **~car** *vt* educate; **~cativo** *a* educational

efeito /e'fejtu/ *m* effect; **fazer ~** have an effect; **para todos os ~s** to all intents and purposes; **~ colateral** side effect; **~ estufa** greenhouse effect

efêmero /e'fẽmeru/ *a* ephemeral

efeminado /efemi'nadu/ *a* effeminate

efervescente /eferve'stʃi/ *a* effervescent

efe|tivar /efetʃi'var/ *vt* bring into effect; (*contratar*) make a permanent member of staff; **~tivo** *a* real, effective; <*cargo, empregado*> permanent; **~tuar** *vt* carry out, effect

efi|cácia /efi'kasia/ *f* effectiveness; **~caz** *a* effective

efici|ência /efisi'ẽsia/ *f* efficiency; **~ente** *a* efficient

efígie /e'figi/ *f* effigy

efusivo /efu'zivu/ *a* effusive

Egeu /e'ʒew/ *a & m* Aegean

égide /'ɛʒidʒi/ *f* aegis

egípcio /e'ʒipsiu/ *a & m* Egyptian

Egito /e'ʒitu/ *m* Egypt

ego /'ɛgu/ *m* ego; **~cêntrico** *a* self-centred, egocentric; **~ísmo** *m* selfishness; **~ísta** *a* selfish □ *m/f* egoist □ *m* (*de rádio etc*) earplug

égua /'ɛgwa/ *f* mare

eis /ejs/ *adv* (*aqui está*) here is/are; (*isso é*) that is

eixo /'ejʃu/ *m* axle; (*mat, entre cidades*) axis; **pôr nos ~s** set straight

ela /'ɛla/ *pron* she; (*coisa*) it; (*com preposição*) her; (*coisa*) it

elaborar /elabo'rar/ *vt* (*fazer*) make, produce; (*desenvolver*) work out

elasticidade /elastʃisi'dadʒi/ *f* (*de coisa*) elasticity; (*de pessoa*) suppleness

elástico /e'lastʃiku/ *a* elastic □ *m* (*de borracha*) elastic band; (*de calcinha etc*) elastic

ele /'eli/ *pron* he; (*coisa*) it; (*com preposição*) him; (*coisa*) it

electr- (*Port*) *veja* **eletr-**

eléctrico /i'lɛktriku/ (*Port*) *m* tram, (*Amer*) streetcar □ *a veja* **elétrico**

elefante /ele'fãtʃi/ *m* elephant

ele|gância /ele'gãsia/ *f* elegance; **~gante** *a* elegant

eleger /ele'ʒer/ *vt* elect; **~-se** *vpr* get elected

elegia /ele'ʒia/ *f* elegy

elei|ção /elej'sãw/ *f* election; **~to** *a* elected, elect; <*povo*> chosen; **~tor** *m* voter; **~torado** *m* electorate; **~toral** (*pl* **~torais**) *a* electoral

elemen|tar /elemẽ'tar/ *a* elementary; **~to** *m* element

elenco /e'lẽku/ *m* (*de filme, peça*) cast

eletri|cidade /eletrisi'dadʒi/ *f* electricity; **~cista** *m/f* electrician

elétrico /e'lɛtriku/ *a* electric

eletri|ficar /eletrifi'kar/ *vt* electrify; **~zar** *vt* electrify

eletro /e'lɛtru/ *m* ECG; **~cutar** *vt* electrocute; **~do** /o/ *m* electrode; **~domésticos** *m pl* electrical appliances

eletrôni|ca /ele'tronika/ *f* electronics; **~co** *a* electronic

ele|vação /eleva'sãw/ *f* elevation; (*aumento*) rise; **~vado** *a* high; <*sentimento, estilo*> elevated; **~vador** *m* lift, (*Amer*) elevator; **~var** *vt* raise; (*promover*) elevate; **~var-se** *vpr* rise

elimi|nar /elimi'nar/ *vt* eliminate; **~natória** *f* heat; **~natório** *a* eliminatory

elipse /e'lipsi/ *f* ellipse

elíptico /e'liptʃiku/ *a* elliptical

eli|te /e'litʃi/ *f* elite; **~tismo** *m* elitism; **~tista** *a & m/f* elitist

elmo /'ɛwmu/ *m* helmet

elo /'ɛlu/ *m* link

elo|giar /eloʒi'ar/ *vt* praise; **~giar alg por** compliment s.o. on; **~gio** *m* (*louvor*) praise; (*um*) compliment; **~gioso** /o/ *a* complimentary

elo|qüência /elo'kwẽsia/ *f* eloquence; **~qüente** *a* eloquent

eluci|dar /elusi'dar/ *vt* elucidate; **~dativo** *a* elucidatory

em /j/ *prep* in; (*sobre*) on; **ela está no Eduardo** she's at Eduardo's (house); **de casa ~ casa** from house to house; **aumentar ~ 10%** increase by 10%

emagre|cer /emagre'ser/ *vi* lose weight, get thinner □ *vt* make thinner; **~cimento** *m* slimming

emanar /ema'nar/ *vi* emanate (**de** from)

emanci|pação /emãsipa'sãw/ *f* emancipation; **~par** *vt* emancipate; **~par-se** *vpr* become emancipated

emara|nhado /emara'ɲadu/ *a* tangled □ *m* tangle; **~nhar** *vt* tangle; (*envolver*) entangle; **~nhar-se** *vpr* get tangled up; (*envolver-se*) become entangled (em in)

embaçar /ĩba'sar/, (*Port*) **embaciar** /ĩbasi'ar/ *vt* steam up <*vidro*> □ *vi* <*vidro*> steam up; <*olhos*> grow misty

embainhar /ĩbaj'ɲar/ *vt* hem <*vestido, calça*>

embaixa|da /ĩba'ʃada/ *f* embassy; **~dor** *m* ambassador; **~triz** *f* ambassador; (*esposa*) ambassador's wife

embaixo /ĩ'baʃu/ *adv* underneath; (*em casa*) downstairs; **~ de** under

emba|lagem /ĩba'laʒẽ/ *f* packaging; **~lar**[1] *vt* pack

emba|lar[2] /ĩba'lar/ *vt* rock <*criança*>; **~lo** *m* (*fig*) excitement, thrill

embalsamar /ĩbawsa'mar/ *vt* embalm

embara|çar /ĩbara'sar/ *vt* embarrass; **~çar-se** *vpr* get embarrassed (com by); **~ço** *m* embarrassment; **~çoso** /o/ *a* embarrassing

embaralhar /ĩbara'ʎar/ *vt* muddle up; shuffle <*cartas*>; **~-se** *vpr* get muddled up

embar|cação /ĩbarka'sãw/ *f* vessel; **~cadouro** *m* wharf; **~car** *vt/i* board, embark

embar|gado /ĩbar'gadu/ *a* <*voz*> faltering; **~go** *m* embargo

embarque /ĩ'barki/ *m* boarding; (*seção do aeroporto*) departures

embasba|cado /ĩbazba'kadu/ *a* open-mouthed; **~car-se** *vpr* be left open-mouthed

embate /ĩ'batʃi/ *m* (*de carros etc*) crash; (*fig*) clash

embebedar /ĩbebe'dar/ *vt* make drunk; **~-se** *vpr* get drunk

embeber /ĩbe'ber/ *vt* soak; **~-se de** soak up; **~-se em** get absorbed in

embele|zador /ĩbeleza'dor/ *a* <*cirurgia*> cosmetic; **~zar** *vt* embellish; spruce up <*casa*>; **~zar-se** *vpr* make o.s. beautiful

embevecer /ĩbeve'ser/ *vt* captivate, engross; **~-se** *vpr* get engrossed, be captivated

emblema /ẽ'blema/ *m* emblem

embocadura /ĩboka'dura/ *f* (*de instrumento*) mouthpiece; (*de freio*) bit; (*de rio*) mouth; (*de rua*) entrance

êmbolo /'ẽbulu/ *m* piston

embolsar /ĩbow'sar/ *vt* pocket; (*reembolsar*) reimburse

embora /ĩ'bɔra/ *adv* away □ *conj* although

emborcar /ĩbor'kar/ *vi* overturn; <*barco*> capsize

emboscada /ĩbos'kada/ *f* ambush

embrai|agem /ẽbraj'aʒẽ/ (*Port*) *f veja* **embreagem**; **~ar** (*Port*) *vi veja* **embrear**

embre|agem /ẽbri'aʒẽ/ *f* clutch; **~ar** *vi* let in the clutch

embria|gar /ẽbria'gar/ *vt* intoxicate; **~gar-se** *vpr* get drunk, become intoxicated; **~guez** /e/ *f* drunkenness; **~guez no volante** drunken driving

embri|ão /ẽbri'ãw/ *m* embryo; **~onário** *a* embryonic

embro|mação /ĩbroma'sãw/ *f* flannel; **~mar** *vt* flannel, string along; (*enganar*) con □ *vi* stall, drag one's feet

embru|lhada /ĩbru'ʎada/ *f* muddle; **~lhar** *vt* wrap up <*pacote*>; upset <*estômago*>; (*confundir*) muddle up; **~lhar-se** *vpr* <*pessoa*> get muddled up; **~lho** *m* parcel; (*fig*) mix-up

embur|rado /ĩbu'xadu/ *a* sulky; **~rar** *vi* sulk

embuste /ĩ'bustʃi/ *m* hoax, put-up job

embu|tido /ĩbu'tʃidu/ *a* built-in, fitted; **~tir** *vt* build in, fit

emen|da /e'mẽda/ *f* correction, improvement; (*de lei*) amendment; **~dar** *vt* correct; amend <*lei*>; **~dar-se** *vpr* mend one's ways

ementa /i'mẽta/ (*Port*) *f* menu

emer|gência /emer'ʒẽsia/ *f* emergency; **~gente** *a* emergent; **~gir** *vi* surface

emi|gração /emigra'sãw/ *f* emigration; (*de aves etc*) migration; **~grado** *a & m* émigré; **~grante** *a & m/f* emigrant; **~grar** *vi* emigrate; <*aves, animais*> migrate

emi|nência /emi'nẽsia/ *f* eminence; **~nente** *a* eminent

emis|são /emi'sãw/ *f* (*de ações etc*) issue; (*na rádio, TV*) transmission, broadcast; (*de som, gases*) emission; **~sário** *m* emissary; **~sor** *m* transmitter; **~sora** *f* (*de rádio*) radio station; (*de TV*) TV station

emitir /emi'tʃir/ *vt* issue <*ações, selos etc*>; emit <*sons*>; (*pela rádio, TV*) transmit, broadcast

emoção /emo'sãw/ *f* emotion; (*excitação*) excitement

emocio|nal /emosio'naw/ (*pl* **~nais**) *a* emotional; **~nante** *a* (*excitante*) exciting; (*comovente*) touching, emotional; **~nar** *vt* (*excitar*) excite; (*comover*) move, touch; **~nar-se** *vpr* get emotional

emoldurar /emowdu'rar/ *vt* frame

emotivo /emo'tʃivu/ *a* emotional

empacar /ĩpa'kar/ *vi* <*cavalo*> baulk; <*negociações etc*> grind to a halt; <*orador*> dry up

empacotar /ĩpako'tar/ *vt* pack up; (*pôr em pacotes*) packet

empa|da /ẽ'pada/ *f* pie; **~dão** *m* (large) pie

empalhar /ĩpa'ʎar/ *vt* stuff

empalidecer /ĩpalide'ser/ *vi* turn pale

empanar[1] /ẽpa'nar/ *vt* tarnish, dull
empanar[2] /ẽpa'nar/ *vt* cook in batter <*carne etc*>
empanturrar /ĩpãtu'xar/ *vt* stuff; **~-se** *vpr* stuff o.s. (de with)
empapar /ĩpa'par/ *vt* soak
empa|tar /ẽpa'tar/ *vt* draw <*jogo*> □ *vi* <*times*> draw; <*corredores*> tie; **~te** *m* (*em jogo*) draw; (*em corrida, votação*) tie; (*em xadrez, fig*) stalemate
empatia /ẽpa'tʃia/ *f* empathy
empecilho /ẽpe'siʎu/ *m* hindrance
empenar /ẽpe'nar/ *vt/i* warp
empe|nhar /ĩpe'ɲar/ *vt* (*penhorar*) pawn; (*prometer*) pledge; **~nhar-se** *vpr* do one's utmost (em to); **~nho** /e/ *m* (*compromisso*) pledge; (*diligência*) effort, commitment
emperrar /ĩpe'xar/ *vt* make stick □ *vi* stick
emperti|gado /ĩpertʃi'gadu/ *a* upright; **~gar-se** *vpr* stand up straight
empilhar /ĩpi'ʎar/ *vt* pile up
empi|nado /ĩpi'nadu/ *a* erect; (*íngreme*) sheer, steep; <*nariz*> turned-up; (*fig*) stuck-up; **~nar** *vt* stand upright; fly <*pipa*>; tip up <*copo*>
empírico /ẽ'piriku/ *a* empirical
emplacar /ĩpla'kar/ *vt* notch up <*pontos, sucessos, anos*>; license <*carro*>
emplastro /ĩ'plastru/ *m* surgical plaster; **~ de nicotina** nicotine patch
empobre|cer /ĩpobre'ser/ *vt* impoverish; **~cimento** *m* impoverishment
empoleirar /ĩpole'rar/ *vt* perch; **~-se** *vpr* perch
empol|gação /ĩpowga'sãw/ *f* fascination; **~gante** *a* fascinating; **~gar** *vt* fascinate
empossar /ĩpo'sar/ *vt* swear in
empreen|dedor /ẽpriẽde'dor/ *a* enterprising □ *m* entrepreneur; **~der** *vt* undertake; **~dimento** *m* undertaking
empre|gada /ĩpre'gada/ *f* (*doméstica*) maid; **~gado** *m* employee; **~gador** *m* employer; **~gar** *vt* employ; **~gar-se** *vpr* get a job; **~gatício** *a* **vínculo ~gatício** contract of employment; **~go** /e/ *m* (*trabalho*) job; (*uso*) use; **~guismo** *m* patronage
emprei|tada /ĩprej'tada/ *f* commission, contract; (*empreendimento*) venture; **~teira** *f* contractor, firm of contractors; **~teiro** *m* contractor
empre|sa /ĩ'preza/ *f* company; **~sariado** *m* business community; **~sarial** (*pl* **~sariais**) *a* business; **~sário** *m* businessman; (*de cantor etc*) manager
empres|tado /ĩpres'tadu/ *a* on loan; **pedir ~tado** (ask to) borrow; **tomar ~tado** borrow; **~tar** *vt* lend
empréstimo /ĩ'prɛstʃimu/ *m* loan
empur|rão /ĩpu'xãw/ *m* push; **~rar** *vt* push
emular /emu'lar/ *vt* emulate
enamorado /enamo'radu/ *a* (*apaixonado*) in love
encabeçar /ĩkabe'sar/ *vt* head
encabu|lado /ĩkabu'ladu/ *a* shy; **~lar** *vt* embarrass; **~lar-se** *vpr* be shy
encadear /ĩkade'ar/ *vt* chain *ou* link together
encader|nação /ĩkaderna'sãw/ *f* binding; **~nado** *a* bound; (*com capa dura*) hardback; **~nar** *vt* bind
encai|xar /ĩka'ʃar/ *vt/i* fit; **~xe** *m* (*cavidade*) socket; (*juntura*) joint
encalço /ĩ'kawsu/ *m* pursuit; **no ~ de** in pursuit of
encalhar /ĩka'ʎar/ *vi* <*barco*> run aground; (*fig*) get bogged down; <*mercadoria*> not sell; (*fam: ficar solteiro*) be left on the shelf
encaminhar /ĩkami'ɲar/ *vt* (*dirigir*) steer, direct; (*remeter*) pass on; set in motion <*processo*>; **~-se** *vpr* set out
encana|dor /ĩkana'dor/ *m* plumber; **~mento** *m* plumbing
encan|tador /ĩkãta'dor/ *a* enchanting; **~tamento** *m* enchantment; **~tar** *vt* enchant; **~to** *m* charm
encaraco|lado /ĩkarako'ladu/ *a* curly; **~lar** *vt* curl; **~lar-se** *vpr* curl up
encarar /ĩka'rar/ *vt* confront, face
encarcerar /ĩkarse'rar/ *vt* imprison
encardido /ĩkar'dʒidu/ *a* grimy
encarecidamente /ĩkaresida'mẽtʃi/ *adv* insistently
encargo /ĩ'kargu/ *m* task, responsibility
encar|nação /ĩkarna'sãw/ *f* (*do espírito*) incarnation; (*de um personagem*) embodiment; **~nar** *vt* embody; play <*papel*>
encarre|gado /ĩkaxe'gadu/ *a* in charge (de of) □ *m* person in charge; (*de operários*) foreman; **~gado de negócios** chargé d'affaires; **~gar** *vt* **~gar alg de** put s.o. in charge of; **~gar-se de** undertake to
encarte /ĩ'kartʃi/ *m* insert
ence|nação /ĩsena'sãw/ *f* (*de peça*) production; (*fingimento*) playacting; **~nar** *vt* put on □ *vi* put it on
ence|radeira /ĩsera'dera/ *f* floor polisher; **~rar** *vt* wax
encer|rado /ĩse'xadu/ *a* <*assunto*> closed; **~ramento** *m* close; **~rar** *vt* close; **~rar-se** *vpr* close
encharcar /ĩʃar'kar/ *vt* soak
en|chente /ẽ'ʃẽtʃi/ *f* flood; **~cher** *vt* fill; (*fam*) annoy □ (*fam*) *vi* be annoying; **~cher-se** *vpr* fill up; (*fam: fartar-se*) get fed up (de with)

enciclopédia /ẽsiklo'pɛdʒia/ *f* encyclopaedia

enco|berto /ĩko'bɛrtu/ *a* <*céu, tempo*> overcast; ~**brir** *vt* cover up □ *vi* <*tempo*> become overcast

encolher /ĩko'ʎer/ *vt* shrug <*ombros*>; pull up <*pernas*>; shrink <*roupa*> □ *vi* <*roupa*> shrink; ~**-se** *vpr* (*de medo*) shrink; (*de frio*) huddle; (*espremer-se*) squeeze up

encomen|da /ĩko'mẽda/ *f* order; **de ou sob** ~**da** to order; ~**dar** *vt* order (a from)

encon|trão /ĩkõ'trãw/ *m* bump; (*empurrão*) shove; ~**trar** *vt* (*achar*) find; (*ver*) meet; ~**trar com** meet; ~**trar-se** *vpr* (*ver-se*) meet; (*estar*) be; ~**tro** *m* meeting; (*mil*) encounter; **ir ao** ~**tro de** go to meet; (*fig*) meet; **ir de** ~**tro a** run into; (*fig*) go against

encorajar /ĩkora'ʒar/ *vt* encourage

encor|pado /ĩkor'padu/ *a* stocky; <*vinho*> full-bodied; ~**par** *vt/i* fill out

encos|ta /ĩ'kɔsta/ *f* slope; ~**tar** *vt* (*apoiar*) lean; park <*carro*>; leave on the latch <*porta*>; (*pôr de lado*) put aside □ *vi* <*carro*> pull in; ~**tar-se** *vpr* lean; ~**to** /o/ *m* back

encra|vado /ĩkra'vadu/ *a* <*unha, pêlo*> ingrowing; ~**var** *vt* stick

encren|ca /ĩ'krẽka/ *f* fix, jam; *pl* trouble; ~**car** *vt* get into trouble <*pessoa*>; complicate <*situação*> □ *vi* <*situação*> get complicated; <*carro*> break down; ~**car-se** *vpr* <*pessoa*> get into trouble; ~**queiro** *m* troublemaker

encres|pado /ĩkres'padu/ *a* <*mar*> choppy; ~**par** *vt* frizz <*cabelo*>; ~**par-se** *vpr* <*cabelo*> go frizzy; <*mar*> get choppy

encruzilhada /ĩkruzi'ʎada/ *f* crossroads

encurralar /ĩkuxa'lar/ *vt* hem in, pen in

encurtar /ĩkur'tar/ *vt* shorten

endere|çar /ĩdere'sar/ *vt* address; ~**ço** /e/ *m* address

endinheirado /ĩdʒiɲe'radu/ *a* well-off

endireitar /ĩdʒirej'tar/ *vt* straighten; ~**-se** *vpr* straighten up

endivi|dado /ĩdʒivi'dadu/ *a* in debt; ~**dar** *vt* put into debt; ~**dar-se** *vpr* get into debt

endoidecer /ĩdojde'ser/ *vi* get mad

endos|sar /ĩdo'sar/ *vt* endorse; ~**so** /o/ *m* endorsement

endurecer /ĩdure'ser/ *vt/i* harden

ener|gético /ener'ʒɛtʃiku/ *a* energy; ~**gia** *f* energy

enérgico /e'nɛrʒiku/ *a* vigorous; <*remédio, discurso*> powerful

enevoado /enevu'adu/ *a* (*com névoa*) misty; (*com nuvens*) cloudy

enfarte /ĩ'fartʃi/ *m* heart attack

ênfase /'ẽfazi/ *f* emphasis; **dar** ~ **a** emphasize

enfático /ẽ'fatʃiku/ *a* emphatic

enfatizar /ẽfatʃi'zar/ *vt* emphasize

enfei|tar /ĩfej'tar/ *vt* decorate; ~**tar-se** *vpr* dress up; ~**te** *m* decoration

enfeitiçar /ĩfejtʃi'sar/ *vt* bewitch

enfer|magem /ĩfer'maʒẽ/ *f* nursing; ~**maria** *f* ward; ~**meira** *f* nurse; ~**meiro** *m* male nurse; ~**midade** *f* illness; ~**mo** *a* sick □ *m* patient

enferru|jado /ĩfexu'ʒadu/ *a* rusty; ~**jar** *vt/i* rust

enfezado /ĩfe'zadu/ *a* bad- tempered

enfiar /ẽfi'ar/ *vt* put; slip on <*roupa*>; thread <*agulha*>; string <*pérolas*>

enfileirar /ĩfilej'rar/ *vt* line up; ~**-se** *vpr* line up

enfim /ẽ'fĩ/ *adv* (*finalmente*) finally; (*resumindo*) anyway

enfo|car /ĩfo'kar/ *vt* tackle; ~**que** *m* approach

enfor|camento /ĩforka'mẽtu/ *m* hanging; ~**car** *vt* hang; ~**car-se** *vpr* hang o.s.

enfraquecer /ĩfrake'ser/ *vt/i* weaken

enfrentar /ĩfrẽ'tar/ *vt* face

enfumaçado /ĩfuma'sadu/ *a* smoky

enfurecer /ĩfure'ser/ *vt* infuriate; ~**-se** *vpr* get furious

enga|jamento /ĩgaʒa'mẽtu/ *m* commitment; ~**jado** *a* committed; ~**jar-se** *vpr* get involved (**em** in)

engalfinhar-se /ĩgawfi'ɲarsi/ *vpr* grapple

enga|nado /ĩga'nadu/ *a* (*errado*) mistaken; ~**nar** *vt* deceive; cheat on <*marido, esposa*>; stave off <*fome*>; ~**nar-se** *vpr* be mistaken; ~**no** *m* (*erro*) mistake; (*desonestidade*) deception

engarra|famento /ĩgaxafa'mẽtu/ *m* traffic jam; ~**far** *vt* bottle <*vinho etc*>; block <*trânsito*>

engas|gar /ĩgaz'gar/ *vt* choke □ *vi* choke; <*motor*> backfire; ~**go** *m* choking

engastar /ĩgaʃ'tar/ *vt* set <*jóias*>

engatar /ĩga'tar/ *vt* hitch <*reboque etc*> (a to); engage <*marcha*>

engatinhar /ĩgatʃi'ɲar/ *vi* crawl; (*fig*) start out

engave|tamento /ĩgaveta'mẽtu/ *m* pile-up; ~**tar** *vt* shelve

engelhar /ĩʒe'ʎar/ *vi* (*pele*) wrinkle

enge|nharia /ĩʒeɲa'ria/ *f* engineering; ~**nheiro** *m* engineer; ~**nho** /e/ *m* (*de pessoa*) ingenuity; (*de açúcar*) sugar mill; (*máquina*) device; ~**nhoca** /ɔ/ *f* gadget; ~**nhoso** *a* ingenious

engessar /ĩʒe'sar/ *vt* put in plaster

engodo /ĩ'godu/ *m* lure

engolir /ĩgo'lir/ *vt/i* swallow; ~ em seco gulp

engomar /ĩgo'mar/ *vt* press; (*com goma*) starch

engordar /ĩgor'dar/ *vt* make fat; fatten <*animais*> □ *vi* <*pessoa*> put on weight; <*comida*> be fattening

engraçado /ĩgra'sadu/ *a* funny

engradado /ĩgra'dadu/ *m* crate

engravidar /ĩgravi'dar/ *vt* make pregnant □ *vi* get pregnant

engraxar /ĩgra'ʃar/ *vt* polish

engre|nado /ĩgre'nadu/ *a* <*carro*> in gear; **~nagem** *f* gear; (*fig*) mechanism; **~nar** *vt* put into gear <*carro*>; strike up <*conversa*>; **~nar-se** *vpr* mesh; (*fig*) <*pessoas*> get on

engrossar /ĩgro'sar/ *vt* thicken; raise <*voz*> □ *vi* thicken; <*pessoa*> turn nasty

enguia /ẽ'gia/ *f* eel

engui|çar /ẽgi'sar/ *vi* break down; **~ço** *m* breakdown

enig|ma /e'nigima/ *m* enigma; **~mático** *a* enigmatic

enjaular /ĩʒaw'lar/ *vt* cage

enjo|ar /ĩʒo'ar/ *vt* sicken □ *vi*, **~ar-se** *vpr* get sick (de of); **~ativo** *a* <*comida*> sickly; <*livro etc*> boring

enjôo /ĩ'ʒou/ *m* sickness

enlameado /ĩlami'adu/ *a* muddy

enlatado /ĩla'tadu/ *a* tinned, canned; **~s** *m pl* tinned foods

enle|var /ẽle'var/ *vt* enthral; **~vo** /e/ *m* rapture

enlouquecer /ĩloke'ser/ *vt* drive mad □ *vi* go mad

enluarado /ĩlua'radu/ *a* moonlit

enor|me /e'nɔrmi/ *a* enormous; **~midade** *f* enormity

enquadrar /ĩkwa'drar/ *vt* fit □ *vi*, **~-se** *vpr* fit in

enquanto /ĩ'kwãtu/ *conj* while; ~ isso meanwhile; por ~ for the time being

enquête /ã'kɛtʃi/ *f* survey

enraivecer /ĩxajve'ser/ *vt* enrage

enredo /ẽ'redu/ *m* plot

enrijecer /ĩxiʒe'ser/ *vt* stiffen; **~-se** *vpr* stiffen

enrique|cer /ĩxike'ser/ *vt* (*dar dinheiro a*) make rich; (*fig*) enrich □ *vi* get rich; **~cimento** *m* enrichment

enro|lado /ĩxo'ladu/ *a* complicated; **~lar** *vt* (*envolver*) roll up; (*complicar*) complicate; (*enganar*) cheat; **~lar-se** *vpr* (*envolver-se*) roll up; (*confundir-se*) get mixed up

enroscar /ĩxos'kar/ *vt* twist

enrouquecer /ĩxoke'ser/ *vi* go hoarse

enrugar /ĩxu'gar/ *vt* wrinkle <*pele, tecido*>; furrow <*testa*>

enrustido /ĩxus'tʃidu/ *a* repressed

ensaboar /ĩsabo'ar/ *vt* soap

ensai|ar /ĩsaj'ar/ *vt* (*provar*) try out; (*repetir*) rehearse; **~o** *m* (*prova*) test; (*repetição*) rehearsal; (*escrito*) essay

ensangüentado /ĩsãgwẽ'tadu/ *a* bloody, bloodstained

enseada /ĩsi'ada/ *f* inlet

ensebado /ĩse'badu/ *a* greasy

ensimesmado /ĩsimez'madu/ *a* lost in thought

ensi|nar /ẽsi'nar/ *vt/i* teach (aco a alg s.o. sth); **~nar alg a nadar** teach s.o. to swim; **~no** *m* teaching; (*em geral*) education

ensolarado /ĩsola'radu/ *a* sunny

enso|pado /ĩso'padu/ *a* soaked □ *m* stew; **~par** *vt* soak

ensurde|cedor /ĩsurdese'dor/ *a* deafening; **~cer** *vt* deafen □ *vi* go deaf

entabular /ĩtabu'lar/ *vt* open, start

entalar /ĩta'lar/ *vt* wedge, jam; (*em apertos*) get; **~-se** *vpr* get wedged, get jammed; (*em apertos*) get caught up

entalhar /ĩta'ʎar/ *vt* carve

entanto /ĩ'tãtu/ *m* no ~ however

então /ĩ'tãw/ *adv* then; (*nesse caso*) so

entardecer /ĩtarde'ser/ *m* sunset

ente /'ẽtʃi/ *m* being

entea|da /ẽtʃi'ada/ *f* stepdaughter; **~do** *m* stepson

entedi|ante /ĩtedʒi'ãtʃi/ *a* boring; **~ar** *vt* bore; **~ar-se** *vpr* get bored

enten|der /ĩtẽ'der/ *vt* understand; **~der-se** *vpr* (*dar-se bem*) get on (com with); dar a **~der** give to understand; **~der de futebol** know about football; **~dimento** *m* understanding

enternecedor /ĩternese'dor/ *a* touching

enter|rar /ĩte'xar/ *vt* bury; **~ro** /e/ *m* burial; (*cerimônia*) funeral

entidade /ẽtʃi'dadʒi/ *f* entity; (*órgão*) body

entornar /ĩtor'nar/ *vt* tip over, spill

entorpe|cente /ĩtorpe'sẽtʃi/ *m* drug, narcotic; **~cer** *vt* numb

entortar /ĩtor'tar/ *vt* make crooked

entrada /ẽ'trada/ *f* entry; (*onde se entra*) entrance; (*bilhete*) ticket; (*prato*) starter; (*pagamento*) deposit; *pl* (*no cabelo*) receding hairline; dar ~ a enter; **~ proibida** no entry

entranhas /ĩ'traɲas/ *f pl* entrails

entrar /ẽ'trar/ *vi* go/come in; **~ com** enter <*dados*>; put in <*dinheiro*>; **~ em detalhes** go into details; **~ em vigor** come into force

entravar /ẽtra'var/ *vt* hamper

entre /'ẽtri/ *prep* between; (*em meio a*) among

entreaberto /ẽtria'bɛrtu/ *a* half-open

entrecortar /ẽtrikor'tar/ *vt* intersperse; (*cruzar*) intersect

entre|ga /ĩ'trɛga/ *f* delivery; (*rendição*) surrender; **~ga a domicílio** home delivery; **~gar** *vt* hand over; deliver <*mercadorias, cartas*>; hand in <*caderno, trabalho escolar*>; **~gar-se** *vpr* give o.s. up (a to); **~gue** *pp de* entregar

entrelaçar /ẽtrela'sar/ *vt* intertwine; clasp <*mãos*>

entrelinhas /ẽtri'liɲas/ *f pl* **ler nas ~** read between the lines

entremear /ẽtrimi'ar/ *vt* intersperse

entreolhar-se /ẽtrio'ʎarsi/ *vpr* look at one another

entretanto /ẽtre'tãtu/ *conj* however

entre|tenimento /ẽtreteni'mẽtu/ *m* entertainment; **~ter** *vt* entertain

entrever /ẽtre'ver/ *vt* glimpse

entrevis|ta /ẽtre'vista/ *f* interview; **~tador** *m* interviewer; **~tar** *vt* interview

entristecer /ĩtriste'ser/ *vt* sadden □ *vi* be saddened (com by)

entroncamento /ĩtrõka'mẽtu/ *m* junction

entrosar /ĩtro'zar/ *vt/i* integrate

entu|lhar /ĩtu'ʎar/ *vt* cram (de with); **~lho** *m* rubble

entupir /ĩtu'pir/ *vt* block; **~pir-se** *vpr* get blocked; (*de comida*) stuff o.s. (de with)

enturmar-se /ĩtur'marsi/ *vpr* mix in, fit in

entusias|mar /ĩtuziaz'mar/ *vt* fill with enthusiasm; **~mar-se** *vpr* get enthusiastic (com about); **~mo** *m* enthusiasm; **~ta** *m/f* enthusiast □ *a* enthusiastic

entusiástico /ĩtuzi'astʃiku/ *a* enthusiastic

enumerar /enume'rar/ *vt* enumerate

envelope /ẽve'lɔpi/ *m* envelope

envelhecer /ĩveʎe'ser/ *vt/i* age

envenenar /ĩvene'nar/ *vt* poison; (*fam*) soup up <*carro*>

envergadura /ĩverga'dura/ *f* wingspan; (*fig*) scale

envergo|nhado /ĩvergo'ɲadu/ *a* ashamed; (*constrangido*) embarrassed; **~nhar** *vt* disgrace; (*constranger*) embarrass; **~nhar-se** *vpr* be ashamed; (*acanhar-se*) get embarrassed

envernizar /ĩverni'zar/ *vt* varnish

en|viado /ẽvi'adu/ *m* envoy; **~viar** *vt* send; **~vio** *m* (*ato*) sending; (*remessa*) consignment

envidraçar /ĩvidra'sar/ *vt* glaze

enviesado /ĩvie'zadu/ *a* (*não vertical*) slanting; (*torto*) crooked

envol|vente /ĩvow'vẽtʃi/ *a* compelling, gripping; **~ver** *vt* (*embrulhar*) wrap; (*enredar*) involve; **~ver-se** *vpr* (*enrolar-se*) wrap o.s.; (*enredar-se*) get involved; **~vimento** *m* involvement

enxada /ẽ'ʃada/ *f* hoe

enxaguar /ẽʃa'gwar/ *vt* rinse

enxame /ẽ'ʃami/ *m* swarm

enxaqueca /ẽʃa'keka/ *f* migraine

enxergar /ĩʃer'gar/ *vt/i* see

enxer|tar /ĩʃer'tar/ *vt* graft; **~to** /e/ *m* graft

enxotar /ĩʃo'tar/ *vt* drive away

enxofre /ẽ'ʃofri/ *m* sulphur

enxo|val /ẽʃo'vaw/ (*pl* **~vais**) *m* (*de noiva*) trousseau; (*de bebê*) layette

enxugar /ĩʃu'gar/ *vt* dry; **~-se** *vpr* dry o.s.

enxurrada /ĩʃu'xada/ *f* torrent; (*fig*) flood

enxuto /ĩ'ʃutu/ *a* dry; <*corpo*> shapely

enzima /ẽ'zima/ *f* enzyme

epicentro /epi'sẽtru/ *m* epicentre

épico /'ɛpiku/ *a* epic

epidemia /epide'mia/ *f* epidemic

epi|lepsia /epilep'sia/ *f* epilepsy; **~léptico** *a & m* epileptic

epílogo /e'pilogu/ *m* epilogue

episódio /epi'zɔdʒiu/ *m* episode

epitáfio /epi'tafiu/ *m* epitaph

época /'ɛpoca/ *f* time; (*da história*) age, period; **fazer ~** make history; **móveis da ~** period furniture

epopéia /epo'pɛja/ *f* epic

equação /ekwa'sãw/ *f* equation

equador /ekwa'dor/ *m* equator; **o Equador** Ecuador

equatori|al /ekwatori'aw/ (*pl* **~ais**) *a* equatorial; **~ano** *a & m* Ecuadorian

equilibrar /ekili'brar/ *vt* balance; **~-se** *vpr* balance

equilíbrio /eki'libriu/ *m* balance

equipa /e'kipa/ (*Port*) *f* team

equi|pamento /ekipa'mẽtu/ *m* equipment; **~par** *vt* equip

equiparar /ekipa'rar/ *vt* equate (com with); **~-se** *vpr* compare (a with)

equipe /e'kipi/ *f* team

equitação /ekita'sãw/ *f* riding

equiva|lência /ekiva'lẽsia/ *f* equivalence; **~lente** *a* equivalent; **~ler** *vi* be equivalent (a to)

equivo|cado /ekivo'kadu/ *a* mistaken; **~car-se** *vpr* make a mistake

equívoco /e'kivoku/ *a* equivocal □ *m* mistake

era /'ɛra/ *f* era

erário /e'rariu/ *m* exchequer

ereção /ere'sãw/ *f* erection

eremita /ere'mita/ *m/f* hermit

ereto /e'rɛtu/ *a* erect

erguer /er'ger/ *vt* raise; erect <*monumento etc*>; **~-se** *vpr* rise

eri|çado /eri'sadu/ *a* bristling; **~çar-se** *vpr* bristle

ermo /'ermu/ *a* deserted □ *m* wilderness

erosão /ero'zãw/ *f* erosion

erótico /e'rɔtʃiku/ *a* erotic

erotismo /ero'tʃizmu/ *m* eroticism

er|rado /e'xadu/ *a* wrong; **~rante** *a* wandering; **~rar** *vt* (*não fazer certo*) get wrong; miss <*alvo*> □ *vi* (*enganar-se*) be wrong; (*vaguear*) wander; **~ro** /e/ *m* mistake; **fazer um ~ro** make a mistake; **~rôneo** *a* erroneous

erudi|ção /erudʒi'sãw/ *f* learning; **~to** *a* learned; <*música*> classical □ *m* scholar

erupção /erup'sãw/ *f* (*vulcânica*) eruption; (*cutânea*) rash

erva /'ɛrva/ *f* herb; **~ daninha** weed; **~-doce** *f* aniseed

ervilha /er'viʎa/ *f* pea

esban|jador /izbãʒa'dor/ *a* extravagant □ *m* spendthrift; **~jar** *vt* squander; burst with <*saúde, imaginação, energia etc*>

esbar|rão /izba'xãw/ *m* bump; **~rar** *vi* **~rar com** *ou* **em** bump into <*pessoa*>; come up against <*problema*>

esbelto /iz'bɛwtu/ *a* svelte

esbo|çar /izbo'sar/ *vt* sketch <*desenho etc*>; outline <*plano etc*>; **~çar um sorriso** give a hint of a smile; **~ço** /o/ *m* (*desenho*) sketch; (*plano*) outline; (*de um sorriso*) hint

esbofetear /izbofetʃi'ar/ *vt* slap

esborrachar /izboxa'ʃar/ *vt* squash; **~-se** *vpr* crash

esbravejar /izbrave'ʒar/ *vi* rant, rail

esbura|cado /izbura'kadu/ *a* full of holes; **~car** *vt* make holes in

esbuga|lhado /izbuga'ʎadu/ *a* <*olhos*> bulging; **~lhar-se** *vpr* <*olhos*> pop out

escabroso /iska'brozu/ *a* (*fig*) difficult, tough

escada /is'kada/ *f* (*dentro de casa*) stairs; (*na rua*) steps; (*de mão*) ladder; **~ de incêndio** fire escape; **~ rolante** escalator; **~ria** *f* staircase

escafan|drista /iskafã'drista/ *m/f* diver; **~dro** *m* diving suit

escala /is'kala/ *f* scale; (*de navio*) port of call; (*de avião*) stopover; **fazer ~** stop over; **sem ~** <*vôo*> non-stop

esca|lada /iska'lada/ *f* (*fig*) escalation; **~lão** *m* echelon, level; **~lar** *vt* (*subir a*) scale; (*designar*) select

escaldar /iskaw'dar/ *vt* scald; blanch <*vegetais*>

escalfar /iskaw'far/ *vt* poach

escalonar /iskalo'nar/ *vt* schedule <*pagamento*>

escama /is'kama/ *f* scale

escanca|rado /iskãka'radu/ *a* wide open; **~rar** *vt* open wide

escandalizar /iskãdali'zar/ *vt* scandalize; **~-se** *vpr* be scandalized

escândalo /is'kãdalu/ *m* (*vexame*) scandal; (*tumulto*) fuss, uproar; **fazer um ~** make a scene

escandaloso /iskãda'lozu/ *a* (*chocante*) scandalous; (*espalhafatoso*) outrageous, loud

Escandinávia /iskãdʒi'navia/ *f* Scandinavia

escandinavo /iskãdʒi'navu/ *a & m* Scandinavian

escanga|lhado /iskãga'ʎadu/ *a* broken; **~lhar** *vt* break up; **~lhar-se** *vpr* fall to pieces; **~lhar-se de rir** split one's sides laughing

escaninho /iska'niɲu/ *m* pigeonhole

escanteio /iskã'teju/ *m* corner

esca|pada /iska'pada/ *f* (*fuga*) escape; (*aventura*) escapade; **~pamento** *m* exhaust; **~par** *vi* **~par a** *ou* **de** (*livrar-se*) escape from; (*evitar*) escape; **~pou-lhe a palavra** the word slipped out; **o copo ~pou-me das mãos** the glass slipped out of my hands; **o nome me ~pa** the name escapes me; **~par de boa** have a narrow escape; **~patória** *f* way out; (*desculpa*) pretext; **~pe** *m* escape; (*de carro etc*) exhaust; **~pulir** *vi* escape (**de** from)

escaramuça /iskara'musa/ *f* skirmish

escaravelho /iskara'vɛʎu/ *m* beetle

escarcéu /iskar'sɛw/ *m* uproar, fuss

escarlate /iskar'latʃi/ *a* scarlet

escarnecer /iskarne'ser/ *vt* mock

escárnio /is'karniu/ *m* derision

escarpado /iskar'padu/ *a* steep

escarrado /iska'xadu/ *m* **ele é o pai ~** he's the spitting image of his father

escarro /is'kaxu/ *m* phlegm

escas|sear /iskasi'ar/ *vi* run short; **~sez** *f* shortage; **~so** *a* (*raro*) scarce; (*ralo*) scant

esca|vadeira /iskava'dera/ *f* digger; **~var** *vt* excavate

esclare|cer /isklare'ser/ *vt* explain <*fatos*>; enlighten <*pessoa*>; **~cer-se** *vpr* <*fato*> be explained; <*pessoa*> find out; **~cimento** *m* (*de pessoas*) enlightenment; (*de fatos*) explanation

esclerosado /isklero'zadu/ *a* senile

escoar /isko'ar/ *vt/i* drain

esco|cês /isko'ses/ *a* (*f* **~cesa**) Scottish □ *m* (*f* **~cesa**) Scot

Escócia /is'kɔsia/ *f* Scotland

esco|la /is'kɔla/ *f* school; **~la de samba** samba school; **~lar** *a* school □ *m/f* schoolchild; **~laridade** *f* schooling

esco|lha /is'koʎa/ *f* choice; **~lher** *vt* choose

escol|ta /is'kɔwta/ *f* escort; **~tar** *vt* escort

escombros /is'kõbrus/ *m pl* debris

escon|de-esconde /iskõdʒis'kõdʒi/ *m* hide-and-seek; **~der** *vt* hide; **~der-se** *vpr* hide; **~derijo** *m* hiding place; (*de bandidos*) hideout; **~didas** *f pl* **às ~didas** secretly

esco|ra /is'kɔra/ *f* prop; **~rar** *vt* prop up; **~rar-se** *vpr* <*argumento etc*> be based (em on)

escore /is'kɔri/ *m* score

escória /is'kɔria/ *f* scum, dross

escori|ação /iskoria'sãw/ *f* graze, abrasion; **~ar** *vt* graze

escorpião /iskorpi'ãw/ *m* scorpion; Escorpião Scorpio

escorredor /iskoxe'dor/ *m* drainer

escorrega /isko'xega/ *m* slide

escorre|gador /iskoxega'dor/ *m* slide; **~gão** *m* slip; **~gar** *vi* slip

escor|rer /isko'xer/ *vt* drain □ *vi* trickle; **~rido** *a* <*cabelo*> straight

escoteiro /isko'teru/ *m* boy scout

escotilha /isko'tʃiʎa/ *f* hatch

esco|va /is'kova/ *f* brush; **fazer ~va no cabelo** blow-dry one's hair; **~va de dentes** toothbrush; **~var** *vt* brush; **~vinha** *f* **cabelo à ~vinha** crew-cut

escra|chado /iskra'ʃadu/ (*fam*) *a* outspoken; **~char** (*fam*) *vt* tell off

escra|vatura /iskrava'tura/ *f* slavery; **~vidão** *f* slavery; **~vizar** *vt* enslave; **~vo** *m* slave

escre|vente /iskre'vẽtʃi/ *m/f* clerk; **~ver** *vt/i* write

escri|ta /is'krita/ *f* writing; **~to** *pp de escrever* □ *a* written; **por ~to** in writing; **~tor** *m* writer; **~tório** *m* office; (*numa casa*) study

escritu|ra /iskri'tura/ *f* (*a Bíblia*) scripture; (*contrato*) deed; **~ração** *f* bookkeeping; **~rar** *vt* keep, write up <*contas*>; draw up <*documento*>

escri|vaninha /iskriva'niɲa/ *f* bureau, writing desk; **~vão** *m* (*f* **~vã**) registrar

escrúpulo /is'krupulu/ *m* scruple

escrupuloso /iskrupu'lozu/ *a* scrupulous

escrutínio /iskru'tʃiniu/ *m* ballot

escu|dar /isku'dar/ *vt* shield; **~deria** *f* team; **~do** *m* shield; (*moeda*) escudo

escula|chado /iskula'ʃadu/ (*fam*) *a* sloppy; **~char** (*fam*) *vt* mess up <*coisa*>; tell off <*pessoa*>; **~cho** (*fam*) *m* (*bagunça*) mess; (*bronca*) telling-off

escul|pir /iskuw'pir/ *vt* sculpt; **~tor** *m* sculptor; **~tura** *f* sculpture; **~tural** (*pl* **~turais**) *a* statuesque

escuma /is'kuma/ *f* scum; **~deira** *f* skimmer

escuna /is'kuna/ *f* schooner

escu|ras /is'kuras/ *f pl* **às ~ras** in the dark; **~recer** *vt* darken □ *vi* get dark; **~ridão** *f* darkness; **~ro** *a* & *m* dark

escuso /is'kuzu/ *a* shady

escu|ta /is'kuta/ *f* listening; **estar à ~ta** be listening; **~ta telefônica** phone tapping; **~tar** *vt* (*perceber*) hear; (*prestar atenção a*) listen to □ *vi* (*poder ouvir*) hear; (*prestar atenção*) listen

esdrúxulo /iz'druʃulu/ *a* weird

esfacelar /isfase'lar/ *vt* wreck

esfalfar /isfaw'far/ *vt* wear out; **~-se** *vpr* get worn out

esfaquear /isfaki'ar/ *vt* stab

esfarelar /isfare'lar/ *vt* crumble; **~-se** *vpr* crumble

esfarrapado /isfaxa'padu/ *a* ragged; <*desculpa*> lame

es|fera /is'fɛra/ *f* sphere; **~férico** *a* spherical

esferográfi|co /isfero'grafiku/ *a* **caneta ~ca** ball-point pen

esfiapar /isfia'par/ *vt* fray; **~-se** *vpr* fray

esfinge /is'fĩʒi/ *f* sphinx

esfolar /isfo'lar/ *vt* skin; (*fig*) overcharge

esfomeado /isfomi'adu/ *a* starving, famished

esfor|çar-se /isfor'sarsi/ *vpr* make an effort; **~ço** /o/ *m* effort; **fazer ~ço** make an effort

esfre|gaço /isfre'gasu/ *m* smear; **~gar** *vt* rub; (*para limpar*) scrub

esfriar /isfri'ar/ *vt* cool □ *vi* cool (down); (*sentir frio*) get cold

esfumaçado /isfuma'sadu/ *a* smoky

esfuziante /isfuzi'ãtʃi/ *a* irrepressible, exuberant

esganar /izga'nar/ *vt* throttle

esganiçado /izgani'sadu/ *a* shrill

esgarçar /izgar'sar/ *vt/i* fray

esgo|tado /izgo'tadu/ *a* exhausted; <*estoque, lotação*> sold out; **~tamento** *m* exhaustion; **~tamento nervoso** nervous breakdown; **~tar** *vt* exhaust; (*gastar*) use up; **~tar-se** *vpr* <*pessoa*> become exhausted; <*estoque, lotação*> sell out; <*recursos, provisões*> run out; **~to** /o/ *m* drain; (*de detritos*) sewer

esgri|ma /iz'grima/ *f* fencing; **~mir** *vt* brandish □ *vi* fence; **~mista** *m/f* fencer

esgrouvinhado /izgrovi'ɲadu/ *a* tousled, dishevelled

esgueirar-se /izge'rarsi/ *vpr* slip, sneak

esguelha /iz'geʎa/ *f* **de ~** askew; <*olhar*> askance

esgui|char /izgi'ʃar/ *vt/i* spurt, squirt; **~cho** *m* jet, spurt

esguio /iz'gio/ *a* slender

eslavo /iz'lavu/ *a* Slavic □ *m* Slav

esmaecer /izmaj'ser/ *vi* fade

esma|gador /izmaga'dor/ *a* <*vitória, maioria*> overwhelming; <*provas*> incontrovertible; **~gar** *vt* crush

esmalte /iz'mawtʃi/ *m* enamel; **~ de unhas** nail varnish

esmeralda /izme'rawda/ *f* emerald

esme|rar-se /izme'rarsi/ *vpr* take great care (em over); **~ro** /e/ *m* great care

esmigalhar /izmiga'ʎar/ *vt* crumble <*pão etc*>; shatter <*vidro, copo*>; **~-se** *vpr* <*pão etc*> crumble; <*vidro, copo*> shatter

esmiuçar /izmiu'sar/ *vt* examine in detail

esmo /'ezmu/ *m* **a ~** <*escolher*> at random; <*andar*> aimlessly; <*falar*> nonsense

esmola /iz'mɔla/ *f* donation; *pl* charity

esmorecer /izmore'ser/ *vi* flag

esmurrar /izmu'xar/ *vt* punch

esno|bar /izno'bar/ *vt* snub □ *vi* be snobbish; **~be** /iz'nɔbi/ *a* snobbish □ *m/f* snob; **~bismo** *m* snobbishness

esotérico /ezo'tɛriku/ *a* esoteric

espa|çar /ispa'sar/ *vt* space out; make less frequent <*visitas, consultas etc*>; **~cial** (*pl* **~ciais**) *a* space; **~ço** *m* space; (*cultural etc*) venue; **~çoso** /o/ *a* spacious

espada /is'pada/ *f* sword; *pl* (*naipe*) spades; **~chim** *m* swordsman

espádua /is'padua/ *f* shoulder blade

espaguete /ispa'gɛtʃi/ *m* spaghetti

espaire|cer /ispajre'ser/ *vt* amuse □ *vi* relax; (*dar uma volta*) go for a walk; **~cimento** *m* recreation

espaldar /ispaw'dar/ *m* back

espalhafato /ispaʎa'fatu/ *m* (*barulho*) fuss, uproar; (*de roupa etc*) extravagance; **~so** /o/ *a* (*barulhento*) noisy, rowdy; (*ostentoso*) extravagant

espalhar /ispa'ʎar/ *vt* scatter; spread <*notícia, terror etc*>; shed <*luz*>; **~-se** *vpr* spread; <*pessoas*> spread out

espa|nador /ispana'dor/ *m* feather duster; **~nar** *vt* dust

espan|camento /ispãka'mẽtu/ *m* beating; **~car** *vt* beat up

Espanha /is'paɲa/ *f* Spain

espa|nhol /ispa'ɲɔw/ (*pl* **~nhóis**) *a* (*f* **~nhola**) Spanish □ *m* (*f* **~nhola**) Spaniard; (*língua*) Spanish; **os ~nhóis** the Spanish

espan|talho /ispã'taʎu/ *m* scarecrow; **~tar** *vt* (*admirar*) amaze; (*assustar*) scare; (*afugentar*) drive away; **~tar-se** *vpr* (*admirar-se*) be amazed; (*assustar-se*) get scared; **~to** *m* (*susto*) fright; (*admiração*) amazement; **~toso** /o/ *a* amazing

esparadrapo /ispara'drapu/ *m* sticking plaster

espargo /is'pargu/ (*Port*) *m* asparagus

esparramar /ispaxa'mar/ *vt* scatter; **~-se** *vpr* be scattered, spread

espartano /ispar'tanu/ *a* spartan

espartilho /ispar'tʃiʎu/ *m* corset

espas|mo /is'pazmu/ *m* spasm; **~módico** *a* spasmodic

espatifar /ispatʃi'far/ *vt* smash; **~-se** *vpr* smash; <*carro, avião*> crash

especi|al /ispesi'aw/ (*pl* **~ais**) *a* special; **~alidade** *f* speciality; **~alista** *m/f* specialist

especiali|zado /ispesiali'zadu/ *a* specialized; <*mão-de-obra*> skilled; **~zar-se** *vpr* specialize (em in)

especiaria /ispesia'ria/ *f* spice

espécie /is'pɛsi/ *f* sort, kind; (*de animais*) species

especifi|cação /ispesifika'sãw/ *f* specification; **~car** *vt* specify

específico /ispe'sifiku/ *a* specific

espécime /is'pesimi/ *m* specimen

espectador /ispekta'dor/ *m* (*de TV*) viewer; (*de jogo, espetáculo*) spectator; (*de acidente etc*) onlooker

espectro /is'pɛktru/ *m* (*fantasma*) spectre; (*de cores*) spectrum

especu|lação /ispekula'sãw/ *f* speculation; **~lador** *m* speculator; **~lar** *vi* speculate (sobre on); **~lativo** *a* speculative

espe|lhar /ispe'ʎar/ *vt* mirror; **~lhar-se** *vpr* be mirrored; **~lho** /e/ *m* mirror; **~lho retrovisor** rear-view mirror

espelunca /ispe'lũka/ (*fam*) *f* dive

espera /is'pɛra/ *f* wait; **à ~ de** waiting for

esperan|ça /ispe'rãsa/ *f* hope; **~çoso** /o/ *a* hopeful

esperar /ispe'rar/ *vt* (*aguardar*) wait for; (*desejar*) hope for; (*contar com*) expect □ *vi* wait (por for); **fazer alg ~** keep s.o. waiting; **espero que ele venha** I hope (that) he comes; **espero que sim/não** I hope so/not

esperma /is'pɛrma/ *m* sperm

espernear /isperni'ar/ *vi* kick; (*fig: reclamar*) kick up

esper|talhão /isperta'ʎãw/ *m* (*f* **~talhona**) wise guy; **~teza** /e/ *f* cleverness; (*uma*) clever move; **~to** /e/ *a* clever

espes|so /is'pesu/ *a* thick; **~sura** *f* thickness

espe|tacular /ispetaku'lar/ *a* spectacular; **~táculo** *m* (*no teatro etc*) show; (*cena impressionante*) spectacle; **~taculoso** /o/ *a* spectacular

espe|tar /ispe'tar/ *vt* (*cravar*) stick; (*furar*) skewer; **~tar-se** *vpr* (*cravar-se*) stick; (*ferir-se*) prick o.s.; **~tinho**

m skewer; (*de carne etc*) kebab; **~to** /e/ *m* spit

espevitado /ispevi'tadu/ *a* cheeky

espezinhar /ispezi'ɲar/ *vt* walk all over

espi|a /is'pia/ *m/f* spy; **~ão** *m* (*f* **~ã**) spy; **~ada** *f* peep; **~ar** *vt* (*observar*) spy on; (*aguardar*) watch for □ *vi* peer, peep

espicaçar /ispika'sar/ *vt* goad <*pessoa*>; excite <*imaginação, curiosidade*>

espichar /ispi'ʃar/ *vt* stretch □ *vi* shoot up; **~-se** *vpr* stretch out

espiga /is'piga/ *f* (*de trigo etc*) ear; (*de milho*) cob

espina|fração /ispinafra'sãw/ (*fam*) *f* telling-off; **~frar** (*fam*) *vt* tell off; **~fre** *m* spinach

espingarda /ispĩ'garda/ *f* rifle, shotgun

espinha /is'piɲa/ *f* (*de peixe*) bone; (*na pele*) spot; **~ dorsal** spine

espinho /is'piɲu/ *m* thorn; **~so** /o/ *a* thorny; (*fig*) difficult, tough

espio|nagem /ispio'naʒẽ/ *f* espionage, spying; **~nar** *vt* spy on □ *vi* spy

espi|ral /ispi'raw/ (*pl* **~rais**) *a & f* spiral

espírita /is'pirita/ *a & m/f* spiritualist

espiritismo /ispiri'tʃizmu/ *m* spiritualism

espírito /is'piritu/ *m* spirit; (*graça*) wit

espiritu|al /ispiritu'aw/ (*pl* **~ais**) *a* spiritual; **~oso** /o/ *a* witty

espir|rar /ispi'xar/ *vt* spurt □ *vi* <*pessoa*> sneeze; <*lama, tinta etc*> spatter; <*fogo, lenha, fritura etc*> spit; **~ro** *m* sneeze

esplêndido /is'plẽdʒidu/ *a* splendid

esplendor /isplẽ'dor/ *m* splendour

espoleta /ispo'leta/ *f* fuse

espoliar /ispoli'ar/ *vt* plunder, pillage

espólio /is'pɔliu/ *m* (*herdado*) estate; (*roubado*) spoils

espon|ja /is'põʒa/ *f* sponge; **~joso** /o/ *a* spongy

espon|taneidade /ispõtanej'dadʒi/ *f* spontaneity; **~tâneo** *a* spontaneous

espora /is'pɔra/ *f* spur

esporádico /ispo'radʒiku/ *a* sporadic

esporear /ispori'ar/ *vt* spur on

espor|te /is'pɔrtʃi/ *m* sport □ *a invar* <*roupa*> casual; **carro ~te** sports car; **~tista** *m/f* sportsman (*f* -woman); **~tiva** *f* sense of humour; **~tivo** *a* sporting

espo|sa /is'poza/ *f* wife; **~so** *m* husband

espregui|çadeira /ispregisa'dera/ *f* (*tipo cadeira*) deckchair; (*tipo cama*) sun lounger; **~çar-se** *vpr* stretch

esprei|ta /is'prejta/ *f* **ficar à ~ta** lie in wait; **~tar** *vt* stalk <*caça, vítima*>; spy on <*vizinhos, inimigos etc*>; look out for <*ocasião*> □ *vi* peep, spy

espre|medor /ispreme'dor/ *m* squeezer; **~mer** *vt* squeeze; wring out <*roupa*>; squash <*pessoa*>; **~mer-se** *vpr* squeeze up

espu|ma /is'puma/ *f* foam; **~ma de borracha** foam rubber; **~mante** *a* <*vinho*> sparkling; **~mar** *vi* foam, froth

espúrio /is'puriu/ *a* spurious

esqua|dra /is'kwadra/ *f* squad; **~dra de polícia** (*Port*) police station; **~drão** *m* squadron; **~dria** *f* doors and windows; **~drinhar** *vt* explore; **~dro** *m* set square

esqualidez /iskwali'des/ *f* squalor

esquálido /is'kwalidu/ *a* squalid

esquartejar /iskwarte'ʒar/ *vt* chop up

esque|cer /iske'ser/ *vt/i* forget; **~cer-se de** forget; **~cido** *a* forgotten; (*com memória fraca*) forgetful; **~cimento** *m* oblivion; (*memória fraca*) forgetfulness

esque|lético /iske'lɛtʃiku/ *a* skinny, skeleton-like; **~leto** /e/ *m* skeleton

esque|ma /is'kema/ *m* outline, draft; (*operação*) scheme; **~ma de segurança** security operation; **~mático** *a* schematic

esquentar /iskẽ'tar/ *vt* warm up □ *vi* warm up; <*roupa*> be warm; **~-se** *vpr* get annoyed; **~ a cabeça** (*fam*) get worked up

esquer|da /is'kerda/ *f* left; **à ~da** (*posição*) on the left; (*direção*) to the left; **~dista** *a* left-wing □ *m/f* left-winger; **~do** /e/ *a* left

esqui /is'ki/ *m* ski; (*esporte*) skiing; **~ aquático** water skiing; **~ador** *m* skier; **~ar** *vi* ski

esquilo /is'kilu/ *m* squirrel

esquina /is'kina/ *f* corner

esquisi|tice /iskizi'tʃisi/ *f* strangeness; (*uma*) strange thing; **~to** *a* strange

esqui|var-se /iski'varsi/ *vpr* dodge out of the way; **~var-se de** dodge; **~vo** *a* elusive; <*pessoa*> aloof, antisocial

esquizo|frenia /iskizofre'nia/ *f* schizophrenia; **~frênico** *a & m* schizophrenic

es|sa /'ɛsa/ *pron* that (one); **~sa é boa** that's a good one; **~sa não** come off it; **por ~sas e outras** for these and other reasons; **~se** /e/ *a* that; *pl* those; (*fam: este*) this; *pl* these □ *pron* that one; *pl* those; (*fam: este*) this one; *pl* these

essência /e'sẽsia/ *f* essence

essenci|al /esẽsi'aw/ (*pl* ~**ais**) *a* essential; **o** ~**al** what is essential
estabele|cer /istabele'ser/ *vt* establish; ~**cer-se** *vpr* establish o.s.; ~**cimento** *m* establishment
estabili|dade /istabili'dadʒi/ *f* stability; ~**zar** *vt* stabilize; ~**zar-se** *vpr* stabilize
estábulo /is'tabulu/ *m* cowshed
estaca /is'taka/ *f* stake; (*de barraca*) peg; **voltar à** ~ **zero** go back to square one
estação /ista'sãw/ *f* (*do ano*) season; (*ferroviária etc*) station; ~ **balneária** seaside resort
estacar /ista'kar/ *vi* stop short
estacio|namento /istasiona'mẽtu/ *m* (*ação*) parking; (*lugar*) car park, (*Amer*) parking lot; ~**nar** *vt/i* park
estada /is'tada/ *f*, **estadia** /ista'dʒia/ *f* stay
estádio /is'tadʒiu/ *m* stadium
esta|dista /ista'dʒista/ *m/f* statesman (*f* -woman); ~**do** *m* state; ~**do civil** marital status; ~**do de espírito** state of mind; **Estados Unidos da América** United States of America; **Estado-Maior** *m* Staff; ~**dual** (*pl* ~**duais**) *a* state
esta|fa /is'tafa/ *f* exhaustion; ~**fante** *a* exhausting; ~**far** *vt* tire out; ~**far-se** *vpr* get tired out
estagi|ar /istaʒi'ar/ *vi* do a traineeship; ~**ário** *m* trainee
estágio /is'taʒiu/ *m* traineeship
estag|nado /istagi'nadu/ *a* stagnant; ~**nar** *vi* stagnate
estalagem /ista'laʒẽ/ *f* inn
estalar /ista'lar/ *vt* (*quebrar*) crack; (*fazer barulho com*) click □ *vi* crack
estaleiro /ista'leru/ *m* shipyard
estalo /is'talu/ *m* crack; (*de dedos, língua*) click; **me deu um** ~ it clicked (in my mind)
estam|pa /is'tãpa/ *f* print; ~**pado** *a* <*tecido*> patterned □ *m* (*desenho*) pattern; (*tecido*) print; ~**par** *vt* print
estampido /istã'pidu/ *m* bang
estancar /istã'kar/ *vt* staunch; ~**-se** *vpr* dry up
estância /is'tãsia/ *f* ~ **hidromineral** spa
estandarte /istã'dartʃi/ *m* banner
estanho /is'taɲu/ *m* tin
estanque /is'tãki/ *a* watertight
estante /is'tãtʃi/ *f* bookcase
estapafúrdio /istapa'furdʒiu/ *a* weird, odd
estar /is'tar/ *vi* be; (~ **em casa**) be in; **está chovendo,** (*Port*) **está a chover** it's raining; ~ **com** have; ~ **com calor/sono** be hot/sleepy; ~ **para terminar** be about to finish; **ele não está para ninguém** he's not available to see anyone; **o trabalho está por terminar** the work is yet to be finished
estardalhaço /istarda'ʎasu/ *m* (*barulho*) fuss; (*ostentação*) extravagance
estarre|cedor /istaxese'dor/ *a* horrifying; ~**cer** *vt* horrify; ~**cer-se** *vpr* be horrified
esta|tal /ista'taw/ (*pl* ~**tais**) *a* state-owned □ *f* state company
estate|lado /istate'ladu/ *a* sprawling; ~**lar** *vt* knock down; ~**lar-se** *vpr* go sprawling
estático /is'tatʃiku/ *a* static
estatísti|ca /ista'tʃistʃika/ *f* statistics; ~**co** *a* statistical
estati|zação /istatʃiza'sãw/ *f* nationalization; ~**zar** *vt* nationalize
estátua /is'tatua/ *f* statue
estatueta /istatu'eta/ *f* statuette
estatura /ista'tura/ *f* stature
estatuto /ista'tutu/ *m* statute
está|vel /is'tavew/ (*pl* ~**veis**) *a* stable
este[1] /'ɛstʃi/ *m a invar & m* east
este[2] /'estʃi/ *a* this; *pl* these □ *pron* this one; *pl* these; (*mencionado por último*) the latter
esteio /is'teju/ *m* prop; (*fig*) mainstay
esteira /is'tera/ *f* (*tapete*) mat; (*rastro*) wake
estelionato /istelio'natu/ *m* fraud
estender /istẽ'der/ *vt* (*desdobrar*) spread out; (*alongar*) stretch; (*ampliar*) extend; hold out <*mão*>; hang out <*roupa*>; roll out <*massa*>; draw out <*conversa*>; ~**-se** *vpr* (*deitar-se*) stretch out; (*ir longe*) stretch, extend; ~**-se sobre** dwell on
esteno|datilógrafo /istenodatʃi'lɔgrafu/ *m* shorthand typist; ~**grafia** *f* shorthand
estepe /is'tɛpi/ *m* spare wheel
esterco /is'terku/ *m* dung
estéreo /is'tɛriu/ *a invar* stereo
estere|otipado /isteriotʃi'padu/ *a* stereotypical; ~**ótipo** *m* stereotype
estéril /is'tɛriw/ (*pl* ~**reis**) *a* sterile
esterili|dade /isterili'dadʒi/ *f* sterility; ~**zar** *vt* sterilize
esterli|no /ister'lino/ *a* **libra** ~**na** pound sterling
esteróide /iste'rɔjdʒi/ *m* steroid
estética /is'tɛtʃika/ *f* aesthetics
esteticista /istetʃi'sista/ *m/f* beautician
estético /is'tɛtʃiku/ *a* aesthetic
estetoscópio /istetos'kɔpiu/ *m* stethoscope
estiagem /istʃi'aʒẽ/ *f* dry spell
estibordo /istʃi'bɔrdu/ *m* starboard
esti|cada /istʃi'kada/ *f* **dar uma** ~**cada** go on; ~**car** *vt* stretch □ (*fam*) *vi* go on; ~**car-se** *vpr* stretch out

estigma /is'tʃigima/ m stigma; ~**tizar** vt brand (de as)

estilha|çar /istʃiʎa'sar/ vt shatter; ~**çar-se** vpr shatter; ~**ço** m shard, fragment

estilingue /istʃi'lĩgi/ m catapult

estilis|mo /istʃi'lizmu/ m fashion design; ~**ta** m/f fashion designer

esti|lístico /istʃi'listʃiku/ a stylistic; ~**lizar** vt stylize; ~**lo** m style; ~**lo de vida** lifestyle

esti|ma /es'tʃima/ f esteem; ~**mação** f estimation; **cachorro de ~mação** pet dog; ~**mado** a esteemed; **Estimado Senhor** Dear Sir; ~**mar** vt value <bens, jóias etc> (em at); estimate <valor, preço etc> (em at); think highly of <pessoa>; ~**mativa** f estimate

estimu|lante /istʃimu'lãtʃi/ a stimulating □ m stimulant; ~**lar** vt stimulate; (*incentivar*) encourage

estímulo /is'tʃimulu/ m stimulus; (*incentivo*) incentive

estio /is'tʃiu/ m summer

estipu|lação /istʃipula'sãw/ f stipulation; ~**lar** vt stipulate

estirar /istʃi'rar/ vt stretch; ~**-se** vpr stretch

estirpe /is'tʃirpi/ f stock, line

estivador /istʃiva'dor/ m docker

estocada /isto'kada/ f thrust

estocar /isto'kar/ vt stock □ vi stock up

Estocolmo /isto'kɔwmu/ f Stockholm

esto|far /isto'far/ vt upholster <móveis>; ~**fo** /o/ m upholstery

estóico /is'tɔjku/ a & m stoic

estojo /is'toʒu/ m case

estômago /is'tomagu/ m stomach

Estônia /is'tonia/ f Estonia

estonte|ante /istõtʃi'ãtʃi/ a stunning, mind-boggling; ~**ar** vt stun

estopim /isto'pĩ/ m fuse; (*fig*) flashpoint

estoque /is'tɔki/ m stock

estore /is'tɔri/ m blind

estória /is'tɔria/ f story

estor|var /istor'var/ vt hinder; obstruct <entrada, trânsito>; ~**vo** /o/ m hindrance

estou|rado /isto'radu/ a <pessoa> explosive; ~**rar** vi <bomba, escândalo, pessoa> blow up; <pneu> burst; <guerra> break out; <moda, cantor etc> make it big; ~**ro** m (*de bomba, moda etc*) explosion; (*de pessoa*) outburst; (*de pneu*) blowout; (*de guerra*) outbreak

estrábico /is'trabiku/ a <olhos> squinty; <pessoa> squint-eyed

estrabismo /istra'bizmu/ m squint

estraçalhar /istrasa'ʎar/ vt tear to pieces

estrada /is'trada/ f road; ~ **de ferro** railway, (*Amer*) railroad; ~ **de rodagem** highway; ~ **de terra** dirt road

estrado /is'tradu/ m podium; (*de cama*) base

estraga-prazeres /istragapra'zeris/ m/f invar spoilsport

estragão /istra'gãw/ m tarragon

estra|gar /istra'gar/ vt (*tornar desagradável*) spoil; (*acabar com*) ruin □ vi (*quebrar*) break; (*apodrecer*) go off; ~**go** m damage; pl damage; (*da guerra, do tempo*) ravages

estrangeiro /istrã'ʒeru/ a foreign □ m foreigner; **do ~** from abroad; **para o/no ~** abroad

estrangular /istrãgu'lar/ vt strangle

estra|nhar /istra'ɲar/ vt (*achar estranho*) find strange; (*não se adaptar a*) find it hard to get used to; (*não se sentir à vontade com*) be shy with; ~**nhar que** find it strange that; **estou te ~nhando** that's not like you; **não é de se ~nhar** it's not surprising; ~**nheza** /e/ f (*esquisitice*) strangeness; (*surpresa*) surprise; ~**nho** a strange □ m stranger

estratagema /istrata'ʒema/ m stratagem

estraté|gia /istra'tɛʒia/ f strategy; ~**gico** a strategic

estrato /is'tratu/ m (*camada*) stratum; (*nuvem*) stratus; ~**sfera** f stratosphere

estre|ante /istri'ãtʃi/ a new □ m/f newcomer; ~**ar** vt première <peça, filme>; embark on <carreira>; wear for the first time <roupa> □ vi <pessoa> make one's début; <filme, peça> open

estrebaria /istreba'ria/ f stable

estréia /is'trɛja/ f (*de pessoa*) début; (*de filme, peça*) première

estrei|tar /istrej'tar/ vt narrow; take in <vestido>; make closer <relações, laços> □ vi narrow; ~**tar-se** vpr <relações> become closer; ~**to** a narrow; <relações, laços> close; <saia> straight □ m strait

estre|la /is'trela/ f star; ~**lado** a <céu> starry; <ovo> fried; ~**lado por** <filme etc> starring; ~**la-do-mar** (pl ~**las-do-mar**) f starfish; ~**lar** vt fry <ovo>; star in <filme, peça>; ~**lato** m stardom; ~**lismo** m star quality

estreme|cer /istreme'ser/ vt shake; strain <relações, amizade> □ vi shudder; <relações, amizade> become strained; ~**cimento** m shudder; (*de relações, amizade*) strain

estrepar-se /istre'parsi/ (*fam*) vpr come a cropper

estrépito /is'trɛpitu/ *m* noise; com ~ noisily
estrepitoso /istrepi'tozu/ *a* noisy; <*sucesso etc*> resounding
estres|sante /istre'sãtʃi/ *a* stressful; **~sar** *vt* stress; **~se** /ɛ/ *m* stress
estria /is'tria/ *f* streak; (*no corpo*) stretch mark
estribeira /istri'bera/ *f* stirrup; **perder as ~s** lose control
estribilho /istri'biʎu/ *m* chorus
estribo /is'tribu/ *m* stirrup
estridente /istri'dẽtʃi/ *a* strident
estripulia /istripu'lia/ *f* antic
estrito /is'tritu/ *a* strict
estrofe /is'trɔfi/ *f* stanza, verse
estrogonofe /istrogo'nɔfi/ *m* stroganoff
estrógeno /is'trɔʒenu/ *m* oestrogen
estron|do /is'trõdu/ *m* crash; **~doso** /o/ *a* loud; <*aplausos*> thunderous; <*sucesso, fracasso*> resounding
estropiar /istropi'ar/ *vt* cripple <*pessoa*>; mangle <*palavras*>
estrume /is'trumi/ *m* manure
estrutu|ra /istru'tura/ *f* structure; **~ral** (*pl* **~rais**) *a* structural; **~rar** *vt* structure
estuário /istu'ariu/ *m* estuary
estudan|te /istu'dãtʃi/ *m/f* student; **~til** (*pl* **~tis**) *a* student
estudar /istu'dar/ *vt/i* study
estúdio /is'tudʒiu/ *m* studio
estu|dioso /istudʒi'ozu/ *a* studious □ *m* scholar; **~do** *m* study
estufa /is'tufa/ *f* (*para plantas*) greenhouse; (*de aquecimento*) stove; **~do** *m* stew
estupefato /istupe'fatu/ *a* dumbfounded
estupendo /iste'pẽdu/ *a* stupendous
estupidez /istupi'des/ *f* (*grosseria*) rudeness; (*uma*) rude thing; (*burrice*) stupidity; (*uma*) stupid thing
estúpido /is'tupidu/ *a* (*grosso*) rude, coarse; (*burro*) stupid □ *m* lout
estupor /istu'por/ *m* stupor
estu|prador /istupra'dor/ *m* rapist; **~prar** *vt* rape; **~pro** *m* rape
esturricar /istuxi'kar/ *vt* parch
esvair-se /izva'irsi/ *vpr* fade; **~ em sangue** bleed to death
esvaziar /izvazi'ar/ *vt* empty; **~-se** *vpr* empty
esverdeado /izverdʒi'adu/ *a* greenish
esvoa|çante /izvoa'sãtʃi/ *a* <*cabelo*> fly-away; **~çar** *vi* flutter
eta /'eta/ *int* what a
etapa /e'tapa/ *f* stage; (*de corrida, turnê etc*) leg
etário /e'tariu/ *a* age
éter /'ɛter/ *m* ether
etéreo /e'tɛriu/ *a* ethereal
eter|nidade /eterni'dadʒi/ *f* eternity; **~no** /ɛ/ *a* eternal
éti|ca /'ɛtʃika/ *f* ethics; **~co** *a* ethical
etimo|logia /etʃimolo'ʒia/ *f* etymology; **~lógico** *a* etymological
etíope /e'tʃiopi/ *a & m/f* Ethiopian
Etiópia /etʃi'ɔpia/ *f* Ethiopia
etique|ta /etʃi'keta/ *f* (*rótulo*) label; (*bons modos*) etiquette; **~tar** *vt* label
étnico /'ɛtʃiniku/ *a* ethnic
eu /ew/ *pron* I □ *m* self; **mais alto do que ~** taller than me; **sou ~** it's me
EUA *m pl* USA
eucalipto /ewka'liptu/ *m* eucalyptus
eufemismo /ewfe'mizmu/ *m* euphemism
euforia /ewfo'ria/ *f* euphoria
Europa /ew'rɔpa/ *f* Europe
euro|peu /ewro'pew/ *a & m* (*f* **~péia**) European
eutanásia /ewta'nazia/ *f* euthanasia
evacu|ação /evakua'sãw/ *f* evacuation; **~ar** *vt* evacuate
evadir /eva'dʒir/ *vt* evade; **~-se** *vpr* escape (de from)
evan|gelho /evã'ʒɛʎu/ *m* gospel; **~gélico** *a* evangelical
evaporar /evapo'rar/ *vt* evaporate; **~-se** *vpr* evaporate
eva|são /eva'zãw/ *f* escape; (*fiscal etc*) evasion; **~são escolar** truancy; **~siva** *f* excuse; **~sivo** *a* evasive
even|to /e'vẽtu/ *m* event; **~tual** (*pl* **~tuais**) *a* possible; **~tualidade** *f* eventuality
evidência /evi'dẽsia/ *f* evidence
eviden|ciar /evidẽsi'ar/ *vt* show up; **~ciar-se** *vpr* show up; **~te** *a* obvious, evident
evi|tar /evi'tar/ *vt* avoid; **~tar de beber** avoid drinking; **~tável** (*pl* **~táveis**) *a* avoidable
evocar /evo'kar/ *vt* call to mind, evoke <*passado etc*>; call up <*espíritos etc*>
evolu|ção /evolu'sãw/ *f* evolution; **~ir** *vi* evolve
exacerbar /ezaser'bar/ *vt* exacerbate
exage|rado /ezaʒe'radu/ *a* over the top; **~rar** *vt* (*atribuir proporções irreais a*) exaggerate; (*fazer em excesso*) overdo □ *vi* (*ao falar*) exaggerate; (*exceder-se*) overdo it; **~ro** /e/ *m* exaggeration
exa|lação /ezala'sãw/ *f* fume; (*agradável*) scent; **~lar** *vt* give off <*perfume etc*>
exal|tação /ezawta'sãw/ *f* (*excitação*) agitation; (*engrandecimento*) exaltation; **~tar** *vt* (*excitar*) agitate; (*enfurecer*) infuriate; (*louvar*) exalt; **~tar-se** *vpr* (*excitar-se*) get agitated; (*enfurecer-se*) get furious
exa|me /e'zami/ *m* examination; (*na escola*) exam(ination); **~me de**

sangue blood test; ~minar *vt* examine

exaspe|ração /ezaspera'sãw/ *f* exasperation; ~rar *vt* exasperate; ~rar-se *vpr* get exasperated

exa|tidão /ezatʃi'dãw/ *f* exactness; ~to *a* exact

exaurir /ezaw'rir/ *vt* exhaust; ~-se *vpr* become exhausted

exaus|tivo /ezaws'tʃivu/ *a* <*estudo*> exhaustive; <*trabalho*> exhausting; ~to *a* exhausted

exceção /ese'sãw/ *f* exception; abrir ~ make an exception; com ~ de with the exception of

exce|dente /ese'dẽtʃi/ *a* & *m* excess, surplus; ~der *vt* exceed; ~der-se *vpr* overdo it

exce|lência /ese'lẽsia/ *f* excellence; (*tratamento*) excellency; ~lente *a* excellent

excentricidade /esẽtrisi'dadʒi/ *f* eccentricity

excêntrico /e'sẽtriku/ *a* & *m* eccentric

excep|ção /iʃsɛ'sãw/ (*Port*) *f veja* exceção; ~cional (*pl* ~cionais) *a* exceptional; (*deficiente*) handicapped

exces|sivo /ese'sivu/ *a* excessive; ~so /ɛ/ *m* excess; ~so de bagagem excess baggage; ~so de velocidade speeding

exce|to /e'sɛtu/ *prep* except; ~tuar *vt* except

exci|tação /esita'sãw/ *f* excitement; ~tante *a* exciting; ~tar *vt* excite; ~tar-se *vpr* get excited

excla|mação /isklama'sãw/ *f* exclamation; ~mar *vt/i* exclaim

exclu|ir /isklu'ir/ *vt* exclude; ~são *f* exclusion; com ~são de with the exclusion of; ~sividade *f* exclusive rights; com ~sividade exclusively; ~sivo *a* exclusive; ~so *a* excluded

excomungar /iskomũ'gar/ *vt* excommunicate

excremento /iskre'mẽtu/ *m* excrement

excur|são /iskur'sãw/ *f* excursion; (*a pé*) hike, walk; ~sionista *m/f* day-tripper; (*a pé*) hiker, walker

execu|ção /ezeku'sãw/ *f* execution; ~tante *m/f* performer; ~tar *vt* carry out <*ordem, plano etc*>; perform <*papel, música*>; execute <*preso, criminoso etc*>; ~tivo *a* & *m* executive

exem|plar /ezẽ'plar/ *a* exemplary □ *m* (*de espécie*) example; (*de livro, jornal etc*) copy; ~plificar *vt* exemplify

exemplo /e'zẽplu/ *m* example; a ~ de following the example of; por ~ for example; dar o ~ set an example

exeqüí|vel /eze'kwivew/ (*pl* ~veis) *a* feasible

exer|cer /ezer'ser/ *vt* exercise; exert <*pressão, influência*>; carry on <*profissão*>; ~cício *m* exercise; (*mil*) drill; (*de profissão*) practice; (*financeiro*) financial year; ~citar *vt* exercise; practise <*ofício*>; ~citar-se *vpr* train

exército /e'zɛrsitu/ *m* army

exibição /ezibi'sãw/ *f* (*de filme, passaporte etc*) showing; (*de talento, força, ostentação*) show

exibicionis|mo /ezibisio'nizmu/ *m* exhibitionism; ~ta *a* & *m/f* exhibitionist

exi|bido /ezi'bidu/ *a* <*pessoa*> pretentious □ *m* show-off; ~bir *vt* show; (*ostentar*) show off; ~bir-se *vpr* (*ostentar-se*) show off

exi|gência /ezi'ʒẽsia/ *f* demand; ~gente *a* demanding; ~gir *vt* demand

exíguo /e'zigwu/ *a* (*muito pequeno*) tiny; (*escasso*) minimal

exi|lado /ezi'lado/ *a* exiled □ *m* exile; ~lar *vt* exile; ~lar-se *vpr* go into exile

exílio /e'ziliu/ *m* exile

exímio /e'zimiu/ *a* distinguished

eximir /ezi'mir/ *vt* exempt (de from); ~-se de get out of

exis|tência /ezis'tẽsia/ *f* existence; ~tencial (*pl* ~tenciais) *a* existential; ~tente *a* existing; ~tir *vi* exist

êxito /'ezitu/ *m* success; (*música, filme etc*) hit; ter ~ succeed

êxodo /'ezodu/ *m* exodus

exonerar /ezone'rar/ *vt* (*de cargo*) dismiss, sack; ~-se *vpr* resign

exorbitante /ezorbi'tãtʃi/ *a* exorbitant

exor|cismo /ezor'sizmu/ *m* exorcism; ~cista *m/f* exorcist; ~cizar *vt* exorcize

exótico /e'zɔtʃiku/ *a* exotic

expan|dir /ispã'dʒir/ *vt* spread; ~dir-se *vpr* spread; <*pessoa*> open up; ~dir-se sobre expand upon; ~são *f* expansion; ~sivo *a* expansive, open

expatri|ado /ispatri'ado/ *a* & *m* expatriate; ~ar-se *vpr* leave one's country

expectativa /ispekta'tʃiva/ *f* expectation; na ~ de expecting; estar na ~ wait to see what happens; ~ de vida life expectancy

expedição /espedʒi'sãw/ *f* (*de encomendas, cartas*) dispatch; (*de passaporte, diploma etc*) issue; (*viagem*) expedition

expediente /ispedʒi'ẽtʃi/ *a* <*pessoa*> resourceful □ *m* (*horário*) working hours; (*meios*) expedient; meio ~ part-time

expe|dir /ispe'dʒir/ *vt* dispatch <*encomendas, cartas*>; issue <*passaporte, diploma*>; **~dito** *a* prompt, quick

expelir /ispe'lir/ *vt* expel

experi|ência /isperi'ẽsia/ *f* experience; (*teste, tentativa*) experiment; **~ente** *a* experienced

experimen|tação /isperimẽta'sãw/ *f* experimentation; **~tado** *a* experienced; **~tar** *vt* (*provar*) try out; try on <*roupa*>; try <*comida*>; (*sentir, viver*) experience; **~to** *m* experiment

expi|ar /espi'ar/ *vt* atone for; **~atório** *a* **bode ~atório** scapegoat

expi|ração /espira'sãw/ *f* (*vencimento*) expiry; (*de ar*) exhalation; **~rar** *vt* exhale □ *vi* (*morrer, vencer*) expire; (*expelir ar*) breath out, exhale

expli|cação /isplika'sãw/ *f* explanation; **~car** *vt* explain; **~car-se** *vpr* explain o.s.; **~cável** (*pl* **~cáveis**) *a* explainable

explicitar /isplisi'tar/ *vt* set out

explícito /is'plisitu/ *a* explicit

explodir /isplo'dʒir/ *vt* explode □ *vi* explode; <*ator etc*> make it big

explo|ração /isplora'sãw/ *f* (*uso, abuso*) exploitation; (*pesquisa*) exploration; **~rar** *vt* (*tirar proveito de*) exploit; (*esquadrinhar*) explore

explo|são /isplo'zãw/ *f* explosion; **~sivo** *a* & *m* explosive

expor /es'por/ *vt* (*sujeitar, arriscar*) expose (a to); display <*mercadorias*>; exhibit <*obras de arte*>; (*explicar*) expound; **~ a vida** risk one's life; **~-se** *vpr* expose o.s. (a to)

expor|tação /isporta'sãw/ *f* export; **~tador** *a* exporting □ *m* exporter; **~tadora** *f* export company; **~tar** *vt* export

exposi|ção /ispozi'sãw/ *f* (*de arte etc*) exhibition; (*de mercadorias*) display; (*de filme fotográfico*) exposure; (*explicação*) exposition; **~tor** *m* exhibitor

exposto /is'postu/ *a* exposed (a to); <*mercadoria, obra de arte*> on display

expres|são /ispre'sãw/ *f* expression; **~sar** *vt* express; **~sar-se** *vpr* express o.s.; **~sivo** *a* expressive; <*número, quantia*> significant; **~so** /ɛ/ *a* & *m* express

exprimir /ispri'mir/ *vt* express; **~-se** *vpr* express o.s.

expropriar /ispropri'ar/ *vt* expropriate

expul|são /ispuw'sãw/ *f* expulsion; (*de jogador*) sending off; **~sar** *vt* (*de escola, partido, país etc*) expel; (*de clube, bar, festa etc*) throw out; (*de jogo*) send off; **~so** *pp de* **expulsar**

expur|gar /ispur'gar/ *vt* purge; expurgate <*livro*>; **~go** *m* purge

êxtase /'estazi/ *f* ecstasy

extasiado /istazi'adu/ *a* ecstatic

exten|são /istẽ'sãw/ *f* extension; (*tamanho, alcance, duração*) extent; (*de terreno*) expanse; **~sivo** *a* extensive; **~so** *a* extensive; **por ~so** in full

extenu|ante /istenu'ãtʃi/ *a* wearing, tiring; **~ar** *vt* tire out; **~ar-se** *vpr* tire o.s. out

exterior /isteri'or/ *a* outside, exterior; <*aparência*> outward; <*relações, comércio etc*> foreign □ *m* outside, exterior; (*de pessoa*) exterior; **o ~** (*outros países*) abroad; **para o/no ~** abroad

exter|minar /istermi'nar/ *vt* exterminate; **~mínio** *m* extermination

exter|nar /ister'nar/ *vt* show; **~na** /ɛ/ *f* location shot; **~no** /ɛ/ *a* external; <*dívida etc*> foreign □ *m* day-pupil

extin|ção /istʃĩ'sãw/ *f* extinction; **~guir** *vt* extinguish <*fogo*>; wipe out <*dívida, animal, povo*>; **~guir-se** *vpr* <*fogo, luz*> go out; <*animal, planta*> become extinct; **~to** *a* extinct; <*organização, pessoa*> defunct; **~tor** *m* fire extinguisher

extirpar /istʃir'par/ *vt* remove <*tumor etc*>; uproot <*ervas daninhas*>; eradicate <*abusos*>

extor|quir /istor'kir/ *vt* extort; **~são** *f* extortion

extra /'ɛstra/ *a* & *m/f* extra; **horas ~s** overtime

extração /istra'sãw/ *f* extraction; (*da loteria*) draw

extraconju|gal /estrakõʒu'gaw/ (*pl* **~gais**) *a* extramarital

extracurricular /estrakuxiku'lar/ *a* extracurricular

extradi|ção /istradʒi'sãw/ *f* extradition; **~tar** *vt* extradite

extrair /istra'ir/ *vt* extract; draw <*números da loteria*>

extrajudici|al /estraʒudʒisi'aw/ (*pl* **~ais**) *a* out-of-court; **~almente** *adv* out of court

extraordinário /istraordʒi'nariu/ *a* extraordinary

extrapolar /istrapo'lar/ *vt* (*exceder*) overstep; (*calcular*) extrapolate □ *vi* overstep the mark, go too far

extra-sensori|al /estrasẽsori'aw/ (*pl* **~ais**) *a* extra-sensory

extraterrestre /estrate'xestri/ *a* & *m* extraterrestrial

extrato /is'trato/ *m* extract; (*de conta*) statement

extrava|gância /istrava'gãsia/ *f* extravagance; **~gante** *a* extravagant

extravasar /istrava'zar/ *vt* release, let out <*emoções, sentimentos*> □ *vi* overflow

extra|viado /istravi'adu/ *a* lost; **~viar** *vt* lose, mislay <*papéis, car-*

ta>; lead astray <*pessoa*>; embezzle <*dinheiro*>; ~viar-se *vpr* go astray; <*carta*> get lost; ~vio *m* (*perda*) misplacement; (*de dinheiro*) embezzlement

extre|midade /estremi'dadʒi/ *f* end; (*do corpo*) extremity; ~mismo *m* extremism; ~mista *a* & *m/f* extremist; ~mo /e/ *a* & *m* extreme; o Extremo Oriente the Far East; ~moso /o/ *a* doting

extrovertido /istrover'tʃido/ *a* & *m* extrovert

exube|rância /ezube'rãsia/ *f* exuberance; ~rante *a* exuberant

exultar /ezuw'tar/ *vi* exult

exumar /ezu'mar/ *vt* exhume <*cadáver*>; dig up <*documentos etc*>

F

fã /fã/ *m/f* fan

fábrica /'fabrika/ *f* factory

fabri|cação /fabrika'sãw/ *f* manufacture; ~cante *m/f* manufacturer; ~car *vt* manufacture; (*inventar*) fabricate

fábula /'fabula/ *f* fable; (*fam: dinheirão*) fortune

fabuloso /fabu'lozu/ *a* fabulous

faca /'faka/ *f* knife; ~da *f* knife blow; dar uma ~da em (*fig*) get some money off

façanha /fa'saɲa/ *f* feat

facção /fak'sãw/ *f* faction

face /'fasi/ *f* face; (*do rosto*) cheek; ~ta /e/ *f* facet

fachada /fa'ʃada/ *f* façade

facho /'faʃu/ *m* beam

faci|al /fasi'aw/ (*pl* ~ais) *a* facial

fá|cil /'fasiw/ (*pl* ~ceis) *a* easy; <*pessoa*> easy-going

facili|dade /fasili'dadʒi/ *f* ease; (*talento*) facility; ~tar *vt* facilitate

fã-clube /fã'klubi/ *m* fan club

fac-símile /fak'simili/ *m* facsimile; (*fax*) fax

fact- (*Port*) *veja* fat-

facul|dade /fakuw'dadʒi/ *f* (*mental etc*) faculty; (*escola*) university, (*Amer*) college; fazer ~dade go to university; ~tativo *a* optional

fada /'fada/ *f* fairy; ~do *a* destined, doomed; ~-madrinha (*pl* ~s-madrinhas) *f* fairy godmother

fadiga /fa'dʒiga/ *f* fatigue

fa|dista /fa'dʒista/ *m/f* fado singer; ~do *m* fado

fagote /fa'gɔtʃi/ *m* bassoon

fagulha /fa'guʎa/ *f* spark

faia /'faja/ *f* beech

faisão /faj'zãw/ *m* pheasant

faísca /fa'iska/ *f* spark

fais|cante /fajs'kãtʃi/ *a* sparkling; ~car *vi* spark; (*cintilar*) sparkle

faixa /'faʃa/ *f* strip; (*cinto*) sash; (*em karatê, judô*) belt; (*da estrada*) lane; (*para pedestres*) zebra crossing, (*Amer*) crosswalk; (*atadura*) bandage; (*de disco*) track; ~ etária age group

fajuto /fa'ʒutu/ (*fam*) *a* fake

fala /'fala/ *f* speech

falácia /fa'lasia/ *f* fallacy

fa|lado /fa'ladu/ *a* <*língua*> spoken; <*caso, pessoa*> talked about; ~lante *a* talkative; ~lar *vt/i* speak; (*dizer*) say; ~lar com talk to; ~lar de ou em talk about; por ~lar em speaking of; sem ~lar em not to mention; ~lou! (*fam*) OK!; ~latório *m* (*boatos*) talk; (*som de vozes*) talking

falaz /fa'las/ *a* fallacious

falcão /faw'kãw/ *m* falcon

falcatrua /fawka'trua/ *f* swindle

fale|cer /fale'ser/ *vi* die, pass away; ~cido *a* & *m* deceased; ~cimento *m* death

falência /fa'lẽsia/ *f* bankruptcy; ir à ~ go bankrupt

falésia /fa'lɛzia/ *f* cliff

fa|lha /'faʎa/ *f* fault; (*omissão*) failure; ~lhar *vi* fail; ~lho *a* faulty

fálico /'faliku/ *a* phallic

fa|lido /fa'lidu/ *a* & *m* bankrupt; ~lir *vi* go bankrupt; ~lível (*pl* ~líveis) *a* fallible

falo /'falu/ *m* phallus

fal|sário /faw'sariu/ *m* forger; ~sear *vt* falsify; ~sete *m* falsetto; ~sidade *f* falseness; (*mentira*) falsehood

falsifi|cação /fawsifika'sãw/ *f* forgery; ~cador *m* forger; ~car *vt* falsify; forge <*documentos, notas*>

falso /'fawsu/ *a* false

fal|ta /'fawta/ *f* lack; (*em futebol*) foul; em ~ta at fault; por ~ta de for lack of; sem ~ta without fail; fazer ~ta be needed; sentir a ~ta de miss; ~tar *vi* be missing; <*aluno*> be absent; ~tam dois dias para it's two days until; me ~ta ... I don't have ...; ~tar a miss <*aula etc*>; break <*palavra, promessa*>; ~to *a* short (de of)

fa|ma /'fama/ *f* reputation; (*celebridade*) fame; ~migerado *a* notorious

família /fa'milia/ *f* family

famili|ar /famili'ar/ *a* familiar; (*de família*) family; ~aridade *f* familiarity; ~arizar *vt* familiarize; ~arizar-se *vpr* familiarize o.s.

faminto /fa'mĩtu/ *a* starving

famoso /fa'mozu/ *a* famous

fanático /fa'natʃiku/ *a* fanatical □ *m* fanatic

fanatismo /fana'tʃizmu/ *m* fanaticism

fanfarrão /fãfa'xãw/ *m* braggart
fanhoso /fa'ɲozu/ *a* nasal; ser ~ talk through one's nose
fanta|sia /fãta'zia/ *f* (*faculdade*) imagination; (*devaneio*) fantasy; (*roupa*) fancy dress; **~siar** *vt* dream up □ *vi* fantasize; **~siar-se** *vpr* dress up (de as); **~sioso** /o/ *a* fanciful; <*pessoa*> imaginative; **~sista** *a* imaginative
fantasma /fã'tazma/ *m* ghost; **~górico** *a* ghostly
fantástico /fã'tastʃiku/ *a* fantastic
fantoche /fã'tɔʃi/ *m* puppet
faqueiro /fa'keru/ *m* canteen of cutlery
fara|ó /fara'ɔ/ *m* pharaoh; **~ônico** *a* (*fig*) of epic proportions
farda /'farda/ *f* uniform; **~do** *a* uniformed
fardo /'fardu/ *m* (*fig*) burden
fare|jador /fareʒa'dor/ *a* **cão ~jador** sniffer dog; **~jar** *vt* sniff out □ *vi* sniff
farelo /fa'rɛlu/ *m* bran; (*de pão*) crumb; (*de madeira*) sawdust
farfalhar /farfa'ʎar/ *vi* rustle
farináceo /fari'nasiu/ *a* starchy; **~s** *m pl* starchy foods
farin|ge /fa'rĩʒi/ *f* pharynx; **~gite** *f* pharyngitis
farinha /fa'riɲa/ *f* flour; **~ de rosca** breadcrumbs
far|macêutico /farma'sewtʃiku/ *a* pharmaceutical □ *m* (*pessoa*) pharmacist; **~mácia** *f* (*loja*) chemist's, (*Amer*) pharmacy; (*ciência*) pharmacy
faro /'faru/ *f* sense of smell; (*fig*) nose
faroeste /faro'ɛstʃi/ *m* (*filme*) western; (*região*) wild west
faro|fa /fa'rɔfa/ *f* fried manioc flour; **~feiro** (*fam*) *m* day-tripper
fa|rol /fa'rɔw/ (*pl* **~róis**) *m* (*de carro*) headlight; (*de trânsito*) traffic light; (*à beira-mar*) lighthouse; **~rol alto** full beam; **~rol baixo** dipped beam; **~roleiro** *a* boastful □ *m* bighead; **~rolete** /e/ *m*, (*Port*) **~rolim** *m* side-light; (*traseiro*) tail-light
farpa /'farpa/ *f* splinter; (*de metal, fig*) barb; **~do** *a* **arame ~do** barbed wire
farra /'faxa/ (*fam*) *f* partying; **cair na ~** go out and party
farrapo /fa'xapu/ *m* rag
far|rear /faxi'ar/ (*fam*) *vi* party; **~rista** (*fam*) *m/f* raver
far|sa /'farsa/ *f* (*peça*) farce; (*fingimento*) pretence; **~sante** *m/f* (*brincalhão*) joker; (*pessoa sem seriedade*) unreliable character
far|tar /far'tar/ *vt* satiate; **~tar-se** *vpr* (*saciar-se*) gorge o.s. (de with); (*cansar*) tire (de of); **~to** *a* (*abundante*) plentiful; (*cansado*) fed up (de with); **~tura** *f* abundance
fascículo /fa'sikulu/ *m* instalment
fasci|nação /fasina'sãw/ *f* fascination; **~nante** *a* fascinating; **~nar** *vt* fascinate
fascínio /fa'siniu/ *m* fascination
fas|cismo /fa'sizmu/ *m* fascism; **~cista** *a* & *m/f* fascist
fase /'fazi/ *f* phase
fa|tal /fa'taw/ (*pl* **~tais**) *a* fatal; **~talismo** *m* fatalism; **~talista** *a* fatalistic □ *m/f* fatalist; **~talmente** *adv* inevitably
fatia /fa'tʃia/ *f* slice
fatídico /fa'tʃidʒiku/ *a* fateful
fati|gante /fatʃi'gãtʃi/ *a* tiring; **~gar** *vt* tire, fatigue
fato[1] /'fatu/ *m* fact; **de ~** as a matter of fact, in fact; **~ consumado** fait accompli
fato[2] /'fatu/ (*Port*) *m* suit
fator /fa'tor/ *m* factor
fátuo /'fatuu/ *a* fatuous
fatu|ra /fa'tura/ *f* invoice; **~ramento** *m* turnover; **~rar** *vt* invoice for <*encomenda*>; make <*dinheiro*>; (*fig: emplacar*) notch up □ *vi* (*fam*) rake it in
fauna /'fawna/ *f* fauna
fava /'fava/ *f* broad bean; **mandar alg às ~s** tell s.o. where to get off
favela /fa'vɛla/ *f* shanty town; **~do** *m* shanty-dweller
favo /'favu/ *m* honeycomb
favor /fa'vor/ *m* favour; **a ~ de** in favour of; **por ~** please; **faça ~** please
favo|rável /favo'ravew/ (*pl* **~ráveis**) *a* favourable; **~recer** *vt* favour; **~ritismo** *m* favouritism; **~rito** *a* & *m* favourite
faxi|na /fa'ʃina/ *f* clean-up; **~neiro** *m* cleaner
fazen|da /fa'zẽda/ *f* (*de café, gado etc*) farm; (*tecido*) fabric, material; (*pública*) treasury; **~deiro** *m* farmer
fazer /fa'zer/ *vt* do; (*produzir*) make; ask <*pergunta*>; **~-se** *vpr* (*tornar-se*) become; **~-se de** make o.s. out to be; **~ anos** have a birthday; **~ 20 anos** be twenty; **faz dois dias que ele está aqui** he's been here for two days; **faz dez anos que ele morreu** it's ten years since he died; **tanto faz** it doesn't matter
faz-tudo /fas'tudu/ *m/f invar* jack of all trades
fé /fɛ/ *f* faith
fe|bre /'fɛbri/ *f* fever; **~bre amarela** yellow fever; **~bre do feno** hay fever; **~bril** (*pl* **~bris**) *a* feverish
fe|chado /fe'ʃadu/ *a* closed; <*curva*> sharp; <*sinal*> red; <*torneira*> off; <*tempo*> overcast; <*cara*> stern; <*pessoa*> reserved; **~chadura** *f*

lock; ~**chamento** *m* closure; ~**char** *vt* close, shut; turn off <*torneira*>; do up <*calça, casaco*>; close <*negócio*> □ *vi* close, shut; <*sinal*> go red; <*tempo*> cloud over; ~**char à chave** lock; ~**char a cara** frown; ~**cho** /e/ *m* fastener; ~**cho ecler** zip

fécula /'fɛkula/ *f* starch

fecun|dar /fekũ'dar/ *vt* fertilize; ~**do** *a* fertile

feder /fe'der/ *vi* stink

fede|ração /federa'sãw/ *f* federation; ~**ral** (*pl* ~**rais**) *a* federal; (*fam*) huge; ~**rativo** *a* federal

fedor /fe'dor/ *m* stink, stench; ~**ento** *a* stinking

feérico /feɛriku/ *a* magical

feições /fej'sõjs/ *f pl* features

fei|jão /fe'ʒãw/ *m* bean; (*coletivo*) beans; ~**joada** *f* bean stew; ~**joeiro** *m* bean plant

feio /'feju/ *a* ugly; <*palavra, situação, tempo*> nasty; <*olhar*> dirty; ~**so** /o/ *a* plain

fei|ra /'fera/ *f* market; (*industrial*) trade fair; ~**rante** *m/f* market trader

feiti|çaria /fejtʃi'sera/ *f* magic; ~**ceira** *f* witch; ~**ceiro** *m* wizard □ *a* bewitching; ~**ço** *m* spell

fei|tio /fej'tʃiu/ *m* (*de pessoa*) make-up; ~**to** *pp de* **fazer** □ *m* (*ato*) deed; (*proeza*) feat □ *conj* like; **bem** ~**to por ele** (it) serves him right; ~**tura** *f* making

feiúra /fej'ura/ *f* ugliness

feixe /'feʃi/ *m* bundle

fel /fɛw/ *f* gall; (*fig*) bitterness

felicidade /felisi'dadʒi/ *f* happiness

felici|tações /felisita'sõjs/ *f pl* congratulations; ~**tar** *vt* congratulate (**por** on)

felino /fe'linu/ *a* feline

feliz /fe'lis/ *a* happy; ~**ardo** *a* lucky; ~**mente** *adv* fortunately

fel|pa /'fewpa/ *f* (*de pano*) nap; (*penugem*) down, fluff; ~**pudo** *a* fluffy

feltro /'fewtru/ *m* felt

fêmea /'femia/ *a & f* female

femi|nil /femi'niw/ (*pl* ~**nis**) *a* feminine; ~**nilidade** *f* femininity; ~**nino** *a* female; <*palavra*> feminine; ~**nismo** *m* feminism; ~**nista** *a & m/f* feminist

fêmur /'femur/ *m* femur

fen|da /'fẽda/ *f* crack; ~**der** *vt/i* split, crack

feno /'fenu/ *m* hay

fenome|nal /fenome'naw/ (*pl* ~**nais**) *a* phenomenal

fenômeno /fe'nomenu/ *m* phenomenon

fera /'fɛra/ *f* wild beast; **ficar uma** ~ get really angry; **ser** ~ **em** (*fam*) be brilliant at

féretro /'fɛretru/ *m* coffin

feriado /feri'adu/ *m* public holiday

férias /'fɛrias/ *f pl* holiday(s), (*Amer*) vacation; **de** ~ on holiday; **tirar** ~ take a holiday

feri|da /fe'rida/ *f* injury; (*com arma*) wound; ~**do** *a* injured; (*mil*) wounded □ *m* injured person; **os** ~**dos** the injured; (*mil*) the wounded; ~**r** *vt* injure; (*com arma*) wound; (*magoar*) hurt

fermen|tar /fermẽ'tar/ *vt/i* ferment; ~**to** *m* yeast; (*fig*) ferment; ~**to em pó** baking powder

fe|rocidade /ferosi'dadʒi/ *f* ferocity; ~**roz** *a* ferocious

fer|rado /fe'xadu/ *a* **estou** ~**rado** (*fam*) I've had it; ~**rado no sono** fast asleep; ~**radura** *f* horseshoe; ~**ragem** *f* ironwork; *pl* hardware; ~**ramenta** *f* tool; (*coletivo*) tools; ~**rão** *m* (*de abelha*) sting; ~**rar** *vt* brand <*gado*>; shoe <*cavalo*>; ~**rar-se** (*fam*) *vpr* come a cropper; ~**reiro** *m* blacksmith; ~**renho** *a* <*partidário etc*> staunch; <*vontade*> iron

férreo /'fɛxiu/ *a* iron

ferro /'fɛxu/ *m* iron; ~**lho** /o/ *m* bolt; ~**-velho** (*pl* ~**s-velhos**) *m* (*pessoa*) scrap-metal dealer; (*lugar*) scrap-metal yard; ~**via** *f* railway, (*Amer*) railroad; ~**viário** *a* railway □ *m* railway worker

ferrugem /fe'xuʒẽ/ *f* rust

fér|til /'fɛrtʃiw/ (*pl* ~**teis**) *a* fertile

fertili|dade /fertʃili'dadʒi/ *f* fertility; ~**zante** *m* fertilizer; ~**zar** *vt* fertilize

fer|vente /fer'vẽtʃi/ *a* boiling; ~**ver** *vi* boil; (*de raiva*) seethe; ~**vilhar** *vi* bubble; ~**vilhar de** swarm with; ~**vor** *m* fervour; ~**vura** *f* boiling

fes|ta /'fɛsta/ *f* party; (*religiosa*) festival; ~**tejar** *vt/i* celebrate; (*acolher*) fete; ~**tejo** /e/ *m* celebration; ~**tim** *m* feast; ~**tival** (*pl* ~**tivais**) *m* festival; ~**tividade** *f* festivity; ~**tivo** *a* festive

feti|che /fe'tʃiʃi/ *m* fetish; ~**chismo** *m* fetishism; ~**chista** *m/f* fetishist □ *a* fetishistic

fétido /'fɛtʃidu/ *a* fetid

feto[1] /'fɛtu/ *m* (*no útero*) foetus

feto[2] /'fɛtu/ (*Port*) *m* (*planta*) fern

feu|dal /few'daw/ (*pl* ~**dais**) *a* feudal; ~**dalismo** *m* feudalism

fevereiro /feve'reru/ *m* February

fezes /'fɛzis/ *f pl* faeces

fiação /fia'sãw/ *f* (*eletr*) wiring; (*fábrica*) mill

fia|do /fi'adu/ *a* <*conversa*> idle □ *adv* <*comprar*> on credit; ~**dor** *m* guarantor

fiambre /fi'ãbri/ *m* cooked ham

fiança /fi'ãsa/ *f* surety; (*jurid*) bail
fiapo /fi'apu/ *m* thread
fiar /fi'ar/ *vt* spin <*lã etc*>
fiasco /fi'asku/ *m* fiasco
fibra /'fibra/ *f* fibre
ficar /fi'kar/ *vi* (*tornar-se*) become; (*estar, ser*) be; (*manter-se*) stay; ~ **fazendo** keep (on) doing; ~ **com** keep; get <*impressão, vontade*>; ~ **com medo** get scared; ~ **de fazer** arrange to do; ~ **para** be left for; ~ **bom** turn out well; (*recuperar-se*) get better; ~ **bem** look good
fic|ção /fik'sãw/ *f* fiction; ~**ção científica** science fiction; ~**cionista** *m/f* fiction writer
fi|cha /'fiʃa/ *f* (*de telefone*) token; (*de jogo*) chip; (*da caixa*) ticket; (*de fichário*) file card; (*na polícia*) record; (*Port: tomada*) plug; ~**chário** *m*, (*Port*) ~**cheiro** *m* file; (*móvel*) filing cabinet
fictício /fik'tʃisiu/ *a* fictitious
fidalgo /fi'dalgu/ *m* nobleman
fide|digno /fide'dʒignu/ *a* trustworthy; ~**lidade** *f* fidelity
fiduciário /fidusi'ariu/ *a* fiduciary □ *m* trustee
fi|el /fi'ɛw/ (*pl* ~**éis**) *a* faithful □ *m* **os** ~**éis** (*na igreja*) the congregation
figa /'figa/ *f* talisman
fígado /'figadu/ *f* liver
fi|go /'figu/ *m* fig; ~**gueira** *f* fig tree
figu|ra /fi'gura/ *f* figure; (*carta de jogo*) face card; (*fam: pessoa*) character; **fazer (má)** ~**ra** make a (bad) impression; ~**rado** *a* figurative; ~**rante** *m/f* extra; ~**rão** *m* big shot; ~**rar** *vi* appear, figure; ~**rativo** *a* figurative; ~**rinha** *f* sticker; ~**rino** *m* fashion plate; (*de filme, peça*) costume design; (*fig*) model; **como manda o** ~**rino** as it should be
fila /'fila/ *f* line; (*de espera*) queue, (*Amer*) line; (*fileira*) row; **fazer** ~ queue up, (*Amer*) stand in line; ~ **indiana** single file
filamento /fila'mẽtu/ *m* filament
filante /fi'lãtʃi/ (*fam*) *m/f* sponger
filan|tropia /filãtro'pia/ *f* philanthropy; ~**trópico** *a* philanthropic; ~**tropo** /o/ *m* philanthropist
filão /fi'lãw/ *m* (*de ouro*) seam; (*fig*) money-spinner
filar /fi'lar/ (*fam*) *vt* sponge, cadge
filar|mônica /filar'monika/ *f* philharmonic (orchestra); ~**mônico** *a* philharmonic
filate|lia /filate'lia/ *f* philately; ~**lista** *m/f* philatelist
filé /fi'lɛ/ *m* fillet
fileira /fi'lera/ *f* row
filete /fi'letʃi/ *m* fillet
fi|lha /'fiʎa/ *f* daughter; ~**lho** *m* son; *pl* (*crianças*) children; ~**lho da puta** (*chulo*) bastard, (*Amer*) son of a bitch; ~**lho de criação** foster child; ~**lho único** only child; ~**lhote** *m* (*de cão*) pup; (*de lobo etc*) cub; *pl* young
fili|ação /filia'sãw/ *f* affiliation; ~**al** (*pl* ~**ais**) *a* filial □ *f* branch
Filipinas /fili'pinas/ *f pl* Philippines
filipino /fili'pinu/ *a* & *m* Filipino
fil|madora /fiwma'dora/ *f* camcorder; ~**magem** *f* filming; ~**mar** *vt/i* film; ~**me** *m* film
fi|lologia /filolo'ʒia/ *f* philology; ~**lólogo** *m* philologist
filo|sofar /filozo'far/ *vi* philosophize; ~**sofia** *f* philosophy; ~**sófico** *a* philosophical
filósofo /fi'lɔzofu/ *m* philosopher
fil|trar /fiw'trar/ *vt* filter; ~**tro** *m* filter
fim /fĩ/ *m* end; **a** ~ **de** (*para*) in order to; **estar a** ~ **de** fancy; **por** ~ finally; **sem** ~ endless; **ter** ~ come to an end; ~ **de semana** weekend
fi|nado /fi'nadu/ *a* & *m* deceased, departed; ~**nal** (*pl* ~**nais**) *a* final □ *m* end □ *f* final; ~**nalista** *m/f* finalist; ~**nalizar** *vt/i* finish
finan|ças /fi'nãsas/ *f pl* finances; ~**ceiro** *a* financial □ *m* financier; ~**ciamento** *m* financing; (*um*) loan; ~**ciar** *vt* finance; ~**cista** *m/f* financier
fincar /fĩ'kar/ *vt* plant; ~ **o pé** (*fig*) dig one's heels in
findar /fĩ'dar/ *vt/i* end
fineza /fi'neza/ *f* finesse; (*favor*) kindness
fin|gido /fĩ'ʒidu/ *a* feigned; <*pessoa*> insincere; ~**gimento** *m* pretence; ~**gir** *vt* pretend; feign <*doença etc*> □ *vi* pretend; ~**gir-se de** pretend to be
finito /fi'nitu/ *a* finite
finlan|dês /fĩlã'des/ *a* (*f* ~**desa**) Finnish □ *m* (*f* ~**desa**) Finn; (*língua*) Finnish
Finlândia /fĩ'lãdʒia/ *f* Finland
fi|ninho /fi'niɲu/ *adv* **sair de** ~**ninho** slip away; ~**no** *a* (*não grosso*) thin; <*areia, pó etc*> fine; (*refinado*) refined; ~**nório** *a* crafty; ~**nura** *f* thinness; fineness
fio /'fiu/ *m* thread; (*elétrico*) wire; (*de sangue, água*) trickle; (*de luz, esperança*) glimmer; (*de navalha etc*) edge; **horas a** ~ hours on end
fir|ma /'firma/ *f* firm; (*assinatura*) signature; ~**mamento** *m* firmament; ~**mar** *vt* fix; (*basear*) base □ *vi* settle; ~**mar-se** *vpr* be based (em on); ~**me** *a* firm; <*tempo*> settled □ *adv* firmly; ~**meza** *f* firmness
fis|cal /fis'kaw/ (*pl* ~**cais**) *m* inspector; ~**calização** *f* inspection;

~calizar *vt* inspect; ~co *m* inland revenue, (*Amer*) internal revenue service

fis|gada /fiz'gada/ *f* stabbing pain; ~gar *vt* hook

físi|ca /'fizika/ *f* physics; ~co *a* physical □ *m* (*pessoa*) physicist; (*corpo*) physique

fisio|nomia /fiziono'mia/ *f* face; ~nomista *m/f* ser ~nomista have a good memory for faces; ~terapeuta *m/f* physiotherapist; ~terapia *f* physiotherapy

fissura /fi'sura/ *f* fissure; (*fam*) craving; ~do *a* ~do em (*fam*) mad about

fita /'fita/ *f* tape; (*fam: encenação*) playacting; fazer ~ (*fam*) put on an act; ~ adesiva (*Port*) adhesive tape; ~ métrica tape measure

fitar /fi'tar/ *vt* stare at

fivela /fi'vɛla/ *f* buckle

fi|xador /fiksa'dor/ *m* (*de cabelo*) setting lotion; (*de fotos*) fixative; ~xar *vt* fix; stick up <*cartaz*>; ~xo *a* fixed

flácido /'flasidu/ *a* flabby

flagelo /fla'ʒɛlu/ *m* scourge

fla|grante /fla'grãtʃi/ *a* flagrant; apanhar em ~grante (delito) catch in the act; ~grar *vt* catch

flame|jante /flame'ʒãtʃi/ *a* blazing; ~jar *vi* blaze

flamengo /fla'mẽgu/ *a* Flemish □ *m* Fleming; (*língua*) Flemish

flamingo /fla'mĩgu/ *m* flamingo

flâmula /'flamula/ *f* pennant

flanco /'flãku/ *m* flank

flanela /fla'nɛla/ *f* flannel

flanquear /flãki'ar/ *vt* flank

flash /flɛʃ/ *m invar* flash

flau|ta /'flawta/ *f* flute; ~tista *m/f* flautist

flecha /'flɛʃa/ *f* arrow

fler|tar /fler'tar/ *vi* flirt; ~te *m* flirtation

fleuma /'flewma/ *f* phlegm

fle|xão /flek'sãw/ *f* press-up, (*Amer*) push-up; (*ling*) inflection; ~xibilidade *f* flexibility; ~xionar *vt/i* flex <*perna, braço*>; (*ling*) inflect; ~xível (*pl* ~xíveis) *a* flexible

fliperama /flipe'rama/ *m* pinball machine

floco /'flɔku/ *m* flake

flor /flor/ *f* flower; a fina ~ the cream; à ~ da pele (*fig*) on edge

flo|ra /'flɔra/ *f* flora; ~reado *a* full of flowers; (*fig*) florid; ~reio *m* clever turn of phrase; ~rescer *vi* flower; ~resta /ɛ/ *f* forest; ~restal (*pl* ~restais) *a* forest; ~rido *a* in flower; (*fig*) florid; ~rir *vi* flower

flotilha /flo'tʃiʎa/ *f* flotilla

flu|ência /flu'ẽsia/ *f* fluency; ~ente *a* fluent

flui|dez /flui'des/ *f* fluidity; ~do *a* & *m* fluid

fluir /flu'ir/ *vi* flow

fluminense /flumi'nẽsi/ *a* & *m* (person) from Rio de Janeiro state

fluorescente /fluore'sẽtʃi/ *a* fluorescent

flutu|ação /flutua'sãw/ *f* fluctuation; ~ante *a* floating; ~ar *vi* float; <*bandeira*> flutter; (*hesitar*) waver

fluvi|al /fluvi'aw/ (*pl* ~ais) *a* river

fluxo /'fluksu/ *m* flow; ~grama *m* flowchart

fobia /fo'bia/ *f* phobia

foca /'fɔka/ *f* seal

focalizar /fokali'zar/ *vt* focus on

focinho /fo'siɲu/ *m* snout

foco /'fɔku/ *m* focus; (*fig*) centre

fofo /'fofu/ *a* soft; <*pessoa*> cuddly

fofo|ca /fo'fɔka/ *f* piece of gossip; *pl* gossip; ~car *vi* gossip; ~queiro *m* gossip □ *a* gossipy

fo|gão /fo'gãw/ *m* stove; (*de cozinhar*) cooker; ~go /o/ *m* fire; tem ~go? have you got a light?; ser ~go (*fam*) (*ser chato*) be a pain in the neck; (*ser incrível*) be amazing; ~gos de artifício fireworks; ~goso /o/ *a* fiery; ~gueira *f* bonfire; ~guete /e/ *m* rocket

foice /'fojsi/ *f* scythe

fol|clore /fow'klɔri/ *m* folklore; ~clórico *a* folk

fole /'fɔli/ *m* bellows

fôlego /'folegu/ *m* breath; (*fig*) stamina

fol|ga /'fɔwga/ *f* rest, break; (*fam: cara-de-pau*) cheek; ~gado *a* <*roupa*> full, loose; <*vida*> leisurely; (*fam: atrevido*) cheeky; ~gar *vt* loosen □ *vi* have time off

fo|lha /'foʎa/ *f* leaf; (*de papel*) sheet; novo em ~lha brand new; ~lha de pagamento payroll; ~lhagem *f* foliage; ~lhear *vt* leaf through; ~lheto /e/ *m* pamphlet; ~lhinha *f* tear-off calendar; ~lhudo *a* leafy

foli|a /fo'lia/ *f* revelry; ~ão *m* (*f* ~ona) reveller

folículo /fo'likulu/ *m* follicle

fome /'fomi/ *f* hunger; estar com ~ be hungry

fomentar /fomẽ'tar/ *vt* foment

fone /'foni/ *m* (*do telefone*) receiver; (*de rádio etc*) headphones

fonema /fo'nema/ *m* phoneme

fonéti|ca /fo'nɛtʃika/ *f* phonetics; ~co *a* phonetic

fonologia /fonolo'ʒia/ *f* phonology

fonte /'fõtʃi/ *f* (*de água*) spring; (*fig*) source

fora /'fɔra/ *adv* outside; (*não em casa*) out; (*viajando*) away □ *prep* except; dar um ~ drop a clanger; dar um

~ em alg cut s.o. dead; chuck <namorado>; por ~ on the outside; ~-de-lei m/f invar outlaw

foragido /fora'ʒidu/ a at large, on the run □ m fugitive

forasteiro /foras'teru/ m outsider

forca /'forka/ f gallows

for|ça /'forsa/ f (vigor) strength; (violência) force; (elétrica) power; dar uma ~ça a alg help s.o. out; fazer ~ça make an effort; ~ças armadas armed forces; ~çar vt force; ~ça-tarefa (pl ~ças-tarefa) f task force

fórceps /'fɔrseps/ m invar forceps

forçoso /for'sozu/ a forced

for|ja /'fɔrʒa/ f forge; ~jar vt forge

forma /'fɔrma/ f form; (contorno) shape; (maneira) way; de qualquer ~ anyway; manter a ~ keep fit

fôrma /'forma/ f mould; (de cozinha) baking tin

for|mação /forma'sãw/ f formation; (educação) education; (profissionalizante) training; ~mado m graduate; ~mal (pl ~mais) a formal; ~malidade f formality; ~malizar vt formalize; ~mar vt form; (educar) educate; ~mar-se vpr be formed; <estudante> graduate; ~mato m format; ~matura f graduation

formidá|vel /formi'davew/ (pl ~veis) a formidable; (muito bom) tremendous

formi|ga /for'miga/ f ant; ~gamento m pins and needles; ~gar vi swarm (de with); <perna, mão etc> tingle; ~gueiro m ants' nest

formosura /formo'zura/ f beauty

fórmula /'fɔrmula/ f formula

formu|lação /formula'sãw/ f formulation; ~lar vt formulate; ~lário m form

fornalha /for'naʎa/ f furnace

forne|cedor /fornese'dor/ m supplier; ~cer vt supply; ~cer aco a alg supply s.o. with sth; ~cimento m supply

forno /'fornu/ m oven; (para louça etc) kiln

foro /'foru/ m forum

forra /'fɔxa/ f ir à ~ get one's own back

for|ragem /fo'xaʒẽ/ f fodder; ~rar vt line <roupa, caixa etc>; cover <sofá etc>; carpet <assoalho, sala etc>; ~ro /o/ m (de roupa, caixa etc) lining; (de sofá etc) cover; (carpete) (fitted) carpet

forró /fo'xɔ/ m type of Brazilian dance

fortale|cer /fortale'ser/ vt strengthen; ~cimento m strengthening; ~za /e/ f fort-ress

for|te /'fɔrtʃi/ a strong; <golpe> hard; <chuva> heavy; <físico> muscular □ adv strongly; <bater, chover> hard □ m (militar) fort; (habilidade) strong point, forte; ~tificação f fortification; ~tificar vt fortify

fortu|ito /for'tuitu/ a chance; ~na f fortune

fosco /'fosku/ a dull; <vidro> frosted

fosfato /fos'fatu/ m phosphate

fósforo /'fɔsforu/ m match; (elemento químico) phosphor

fossa /'fɔsa/ f pit; na ~ (fig) miserable, depressed

fós|sil /'fɔsiw/ (pl ~seis) m fossil

fosso /'fosu/ m ditch; (de castelo) moat

foto /'fɔtu/ f photo; ~cópia f photocopy; ~copiadora f photocopier; ~copiar vt photocopy; ~gênico a photogenic; ~grafar vt photograph; ~grafia f photography; ~gráfico a photographic

fotógrafo /fo'tɔgrafu/ m photographer

foz /fɔs/ f mouth

fração /fra'sãw/ f fraction

fracas|sado /fraka'sadu/ a failed □ m failure; ~sar vi fail; ~so m failure

fracionar /frasio'nar/ vt break up

fraco /'fraku/ a weak; <luz, som> faint; <medíocre> poor □ m weakness, weak spot

fract- (Port) veja frat-

frade /'fradʒi/ m friar

fragata /fra'gata/ f frigate

frá|gil /'fraʒiw/ (pl ~geis) a fragile; <pessoa> frail

fragilidade /fraʒili'dadʒi/ f fragility; (de pessoa) frailty

fragmen|tar /fragmẽ'tar/ vt fragment; ~tar-se vpr fragment; ~to m fragment

fra|grância /fra'grãsia/ f fragrance; ~grante a fragrant

fralda /'frawda/ f nappy, (Amer) diaper

framboesa /frãbo'eza/ f raspberry

França /'frãsa/ f France

fran|cês /frã'ses/ a (f ~cesa) French □ m (f ~cesa) Frenchman (f -woman); (língua) French; os ~ceses the French

franco /'frãku/ a (honesto) frank; (óbvio) clear; (gratuito) free □ m franc; ~-atirador (pl ~-atiradores) m sniper; (fig) maverick

frangalho /frã'gaʎu/ m tatter

frango /'frãgu/ m chicken

franja /'frãʒa/ f fringe; (do cabelo) fringe, (Amer) bangs

fran|quear /frãki'ar/ vt frank <carta>; ~queza /e/ f frankness; ~quia f (de cartas) franking; (jur) franchise

fran|zino /frã'zinu/ a skinny; ~zir vt gather <tecido>; wrinkle <testa>

fraque /'fraki/ m morning suit

fraqueza /fra'keza/ *f* weakness; (*de luz, som*) faintness

frasco /'frasku/ *m* bottle

frase /'frazi/ *f* (*oração*) sentence; (*locução*) phrase; **~ado** *m* phrasing

frasqueira /fras'kera/ *f* vanity case

frater|nal /frater'naw/ (*pl* **~nais**) *a* fraternal; **~nidade** *f* fraternity; **~nizar** *vi* fraternize; **~no** *a* fraternal

fratu|ra /fra'tura/ *f* fracture; **~rar** *vt* fracture; **~rar-se** *vpr* fracture

frau|dar /fraw'dar/ *vt* defraud; **~de** *f* fraud; **~dulento** *a* fraudulent

frear /fri'ar/ *vt/i* brake

freezer /'frizer/ *m* freezer

fre|guês /fre'ges/ *m* (*f* **~guesa**) customer; **~guesia** *f* (*de loja etc*) clientele; (*paróquia*) parish

frei /frej/ *m* brother

freio /'freju/ *m* brake; (*de cavalo*) bit

freira /'frera/ *f* nun

freixo /'freʃu/ *m* ash

fremir /fre'mir/ *vi* shake

frêmito /'fremitu/ *m* wave

frenesi /frene'zi/ *m* frenzy

frenético /fre'nɛtʃiku/ *a* frantic

frente /'frẽtʃi/ *f* front; **em ~ a** *ou* **de** in front of; **para a ~** forward; **pela ~** ahead; **fazer ~ a** face

freqüência /fre'kwẽsia/ *f* frequency; (*assiduidade*) attendance; **com muita ~** often

freqüen|tador /frekwẽta'dor/ *m* regular visitor (de to); **~tar** *vt* frequent; (*cursar*) attend; **~te** *a* frequent

fres|cão /fres'kãw/ *m* air-conditioned coach; **~co** /e/ *a* <*comida etc*> fresh; <*vento, água, quarto*> cool; (*fam*) (*afetado*) affected; (*exigente*) fussy; **~cobol** *m* kind of racquetball; **~cor** *m* freshness; **~cura** *f* (*fam*) (*afetação*) affectation; (*ser exigente*) fussiness; (*coisa sem importância*) trifle

fresta /'frɛsta/ *f* slit

fre|tar /fre'tar/ *vt* charter <*avião*>; hire <*caminhão*>; **~te** /ɛ/ *m* freight; (*aluguel de avião*) charter; (*de caminhão*) hire

frevo /'frevu/ *m* type of Brazilian dance

fria /'fria/ (*fam*) *f* difficult situation, spot; **~gem** *f* chill

fric|ção /frik'sãw/ *f* friction; **~cionar** *vt* rub

fri|eira /fri'era/ *f* chilblain; **~eza** /e/ *f* coldness

frigideira /friʒi'dera/ *f* frying pan

frígido /'friʒidu/ *a* frigid

frigorífico /frigo'rifiku/ *m* cold store, refrigerator, fridge

frincha /'frĩʃa/ *f* chink

frio /'friu/ *a & m* cold; **estar com ~** be cold; **~rento** *a* sensitive to the cold

frisar /fri'zar/ *vt* (*enfatizar*) stress; crimp <*cabelo*>

friso /'frizu/ *m* frieze

fri|tada /fri'tada/ *f* fry-up; **~tar** *vt* fry; **~tas** *f pl* chips, (*Amer*) French fries; **~to** *a* fried; **está ~to** (*fam*) he's had it; **~tura** *f* fried food

frivolidade /frivoli'dadʒi/ *f* frivolity; **frívolo** *a* frivolous

fronha /'froɲa/ *f* pillowcase

fronte /'frõtʃi/ *f* forehead, brow

frontei|ra /frõ'tera/ *f* border; **~riço** *a* border

frota /'frɔta/ *f* fleet

frou|xidão /froʃi'dãw/ *f* looseness; (*moral*) laxity; **~xo** *a* loose; <*regulamento*> lax; <*pessoa*> lackadaisical

fru|gal /fru'gaw/ (*pl* **~gais**) *a* frugal; **~galidade** *f* frugality

frus|tração /frustra'sãw/ *f* frustration; **~trante** *a* frustrating; **~trar** *vt* frustrate

fru|ta /'fruta/ *f* fruit; **~ta-do-conde** (*pl* **~tas-do-conde**) *f* sweetsop; **~ta-pão** (*pl* **~tas-pão**) *f* breadfruit; **~teira** *f* fruitbowl; **~tífero** *a* (*fig*) fruitful; **~to** *m* fruit

fubá /fu'ba/ *m* maize flour

fu|çar /fu'sar/ *vi* nose around; **~ças** (*fam*) *f pl* face, chops

fu|ga /'fuga/ *f* escape; **~gaz** *a* fleeting; **~gida** *f* escape; **~gir** *vi* run away; (*soltar-se*) escape; **~gir a** avoid; **~gitivo** *a & m* fugitive

fulano /fu'lanu/ *m* whatever his name is

fuleiro /fu'leru/ *a* down-market, cheap and cheerful

fulgor /fuw'gor/ *m* brightness; (*fig*) splendour

fuligem /fu'liʒẽ/ *f* soot

fulmi|nante /fuwmi'nãtʃi/ *a* devastating; **~nar** *vt* strike down; (*fig*) devastate; **~nado por um raio** struck by lightning □ *vi* (*criticar*) rail

fu|maça /fu'masa/ *f* smoke; **~maceira** *f* cloud of smoke; **~mante**, (*Port*) **~mador** *m* smoker; **~mar** *vt/i* smoke; **~mê** *a invar* smoked; **~megar** *vi* smoke; **~mo** *m* (*tabaco*) tobacco; (*Port: fumaça*) smoke; (*fumar*) smoking

função /fũ'sãw/ *f* function; **em ~ de** as a result of; **fazer as funções de** function as

funcho /'fũʃu/ *m* fennel

funcio|nal /fũsio'naw/ (*pl* **~nais**) *a* functional; **~nalismo** *m* civil service; **~namento** *m* working; **~nar** *vi* work; **~nário** *m* employee; **~nário público** civil servant

fun|dação /fũda'sãw/ *f* foundation; **~dador** *m* founder □ *a* founding

fundamen|tal /fũdamẽ'taw/ (*pl* **~tais**) *a* fundamental; **~tar** *vt* (*basear*) base; (*justificar*) substantiate; **~to** *m* foundation

fun|dar /fũ'dar/ *vt* (*criar*) found; (*basear*) base; **~dar-se** *vpr* be based (em on); **~dear** *vi* drop anchor, anchor; **~dilho** *m* seat

fundir /fũ'dʒir/ *vt* melt <*ouro, ferro*>; cast <*sino, estátua*>; (*juntar*) merge; **~-se** *vpr* <*ouro, ferro*> melt; (*juntar-se*) merge

fundo /'fũdu/ *a* deep □ *m* (*parte de baixo*) bottom; (*parte de trás*) back; (*de quadro, foto*) background; (*de dinheiro*) fund; **no ~** basically; **~s** *m pl* (*da casa etc*) back; (*recursos*) funds

fúnebre /'funebri/ *a* funereal

funerário /fune'rariu/ *a* funeral

funesto /fu'nɛstu/ *a* fatal

fungar /fũ'gar/ *vt/i* sniff

fungo /'fũgu/ *m* fungus

fu|nil /fu'niw/ (*pl* **~nis**) *m* funnel; **~nilaria** *f* panel-beating; (*oficina*) bodyshop

furacão /fura'kãw/ *m* hurricane

furado /fu'radu/ *a* **papo ~** (*fam*) hot air

furão /fu'rãw/ *m* (*animal*) ferret

furar /fu'rar/ *vt* pierce <*orelha etc*>; puncture <*pneu*>; make a hole in <*roupa etc*>; jump <*fila*>; break <*greve*> □ *vi* <*roupa etc*> go into a hole; <*pneu*> puncture; (*fam*) <*programa*> fall through

fur|gão /fur'gãw/ *m* van; **~goneta** /e/ (*Port*) *f* van

fúria /'furia/ *f* fury

furioso /furi'ozu/ *a* furious

furo /'furu/ *m* hole; (*de pneu*) puncture; (*jornalístico*) scoop; (*fam: gafe*) blunder, faux pas; **dar um ~** put one's foot in it

furor /fu'ror/ *m* furore

fur|ta-cor /furta'kor/ *a invar* iridescent; **~tar** *vt* steal; **~tivo** *a* furtive; **~to** *m* theft

furúnculo /fu'rũkulu/ *m* boil

fusão /fu'zãw/ *f* fusion; (*de empresas*) merger

fusca /'fuska/ *f* VW beetle

fuselagem /fuze'laʒẽ/ *f* fuselage

fusí|vel /fu'zivew/ (*pl* **~veis**) *m* fuse

fuso /'fuzu/ *m* spindle; **~ horário** time zone

fustigar /fustʃi'gar/ *vt* lash; (*fig: com palavras*) lash out at

futebol /futʃi'bɔw/ *m* football; **~ístico** *a* football

fú|til /'futʃiw/ (*pl* **~teis**) *a* frivolous, inane

futilidade /futʃili'dadʒi/ *f* frivolity, inanity; (*uma*) frivolous thing

futu|rismo /futu'rizmu/ *m* futurism; **~rista** *a & m* futurist; **~rístico** *a* futuristic; **~ro** *a & m* future

fu|zil /fu'ziw/ (*pl* **~zis**) *m* rifle; **~zilamento** *m* shooting; **~zilar** *vt* shoot □ *vi* flash; **~zileiro** *m* rifleman; **~zileiro naval** marine

fuzuê /fuzu'e/ *m* commotion

G

gabar-se /ga'barsi/ *vpr* boast (de of)

gabarito /gaba'ritu/ *m* calibre

gabinete /gabi'netʃi/ *m* (*em casa*) study; (*escritório*) office; (*ministros*) cabinet

gado /'gadu/ *m* livestock; (*bovino*) cattle

gaélico /ga'ɛliku/ *a & m* Gaelic

gafanhoto /gafa'ɲotu/ *m* (*pequeno*) grasshopper; (*grande*) locust

gafe /'gafi/ *f* faux pas, gaffe

gafieira /gafi'era/ *f* dance; (*salão*) dance hall

gagá /ga'ga/ *a* (*fam*) senile

ga|go /'gagu/ *a* stuttering □ *m* stutterer; **~gueira** *f* stutter; **~guejar** *vi* stutter

gaiato /gaj'atu/ *a* funny

gaiola /gaj'ɔla/ *f* cage

gaita /'gajta/ *f* **~ de foles** bagpipes

gaivota /gaj'vɔta/ *f* seagull

gajo /'gaʒu/ *m* (*Port*) guy, bloke

gala /'gala/ *f* **festa de ~** gala; **roupa de ~** formal dress

galã /ga'lã/ *m* leading man

galan|tear /galãtʃi'ar/ *vt* woo; **~teio** *m* wooing; (*um*) courtesy

galão /ga'lãw/ *m* (*enfeite*) braid; (*mil*) stripe; (*medida*) gallon; (*Port: café*) white coffee

galáxia /ga'laksia/ *f* galaxy

galé /ga'lɛ/ *f* galley

galego /ga'legu/ *a & m* Galician

galera /ga'lɛra/ *f* (*fam*) crowd

galeria /gale'ria/ *f* gallery

Gales /'galis/ *m* **País de ~** Wales

ga|lês /ga'les/ *a* (*f* **~lesa**) Welsh □ *m* (*f* **~lesa**) Welshman (*f* -woman); (*língua*) Welsh

galeto /ga'letu/ *m* spring chicken

galgar /gaw'gar/ *vt* (*transpor*) jump over; climb <*escada*>

galgo /'gawgu/ *m* greyhound

galheteiro /gaʎe'teru/ *m* cruet stand

galho /'gaʎu/ *m* branch; **quebrar um ~** (*fam*) help out

galináceos /gali'nasius/ *m pl* poultry

gali|nha /ga'liɲa/ *f* chicken; **~nheiro** *m* chicken coop

galo /'galu/ *m* cock; (*inchação*) bump

galocha /ga'lɔʃa/ *f* Wellington boot

galo|pante /galo'pãtʃi/ *a* galloping; **~par** *vi* gallop; **~pe** /ɔ/ *m* gallop

galpão /gaw'pãw/ *m* shed

galvanizar /gawvani'zar/ *vt* galvanize

gama /'gama/ *f* (*musical*) scale; (*fig*) range

gamado /ga'madu/ *a* besotted (**por** with)

gamão /ga'mãw/ *m* backgammon

gamar /ga'mar/ *vi* fall in love (**por** with)

gana /'gana/ *f* desire

ganância /ga'nãsia/ *f* greed

ganancioso /ganãsi'ozu/ *a* greedy

gancho /'gãʃu/ *m* hook

gangorra /gã'goxa/ *f* seesaw

gangrena /gã'grena/ *f* gangrene

gangue /'gãgi/ *m* gang

ga|nhador /gaɲa'dor/ *m* winner □ *a* winning; **~nhar** *vt* win <*corrida, prêmio*>; earn <*salário*>; get <*presente*>; gain <*vantagem, tempo, amigo*> □ *vi* win; **~nhar a vida** earn a living; **~nha-pão** *m* livelihood; **~nho** *m* gain; *pl* (*no jogo*) winnings □ *pp de* **ganhar**

ga|nido *m* squeal; (*de cachorro*) yelp; **~nir** *vi* squeal; <*cachorro*> yelp

ganso /'gãsu/ *m* goose

gara|gem /ga'raʒẽ/ *f* garage; **~gista** *m/f* garage attendant

garanhão /gara'ɲãw/ *m* stallion

garan|tia /garã'tʃia/ *f* guarantee; **~tir** *vt* guarantee

garatujar /garatu'ʒar/ *vt* scribble

gar|bo /'garbu/ *m* grace; **~boso** *a* graceful

garça /'garsa/ *f* heron

gar|çom /gar'sõ/ *m* waiter; **~çonete** /ɛ/ *f* waitress

gar|fada /gar'fada/ *f* forkful; **~fo** *m* fork

gargalhada /garga'ʎada/ *f* gale of laughter; **rir às ~s** roar with laughter

gargalo /gar'galu/ *m* bottleneck; **tomar no ~** drink out of the bottle

garganta /gar'gãta/ *f* throat

gargare|jar /gargare'ʒar/ *vi* gargle; **~jo** /e/ *m* gargle

gari /ga'ri/ *m/f* (*lixeiro*) dustman, (*Amer*) garbage collector; (*varredor de rua*) roadsweeper, (*Amer*) streetsweeper

garim|par /garĩ'par/ *vi* prospect; **~peiro** *m* prospector; **~po** *m* mine

garo|a /ga'roa/ *f* drizzle; **~ar** *vi* drizzle

garo|ta /ga'rota/ *f* girl; **~to** /o/ *m* boy; (*Port: café*) coffee with milk

garoupa /ga'ropa/ *f* grouper

garra /'gaxa/ *f* claw; (*fig*) drive, determination; *pl* (*poder*) clutches

garra|fa /ga'xafa/ *f* bottle; **~fada** *f* blow with a bottle; **~fão** *m* flagon

garrancho /ga'xãʃu/ *m* scrawl

garrido /ga'xidu/ *a* (*alegre*) lively

garupa /ga'rupa/ *f* (*de animal*) rump; (*de moto*) pillion seat

gás /gas/ *m* gas; *pl* (*intestinais*) wind, (*Amer*) gas; **~ lacrimogêneo** tear gas

gasóleo /ga'zɔliu/ *m* diesel oil

gasolina /gazo'lina/ *f* petrol

gaso|sa /ga'zɔza/ *f* fizzy lemonade, (*Amer*) soda; **~so** *a* gaseous; <*bebida*> fizzy

gáspea /'gaspia/ *f* upper

gas|tador /gasta'dor/ *a & m* spendthrift; **~tar** *vt* spend <*dinheiro, tempo*>; use up <*energia*>; wear out <*roupa, sapatos*>; **~to** *m* expense; *pl* spending, expenditure; **dar para o ~to** do

gastrenterite /gastrẽte'ritʃi/ *f* gastroenteritis

gástrico /'gastriku/ *a* gastric

gastrite /gas'tritʃi/ *f* gastritis

gastronomia /gastrono'mia/ *f* gastronomy

ga|ta /'gata/ *f* cat; (*fam*) sexy woman; **~tão** *m* (*fam*) hunk

gatilho /ga'tʃiʎu/ *m* trigger

ga|tinha /ga'tʃiɲa/ *f* (*fam*) sexy woman; **~to** *m* cat; (*fam*) hunk; **fazer alg de ~to-sapato** treat s.o. like a doormat

gatuno /ga'tunu/ *m* crook □ *a* crooked

gaúcho /ga'uʃu/ *a & m* (person) from Rio Grande do Sul

gaveta /ga'veta/ *f* drawer

gavião /gavi'ãw/ *m* hawk

gaze /'gazi/ *f* gauze

gazela /ga'zɛla/ *f* gazelle

gazeta /ga'zeta/ *f* gazette

geada /ʒi'ada/ *f* frost

ge|ladeira /ʒela'dera/ *f* fridge; **~lado** *a* frozen; (*muito frio*) freezing □ *m* (*Port*) ice cream; **~lar** *vt/i* freeze

gelati|na /ʒela'tʃina/ *f* (*sobremesa*) jelly; (*pó*) gelatine; **~noso** /o/ *a* gooey

geléia /ʒe'lɛja/ *f* jam

ge|leira /ʒe'lera/ *f* glacier; **~lo** /e/ *m* ice

gema /'ʒema/ *f* (*de ovo*) yolk; (*pedra*) gem; **carioca da ~** carioca born and bred; **~da** *f* egg yolk whisked with sugar

gêmeo /'ʒemiu/ *a & m* twin; **Gêmeos** (*signo*) Gemini

ge|mer /ʒe'mer/ *vi* moan, groan; **~mido** *m* moan, groan

gene /'ʒɛni/ *m* gene; **~alogia** *f* genealogy; **~alógico** *a* genealogical; **árvore ~alógica** family tree

Genebra /ʒe'nɛbra/ *f* Geneva

gene|ral /ʒene'raw/ (*pl* **~rais**) *m* general; **~ralidade** *f* generality; **~ralização** *f* generalization;

~ralizar *vt/i* generalize; ~ralizar-se *vpr* become generalized
genérico /ʒe'nɛriku/ *a* generic
gênero /'ʒeneru/ *m* type, kind; (*gramatical*) gender; (*literário*) genre; *pl* goods; ~s alimentícios foodstuffs; ela não faz o meu ~ she's not my type
gene|rosidade /ʒenerozi'dadʒi/ *f* generosity; ~roso /o/ *a* generous
genéti|ca /ʒe'nɛtʃika/ *f* genetics; ~co *a* genetic
gengibre /ʒẽ'ʒibri/ *m* ginger
gengiva /ʒẽ'ʒiva/ *f* gum
geni|al /ʒeni'aw/ (*pl* ~ais) *a* brilliant
gênio /'ʒeniu/ *m* genius; (*temperamento*) temperament
genioso /ʒeni'ozu/ *a* temperamental
geni|tal /ʒeni'taw/ (*pl* ~tais) *a* genital
genitivo /ʒeni'tʃivu/ *a & m* genitive
genocídio /ʒeno'sidʒiu/ *m* genocide
genro /'ʒẽxu/ *m* son-in-law
gente /'ʒẽtʃi/ *f* people; (*fam*) folks; a ~ (*sujeito*) we; (*objeto*) us □ *interj* (*fam*) gosh
gen|til /ʒẽ'tʃiw/ (*pl* ~tis) *a* kind; ~tileza /e/ *f* kindness
genuíno /ʒenu'inu/ *a* genuine
geo|grafia /ʒeogra'fia/ *f* geography; ~gráfico *a* geographical
geógrafo /ʒe'ɔgrafu/ *m* geographer
geo|logia /ʒeolo'ʒia/ *f* geology; ~lógico *a* geological
geólogo /ʒe'ɔlogu/ *m* geologist
geo|metria /ʒeome'tria/ *f* geometry; ~métrico *a* geometrical; ~político *a* geopolitical
Geórgia /ʒi'ɔrʒia/ *f* Georgia
georgiano /ʒiorʒi'anu/ *a & m* Georgian
gera|ção /ʒera'sãw/ *f* generation; ~dor *m* generator
ge|ral /ʒe'raw/ (*pl* ~rais) *a* general □ *f* (*limpeza*) spring-clean; em ~ral in general
gerânio /ʒe'raniu/ *m* geranium
gerar /ʒe'rar/ *vt* create; generate <*eletricidade*>
gerência /ʒe'rẽsia/ *f* management
gerenci|ador /ʒerẽsia'dor/ *m* manager; ~al (*pl* ~ais) *a* management; ~ar *vt* manage
gerente /ʒe'rẽtʃi/ *m* manager □ *a* managing
gergelim /ʒerʒe'lĩ/ *m* sesame
geri|atria /ʒeria'tria/ *f* geriatrics; ~átrico *a* geriatric
geringonça /ʒerĩ'gõsa/ *f* contraption
gerir /ʒe'rir/ *vt* manage
germânico /ʒer'maniku/ *a* Germanic
ger|me /'ʒɛrmi/ *m* germ; ~me de trigo wheatgerm; ~minar *vi* germinate
gerúndio /ʒe'rũdʒiu/ *m* gerund
gesso /'ʒesu/ *m* plaster
ges|tação /ʒesta'sãw/ *f* gestation; ~tante *f* pregnant woman
gestão /ʒes'tãw/ *f* management
ges|ticular *vi* gesticulate; ~to /'ʒɛstu/ *m* gesture
gibi /ʒi'bi/ *m* (*fam*) comic
Gibraltar /ʒibraw'tar/ *f* Gibraltar
gigan|te /ʒi'gãtʃi/ *a & m* giant; ~tesco /e/ *a* gigantic
gilete /ʒi'lɛtʃi/ *f* razor blade □ *a & m/f* (*fam*) bisexual
gim /ʒĩ/ *m* gin
ginásio /ʒi'naziu/ *m* (*escola*) secondary school; (*de ginástica*) gymnasium
ginasta /ʒi'nasta/ *m/f* gymnast
ginásti|ca /ʒi'nastʃika/ *f* gymnastics; (*aeróbica*) aerobics; ~co *a* gymnastic
ginecolo|gia /ʒinekolo'ʒia/ *f* gynaecology; ~gista *m/f* gynaecologist
gingar /ʒĩ'gar/ *vi* sway
gira-discos /ʒira'diʃkuʃ/ *m invar* (*Port*) record player
girafa /ʒi'rafa/ *f* giraffe
gi|rar /ʒi'rar/ *vt/i* spin, revolve; ~rassol (*pl* ~rassóis) *m* sunflower; ~ratório *a* revolving
gíria /'ʒiria/ *f* slang; (*uma* ~) slang expression
giro /'ʒiru/ *m* spin, turn □ *a* (*Port fam*) great
giz /ʒis/ *m* chalk
gla|cê /gla'se/ *m* icing; ~cial (*pl* ~ciais) *a* icy
glamour /gla'mur/ *m* glamour; ~oso /o/ *a* glamorous
glândula /'glãdula/ *f* gland
glandular /glãdu'lar/ *a* glandular
glicerina /glise'rina/ *f* glycerine
glicose /gli'kɔzi/ *f* glucose
glo|bal /glo'baw/ (*pl* ~bais) *a* (*mundial*) global; <*preço etc*> overall; ~bo /o/ *m* globe; ~bo ocular eyeball
glóbulo /'glɔbulu/ *m* globule; (*do sangue*) corpuscle
glória /'glɔria/ *f* glory
glori|ficar /glorifi'kar/ *vt* glorify; ~oso /o/ *a* glorious
glossário /glo'sariu/ *m* glossary
glu|tão /glu'tãw/ *m* (*f* ~tona) glutton □ *a* (*f* ~tona) greedy
gnomo /gi'nomu/ *m* gnome
godê /go'de/ *a* flared
goela /go'ɛla/ *f* gullet
gogó /go'gɔ/ *m* (*fam*) Adam's apple
goia|ba /goj'aba/ *f* guava; ~bada *f* guava jelly; ~beira *f* guava tree
gol /'gow/ (*pl* ~s) *m* goal
gola /'gɔla/ *f* collar
gole /'gɔli/ *m* mouthful
go|lear /goli'ar/ *vt* thrash; ~leiro *m* goalkeeper
golfe /'gowfi/ *m* golf
golfinho /gow'fiɲu/ *m* dolphin

golfista /gow'fista/ *m/f* golfer

golo /'golu/ *m* (*Port*) goal

golpe /'gɔwpi/ *m* blow; (*manobra*) trick; ~ **(de estado)** coup (d'état); ~ **de mestre** masterstroke; ~ **de vento** gust of wind; ~ **de vista** glance; ~**ar** *vt* hit

goma /'goma/ *f* gum; (*para roupa*) starch

gomo /'gomu/ *m* segment

gôndola /'gõdola/ *f* rack

gongo /'gõgu/ *m* gong

gonorréia /gono'xɛja/ *f* gonorrhea

gonzo /'gõzu/ *m* hinge

gorar /go'rar/ *vi* go wrong, fail

gor|do /'gordu/ *a* fat; ~**ducho** *a* plump

gordu|ra /gor'dura/ *f* fat; ~**rento** *a* greasy; ~**roso** /u/ *a* fatty; <*pele*> greasy, oily

gorgolejar /gorgole'ʒar/ *vi* gurgle

gorila /go'rila/ *m* gorilla

gor|jear /gorʒi'ar/ *vi* twitter; ~**jeio** *m* twittering

gorjeta /gor'ʒeta/ *f* tip

gorro /'goxu/ *m* hat

gos|ma /'gɔzma/ *f* slime; ~**mento** *a* slimy

gos|tar /gos'tar/ *vi* ~**tar de** like; ~**to** /o/ *m* taste; (*prazer*) pleasure; **para o meu** ~**to** for my taste; **ter** ~**to de** taste of; ~**toso** *a* nice; <*comida*> nice, tasty; (*fam*) <*pessoa*> gorgeous

go|ta /'gota/ *f* drop; (*que cai*) drip; (*doença*) gout; **foi a** ~**ta d'água** (*fig*) it was the last straw; ~**teira** *f* (*buraco*) leak; (*cano*) gutter; ~**tejar** *vi* drip; <*telhado*> leak □ *vt* drip

gótico /'gɔtʃiku/ *a* Gothic

gotícula /go'tʃicula/ *f* droplet

gover|nador /governa'dor/ *m* governor; ~**namental** (*pl* ~**namentais**) *a* government; ~**nanta** *f* housekeeper; ~**nante** *a* ruling □ *m/f* ruler; ~**nar** *vt* govern; ~**nista** *a* government □ *m/f* government supporter; ~**no** /e/ *m* government

go|zação /goza'sãw/ *f* joking; (*uma*) send-up; ~**zado** *a* funny; ~**zar** *vt* ~**zar (de)** enjoy; (*fam: zombar de*) make fun of □ *vi* (*ter orgasmo*) come; ~**zo** *m* (*prazer*) enjoyment; (*posse*) possession; (*orgasmo*) orgasm; **ser um** ~**zo** be funny

Grã-Bretanha /grãbre'taɲa/ *f* Great Britain

graça /'grasa/ *f* grace; (*piada*) joke; (*humor*) humour, funny side; (*jur*) pardon; **de** ~ for nothing; **sem** ~ (*enfadonho*) dull; (*não engraçado*) unfunny; (*envergonhado*) embarrassed; **ser uma** ~ be lovely; **ter** ~ be funny; **não tem** ~ **sair sozinho** it's no fun to go out alone; ~**s a** thanks to

grace|jar /grase'ʒar/ *vi* joke; ~**jo** /e/ *m* joke

graci|nha /gra'siɲa/ *f* **ser uma** ~**nha** be sweet; ~**oso** /o/ *a* gracious

grada|ção /grada'sãw/ *f* gradation; ~**tivo** *a* gradual

grade /'gradʒi/ *f* grille, grating; (*cerca*) railings; **atrás das** ~**s** behind bars; ~**ado** *a* <*janela*> barred

grado /'gradu/ *m* **de bom/mau** ~ willingly/unwillingly

gradu|ação /gradua'sãw/ *f* graduation; (*mil*) rank; (*variação*) gradation; ~**ado** *a* <*escala*> graduated; <*estudante*> graduate; <*militar*> high-ranking; (*eminente*) respected; ~**al** (*pl* ~**ais**) *a* gradual; ~**ar** *vt* graduate <*escala*>; (*ordenar*) grade; (*regular*) regulate; ~**ar-se** *vpr* <*estudante*> graduate

grafia /gra'fia/ *f* spelling

gráfi|ca /'grafika/ *f* (*arte*) graphics; (*oficina*) print shop; ~**co** *a* graphic □ *m* (*pessoa*) printer; (*diagrama*) graph; *pl* (*de computador*) graphics

grã-fino /grã'finu/ (*fam*) *a* posh, upper-class □ *m* posh person

grafite /gra'fitʃi/ *f* (*mineral*) graphite; (*de lápis*) lead; (*pichação*) piece of graffiti

gra|fologia /grafolo'ʒia/ *f* graphology; ~**fólogo** *m* graphologist

grama[1] /'grama/ *m* gramme

grama[2] /'grama/ *f* grass; ~**do** *m* lawn; (*campo de futebol*) field

gramática /gra'matʃika/ *f* grammar

gramati|cal /gramatʃi'kaw/ (*pl* ~**cais**) *a* grammatical

gram|peador /grãpia'dor/ *m* stapler; ~**pear** *vt* staple <*papéis etc*>; tap <*telefone*>; ~**po** *m* (*de cabelo*) hairclip; (*para papéis etc*) staple; (*ferramenta*) clamp

grana /'grana/ *f* (*fam*) cash

granada /gra'nada/ *f* (*projétil*) grenade; (*pedra*) garnet

gran|dalhão /grãda'ʎãw/ *a* (*f* ~**dalhona**) enormous; ~**dão** *a* (*f* ~**dona**) huge; ~**de** *a* big; (*fig*) <*escritor, amor etc*> great; ~**deza** /e/ *f* greatness; (*tamanho*) magnitude; ~**dioso** /o/ *a* grand

granel /gra'nɛw/ *m* **a** ~ in bulk

granito /gra'nitu/ *m* granite

granizo /gra'nizu/ *m* hail

gran|ja /'grãʒa/ *f* farm; ~**jear** *vt* win, gain

granulado /granu'ladu/ *a* granulated

grânulo /'granulu/ *m* granule

grão /grãw/ (*pl* ~**s**) *m* grain; (*de café*) bean; ~**-de-bico** (*pl* ~**s-de-bico**) *m* chickpea

grasnar /graz'nar/ *vi* <*pato*> quack; <*rã*> croak; <*corvo*> caw

grati|dão /gratʃi'dãw/ *f* gratitude; **~ficação** *f* (*dinheiro a mais*) gratuity; (*recompensa*) gratification; **~ficante** *a* gratifying; **~ficar** *vt* (*dar dinheiro a*) give a gratuity to; (*recompensar*) gratify
gratinado /gratʃi'nadu/ *a* & *m* gratin
grátis /'gratʃis/ *adv* free
grato /'gratu/ *a* grateful
gratuito /gra'tuito/ *a* (*de graça*) free; (*sem motivo*) gratuitous
grau /graw/ *m* degree; **escola de 1º/ 2º ~** primary/secondary school
graúdo /gra'udu/ *a* big; (*importante*) important
gra|vação /grava'sãw/ *f* (*de som*) recording; (*de desenhos etc*) engraving; **~vador** *m* (*pessoa*) engraver; (*máquina*) tape recorder; **~vadora** *f* record company; **~var** *vt* record <*música, disco*>; (*fixar na memória*) memorize; (*estampar*) engrave
gravata /gra'vata/ *f* tie; (*golpe*) stranglehold; **~ borboleta** bowtie
grave /'gravi/ *a* serious; <*voz, som*> deep; <*acento*> grave
grávida /'gravida/ *f* pregnant
gravidade /gravi'dadʒi/ *f* gravity
gravidez /gravi'des/ *f* pregnancy
gravura /gra'vura/ *f* engraving; (*em livro*) illustration
graxa /'graʃa/ *f* (*de sapatos*) polish; (*de lubrificar*) grease
Grécia /'grɛsia/ *f* Greece
grego /'gregu/ *a* & *m* Greek
grei /grej/ *f* flock
gre|lha /'grɛʎa/ *f* grill; **~lhado** *a* grilled □ *m* grill; **~lhar** *vt* grill
grêmio /'gremiu/ *m* guild, association
grená /gre'na/ *a* & *m* dark red
gre|ta /'greta/ *f* crack; **~tar** *vt/i* crack
gre|ve /'grɛvi/ *f* strike; **entrar em ~ve** go on strike; **~ve de fome** hunger strike; **~vista** *m/f* striker
gri|fado /gri'fadu/ *a* in italics; **~far** *vt* italicize
griffe /'grifi/ *f* label, line
gri|lado /gri'ladu/ *a* (*fam*) hung-up; **~lar** (*fam*) *vt* bug; **~lar-se** *vpr* get hung-up (**com** about)
grilhão /gri'ʎãw/ *m* fetter
grilo /'grilu/ *m* (*bicho*) cricket; (*fam*) (*preocupação*) hang-up; (*problema*) hassle; (*barulho*) squeak
grinalda /gri'nawda/ *f* garland
gringo /'grĩgu/ (*fam*) *a* foreign □ *m* foreigner
gri|pado /gri'padu/ *a* **estar/ficar ~pado** have/get the flu; **~par-se** *vpr* get the flu; **~pe** *f* flu, influenza
grisalho /gri'zaʎu/ *a* grey
gri|tante /gri'tãtʃi/ *a* <*erro*> glaring, gross; <*cor*> loud, garish; **~tar** *vt/i* shout; (*de medo*) scream; **~taria** *f* shouting; **~to** *m* shout; (*de medo*) scream; **aos ~tos** in a loud voice; **no ~to** (*fam*) by force
grogue /'grɔgi/ *a* groggy
grosa /'grɔza/ *f* gross
groselha /gro'zɛʎa/ *f* (*vermelha*) redcurrant; (*espinhosa*) gooseberry; **~ negra** blackcurrant
gros|seiro /gro'seru/ *a* rude; (*tosco, malfeito*) rough; **~seria** *f* rudeness; (*uma*) rude thing; **~so** /o/ *a* thick; <*voz*> deep; (*fam*) <*pessoa, atitude*> rude; **~sura** *f* thickness; (*fam: grosseria*) rudeness
grotesco /gro'tesku/ *a* grotesque
grua /'grua/ *f* crane
gru|dado /gru'dadu/ *a* stuck; (*fig*) very attached (**em** to); **~dar** *vt/i* stick; **~de** *m* glue; **~dento** *a* sticky
gru|nhido /gru'ɲidu/ *m* grunt; **~nhir** *vi* grunt
grupo /'grupu/ *m* group
gruta /'gruta/ *f* cave
guaraná /gwara'na/ *m* guarana
guarani /gwara'ni/ *a* & *m/f* Guarani
guarda /'gwarda/ *f* guard □ *m/f* guard; (*policial*) policeman (*f* -woman); **~ costeira** coastguard; **~-chuva** *m* umbrella; **~-costas** *m invar* bodyguard; **~dor** *m* parking attendant; **~-florestal** (*pl* **~s-florestais**) *m/f* forest ranger; **~-louça** *m* china cupboard; **~napo** *m* napkin, serviette; **~-noturno** (*pl* **~s-noturnos**) *m* night watchman
guardar /gwar'dar/ *vt* (*pôr no lugar*) put away; (*conservar*) keep; (*vigiar*) guard; (*não esquecer*) remember; **~-se de** guard against
guarda|-redes /'gwarda-'xedʃ/ *m invar* (*Port*) goalkeeper; **~-roupa** *m* wardrobe; **~-sol** (*pl* **~-sóis**) *m* sunshade
guardi|ão /gwardʒi'ãw/ (*pl* **~ães** *ou* **~ões**) *m* (*f* **~ã**) guardian
guarita /gwa'rita/ *f* sentry box
guar|necer /gwarne'ser/ *vt* (*fortificar*) garrison; (*munir*) equip; (*enfeitar*) garnish; **~nição** *f* (*mil*) garrison; (*enfeite*) garnish
Guatemala /gwate'mala/ *f* Guatemala
guatemalteco /gwatemal'tɛku/ *a* & *m* Guatemalan
gude /'gudʒi/ *m* **bola de ~** marble
guelra /'gɛwxa/ *f* gill
guer|ra /'gɛxa/ *f* war; **~reiro** *m* warrior □ *a* warlike; **~rilha** *f* guerrilla war; **~rilheiro** *a* & *m* guerrilla
gueto /'getu/ *m* ghetto
guia /'gia/ *m/f* guide □ *m* guide(book) □ *f* delivery note
Guiana /gi'ana/ *f* Guyana
guianense /gia'nẽsi/ *a* & *m/f* Guyanan

guiar /gi'ar/ *vt* guide; drive <*veículo*> □ *vi* drive; ~-se *vpr* be guided
guichê /gi'ʃe/ *m* window
guidom /gi'dõ/, (*Port*) **guidão** /gi'dãw/ *m* handlebars
guilhotina /giʎo'tʃina/ *f* guillotine
guimba /'gĩba/ *f* butt
guinada /gi'nada/ *f* change of direction; **dar uma** ~ change direction
guinchar[1] /gĩ'ʃar/ *vi* squeal; <*freios*> screech
guinchar[2] /gĩ'ʃar/ *vt* tow <*carro*>; (*içar*) winch
guincho[1] /'gĩʃu/ *m* squeal; (*de freios*) screech
guincho[2] /'gĩʃu/ *m* (*máquina*) winch; (*veículo*) tow truck
guin|dar /gĩ'dar/ *vt* hoist; ~**daste** *m* crane
Guiné /gi'nɛ/ *f* Guinea
gui|sado /gi'zadu/ *m* stew; ~**sar** *vt* stew
guitar|ra /gi'taxa/ *f* (electric) guitar; ~**rista** *m/f* guitarist
guizo /'gizu/ *m* bell
gu|la /'gula/ *f* greed; ~**lodice** *f* greed; ~**loseima** *f* delicacy; ~**loso** /o/ *a* greedy
gume /'gumi/ *m* cutting edge
guri /gu'ri/ *m* boy; ~**a** *f* girl
guru /gu'ru/ *m* guru
gutu|ral /gutu'raw/ (*pl* ~**rais**) *a* guttural

H

há|bil /'abiw/ (*pl* ~**beis**) *a* clever, skilful
habili|dade /abili'dadʒi/ *f* skill; **ter** ~**dade com** be good with; ~**doso** /o/ *a* skilful; ~**tação** *f* qualification; ~**tar** *vt* qualify
habi|tação /abita'sãw/ *f* housing; (*casa*) dwelling; ~**tacional** (*pl* ~**tacionais**) *a* housing; ~**tante** *m/f* inhabitant; ~**tar** *vt* inhabit □ *vi* live; ~**tável** (*pl* ~**táveis**) *a* habitable
hábito /'abitu/ *m* habit
habitu|al /abitu'aw/ (*pl* ~**ais**) *a* habitual; ~**ar** *vt* accustom (**a** to); ~**ar-se** *vpr* get accustomed (**a** to)
hadoque /a'dɔki/ *m* haddock
Haia /'aja/ *f* the Hague
Haiti /aj'tʃi/ *m* Haiti
haitiano /ajtʃi'anu/ *a* & *m* Haitian
hálito /'alitu/ *m* breath
halitose /ali'tɔzi/ *f* halitosis
hall /xɔw/ (*pl* ~**s**) *m* hall; (*de hotel*) foyer
halte|re /aw'tɛri/ *m* dumbbell; ~**rofilismo** *m* weight lifting; ~**rofilista** *m/f* weight lifter
hambúrguer /ã'burger/ *m* hamburger
hangar /ã'gar/ *m* hangar
haras /'aras/ *m invar* stud farm
hardware /'xarduɛr/ *m* hardware
harmo|nia /armo'nia/ *f* harmony; ~**nioso** /o/ *a* harmonious; ~**nizar** *vt* harmonize; (*conciliar*) reconcile; ~**nizar-se** *vpr* (*combinar*) tone in; (*concordar*) coincide
har|pa /'arpa/ *f* harp; ~**pista** *m/f* harpist
haste /'astʃi/ *m* pole; (*de planta*) stem, stalk; ~**ar** *vt* hoist, raise
Havaí /ava'i/ *m* Hawaii
havaiano /avaj'anu/ *a* & *m* Hawaiian
haver /a'ver/ *m* credit; *pl* possessions □ *vt* (*auxiliar*) **havia sido** it had been; (*impessoal*) **há** there is/are; **ele trabalha aqui há anos** he's been working here for years; **ela morreu há vinte anos (atrás)** she died twenty years ago
haxixe /a'ʃiʃi/ *m* hashish
he|braico /e'brajku/ *a* & *m* Hebrew; ~**breu** *a* & *m* (*f* ~**bréia**) Hebrew
hectare /ek'tari/ *m* hectare
hediondo /edʒi'õdu/ *a* hideous
hein /ẽj/ *int* eh
hélice /'ɛlisi/ *f* propeller
helicóptero /eli'kɔpteru/ *m* helicopter
hélio /'ɛliu/ *m* helium
heliporto /eli'portu/ *m* heliport
hem /ẽj/ *int* eh
hematoma /ema'toma/ *m* bruise
hemisfério /emis'fɛriu/ *m* hemisphere; **Hemisfério Norte/Sul** Northern/Southern Hemisphere
hemo|filia /emofi'lia/ *f* haemophilia; ~**fílico** *a* & *m* haemophiliac; ~**globina** *f* haemoglobin; ~**grama** *m* blood count
hemor|ragia /emoxa'ʒia/ *f* haemorrhage; ~**róidas** *f pl* haemorrhoids
henê /e'ne/ *m* henna
hepatite /epa'tʃitʃi/ *f* hepatitis
hera /'ɛra/ *f* ivy
heráldi|ca /e'rawdʒika/ *f* heraldry; ~**co** *a* heraldic
herança /e'rãsa/ *f* inheritance; (*de um povo etc*) heritage
her|bicida /erbi'sida/ *m* weedkiller; ~**bívoro** *a* herbivorous □ *m* herbivore
her|dar /er'dar/ *vt* inherit; ~**deiro** *m* heir
hereditário /eredʒi'tariu/ *a* hereditary
here|ge /e'rɛʒi/ *m/f* heretic; ~**sia** *f* heresy
herético /e'rɛtʃiku/ *a* heretical
hermético /er'mɛtʃiku/ *a* airtight; (*fig*) obscure
hérnia /'ɛrnia/ *f* hernia
herói /e'rɔj/ *m* hero; ~**co** *a* heroic

hero|ína /ero'ina/ *f* (*mulher*) heroine; (*droga*) heroin; **~ismo** *m* heroism
herpes /'ɛrpis/ *m invar* herpes; **~-zoster** *m* shingles
hesi|tação /ezita'sãw/ *f* hesitation; **~tante** *a* hesitant; **~tar** *vi* hesitate
hetero|doxo /etero'dɔksu/ *a* unorthodox; **~gêneo** *a* heterogeneous
heterossexu|al /eteroseksu'aw/ (*pl* **~ais**) *a & m* heterosexual
hexago|nal /eksago'naw/ (*pl* **~nais**) *a* hexagonal
hexágono /ek'sagonu/ *m* hexagon
hiato /i'atu/ *m* hiatus
hiber|nação /iberna'sãw/ *f* hibernation; **~nar** *vi* hibernate
híbrido /'ibridu/ *a & m* hybrid
hidrante /i'drãtʃi/ *m* fire hydrant
hidra|tante /idra'tãtʃi/ *a* moisturising □ *m* moisturizer; **~tar** *vt* moisturize <*pele*>; **~to** *m* **~to de carbono** carbohydrate
hidráuli|ca /i'drawlika/ *f* hydraulics; **~co** *a* hydraulic
hidrelétri|ca /idre'lɛtrika/ *f* hydroelectric power station; **~co** *a* hydroelectric
hidro|avião /idroavi'ãw/ *m* seaplane; **~carboneto** /e/ *m* hydrocarbon
hidrófilo /i'drɔfilu/ *a* absorbent; **algodão ~** cotton wool, (*Amer*) absorbent cotton
hidrofobia /idrofo'bia/ *f* rabies
hidro|gênio /idro'ʒeniu/ *m* hydrogen; **~massagem** *f* **banheira de ~massagem** jacuzzi; **~via** *f* waterway
hiena /i'ena/ *f* hyena
hierarquia /ierar'kia/ *f* hierarchy
hieróglifo /ie'rɔglifu/ *m* hieroglyphic
hífen /'ifẽ/ *m* hyphen
higi|ene /iʒi'eni/ *f* hygiene; **~ênico** *a* hygienic
hilari|ante /ilari'ãtʃi/ *a* hilarious; **~dade** *f* hilarity
Himalaia /ima'laja/ *m* Himalayas
hin|di /ĩ'dʒi/ *m* Hindi; **~du** *a & m/f* Hindu; **~duísmo** *m* Hinduism; **~duísta** *a & m/f* Hindu
hino /'inu/ *m* hymn; **~ nacional** national anthem
hipermercado /ipermer'kadu/ *m* hypermarket
hipersensí|vel /ipersẽ'sivew/ (*pl* **~veis**) *a* hypersensitive
hipertensão /ipertẽ'sãw/ *f* hypertension
hípico /'ipiku/ *a* horseriding
hipismo /i'pizmu/ *m* horseriding; (*corridas*) horseracing
hip|nose /ipi'nɔzi/ *f* hypnosis; **~nótico** *a* hypnotic; **~notismo** *m* hypnotism; **~notizador** *m* hypnotist; **~notizar** *vt* hypnotize
hipocondríaco /ipokõ'driaku/ *a & m* hypochondriac
hipocrisia /ipokri'zia/ *f* hypocrisy
hipócrita /i'pɔkrita/ *m/f* hypocrite □ *a* hypocritical
hipódromo /i'pɔdromu/ *m* race course, (*Amer*) race track
hipopótamo /ipo'pɔtamu/ *m* hippopotamus
hipote|ca /ipo'tɛka/ *f* mortgage; **~car** *vt* mortgage; **~cário** *a* mortgage
hipotermia /ipoter'mia/ *f* hypothermia
hipótese /i'pɔtezi/ *f* hypothesis; **na ~ de** in the event of; **na pior das ~s** at worst
hipotético /ipo'tɛtʃiku/ *a* hypothetical
hirto /'irtu/ *adj* rigid, stiff
hispânico /is'paniku/ *a* Hispanic
histamina /ista'mina/ *f* histamine
his|terectomia /isterekto'mia/ *f* hysterectomy; **~teria** *f* hysteria; **~térico** *a* hysterical; **~terismo** *m* hysteria
his|tória /is'tɔria/ *f* (*do passado*) history; (*conto*) story; *pl* (*amolação*) trouble; **~toriador** *m* historian; **~tórico** *a* historical; (*marcante*) historic □ *m* history
hoje /'oʒi/ *adv* today; **~ em dia** nowadays; **~ de manhã** this morning; **~ à noite** tonight
Holanda /o'lãda/ *f* Holland
holan|dês /olã'des/ *a* (*f* **~desa**) Dutch □ *m* (*f* **~desa**) Dutchman (*f* -woman); (*língua*) Dutch; **os ~deses** the Dutch
holding /'xɔwdʒĩ/ (*pl* **~s**) *f* holding company
holerite /ole'ritʃi/ *m* pay slip
holo|causto /olo'kawstu/ *m* holocaust; **~fote** /ɔ/ *m* spotlight; **~grama** *m* hologram
homem /'omẽ/ *m* man; **~ de negócios** businessman; **~-rã** (*pl* **homens-rã**) *m* frogman
homena|gear /omenaʒi'ar/ *vt* pay tribute to; **~gem** *f* tribute; **em ~gem a** in honour of
homeo|pata /omio'pata/ *m/f* homoeopath; **~patia** *f* homoeopathy; **~pático** *a* homoeopathic
homérico /o'mɛriku/ *a* (*estrondoso*) booming; (*extraordinário*) phenomenal
homi|cida /omi'sida/ *a* homicidal □ *m/f* murderer; **~cídio** *m* homicide; **~cídio involuntário** manslaughter
homo|geneizado /omoʒenej'zadu/ *a* <*leite*> homogenized; **~gêneo** *a* homogeneous
homologar /omolo'gar/ *vt* ratify

homólogo /o'mɔlogu/ *m* opposite number □ *a* equivalent
homônimo /o'monimu/ *m* (*xará*) namesake; (*vocábulo*) homonym
homossexu|al /omoseksu'aw/ (*pl* ~**ais**) *a* & *m* homosexual; ~**alismo** *m* homosexuality
Honduras /õ'duras/ *f* Honduras
hondurenho /õdu'reɲu/ *a* & *m* Honduran
hones|tidade /onestʃi'dadʒi/ *f* honesty; ~**to** /ɛ/ *a* honest
hono|rário /ono'rariu/ *a* honorary; ~**rários** *m pl* fees; ~**rífico** *a* honorific
hon|ra /'õxa/ *f* honour; ~**radez** *f* honesty, integrity; ~**rado** *a* honourable; ~**rar** *vt* honour; ~**roso** /o/ *a* honourable
hóquei /'ɔkej/ *m* (field) hockey; ~ **sobre gelo** ice hockey; ~ **sobre patins** roller hockey
hora /'ɔra/ *f* (*unidade de tempo*) hour; (*ocasião*) time; **que** ~**s são?** what's the time?; **a que** ~**s?** at what time?; **às três** ~**s** at three o'clock; **dizer as** ~**s** tell the time; **tem** ~**s?** do you have the time?; **de** ~ **em** ~ every hour; **em cima da** ~ at the last minute; **na** ~ (*naquele momento*) at the time; (*no ato*) on the spot; (*a tempo*) on time; **está na** ~ **de ir** it's time to go; **na** ~ **H** (*no momento certo*) at just the right moment; (*no momento crítico*) at the crucial moment; **meia** ~ half an hour; **toda** ~ all the time; **fazer** ~ kill time; **marcar** ~ make an appointment; **perder a** ~ lose track of time; **não tenho** ~ my time is my own; **não vejo a** ~ **de ir** I can't wait to go; ~**s extras** overtime; ~**s vagas** spare time
horário /o'rariu/ *a* hourly; **km** ~**s** km per hour □ *m* (*hora*) time; (*tabela*) timetable; (*de trabalho etc*) hours; ~ **nobre** prime time
horda /'ɔrda/ *f* horde
horista /o'rista/ *a* paid by the hour □ *m/f* worker paid by the hour
horizon|tal /orizõ'taw/ (*pl* ~**tais**) *a* & *f* horizontal; ~**te** *m* horizon
hor|monal /ormo'naw/ (*pl* ~**monais**) *a* hormonal; ~**mônio** *m* hormone
horóscopo /o'rɔskopu/ *m* horoscope
horrendo /o'xẽdu/ *a* horrid
horripi|lante /oxipi'lãtʃi/ *a* horrifying; ~**lar** *vt* horrify
horrí|vel /o'xivew/ (*pl* ~**veis**) *a* horrible, awful
horror /o'xor/ *m* horror (**a** of); (*coisa horrorosa*) horrible thing; **ser um** ~ be awful; **que** ~! how awful!
horro|rizar /oxori'zar/ *vt/i* horrify; ~**rizar-se** *vpr* be horrified; ~**roso** /o/ *a* horrible
horta /'ɔrta/ *f* vegetable plot; ~ **comercial** market garden, (*Amer*) truck farm; ~**liça** *f* vegetable
hortelã /orte'lã/ *f* mint; ~**-pimenta** peppermint
horti|cultor /ortʃikuw'tor/ *m* horticulturalist; ~**cultura** *f* horticulture; ~**frutigranjeiros** *m pl* fruit and vegetables; ~**granjeiros** *m pl* vegetables
horto /'ortu/ *m* market garden; (*viveiro*) nursery
hospe|dagem /ospe'daʒẽ/ *f* accommodation; ~**dar** *vt* put up; ~**dar-se** *vpr* stay
hóspede /'ɔspidʒi/ *m/f* guest
hospedei|ra /ospe'dera/ *f* landlady; ~**ra de bordo** (*Port*) stewardess; ~**ro** *m* landlord
hospício /os'pisiu/ *m* (*de loucos*) asylum
hospi|tal /ospi'taw/ (*pl* ~**tais**) *m* hospital; ~**talar** *a* hospital; ~**taleiro** *a* hospitable; ~**talidade** *f* hospitality; ~**talizar** *vt* hospitalize
hóstia /'ɔstʃia/ *f* Host, Communion wafer
hos|til /os'tʃiw/ (*pl* ~**tis**) *a* hostile; ~**tilidade** *f* hostility; ~**tilizar** *vt* antagonize
ho|tel /o'tɛw/ (*pl* ~**téis**) *m* hotel; ~**teleiro** *a* hotel □ *m* hotelier
huma|nidade /umani'dadʒi/ *f* humanity; ~**nismo** *m* humanism; ~**nista** *a* & *m/f* humanist; ~**nitário** *a* & *m* humanitarian; ~**nizar** *vt* humanize; ~**no** *a* human; (*compassivo*) humane; ~**nos** *m pl* humans
húmido /'umidu/ *adj* (*Port*) humid
humil|dade /umiw'dadʒi/ *f* humility; ~**de** *a* humble
humi|lhação /umiʎa'sãw/ *f* humiliation; ~**lhante** *a* humiliating; ~**lhar** *vt* humiliate
humor /u'mor/ *m* humour; (*disposição do espírito*) mood; **de bom/mau** ~ in a good/bad mood
humo|rismo /umo'rizmu/ *m* humour; ~**rista** *m/f* (*no palco*) comedian; (*escritor*) humorist; ~**rístico** *a* humorous
húngaro /'ũgaru/ *a* & *m* Hungarian
Hungria /ũ'gria/ *f* Hungary
hurra /'uxa/ *int* hurrah □ *m* cheer

I

ia|te /i'atʃi/ *m* yacht; ~**tismo** *m* yachting; ~**tista** *m/f* yachtsman (*f* -woman)

ibérico /i'bɛriku/ *a & m* Iberian
ibope /i'bɔpi/ *m* dar ~ (*fam*) be popular
içar /i'sar/ *vt* hoist
iceberg /ajs'bɛrgi/ (*pl* ~s) *m* iceberg
ícone /'ikoni/ *m* icon
iconoclasta /ikono'klasta/ *m/f* iconoclast □ *a* iconoclastic
icterícia /ikte'risia/ *f* jaundice
ida /'ida/ *f* going; **na ~** on the way there; **~ e volta** return, (*Amer*) round trip
idade /i'dadʒi/ *f* age; **meia ~** middle age; **homem de meia ~** middle-aged man; **senhor de ~** elderly man; **Idade Média** Middle Ages
ide|al /ide'aw/ (*pl* ~ais) *a & m* ideal; **~alismo** *m* idealism; **~alista** *m/f* idealist □ *a* idealistic; **~alizar** *vt* (*criar*) devise; (*sublimar*) idealize; **~ar** *vt* devise; **~ário** *m* ideas
idéia /i'dɛja/ *f* idea; **mudar de ~** change one's mind
idem /'idẽ/ *adv* ditto
idêntico /i'dẽtʃiku/ *a* identical
identi|dade /idẽtʃi'dadʒi/ *f* identity; **~ficar** *vt* identify; **~ficar-se** *vpr* identify (com with)
ideo|logia /ideolo'ʒia/ *f* ideology; **~lógico** *a* ideological
idílico /i'dʒiliku/ *a* idyllic
idílio /i'dʒiliu/ *m* idyll
idio|ma /idʒi'oma/ *m* language; **~mático** *a* idiomatic
idio|ta /idʒi'ɔta/ *m/f* idiot □ *a* idiotic; **~tice** *f* stupidity; (*uma*) stupid thing
idola|trar /idola'trar/ *vt* idolize; **~tria** *f* idolatry
ídolo /'idulu/ *m* idol
idôneo /i'doniu/ *a* suitable
idoso /i'dozu/ *a* elderly
Iêmen /i'emẽ/ *m* Yemen
iemenita /ieme'nita/ *a & m/f* Yemeni
iene /i'ɛni/ *m* yen
iglu /i'glu/ *m* igloo
ignição /igni'sãw/ *f* ignition
ignomínia /igno'minia/ *f* ignominy
igno|rância /igno'rãsia/ *f* ignorance; **~rante** *a* ignorant; **~rar** (*desconsiderar*) ignore; (*desconhecer*) not know
igreja /i'greʒa/ *f* church
igu|al /i'gwaw/ (*pl* ~ais) *a* equal; (*em aparência*) identical; (*liso*) even □ *m/f* equal; **por ~al** equally; **~alar** *vt* equal; level <*terreno*>; **~alar(-se)** *a* be equal to; **~aldade** *f* equality; **~alitário** *a* egalitarian; **~almente** *adv* equally; (*como resposta*) the same to you; **~alzinho** *a* exactly the same (a as)
iguaria /igwa'ria/ *f* delicacy
iídiche /i'idiʃi/ *m* Yiddish
ile|gal /ile'gaw/ (*pl* ~gais) *a* illegal; **~galidade** *f* illegality
ilegítimo /ile'ʒitʃimu/ *a* illegitimate
ilegí|vel /ile'ʒivew/ (*pl* ~veis) *a* illegible
ileso /i'lɛzu/ *a* unhurt
iletrado /ile'tradu/ *adj & m* illiterate
ilha /'iʎa/ *f* island
ilharga /i'ʎarga/ *f* side
ilhéu /i'ʎɛw/ *m* (*f* **ilhoa**) islander
ilhós /i'ʎɔs/ *m invar* eyelet
ilhota /i'ʎɔta/ *f* small island
ilícito /i'lisitu/ *a* illicit
ilimitado /ilimi'tadu/ *a* unlimited
ilógico /i'lɔʒiku/ *a* illogical
iludir /ilu'dʒir/ *vt* delude; **~-se** *vpr* delude o.s.
ilumi|nação /ilumina'sãw/ *f* lighting; (*inspiração*) enlightenment; **~nar** *vt* light up, illuminate; (*inspirar*) enlighten
ilu|são /ilu'zãw/ *f* illusion; (*sonho*) delusion; **~sionista** *m/f* illusionist; **~sório** *a* illusory
ilus|tração /ilustra'sãw/ *f* illustration; (*erudição*) learning; **~trador** *m* illustrator; **~trar** *vt* illustrate; **~trativo** *a* illustrative; **~tre** *a* illustrious; **~tríssimo senhor** Dear Sir
ímã /'imã/ *m* magnet
imaculado /imaku'ladu/ *a* immaculate
imagem /i'maʒẽ/ *f* image; (*da TV*) picture
imagi|nação /imaʒina'sãw/ *f* imagination; **~nar** *vt* imagine; **~nário** *a* imaginary; **~nativo** *a* imaginative; **~nável** (*pl* ~**náveis**) *a* imaginable; **~noso** /o/ *a* imaginative
imatu|ridade /imaturi'dadʒi/ *f* immaturity; **~ro** *a* immature
imbatí|vel /ĩba'tʃivew/ (*pl* ~veis) *a* unbeatable
imbe|cil /ĩbe'siw/ (*pl* ~cis) *a* stupid □ *m/f* imbecile
imberbe /ĩ'berbi/ *adj* (*sem barba*) beardless
imbricar /ĩbri'kar/ *vt* overlap; **~-se** *vpr* overlap
imedia|ções /imedʒia'sõjs/ *f pl* vicinity; **~tamente** *adv* immediately; **~to** *a* immediate
imemori|al /imemori'aw/ (*pl* ~ais) *a* immemorial
imen|sidão /imẽsi'dãw/ *f* vastness; **~so** *a* immense
imergir /imer'ʒir/ *vt* immerse
imi|gração /imigra'sãw/ *f* immigration; **~grante** *a & m/f* immigrant; **~grar** *vi* immigrate
imi|nência /imi'nẽsia/ *f* imminence; **~nente** *a* imminent
imiscuir-se /imisku'irsi/ *vpr* interfere
imi|tação /imita'sãw/ *f* imitation; **~tador** *m* imitator; **~tar** *vt* imitate

imobili|ária /imobili'aria/ *f* estate agent's, (*Amer*) realtor; **~ário** *a* property; **~dade** *f* immobility; **~zar** *vt* immobilize

imo|ral /imo'raw/ (*pl* **~rais**) *a* immoral; **~ralidade** *f* immorality

imor|tal /imor'taw/ (*pl* **~tais**) *a* immortal □ *m/f* member of the Brazilian Academy of Letters; **~talidade** *f* immortality; **~talizar** *vt* immortalize

imó|vel /i'mɔvew/ (*pl* **~veis**) *a* motionless, immobile □ *m* building, property; *pl* property, real estate

impaci|ência /ĩpasi'ẽsia/ *f* impatience; **~entar-se** *vpr* get impatient; **~ente** *a* impatient

impacto /ĩ'paktu/, (*Port*) **impacte** /ĩ'paktʃi/ *m* impact

impagá|vel /ĩpa'gavew/ (*pl* **~veis**) *a* priceless

ímpar /'ĩpar/ *a* unique; <*número*> odd

imparci|al /ĩparsi'aw/ (*pl* **~ais**) *a* impartial; **~alidade** *f* impartiality

impasse /ĩ'pasi/ *m* impasse

impassí|vel /ĩpa'sivew/ (*pl* **~veis**) *a* impassive

impecá|vel /ĩpe'kavew/ (*pl* **~veis**) *a* impeccable

impe|dido /ĩpe'dʒidu/ *a* <*rua*> blocked; (*Port: ocupado*) engaged, (*Amer*) busy; (*no futebol*) offside; **~dimento** *m* prevention; (*estorvo*) obstruction; (*no futebol*) offside position; **~dir** *vt* stop; (*estorvar*) hinder; block <*rua*>; **~dir alg de ir** *ou* **que alg vá** stop s.o. going

impelir /ĩpe'lir/ *vt* drive

impenetrá|vel /ĩpene'travew/ (*pl* **~veis**) *a* impenetrable

impensá|vel /ĩpẽ'savew/ (*pl* **~veis**) *a* unthinkable

impe|rador /ĩpera'dor/ *m* emperor; **~rar** *vi* reign, rule; **~rativo** *a* & *m* imperative; **~ratriz** *f* empress

imperceptí|vel /ĩpersep'tʃivew/ (*pl* **~veis**) *a* imperceptible

imperdí|vel /ĩper'dʒivew/ (*pl* **~veis**) *a* unmissable

imperdoá|vel /ĩperdo'avew/ (*pl* **~veis**) *a* unforgivable

imperfei|ção /ĩperfej'sãw/ *f* imperfection; **~to** *a* & *m* imperfect

imperi|al /ĩperi'aw/ (*pl* **~ais**) *a* imperial; **~alismo** *m* imperialism; **~alista** *a* & *m/f* imperialist

império /ĩ'pɛriu/ *m* empire

imperioso /ĩperi'ozu/ *a* imperious; <*necessidade*> pressing

imperme|abilizar /ĩpermiabili'zar/ *vt* waterproof; **~ável** (*pl* **~áveis**) *a* waterproof; (*fig*) impervious (a to) □ *m* raincoat

imperti|nência /ĩpertʃi'nẽsia/ *f* impertinence; **~nente** *a* impertinent

impesso|al /ĩpeso'aw/ (*pl* **~ais**) *a* impersonal

ímpeto /'ĩpetu/ *m* (*vontade*) urge, impulse; (*de emoção*) surge; (*movimento*) start; (*na física*) impetus

impetuo|sidade /ĩpetuozi'dadʒi/ *f* impetuosity; **~so** /o/ *a* impetuous

impiedoso /ĩpie'dozu/ *a* merciless

impingir /ĩpĩ'ʒir/ *vt* foist (a on)

implacá|vel /ĩpla'kavew/ (*pl* **~veis**) *a* implacable

implan|tar /ĩplã'tar/ *vt* introduce; (*no corpo*) implant; **~te** *m* implant

implemen|tar /ĩplemẽ'tar/ *vt* implement; **~to** *m* implement

impli|cação /ĩplika'sãw/ *f* implication; **~cância** *f* (*ato*) harassment; (*antipatia*) grudge; **estar de ~cância com** have it in for; **~cante** *a* troublesome □ *m/f* troublemaker; **~car** *vt* (*comprometer*) implicate; **~car (em)** (*dar a entender*) imply; (*acarretar, exigir*) involve; **~car com** (*provocar*) pick on; (*antipatizar*) not get on with

implícito /ĩ'plisitu/ *a* implicit

implorar /ĩplo'rar/ *vt* plead for (a from)

imponente /ĩpo'nẽtʃi/ *a* imposing

impopular /ĩpopu'lar/ *a* unpopular

impor /ĩ'por/ *vt* impose (a on); command <*respeito*>; **~-se** *vpr* assert o.s.

impor|tação /ĩporta'sãw/ *f* import; **~tador** *m* importer; **~tadora** *f* import company; **~tados** *m pl* imported goods; **~tância** *f* importance; (*quantia*) amount; **ter ~tância** be important; **~tante** *a* important; **~tar** *vt* import <*mercadorias*> □ *vi* matter; **~tar em** (*montar a*) amount to; (*resultar em*) lead to; **~tar-se (com)** mind

importu|nar /ĩportu'nar/ *vt* bother; **~no** *a* annoying

imposição /ĩpozi'sãw/ *f* imposition

impossibili|dade /ĩposibili'dadʒi/ *f* impossibility; **~tar** *vt* make impossible; **~tar alg de ir, ~tar a alg ir** prevent s.o. from going, make it impossible for s.o. to go

impossí|vel /ĩpo'sivew/ (*pl* **~veis**) *a* impossible

impos|to /ĩ'postu/ *m* tax; **~to de renda** income tax; **~to sobre o valor acrescentado** (*Port*) VAT; **~tor** *m* impostor; **~tura** *f* deception

impo|tência /ĩpo'tẽsia/ *f* impotence; **~tente** *a* impotent

impreci|são /ĩpresi'zãw/ *f* imprecision; **~so** *a* imprecise

impregnar /ĩpreg'nar/ *vt* impregnate

imprensa /ĩ'prẽsa/ *f* press; **~ marrom** gutter press

imprescindí|vel /ĩpresĩ'dʒivew/ (*pl* **~veis**) *a* essential

impres|são /ĩpre'sãw/ *f* impression; (*no prelo*) printing; **~são digital** fingerprint; **~sionante** *a* (*imponente*) impressive; (*comovente*) striking; **~sionar** *vt* (*causar admiração*) impress; (*comover*) make an impression on; **~sionar-se** *vpr* be impressed (**com** by); **~sionável** (*pl* **~sionáveis**) *a* impressionable; **~sionismo** *m* impressionism; **~sionista** *a & m/f* impressionist; **~so** *a* printed □ *m* printed sheet; *pl* printed matter; **~sor** *m* printer; **~sora** *f* printer

imprestá|vel /ĩpres'tavew/ (*pl* **~veis**) *a* useless

impre|visível /ĩprevi'zivew/ (*pl* **~visíveis**) *a* unpredictable; **~visto** *a* unforeseen □ *m* unforeseen circumstance

imprimir /ĩpri'mir/ *vt* print

impropério /ĩpro'pɛriu/ *m* term of abuse; *pl* abuse

impróprio /ĩ'prɔpriu/ *a* improper; (*inadequado*) unsuitable (**para** for)

imprová|vel /ĩpro'vavew/ (*pl* **~veis**) *a* unlikely

improvi|sação /ĩproviza'sãw/ *f* improvisation; **~sar** *vt/i* improvise; **~so** *m* **de ~so** on the spur of the moment

impru|dência /ĩpru'dẽsia/ *f* recklessness; **~dente** *a* reckless

impul|sionar /ĩpuwsio'nar/ *vt* drive; **~sivo** *a* impulsive; **~so** *m* impulse

impu|ne /ĩ'puni/ *a* unpunished; **~nidade** *f* impunity

impu|reza /ĩpu'reza/ *f* impurity; **~ro** *a* impure

imun|dície /imũ'dʒisi/ *f* filth; **~do** *a* filthy

imu|ne /i'muni/ *a* immune (**a** to); **~nidade** *f* immunity; **~nizar** *vt* immunize

inabalá|vel /inaba'lavew/ (*pl* **~veis**) *a* unshakeable

iná|bil /i'nabiw/ (*pl* **~bis**) *a* (*desafeitado*) clumsy

inabitado /inabi'tadu/ *a* uninhabited

inacabado /inaka'badu/ *a* unfinished

inaceitá|vel /inasej'tavew/ (*pl* **~veis**) *a* unacceptable

inacessí|vel /inase'sivew/ (*pl* **~veis**) *a* inaccessible

inacreditá|vel /inakredʒi'tavew/ (*pl* **~veis**) *a* unbelievable

inadequado /inade'kwadu/ *a* unsuitable

inadmissí|vel /inadʒimi'sivew/ (*pl* **~veis**) *a* inadmissible

inadvertência /inadʒiver'tẽsia/ *f* oversight

inalar /ina'lar/ *vt* inhale

inalcançá|vel /inawkã'savew/ (*pl* **~veis**) *a* unattainable

inalterá|vel /inawte'ravew/ (*pl* **~veis**) *a* unchangeable

inanição /inani'sãw/ *f* starvation

inanimado /inani'madu/ *a* inanimate

inapto /i'naptu/ *a* (*incapaz*) unfit

inati|vidade /inatʃivi'dadʒi/ *f* inactivity; **~vo** *a* inactive

inato /i'natu/ *a* innate

inaudito /inaw'dʒitu/ *a* unheard of

inaugu|ração /inawgura'sãw/ *f* inauguration; **~ral** (*pl* **~rais**) *a* inaugural; **~rar** *vt* inaugurate

incabí|vel /ĩka'bivew/ (*pl* **~veis**) *a* inappropriate

incalculá|vel /ĩkawku'lavew/ (*pl* **~veis**) *a* incalculable

incandescente /ĩkãde'sẽtʃi/ *a* red-hot

incansá|vel /ĩkã'savew/ (*pl* **~veis**) *a* tireless

incapaci|tado /ĩkapasi'tadu/ *a* <*pessoa*> disabled; **~tar** *vt* incapacitate

incauto /ĩ'kawtu/ *a* reckless

incendi|ar /ĩsẽdʒi'ar/ *vt* set alight; **~ar-se** *vpr* catch fire; **~ário** *a* incendiary; (*fig*) <*discurso*> inflammatory □ *m* arsonist; (*fig*) agitator

incêndio /ĩ'sẽdʒiu/ *m* fire

incenso /ĩ'sẽsu/ *m* incense

incenti|var /ĩsẽtʃi'var/ *vt* encourage; **~vo** *m* incentive

incer|teza /ĩser'teza/ *f* uncertainty; **~to** /ɛ/ *a* uncertain

inces|to /ĩ'sɛstu/ *m* incest; **~tuoso** /o/ *a* incestuous

in|chação /ĩʃa'sãw/ *f* swelling; **~char** *vt/i* swell

inci|dência /ĩsi'dẽsia/ *f* incidence; **~dente** *m* incident; **~dir** *vi* **~dir em** <*luz*> shine on; <*imposto*> be payable on

incinerar /ĩsine'rar/ *vt* incinerate

inci|são /ĩsi'zãw/ *f* incision; **~sivo** *a* incisive

incitar /ĩsi'tar/ *vt* incite

incli|nação /ĩklina'sãw/ *f* (*do chão*) incline; (*da cabeça*) nod; (*propensão*) inclination; **~nado** *a* <*chão*> sloping; <*edifício*> leaning; (*propenso*) inclined (**a** to); **~nar** *vt* tilt; nod <*cabeça*> □ *vi* <*chão*> slope; <*edifício*> lean; (*tender*) incline (**para** towards); **~nar-se** *vpr* lean

inclu|ir /ĩklu'ir/ *vt* include; **~são** *f* inclusion; **~sive** *prep* including □ *adv* inclusive; (*até*) even; **~so** *a* included

incoe|rência /ĩkoe'rẽsia/ *f* (*falta de nexo*) incoherence; (*inconseqüência*) inconsistency; **~rente** *a* (*sem nexo*) incoherent; (*inconseqüente*) inconsistent

incógni|ta /ĩ'kɔgnita/ *f* unknown; **~to** *adv* incognito
incolor /ĩko'lor/ *a* colourless
incólume /ĩ'kɔlumi/ *a* unscathed
incomodar /ĩkomo'dar/ *vt* bother □ *vi* be a nuisance; **~-se** *vpr* (*dar-se ao trabalho*) bother (**em** to); **~-se (com)** be bothered (by), mind
incômodo /ĩ'komodu/ *a* (*desagradável*) tiresome; (*sem conforto*) uncomfortable □ *m* nuisance
incompa|rável /ĩkõpa'ravew/ (*pl* **~ráveis**) *a* incomparable; **~tível** (*pl* **~tíveis**) *a* incompatible
incompe|tência /ĩkõpe'tẽsia/ *f* incompetence; **~tente** *a* incompetent
incompleto /ĩkõ'plɛtu/ *a* incomplete
incompreensí|vel /ĩkõpriẽ'sivew/ (*pl* **~veis**) *a* incomprehensible
inconcebí|vel /ĩkõse'bivew/ (*pl* **~veis**) *a* inconceivable
incondicio|nal /ĩkõdʒisio'naw/ (*pl* **~nais**) *a* unconditional; <*fã, partidário*> firm
inconformado /ĩkõfor'madu/ *a* unreconciled (**com** to)
inconfundí|vel /ĩkõfũ'dʒivew/ (*pl* **~veis**) *a* unmistakeable
inconsciente /ĩkõsi'ẽtʃi/ *a & m* unconscious
inconseqüente /ĩkõse'kwẽtʃi/ *a* inconsistent
incons|tância /ĩkõs'tãsia/ *f* changeability; **~tante** *a* changeable
inconstitucio|nal /ĩkõstʃitusio'naw/ (*pl* **~nais**) *a* unconstitutional
incontestá|vel /ĩkõtes'tavew/ (*pl* **~veis**) *a* indisputable
inconveniente /ĩkõveni'ẽtʃi/ *a* (*difícil*) inconvenient; (*desagradável*) annoying, tiresome; (*indecente*) unseemly □ *m* drawback
incorporar /ĩkorpo'rar/ *vt* incorporate
incorrer /ĩko'xer/ *vi* **~ em** <*multa etc*> incur
incorrigí|vel /ĩkoxi'ʒivew/ (*pl* **~veis**) *a* incorrigible
incrédulo /ĩ'krɛdulu/ *a* incredulous
incremen|tado /ĩkremẽ'tadu/ *a* (*fam*) stylish; **~tar** *vt* build up; (*fam*) jazz up; **~to** *m* development, growth
incriminar /ĩkrimi'nar/ *vt* incriminate
incrí|vel /ĩ'krivew/ (*pl* **~veis**) *a* incredible
incu|bação /ĩkuba'sãw/ *f* incubation; **~badora** *f* incubator; **~bar** *vt/i* incubate
inculto /ĩ'kuwtu/ *a* <*pessoa*> uneducated; <*terreno*> uncultivated
incum|bência /ĩkũ'bẽsia/ *f* task; **~bir** *vt* **~bir alg de aco/de ir** assign s.o. sth/to go □ *vi* **~bir a** be up to; **~bir-se de** take on
incurá|vel /ĩku'ravew/ (*pl* **~veis**) *a* incurable
incursão /ĩkur'sãw/ *f* incursion
incutir /ĩku'tʃir/ *vt* instil (**em** in)
indagar /ĩda'gar/ *vt* inquire (into)
inde|cência /ĩde'sẽsia/ *f* indecency; **~cente** *a* indecent
indecifrá|vel /ĩdesi'fravew/ (*pl* **~veis**) *a* indecipherable
indeciso /ĩde'sizu/ *a* undecided
indecoroso /ĩdeko'rozu/ *a* indecorous
indefi|nido /ĩdefi'nidu/ *a* indefinite; **~nível** (*pl* **~níveis**) *a* indefinable
indelé|vel /ĩde'lɛvew/ (*pl* **~veis**) *a* indelible
indelica|deza /ĩdelika'deza/ *f* impoliteness; (*uma*) impolite thing; **~do** *a* impolite
indeni|zação /ĩdeniza'sãw/ *f* compensation; **~zar** *vt* compensate
indepen|dência /ĩdepẽ'dẽsia/ *f* independence; **~dente** *a* independent
indescrití|vel /ĩdʒiskri'tʃivew/ (*pl* **~veis**) *a* indescribable
indesculpá|vel /ĩdʒiskuw'pavew/ (*pl* **~veis**) *a* inexcusable
indesejá|vel /ĩdeze'ʒavew/ (*pl* **~veis**) *a* undesirable
indestrutí|vel /ĩdʒistru'tʃivew/ (*pl* **~veis**) *a* indestructible
indeterminado /ĩdetermi'nadu/ *a* indeterminate
indevido /ĩde'vidu/ *a* undue
indexar /ĩdek'sar/ *vt* index; index-link <*salário, preços*>
Índia /'ĩdʒia/ *f* India
indiano /ĩdʒi'anu/ *a & m* Indian
indi|cação /ĩdʒika'sãw/ *f* indication; (*do caminho*) directions; (*nomeação*) nomination; (*recomendação*) recommendation; **~cador** *m* indicator; (*dedo*) index finger □ *a* indicative (**de** of); **~car** *vt* indicate; (*para cargo, prêmio*) nominate (**para** for); (*recomendar*) recommend; **~cativo** *a & m* indicative
índice /'ĩdʒisi/ *m* (*taxa*) rate; (*em livro etc*) index; **~ de audiência** ratings
indiciar /ĩdʒisi'ar/ *vt* charge
indício /ĩ'dʒisiu/ *m* sign, indication; (*de crime*) clue
indife|rença /ĩdʒife'rẽsa/ *f* indifference; **~rente** *a* indifferent
indígena /ĩ'dʒiʒena/ *a* indigenous, native □ *m/f* native
indiges|tão /ĩdʒiʒes'tãw/ *f* indigestion; **~to** *a* indigestible; (*fig*) heavy-going
indig|nação /ĩdʒigna'sãw/ *f* indignation; **~nado** *a* indignant; **~nar** *vt*

make indignant; ~nar-se *vpr* get indignant (com about)
indig|nidade /ĩdʒigni'dadʒi/ *f* indignity; ~no *a* <*pessoa*> unworthy; <*ato*> despicable
índio /'ĩdʒiu/ *a & m* Indian
indire|ta /ĩdʒi'rɛta/ *f* hint; ~to /ɛ/ *a* indirect
indis|creto /ĩdʒis'krɛtu/ *a* indiscreet; ~crição *f* indiscretion
indiscriminado /ĩdʒiskrimi'nadu/ *a* indiscriminate
indiscutí|vel /ĩdʒisku'tʃivew/ (*pl* ~veis) *a* unquestionable
indispensá|vel /ĩdʒispẽ'savew/ (*pl* ~veis) *a* indispensable
indisponí|vel /ĩdʒispo'nivew/ (*pl* ~veis) *a* unavailable
indis|por /ĩdʒis'por/ *vt* upset; ~por alg contra turn s.o. against; ~por-se *vpr* fall out (com with); ~posição *f* indisposition; ~posto *a* (*doente*) indisposed
indistinto /ĩdʒis'tʃĩtu/ *a* indistinct
individu|al /ĩdʒividu'aw/ (*pl* ~ais) *a* individual; ~alidade *f* individuality; ~alismo *m* individualism; ~alista *a & m/f* individualist
indivíduo /ĩdʒi'viduu/ *m* individual
indizí|vel /ĩdʒi'zivew/ (*pl* ~veis) *a* unspeakable
índole /'ĩdoli/ *f* nature
indo|lência /ĩdo'lẽsia/ *f* indolence; ~lente *a* indolent
indolor /ĩdo'lor/ *a* painless
Indonésia /ĩdo'nɛzia/ *f* Indonesia
indonésio /ĩdo'nɛziu/ *a & m* Indonesian
indubitá|vel /ĩdubi'tavew/ (*pl* ~veis) *a* undoubted
indul|gência /ĩduw'ʒẽsia/ *f* indulgence; ~gente *a* indulgent
indulto /ĩ'duwtu/ *m* pardon
indumentária /ĩdumẽ'taria/ *f* outfit
indústria /ĩ'dustria/ *f* industry
industri|al /ĩdustri'aw/ (*pl* ~ais) *a* industrial □ *m/f* industrialist; ~alizado *a* <*país*> industrialized; <*mercadoria*> manufactured; <*comida*> processed; ~alizar *vt* industrialize <*país, agricultura etc*>; process <*comida, lixo etc*>; ~oso /o/ *a* industrious
induzir /ĩdu'zir/ *vt* (*persuadir*) induce; (*inferir*) infer (de from); ~ em erro lead astray, mislead s.o.
inebriante /inebri'ãtʃi/ *a* intoxicating
inédito /i'nɛdʒitu/ *a* unheard-of, unprecedented; (*não publicado*) unpublished
ineficaz /inefi'kas/ *a* ineffective
inefici|ência /inefisi'ẽsia/ *f* inefficiency; ~ente *a* inefficient
inegá|vel /ine'gavew/ (*pl* ~veis) *a* undeniable
inépcia /i'nɛpsia/ *f* ineptitude
inepto /i'nɛptu/ *a* inept
inequívoco /ine'kivoku/ *a* unmistakeable
inércia /i'nɛrsia/ *f* inertia
inerente /ine'rẽtʃi/ *a* inherent (a in)
inerte /i'nɛrtʃi/ *a* inert
inesgotá|vel /inezgo'tavew/ (*pl* ~veis) *a* inexhaustible
inesperado /inespe'radu/ *a* unexpected
inesquecí|vel /ineske'sivew/ (*pl* ~veis) *a* unforgettable
inevitá|vel /inevi'tavew/ (*pl* ~veis) *a* inevitable
inexato /ine'zatu/ *a* inaccurate
inexis|tência /inezis'tẽsia/ *f* lack; ~tente *a* non-existent
inexperi|ência /inisperi'ẽsia/ *f* inexperience; ~ente *a* inexperienced
inexpressivo /inespre'sivu/ *a* expressionless
infalí|vel /ĩfa'livew/ (*pl* ~veis) *a* infallible
infame /ĩ'fami/ *a* despicable; (*péssimo*) dreadful
infâmia /ĩ'famia/ *f* disgrace
infância /ĩ'fãsia/ *f* childhood
infantaria /ĩfãta'ria/ *f* infantry
infan|til /ĩfã'tʃiw/ *a* <*roupa, livro*> children's; (*bobo*) childish; ~tilidade *f* childishness; (*uma*) childish thing
infarto /ĩ'fartu/ *m* heart attack
infec|ção /ĩfek'sãw/ *f* infection; ~cionar *vt* infect; ~cioso *a* infectious
infeliz /ĩfe'lis/ *a* (*não contente*) unhappy; (*inconveniente*) unfortunate; (*desgraçado*) wretched □ *m* (*desgraçado*) wretch; ~mente *adv* unfortunately
inferi|or /ĩferi'or/ *a* lower; (*em qualidade*) inferior (a to); ~oridade *f* inferiority
inferir /ĩfe'rir/ *vt* infer
infer|nal /ĩfer'naw/ (*pl* ~nais) *a* infernal; ~nizar *vt* ~nizar a vida dele make his life hell; ~no /ɛ/ *m* hell
infér|til /ĩ'fɛrtʃiw/ (*pl* ~teis) *a* infertile
infertilidade /ĩfertʃili'dadʒi/ *f* infertility
infestar /ĩfes'tar/ *vt* infest
infetar /ĩfe'tar/ *vt* infect
infidelidade /ĩfideli'dadʒi/ *f* infidelity
infi|el /ĩfi'ɛw/ (*pl* ~éis) *a* unfaithful
infiltrar /ĩfiw'trar/ *vt* infiltrate; ~-se em infiltrate
ínfimo /'ĩfimu/ *a* lowest; (*muito pequeno*) tiny
infindá|vel /ĩfĩ'davew/ (*pl* ~veis) *a* unending

infinidade /ĩfini'dadʒi/ *f* infinity; **uma ~ de** an infinite number of
infini|tesimal /ĩfinitezi'maw/ (*pl* **~tesimais**) *a* infinitesimal; **~tivo** *a & m* infinitive; **~to** *a* infinite □ *m* infinity
infla|ção /ĩfla'sãw/ *f* inflation; **~cionar** *vt* inflate; **~cionário** *a* inflationary; **~cionista** *a & m/f* inflationist
infla|mação /ĩflama'sãw/ *f* inflammation; **~mar** *vt* inflame; **~mar-se** *vpr* become inflamed; **~matório** *a* inflammatory; **~mável** (*pl* **~máveis**) *a* inflammable
in|flar *vt* inflate; **~flar-se** *vpr* inflate; **~flável** (*pl* **~fláveis**) *a* inflatable
infle|xibilidade /ĩfleksibili'dadʒi/ *f* inflexibility; **~xível** (*pl* **~xíveis**) *a* inflexible
infligir /ĩfli'ʒir/ *vt* inflict (**a** on)
influência /ĩflu'ẽsia/ *f* influence
influen|ciar /ĩfluẽsi'ar/ *vt* **~ciar (em)** influence; **~ciar-se** *vpr* be influenced; **~ciável** (*pl* **~ciáveis**) *a* open to influence; **~te** *a* influential
influir /ĩflu'ir/ *vi* **~ em** *ou* **sobre** influence
informação /ĩforma'sãw/ *f* information; (*uma*) a piece of information; (*mil*) intelligence; *pl* information
infor|mal /ĩfor'maw/ (*pl* **~mais**) *a* informal; **~malidade** *f* informality
infor|mar /ĩfor'mar/ *vt* inform; **~mar-se** *vpr* find out (**de** about); **~mática** *f* information technology; **~mativo** *a* informative; **~matizar** *vt* computerize; **~me** *m* (*mil*) piece of intelligence
infortúnio /ĩfor'tuniu/ *m* misfortune
infração /ĩfra'sãw/ *f* infringement
infra-estrutura /ĩfraistru'tura/ *f* infrastructure
infrator /ĩfra'tor/ *m* offender
infravermelho /ĩfraver'meʎu/ *a* infrared
infringir /ĩfrĩ'ʒir/ *vt* infringe
infrutífero /ĩfru'tʃiferu/ *a* fruitless
infundado /ĩfũ'dadu/ *a* unfounded
infundir /ĩfũ'dʒir/ *vt* (*insuflar*) infuse; (*incutir*) instil
infusão /ĩfu'zãw/ *f* infusion
ingenuidade /ĩʒenui'dadʒi/ *f* naivety
ingênuo /ĩ'ʒenuu/ *a* naive
Inglaterra /ĩgla'tɛxa/ *f* England
ingerir /ĩʒe'rir/ *vt* ingest; (*engolir*) swallow
in|glês /ĩ'gles/ *a* (*f* **~glesa**) English □ *m* (*f* **~glesa**) Englishman (*f* -woman); (*língua*) English; **os ~gleses** the English
ingra|tidão /ĩgratʃi'dãw/ *f* ingratitude; **~to** *a* ungrateful
ingrediente /ĩgredʒi'ẽtʃi/ *m* ingredient
íngreme /'ĩgrimi/ *a* steep
ingres|sar /ĩgre'sar/ *vi* **~sar em** join; **~so** *m* entry; (*bilhete*) ticket
inhame /i'ɲami/ *m* yam
ini|bição /inibi'sãw/ *f* inhibition; **~bir** *vt* inhibit
inici|ado /inisi'adu/ *m* initiate; **~al** (*pl* **~ais**) *a & f* initial; **~ar** *vt* (*começar*) begin; (*em ciência, seita etc*) initiate (**em** into) □ *vi* begin; **~ativa** *f* initiative
início /i'nisiu/ *m* beginning
inigualá|vel /inigwa'lavew/ (*pl* **~veis**) *a* unparalleled
inimaginá|vel /inimaʒi'navew/ (*pl* **~veis**) *a* unimaginable
inimi|go /ini'migu/ *a & m* enemy; **~zade** *f* enmity
ininterrupto /inĩte'xuptu/ *a* continuous
inje|ção /ĩʒe'sãw/ *f* injection; **~tado** *a* <*olhos*> bloodshot; **~tar** *vt* inject; **~tável** (*pl* **~táveis**) *a* <*droga*> intravenous
injúria /ĩ'ʒuria/ *f* insult
injuriar /ĩʒuri'ar/ *vt* insult
injus|tiça /ĩʒus'tʃisa/ *f* injustice; **~tiçado** *a* wronged; **~to** *a* unfair, unjust
ino|cência /ino'sẽsia/ *f* innocence; **~centar** *vt* clear (**de** of); **~cente** *a* innocent
inocular /inoku'lar/ *vt* inoculate
inócuo /i'nɔkuu/ *a* harmless
inodoro /ino'dɔru/ *a* odourless
inofensivo /inofẽ'sivu/ *a* harmless
inoportuno /inopor'tunu/ *a* inopportune
inorgânico /inor'ganiku/ *a* inorganic
inóspito /i'nɔspitu/ *a* inhospitable
ino|vação /inova'sãw/ *f* innovation; **~var** *vt/i* innovate
inoxidá|vel /inoksi'davew/ (*pl* **~veis**) *a* <*aço*> stainless
inquérito /ĩ'kɛritu/ *m* inquiry
inquie|tação /ĩkieta'sãw/ *f* concern; **~tador**, **~tante** *a* worrying; **~tar** *vt* worry; **~tar-se** *vpr* worry; **~to** /ɛ/ *a* uneasy
inquili|nato /ĩkili'natu/ *m* tenancy; **~no** *m* tenant
inquirir /ĩki'rir/ *vt* cross-examine <*testemunha*>
Inquisição /ĩkizi'sãw/ *f* **a ~** the Inquisition
insaciá|vel /ĩsasi'avew/ (*pl* **~veis**) *a* insatiable
insalubre /ĩsa'lubri/ *a* unhealthy
insatis|fação /ĩsatʃisfa'sãw/ *f* dissatisfaction; **~fatório** *a* unsatisfactory; **~feito** *a* dissatisfied

ins|crever /ĩskre'ver/ *vt* (*registrar*) register; (*gravar*) inscribe; **~crever-se** *vpr* register; (*em escola etc*) enrol; **~crição** *f* (*registro*) registration; (*em clube, escola*) enrolment; (*em monumento etc*) inscription

insegu|rança /ĩsegu'rãsa/ *f* insecurity; **~ro** *a* insecure

insemi|nação /ĩsemina'sãw/ *f* insemination; **~nar** *vt* inseminate

insen|satez /ĩsẽsa'tes/ *f* folly; **~sato** *a* foolish; **~sibilidade** *f* insensitivity; **~sível** (*pl* **~síveis**) *a* insensitive

insepará|vel /ĩsepa'ravew/ (*pl* **~veis**) *a* inseparable

inserção /ĩser'sãw/ *f* insertion

inserir /ĩse'rir/ *vt* insert; enter <*dados*>

inse|ticida /ĩsetʃi'sida/ *m* insecticide; **~to** /ɛ/ *m* insect

insígnia /ĩ'signia/ *f* insignia

insignifi|cância /ĩsignifi'kãsia/ *f* insignificance; **~cante** *a* insignificant

insincero /ĩsĩ'sɛru/ *a* insincere

insinu|ante /ĩsinu'ãtʃi/ *a* suggestive; **~ar** *vt/i* insinuate

insípido /ĩ'sipidu/ *a* insipid

insis|tência /ĩsis'tẽsia/ *f* insistence; **~tente** *a* insistent; **~tir** *vt/i* insist (**em** on)

insolação /ĩsola'sãw/ *f* sunstroke

inso|lência /ĩso'lẽsia/ *f* insolence; **~lente** *a* insolent

insólito /ĩ'sɔlitu/ *a* unusual

insolú|vel /ĩso'luvew/ (*pl* **~veis**) *a* insoluble

insone /ĩ'sɔni/ *a* <*noite*> sleepless; <*pessoa*> insomniac □ *m/f* insomniac

insônia /ĩ'sonia/ *f* insomnia

insosso /ĩ'sosu/ *a* bland; (*sem sabor*) tasteless; (*sem sal*) unsalted

inspe|ção /ĩspe'sãw/ *f* inspection; **~cionar** *vt* inspect; **~tor** *m* inspector

inspi|ração /ĩspira'sãw/ *f* inspiration; **~rar** *vt* inspire; **~rar-se** *vpr* take inspiration (**em** from)

instabilidade /ĩstabili'dadʒi/ *f* instability

insta|lação /ĩstala'sãw/ *f* installation; **~lar** *vt* install; **~lar-se** *vpr* install o.s.

instan|tâneo /ĩstã'taniu/ *a* instant; **~te** *m* instant

instaurar /ĩstaw'rar/ *vt* set up

instá|vel /ĩ'stavew/ (*pl* **~veis**) *a* unstable; <*tempo*> unsettled

insti|gação /ĩstʃiga'sãw/ *f* instigation; **~gante** *a* stimulating; **~gar** *vt* incite

instin|tivo /ĩstʃĩ'tʃivu/ *a* instinctive; **~to** *m* instinct

institu|cional /ĩstʃitusio'naw/ (*pl* **~cionais**) *a* institutional; **~ição** *f* institution; **~ir** *vt* set up; set <*prazo*>; **~to** *m* institute

instru|ção /ĩstru'sãw/ *f* instruction; **~ir** *vt* instruct; train <*recrutas*>; (*informar*) advise (**sobre** of)

instrumen|tal /ĩstrumẽ'taw/ (*pl* **~tais**) *a* instrumental; **~tista** *m/f* instrumentalist; **~to** *m* instrument

instru|tivo /ĩstru'tʃivu/ *a* instructive; **~tor** *m* instructor

insubstituí|vel /ĩsubistʃitu'ivew/ (*pl* **~veis**) *a* irreplaceable

insucesso /ĩsu'sesu/ *m* failure

insufici|ência /ĩsufisi'ẽsia/ *f* insufficiency; (*dos órgãos*) failure; **~ente** *a* insufficient

insulina /ĩsu'lina/ *f* insulin

insul|tar /ĩsuw'tar/ *vt* insult; **~to** *m* insult

insuperá|vel /ĩsupe'ravew/ (*pl* **~veis**) *a* <*problema*> insurmountable; <*qualidade*> unsurpassed

insuportá|vel /ĩsupor'tavew/ (*pl* **~veis**) *a* unbearable

insur|gente /ĩsur'ʒẽtʃi/ *a* & *m/f* insurgent; **~gir-se** *vpr* rise up, revolt; **~reição** *f* insurrection

intato /ĩ'tatu/ *a* intact

íntegra /'ĩtegra/ *f* full text; **na ~** in full

inte|gração /ĩtegra'sãw/ *f* integration; **~gral** (*pl* **~grais**) *a* whole; **arroz/pão ~gral** brown rice/bread; **~grante** *a* integral □ *m/f* member; **~grar** *vt* make up, form; **~grar-se em** become a part of; **~gridade** *f* integrity

íntegro /'ĩtegru/ *a* honest

intei|ramente /ĩtera'mẽtʃi/ *adv* completely; **~rar** *vt* (*informar*) fill in, inform (**de** about); **~rar-se** *vpr* find out (**de** about); **~riço** *a* in one piece; **~ro** *a* whole

intelec|to /ĩte'lɛktu/ *m* intellect; **~tual** (*pl* **~tuais**) *a* & *m/f* intellectual

inteli|gência /ĩteli'ʒẽsia/ *f* intelligence; **~gente** *a* clever, intelligent; **~gível** (*pl* **~gíveis**) *a* intelligible

intem|périe /ĩtẽ'pɛri/ *f* bad weather; **~pestivo** *a* ill-timed

inten|ção /ĩtẽ'sãw/ *f* intention; **segundas ~ções** ulterior motives

intencio|nado /ĩtẽsio'nadu/ *a* **bem ~nado** well-meaning; **~nal** (*pl* **~nais**) *a* intentional; **~nar** *vt* intend

inten|sidade /ĩtẽsi'dadʒi/ *f* intensity; **~sificar** *vt* intensify; **~sificar-se** *vpr* intensify; **~sivo** *a* intensive; **~so** *a* intense

intento /ĩ'tẽtu/ *m* intention

intera|ção /ĩtera'sãw/ *f* interaction; **~gir** *vi* interact; **~tivo** *a* interactive

inter|calar /ĩterka'lar/ *vt* insert; **~câmbio** *m* exchange; **~ceptar** *vt* intercept
intercontinen|tal /ĩterkõtʃinẽ'taw/ (*pl* **~tais**) *a* intercontinental
interdepen|dência /ĩterdepẽ'dẽsia/ *f* interdependence; **~dente** *a* interdependent
interdi|ção /ĩterdʒi'sãw/ *f* closure; (*jurid*) injunction; **~tar** *vt* close <*rua etc*>; (*proibir*) ban
interes|sante /ĩtere'sãtʃi/ *a* interesting; **~sar** *vt* interest □ *vi* be relevant; **~sar-se** *vpr* be interested (em *ou* por in); **~se** /e/ *m* interest; (*próprio*) self-interest; **~seiro** *a* self-seeking
interestadu|al /ĩteristadu'aw/ (*pl* **~ais**) *a* interstate
interface /ĩter'fasi/ *f* interface
interfe|rência /ĩterfe'rẽsia/ *f* interference; **~rir** *vi* interfere
interfone /ĩter'fɔni/ *m* intercom
ínterim /'ĩterĩ/ *m* interim; **nesse ~** in the interim
interino /ĩte'rinu/ *a* temporary
interior /ĩteri'or/ *a* inner; (*dentro do país*) internal, domestic □ *m* inside; (*do país*) country, interior
inter|jeição /ĩterʒej'sãw/ *f* interjection; **~ligar** *vt* interconnect; **~locutor** *m* interlocutor; **~mediário** *a* & *m* intermediary
intermédio /ĩter'mɛdʒiu/ *m* **por ~ de** through
interminá|vel /ĩtermi'navew/ (*pl* **~veis**) *a* interminable
intermitente /ĩtermi'tẽtʃi/ *a* intermittent
internacio|nal /ĩternasio'naw/ (*pl* **~nais**) *a* international
inter|nar *vt* intern <*preso*>; admit to hospital <*doente*>; **~nato** *m* boarding school; **~no** *a* internal
interpelar /ĩterpe'lar/ *vt* question
interpor /ĩter'por/ *vt* interpose; **~-se** *vpr* intervene
interpre|tação /ĩterpreta'sãw/ *f* interpretation; **~tar** *vt* interpret; perform <*papel, música*>; **intérprete** *m/f* (*de línguas*) interpreter; (*de teatro etc*) performer
interro|gação /ĩtexoga'sãw/ *f* interrogation; **~gar** *vt* interrogate, question; **~gativo** *a* interrogative; **~gatório** *m* interrogation
inter|romper /ĩtexõ'per/ *vt* interrupt; **~rupção** *f* interruption; **~ruptor** *m* switch
interurbano /ĩterur'banu/ *a* long-distance □ *m* trunk call
intervalo /ĩter'valu/ *m* interval
inter|venção /ĩtervẽ'sãw/ *f* intervention; **~vir** *vi* intervene
intesti|nal /ĩtestʃi'naw/ (*pl* **~nais**) *a* intestinal; **~no** *m* intestine
inti|mação /ĩtʃima'sãw/ *f* (*da justiça*) summons; **~mar** *vt* order; (*à justiça*) summon
intimidade /ĩtʃimi'dadʒi/ *f* intimacy; (*entre amigos*) closeness; (*vida íntima*) private life; **ter ~ com** be close to
intimidar /ĩtʃimi'dar/ *vt* intimidate; **~-se** *vpr* be intimidated
íntimo /'ĩtʃimu/ *a* intimate; <*amigo*> close; <*vida*> private □ *m* close friend
intitular /ĩtʃitu'lar/ *vt* entitle
intocá|vel /ĩto'kavew/ (*pl* **~veis**) *a* untouchable
intole|rância /ĩtole'rãsia/ *f* intolerance; **~rante** *a* intolerant; **~rável** (*pl* **~ráveis**) *a* intolerable
intoxi|cação /ĩtoksika'sãw/ *f* poisoning; **~cação alimentar** food poisoning; **~car** *vt* poison
intragá|vel /ĩtra'gavew/ (*pl* **~veis**) *a* <*comida*> inedible; <*pessoa*> unbearable
intransigente /ĩtrãzi'ʒẽtʃi/ *a* uncompromising
intransi|tável /ĩtrãzi'tavew/ (*pl* **~táveis**) *a* impassable; **~tivo** *a* intransitive
intratá|vel /ĩtra'tavew/ (*pl* **~veis**) *a* <*pessoa*> difficult
intra-uterino /ĩtraute'rinu/ *a* **dispositivo ~** intra-uterine device, IUD
intrépido /ĩ'trɛpidu/ *a* intrepid
intri|ga /ĩ'triga/ *f* intrigue; (*enredo*) plot; **~gante** *a* intriguing; **~gar** *vt* intrigue
intrincado /ĩtrĩ'kadu/ *a* intricate
intrínseco /ĩ'trĩsiku/ *a* intrinsic
introdu|ção /ĩtrodu'sãw/ *f* introduction; **~tório** *a* introductory; **~zir** *vt* introduce
intrometer-se /ĩtrome'tersi/ *vpr* interfere; **~tido** *a* interfering □ *m* busybody
introspec|ção /ĩtrospek'sãw/ *f* introspection; **~tivo** *a* introspective
introvertido /ĩtrover'tʃidu/ *a* introverted □ *m* introvert
intruso /ĩ'truzu/ *a* intrusive □ *m* intruder
intu|ição /ĩtui'sãw/ *f* intuition; **~ir** *vt* intuit; **~itivo** *a* intuitive; **~to** *m* purpose
inumano /inu'manu/ *a* inhuman
inumerá|vel /inume'ravew/ (*pl* **~veis**) *a* innumerable
inúmero /i'numeru/ *a* countless
inun|dação /inũda'sãw/ *f* flood; **~dar** *vt/i* flood
inusitado /inuzi'tadu/ *a* unusual
inú|til /i'nutʃiw/ (*pl* **~teis**) *a* useless

inutilmente /inutʃiw'mẽtʃi/ *adv* in vain

inutilizar /inutʃili'zar/ *vt* render useless; damage <*aparelho*>; thwart <*esforços*>

invadir /ĩva'dʒir/ *vt* invade

invali|dar /ĩvali'dar/ *vt* invalidate; disable <*pessoa*>; **~dez** /e/ *f* disability

inválido /ĩ'validu/ *a & m* invalid

invariá|vel /ĩvari'avew/ (*pl* **~veis**) *a* invariable

inva|são /ĩva'zãw/ *f* invasion; **~sor** *m* invader □ *a* invading

inve|ja /ĩ'vɛʒa/ *f* envy; **~jar** *vt* envy; **~jável** (*pl* **~jáveis**) *a* enviable; **~joso** /o/ *a* envious

inven|ção /ĩvẽ'sãw/ *f* invention; **~tar** *vt* invent; **~tário** *m* inventory; **~tivo** *a* inventive; **~tor** *m* inventor

inver|nar /ĩver'nar/ *vi* winter, spend the winter; **~no** /ɛ/ *m* winter

inverossí|mil /ĩvero'simiw/ (*pl* **~meis**) *a* improbable

inver|são /ĩver'sãw/ *f* inversion; **~so** *a* inverse; <*ordem*> reverse □ *m* reverse; **~ter** *vt* reverse; (*colocar de cabeça para baixo*) invert

invertebrado /ĩverte'bradu/ *a & m* invertebrate

invés /ĩ'vɛs/ *m* ao **~** de instead of

investida /ĩves'tʃida/ *f* attack

investidura /ĩvestʃi'dura/ *f* investiture

investi|gação /ĩvestʃiga'sãw/ *f* investigation; **~gar** *vt* investigate

inves|timento /ĩvestʃi'mẽtu/ *m* investment; **~tir** *vt/i* invest; **~tir contra** attack

inveterado /ĩvete'radu/ *a* inveterate

inviá|vel /ĩvi'avew/ (*pl* **~veis**) *a* impracticable

invicto /ĩ'viktu/ *a* unbeaten

invisí|vel /ĩvi'zivew/ (*pl* **~veis**) *a* invisible

invocar /ĩvo'kar/ *vt* invoke; (*fam*) pester

invólucro /ĩ'vɔlukru/ *m* covering

involuntário /ĩvolũ'tariu/ *a* involuntary

invulnerá|vel /ĩvuwne'ravew/ (*pl* **~veis**) *a* invulnerable

iodo /i'odu/ *m* iodine

ioga /i'ɔga/ *f* yoga

iogurte /io'gurtʃi/ *m* yoghurt

ir /ir/ *vi* go; **~-se** *vpr* go away; **vou voltar** I will come back; **vou melhorando** I am (gradually) getting better

ira /'ira/ *f* wrath

Irã /i'rã/ *m* Iran

iraniano /irani'anu/ *a & m* Iranian

Irão /i'rãw/ *m* (*Port*) Iran

Iraque /i'raki/ *m* Iraq

iraquiano /iraki'anu/ *a & m* Iraqui

Irlanda /ir'lãda/ *f* Ireland

irlan|dês /irlã'des/ *a* (*f* **~desa**) Irish □ *m* (*f* **~desa**) Irishman (*f* -woman); (*língua*) Irish; os **~deses** the Irish

irmã /ir'mã/ *f* sister

irmandade /irmã'dadʒi/ *f* (*associação*) brotherhood

irmão /ir'mãw/ (*pl* **~s**) *m* brother

ironia /iro'nia/ *f* irony

irônico /i'roniku/ *a* ironic

irracio|nal /ixasio'naw/ (*pl* **~nais**) *a* irrational

irradiar /ixadʒi'ar/ *vt* radiate; (*pelo rádio*) broadcast □ *vi* shine; **~-se** *vpr* spread, radiate

irre|al /ixe'aw/ (*pl* **~ais**) *a* unreal

irreconhecí|vel /ixekoɲe'sivew/ (*pl* **~veis**) *a* unrecognizable

irrecuperá|vel /ixekupe'ravew/ (*pl* **~veis**) *a* irretrievable

irrefletido /ixefle'tʃidu/ *a* rash

irregu|lar /ixegu'lar/ *a* irregular; (*inconstante*) erratic; **~laridade** *f* irregularity

irrelevante /ixele'vãtʃi/ *a* irrelevant

irrepará|vel /ixepa'ravew/ (*pl* **~veis**) *a* irreparable

irrepreensí|vel /ixepriẽ'sivew/ (*pl* **~veis**) *a* irreproachable

irrequieto /ixeki'ɛtu/ *a* restless

irresistí|vel /ixezis'tʃivew/ (*pl* **~veis**) *a* irresistible

irresoluto /ixezo'lutu/ *a* <*questão*> unresolved; <*pessoa*> indecisive

irresponsá|vel /ixespõ'savew/ (*pl* **~veis**) *a* irresponsible

irreverente /ixeve'rẽtʃi/ *a* irreverent

irri|gação /ixiga'sãw/ *f* irrigation; **~gar** *vt* irrigate

irrisório /ixi'zɔriu/ *a* derisory

irri|tação /ixita'sãw/ *f* irritation; **~tadiço** *a* irritable; **~tante** *a* irritating; **~tar** *vt* irritate; **~tar-se** *vpr* get irritated

irromper /ixõ'per/ *vi* **~ em** burst into

isca /'iska/ *f* bait

isen|ção /izẽ'sãw/ *f* exemption; **~tar** *vt* exempt; **~to** *a* exempt

Islã /iz'lã/ *m* Islam

islâmico /iz'lamiku/ *a* Islamic

isla|mismo /izla'mizmu/ *m* Islam; **~mita** *a & m/f* Muslim

islan|dês /izlã'des/ *a* (*f* **~desa**) Icelandic □ *m* (*f* **~desa**) Icelander; (*língua*) Icelandic

Islândia /iz'lãdʒia/ *f* Iceland

iso|lamento /izola'mẽtu/ *m* isolation; (*eletr*) insulation; **~lante** *a* insulating; **~lar** *vt* isolate; (*eletr*) insulate □ *vi* (*contra azar*) touch wood, (*Amer*) knock on wood

isopor /izo'por/ *m* polystyrene

isqueiro /is'keru/ *m* lighter

Israel /izxa'ɛw/ *m* Israel
israe|lense /izraj'lẽsi/ *a & m/f* Israeli; ~**lita** *a & m/f* Israelite
isso /'isu/ *pron* that; **por ~** therefore
isto /'istu/ *pron* this; ~ **é** that is
Itália /i'talia/ *f* Italy
italiano /itali'anu/ *a & m* Italian
itálico /i'taliku/ *a & m* italic
item /'itẽ/ *m* item
itine|rante /itʃine'rãtʃi/ *a* itinerant; ~**rário** *m* itinerary
Iugoslávia /iugoz'lavia/ *f* Yugoslavia
iugoslavo /iugoz'lavu/ *a & m* Yugoslavian

J

já /ʒa/ *adv* already; (*agora*) right away □ *conj* on the other hand; **desde ~** from now on; ~ **não** no longer; ~ **que** since; ~, ~ in no time
jabuticaba /ʒabutʃi'kaba/ *f* jaboticaba
jaca /'ʒaka/ *f* jack fruit
jacaré /ʒaka'rɛ/ *m* alligator
jacinto /ʒa'sĩtu/ *m* hyacinth
jactância /ʒak'tãsia/ *f* boasting
jade /'ʒadʒi/ *m* jade
jaguar /ʒagu'ar/ *m* jaguar
jagunço /ʒa'gũsu/ *m* hired gunman
jamais /ʒa'majs/ *adv* never
Jamaica /ʒa'majka/ *f* Jamaica
jamaicano /ʒamaj'kanu/ *a & m* Jamaican
jamanta /ʒa'mãta/ *f* juggernaut
janeiro /ʒa'neru/ *m* January
janela /ʒa'nɛla/ *f* window
jangada /ʒã'gada/ *f* (fishing) raft
janta /'ʒãta/ *f* (*fam*) dinner
jantar /ʒã'tar/ *m* dinner □ *vi* have dinner □ *vt* have for dinner
Japão /ʒa'pãw/ *m* Japan
japo|na /ʒa'pɔna/ *f* pea jacket □ *m/f* (*fam*) Japanese; ~**nês** *a & m* (*f* ~**nesa**) Japanese
jaqueira /ʒa'kera/ *f* jack-fruit tree
jaqueta /ʒa'keta/ *f* jacket
jarda /'ʒarda/ *f* yard
jar|dim /ʒar'dʒĩ/ *m* garden; ~**dim-de-infância** (*pl* ~**dins-de-infância**) *f* kindergarten
jardi|nagem /ʒardʒi'naʒẽ/ *f* gardening; ~**nar** *vi* garden; ~**neira** *f* (*calça*) dungarees; (*vestido*) pinafore dress, (*Amer*) jumper; (*ônibus*) open-sided bus; (*para flores*) flower stand; ~**neiro** *m* gardener
jargão /ʒar'gãw/ *m* jargon
jar|ra /'ʒaxa/ *f* pot; ~**ro** *m* jug
jasmim /ʒaz'mĩ/ *m* jasmine
jato /'ʒatu/ *m* jet
jaula /'ʒawla/ *f* cage
ja|zer /ʒa'zer/ *vi* lie; ~**zida** *f* deposit; ~**zigo** *m* grave
jazz /dʒaz/ *m* jazz; ~**ista** *m/f* jazz artist; ~**ístico** *a* jazzy
jeca /'ʒɛka/ *m/f* country bumpkin □ *a* countrified; (*cafona*) tacky; ~**-tatu** *m/f* country bumpkin
jei|tão /ʒej'tãw/ *m* (*fam*) individual style; ~**tinho** *m* knack; ~**to** *m* way; (*de pessoa*) manner; (*habilidade*) skill; **de qualquer ~to** anyway; **de ~to nenhum** no way; **pelo ~to** by the looks of things; **sem ~to** awkward; **dar um ~to** find a way; **dar um ~to em** (*arrumar*) tidy up; (*consertar*) fix; (*torcer*) twist <*pé etc*>; **ter ~to de** look like; **ter** *ou* **levar ~to para** be good at; **tomar ~to** pull one's socks up; ~**toso** /o/ *a* skilful; (*de aparência*) elegant
je|juar /ʒeʒu'ar/ *vi* fast; ~**jum** *m* fast
Jeová /ʒio'va/ *m* **testemunha de ~** Jehovah's witness
jérsei /'ʒersej/ *m* jersey
jesuíta /ʒezu'ita/ *a & m/f* Jesuit
Jesus /ʒe'zus/ *m* Jesus
jibóia /ʒi'bɔja/ *f* boa constrictor
jiboiar /ʒiboj'ar/ *vi* have a rest to let one's dinner go down
jiló /ʒi'lɔ/ *m* okra
jipe /'ʒipi/ *m* jeep
jiu-jitsu /ʒiu'ʒitsu/ *m* jiu-jitsu
joa|lheiro /ʒoa'ʎeru/ *m* jeweller; ~**lheria** *f* jeweller's (shop)
joaninha /ʒoa'niɲa/ *f* ladybird, (*Amer*) ladybug; (*alfinete*) safety pin
joão-ninguém /ʒoãwnĩ'gẽj/ (*pl* **joões-ninguém**) *m* nobody
jocoso /ʒo'kozu/ *a* jocular
joe|lhada /ʒoe'ʎada/ *f* blow with the knee; ~**lheira** *f* kneepad; ~**lho** /e/ *m* knee; **de ~lhos** kneeling
jo|gada /ʒo'gada/ *f* move; ~**gado** *a* <*pessoa*> flat out; <*papéis, roupa etc*> lying around; ~**gador** *m* player; (*no cassino etc*) gambler; ~**gar** *vt* play; (*atirar*) throw; (*arriscar no jogo*) gamble □ *vi* play; (*no cassino etc*) gamble; (*balançar*) toss; ~**gar fora** throw away; ~**gatina** *f* gambling
jogging /'ʒɔgĩ/ *m* (*cooper*) jogging; (*roupa*) track suit
jogo /'ʒogu/ *m* (*partida*) game; (*ação de jogar*) play; (*jogatina*) gambling; (*conjunto*) set; **em ~** at stake; ~ **de cintura** (*fig*) flexibility, room to manoeuvre; ~ **de luz** lighting effects; ~ **do bicho** illegal numbers game; **Jogos Olímpicos** Olympic Games; ~**da-velha** *m* noughts and crosses
joguete /ʒo'getʃi/ *m* plaything
jóia /'ʒɔja/ *f* jewel; (*propina*) entry fee □ *a* (*fam*) great

joio /'ʒoju/ *m* chaff; **separar o ~ do trigo** separate the wheat from the chaff

jóquei /'ʒɔkej/ *m* (*pessoa*) jockey; (*lugar*) race course

Jordânia /ʒor'dania/ *f* Jordan

jordaniano /ʒordani'anu/ *a & m* Jordanian

jor|nada /ʒor'nada/ *f* (*viagem*) journey; **~nada de trabalho** working day; **~nal** (*pl* **~nais**) *m* newspaper; (*na TV*) news

jorna|leco /ʒorna'lɛku/ *m* rag, scandal sheet; **~leiro** *m* (*vendedor*) newsagent, (*Amer*) newsdealer; (*entregador*) paperboy; **~lismo** *m* journalism; **~lista** *m/f* journalist; **~lístico** *a* journalistic

jor|rar /ʒo'xar/ *vi* gush, spurt; **~ro** /'ʒoxu/ *m* spurt

jota /'ʒɔta/ *m* letter J

jovem /'ʒɔvẽ/ *a* young; (*criado por jovens*) youth □ *m/f* young man (*f* -woman); *pl* young people

jovi|al /ʒovi'aw/ (*pl* **~ais**) *a* jovial

juba /'ʒuba/ *f* mane

jubileu /ʒubi'lew/ *m* jubilee

júbilo /'ʒubilu/ *m* joy

ju|daico /ʒu'dajku/ *a* Jewish; **~daísmo** *m* Judaism; **~deu** *a* (*f* **~dia**) Jewish □ *m* (*f* **~dia**) Jew; **~diação** *f* ill-treatment; (*uma*) terrible thing; **~diar** *vi* **~diar de** ill-treat

judici|al /ʒudʒisi'aw/ (*pl* **~ais**) *a* judicial; **~ário** *a* judicial □ *m* judiciary; **~oso** /o/ *a* judicious

judô /ʒu'do/ *m* judo

judoca /ʒu'dɔka/ *m/f* judo player

jugo /'ʒugu/ *m* yoke

juiz /ʒu'is/ *m* (*f* **juíza**) judge; (*em jogos*) referee

juizado /ʒui'zadu/ *m* court

juízo /ʒu'izu/ *m* judgement; (*tino*) sense; (*tribunal*) court; **perder o ~** lose one's head; **ter ~** be sensible; **tomar** *ou* **criar ~** come to one's senses

jujuba /ʒu'ʒuba/ *f* (*bala*) fruit jelly

jul|gamento /ʒuwga'mẽtu/ *m* judgement; **~gar** *vt* judge; pass judgement on <*réu*>; (*imaginar*) think; **~gar-se** *vpr* consider o.s.

julho /'ʒuʎu/ *m* July

jumento /ʒu'mẽtu/ *m* donkey

junção /ʒũ'sãw/ *f* join; (*ação*) joining

junco /'ʒũku/ *m* reed

junho /'ʒuɲu/ *m* June

juni|no /ʒu'ninu/ *a* **festa ~na** St John's Day festival

júnior /'ʒunior/ *a & m* junior

jun|ta /'ʒũta/ *f* board; (*pol*) junta; **~tar** *vt* (*acrescentar*) add; (*uma coisa a outra*) join; (*uma coisa com outra*) combine; save up <*dinheiro*>; gather up <*papéis, lixo etc*> □ *vi* gather; **~tar-se** *vpr* join together; <*multidão*> gather; <*casal*> live together; **~tar-se a** join; **~to** *a* together □ *adv* together; **~to a** next to; **~to com** together with

ju|ra /'ʒura/ *f* vow; **~rado** *m* juror; **~ramentado** *a* accredited; **~ramento** *m* oath; **~rar** *vt/i* swear; **~ra?** (*fam*) really?

júri /'ʒuri/ *m* jury

jurídico /ʒu'ridʒiku/ *a* legal

juris|consulto /ʒuriskõ'suwtu/ *m* legal advisor; **~dição** *f* jurisdiction; **~prudência** *f* jurisprudence; **~ta** *m/f* jurist

juros /'ʒurus/ *m pl* interest

jus /ʒus/ *m* **fazer ~ a** live up to

jusante /ʒu'zãtʃi/ *f* **a ~** downstream

justamente /ʒusta'mẽtʃi/ *adv* exactly; (*com justiça*) fairly

justapor /ʒusta'por/ *vt* juxtapose

justi|ça /ʒus'tʃisa/ *f* (*perante a lei*) justice; (*para com outros*) fairness; (*tribunal*) court; **~ceiro** *a* fair-minded □ *m* vigilante

justifi|cação /ʒustʃifika'sãw/ *f* justification; **~car** *vt* justify; **~cativa** *f* justification; **~cável** (*pl* **~cáveis**) *a* justifiable

justo /'ʒustu/ *a* fair; (*apertado*) tight □ *adv* just

juve|nil /ʒuve'niw/ (*pl* **~nis**) *a* youthful; (*para jovens*) for young people; <*time, torneio*> junior □ *m* junior championship

juventude /ʒuvẽ'tudʒi/ *f* youth

K

karaokê /karao'ke/ *m* karaoke

kart /'kartʃi/ (*pl* **~s**) *m* go-kart

ketchup /ke'tʃupi/ *m* ketchup

kit /'kitʃi/ (*pl* **~s**) *m* kit

kitchenette /kitʃe'nɛtʃi/ *f* bedsitter

Kuwait /ku'wajtʃi/ *m* Kuwait

kuwaitiano /kuwajtʃi'anu/ *a & m* Kuwaiti

L

lá /la/ *adv* there; **até ~** <*ir*> there; <*esperar etc*> until then; **por ~** (*naquela direção*) that way; (*naquele lugar*) around there; **~ fora** outside; **sei ~** how should I know?

lã /lã/ *f* wool

labareda /laba'reda/ *f* flame

lábia /'labia/ *f* flannel; **ter ~** have the gift of the gab

lábio /'labio/ *m* lip

labirinto /labi'rĩtu/ *m* labyrinth
laboratório /labora'tɔriu/ *m* laboratory
laborioso /labori'ozu/ *a* hard-working
labu|ta /la'buta/ *f* drudgery; ~**tar** *vi* slog
laca /'laka/ *f* lacquer
laçada /la'sada/ *f* slipknot
lacaio /la'kaju/ *m* lackey
la|çar /la'sar/ *vt* lasso <*boi*>; ~**ço** *m* bow; (*de vaqueiro*) lasso; (*vínculo*) tie
lacônico /la'koniku/ *a* laconic
lacraia /la'kraja/ *f* centipede
la|crar /la'krar/ *vt* seal; ~**cre** *m* (*substância*) sealing wax; (*fechamento*) seal
lacri|mejar /lakrime'ʒar/ *vi* water; ~**mogêneo** *a* <*gás*> tear; <*filme*> tearjerking; ~**moso** /o/ *a* tearful
lácteo /'laktʃiu/ *a* milk; **Via Láctea** Milky Way
lacticínio /laktʃi'siniu/ *m veja* laticínio
lacuna /la'kuna/ *f* gap
ladainha /lada'iɲa/ *f* litany
la|dear /ladʒi'ar/ *vt* flank; sidestep <*dificuldade*>; ~**deira** *f* slope
lado /'ladu/ *m* side; **o ~ de cá/lá** this/that side; **ao ~ de** beside; **~ a ~** side by side; **para este ~** this way; **por outro ~** on the other hand
la|drão /la'drãw/ *m* (*f* ~**dra**) thief; (*tubo*) overflow pipe □ *a* thieving
ladrar /la'drar/ *vi* bark
ladri|lhar /ladri'ʎar/ *vt* tile; ~**lho** *m* tile
ladroagem /ladro'aʒẽ/ *f* stealing
lagar|ta /la'garta/ *f* caterpillar; (*numa roda*) caterpillar track; ~**tear** *vi* bask in the sun; ~**tixa** *f* gecko; ~**to** *m* lizard
lago /'lagu/ *m* lake
lagoa /la'goa/ *f* lagoon
lagos|ta /la'gosta/ *f* lobster; ~**tim** *m* crayfish, (*Amer*) crawfish
lágrima /'lagrima/ *f* tear
laia /'laja/ *f* kind
laico /'lajku/ *adj* <*pessoa*> lay; <*ensino*> secular
laivos /'lajvus/ *m pl* traces
laje /'laʒi/ *m* flagstone; ~**ar** *vt* pave
lajota /la'ʒɔta/ *f* small paving stone
lama /'lama/ *f* mud; ~**çal** (*pl* ~**çais**) *m* bog; ~**cento** *a* muddy
lamba|da /lã'bada/ *f* lambada; ~**teria** *f* lambada club
lam|ber /lã'ber/ *vt* lick; ~**bida** *f* lick
lambreta /lã'breta/ *f* moped
lambris /lã'bris/ *m pl* panelling
lambuzar /lãbu'zar/ *vt* smear; ~**-se** *vpr* get sticky
lamen|tar /lamẽ'tar/ *vt* (*lastimar*) lament; (*sentir*) be sorry; ~**tar-se de** lament; ~**tável** (*pl* ~**táveis**) *a* lamentable; ~**to** *m* lament
lâmina /'lamina/ *f* blade; (*de persiana*) slat
laminar /lami'nar/ *vt* laminate
lâmpada /'lãpada/ *f* light bulb; (*abajur*) lamp
lampe|jar /lãpe'ʒar/ *vi* flash; ~**jo** /e/ *m* flash
lampião /lãpi'ãw/ *m* lantern
lamúria /la'muria/ *f* moaning
lamuriar-se /lamuri'arsi/ *vpr* moan (de about)
lan|ça /'lãsa/ *f* spear; ~**çamento** *m* (*de navio, foguete, produto*) launch; (*de filme, disco*) release; (*novo produto*) new line; (*novo filme, disco*) release; (*novo livro*) new title; (*em livro comercial*) entry; ~**çar** *vt* (*atirar*) throw; launch <*navio, foguete, novo produto, livro*>; release <*filme, disco*>; (*em livro comercial*) enter; (*em leilão*) bid; ~**çar mão de** make use of; ~**ce** *m* (*num filme, jogo*) bit, moment; (*episódio*) episode; (*questão*) matter; (*jogada*) move; (*em leilão*) bid; (*de escada*) flight; (*de casas*) row
lancha /'lãʃa/ *f* launch
lan|char /lã'ʃar/ *vi* have a snack □ *vt* have a snack of; ~**che** *m* snack; ~**chonete** /ɛ/ *f* snack bar
lancinante /lãsi'nãtʃi/ *a* <*dor*> shooting; <*grito*> piercing
lânguido /'lãgidu/ *a* languid
lantejoula /lãte'ʒola/ *f* sequin
lanter|na /lã'tɛrna/ *f* lantern; (*de bolso*) torch, (*Amer*) flashlight; ~**nagem** *f* panel-beating; (*oficina*) body-shop; ~**ninha** *m/f* usher (*f* usherette)
lanugem /la'nuʒẽ/ *f* down
lapela /la'pɛla/ *f* lapel
lapidar /lapi'dar/ *vt* cut <*pedra preciosa*>; (*fig*) polish
lápide /'lapidʒi/ *f* tombstone
lápis /'lapis/ *m invar* pencil
lapiseira /lapi'zera/ *f* propelling pencil; (*caixa*) pencil box
Lapônia /la'ponia/ *f* Lappland
lapso /'lapsu/ *m* lapse
la|quê /la'ke/ *m* lacquer; ~**quear** *vt* lacquer
lar /lar/ *m* home
laran|ja /la'rãʒa/ *f* orange □ *a invar* orange; ~**jada** *f* orangeade; ~**jeira** *f* orange tree
lareira /la'rera/ *f* hearth, fireplace
lar|gada /lar'gada/ *f* start; **dar a ~gada** start off; ~**gar** *vt* (*soltar*) let go of; give up <*estudos, emprego etc*>; ~**gar de fumar** give up smoking; ~**go** *a* wide; <*roupa*> loose □ *m* (*praça*) square; **ao ~go** (*no alto-mar*) out at sea; ~**gura** *f* width
larin|ge /la'rĩʒi/ *f* larynx; ~**gite** *f* laryngitis
larva /'larva/ *f* larva

lasanha /la'zaɲa/ *f* lasagna
las|ca /'laska/ *f* chip; **~car** *vt/i* chip; **de ~car** (*fam*) awful
lástima /'lastʃima/ *f* shame
lastro /'lastru/ *m* ballast
la|ta /'lata/ *f* (*material*) tin; (*recipiente*) tin, (*Amer*) can; **~ta de lixo** dustbin, (*Amer*) trash can; **~tão** *m* brass
late|jante /late'ʒãtʃi/ *a* throbbing; **~jar** *vi* throb
latente /la'tẽtʃi/ *a* latent
late|ral /late'raw/ (*pl* **~rais**) *a* side, lateral
laticínio /latʃi'siniu/ *m* dairy product
latido /la'tʃidu/ *m* bark
lati|fundiário /latʃifũdʒi'ariu/ *a* landowning □ *m* landowner; **~fúndio** *m* estate
latim /la'tʃĩ/ *m* Latin
latino /la'tʃinu/ *a* & *m* Latin; **~-americano** *a* & *m* Latin American
latir /la'tʃir/ *vi* bark
latitude /latʃi'tudʒi/ *f* latitude
lauda /'lawda/ *f* side
laudo /'lawdu/ *m* report, findings
lava /'lava/ *f* lava
lava|bo /la'vabu/ *m* toilet; **~dora** *f* washing machine; **~gem** *f* washing; **~gem a seco** dry cleaning; **~gem cerebral** brainwashing
lavanda /la'vãda/ *f* lavender
lavanderia /lavãde'ria/ *f* laundry
lavar /la'var/ *vt* wash; **~ a seco** dry-clean; **~-se** *vpr* wash
lavatório /lava'tɔriu/ *m* (*Port*) washbasin
lavoura /la'vora/ *f* (*agricultura*) farming; (*terreno*) field
lav|rador /lavra'dor/ *m* farmhand; **~rar** *vt* work; draw up <*documento*>
laxante /la'ʃãtʃi/ *a* & *m* laxative
lazer /la'zer/ *m* leisure
le|al /le'aw/ (*pl* **~ais**) *a* loyal; **~aldade** *f* loyalty
leão /le'ãw/ *m* lion; **Leão** (*signo*) Leo; **~-de-chácara** (*pl* **leões-de-chácara**) *m* bouncer
lebre /'lɛbri/ *f* hare
lecionar /lesio'nar/ *vt/i* teach
le|gação /lega'sãw/ *f* legation; **~gado** *m* (*pessoa*) legate; (*herança*) legacy
le|gal /le'gaw/ (*pl* **~gais**) *a* legal; (*fam*) good; <*pessoa*> nice; **tá ~gal** OK; **~galidade** *f* legality; **~galizar** *vt* legalize
legar /le'gar/ *vt* bequeath
legenda /le'ʒẽda/ *f* (*de quadro*) caption; (*de filme*) subtitle; (*inscrição*) inscription
legi|ão /leʒi'ãw/ *f* legion; **~onário** *m* (*romano*) legionary; (*da legião estrangeira*) legionnaire
legis|lação /leʒizla'sãw/ *f* legislation; **~lador** *m* legislator; **~lar** *vi* legislate; **~lativo** *a* legislative □ *m* legislature; **~latura** *f* legislature; **~ta** *m/f* legal expert
legiti|mar /leʒitʃi'mar/ *vt* legitimize; **~midade** *f* legitimacy
legítimo /le'ʒitʃimu/ *a* legitimate
legí|vel /le'ʒivew/ (*pl* **~veis**) *a* legible
légua /'lɛgwa/ *f* league
legume /le'gumi/ *m* vegetable
lei /lej/ *f* law
leigo /'lejgu/ *a* lay □ *m* layman
lei|lão /lej'lãw/ *m* auction; **~loar** *vt* auction; **~loeiro** *m* auctioneer
leitão /lej'tãw/ *m* sucking pig
lei|te /'lejtʃi/ *m* milk; **~te condensado/desnatado** condensed/skimmed milk; **~teira** *f* (*jarro*) milk jug; (*panela*) milk saucepan; **~teiro** *m* milkman □ *a* <*vaca*> dairy
leito /'lejtu/ *m* bed
leitor /lej'tor/ *m* reader
leitoso /lej'tozu/ *a* milky
leitura /lej'tura/ *f* (*ação*) reading; (*material*) reading matter
lema /'lema/ *m* motto
lem|brança /lẽ'brãsa/ *f* memory; (*presente*) souvenir; **~brar** *vt/i* remember; **~brar-se de** remember; **~brar aco a alg** remind s.o. of sth; **~brete** /e/ *m* reminder
leme /'lemi/ *m* rudder
len|ço /'lẽsu/ *m* (*para o nariz*) handkerchief; (*para vestir*) scarf; **~çol** /ɔ/ (*pl* **~çóis**) *m* sheet
len|da /'lẽda/ *f* legend; **~dário** *a* legendary
lenha /'leɲa/ *f* firewood; (*uma*) log; **~dor** *m* woodcutter
lente /'lẽtʃi/ *f* lens; **~ de contato** contact lens
lentidão /lẽtʃi'dãw/ *f* slowness
lentilha /lẽ'tʃiʎa/ *f* lentil
lento /'lẽtu/ *a* slow
leoa /le'oa/ *f* lioness
leopardo /lio'pardu/ *m* leopard
le|pra /'lɛpra/ *f* leprosy; **~proso** /o/ *a* leprous □ *m* leper
leque /'lɛki/ *m* fan; (*fig*) array
ler /ler/ *vt/i* read
ler|deza /ler'deza/ *f* sluggishness; **~do** /ɛ/ *a* sluggish
le|são /le'zãw/ *f* lesion, injury; **~sar** *vt* damage
lésbi|ca /'lɛzbika/ *f* lesbian; **~co** *a* lesbian
lesionar /lezio'nar/ *vt* injure
lesma /'lezma/ *f* slug
leste /'lɛstʃi/ *m* east
le|tal /le'taw/ (*pl* **~tais**) *a* lethal
le|tão /le'tãw/ *a* & *m* (*f* **~tã**) Latvian
letargia /letar'ʒia/ *f* lethargy
letivo /le'tʃivu/ *a* **ano ~** academic year

Letônia /le'tonia/ *f* Latvia
letra /'letra/ *f* letter; (*de música*) lyrics, words; (*caligrafia*) writing; **Letras** Modern Languages; **ao pé da ~** literally; **com todas as ~s** in no uncertain terms; **tirar de ~** take in one's stride; **~ de fôrma** block letter
letreiro /le'treru/ *m* sign
leucemia /lewse'mia/ *f* leukaemia
leva /ɛ/ *f* batch
levado /le'vadu/ *a* naughty
levan|tamento /levãta'mẽtu/ *m* (*enquete*) survey; (*rebelião*) uprising; **~tamento de pesos** weightlifting; **~tar** *vt* raise; lift <*peso*> □ *vi* get up; **~tar-se** *vpr* get up; (*revoltar-se*) rise up
levante /le'vãtʃi/ *m* east
levar /le'var/ *vt* take; lead <*vida*>; get <*tapa, susto etc*> □ *vi* lead (a to)
leve /'lɛvi/ *a* light; (*não grave*) slight; **de ~** lightly
levedura /leve'dura/ *f* yeast
leveza /le'veza/ *f* lightness
levi|andade /leviã'dadʒi/ *f* frivolity; **~ano** *a* frivolous
levitar /levi'tar/ *vi* levitate
lexi|cal /leksi'kaw/ (*pl* **~cais**) *a* lexical
léxico /'leksiku/ *m* lexicon
lexicografia /leksikogra'fia/ *f* lexicography
lhe /ʎi/ *pron* (*a ele*) to him; (*a ela*) to her; (*a você*) to you; **~s** *pron* to them; (*a vocês*) to you
liba|nês /liba'nes/ *a & m* (*f* **~nesa**) Lebanese
Líbano /'libanu/ *m* Lebanon
libélula /li'bɛlula/ *f* dragonfly
libe|ração /libera'sãw/ *f* release; **~ral** (*pl* **~rais**) *a & m* liberal; **~ralismo** *m* liberalism; **~ralizar** *vt* liberalize; **~rar** *vt* release
liberdade /liber'dadʒi/ *f* freedom; **pôr em ~** set free; **~ condicional** probation
líbero /'liberu/ *m* sweeper
liber|tação /liberta'sãw/ *f* liberation; **~tar** *vt* free
Líbia /'libia/ *f* Libya
líbio /'libiu/ *a & m* Libyan
libi|dinoso /libidʒi'nozu/ *a* lecherous; **~do** *f* libido
li|bra /'libra/ *f* pound; **Libra** (*signo*) Libra; **~briano** *a & m* Libran
lição /li'sãw/ *f* lesson
licen|ça /li'sẽsa/ *f* leave; (*documento*) licence; **com ~ça** excuse me; **de ~ça** on leave; **sob ~ça** under licence; **~ciar** *vt* (*autorizar*) license; (*dar férias a*) give leave to; **~ciar-se** *vpr* (*tirar férias*) take leave; (*formar-se*) graduate; **~ciatura** *f* degree; **~cioso** /o/ *a* licentious
liceu /li'sew/ *m* (*Port*) secondary school, (*Amer*) high school
licor /li'kor/ *m* liqueur
lida /'lida/ *f* slog, grind; (*leitura*) read
lidar /li'dar/ *vt/i* **~ com** deal with
lide /'lidʒi/ *f* (*trabalho*) work
líder /'lider/ *m/f* leader
lide|rança /lide'rãsa/ *f* (*de partido etc*) leadership; (*em corrida, jogo etc*) lead; **~rar** *vt* lead
lido /'lidu/ *a* well-read
liga /'liga/ *f* (*aliança*) league; (*tira*) garter; (*presilha*) suspender; (*de metais*) alloy
li|gação /liga'sãw/ *f* connection; (*telefônica*) call; (*amorosa*) liaison; **~gada** *f* call, ring; **~gado** *a* <*luz, TV*> on; **~gado em** attached to <*pessoa*>; hooked on <*droga*>; **~gamento** *m* ligament; **~gar** *vt* join, connect; switch on <*luz, TV etc*>; start up <*carro*>; bind <*amigos*> □ *vi* ring up, call; **~gar para** (*telefonar*) ring, call; (*dar importância*) care about; (*dar atenção*) pay attention to; **~gar-se** *vpr* join
ligeiro /li'ʒeru/ *a* light; <*ferida, melhora*> slight; (*ágil*) nimble
lilás /li'las/ *m* lilac □ *a invar* mauve
lima[1] /'lima/ *f* (*ferramenta*) file
lima[2] /'lima/ *f* (*fruta*) sweet orange
limão /li'mãw/ *m* lime; (*amarelo*) lemon
limar /li'mar/ *vt* file
limeira /li'mera/ *f* sweet orange tree
limiar /limi'ar/ *m* threshold
limi|tação /limita'sãw/ *f* limitation; **~tar** *vt* limit; **~tar-se** *vpr* limit o.s.; **~tar(-se) com** border on; **~te** *m* limit; (*de terreno*) boundary; **passar dos ~tes** go too far; **~te de velocidade** speed limit
limo|eiro /limo'eru/ *m* lime tree; **~nada** *f* lemonade
lim|pador /lĩpa'dor/ *m* **~pador de pára-brisas** windscreen wiper; **~par** *vt* clean; wipe <*lágrimas, suor*>; (*fig*) clean up <*cidade, organização*>; **~peza** /e/ *f* (*ato*) cleaning; (*qualidade*) cleanness; (*fig*) clean-up; **~peza pública** sanitation; **~po** *a* clean; <*céu, consciência*> clear; <*lucro*> net, clear; (*fig*) pure; **passar a ~po** write up <*trabalho*>; (*fig*) sort out <*vida*>; **tirar a ~po** get to the bottom of <*caso*>
limusine /limu'zini/ *f* limousine
lince /'lĩsi/ *m* lynx
lindo /'lĩdu/ *a* beautiful
linear /lini'ar/ *a* linear
lingote /lĩ'gɔtʃi/ *m* ingot
língua /'lĩgwa/ *f* (*na boca*) tongue; (*idioma*) language; **~ materna** mother tongue

linguado /lĩ'gwadu/ *m* sole

lingua|gem /lĩ'gwaʒẽ/ *f* language; **~jar** *m* speech, dialect

lingüeta /lĩ'gweta/ *f* bolt

lingüiça /lĩ'gwisa/ *f* pork sausage

lin|güista /lĩ'gwiʃta/ *m/f* linguist; **~güística** *f* linguistics; **~güístico** *a* linguistic

linha /'liɲa/ *f* line; (*fio*) thread; **perder a ~** lose one's cool; **~ aérea** airline; **~ de fogo** firing line; **~ de montagem** assembly line; **~gem** *f* lineage

linho /'liɲu/ *m* linen; (*planta*) flax

linóleo /li'nɔliu/ *m* lino(leum)

lipoaspiração /lipoaspira'sãw/ *f* liposuction

liqui|dação /likida'sãw/ *f* liquidation; (*de loja*) clearance sale; (*de conta*) settlement; **~dar** *vt* liquidate; settle <*conta*>; pay off <*dívida*>; sell off, clear <*mercadorias*>

liqüidificador /likwidʒifika'dor/ *m* liquidizer

líquido /'likidu/ *a* liquid; <*lucro, salário*> net □ *m* liquid

líri|ca /'lirika/ *f* (*mus*) lyrics; (*poesia*) lyric poetry; **~co** *a* lyrical; <*poesia*> lyric

lírio /'liriu/ *m* lily

Lisboa /liz'boa/ *f* Lisbon

lisboeta /lizbo'eta/ *a & m/f* (person) from Lisbon

liso /'lizu/ *a* smooth; (*sem desenho*) plain; <*cabelo*> straight; (*fam: duro*) broke

lison|ja /li'zõʒa/ *f* flattery; **~jear** *vt* flatter

lista /'lista/ *f* list; (*listra*) stripe; **~ telefônica** telephone directory

listra /'listra/ *f* stripe; **~do** *a* striped, stripey

lite|ral /lite'raw/ (*pl* **~rais**) *a* literal; **~rário** *a* literary; **~ratura** *f* literature

litígio /li'tʃiʒiu/ *m* dispute; (*jurid*) lawsuit

lito|ral /lito'raw/ (*pl* **~rais**) *m* coastline; **~râneo** *a* coastal

litro /'litru/ *m* litre

Lituânia /litu'ania/ *f* Lithuania

lituano /litu'anu/ *a & m* Lithuanian

living /'livĩ/ (*pl* **~s**) *m* living room

livrar /li'vrar/ *vt* free; (*salvar*) save; **~-se** *vpr* escape; **~-se de** get rid of

livraria /livra'ria/ *f* bookshop

livre /'livri/ *a* free; **~ de impostos** tax-free; **~-arbítrio** *m* free will

liv|reiro /li'vreru/ *m* bookseller; **~ro** *m* book; **~ro de consulta** reference book; **~ro de cozinha** cookery book; **~ro de texto** text book

li|xa /'liʃa/ *f* (*de unhas*) emery board; (*para madeira etc*) sandpaper; **~xar** *vt* sand <*madeira*>; file <*unhas*>; **estou me ~xando** (*fam*) I couldn't care less

li|xeira /li'ʃera/ *f* dustbin, (*Amer*) garbage can; **~xeiro** *m* dustman, (*Amer*) garbage collector; **~xo** rubbish, (*Amer*) garbage; (*atômico*) waste

lobisomem /lobi'zomẽ/ *m* werewolf

lobo /'lobu/ *m* wolf; **~-marinho** (*pl* **~s-marinhos**) *m* sea lion

lóbulo /'lɔbulu/ *m* lobe

lo|cação /loka'sãw/ *f* (*de imóvel*) lease; (*de carro*) rental; **~cador** *m* (*de casa*) landlord; **~cadora** *f* rental company; (*de vídeos*) video shop

lo|cal /lo'kaw/ (*pl* **~cais**) *a* local □ *m* site; (*de um acidente etc*) scene; **~calidade** *f* locality; **~calização** *f* location; **~calizar** *vt* locate; **~calizar-se** *vpr* (*orientar-se*) get one's bearings

loção /lo'sãw/ *f* lotion; **~ apósbarba** aftershave lotion

locatário /loka'tariu/ *m* (*de imóvel*) tenant; (*de carro etc*) hirer

locomo|tiva /lokomo'tʃiva/ *f* locomotive; **~ver-se** *vpr* get around

locu|ção /loku'sãw/ *f* phrase; **~tor** *m* announcer

lodo /'lodu/ *m* mud; **~so** /o/ *a* muddy

logaritmo /loga'ritʃimu/ *m* logarithm

lógi|ca /'lɔʒika/ *f* logic; **~co** *a* logical

logo /'lɔgu/ *adv* (*em seguida*) straightaway; (*em breve*) soon; (*justamente*) just; **~ mais** later; **~ antes/depois** just before/straight after; **~ que** as soon as; **até ~** goodbye

logotipo /logo'tʃipu/ *m* logo

logradouro /logra'doru/ *m* public place

loiro /'lojru/ *a veja* **louro**

lo|ja /'lɔja/ *f* shop, (*Amer*) store; **~ja de departamentos** department store; **~ja maçônica** masonic lodge; **~jista** *m/f* shopkeeper

lom|bada /lõ'bada/ *f* (*de livro*) spine; (*na rua*) speed bump; **~binho** *m* tenderloin; **~bo** *m* back; (*carne*) loin

lona /'lona/ *f* canvas

Londres /'lõdris/ *f* London

londrino /lõ'drinu/ *a* London □ *m* Londoner

longa-metragem /lõgame'traʒẽ/ (*pl* **longas-metragens**) *m* feature film

longe /'lõʒi/ *adv* far, a long way; **de ~** from a distance; (*por muito*) by far; **~ disso** far from it

longevidade /lõʒevi'dadʒi/ *f* longevity

longínquo /lõ'ʒĩkwu/ *a* distant

longitude /lõʒi'tudʒi/ *f* longitude

longo /'lõgu/ *a* long □ *m* long dress; **ao ~ de** along; (*durante*) through, over

lontra /'lõtra/ *f* otter
lorde /'lɔrdʒi/ *m* lord
lorota /lo'rɔta/ (*fam*) *f* fib
losango /lo'zãgu/ *m* diamond
lo|tação /lota'sãw/ *f* capacity; (*ônibus*) bus; ~**tação esgotada** full house; ~**tado** *a* crowded; <*teatro, ônibus*> full; ~**tar** *vt* fill □ *vi* fill up
lote /'lɔtʃi/ *m* (*quinhão*) portion; (*de terreno*) plot, (*Amer*) lot; (*em leilão*) lot; (*porção de coisas*) batch
loteria /lote'ria/ *f* lottery
louça /'losa/ *f* china; (*pratos etc*) crockery; **lavar a** ~ wash up, (*Amer*) do the dishes
lou|co /'loku/ *a* mad, crazy □ *m* madman; **estou** ~**co para ir** (*fam*) I'm dying to go; ~**cura** *f* madness; (*uma*) crazy thing
louro /'loru/ *a* blond □ *m* laurel; (*condimento*) bayleaf
lou|var /lo'var/ *vt* praise; ~**vável** (*pl* ~**váveis**) *a* praiseworthy; ~**vor** /o/ *m* praise
lua /'lua/ *f* moon; ~**-de-mel** *f* honeymoon
lu|ar /lu'ar/ *m* moonlight; ~**arento** *a* moonlit
lubrifi|cação /lubrifika'sãw/ *f* lubrication; ~**cante** *a* lubricating □ *m* lubricant; ~**car** *vt* lubricate
lucidez /lusi'des/ *f* lucidity
lúcido /'lusidu/ *a* lucid
lu|crar /lu'krar/ *vi* profit (**com** by); ~**cratividade** *f* profitability; ~**crativo** *a* profitable, lucrative; ~**cro** *m* profit
ludibriar /ludʒibri'ar/ *vt* cheat
lúdico /'ludʒiku/ *a* playful
lugar /lu'gar/ *m* place; (*espaço*) room; **em** ~ **de** in place of; **em primeiro** ~ in the first place; **em algum** ~ somewhere; **em todo** ~ everywhere; **dar** ~ **a** give rise to; **ter** ~ take place
lugarejo /luga'reʒu/ *m* village
lúgubre /'lugubri/ *a* gloomy, dismal
lula /'lula/ *f* squid
lume /'lumi/ *m* fire
luminária /lumi'naria/ *f* light, lamp; *pl* illuminations
luminoso /lumi'nozu/ *a* luminous; <*idéia*> brilliant
lunar /lu'nar/ *a* lunar □ *m* mole
lupa /'lupa/ *f* magnifying glass
lusco-fusco /lusku'fusku/ *m* twilight
lusitano /luzi'tanu/, **luso** /'luzu/ *a* & *m* Portuguese
lus|trar /lus'trar/ *vt* shine, polish; ~**tre** *m* shine; (*fig*) lustre; (*luminária*) light, lamp; ~**troso** /o/ *a* shiny
lu|ta /'luta/ *f* fight, struggle; ~**ta livre** wrestling; ~**tador** *m* fighter; (*de luta livre*) wrestler; ~**tar** *vi* fight □ *vt* do <*judô etc*>
luto /'lutu/ *m* mourning
luva /'luva/ *f* glove
luxação /luʃa'sãw/ *f* dislocation
Luxemburgo /luʃẽ'burgu/ *m* Luxembourg
luxembur|guês /luʃẽbur'ges/ *a* (*f* ~**guesa**) Luxemburg □ *m* (*f* ~**guesa**) Luxemburger; (*língua*) Luxemburgish
luxo /'luʃu/ *m* luxury; **hotel de** ~ luxury hotel; **cheio de** ~ (*fam*) fussy
luxuoso /luʃu'ozu/ *a* luxurious
luxúria /lu'ʃuria/ *f* lust
luxuriante /luʃuri'ãtʃi/ *a* lush
luz /lus/ *f* light; **à** ~ **de** by the light of <*velas etc*>; in the light of <*fatos etc*>; **dar à** ~ give birth to
luzidio /luzi'dʒio/ *a* shiny
luzir /lu'zir/ *vi* shine

M

maca /'maka/ *f* stretcher
maçã /ma'sã/ *f* apple
macabro /ma'kabru/ *a* macabre
maca|cão /maka'kãw/ *m* (*de trabalho*) overalls, (*Amer*) coveralls; (*tipo de calça*) dungarees; (*roupa inteiriça*) jumpsuit; (*para bebê*) romper suit; ~**co** *m* monkey; (*aparelho*) jack
maçada /ma'sada/ *f* bore
maçaneta /masa'neta/ *f* doorknob
maçante /ma'sãtʃi/ *a* boring
macar|rão /maka'xãw/ *m* pasta; (*espaguete*) spaghetti; ~**ronada** *f* pasta with tomato sauce and cheese
macarrônico /maka'xoniku/ *a* broken
macete /ma'setʃi/ *m* trick
machado /ma'ʃadu/ *m* axe
ma|chão /ma'ʃãw/ *a* tough □ *m* tough guy; ~**chismo** *m* machismo; ~**chista** *a* chauvinistic □ *m* male chauvinist; ~**cho** *a* male; <*homem*> macho □ *m* male
machu|cado /maʃu'kadu/ *m* injury; (*na pele*) sore patch; ~**car** *vt/i* hurt; ~**car-se** *vpr* hurt o.s.
maciço /ma'sisu/ *a* solid; <*dose etc*> massive □ *m* massif
macieira /masi'era/ *f* apple tree
maciez /masi'es/ *f* softness
macilento /masi'lẽtu/ *a* haggard
macio /ma'siu/ *a* soft; <*carne*> tender
maço /'masu/ *m* (*de cigarros*) packet; (*de notas*) bundle
ma|çom /ma'sõ/ *m* freemason; ~**çonaria** *f* freemasonry
maconha /ma'koɲa/ *f* marijuana
maçônico /ma'soniku/ *a* masonic
má-criação /makria'sãw/ *f* rudeness
macrobiótico /makrobi'ɔtʃiku/ *a* macrobiotic

macum|ba /ma'kũba/ *f* Afro-Brazilian cult; (*uma*) spell; **~beiro** *m* follower of macumba □ *a* macumba

madame /ma'dami/ *f* lady

Madeira /ma'dera/ *f* Madeira

madeira /ma'dera/ *f* wood □ *m* (*vinho*) Madeira; **~ de lei** hardwood

madeirense /made'rẽsi/ *a & m* Madeiran

madeixa /ma'deʃa/ *f* lock

madrasta /ma'drasta/ *f* stepmother

madrepérola /madre'pɛrola/ *f* mother of pearl

madressilva /madre'siwva/ *f* honeysuckle

Madri /ma'dri/ *f* Madrid

madrinha /ma'driɲa/ *f* (*de batismo*) godmother; (*de casamento*) bridesmaid

madru|gada /madru'gada/ *f* early morning; **~gador** *m* early riser; **~gar** *vi* get up early

maduro /ma'duru/ *a* <*fruta*> ripe; <*pessoa*> mature

mãe /mãj/ *f* mother; **~-de-santo** (*pl* **~s-de-santo**) *f* macumba priestess

maes|tria /majs'tria/ *f* expertise; **~tro** *m* conductor

máfia /'mafia/ *f* mafia

magazine /maga'zini/ *m* department store

magia /ma'ʒia/ *f* magic

mági|ca /'maʒika/ *f* magic; (*uma*) magic trick; **~co** *a* magic □ *m* magician

magis|tério /maʒis'tɛriu/ *m* teaching; (*professores*) teachers; **~trado** *m* magistrate

magnânimo /mag'nanimu/ *a* magnanimous

magnata /mag'nata/ *m* magnate

magnésio /mag'nɛziu/ *m* magnesium

mag|nético /mag'nɛtʃiku/ *a* magnetic; **~netismo** *m* magnetism; **~netizar** *vt* magnetize; (*fig*) mesmerize

mag|nificência /magnifi'sẽsia/ *f* magnificence; **~nífico** *a* magnificent

magnitude /magni'tudʒi/ *f* magnitude

mago /'magu/ *m* magician; **os reis ~s** the Three Wise Men

mágoa /'magoa/ *f* sorrow

magoar /mago'ar/ *vt/i* hurt; **~-se** *vpr* be hurt

ma|gricela /magri'sɛla/ *a* skinny; **~gro** *a* thin; <*leite*> skimmed; <*carne*> lean; (*fig*) meagre

maio /'maju/ *m* May

maiô /ma'jo/ *m* swimsuit

maionese /majo'nɛzi/ *f* mayonnaise

maior /ma'jɔr/ *a* bigger; <*escritor, amor etc*> greater; **o ~ carro** the biggest car; **o ~ escritor** the greatest writer; **~ de idade** of age

Maiorca /ma'jɔrka/ *f* Majorca

maio|ria /majo'ria/ *f* majority; **a ~ria dos brasileiros** most Brazilians; **~ridade** *f* majority, adulthood

mais /majs/ *adv & pron* more; **~ dois** two more; **dois dias a ~** two more days; **não trabalho ~** I don't work any more; **~ ou menos** more or less

maisena /maj'zɛna/ *f* cornflour, (*Amer*) cornstarch

maître /mɛtr/ *m* head waiter

maiúscula /ma'juskula/ *f* capital letter

majes|tade /maʒes'tadʒi/ *f* majesty; **~toso** *a* majestic

major /ma'jɔr/ *m* major

majoritário /maʒori'tariu/ *a* majority

mal /maw/ *adv* badly; (*quase não*) hardly □ *conj* hardly □ *m* evil; (*doença*) sickness; **não faz ~** never mind; **levar a ~** take offence at; **passar ~** be sick

mala /'mala/ *f* suitcase; (*do carro*) boot, (*Amer*) trunk; **~ aérea** air courier

malabaris|mo /malaba'rizmu/ *m* juggling act; **~ta** *m/f* juggler

malagradecido /malagrade'sidu/ *a* ungrateful

malagueta /mala'geta/ *f* chilli pepper

malaio /ma'laju/ *a & m* Malay

Malaísia /mala'izia/ *f* Malaysia

malaísio /mala'iziu/ *a & m* Malaysian

malan|dragem /malã'draʒẽ/ *f* hustling; (*uma*) clever trick; **~dro** *a* cunning □ *m* hustler

malária /ma'laria/ *f* malaria

mal-assombrado /malasõ'bradu/ *a* haunted

Malavi /mala'vi/ *m* Malawi

malcriado /mawkri'adu/ *a* rude

mal|dade /maw'dadʒi/ *f* wickedness; (*uma*) wicked thing; **por ~dade** out of spite; **~dição** *f* curse; **~dito** *a* cursed, damned; **~doso** /o/ *a* wicked

maleá|vel /mali'avew/ (*pl* **~veis**) *a* malleable

maledicência /maledi'sẽsia/ *f* malicious gossip

maléfico /ma'lɛfiku/ *a* evil; (*prejudicial*) harmful

mal-encarado /malĩka'radu/ *a* shady, dubious □ *m* shady character

mal-entendido /malĩtẽ'dʒidu/ *m* misunderstanding

mal-estar /malis'tar/ *m* (*doença*) ailment; (*constrangimento*) discomfort

maleta /ma'leta/ *f* overnight bag

malévolo /ma'lɛvolu/ *a* malevolent

malfei|to /maw'fejtu/ *a* badly done; <*roupa etc*> badly made; (*fig*) wrongful; **~tor** *m* wrongdoer; **~toria** *f* wrongdoing

ma|lha /'maʎa/ *f* (*ponto*) stitch; (*tricô*) knitting; (*tecido*) jersey; (*casaco*) jumper, (*Amer*) sweater; (*para ginástica*) leotard; (*de rede*) mesh; **fazer ~lha** knit; **~lhado** *a* <*animal*> dappled; <*roque*> heavy; **~lhar** *vt* beat; thresh <*trigo etc*> □ *vi* (*fam*) work out

mal-humorado /malumo'radu/ *a* in a bad mood, grumpy

malícia /ma'lisia/ *f* (*má índole*) malice; (*astúcia*) guile; (*humor*) innuendo

malicioso /malisi'ozu/ *a* (*mau*) malicious; (*astuto*) crafty; (*que põe malícia*) dirty-minded

maligno /ma'liginu/ *a* malignant

malmequer /mawme'ker/ *m* marigold

maloca /ma'lɔka/ *f* Indian village

malo|grar-se /malo'grarsi/ *vpr* go wrong, fail; **~gro** /o/ *m* failure

mal-passado /mawpa'sadu/ *a* <*carne*> rare

Malta /'mawta/ *f* Malta

malte /'mawtʃi/ *m* malt

maltrapilho /mawtra'piʎu/ *a* scruffy

maltratar /mawtra'tar/ *vt* ill-treat, mistreat

malu|co /ma'luku/ *a* mad, crazy □ *m* madman; **~quice** *f* madness; (*uma*) crazy thing

malvado /maw'vadu/ *a* wicked

malver|sação /mawversa'sãw/ *f* mismanagement; (*de fundos*) misappropriation; **~sar** *vt* mismanage; misappropriate <*dinheiro*>

Malvinas /maw'vinas/ *f pl* Falklands

mamadeira /mama'dera/ *f* (baby's) bottle

mamãe /ma'mãj/ *f* mum

mamão /ma'mãw/ *m* papaya

ma|mar /ma'mar/ *vi* suckle; **~mata** *f* (*fam*) fiddle

mamífero /ma'miferu/ *m* mammal

mamilo /ma'milu/ *m* nipple

mamoeiro /mamo'eru/ *m* papaya tree

manada /ma'nada/ *f* herd

mananci|al /manãsi'aw/ (*pl* **~ais**) *m* spring; (*fig*) rich source

man|cada /mã'kada/ *f* blunder; **~car** *vi* limp; **~car-se** *vpr* (*fam*) take the hint, get the message

Mancha /'mãʃa/ *f* **o canal da ~** the English Channel

man|cha /'mãʃa/ *f* stain; (*na pele*) mark; **~char** *vt* stain

manchete /mã'ʃɛtʃi/ *f* headline

manco /'mãku/ *a* lame □ *m* cripple

mandachuva /mãda'ʃuva/ *m* (*fam*) bigwig; (*chefe*) boss

man|dado /mã'dadu/ *m* order; **~dado de busca** search warrant; **~dado de prisão** arrest warrant; **~damento** *m* commandment; **~dante** *m/f* person in charge; **~dão** *a* (*f* **~dona**) bossy; **~dar** *vt* (*pedir*) order; (*enviar*) send □ *vi* be in charge; **~dar-se** *vpr* (*fam*) take off; **~dar buscar** fetch; **~dar dizer** send word; **~dar alg ir** tell s.o. to go; **~dar ver** (*fam*) go to town; **~dar em alg** order s.o. about; **~dato** *m* mandate

mandíbula /mã'dʒibula/ *f* (lower) jaw

mandioca /mãdʒi'ɔka/ *f* manioc

maneira /ma'nera/ *f* way; *pl* (*boas*) manners; **desta ~** in this way; **de qualquer ~** anyway

mane|jar /mane'ʒar/ *vt* handle; operate <*máquina*>; **~jável** (*pl* **~jáveis**) *a* manageable; **~jo** /e/ *m* handling

manequim /mane'kĩ/ *m* (*boneco*) dummy; (*medida*) size □ *m/f* mannequin, model

maneta /ma'neta/ *a* one-armed □ *m/f* person with one arm

manga[1] /'mãga/ *f* (*de roupa*) sleeve

manga[2] /'mãga/ *f* (*fruta*) mango

manganês /mãga'nes/ *m* manganese

mangue /'mãgi/ *m* mangrove swamp

mangueira[1] /mã'gera/ *f* (*tubo*) hose

mangueira[2] /mã'gera/ *f* (*árvore*) mango tree

manha /'maɲa/ *f* tantrum

manhã /ma'ɲã/ *f* morning; **de ~** in the morning

manhoso /ma'ɲozu/ *a* wilful

mania /ma'nia/ *f* (*moda*) craze; (*doença*) mania

maníaco /ma'niaku/ *a* manic □ *m* maniac; **~-depressivo** *a & m* manic depressive

manicômio /mani'komiu/ *m* lunatic asylum

manicura /mani'kura/ *f* manicure; (*pessoa*) manicurist

manifes|tação /manifesta'sãw/ *f* manifestation; (*passeata*) demonstration; **~tante** *m/f* demonstrator; **~tar** *vt* manifest, demonstrate; **~tar-se** *vpr* (*revelar-se*) manifest o.s.; (*exprimir-se*) express an opinion; **~to** /ɛ/ *a* manifest, clear □ *m* manifesto

manipular /manipu'lar/ *vt* manipulate

manjedoura /mãʒe'dora/ *f* manger

manjericão /mãʒeri'kãw/ *m* basil

mano|bra /ma'nɔbra/ *f* manoeuvre; **~brar** *vt* manoeuvre; **~brista** *m/f* parking valet

mansão /mã'sãw/ *f* mansion

man|sidão /mãsi'dãw/ *f* gentleness; (*do mar*) calm; **~sinho** *adv* **de ~sinho** (*devagar*) slowly; (*de leve*) gently; (*de fininho*) stealthily; **~so** *a* gentle; <*mar*> calm; <*animal*> tame

manta /'mãta/ *f* blanket; (*casaco*) cloak

mantei|ga /mã'tejga/ *f* butter; **~gueira** *f* butter dish

manter /mã'ter/ *vt* keep; **~-se** *vpr* keep; (*sustentar-se*) keep o.s.

mantimentos /mãtʃi'mẽtus/ *m pl* provisions

manto /'mãtu/ *m* mantle

manu|al /manu'aw/ (*pl* **~ais**) *a & m* manual; **~fatura** *f* manufacture; (*fábrica*) factory; **~faturar** *vt* manufacture

manuscrito /manus'kritu/ *a* handwritten □ *m* manuscript

manu|sear /manuzi'ar/ *vt* handle; **~seio** *m* handling

manutenção /manutẽ'sãw/ *f* maintenance; (*de prédio*) upkeep

mão /mãw/ (*pl* **~s**) *f* hand; (*do trânsito*) direction; (*de tinta*) coat; **abrir ~ de** give up; **agüentar a ~** hang on; **dar a ~ a alg** hold s.o.'s hand; (*cumprimentando*) shake s.o.'s hand; **deixar alg na ~** let s.o. down; **enfiar** *ou* **meter a ~ em** hit, slap; **lançar ~ de** make use of; **escrito à ~** written by hand; **ter à ~** have to hand; **de ~s dadas** hand in hand; **em segunda ~** second-hand; **fora de ~** out of the way; **~ única** one way; **~-de-obra** *f* labour

mapa /'mapa/ *m* map

maquete /ma'kɛtʃi/ *f* model

maqui|agem /maki'aʒẽ/ *f* make-up; **~ar** *vt* make up; **~ar-se** *vpr* put on make-up

maquiavélico /makia'vɛliku/ *a* Machiavellian

maqui|lagem, ~lar, (*Port*) **~lhagem, ~lhar** *veja* **maqui|agem, ~ar**

máquina /'makina/ *f* machine; (*ferroviária*) engine; **escrever à ~** type; **~ de costura** sewing machine; **~ de escrever** typewriter; **~ de lavar (roupa)** washing machine; **~ de lavar pratos** dishwasher; **~ fotográfica** camera

maqui|nação /makina'sãw/ *f* machination; **~nal** (*pl* **~nais**) *a* mechanical; **~nar** *vt/i* plot; **~naria** *f* machinery; **~nista** *m/f* (*ferroviário*) engine driver; (*de navio*) engineer

mar /mar/ *m* sea

maracu|já /maraku'ʒa/ *m* passion fruit; **~jazeiro** *m* passion-fruit plant

marasmo /ma'razmu/ *f* stagnation

marato|na /mara'tona/ *f* marathon; **~nista** *m/f* marathon runner

maravi|lha /mara'viʎa/ *f* marvel; **às mil ~lhas** wonderfully; **~lhar** *vt* amaze; **~lhar-se** *vpr* marvel (de at); **~lhoso** /o/ *a* marvellous

mar|ca /'marka/ *f* (*sinal*) mark; (*de carro, máquina*) make; (*de cigarro, sabão etc*) brand; **~ca registrada** registered trademark; **~cação** *f* marking; (*Port: discagem*) dialling; **~cador** *m* marker; (*em livro*) bookmark; (*placar*) scoreboard; (*jogador*) scorer; **~cante** *a* outstanding; **~capasso** *m* pacemaker; **~car** *vt* mark; arrange <*hora, encontro, jantar etc*>; score <*gol, ponto*>; (*Port: discar*) dial; <*relógio, termômetro*> show; brand <*gado*>; (*observar*) keep a close eye on; (*impressionar*) leave one's mark on □ *vi* make one's mark; **~car época** make history; **~car hora** make an appointment; **~car o compasso** beat time; **~car os pontos** keep the score

marce|naria /marsena'ria/ *f* cabinet-making; (*oficina*) cabinet maker's workshop; **~neiro** *m* cabinet maker

mar|cha /'marʃa/ *f* march; (*de carro*) gear; **pôr-se em ~cha** get going; **~cha à ré,** (*Port*) **~cha atrás** reverse; **~char** *vi* march

marci|al /marsi'aw/ (*pl* **~ais**) *a* martial; **~ano** *a & m* Martian

marco[1] /'marku/ *m* (*sinal*) landmark

marco[2] /'marku/ *m* (*moeda*) mark

março /'marsu/ *m* March

maré /ma'rɛ/ *f* tide

mare|chal /mare'ʃaw/ (*pl* **~chais**) *m* marshal

maresia /mare'zia/ *f* smell of the sea

marfim /mar'fĩ/ *m* ivory

margarida /marga'rida/ *f* daisy; (*para impressora*) daisywheel

margarina /marga'rina/ *f* margarine

mar|gem /'marʒẽ/ *f* (*de rio*) bank; (*de lago*) shore; (*parte em branco, fig*) margin; **~ginal** (*pl* **~ginais**) *a* marginal; (*delinqüente*) delinquent □ *m/f* delinquent □ *f* (*rua*) riverside road; **~ginalidade** *f* delinquency; **~ginalizar** *vt* marginalize

marido /ma'ridu/ *m* husband

marimbondo /marĩ'bõdu/ *m* hornet

marina /ma'rina/ *f* marina

mari|nha /ma'riɲa/ *f* navy; **~nha mercante** merchant navy; **~nheiro** *m* sailor; **~nho** *a* marine

marionete /mario'nɛtʃi/ *f* puppet

mariposa /mari'poza/ *f* moth

mariscos /ma'riskus/ *m* seafood

mari|tal /mari'taw/ (*pl* **~tais**) *a* marital

marítimo /ma'ritʃimu/ *a* sea; <*cidade*> seaside

marmanjo /mar'mãʒu/ *m* grown-up

marme|lada /marme'lada/ *f* (*fam*) fix; **~lo** /ɛ/ *m* quince

marmita /mar'mita/ *f* (*de soldado*) mess tin; (*de trabalhador*) lunchbox

mármore /'marmori/ *m* marble

marmóreo /mar'mɔriu/ *a* marble

marquise /mar'kizi/ *f* awning

marreco /ma'xɛku/ *m* wild duck

Marrocos /ma'xɔkus/ *m* Morocco
marrom /ma'xõ/ *a & m* brown
marroquino /maxo'kinu/ *a & m* Moroccan
Marte /'martʃi/ *m* Mars
marte|lada /marte'lada/ *f* hammer blow; ~**lar** *vt/i* hammer; ~**lar em** (*fig*) go on and on about; ~**lo** /ɛ/ *m* hammer
mártir /'martʃir/ *m/f* martyr
mar|tírio /mar'tʃiriu/ *m* martyrdom; (*fig*) torture; ~**tirizar** *vt* martyr; (*fig*) torture
marujo /ma'ruʒu/ *m* sailor
mar|xismo /mark'sizmu/ *m* Marxism; ~**xista** *a & m/f* Marxist
mas /mas/ *conj* but
mascar /mas'kar/ *vt* chew
máscara /'maskara/ *f* mask; (*tratamento facial*) face-pack
mascarar /maska'rar/ *vt* mask
mascate /mas'katʃi/ *m* street vendor
mascavo /mas'kavu/ *a* **açúcar** ~ brown sugar
mascote /mas'kɔtʃi/ *f* mascot
masculino /masku'linu/ *a* male; (*para homens*) men's; <*palavra*> masculine □ *m* masculine
másculo /'maskulu/ *a* masculine
masmorra /maz'moxa/ *f* dungeon
masoquis|mo /mazo'kizmu/ *m* masochism; ~**ta** *m/f* masochist □ *a* masochistic
massa /'masa/ *f* mass; (*de pão*) dough; (*de torta, empada*) pastry; (*macarrão etc*) pasta; **cultura de** ~ mass culture; **em** ~ en masse; **as** ~**s** the masses
massa|crante /masa'krãtʃi/ *a* gruelling; ~**crar** *vt* massacre; (*fig: maçar*) wear out; ~**cre** *m* massacre
massa|gear /masaʒi'ar/ *vt* massage; ~**gem** *f* massage; ~**gista** *m/f* masseur (*f* masseuse)
mastigar /mastʃi'gar/ *vt* chew; (*ponderar*) chew over
mastro /'mastru/ *m* mast; (*de bandeira*) flagpole
mastur|bação /masturba'sãw/ *f* masturbation; ~**bar-se** *vpr* masturbate
mata /'mata/ *f* forest
mata-borrão /matabo'xãw/ *m* blotting paper
matadouro /mata'doru/ *m* slaughterhouse
mata|gal /mata'gaw/ (*pl* ~**gais**) *m* thicket
mata-moscas /mata'moskas/ *m invar* fly spray
ma|tança /ma'tãsa/ *f* slaughter; ~**tar** *vt* kill; satisfy <*fome*>; quench <*sede*>; guess <*charada*>; (*fazer nas coxas*) dash off; (*fam*) skive off <*aula, serviço*> □ *vi* kill
mata-ratos /mata'xatus/ *m invar* rat poison
mate[1] /'matʃi/ *m* (*chá*) maté
mate[2] /'matʃi/ *a invar* matt
matemáti|ca /mate'matʃika/ *f* mathematics; ~**co** *a* mathematical □ *m* mathematician
matéria /ma'tɛria/ *f* (*assunto, disciplina*) subject; (*no jornal*) article; (*substância*) matter; (*usada para fazer algo*) material; **em** ~ **de** in the way of
materi|al /materi'aw/ (*pl* ~**ais**) *m* materials □ *a* material; ~**alismo** *m* materialism; ~**alista** *a* materialistic □ *m/f* materialist; ~**alizar-se** *vpr* materialize
matéria-prima /matɛria'prima/ (*pl* **matérias-primas**) *f* raw material
mater|nal /mater'naw/ (*pl* ~**nais**) *a* maternal; ~**nidade** *f* maternity; (*clínica*) maternity hospital; ~**no** /ɛ/ *a* maternal; **língua** ~**na** mother tongue
mati|nal /matʃi'naw/ (*pl* ~**nais**) *a* morning; ~**nê** *f* matinée
matiz /ma'tʃis/ *m* shade; (*político*) colouring; (*pontinha: de ironia etc*) tinge
matizar /matʃi'zar/ *vt* tinge (**de** with)
mato /'matu/ *m* scrubland, bush
matraca /ma'traka/ *f* rattle; (*tagarela*) chatterbox
matreiro /ma'treru/ *a* cunning
matriar|ca /matri'arka/ *f* matriarch; ~**cal** (*pl* ~**cais**) *a* matriarchal
matrícula /ma'trikula/ *f* enrolment; (*taxa*) enrolment fee; (*Port: de carro*) number plate, (*Amer*) license plate
matricular /matriku'lar/ *vt* enrol; ~-**se** *vpr* enrol
matri|monial /matrimoni'aw/ (*pl* ~**moniais**) *a* marriage; ~**mônio** *m* marriage
matriz /ma'tris/ *f* matrix; (*útero*) womb; (*sede*) head office
maturidade /maturi'dadʒi/ *f* maturity
matutino /matu'tʃinu/ *a* morning □ *m* morning paper
matuto /ma'tutu/ *a* countrified □ *m* country bumpkin
mau /maw/ *a* (*f* **má**) bad; ~-**caráter** *m invar* bad lot □ *a invar* no-good; ~-**olhado** *m* evil eye
mausoléu /mawzo'lɛw/ *m* mausoleum
maus-tratos /maws'tratus/ *m pl* ill-treatment
maxilar /maksi'lar/ *m* jaw
máxima /'masima/ *f* maxim
maximizar /masimi'zar/ *vt* maximize; (*exagerar*) play up
máximo /'masimu/ *a* (*antes do substantivo*) utmost, greatest; (*depois do substantivo*) maximum □ *m*

maximum; o ~ (*fam: o melhor*) really something; ao ~ to the maximum; no ~ at most

maxixe /ma'ʃiʃi/ *m* gherkin

me /mi/ *pron* me; (*indireto*) (to) me; (*reflexivo*) myself

meada /mi'ada/ *f* skein; **perder o fio da ~** lose one's thread

meados /mi'adus/ *m pl* **~ de maio** mid-May

meandro /mi'ãdru/ *f* meander; *pl* (*fig*) twists and turns

mecâni|ca /me'kanika/ *f* mechanics; **~co** *a* mechanical □ *m* mechanic

meca|nismo /meka'nizmu/ *m* mechanism; **~nizar** *vt* mechanize

mecenas /me'sɛnas/ *m invar* patron

mecha /'mɛʃa/ *f* (*de vela*) wick; (*de bomba*) fuse; (*porção de cabelos*) lock; (*cabelo tingido*) highlight; **~do** *a* highlighted

meda|lha /me'daʎa/ *f* medal; **~lhão** *m* medallion; (*jóia*) locket

média /'mɛdʒia/ *f* average; (*café*) white coffee; **em ~** on average

medi|ação /medʒia'sãw/ *f* mediation; **~ador** *m* mediator; **~ante** *prep* through, by; **~ar** *vi* mediate

medica|ção /medʒika'sãw/ *f* medication; **~mento** *m* medicine

medição /medʒi'sãw/ *f* measurement

medicar /medʒi'kar/ *vt* treat □ *vi* practise medicine; **~-se** *vpr* dose o.s. up

medici|na /medʒi'sina/ *f* medicine; **~na legal** forensic medicine; **~nal** (*pl* **~nais**) *a* medicinal

médico /'mɛdʒiku/ *m* doctor □ *a* medical; **~-legal** (*pl* **~-legais**) *a* forensic; **~-legista** (*pl* **~s-legistas**) *m/f* forensic scientist

medi|da /me'dʒida/ *f* measure; (*dimensão*) measurement; **à ~da que** as; **sob ~da** made to measure; **tirar as ~das de alg** take s.o.'s measurements; **~dor** *m* meter

medie|val /medʒie'vaw/ (*pl* **~vais**) *a* medieval

médio /'mɛdʒiu/ *a* (*típico*) average; <*tamanho, prazo*> medium; <*classe, dedo*> middle

medíocre /me'dʒiokri/ *a* mediocre

mediocridade /medʒiokri'dadʒi/ *f* mediocrity

medir /me'dʒir/ *vt* measure; weigh <*palavras*> □ *vi* measure; **~-se** *vpr* measure o.s.; **quanto você mede?** how tall are you?

medi|tação /medʒita'sãw/ *f* meditation; **~tar** *vi* meditate

mediterrâneo /medʒite'xaniu/ *a* Mediterranean □ *m* **o Mediterrâneo** the Mediterranean

médium /'mɛdʒiũ/ *m/f* medium

medo /'medu/ *m* fear; **ter ~ de** be afraid of; **com ~** afraid; **~nho** /o/ *a* frightful

medroso /me'drozu/ *a* fearful, timid

medula /me'dula/ *f* marrow

megalomania /megaloma'nia/ *f* megalomania

meia /'meja/ *f* (*comprida*) stocking; (*curta*) sock; (*seis*) six; **~-calça** (*pl* **~s-calças**) *f* tights, (*Amer*) pantihose; **~-idade** *f* middle age; **~-noite** *f* midnight; **~-volta** (*pl* **~s-voltas**) *f* about-turn

mei|go /'mejgu/ *a* sweet; **~guice** *f* sweetness

meio /'meju/ *a* half □ *adv* rather □ *m* (*centro*) middle; (*ambiente*) environment; (*recurso*) means; **~ litro** half a litre; **dois meses e ~** two and a half months; **em ~ a** amid; **por ~ de** through; **o ~ ambiente** the environment; **os ~s de comunicação** the media; **~-dia** *m* midday; **~-fio** *m* kerb; **~-termo** *m* (*acordo*) compromise

mel /mɛw/ *m* honey

mela|ço /me'lasu/ *m* molasses; **~do** *a* sticky □ *m* treacle

melancia /melã'sia/ *f* watermelon

melan|colia /melãko'lia/ *f* melancholy; **~cólico** *a* melancholy

melão /me'lãw/ *m* melon

melar /me'lar/ *vt* make sticky

melhor /me'ʎɔr/ *a & adv* better; **o ~** the best

melho|ra /me'ʎɔra/ *f* improvement; **~ras!** get well soon!; **~ramento** *m* improvement; **~rar** *vt* improve □ *vi* improve; <*doente*> get better

melin|drar /melĩ'drar/ *vt* hurt; **~drar-se** *vpr* be hurt; **~droso** /o/ *a* delicate; <*pessoa*> sensitive

melodi|a /melo'dʒia/ *f* melody; **~oso** /o/ *a* melodious

melodra|ma /melo'drama/ *m* melodrama; **~mático** *a* melodramatic

meloso /me'lozu/ *a* sickly sweet

melro /'mɛwxu/ *m* blackbird

membrana /mẽ'brana/ *f* membrane

membro /'mẽbru/ *m* member; (*braço, perna*) limb

memo|rando /memo'rãdu/ *m* memo; **~rável** (*pl* **~ráveis**) *a* memorable

memória /me'mɔria/ *f* memory; *pl* (*autobiografia*) memoirs

men|ção /mẽ'sãw/ *f* mention; **fazer ~ção de** mention; **~cionar** *vt* mention

mendi|cância /mẽdʒi'kãsia/ *f* begging; **~gar** *vi* beg; **~go** *m* beggar

menina /me'nina/ *f* girl; **a ~ dos olhos de alg** the apple of s.o.'s eye

meningite /menĩ'ʒitʃi/ *f* meningitis

meni|nice /meni'nisi/ *f* (*idade*) childhood; **~no** *m* boy

menopausa /meno'pawza/ *f* menopause

menor /me'nɔr/ *a* smaller □ *m/f* minor; **o/a ~** the smallest; (*mínimo*) the slightest, the least

menos /'menos/ *adv & pron* less □ *prep* except; **dois dias a ~** two days less; **a ~ que** unless; **ao** *ou* **pelo ~** at least; **o ~ bonito** the least pretty; **~prezar** *vt* look down upon; **~prezo** /e/ *m* disdain

mensa|geiro /mẽsa'ʒeru/ *m* messenger; **~gem** *f* message

men|sal /mẽ'saw/ (*pl* **~sais**) *a* monthly; **~salidade** *f* monthly payment; **~salmente** *adv* monthly

menstru|ação /mẽstrua'sãw/ *f* menstruation; **~ada** *a* **estar ~ada** be having one's period; **~al** (*pl* **~ais**) *a* menstrual; **~ar** *vi* menstruate

menta /'mẽta/ *f* mint

men|tal /mẽ'taw/ (*pl* **~tais**) *a* mental; **~talidade** *f* mentality; **~te** *f* mind

men|tir /mẽ'tʃir/ *vi* lie; **~tira** *f* lie; **~tiroso** /o/ *a* lying □ *m* liar

mentor /mẽ'tor/ *m* mentor

mercado /mer'kadu/ *m* market; **~ria** *f* commodity; *pl* goods

mercan|te /mer'kãtʃi/ *a* merchant; **~til** (*pl* **~tis**) *a* mercantile; **~tilismo** *m* commercialism

mercê /mer'se/ *f* **à ~ de** at the mercy of

merce|aria /mersia'ria/ *f* grocer's; **~eiro** *m* grocer

mercenário /merse'nariu/ *a & m* mercenary

mercúrio /mer'kuriu/ *m* mercury; **Mercúrio** Mercury

merda /'mɛrda/ *f* (*chulo*) shit

mere|cedor /merese'dor/ *a* deserving; **~cer** *vt* deserve □ *vi* be deserving; **~cimento** *m* merit

merenda /me'rẽda/ *f* packed lunch; **~ escolar** school dinner

mere|trício /mere'trisiu/ *m* prostitution; **~triz** *f* prostitute

mergu|lhador /merguʎa'dor/ *m* diver; **~lhar** *vt* dip (**em** into) □ *vi* (*na água*) dive; (*no trabalho*) bury o.s.; **~lho** *m* dive; (*esporte*) diving; (*banho de mar*) dip

meridi|ano /meridʒi'anu/ *m* meridian; **~onal** (*pl* **~onais**) *a* southern

mérito /'mɛritu/ *m* merit

merluza /mer'luza/ *f* hake

mero /'mɛru/ *a* mere

mês /mes/ (*pl* **meses**) *m* month

mesa /'meza/ *f* table; (*de trabalho*) desk; **~ de centro** coffee table; **~ de jantar** dining table; **~ telefônica** switchboard

mesada /me'zada/ *f* monthly allowance

mescla /'mɛskla/ *f* mixture, blend

mesmice /mez'misi/ *f* sameness

mesmo /'mezmu/ *a* same □ *adv* (*até*) even; (*justamente*) right; (*de verdade*) really; **você ~** you yourself; **hoje ~** this very day; **~ assim** even so; **~ que** even if; **dá no ~** it comes to the same thing; **fiquei na mesma** I'm none the wiser

mesqui|nharia /meskiɲa'ria/ *f* meanness; (*uma*) mean thing; **~nho** *a* mean

mesquita /mes'kita/ *f* mosque

Messias /me'sias/ *m* Messiah

mesti|çagem /mestʃi'saʒẽ/ *f* interbreeding; **~ço** *a* <*pessoa*> of mixed race; <*animal*> crossbred □ *m* (*pessoa*) person of mixed race; (*animal*) mongrel

mes|trado /mes'tradu/ *m* master's degree; **~tre** /ɛ/ *m* (*f* **~tra**) master (*f* mistress); (*de escola*) teacher □ *a* main; <*chave*> master; **~tre-de-obras** (*pl* **~tres-de-obras**) *m* foreman; **~tre-sala** (*pl* **~tres-salas**) *m* master of ceremonies (*in carnival procession*); **~tria** *f* expertise

meta /'mɛta/ *f* (*de corrida*) finishing post; (*gol, fig*) goal

meta|bólico /meta'bɔliku/ *a* metabolic; **~bolismo** *m* metabolism

metade /me'tadʒi/ *f* half; **pela ~** halfway

metafísi|ca /meta'fizika/ *f* metaphysics; **~co** *a* metaphysical

metáfora /me'tafora/ *f* metaphor

metafórico /meta'fɔriku/ *a* metaphorical

me|tal /me'taw/ (*pl* **~tais**) *m* metal; *pl* (*numa orquestra*) brass; **~tálico** *a* metallic

meta|lurgia /metalur'ʒia/ *f* metallurgy; **~lúrgica** *f* metal works; **~lúrgico** *a* metallurgical □ *m* metalworker

metamorfose /metamor'fɔzi/ *f* metamorphosis

metano /me'tanu/ *m* methane

meteórico /mete'ɔriku/ *a* meteoric

meteoro /mete'ɔru/ *m* meteor; **~logia** *f* meteorology; **~lógico** *a* meteorological; **~logista** *m/f* (*cientista*) meteorologist; (*na TV*) weather forecaster

meter /me'ter/ *vt* put; **~-se** *vpr* (*envolver-se*) get (**em** into); (*intrometer-se*) meddle (**em** in); **~ medo** be frightening

meticuloso /metʃiku'lozu/ *a* meticulous

metido /me'tʃidu/ *a* snobbish; **ele é ~ a perito** he thinks he's an expert

metódico /me'tɔdʒiku/ *a* methodical

metodista /meto'dʒista/ *a & m/f* Methodist

método /'mɛtodu/ *m* method
metra|lhadora /metraʎa'dora/ *f* machine gun; **~lhar** *vt* machine-gun
métri|co /'mɛtriku/ *a* metric; **fita ~ca** tape measure
metro[1] /'mɛtru/ *m* metre
metro[2] /'mɛtru/ *m* (*Port: metropolitano*) underground, (*Amer*) subway
metrô /me'tro/ *m* underground, (*Amer*) subway
metrópole /me'trɔpoli/ *f* metropolis
metropolitano /metropoli'tanu/ *a* metropolitan □ *m* (*Port*) underground, (*Amer*) subway
meu /mew/ *a* (*f* **minha**) my □ *pron* (*f* **minha**) mine; **um amigo ~** a friend of mine; **fico na minha** (*fam*) I keep myself to myself
mexer /me'ʃer/ *vt* move; (*com colher etc*) stir □ *vi* move; **~-se** *vpr* move; (*apressar-se*) get a move on; **~ com** (*comover*) affect, get to; (*brincar com*) tease; (*trabalhar com*) work with; **~ em** touch
mexeri|ca /meʃe'rika/ *f* tangerine; **~car** *vi* gossip; **~co** *m* piece of gossip; *pl* gossip; **~queiro** *a* gossiping □ *m* gossip
mexicano /meʃi'kanu/ *a & m* Mexican
México /'mɛʃiku/ *m* Mexico
mexido /me'ʃidu/ *a* **ovos ~s** scrambled eggs
mexilhão /meʃi'ʎãw/ *m* mussel
mi|ado /mi'adu/ *m* miaow; **~ar** *vi* miaow
micróbio /mi'krɔbiu/ *m* microbe
micro|cosmo /mikro'kɔzmu/ *m* microcosm; **~empresa** /e/ *f* small business; **~empresário** *m* small businessman; **~filme** *m* microfilm; **~fone** *m* microphone; **~onda** *f* microwave; **(forno de) ~s** *m* microwave (oven); **~ônibus** *m invar* minibus; **~processador** *m* microprocessor
microrganismo /mikrorga'nizmu/ *m* microorganism
microscó|pico /mikros'kɔpiku/ *a* microscopic; **~pio** *m* microscope
mídia /'midʒia/ *f* media
migalha /mi'gaʎa/ *f* crumb
mi|gração /migra'sãw/ *f* migration; **~grar** *vi* migrate; **~gratório** *a* migratory
mi|jar /mi'ʒar/ *vi* (*fam*) pee; **~jar-se** *vpr* wet o.s.; **~jo** *m* (*fam*) pee
mil /miw/ *a & m invar* thousand; **estar a ~** be on top form
mila|gre /mi'lagri/ *m* miracle; **~groso** /o/ *a* miraculous
milênio /mi'leniu/ *m* millennium
milésimo /mi'lɛzimu/ *a* thousandth
milha /'miʎa/ *f* mile
milhão /mi'ʎãw/ *m* million; **um ~ de dólares** a million dollars
milhar /mi'ʎar/ *m* thousand; **~es de vezes** thousands of times; **aos ~es** in their thousands
milho /'miʎo/ *m* maize, (*Amer*) corn
milico /mi'liku/ *m* (*fam*) military man; **os ~s** the military
mili|grama /mili'grama/ *m* milligram; **~litro** *m* millilitre; **~metro** /e/ *m* millimetre
milionário /milio'nariu/ *a & m* millionaire
mili|tante /mili'tãtʃi/ *a & m* militant; **~tar** *a* military □ *m* soldier
mim /mĩ/ *pron* me
mimar /mi'mar/ *vt* spoil
mímica /'mimika/ *f* mime; (*brincadeira*) charades
mi|na /'mina/ *f* mine; **~nar** *vt* mine; (*fig: prejudicar*) undermine
mindinho /mĩ'dʒiɲu/ *m* little finger, (*Amer*) pinkie
mineiro /mi'neru/ *a* mining; (*de MG*) from Minas Gerais □ *m* miner; (*de MG*) person from Minas Gerais
mine|ração /minera'sãw/ *f* mining; **~ral** (*pl* **~rais**) *a & m* mineral; **~rar** *vt/i* mine
minério /mi'nɛriu/ *m* ore
mingau /mĩ'gaw/ *m* porridge
mingua /'mĩgwa/ *f* lack
minguante /mĩ'gwãtʃi/ *a* **quarto ~** last quarter
minguar /mĩ'gwar/ *vi* dwindle
minha /'miɲa/ *a & pron veja* **meu**
minhoca /mi'ɲɔka/ *f* worm
miniatura /minia'tura/ *f* miniature
mini|malista /minima'lista/ *a & m/f* minimalist; **~mizar** *vt* minimize; (*subestimar*) play down
mínimo /'minimu/ *a* (*muito pequeno*) tiny; (*mais baixo*) minimum □ *m* minimum; **a mínima idéia** the slightest idea; **no ~** at least
minissaia /mini'saja/ *f* miniskirt
minis|terial /ministeri'aw/ (*pl* **~teriais**) *a* ministerial; **~tério** *m* ministry; **Ministério do Interior** Home Office, (*Amer*) Department of the Interior
minis|trar /minis'trar/ *vt* administer; **~tro** *m* minister; **primeiro ~tro** prime minister
Minorca /mi'nɔrka/ *f* Menorca
mino|ritário /minori'tariu/ *a* minority; **~ria** *f* minority
minúcia /mi'nusia/ *f* detail
minucioso /minusi'ozu/ *a* thorough
minúscu|la /mi'nuskula/ *f* small letter; **~lo** *a* <*letra*> small; (*muito pequeno*) minuscule
minuta /mi'nuta/ *f* (*rascunho*) rough draft

minuto /mi'nutu/ *m* minute

miolo /mi'olu/ *f* (*de fruta*) flesh; (*de pão*) crumb; *pl* brains

míope /'miopi/ *a* short-sighted

miopia /mio'pia/ *f* myopia

mira /'mira/ *f* sight; **ter em ~** have one's sights on

mirabolante /mirabo'lãtʃi/ *a* amazing; <*idéias, plano*> grandiose

mi|ragem /mi'raʒẽ/ *f* mirage; **~rante** *m* lookout; **~rar** *vt* look at; **~rar-se** *vpr* look at o.s.

mirim /mi'rĩ/ *a* little

miscelânea /mise'lania/ *f* miscellany

miscigenação /misiʒena'sãw/ *f* interbreeding

mise-en-plis /mizã'pli/ *m* shampoo and set

miserá|vel /mize'ravew/ (*pl* **~veis**) *a* miserable

miséria /mi'zɛria/ *f* misery; (*pobreza*) poverty; **uma ~** (*pouco dinheiro*) a pittance; **chorar ~** claim poverty

miseri|córdia /mizeri'kɔrdʒia/ *f* mercy; **~cordioso** *a* merciful

misógino /mi'zɔʒinu/ *m* misogynist □ *a* misogynistic

miss /'misi/ *f* beauty queen

missa /'misa/ *f* mass

missão /mi'sãw/ *f* mission

mís|sil /'misiw/ (*pl* **~seis**) *m* missile; **~sil de longo alcance** long-range missile

missionário /misio'nariu/ *m* missionary

missiva /mi'siva/ *f* missive

mis|tério /mis'tɛriu/ *m* mystery; **~terioso** /o/ *a* mysterious; **~ticismo** *m* mysticism

místico /'mistʃiku/ *m* mystic □ *a* mystical

misto /'mistu/ *a* mixed □ *m* mix; **~ quente** toasted ham and cheese sandwich

mistu|ra /mis'tura/ *f* mixture; **~rar** *vt* mix; (*confundir*) mix up; **~rar-se** *vpr* mix (**com** with)

mítico /'mitʃiku/ *a* mythical

mito /'mitu/ *m* myth; **~logia** *f* mythology; **~lógico** *a* mythological

miudezas /miu'dezas/ *f pl* odds and ends

miúdo /mi'udu/ *a* tiny, minute; <*chuva*> fine; <*despesas*> minor □ *m* (*criança*) child, little one; *pl* (*de galinha*) giblets; **trocar em ~s** go into detail

mixaria /miʃa'ria/ *f* (*fam*) (*soma irrisória*) pittance

mixórdia /mi'ʃɔrdʒia/ *f* muddle

mnemônico /ne'moniku/ *a* mnemonic

mobilar /mobi'lar/ *vt* (*Port*) furnish

mobília /mo'bilia/ *f* furniture

mobili|ar /mobili'ar/ *vt* furnish; **~ário** *m* furniture

mobili|dade /mobili'dadʒi/ *f* mobility; **~zar** *vt* mobilize

moça /'mosa/ *f* girl

moçambicano /mosãbi'kanu/ *a* & *m* Mozambican

Moçambique /mosã'biki/ *m* Mozambique

moção /mo'sãw/ *f* motion

mochila /mo'ʃila/ *f* rucksack

moço /'mosu/ *a* young □ *m* boy, lad

moda /'mɔda/ *f* fashion; **na ~** fashionable

modalidade /modali'dadʒi/ *f* (*esporte*) event

mode|lagem /mode'laʒẽ/ *f* modelling; **~lar** *vt* model (**a** on); **~lar-se** *vpr* model o.s. (**a** on) □ *a* model; **~lo** /e/ *m* model

mode|ração /modera'sãw/ *f* moderation; **~rado** *a* moderate; **~rar** *vt* moderate; reduce <*velocidade, despesas*>; **~rar-se** *vpr* restrain oneself

moder|nidade /moderni'dadʒi/ *f* modernity; **~nismo** *m* modernism; **~nista** *a* & *m/f* modernist; **~nizar** *vt* modernize; **~no** /ɛ/ *a* modern

modess /'mɔdʒis/ *m invar* sanitary towel

modéstia /mo'dɛstʃia/ *f* modesty

modesto /mo'dɛstu/ *a* modest

módico /'mɔdʒiku/ *a* modest

modifi|cação /modʒifika'sãw/ *f* modification; **~car** *vt* modify

mo|dismo /mo'dʒizmu/ *m* idiom; **~dista** *f* dressmaker

modo /'mɔdu/ *m* way; (*ling*) mood; *pl* (*maneiras*) manners

modular /modu'lar/ *vt* modulate □ *a* modular

módulo /'mɔdulu/ *m* module

moeda /mo'ɛda/ *f* (*peça de metal*) coin; (*dinheiro*) currency

mo|edor /moe'dor/ *m* **~edor de café** coffee-grinder; **~edor de carne** mincer; **~er** *vt* grind <*café, trigo*>; squeeze <*cana*>; mince <*carne*>; (*bater*) beat

mo|fado /mo'fadu/ *a* mouldy; **~far** *vi* moulder; **~fo** /o/ *m* mould

mogno /'mɔgnu/ *m* mahogany

moinho /mo'iɲu/ *m* mill; **~ de vento** windmill

moisés /moj'zɛs/ *m invar* carry-cot

moita /'mojta/ *f* bush

mola /'mɔla/ *f* spring

mol|dar /mow'dar/ *vt* mould; cast <*metal*>; **~de** /ɔ/ *m* mould; (*para costura etc*) pattern

moldu|ra /mow'dura/ *f* frame; **~rar** *vt* frame

mole /'mɔli/ *a* soft; <*pessoa*> listless; (*fam*) (*fácil*) easy □ *adv* easily; é ~? (*fam*) can you believe it?

molécula /mo'lɛkula/ *f* molecule

moleque /mo'lɛki/ *m* (*menino*) lad; (*de rua*) urchin; (*homem*) scoundrel

molestar /moles'tar/ *vt* bother

moléstia /mo'lɛstʃia/ *f* disease

moletom /mole'tõ/ *m* (*tecido*) knitted cotton; (*blusa*) sweatshirt

moleza /mo'leza/ *f* softness; (*de pessoa*) laziness; **viver na ~** lead a cushy life; **ser ~** be easy

mo|lhado /mo'ʎadu/ *a* wet; **~lhar** *vt* wet; **~lhar-se** *vpr* get wet

molho[1] /'mɔʎu/ *m* (*de chaves*) bunch; (*de palha*) sheaf

molho[2] /'moʎu/ *m* sauce; (*para salada*) dressing; **deixar de ~** leave in soak <*roupa*>; **~ inglês** Worcester sauce

molusco /mo'lusku/ *m* mollusc

momen|tâneo /momẽ'taniu/ *a* momentary; **~to** *m* moment; (*força*) momentum

Mônaco /'monaku/ *m* Monaco

monar|ca /mo'narka/ *m/f* monarch; **~quia** *f* monarchy; **~quista** *a & m/f* monarchist

monástico /mo'nastʃiku/ *a* monastic

monção /mõ'sãw/ *f* monsoon

mone|tário /mone'tariu/ *a* monetary; **~tarismo** *m* monetarism; **~tarista** *a & m/f* monetarist

monge /'mõʒi/ *m* monk

monitor /moni'tor/ *m* monitor; **~ de vídeo** VDU

monitorar /monito'rar/ *vt* monitor

mono|cromo /mono'krɔmu/ *a* monochrome; **~gamia** *f* monogamy

monógamo /mo'nɔgamu/ *a* monogamous

monograma /mono'grama/ *m* monogram

monólogo /mo'nɔlogu/ *m* monologue

mononucleose /mononukli'ɔzi/ *f* glandular fever

mono|pólio /mono'pɔliu/ *m* monopoly; **~polizar** *vt* monopolize

monossílabo /mono'silabu/ *a* monosyllabic □ *m* monosyllable

monotonia /monoto'nia/ *f* monotony

monótono /mo'nɔtonu/ *a* monotonous

monóxido /mo'nɔksidu/ *m* **~ de carbono** carbon monoxide

mons|tro /'mõstru/ *m* monster; **~truosidade** *f* monstrosity; **~truoso** /o/ *a* monstrous

monta|dor /mõta'dor/ *m* (*de cinema*) editor; **~dora** *f* assembly company; **~gem** *f* assembly; (*de filme*) editing; (*de peça teatral*) production

monta|nha /mõ'taɲa/ *f* mountain; **~nha-russa** (*pl* **~nhas-russas**) *f* roller coaster; **~nhismo** *m* mountaineering; **~nhoso** /o/ *a* mountainous

mon|tante /mõ'tãtʃi/ *m* amount □ *a* rising; **a ~tante** upstream; **~tão** *m* heap; **~tar** *vt* ride <*cavalo, bicicleta*>; assemble <*peças, máquina*>; put up <*barraca*>; set up <*empresa, escritório*>; mount <*guarda, diamante*>; put on <*espetáculo, peça*>; edit <*filme*> □ *vi* ride; **~tar a** <*dívidas etc*> amount to; **~tar em** (*subir em*) mount; **~taria** *f* mount; **~te** *m* heap; **um ~te de coisas** (*fam*) loads of things; **o Monte Branco** Mont Blanc

Montevidéu /mõtʃivi'dɛw/ *f* Montevideo

montra /'mõtra/ *f* (*Port*) shop window

monumen|tal /monumẽ'taw/ (*pl* **~tais**) *a* monumental; **~to** *m* monument

mora|da /mo'rada/ *f* dwelling; (*Port*) address; **~dia** *f* dwelling; **~dor** *m* resident

mo|ral /mo'raw/ (*pl* **~rais**) *a* moral □ *f* (*ética*) morals; (*de uma história*) moral □ *m* (*ânimo*) morale; (*de pessoa*) moral sense; **~ralidade** *f* morality; **~ralista** *a* moralistic □ *m/f* moralist; **~ralizar** *vi* moralize

morango /mo'rãgu/ *m* strawberry

morar /mo'rar/ *vi* live

moratória /mora'tɔria/ *f* moratorium

mórbido /'mɔrbidu/ *a* morbid

morcego /mor'segu/ *m* bat

mor|daça /mor'dasa/ *f* gag; (*para cão*) muzzle; **~daz** *a* scathing; **~der** *vt/i* bite; **~dida** *f* bite

mordo|mia /mordo'mia/ *f* (*no emprego*) perk; (*de casa etc*) comfort; **~mo** /o/ *m* butler

more|na /mo'rena/ *f* brunette; **~no** *a* dark; (*bronzeado*) brown □ *m* dark person

morfina /mor'fina/ *f* morphine

moribundo /mori'bũdu/ *a* dying

moringa /mo'rĩga/ *f* water jug

morma|cento /morma'sẽtu/ *a* sultry; **~ço** *m* sultry weather

morno /'mornu/ *a* lukewarm

moro|sidade /morozi'dadʒi/ *f* slowness; **~so** /o/ *a* slow

morrer /mo'xer/ *vi* die; <*luz, dia, ardor, esperança etc*> fade; <*carro*> stall

morro /'moxu/ *m* hill; (*fig: favela*) slum

mortadela /morta'dɛla/ *f* mortadella, salami

mor|tal /mor'taw/ (*pl* **~tais**) *a & m* mortal; **~talha** *f* shroud; **~talidade** *f* mortality; **~tandade** *f* slaughter; **~te** /ɔ/ *f* death; **~tífero** *a* deadly; **~tificar** *vt* mortify; **~to** /o/ *a* dead

mosaico /mo'zajku/ *m* mosaic

mosca /'moska/ *f* fly

Moscou /mos'ku/, (*Port*) **Moscovo** /moʃ'kovu/ *f* Moscow

mosquito /mos'kitu/ *m* mosquito

mostarda /mos'tarda/ *f* mustard

mosteiro /mos'teru/ *m* monastery

mos|tra /'mɔstra/ *f* display; **dar ~tras de** show signs of; **pôr à ~tra** show up; **~trador** *m* face, dial; **~trar** *vt* show; **~trar-se** *vpr* (*revelar-se*) show o.s. to be; (*exibir-se*) show off; **~truário** *m* display case

mo|tel /mo'tɛw/ (*pl* **~téis**) *m* motel

motim /mo'tʃĩ/ *m* riot; (*na marinha*) mutiny

moti|vação /motʃiva'sãw/ *f* motivation; **~var** *vt* (*incentivar*) motivate; (*provocar*) cause; **~vo** *m* (*razão*) reason; (*estímulo*) motive; (*na arte, música*) motif; **dar ~vo de** give cause for

moto /'mɔtu/ *f* motorbike; **~ca** /mo'tɔka/ *f* (*fam*) motorbike

motoci|cleta /motosi'klɛta/ *f* motorcycle; **~clismo** *m* motorcycling; **~clista** *m/f* motorcyclist

motoqueiro /moto'keru/ *m* (*fam*) biker

motor /mo'tor/ *m* (*de carro, avião etc*) engine; (*elétrico*) motor □ *a* (*f* **motriz**) <*força*> driving; (*anat*) motor; **~ de arranque** starter motor; **~ de popa** outboard motor

moto|rista /moto'rista/ *m/f* driver; **~rizado** *a* motorized; **~rizar** *vt* motorize

movedi|ço /move'dʒisu/ *a* unstable, moving; **areia ~ça** quicksand

mó|vel /'mɔvew/ (*pl* **~veis**) *a* <*peça, parte*> moving; <*tropas*> mobile; <*festa*> movable □ *m* piece of furniture; *pl* furniture

mo|ver /mo'ver/ *vt* move; (*impulsionar, fig*) drive; **~ver-se** *vpr* move; **~vido** *a* driven; **~vido a álcool** alcohol-powered

movimen|tação /movimẽta'sãw/ *f* bustle; **~tado** *a* <*rua, loja*> busy; <*música*> up-beat, lively; <*pessoa, sessão*> lively; **~tar** *vt* liven up; **~tar-se** *vpr* move; **~to** *m* movement; (*tecn*) motion; (*na rua etc*) activity

muam|ba /mu'ãba/ *f* contraband; **~beiro** *m* smuggler

muco /'muku/ *m* mucus

muçulmano /musuw'manu/ *a* & *m* Muslim

mu|da /'muda/ *f* (*planta*) seedling; **~da de roupa** change of clothes; **~dança** *f* change; (*de casa*) move; (*de carro*) transmission; **~dar** *vt/i* change; **~dar de assunto** change the subject; **~dar (de casa)** move (house); **~dar de cor** change colour; **~dar de idéia** change one's mind; **~dar de lugar** change places; **~dar de roupa** change (clothes); **~dar-se** *vpr* move

mu|dez /mu'des/ *f* silence; **~do** *a* silent; (*deficiente*) dumb; <*telefone*> dead □ *m* mute

mu|gido /mu'ʒidu/ *m* moo; **~gir** *vi* moo

muito /'mũitu/ *a* a lot of; *pl* many □ *pron* a lot □ *adv* (*com adjetivo, advérbio*) very; (*com verbo*) a lot; **~ maior** much bigger; **~ tempo** a long time

mula /'mula/ *f* mule

mulato /mu'latu/ *a* & *m* mulatto

muleta /mu'leta/ *f* crutch

mulher /mu'ʎɛr/ *f* woman; (*esposa*) wife

mulherengo /muʎe'rẽgu/ *a* womanizing □ *m* womanizer, ladies' man

mul|ta /'muwta/ *f* fine; **~tar** *vt* fine

multicolor /muwtʃiko'lor/ *a* multicoloured

multidão /muwtʃi'dãw/ *f* crowd

multinacio|nal /muwtʃinasio-'naw/ (*pl* **~nais**) *a* & *f* multinational

multipli|cação /muwtʃiplika-'sãw/ *f* multiplication; **~car** *vt* multiply; **~car-se** *vpr* multiply; **~cidade** *f* multiplicity

múltiplo /'muwtʃiplu/ *a* & *m* multiple

multirraci|al /muwtʃixasi'aw/ (*pl* **~ais**) *a* multiracial

múmia /'mumia/ *f* mummy

mun|dano /mũ'danu/ *a* <*prazeres etc*> worldly; <*vida, mulher*> society; **~dial** (*pl* **~diais**) *a* world □ *m* world championship; **~do** *m* world; **todo (o) ~do** everybody

munição /muni'sãw/ *f* ammunition

muni|cipal /munisi'paw/ (*pl* **~cipais**) *a* municipal; **~cípio** *m* (*lugar*) borough, community; (*prédio*) town hall; (*autoridade*) local authority

munir /mu'nir/ *vt* provide (**de** with); **~-se** *vpr* equip o.s. (**de** with)

mu|ral /mu'raw/ (*pl* **~rais**) *a* & *m* mural; **~ralha** *f* wall

mur|char /mur'ʃar/ *vi* <*planta*> wither, wilt; <*salada*> go limp; <*beleza*> fade □ *vt* wither, wilt <*planta*>; **~cho** *a* <*planta*> wilting; <*pessoa*> broken

mur|murar /murmu'rar/ *vi* murmur; (*queixar-se*) mutter □ *vt* murmur; **~múrio** *m* murmur

muro /'muru/ *m* wall

murro /'muxu/ *m* punch

musa /'muza/ *f* muse

muscu|lação /muskula'sãw/ *f* weight-training; **~lar** *a* muscular; **~latura** *f* musculature

músculo /'muskulu/ *m* muscle

musculoso /musku'lozu/ *a* muscular

museu /mu'zew/ *m* museum

musgo /'muzgu/ *m* moss

música /'muzika/ *f* music; (*uma*) song; ~ de câmara chamber music; ~ de fundo background music; ~ clássica *ou* erudita classical music

musi|cal /muzi'kaw/ (*pl* ~cais) *a* & *m* musical; ~car *vt* set to music

músico /'muziku/ *m* musician □ *a* musical

musse /'musi/ *f* mousse

mutilar /mutʃi'lar/ *vt* mutilate; maim <*pessoa*>

mutirão /mutʃi'rãw/ *m* joint effort

mútuo /'mutuu/ *a* mutual

muxoxo /mu'ʃoʃu/ *m* fazer ~ tut

N

na = em + a

nabo /'nabu/ *m* turnip

nação /na'sãw/ *f* nation

nacio|nal /nasio'naw/ (*pl* ~nais) *a* national; (*brasileiro*) home-produced; ~nalidade *f* nationality; ~nalismo *m* nationalism; ~nalista *a* & *m/f* nationalist; ~nalizar *vt* nationalize

naco /'naku/ *m* chunk

nada /'nada/ *pron* nothing □ *adv* not at all; de ~ (*não há de quê*) don't mention it; que ~!, ~ disso! no way!

na|dadeira /nada'dera/ *f* (*de peixe*) fin; (*de mergulhador*) flipper; ~dador *m* swimmer; ~dar *vi* swim

nádegas /'nadegas/ *f pl* buttocks

nado /'nadu/ *m* ~ borboleta butterfly stroke; ~ de costas backstroke; ~ de peito breaststroke; atravessar a ~ swim across

náilon /'najlõ/ *m* nylon

naipe /'najpi/ *m* (*em jogo de cartas*) suit

namo|rada /namo'rada/ *f* girlfriend; ~rado *m* boyfriend; ~rador *a* amorous □ *m* ladies' man; ~rar *vt* (*ter relação com*) go out with; (*cobiçar*) eye up □ *vi* <*casal*> (*ter relação*) go out together; (*beijar-se etc*) kiss and cuddle; <*homem*> have a girlfriend; <*mulher*> have a boyfriend; ~ro /o/ *m* relationship

nanar /na'nar/ *vi* (*col*) sleep

nanico /na'niku/ *a* tiny

não /nãw/ *adv* not; (*resposta*) no □ *m* no; ~-alinhado *a* non-aligned; ~-conformista *a* & *m/f* non-conformist

naquela, naquele, naquilo = em + aquela, aquele, aquilo

narci|sismo /narsi'zizmu/ *m* narcissism; ~sista *m/f* narcissist □ *a* narcissistic; ~so *m* narcissus

narcótico /nar'kɔtʃiku/ *a* & *m* narcotic

nari|gudo /nari'gudu/ *a* with a big nose; ser ~gudo have a big nose; ~na *f* nostril

nariz /na'ris/ *m* nose

nar|ração /naxa'sãw/ *f* narration; ~rador *m* narrator; ~rar *vt* narrate; ~rativa *f* narrative; ~rativo *a* narrative

nas = em + as

na|sal /na'zaw/ (*pl* ~sais) *a* nasal; ~salizar *vt* nasalize

nas|cença /na'sẽsa/ *f* birth; ~cente *a* nascent □ *f* source; ~cer *vi* be born; <*dente, espinha*> grow; <*planta*> sprout; <*sol, lua*> rise; <*dia*> dawn; (*fig*) <*empresa, projeto etc*> come into being □ *m* o ~cer do sol sunrise; ~cimento *m* birth

nata /'nata/ *f* cream

natação /nata'sãw/ *f* swimming

Natal /na'taw/ *m* Christmas

na|tal /na'taw/ (*pl* ~tais) *a* <*país, terra*> native

nata|lício /nata'lisiu/ *a* & *m* birthday; ~lidade *f* índice de ~lidade birth rate; ~lino *a* Christmas

nati|vidade /natʃivi'dadʒi/ *f* nativity; ~vo *a* & *m* native

nato /'natu/ *a* born

natu|ral /natu'raw/ (*pl* ~rais) *a* natural; (*oriundo*) originating (de from) □ *m* native (de of)

natura|lidade /naturali'dadʒi/ *f* naturalness; com ~lidade matter-of-factly; de ~lidade carioca born in Rio de Janeiro; ~lismo *m* naturalism; ~lista *a* & *m/f* naturalist; ~lizar *vt* naturalize; ~lizar-se *vpr* become naturalized

natureza /natu'reza/ *f* nature; ~ morta still life

naturis|mo /natu'rizmu/ *m* naturism; ~ta *m/f* naturist

nau|fragar /nawfra'gar/ *vi* <*navio*> be wrecked; <*tripulação*> be shipwrecked; (*fig*) <*plano, casamento etc*> founder; ~frágio *m* shipwreck; (*fig*) failure

náufrago /'nawfragu/ *m* castaway

náusea /'nawzia/ *f* nausea

nauseabundo /nawzia'bũdu/ *a* nauseating

náuti|ca /'nawtʃika/ *f* navigation; ~co *a* nautical

na|val /na'vaw/ (*pl* ~vais) *a* naval; construção ~val shipbuilding

navalha /na'vaʎa/ *f* razor; ~da *f* cut with a razor

nave /'navi/ *f* nave; ~ espacial spaceship

nave|gação /navega'sãw/ *f* navigation; (*tráfego*) shipping; ~gador *m* navigator; ~gante *m/f* seafarer; ~gar *vt* navigate; sail <*mar*> □ *vi* sail; (*traçar o rumo*) navigate; **~gável** (*pl* **~gáveis**) *a* navigable

navio /na'viu/ *m* ship; **~ cargueiro** cargo ship; **~ de guerra** warship; **~ petroleiro** oil tanker

nazista /na'zista/, (*Port*) **nazi** /na'zi/ *a & m/f* Nazi

neblina /ne'blina/ *f* mist

nebulo|sa /nebu'lɔza/ *f* nebula; **~sidade** *f* cloud; **~so** /o/ *a* cloudy; (*fig*) obscure

neces|saire /nese'sɛr/ *m* toilet bag; **~sário** *a* necessary; **~sidade** *f* necessity; (*que se impõe*) need; (*pobreza*) need; **~sitado** *a* needy □ *m* person in need; **~sitar** *vt* require; (*tornar necessário*) necessitate; **~sitar de** need

necro|lógio /nekro'lɔʒiu/ *m* obituary column; **~tério** *m* mortuary, (*Amer*) morgue

néctar /'nɛktar/ *m* nectar

nectarina /nekta'rina/ *f* nectarine

nefasto /ne'fastu/ *a* fatal

ne|gação /nega'sãw/ *f* denial; (*ling*) negation; **ser uma ~gação em** be hopeless at; **~gar** *vt* deny; **~gar-se a** refuse to; **~gativa** *f* refusal; (*ling*) negative; **~gativo** *a & m* negative

negli|gência /negli'ʒẽsia/ *f* negligence; **~genciar** *vt* neglect; **~gente** *a* negligent

negoci|ação /negosia'sãw/ *f* negotiation; **~ador** *m* negotiator; **~ante** *m/f* dealer (**de** in); **~ar** *vt/i* negotiate; **~ar em** deal in; **~ata** *f* shady deal; **~ável** (*pl* **~áveis**) *a* negotiable

negócio /ne'gɔsiu/ *m* deal; (*fam: coisa*) thing; *pl* business; **a** *ou* **de ~s** <*viajar*> on business

negocista /nego'sista/ *m* wheeler-dealer □ *a* wheeler-dealing

ne|grito /ne'gritu/ *m* bold; **~gro** /e/ *a & m* black; (*de raça*) Negro

nela, nele = **em** + **ela, ele**

nem /nẽj/ *adv* not even □ *conj* **~ ... ~ ...** neither ... nor ...; **~ sempre** not always; **~ todos** not all; **~ que** not even if; **que ~** like; **~ eu** nor do I

nenê /ne'ne/, **neném** /ne'nẽj/ *m* baby

nenhum /ne'ɲũ/ *a* (*f* **nenhuma**) no □ *pron* (*f* **nenhuma**) not one; **~ dos dois** neither of them; **~ erro** no mistakes; **erro ~** no mistakes at all, not a single mistake; **~ lugar** nowhere

nenúfar /ne'nufar/ *m* waterlily

neologismo /neolo'ʒizmu/ *m* neologism

néon /'nɛõ/ *m* neon

neozelan|dês /neozelã'des/ *a* (*f* **~desa**) New Zealand □ *m* (*f* **~desa**) New Zealander

Nepal /ne'paw/ *m* Nepal

nervo /'nervu/ *m* nerve; **~sismo** *m* (*chateação*) annoyance; (*medo*) nervousness; **~so** /o/ *a* <*sistema, doença*> nervous; (*chateado*) annoyed; (*medroso*) nervous; **deixar alg ~so** get on s.o.'s nerves

nessa(s), nesse(s) = **em** + **essa(s), esse(s)**

nesta(s), neste(s) = **em** + **esta(s), este(s)**

ne|ta /'nɛta/ *f* granddaughter; **~to** /ɛ/ *m* grandson; *pl* grandchildren

neuro|logia /newrolo'ʒia/ *f* neurology; **~lógico** *a* neurological; **~logista** *m/f* neurologist

neu|rose /new'rɔzi/ *f* neurosis; **~rótico** *a* neurotic

neutrali|dade /newtrali'dadʒi/ *f* neutrality; **~zar** *vt* neutralize

neutrão /new'trãw/ *m* (*Port*) *veja* **nêutron**

neutro /'newtru/ *a* neutral

nêutron /'newtrõ/ *m* neutron

ne|vada /ne'vada/ *f* snowfall; **~vado** *a* snow-covered; **~var** *vi* snow; **~vasca** *f* snowstorm; **~ve** /ɛ/ *f* snow

névoa /'nɛvoa/ *f* haze

nevoeiro /nevo'eru/ *m* fog

nexo /'nɛksu/ *m* connection; **sem ~** incoherent

Nicarágua /nika'ragwa/ *f* Nicaragua

nicaragüense /nikara'gwẽsi/ *a & m/f* Nicaraguan

nicho /'niʃu/ *m* niche

nicotina /niko'tʃina/ *f* nicotine

Níger /'niʒer/ *m* Niger

Nigéria /ni'ʒɛria/ *f* Nigeria

nigeriano /niʒeri'anu/ *a & m* Nigerian

Nilo /'nilu/ *m* Nile

ninar /ni'nar/ *vt* lull to sleep

ninfa /'nĩfa/ *f* nymph

ninguém /nĩ'gẽj/ *pron* no-one, nobody

ninhada /ni'ɲada/ *f* brood

ninharia /niɲa'ria/ *f* trifle

ninho /'niɲu/ *m* nest

níquel /'nikew/ *m* nickel

nisei /ni'sej/ *a & m/f* Japanese Brazilian

nisso = **em** + **isso**

nisto = **em** + **isto**

nitidez /nitʃi'des/ *f* (*de imagem etc*) sharpness

nítido /'nitʃidu/ *a* <*imagem, foto*> sharp; <*diferença, melhora*> distinct, clear

nitrogênio /nitro'ʒeniu/ *m* nitrogen

ní|vel /'nivew/ (*pl* **~veis**) *m* level; **a ~vel de** in terms of

nivelamento /nivela'mẽtu/ *m* levelling

nivelar /nive'lar/ *vt* level

no = **em** + **o**

nó /nɔ/ *m* knot; **dar um ~** tie a knot; **~ dos dedos** knuckle; **um ~ na garganta** a lump in one's throat

nobre /'nɔbri/ *a* noble; <*bairro*> exclusive □ *m/f* noble; **~za** /e/ *f* nobility
noção /no'sãw/ *f* notion; *pl* (*rudimentos*) elements
nocaute /no'kawtʃi/ *m* knockout; **pôr alg ~** knock s.o. out; **~ar** *vt* knock out
nocivo /no'sivu/ *a* harmful
nódoa /'nodoa/ *f* (*Port*) stain
nogueira /no'gera/ *f* (*árvore*) walnut tree
noi|tada /noj'tada/ *f* night; **~te** *f* night; (*antes de dormir*) evening; **à** *ou* **de ~te** at night; (*antes de dormir*) in the evening; **hoje à ~te** tonight; **ontem à ~te** last night; **boa ~te** (*ao chegar*) good evening; (*ao despedir-se*) good night; **~te em branco** *ou* **claro** sleepless night
noi|vado /noj'vadu/ *m* engagement; **~va** *f* fiancée; (*no casamento*) bride; **~vo** *m* fiancé; (*no casamento*) bridegroom; **os ~vos** the engaged couple; (*no casamento*) the bride and groom; **ficar ~vo** get engaged
no|jento /no'ʒẽtu/ *a* disgusting; **~jo** /o/ *m* disgust
nômade /'nomadʒi/ *m/f* nomad □ *a* nomadic
nome /'nomi/ *m* name; **de ~** by name; **em ~ de** in the name of; **~ comercial** trade name; **~ de batismo** Christian name; **~ de guerra** professional name
nome|ação /nomia'sãw/ *f* appointment; **~ar** *vt* (*para cargo*) appoint; (*chamar pelo nome*) name
nomi|nal /nomi'naw/ (*pl* **~nais**) *a* nominal
nonagésimo /nona'ʒɛzimu/ *a* ninetieth
nono /'nonu/ *a & m* ninth
nora /'nɔra/ *f* daughter-in-law
nordes|te /nor'dɛstʃi/ *m* northeast; **~tino** *a* Northeastern □ *m* person from the Northeast (*of Brazil*)
nórdico /'nɔrdʒiku/ *a* Nordic
nor|ma /'nɔrma/ *f* norm; **~mal** (*pl* **~mais**) *a* normal
normali|dade /normali'dadʒi/ *f* normality; **~zar** *vt* bring back to normal; normalize <*relações diplomáticas*>; **~zar-se** *vpr* return to normal
noroeste /noro'ɛstʃi/ *a & m* northwest
norte /'nɔrtʃi/ *a & m* north; **~-africano** *a & m* North African; **~-americano** *a & m* North American; **~-coreano** *a & m* North Korean
nortista /nor'tʃista/ *a* Northern □ *m/f* Northerner
Noruega /noru'ɛga/ *f* Norway
norue|guês /norue'ges/ *a & m* (*f* **~guesa**) Norwegian
nos[1] = **em** + **os**
nos[2] /nus/ *pron* us; (*indireto*) (to) us; (*reflexivo*) ourselves
nós /nɔs/ *pron* we; (*depois de preposição*) us
nos|sa /'nɔsa/ *int* gosh; **~so** /ɔ/ *a* our □ *pron* ours
nos|talgia /nostaw'ʒia/ *f* nostalgia; **~tálgico** *a* nostalgic
nota /'nɔta/ *f* note; (*na escola etc*) mark; (*conta*) bill; **custar uma ~ (preta)** (*fam*) cost a bomb; **tomar ~** take note (**de** of); **~ fiscal** receipt
no|tação /nota'sãw/ *f* notation; **~tar** *vt* notice, note; **fazer ~tar** point out; **~tável** (*pl* **~táveis**) *a & m/f* notable
notícia /no'tʃisia/ *f* piece of news; *pl* news
notici|ar /notʃi'sjar/ *vt* report; **~ário** *m* (*na TV*) news; (*em jornal*) news section; **~arista** *m/f* (*na TV*) newsreader; (*em jornal*) news reporter; **~oso** /o/ *a* **agência ~osa** news agency
notifi|cação /notʃifika'sãw/ *f* notification; **~car** *vt* notify
notívago /no'tʃivagu/ *a* nocturnal □ *m* night person
notório /no'tɔriu/ *a* well-known
noturno /no'turnu/ *a* night; <*animal*> nocturnal
nova /'nɔva/ *f* piece of news; **~mente** *adv* again
novato /no'vatu/ *m* novice
nove /'nɔvi/ *a & m* nine; **~centos** *a & m* nine hundred
novela /no'vɛla/ *f* (*na TV*) soap opera; (*livro*) novella
novembro /no'vẽbru/ *m* November
noventa /no'vẽta/ *a & m* ninety
noviço /no'visu/ *m* novice
novidade /novi'dadʒi/ *f* novelty; (*notícia*) piece of news; *pl* (*notícias*) news
novilho /no'viʎu/ *m* calf
novo /'novu/ *a* new; (*jovem*) young; **de ~** again; **~ em folha** brand new
noz /nɔs/ *f* walnut; **~ moscada** nutmeg
nu /nu/ *a* (*f* **~a**) <*corpo, pessoa*> naked; <*braço, parede, quarto*> bare □ *m* nude; **~ em pêlo** stark naked; **a verdade ~a e crua** the plain truth
nuança /nu'ãsa/ *f* nuance
nu|blado /nu'bladu/ *a* cloudy; **~blar** *vt* cloud; **~blar-se** *vpr* cloud over
nuca /'nuka/ *f* nape of the neck
nuclear /nukli'ar/ *a* nuclear
núcleo /'nukliu/ *m* nucleus
nu|dez /nu'des/ *f* nakedness; (*na TV etc*) nudity; (*da parede etc*) bareness; **~dismo** *m* nudism; **~dista** *m/f* nudist
nulo /'nulu/ *a* void
num, numa(s) = **em** + **um, uma(s)**

nume|ral /nume'raw/ (*pl* **~rais**) *a* & *m* numeral; **~rar** *vt* number
numérico /nu'mɛriku/ *a* numerical
número /'numeru/ *m* number; (*de jornal, revista*) issue; (*de sapatos*) size; (*espetáculo*) act; **fazer ~** make up the numbers
numeroso /nume'rozu/ *a* numerous
nunca /'nũka/ *adv* never; **~ mais** never again
nuns = em + uns
nupci|al /nupsi'aw/ (*pl* **~ais**) *a* bridal
núpcias /'nupsias/ *f pl* marriage
nu|trição /nutri'sãw/ *f* nutrition; **~trir** *vt* nourish; (*fig*) harbour <*ódio, esperança*>; **~tritivo** *a* nourishing; <*valor*> nutritional
nuvem /'nuvẽ/ *f* cloud

O

o /u/ *artigo* the □ *pron* (*homem*) him; (*coisa*) it; (*você*) you; **~ que** (*a coisa que*) what; (*aquele que*) the one that; **~ quê?** what?; **meu livro e ~ do João** my book and John's (one)
ó /ɔ/ *int* (*fam*) look
ô /o/ *int* oh
oásis /o'azis/ *m invar* oasis
oba /'oba/ *int* great
obcecar /obise'kar/ *vt* obsess
obe|decer /obede'ser/ *vt* **~decer a** obey; **~diência** *f* obedience; **~diente** *a* obedient
obe|sidade /obezi'dadʒi/ *f* obesity; **~so** /e/ *a* obese
óbito /'ɔbitu/ *m* death
obituário /obitu'ariu/ *m* obituary
obje|ção /obiʒe'sãw/ *f* objection; **~tar** *vt/i* object (a to)
objeti|va /obiʒe'tʃiva/ *f* lens; **~vidade** *f* objectivity; **~vo** *a* & *m* objective
objeto /obi'ʒɛtu/ *m* object
oblíquo /o'blikwu/ *a* oblique; <*olhar*> sidelong
obliterar /oblite'rar/ *vt* obliterate
oblongo /o'blõgu/ *a* oblong
obo|é /obo'ɛ/ *m* oboe; **~ísta** *m/f* oboist
obra /'ɔbra/ *f* work; **em ~s** being renovated; **~ de arte** work of art; **~ de caridade** charity; **~-prima** (*pl* **~s-primas**) *f* masterpiece
obri|gação /obriga'sãw/ *f* obligation; (*título*) bond; **~gado** *int* thank you; (*não querendo*) no thank you; **~gar** *vt* force, oblige (a to); **~gar-se** *vpr* undertake (a to); **~gatório** *a* obligatory, compulsory
obsce|nidade /obiseni'dadʒi/ *f* obscenity; **~no** /e/ *a* obscene
obscu|ridade /obiskuri'dadʒi/ *f* obscurity; **~ro** *a* obscure
obséquio /obi'sɛkiu/ *m* favour
obsequioso /obiseki'ozu/ *a* obsequious
obser|vação /obiserva'sãw/ *f* observation; **~vador** *a* observant □ *m* observer; **~vância** *f* observance; **~var** *vt* observe; **~vatório** *m* observatory
obses|são /obise'sãw/ *f* obsession; **~sivo** *a* obsessive
obsoleto /obiso'letu/ *a* obsolete
obstáculo /obis'takulu/ *m* obstacle
obstar /obis'tar/ *vt* stand in the way (a of)
obs|tetra /obis'tɛtra/ *m/f* obstetrician; **~tetrícia** *f* obstetrics; **~tétrico** *a* obstetric
obsti|nação /obistina'sãw/ *f* obstinacy; **~nado** *a* obstinate; **~nar-se** *vpr* insist (em on)
obstru|ção /obistru'sãw/ *f* obstruction; **~ir** *vt* obstruct
ob|tenção /obitẽ'sãw/ *f* obtaining; **~ter** *vt* obtain
obtu|ração /obitura'sãw/ *f* filling; **~rador** *m* shutter; **~rar** *vt* fill <*dente*>
obtuso /obi'tuzu/ *a* obtuse
óbvio /'ɔbviu/ *a* obvious
ocasi|ão /okazi'ãw/ *f* occasion; (*oportunidade*) opportunity; (*compra*) bargain; **~onal** (*pl* **~onais**) *a* chance; **~onar** *vt* cause
Oceania /osia'nia/ *f* Oceania
oce|ânico /osi'aniku/ *a* ocean; **~ano** *m* ocean
ociden|tal /osidẽ'taw/ (*pl* **~tais**) *a* western □ *m/f* Westerner; **~te** *m* West
ócio /'ɔsiu/ *m* (*lazer*) leisure; (*falta de trabalho*) idleness
ocioso /osi'ozu/ *a* idle □ *m* idler
oco /'oku/ *a* hollow; <*cabeça*> empty
ocor|rência /oko'xẽsia/ *f* occurrence; **~rer** *vi* occur (a to)
ocu|lar /oku'lar/ *a* **testemunha ~lar** eye witness; **~lista** *m/f* optician
óculos /'ɔkulus/ *m pl* glasses; **~ de sol** sunglasses
ocul|tar /okuw'tar/ *vt* conceal; **~to** *a* hidden; (*sobrenatural*) occult
ocu|pação /okupa'sãw/ *f* occupation; **~pado** *a* <*pessoa*> busy; <*cadeira*> taken; <*telefone*> engaged, (*Amer*) busy; **~par** *vt* occupy; take up <*tempo, espaço*>; hold <*cargo*>; **~par-se** *vpr* keep busy; **~par-se com** *ou* **de** be involved with <*política, literatura etc*>; take care of <*cliente, doente, problema*>; occupy one's time with <*leitura, palavras cruzadas etc*>
ode /'ɔdʒi/ *f* ode

odiar /odʒi'ar/ *vt* hate
ódio /'ɔdʒiu/ *m* hatred, hate; (*raiva*) anger
odioso /odʒi'ozu/ *a* hateful
odontologia /odõtolo'ʒia/ *f* dentistry
odor /o'dor/ *m* odour
oeste /o'ɛstʃi/ *a & m* west
ofe|gante /ofe'gãtʃi/ *a* panting; **~gar** *vi* pant
ofen|der /ofẽ'der/ *vt* offend; **~der-se** *vpr* take offence; **~sa** *f* insult; **~siva** *f* offensive; **~sivo** *a* offensive
ofere|cer /ofere'ser/ *vt* offer; **~cer-se** *vpr* <*pessoa*> offer o.s. (como as); <*ocasião*> arise; **~cer-se para ajudar** offer to help; **~cimento** *m* offer
oferenda /ofe'rẽda/ *f* offering
oferta /o'fɛrta/ *f* offer; **em ~** on offer; **a ~ e a demanda** supply and demand
ofici|al /ofisi'aw/ (*pl* **~ais**) *a* official □ *m* officer; **~alizar** *vt* make official; **~ar** *vi* officiate
oficina /ofi'sina/ *f* workshop; (*para carros*) garage, (*Amer*) shop
ofício /o'fisiu/ *m* (*profissão*) trade; (*na igreja*) service
oficioso /ofisi'ozu/ *a* unofficial
ofus|cante /ofus'kãtʃi/ *a* dazzling; **~car** *vt* dazzle <*pessoa*>; obscure <*sol etc*>; (*fig: eclipsar*) outshine
oi /oj/ *int* (*cumprimento*) hi; (*resposta*) yes?
oi|tavo /oi'tavu/ *a & m* eighth; **~tenta** *a & m* eighty; **~to** *a & m* eight; **~tocentos** *a & m* eight hundred
olá /o'la/ *int* hello
olaria /ola'ria/ *f* pottery
óleo /'ɔliu/ *m* oil
oleo|duto /oliu'dutu/ *m* oil pipeline; **~so** /o/ *a* oily
olfato /ow'fatu/ *m* sense of smell
olhada /o'ʎada/ *f* look; **dar uma ~** have a look
olhar /o'ʎar/ *vt* look at; (*assistir*) watch □ *vi* look □ *m* look; **~ para** look at; **~ por** look after; **e olhe lá** (*fam*) and that's pushing it
olheiras /o'ʎeras/ *f pl* dark rings under one's eyes
olho /'oʎu/ *m* eye; **a ~ nu** with the naked eye; **custar os ~s da cara** cost a fortune; **ficar de ~** keep an eye out; **ficar de ~ em** keep an eye on; **pôr alg no ~ da rua** throw s.o. out; **não pregar o ~** not sleep a wink; **~ gordo** *ou* **grande** envy; **~ mágico** peephole; **~ roxo** black eye
Olimpíada /olĩ'piada/ *f* Olympic Games
olímpico /o'lĩpiku/ *a* <*jogos, vila*> Olympic; (*fig*) blithe
oliveira /oli'vera/ *f* olive tree
olmo /'owmu/ *m* elm
om|breira /õ'brera/ *f* (*para roupa*) shoulder pad; **~bro** *m* shoulder; **dar de ~bros** shrug one's shoulders
omelete /ome'lɛtʃi/, (*Port*) **omeleta** /ome'leta/ *f* omelette
omis|são /omi'sãw/ *f* omission; **~so** *a* negligent, remiss
omitir /omi'tʃir/ *vt* omit
omni- (*Port*) *veja* **oni-**
omoplata /omo'plata/ *f* shoulder blade
onça[1] /'õsa/ *f* (*peso*) ounce
onça[2] /'õsa/ *f* (*animal*) jaguar
onda /'õda/ *f* wave; **pegar ~** (*fam*) surf
onde /'õdʒi/ *adv* where; **por ~?** which way?; **~ quer que** wherever
ondu|lação /õdula'sãw/ *f* undulation; (*do cabelo*) wave; **~lado** *a* wavy; **~lante** *a* undulating; **~lar** *vt* wave <*cabelo*> □ *vi* undulate
onerar /one'rar/ *vt* burden
ônibus /'onibus/ *m invar* bus; **~ espacial** space shuttle
onipotente /onipo'tẽtʃi/ *a* omnipotent
onírico /o'niriku/ *a* dreamlike
onisciente /onisi'ẽtʃi/ *a* omniscient
onomatopéia /onomato'pɛja/ *f* onomatopoeia
ontem /'õtẽ/ *adv* yesterday
onze /'õzi/ *a & m* eleven
opaco /o'paku/ *a* opaque
opala /o'pala/ *f* opal
opção /opi'sãw/ *f* option
ópera /'ɔpera/ *f* opera
ope|ração /opera'sãw/ *f* operation; (*bancária etc*) transaction; **~rador** *m* operator; **~rar** *vt* operate; operate on <*doente*>; work <*milagre*> □ *vi* operate; **~rar-se** *vpr* (*acontecer*) come about; (*fazer operação*) have an operation; **~rário** *a* working □ *m* worker
opereta /ope'reta/ *f* operetta
opinar /opi'nar/ *vt* think □ *vi* express one's opinion
opinião /opini'ãw/ *f* opinion; **na minha ~** in my opinion; **~ pública** public opinion
ópio /'ɔpiu/ *m* opium
opor /o'por/ *vt* put up <*resistência, argumento*>; (*pôr em contraste*) contrast (a with); **~-se a** (*não aprovar*) oppose; (*ser diferente*) contrast with
oportu|nidade /oportuni'dadʒi/ *f* opportunity; **~nista** *a & m/f* opportunist; **~no** *a* opportune
oposi|ção /opozi'sãw/ *f* opposition (a to); **~cionista** *a* opposition □ *m/f* opposition politician
oposto /o'postu/ *a & m* opposite

opres|são /opre'sãw/ *f* oppression; (*no peito*) tightness; **~sivo** *a* oppressive; **~sor** *m* oppressor
oprimir /opri'mir/ *vt* oppress; (*com trabalho*) weigh down □ *vi* be oppressive
optar /opi'tar/ *vi* opt (**por** for); **~ por ir** opt to go
óptica, óptico *veja* **ótica, ótico**
opu|lência /opu'lẽsia/ *f* opulence; **~lento** *a* opulent
ora /'ɔra/ *adv & conj* now □ *int* come; **~ essa!** come now!; **~ ..., ~ ...** first ..., then
oração /ora'sãw/ *f* (*prece*) prayer; (*discurso*) oration; (*frase*) clause
oráculo /o'rakulu/ *m* oracle
orador /ora'dor/ *m* orator
oral /o'raw/ (*pl* **orais**) *a & f* oral
orar /o'rar/ *vi* pray
órbita /'ɔrbita/ *f* orbit; (*do olho*) socket
orçamen|tário /orsamẽ'tariu/ *a* budgetary; **~to** *m* (*plano financeiro*) budget; (*previsão dos custos*) estimate
orçar /or'sar/ *vt* estimate (**em** at)
ordeiro /or'deru/ *a* orderly
ordem /'ɔrdẽ/ *f* order; **por ~ alfabética** in alphabetical order; **~ de pagamento** banker's draft; **~ do dia** agenda
orde|nação /ordena'sãw/ *f* ordering; (*de padre*) ordination; **~nado** *a* ordered □ *m* wages; **~nar** *vt* order; put in order <*papéis, livros etc*>; ordain <*padre*>
ordenhar /orde'ɲar/ *vt* milk
ordinário /ordʒi'nariu/ *a* (*normal*) ordinary; (*grosseiro*) vulgar; (*de má qualidade*) inferior; (*sem caráter*) rough
orégano /o'rɛganu/ *m* oregano
ore|lha /o'reʎa/ *f* ear; **~lhão** *m* phone booth; **~lhudo** *a* with big ears; **ser ~lhudo** have big ears
orfanato /orfa'natu/ *m* orphanage
ór|fão /'ɔrfãw/ (*pl* **~fãos**) *a & m* (*f* **~fã**) orphan
orgânico /or'ganiku/ *a* organic
orga|nismo /orga'nizmu/ *m* organism; (*do Estado etc*) institution; **~nista** *m/f* organist
organi|zação /organiza'sãw/ *f* organization; **~zador** *a* organizing □ *m* organizer; **~zar** *vt* organize
órgão /'ɔrgãw/ (*pl* **~s**) *m* organ; (*do Estado etc*) body
orgasmo /or'gazmu/ *m* orgasm
orgia /or'ʒia/ *f* orgy
orgu|lhar /orgu'ʎar/ *vt* make proud; **~lhar-se** *vpr* be proud (**de** of); **~lho** *m* pride; **~lhoso** /o/ *a* proud
orien|tação /oriẽta'sãw/ *f* orientation; (*direção*) direction; (*vocacional etc*) guidance; **~tador** *m* advisor; **~tal** (*pl* **~tais**) *a* eastern; (*da Asia*) oriental; **~tar** *vt* direct; (*aconselhar*) advise; (*situar*) position; **~tar-se** *vpr* get one's bearings; **~tar-se por** be guided by; **~te** *m* east; **Oriente Médio** Middle East; **Extremo Oriente** Far East
orifício /ori'fisiu/ *m* opening; (*no corpo*) orifice
origem /o'riʒẽ/ *f* origin; **dar ~ a** give rise to; **ter ~** originate
origi|nal /oriʒi'naw/ (*pl* **~nais**) *a & m* original; **~nalidade** *f* originality; **~nar** *vt* give rise to; **~nar-se** *vpr* originate; **~nário** *a* <*planta, animal*> native (**de** to); <*pessoa*> originating (**de** from)
oriundo /o'rjũdu/ *a* originating (**de** from)
orla /'ɔrla/ *f* border; **~ marítima** seafront
ornamen|tação /ornamẽta'sãw/ *f* ornamentation; **~tal** (*pl* **~tais**) *a* ornamental; **~tar** *vt* decorate; **~to** *m* ornament
orques|tra /or'kɛstra/ *f* orchestra; **~tra sinfônica** symphony orchestra; **~tral** (*pl* **~trais**) *a* orchestral; **~trar** *vt* orchestrate
orquídea /or'kidʒia/ *f* orchid
ortodoxo /orto'dɔksu/ *a* orthodox
orto|grafia /ortogra'fia/ *f* spelling, orthography; **~gráfico** *a* orthographic
orto|pedia /ortope'dʒia/ *f* orthopaedics; **~pédico** *a* orthopaedic; **~pedista** *m/f* orthopaedic surgeon
orvalho /or'vaʎu/ *m* dew
os /us/ *artigo & pron veja* **o**
oscilar /osi'lar/ *vi* oscillate
ósseo /'ɔsiu/ *a* bone
os|so /'osu/ *m* bone; **~sudo** *a* bony
ostensivo /ostẽ'sivu/ *a* ostensible
osten|tação /ostẽta'sãw/ *f* ostentation; **~tar** *vt* show off; **~toso** *a* showy, ostentatious
osteopata /ostʃio'pata/ *m/f* osteopath
ostra /'ostra/ *f* oyster
ostracismo /ostra'sizmu/ *m* ostracism
otário /o'tariu/ *m* (*fam*) fool
óti|ca /'ɔtʃika/ *f* (*ciência*) optics; (*loja*) optician's; (*ponto de vista*) viewpoint; **~co** *a* optical
otimis|mo /otʃi'mizmu/ *m* optimism; **~ta** *m/f* optimist □ *a* optimistic
ótimo /'ɔtʃimu/ *a* excellent
otorrino /oto'xinu/ *m* ear, nose and throat specialist
ou /o/ *conj* or; **~ ... ~ ...** either ... or ...; **~ seja** in other words
ouriço /o'risu/ *m* hedgehog; **~-do-mar** (*pl* **~s-do-mar**) *m* sea urchin

ouri|ves /o'rivis/ *m/f invar* jeweller; **~vesaria** *f* (*loja*) jeweller's

ouro /'oru/ *m* gold; *pl* (*naipe*) diamonds; **de ~** golden

ou|sadia /oza'dʒia/ *f* daring; (*uma*) daring step; **~sado** *a* daring; **~sar** *vt/i* dare

outdoor /'awtdor/ (*pl* **~s**) *m* billboard

outo|nal /oto'naw/ (*pl* **~nais**) *a* autumnal; **~no** /o/ *m* autumn, (*Amer*) fall

outorgar /otor'gar/ *vt* grant

ou|trem /o'trẽj/ *pron* (*outro*) someone else; (*outros*) others; **~tro** *a* other □ *pron* (*um*) another (one); *pl* others; **~tro copo** another glass; **~tra coisa** something else; **~tro dia** the other day; **no ~tro dia** the next day; **~tra vez** again; **~trora** *adv* once upon a time; **~trossim** *adv* equally

outubro /o'tubru/ *m* October

ou|vido /o'vidu/ *m* ear; **de ~vido** by ear; **dar ~vidos a** listen to; **~vinte** *m/f* listener; **~vir** *vt* hear; (*atentamente*) listen to □ *vi* hear; **~vir dizer que** hear that; **~vir falar de** hear of

ovação /ova'sãw/ *f* ovation

oval /o'vaw/ (*pl* **ovais**) *a & f* oval

ovário /o'variu/ *m* ovary

ovelha /o'veʎa/ *f* sheep

óvni /'ɔvni/ *m* UFO

ovo /'ovu/ *m* egg; **~ cozido/frito/mexido/pochê** boiled/fried/scrambled/poached egg

oxi|genar /oksiʒe'nar/ *vt* bleach <*cabelo*>; **~gênio** *m* oxygen

ozônio /o'zoniu/ *m* ozone

P

pá /pa/ *f* spade; (*de hélice*) blade; (*de moinho*) sail □ *m* (*Port: fam*) mate

pacato /pa'katu/ *a* quiet

paci|ência /pasi'ẽsia/ *f* patience; **~ente** *a & m/f* patient

pacificar /pasifi'kar/ *vt* pacify

pacífico /pa'sifiku/ *a* peaceful; **Oceano Pacífico** Pacific Ocean; **ponto ~** undisputed point

pacifis|mo /pasi'fizmu/ *m* pacifism; **~ta** *a & m/f* pacifist

paço /'pasu/ *m* palace

pacote /pa'kɔtʃi/ *m* (*de biscoitos etc*) packet; (*mandado pelo correio*) parcel; (*econômico, turístico, software*) package

pacto /'paktu/ *m* pact

padaria /pada'ria/ *f* baker's (shop), bakery

padecer /pade'ser/ *vt/i* suffer

padeiro /pa'deru/ *m* baker

padiola /padʒi'ɔla/ *f* stretcher

padrão /pa'drãw/ *m* standard; (*desenho*) pattern

padrasto /pa'drastu/ *m* stepfather

padre /'padri/ *m* priest

padrinho /pa'driɲu/ *m* (*de batismo*) godfather; (*de casamento*) best man

padroeiro /padro'eru/ *m* patron saint

padronizar /padroni'zar/ *vt* standardize

paetê /paj'te/ *m* sequin

paga /'paga/ *f* pay; **~mento** *m* payment

pa|gão /pa'gãw/ (*pl* **~gãos**) *a & m* (*f* **~gã**) pagan

pagar /pa'gar/ *vt* pay for <*compra, erro etc*>; pay <*dívida, conta, empregado etc*>; pay back <*empréstimo*>; repay <*gentileza etc*> □ *vi* pay; **eu pago para ver** I'll believe it when I see it

página /'paʒina/ *f* page

pago /'pagu/ *a* paid □ *pp de* **pagar**

pagode /pa'gɔdʒi/ *m* (*torre*) pagoda; (*fam*) singalong

pai /paj/ *m* father; *pl* (*pai e mãe*) parents; **~-de-santo** (*pl* **~s-de-santo**) *m* macumba priest

pai|nel /paj'nɛw/ (*pl* **~néis**) *m* panel; (*de carro*) dashboard

paio /'paju/ *m* pork sausage

pairar /paj'rar/ *vi* hover

país /pa'is/ *m* country; **País de Gales** Wales; **Países Baixos** Netherlands

paisa|gem /paj'zaʒẽ/ *f* landscape; **~gista** *m/f* landscape gardener

paisana /paj'zana/ *f* **à ~** <*policial*> in plain clothes; <*soldado*> in civilian clothes

paixão /pa'ʃãw/ *f* passion

pala /'pala/ *f* (*de boné*) peak; (*de automóvel*) sun visor

palácio /pa'lasiu/ *m* palace

paladar /pala'dar/ *m* palate, taste

palanque /pa'lãki/ *m* stand

palavra /pa'lavra/ *f* word; **pedir a ~** ask to speak; **ter ~** be reliable; **tomar a ~** start to speak; **sem ~** <*pessoa*> unreliable; **~ de ordem** watchword; **~s cruzadas** crossword

palavrão /pala'vrãw/ *m* swearword

palco /'pawku/ *m* stage

palestino /pales'tʃinu/ *a & m* Palestinian

palestra /pa'lɛstra/ *f* lecture

paleta /pa'leta/ *f* palette

paletó /pale'tɔ/ *m* jacket

palha /'paʎa/ *f* straw

palha|çada /paʎa'sada/ *f* joke; **~ço** *m* clown

paliativo /palia'tʃivu/ *a & m* palliative

palidez /pali'des/ *f* paleness

pálido /'palidu/ *a* pale

pali|tar /pali'tar/ *vt* pick □ *vi* pick one's teeth; **~teiro** *m* toothpick holder; **~to** *m* (*para dentes*) toothpick; (*de fósforo*) matchstick; (*pessoa magra*) beanpole

pal|ma /'pawma/ *f* palm; *pl* (*aplauso*) clapping; **bater ~mas** clap; **~meira** *f* palm tree; **~mito** *m* palm heart; **~mo** *m* span; **~mo a ~mo** inch by inch

palpá|vel /paw'pavew/ (*pl* **~veis**) *a* palpable

pálpebra /'pawpebra/ *f* eyelid

palpi|tação /pawpita'sãw/ *f* palpitation; **~tante** *a* (*fig*) thrilling; **~tar** *vi* <*coração*> flutter; <*pessoa*> tremble; (*dar palpite*) stick one's oar in; **~te** *m* (*pressentimento*) hunch; (*no jogo etc*) tip; **dar ~te** stick one's oar in

panacéia /pana'sɛja/ *f* panacea

Panamá /pana'ma/ *m* Panama

panamenho /pana'meɲu/ *a & m* Panamanian

pan-americano /panameri'kanu/ *a* Pan-American

pança /'pãsa/ *f* paunch

pancada /pã'kada/ *f* blow; **~ d'água** downpour; **~ria** *f* fight, punch-up

pâncreas /'pãkrias/ *m invar* pancreas

pançudo /pã'sudu/ *a* paunchy

panda /'pãda/ *f* panda

pandarecos /pãda'rɛkus/ *m pl* **aos** *ou* **em ~** battered

pandeiro /pã'deru/ *m* tambourine

pandemônio /pãde'moniu/ *m* pandemonium

pane /'pani/ *f* breakdown

panela /pa'nɛla/ *f* saucepan; **~ de pressão** pressure cooker

panfleto /pã'fletu/ *m* pamphlet

pânico /'paniku/ *m* panic; **em ~** in a panic; **entrar em ~** panic

panifica|ção /panifika'sãw/ *f* bakery; **~dora** *f* bakery

pano /'panu/ *m* cloth; **~ de fundo** backdrop; **~ de pó** duster; **~ de pratos** tea towel

pano|rama /pano'rama/ *m* panorama; **~râmico** *a* panoramic

panqueca /pã'kɛka/ *f* pancake

panta|nal /pãta'naw/ (*pl* **~nais**) *m* marshland

pântano /'pãtanu/ *m* marsh

pantanoso /pãta'nozu/ *a* marshy

pantera /pã'tɛra/ *f* panther

pão /pãw/ (*pl* **pães**) *m* bread; **~ de fôrma** sliced loaf; **~ integral** brown bread; **~-de-ló** *m* sponge cake; **~-duro** (*pl* **pães-duros**) (*fam*) *a* stingy, tight-fisted □ *m/f* skinflint; **~zinho** *m* bread roll

Papa /'papa/ *m* Pope

papa /'papa/ *f* (*de nenem*) food; (*arroz etc*) mush

papagaio /papa'gaju/ *m* parrot

papai /pa'paj/ *m* dad, daddy; **Papai Noël** Father Christmas

papar /pa'par/ *vt/i* (*fam*) eat

papari|car /papari'kar/ *vt* pamper; **~cos** *m pl* pampering

pa|pel /pa'pɛw/ (*pl* **~péis**) *m* (*de escrever etc*) paper; (*um*) piece of paper; (*numa peça, filme*) part; (*fig: função*) role; **de ~pel passado** officially; **~pel de alumínio** aluminium foil; **~pel higiênico** toilet paper; **~pelada** *f* paperwork; **~pelão** *m* cardboard; **~pelaria** *f* stationer's (shop); **~pelzinho** *m* scrap of paper

papo /'papu/ *f* (*fam: conversa*) talk; (*do rosto*) double chin; **bater um ~** (*fam*) have a chat; **~ furado** idle talk

papoula /pa'pola/ *f* poppy

páprica /'paprika/ *f* paprika

paque|ra /pa'kɛra/ *f* (*fam*) pick-up; **~rador** *a* flirtatious □ *m* flirt; **~rar** *vt* flirt with <*pessoa*>; eye up <*vestido, carro etc*> □ *vi* flirt

paquista|nês /pakista'nes/ *a & m* (*f* **~nesa**) Pakistani

Paquistão /pakis'tãw/ *m* Pakistan

par /par/ *a* even □ *m* pair; (*parceiro*) partner; **a ~ de** up to date with <*notícias etc*>; **sem ~** unequalled

para /'para/ *prep* for; (*a*) to; **~ que** so that; **~ quê?** what for?; **~ casa** home; **estar ~ sair** be about to leave; **era ~ eu ir** I was supposed to go

para|benizar /parabeni'zar/ *vt* congratulate (**por** on); **~béns** *m pl* congratulations

parábola /pa'rabola/ *f* (*conto*) parable; (*curva*) parabola

parabóli|co /para'bɔliku/ *a* **antena ~ca** satellite dish

pára|-brisa /para'briza/ *m* windscreen, (*Amer*) windshield; **~-choque** *m* bumper

para|da /pa'rada/ *f* stop; (*interrupção*) stoppage; (*militar*) parade; (*fam: coisa difícil*) ordeal, challenge; **~da cardíaca** cardiac arrest; **~deiro** *m* whereabouts

paradisíaco /paradʒi'ziaku/ *a* idyllic

parado /pa'radu/ *a* <*trânsito, carro*> at a standstill, stopped; (*fig*) <*pessoa*> dull; **ficar ~** <*pessoa*> stand still; <*trânsito*> come to a standstill; (*fig: deixar de trabalhar*) stop work

parado|xal /paradok'saw/ (*pl* **~xais**) *a* paradoxical; **~xo** /ɔ/ *m* paradox

parafina /para'fina/ *f* paraffin

paráfrase /pa'rafrazi/ *f* paraphrase

parafrasear /parafrazi'ar/ *vt* paraphrase

parafuso /para'fuzu/ *f* screw; **entrar em ~** get into a state

para|gem /pa'raʒẽ/ *f* (*Port: parada*) stop; **nestas ~gens** in these parts

parágrafo /pa'ragrafu/ *m* paragraph

Paraguai /para'gwaj/ *m* Paraguay

paraguaio /para'gwaju/ *a & m* Paraguayan

paraíso /para'izu/ *m* paradise

pára-lama /para'lama/ *m* (*de carro*) wing, (*Amer*) fender; (*de bicicleta*) mudguard

parale|la /para'lɛla/ *f* parallel; *pl* (*aparelho*) parallel bars; **~lepípedo** *m* paving stone; **~lo** /ɛ/ *a & m* parallel

para|lisar /parali'zar/ *vt* paralyse; bring to a halt <*fábrica, produção*>; **~lisar-se** *vpr* become paralysed; <*fábrica, produção*> grind to a halt; **~lisia** *f* paralysis; **~lítico** *a & m* paralytic

paranói|a /para'nɔja/ *f* paranoia; **~co** *a* paranoid

parapeito /para'pejtu/ *m* (*muro*) parapet; (*da janela*) window-sill

pára-que|das /para'kɛdas/ *m invar* parachute; **~dista** *m/f* parachutist; (*militar*) paratrooper

parar /pa'rar/ *vt/i* stop; **~ de fumar** stop smoking; **ir ~** end up

pára-raios /para'xajus/ *m invar* lightning conductor

parasita /para'zita/ *a & m/f* parasite

parceiro /par'seru/ *m* partner

parce|la /par'sɛla/ *f* (*de terreno*) plot; (*prestação*) instalment; **~lar** *vt* spread <*pagamento*>

parceria /parse'ria/ *f* partnership

parci|al /parsi'aw/ (*pl* **~ais**) *a* partial; (*partidário*) biased; **~alidade** *f* bias

parco /'parku/ *a* frugal; <*recursos*> scant

par|dal /par'daw/ (*pl* **~dais**) *m* sparrow; **~do** *a* <*papel*> brown; <*pessoa*> mulatto

pare|cer /pare'ser/ *vi* (*ter aparência de*) seem; (*ter semelhança com*) be like; **~cer-se com** look like, resemble □ *m* opinion; **~cido** *a* similar (**com** to)

parede /pa'redʒi/ *f* wall

paren|te /pa'rẽtʃi/ *m/f* relative, relation; **~tesco** /e/ *m* relationship

parêntese /pa'rẽtʃizi/ *f* parenthesis; *pl* (*sinais*) brackets, parentheses

paridade /pari'dadʒi/ *f* parity

parir /pa'rir/ *vt* give birth to □ *vi* give birth

parlamen|tar /parlamẽ'tar/ *a* parliamentary □ *m/f* member of parliament; **~tarismo** *m* parliamentary system; **~to** *m* parliament

parmesão /parme'zãw/ *a & m* (**queijo**) **~** Parmesan (cheese)

paródia /pa'rɔdʒia/ *f* parody

parodiar /parodʒi'ar/ *vt* parody

paróquia /pa'rɔkia/ *f* parish

parque /'parki/ *m* park

parte /'partʃi/ *f* part; (*quinhão*) share; (*num litígio, contrato*) party; **a maior ~ de** most of; **à ~** (*de lado*) aside; (*separadamente*) separately; **um erro da sua ~** a mistake on your part; **em ~** in part; **em alguma ~** somewhere; **por toda ~** everywhere; **por ~ do pai** on one's father's side; **fazer ~ de** be part of; **tomar ~ em** take part in

parteira /par'tera/ *f* midwife

partici|pação /partʃisipa'sãw/ *f* participation; (*numa empresa, nos lucros*) share; **~pante** *a* participating □ *m/f* participant; **~par** *vi* take part (**de** *ou* **em** in)

particípio /partʃi'sipiu/ *m* participle

partícula /par'tʃikula/ *f* particle

particu|lar /partʃiku'lar/ *a* private; (*especial*) unusual □ *m* (*pessoa*) private individual; *pl* (*detalhes*) particulars; **em ~lar** (*especialmente*) in particular; (*a sós*) in private; **~laridade** *f* peculiarity

partida /par'tʃida/ *f* (*saída*) departure; (*de corrida*) start; (*de futebol, xadrez etc*) match; **dar ~ em** start up

par|tidário /partʃi'dariu/ *a* partisan □ *m* supporter; **~tido** *a* broken □ *m* (*político*) party; (*casamento, par*) match; **tirar ~tido de** benefit from; **tomar o ~tido de** side with; **~tilha** *f* division; **~tir** *vi* (*sair*) depart; <*corredor*> start □ *vt* break; **~tir-se** *vpr* break; **a ~tir de ...** from ... onwards; **~tir para** (*fam*) resort to; **~tir para outra** do something different, change direction; **~titura** *f* score

parto /'partu/ *m* birth

parvo /'parvu/ *a* (*Port*) stupid

Páscoa /'paskoa/ *f* Easter

pas|mar /paz'mar/ *vt* amaze; **~mar-se** *vpr* be amazed (**com** at); **~mo** *a* amazed □ *m* amazement

passa /'pasa/ *f* raisin

pas|sada /pa'sada/ *f* **dar uma ~sada em** call in at; **~sadeira** *f* (*mulher*) woman who irons; (*Port: faixa*) zebra crossing, (*Amer*) crosswalk; **~sado** *a* <*ano, mês, semana*> last; <*tempo, particípio etc*> past; <*fruta, comida*> off □ *m* past; **são duas horas ~sadas** it's gone two o'clock; **bem/mal ~sado** <*bife*> well done/rare

passa|geiro /pasa'ʒeru/ *m* passenger □ *a* passing; **~gem** *f* passage; (*bilhete*) ticket; **de ~gem** <*dizer etc*> in passing; **estar de ~gem** be passing through; ~**gem de ida e volta** return ticket, (*Amer*) round trip ticket

passaporte /pasa'pɔrtʃi/ *m* passport

passar /pa'sar/ *vt* pass; spend <*tempo*>; cross <*ponte, rio*>; (*a ferro*) iron <*roupa etc*>; (*aplicar*) put on <*creme, batom etc*> □ *vi* pass; <*dor, medo, chuva etc*> go; (*ser aceitável*) be passable □ *m* passing; ~**-se** *vpr* happen; **passou a beber muito** he started to drink a lot; **passei dos 30 anos** I'm over thirty; **não passa de um boato** it's nothing more than a rumour; ~ **por** go through; go along <*rua*>; (*ser considerado*) be taken for; **fazer-se** ~ **por** pass o.s. off as; ~ **por cima de** (*fig*) overlook; ~ **sem** do without

passarela /pasa'rɛla/ *f* (*sobre rua*) footbridge; (*para desfile de moda*) catwalk

pássaro /'pasaru/ *m* bird

passatempo /pasa'tẽpu/ *m* pastime

passe /'pasi/ *m* pass

pas|sear /pasi'ar/ *vi* go out and about; (*viajar*) travel around □ *vt* take for a walk; ~**seata** *f* protest march; ~**seio** *m* outing; (*volta a pé*) walk; (*volta de carro*) drive; **dar um** ~**seio** (*a pé*) go for a walk; (*de carro*) go for a drive

passio|nal /pasio'naw/ (*pl* ~**nais**) *a* **crime** ~**nal** crime of passion

passista /pa'sista/ *m/f* dancer

passí|vel /pa'sivew/ (*pl* ~**veis**) *a* ~**vel de** subject to

passi|vidade /pasivi'dadʒi/ *f* passivity; ~**vo** *a* passive □ *m* (*com*) liabilities; (*ling*) passive

passo /'pasu/ *m* step; (*velocidade*) pace; (*barulho*) footstep; ~ **a** ~ step by step; **a dois** ~**s de** a stone's throw from; **dar um** ~ take a step

pasta /'pasta/ *f* (*matéria*) paste; (*bolsa*) briefcase; (*fichário*) folder; **ministro sem** ~ minister without portfolio; ~ **de dentes** toothpaste

pas|tagem /pas'taʒẽ/ *f* pasture; ~**tar** *vi* graze

pas|tel /pas'tɛw/ (*pl* ~**téis**) *m* (*para comer*) samosa; (*Port: doce*) pastry; (*para desenhar*) pastel; ~**telão** *m* (*comédia*) slapstick; ~**telaria** *f* (*loja*) samosa vendor, (*Port*) pastry shop; (*Port: pastéis*) pastries

pasteurizado /pastewri'zadu/ *a* pasteurized

pastilha /pas'tʃiʎa/ *f* pastille

pas|to /'pastu/ *m* (*erva*) fodder, feed; (*lugar*) pasture; ~**tor** *m* (*de gado*) shepherd; (*clérigo*) vicar; ~**tor alemão** (*cachorro*) Alsatian; ~**toral** (*pl* ~**torais**) *a* pastoral

pata /'pata/ *f* paw; ~**da** *f* kick

patamar /pata'mar/ *m* landing; (*fig*) level

patê /pa'te/ *m* pâté

patente /pa'tẽtʃi/ *a* obvious □ *f* (*mil*) rank; (*de invenção*) patent; ~**ar** *vt* patent <*produto, invenção*>

pater|nal /pater'naw/ (*pl* ~**nais**) *a* paternal; ~**nidade** *f* paternity; ~**no** /ɛ/ *a* paternal

pate|ta /pa'tɛta/ *a* daft, silly □ *m/f* fool; ~**tice** *f* stupidity; (*uma*) silly thing

patético /pa'tɛtʃiku/ *a* pathetic

patíbulo /pa'tʃibulu/ *m* gallows

pati|faria /patʃifa'ria/ *f* roguishness; (*uma*) dirty trick; ~**fe** *m* scoundrel

patim /pa'tʃĩ/ *m* skate; ~ **de rodas** roller skate

pati|nação /patʃina'sãw/ *f* skating; (*rinque*) skating rink; ~**nador** *m* skater; ~**nar** *vi* skate; <*carro*> skid; ~**nete** /ɛ/ *m* skateboard

pátio /'patʃiu/ *m* courtyard; (*de escola*) playground

pato /'patu/ *m* duck

pato|logia /patolo'ʒia/ *f* pathology; ~**lógico** *a* pathological; ~**logista** *m/f* pathologist

patrão /pa'trãw/ *m* boss

pátria /'patria/ *f* homeland

patriar|ca /patri'arka/ *m* patriarch; ~**cal** (*pl* ~**cais**) *a* patriarchal

patrimônio /patri'moniu/ *m* (*bens*) estate, property; (*fig: herança*) heritage

patri|ota /patri'ɔta/ *m/f* patriot; ~**ótico** *a* patriotic; ~**otismo** *m* patriotism

patroa /pa'troa/ *f* boss; (*fam: esposa*) missus, wife

patro|cinador /patrosina'dor/ *m* sponsor; ~**cinar** *vt* sponsor; ~**cínio** *m* sponsorship

patru|lha /pa'truʎa/ *f* patrol; ~**lhar** *vt/i* patrol

pau /paw/ *m* stick; (*fam: cruzeiro*) cruzeiro; (*chulo: pênis*) prick; *pl* (*naipe*) clubs; **a meio** ~ at half mast; **rachar** ~ (*fam: brigar*) row, fight like cat and dog; ~**lada** *f* blow with a stick

paulista /paw'lista/ *a & m/f* (person) from (the state of) São Paulo; ~**no** *a & m* (person) from (the city of) São Paulo

pausa /'pawza/ *f* pause; ~**do** *a* slow

pauta /'pawta/ *f* (*em papel*) lines; (*de música*) stave; (*fig: de discussão etc*) agenda; ~**do** *a* <*papel*> lined

pavão /pa'vãw/ *m* peacock

pavilhão /pavi'ʎãw/ *m* pavilion; (*no jardim*) summerhouse

pavimen|tar /pavimẽ'tar/ *vt* pave; ~**to** *m* floor; (*de rua etc*) surface

pavio /pa'viu/ *m* wick

pavor /pa'vor/ *m* terror; **ter** ~ **de** be terrified of; ~**oso** /o/ *a* dreadful

paz /pas/ *f* peace; fazer as ~es make up

pé /pɛ/ *m* foot; (*planta*) plant; (*de móvel*) leg; a ~ on foot; ao ~ da letra literally; estar de ~ <*festa etc*> be on; ficar de ~ stand up; em ~ standing (up); em ~ de igualdade on an equal footing

peão /pi'ãw/ *m* (*Port: pedestre*) pedestrian; (*no xadrez*) pawn

peça /'pɛsa/ *f* piece; (*de máquina, carro etc*) part; (*teatral*) play; pregar uma ~ em play a trick on; ~ de reposição spare part; ~ de vestuário item of clothing

pe|cado /pe'kadu/ *m* sin; ~**cador** *m* sinner; ~**caminoso** /o/ *a* sinful; ~**car** *vi* (*contra a religião*) sin; (*fig*) fall down

pechin|cha /pe'ʃĩʃa/ *f* bargain; ~**char** *vi* bargain, haggle

peçonhento /peso'ɲẽtu/ *a* animais ~s vermin

pecu|ária /peku'aria/ *f* livestock-farming; ~**ário** *a* livestock; ~**arista** *m/f* livestock farmer

peculi|ar /pekuli'ar/ *a* peculiar; ~**aridade** *f* peculiarity

pecúlio /pe'kuliu/ *m* savings

pedaço /pe'dasu/ *m* piece; aos ~s in pieces; cair aos ~s fall to pieces

pedágio /pe'daʒiu/ *m* toll; (*cabine*) tollbooth

peda|gogia /pedago'ʒia/ *f* education; ~**gógico** *a* educational; ~**gogo** /o/ *m* educationalist

pe|dal /pe'daw/ (*pl* ~**dais**) *m* pedal; ~**dalar** *vt/i* pedal

pedante /pe'dãtʃi/ *a* pretentious □ *m/f* pseud

pé|-de-atleta /pɛdʒiat'lɛta/ *m* athlete's foot; ~**-de-meia** (*pl* ~**s-de-meia**) *m* nest egg; ~**-de-pato** (*pl* ~**s-de-pato**) *m* flipper

pederneira /peder'nera/ *f* flint

pedes|tal /pedes'taw/ (*pl* ~**tais**) *m* pedestal

pedestre /pe'dɛstri/ *a* & *m/f* pedestrian

pé|-de-vento /pɛdʒi'vẽtu/ (*pl* ~**s-de-vento**) *m* gust of wind

pedia|tra /pedʒi'atra/ *m/f* paediatrician; ~**tria** *f* paediatrics

pedicuro /pedʒi'kuru/ *m* chiropodist, (*Amer*) podiatrist

pe|dido /pe'dʒidu/ *m* request; (*encomenda*) order; a ~**dido** de at the request of; ~**dido** de demissão resignation; ~**dido** de desculpa apology; ~**dir** *vt* ask for; (*num restaurante etc*) order □ *vi* ask; (*num restaurante etc*) order; ~**dir** aco a alg ask s.o. for sth; ~**dir** para alg ir ask s.o. to go; ~**dir** desculpa apologize; ~**dir** em casamento propose to

pedinte /pe'dʒĩtʃi/ *m/f* beggar

pedra /'pɛdra/ stone; ~ de gelo ice cube; chuva de ~ hail; ~ pomes pumice stone

pedregoso /pedre'gozu/ *a* stony

pedreiro /pe'dreru/ *m* builder

pegada /pe'gada/ *f* footprint; (*de goleiro*) save

pegajoso /pega'ʒozu/ *a* sticky

pegar /pe'gar/ *vt* get; catch <*bola, doença, ladrão, ônibus*>; (*segurar*) get hold of; pick up <*emissora, hábito, mania*> □ *vi* (*aderir*) stick; <*doença*> be catching; <*moda*> catch on; <*carro, motor*> start; <*mentira, desculpa*> stick; ~**-se** *vpr* come to blows; ~ bem/mal go down well/badly; ~ fogo catch fire; pega essa rua take that street; ~ em grab; ~ no sono get to sleep

pego /'pɛgu/ *pp de* pegar

pei|dar /pej'dar/ *vi* (*chulo*) fart; ~**do** *m* (*chulo*) fart

pei|to /'pejtu/ *m* chest; (*seio*) breast; (*fig: coragem*) guts; ~**toril** (*pl* ~**toris**) *m* window-sill; ~**tudo** *a* <*mulher*> busty; (*fig: corajoso*) gutsy

pei|xaria /peʃa'ria/ *f* fishmonger's; ~**xe** *m* fish; Peixes (*signo*) Pisces; ~**xeiro** *m* fishmonger

pela = por + a

pelado /pe'ladu/ *a* (*nu*) naked, in the nude

pelan|ca /pe'lãka/ *f* roll of fat; *pl* flab; ~**cudo** *a* flabby

pelar /pe'lar/ *vt* peel <*fruta, batata*>; skin <*animal*>; (*fam: tomar dinheiro de*) fleece

pelas = por + as

pele /'pɛli/ *f* skin; (*como roupa*) fur; ~**teiro** *m* furrier; ~**teria** *f* furrier's

pelica /pe'lika/ *f* luvas de ~ kid gloves

pelicano /peli'kanu/ *m* pelican

película /pe'likula/ *f* skin

pelo = por + o

pêlo /'pelu/ *m* hair; (*de animal*) coat; nu em ~ stark naked; montar em ~ ride bareback

pelos = por + os

pelotão /pelo'tãw/ *m* platoon

pelúcia /pe'lusia/ *f* bicho de ~ soft toy, fluffy animal

peludo /pe'ludu/ *a* hairy

pena[1] /'pena/ *f* (*de ave*) feather; (*de caneta*) nib

pena[2] /'pena/ *f* (*castigo*) penalty; (*de amor etc*) pang; é uma ~ que it's a pity that; que ~! what a pity!; dar ~ be upsetting; estar com *ou* ter ~ de feel sorry for; (não) vale a ~ it's (not) worth it; vale a ~ tentar it's worth trying; ~ **de morte** death penalty

penada /pe'nada/ *f* stroke of the pen

pe|nal /pe'naw/ (*pl* **~nais**) *a* penal; **~nalidade** *f* penalty; **~nalizar** *vt* penalize

pênalti /'penawtʃi/ *m* penalty

penar /pe'nar/ *vi* suffer

pen|dente /pẽ'dẽtʃi/ *a* hanging; (*fig: causa*) pending; **~der** *vi* hang; (*inclinar-se*) slope; (*tender*) be inclined (a to); **~dor** *m* inclination

pêndulo /'pẽdulu/ *m* pendulum

pendu|rado /pẽdu'radu/ *a* hanging; (*fam: por fazer, pagar*) outstanding; **~rar** *vt* hang (up); (*fam*) put on the slate <*compra*> □ *vi* (*fam*) pay later; **~ricalho** *m* pendant

penedo /pe'nedu/ *m* rock

penei|ra /pe'nera/ *f* sieve; **~rar** *vt* sieve, sift □ *vi* drizzle

pene|tra /pe'nɛtra/ *m/f* (*fam*) gatecrasher; **~tração** *f* penetration; (*fig*) perspicacity; **~trante** *a* <*som, olhar*> piercing; <*dor*> sharp; <*ferida*> deep; <*frio*> biting; <*análise, espírito*> incisive, perceptive; **~trar** *vt* penetrate □ *vi* **~trar em** enter <*casa*>; (*fig*) penetrate

penhasco /pe'ɲasku/ *m* cliff

penhoar /peɲo'ar/ *m* dressing gown

penhor /pe'ɲor/ *m* pledge; **casa de ~es** pawnshop

penicilina /penisi'lina/ *f* penicillin

penico /pe'niku/ *m* potty

península /pe'nĩsula/ *f* peninsula

pênis /'penis/ *m invar* penis

penitência /peni'tẽsia/ *f* (*arrependimento*) penitence; (*expiação*) penance

penitenciá|ria /penitẽsi'aria/ *f* prison; **~rio** *a* prison □ *m* prisoner

penoso /pe'nozu/ *a* <*experiência, tarefa, assunto*> painful; <*trabalho, viagem*> hard, difficult

pensa|dor /pẽsa'dor/ *m* thinker; **~mento** *m* thought

pensão /pẽ'sãw/ *f* (*renda*) pension; (*hotel*) guesthouse; ~ **(alimentícia)** (*paga por ex-marido*) alimony; ~ **completa** full board

pen|sar /pẽ'sar/ *vt/i* think (em of *ou* about); **~sativo** *a* thoughtful, pensive

pên|sil /'pẽsiw/ (*pl* **~seis**) *a* **ponte ~sil** suspension bridge

penso /'pẽsu/ *m* (*curativo*) dressing

pentágono /pẽ'tagonu/ *m* pentagon

pentatlo /pẽ'tatlu/ *m* pentathlon

pente /'pẽtʃi/ *m* comb; **~adeira** *f* dressing table; **~ado** *m* hairstyle, hairdo; **~ar** *vt* comb; **~ar-se** *vpr* do one's hair; (*com pente*) comb one's hair

Pentecostes /pẽte'kɔstʃis/ *m* Whitsun

pente-fino /pẽtʃi'finu/ *m* **passar a ~** go over with a fine-tooth comb

pente|lhar /pẽte'ʎar/ *vt* (*fam*) bother; **~lho** /e/ *m* pubic hair; (*fam: pessoa inconveniente*) pain (in the neck)

penugem /pe'nuʒẽ/ *f* down

penúltimo /pe'nuwtʃimu/ *a* last but one, penultimate

penumbra /pe'nũbra/ *f* half-light

penúria /pe'nuria/ *f* penury, extreme poverty

pepino /pe'pinu/ *m* cucumber

pepita /pe'pita/ *f* nugget

peque|nez /peke'nes/ *f* smallness; (*fig*) pettiness; **~nininho** *a* tiny; **~no** /e/ *a* small; (*mesquinho*) petty

Pequim /pe'kĩ/ *f* Peking, Beijing

pequinês /peki'nes/ *m* Pekinese

pêra /'pera/ *f* pear

perambular /perãbu'lar/ *vi* wander

perante /pe'rãtʃi/ *prep* before

percalço /per'kawsu/ *m* pitfall

perceber /perse'ber/ *vt* realize; (*Port: entender*) understand; (*psiqu*) perceive

percen|tagem /persẽ'taʒẽ/ *f* percentage; **~tual** (*pl* **~tuais**) *a* & *m* percentage

percep|ção /persep'sãw/ *f* perception; **~tível** (*pl* **~tíveis**) *a* perceptible

percevejo /perse'veʒu/ *m* (*bicho*) bedbug; (*tachinha*) drawing pin, (*Amer*) thumbtack

per|correr /perko'xer/ *vt* cross; cover <*distância*>; (*viajar por*) travel through; **~curso** *m* journey

percus|são /perku'sãw/ *f* percussion; **~sionista** *m/f* percussionist

percutir /perku'tʃir/ *vt* strike

perda /'perda/ *f* loss; ~ **de tempo** waste of time

perdão /per'dãw/ *f* pardon

perder /per'der/ *vt* lose; (*não chegar a ver, pegar*) miss <*ônibus, programa na TV etc*>; waste <*tempo*> □ *vi* lose; **~-se** *vpr* get lost; **~-se de alg** lose s.o.; ~ **aco de vista** lose sight of sth

perdiz /per'dʒis/ *f* partridge

perdoar /perdo'ar/ *vt* forgive (aco a alg s.o. for sth)

perdulário /perdu'lariu/ *a* & *m* spendthrift

perdurar /perdu'rar/ *vi* endure; <*coisa ruim*> persist

pere|cer /pere'ser/ *vi* perish; **~cível** (*pl* **~cíveis**) *a* perishable

peregri|nação /peregrina'sãw/ *f* peregrination; (*romaria*) pilgrimage; **~nar** *vi* roam; (*por motivos religiosos*) go on a pilgrimage; **~no** *m* pilgrim

pereira /pe'rera/ *f* pear tree

peremptório /perẽp'tɔriu/ *a* peremptory

perene /pe'reni/ *a* perennial

perereca /pere'rɛka/ *f* tree frog

perfazer /perfa'zer/ *vt* make up

perfeccionis|mo /perfeksio'nizmu/ *m* perfectionism; **~ta** *a & m/f* perfectionist

perfei|ção /perfej'sãw/ *f* perfection; **~to** *a & m* perfect

per|fil /per'fiw/ (*pl* **~fis**) *m* profile; **~filar** *vt* line up; **~filar-se** *vpr* line up

perfu|mado /perfu'madu/ *a* <*flor, ar*> fragrant; <*sabonete etc*> scented; <*pessoa*> with perfume on; **~mar** *vt* perfume; **~mar-se** *vpr* put perfume on; **~maria** *f* perfumery; (*fam*) trimmings, frills; **~me** *m* perfume

perfu|rador /perfura'dor/ *m* punch; **~rar** *vt* punch <*papel, bilhete*>; drill through <*chão*>; perforate <*úlcera, pulmão etc*>; **~ratriz** *f* drill

pergaminho /perga'miɲu/ *m* parchment

pergun|ta /per'gũta/ *f* question; fazer uma **~ta** ask a question; **~tar** *vt/i* ask; **~tar** aco a alg ask s.o. sth; **~tar** por ask after

perícia /pe'risia/ *f* (*mestria*) expertise; (*inspeção*) investigation; (*peritos*) experts

perici|al /perisi'aw/ (*pl* **~ais**) *a* expert

pericli|tante /perikli'tãtʃi/ *a* precarious; **~tar** *vi* be at risk

peri|feria /perife'ria/ *f* periphery; (*da cidade*) outskirts; **~férico** *a & m* peripheral

perigo /pe'rigu/ *m* danger; **~so** /o/ *a* dangerous

perímetro /pe'rimetru/ *m* perimeter

periódico /peri'ɔdʒiku/ *a* periodic □ *m* periodical

período /pe'riodu/ *m* period; trabalhar meio **~** work part-time

peripécias /peri'pɛsias/ *f pl* ups and downs, vicissitudes

periquito /peri'kitu/ *m* parakeet; (*de estimação*) budgerigar

periscópio /peris'kɔpiu/ *m* periscope

perito /pe'ritu/ *a & m* expert (em at)

per|jurar /perʒu'rar/ *vi* commit perjury; **~júrio** *m* perjury; **~juro** *m* perjurer

perma|necer /permane'ser/ *vi* remain; **~nência** *f* permanence; (*estadia*) stay; **~nente** *a* permanent □ *f* perm

permeá|vel /permi'avew/ (*pl* **~veis**) *a* permeable

permis|são /permi'sãw/ *f* permission; **~sível** (*pl* **~síveis**) *a* permissible; **~sivo** *a* permissive

permitir /permi'tʃir/ *vt* allow, permit; **~** a alg ir allow s.o. to go

permutar /permu'tar/ *vt* exchange

perna /'pɛrna/ *f* leg

pernicioso /pernisi'ozu/ *a* pernicious

per|nil /per'niw/ (*pl* **~nis**) *m* leg

pernilongo /perni'lõgu/ *m* (large) mosquito

pernoi|tar /pernoj'tar/ *vi* spend the night; **~te** *m* overnight stay

pérola /'pɛrola/ *f* pearl

perpendicular /perpẽdʒiku'lar/ *a* perpendicular

perpetrar /perpe'trar/ *vt* perpetrate

perpetu|ar /perpetu'ar/ *vt* perpetuate; **~idade** *f* perpetuity

perpétu|o /per'pɛtuu/ *a* perpetual; prisão **~a** life imprisonment

perple|xidade /perpleksi'dadʒi/ *f* puzzlement; **~xo** /ɛ/ *a* puzzled

persa /'pɛrsa/ *a & m/f* Persian

perse|guição /persegi'sãw/ *f* pursuit; (*de minorias etc*) persecution; **~guidor** *m* pursuer; (*de minorias etc*) persecutor; **~guir** *vt* pursue; persecute <*minoria, seita etc*>

perseve|rança /perseve'rãsa/ *f* perseverance; **~rante** *a* persevering; **~rar** *vi* persevere

persiana /persi'ana/ *f* blind

pérsico /'pɛrsiku/ *a* Golfo Pérsico Persian Gulf

persignar-se /persig'narsi/ *vt* cross o.s.

persis|tência /persis'tẽsia/ *f* persistence; **~tente** *a* persistent; **~tir** *vi* persist

perso|nagem /perso'naʒẽ/ *m/f* (*pessoa famosa*) personality; (*em livro, filme etc*) character; **~nalidade** *f* personality; **~nalizar** *vt* personalize; **~nificar** *vt* personify

perspectiva /perspek'tʃiva/ *f* (*na arte, ponto de vista*) perspective; (*possibilidade*) prospect

perspi|cácia /perspi'kasia/ *f* insight, perceptiveness; **~caz** *a* perceptive

persua|dir /persua'dʒir/ *vt* persuade (alg a s.o. to); **~são** *f* persuasion; **~sivo** *a* persuasive

perten|cente /pertẽ'sẽtʃi/ *a* belonging (a to); (*que tem a ver com*) pertaining (a to); **~cer** *vi* belong (a to); (*referir-se*) pertain (a to); **~ces** *m pl* belongings

perto /'pɛrtu/ *adv* near (de to); aqui **~** near here, nearby; de **~** closely; <*ver*> close up

pertur|bação /perturba'sãw/ *f* disturbance; (*do espírito*) anxiety; **~bado** *a* <*pessoa*> unsettled, troubled; **~bar** *vt* disturb; **~bar-se** *vpr* get upset, be perturbed

Peru /pe'ru/ *m* Peru

peru /pe'ru/ *m* turkey

perua /pe'rua/ *f* (*carro grande*) estate car, (*Amer*) station wagon; (*caminho-*

nete) van; (*para escolares etc*) minibus; (*fam: mulher*) brassy woman

peruano /peru'ano/ *a & m* Peruvian

peruca /pe'ruka/ *f* wig

perver|são /perver'sãw/ *f* perversion; **~so** *a* perverse; **~ter** *vt* pervert

pesadelo /peza'delu/ *m* nightmare

pesado /pe'zadu/ *a* heavy; <*estilo, livro*> heavy-going □ *adv* heavily

pêsames /'pezamis/ *m pl* condolences

pesar[1] /pe'zar/ *vt* weigh; (*fig: avaliar*) weigh up □ *vi* weigh; (*influir*) carry weight; **~ sobre** <*ameaça etc*> hang over; **~-se** *vpr* weigh o.s.

pesar[2] /pe'zar/ *m* sorrow; **~oso** /o/ *a* sorry, sorrowful

pes|ca /'pɛska/ *f* fishing; **ir à ~ca** go fishing; **~cador** *m* fisherman; **~car** *vt* catch; (*retirar da água*) fish out □ *vi* fish; (*fam*) (*entender*) understand; (*cochilar*) nod off; **~car de** (*fam*) know all about

pescoço /pes'kosu/ *m* neck

peseta /pe'zeta/ *f* peseta

peso /'pezu/ *m* weight; **de ~** (*fig*) <*pessoa*> influential; <*livro, argumento*> authoritative

pesqueiro /pes'keru/ *a* fishing

pesqui|sa /pes'kiza/ *f* research; (*uma*) study; *pl* research; **~sa de mercado** market research; **~sador** *m* researcher; **~sar** *vt/i* research

pêssego /'pesigu/ *m* peach

pessegueiro /pesi'geru/ *m* peach tree

pessimis|mo /pesi'mizmu/ *m* pessimism; **~ta** *a* pessimistic □ *m/f* pessimist

péssimo /'pɛsimu/ *a* terrible, awful

pesso|a /pe'soa/ *f* person; *pl* people; **em ~a** in person; **~al** (*pl* **~ais**) *a* personal □ *m* staff; (*fam*) folks

pesta|na /pes'tana/ *f* eyelash; **tirar uma ~na** (*fam*) have a nap; **~nejar** *vi* blink; **sem ~nejar** (*fig*) without batting an eyelid

pes|te /'pɛstʃi/ *f* (*doença*) plague; (*criança etc*) pest; **~ticida** *m* pesticide

pétala /'pɛtala/ *f* petal

peteca /pe'tɛka/ *f* kind of shuttlecock; (*jogo*) kind of badminton played with the hand

peteleco /pete'lɛku/ *m* flick

petição /petʃi'sãw/ *f* petition

petisco /pe'tʃisku/ *m* savoury, titbit

petrificar /petrifi'kar/ *vt* petrify; (*de surpresa*) stun; **~-se** *vpr* be petrified; (*de surpresa*) be stunned

petroleiro /petro'leru/ *a* oil □ *m* oil tanker

petróleo /pe'trɔliu/ *m* oil, petroleum; **~ bruto** crude oil

petrolífero /petro'liferu/ *a* oil-producing

petroquími|ca /petro'kimika/ *f* petrochemicals; **~co** *a* petrochemical

petu|lância /petu'lãsia/ *f* cheek; **~lante** *a* cheeky

peúga /pi'uga/ *f* (*Port*) sock

pevide /pe'vidʒi/ *f* (*Port*) pip

pia /'pia/ *f* (*do banheiro*) washbasin; (*da cozinha*) sink; **~ batismal** font

piada /pi'ada/ *f* joke

pia|nista /pia'nista/ *m/f* pianist; **~no** *m* piano; **~no de cauda** grand piano

piar /pi'ar/ *vi* <*pinto*> cheep; <*coruja*> hoot

picada /pi'kada/ *f* (*de agulha, alfinete etc*) prick; (*de abelha, vespa*) sting; (*de mosquito, cobra*) bite; (*de heroína*) shot; (*de avião*) nosedive; **o fim da ~** (*fig*) the limit

picadeiro /pika'deru/ *m* ring

picante /pi'kãtʃi/ *a* <*comida*> hot, spicy; <*piada*> risqué; <*filme, livro*> raunchy

pica-pau /pika'paw/ *m* woodpecker

picar /pi'kar/ *vt* (*com agulha, alfinete etc*) prick; <*abelha, vespa, urtiga*> sting; <*mosquito, cobra*> bite; <*pássaro*> peck; chop <*carne, alho etc*>; shred <*papel*> □ *vi* <*peixe*> bite; <*lã, cobertor*> prickle

picareta /pika'reta/ *f* pickaxe

pi|chação /piʃa'sãw/ *f* piece of graffiti; *pl* graffiti; **~char** *vt* spray with graffiti <*muro, prédio*>; spray <*grafite, desenho*>; **~che** *m* pitch

picles /'piklis/ *m pl* pickles

pico /'piku/ *m* peak; **20 anos e ~** (*Port*) just over 20

picolé /piko'lɛ/ *m* ice lolly

pico|tar /piko'tar/ *vt* perforate; **~te** /ɔ/ *m* perforations

pie|dade /pie'dadʒi/ *f* (*religiosidade*) piety; (*compaixão*) pity; **~doso** /o/ *a* merciful, compassionate

pie|gas /pi'ɛgas/ *a invar* <*filme, livro*> sentimental, schmaltzy; <*pessoa*> soppy; **~guice** *f* sentimentality

pifar /pi'far/ *vi* (*fam*) break down, go wrong

pigar|rear /pigaxi'ar/ *vi* clear one's throat; **~ro** *m* frog in the throat

pigmento /pig'mẽtu/ *m* pigment

pig|meu /pig'mew/ *a & m* (*f* **~méia**) pygmy

pijama /pi'ʒama/ *m* pyjamas

pilantra /pi'lãtra/ *m/f* (*fam*) crook

pilão /pi'lãw/ *m* (*na cozinha*) pestle; (*na construção*) ram

pilar /pi'lar/ *m* pillar

pilastra /pi'lastra/ *f* pillar

pileque /pi'lɛki/ *m* drinking session; **tomar um ~** get drunk

pilha /'piʎa/ *f* (*monte*) pile; (*elétrica*) battery

pilhar /pi'ʎar/ *vt* pillage

pilhéria /pi'ʎɛria/ *f* joke
pilotar /pilo'tar/ *vt* fly, pilot <*avião*>; drive <*carro*>
pilotis /pilo'tʃis/ *m pl* pillars
piloto /pi'lotu/ *m* pilot; (*de carro*) driver; (*de gás*) pilot light □ *a invar* pilot
pílula /'pilula/ *f* pill
pimen|ta /pi'mẽta/ *f* pepper; **~ta de Caiena** cayenne pepper; **~ta-do-reino** *f* black pepper; **~ta-malagueta** (*pl* **~tas-malagueta**) *f* chilli pepper; **~tão** *m* (bell) pepper; **~teira** *f* pepper pot
pinacoteca /pinako'tɛka/ *f* art gallery
pin|ça /'pĩsa/ (*para tirar pêlos*) tweezers; (*para segurar*) tongs; (*de siri etc*) pincer; **~çar** *vt* pluck <*sobrancelhas*>
pin|cel /pĩ'sɛw/ (*pl* **~céis**) *m* brush; **~celada** *f* brush stroke; **~celar** *vt* paint
pin|ga /'pĩga/ *f* Brazilian rum; **~gado** *a* <*café*> with a dash of milk; **~gar** *vi* drip; (*começar a chover*) spit (with rain) □ *vt* drip; **~gente** *m* pendant; **~go** *m* drop; (*no i*) dot
pingue-pongue /pĩgi'põgi/ *m* table tennis
pingüim /pĩ'gwĩ/ *m* penguin
pi|nha /'piɲa/ *f* pine cone; **~nheiro** *f* pine tree; **~nho** *m* pine
pino /'pinu/ *m* pin; (*para trancar carro*) lock; **a ~** upright; **bater ~** <*carro*> knock
pin|ta /'pĩta/ *f* (*sinal*) mole; (*fam: aparência*) look; **~tar** *vt* paint; dye <*cabelo*>; put make-up on <*rosto, olhos*> □ *vi* paint; (*fam*) <*pessoa*> show up; <*problema, oportunidade*> crop up; **~tar-se** *vpr* put on make-up
pintarroxo /pĩta'xoʃu/ *m* robin
pinto /'pĩtu/ *m* chick
pin|tor /pĩ'tor/ *m* painter; **~tura** *f* painting
pio[1] /'piu/ *m* (*de pinto*) cheep; (*de coruja*) hoot
pio[2] /'piu/ *a* pious
piolho /pi'oʎu/ *m* louse
pioneiro /pio'neru/ *m* pioneer □ *a* pioneering
pior /pi'ɔr/ *a & adv* worse; **o ~** the worst
pio|ra /pi'ɔra/ *f* worsening; **~rar** *vt* make worse, worsen □ *vi* get worse, worsen
pipa /'pipa/ *f* (*que voa*) kite; (*de vinho*) cask
pipilar /pipi'lar/ *vi* chirp
pipo|ca /pi'pɔka/ *f* popcorn; **~car** *vi* spring up; **~queiro** *m* popcorn seller
pique /'piki/ *m* (*disposição*) energy; **a ~** vertically; **ir a ~** <*navio*> sink
piquenique /piki'niki/ *m* picnic
pique|te /pi'ketʃi/ *m* picket; **~teiro** *m* picket
pirado /pi'radu/ *a* (*fam*) crazy
pirâmide /pi'ramidʒi/ *f* pyramid
piranha /pi'raɲa/ *f* piranha; (*fam: mulher*) maneater
pirar /pi'rar/ (*fam*) *vi* flip out, go mad
pirata /pi'rata/ *a & m/f* pirate; **~ria** *f* piracy
pires /'piris/ *m invar* saucer
pirilampo /piri'lãpu/ *m* glow-worm
Pirineus /piri'news/ *m pl* Pyrenees
pirra|ça /pi'xasa/ *f* spiteful act; **fazer ~ça** be spiteful; **~cento** *a* spiteful
pirueta /piru'eta/ *f* pirouette
pirulito /piru'litu/ *m* lollipop
pi|sada /pi'zada/ *f* step; (*rastro*) footprint; **~sar** *vt* tread on; tread <*uvas, palco*>; (*esmagar*) trample on □ *vi* step; **~sar em** step on; (*entrar*) set foot in
pis|cadela /piska'dɛla/ *f* wink; **~ca-pisca** *m* indicator; **~car** *vi* (*com o olho*) wink; (*pestanejar*) blink; <*estrela, luz*> twinkle; <*motorista*> indicate □ *m* **num ~car de olhos** in a flash
piscicultura /pisikuw'tura/ *f* fish farming; (*lugar*) fish farm
piscina /pi'sina/ *f* swimming pool
piso /'pizu/ *m* floor
pisotear /pizotʃi'ar/ *vt* trample
pista /'pista/ *f* track; (*da estrada*) carriageway; (*para aviões*) runway; (*de circo*) ring; (*dica*) clue; **~ de dança** dancefloor
pistache /pis'taʃi/ *m*, **pistacho** /pis'taʃu/ *m* pistachio (nut)
pisto|la /pis'tɔla/ *f* pistol; (*para pintar*) spray gun; **~lão** *m* influential contact; **~leiro** *m* gunman
pitada /pi'tada/ *f* pinch
piteira /pi'tera/ *f* cigarette-holder
pitoresco /pito'resku/ *a* picturesque
pitu /pi'tu/ *m* crayfish
pivete /pi'vɛtʃi/ *m/f* child thief
pivô /pi'vo/ *m* pivot
pixaim /piʃa'ĩ/ *a* frizzy
pizza /'pitsa/ *f* pizza; **~ria** *f* pizzeria
placa /'plaka/ *f* plate; (*de carro*) number plate, (*Amer*) license plate; (*comemorativa*) plaque; (*em computador*) board; **~ de sinalização** roadsign
placar /pla'kar/ *m* scoreboard; (*escore*) scoreline
plácido /'plasidu/ *a* placid
plagi|ário /plaʒi'ariu/ *m* plagiarist; **~ar** *vt* plagiarize
plágio /'plaʒiu/ *m* plagiarism
plaina /'plajna/ *f* plane
planador /plana'dor/ *m* glider
planalto /pla'nawtu/ *m* plateau
planar /pla'nar/ *vi* glide

planeamento, planear (*Port*) *veja* planejamento, planejar
plane|jamento /planeʒa'mẽtu/ *m* planning; ~**jamento familiar** family planning; ~**jar** *vt* plan
planeta /pla'neta/ *m* planet
planície /pla'nisi/ *f* plain
planificar /planifi'kar/ *vt* (*programar*) plan (out)
planilha /pla'niʎa/ *f* spreadsheet
plano /'planu/ *a* flat □ *m* plan; (*superfície, nível*) plane; **primeiro** ~ foreground
planta /'plãta/ *f* plant; (*do pé*) sole; (*de edifício*) ground plan; ~**ção** *f* (*ato*) planting; (*terreno*) plantation; ~**do** *a* **deixar alg** ~**do** (*fam*) keep s.o. waiting around
plantão /plã'tãw/ *m* duty; (*noturno*) night duty; **estar de** ~ be on duty
plantar /plã'tar/ *vt* plant
plas|ma /'plazma/ *m* plasma; ~**mar** *vt* mould, shape
plásti|ca /'plastʃika/ *f* face-lift; ~**co** *a* & *m* plastic
plataforma /plata'fɔrma/ *f* platform
plátano /'platanu/ *m* plane tree
platéia /pla'tɛja/ *f* audience; (*parte do teatro*) stalls, (*Amer*) orchestra
platina /pla'tʃina/ *f* platinum; ~**dos** *m pl* points
platônico /pla'toniku/ *a* platonic
plausí|vel /plaw'zivew/ (*pl* ~**veis**) *a* plausible
ple|be /'plɛbi/ *f* common people; ~**beu** *a* (*f* ~**béia**) plebeian □ *m* (*f* ~**béia**) commoner; ~**biscito** *m* plebiscite
plei|tear /plejtʃi'ar/ *vt* contest; ~**to** *m* (*litígio*) case; (*eleitoral*) contest
ple|namente /plena'mẽtʃi/ *adv* fully; ~**nário** *a* plenary □ *m* plenary assembly; ~**no** /e/ *a* full; **em** ~**no verão** in the middle of summer
plissado /pli'sadu/ *a* pleated
pluma /'pluma/ *f* feather; ~**gem** *f* plumage
plu|ral /plu'raw/ (*pl* ~**rais**) *a* & *m* plural
plutônio /plu'toniu/ *m* plutonium
pluvi|al /pluvi'aw/ (*pl* ~**ais**) *a* rain
pneu /pi'new/ *m* tyre; ~**mático** *a* pneumatic □ *m* tyre
pneumonia /pineumo'nia/ *f* pneumonia
pó /pɔ/ *f* powder; (*poeira*) dust; **leite em** ~ powdered milk
pobre /'pɔbri/ *a* poor □ *m/f* poor man (*f* woman); **os** ~**s** the poor; ~**za** /e/ *f* poverty
poça /'posa/ *f* pool; (*deixada pela chuva*) puddle
poção /po'sãw/ *f* potion
pocilga /po'siwga/ *f* pigsty
poço /'posu/ *f* (*de água, petróleo*) well; (*de mina, elevador*) shaft
podar /po'dar/ *vt* prune
pó-de-arroz /pɔdʒia'xoz/ *m* (face) powder
poder /po'der/ *m* power □ *v aux* can, be able; (*eventualidade*) may; **ele pode/podia/poderá vir** he can/could/might come; **ele pôde vir** he was able to come; **pode ser que** it may be that; ~ **com** stand up to; **em** ~ **de alg** in sb's possession; **estar no** ~ be in power
pode|rio /pode'riu/ *m* might; ~**roso** /o/ *a* powerful
pódio /'pɔdʒiu/ *m* podium
podre /'podri/ *a* rotten; (*fam*) (*cansado*) exhausted; (*doente*) grotty; ~ **de rico** filthy rich; ~**s** *m pl* faults
poei|ra /po'era/ *f* dust; ~**rento** *a* dusty
poe|ma /po'ema/ *m* poem; ~**sia** *f* (*arte*) poetry; (*poema*) poem; ~**ta** *m* poet
poético /po'ɛtʃiku/ *a* poetic
poetisa /poe'tʃiza/ *f* poetess
pois /pojs/ *conj* as, since; ~ **é** that's right; ~ **não** of course; ~ **não?** can I help you?; ~ **sim** certainly not
polaco /pu'laku/ (*Port*) *a* Polish □ *m* Pole; (*língua*) Polish
polar /po'lar/ *a* polar
polarizar /polari'zar/ *vt* polarize; ~-**se** *vpr* polarize
pole|gada /pole'gada/ *f* inch; ~**gar** *m* thumb
poleiro /po'leru/ *m* perch
polêmi|ca /po'lemika/ *f* controversy, debate; ~**co** *a* controversial
pólen /'pɔlẽ/ *m* pollen
polícia /po'lisia/ *f* police □ *m/f* policeman (*f* -woman)
polici|al /polisi'aw/ (*pl* ~**ais**) *a* <*carro, inquérito etc*> police; <*romance, filme*> detective □ *m/f* policeman (*f* -woman); ~**amento** *m* policing; ~**ar** *vt* police
poli|dez /poli'des/ *f* politeness; ~**do** *a* polite
poli|gamia /poliga'mia/ *f* polygamy; ~**glota** *a* & *m/f* polyglot
Polinésia /poli'nɛzia/ *f* Polynesia
polinésio /poli'nɛziu/ *a* & *m* Polynesian
pólio /'pɔliu/ *f* polio
polir /po'lir/ *vt* polish
polissílabo /poli'silabu/ *m* polysyllable
políti|ca /po'litʃika/ *f* politics; (*uma*) policy; ~**co** *a* political □ *m* politician
pólo[1] /'pɔlu/ *m* pole
pólo[2] /'pɔlu/ *m* (*jogo*) polo; ~ **aquático** water polo

polo|nês /polo'nes/ *a* (*f* ~**nesa**) Polish □ *m* (*f* ~**nesa**) Pole; (*língua*) Polish
Polônia /po'lonia/ *f* Poland
polpa /'powpa/ *f* pulp
poltrona /pow'trona/ *f* armchair
polu|ente /polu'ẽtʃi/ *a & m* pollutant; ~**ição** *f* pollution; ~**ir** *vt* pollute
polvilhar /powvi'ʎar/ *vt* sprinkle
polvo /'powvu/ *m* octopus
pólvora /'pɔwvora/ *f* gunpowder
polvorosa /powvo'rɔza/ *f* uproar; **em** ~ in uproar; <*pessoa*> in a flap
pomada /po'mada/ *f* ointment
pomar /po'mar/ *m* orchard
pom|ba /'põba/ *f* dove; ~**bo** *m* pigeon
pomo-de-Adão /pomudʒia'dãw/ *m* Adam's apple
pom|pa /'põpa/ *f* pomp; ~**poso** /o/ *a* pompous
ponche /'põʃi/ *m* punch
ponderar /põde'rar/ *vt/i* ponder
pônei /'ponej/ *m* pony
ponta /'põta/ *f* end; (*de faca, prego*) point; (*de nariz, dedo, língua*) tip; (*de sapato*) toe; (*Cin, Teat: papel curto*) walk-on part; (*no campo de futebol*) wing; (*jogador*) winger; **na** ~ **dos pés** on tip-toe; **uma** ~ **de** a touch of <*ironia etc*>; **agüentar as** ~**s** (*fam*) hold on; ~**-cabeça** /e/ *f* **de** ~**-cabeça** upside down
pontada /põ'tada/ *f* (*dor*) twinge
pontapé /põta'pɛ/ *m* kick; ~ **inicial** kick-off
pontaria /põta'ria/ *f* aim; **fazer** ~ take aim
ponte /'põtʃi/ *f* bridge; ~ **aérea** shuttle; (*em tempo de guerra*) airlift; ~ **de safena** heart bypass; ~ **pênsil** suspension bridge
ponteiro /põ'teru/ *m* pointer; (*de relógio*) hand
pontiagudo /põtʃia'gudu/ *a* sharp
pontilhado /põtʃi'ʎadu/ *a* dotted
ponto /'põtu/ *m* point; (*de costura, tricô*) stitch; (*no final de uma frase*) full stop, (*Amer*) period; (*sinalzinho, no i*) dot; (*de ônibus*) stop; (*no teatro*) prompter; **a** ~ **de** on the point of; **ao** ~ <*carne*> medium; **até certo** ~ to a certain extent; **às duas em** ~ at exactly two o'clock; **dormir no** ~ (*fam*) miss the boat; **entregar os** ~**s** (*fam*) give up; **fazer** ~ (*fam*) hang out; **dois** ~**s** colon; ~ **de exclamação/interrogação** exclamation/question mark; ~ **de táxi** taxi rank, (*Amer*) taxi stand; ~ **de vista** point of view; ~ **morto** neutral; ~**-e-vírgula** *m* semicolon
pontu|ação /põtua'sãw/ *f* punctuation; ~**al** (*pl* ~**ais**) *a* punctual; ~**alidade** *f* punctuality; ~**ar** *vt* punctuate
pontudo /põ'tudu/ *a* pointed
popa /'popa/ *f* stern
popu|lação /popula'sãw/ *f* population; ~**lacional** (*pl* ~**lacionais**) *a* population; ~**lar** *a* popular; ~**laridade** *f* popularity; ~**larizar** *vt* popularize; ~**larizar-se** *vpr* become popular
pôquer /'poker/ *m* poker
por /por/ *prep* for; (*através de*) through; (*indicando meio, agente*) by; (*motivo*) out of; ~ **ano/mês/** *etc* per year/month/*etc*; ~ **cento** per cent; ~ **aqui** (*nesta área*) around here; (*nesta direção*) this way; ~ **dentro/fora** on the inside/outside; ~ **isso** for this reason; ~ **sorte** luckily; ~ **que** why; ~ **mais caro que seja** however expensive it may be; **está** ~ **acontecer/fazer** it is yet to happen/to be done
pôr /por/ *vt* put; put on <*roupa, chapéu, óculos*>; lay <*mesa, ovos*> □ *m* **o** ~ **do sol** sunset; ~**-se** *vpr* <*sol*> set; ~**-se a** start to; ~**-se a caminho** set off
porão /po'rãw/ *m* (*de prédio*) basement; (*de casa*) cellar; (*de navio*) hold
porca /'pɔrka/ *f* (*de parafuso*) nut; (*animal*) sow
porção /por'sãw/ *f* portion; **uma** ~ **de** (*muitos*) a lot of
porcaria /porka'ria/ *f* (*sujeira*) filth; (*coisa malfeita*) piece of trash; *pl* trash
porcelana /porse'lana/ *f* china
porcentagem /porsẽ'taʒẽ/ *f* percentage
porco /'porku/ *a* filthy □ *m* (*animal, fig*) pig; (*carne*) pork; ~**-espinho** (*pl* ~**s-espinhos**) *m* porcupine
porém /po'rẽj/ *conj* however
pormenor /porme'nɔr/ *m* detail
por|nô /por'no/ *a* porn □ *m* porn film; ~**nografia** *f* pornography; ~**nográfico** *a* pornographic
poro /'pɔru/ *m* pore; ~**so** /o/ *a* porous
por|quanto /por'kwãtu/ *conj* since; ~**que** /por'ki/ *conj* because; (*Port: por quê?*) why; ~**quê** /por'ke/ *adv* (*Port*) why □ *m* reason why
porquinho|-da-índia /porkiɲuda-'ĩdʒia/ (*pl* ~**s-da-índia**) *m* guinea pig
porrada /po'xada/ *f* (*fam*) beating
porre /'pɔxi/ *m* (*fam*) drinking session, booze-up; **de** ~ drunk; **tomar um** ~ get drunk
porta /'pɔrta/ *f* door
porta-aviões /pɔrtavi'õjs/ *m invar* aircraft carrier
portador /porta'dor/ *m* bearer
portagem /por'taʒẽ/ *f* (*Port*) toll
porta|chaves /pɔrta'ʃavis/ *m invar* key-holder *ou* key-ring; ~**-jóias** *m in-*

var jewellery box; ~**-lápis** *m invar* pencil holder; ~**-luvas** *m invar* glove compartment; ~**-malas** *m invar* boot, (*Amer*) trunk; ~**-níqueis** *m invar* purse

portanto /por'tãtu/ *conj* therefore

portão /por'tãw/ *m* gate

portar /por'tar/ *vt* carry; ~**-se** *vpr* behave

porta|-retrato /pɔrtaxe'tratu/ *m* photo frame; ~**-revistas** *m invar* magazine rack

portaria /porta'ria/ *f* (*entrada*) entrance; (*decreto*) decree

portá|til (*pl* ~**teis**) *a* portable

porta|-toalhas /pɔrtato'aʎas/ *m invar* towel rail; ~**-voz** *m/f* spokesman (*f* -woman)

porte /'pɔrtʃi/ *m* (*frete*) carriage; (*de cartas etc*) postage; (*de pessoa*) bearing; (*dimensão*) scale; **de grande/pequeno** ~ large-/small-scale

porteiro /por'teru/ *m* doorman; ~ **eletrônico** entryphone

porto /'portu/ *m* port; **o Porto** Oporto; ~ **de escala** port of call; **Porto Rico** *m* Puerto Rico; ~**-riquenho** /e/ *a & m* Puertorican

portuense /portu'ẽsi/ *a & m/f* (person) from Oporto

Portugal /portu'gaw/ *m* Portugal

portu|guês /portu'ges/ *a & m* (*f* ~**guesa**) Portuguese

portuário /portu'ariu/ *a* port □ *m* dock worker, docker

po|sar /po'zar/ *vi* pose; ~**se** /o/ *f* pose; (*de filme*) exposure

pós-datar /pɔzda'tar/ *vt* postdate

pós-escrito /pɔzis'kritu/ *m* postscript

pós-gradua|ção /pɔzgradua'sãw/ *f* postgraduation; ~**do** *a & m* postgraduate

pós-guerra /pɔz'gɛxa/ *m* post-war period; **a Europa do** ~ post-war Europe

posi|ção /pozi'sãw/ *f* position; ~**cionar** *vt* position; ~**tivo** *a & m* positive

posologia /pozolo'ʒia/ *f* dosage

pos|sante /po'sãtʃi/ *a* powerful; ~**se** /ɔ/ *f* (*de casa etc*) possession, ownership; (*do presidente etc*) swearing in; *pl* (*pertences*) possessions; **tomar** ~**se** take office; **tomar** ~**se de** take possession of

posses|são /pose'sãw/ *f* possession; ~**sivo** *a* possessive; ~**so** /ɛ/ *a* possessed; (*com raiva*) furious

possibili|dade /posibili'dadʒi/ *f* possibility; ~**tar** *vt* make possible

possí|vel /po'sivew/ (*pl* ~**veis**) *a* possible; **fazer todo o** ~**vel** do one's best

possuir /posu'ir/ *vt* possess; (*ser dono de*) own

posta /'pɔsta/ *f* (*de peixe*) steak

pos|tal /pos'taw/ (*pl* ~**tais**) *a* postal □ *m* postcard

postar /pos'tar/ *vt* place; ~**-se** *vpr* position o.s.

poste /'pɔstʃi/ *m* post

pôster /'poster/ *m* poster

posteri|dade /posteri'dadʒi/ *f* posterity; ~**or** *a* (*no tempo*) subsequent, later; (*no espaço*) rear; ~**ormente** *adv* subsequently

postiço /pos'tʃisu/ *a* false

posto /'postu/ *m* post; ~ **de gasolina** petrol station, (*Amer*) gas station; ~ **de saúde** health centre □ *pp de* **pôr**; ~ **que** although

póstumo /'pɔstumu/ *a* posthumous

postura /pos'tura/ *f* posture

potá|vel /po'tavew/ (*pl* ~**veis**) *a* **água** ~**vel** drinking water

pote /'pɔtʃi/ *m* pot; (*de vidro*) jar

potência /po'tẽsia/ *f* power

poten|cial /potẽsi'aw/ (*pl* ~**ciais**) *a & m* potential; ~**te** *a* potent

potro /'potru/ *m* foal

pouco /'poku/ *a & pron* little; *pl* few □ *adv* not much □ *m* **um** ~ a little; ~ **a** ~ little by little; **aos** ~**s** gradually; **daqui a** ~ shortly; **por** ~ almost; ~ **tempo** a short time

pou|pança /po'pãsa/ *f* saving; (*conta*) savings account; ~**par** *vt* save; spare <*vida*>

pouquinho /po'kiɲu/ *m* **um** ~ **(de)** a little

pou|sada /po'zada/ *f* inn; ~**sar** *vi* land; ~**so** *m* landing

po|vão /po'vãw/ *m* common people; ~**vo** /o/ *m* people

povo|ação /povoa'sãw/ *f* settlement; ~**ar** *vt* populate

poxa /'poʃa/ *int* gosh

pra /pra/ *prep* (*fam*) *veja* **para**

praça /'prasa/ *f* (*largo*) square; (*mercado*) market □ *m* (*soldado*) private

prado /'pradu/ *m* meadow

pra-frente /pra'frẽtʃi/ *a invar* (*fam*) with it, modern

praga /'praga/ *f* curse; (*inseto, doença, pessoa*) pest

prag|mático /prag'matʃiku/ *a* pragmatic; ~**matismo** *m* pragmatism

praguejar /prage'ʒar/ *vt/i* curse

praia /'praja/ *f* beach

pran|cha /'prãʃa/ *f* plank; (*de surfe*) board; ~**cheta** /e/ *f* drawing board

pranto /'prãtu/ *m* weeping

pra|ta /'prata/ *f* silver; ~**taria** *f* (*coisas de prata*) silverware; ~**teado** *a* silver-plated; (*cor*) silver

prateleira /prate'lera/ *f* shelf

prática /'pratʃika/ *f* practice; **na** ~ in practice

prati|cante /pratʃi'kãtʃi/ *a* practising □ *m/f* apprentice; (*de esporte etc*) player; ~**car** *vt* practise; (*cometer, executar*) carry out □ *vi* practise; ~**cável** (*pl* ~**cáveis**) *a* practicable
prático /'pratʃiku/ *a* practical
prato /'pratu/ *m* (*objeto*) plate; (*comida*) dish; (*parte de uma refeição*) course; (*do toca-discos*) turntable; *pl* (*instrumento*) cymbals; ~ **fundo** dish; ~ **principal** main course
praxe /'praʃi/ *f* normal practice; **de** ~ usually
prazer /pra'zer/ *m* pleasure; **muito** ~ (**em conhecê-lo**) pleased to meet you; ~**oso** /o/ *a* pleasurable
prazo /'prazu/ *m* term, time; **a** ~ <*compra etc*> on credit; **a curto/longo** ~ in the short/long term; **último** ~ deadline
preâmbulo /pri'ãbulu/ *m* preamble
precário /pre'kariu/ *a* precarious
precaução /prekaw'sãw/ *f* precaution
preca|ver-se /preka'versi/ *vpr* take precautions (**de** against); ~**vido** *a* cautious
prece /'prɛsi/ *f* prayer
prece|dência /prese'dẽsia/ *f* precedence; ~**dente** *a* preceding □ *m* precedent; ~**der** *vt/i* precede
preceito /pre'sejtu/ *m* precept
precioso /presi'ozu/ *a* precious
precipício /presi'pisiu/ *m* precipice
precipi|tação /presipita'sãw/ *f* haste; (*chuva etc*) precipitation; ~**tado** *a* <*fuga*> headlong; <*decisão, ato*> hasty, rash; ~**tar** *vt* (*lançar*) throw; (*antecipar*) hasten; ~**tar-se** *vpr* (*lançar-se*) throw o.s.; (*apressar-se*) rush; (*agir sem pensar*) act rashly
precisão /presi'zãw/ *f* precision, accuracy
precisamente /presiza'mẽtʃi/ *adv* precisely
preci|sar /presi'zar/ *vt* (*necessitar*) need; (*indicar com exatidão*) specify □ *vi* be necessary; ~**sar de** need; ~**so ir** I have to go; ~**sa-se** wanted; ~**so** *a* (*exato*) precise; (*necessário*) necessary
preço /'presu/ *m* price; ~ **de custo** cost price; ~ **fixo** set price
precoce /pre'kɔsi/ *a* <*fruto*> early; <*velhice, calvície etc*> premature; <*criança*> precocious
precon|cebido /prekõse'bidu/ *a* preconceived; ~**ceito** *m* prejudice; ~**ceituoso** *a* prejudiced
preconizar /prekoni'zar/ *vt* advocate
precursor /prekur'sor/ *m* forerunner
preda|dor /preda'dor/ *m* predator; ~**tório** *a* predatory
predecessor /predese'sor/ *m* predecessor
predestinar /predestʃi'nar/ *vt* predestine
predeterminar /predetermi'nar/ *vt* predetermine
predição /predʒi'sãw/ *f* prediction
predile|ção /predʒile'sãw/ *f* preference; ~**to** /ɛ/ *a* favourite
prédio /'prɛdʒiu/ *m* building
predis|por /predʒis'por/ *vt* prepare (**para** for); (*tornar parcial*) prejudice (**contra** against); ~**por-se** *vpr* prepare o.s.; ~**posto** *a* predisposed; (*contra*) prejudiced
predizer /predʒi'zer/ *vt* predict, foretell
predomi|nância /predomi'nãsia/ *f* predominance; ~**nante** *a* predominant; ~**nar** *vi* predominate
predomínio /predo'miniu/ *m* predominance
preencher /priẽ'ʃer/ *vt* fill; fill in, (*Amer*) fill out <*formulário*>; meet <*requisitos*>
pré|-escola /prɛis'kɔla/ *f* infant school, (*Amer*) preschool; ~**-escolar** *a* pre-school; ~**-estréia** *f* preview; ~**-fabricado** *a* prefabricated
prefácio /pre'fasiu/ *m* preface
prefei|to /pre'fejtu/ *m* mayor; ~**tura** *f* prefecture; (*prédio*) town hall
prefe|rência /prefe'rẽsia/ *f* preference; (*direito no trânsito*) right of way; **de** ~**rência** preferably; ~**rencial** (*pl* ~**renciais**) *a* preferential; <*rua*> main; ~**rido** *a* favourite; ~**rir** *vt* prefer (**a** to); ~**rível** (*pl* ~**ríveis**) *a* preferable
prefixo /pre'fiksu/ *m* prefix
prega /'prɛga/ *f* pleat
pregador[1] /prega'dor/ *m* (*de roupa*) peg
pre|gador[2] /prega'dor/ *m* (*quem prega*) preacher; ~**gão** *m* (*de vendedor*) cry; **o** ~**gão** (*na bolsa de valores*) trading; (*em leilão*) bidding
pregar[1] /pre'gar/ *vt* fix; (*com prego*) nail; sew on <*botão*>; **não** ~ **olho** not sleep a wink; ~ **uma peça em** play a trick on; ~ **um susto em alg** give s.o. a fright
pregar[2] /pre'gar/ *vt/i* preach
prego /'prɛgu/ *m* nail
pregui|ça /pre'gisa/ *f* laziness; (*bicho*) sloth; **estou com** ~**ça de ir** I can't be bothered to go; ~**çoso** *a* lazy
pré-histórico /prɛjs'tɔriku/ *a* prehistoric
preia-mar /preja'mar/ *f* high tide
prejudi|car /preʒudʒi'kar/ *vt* harm; damage <*saúde*>; ~**car-se** *vpr* harm o.s.; ~**cial** (*pl* ~**ciais**) *a* harmful, damaging (**a** to)

prejuízo /preʒu'izu/ *m* damage; (*financeiro*) loss; em ~ de to the detriment of

prejulgar /preʒuw'gar/ *vt* prejudge

preliminar /prelimi'nar/ *a & m/f* preliminary

prelo /'prɛlu/ *m* printing press; no ~ being printed

prelúdio /pre'ludʒiu/ *m* prelude

prematuro /prema'turu/ *a* premature

premeditar /premedʒi'tar/ *vt* premeditate

premente /pre'mẽtʃi/ *a* pressing

premi|ado /premi'adu/ *a* <*romance, atleta etc*> prize-winning; <*bilhete, número etc*> winning □ *m* prizewinner; **~ar** *vt* award a prize to <*romance, atleta etc*>; reward <*honestidade, mérito*>

prêmio /'premiu/ *m* prize; (*de seguro*) premium; **Grande Prêmio** (*de F1*) Grand Prix

premissa /pre'misa/ *f* premiss

premonição /premoni'sãw/ *f* premonition

pré-na|tal /prɛna'taw/ (*pl* **~tais**) *a* antenatal, (*Amer*) prenatal

prenda /'prẽda/ *f* (*Port*) present; **~s domésticas** household chores; **~do** *a* domesticated

pren|dedor /prẽde'dor/ *m* clip; **~dedor de roupa** clothes peg; **~der** *vt* (*pregar*) fix; (*capturar*) arrest; (*atar*) tie up <*cachorro*>; tie back <*cabelo*>; (*restringir*) restrict; (*ligar afetivamente*) bind; **~der (a atenção de)** alg grab s.o.('s attention)

prenhe /'preɲi/ *a* pregnant

prenome /pre'nomi/ *m* first name

pren|sa /'prẽsa/ *f* press; **~sar** *vt* press

preocu|pação /preokupa'sãw/ *f* concern; **~pante** *a* worrying; **~par** *vt* worry; **~par-se** *vpr* worry (com about)

prepa|ração /prepara'sãw/ *f* preparation; **~rado** *m* preparation; **~rar** *vt* prepare; **~rar-se** *vpr* prepare, get ready; **~rativos** *m pl* preparations; **~ro** *m* preparation; (*competência*) knowledge; **~ro físico** physical fitness

preponderar /prepõde'rar/ *vi* prevail (sobre over)

preposição /prepozi'sãw/ *f* preposition

prerrogativa /prexoga'tʃiva/ *f* prerogative

presa /'preza/ *f* (*de caça*) prey; (*de cobra*) fang; (*de elefante*) tusk; **~ de guerra** spoils of war

prescin|dir /presĩ'dʒir/ *vi* **~dir de** dispense with; **~dível** (*pl* **~díveis**) *a* dispensable

pres|crever /preskre'ver/ *vt* prescribe; **~crição** *f* prescription; (*norma*) rule

presen|ça /pre'zẽsa/ *f* presence; **~ça de espírito** presence of mind; **~ciar** *vt* (*estar presente a*) be present at; (*testemunhar*) witness; **~te** *a & m* present; **~tear** *vt* **~tear alg (com aco)** give s.o. (sth as) a present

presépio /pre'zɛpiu/ *m* crib

preser|vação /prezerva'sãw/ *f* preservation; **~var** *vt* preserve, protect; **~vativo** *m* (*em comida*) preservative; (*camisinha*) condom

presi|dência /prezi'dẽsia/ *f* presidency; (*de uma reunião*) chair; **~dencial** (*pl* **~denciais**) *a* presidential; **~dencialismo** *m* presidential system; **~dente** *m* (*f* **~denta**) president; (*de uma reunião*) chairperson

presidiário /prezidʒi'ariu/ *m* convict

presídio /pre'zidʒiu/ *m* prison

presidir /prezi'dʒir/ *vi* preside (a over)

presilha /pre'ziʎa/ *f* fastener; (*de cabelo*) slide

preso /'prezu/ *pp de* **prender** □ *m* prisoner; **ficar ~** get stuck; <*saia, corda etc*> get caught

pressa /'prɛsa/ *f* hurry; **às ~s** in a hurry, hurriedly; **estar com** *ou* **ter ~** be in a hurry

presságio /pre'saʒiu/ *m* omen

pressão /pre'sãw/ *f* pressure; **fazer ~ sobre** put pressure on; **~ arterial** blood pressure

pressen|timento /presẽtʃi'mẽtu/ *m* premonition, feeling; **~tir** *vt* sense

pressionar /presio'nar/ *vt* press <*botão*>; pressure <*pessoa*>

pressupor /presu'por/ *vt* <*pessoa*> presume; <*coisa*> presuppose

pressurizado /presuri'zadu/ *a* pressurized

pres|tação /presta'sãw/ *f* repayment, instalment; **~tar** *vt* render <*contas, serviço*> □ *vi* be of use; **não ~ta** he/it is no good; **~tar atenção** pay attention; **~tar juramento** take an oath; **~tativo** *a* helpful; **~tável** (*pl* **~táveis**) *a* serviceable

prestes /'prɛstʃis/ *a invar* **~ a** about to

prestidigita|ção /prestʃidʒiʒita'sãw/ *f* conjuring; **~dor** *m* conjurer

pres|tigiar /prestʃiʒi'ar/ *vt* give prestige to; **~tígio** *m* prestige; **~tigioso** /o/ *a* prestigious

préstimo /'prɛstʃimu/ *m* merit

presumir /prezu'mir/ *vt* presume

presun|ção /prezũ'sãw/ *f* presumption; **~çoso** /o/ *a* presumptuous

presunto /pre'zũtu/ *m* ham

pretendente /pretẽ'dẽtʃi/ *m/f* (*candidato*) candidate, applicant

preten|der /pretẽ'der/ *vt* intend; **~são** *f* pretension; **~sioso** /o/ *a* pretentious

preterir /prete'rir/ *vt* disregard

pretérito /pre'tɛritu/ *m* preterite

pretexto /pre'testu/ *m* pretext

preto /'pretu/ *a & m* black; **~-e-branco** *a invar* black and white

prevalecer /prevale'ser/ *vi* prevail

prevenção /prevẽ'sãw/ *f* (*impedimento*) prevention; (*parcialidade*) bias

prevenir /preve'nir/ *vt* (*evitar*) prevent; (*avisar*) warn; **~-se** *vpr* take precautions

preventivo /prevẽ'tʃivu/ *a* preventive

prever /pre'ver/ *vt* foresee, predict

previdência /previ'dẽsia/ *f* foresight; **~ social** social security

prévio /'prɛviu/ *a* prior

previ|são /previ'zãw/ *f* prediction, forecast; **~são do tempo** weather forecast; **~sível** (*pl* **~síveis**) *a* predictable

pre|zado /pre'zadu/ *a* esteemed; **Prezado Senhor** Dear Sir; **~zar** *vt* think highly of; **~zar-se** *vpr* have self-respect

prima /'prima/ *f* cousin

primário /pri'mariu/ *a* primary; (*fundamental*) basic

primata /pri'mata/ *m* primate

primave|ra /prima'vɛra/ *f* spring; (*flor*) primrose; **~ril** (*pl* **~ris**) *a* spring

primazia /prima'zia/ *f* primacy

primei|ra /pri'mera/ *f* (*marcha*) first (gear); **de ~ra** first-rate; <*carne*> prime; **~ra-dama** (*pl* **~ras-damas**) *f* first lady; **~ranista** *m/f* first-year (student); **~ro** *a & adv* first; **no dia ~ro de maio** on the first of May; **em ~ro lugar** (*para começar*) in the first place; (*numa corrida, competição*) in first place; **~ro de tudo** first of all; **~ros socorros** first aid; **~ro-ministro** (*pl* **~ros-ministros**) *m* (*f* **~ra-ministra**) prime-minister

primitivo /primi'tʃivu/ *a* primitive

primo /'primu/ *m* cousin □ *a* **número ~** prime number; **~gênito** *a & m* first-born

primor /pri'mor/ *m* perfection

primordi|al /primordʒi'aw/ (*pl* **~ais**) *a* (*primitivo*) primordial; (*fundamental*) fundamental

primoroso /primo'rozu/ *a* exquisite

princesa /prĩ'seza/ *f* princess

princi|pado /prĩsipi'adu/ *m* principality; **~pal** (*pl* **~pais**) *a* main □ *m* principal

príncipe /'prĩsipi/ *m* prince

principiante /prĩsipi'ãtʃi/ *m/f* beginner

princípio /prĩ'sipiu/ *m* (*início*) beginning; (*regra*) principle; **em ~** in principle; **por ~** on principle

priori|dade /priori'dadʒi/ *f* priority; **~tário** *a* priority

prisão /pri'zãw/ *f* (*ato de prender*) arrest; (*cadeia*) prison; (*encarceramento*) imprisonment; **~ perpétua** life imprisonment; **~ de ventre** constipation

prisioneiro /prizio'neru/ *m* prisoner

prisma /'prizma/ *m* prism

privação /priva'sãw/ *f* deprivation

privacidade /privasi'dadʒi/ *f* privacy

pri|vada /pri'vada/ *f* toilet; **~vado** *a* private; **~vado de** deprived of; **~var** *vt* deprive (**de** of); **~var-se** *vpr* deprive o.s. (**de** of)

privati|vo /priva'tʃivu/ *a* private; **~zar** *vt* privatize

privi|legiado /privileʒi'adu/ *a* privileged; <*tratamento*> preferential; **~legiar** *vt* favour; **~légio** *m* privilege

pro (*fam*) = **para** + **o**

pró /prɔ/ *adv* for □ *m* **os ~s e os contras** the pros and cons

proa /'proa/ *f* bow, prow

probabilidade /probabili'dadʒi/ *f* probability

proble|ma /pro'blema/ *m* problem; **~mático** *a* problematic

proce|dência /prose'dẽsia/ *f* origin; **~dente** *a* logical; **~dente de** coming from; **~der** *vi* proceed; (*comportar-se*) behave; (*na justiça*) take legal action; **~der de** come from; **~dimento** *m* procedure; (*comportamento*) behaviour; (*na justiça*) proceedings

proces|sador /prosesa'dor/ *m* processor; **~sador de texto** word processor; **~samento** *m* processing; (*na justiça*) prosecution; **~samento de dados** data processing; **~sar** *vt* process; (*por crime*) prosecute; (*por causa civil*) sue; **~so** /ɛ/ *m* process; (*criminal*) trial; (*civil*) lawsuit

procla|mação /proklama'sãw/ *f* proclamation; **~mar** *vt* proclaim

procri|ação /prokria'sãw/ *f* procreation; **~ar** *vt/i* procreate

procu|ra /pro'kura/ *f* search; (*de produto*) demand; **à ~ra de** in search of; **~ração** *f* power of attorney; **~rado** *a* sought after, in demand; **~rado pela polícia** wanted by the police; **~rador** *m* (*mandatário*) proxy; (*advogado*) public prosecutor; **~rar** *vt* look for; (*contatar*) get in touch with; (*ir visitar*) look up; **~rar saber** try to find out

prodígio /pro'dʒiʒiu/ *m* wonder; (*pessoa*) prodigy

prodigioso /prodʒiʒi'ozu/ *a* prodigious

pródigo /'prɔdigu/ *a* lavish, extravagant

produ|ção /produ'sãw/ *f* production; **~tividade** *f* productivity; **~tivo** *a* productive; **~to** *m* product; (*renda*) proceeds; **~to nacional bruto** gross national product; **~tos agrícolas** agricultural produce; **~tor** *m* producer □ *a* **país ~tor de trigo** wheat-producing country; **~zido** *a* (*fam: arrumado*) done up; **~zir** *vt* produce

proeminente /proemi'nẽtʃi/ *a* prominent

proeza /pro'eza/ *f* achievement

profa|nar /profa'nar/ *vt* desecrate; **~no** *a* profane

profecia /profe'sia/ *f* prophecy

proferir /profe'rir/ *vt* utter; give <*discurso, palestra*>; pass <*sentença*>

profes|sar /profe'sar/ *vt* profess; **~so** /ɛ/ *a* professed; <*político etc*> seasoned; **~sor** *m* teacher; **~sor catedrático** professor

pro|feta /pro'fɛta/ *m* prophet; **~fético** *a* prophetic; **~fetizar** *vt* prophesy

profissão /profi'sãw/ *f* profession

profissio|nal /profisio'naw/ (*pl* **~nais**) *a* & *m/f* professional; **~nalismo** *m* professionalism; **~nalizante** *a* vocational; **~nalizar-se** *vpr* <*esportista etc*> turn professional

profun|didade /profũdʒi'dadʒi/ *f* depth; **~do** *a* deep; <*sentimento etc*> profound

profusão /profu'zãw/ *f* profusion

prog|nosticar /prognostʃi'kar/ *vt* forecast; **~nóstico** *m* forecast; (*med*) prognosis

progra|ma /pro'grama/ *m* programme; (*de computador*) program; (*diversão*) thing to do; **~mação** *f* programming; **~mador** *m* programmer; **~mar** *vt* plan; program <*computador etc*>; **~mável** (*pl* **~máveis**) *a* programmable

progredir /progre'dʒir/ *vi* progress

progres|são /progre'sãw/ *f* progression; **~sista** *a* & *m/f* progressive; **~sivo** *a* progressive; **~so** /ɛ/ *m* progress

proi|bição /proibi'sãw/ *f* ban (de on); **~bido** *a* forbidden; **~bir** *vt* forbid (**alg de** s.o. to); ban <*livro, importações etc*>; **~bitivo** *a* prohibitive

proje|ção /proʒe'sãw/ *f* projection; **~tar** *vt* plan <*viagem, estrada etc*>; design <*casa, carro etc*>; project <*filme, luz*>

projé|til /pro'ʒɛtʃiw/ (*pl* **~teis**) *m* projectile

proje|tista /proʒe'tʃista/ *m/f* designer; **~to** /ɛ/ *m* project; (*de casa, carro*) design; **~to de lei** bill; **~tor** *m* projector

prol /prɔw/ *m* **em ~ de** on behalf of

prole /'prɔli/ *f* offspring; **~tariado** *m* proletariat; **~tário** *a* & *m* proletarian

prolife|ração /prolifera'sãw/ *f* proliferation; **~rar** *vi* proliferate

prolífico /pro'lifiku/ *a* prolific

prolixo /pro'liksu/ *a* verbose, long-winded

prólogo /'prɔlogu/ *m* prologue

prolon|gado /prolõ'gadu/ *a* prolonged; **~gar** *vt* prolong; **~gar-se** *vpr* go on

promessa /pro'mɛsa/ *f* promise

prome|tedor /promete'dor/ *a* promising; **~ter** *vt* promise □ *vi* (*dar esperança*) show promise; **~ter voltar** promise to return

promíscuo /pro'miskuu/ *a* promiscuous

promis|sor /promi'sor/ *a* promising; **~sória** *f* promissory note

promoção /promo'sãw/ *f* promotion

promontório /promõ'tɔriu/ *m* promontory

promo|tor /promo'tor/ *m* promoter; (*advogado*) prosecutor; **~ver** *vt* promote

promulgar /promuw'gar/ *vt* promulgate

prono|me /pro'nomi/ *m* pronoun; **~minal** (*pl* **~minais**) *a* pronominal

pron|tidão /prõtʃi'dãw/ *f* readiness; **com ~tidão** promptly; **estar de ~tidão** be at the ready; **~tificar** *vt* get ready; **~tificar-se** *vpr* volunteer (**a** to; **para** for); **~to** *a* ready; (*rápido*) prompt □ *int* that's that; **~to-socorro** (*pl* **~tos-socorros**) *m* casualty department; (*Port: reboque*) towtruck; **~tuário** *m* (*manual*) manual, handbook; (*médico*) notes; (*policial*) record, file

pronúncia /pro'nũsia/ *f* pronunciation

pronunci|ado /pronũsi'adu/ *a* pronounced; **~amento** *m* pronouncement; **~ar** *vt* pronounce

propagar /propa'gar/ *vt* propagate <*espécie*>; spread <*notícia, idéia, fé*>; **~-se** *vpr* spread; <*espécie*> propagate

propen|são /propẽ'sãw/ *f* propensity; **~so** *a* inclined (**a** to)

pro|piciar /propisi'ar/ *vt* provide; **~pício** *a* propitious

propina /pro'pina/ *f* bribe; (*Port: escolar*) fee

propor /pro'por/ *vt* propose; **~-se** *vpr* set o.s. <*objetivo*>; **~-se a estudar** set out to study

proporção /propor'sãw/ *f* proportion

proporcio|nado /proporsio'nadu/ *a* proportionate (a to); **bem ~nado** well proportioned; **~nal** (*pl* **~nais**) *a* proportional; **~nar** *vt* provide

proposi|ção /propozi'sãw/ *f* proposition; **~tado** *a*, **~tal** (*pl* **~tais**) *a* intentional

propósito /pro'pɔzitu/ *m* intention; **a ~** by the way; **a ~ de** on the subject of; **chegar a ~** arrive at the right time; **de ~** on purpose

proposta /pro'pɔsta/ *f* proposal

propriamente /propria'mẽtʃi/ *adv* strictly; **a casa ~ dita** the house proper

proprie|dade /proprie'dadʒi/ *f* property; (*direito sobre bens*) ownership; **~tário** *m* owner; (*de casa alugada*) landlord

próprio /'prɔpriu/ *a* (*de si*) own; <*sentido*> literal; <*nome*> proper; **meu ~ carro** my own car; **um carro ~** a car of my own; **o ~ rei** the king himself; **~ a** peculiar to; **~ para** suited to

prorro|gação /proxoga'sãw/ *f* extension; (*de dívida*) deferment; (*em futebol etc*) extra time; **~gar** *vt* extend <*prazo*>; defer <*pagamento*>

pro|sa /'prɔza/ *f* prose; **~sador** *m* prose writer; **~saico** *a* prosaic

proscrever /proskre'ver/ *vt* proscribe

prospecto /pros'pɛktu/ *m* (*livro*) brochure; (*folheto*) leaflet

prospe|rar /prospe'rar/ *vi* prosper; **~ridade** *f* prosperity

próspero /'prɔsperu/ *a* prosperous

prosse|guimento /prosegi'mẽtu/ *m* continuation; **~guir** *vt* continue □ *vi* proceed, go on

prostitu|ição /prostʃitui'sãw/ *f* prostitution; **~ta** *f* prostitute

pros|tração /prostra'sãw/ *f* debility; **~trado** *a* prostrate; **~trar** *vt* prostrate; (*enfraquecer*) debilitate; **~trar-se** *vpr* prostrate o.s.

protago|nista /protago'nista/ *m/f* protagonist; **~nizar** *vt* be at the centre of <*acontecimento*>; feature in <*peça, filme*>

prote|ção /prote'sãw/ *f* protection; **~cionismo** *m* protectionism; **~cionista** *a* & *m/f* protectionist; **~ger** *vt* protect; **~gido** *m* protégé

proteína /prote'ina/ *f* protein

protelar /prote'lar/ *vt* put off

protes|tante /protes'tãtʃi/ *a* & *m/f* Protestant; **~tar** *vt/i* protest; **~to** /ɛ/ *m* protest

protetor /prote'tor/ *m* protector □ *a* protective

protocolo /proto'kɔlu/ *m* protocol; (*registro*) register

protótipo /pro'tɔtʃipu/ *m* prototype

protuberância /protube'rãsia/ *f* bulge

pro|va /'prɔva/ *f* (*que comprova*) proof; (*teste*) trial; (*exame*) exam; (*esportiva*) competition; (*de livro etc*) proof; *pl* (*na justiça*) evidence; **à ~va de bala** bulletproof; **pôr à ~va** put to the test; **~vado** *a* proven; **~var** *vt* try <*comida*>; try on <*roupa*>; try out <*carro, novo sistema etc*>; (*comprovar*) prove

prová|vel /pro'vavew/ (*pl* **~veis**) *a* probable

proveito /pro'vejtu/ *m* profit, advantage; **tirar ~ de** (*beneficiar-se*) profit from; (*explorar*) take advantage of; **~so** /o/ *a* useful

proveni|ência /proveni'ẽsia/ *f* origin; **~ente** *a* originating (**de** from)

proventos /pro'vẽtus/ *m pl* proceeds

prover /pro'ver/ *vt* provide (**de** with)

provérbio /pro'vɛrbiu/ *m* proverb

proveta /pro'veta/ *f* test tube; **bebê de ~** test-tube baby

provi|dência /provi'dẽsia/ *f* (*medida*) measure, step; (*divina*) providence; **tomar ~dências** take steps, take action; **~denciar** *vt* (*prover*) get hold of, provide; (*resolver*) see to, take care of □ *vi* take action

província /pro'vĩsia/ *f* province; (*longe da cidade*) provinces

provinci|al /provĩsi'aw/ (*pl* **~ais**) *a* provincial; **~ano** *a* & *m* provincial

provir /pro'vir/ *vi* come (**de** from); (*resultar*) be due (**de** to)

provi|são /provi'zãw/ *f* provision; **~sório** *a* provisional

provo|cação /provoka'sãw/ *f* provocation; **~cador**, **~cante** *a* provocative; **~car** *vt* provoke; (*ocasionar*) cause

proximidade /prosimi'dadʒi/ *f* closeness; *pl* (*imediações*) vicinity

próximo /'prɔsimo/ *a* (*no tempo*) next; (*perto*) near, close (**de** to); <*parente*> close; <*futuro*> near □ *m* neighbour, fellow man

pru|dência /pru'dẽsia/ *f* prudence; **~dente** *a* prudent

prumo /'prumu/ *m* plumb line; **a ~** vertically

prurido /pru'ridu/ *m* itch

pseudônimo /pisew'donimu/ *m* pseudonym

psica|nálise /pisika'nalizi/ *f* psychoanalysis; **~nalista** *m/f* psychoanalyst

psi|cologia /pisikolo'ʒia/ *f* psychology; **~cológico** *a* psychological; **~cólogo** *m* psychologist

psico|pata /pisiko'pata/ *m/f* psychopath; **~se** /ɔ/ *f* psychosis; **~terapeuta** *m/f* psychotherapist; **~terapia** *f* psycho-therapy

psicótico /pisi'kɔtʃiku/ *a & m* psychotic

psique /pi'siki/ *f* psyche

psiqui|atra /pisiki'atra/ *m/f* psychiatrist; **~atria** *f* psychiatry; **~átrico** *a* psychiatric

psíquico /pi'sikiku/ *a* psychological

pua /'pua/ *f* bit

puberdade /puber'dadʒi/ *f* puberty

publi|cação /publika'sãw/ *f* publication; **~car** *vt* publish

publici|dade /publisi'dadʒi/ *f* publicity; (*reclame*) advertising; **~tário** *a* publicity; (*de reclame*) advertising □ *m* advertising executive

público /'publiku/ *a* public □ *m* public; (*platéia*) audience; **em ~** in public; **o grande ~** the general public

pudera /pu'dɛra/ *int* no wonder!

pudico /pu'dʒiku/ *a* prudish

pudim /pu'dʒĩ/ *m* pudding

pudor /pu'dor/ *m* modesty, shame

pue|ril /pue'riw/ (*pl* **~ris**) *a* puerile

pugilis|mo /puʒi'lizmu/ *m* boxing; **~ta** *m* boxer

pu|ído /pu'idu/ *a* worn through; **~ir** *vt* wear through

pujan|ça /pu'ʒãsa/ *f* power; **~te** *a* powerful; (*de saúde*) robust

pular /pu'lar/ *vt* jump (over); (*omitir*) skip □ *vi* jump; **~ de contente** jump for joy; **~ carnaval** celebrate Carnival; **~ corda** skip

pulga /'puwga/ *f* flea

pulmão /puw'mãw/ *m* lung

pulo /'pulu/ *m* jump; **dar um ~ em** drop by; **dar ~s** jump up and down

pulôver /pu'lover/ *m* pullover

púlpito /'puwpitu/ *m* pulpit

pul|sar /puw'sar/ *vi* pulsate; **~seira** *f* bracelet; **~so** *m* (*do braço*) wrist; (*batimento arterial*) pulse

pulular /pulu'lar/ *vi* swarm (**de** with)

pulveri|zador /puwveriza'dor/ *m* spray; **~zar** *vt* spray <*líquido*>; (*reduzir a pó, fig*) pulverize

pun|gente /pũ'ʒẽtʃi/ *a* consuming; **~gir** *vt* afflict

pu|nhado /pu'ɲadu/ *m* handful; **~nhal** (*pl* **~nhais**) *m* dagger; **~nhalada** *f* stab wound; **~nho** *m* fist; (*de camisa etc*) cuff; (*de espada*) hilt

pu|nição /puni'sãw/ *f* punishment; **~nir** *vt* punish; **~nitivo** *a* punitive

pupila /pu'pila/ *f* pupil

purê /pu're/ *m* purée; **~ de batata** mashed potato

pureza /pu'reza/ *f* purity

pur|gante /pur'gãtʃi/ *a & m* purgative; **~gar** *vt* purge; **~gatório** *m* purgatory

purificar /purifi'kar/ *vt* purify

puritano /puri'tanu/ *a & m* puritan

puro /'puru/ *a* pure; <*aguardente*> neat; **~ e simples** pure and simple; **~-sangue** (*pl* **~s-sangues**) *a & m* thoroughbred

púrpura /'purpura/ *a* purple

purpurina /purpu'rina/ *f* glitter

purulento /puru'lẽtu/ *a* festering

pus /pus/ *m* pus

pusilânime /puzi'lanimi/ *a* faint-hearted

pústula /'pustula/ *f* pimple

puta /'puta/ *f* whore □ *a invar* (*fam*) **um ~ carro** one hell of a car; **filho da ~** (*chulo*) bastard; **~ que (o) pariu!** (*chulo*) fucking hell!

puto /'putu/ *a* (*fam*) furious

putrefazer /putrefa'zer/ *vi* putrefy

puxa /'puʃa/ *int* gosh

pu|xado /pu'ʃadu/ *a* (*fam*) <*exame*> tough; <*trabalho*> hard; <*aluguel, preço*> steep; **~xador** *m* handle; **~xão** *m* pull, tug; **~xa-puxa** *m* toffee; **~xar** *vt* pull; strike up <*conversa*>; bring up <*assunto*>; **~xar de uma perna** limp; **~xar para** (*parecer com*) take after; **~xar por** (*exigir muito de*) push (hard); **~xa-saco** *m* (*fam*) creep

Q

QI /ke i/ *m* IQ

quadra /'kwadra/ *f* (*de tênis etc*) court; (*quarteirão*) block; **~do** *a & m* square

quadragésimo /kwadra'ʒɛzimu/ *a* fortieth

qua|dril /kwa'driw/ (*pl* **~dris**) *m* hip

quadrilha /kwa'driʎa/ *f* (*bando*) gang; (*dança*) square dance

quadrinho /kwa'driɲu/ *m* frame; **história em ~s** comic strip

quadro /'kwadru/ *m* picture; (*pintado*) painting; (*tabela*) table; (*pessoal*) staff; (*equipe*) team; (*de uma peça*) scene; **~-negro** (*pl* **~s-negros**) *m* blackboard

quadruplicar /kwadrupli'kar/ *vt/i* quadruple

quádruplo /'kwadruplu/ *a* quadruple; **~s** *m pl* (*crianças*) quads

qual /kwaw/ (*pl* **quais**) *pron* which (one); **o/a ~** (*coisa*) that, which; (*pessoa*) that, who; **~ é o seu nome?** what's your name?; **seja ~ for a decisão** whatever the decision may be

qualidade /kwali'dadʒi/ *f* quality; **na ~ de** in one's capacity as, as

qualifi|cação /kwalifika'sãw/ *f* qualification; **~car** *vt* qualify; (*descrever*) describe (**de** as); **~car-se** *vpr* qualify

qualitativo /kwalita'tʃivu/ *a* qualitative

qualquer /kwaw'kɛr/ (*pl* **quaisquer**) *a* any; **um livro ~** any old book; **~ um** any one

quando /'kwãdu/ *adv & conj* when; **~ quer que** whenever; **~ de** at the time of; **~ muito** at most

quantia /kwã'tʃia/ *f* amount

quanti|dade /kwãtʃi'dadʒi/ *f* quantity; **uma ~dade de** a lot of; **em ~dade** in large amounts; **~ficar** *vt* quantify; **~tativo** *a* quantitative

quanto /'kwãtu/ *adv & pron* how much; *pl* how many; **~ tempo?** how long?; **~ mais barato melhor** the cheaper the better; **tão alto ~ eu** as tall as me; **~ ri!** how I laughed!; **~ a** as for; **~ antes** as soon as possible

quaren|ta /kwa'rẽta/ *a & m* forty; **~tão** *a & m* (*f* **~tona**) forty-year-old; **~tena** /e/ *f* quarantine

quaresma /kwa'rɛzma/ *f* Lent

quarta /'kwarta/ *f* (*dia*) Wednesday; (*marcha*) fourth (gear); **~-de-final** (*pl* **~s-de-final**) *f* quarter final; **~-feira** (*pl* **~s-feiras**) *f* Wednesday

quartanista /kwarta'nista/ *m/f* fourth-year (student)

quarteirão /kwarte'rãw/ *m* block

quar|tel /kwar'tɛw/ (*pl* **~téis**) *m* barracks; **~tel-general** (*pl* **~téis-generais**) *m* headquarters

quarteto /kwar'tetu/ *m* quartet; **~ de cordas** string quartet

quarto /'kwartu/ *a* fourth □ *m* (*parte*) quarter; (*aposento*) bedroom; (*guarda*) watch; **são três e/menos um ~** (*Port*) it's quarter past/to three; **~ de banho** (*Port*) bathroom; **~ de hora** quarter of an hour; **~ de hóspedes** guest room

quartzo /'kwartzu/ *m* quartz

quase /'kwazi/ *adv* almost, nearly; **~ nada/nunca** hardly anything/ever

quatro /'kwatru/ *a & m* four; **de ~** (*no chão*) on all fours; **~centos** *a & m* four hundred

que /ki/ *a* which, what; **~ dia é hoje?** what's the date today?; **~ homem!** what a man!; **~ triste!** how sad! □ *pron* what; **~ é ~ é?** what is it? □ *pron rel* (*coisa*) which, that; (*pessoa*) who, that; (*interrogativo*) what; **o dia em ~** ... the day when/that ... □ *conj* that; (*porque*) because; **espero ~ sim/não** I hope so/not

quê /ke/ *pron* what □ *m* **um ~** something; **não tem de ~** don't mention it

quebra /'kɛbra/ *f* break; (*de empresa, banco*) crash; (*de força*) cut; **de ~** in addition; **~-cabeça** *m* jigsaw (puzzle); (*fig*) puzzle; **~diço** *a* breakable; **~do** *a* broken; <*carro*> broken down; **~dos** *m pl* small change; **~-galho** (*fam*) *m* stopgap; **~-mar** *m* breakwater; **~-molas** *m invar* speed bump; **~-nozes** *m invar* nutcrackers; **~-pau** (*fam*) *m* row; **~-quebra** *m* riot

quebrar /ke'brar/ *vt* break □ *vi* break; <*carro etc*> break down; <*banco, empresa etc*> crash, go bust; **~-se** *vpr* break

queda /'kɛda/ *f* fall; **ter uma ~ por** have a soft spot for; **~-de-braço** *f* arm wrestling

quei|jeira /ke'ʒera/ *f* cheese dish; **~jo** *m* cheese; **~jo prato** cheddar; **~jo-de-minas** *m* Cheshire cheese

queima /'kejma/ *f* burning; **~da** *f* forest fire; **~do** *a* burnt; (*bronzeado*) tanned, brown; **cheiro de ~do** smell of burning

queimar /kej'mar/ *vt* burn; (*bronzear*) tan □ *vi* burn; <*lâmpada*> go; <*fusível*> blow; **~-se** *vpr* burn o.s.; (*bronzear-se*) go brown

queima-roupa /kejma'xopa/ *f* **à ~** point-blank

quei|xa /'keʃa/ *f* complaint; **~xar-se** *vpr* complain (**de** about)

queixo /'keʃu/ *m* chin; **bater o ~** shiver

queixoso /ke'ʃozu/ *a* plaintive □ *m* plaintiff

quem /kẽj/ *pron* who; (*a pessoa que*) anyone who, he who; **de ~ é este livro?** whose is this book?; **~ quer que** whoever; **seja ~ for** whoever it is; **~ falou isso fui eu** it was me who said that; **~ me dera (que)** ... I wish ..., if only

Quênia /'kenia/ *m* Kenya

queniano /keni'anu/ *a & m* Kenyan

quen|tão /kẽ'tãw/ *m* mulled wine; **~te** *a* hot; (*com calor agradável*) warm; **~tura** *f* heat

quepe /'kɛpi/ *m* cap

quer /kɛr/ *conj* **~ ... ~ ...** whether ... or ...

querer /ke'rer/ *vt/i* want; **quero ir** I want to go; **quero que você vá** I want you to go; **eu queria falar com o Sr X** I'd like to speak to Mr X; **vai ~ vir amanhã?** do you want to come tomorrow?; **vou ~ um cafezinho** I'd like a coffee; **se você quiser** if you want; **queira sentar** do sit down; **~ dizer** mean; **quer dizer** (*isto é*) that is to say, I mean

querido /ke'ridu/ *a* dear □ *m* darling

quermesse /ker'mɛsi/ *f* fête, fair

querosene /kero'zeni/ *m* kerosene

questão /kes'tãw/ *m* question; (*assunto*) matter; **em ~** in question; **fazer ~ de** really want to; **não faço ~ de ir** I don't mind not going

questio|nar /kestʃio'nar/ *vt/i* question; ~**nário** *m* questionnaire; ~**nável** (*pl* ~**náveis**) *a* questionable
quiabo /ki'abu/ *m* okra
quibe /'kibi/ *m* savoury meatball
quicar /ki'kar/ *vt/i* bounce
quiche /'kiʃi/ *f* quiche
quie|to /ki'ɛtu/ *a* (*calado*) quiet; (*imóvel*) still; ~**tude** *f* quiet
quilate /ki'latʃi/ *m* carat; (*fig*) calibre
quilha /'kiʎa/ *f* keel
quilo /'kilo/ *m* kilo; ~**grama** *m* kilogram; ~**metragem** *f* mileage; ~**métrico** *a* mile-long
quilômetro /ki'lometru/ *m* kilometre
quimbanda /kĩ'bãda/ *m* Afro-Brazilian cult
qui|mera /ki'mɛra/ *f* fantasy; ~**mérico** *a* fanciful
quími|ca /'kimika/ *f* chemistry; ~**co** *a* chemical □ *m* chemist
quimioterapia /kimiotera'pia/ *f* chemotherapy
quimono /ki'mɔnu/ *m* kimono
quina /'kina/ *f* de ~ edgeways
quindim /kĩ'dʒĩ/ *m* sweet made of coconut, sugar and egg yolks
quinhão /ki'ɲãw/ *m* share
quinhentos /ki'ɲẽtus/ *a* & *m* five hundred
quinina /ki'nina/ *f* quinine
qüinquagésimo /kwĩkwa'ʒɛzimu/ *a* fiftieth
quinquilharias /kĩkiʎa'rias/ *f pl* knick-knacks
quinta[1] /'kĩta/ *f* (*fazenda*) farm
quinta[2] /'kĩta/ *f* (*dia*) Thursday; ~-**feira** (*pl* ~**s-feiras**) *f* Thursday
quin|tal /kĩ'taw/ (*pl* ~**tais**) *m* back yard
quinteiro /kĩ'tajru/ *m* (*Port*) farmer
quinteto /kĩ'tetu/ *m* quintet
quin|to /'kĩtu/ *a* & *m* fifth; ~**tuplo** *a* fivefold; ~**tuplos** *m pl* (*crianças*) quins
quinze /'kĩzi/ *a* & *m* fifteen; **às dez e** ~ at quarter past ten; **são** ~ **para as dez** it's quarter to ten; ~**na** /e/ *f* fortnight; ~**nal** (*pl* ~**nais**) *a* fortnightly; ~**nalmente** *adv* fortnightly
quiosque /ki'ɔski/ *m* (*banca*) kiosk; (*no jardim*) gazebo
quiro|mância /kiro'mãsia/ *f* palmistry; ~**mante** *m/f* palmist
quisto /'kistu/ *m* cyst
quitan|da /ki'tãda/ *f* grocer's (shop); ~**deiro** *m* grocer
qui|tar /ki'tar/ *vt* pay off <*dívida*>; ~**te** *a* **estar** ~**te** be quits
quociente /kwosi'ẽtʃi/ *m* quotient
quórum /'kwɔrũ/ *m* quorum

R

rã /xã/ *f* frog
rabanete /xaba'netʃi/ *m* radish
rabear /xabi'ar/ *vi* <*caminhão*> jack-knife
rabino /xa'binu/ *m* rabbi
rabis|car /xabis'kar/ *vt* scribble □ *vi* (*escrever mal*) scribble; (*fazer desenhos*) doodle; ~**co** *m* doodle
rabo /'xabu/ *m* (*de animal*) tail; **com o** ~ **do olho** out of the corner of one's eye; ~-**de-cavalo** (*pl* ~**s-de-cavalo**) *m* pony tail
rabugento /xabu'ʒẽtu/ *a* grumpy
raça /'xasa/ *f* (*de homens*) race; (*de animais*) breed
ração /xa'sãw/ *f* (*de comida*) ration; (*para animal*) food
racha /'xaʃa/ *f* crack; ~**dura** *f* crack
rachar /xa'ʃar/ *vt* (*dividir*) split; (*abrir fendas em*) crack; chop <*lenha*>; split <*despesas*> □ *vi* (*dividir-se*) split; (*apresentar fendas*) crack; (*ao pagar*) split the cost
raci|al /xasi'aw/ (*pl* ~**ais**) *a* racial
racio|cinar /xasiosi'nar/ *vi* reason; ~**cínio** *m* reasoning; ~**nal** (*pl* ~**nais**) *a* rational; ~**nalizar** *vt* rationalize
racio|namento /xasiona'mẽtu/ *m* rationing; ~**nar** *vt* ration
racis|mo /xa'sizmu/ *m* racism; ~**ta** *a* & *m/f* racist
radar /xa'dar/ *m* radar
radia|ção /xadʒia'sãw/ *f* radiation; ~**dor** *m* radiator
radialista /radʒia'lista/ *m/f* radio announcer
radiante /xadʒi'ãtʃi/ *a* (*de alegria*) overjoyed
radi|cal /xadʒi'kaw/ (*pl* ~**cais**) *a* & *m* radical; ~**car-se** *vpr* settle
rádio[1] /'xadʒiu/ *m* radio □ *f* radio station
rádio[2] /'xadʒiu/ *m* (*elemento*) radium
radioati|vidade /xadioatʃivi'dadʒi/ *f* radioactivity; ~**vo** *a* radioactive
radiodifusão /xadʒiodʒifu'zãw/ *f* broadcasting
radiogra|far /radʒiogra'far/ *vt* X-ray <*pulmões, osso etc*>; radio <*mensagem*>; ~**fia** *f* X-ray
radiolo|gia /radʒiolo'ʒia/ *f* radiology; ~**gista** *m/f* radiologist
radio|novela /xadʒiono'vɛla/ *f* radio serial; ~**patrulha** *f* patrol car; ~**táxi** *m* radio taxi; ~**terapia** *f* radiotherapy, ray treatment
raia /'xaja/ *f* (*em corrida*) lane; (*peixe*) ray

rainha /xa'iɲa/ *f* queen; **~-mãe** *f* queen mother

raio /'xaju/ *m* (*de luz etc*) ray; (*de círculo*) radius; (*de roda*) spoke; (*relâmpago*) bolt of lightning; **~ de ação** range

rai|va /'xajva/ *f* rage; (*doença*) rabies; **estar com ~va** be furious (de with); **ter ~va de alg** have it in for s.o.; **~voso** *a* furious; <*cachorro*> rabid

raiz /xa'iz/ *f* root; **~ quadrada/cúbica** square/cube root

rajada /xa'ʒada/ *f* (*de vento*) gust; (*de tiros*) burst

ra|lador /xala'dor/ *m* grater; **~lar** *vt* grate

ralé /xa'lɛ/ *f* rabble

ralhar /xa'ʎar/ *vi* scold

ralo[1] /'xalu/ *m* (*ralador*) grater; (*de escoamento*) drain

ralo[2] /'xalu/ *a* <*cabelo*> thinning; <*sopa, tecido*> thin; <*vegetação*> sparse; <*café*> weak

ra|mal /xa'maw/ (*pl* **~mais**) *m* (*telefone*) extension; (*de ferrovia*) branch line

ramalhete /xama'ʎetʃi/ *m* posy, bouquet

ramifi|cação /xamifika'sãw/ *f* branch; **~car-se** *vi* branch off

ramo /'xamu/ *m* branch; (*profissional etc*) field; (*buquê*) bunch; **Domingo de Ramos** Palm Sunday

rampa /'xãpa/ *f* ramp

rancor /xã'kor/ *m* resentment; **~oso** /o/ *a* resentful

rançoso /xã'sozu/ *a* rancid

ran|ger /xã'ʒer/ *vt* grind <*dentes*> □ *vi* creak; **~gido** *m* creak

ranhura /xa'ɲura/ *f* groove; (*para moedas*) slot

ranzinza /xã'zĩza/ *a* cantankerous

rapariga /xapa'riga/ *f* (*Port*) girl

rapaz /xa'pas/ *m* boy

rapé /xa'pɛ/ *m* snuff

rapidez /xapi'des/ *f* speed

rápido /'xapidu/ *a* fast □ *adv* <*fazer*> quickly; <*andar*> fast

rapina /xa'pina/ *f* **ave de ~** bird of prey

rapo|sa /xa'poza/ *f* vixen; **~so** *m* fox

rapsódia /xap'sɔdʒia/ *f* rhapsody

rap|tar /xap'tar/ *vt* abduct, kidnap <*criança*>; **~to** *m* abduction, kidnapping (*de criança*)

raquete /xa'kɛtʃi/ *f*, (*Port*) **raqueta** /xa'keta/ *f* racquet

raquítico /xa'kitʃiku/ *a* puny

ra|ramente /xara'mẽtʃi/ *adv* rarely; **~ridade** *f* rarity; **~ro** *a* rare □ *adv* rarely

rascunho /xas'kuɲu/ *m* rough version, draft

ras|gado /xaz'gadu/ *a* torn; (*fig*) <*elogios etc*> effusive; **~gão** *m* tear; **~gar** *vt* tear; (*em pedaços*) tear up □ *vi*, **~gar-se** *vpr* tear; **~go** *m* tear; (*fig*) burst

raso /'xazu/ *a* <*água*> shallow; <*sapato*> flat; <*colher etc*> level

ras|pão /xas'pãw/ *m* graze; **atingir de ~pão** graze; **~par** *vt* shave <*cabeça, pêlos*>; plane <*madeira*>; (*para limpar*) scrape; (*tocar de leve*) graze; **~par em** scrape

ras|teiro /xas'teru/ *a* <*planta*> creeping; <*animal*> crawling; **~tejante** *a* crawling; <*voz*> slurred; **~tejar** *vi* crawl

rasto /'xastu/ *m veja* rastro

ras|trear /xastri'ar/ *vt* track <*satélite etc*>; scan <*céu, corpo etc*>; **~tro** *m* trail

ratear[1] /xatʃi'ar/ *vi* <*motor*> miss

ra|tear[2] /xatʃi'ar/ *vt* share; **~teio** *m* sharing

ratifi|cação /xatʃifika'sãw/ *f* ratification; **~car** *vt* ratify

rato /'xatu/ *m* rat; (*camundongo*) mouse; **~eira** *f* mousetrap

ravina /xa'vina/ *f* ravine

razão /xa'zãw/ *f* reason; (*proporção*) ratio □ *m* ledger; **à ~ de** at the rate of; **em ~ de** on account of; **ter ~** be right; **não ter ~** be wrong

razoá|vel /xazo'avew/ (*pl* **~veis**) *a* reasonable

ré[1] /xɛ/ *f* (*na justiça*) defendant

ré[2] /xɛ/ *f* (*marcha*) reverse; **dar ~** reverse

reabastecer /xeabaste'ser/ *vt/i* refuel

reabilitar /xeabili'tar/ *vt* rehabilitate

rea|ção /xea'sãw/ *f* reaction; **~ção em cadeia** chain reaction; **~cionário** *a* & *m* reactionary

readmitir /xeadʒimi'tʃir/ *vt* reinstate <*funcionário*>

reagir /xea'ʒir/ *vi* react; <*doente*> respond

reajus|tar /xeaʒus'tar/ *vt* readjust; **~te** *m* adjustment

re|al /xe'aw/ (*pl* **~ais**) *a* (*verdadeiro*) real; (*da realeza*) royal

real|çar /xeaw'sar/ *vt* highlight; **~ce** *m* prominence

realejo /xea'leʒu/ *m* barrel organ

realeza /xea'leza/ *f* royalty

realidade /xeali'dadʒi/ *f* reality

realimentação /xealimẽta'sãw/ *f* feedback

realis|mo /xea'lizmu/ *m* realism; **~ta** *a* realistic □ *m/f* realist

reali|zado /xeali'zadu/ *a* <*pessoa*> fulfilled; **~zar** *vt* (*fazer*) carry out; (*tornar real*) realize <*sonho, capital*>; **~zar-se** *vpr* <*sonho*> come true; <*pessoa*> fulfil o.s.; <*casamento, reunião etc*> take place

realmente /xeaw'mẽtʃi/ *adv* really

reaparecer /xeapare'ser/ *vi* reappear

reativar /xeatʃi'var/ *vt* reactivate

reaver /xea'ver/ *vt* get back

reavivar /xeavi'var/ *vt* revive

rebaixar /xeba'ʃar/ *vt* lower <*preço*>; (*fig*) demean □ *vi* <*preços*> drop; **~-se** *vpr* demean o.s.

rebanho /xe'baɲu/ *m* herd; (*fiéis*) flock

reba|te /xe'batʃi/ *m* alarm; **~ter** *vt* return <*bola*>; refute <*acusação*>; (*à máquina*) retype

rebelar-se /xebe'larsi/ *vpr* rebel

rebel|de /xe'bɛwdʒi/ *a* rebellious □ *m/f* rebel; **~dia** *f* rebelliousness

rebelião /xebeli'ãw/ *f* rebellion

reben|tar /xebẽ'tar/ *vt/i veja* arrebentar; **~to** *m* (*de planta*) shoot; (*descendente*) offspring

rebite /xe'bitʃi/ *m* rivet

rebobinar /xebobi'nar/ *vt* rewind

rebo|cador /xeboka'dor/ *m* tug; **~car** *vt* (*tirar*) tow; (*cobrir com reboco*) plaster; **~co** /o/ *m* plaster

rebolar /xebo'lar/ *vi* swing one's hips

reboque /xe'bɔki/ *m* towing; (*veículo a* **~**) trailer; (*com guindaste*) tow-truck; a **~** on tow

rebuçado /xebu'sadu/ *m* (*Port*) sweet, (*Amer*) candy

rebuliço /xebu'lisu/ *m* commotion

rebuscado /xebus'kadu/ *a* récherché

recado /xe'kadu/ *m* message

reca|ída /xeka'ida/ *f* relapse; **~ir** *vi* relapse; <*acento, culpa*> fall

recal|cado /xekaw'kadu/ *a* repressed; **~car** *vt* repress

recanto /xe'kãtu/ *m* nook, recess

recapitular /xekapitu'lar/ *vt* review □ *vi* recap

reca|tado /xeka'tadu/ *a* reserved, withdrawn; **~to** *m* reserve

recear /xesi'ar/ *vt/i* fear (*por* for)

rece|ber /xese'ber/ *vt* receive; entertain <*convidados*> □ *vi* (**~***ber salário*) get paid; (**~***ber convidados*) entertain; **~bimento** *m* receipt

receio /xe'seju/ *m* fear

recei|ta /xe'sejta/ *f* (*de cozinha*) recipe; (*médica*) prescription; (*dinheiro*) revenue; **~tar** *vt* prescribe

recém|-casados /xesẽjka'zadus/ *m pl* newly-weds; **~-chegado** *m* newcomer; **~-nascido** *a* newborn □ *m* newborn child, baby

recente /xe'sẽtʃi/ *a* recent; **~mente** *adv* recently

receoso /xese'ozu/ *a* (*apreensivo*) afraid

recep|ção /xesep'sãw/ *f* reception; (*Port: de carta*) receipt; **~cionar** *vt* receive; **~cionista** *m/f* receptionist; **~táculo** *m* receptacle; **~tivo** *a* receptive; **~tor** *m* receiver

reces|são /xese'sãw/ *f* recession; **~so** /ɛ/ *m* recess

re|chear /xeʃi'ar/ *vt* stuff <*frango, assado*>; fill <*empada*>; **~cheio** *m* (*para frango etc*) stuffing; (*de empada etc*) filling

rechonchudo /xeʃõ'ʃudu/ *a* plump

recibo /xe'sibu/ *m* receipt

reciclar /xesik'lar/ *vt* recycle

recife /xe'sifi/ *m* reef

recinto /xe'sĩtu/ *m* enclosure

recipiente /xesipi'ẽtʃi/ *m* container

reciprocar /xesipro'kar/ *vt* reciprocate

recíproco /xe'siproku/ *a* reciprocal; <*sentimento*> mutual

reci|tal /xesi'taw/ (*pl* **~tais**) *m* recital; **~tar** *vt* recite

recla|mação /xeklama'sãw/ *f* complaint; (*no seguro*) claim; **~mar** *vt* claim □ *vi* complain (de about); (*no seguro*) claim; **~me** *m*, (*Port*) **~mo** *m* advertising

reclinar-se /xekli'narsi/ *vpr* recline

recluso /xe'kluzu/ *a* reclusive □ *m* recluse

recobrar /xeko'brar/ *vt* recover; **~-se** *vpr* recover

recolher /xeko'ʎer/ *vt* collect; (*retirar*) withdraw; **~-se** *vpr* retire

recomeçar /xekome'sar/ *vt/i* start again

recomen|dação /xekomẽda'sãw/ *f* recommendation; **~dar** *vt* recommend; **~dável** (*pl* **~dáveis**) *a* advisable

recompen|sa /xekõ'pẽsa/ *f* reward; **~sar** *vt* reward

reconcili|ação /xekõsilia'sãw/ *f* reconciliation; **~ar** *vt* reconcile; **~ar-se** *vpr* be reconciled

reconhe|cer /xekoɲe'ser/ *vt* recognize; (*admitir*) acknowledge; (*mil*) reconnoitre; identify <*corpo*>; **~cimento** *m* recognition; (*gratidão*) gratitude; (*mil*) reconnaissance; (*de corpo*) identification; **~cível** (*pl* **~cíveis**) *a* recognizable

reconsiderar /xekõside'rar/ *vt/i* reconsider

reconstituinte /xekõstʃitu'ĩtʃi/ *m* tonic

reconstituir /xekõstʃitu'ir/ *vt* reform; reconstruct <*crime, cena*>

reconstruir /xekõstru'ir/ *vt* rebuild

recor|dação /xekorda'sãw/ *f* recollection; (*objeto*) memento; **~dar** *vt* recollect; **~dar-se (de)** recall

recor|de /xe'kɔrdʒi/ *a invar & m* record; **~dista** *a* record-breaking □ *m/f* record-holder

recorrer /xeko'xer/ *vi* **~** a turn to <*médico, amigo*>; resort to <*violência, tática*>; **~** de appeal against

recor|tar /xekor'tar/ *vt* cut out; **~te** /ɔ/ *m* cutting, (*Amer*) clipping

recostar /xekos'tar/ *vt* lean back; **~-se** *vpr* lean back

recreio /xe'kreju/ *m* recreation; (*na escola*) break

recriar /xekri'ar/ *vt* recreate

recriminação /xekrimina'sãw/ *f* recrimination

recrudescer /xekrude'ser/ *vi* intensify

recru|ta /xe'kruta/ *m/f* recruit; **~tamento** *m* recruitment; **~tar** *vt* recruit

recu|ar /xeku'ar/ *vi* move back; <*tropas*> retreat; (*no tempo*) go back; (*ceder*) back down; (*não cumprir*) back out (de of) □ *vt* move back; **~o** *m* retreat; (*fig: de intento*) climbdown

recupe|ração /xekupera'sãw/ *f* recovery; **~rar** *vt* recover; make up <*atraso, tempo perdido*>; **~rar-se** *vpr* recover (de from)

recurso /xe'kursu/ *m* resort; (*coisa útil*) resource; (*na justiça*) appeal; *pl* resources

recu|sa /xe'kuza/ *f* refusal; **~sar** *vt* refuse; turn down <*convite, oferta*>; **~sar-se** *vpr* refuse (a to)

reda|ção /xeda'sãw/ *f* (*de livro, contrato*) draft; (*pessoal*) editorial staff; (*seção*) editorial department; (*na escola*) composition; **~tor** *m* editor

rede /'xedʒi/ *f* net; (*para deitar*) hammock; (*fig: sistema*) network

rédea /'xɛdʒia/ *f* rein

redemoinho /xedemo'iɲu/ *m veja* **rodamoinho**

reden|ção /xedẽ'sãw/ *f* redemption; **~tor** *a* redeeming □ *m* redeemer

redigir /xedʒi'ʒir/ *vt* draw up <*contrato*>; write <*artigo*>; edit <*dicionário*>

redimir /xedʒi'mir/ *vt* redeem

redobrar /xedo'brar/ *vt* redouble

redon|deza /xedõ'deza/ *f* roundness; *pl* vicinity; **~do** *a* round

redor /xe'dɔr/ *m* ao *ou* em **~** de around

redução /xedu'sãw/ *f* reduction

redun|dante /xedũ'dãtʃi/ *a* redundant; **~dar** *vi* **~dar** em develop into

redu|zido /xedu'zidu/ *a* limited; (*pequeno*) small; **~zir** *vt* reduce; **~zir-se** *vpr* (*ficar reduzido*) be reduced (a to); (*resumir-se*) come down (a to)

reeleger /xeele'ʒer/ *vt* re-elect; **~-se** *vpr* be re-elected

reeleição /xeelej'sãw/ *f* re-election

reembol|sar /xeẽbow'sar/ *vt* reimburse <*pessoa*>; refund <*dinheiro*>; **~so** /o/ *m* refund; **~so postal** cash on delivery

reencarnação /xeẽkarna'sãw/ *f* reincarnation

reentrância /xeẽ'trãsia/ *f* recess

reescalonar /xeeskalo'nar/ *vt* reschedule

reescrever /xeeskre'ver/ *vt* rewrite

refastelar-se /xefaste'larsi/ *vpr* stretch out

refazer /xefa'zer/ *vt* redo; rebuild <*vida*>; **~-se** *vpr* recover (de from)

refei|ção /xefej'sãw/ *f* meal; **~tório** *m* dining hall

refém /xe'fẽj/ *m* hostage

referência /xefe'rẽsia/ *f* reference; com **~** a with reference to

referendum /xefe'rẽdũ/ *m* referendum

refe|rente /xefe'rẽtʃi/ *a* **~rente a** regarding; **~rir** *vt* report; **~rir-se** *vpr* refer (a to)

refestelar-se /xefeste'larsi/ *vpr* (*Port*) *veja* **refastelar-se**

re|fil /xe'fiw/ (*pl* **~fis**) *m* refill

refi|nado /xefi'nadu/ *a* refined; **~namento** *m* refinement; **~nar** *vt* refine; **~naria** *f* refinery

refle|tido /xefle'tʃidu/ *a* <*decisão*> well-thought-out; <*pessoa*> thoughtful; **~tir** *vt/i* reflect; **~tir-se** *vpr* be reflected; **~xão** /ks/ *f* reflection; **~xivo** /ks/ *a* reflexive; **~xo** /ɛks/ *a* <*luz*> reflected; <*ação*> reflex □ *m* (*de luz etc*) reflection; (*físico*) reflex; (*no cabelo*) streak

refluxo /xe'fluksu/ *m* ebb

refo|gado /xefo'gadu/ *m* lightly fried mixture of onions and garlic; **~gar** *vt* fry lightly

refor|çar /xefor'sar/ *vt* reinforce; **~ço** /o/ *m* reinforcement

refor|ma /xe'fɔrma/ *f* (*da lei etc*) reform; (*na casa etc*) renovation; (*de militar*) discharge; (*pensão*) pension; **~ma ministerial** cabinet reshuffle; **~mado** *a* reformed; (*Port: aposentado*) retired □ *m* (*Port*) pensioner; **~mar** *vt* reform <*lei, sistema etc*>; renovate <*casa, prédio*>; (*Port: aposentar*) retire; **~mar-se** *vpr* (*Port: aposentar-se*) retire; <*criminoso*> reform; **~matório** *m* reform school; **~mista** *a & m/f* reformist

refratário /xefra'tariu/ *a* <*tigela etc*> ovenproof, heatproof

refrear /xefri'ar/ *vt* rein in <*cavalo*>; (*fig*) curb, keep in check <*paixões etc*>; **~-se** *vpr* restrain o.s.

refrega /xe'frɛga/ *f* clash, fight

refres|cante /xefres'kãtʃi/ *a* refreshing; **~car** *vt* freshen, cool <*ar*>; refresh <*pessoa, memória etc*> □ *vi* get cooler; **~car-se** *vpr* refresh o.s.; **~co** /e/ *m* (*bebida*) soft drink; *pl* refreshments

refrige|rado /xefriʒe'radu/ *a* cooled; <*casa etc*> air-conditioned; (*na geladeira*) refrigerated; **~rador** *m* refrigerator; **~rante** *m* soft drink; **~rar** *vt* keep cool; (*na geladeira*) refrigerate

refugi|ado /xefuʒi'adu/ *m* refugee; **~ar-se** *vpr* take refuge

refúgio /xe'fuʒiu/ *m* refuge

refugo /xe'fugu/ *m* waste, refuse

refutar /xefu'tar/ *vt* refute

regaço /xe'gasu/ *m* lap

regador /xega'dor/ *m* watering can

regalia /xega'lia/ *f* privilege

regar /xe'gar/ *vt* water

regata /xe'gata/ *f* regatta

regatear /xegatʃi'ar/ *vi* bargain, haggle

re|gência /xe'ʒẽsia/ *f* (*de verbo etc*) government; **~gente** *m/f* (*de orquestra*) conductor; **~ger** *vt* govern □ *vi* rule

região /xeʒi'ãw/ *f* region; (*de cidade etc*) area

regi|me /xe'ʒimi/ *m* regime; (*dieta*) diet; **fazer ~me** diet; **~mento** *m* (*militar*) regiment; (*regulamento*) regulations

régio /'xɛʒiu/ *a* regal

regio|nal /xeʒio'naw/ (*pl* **~nais**) *a* regional

regis|trador /xeʒistra'dor/ *a* **caixa ~tradora** cash register; **~trar** *vt* register; (*anotar*) record; **~tro** *m* (*lista*) register; (*de um fato, em banco de dados*) record; (*ato de ~trar*) registration

rego /'xegu/ *m* (*de arado*) furrow; (*de roda*) rut; (*para escoamento*) ditch

regozi|jar /xegozi'ʒar/ *vt* delight; **~jar-se** *vpr* be delighted; **~jo** *m* delight

regra /'xɛgra/ *f* rule; *pl* (*menstruações*) periods; **em ~** as a rule

regres|sar /xegre'sar/ *vi* return; **~sivo** *a* regressive; **contagem ~siva** countdown; **~so** /ɛ/ *m* return

régua /'xɛgwa/ *f* ruler

regu|lagem /xegu'laʒẽ/ *f* (*de carro*) tuning; **~lamento** *m* regulations; **~lar** *a* regular; <*estatura, qualidade etc*> average □ *vt* regulate; tune <*carro, motor*>; set <*relógio*> □ *vi* work; **~lar-se por** go by, be guided by; **~laridade** *f* regularity; **~larizar** *vt* regularize

regurgitar /xegurʒi'tar/ *vt* bring up

rei /xej/ *m* king; **~nado** *m* reign

reincidir /xeĩsi'dʒir/ *vi* <*criminoso*> reoffend

reino /'xejnu/ *m* kingdom; (*fig: da fantasia etc*) realm; **Reino Unido** United Kingdom

reiterar /xejte'rar/ *vt* reiterate

reitor /xej'tor/ *m* chancellor, (*Amer*) president

reivindi|cação /xejvĩdʒika'sãw/ *f* demand; **~car** *vt* claim, demand

rejei|ção /xeʒej'sãw/ *f* rejection; **~tar** *vt* reject

rejuvenescer /xeʒuvene'ser/ *vt* rejuvenate □ *vi* be rejuvenated

relação /xela'sãw/ *f* relationship; (*relatório*) account; (*lista*) list; *pl* relations; **com ou em ~ a** in relation to, regarding

relacio|namento /xelasiona'mẽtu/ *m* relationship; **~nar** *vt* relate (**com** to); (*listar*) list; **~nar-se** *vpr* relate (**com** to)

relações-públicas /xelasõjs-'publikas/ *m/f invar* public-relations person

relâmpago /xe'lãpagu/ *m* flash of lightning; *pl* lightning □ *a* lightning; **num ~** in a flash

relampejar /xelãpe'ʒar/ *vi* flash; **relampejou** there was a flash of lightning

relance /xe'lãsi/ *m* glance; **olhar de ~** glance (at)

rela|tar /xela'tar/ *vt* relate; **~tivo** *a* relative; **~to** *m* account; **~tório** *m* report

rela|xado /xela'ʃadu/ *a* relaxed; <*disciplina*> lax; <*pessoa*> lazy, complacent; **~xamento** *m* (*físico*) relaxation; (*de pessoa*) complacency; **~xante** *a* relaxing □ *m* tranquillizer; **~xar** *vt* relax □ *vi* (*descansar*) relax; (*tornar-se omisso*) get complacent; **~xar-se** *vpr* relax; **~xe** *m* relaxation

reles /'xɛlis/ *a invar* <*gente*> common; <*ação*> despicable

rele|vância /xele'vãsia/ *f* relevance; **~vante** *a* relevant; **~var** *vt* emphasize; **~vo** /e/ *m* relief; (*importância*) prominence

religi|ão /xeliʒi'ãw/ *f* religion; **~oso** /o/ *a* religious

relin|char /xelĩ'ʃar/ *vi* neigh; **~cho** *m* neighing

relíquia /xe'likia/ *f* relic

relógio /xe'lɔʒiu/ *m* clock; (*de pulso*) watch

relu|tância /xelu'tãsia/ *f* reluctance; **~tante** *a* reluctant; **~tar** *vi* be reluctant (**em** to)

reluzente /xelu'zẽtʃi/ *a* shining, gleaming

relva /'xɛwva/ *f* grass; **~do** *m* lawn

remador /xema'dor/ *m* rower

remanescente /xemane'sẽtʃi/ *a* remaining □ *m* remainder

remar /xe'mar/ *vt/i* row

rema|tar /xema'tar/ *vt* finish off; **~te** *m* finish; (*adorno*) finishing touch; (*de piada*) punch line

remediar /xemedʒi'ar/ *vt* remedy

remédio /xe'mɛdʒiu/ *m* (*contra doença*) medicine, drug; (*a problema etc*) remedy

remelento /xeme'lẽtu/ *a* bleary

remen|dar /xemẽ'dar/ *vt* mend; (*com pedaço de pano*) patch; **~do** *m* mend; (*pedaço de pano*) patch

remessa /xe'mɛsa/ *f* (*de mercadorias*) shipment; (*de dinheiro*) remittance

reme|tente /xeme'tẽtʃi/ *m/f* sender; **~ter** *vt* send <*mercadorias, dinheiro etc*>; refer <*leitor*> (a to)

remexer /xeme'ʃer/ *vt* shuffle <*papéis*>; stir up <*poeira, lama*>; wave <*braços*> □ *vi* rummage; **~-se** *vpr* move around

reminiscência /xemini'sẽsia/ *f* reminiscence

remir /xe'mir/ *vt* redeem; **~-se** *vpr* redeem o.s.

remissão /xemi'sãw/ *f* (*de pecados*) redemption; (*de doença, pena*) remission; (*num livro*) cross-reference

remo /'xemu/ *m* oar; (*esporte*) rowing

remoção /xemo'sãw/ *f* removal

remoinho /xemo'iɲu/ *m* (*Port*) *veja* **rodamoinho**

remontar /xemõ'tar/ *vi* **~** a <*coisa*> date back to; <*pessoa*> think back to

remorso /xe'mɔrsu/ *m* remorse

remo|to /xe'mɔtu/ *a* remote; **~ver** *vt* remove

remune|ração /xemunera'sãw/ *f* payment; **~rador** *a* profitable; **~rar** *vt* pay

rena /'xena/ *f* reindeer

re|nal /xe'naw/ (*pl* **~nais**) *a* renal, kidney

Renascença /xena'sẽsa/ *f* Renaissance

renas|cer /xena'ser/ *vi* be reborn; **~cimento** *m* rebirth

renda[1] /'xẽda/ *f* (*tecido*) lace

ren|da[2] /'xẽda/ *f* income; (*Port: aluguel*) rent; **~der** bring in, yield <*lucro*>; earn <*juros*>; fetch <*preço*>; bring <*resultado*> □ *vi* <*investimento, trabalho, ação*> pay off; <*comida*> go a long way; <*produto comprado*> give value for money; **~der-se** *vpr* surrender; **~dição** *f* surrender; **~dimento** *m* (*renda*) income; (*de investimento, terreno*) yield; (*de motor etc*) output; (*de produto comprado*) value for money; **~doso** /o/ *a* profitable

rene|gado /xene'gadu/ *a* & *m* renegade; **~gar** *vt* renounce

renhido /xe'ɲidu/ *a* hard-fought

Reno /'xenu/ *m* Rhine

reno|mado /xeno'madu/ *a* renowned; **~me** /o/ *m* renown

reno|vação /xenova'sãw/ *f* renewal; **~var** *vt* renew

renque /'xẽki/ *m* row

ren|tabilidade /xẽtabili'dadʒi/ *f* profitability; **~tável** (*pl* **~táveis**) *a* profitable

rente /'xẽtʃi/ *adv* **~** a close to □ *a* <*cabelo*> cropped

renúncia /xe'nũsia/ *f* renunciation (a of); (*a cargo*) resignation (a from)

renunciar /xenũsi'ar/ *vi* <*presidente etc*> resign; **~** a give up; waive <*direito*>

reorganizar /xeorgani'zar/ *vt* reorganize

repa|ração /xepara'sãw/ *f* reparation; (*conserto*) repair; **~rar** *vt* (*consertar*) repair; make up for <*ofensa, injustiça, erro*>; make good <*danos, prejuízo*> □ *vi* **~rar** (em) notice; **~ro** *m* (*conserto*) repair

repar|tição /xepartʃi'sãw/ *f* division; (*seção do governo*) department; **~tir** *vt* divide up

repassar /xepa'sar/ *vt* revise <*matéria, lição*>

repatriar /xepatri'ar/ *vt* repatriate

repe|lente /xepe'lẽtʃi/ *a* & *m* repellent; **~lir** *vt* repel; reject <*idéia, proposta etc*>

repensar /xepẽ'sar/ *vt/i* rethink

repen|te /xe'pẽtʃi/ *m* **de ~te** suddenly; (*fam: talvez*) maybe; **~tino** *a* sudden

reper|cussão /xeperku'sãw/ *f* repercussion; **~cutir** *vi* <*som*> reverberate; (*fig: ter efeito*) have repercussions

repertório /xeper'tɔriu/ *m* (*músico etc*) repertoire; (*lista*) list

repe|tição /xepetʃi'sãw/ *f* repetition; **~tido** *a* repeated; **~tidas vezes** repeatedly; **~tir** *vt* repeat □ *vi* (*ao comer*) have seconds; **~tir-se** *vpr* <*pessoa*> repeat o.s.; <*fato, acontecimento*> recur; **~titivo** *a* repetitive

repi|car /xepi'kar/ *vt/i* ring; **~que** *m* ring

replay /xe'plej/ (*pl* **~s**) *m* action replay

repleto /xe'plɛtu/ *a* full up

réplica /'xɛplika/ *f* reply; (*cópia*) replica

replicar /xepli'kar/ *vt* answer □ *vi* reply

repolho /xe'poʎu/ *m* cabbage

repor /xe'por/ *vt* (*num lugar*) put back; (*substituir*) replace

reportagem /xepor'taʒẽ/ *f* (*uma*) report; (*ato*) reporting

repórter /xe'pɔrter/ *m/f* reporter

reposição /xepozi'sãw/ *f* replacement

repou|sar /xepo'sar/ *vt/i* rest; **~so** *m* rest

repreen|der /xepriẽ'der/ *vt* rebuke, reprimand; **~são** *f* rebuke, reprimand; **~sível** (*pl* **~síveis**) *a* reprehensible

represa /xe'preza/ *f* dam

represália /xepre'zalia/ *f* reprisal

represen|tação /xeprezẽta'sãw/ *f* representation; (*espetáculo*) performance; (*ofício de ator*) acting; **~tante** *m/f* representative; **~tar** *vt* represent; (*no teatro*) perform <*peça*>; play <*papel, personagem*> □ *vi* <*ator*> act; **~tativo** *a* representative

repres|são /xepre'sãw/ *f* repression; **~sivo** *a* repressive

repri|mido /xepri'midu/ *a* repressed; **~mir** *vt* repress

reprise /xe'prizi/ *f* (*na TV*) repeat; (*de filme*) rerun

reprodu|ção /xeprodu'sãw/ *f* reproduction; **~zir** *vt* reproduce; **~zir-se** *vpr* (*multiplicar-se*) reproduce; (*repetir-se*) recur

repro|vação /xeprova'sãw/ *f* disapproval; (*em exame*) failure; **~var** *vt* (*rejeitar*) disapprove of; (*em exame*) fail; **ser ~vado** <*aluno*> fail

rép|til /'xɛptʃiw/ (*pl* **~teis**) *m* reptile

república /xe'publika/ *f* republic; (*de estudantes*) hall of residence

republicano /xepubli'kanu/ *a* & *m* republican

repudiar /xepudʒi'ar/ *vt* disown; repudiate <*esposa*>

repug|nância /xepug'nãsia/ *f* repugnance; **~nante** *a* repugnant

repul|sa /xe'puwsa/ *f* repulsion; (*recusa*) rejection; **~sivo** *a* repulsive

reputação /xeputa'sãw/ *f* reputation

requebrar /xeke'brar/ *vt* swing; **~-se** *vpr* sway

requeijão /xeke'ʒãw/ *m* cheese spread, cottage cheese

reque|rer /xeke'rer/ *vt* (*pedir*) apply for; (*exigir*) require; **~rimento** *m* application

requin|tado /xekĩ'tadu/ *a* refined; **~tar** *vt* refine; **~te** *m* refinement

requisi|ção /xekizi'sãw/ *f* requisition; **~tar** *vt* requisition; **~to** *m* requirement

rês /xes/ (*pl* **reses**) *m* head of cattle; *pl* cattle

rescindir /xesĩ'dʒir/ *vt* rescind

rés-do-chão /xɛzdu'ʃãw/ *m invar* (*Port*) ground floor, (*Amer*) first floor

rese|nha /xe'zeɲa/ *f* review; **~nhar** *vt* review

reser|va /xe'zɛrva/ *f* reserve; (*em hotel, avião etc, ressalva*) reservation; **~var** *vt* reserve; **~vatório** *m* reservoir; **~vista** *m/f* reservist

resfri|ado /xesfri'ado/ *a* **estar ~ado** have a cold □ *m* cold; **~ar** *vt* cool □ *vi* get cold; (*tornar-se morno*) cool down; **~ar-se** *vpr* catch a cold

resga|tar /xezga'tar/ *vt* (*salvar*) rescue; (*remir*) redeem; **~te** *m* (*salvamento*) rescue; (*pago por refém*) ransom; (*remissão*) redemption

resguardar /xezgwar'dar/ *vt* protect; **~-se** *vpr* protect o.s. (**de** from)

residência /xezi'dẽsia/ *f* residence

residen|cial /xezidẽsi'aw/ (*pl* **~ciais**) *a* <*bairro*> residential; <*telefone etc*> home; **~te** *a* & *m/f* resident

residir /xezi'dʒir/ *vi* reside

resíduo /xe'ziduu/ *m* residue

resig|nação /xezigna'sãw/ *f* resignation; **~nado** *a* resigned; **~nar-se** *vpr* resign o.s. (**com** to)

resina /xe'zina/ *f* resin

resis|tência /xezis'tẽsia/ *f* resistance; (*de atleta, mental*) endurance; (*de material, objeto*) toughness; **~tente** *a* strong, tough; <*tecido, roupa*> hard-wearing; <*planta*> hardy; **~tente a** resistant to; **~tir** *vi* (*opor ~tência*) resist; (*agüentar*) <*pessoa*> hold out; <*objeto*> hold; **~tir a** (*combater*) resist; (*agüentar*) withstand; **~tir ao tempo** stand the test of time

resmun|gar /xezmũ'gar/ *vi* grumble; **~go** *m* grumbling

resolu|ção /xezolu'sãw/ *f* resolution; (*firmeza*) resolve; (*de problema*) solution; **~to** *a* resolute; **~to a** resolved to

resolver /xezow'ver/ *vt* (*esclarecer*) sort out; solve <*problema, enigma*>; (*decidir*) decide; **~-se** *vpr* make up one's mind (**a** to)

respaldo /xes'pawdu/ *m* (*de cadeira*) back; (*fig: apoio*) backing

respectivo /xespek'tʃivu/ *a* respective

respei|tabilidade /xespejtabili'dadʒi/ *f* respectability; **~tador** *a* respectful; **~tar** *vt* respect; **~tável** (*pl* **~táveis**) *a* respectable; **~to** *m* respect (**por** for); **a ~to de** about; **a este ~to** in this respect; **com ~to a** with regard to; **dizer ~to a** concern; **~toso** /o/ *a* respectful

respin|gar /xespĩ'gar/ *vt/i* splash; **~go** *m* splash

respi|ração /xespira'sãw/ *f* breathing; **~rador** *m* respirator; **~rar** *vt/i* breathe; **~ratório** *a* respiratory; **~ro** *m* breath; (*descanso*) break, breather

resplande|cente /xesplãde'sẽtʃi/ *a* resplendent; **~cer** *vi* shine

resplendor /xesplẽ'dor/ *m* brilliance; (*fig*) glory

respon|dão /xespõ'dãw/ *a* (*f* **~dona**) cheeky; **~der** *vt/i* answer; (*com insolência*) answer back; **~der a** answer; **~der por** answer for, take responsibility for

responsabili|dade /xespõsabili'dadʒi/ *f* responsibility; **~zar** *vt* hold responsible (por for); **~zar-se** *vpr* take responsibility (por for)

responsá|vel /xespõ'savew/ (*pl* **~veis**) *a* responsible (por for)

resposta /xes'pɔsta/ *f* answer

resquício /xes'kisiu/ *m* vestige, remnant

ressabiado /xesabi'adu/ *a* wary, suspicious

ressaca /xe'saka/ *f* (*depois de beber*) hangover; (*do mar*) undertow

ressaltar /xesaw'tar/ *vt* emphasize □ *vi* stand out

ressalva /xe'sawva/ *f* reservation, proviso; (*proteção*) safeguard

ressarcir /xesar'sir/ *vt* refund

resse|cado /xese'kadu/ *a* <*terra*> parched; <*pele*> dry; **~car** *vt/i* dry up

ressen|tido /xesẽ'tʃidu/ *a* resentful; **~timento** *m* resentment; **~tir-se de** (*ofender-se*) resent; (*ser influenciado*) show the effects of

ressequido /xese'kidu/ *a veja* ressecado

resso|ar /xeso'ar/ *vi* resound; **~nância** *f* resonance; **~nante** *a* resonant; **~nar** *vi* (*Port*) snore

ressurgimento /xesurʒi'mẽtu/ *m* resurgence

ressurreição /xesuxej'sãw/ *f* resurrection

ressuscitar /xesusi'tar/ *vt* revive

restabele|cer /xestabele'ser/ *vt* restore; restore to health <*doente*>; **~cer-se** *vpr* recover; **~cimento** *m* restoration; (*de doente*) recovery

res|tante /xes'tãtʃi/ *a* remaining □ *m* remainder; **~tar** *vi* remain; **~ta-me dizer que ...** it remains for me to say that

restau|ração /xestawra'sãw/ *f* restoration; **~rante** *m* restaurant; **~rar** *vt* restore

restitu|ição /xestʃitui'sãw/ *f* return, restitution; **~ir** *vt* (*devolver*) return; restore <*forma, força etc*>; reinstate <*funcionário*>

resto /'xɛstu/ *m* rest; *pl* (*de comida*) left-overs; (*de cadáver*) remains; **de ~** besides

restrição /xestri'sãw/ *f* restriction

restringir /xestrĩ'ʒir/ *vt* restrict

restrito /xes'tritu/ *a* restricted

resul|tado /xezuw'tadu/ *m* result; **~tante** *a* resulting (de from); **~tar** *vi* result (de from; em in)

resu|mir /xezu'mir/ *vt* (*abreviar*) summarize; (*conter em poucas palavras*) sum up; **~mir-se** *vpr* (*ser expresso em poucas palavras*) be summed up; **~mir-se em** (*ser apenas*) come down to; **~mo** *m* summary; **em ~mo** briefly

resvalar /xezva'lar/ *vi* (*sem querer*) slip; (*deslizar*) slide

reta /'xɛta/ *f* (*linha*) straight line; (*de pista etc*) straight; **~ final** home straight

retaguarda /xeta'gwarda/ *f* rearguard

retalho /xe'taʎu/ *m* scrap; **a ~** (*Port*) retail

retaliação /xetalia'sãw/ *f* retaliation

retangular /xetãgu'lar/ *a* rectangular

retângulo /xe'tãgulu/ *m* rectangle

retar|dado /xetar'dadu/ *a* retarded □ *m* retard; **~dar** *vt* delay; **~datário** *m* latecomer

retenção /xetẽ'sãw/ *f* retention

reter /xe'ter/ *vt* keep <*pessoa*>; hold back <*águas, riso, lágrimas*>; (*na memória*) retain; **~-se** *vpr* restrain o.s.

rete|sado /xete'zadu/ *a* taut; **~sar** *vt* pull taut

reticência /xetʃi'sẽsia/ *f* reticence

reti|dão /xetʃi'dãw/ *f* rectitude; **~ficar** *vt* rectify

reti|rada /xetʃi'rada/ *f* (*de tropas*) retreat; (*de dinheiro*) withdrawal; **~rado** *a* secluded; **~rar** *vt* withdraw; (*afastar*) move away; **~rar-se** *vpr* <*tropas*> retreat; (*afastar-se*) withdraw; (*de uma atividade*) retire; **~ro** *m* retreat

reto /'xɛtu/ *a* <*linha etc*> straight; <*pessoa*> honest

retocar /xeto'kar/ *vt* touch up <*desenho, maquiagem etc*>; alter <*texto*>

reto|mada /xeto'mada/ *f* (*continuação*) resumption; (*reconquista*) retaking; **~mar** *vt* (*continuar com*) resume; (*conquistar de novo*) retake

retoque /xe'tɔki/ *m* finishing touch

retorcer /xetor'ser/ *vt* twist; **~-se** *vpr* writhe

retóri|ca /xe'tɔrika/ *f* rhetoric; **~co** *a* rhetorical

retor|nar /xetor'nar/ *vi* return; **~no** *m* return; (*na estrada*) turning place; **dar ~no** do a U-turn

retrair /xetra'ir/ *vt* retract, withdraw; **~-se** *vpr* (*recuar*) withdraw; (*encolher-se*) retract

retrasa|do /xetra'zadu/ *a* **a semana ~da** the week before last

retratar[1] /xetra'tar/ *vt* (*desdizer*) retract

retra|tar[2] /xetra'tar/ *vt* (*em quadro, livro*) portray, depict; **~to** *m* portrait; (*foto*) photo; (*representação*) portrayal; **~to falado** identikit picture

retribuir /xetribu'ir/ *vt* return <*favor, visita*>; repay <*gentileza*>

retroativo /xetroa'tʃivu/ *a* retroactive; <*pagamento*> backdated

retro|ceder /xetrose'der/ *vi* retreat; (*desistir*) back down; **~cesso** /ɛ/ *m* retreat; (*ao passado*) regression

retrógrado /xe'trɔgradu/ *a* retrograde

retrospec|tiva /xetrospek'tʃiva/ *f* retrospective; **~tivo** *a* retrospective; **~to** /ɛ/ *m* look back; em **~to** in retrospect

retrovisor /xetrovi'zor/ *a* & *m* (**espelho**) **~** rear-view mirror

retrucar /xetru'kar/ *vt/i* retort

retum|bante /xetũ'bãtʃi/ *a* resounding; **~bar** *vi* resound

réu /'xɛw/ *m* (*f* **ré**) defendant

reumatismo /xewma'tʃizmu/ *m* rheumatism

reu|nião /xeuni'ãw/ *f* meeting; (*descontraída*) get-together; (*de família*) reunion; **~nião de cúpula** summit meeting; **~nir** *vt* bring together <*pessoas*>; combine <*qualidades*>; **~nir-se** *vpr* meet; <*amigos, familiares*> get together; **~nir-se a** join

revanche /xe'vãʃi/ *f* revenge; (*jogo*) return match

reveillon /xeve'jõ/ (*pl* **~s**) *m* New Year's Eve

reve|lação /xevela'sãw/ *f* revelation; (*de fotos*) developing; (*novo talento*) promising newcomer; **~lar** *vt* reveal; develop <*filme, fotos*>; **~lar-se** *vpr* (*vir a ser*) turn out to be

revelia /xeve'lia/ *f* **à ~** by default; **à ~ de** without the knowledge of

reven|dedor /xevẽde'dor/ *m* dealer; **~der** *vt* resell

rever /xe'ver/ *vt* (*ver de novo*) see again; (*revisar*) revise; (*examinar*) check

reve|rência /xeve'resia/ *f* reverence; (*movimento do busto*) bow; (*dobrando os joelhos*) curtsey; **~rente** *a* reverent

reverso /xe'vɛrsu/ *m* reverse; **o ~ da medalha** the other side of the coin

revés /xe'vɛs/ (*pl* **reveses**) *m* setback

reves|timento /xevestʃi'mẽtu/ *m* covering; **~tir** *vt* cover

reve|zamento /xeveza'mẽtu/ *m* alternation; **~zar** *vt/i* alternate; **~zar-se** *vpr* alternate

revi|dar /xevi'dar/ *vt* return <*golpe, insulto*>; refute <*crítica*>; (*retrucar*) retort □ *vi* hit back; **~de** *m* response

revigorar /xevigo'rar/ *vt* strengthen □ *vi*, **~-se** *vpr* regain one's strength

revi|rar /xevi'rar/ *vt* turn out <*bolsos, gavetas*>; turn over <*terra*>; turn inside out <*roupa*>; roll <*olhos*>; **~rar-se** *vpr* toss and turn; **~ravolta** /ɔ/ *f* (*na política etc*) about-face, about-turn; (*da situação*) turnabout, dramatic change

revi|são /xevi'zãw/ *f* (*de lições etc*) revision; (*de máquina, motor*) overhaul; (*de carro*) service; **~são de provas** proofreading; **~sar** *vt* revise <*provas, lições*>; service <*carro*>; **~sor** *m* (*de bilhetes*) ticket inspector; **~sor de provas** proofreader

revis|ta /xe'vista/ *f* (*para ler*) magazine; (*teatral*) revue; (*de tropas etc*) review; **passar ~ta a** review; **~tar** *vt* search

reviver /xevi'ver/ *vt* relive □ *vi* revive

revogar /xevo'gar/ *vt* revoke <*lei*>; cancel <*ordem*>

revol|ta /xe'vɔwta/ *f* (*rebelião*) revolt; (*indignação*) disgust; **~tante** *a* disgusting; **~tar** *vt* disgust; **~tar-se** *vpr* (*rebelar-se*) revolt; (*indignar-se*) be disgusted; **~to** /o/ *a* <*casa, gaveta*> upside down; <*cabelo*> dishevelled; <*mar*> rough; <*mundo, região*> troubled; <*anos*> turbulent

revolu|ção /xevolu'sãw/ *f* revolution; **~cionar** *vt* revolutionize; **~cionário** *a* & *m* revolutionary

revolver /xevow'ver/ *vt* turn over <*terra*>; roll <*olhos*>; go through <*gavetas, arquivos*>

revólver /xe'vɔwver/ *m* revolver

re|za /'xɛza/ *f* prayer; **~zar** *vi* pray □ *vt* say <*missa, oração*>; (*dizer*) state

riacho /xi'aʃu/ *m* stream

ribalta /xi'bawta/ *f* footlights

ribanceira /xibã'sera/ *f* embankment

ribombar /xibõ'bar/ *vi* rumble

rico /'xiku/ *a* rich □ *m* rich man; **os ~s** the rich

ricochete /xiko'ʃetʃi/ *m* ricochet; **~ar** *vi* ricochet

ricota /xi'kɔta/ *f* curd cheese, ricotta

ridicularizar /xidʒikulari'zar/ *vt* ridicule

ridículo /xi'dʒikulu/ *a* ridiculous

ri|fa /'xifa/ *f* raffle; **~far** *vt* raffle

rifão /xi'fãw/ *m* saying

rifle /'xifli/ *m* rifle

rigidez /xiʒi'des/ *f* rigidity

rígido /'xiʒidu/ *a* rigid

rigor /xi'gor/ *m* severity; (*meticulosidade*) rigour; **vestido a ~** evening dress; **de ~** essential

rigoroso /xigo'rozu/ *a* strict; <*inverno, pena*> severe, harsh; <*lógica, estudo*> rigorous

rijo /'xiʒu/ *a* stiff; <*músculos*> firm

rim /xĩ/ *m* kidney; *pl* (*parte das costas*) small of the back

ri|ma /'xima/ *f* rhyme; **~mar** *vt/i* rhyme

rí|mel /'ximew/ (*pl* **~meis**) *m* mascara

ringue /'xĩgi/ *m* ring

rinoceronte /xinose'rõtʃi/ *m* rhinoceros
rinque /'xĩki/ *m* rink
rio /'xio/ *m* river
riqueza /xi'keza/ *f* wealth; (*qualidade*) richness; *pl* riches
rir /xir/ *vi* laugh (**de** at)
risada /xi'zada/ *f* laugh, laughter; **dar ~** laugh
ris|ca /'xiska/ *f* stroke; (*listra*) stripe; (*do cabelo*) parting; **à ~ca** to the letter; **~car** *vt* (*apagar*) cross out <*erro*>; strike <*fósforo*>; scratch <*mesa, carro etc*>; write off <*amigo etc*>; **~co**[1] *m* (*na parede etc*) scratch; (*no papel*) line; (*esboço*) sketch
risco[2] /'xisku/ *m* risk
riso /'xizu/ *m* laugh; **~nho** /o/ *a* smiling
ríspido /'xispidu/ *a* harsh
rítmico /'xitʃmiku/ *a* rhythmic
ritmo /'xitʃimu/ *m* rhythm
rito /'xitu/ *m* rite
ritu|al /xitu'aw/ (*pl* **~ais**) *a & m* ritual
ri|val /xi'vaw/ (*pl* **~vais**) *a & m/f* rival; **~validade** *f* rivalry; **~valizar** *vt* rival □ *vi* vie (**com** with)
rixa /'xiʃa/ *f* fight
robô /xo'bo/ *m* robot
robusto /xo'bustu/ *a* robust
roça /'xɔsa/ *f* (*campo*) country
rocambole /xokã'bɔli/ *m* roll
roçar /xo'sar/ *vt* graze; **~ em** brush against
ro|cha /'xɔʃa/ *f* rock; **~chedo** /e/ *m* cliff
roda /'xɔda/ *f* (*de carro etc*) wheel; (*de amigos etc*) circle; **~ dentada** cog; **~da** *f* round; **~do** *a* **saia ~da** full skirt; **~-gigante** (*pl* **~s-gigantes**) *f* big wheel, (*Amer*) ferris wheel; **~moinho** *m* (*de vento*) whirlwind; (*na água*) whirlpool; (*fig*) whirl, swirl; **~pé** *m* skirting board, (*Amer*) baseboard
rodar /xo'dar/ *vt* (*fazer girar*) spin; (*viajar por*) go round; do <*quilometragem*>; shoot <*filme*>; run <*programa*> □ *vi* (*girar*) spin; (*de carro*) drive round
rodear /xodʒi'ar/ *vt* (*circundar*) surround; (*andar ao redor de*) go round
rodeio /xo'deju/ *m* (*ao falar*) circumlocution; (*de gado*) round-up; **falar sem ~s** talk straight
rodela /xo'dɛla/ *f* (*de limão etc*) slice; (*peça de metal*) washer
rodízio /xo'dʒiziu/ *m* rota
rodo /'xodu/ *m* rake
rodopiar /xodopi'ar/ *vi* spin round
rodovi|a /xodo'via/ *f* highway; **~ária** *f* bus station; **~ário** *a* road; **polícia ~ária** traffic police
ro|edor /xoe'dor/ *m* rodent; **~er** *vt* gnaw; bite <*unhas*>; (*fig*) eat away
rogar /xo'gar/ *vi* request
rojão /xo'ʒãw/ *m* rocket
rol /xɔw/ (*pl* **róis**) *m* roll
rolar /xo'lar/ *vt* roll □ *vi* roll; (*fam*) (*acontecer*) happen
roldana /xow'dana/ *f* pulley
roleta /xo'leta/ *f* (*jogo*) roulette; (*borboleta*) turnstile
rolha /'xoʎa/ *f* cork
roliço /xo'lisu/ *a* <*objeto*> cylindrical; <*pessoa*> plump
rolo /'xolu/ *m* (*de filme, tecido etc*) roll; (*máquina, bobe*) roller; **~ compressor** steamroller; **~ de massa** rolling pin
Roma /'xoma/ *f* Rome
romã /xo'mã/ *f* pomegranate
roman|ce /xo'mãsi/ *m* (*livro*) novel; (*caso*) romance; **~cista** *m/f* novelist
romano /xo'manu/ *a & m* Roman
romântico /xo'mãtʃiku/ *a* romantic
romantismo /xomã'tʃizmu/ *m* (*amor*) romance; (*idealismo*) romanticism
romaria /xoma'ria/ *f* pilgrimage
rombo /'xõbu/ *m* hole
Romênia /xo'menia/ *f* Romania
romeno /xo'menu/ *a & m* Romanian
rom|per /xõ'per/ *vt* break; break off <*relações*> □ *vi* <*dia*> break; <*sol*> rise; **~per com** break up with; **~pimento** *m* break; (*de relações*) breaking off
ron|car /xõ'kar/ *vi* (*ao dormir*) snore; <*estômago*> rumble; **~co** *m* snoring; (*um*) snore; (*de motor*) roar
ron|da /'xõda/ *f* round, patrol; **~dar** *vt* (*patrulhar*) patrol; (*espreitar*) prowl around □ *vi* <*vigia etc*> patrol; <*animal, ladrão*> prowl around
ronronar /xõxo'nar/ *vi* purr
roque[1] /'xɔki/ *m* (*em xadrez*) rook
ro|que[2] /'xɔki/ *m* (*música*) rock; **~queiro** *m* rock musician
rosa /'xɔza/ *f* rose □ *a invar* pink; **~do** *a* rosy; <*vinho*> rosé
rosário /xo'zariu/ *m* rosary
rosbife /xoz'bifi/ *m* roast beef
rosca /'xoska/ *f* (*de parafuso*) thread; (*biscoito*) rusk; **farinha de ~** breadcrumbs
roseira /xo'zera/ *f* rosebush
roseta /xo'zeta/ *f* rosette
rosnar /xoz'nar/ *vi* <*cachorro*> growl; <*pessoa*> snarl
rosto /'xostu/ *m* face
rota /'xɔta/ *f* route
rota|ção /xota'sãw/ *f* rotation; **~tividade** *f* turnround; **~tivo** *a* rotating
rotei|rista /xote'rista/ *m/f* scriptwriter; **~ro** *m* (*de viagem*) itinerary;

(*de filme, peça*) script; (*de discussão etc*) outline
roti|na /xo'tʃina/ *f* routine; **~neiro** *a* routine
rótula /'xɔtula/ *f* kneecap
rotular /xotu'lar/ *vt* label (de as)
rótulo /'xɔtulu/ *m* label
rou|bar /xo'bar/ *vt* steal <*dinheiro, carro etc*>; rob <*pessoa, loja etc*> □ *vi* steal; (*em jogo*) cheat; **~bo** *m* theft, robbery
rouco /'xoku/ *a* hoarse; <*voz*> gravelly
rou|pa /'xopa/ *f* clothes; (*uma*) outfit; **~pa de baixo** underwear; **~pa de cama** bedclothes; **~pão** *m* dressing gown
rouquidão /xoki'dãw/ *f* hoarseness
rouxi|nol /xoʃi'nɔw/ (*pl* **~nóis**) *m* nightingale
roxo /'xoʃu/ *a* purple
rua /'xua/ *f* street
rubéola /xu'bɛola/ *f* German measles
rubi /xu'bi/ *m* ruby
rude /'xudʒi/ *a* rude
rudimentos /xudʒi'mẽtus/ *m pl* rudiments, basics
ruela /xu'ɛla/ *f* backstreet
rufar /xu'far/ *vi* <*tambor*> roll □ *m* roll
ruga /'xuga/ *f* (*na pele*) wrinkle; (*na roupa*) crease
ru|gido /xu'ʒidu/ *m* roar; **~gir** *vi* roar
ruibarbo /xui'barbu/ *m* rhubarb
ruído /xu'idu/ *m* noise
ruidoso /xui'dozu/ *a* noisy
ruim /xu'ĩ/ *a* bad
ruína /xu'ina/ *f* ruin
ruivo /'xuivu/ *a* <*cabelo*> red; <*pessoa*> red-haired □ *m* redhead
rulê /xu'le/ *a* **gola ~** roll-neck
rum /xũ/ *m* rum
ru|mar /xu'mar/ *vi* head (para for); **~mo** *m* course; **~mo a** heading for; **sem ~mo** <*vida*> aimless; <*andar*> aimlessly
rumor /xu'mor/ *m* (*da rua, de vozes*) hum; (*do trânsito*) rumble; (*boato*) rumour
ru|ral /xu'raw/ (*pl* **~rais**) *a* rural
rusga /'xuzga/ *f* quarrel, disagreement
rush /xaʃ/ *m* rush hour
Rússia /'xusia/ *f* Russia
russo /'xusu/ *a* & *m* Russian
rústico /'xustʃiku/ *a* rustic

S

Saará /saa'ra/ *m* Sahara
sábado /'sabadu/ *m* Saturday
sabão /sa'bãw/ *m* soap; **~ em pó** soap powder
sabatina /saba'tʃina/ *f* test
sabedoria /sabedo'ria/ *f* wisdom
saber /sa'ber/ *vt/i* know (de about); (*descobrir*) find out (de about) □ *m* knowledge; **eu sei cantar** I know how to sing, I can sing; **sei lá** I've no idea; **que eu saiba** as far as I know
sabiá /sabi'a/ *m* thrush
sabi|chão /sabi'ʃãw/ *a* & *m* (*f* **~chona**) know-it-all
sábio /'sabiu/ *a* wise □ *m* wise man
sabone|te /sabo'netʃi/ *m* bar of soap; **~teira** *f* soapdish
sabor /sa'bor/ *m* flavour; **ao ~ de** at the mercy of
sabo|rear /sabori'ar/ *vt* savour; **~roso** *a* tasty
sabo|tador /sabota'dor/ *m* saboteur; **~tagem** *f* sabotage; **~tar** *vt* sabotage
saca /'saka/ *f* sack
sacada /sa'kada/ *f* balcony
sa|cal /sa'kaw/ (*pl* **~cais**) *a* (*fam*) boring
saca|na /sa'kana/ (*fam*) *a* (*desonesto*) devious; (*lascivo*) dirty-minded, naughty □ *m/f* rogue; **~nagem** (*fam*) *f* (*esperteza*) trickery; (*sexo*) sex; (*uma*) dirty trick; **~near** (*fam*) *vt* (*enganar*) do the dirty on; (*amolar*) take the mickey out of
sacar /sa'kar/ *vt/i* withdraw <*dinheiro*>; draw <*arma*>; (*em tênis, vôlei etc*) serve; (*fam*) (*entender*) understand
saçaricar /sasari'kar/ *vi* play around
sacarina /saka'rina/ *f* saccharine
saca-rolhas /saka'xoʎas/ *m invar* corkscrew
sacer|dócio /saser'dɔsiu/ *m* priesthood; **~dote** /ɔ/ *m* priest; **~dotisa** *f* priestess
sachê /sa'ʃe/ *m* sachet
saciar /sasi'ar/ *vt* satisfy
saco /'saku/ *m* bag; **que ~!** (*fam*) what a pain!; **estar de ~ cheio (de)** (*fam*) be fed up (with), be sick (of); **encher o ~ de alg** (*fam*) get on s.o.'s nerves; **puxar o ~ de alg** (*fam*) suck up to s.o.; **~ de dormir** sleeping bag; **~la** /ɔ/ *f* bag; **~lão** *m* wholesale fruit and vegetable market; **~lejar** *vt* shake
sacramento /sakra'mẽtu/ *m* sacrament
sacri|ficar /sakrifi'kar/ *vt* sacrifice; have put down <*cachorro etc*>; **~fício** *m* sacrifice; **~légio** *m* sacrilege
sacrílego /sa'krilegu/ *a* sacrilegious
sacro /'sakru/ *a* <*música*> religious
sacrossanto /sakro'sãtu/ *a* sacrosanct
sacu|dida /saku'dʒida/ *f* shake; **~dir** *vt* shake

sádico /'sadʒiku/ *a* sadistic □ *m* sadist

sadio /sa'dʒiu/ *a* healthy

sadismo /sa'dʒizmu/ *m* sadism

safa|deza /safa'deza/ *f* (*desonestidade*) deviousness; (*libertinagem*) indecency; (*uma*) dirty trick; **~do** *a* (*desonesto*) devious; (*lascivo*) dirty-minded; (*esperto*) quick; <*criança*> naughty

safena /sa'fɛna/ *f* **ponte de ~** heart bypass; **~do** *m* bypass patient

safira /sa'fira/ *f* sapphire

safra /'safra/ *f* crop

sagitariano /saʒitari'anu/ *a* & *m* Sagittarian

Sagitário /saʒi'tariu/ *m* Sagittarius

sagrado /sa'gradu/ *a* sacred

saguão /sa'gwãw/ *m* (*de teatro, hotel*) foyer, (*Amer*) lobby; (*de estação, aeroporto*) concourse

saia /'saja/ *f* skirt; **~-calça** (*pl* **~s-calças**) *f* culottes

saída /sa'ida/ *f* (*partida*) departure; (*porta, fig*) way out; **de ~** at the outset; **estar de ~** be on one's way out

sair /sa'ir/ *vi* (*de dentro*) go/come out; (*partir*) leave; (*desprender-se*) come off; <*mancha*> come out; (*resultar*) turn out; **~-se** *vpr* fare; **~-se com** (*dizer*) come out with; **~ mais barato** work out cheaper

sal /saw/ (*pl* **sais**) *m* salt; **~ de frutas** Epsom salts

sala /'sala/ *f* (*numa casa*) lounge; (*num lugar público*) hall; (*classe*) class; **fazer ~ a** entertain; **~ (de aula)** classroom; **~ de embarque** departure lounge; **~ de espera** waiting room; **~ de jantar** dining room; **~ de operação** operating theatre

sala|da /sa'lada/ *f* salad; (*fig*) jumble, mishmash; **~da de frutas** fruit salad; **~deira** *f* salad bowl

sala-e-quarto /sali'kwartu/ *m* two-room flat

sala|me /sa'lami/ *m* salami; **~minho** *m* pepperoni

salão /sa'lãw/ *m* hall; (*de cabeleireiro*) salon; (*de carros*) show; **~ de beleza** beauty salon

salari|al /salari'aw/ (*pl* **~ais**) *a* wage

salário /sa'lariu/ *m* salary

sal|dar /saw'dar/ *vt* settle; **~do** *m* balance

saleiro /sa'leru/ *m* salt cellar

sal|gadinhos /sawga'dʒiɲus/ *m pl* snacks; **~gado** *a* salty; <*preço*> exorbitant; **~gar** *vt* salt

salgueiro /saw'geru/ *m* willow; **~ chorão** weeping willow

saliência /sali'ẽsia/ *f* projection

salien|tar /saliẽ'tar/ *vt* (*deixar claro*) point out; (*acentuar*) highlight; **~tar-se** *vpr* distinguish o.s.; **~te** *a* prominent

saliva /sa'liva/ *f* saliva

salmão /saw'mãw/ *m* salmon

salmo /'sawmu/ *m* psalm

salmonela /sawmo'nɛla/ *f* salmonella

salmoura /saw'mora/ *f* brine

salpicar /sawpi'kar/ *vt* sprinkle; (*sem querer*) spatter

salsa /'sawsa/ *f* parsley

salsicha /saw'siʃa/ *f* sausage

saltar /saw'tar/ *vt* (*pular*) jump; (*omitir*) skip □ *vi* jump; **~ à vista** be obvious; **~ do ônibus** get off the bus

saltear /sawtʃi'ar/ *vt* sauté <*batatas etc*>

saltitar /sawtʃi'tar/ *vi* hop

salto /'sawtu/ *m* (*pulo*) jump; (*de sapato*) heel; **~ com vara** pole vault; **~ em altura** high jump; **~ em distância** long jump; **~-mortal** (*pl* **~s-mortais**) *m* somersault

salu|bre /sa'lubri/ *a* healthy; **~tar** *a* salutary

salva[1] /'sawva/ *f* (*de canhões*) salvo; (*bandeja*) salver; **~ de palmas** round of applause

salva[2] /'sawva/ *f* (*erva*) sage

salva|ção /sawva'sãw/ *f* salvation; **~dor** *m* saviour

salvaguar|da /sawva'gwarda/ *f* safeguard; **~dar** *vt* safeguard

sal|vamento /sawva'mẽtu/ *m* rescue; (*de navio*) salvage; **~var** *vt* save; **~var-se** *vpr* escape; **~va-vidas** *m invar* (*bóia*) lifebelt □ *m/f* (*pessoa*) lifeguard □ *a* **barco ~va-vidas** lifeboat; **~vo** *a* safe □ *prep* save; **a ~vo** safe

samambaia /samã'baja/ *f* fern

sam|ba /'sãba/ *m* samba; **~ba-canção** (*pl* **~bas-canção**) *m* slow samba □ *a invar* **cueca ~ba-canção** boxer shorts; **~ba-enredo** (*pl* **~bas-enredo**) *m* samba story; **~bar** *vi* samba; **~bista** *m/f* (*dançarino*) samba dancer; (*compositor*) composer of sambas; **~bódromo** *m* Carnival parade ground

samovar /samo'var/ *m* tea urn

sanar /sa'nar/ *vt* cure

san|ção /sã'sãw/ *f* sanction; **~cionar** *vt* sanction

sandália /sã'dalia/ *f* sandal

sandes /'sãdiʃ/ *f invar* (*Port*) sandwich

sanduíche /sãdu'iʃi/ *m* sandwich

sane|amento /sania'mẽtu/ *m* (*esgotos*) sanitation; (*de finanças*) rehabilitation; **~ar** *vt* set straight <*finanças*>

sanfona /sã'fona/ *f* (*instrumento*) accordion; (*tricô*) ribbing; **~do** *a* <*porta*> folding; <*pulôver*> ribbed

san|grar /sã'grar/ *vt/i* bleed; **~grento** *a* bloody; <*carne*> rare;

~gria *f* bloodshed; (*de dinheiro*) extortion
sangue /'sãgi/ *m* blood; ~ **pisado** bruise; ~**-frio** *m* cool, coolness
sanguessuga /sãgi'suga/ *f* leech
sanguinário /sãgi'nariu/ *a* bloodthirsty
sanguíneo /sã'giniu/ *a* blood
sanidade /sani'dadʒi/ *f* sanity
sanitário /sani'tariu/ *a* sanitary; ~**s** *mpl* toilets
san|tidade /sãtʃi'dadʒi/ *f* sanctity; ~**tificar** *vt* sanctify; ~**to** *a* holy □ *m* saint; **todo** ~**to dia** every single day; ~**tuário** *m* sanctuary
São /sãw/ *a* Saint
são /sãw/ (*pl* ~**s**) *a* (*f* **sã**) healthy; (*mentalmente*) sane; <*conselho*> sound
sapata /sa'pata/ *f* shoe; ~**ria** *f* shoe shop
sapate|ado /sapatʃi'adu/ *m* tap dancing; ~**ador** *m* tap dancer; ~**ar** *vi* tap one's feet; (*dançar*) tap-dance
sapa|teiro /sapa'teru/ *m* shoemaker; ~**tilha** *f* pump; ~**tilha de balé** ballet shoe; ~**to** *m* shoe
sapeca /sa'pɛka/ *a* saucy
sa|pinho /sa'piɲu/ *m* thrush; ~**po** *m* toad
saque[1] /'saki/ *m* (*do banco*) withdrawal; (*em tênis, vôlei etc*) serve
saque[2] /'saki/ *m* (*de loja etc*) looting; ~**ar** *vt* loot
saraiva /sa'rajva/ *f* hail; ~**da** *f* hailstorm; **uma** ~**da de** a hail of
sarampo /sa'rãpu/ *m* measles
sarar /sa'rar/ *vt* cure □ *vi* get better; <*ferida*> heal
sar|casmo /sar'kazmu/ *m* sarcasm; ~**cástico** *a* sarcastic
sarda /'sarda/ *f* freckle
Sardenha /sar'deɲa/ *f* Sardinia
sardento /sar'dẽtu/ *a* freckled
sardinha /sar'dʒiɲa/ *f* sardine
sardônico /sar'doniku/ *a* sardonic
sargento /sar'ʒẽtu/ *m* sergeant
sarjeta /sar'ʒeta/ *f* gutter
Satanás /sata'nas/ *m* Satan
satânico /sa'taniku/ *a* satanic
satélite /sa'tɛlitʃi/ *a* & *m* satellite
sátira /'satʃira/ *f* satire
satírico /sa'tʃiriku/ *a* satirical
satirizar /satʃiri'zar/ *vt* satirize
satisfa|ção /satʃisfa'sãw/ *f* satisfaction; **dar** ~**ções a** answer to; ~**tório** *a* satisfactory; ~**zer** *vt* ~**zer (a)** satisfy □ *vi* be satisfactory; ~**zer-se** *vpr* be satisfied
satisfeito /satʃis'fejtu/ *a* satisfied; (*contente*) content; (*de comida*) full
saturar /satu'rar/ *vt* saturate
Saturno /sa'turnu/ *m* Saturn
saudação /sawda'sãw/ *f* greeting
saudade /saw'dadʒi/ *f* longing; (*lembrança*) nostalgia; **estar com** ~**s de** miss; **matar** ~**s** catch up
saudar /saw'dar/ *vt* greet
saudá|vel /saw'davew/ (*pl* ~**veis**) *a* healthy
saúde /sa'udʒi/ *f* health □ *int* (*ao beber*) cheers; (*ao espirrar*) bless you
saudo|sismo /sawdo'zizmu/ *m* nostalgia; ~**so** /o/ *a* longing; **estar** ~**so de** miss; **o nosso** ~**so amigo** our much-missed friend
sauna /'sawna/ *f* sauna
saxofo|ne /sakso'foni/ *m* saxophone; ~**nista** *m/f* saxophonist
sazo|nado /sazo'nadu/ *a* seasoned; ~**nal** (*pl* ~**nais**) *a* seasonal
se[1] /si/ *conj* if; **não sei** ~ ... I don't know if/whether
se[2] /si/ *pron* (*ele mesmo*) himself; (*ela mesma*) herself; (*você mesmo*) yourself; (*eles/elas*) themselves; (*vocês*) yourselves; (*um ao outro*) each other; **dorme-**~ **tarde no Brasil** people go to bed late in Brazil; **aqui** ~ **fala inglês** English is spoken here
sebo /'sebu/ *m* (*sujeira*) grease; (*livraria*) secondhand bookshop; ~**so** /o/ *a* greasy; <*pessoa*> slimy
seca /'seka/ *f* drought; ~**dor** *m* ~**dor de cabelo** hairdryer; ~**dora** *f* tumble dryer
seção /se'sãw/ *f* section; (*de loja*) department
secar /se'kar/ *vt/i* dry
sec|ção /sek'sãw/ *f* *veja* **seção**; ~**cionar** *vt* split up
seco /'seku/ *a* dry; <*resposta, tom*> curt; <*pessoa, caráter*> cold; <*barulho, pancada*> dull; **estar** ~ **por** I'm dying for
secretaria /sekreta'ria/ *f* (*de empresa*) general office; (*ministério*) department
secretá|ria /sekre'taria/ *f* secretary; ~**ria eletrônica** ansaphone; ~**rio** *m* secretary
secreto /se'krɛtu/ *a* secret
secular /seku'lar/ *a* (*não religioso*) secular; (*antigo*) age-old
século /'sɛkulu/ *m* century; *pl* (*muito tempo*) ages
secundário /sekũ'dariu/ *a* secondary
secura /se'kura/ *f* dryness; **estar com uma** ~ **de** be longing for/to
seda /'seda/ *f* silk
sedativo /seda'tʃivu/ *a* & *m* sedative
sede[1] /'sɛdʒi/ *f* headquarters; (*local do governo*) seat
sede[2] /'sedʒi/ *f* thirst (**de** for); **estar com** ~ be thirsty
sedentário /sedẽ'tariu/ *a* sedentary
sedento /se'dẽtu/ *a* thirsty (**de** for)
sediar /sedʒi'ar/ *vt* host

sedimen|tar /sedʒimẽ'tar/ *vt* consolidate; **~to** *m* sediment
sedoso /se'dozu/ *a* silky
sedu|ção /sedu'sãw/ *f* seduction; **~tor** *a* seductive; **~zir** *vt* seduce
segmento /seg'mẽtu/ *m* segment
segredo /se'gredu/ *m* secret; (*de cofre etc*) combination
segregar /segre'gar/ *vt* segregate
segui|da /se'gida/ *f* em **~da** (*imediatamente*) straight away; (*depois*) next; **~do** *a* followed (de by); **cinco horas ~das** five hours running; **~dor** *m* follower; **~mento** *m* continuation; **dar ~mento a** go on with
se|guinte /se'gĩtʃi/ *a* following; <*dia, semana etc*> next; **~guir** *vt/i* follow; (*continuar*) continue; **~guir-se** *vpr* follow; **~guir em frente** (*ir embora*) go; (*indicação na rua*) go straight ahead
segun|da /se'gũda/ *f* (*dia*) Monday; (*marcha*) second; **de ~da** second-rate; **~da-feira** (*pl* **~das-feiras**) *f* Monday; **~do** *a* & *m* second □ *adv* secondly □ *prep* according to □ *conj* according to what; **~das intenções** ulterior motives; **de ~da mão** second-hand
segu|rança /segu'rãsa/ *f* security; (*estado de seguro*) safety; (*certeza*) assurance □ *m/f* security guard; **~rar** *vt* hold; **~rar-se** *vpr* (*controlar-se*) control o.s.; **~rar-se em** hold on to; **~ro** *a* secure; (*fora de perigo*) safe; (*com certeza*) sure □ *m* insurance; **estar no ~ro** <*bens*> be insured; **fazer ~ro de** insure; **~ro-desemprego** *m* unemployment benefit
seio /'seju/ *m* breast, bosom; **no ~ de** within
seis /sejs/ *a* & *m* six; **~centos** *a* & *m* six hundred
seita /'sejta/ *f* sect
seixo /'sejʃu/ *m* pebble
sela /'sɛla/ *f* saddle
selar[1] /se'lar/ *vt* saddle <*cavalo*>
selar[2] /se'lar/ *vt* seal; (*franquear*) stamp
sele|ção /sele'sãw/ *f* selection; (*time*) team; **~cionar** *vt* select; **~to** /ɛ/ *a* select
selim /se'lĩ/ *m* saddle
selo /'selu/ *m* seal; (*postal*) stamp; (*de discos*) label
selva /'sɛwva/ *f* jungle; **~gem** *a* wild; **~geria** *f* savagery
sem /sẽj/ *prep* without; **~ eu saber** without me knowing; **ficar ~ dinheiro** run out of money
semáforo /se'maforu/ *m* (*na rua*) traffic lights; (*de ferrovia*) signal
sema|na /se'mana/ *f* week; **~nal** (*pl* **~nais**) *a* weekly; **~nalmente** *adv* weekly; **~nário** *m* weekly
semear /semi'ar/ *vt* sow
semelhan|ça /seme'ʎãsa/ *f* similarity; **~te** *a* similar; (*tal*) such
sêmen /'semẽ/ *m* semen
semente /se'mẽtʃi/ *f* seed; (*em fruta*) pip
semestre /se'mɛstri/ *m* six months; (*da faculdade etc*) term, (*Amer*) semester
semi|círculo /semi'sirkulu/ *m* semicircle; **~final** (*pl* **~finais**) *f* semifinal
seminário /semi'nariu/ *m* (*aula*) seminar; (*colégio religioso*) seminary
sem-número /sẽ'numeru/ *m* **um ~ de** innumerable
sempre /'sẽpri/ *adv* always; **como ~** as usual; **para ~** for ever; **~ que** whenever
sem|-terra /sẽ'tɛxa/ *m/f invar* landless labourer; **~-teto** *a* homeless □ *m/f* homeless person; **~-vergonha** *a invar* brazen □ *m/f invar* scoundrel
sena|do /se'nadu/ *m* senate; **~dor** *m* senator
senão /si'nãw/ *conj* otherwise; (*mas antes*) but rather □ *m* snag
senda /'sẽda/ *f* path
senha /'seɲa/ *f* (*palavra*) password; (*número*) code; (*sinal*) signal
senhor /se'ɲor/ *m* gentleman; (*homem idoso*) older man; (*tratamento*) sir □ *a* (*f* **~a**) mighty; **Senhor** (*com nome*) Mr; (*Deus*) Lord; **o ~** (*você*) you
senho|ra /se'ɲɔra/ *f* lady; (*mulher idosa*) older woman; (*tratamento*) madam; **Senhora** (*com nome*) Mrs; **a ~ra** (*você*) you; **nossa ~ra!** (*fam*) gosh; **~ria** *f* **Vossa Senhoria** you; **~rita** *f* young lady; (*tratamento*) miss; **Senhorita** (*com nome*) Miss
se|nil (*pl* **~nis**) *a* senile; **~nilidade** *f* senility
sensação /sẽsa'sãw/ *f* sensation
sensacio|nal /sẽsasio'naw/ (*pl* **~nais**) *a* sensational; **~nalismo** *m* sensationalism; **~nalista** *a* sensationalist
sen|sato /sẽ'satu/ *a* sensible; **~sibilidade** *f* sensitivity; **~sível** (*pl* **~síveis**) *a* sensitive; (*que se pode sentir*) noticeable; **~so** *m* sense; **~sual** (*pl* **~suais**) *a* sensual
sen|tado /sẽ'tadu/ *a* sitting; **~tar** *vt/i* sit; **~tar-se** *vpr* sit down
sentença /sẽ'tẽsa/ *f* sentence
sentido /sẽ'tʃidu/ *m* sense; (*direção*) direction □ *a* hurt; **fazer** *ou* **ter ~** make sense
sentimen|tal /sẽtʃimẽ'taw/ (*pl* **~tais**) *a* sentimental; **vida ~tal** love life; **~to** *m* feeling

sentinela /sẽtʃi'nɛla/ *f* sentry

sentir /sẽ'tʃir/ *vt* feel; (*notar*) sense; smell <*cheiro*>; taste <*gosto*>; tell <*diferença*>; (*ficar magoado por*) be hurt by □ *vi* feel; **~-se** *vpr* feel; **sinto muito** I'm very sorry

sepa|ração /separa'sãw/ *f* separation; **~rado** *a* separate; <*casal*> separated; **~rar** *vt* separate; **~rar-se** *vpr* separate

séptico /'sɛptʃiku/ *a* septic

sepul|tar /sepuw'tar/ *vt* bury; **~tura** *f* grave

seqüência /se'kwẽsia/ *f* sequence

sequer /se'kɛr/ *adv* **nem ~** not even

seqües|trador /sekwestra'dor/ *m* kidnapper; (*de avião*) hijacker; **~trar** *vt* kidnap <*pessoa*>; hijack <*avião*>; sequestrate <*bens*>; **~tro** /ɛ/ *m* (*de pessoa*) kidnapping; (*de avião*) hijack; (*de bens*) sequestration

ser /ser/ *vi* be □ *m* being; **é** (*como resposta*) yes; **você gosta, não é?** you like it, don't you?; **ele foi morto** he was killed; **será que ele volta?** I wonder if he's coming back; **ou seja** in other words; **a não ~** except; **a não ~ que** unless; **não sou de fofocar** I'm not one to gossip

sereia /se'reja/ *f* mermaid

serenata /sere'nata/ *f* serenade

sereno /se'renu/ *a* serene; <*tempo*> fine

série /'sɛri/ *f* series; (*na escola*) grade; **fora de ~** (*fam*) incredible

seriedade /serie'dadʒi/ *f* seriousness

serin|ga /se'rĩga/ *f* syringe; **~gueiro** *m* rubber tapper

sério /'sɛriu/ *a* serious; (*responsável*) responsible; **~?** really?; **falar ~** be serious; **levar a ~** take seriously

sermão /ser'mãw/ *m* sermon

serpen|te /ser'pẽtʃi/ *f* serpent; **~tear** *vi* wind; **~tina** *f* streamer

serra[1] /'sɛxa/ *f* (*montanhas*) mountain range

serra[2] /'sɛxa/ *f* (*de serrar*) saw; **~gem** *f* sawdust; **~lheiro** *m* locksmith

serrano /se'xanu/ *a* mountain

serrar /se'xar/ *vt* saw

ser|tanejo /serta'neʒu/ *a* from the backwoods □ *m* backwoodsman; **~tão** *m* backwoods

servente /ser'vẽtʃi/ *m/f* labourer

Sérvia /'sɛrvia/ *f* Serbia

servi|çal /servi'saw/ (*pl* **~çais**) *a* helpful □ *m/f* servant; **~ço** *m* service; (*trabalho*) work; (*tarefa*) job; **estar de ~ço** be on duty; **~dor** *m* servant

ser|vil /ser'viw/ (*pl* **~vis**) *a* servile

sérvio /'sɛrviu/ *a & m* Serbian

servir /ser'vir/ *vt* serve □ *vi* serve; (*ser adequado*) do; (*ser útil*) be of use; <*roupa, sapato etc*> fit; **~-se** *vpr* (*ao comer etc*) help o.s. (**de** to); **~-se de** make use of; **~ como** *ou* **de** serve as; **para que serve isso?** what is this (used) for?

sessão /se'sãw/ *f* session; (*no cinema*) showing, performance

sessenta /se'sẽta/ *a & m* sixty

seta /'sɛta/ *f* arrow; (*de carro*) indicator

sete /'sɛtʃi/ *a & m* seven; **~centos** *a & m* seven hundred

setembro /se'tẽbru/ *m* September

setenta /se'tẽta/ *a & m* seventy

sétimo /'sɛtʃimu/ *a* seventh

setuagésimo /setua'ʒɛzimu/ *a* seventieth

setor /se'tor/ *m* sector

seu /sew/ *a* (*f* **sua**) (*dele*) his; (*dela*) her; (*de coisa*) its; (*deles*) their; (*de você, de vocês*) your □ *pron* (*dele*) his; (*dela*) hers; (*deles*) theirs; (*de você, de vocês*) yours; **~ idiota!** you idiot!; **seu João** Mr John

seve|ridade /severi'dadʒi/ *f* severity; **~ro** /ɛ/ *a* severe

sexagésimo /seksa'ʒɛzimu/ *a* sixtieth

sexo /'sɛksu/ *m* sex; **fazer ~** have sex

sex|ta /'sesta/ *f* Friday; **~ta-feira** (*pl* **~tas-feiras**) *f* Friday; **Sexta-feira Santa** Good Friday; **~to** /e/ *a & m* sixth

sexu|al /seksu'aw/ (*pl* **~ais**) *a* sexual; **vida ~al** sex life

sexy /'sɛksi/ *a invar* sexy

shopping /'ʃɔpĩ/ (*pl* **~s**) *m* shopping centre, (*Amer*) mall

short /'ʃɔrtʃi/ *m* (*pl* **~s**) shorts; **um ~** a pair of shorts

show /'ʃou/ (*pl* **~s**) *m* show; (*de música*) concert

si /si/ *pron* (*ele*) himself; (*ela*) herself; (*coisa*) itself; (*você*) yourself; (*eles*) themselves; (*vocês*) yourselves; (*qualquer pessoa*) oneself; **em ~** in itself; **fora de ~** beside o.s.; **cheio de ~** full of o.s.; **voltar a ~** come round

sibilar /sibi'lar/ *vi* hiss

SIDA /'sida/ *f* (*Port*) AIDS

side|ral /side'raw/ (*pl* **~rais**) *a* **espaço ~ral** outer space.

siderurgia /siderur'ʒia/ *f* iron and steel industry

siderúrgi|ca /side'rurʒika/ *f* steelworks; **~co** *a* iron and steel □ *m* steelworker

sifão /si'fãw/ *m* syphon

sífilis /'sifilis/ *f* syphilis

sigilo /si'ʒilu/ *m* secrecy; **~so** /o/ *a* secret

sigla /'sigla/ *f* acronym

signatário /signa'tariu/ *m* signatory

signifi|cação /signifika'sãw/ *f* significance; **~cado** *m* meaning; **~car** *vt* mean; **~cativo** *a* significant

signo /'signu/ *m* sign
sílaba /'silaba/ *f* syllable
silenciar /silẽsi'ar/ *vt* silence
silêncio /si'lẽsiu/ *m* silence
silencioso /silẽsi'ozu/ *a* silent □ *m* silencer, (*Amer*) muffler
silhueta /siʎu'eta/ *f* silhouette
silício /si'lisiu/ *m* silicon
silicone /sili'kɔni/ *m* silicone
silo /'silu/ *m* silo
silvar /siw'var/ *vi* hiss
sil|vestre /siw'vɛstri/ *a* wild; **~vicultura** *f* forestry
sim /sĩ/ *adv* yes; **acho que ~** I think so
simbólico /sĩ'bɔliku/ *a* symbolic
simbo|lismo /sĩbo'lizmu/ *m* symbolism; **~lizar** *vt* symbolize
símbolo /'sĩbolu/ *m* symbol
si|metria /sime'tria/ *f* symmetry; **~métrico** *a* symmetrical
similar /simi'lar/ *a* similar
sim|patia /sĩpa'tʃia/ *f* (*qualidade*) pleasantness; (*afeto*) fondness (**por** for); (*compreensão, apoio*) sympathy; *pl* sympathies; **ter ~patia por** be fond of; **~pático** *a* nice
simpati|zante /sĩpatʃi'zãtʃi/ *a* sympathetic □ *m/f* sympathizer; **~zar** *vi* **~zar com** take a liking to <*pessoa*>; sympathize with <*idéias, partido etc*>
simples /'sĩplis/ *a invar* simple; (*único*) single □ *f* (*no tênis etc*) singles; **~mente** *adv* simply
simpli|cidade /sĩplisi'dadʒi/ *f* simplicity; **~ficar** *vt* simplify
simplório /sĩ'plɔriu/ *a* simple
simpósio /sĩ'pɔziu/ *m* symposium
simu|lação /simula'sãw/ *f* simulation; **~lar** *vt* simulate
simultâneo /simuw'taniu/ *a* simultaneous
sina /'sina/ *f* fate
sinagoga /sina'gɔga/ *f* synagogue
si|nal /si'naw/ (*pl* **~nais**) *m* sign; (*aviso, de rádio etc*) signal; (*de trânsito*) traffic light; (*no telefone*) tone; (*dinheiro*) deposit; (*na pele*) mole; **por ~nal** as a matter of fact; **~nal de pontuação** punctuation mark; **~naleira** *f* traffic lights; **~nalização** *f* (*na rua*) road signs; **~nalizar** *vt* signal; signpost <*rua, cidade*>
since|ridade /sĩseri'dadʒi/ *f* sincerity; **~ro** /ɛ/ *a* sincere
sincro|nia /sĩkro'nia/ *f* synchronization; **~nizar** *vt* synchronize
sindi|cal /sĩdʒi'kaw/ (*pl* **~cais**) *a* trade union; **~calismo** *m* trade unionism; **~calista** *m/f* trade unionist; **~calizar** *vt* unionize; **~cato** *m* trade union
síndico /'sĩdʒiku/ *m* house manager
síndrome /'sĩdromi/ *f* syndrome
sineta /si'neta/ *f* bell
sin|fonia /sĩfo'nia/ *f* symphony; **~fônica** *f* symphony orchestra
singe|leza /sĩʒe'leza/ *f* simplicity; **~lo** /ɛ/ *a* simple
singu|lar /sĩgu'lar/ *a* singular; (*estranho*) peculiar; **~larizar** *vt* single out
sinis|trado /sinis'tradu/ *a* damaged; **~tro** *a* sinister □ *m* accident
sino /'sinu/ *m* bell
sinônimo /si'nonimu/ *a* synonymous □ *m* synonym
sintaxe /sĩ'taksi/ *f* syntax
síntese /'sĩtezi/ *f* synthesis
sin|tético /sĩ'tɛtʃiku/ *a* (*artificial*) synthetic; (*resumido*) concise; **~tetizar** *vt* summarize
sinto|ma /sĩ'toma/ *m* symptom; **~mático** *a* symptomatic
sintoni|zador /sĩtoniza'dor/ *m* tuner; **~zar** *vt* tune <*rádio, TV*>; tune in to <*emissora*> □ *vi* be in tune (**com** with)
sinuca /si'nuka/ *f* snooker
sinuoso /sinu'ozu/ *a* winding
sinusite /sinu'zitʃi/ *f* sinusitis
sirene /si'rɛni/ *f* siren
siri /si'ri/ *m* crab
Síria /'siria/ *f* Syria
sírio /'siriu/ *a & m* Syrian
siso /'sizu/ *m* good sense
siste|ma /sis'tema/ *m* system; **~mático** *a* systematic
sisudo /si'zudu/ *a* serious
sítio /'sitʃiu/ *m* (*chácara*) farm; (*Port: local*) place; **estado de ~** state of siege
situ|ação /situa'sãw/ *f* situation; (*no governo*) party in power; **~ar** *vt* situate; **~ar-se** *vpr* be situated; <*pessoa*> position o.s.
smoking /iz'mokĩ/ (*pl* **~s**) *m* dinner jacket, (*Amer*) tuxedo
só /sɔ/ *a* alone; (*sentindo solidão*) lonely □ *adv* only; **um ~ voto** one single vote; **~ um carro** only one car; **a ~s** alone; **imagina ~** just imagine; **~ que** except (that)
soalho /so'aʎu/ *m* floor
soar /so'ar/ *vt/i* sound
sob /'sobi/ *prep* under
sobera|nia /sobera'nia/ *f* sovereignty; **~no** *a & m* sovereign
soberbo /so'berbu/ *a* <*pessoa*> haughty; (*magnífico*) splendid
sobra /'sɔbra/ *f* surplus; *pl* leftovers; **tempo de ~** (*muito*) plenty of time; **ficar de ~** be left over; **ter aco de ~** (*sobrando*) have sth left over
sobraçar /sobra'sar/ *vt* carry under one's arm
sobrado /so'bradu/ *m* (*casa*) house; (*andar*) upper floor

sobrancelha /sobrã'seʎa/ *f* eyebrow

so|brar /so'brar/ *vi* be left; **~bram-me dois** I have two left

sobre /'sobri/ *prep* (*em cima de*) on; (*por cima de, acima de*) over; (*acerca de*) about

sobreaviso /sobria'vizu/ *m* **estar de ~** be on one's guard

sobrecapa /sobri'kapa/ *f* dust jacket

sobrecarregar /sobrikaxe'gar/ *vt* overload

sobreloja /sobri'lɔʒa/ *f* mezzanine

sobremesa /sobri'meza/ *f* dessert

sobrenatu|ral /sobrinatu'raw/ (*pl* **~rais**) *a* supernatural

sobrenome /sobri'nomi/ *m* surname

sobrepor /sobri'por/ *vt* superimpose

sobrepujar /sobripu'ʒar/ *vt* (*em altura*) tower over; (*em valor, número etc*) surpass; overwhelm <*adversário*>; overcome <*problemas*>

sobrescritar /sobriskri'tar/ *vt* address

sobressair /sobrisa'ir/ *vi* stand out; **~-se** *vpr* stand out

sobressalente /sobrisa'lẽtʃi/ *a* spare

sobressal|tar /sobrisaw'tar/ *vt* startle; **~tar-se** *vpr* be startled; **~to** *m* (*movimento*) start; (*susto*) fright

sobretaxa /sobri'taʃa/ *f* surcharge

sobretudo /sobri'tudu/ *adv* above all □ *m* overcoat

sobrevir /sobri'vir/ *vi* happen suddenly; (*seguir*) ensue; **~ a** follow

sobrevi|vência /sobrivi'vẽsia/ *f* survival; **~vente** *a* surviving □ *m/f* survivor; **~ver** *vt/i* **~ver (a)** survive

sobrevoar /sobrivo'ar/ *vt* fly over

sobri|nha /so'briɲa/ *f* niece; **~nho** *m* nephew

sóbrio /'sɔbriu/ *a* sober

socar /so'kar/ *vt* (*esmurrar*) punch; (*amassar*) crush

soci|al /sosi'aw/ (*pl* **~ais**) *a* social; **camisa ~al** dress shirt; **~alismo** *m* socialism; **~alista** *a & m/f* socialist; **~alite** /-a'lajtʃi/ *m/f* socialite; **~ável** (*pl* **~áveis**) *a* sociable

sociedade /sosie'dadʒi/ *f* society; (*parceria*) partnership; **~ anônima** limited company

sócio /'sɔsiu/ *m* (*de empresa*) partner; (*de clube*) member

socio-econômico /sosioeko'nomiku/ *a* socio-economic

soci|ologia /sosiolo'ʒia/ *f* sociology; **~ológico** *a* sociological; **~ólogo** *m* sociologist

soco /'soku/ *m* punch; **dar um ~ em** punch

socor|rer /soko'xer/ *vt* help; **~ro** *m* aid □ *int* help; **primeiros ~ros** first aid

soda /'sɔda/ *f* (*água*) soda water; **~ cáustica** caustic soda

sódio /'sɔdʒiu/ *m* sodium

sofá /so'fa/ *m* sofa; **~-cama** (*pl* **~s-camas**) *m* sofa-bed

sofisticado /sofistʃi'kadu/ *a* sophisticated

so|fredor /sofre'dor/ *a* martyred; **~frer** *vt* suffer <*dor, derrota, danos etc*>; have <*acidente*>; undergo <*operação, mudança etc*> □ *vi* suffer; **~frer de** suffer from <*doença*>; have trouble with <*coração etc*>; **~frido** *a* long-suffering; **~frimento** *m* suffering; **~frível** (*pl* **~fríveis**) *a* passable

soft /'sɔftʃi/ (*pl* **~s**) *m* software package; **~ware** *m* software; (*um*) software package

so|gra /'sɔgra/ *f* mother-in-law; **~gro** /o/ *m* father-in-law; **~gros** /ɔ/ *m pl* in-laws

soja /'sɔʒa/ *f* soya, (*Amer*) soy

sol /sɔw/ (*pl* **sóis**) *m* sun; **faz ~** it's sunny

sola /'sɔla/ *f* sole; **~do** *a* <*bolo*> flat

solapar /sola'par/ *vt* undermine

solar[1] /so'lar/ *a* solar

solar[2] /so'lar/ *vt* sole <*sapato*> □ *vi* <*bolo*> go flat

solavanco /sola'vãku/ *m* jolt; **dar ~s** jolt

soldado /sow'dadu/ *m* soldier

sol|dadura /sowda'dura/ *f* weld; **~dar** *vt* weld

soldo /'sowdu/ *m* pay

soleira /so'lera/ *f* doorstep

sole|ne /so'leni/ *a* solemn; **~nidade** *f* (*cerimônia*) ceremony; (*qualidade*) solemnity

soletrar /sole'trar/ *vt* spell

solici|tação /solisita'sãw/ *f* request (**de** for); (*por escrito*) application (**de** for); **~tante** *m/f* applicant; **~tar** *vt* request; (*por escrito*) apply for

solícito /so'lisitu/ *a* helpful

solidão /soli'dãw/ *f* loneliness

soli|dariedade /solidarie'dadʒi/ *f* solidarity; **~dário** *a* supportive (**com** of)

soli|dez /soli'des/ *f* solidity; **~dificar** *vt* solidify; **~dificar-se** *vpr* solidify

sólido /'sɔlidu/ *a & m* solid

solista /so'lista/ *m/f* soloist

solitá|ria /soli'taria/ *f* (*verme*) tapeworm; (*cela*) solitary confinement; **~rio** *a* solitary

solo[1] /'sɔlu/ *m* (*terra*) soil; (*chão*) ground

solo[2] /'sɔlu/ *m* solo

soltar /sow'tar/ *vt* let go <*prisioneiros, animal etc*>; let loose <*cães*>; (*deixar de segurar*) let go of; loosen <*gravata, corda etc*>; let down

<*cabelo*>; let out <*grito, suspiro etc*>; let off <*foguetes*>; tell <*piada*>; take off <*freio*>; **~-se** *vpr* <*peça, parafuso*> come loose; <*pessoa*> let o.s. go

soltei|ra /sow'tera/ *f* single woman; **~rão** *m* bachelor; **~ro** *a* single □ *m* single man; **~rona** *f* spinster

solto /'sowtu/ *a* (*livre*) free; <*cães*> loose; <*cabelo*> down; <*arroz*> fluffy; (*frouxo*) loose; (*à vontade*) relaxed; (*abandonado*) abandoned; **correr ~** run wild

solução /solu'sãw/ *f* solution

soluçar /solu'sar/ *vi* (*ao chorar*) sob; (*engasgar*) hiccup

solucionar /solusio'nar/ *vt* solve

soluço /so'lusu/ *m* (*ao chorar*) sob; (*engasgo*) hiccup; **estar com ~s** have the hiccups

solú|vel /so'luvew/ (*pl* **~veis**) *a* soluble

solvente /sow'vẽtʃi/ *a & m* solvent

som /sõ/ *m* sound; (*aparelho*) stereo; **um ~** (*fam*) (*música*) a bit of music

so|ma /'soma/ *f* sum; **~mar** *vt* add up <*números etc*>; (*ter como soma*) add up to

sombra /'sõbra/ *f* shadow; (*área abrigada do sol*) shade; **à ~ de** in the shade of; **sem ~ de dúvida** without a shadow of a doubt

sombre|ado /sõbri'adu/ *a* shady □ *m* shading; **~ar** *vt* shade

sombrinha /sõ'briɲa/ *f* parasol

sombrio /sõ'briu/ *a* gloomy

somente /so'mẽtʃi/ *adv* only

sonâmbulo /so'nãbulu/ *m* sleepwalker

sonante /so'nãtʃi/ *a* **moeda ~** hard cash

sonata /so'nata/ *f* sonata

son|da /'sõda/ *f* probe; **~dagem** *f* (*no mar*) sounding; (*de terreno*) survey; **~dagem de opinião** opinion poll; **~dar** *vt* probe; sound <*profundeza*>; (*fig*) sound out <*pessoas, opiniões etc*>

soneca /so'nɛka/ *f* nap; **tirar uma ~** have a nap

sone|gação /sonega'sãw/ *f* (*de impostos*) tax evasion; **~gador** *m* tax dodger; **~gar** *vt* withhold

soneto /so'netu/ *m* sonnet

so|nhador /soɲa'dor/ *a* dreamy □ *m* dreamer; **~nhar** *vt/i* dream (**com** about); **~nho** /'soɲu/ *m* dream; (*doce*) doughnut

sono /'sonu/ *m* sleep; **estar com ~** be sleepy; **pegar no ~** get to sleep; **~lento** *a* sleepy

sono|plastia /sonoplas'tʃia/ *f* sound effects; **~ridade** *f* sound quality; **~ro** /ɔ/ *a* sound; <*voz*> sonorous; <*consoante*> voiced

sonso /'sõsu/ *a* devious

sopa /'sopa/ *f* soup

sopapo /so'papu/ *m* slap; **dar um ~ em** slap

sopé /so'pɛ/ *m* foot

sopeira /so'pera/ *f* soup tureen

soprano /so'pranu/ *m/f* soprano

so|prar /so'prar/ *vt* blow <*folhas etc*>; blow up <*balão*>; blow out <*vela*> □ *vi* blow; **~pro** *m* blow; (*de vento*) puff; **instrumento de ~pro** wind instrument

soquete[1] /so'kɛtʃi/ *f* ankle sock

soquete[2] /so'ketʃi/ *m* socket

sordidez /sordʒi'des/ *f* sordidness; (*imundície*) squalor

sórdido /'sɔrdʒidu/ *a* (*reles*) sordid; (*imundo*) squalid

soro /'soru/ *m* (*remédio*) serum; (*de leite*) whey

sorrateiro /soxa'teru/ *a* crafty

sor|ridente /soxi'dẽtʃi/ *a* smiling; **~rir** *vi* smile; **~riso** *m* smile

sorte /'sɔrtʃi/ *f* luck; (*destino*) fate; **pessoa de ~** lucky person; **por ~** luckily; **ter** *ou* **dar ~** be lucky; **tive a ~ de conhecê-lo** I was lucky enough to meet him; **tirar a ~** draw lots; **trazer** *ou* **dar ~** bring good luck

sor|tear /sortʃi'ar/ *vt* draw for <*prêmio*>; select in a draw <*pessoa*>; **~teio** *m* draw

sorti|do /sor'tʃidu/ *a* assorted; **~mento** *m* assortment

sorumbático /sorũ'batʃiku/ *a* sombre, gloomy

sorver /sor'ver/ *vt* sip <*bebida*>

sósia /'sɔzia/ *m/f* double

soslaio /soz'laju/ *m* **de ~** sideways; <*olhar*> askance

sosse|gado /sose'gadu/ *a* <*vida*> quiet; **ficar ~gado** <*pessoa*> rest assured; **~gar** *vt* reassure □ *vi* rest; **~go** /e/ *m* peace

sótão /'sɔtãw/ (*pl* **~s**) *m* attic, loft

sotaque /so'taki/ *m* accent

soterrar /sote'xar/ *vt* bury

soutien /suti'ã/ (*pl* **~s**) *m* (*Port*) bra

sova|co /so'vaku/ *m* armpit; **~queira** *f* BO, body odour

soviético /sovi'ɛtʃiku/ *a & m* Soviet

sovi|na /so'vina/ *a* stingy, mean, (*Amer*) cheap □ *m/f* cheapskate; **~nice** *f* stinginess, meanness, (*Amer*) cheapness

sozinho /so'ziɲu/ *a* (*sem ninguém*) alone, on one's own; (*por si próprio*) by o.s.; **falar ~** talk to o.s.

spray /is'prej/ (*pl* **~s**) *m* spray

squash /is'kwɛʃ/ *m* squash

stand /is'tãdʒi/ (*pl* **~s**) *m* stand

status /is'tatus/ *m* status

stripper /is'triper/ (*pl* **~s**) *m/f* stripper

strip-tease /istripi'tʃizi/ *m* striptease

sua /'sua/ *a & pron veja* seu

su|ado /su'adu/ *a* <*pessoa, roupa*> sweaty; (*fig*) hard-earned; **~ar** *vt/i* sweat; **~ar por/para** (*fig*) work hard for/to; **~ar frio** come out in a cold sweat

sua|ve /su'avi/ *a* <*toque, subida*> gentle; <*gosto, cheiro, dor, inverno*> mild; <*música, voz*> soft; <*vinho*> smooth; <*trabalho*> light; <*prestações*> easy; **~vidade** *f* gentleness; mildness; softness; smoothness; *veja* suave; **~vizar** *vt* soften; soothe <*dor, pessoa*>

subalterno /subaw'tɛrnu/ *a & m* subordinate

subconsciente /subikõsi'ẽtʃi/ *a & m* subconscious

subdesenvolvido /subidʒizĩvow'vidu/ *a* underdeveloped

súbdito /'subditu/ *m* (*Port*) *veja* súdito

subdividir /subidʒivi'dʒir/ *vt* subdivide

subemprego /subĩ'pregu/ *m* menial job

subemprei|tar /subĩprej'tar/ *vt* subcontract; **~teiro** *m* subcontractor

subenten|der /subĩtẽ'der/ *vt* infer; **~dido** *a* implied □ *m* insinuation

subestimar /subestʃi'mar/ *vt* underestimate

su|bida /su'bida/ *f* (*ação*) ascent; (*ladeira*) incline; (*de preços etc, fig*) rise; **~bir** *vi* go up; <*rio, águas*> rise □ *vt* go up, climb; **~bir em** climb <*árvore*>; get up onto <*mesa*>; get on <*ônibus*>

súbito /'subitu/ *a* sudden; (de) **~** suddenly

subjacente /subiʒa'sẽtʃi/ *a* underlying

subjeti|vidade /subiʒetʃivi'dadʒi/ *f* subjectivity; **~vo** *a* subjective

subjugar /subiʒu'gar/ *vt* subjugate

subjuntivo /subiʒũ'tʃivu/ *a & m* subjunctive

sublevar-se /suble'varsi/ *vpr* rise up

sublime /su'blimi/ *a* sublime

subli|nhado /subli'ɲadu/ *m* underlining; **~nhar** *vt* underline

sublocar /sublo'kar/ *vt/i* sublet

submarino /subima'rinu/ *a* underwater □ *m* submarine

submer|gir /subimer'ʒir/ *vt* submerge; **~gir-se** *vpr* submerge; **~so** *a* submerged

submeter /subime'ter/ *vt* subject (a to); put down, subdue <*povo, rebeldes etc*>; submit <*projeto*>; **~-se** *vpr* (*render-se*) submit; **~-se a** (*sofrer*) undergo

submis|são /subimi'sãw/ *f* submission; **~so** *a* submissive

submundo /subi'mũdu/ *m* underworld

subnutrição /subinutri'sãw/ *f* malnutrition

subordi|nado /subordʒi'nadu/ *a & m* subordinate; **~nar** *vt* subordinate (a to)

subor|nar /subor'nar/ *vt* bribe; **~no** /o/ *m* bribe

subproduto /subipro'dutu/ *m* by-product

subs|crever /subiskre'ver/ *vt* sign <*carta etc*>; subscribe to <*opinião*>; subscribe <*dinheiro*> (para to); **~crever-se** *vpr* sign one's name; **~crição** *f* subscription; **~crito** *pp de* **~crever**

subseqüente /subise'kwẽtʃi/ *a* subsequent

subserviente /subiservi'ẽtʃi/ *a* subservient

subsidiar /subisidʒi'ar/ *vt* subsidize

subsidiá|ria /subisidʒi'aria/ *f* subsidiary; **~rio** *a* subsidiary

subsídio /subi'sidʒiu/ *m* subsidy

subsistência /subisis'tẽsia/ *f* subsistence

subsolo /subi'sɔlu/ *m* (*porão*) basement

substância /subis'tãsia/ *f* substance

substan|cial /subistãsi'aw/ (*pl* **~ciais**) *a* substantial; **~tivo** *m* noun

substitu|ição /subistʃitui'sãw/ *f* replacement; substitution; **~ir** *vt* (*pôr B no lugar de A*) replace (A por B A with B); (*usar B em vez de A*) substitute (A por B B for A); **~to** *a & m* substitute

subterfúgio /subiter'fuʒiu/ *m* subterfuge

subterrâneo /subite'xaniu/ *a* underground

sub|til /sub'til/ (*pl* **~tis**) *a* (*Port*) *veja* sutil

subtra|ção /subitra'sãw/ *f* subtraction; **~ir** *vt* subtract <*números*>; (*roubar*) steal

suburbano /subur'banu/ *a* suburban

subúrbio /su'burbiu/ *m* suburbs

subven|ção /subivẽ'sãw/ *f* grant, subsidy; **~cionar** *vt* subsidize

subver|são /subiver'sãw/ *f* subversion; **~sivo** *a & m* subversive

suca|ta /su'kata/ *f* scrap metal; **~tear** *vt* scrap

sucção /suk'sãw/ *f* suction

suce|der /suse'der/ *vi* (*acontecer*) happen □ *vt* **~der a** succeed <*rei etc*>; (*vir depois*) follow; **~der-se** *vpr* follow on from one another; **~dido** *a* **bem ~dido** successful

suces|são /suse'sãw/ *f* succession; **~sivo** *a* successive; **~so** /ɛ/ *m* success; (*música*) hit; **fazer** *ou* **ter ~so** be successful; **~sor** *m* successor
sucinto /su'sĩtu/ *a* succinct
suco /'suku/ *m* juice
suculento /suku'lẽtu/ *a* juicy
sucumbir /sukũ'bir/ *vi* succumb (a to)
sucur|sal /sukur'saw/ (*pl* **~sais**) *f* branch
Sudão /su'dãw/ *m* Sudan
sudário /su'dariu/ *m* shroud
sudeste /su'dɛstʃi/ *a* & *m* southeast; **o Sudeste Asiático** Southeast Asia
súdito /'sudʒitu/ *m* subject
sudoeste /sudo'ɛstʃi/ *a* & *m* southwest
Suécia /su'ɛsia/ *f* Sweden
sueco /su'ɛku/ *a* & *m* Swedish
suéter /su'ɛter/ *m/f* sweater
sufici|ência /sufisi'ẽsia/ *f* sufficiency; **~ente** *a* enough, sufficient; **o ~ente** enough
sufixo /su'fiksu/ *m* suffix
suflê /su'fle/ *m* soufflé
sufo|cante /sufo'kãtʃi/ *a* stifling; **~car** *vt* (*asfixiar*) suffocate; (*fig*) stifle □ *vi* suffocate; **~co** /o/ *m* hassle; **estar num ~co** be having a tough time
sufrágio /su'fraʒiu/ *m* suffrage
sugar /su'gar/ *vt* suck
sugerir /suʒe'rir/ *vt* suggest
suges|tão /suʒes'tãw/ *f* suggestion; **dar uma ~tão** make a suggestion; **~tivo** *a* suggestive
Suíça /su'isa/ *f* Switzerland
suíças /su'isas/ *f pl* sideburns
sui|cida /sui'sida/ *a* suicidal □ *m/f* suicide (victim); **~cidar-se** *vpr* commit suicide; **~cídio** *m* suicide
suíço /su'isu/ *a* & *m* Swiss
suíno /su'inu/ *a* & *m* pig
suíte /su'itʃi/ *f* suite
su|jar /su'ʒar/ *vt* dirty; (*fig*) sully <*reputação etc*> □ *vi*, **~jar-se** *vpr* get dirty; **~jar-se com alg** queer one's pitch with s.o.; **~jeira** *f* dirt; (*uma*) dirty trick
sujei|tar /suʒej'tar/ *vt* subject (a to); **~tar-se** *vpr* subject o.s. (a to); **~to** *a* subject (a to) □ *m* (*de oração*) subject; (*pessoa*) person
su|jidade /suʒi'dadʒi/ *f* (*Port*) dirt; **~jo** *a* dirty
sul /suw/ *a invar* & *m* south; **~-africano** *a* & *m* South African; **~-americano** *a* & *m* South American; **~-coreano** *a* & *m* South Korean
sul|car /suw'kar/ *vt* furrow <*testa*>; **~co** *m* furrow
sulfúrico /suw'furiku/ *a* sulphuric
sulista /su'lista/ *a* southern □ *m/f* southerner
sultão /suw'tãw/ *m* sultan
sumário /su'mariu/ *a* <*justiça*> summary; <*roupa*> skimpy, brief
su|miço /su'misu/ *m* disappearance; **dar ~miço em** spirit away; **tomar chá de ~miço** disappear; **~mido** *a* <*cor, voz*> faint; **ele anda ~mido** he's disappeared; **~mir** *vi* disappear
sumo /'sumu/ *m* (*Port*) juice
sumptuoso /sũtu'ozu/ *a* (*Port*) *veja* **suntuoso**
sunga /'sũga/ *f* swimming trunks
suntuoso /sũtu'ozu/ *a* sumptuous
suor /su'or/ *m* sweat
superar /supe'rar/ *vt* overcome <*dificuldade etc*>; surpass <*expectativa, pessoa*>
superá|vel /supe'ravew/ (*pl* **~veis**) *a* surmountable; **~vit** (*pl* **~vits**) *m* surplus
superestimar /superestʃi'mar/ *vt* overestimate
superestrutura /superistru'tura/ *f* superstructure
superfici|al /superfisi'aw/ (*pl* **~ais**) *a* superficial
superfície /super'fisi/ *f* surface; (*medida*) area
supérfluo /su'pɛrfluu/ *a* superfluous
superintendência /superĩtẽ'dẽsia/ *f* bureau
superi|or /superi'or/ *a* (*de cima*) upper; <*ensino*> higher; <*número, temperatura etc*> greater (a than); (*melhor*) superior (a to) □ *m* superior; **~oridade** *f* superiority
superlativo /superla'tʃivu/ *a* & *m* superlative
superlota|ção /superlota'sãw/ *f* overcrowding; **~do** *a* overcrowded
supermercado /supermer'kadu/ *m* supermarket
superpotência /superpo'tẽsia/ *f* superpower
superpovoado /superpovo'adu/ *a* overpopulated
supersecreto /superse'krɛtu/ *a* top secret
supersensí|vel /supersẽ'sivew/ (*pl* **~veis**) *a* oversensitive
supersônico /super'soniku/ *a* supersonic
supersti|ção /superstʃi'sãw/ *f* superstition; **~cioso** /o/ *a* superstitious
supervi|são /supervi'zãw/ *f* supervision; **~sionar** *vt* supervise; **~sor** *m* supervisor
supetão /supe'tãw/ *m* **de ~** all of a sudden
suplantar /suplã'tar/ *vt* supplant
suplemen|tar /suplemẽ'tar/ *a* supplementary □ *vt* supplement; **~to** *m* supplement

suplente /su'plẽtʃi/ *a & m/f* substitute
supletivo /suple'tʃivu/ *a* supplementary; **ensino ~** adult education
súplica /'suplika/ *f* plea; **tom de ~** pleading tone
suplicar /supli'kar/ *vt* plead for; (*em juízo*) petition for
suplício /su'plisiu/ *m* torture; (*fig: aflição*) torment
supor /su'por/ *vt* suppose
supor|tar /supor'tar/ *vt* (*sustentar*) support; (*tolerar*) stand, bear; **~tável** (*pl* **~táveis**) *a* bearable; **~te** /ɔ/ *m* support
suposição /supozi'sãw/ *f* supposition
supositório /supozi'tɔriu/ *m* suppository
supos|tamente /suposta'mẽtʃi/ *adv* supposedly; **~to** /o/ *a* supposed; **~to que** supposing that
supre|macia /suprema'sia/ *f* supremacy; **~mo** /e/ *a* supreme
supressão /supre'sãw/ *f* (*de lei, cargo, privilégio*) abolition; (*de jornal, informação, nomes*) suppression; (*de palavras, cláusula*) deletion
suprimento /supri'mẽtu/ *m* supply
suprimir /supri'mir/ *vt* abolish <*lei, cargo, privilégio*>; suppress <*jornal, informação, nomes*>; delete <*palavras, cláusula*>
suprir /su'prir/ *vt* provide for <*família, necessidades*>; make up for <*falta*>; make up <*quantia*>; supply <*o que falta*>; (*substituir*) take the place of; **~ alg de** provide s.o. with; **~ A por B** substitute B for A
supurar /supu'rar/ *vi* turn septic
sur|dez /sur'des/ *f* deafness; **~do** *a* deaf; <*consoante*> voiceless □ *m* deaf person; **os ~dos** the deaf; **~do-mudo** (*pl* **~dos-mudos**) *a* deaf and dumb □ *m* deaf-mute
sur|fe /'surfi/ *m* surfing; **~fista** *m/f* surfer
sur|gimento /surʒi'mẽtu/ *m* appearance; **~gir** *vi* arise; **~gir à mente** spring to mind
Suriname /suri'nami/ *m* Surinam
surpreen|dente /surpriẽ'dẽtʃi/ *a* surprising; **~der** *vt* surprise □ *vi* be surprising; **~der-se** *vpr* be surprised (de at)
surpre|sa /sur'preza/ *f* surprise; **de ~sa** by surprise; **~so** /e/ *a* surprised
sur|ra /'suxa/ *f* thrashing; **~rado** *a* <*roupa*> worn-out; **~rar** *vt* thrash <*pessoa*>; wear out <*roupa*>
surrealis|mo /suxea'lizmu/ *m* surrealism; **~ta** *a & m/f* surrealist
surtir /sur'tʃir/ *vt* produce; **~ efeito** be effective
surto /'surtu/ *m* outbreak
suscept- (*Port*) *veja* **suscet-**
susce|tibilidade /susetʃibili'dadʒi/ *f* (*de pessoa*) sensitivity; **~tível** (*pl* **~tíveis**) *a* <*pessoa*> touchy, sensitive; **~tível de** open to
suscitar /susi'tar/ *vt* cause; raise <*dúvida, suspeita*>
suspei|ta /sus'pejta/ *f* suspicion; **~tar** *vt/i* **~tar (de)** suspect; **~to** *a* suspicious; (*duvidoso*) suspect □ *m* suspect; **~toso** /o/ *a* suspicious
suspen|der /suspẽ'der/ *vt* suspend; **~são** *f* suspension; **~se** *m* suspense; **~so** *a* suspended; **~sórios** *m pl* braces, (*Amer*) suspenders
suspi|rar /suspi'rar/ *vi* sigh; **~rar por** long for; **~ro** *m* sigh; (*doce*) meringue
sussur|rar /susu'xar/ *vt/i* whisper; **~ro** *m* whisper
sustar /sus'tar/ *vt/i* stop
susten|táculo /sustẽ'takulu/ *m* mainstay; **~tar** *vt* support; (*afirmar*) maintain; **~to** *m* support; (*ganha-pão*) livelihood
susto /'sustu/ *m* fright
sutiã /sutʃi'ã/ *m* bra
su|til /su'tʃiw/ (*pl* **~tis**) *a* subtle; **~tileza** /e/ *f* subtlety
sutu|ra /su'tura/ *f* suture; **~rar** *vt* suture

T

tá /ta/ *int* (*fam*) OK; *veja* **estar**
taba|caria /tabaka'ria/ *f* tobacconist's; **~co** *m* tobacco
tabefe /ta'bɛfi/ *m* slap
tabe|la /ta'bɛla/ *f* table; **~lar** *vt* tabulate
tablado /ta'bladu/ *m* platform
tabu /ta'bu/ *a & m* taboo
tábua /'tabua/ *f* board; **~ de passar roupa** ironing board
tabuleiro /tabu'leru/ *m* (*de xadrez etc*) board
tabuleta /tabu'lɛta/ *f* (*letreiro*) sign
taça /'tasa/ *f* (*prêmio*) cup; (*de champanhe etc*) glass
ta|cada /ta'kada/ *f* shot; **de uma ~cada** in one go; **~car** *vt* hit <*bola*>; (*fam*) throw
tacha /'taʃa/ *f* tack
tachar /ta'ʃar/ *vt* brand (de as)
tachinha /ta'ʃiɲa/ *f* drawing pin, (*Amer*) thumbtack
tácito /'tasitu/ *a* tacit
taciturno /tasi'turnu/ *a* taciturn
taco /'taku/ *m* (*de golfe*) club; (*de bilhar*) cue; (*de hóquei*) stick
tact- (*Port*) *veja* **tat-**
tagare|la /taga'rɛla/ *a* chatty, talkative □ *m/f* chatterbox; **~lar** *vi* chatter

tailan|dês /tajlã'des/ *a & m* (*f* ~**desa**) Thai

Tailândia /taj'lãdʒia/ *f* Thailand

tailleur /ta'jɛr/ (*pl* ~ s) *m* suit

Taiti /taj'tʃi/ *m* Tahiti

tal /taw/ (*pl* tais) *a* such; **que** ~? what do you think?, (*Port*) how are you?; **que** ~ **uma cerveja?** how about a beer?; ~ **como** such as; ~ **qual** just like; **um** ~ **de João** someone called John; **e** ~ and so on

tala /'tala/ *f* splint

talão /ta'lãw/ *m* stub; ~ **de cheques** chequebook

talco /'tawku/ *m* talc

talen|to /ta'lẽtu/ *m* talent; ~**toso** /o/ *a* talented

talhar /ta'ʎar/ *vt* slice <*dedo, carne*>; carve <*pedra, imagem*>

talharim /taʎa'rĩ/ *m* tagliatelle

talher /ta'ʎɛr/ *m* set of cutlery; *pl* cutlery

talho /'taʎu/ *m* (*Port*) butcher's

talismã /taliz'mã/ *m* charm, talisman

talo /'talu/ *m* stalk

talvez /taw'ves/ *adv* perhaps; ~ **ele venha amanhã** he may come tomorrow

tamanco /ta'mãku/ *m* clog

tamanho /ta'maɲu/ *m* size □ *adj* such

tâmara /'tamara/ *f* date

tamarindo /tama'rĩdu/ *m* tamarind

também /tã'bẽj/ *adv* also; ~ **não** not ... either, neither

tam|bor /tã'bor/ *m* drum; ~**borilar** *vi* <*dedos*> drum; <*chuva*> patter; ~**borim** *m* tambourine

Tâmisa /'tamiza/ *m* Thames

tam|pa /'tãpa/ *f* lid; ~**pão** *m* (*vaginal*) tampon; ~**par** *vt* put the lid on <*recipiente*>; (*tapar*) cover; ~**pinha** *f* top□ *m/f* (*fam*) shorthouse

tampouco /tã'poku/ *adv* nor, neither

tanga /'tãga/ *f* G-string; (*avental*) loincloth

tangente /tã'ʒẽtʃi/ *f* tangent; **pela** ~ (*fig*) narrowly

tangerina /tãʒe'rina/ *f* tangerine

tango /'tãgu/ *m* tango

tanque /'tãki/ *m* tank; (*para lavar roupa*) sink

tanto /'tãtu/ *a & pron* so much; *pl* so many □ *adv* so much; ~ ... **como** ... both ... and ...; ~ (...) **quanto** as much (...) as; ~ **melhor** so much the better; ~ **tempo** so long; **vinte e** ~**s anos** twenty odd years; **nem** ~ not as much; **um** ~ **difícil** somewhat difficult; ~ **que** to the extent that

Tanzânia /tã'zania/ *f* Tanzania

tão /tãw/ *adv* so; ~ **grande quanto** as big as; ~**-somente** *adv* solely

tapa /'tapa/ *m ou f* slap; **dar um** ~ **em** slap

tapar /ta'par/ *vt* (*cobrir*) cover; block <*luz, vista*>; cork <*garrafa*>

tapeçaria /tapesa'ria/ *f* (*pano*) tapestry; (*loja*) carpet shop

tape|tar /tape'tar/ *vt* carpet; ~**te** /e/ *m* carpet

tapioca /tapi'ɔka/ *f* tapioca

tapume /ta'pumi/ *m* fence

taquicardia /takikar'dʒia/ *f* palpitations

taquigra|far /takigra'far/ *vt/i* write in shorthand; ~**fia** *f* shorthand

tara /'tara/ *f* fetish; ~**do** *a* sex-crazed □ *m* sex maniac; **ser** ~**do por** be crazy about

tar|dar /tar'dar/ *vi* (*atrasar*) be late; (*demorar muito*) be long □ *vt* delay; ~**dar a responder** take a long time to answer, be a long time answering; **o mais** ~**dar** at the latest; **sem mais** ~**dar** without further delay; ~**de** *adv* late □ *f* afternoon; **hoje à** ~**de** this afternoon; ~**de da noite** late at night; ~**dinha** *f* late afternoon; ~**dio** *a* late

tarefa /ta'rɛfa/ *f* task, job

tarifa /ta'rifa/ *f* tariff; ~ **de embarque** airport tax

tarimbado /tarĩ'badu/ *a* experienced

tarja /'tarʒa/ *f* strip

ta|rô /ta'ro/ *m* tarot; ~**rólogo** *m* tarot reader

tartamu|dear /tartamudʒi'ar/ *vi* stammer; ~**do** *a* stammering □ *m* stammerer

tártaro /'tartaru/ *m* tartar

tartaruga /tarta'ruga/ *f* (*bicho*) turtle; (*material*) tortoiseshell

tatear /tatʃi'ar/ *vt* feel □ *vi* feel one's way

táti|ca /'tatʃika/ *f* tactics; ~**co** *a* tactical

tá|til /'tatʃiw/ (*pl* ~**teis**) *a* tactile

tato /'tatu/ *m* (*sentido*) touch; (*diplomacia*) tact

tatu /ta'tu/ *m* armadillo

tatu|ador /tatua'dor/ *m* tattooist; ~**agem** *f* tattoo; ~**ar** *vt* tattoo

tauromaquia /tawroma'kia/ *f* bullfighting

taxa /'taʃa/ *f* (*a pagar*) charge; (*índice*) rate; ~ **de câmbio** exchange rate; ~ **de juros** interest rate; ~ **rodoviária** road tax

taxar /ta'ʃar/ *vt* tax

taxativo /taʃa'tʃivu/ *a* firm, categorical

táxi /'taksi/ *m* taxi

taxiar /taksi'ar/ *vi* taxi

taxímetro /tak'simetru/ *m* taxi meter

taxista /tak'sista/ *m/f* taxi driver

tchã /tʃã/ *m* (*fam*) special something

tchau /tʃaw/ *int* goodbye, bye

tcheco /'tʃɛku/ *a & m* Czech

Tchecoslováquia /tʃekoslo'vakia/ *f* Czechoslovakia
te /tʃi/ *pron* you; (*a ti*) to you
tear /tʃi'ar/ *m* loom
tea|tral /tʃia'traw/ (*pl* **~trais**) *a* theatrical; <*grupo*> theatre; **~tro** *m* theatre; **~trólogo** *m* playwright
tece|lagem /tese'laʒẽ/ *f* (*trabalho*) weaving; (*fábrica*) textile factory; **~lão** *m* (*f* **~lã**) weaver
te|cer /te'ser/ *vt/i* weave; **~cido** *m* cloth; (*no corpo*) tissue
te|cla /'tɛkla/ *f* key; **~cladista** *m/f* (*músico*) keyboard player; (*de computador*) keyboard operator; **~clado** *m* keyboard; **~clar** *vt* key (in)
técni|ca /'tɛknika/ *f* technique; **~co** *a* technical □ *m* specialist; (*de time*) manager; (*que mexe com máquinas*) technician
tecno|crata /tekno'krata/ *m/f* technocrat; **~logia** *f* technology; **~lógico** *a* technological
teco-teco /tɛku'tɛku/ *m* light aircraft
tecto /'tɛtu/ *m* (*Port*) *veja* **teto**
tédio /'tɛdʒiu/ *m* boredom
tedioso /tedʒi'ozu/ *a* boring, tedious
Teerã /tee'rã/ *f* Teheran
teia /'teja/ *f* web
tei|ma /'tejma/ *f* persistence; **~mar** *vi* insist; **~mar em ir** insist on going; **~mosia** *f* stubbornness; **~moso** /o/ *a* stubborn; <*ruído*> insistent
teixo /'tejʃu/ *m* yew
Tejo /'teʒu/ *m* Tagus
tela /'tɛla/ *f* (*de cinema, TV etc*) screen; (*tecido, pintura*) canvas
telecoman|dado /telekomã'dadu/ *a* remote-controlled; **~do** *m* remote control
telecomunicação /telekomunika'sãw/ *f* telecommunication
teleférico /tele'fɛriku/ *m* cable car
telefo|nar /telefo'nar/ *vi* telephone; **~nar para alg** phone s.o.; **~ne** /o/ *m* telephone; (*número*) phone number; **~ne celular** cell phone; **~ne sem fio** cordless phone; **~nema** /e/ *m* phone call; **~nia** *f* telephone technology
telefôni|co /tele'foniku/ *a* telephone; **cabine ~ca** phone box, (*Amer*) phone booth; **mesa ~ca** switchboard
telefonista /telefo'nista/ *m/f* (*da companhia telefônica*) operator; (*dentro de empresa etc*) telephonist
tele|grafar /telegra'far/ *vt/i* telegraph; **~gráfico** *a* telegraphic
telégrafo /te'lɛgrafu/ *m* telegraph
tele|grama /tele'grama/ *m* telegram; **~guiado** *a* remote- controlled
telejor|nal /teleʒor'naw/ (*pl* **~nais**) *m* television news
tele|novela /teleno'vɛla/ *f* TV soap opera; **~objetiva** *f* telephoto lens
tele|patia /telepa'tʃia/ *f* telepathy; **~pático** *a* telepathic
telescó|pico /teles'kɔpiku/ *a* telescopic; **~pio** *m* telescope
telespectador /telespekta'dor/ *m* television viewer □ *a* viewing
televi|são /televi'zãw/ *f* television; **~são a cabo** cable television; **~sionar** *vt* televise; **~sivo** *a* television; **~sor** *m* television set
telex /te'lɛks/ *m invar* telex
telha /'teʎa/ *f* tile; **~do** *m* roof
te|ma /'tema/ *m* theme; **~mático** *a* thematic
temer /te'mer/ *vt* fear □ *vi* be afraid; **~ por** fear for
teme|rário /teme'rariu/ *a* reckless; **~ridade** *f* recklessness; **~roso** /o/ *a* fearful
te|mido /te'midu/ *a* feared; **~mível** (*pl* **~míveis**) *a* fearsome; **~mor** *m* fear
tempão /tẽ'pãw/ *m* **um ~** a long time
temperado /tẽpe'radu/ *a* <*clima*> temperate □ *pp de* **temperar**
temperamen|tal /tẽperamẽ'taw/ (*pl* **~tais**) *a* temperamental; **~to** *m* temperament
temperar /tẽpe'rar/ *vt* season <*comida*>; temper <*aço*>
temperatura /tẽpera'tura/ *f* temperature
tempero /tẽ'peru/ *m* seasoning
tempes|tade /tẽpes'tadʒi/ *f* storm; **~tuoso** /o/ *a* stormy; (*fig*) tempestuous
templo /'tẽplu/ *m* temple
tempo /'tẽpu/ *m* (*período*) time; (*atmosférico*) weather; (*do verbo*) tense; (*de jogo*) half; **ao mesmo ~** at the same time; **nesse meio ~** in the meantime; **o ~ todo** all the time; **de todos os ~s** of all time; **quanto ~** how long; **muito/pouco ~** a long/ short time; **~ integral** full time
têmpora /'tẽpora/ *f* temple
tempo|rada /tẽpo'rada/ *f* (*sazão*) season; (*tempo*) while; **~ral** (*pl* **~rais**) *a* temporal □ *m* storm; **~rário** *a* temporary
te|nacidade /tenasi'dadʒi/ *f* tenacity; **~naz** *a* tenacious □ *f* tongs
tenção /tẽ'sãw/ *f* intention
tencionar /tẽsio'nar/ *vt* intend
tenda /'tẽda/ *f* tent
tendão /tẽ'dãw/ *m* tendon; **~ de Aquiles** Achilles tendon
tendência /tẽ'dẽsia/ *f* (*moda*) trend; (*propensão*) tendency
tendencioso /tẽdẽsi'ozu/ *a* tendentious

ten|der /tẽ'der/ *vi* tend (para towards); **~de a engordar** he tends to get fat; **o tempo ~de a ficar bom** the weather is improving

tenebroso /tene'brozu/ *a* dark; (*fig: terrível*) dreadful

tenente /te'nẽtʃi/ *m/f* lieutenant

tênis /'tenis/ *m invar* (*jogo*) tennis; (*sapato*) trainer; **um ~** (*par*) a pair of trainers; **~ de mesa** table tennis

tenista /te'nista/ *m/f* tennis player

tenor /te'nor/ *m* tenor

tenro /'tẽxu/ *a* tender

ten|são /tẽ'sãw/ *f* tension; **~são (arterial)** blood pressure; **~so** *a* tense

tentação /tẽta'sãw/ *f* temptation

tentáculo /tẽ'taculu/ *m* tentacle

ten|tador /tẽta'dor/ *a* tempting; **~tar** *vt* try; (*seduzir*) tempt □ *vi* try; **~tativa** *f* attempt; **~tativo** *a* tentative

tênue /'tenui/ *a* faint

teo|logia /teolo'ʒia/ *f* theology; **~lógico** *a* theological

teólogo /te'ɔlogu/ *m* theologian

teor /te'or/ *m* (*de gordura etc*) content; (*de carta, discurso*) drift

teo|rema /teo'rema/ *m* theorem; **~ria** *f* theory

teórico /te'ɔriku/ *a* theoretical

teorizar /teori'zar/ *vt* theorize

tépido /'tɛpidu/ *a* tepid

ter /ter/ *vt* have; **tenho vinte anos** I am twenty (years old); **~ medo/sede** be afraid/thirsty; **tenho que** *ou* **de ir** I have to go; **tem** (*há*) there is/are; **não tem de quê** don't mention it; **~ a ver com** have to do with

tera|peuta /tera'pewta/ *m/f* therapist; **~pêutico** *a* therapeutic; **~pia** *f* therapy

terça /'tersa/ *f* Tuesday; **~-feira** (*pl* **~s-feiras**) *f* Tuesday; **Terça-Feira Gorda** Shrove Tues- day

tercei|ra /ter'sera/ *f* (*marcha*) third; **~ranista** *m/f* third-year; **~ro** *a* third □ *m* third party

terço /'tersu/ *m* third

ter|çol (*pl* **~çóis**) *m* stye

tergal /ter'gaw/ *m* Terylene

térmi|co /'tɛrmiku/ *a* thermal; **garrafa ~ca** Thermos flask

termi|nal /termi'naw/ (*pl* **~nais**) *a* & *m* terminal; **~nal de vídeo** VDU; **~nante** *a* definite; **~nar** *vt* finish □ *vi* <*pessoa, coisa*> finish; <*coisa*> end; **~nar com alg** (*cortar relação*) break up with s.o.

ter|minologia /terminolo'ʒia/ *f* terminology; **~mo**[1] /'termu/ *m* term; **pôr ~mo a** put an end to; **meio ~mo** compromise

termo[2] /'termu / *m* (*Port*) Thermos flask

ter|mômetro /ter'mometru/ *m* thermometer; **~mostato** *m* thermostat

terno[1] /'tɛrnu/ *m* suit

ter|no[2] /'tɛrnu/ *a* tender; **~nura** *f* tenderness

terra /'tɛxa/ *f* land; (*solo, elétrico*) earth; (*chão*) ground; **a Terra** Earth; **por ~** on the ground; **~ natal** homeland

terraço /te'xasu/ *m* terrace

terra|cota /texa'kɔta/ *f* terracotta; **~moto** /texa'mɔtu/ *m* (*Port*) earthquake; **~plenagem** *f* earth moving

terreiro /te'xeru/ *m* meeting place for Afro-Brazilian cults

terremoto /texe'mɔtu/ *m* earthquake

terreno /te'xenu/ *a* earthly □ *m* ground; (*geog*) terrain; (*um*) piece of land; **~ baldio** piece of waste ground

térreo /'tɛxiu/ *a* ground-floor; **(andar) ~** ground floor, (*Amer*) first floor

terrestre /te'xɛstri/ *a* <*animal, batalha, forças*> land; (*da Terra*) of the Earth, the Earth's; <*alegrias etc*> earthly

terrificante /texifi'kãtʃi/ *a* terrifying

terrina /te'xina/ *f* tureen

territori|al /texitori'aw/ (*pl* **~ais**) *a* territorial

território /texi'tɔriu/ *m* territory

terrí|vel /te'xivew/ (*pl* **~veis**) *a* terrible

terror /te'xor/ *m* terror; **filme de ~** horror film

terroris|mo /texo'rizmu/ *m* terrorism; **~ta** *a* & *m/f* terrorist

tese /'tɛzi/ *f* theory; (*escrita*) thesis

teso /'tezu/ *a* (*apertado*) taut; (*rígido*) stiff

tesoura /te'zora/ *f* scissors; **uma ~** a pair of scissors

tesou|reiro /tezo'reru/ *m* treasurer; **~ro** *m* treasure; (*do Estado*) treasury

testa /'tɛsta/ *f* forehead; **~-de-ferro** (*pl* **~s-de-ferro**) *m* frontman

testamento /testa'mẽtu/ *m* will; (*na Bíblia*) testament

tes|tar /tes'tar/ *vt* test; **~te** /ɛ/ *m* test

testemu|nha /teste'muɲa/ *f* witness; **~nha ocular** eye witness; **~nhar** *vt* bear witness to □ *vi* testify; **~nho** *m* evidence, testimony

testículo /tes'tʃikulu/ *m* testicle

teta /'teta/ *f* teat

tétano /'tɛtanu/ *m* tetanus

teto /'tɛtu/ *m* ceiling; **~ solar** sun roof

tétrico /'tɛtriku/ *a* (*triste*) dismal; (*medonho*) horrible

teu /tew/ (*f* **tua**) *a* your □ *pron* yours

têx|til /'testʃiw/ (*pl* **~teis**) *m* textile

tex|to /'testu/ *m* text; **~tura** *f* texture

texugo /te'ʃugu/ *m* badger

tez /tes/ *f* complexion

ti /tʃi/ *pron* you

tia /'tʃia/ *f* aunt; **~-avó** (*pl* **~s-avós**) *f* great aunt

tiara /tʃi'ara/ *f* tiara

tíbia /'tʃibia/ *f* shinbone

ticar /tʃi'kar/ *vt* tick

tico /'tʃiku/ *m* **um ~ de** a little bit of

tiete /tʃi'ɛtʃi/ *m/f* fan

tifo /'tʃifu/ *m* typhoid

tigela /tʃi'ʒɛla/ *f* bowl; **de meia ~** smalltime

tigre /'tʃigri/ *m* tiger; **~sa** /e/ *f* tigress

tijolo /tʃi'ʒolu/ *m* brick

til /tʃiw/ (*pl* **tis**) *m* tilde

tilintar /tʃilĩ'tar/ *vi* jingle □ *m* jingling

timão /tʃi'mãw/ *m* tiller

timbre /'tʃĩbri/ *m* (*insígnia*) crest; (*em papel*) heading; (*de som*) tone; (*de vogal*) quality

time /'tʃimi/ *m* team

timidez /tʃimi'des/ *f* shyness

tímido /'tʃimidu/ *a* shy

tímpano /'tʃĩpanu/ *m* (*tambor*) kettledrum; (*no ouvido*) eardrum

tina /'tʃina/ *f* vat

tingir /tʃĩ'ʒir/ *vt* dye <*tecido, cabelo*>; (*fig*) tinge

ti|nido /tʃi'nidu/ *m* tinkling; **~nir** *vi* tinkle; <*ouvidos*> ring; (*tremer*) tremble; **estar ~nindo** (*fig*) be in peak condition

tino /'tʃinu/ *m* sense, judgement; **ter ~ para** have a flair for

tin|ta /'tʃĩta/ *f* (*para pintar*) paint; (*para escrever*) ink; (*para tingir*) dye; **~teiro** *m* inkwell

tintim /tʃĩ'tʃĩ/ *m* **contar ~ por ~** give a blow-by-blow account of

tin|to /'tʃĩtu/ *a* dyed; <*vinho*> red; **~tura** *f* dye; (*fig*) tinge; **~turaria** *f* dry cleaner's

tio /'tʃiu/ *m* uncle; *pl* (**~** *e tia*) uncle and aunt; **~-avô** (*pl* **~s-avôs**) *m* great uncle

típico /'tʃipiku/ *a* typical

tipo /'tʃipu/ *m* type

tipóia /tʃi'pɔja/ *f* sling

tique /'tʃiki/ *m* (*sinal*) tick; (*do rosto etc*) twitch

tíquete /'tʃiketʃi/ *m* ticket

tiquinho /tʃi'kiɲu/ *m* **um ~ de** a tiny bit of

tira /'tʃira/ *f* strip □ *m/f* (*fam*) copper, (*Amer*) cop

tiracolo /tʃira'kɔlu/ *m* **a ~** <*bolsa*> over one's shoulder; <*pessoa*> in tow

tiragem /tʃi'raʒẽ/ *f* (*de jornal*) circulation

tira|-gosto /tʃira'gostu/ *m* snack; **~-manchas** *m invar* stain remover

ti|rania /tʃira'nia/ *f* tyranny; **~rânico** *a* tyrannical; **~rano** *m* tyrant

tirar /tʃi'rar/ *vt* (*afastar*) take away; (*de dentro*) take out; take off <*roupa, sapato, tampa*>; take <*foto, cópia, férias*>; clear <*mesa*>; get <*nota, diploma, salário*>; get out <*mancha*>

tiritar /tʃiri'tar/ *vi* shiver

tiro /'tʃiru/ *m* shot; **~ ao alvo** shooting; **é ~ e queda** (*fam*) it can't fail; **~teio** *m* shoot-out

titânio /tʃi'taniu/ *m* titanium

títere /'tʃiteri/ *m* puppet

ti|tia /tʃi'tʃia/ *f* auntie; **~tio** *m* uncle

tititi /tʃitʃi'tʃi/ *m* (*fam*) talk

titubear /tʃitubi'ar/ *vi* stagger, totter; (*fig: hesitar*) waver

titular /tʃitu'lar/ *m/f* title holder; (*de time*) captain □ *vt* title

título /'tʃitulu/ *m* title; (*obrigação*) bond; **a ~ de** on the basis of; **a ~ pessoal** on a personal basis

toa /'toa/ *f* **à ~** (*sem rumo*) aimlessly; (*ao acaso*) at random; (*sem motivo*) without reason; (*em vão*) for nothing; (*desocupado*) at a loose end; (*de repente*) out of the blue

toada /to'ada/ *f* melody

toalete /toa'lɛtʃi/ *m* toilet

toalha /to'aʎa/ *f* towel; **~ de mesa** tablecloth

tobogã /tobo'gã/ *m* (*rampa*) slide; (*trenó*) toboggan

toca /'tɔka/ *f* burrow

toca|-discos /toka'dʒiskus/ *m invar* record player; **~-fitas** *m invar* tape player

tocaia /to'kaja/ *f* ambush

tocante /to'kãtʃi/ *a* (*enternecedor*) moving

tocar /to'kar/ *vt* touch; play <*piano, música, disco etc*>; ring <*campainha*> □ *vi* touch; <*pianista, música, disco etc*> play; <*campainha, telefone, sino*> ring; **~-se** *vpr* touch; (*mancar-se*) take the hint; **~ a** (*dizer respeito*) concern; **~ em** touch; touch on <*assunto*>

tocha /'tɔʃa/ *f* torch

toco /'toku/ *m* (*de árvore*) stump; (*de cigarro*) butt

toda /'toda/ *f* **a ~** at full speed

todavia /toda'via/ *conj* however

todo /'todu/ *a* all; (*cada*) every; *pl* all; **~ o dinheiro** all the money; **~ dia, ~s os dias** every day; **~s os alunos** all the pupils; **o dia ~** all day; **em ~ lugar** everywhere; **~ mundo, ~s** everyone; **~s nós** all of us; **ao ~** in all; **~-poderoso** *a* almighty

tofe /'tɔfi/ *m* toffee

toga /'tɔga/ *f* gown; (*de romano*) toga

toicinho /toj'siɲu/ *m* bacon

toldo /'towdu/ *m* awning

tole|rância /tole'rãsia/ *f* tolerance; **~rante** *a* tolerant; **~rar** *vt* tolerate; **~rável** (*pl* **~ráveis**) *a* tolerable

to|lice /to'lisi/ *f* foolishness; (*uma*) foolish thing; **~lo** /o/ *a* foolish □ *m* fool

tom /tõ/ *m* tone

to|mada /to'mada/ *f* (*conquista*) capture; (*elétrica*) plughole; (*de filme*) shot; **~mar** *vt* take; (*beber*) drink; **~mar café** have breakfast

tomara /to'mara/ *int* I hope so; **~ que** let's hope that; **~-que-caia** *a invar* <*vestido*> strapless

tomate /to'matʃi/ *m* tomato

tom|bar /tõ'bar/ *vt* (*derrubar*) knock down; list <*edifício*> □ *vi* fall over; **~bo** *m* fall; **levar um ~bo** have a fall

tomilho /to'miʎu/ *m* thyme

tomo /'tomu/ *m* volume

tona /'tona/ *f* **trazer à ~** bring up; **vir à ~** emerge

tonalidade /tonali'dadʒi/ *f* (*de música*) key; (*de cor*) shade

to|nel /to'nɛw/ (*pl* **~néis**) *m* cask; **~nelada** *f* tonne

tôni|ca /'tonika/ *f* tonic; (*fig: assunto*) keynote; **~co** *a* & *m* tonic

tonificar /tonifi'kar/ *vt* tone up

ton|tear /tõtʃi'ar/ *vt* **~tear alg** make s.o.'s head spin; **~teira** *f* dizziness; **~to** *a* (*zonzo*) dizzy; (*bobo*) stupid; (*atrapalhado*) flustered; **~tura** *f* dizziness

to|pada /to'pada/ *f* trip; **dar uma ~pada em** stub one's toe on; **~par** *vt* agree to, accept; **~par com** bump into <*pessoa*>; come across <*coisa*>

topázio /to'paziu/ *m* topaz

topete /to'pɛtʃi/ *m* quiff

tópico /'tɔpiku/ *a* topical □ *m* topic

topless /topi'lɛs/ *a invar* & *adv* topless

topo /'topu/ *m* top

topografia /topogra'fia/ *f* topography

topônimo /to'ponimu/ *m* place name

toque /'tɔki/ *m* touch; (*da campainha, do telefone*) ring; (*de instrumento*) playing; **dar um ~ em** (*fam*) have a word with

Tóquio /'tɔkiu/ *f* Tokyo

tora /'tɔra/ *f* log

toranja /to'rãʒa/ *f* grapefruit

tórax /'tɔraks/ *m invar* thorax

tor|ção /tor'sãw/ *f* (*do braço etc*) sprain; **~cedor** *m* supporter; **~cer** *vt* twist; (*machucar*) sprain; (*espremer*) wring <*roupa*>; (*centrifugar*) spin <*roupa*> □ *vi* (*gritar*) cheer (por for); (*desejar sucesso*) keep one's fingers crossed (por for; **para que** that); **~cer-se** *vpr* twist about; **~cicolo** /ɔ/ *m* stiff neck; **~cida** *f* (*torção*) twist; (*torcedores*) supporters; (*gritaria*) cheering

tormen|ta /tor'mẽta/ *f* storm; **~to** *m* torment; **~toso** /o/ *a* stormy

tornado /tor'nadu/ *m* tornado

tornar /tor'nar/ *vt* make; **~-se** *vpr* become

torne|ado /torni'adu/ *a* **bem ~ado** shapely; **~ar** *vt* turn

torneio /tor'neju/ *m* tournament

torneira /tor'nera/ *f* tap, (*Amer*) faucet

torniquete /torni'ketʃi/ *m* (*para ferido*) tourniquet; (*Port: de entrada*) turnstile

torno /'tornu/ *m* lathe; (*de ceramista*) wheel; **em ~ de** around

tornozelo /torno'zelu/ *m* ankle

toró /to'rɔ/ *m* downpour

torpe /'torpi/ *a* dirty

torpe|dear /torpedʒi'ar/ *vt* torpedo; **~do** /e/ *m* torpedo

torpor /tor'por/ *m* torpor

torra|da /to'xada/ *f* piece of toast; *pl* toast; **~deira** *f* toaster

torrão /to'xãw/ *m* (*de terra*) turf; (*de açúcar*) lump

torrar /to'xar/ *vt* toast <*pão*>; roast <*café*>; blow <*dinheiro*>; sell off <*mercadorias*>

torre /'toxi/ *f* tower; (*em xadrez*) rook; **~ de controle** control tower; **~ão** *m* turret

torrefação /toxefa'sãw/ *f* (*ação*) roasting; (*fábrica*) coffee-roasting plant

torren|cial /toxẽsi'aw/ (*pl* **~ciais**) *a* torrential; **~te** *f* torrent

torresmo /to'xezmu/ *m* crackling

tórrido /'tɔxidu/ *a* torrid

torrone /to'xoni/ *m* nougat

torso /'torsu/ *m* torso

torta /'tɔrta/ *f* pie, tart

tor|to /'tortu/ *a* crooked; **a ~ e a direito** left, right and centre; **~tuoso** *a* winding

tortu|ra /tor'tura/ *f* torture; **~rador** *m* torturer; **~rar** *vt* torture

to|sa /'tɔza/ *f* (*de cachorro*) clipping; (*de ovelhas*) shearing; **~são** *m* fleece; **~sar** *vt* clip <*cachorro*>; shear <*ovelhas*>; crop <*cabelo*>

tosco /'tosku/ *a* rough, coarse

tosquiar /toski'ar/ *vt* shear <*ovelha*>

tos|se /'tɔsi/ *f* cough; **~se de cachorro** whooping cough; **~sir** *vi* cough

tostão /tos'tãw/ *m* penny

tostar /tos'tar/ *vt* brown <*carne*>; tan < *pele, pessoa*>; **~-se** *vpr* (*ao sol*) go brown

to|tal /to'taw/ (*pl* **~tais**) *a* & *m* total

totali|dade /totali'dadʒi/ *f* entirety; **~tário** *a* totalitarian; **~zar** *vt* total

touca /'toka/ *f* bonnet; (*de freira*) wimple; **~ de banho** bathing cap; **~dor** *m* dressing table

toupeira /to'pera/ *f* mole

tou|rada /to'rada/ *f* bullfight; **~reiro** *m* bullfighter; **~ro** *m* bull; **Touro** (*signo*) Taurus

tóxico /'tɔksiku/ *a* toxic □ *m* toxic substance

toxicômano /toksi'komanu/ *m* drug addict

toxina /tok'sina/ *f* toxin

traba|lhador /trabaʎa'dor/ *a* <*pessoa*> hard-working; <*classe*> working □ *m* worker; **~lhar** *vt* work □ *vi* work; (*numa peça, filme*) act; **~lheira** *f* big job; **~lhista** *a* labour; **~lho** *m* work; (*um*) job; (*na escola*) assignment; **dar-se o ~lho de** go to the trouble of; **~lho de parto** labour; **~lhos forçados** hard labour; **~lhoso** *a* laborious

traça /'trasa/ *f* moth

tração /tra'sãw/ *f* traction

tra|çar /tra'sar/ *vt* draw; draw up <*plano*>; set out <*ordens*>; **~ço** *m* stroke; (*entre frases*) dash; (*vestígio*) trace; (*característica*) trait; *pl* (*do rosto*) features

tractor /tra'tor/ *m* (*Port*) *veja* trator

tradi|ção /tradʒi'sãw/ *f* tradition; **~cional** (*pl* **~cionais**) *a* traditional

tradu|ção /tradu'sãw/ *f* translation; **~tor** *m* translator; **~zir** *vt/i* translate (**de** from; **para** into)

trafe|gar /trafe'gar/ *vi* run; **~gável** (*pl* **~gáveis**) *a* open to traffic

tráfego /'trafegu/ *m* traffic

trafi|cância /trafi'kãsia/ *f* trafficking; **~cante** *m/f* trafficker; **~car** *vt/i* traffic (**com** in)

tráfico /'trafiku/ *m* traffic

tra|gada /tra'gada/ *f* (*de bebida*) swallow; (*de cigarro*) drag; **~gar** *vt* swallow; inhale <*fumaça*>

tragédia /tra'ʒɛdʒia/ *f* tragedy

trágico /'traʒiku/ *a* tragic

trago /'tragu/ *m* (*de bebida*) swallow; (*de cigarro*) drag; **de um ~** in one go

trai|ção /traj'sãw/ *f* (*ato*) betrayal; (*deslealdade*) treachery; (*da pátria*) treason; **~çoeiro** *a* treacherous; **~dor** *a* treacherous □ *m* traitor

trailer /'trejler/ (*pl* **~s**) *m* (*de filme etc*) trailer; (*casa móvel*) caravan, (*Amer*) trailer

traineira /traj'nera/ *f* trawler

training /'trejnĩ/ (*pl* **~s**) *m* track suit

trair /tra'ir/ *vt* betray; be unfaithful to <*marido, mulher*>; **~-se** *vpr* give o.s. away

tra|jar /tra'ʒar/ *vt* wear; **~jar-se** *vpr* dress (**de** in); **~je** *m* outfit; **~je a rigor** evening dress; **~je espacial** space suit

traje|to /tra'ʒɛtu/ *m* (*percurso*) journey; (*caminho*) route; **~tória** *f* trajectory; (*fig*) course

tralha /'traʎa/ *f* (*trastes*) junk

tra|ma /'trama/ *f* plot; **~mar** *vt/i* plot

trambi|que /trã'biki/ (*fam*) *m* con; **~queiro** (*fam*) *m* con artist

tramitar /trami'tar/ *vi* be processed

trâmites /'tramitʃis/ *m pl* channels

tramóia /tra'mɔja/ *f* scheme

trampolim /trãpo'lĩ/ *m* (*de ginástica*) trampoline; (*de piscina, fig*) springboard

tranca /'trãka/ *f* bolt; (*em carro*) lock

trança /'trãsa/ *f* (*de cabelo*) plait

tran|cafiar /trãkafi'ar/ *vt* lock up; **~car** *vt* lock; cancel <*matrícula*>

trançar /trã'sar/ *vt* plait <*cabelo*>; weave <*palha etc*>

tranco /'trãku/ *m* jolt; **aos ~s e barrancos** in fits and starts

tranqueira /trã'kera/ *f* junk

tranqüi|lidade /trãkwili'dadʒi/ *f* tranquillity; **~lizador** *a* reassuring; **~lizante** *m* tranquillizer □ *a* reassuring; **~lizar** *vt* reassure; **~lizar-se** *vpr* be reassured; **~lo** *a* <*bairro, sono*> peaceful; <*pessoa, voz, mar*> calm; <*consciência*> clear; <*sucesso, lucro*> sure-fire □ *adv* with no trouble

transa /'trãza/ *f* (*fam*) (*negócio*) deal; (*caso*) affair; **~ção** *f* transaction; **~do** *a* (*fam*) <*roupa, pessoa, casa*> stylish; <*relação*> healthy

Transamazônica /tranzama'zonika/ *f* trans-Amazonian highway

transar /trã'zar/ (*fam*) *vt* set up; do <*drogas*> □ *vi* (*negociar*) deal; (*fazer sexo*) have sex

transatlântico /trãzat'lãtʃiku/ *a* transatlantic □ *m* liner

transbordar /trãzbor'dar/ *vi* overflow

transcen|dental /trãsẽdẽ'taw/ (*pl* **~dentais**) *a* transcendental; **~der** *vt/i* **~der (a)** transcend

trans|crever /trãskre'ver/ *vt* transcribe; **~crição** *f* transcription; **~crito** *a* transcribed □ *m* transcript

transe /'trãzi/ *m* trance

transeunte /trãzi'ũtʃi/ *m/f* passer-by

transfe|rência /trãsfe'rẽsia/ *f* transfer; **~ridor** *m* protractor; **~rir** *vt* transfer; **~rir-se** *vpr* transfer

transfor|mação /trãsforma'sãw/ *f* transformation; **~mador** *m* transformer; **~mar** *vt* transform; **~mar-se** *vpr* be transformed

trânsfuga /'trãsfuga/ *m/f* deserter; (*de um país*) defector

transfusão /trãsfu'zãw/ *f* transfusion
trans|gredir /trãzgre'dʒir/ *vt* infringe; ~**gressão** *f* infringement
transi|ção /trãzi'sãw/ *f* transition; ~**cional** (*pl* ~**cionais**) *a* transitional
transi|gente /trãzi'ʒẽtʃi/ *a* open to compromise; ~**gir** *vi* compromise
transis|tor /trãzis'tor/ *m* transistor; ~**torizado** *a* transistorized
transi|tar /trãzi'tar/ *vi* pass; ~**tável** (*pl* ~**táveis**) *a* passable; ~**tivo** *a* transitive
trânsito /'trãzitu/ *m* traffic; **em** ~ in transit
transitório /trãzi'tɔriu/ *a* transitory
translúcido /trãz'lusidu/ *a* translucent
transmis|são /trãzmi'sãw/ *f* transmission; ~**sor** *m* transmitter
transmitir /trãzmi'tʃir/ *vt* transmit <*programa, calor, doença*>; convey <*notícia, ordens*>; transfer <*herança, direito*>; ~**-se** *vpr* <*doença*> be transmitted
transpa|recer /trãspare'ser/ *vi* be visible; (*fig*) <*emoção, verdade*> come out; ~**rência** *f* transparency; ~**rente** *a* transparent
transpi|ração /trãspira'sãw/ *f* perspiration; ~**rar** *vt* exude □ *vi* (*suar*) perspire; <*notícia*> trickle through; <*verdade*> come out
transplan|tar /trãsplã'tar/ *vt* transplant; ~**te** *m* transplant
transpor /trãs'por/ *vt* cross <*rio, fronteira*>; get over <*obstáculo, dificuldade*>; transpose <*letras, música*>
transpor|tadora /trãsporta'dora/ *f* transport company; ~**tar** *vt* transport; (*em contas*) carry forward; ~**te** *m* transport; ~**te coletivo** public transport
transposto /trãs'postu/ *pp de* **transpor**
transtor|nar /trãstor'nar/ *vt* mess up <*papéis, casa*>; disrupt <*rotina, ambiente*>; disturb, upset <*pessoa*>; ~**nar-se** *vpr* <*pessoa*> be rattled; ~**no** /o/ *m* (*de casa, rotina*) disruption; (*de pessoa*) disturbance; (*contratempo*) upset
transver|sal /trãzver'saw/ (*pl* ~**sais**) *a* (**rua**) ~**sal** cross street; ~**so** /ɛ/ *a* transverse
transvi|ado /trãzvi'adu/ *a* wayward; ~**ar** *vt* lead astray
trapa|ça /tra'pasa/ *f* swindle; ~**cear** *vi* cheat; ~**ceiro** *a* crooked □ *m* cheat
trapa|lhada /trapa'ʎada/ *f* bungle; ~**lhão** *a* (*f* ~**lhona**) bungling □ *m* (*f* ~**lhona**) bungler
trapézio /tra'pɛziu/ *m* trapeze
trapezista /trape'zista/ *m/f* trapeze artist
trapo /'trapu/ *m* rag
traquéia /tra'kɛja/ *f* windpipe, trachea
traquejo /tra'keʒu/ *m* knack
traquinas /tra'kinas/ *a invar* mischievous
trás /tras/ *adv* **de** ~ from behind; **a roda de** ~ the back wheel; **de** ~ **para frente** back to front; **para** ~ backwards; **deixar para** ~ leave behind; **por** ~ **de** behind
traseiro /tra'zeru/ *a* rear, back □ *m* bottom
trasladar /trazla'dar/ *vt* transport
traspas|sado /traspa'sadu/ *a* <*paletó*> double-breasted; ~**sar** *vt* pierce
traste /'trastʃi/ *m* (*pessoa*) pain; (*coisa*) piece of junk
tra|tado /tra'tadu/ *m* (*pacto*) treaty; (*estudo*) treatise; ~**tamento** *m* treatment; (*título*) title; ~**tar** *vt* treat; negotiate <*preço, venda*> □ *vi* (*manter relações*) have dealings (**com** with); (*combinar*) negotiate (**com** with); ~**tar de** deal with; ~**tar alg de** *ou* **por** address s.o. as; ~**tar de voltar** (*tentar*) seek to return; (*resolver*) decide to return; ~**tar-se de** be a matter of; ~**tável** (*pl* ~**táveis**) *a* <*doença*> treatable; <*pessoa*> accommodating; ~**tos** *m pl* **maus** ~**tos** illtreatment
trator /tra'tor/ *m* tractor
trauma /'trawma/ *m* trauma; ~**tizante** *a* traumatic; ~**tizar** *vt* traumatize
tra|vão /tra'vãw/ *m* (*Port*) brake; ~**var** *vt* lock <*rodas, músculos*>; stop <*carro*>; block <*passagem*>; strike up <*amizade, conversa*>; wage <*luta, combate*> □ *vi* (*Port*) brake
trave /'travi/ *f* beam, joist; (*do gol*) crossbar
traves|sa /tra'vɛsa/ *f* (*trave*) crossbar; (*rua*) side street; (*prato*) dish; (*pente*) slide; ~**são** *m* dash; ~**seiro** *m* pillow; ~**sia** *f* crossing; ~**so** /e/ *a* <*criança*> naughty; ~**sura** *f* prank; *pl* mischief
travesti /traves'tʃi/ *m* transvestite; (*artista*) drag artist; ~**do** *a* in drag
trazer /tra'zer/ *vt* bring; bear <*nome, ferida*>; wear <*barba, chapéu, cabelo curto*>
trecho /'treʃu/ *m* (*de livro etc*) passage; (*de rua etc*) stretch
treco /'trɛku/ (*fam*) *m* (*coisa*) thing; (*ataque*) turn
trégua /'trɛgwa/ *f* truce; (*fig*) respite
trei|nador /trejna'dor/ *m* trainer; ~**namento** *m* training; ~**nar** *vt* train <*atleta, animal*>; practise <*língua etc*> □ *vi* <*atleta*> train;

<*pianista, principiante*> practise; ~**no** *m* training; (*um*) training session

trejeito /tre'ʒejtu/ *m* grimace

trela /'trɛla/ *f* lead, (*Amer*) leash

treliça /tre'lisa/ *f* trellis

trem /trẽj/ *m* train; ~ **de aterrissagem** undercarriage; ~ **de carga** goods train, (*Amer*) freight train

trema /'trema/ *m* dieresis

treme|deira /treme'dera/ *f* shiver; ~**licar** *vi* tremble; ~**luzir** *vi* glimmer, flicker

tremendo /tre'mẽdu/ *a* tremendous

tre|mer /tre'mer/ *vi* tremble; <*terra*> shake; ~**mor** *m* tremor; (*tremedeira*) shiver; ~**mular** *vi* <*bandeira*> flutter; <*luz, estrela*> glimmer, flicker

trêmulo /'tremulu/ *a* trembling; <*luz*> flickering

trena /'trena/ *f* tape measure

trenó /tre'nɔ/ *m* sledge, (*Amer*) sled; (*puxado a cavalos etc*) sleigh

tre|padeira /trepa'dera/ *f* climbing plant; ~**par** *vt* climb □ *vi* climb; (*chulo*) fuck

três /tres/ *a & m* three

tresloucado /trezlo'kadu/ *a* deranged

trevas /'trɛvas/ *f pl* darkness

trevo /'trevu/ *m* (*planta*) clover; (*rodoviário*) interchange

treze /'trezi/ *a & m* thirteen

trezentos /tre'zẽtus/ *a & m* three hundred

triagem /tri'aʒẽ/ *f* (*escolha*) selection; (*separação*) sorting; **fazer uma** ~ **de** sort

tri|angular /triãgu'lar/ *a* triangular; ~**ângulo** *m* triangle

tri|bal /tri'baw/ (*pl* ~**bais**) *a* tribal; ~**bo** *f* tribe

tribu|na /tri'buna/ *f* rostrum; ~**nal** (*pl* ~**nais**) *m* court

tribu|tação /tributa'sãw/ *f* taxation; ~**tar** *vt* tax; ~**tário** *a* tax □ *m* tributary; ~**to** *m* tribute

tri|cô /tri'ko/ *m* knitting; **artigos de** ~**cô** knitwear; ~**cotar** *vt/i* knit

tridimensio|nal /tridʒimẽsio'naw/ (*pl* ~**nais**) *a* three- dimensional

trigêmeo /tri'ʒemiu/ *m* triplet

trigésimo /tri'ʒɛzimu/ *a* thirtieth

tri|go /'trigu/ *m* wheat; ~**gueiro** *a* dark

trilha /'triʎa/ *f* path; (*pista, de disco*) track; ~ **sonora** soundtrack

trilhão /tri'ʎãw/ *m* billion, (*Amer*) trillion

trilho /'triʎu/ *m* track

trilogia /trilo'ʒia/ *f* trilogy

trimes|tral /trimes'traw/ (*pl* ~**trais**) *a* quarterly; ~**tre** /ɛ/ *m* quarter; (*do ano letivo*) term

trincar /trĩ'kar/ *vt/i* crack

trincheira /trĩ'ʃera/ *f* trench

trinco /'trĩku/ *m* latch

trindade /trĩ'dadʒi/ *f* trinity

trinta /'trĩta/ *a & m* thirty

trio /'triu/ *m* trio; ~ **elétrico** music float

tripa /'tripa/ *f* gut

tripé /tri'pɛ/ *m* tripod

tripli|car /tripli'kar/ *vt/i*, ~**car-se** *vpr* treble; ~**cata** *f* triplicate

triplo /'triplu/ *a & m* triple

tripu|lação /tripula'sãw/ *f* crew; ~**lante** *m/f* crew member; ~**lar** *vt* man

triste /'tristʃi/ *a* sad; ~**za** /e/ *f* sadness; **é uma** ~**za** (*fam*) it's pathetic

tritu|rador /tritura'dor/ *m* (*de papel*) shredder; ~**rador de lixo** waste disposal unit; ~**rar** *vt* shred <*legumes, papel*>; grind up <*lixo*>

triun|fal /triũ'faw/ (*pl* ~**fais**) *a* triumphal; ~**fante** *a* triumphant; ~**far** *vi* triumph; ~**fo** *m* triumph

trivi|al /trivi'aw/ (*pl* ~**ais**) *a* trivial; ~**alidade** *f* triviality; *pl* trivia

triz /tris/ *m* **por um** ~ narrowly, by a hair's breadth; **não foi atropelado por um** ~ he narrowly missed being knocked down

tro|ca /'trɔka/ *f* exchange; **em** ~**ca de** in exchange for; ~**cadilho** *m* pun; ~**cado** *m* change; ~**cador** *m* conductor; ~**car** *vt* (*dar e receber*) exchange (**por** for); change <*dinheiro, lençóis, lâmpada, lugares etc*>; (*transpor*) change round; (*confundir*) mix up; ~**car-se** *vpr* change; ~**car de roupa/trem/lugar** change clothes/trains/places; ~**ca-troca** *m* swap; ~**co** /o/ *m* change; **a** ~**co de quê?** what for?; **dar o** ~**co em alg** pay s.o. back

troço /'trɔsu/ (*fam*) *m* (*coisa*) thing; (*ataque*) turn; **me deu um** ~ I had a funny turn

troféu /tro'fɛw/ *m* trophy

trólebus /'trɔlebus/ *m invar* trolley bus

trom|ba /'trõba/ *f* (*de elefante*) trunk; (*cara amarrada*) long face; ~**bada** *f* crash; ~**ba-d'água** (*pl* ~**bas-d'água**) *f* downpour; ~**badinha** *m* bag snatcher; ~**bar** *vi* ~**bar com** crash into <*poste, carro*>; bump into <*pessoa*>

trombo|ne /trõ'bɔni/ *m* trombone; ~**nista** *m/f* trombonist

trompa /'trõpa/ *f* French horn; ~ **de Falópio** fallopian tube

trompe|te /trõ'pɛtʃi/ *m* trumpet; ~**tista** *m/f* trumpeter

tron|co /'trõku/ *m* trunk; ~**cudo** *a* stocky

trono /'tronu/ *m* throne

tropa /'trɔpa/ *f* troop; (*exército*) army; *pl* troops; ~ **de choque** riot police
trope|ção /trope'sãw/ *m* trip; (*erro*) slip-up; ~**çar** *vi* trip; (*errar*) slip up; ~**ço** /e/ *m* stumbling block
trôpego /'tropegu/ *a* unsteady
tropi|cal /tropi'kaw/ (*pl* ~**cais**) *a* tropical
trópico /'trɔpiku/ *m* tropic
tro|tar /tro'tar/ *vi* trot; ~**te** /ɔ/ *m* (*de cavalo*) trot; (*de estudantes*) practical joke; (*mentira*) hoax
trouxa /'troʃa/ *f* (*de roupa etc*) bundle □ *m/f* (*fam*) sucker □ *a* (*fam*) gullible
tro|vão /tro'vãw/ *m* clap of thunder; *pl* thunder; ~**vejar** *vi* thunder; ~**voada** *f* thunderstorm; ~**voar** *vi* thunder
trucidar /trusi'dar/ *vt* slaughter
trucu|lência /truku'lẽsia/ *f* barbarity; ~**lento** *a* (*cruel*) barbaric; (*brigão*) belligerent
trufa /'trufa/ *f* truffle
trunfo /'trũfu/ *m* trump; (*fig*) trump card
truque /'truki/ *m* trick
truta /'truta/ *f* trout
tu /tu/ *pron* you
tua /'tua/ *veja* **teu**
tuba /'tuba/ *f* tuba
tubarão /tuba'rãw/ *m* shark
tubá|rio /tu'bariu/ *a* **gravidez** ~**ria** ectopic pregnancy
tuberculose /tubercu'lɔzi/ *f* tuberculosis
tubo /'tubu/ *m* tube; (*no corpo*) duct
tubulação /tubula'sãw/ *f* ducting
tucano /tu'kanu/ *m* toucan
tudo /'tudu/ *pron* everything; ~ **bem?** (*cumprimento*) how are things?; ~ **de bom** all the best; **em** ~ **quanto é lugar** all over the place
tufão /tu'fãw/ *m* typhoon
tulipa /tu'lipa/ *f* tulip
tumba /'tũba/ *f* tomb
tumor /tu'mor/ *m* tumour; ~ **cerebral** brain tumour
túmulo /'tumulu/ *m* grave
tumul|to /tu'muwtu/ *m* commotion; (*motim*) riot; ~**tuado** *a* disorderly, rowdy; ~**tuar** *vt* disrupt □ *vi* cause a commotion; ~**tuoso** *a* tumultuous
tú|nel /'tunew/ (*pl* ~**neis**) *m* tunnel
túnica /'tunika/ *f* tunic
Tunísia /tu'nizia/ *f* Tunisia
tupiniquim /tupini'kĩ/ *a* Brazilian
turbante /tur'bãtʃi/ *m* turban
turbilhão /turbi'ʎãw/ *m* whirlwind
turbina /tur'bina/ *f* turbine
turbu|lência /turbu'lẽsia/ *f* turbulence; ~**lento** *a* turbulent
turco /'turku/ *a* & *m* Turkish
turfa /'turfa/ *f* peat
turfe /'turfe/ *m* horse-racing
turis|mo /tu'rizmu/ *m* tourism; **fazer** ~**mo** go sightseeing; ~**ta** *m/f* tourist
turístico /tu'ristʃiku/ *a* <*ponto, indústria*> tourist; <*viagem*> sightseeing
turma /'turma/ *f* group; (*na escola*) class
turnê /tur'ne/ *f* tour
turno /'turnu/ *m* (*de trabalho*) shift; (*de competição, eleição*) round
turquesa /tur'keza/ *m/f* & *a invar* turquoise
Turquia /tur'kia/ *f* Turkey
turra /'tuxa/ *f* **às** ~**s com** at loggerheads with
tur|var /tur'var/ *vt* cloud; ~**vo** *a* cloudy
tutano /tu'tanu/ *m* marrow
tutela /tu'tɛla/ *f* guardianship
tutor /tu'tor/ *m* guardian
tutu /tu'tu/ *m* (*vestido*) tutu; (*prato*) beans with bacon and manioc flour
TV /te've/ *f* TV

U

ubíquo /u'bikwu/ *a* ubiquitous
Ucrânia /u'krania/ *f* Ukraine
ucraniano /ukrani'anu/ *a* & *m* Ukrainian
ué /u'ɛ/ *int* hang on
ufa /'ufa/ *int* phew
ufanis|mo /ufa'nizmu/ *m* chauvinism; ~**ta** *a* & *m/f* chauvinist
Uganda /u'gãda/ *m* Uganda
ui /ui/ *int* (*de dor*) ouch; (*de nojo*) ugh; (*de espanto*) oh
uísque /u'iski/ *m* whisky
ui|var /ui'var/ *vi* howl; ~**vo** *m* howl
úlcera /'uwsera/ *f* ulcer
ulterior /uwteri'or/ *a* further
ulti|mamente /uwtʃima'mẽtʃi/ *adv* recently; ~**mar** *vt* finalize; ~**mato** *m* ultimatum
último /'uwtʃimu/ *a* last; <*moda, notícia etc*> latest; **em** ~ **caso** as a last resort; **nos** ~**s anos** in recent years; **por** ~ last
ultra|jante /uwtra'ʒãtʃi/ *a* offensive; ~**jar** *vt* offend; ~**je** *m* outrage
ultraleve /uwtra'lɛvi/ *m* microlite
ultra|mar /uwtra'mar/ *m* overseas; ~**marino** *a* overseas
ultrapas|sado /uwtrapa'sadu/ *a* outdated; ~**sagem** *f* overtaking, (*Amer*) passing; ~**sar** *vt* (*de carro*) overtake, (*Amer*) pass; (*ser superior a*) surpass; (*exceder*) exceed; (*extrapolar*) go beyond □ *vi* overtake, (*Amer*) pass
ultra-sonografia /uwtrasonogra'fia/ *f* ultrasound scan
ultravioleta /uwtravio'leta/ *a* ultraviolet

ulu|lante /ulu'lãtʃi/ *a* (*fig*) blatant; ~**lar** *vi* wail

um /ũ/ (*f* **uma**; *m pl* **uns**, *f pl* **umas**) *art* a, an; *pl* some □ *a & pron* one; ~ **ao outro** one another; **vieram umas 20 pessoas** about 20 people came

umbanda /ũ'bãda/ *m* Afro-Brazilian cult

umbigo /ũ'bigu/ *m* navel

umbili|cal /ũbili'kaw/ (*pl* ~**cais**) *a* umbilical

umedecer /umede'ser/ *vt* moisten; ~-**se** *vpr* moisten

umidade /umi'dadʒi/ *f* moisture; (*desagradável*) damp; (*do ar*) humidity

úmido /'umidu/ *a* moist; <*parede, roupa etc*> damp; <*ar, clima*> humid

unânime /u'nanimi/ *a* unanimous

unanimidade /unanimi'dadʒi/ *f* unanimity

undécimo /ũ'dɛsimu/ *a* eleventh

ungüento /ũ'gwẽtu/ *m* ointment

unha /'uɲa/ *f* nail; (*de animal, utensílio*) claw

unhar /u'ɲar/ *vt* claw

união /uni'ãw/ *f* union; (*concórdia*) unity; (*ato de unir*) joining

unicamente /unika'mẽtʃi/ *adv* only

único /'uniku/ *a* only; (*ímpar*) unique

uni|dade /uni'dadʒi/ *f* unit; ~**do** *a* united; <*família*> close

unifi|cação /unifika'sãw/ *f* unification; ~**car** *vt* unify

unifor|me /uni'fɔrmi/ *a* uniform; <*superfície*> even □ *m* uniform; ~**midade** *f* uniformity; ~**mizado** *a* <*policial etc*> uniformed; (*padronizado*) standardized; ~**zar** *vt* (*padronizar*) standardize

unilate|ral /unilate'raw/ (*pl* ~**rais**) *a* unilateral

unir /u'nir/ *vt* unite <*povo, nações, família etc*>; (*ligar, casar*) join; (*combinar*) combine (**a** *ou* **com** with); ~-**se** *vpr* (*aliar-se*) unite (**a** with); (*juntar-se*) join together; (*combinar-se*) combine (**a** *ou* **com** with)

unissex /uni'sɛks/ *a invar* unisex

uníssono /u'nisonu/ *m* **em** ~ in unison

univer|sal /univer'saw/ (*pl* ~**sais**) *a* universal

universi|dade /universi'dadʒi/ *f* university; ~**tário** *a* university □ *m* university student

universo /uni'vɛrsu/ *m* universe

untar /ũ'tar/ *vt* grease <*fôrma*>; spread <*pão*>; smear <*corpo, rosto etc*>

upa /'upa/ *int* (*incentivando*) upsadaisy; (*ao cair algo etc*) whoops

urânio /u'raniu/ *m* uranium

Urano /u'ranu/ *m* Uranus

urbanis|mo /urba'nizmu/ *m* town planning; ~**ta** *m/f* town planner

urbani|zado /urbani'zadu/ *a* built-up; ~**zar** *vt* urbanize

urbano /ur'banu/ *a* (*da cidade*) urban; (*refinado*) urbane

urdir /ur'dʒir/ *vt* weave; (*maquinar*) hatch

urdu /ur'du/ *m* Urdu

ur|gência /ur'ʒẽsia/ *f* urgency; ~**gente** *a* urgent; ~**gir** *vi* be urgent; <*tempo*> press; ~**ge irmos** we must go urgently

uri|na /u'rina/ *f* urine; ~**nar** *vt* pass □ *vi* urinate; ~**nol** (*pl* ~**nóis**) *m* (*penico*) chamber pot; (*em banheiro*) urinal

urna /'urna/ *f* (*para cinzas*) urn; (*para votos*) ballot box; *pl* (*fig*) polls

ur|rar /u'xar/ *vt/i* roar; ~**ro** *m* roar

urso /'ursu/ *m* bear; ~-**branco** (*pl* ~**s-brancos**) *m* polar bear

urti|cária /urtʃi'karia/ *f* nettle rash; ~**ga** *f* nettle

urubu /uru'bu/ *m* black vulture

Uruguai /uru'gwaj/ *m* Uruguay

uruguaio /uru'gwaju/ *a & m* Uruguayan

urze /'urzi/ *f* heather

usado /u'zadu/ *a* used; <*roupa*> worn; <*palavra*> common

usar /u'zar/ *vt* wear <*roupa, óculos, barba etc*>; ~ (**de**) (*utilizar*) use

usina /u'zina/ *f* plant; ~ **termonuclear** nuclear power station

uso /'uzu/ *m* use; (*de palavras, linguagem*) usage; (*praxe*) practice

usu|al /uzu'aw/ (*pl* ~**ais**) *a* common; ~**ário** *m* user; ~**fruir** *vt* enjoy <*coisas boas*>; have the use of <*prédio, jardim etc*>; ~**fruto** *m* use

usurário /uzu'rariu/ *a* money-grubbing □ *m* money-lender

usurpar /uzur'par/ *vt* usurp

uten|sílio /utẽ'siliu/ *m* utensil; ~**te** *m/f* (*Port*) user

útero /'uteru/ *m* uterus, womb

UTI /ute'i/ *f* intensive care unit

útil /'utʃiw/ (*pl* **úteis**) *a* useful; **dia** ~ workday

utili|dade /utʃili'dadʒi/ *f* usefulness; (*uma*) utility; ~**tário** *a* utilitarian; ~**zar** *vt* (*empregar*) use; (*tornar útil*) utilize; ~**zável** (*pl* ~**záveis**) *a* usable

utopia /uto'pia/ *f* Utopia

utópico /u'tɔpiku/ *a* Utopian

uva /'uva/ *f* grape

úvula /'uvula/ *f* uvula

V

vaca /'vaka/ *f* cow

vaci|lante /vasi'lãtʃi/ *a* wavering; <*luz*> flickering; ~**lar** *vi* waver;

<luz> flicker; (*fam: bobear*) slip up

vaci|na /va'sina/ *f* vaccine; **~nação** *f* vaccination; **~nar** *vt* vaccinate

vácuo /'vakuu/ *m* vacuum

va|diar /vadʒi'ar/ *vi* (*viver ocioso*) laze around; (*fazer cera*) mess about; **~dio** *a* idle □ *m* idler

vaga /'vaga/ *f* (*posto*) vacancy; (*para estacionar*) parking place

vagabun|dear /vagabũdʒi'ar/ *vi* (*perambular*) roam; (*vadiar*) laze around; **~do** *a* *<pessoa, vida>* idle; *<produto, objeto>* shoddy □ *m* tramp; (*pessoa vadia*) bum

vaga-lume /vaga'lumi/ *m* glow-worm

va|gão /va'gãw/ *m* (*de passageiros*) carriage, (*Amer*) car; (*de carga*) wagon; **~gão-leito** (*pl* **~gões-leitos**) *m* sleeping car; **~gão-restaurante** (*pl* **~gões-restaurantes**) *m* dining car

vagar[1] /va'gar/ *vi* *<pessoa>* wander about; *<barco>* drift

vagar[2] /va'gar/ *vi* *<cargo, apartamento>* become vacant

vagaroso /vaga'rozu/ *a* slow

vagem /'vaʒẽ/ *f* green bean

vagi|na /va'ʒina/ *f* vagina; **~nal** (*pl* **~nais**) *a* vaginal

vago[1] /'vagu/ *a* (*indefinido*) vague

vago[2] /'vagu/ *a* (*desocupado*) vacant; *<tempo>* spare

vaguear /vagi'ar/ *vi* roam

vai|a /'vaja/ *f* boo; **~ar** *vi* boo

vai|dade /vaj'dadʒi/ *f* vanity; **~doso** *a* vain

vaivém /vaj'vẽj/ *m* comings and goings, toing and froing

vala /'vala/ *f* ditch; **~ comum** mass grave

vale[1] /'vali/ *m* (*de rio etc*) valley

vale[2] /'vali/ *m* (*ficha*) voucher; **~ postal** postal order

valen|tão /valẽ'tãw/ *a* (*f* **~tona**) tough □ *m* tough guy; **~te** *a* brave; **~tia** *f* bravery; (*uma*) feat

valer /va'ler/ *vt* be worth □ *vi* be valid; **~ aco a alg** earn s.o. sth; **~-se de** avail o.s. of; **~ a pena** be worth it; **vale a pena tentar** it's worth trying; **mais vale desistir** it's better to give up; **vale tudo** anything goes; **fazer ~** enforce *<lei>*; stand up for *<direitos>*; **para ~** (*a sério*) for real; (*muito*) really

vale|-refeição /valirefej'sãw/ (*pl* **~s-refeição**) *m* luncheon voucher

valeta /va'leta/ *f* gutter

valete /va'lɛtʃi/ *m* jack

valia /va'lia/ *f* value

validar /vali'dar/ *vt* validate

válido /'validu/ *a* valid

valioso /vali'ozu/ *a* valuable

valise /va'lizi/ *f* travelling bag

valor /va'lor/ *m* value; (*valentia*) valour; *pl* (*títulos*) securities; **no ~ de** to the value of; **sem ~** worthless; **objetos de ~** valuables; **~ nominal** face value

valori|zação /valoriza'sãw/ *f* (*apreciação*) valuing; (*aumento no valor*) increase in value; **~zado** *a* highly valued; **~zar** *vt* (*apreciar*) value; (*aumentar o valor de*) increase the value of; **~zar-se** *vt* *<coisa>* increase in value; *<pessoa>* value o.s.

val|sa /'vawsa/ *f* waltz; **~sar** *vi* waltz

válvula /'vawvula/ *f* valve

vampiro /vã'piru/ *m* vampire

vandalismo /vãda'lizmu/ *m* vandalism

vândalo /'vãdalu/ *m* vandal

vangloriar-se /vãglori'arsi/ *vpr* brag (de about)

vanguarda /vã'gwarda/ *f* vanguard; (*de arte*) avant-garde

vanta|gem /vã'taʒẽ/ *f* advantage; **contar ~gem** boast; **levar ~gem** have the advantage (a over); **tirar ~gem de** take advantage of; **~joso** /o/ *a* advantageous

vão /vãw/ (*pl* **~s**) *a* (*f* **vã**) vain □ *m* gap; **em ~** in vain

vapor /va'por/ *m* (*fumaça*) steam; (*gás*) vapour; (*barco*) steamer; **máquina a ~** steam engine; **a todo ~** at full blast

vaporizar /vapori'zar/ *vt* vaporize; (*com spray*) spray

vaqueiro /va'keru/ *m* cowboy

vaquinha /va'kiɲa/ *f* collection, whip-round

vara /'vara/ *f* rod; **~ cível** civil district; **~ mágica** *ou* **de condão** magic wand

va|ral /va'raw/ (*pl* **~rais**) *m* washing line

varanda /va'rãda/ *f* veranda

varão /va'rãw/ *m* male

varar /va'rar/ *vt* (*furar*) pierce; (*passar por*) sweep through

varejão /vare'ʒão/ *m* wholesale store

varejeira /vare'ʒera/ *f* bluebottle

vare|jista /vare'ʒista/ *a* retail □ *m/f* retailer; **~jo** /e/ *m* retail trade; **vender a ~jo** sell retail

vari|ação /varia'sãw/ *f* variation; **~ado** *a* varied; **~ante** *a* & *f* variant; **~ar** *vt/i* vary; **para ~ar** for a change; **~ável** (*pl* **~áveis**) *a* variable; *<tempo>* changeable

varicela /vari'sɛla/ *f* chickenpox

variedade /varie'dadʒi/ *f* variety

vários /'varius/ *a pl* several

varíola /va'riola/ *f* smallpox

variz /va'ris/ *f* varicose vein

varo|nil /varo'niw/ (*pl* **~nis**) *a* manly

var|rer /va'xer/ *vt* sweep; (*fig*) sweep away; **~rido** *a* **um doido ~rido** a raving lunatic

Varsóvia /var'sɔvia/ *f* Warsaw

vasculhar /vasku'ʎar/ *vt* search through

vasectomia /vazekto'mia/ *f* vasectomy

vaselina /vaze'lina/ *f* vaseline

vasilha /va'ziʎa/ *f* jug

vaso /'vazu/ *m* pot; (*para flores*) vase; **~ sanguíneo** blood vessel

vassoura /va'sora/ *f* broom

vas|tidão /vastʃi'dãw/ *f* vastness; **~to** *a* vast

vatapá /vata'pa/ *m* spicy North-Eastern dish

Vaticano /vatʃi'kanu/ *m* Vatican

vati|cinar /vatʃisi'nar/ *vt* prophesy; **~cínio** *m* prophecy

va|zamento /vaza'mẽtu/ *m* leak; **~zante** *f* ebb tide; **~zão** *m* outflow; **dar ~zão a** (*fig*) give vent to; **~zar** *vt/i* leak

vazio /va'ziu/ *a* empty □ *m* emptiness; (*um*) void

veado /vi'adu/ *m* deer

ve|dação /veda'sãw/ *f* (*de casa, janela*) insulation; (*em motor etc*) gasket; **~dar** *vt* seal <*recipiente, abertura*>; stanch <*sangue*>; seal off <*saída, área*>; **~dar aco (a alg)** prohibit sth (for s.o.)

vedete /ve'dɛte/ *f* star

vee|mência /vee'mẽsia/ *f* vehemence; **~mente** *a* vehement

vege|tação /veʒeta'sãw/ *f* vegetation; **~tal** (*pl* **~tais**) *a & m* vegetable; **~tar** *vi* vegetate; **~tariano** *a & m* vegetarian

veia /'veja/ *f* vein

veicular /veiku'lar/ *vt* convey; place <*anúncios*>

veículo /ve'ikulu/ *m* vehicle; (*de comunicação etc*) medium

vela[1] /'vɛla/ *f* (*de barco*) sail; (*esporte*) sailing

vela[2] /'vɛla/ *f* candle; (*em motor*) spark plug; **segurar a ~** (*fam*) play gooseberry

velar[1] /ve'lar/ *vt* (*cobrir*) veil

velar[2] /ve'lar/ *vt* watch over □ *vi* keep vigil

veleidade /velej'dadʒi/ *f* whim

ve|leiro /ve'leru/ *m* sailing boat; **~lejar** *vi* sail

velhaco /ve'ʎaku/ *a* crooked □ *m* crook

ve|lharia /veʎa'ria/ *f* old thing; **~lhice** *f* old age; **~lho** /ɛ/ *a* old □ *m* old man; **~lhote** /ɔ/ *m* old man

velocidade /velosi'dadʒi/ *f* speed; (*Port: marcha*) gear; **a toda ~** at full speed; **~ máxima** speed limit

velocímetro /velo'simetru/ *m* speedometer

velocista /velo'sista/ *m/f* sprinter

velório /ve'lɔriu/ *m* wake

veloz /ve'los/ *a* fast

veludo /ve'ludu/ *m* velvet; **~ cotelê** corduroy

ven|cedor /vẽse'dor/ *a* winning □ *m* winner; **~cer** *vt* win over <*adversário etc*>; win <*partida, corrida, batalha*> □ *vi* (*triunfar*) win; <*prestação, aluguel, dívida*> fall due; <*contrato, passaporte, prazo*> expire; <*apólice*> mature; **~cido** *a* **dar-se por ~cido** give in; **~cimento** *m* (*de dívida, aluguel*) due date; (*de contrato, prazo*) expiry date; (*de alimento, remédio etc*) best before date; (*salário*) payment; *pl* earnings

venda[1] /'vẽda/ *f* sale; (*loja*) general store; **à ~** on sale; **pôr à ~** put up for sale

ven|da[2] /'vẽda/ *f* blindfold; **~dar** *vt* blindfold

venda|val /vẽda'vaw/ (*pl* **~vais**) *m* gale, storm

ven|dável /vẽ'davew/ (*pl* **~dáveis**) *a* saleable; **~dedor** *m* (*de loja*) shop assistant; (*em geral*) seller; **~der** *vt/i* sell; **estar ~dendo saúde** be bursting with health

vendeta /vẽ'deta/ *f* vendetta

veneno /ve'nenu/ *m* poison; (*de cobra etc, malignidade*) venom; **~so** /o/ *a* poisonous; (*maldoso*) venomous

vene|ração /venera'sãw/ *f* reverence; (*de Deus etc*) worship; **~rar** *vt* revere; worship <*Deus etc*>

vené|reo /ve'nɛriu/ *a* **doença ~rea** venereal disease

Veneza /ve'neza/ *f* Venice

veneziana /venezi'ana/ *f* shutter

Venezuela /venezu'ɛla/ *f* Venezuela

venezuelano /venezue'lanu/ *a & m* Venezuelan

venta /'vẽta/ *f* nostril

ven|tania /vẽta'nia/ *f* gale; **~tar** *vi* be windy; **~tarola** /ɔ/ *f* fan

venti|lação /vẽtʃila'sãw/ *f* ventilation; **~lador** *m* fan; **~lar** *vt* ventilate; air <*sala, roupa*>

ven|to /'vẽtu/ *m* wind; **de ~to em popa** smoothly; **~toinha** *f* (*cata-vento*) weather vane; (*Port: ventilador*) fan; **~tosa** /ɔ/ *f* sucker; **~toso** /o/ *a* windy

ven|tre /'vẽtri/ *m* belly; **~tríloquo** *m* ventriloquist

Vênus /'venus/ *f* Venus

ver /ver/ *vt* see; watch <*televisão*>; (*resolver*) see to □ *vi* see □ *m* **a meu ~** in my view; **~-se** *vpr* (*no espelho* *etc*) see o.s.; (*em estado, condição*) find o.s.; (*um ao outro*) see each other; **ter a ~ com** have to do with; **vai ~ que ela não sabe** (*fam*) I bet she doesn't know; **vê se você não volta tarde** see you don't get back late; **viu?** (*fam*) right?

veracidade /verasi'dadʒi/ *f* truthfulness

vera|near /verani'ar/ *vi* spend the summer; **~neio** *m* summer holiday, (*Amer*) summer vacation; **~nista** *m/f* holidaymaker, (*Amer*) vacationer

verão /ve'rãw/ *m* summer

veraz /ve'ras/ *a* truthful

verbas /'vɛrbas/ *f pl* funds

ver|bal /ver'baw/ (*pl* **~bais**) *a* verbal; **~bete** /e/ *m* entry; **~bo** *m* verb; **~borragia** *f* waffle; **~boso** /o/ *a* verbose

verda|de /ver'dadʒi/ *f* truth; **de ~de** <*coisa*> real; <*fazer*> really; **na ~de** actually; **para falar a ~de** to tell the truth; **~deiro** *a* <*declaração, pessoa*> truthful; (*real*) true

verde /'verdʒi/ *a & m* green; **jogar ~ para colher maduro** fish for information; **~-abacate** *a invar* avocado; **~-amarelo** *a* yellow and green; (*brasileiro*) Brazilian; (*nacionalista*) nationalistic; **~-esmeralda** *a invar* emerald green; **~jar** *vi* turn green

verdu|ra /ver'dura/ *f* (*para comer*) greens; (*da natureza*) greenery; **~reiro** *m* greengrocer, (*Amer*) produce dealer

vereador /veria'dor/ *m* councillor

vereda /ve'reda/ *f* path

veredito /vere'dʒitu/ *m* verdict

vergar /ver'gar/ *vt/i* bend

vergo|nha /ver'goɲa/ *f* (*pudor*) shame; (*constrangimento*) embarrassment; (*timidez*) shyness; (*uma*) disgrace; **ter ~nha** be ashamed; be embarrassed; be shy; **cria** *ou* **tome ~nha na cara!** you should be ashamed of yourself!; **~nhoso** *a* shameful

verídico /ve'ridʒiku/ *a* true

verificar /verifi'kar/ *vt* check, verify <*fatos, dados etc*>; **~ que** ascertain that; **~ se** check that; **~-se** *vpr* <*previsão etc*> come true; <*acidente etc*> happen

verme /'vɛrmi/ *m* worm

verme|lhidão /vermeʎi'dãw/ *f* redness; **~lho** /e/ *a & m* red; **no ~lho** (*endividado*) in the red

vernáculo /ver'nakulu/ *a & m* vernacular

verniz /ver'nis/ *f* varnish; (*couro*) patent leather

veros|símil /vero'simiw/ (*pl* **~símeis**) *a* plausible; **~similhança** *f* plausibility

verruga /ve'xuga/ *f* wart

ver|sado /ver'sadu/ *a* well-versed (**em** in); **~são** *f* version; **~sar** *vi* **~sar sobre** concern; **~sátil** (*pl* **~sáteis**) *a* versatile; **~satilidade** *f* versatility; **~sículo** *m* (*da Bíblia*) verse; **~so**[1] /ɛ/ *m* verse

verso[2] /ɛ/ *m* (*de página*) reverse, other side; **vide ~** see over

vértebra /'vɛrtebra/ *f* vertebra

verte|brado /verte'bradu/ *a & m* vertebrate; **~bral** (*pl* **~brais**) *a* spinal

ver|tente /ver'tẽtʃi/ *f* slope; **~ter** *vt* (*derramar*) pour; shed <*lágrimas, sangue*>; (*traduzir*) render (**para** into)

verti|cal /vertʃi'kaw/ (*pl* **~cais**) *a & f* vertical; **~gem** *f* dizziness; **~ginoso** /o/ *a* dizzy

vesgo /'vezgu/ *a* cross-eyed

vesícula /ve'zikula/ *f* gall bladder

vespa /'vespa/ *f* wasp

véspera /'vɛspera/ *f* **a ~** the day before; **a ~ de** the eve of; **a ~ de Natal** Christmas Eve; **nas ~s de** on the eve of

vespertino /vesper'tʃinu/ *a* evening

ves|te /'vɛstʃi/ *f* robe; **~tiário** *m* (*para se trocar*) changing room; (*para guardar roupa*) cloakroom

vestibular /vestʃibu'lar/ *m* university entrance exam

vestíbulo /ves'tʃibulu/ *m* hall(way); (*do teatro*) foyer

vestido /ves'tʃidu/ *m* dress □ *a* dressed (**de** in)

vestígio /ves'tʃiʒiu/ *m* trace

ves|timenta /vestʃi'mẽta/ *f* (*de sacerdote*) vestments; **~tir** *vt* (*pôr*) put on; (*usar*) wear; (*pôr roupa em*) dress; (*dar roupa a*) clothe; **~tir-se** *vpr* dress; **~tir-se de branco/de padre** dress in white/as a priest; **~tuário** *m* clothing

vetar /ve'tar/ *vt* veto

veterano /vete'ranu/ *a & m* veteran

veterinário /veteri'nariu/ *a* veterinary □ *m* vet

veto /'vɛtu/ *m* veto

véu /vɛw/ *m* veil

vexa|me /ve'ʃami/ *m* disgrace; **dar um ~me** make a fool of o.s.; **~minoso** /o/ *a* disgraceful

vexar /ve'ʃar/ *vt* shame; **~-se** *vpr* be ashamed (**de** of)

vez /ves/ *f* (*ocasião*) time; (*turno*) turn; **às ~es** sometimes; **cada ~ mais** more and more; **de ~** for good; **desta ~** this time; **de ~ em quando** now and again, from time to time; **de uma ~** (*ao mesmo tempo*) at once; (*de um *golpe*) in one go; de uma ~ por todas once and for all; duas ~es twice; em ~ de instead of; fazer as ~es de take the place of; mais uma ~, outra ~ again; muitas ~es (*com muita freqüência*) often; (*repetidamente*) many times; raras ~es seldom; repetidas ~es repeatedly; uma ~ once; uma ~ que since

via /'via/ *f* (*estrada*) road; (*rumo, meio*) way; (*exemplar*) copy; *pl* (*trâmites*) channels □ *prep* via; em ~s de on the point of; por ~ aérea/marítima by air/sea; por ~ das dúvidas just in case; por ~ de regra as a rule; Via Láctea Milky Way

viabili|dade /viabili'dadʒi/ *f* feasibility; ~**zar** *vt* make feasible

viação /via'sãw/ *f* (*transporte*) road transport; (*estradas*) road network; (*companhia*) bus company

viaduto /via'dutu/ *m* viaduct; (*rodoviário*) flyover, (*Amer*) overpass

via|gem /vi'aʒẽ/ *f* (*uma*) trip, journey; (*em geral*) travelling; *pl* (*de uma pessoa*) travels; (*em geral*) travel; boa ~gem! have a good trip!; ~gem de negócios business trip; ~**jado** *a* well-travelled; ~**jante** *a* travelling □ *m/f* traveller; ~**jar** *vi* travel; estar ~jando (*fam*) (*com o pensamento longe*) be miles away

viário /vi'ariu/ *a* road; anel ~ ring road

viatura /via'tura/ *f* vehicle

viá|vel /vi'avew/ (*pl* ~veis) *a* feasible

víbora /'vibora/ *f* viper

vi|bração /vibra'sãw/ *f* vibration; (*fig*) thrill; ~**brante** *a* vibrant; ~**brar** *vt* shake □ *vi* vibrate; (*fig*) be thrilled (com by)

vice /'visi/ *m/f* deputy

vice-cam|peão /visikãpi'ãw/ *m* (*f* ~peã) runner-up

vicejar /vise'ʒar/ *vi* flourish

vice-presiden|te /visiprezi'dẽtʃi/ *m* (*f* ~ta) vice-president

vice-rei /visi'xej/ *m* viceroy

vice-versa /visi'vɛrsa/ *adv* vice-versa

vici|ado /visi'adu/ *a* addicted (em to) □ *m* addict; um ~ado em drogas a drug addict; ~**ar** *vt* (*falsificar*) tamper with; (*estragar*) ruin □ *vi* <*droga*> be addictive; ~**ar-se** *vpr* get addicted (em to)

vício /'visiu/ *m* vice

vicioso /visi'ozu/ *a* círculo ~ vicious circle

vicissitudes /visisi'tudʒis/ *f pl* ups and downs

viço /'visu/ *m* (*de plantas*) exuberance; (*de pessoa, pele*) freshness; ~**so** /o/ *a* <*planta*> lush; <*pele, pessoa*> fresh

vida /'vida/ *f* life; sem ~ lifeless; dar ~ a liven up

videira /vi'dera/ *f* vine

vidente /vi'dẽtʃi/ *m/f* clairvoyant

vídeo /'vidʒiu/ *m* video; (*tela*) screen

video|cassete /vidʒiuka'sɛtʃi/ *m* (*fita*) video tape; (*aparelho*) video, (*Amer*) VCR; ~**clipe** *m* video; ~**clube** *m* video club; ~**game** *m* videogame; ~**teipe** *m* video tape

vidra|ça /vi'drasa/ *f* window pane; ~**çaria** *f* (*fábrica*) glassworks; (*vidraças*) glazing; ~**ceiro** *m* glazier

vi|drado /vi'dradu/ *a* glazed; estar ~drado em *ou* por (*fam*) love; ~**drar** *vt* glaze □ *vi* (*fam*) fall in love (em *ou* por with); ~**dro** *m* (*material*) glass; (*pote*) jar; (*janela*) window; ~dro fumê tinted glass

viela /vi'ɛla/ *f* alley

Viena /vi'ɛna/ *f* Vienna

Vietnã /vietʃi'nã/ *m*, (*Port*) **Vietname** /viet'nam/ *m* Vietnam

vietnamita /vietna'mita/ *a* & *m/f* Vietnamese

viga /'viga/ *f* joist

vigarice /viga'risi/ *f* swindle

vigário /vi'gariu/ *m* vicar

vigarista /viga'rista/ *m/f* swindler, con artist

vi|gência /vi'ʒẽsia/ *f* (*qualidade*) force; (*tempo*) period in force; ~**gente** *a* in force

vigésimo /vi'ʒɛzimu/ *a* twentieth

vigi|a /vi'ʒia/ *f* (*guarda*) watch; (*em navio*) porthole □ *m* night watchman; ~**ar** *vt* (*observar*) watch; (*cuidar de*) watch over; (*como sentinela*) guard □ *vi* keep watch

vigi|lância /viʒi'lãsia/ *f* vigilance; ~**lante** *a* vigilant

vigília /vi'ʒilia/ *f* vigil

vigor /vi'gor/ *m* vigour; em ~ in force

vigo|rar /vigo'rar/ *vi* be in force; ~**roso** *a* vigorous

vil /viw/ (*pl* vis) *a* base, despicable

vila /'vila/ *f* (*cidadezinha*) small town; (*casa elegante*) villa; (*conjunto de casas*) housing estate; ~ olímpica Olympic village

vi|lania /vila'nia/ *f* villainy; ~**lão** *m* (*f* ~lã) villain

vilarejo /vila'reʒu/ *m* village

vilipendiar /vilipẽdʒi'ar/ *vt* disparage

vime /'vimi/ *m* wicker

vina|gre /vi'nagri/ *m* vinegar; ~**grete** /ɛ/ *m* vinaigrette

vin|car /vĩ'kar/ *vt* crease; line <*rosto*>; ~**co** *m* crease; (*no rosto*) line

vincular /vĩku'lar/ *vt* bond, tie

vínculo /'vĩkulu/ *m* link, bond; ~ empregatício contract of employment

vinda /'vĩda/ *f* coming; **dar as boas ~s** a welcome

vindicar /vĩdʒi'kar/ *vt* vindicate

vindima /vĩ'dʒima/ *f* vintage

vin|do /'vĩdu/ *pp e pres de* vir; **~douro** *a* coming

vin|gança /vĩ'gãsa/ *f* vengeance, revenge; **~gar** *vt* revenge □ *vi* <*flores*> thrive; <*criança*> survive; <*plano, empreendimento*> be successful; **~gar-se** *vpr* take one's revenge (**de** for; **em** on); **~gativo** *a* vindictive

vinha /'viɲa/ *f* vineyard

vinhedo /vi'ɲedu/ *m* vineyard

vinheta /vi'ɲeta/ *f* (*na TV etc*) sequence

vinho /'viɲu/ *m* wine □ *a invar* maroon; **~ do Porto** port

vinícola /vi'nikola/ *a* wine-growing

vinicul|tor /vinikuw'tor/ *m* wine grower; **~tura** *f* wine growing

vinil /vi'niw/ *m* vinyl

vinte /'vĩtʃi/ *a & m* twenty; **~na** /e/ *f* score

viola /vi'ɔla/ *f* viola

violação /viola'sãw/ *f* violation

violão /vio'lãw/ *m* guitar

violar /vio'lar/ *vt* violate

vio|lência /vio'lẽsia/ *f* violence; (*uma*) act of violence; **~lentar** *vt* rape <*mulher*>; **~lento** *a* violent

violeta /vio'leta/ *f* violet □ *a invar* violet

violi|nista /violi'nista/ *m/f* violinist; **~no** *m* violin

violonce|lista /violõse'lista/ *m/f* cellist; **~lo** /ɛ/ *m* cello

vir /vir/ *vi* come; **o ano que vem** next year; **venho lendo os jornais** I have been reading the papers; **vem cá** come here; (*fam*) listen; **isso não vem ao caso** that's irrelevant; **~ a ser** turn out to be; **~ com** give <*argumento etc*>

virabrequim /virabre'kĩ/ *m* crankshaft

viração /vira'sãw/ *f* breeze

vira-casaca /viraka'zaka/ *m/f* turncoat

vira|da /vi'rada/ *f* turn; **~do** *a* <*roupa*> inside out; (*de cabeça para baixo*) upside down; **~do para** facing

vira-lata /vira'lata/ *m* mongrel

virar /vi'rar/ *vt* turn; turn over <*disco, barco etc*>; turn inside out <*roupa*>; turn out <*bolsos*>; tip <*balde, água etc*> □ *vi* turn; <*barco*> turn over; (*tornar-se*) become; **~-se** *vpr* turn round; (*na vida*) get by, cope; **~-se para** turn to; **vira e mexe** every so often

viravolta /vira'vɔwta/ *f* about-turn

virgem /'virʒẽ/ *a* <*fita*> blank; <*floresta, noiva etc*> virgin □ *f* virgin; **Virgem** (*signo*) Virgo

virgindade /virʒĩ'dadʒi/ *f* virginity

vírgula /'virgula/ *f* comma; (*decimal*) point

vi|ril /vi'riw/ (*pl* **~ris**) *a* virile

virilha /vi'riʎa/ *f* groin

virilidade /virili'dadʒi/ *f* virility

virtu|al /virtu'aw/ (*pl* **~ais**) *a* virtual

virtude /vir'tudʒi/ *f* virtue

virtuo|sismo /virtuo'zizmu/ *m* virtuosity; **~so** /o/ *a* virtuous □ *m* virtuoso

virulento /viru'lẽtu/ *a* virulent

vírus /'virus/ *m invar* virus

visão /vi'zãw/ *f* vision; (*aspecto, ponto de vista*) view

visar /vi'zar/ *vt* aim at <*caça, alvo*>; **~ (a)** aim for <*objetivo*>; <*medida, ação*> be aimed at

vísceras /'viseras/ *f pl* innards

viscon|de /vis'kõdʒi/ *m* viscount; **~dessa** /e/ *f* viscountess

viscoso /vis'kozu/ *a* viscous

viseira /vi'zera/ *f* visor

visibilidade /vizibili'dadʒi/ *f* visibility

visionário /vizio'nariu/ *a & m* visionary

visi|ta /vi'zita/ *f* visit; (*visitante*) visitor; **fazer uma ~ta a alg** pay s.o. a visit; **~tante** *a* visiting □ *m/f* visitor; **~tar** *vt* visit

visí|vel /vi'zivew/ (*pl* **~veis**) *a* visible

vislum|brar /vizlũ'brar/ *vt* (*entrever*) glimpse; (*imaginar*) envisage; **~bre** *m* glimpse

visom /vi'zõ/ *m* mink

visor /vi'zor/ *m* viewfinder

vis|ta /'vista/ *f* sight; (*dos olhos*) eyesight; (*panorama*) view; **à ~ta** (*visível*) in view; (*em dinheiro*) in cash; **à primeira ~ta** at first sight; **pôr à ~ta** put on show; **de ~ta** <*conhecer*> by sight; **em ~ta de** in view of; **ter em ~ta** have in view; **dar na ~ta** attract attention; **fazer ~ta** look nice; **fazer ~ta grossa** turn a blind eye (**a** to); **perder de ~ta** lose sight of; **a perder de ~ta** as far as the eye can see; **uma ~ta de olhos** a quick look; **~to** *a* seen □ *m* visa; **pelo ~to** by the looks of things; **~to que** seeing that

visto|ria /visto'ria/ *f* inspection; **~riar** *vt* inspect

vistoso /vis'tozu/ *a* eye-catching

visu|al /vizu'aw/ (*pl* **~ais**) *a* visual □ *m* look; **~alizar** *vt* visualize

vi|tal /vi'taw/ (*pl* **~tais**) *a* vital; **~talício** *a* for life; **~talidade** *f* vitality

vita|mina /vita'mina/ *f* vitamin; (*bebida*) liquidized fruit drink; **~minado** *a* with added vitamins; **~mínico** *a* vitamin
vitela /vi'tɛla/ *f* (*carne*) veal
viticultura /vitʃikuw'tura/ *f* viticulture
vítima /'vitʃima/ *f* victim
viti|mar /vitʃi'mar/ *vt* (*matar*) claim the life of; **ser ~mado por** fall victim to
vitória /vi'tɔria/ *f* victory
vitorioso /vitori'ozu/ *a* victorious
vi|tral /vi'traw/ (*pl* **~trais**) *m* stained glass window
vitrine /vi'trini/ *f* shop window
vitrola /vi'trɔla/ *f* jukebox
viú|va /vi'uva/ *f* widow; **~vo** *a* widowed □ *m* widower
viva /'viva/ *f* cheer □ *int* hurray; **~ a rainha** long live the queen
vivacidade /vivasi'dadʒi/ *f* vivacity
vivalma /vi'vawma/ *f* **não há ~ lá fora** there's not a soul outside
vivar /vi'var/ *vt/i* cheer
vivaz /vi'vas/ *a* lively, vivacious; <*planta*> hardy
viveiro /vi'veru/ *m* (*de plantas*) nursery; (*de peixes*) fishpond; (*de aves*) aviary; (*fig*) breeding ground
vivência /vi'vẽsia/ *f* experience
vívido /'vividu/ *a* vivid
viver /vi'ver/ *vt/i* live (de on) □ *m* life; **ele vive reclamando** he's always complaining
víveres /'viveris/ *m pl* provisions
vivissecção /vivisek'sãw/ *f* vivisection
vivo /'vivu/ *a* (*que vive*) living; (*animado*) lively; <*cor*> bright □ *m* **os ~s** the living; **ao ~** live; **estar ~** be alive; **dinheiro ~** cash
vizi|nhança /vizi'ɲãsa/ *f* neighbourhood; **~nho** *a* neighbouring □ *m* neighbour
vo|ador /voa'dor/ *a* flying; **~ar** *vi* fly; (*explodir*) blow up; **sair ~ando** rush off
vocabulário /vokabu'lariu/ *m* vocabulary
vocábulo /vo'kabulu/ *m* word
voca|ção /voka'sãw/ *f* vocation; **~cional** (*pl* **~cionais**) *a* vocational; **orientação ~cional** careers guidance
vo|cal /vo'kaw/ (*pl* **~cais**) *a* vocal
você /vo'se/ *pron* you; **~s** *pron* you
vociferar /vosife'rar/ *vi* shout abuse
vodca /'vɔdʒka/ *f* vodka
voga /'vɔga/ *f* (*moda*) vogue
vo|gal /vo'gaw/ (*pl* **~gais**) *f* vowel
volante /vo'lãtʃi/ *m* (*de carro*) steering wheel
volá|til /vo'latʃiw/ (*pl* **~teis**) *a* volatile
vôlei /'volej/ *m*, **voleibol** /volej'bɔw/ *m* volleyball
volt /'vɔwtʃi/ (*pl* **~s**) *m* volt
volta /'vɔwta/ *f* (*retorno*) return; (*da pista*) lap; (*resposta*) response; **às ~s com** tied up with; **de ~** back; **em ~ de** around; **na ~** on the way back; **na ~ do correio** by return of post; **por ~ de** around; **dar a ~ ao mundo** go round the world; **dar a ~ por cima** make a comeback; **dar meia ~** turn round; **dar uma ~** (*a pé*) go for a walk; (*de carro*) go for a drive; **dar uma ~ em** turn round; **dar ~s** spin round; **ter ~** get a response; **~ e meia** every so often; **~do** *a* **~do para** geared towards
voltagem /vow'taʒẽ/ *f* voltage
voltar /vow'tar/ *vi* go/come back, return □ *vt* rewind <*fita*>; **~-se** *vpr* turn round; **~-se para/contra** turn to/against; **~ a si** come to; **~ a fazer** do again; **~ atrás** backtrack
volu|me /vo'lumi/ *m* volume; **~moso** *a* sizeable; <*som*> loud
voluntário /volũ'tariu/ *a & m* volunteer
volúpia /vo'lupia/ *f* sensuality, lust
voluptuoso /voluptu'ozu/ *a* sensual; <*mulher*> voluptuous
volú|vel /vo'luvew/ (*pl* **~veis**) *a* fickle
vomitar /vomi'tar/ *vt/i* vomit
vômito /'vomitu/ *m* vomit; *pl* vomiting
vontade /võ'tadʒi/ *f* will; **à ~** (*bem*) at ease; (*quanto quiser*) as much as one likes; **fique à ~** make yourself at home; **tem comida à ~** there's plenty of food; **estar com ~ de** feel like; **isso me dá ~ de chorar** it makes me feel like crying; **fazer a ~ de alg** do what s.o. wants
vôo /'vou/ *m* flight; **levantar ~** take off; **~ livre** hang-gliding
voraz /vo'ras/ *a* voracious
vos /vus/ *pron* you; (*a vocês*) to you
vós /vɔs/ *pron* you
vosso /'vɔsu/ *a* your □ *pron* yours
vo|tação /vota'sãw/ *f* vote; **~tante** *m/f* voter; **~tar** *vt* vote on <*lei etc*>; (*dedicar*) devote; (*prometer*) vow □ *vi* vote (em for)
voto /'vɔtu/ *m* (*em votação*) vote; (*promessa*) vow; *pl* (*desejos*) wishes
vo|vó /vo'vɔ/ *f* grandma; **~vô** *m* grandpa
voz /vɔs/ *f* voice; **dar ~ de prisão a alg** place s.o. under arrest
vozeirão /voze'rãw/ *m* loud voice
vozerio /voze'riu/ *m* shouting
vul|cânico /vuw'kaniku/ *a* volcanic; **~cão** *m* volcano

vul|gar /vuw'gar/ *a* ordinary; (*baixo*) vulgar; ~**garizar** *vt* popularize; (*tornar baixo*) vulgarize; ~**go** *adv* commonly known as
vulne|rabilidade /vuwnerabili'dadʒi/ *f* vulnerability; ~**rável** (*pl* ~**ráveis**) *a* vulnerable
vul|to /'vuwtu/ *m* (*figura*) figure; (*tamanho*) bulk; (*importância*) importance; de ~to important; ~**toso** /o/ *a* bulky; (*importante*) important

W

walkie-talkie /uɔki'tɔki/ (*pl* ~s) *m* walkie-talkie
walkman /uɔk'mɛn/ *m invar* walkman
watt /u'ɔtʃi/ (*pl* ~s) *m* watt
windsur|fe /uĩ'surfi/ *m* windsurfing; ~**fista** *m/f* windsurfer

X

xadrez /ʃa'dres/ *m* (*jogo*) chess; (*desenho*) check; (*fam: prisão*) prison □ *a invar* check
xale /'ʃali/ *m* shawl
xampu /ʃã'pu/ *m* shampoo
xará /ʃa'ra/ *m/f* namesake
xarope /ʃa'rɔpi/ *m* syrup
xaxim /ʃa'ʃĩ/ *m* plant fibre
xenofobia /ʃenofo'bia/ *f* xenophobia
xenófobo /ʃe'nɔfobu/ *a* xenophobic □ *m* xenophobe
xepa /'ʃepa/ *f* scraps
xeque[1] /'ʃɛki/ *m* (*árabe*) sheikh
xeque[2] /'ʃɛki/ *m* (*no xadrez*) check; ~**-mate** *m* checkmate
xere|ta /ʃe'reta/ (*fam*) *a* nosy □ *m/f* nosy parker; ~**tar** (*fam*) *vi* nose around
xerez /ʃe'res/ *m* sherry
xerife /ʃe'rifi/ *m* sheriff
xerocar /ʃero'kar/ *vt* photocopy
xerox /ʃe'rɔks/ *m invar* photocopy
xexelento /ʃeʃe'lẽtu/ (*fam*) *a* scruffy □ *m* scruff
xícara /'ʃikara/ *f* cup
xiita /ʃi'ita/ *a* & *m/f* Shiite
xilofone /ʃilo'foni/ *m* xylophone
xingar /ʃĩ'gar/ *vt* swear at □ *vi* swear
xis /ʃis/ *m invar* letter X; o ~ do problema the crux of the problem
xixi /ʃi'ʃi/ (*fam*) *m* wee; fazer ~ do a wee
xô /ʃo/ *int* shoo
xucro /'ʃukru/ *a* ignorant

Z

zagueiro /za'geru/ *m* fullback
Zaire /'zajri/ *m* Zaire
Zâmbia /'zãbia/ *f* Zambia
zan|gado /zã'gadu/ *a* cross, annoyed; ~**gar** *vt* annoy; ~**garse** *vpr* get cross, get annoyed (com with)
zanzar /zã'zar/ *vi* wander
zarpar /zar'par/ *vi* set off; (*de navio*) set sail
zebra /'zebra/ *f* zebra; (*pessoa*) fool; (*resultado*) upset
ze|lador /zela'dor/ *m* caretaker, (*Amer*) janitor; ~**lar** *vt* ~lar (por) take care of; ~**lo** /e/ *m* zeal; ~lo por devotion to; ~**loso** /o/ *a* zealous
zero /'zɛru/ *m* zero; (*em escores*) nil; ~**-quilômetro** *a invar* brand new
ziguezague /zigi'zagi/ *m* zigzag; ~**ar** *vi* zigzag
Zimbábue /zĩ'babui/ *m* Zimbabwe
zinco /'zĩku/ *m* zinc
zíper /'ziper/ *m* zip, zipper
zodíaco /zo'dʒiaku/ *m* zodiac
zoeira /zo'era/ *f* din
zom|bador /zõba'dor/ *a* mocking; ~**bar** *vi* ~bar (de) mock; ~**baria** *f* mockery
zona /'zona/ *f* (*área*) zone; (*de cidade*) district; (*desordem*) mess; (*tumulto*) commotion; (*bairro do meretrício*) red-light district
zonzo /'zõzu/ *a* dizzy
zôo /'zou/ *m* zoo
zoo|logia /zoolo'ʒia/ *f* zoology; ~**lógico** *a* zoological
zoólogo /zo'ɔlogu/ *m* zoologist
zulu /zu'lu/ *a* & *m/f* Zulu
zum /zũ/ *m* zoom lens
zumbi /zũ'bi/ *m* zombie
zum|bido /zũ'bidu/ *m* buzz; (*no ouvido*) ringing; ~**bir** *vi* buzz
zu|nido /zu'nidu/ *m* (*de vento, bala*) whistle; (*de inseto*) buzz; ~**nir** *vi* <*vento, bala*> whistle; <*inseto*> buzz
zunzum /zũ'zũ/ *m* rumour
Zurique /zu'riki/ *f* Zurich
zurrar /zu'xar/ *vi* bray

ENGLISH-PORTUGUESE
INGLÊS-PORTUGUÊS

A

a /ə/; *emphatic* /eɪ/ (*before vowel* an /ən/; *emphatic* /æn/) *a* um. **two pounds a metre** duas libras o metro. **sixty miles an hour** sessenta milhas por hora, (*P*) à hora. **once a year** uma vez por ano
aback /ə'bæk/ *adv* **taken ~** desconcertado, (*P*) surpreendido
abandon /ə'bændən/ *vt* abandonar □ *n* abandono *m*. **~ed** *a* abandonado; (*behaviour*) livre, dissoluto. **~ment** *n* abandono *m*
abashed /ə'bæʃt/ *a* confuso, (*P*) atrapalhado
abate /ə'beɪt/ *vt/i* abater, abrandar, diminuir. **~ment** *n* abrandamento *m*, diminuição *f*
abattoir /'æbətwa:(r)/ *n* matadouro *m*
abbey /'æbɪ/ *n* abadia *f*, mosteiro *m*
abbreviat|e /ə'bri:vɪeɪt/ *vt* abreviar. **~ion** /-'eɪʃn/ *n* abreviação *f*; (*short form*) abreviatura *f*
abdicat|e /'æbdɪkeɪt/ *vt/i* abdicar. **~ion** /-'keɪʃn/ *n* abdicação *f*
abdom|en /'æbdəmən/ *n* abdômen *m*, (*P*) abdómen *m*. **~inal** /-'dɒmɪnl/ *a* abdominal
abduct /æb'dʌkt/ *vt* raptar. **~ion** /-ʃn/ *n* rapto *m*. **~or** *n* raptor, -a *mf*
aberration /æbə'reɪʃn/ *n* aberração *f*
abet /ə'bet/ *vt* (*pt* **abetted**) (*jur*) instigar; (*aid*) auxiliar
abeyance /ə'beɪəns/ *n* **in ~** (*matter*) em suspenso; (*custom*) em desuso
abhor /əb'hɔ:(r)/ *vt* (*pt* **abhorred**) abominar, ter horror a. **~rence** /-'hɒrəns/ *n* horror *m*. **~rent** /-'hɒrənt/ *a* abominável, execrável
abide /ə'baɪd/ *vt* (*pt* **abided**) suportar, tolerar. **~ by** (*promise*) manter; (*rules*) acatar
abiding /ə'baɪdɪŋ/ *a* eterno, perpétuo
ability /ə'bɪlətɪ/ *n* capacidade *f* (to do para *or* de fazer); (*cleverness*) habilidade *f*, esperteza *f*
abject /'æbdʒekt/ *a* abjeto, (*P*) abjecto
ablaze /ə'bleɪz/ *a* em chamas; (*fig*) aceso, (*P*) excitado
abl|e /'eɪbl/ *a* (**~er**, **~est**) capaz (to de). **be ~e to** (*have power, opportunity*) ser capaz de, poder; (*know how to*) ser capaz de, saber. **~y** *adv* habilmente
ablutions /ə'blu:ʃnz/ *npl* ablução *f*, abluções *fpl*
abnormal /æb'nɔ:ml/ *a* anormal. **~ity** /-'mælətɪ/ *n* anormalidade *f*. **~ly** *adv* (*unusually*) excepcionalmente
aboard /ə'bɔ:d/ *adv* a bordo □ *prep* a bordo de
abode /ə'bəʊd/ *n* (*old use*) habitação *f*. **place of ~** domicílio *m*
aboli|sh /ə'bɒlɪʃ/ *vt* abolir, extinguir. **~tion** /æbə'lɪʃn/ *n* abolição *f*, extinção *f*
abominable /ə'bɒmɪnəbl/ *a* abominável, detestável
abominat|e /ə'bɒmɪneɪt/ *vt* abominar, detestar. **~ion** /-'neɪʃn/ *n* abominação *f*
abort /ə'bɔ:t/ *vt/i* (fazer) abortar. **~ive** *a* (*attempt etc*) abortado, malogrado
abortion /ə'bɔ:ʃn/ *n* aborto *m*. **have an ~** fazer um aborto, ter um aborto. **~ist** *n* abortad/or, -eira *mf*
abound /ə'baʊnd/ *vi* abundar (in em)
about /ə'baʊt/ *adv* (*approximately*) aproximadamente, cerca de; (*here and there*) aqui e ali; (*all round*) por todos os lados, em roda, em volta; (*in existence*) por aí □ *prep* acerca de, sobre; (*round*) em torno de; (*somewhere in*) em, por. **~-face**, **~-turn** *ns* reviravolta *f*. **~ here** por aqui. **be ~ to** estar prestes a. **he was ~ to eat** ia comer. **how** *or* **what ~ leaving?** e se nós fôssemos embora? **know/talk ~** saber/falar sobre
above /ə'bʌv/ *adv* acima, por cima □ *prep* sobre. **he's not ~ lying** ele não é de mentir. **~ all** sobretudo. **~-board** *a* franco, honesto □ *adv* com lisura. **~-mentioned** *a* acima, supracitado
abrasion /ə'breɪʒn/ *n* atrito *m*; (*injury*) escoriação *f*, esfoladura *f*
abrasive /ə'breɪsɪv/ *a* abrasivo; (*fig*) agressivo □ *n* abrasivo *m*
abreast /ə'brest/ *adv* lado a lado. **keep ~ of** manter-se a par de
abridge /ə'brɪdʒ/ *vt* abreviar. **~ment**

n abreviação *f*, abreviatura *f*, redução *f*; (*abridged text*) resumo *m*

abroad /ə'brɔ:d/ *adv* no estrangeiro; (*far and wide*) por todo o lado. **go ~** ir para o estrangeiro

abrupt /ə'brʌpt/ *a* (*sudden, curt*) brusco; (*steep*) abrupto. **~ly** *adv* (*suddenly*) bruscamente; (*curtly*) com brusquidão. **~ness** *n* brusquidão *f*; (*steepness*) declive *m*

abscess /'æbsɪs/ *n* abscesso *m*, (*P*) abcesso *m*

abscond /əb'skɒnd/ *vi* evadir-se, andar fugido

absen|t[1] /'æbsənt/ *a* ausente; (*look etc*) distraído. **~ce** *n* ausência *f*; (*lack*) falta *f*. **~t-minded** *a* distraído. **~t-mindedness** *n* distração *f*, (*P*) distracção *f*

absent[2] /əb'sent/ *v refl* **~ o.s.** ausentar-se

absentee /æbsən'ti:/ *n* ausente *mf*, (*P*) absentista *mf*. **~ism** *n* absenteísmo *m*, (*P*) absentismo *m*

absolute /'æbsəlu:t/ *a* absoluto; (*colloq: coward etc*) autêntico, (*P*) verdadeiro. **~ly** *adv* absolutamente

absolution /æbsə'lu:ʃn/ *n* absolvição *f*

absolve /əb'zɒlv/ *vt* (*from sin*) absolver (**from** de); (*from vow*) desligar (**from** de)

absor|b /əb'sɔ:b/ *vt* absorver. **~ption** *n* absorção *f*

absorbent /əb'sɔ:bənt/ *a* absorvente. **~ cotton** (*Amer*) algodão hidrófilo *m*

abst|ain /əb'stem/ *vi* abster-se (**from** de). **~ention** /-'stenʃn/ *n* abstenção *f*

abstemious /əb'sti:mɪəs/ *a* abstêmio, (*P*) abstémio, sóbrio

abstinen|ce /'æbstɪnəns/ *n* abstinência *f*. **~t** *a* abstinente

abstract[1] /'æbstrækt/ *a* abstrato, (*P*) abstracto

abstract[2] /əb'strækt/ *vt* (*take out*) extrair; (*separate*) abstrair. **~ed** *a* distraído. **~ion** /-ʃn/ *n* (*of mind*) distração *f*, (*P*) distracção *f*; (*idea*) abstração *f*, (*P*) abstracção *f*

absurd /əb'sɜ:d/ *a* absurdo. **~ity** *n* absurdo *m*

abundan|t /ə'bʌndənt/ *a* abundante. **~ce** *n* abundância *f*

abuse[1] /ə'bju:z/ *vt* (*misuse*) abusar de; (*ill-treat*) maltratar; (*insult*) injuriar, insultar

abus|e[2] /ə'bju:s/ *n* (*wrong use*) abuso *m* (**of** de); (*insults*) insultos *m pl*. **~ive** *a* injurioso, ofensivo

abysmal /ə'bɪzməl/ *a* abismal; (*colloq: bad*) abissal

abyss /ə'bɪs/ *n* abismo *m*

academic /ækə'demɪk/ *a* acadêmico, (*P*) académico, universitário; (*scholarly*) intelectual; (*pej*) acadêmico, (*P*) teórico □ *n* universitário

academy /ə'kædəmɪ/ *n* academia *f*

accede /ək'si:d/ *vi* **~ to** (*request*) aceder a; (*post*) assumir; (*throne*) ascender a, subir a

accelerat|e /ək'seləreɪt/ *vt* acelerar □ *vi* acelerar-se; (*auto*) acelerar. **~ion** /-'reɪʃn/ *n* aceleração *f*

accelerator /ək'seləreɪtə(r)/ *n* (*auto*) acelerador *m*

accent[1] /'æksənt/ *n* acento *m*; (*local pronunciation*) sotaque *m*

accent[2] /æk'sent/ *vt* acentuar

accentuate /æk'sentʃʊeɪt/ *vt* acentuar

accept /ək'sept/ *vt* aceitar. **~able** *a* aceitável. **~ance** *n* aceitação *f*; (*approval*) aprovação *f*

access /'ækses/ *n* acesso *m* (**to** a). **~ible** /ək'sesəbl/ *a* acessível

accessory /ək'sesərɪ/ *a* acessório □ *n* acessório *m*; (*jur: person*) cúmplice *m*

accident /'æksɪdənt/ *n* acidente *m*, desastre *m*; (*chance*) acaso *m*. **~al** /-'dentl/ *a* acidental, fortuito. **~ally** /-'dentəlɪ/ *adv* acidentalmente, por acaso

acclaim /ə'kleɪm/ *vt* aclamar □ *n* aplauso *m*, aclamações *fpl*

acclimatiz|e /ə'klaɪmətaɪz/ *vt/i* aclimatar(-se). **~ation** /-'zeɪʃn/ *n* aclimatação *f*

accommodat|e /ə'kɒmədeɪt/ *vt* acomodar; (*lodge*) alojar; (*adapt*) adaptar; (*supply*) fornecer; (*oblige*) fazer a vontade de. **~ing** *a* obsequioso, amigo de fazer vontades. **~ion** /-'deɪʃn/ *n* acomodação *f*, (*rooms*) alojamento *m*, quarto *m*

accompan|y /ə'kʌmpənɪ/ *vt* acompanhar. **~iment** *n* acompanhamento *m*. **~ist** *n* (*mus*) acompanhad/or, (*B*) -eira *mf*

accomplice /ə'kʌmplɪs/ *n* cúmplice *mf*

accomplish /ə'kʌmplɪʃ/ *vt* (*perform*) executar, realizar; (*achieve*) realizar, conseguir fazer. **~ed** *a* acabado. **~ment** *n* realização *f*, (*ability*) talento *m*, dote *m*

accord /ə'kɔ:d/ *vi* concordar □ *vt* conceder □ *n* acordo *m*. **of one's own ~** por vontade própria, espontaneamente. **~ance** *n* **in ~ance with** em conformidade com, de acordo com

according /ə'kɔ:dɪŋ/ *adv* **~ to** conforme. **~ly** *adv* (*therefore*) por conseguinte, por consequência; (*appropriately*) conformemente

accordion /ə'kɔ:dɪən/ *n* acordeão *m*

accost /ə'kɒst/ *vt* abordar, abeirar-se de

account /ə'kaʊnt/ *n* (*comm*) conta *f*; (*description*) relato *m*; (*importance*) importância *f* □ *vt* considerar. ~ **for** dar contas de, explicar. **on** ~ **of** por causa de. **on no** ~ em caso algum. **take into** ~ ter *or* levar em conta. ~**able** /-əbl/ *a* responsável (**for** por). ~**ability** /-ə'bɪlətɪ/ *n* responsabilidade *f*

accountant /ə'kaʊntənt/ *n* contador(a) *m/f*, (*P*) contabilista *mf*

accrue /ə'kru:/ *vi* acumular-se. ~ **to** reverter em favor de

accumulat|e /ə'kju:mjʊleɪt/ *vt/i* acumular(-se). ~**ion** /-'leɪʃn/ *n* acumulação *f*, acréscimo *m*

accumulator /ə'kju:mjʊleɪtə(r)/ *n* (*electr*) acumulador *m*

accura|te /'ækjərət/ *a* exato, (*P*) exacto, preciso. ~**cy** *n* exatidão *f*, (*P*) exactidão *f*, precisão *f*. ~**tely** *adv* com exatidão, (*P*) exactidão

accus|e /ə'kju:z/ *vt* acusar. **the** ~**ed** o acusado. ~**ation** /ækju:'zeɪʃn/ *n* acusação *f*

accustom /ə'kʌstəm/ *vt* acostumar, habituar. ~**ed** *a* acostumado, habituado. **get** ~**ed to** acostumar-se a, habituar-se a

ace /eɪs/ *n* ás *m*

ache /eɪk/ *n* dor *f* □ *vi* doer. **my leg** ~**s** dói-me a perna, tenho dores na perna

achieve /ə'tʃi:v/ *vt* realizar, efetuar; (*success*) alcançar. ~**ment** *n* realização *f*; (*feat*) feito *m*, façanha *f*, sucesso *m*

acid /'æsɪd/ *a* ácido; (*wine*) azedo; (*words*) áspero □ *n* ácido *m*. ~**ity** /ə'sɪdətɪ/ *n* acidez *f*

acknowledge /ək'nɒlɪdʒ/ *vt* reconhecer. ~ **(receipt of)** acusar a recepção de. ~**ment** *n* reconhecimento *m*; (*letter etc*) acusação *f* de recebimento, (*P*) aviso *m* de recepção

acne /'æknɪ/ *n* acne *mf*

acorn /'eɪkɔ:n/ *n* bolota *f*, glande *f*

acoustic /ə'ku:stɪk/ *a* acústico. ~**s** *npl* acústica *f*

acquaint /ə'kweɪnt/ *vt* ~ **s.o. with sth** pôr alg a par de alg coisa. **be** ~**ed with** (*person, fact*) conhecer. ~**ance** *n* (*knowledge, person*) conhecimento *m*; (*person*) conhecido *m*

acquiesce /ækwɪ'es/ *vi* consentir. ~**nce** /ækwɪ'esns/ *n* aquiescência *f*, consentimento *m*

acqui|re /ə'kwaɪə(r)/ *vt* adquirir. ~**sition** /ækwɪ'zɪʃn/ *n* aquisição *f*

acquit /ə'kwɪt/ *vt* (*pt* **acquitted**) absolver. ~ **o.s. well** sair-se bem. ~**tal** *n* absolvição *f*

acrid /'ækrɪd/ *a* acre

acrimon|ious /ækrɪ'məʊnɪəs/ *a* acrimonioso. ~**y** /'ækrɪmənɪ/ *n* acrimônia *f*, (*P*) acrimónia *f*

acrobat /'ækrəbæt/ *n* acrobata *mf*. ~**ic** /-'bætɪk/ *a* acrobático. ~**ics** /-'bætɪks/ *npl* acrobacia *f*

acronym /'ækrənɪm/ *n* sigla *f*

across /ə'krɒs/ *adv & prep* (*side to side*) de lado a lado (de), de um lado para o outro (de); (*on the other side*) do outro lado (de); (*crosswise*) através (de), de través. **go** *or* **walk** ~ atravessar. **swim** ~ atravessar a nado

act /ækt/ *n* (*deed, theatr*) ato *m*, (*P*) acto *m*; (*in variety show*) número *m*; (*decree*) lei *f* □ *vi* agir, atuar, (*P*) actuar; (*theatr*) representar; (*function*) funcionar; (*pretend*) fingir □ *vt* (*part, role*) desempenhar. ~ **as** servir de. ~**ing** *a* interino □ *n* (*theatr*) desempenho *m*

action /'ækʃn/ *n* ação *f*, (*P*) acção *f*; (*mil*) combate *m*. **out of** ~ fora de combate; (*techn*) avariado. **take** ~ agir, atuar, (*P*) actuar

activ|e /'æktɪv/ *a* ativo, (*P*) activo; (*interest*) vivo; (*volcano*) em atividade, (*P*) actividade. ~**ity** /-'tɪvətɪ/ *n* atividade *f*, (*P*) actividade *f*

ac|tor /'æktə(r)/ *n* ator *m*, (*P*) actor *m*. ~**tress** *n* atriz *f*, (*P*) actriz *f*

actual /'æktʃʊəl/ *a* real, verdadeiro; (*example*) concreto. **the** ~ **pen which** a própria caneta que. ~**ity** /-'ælətɪ/ *n* realidade *f*. ~**ly** *adv* (*in fact*) na realidade

acumen /ə'kju:men/ *n* agudeza *f*, perspicácia *f*

acupunctur|e /'ækjʊpʌŋktʃə(r)/ *n* acupuntura *f*, (*P*) acupunctura *f*. ~**ist** *n* acupunturador *m*, (*P*) acupuncturista *mf*

acute /ə'kju:t/ *a* agudo; (*mind*) perspicaz; (*emotion*) intenso, vivo; (*shortage*) grande. ~**ly** *adv* vivamente.

ad /æd/ *n* (*colloq*) anúncio *m*

AD *abbr* dC

adamant /'ædəmənt/ *a* inflexível

adapt /ə'dæpt/ *vt/i* adaptar(-se). ~**ation** /ædæp'teɪʃn/ *n* adaptação *f*. ~**or** (*electr*) *n* adaptador *m*

adaptab|le /ə'dæptəbl/ *a* adaptável. ~**ility** /-'bɪlətɪ/ *n* adaptabilidade *f*

add /æd/ *vt/i* acrescentar. ~ **(up)** somar. ~ **up to** (*total*) elevar-se a

adder /'ædə(r)/ *n* víbora *f*

addict /'ædɪkt/ *n* viciado *m*. **drug** ~ (*B*) viciado em droga, viciado da droga, (*P*) toxicodependente *mf*

addict|ed /ə'dɪktɪd/ *a* **be** ~**ed to** (*drink, drugs; fig*) ter o vício de. ~**ion** /-ʃn/ *n* (*med*) dependência *f*; (*fig*) vício *m*. ~**ive** *a* que produz dependência

addition /ə'dɪʃn/ *n* adição *f*. **in** ~ além disso. **in** ~ **to** além de. ~**al** /-ʃənl/ *a* adicional, suplementar

address /ə'dres/ *n* endereço *m*; (*speech*) discurso *m* □ *vt* endereçar; (*speak to*) dirigir-se a
adenoids /'ædɪnɔɪdz/ *npl* adenóides *mpl*
adept /'ædept/ *a* & *n* especialista (*mf*), perito (*m*) (at em)
adequa|te /'ædɪkwət/ *a* adequado; (*satisfactory*) satisfatório. **~cy** *n* adequação *f*; (*of person*) competência *f*. **~tely** *adv* adequadamente
adhere /əd'hɪə(r)/ *vi* aderir (to a)
adhesive /əd'hi:sɪv/ *a* & *n* adesivo (*m*). **~ plaster** esparadrapo *m*, (*P*) adesivo *m*
adjacent /ə'dʒeɪsnt/ *a* adjacente, contíguo (to a)
adjective /'ædʒektɪv/ *n* adjetivo *m*, (*P*) adjectivo *m*
adjoin /ə'dʒɔɪn/ *vt* confinar com, ficar contíguo a
adjourn /ə'dʒɜ:n/ *vt* adiar □ *vi* suspender a sessão. **~ to** (*go*) passar a, ir para
adjudicate /ə'dʒu:dɪkeɪt/ *vt/i* julgar; (*award*) adjudicar
adjust /ə'dʒʌst/ *vt/i* (*alter*) ajustar, regular; (*arrange*) arranjar. **~ (o.s.) to** adaptar-se a. **~able** *a* regulável. **~ment** *n* (*techn*) regulação *f*, afinação *f*; (*of person*) adaptação *f*
ad lib /æd'lɪb/ *vi* (*pt* **ad libbed**) (*colloq*) improvisar □ *adv* à vontade
administer /əd'mɪnɪstə(r)/ *vt* administrar
administrat|e /əd'mɪnɪstreɪt/ *vt* administrar, gerir. **~ion** /-'streɪʃn/ *n* administração *f*. **~or** *n* administrador *m*
administrative /əd'mɪnɪstrətɪv/ *a* administrativo
admirable /'ædmərəbl/ *a* admirável
admiral /'ædmərəl/ *n* almirante *m*
admir|e /əd'maɪə(r)/ *vt* admirar. **~ation** /-mɪ'reɪʃn/ *n* admiração *f*. **~er** /-'maɪərə(r)/ *n* admirador *m*
admission /əd'mɪʃn/ *n* admissão *f*; (*to museum, theatre, etc*) ingresso *m*, (*P*) entrada *f*; (*confession*) confissão *f*
admit /əd'mɪt/ *vt* (*pt* **admitted**) (*let in*) admitir, permitir a entrada a; (*acknowledge*) reconhecer, admitir. **~ to** confessar. **~tance** *n* admissão *f*
admoni|sh /əd'mɒnɪʃ/ *vt* admoestar. **~tion** /-ə'nɪʃn/ *n* admoestação *f*
adolescen|t /ædə'lesnt/ *a* & *n* adolescente (*mf*). **~ce** *n* adolescência *f*
adopt /ə'dɒpt/ *vt* adotar, (*P*) adoptar. **~ed child** filho adotivo, (*P*) adoptivo. **~ion** /-ʃn/ *n* adoção *f*, (*P*) adopção *f*
ador|e /ə'dɔ:(r)/ *vt* adorar. **~able** *a* adorável. **~ation** /ædə'reɪʃn/ *n* adoração *f*
adorn /ə'dɔ:n/ *vt* adornar, enfeitar
adrenalin /ə'drenəlɪn/ *n* adrenalina *f*
adrift /ə'drɪft/ *a* & *adv* à deriva
adult /'ædʌlt/ *a* & *n* adulto (*m*). **~hood** *n* idade *f* adulta, (*P*) maioridade *f*
adulterat|e /ə'dʌltəreɪt/ *vt* adulterar. **~ion** /'reɪʃn/ *n* adulteração *f*
adulter|y /ə'dʌltərɪ/ *n* adultério *m*. **~er**, **~ess** *ns* adúlter/o, -a *mf*. **~ous** *a* adúltero
advance /əd'va:ns/ *vt/i* avançar □ *n* avanço *m*; (*payment*) adiantamento *m* □ *a* (*payment, booking*) adiantado. **in ~** com antecedência. **~d** *a* avançado. **~ment** *n* promoção *f*, ascensão *f*
advantage /əd'va:ntɪdʒ/ *n* vantagem *f*. **take ~ of** aproveitar-se de, tirar partido de; (*person*) explorar. **~ous** /ædvən'teɪdʒəs/ *a* vantajoso
adventur|e /əd'ventʃə(r)/ *n* aventura *f*. **~er** *n* aventureiro *m*, explorador *m*. **~ous** *a* aventuroso
adverb /'ædvɜ:b/ *n* advérbio *m*
adversary /'ædvəsərɪ/ *n* adversário *m*, antagonista *mf*
advers|e /'ædvɜ:s/ *a* (*contrary*) adverso; (*unfavourable*) desfavorável. **~ity** /əd'vɜ:sətɪ/ *n* adversidade *f*
advert /'ædvɜ:t/ *n* (*colloq*) anúncio *m*
advertise /'ædvətaɪz/ *vt/i* anunciar, fazer publicidade (de); (*sell*) pôr um anúncio (para). **~ for** procurar; **~r** /-ə(r)/ *n* anunciante *mf*
advertisement /əd'vɜ:tɪsmənt/ *n* anúncio *m*; (*advertising*) publicidade *f*
advice /əd'vaɪs/ *n* conselho(s) *mpl*; (*comm*) aviso *m*
advis|e /əd'vaɪz/ *vt* aconselhar; (*inform*) avisar, informar. **~e against** desaconselhar. **~able** *a* aconselhável. **~er** *n* conselheiro *m*; (*in business*) consultor *m*. **~ory** *a* consultivo
advocate[1] /'ædvəkət/ *n* (*jur*) advogado *m*; (*supporter*) defensor(a) *m/f*
advocate[2] /'ædvəkeɪt/ *vt* advogar, defender
aerial /'eərɪəl/ *a* aéreo □ *n* antena *f*
aerobatics /eərə'bætɪks/ *npl* acrobacia *f* aérea
aerobics /eə'rəʊbɪks/ *n* ginástica *f* aeróbica
aerodynamic /eərəʊdaɪ'næmɪk/ *a* aerodinâmico
aeroplane /'eərəpleɪn/ *n* avião *m*
aerosol /'eərəsɒl/ *n* aerossol *m*
aesthetic /i:s'θetɪk/ *a* estético.
affair /ə'feə(r)/ *n* (*business*) negócio *m*; (*romance*) ligação *f*, aventura *f*; (*matter*) asunto *m*. **love ~** paixão *f*
affect /ə'fekt/ *vt* afetar, (*P*) afectar. **~ation** /æfek'teɪʃn/ *n* afetação *f*, (*P*)

afectação *f*. ~**ed** *a* afetado, (*P*) afectado, pretencioso
affection /ə'fekʃn/ *n* afeição *f*, afeto *m*, (*P*) afecto *m*
affectionate /ə'fekʃənət/ *a* afetuoso, (*P*) afectuoso, carinhoso
affiliat|e /ə'fɪlɪeɪt/ *vt* afiliar. ~**ed company** filial *f*. ~**ion** /-'eɪʃn/ *n* afiliação *f*
affirm /ə'fɜ:m/ *vt* afirmar. ~**ation** /æfə'meɪʃn/ *n* afirmação *f*
affirmative /ə'fɜ:mətɪv/ *a* afirmativo □ *n* afirmativa *f*
afflict /ə'flɪkt/ *vt* afligir. ~**ion** /-ʃn/ *n* aflição *f*
affluen|t /'æflʊənt/ *a* rico, afluente. ~**ce** *n* riqueza *f*, afluência *f*
afford /ə'fɔ:d/ *vt* (*have money for*) permitir-se, ter meios (para). **can you afford the time?** você teria tempo? **I can't afford a car** eu não posso comprar um carro. **we can't afford to lose** não podemos perder
affront /ə'frʌnt/ *n* afronta *f* □ *vt* insultar
afield /ə'fi:ld/ *adv* **far** ~ longe
afloat /ə'fləʊt/ *adv* & *a* à tona, a flutuar; (*at sea*) no mar; (*business*) lançado, (*P*) sem dívidas
afraid /ə'freɪd/ *a* **be** ~ ter medo (**of**, **to** de; **that** que); (*be sorry*) lamentar, ter muita pena. **I'm** ~ (**that**) (*regret to say*) lamento *or* tenho muita pena de dizer que
afresh /ə'freʃ/ *adv* de novo
Africa /'æfrɪkə/ *n* áfrica *f*. ~**n** *a* & *n* africano (*m*)
after /a:ftə(r)/ *adv* depois □ *prep* depois de □ *conj* depois que. ~ **all** afinal de contas. ~ **doing**, depois de fazer. **be** ~ (*seek*) querer, pretender. ~-**effect** *n* seqüela *f*, (*P*) sequela *f*, efeito *m* retardado; (*of drug*) efeito *m* secundário
aftermath /'a:ftəmæθ/ *n* conseqüências *fpl*
afternoon /a:ftə'nu:n/ *n* tarde *f*
aftershave /'a:ftəʃeɪv/ *n* loção *f* apósbarba, (*P*) loção *f* para a barba
afterthought /'a:ftəθɔ:t/ *n* reflexão *f* posterior. **as an** ~ pensando melhor
afterwards /'a:ftəwədz/ *adv* depois, mais tarde
again /ə'gen/ *adv* de novo, outra vez; (*on the other hand*) por outro lado. **then** ~ além disso
against /ə'genst/ *prep* contra
age /eɪdʒ/ *n* idade *f*; (*period*) época *f*, idade *f* □ *vt/i* (*pres p* **ageing**) envelhecer. ~**s** (*colloq: very long time*) há séculos *mpl*. **of** ~ (*jur*) maior. **ten years of** ~ com/de dez anos. **under** ~ menor. ~-**group** *n* faixa etária *f*. ~**less** *a* sempre jovem
aged[1] /eɪdʒd/ *a* ~ **six** de seis anos de idade
aged[2] /'eɪdʒɪd/ *a* idoso, velho
agen|cy /'eɪdʒənsɪ/ *n* agência *f*; (*means*) intermédio *m*. ~**t** *n* agente *mf*
agenda /ə'dʒendə/ *n* ordem *f* do dia
aggravat|e /'ægrəveɪt/ *vt* agravar; (*colloq: annoy*) irritar. ~**ion** /-'veɪʃn/ *n* (*worsening*) agravamento *m*; (*exasperation*) irritação *f*; (*colloq: trouble*) aborrecimentos *mpl*
aggregate /'ægrɪgeɪt/ *vt/i* agregar (-se) □ *a* /'ægrɪgət/ total, global □ *n* (*total, mass, materials*) agregado *m*. **in the** ~ no todo
aggress|ive /ə'gresɪv/ *a* agressivo; (*weapons*) ofensivo. ~**ion** /-ʃn/ *n* agressão *f*. ~**iveness** *n* agressividade *f*. ~**or** *n* agressor *m*
aggrieved /ə'gri:vd/ *a* (*having a grievance*) lesado
agil|e /'ædʒaɪl/ *a* ágil. ~**ity** /ə'dʒɪlətɪ/ *n* agilidade *f*
agitat|e /'ædʒɪteɪt/ *vt* agitar. ~**ion** /-'teɪʃn/ *n* agitação *f*. ~**or** *n* agitador *m*
agnostic /æg'nɒstɪk/ *a* & *n* agnóstico (*m*)
ago /ə'gəʊ/ *adv* há. **a month** ~ há um mês. **long** ~ há muito tempo
agon|y /'ægənɪ/ *n* agonia *f*; (*mental*) angústia *f*. ~**ize** *vi* atormentar-se, torturar-se. ~**izing** *a* angustiante, (*P*) doloroso
agree /ə'gri:/ *vt/i* concordar; (*of figures*) acertar. ~ **that** reconhecer que. ~ **to do** concordar em *or* aceitar fazer. ~ **to sth** concordar com alguma coisa. **seafood doesn't** ~ **with me** não me dou bem com mariscos. ~**d** *a* (*time, place*) combinado. **be** ~**d** estar de acordo
agreeable /ə'gri:əbl/ *a* agradável. **be** ~ **to** estar de acordo com
agreement /ə'gri:mənt/ *n* acordo *m*; (*gramm*) concordância *f*; (*contract*) contrato *m*. **in** ~ de acordo
agricultur|e /'ægrɪkʌltʃə(r)/ *n* agricultura *f*. ~**al** /-'kʌltʃərəl/ *a* agrícola
aground /ə'graʊnd/ *adv* **run** ~ (*of ship*) encalhar
ahead /ə'hed/ *adv* à frente, adiante; (*in advance*) adiantado. ~ **of sb** diante de alguém, à frente de alguém. ~ **of time** antes da hora, adiantado. **straight** ~ sempre em frente
aid /eɪd/ *vt* ajudar □ *n* ajuda *f*. ~ **and abet** ser cúmplice de. **in** ~ **of** em auxílio de, a favor de
AIDS /eɪdz/ *n* (*med*) AIDS *f*, (*P*) sida *m*
ail /eɪl/ *vt* **what** ~**s you?** o que é que você tem? ~**ing** *a* doente. ~**ment** *n* doença *f*, achaque *m*

aim /eɪm/ *vt* (*gun*) apontar; (*efforts*) dirigir; (*send*) atirar (at para) □ *vi* visar □ *n* alvo *m*. ~ **at** visar. ~ **to** aspirar a, tencionar. **take** ~ fazer pontaria. ~**less** *a*, ~**lessly** *adv* sem objetivo, (*P*) objectivo

air /eə(r)/ *n* ar *m* □ *vt* arejar; (*views*) expor □ *a* (*base etc*) aéreo. **in the** ~ (*rumour*) espalhado; (*plans*) no ar. **on the** ~ (*radio*) no ar. ~**-conditioned** *a* com ar condicionado. ~**-conditioning** *n* condicionamento *m* do ar, (*P*) ar *m* condicionado. ~ **force** Força *f* Aérea. ~ **hostess** aeromoça *f*, (*P*) hospedeira *f* de bordo. ~ **raid** ataque *m* aéreo

airborne /'eəbɔ:n/ *a* (*aviat: in flight*) no ar; (*diseases*) levado pelo ar; (*freight*) por transporte aéreo

aircraft /'eəkra:ft/ *n* (*pl invar*) avião *m*. ~**-carrier** *n* porta-aviões *m*

airfield /'eəfi:ld/ *n* campo *m* de aviação

airgun /'eəgʌn/ *n* espingarda *f* de pressão

airlift /'eəlɪft/ *n* ponte *f* aérea □ *vt* transportar em ponte aérea

airline /'eəlaɪn/ *n* linha *f* aérea

airlock /'eəlɒk/ *n* câmara *f* de vácuo; (*in pipe*) bolha *f* de ar

airmail /'eəmeɪl/ *n* correio *m* aéreo. **by** ~ por avião

airport /'eəpɔ:t/ *n* aeroporto *m*

airsick /'eəsɪk/ *a* enjoado. ~**ness** /-nɪs/ *n* enjôo *m*, (*P*) enjoo *m*

airstrip /'eəstrɪp/ *n* pista *f* de aterrissagem, (*P*) pista *f* de aterragem

airtight /'eətaɪt/ *a* hermético

airy /'eərɪ/ *a* (-ier, -iest) arejado; (*manner*) desenvolto

aisle /aɪl/ *n* (*of church*) nave *f* lateral; (*gangway*) coxia *f*

ajar /ə'dʒa:(r)/ *adv* & *a* entreaberto

alabaster /'æləba:stə(r)/ *n* alabastro *m*

à la carte /a:la:'ka:t/ *adv* & *a* à la carte, (*P*) à lista

alarm /ə'la:m/ *n* alarme *m*; (*clock*) campainha *f* □ *vt* alarmar. ~**-clock** *n* despertador *m*. ~**-bell** *n* campainha *f* de alarme. ~**ing** *a* alarmante. ~**ist** *n* alarmista *mf*

alas /ə'læs/ *int* ai! ai de mim!

albatross /'ælbətrɒs/ *n* albatroz *m*

album /'ælbəm/ *n* álbum *m*

alcohol /'ælkəhɒl/ *n* álcool *m*. ~**ic** /-'hɒlɪk/ *a* (*person, drink*) alcoólico □ *n* alcoólico *m*. ~**ism** *n* alcoolismo *m*

alcove /'ælkəʊv/ *n* recesso *m*, alcova *f*

ale /eɪl/ *n* cerveja *f* inglesa

alert /ə'lɜ:t/ *a* (*lively*) vivo; (*watchful*) vigilante □ *n* alerta *m* □ *vt* alertar. **be on the** ~ estar alerta

algebra /'ældʒɪbrə/ *n* álgebra *f*. ~**ic** /-'breɪɪk/ *a* algébrico

Algeria /æl'dʒɪərɪə/ *n* Argélia *f*. ~**n** *a* & *n* argelino (*m*)

alias /'eɪlɪəs/ *n* (*pl* -ases) outro nome *m*, nome falso *m*, (*P*) pseudónimo *m* □ *adv* aliás

alibi /'ælɪbaɪ/ *n* (*pl* -is) álibi *m*, (*P*) alibi *m*

alien /'eɪlɪən/ *n* & *a* estrangeiro (*m*). ~ **to** (*contrary*) contrário a; (*differing*) alheio a, estranho a

alienat|e /'eɪlɪəneɪt/ *vt* alienar. ~**ion** /-'neɪʃn/ *n* alienação *f*

alight[1] /ə'laɪt/ *vi* descer; (*bird*) pousar

alight[2] /ə'laɪt/ *a* (*on fire*) em chamas; (*lit up*) aceso

align /ə'laɪn/ *vt* alinhar. ~**ment** *n* alinhamento *m*

alike /ə'laɪk/ *a* semelhante, parecido □ *adv* da mesma maneira. **look** *or* **be** ~ parecer-se

alimony /'ælɪmənɪ/ *n* pensão *f* alimentar, (*P*) de alimentos

alive /ə'laɪv/ *a* vivo. ~ **to** sensível a. ~ **with** fervilhando de, (*P*) a fervilhar de

alkali /'ælkəlaɪ/ *n* (*pl* -is) álcali *m*, (*P*) alcali *m*

all /ɔ:l/ *a* & *pron* todo (*f* & *pl* -a, -os, -as) □ *pron* (*everything*) tudo □ *adv* completamente, de todo □ *n* tudo *m*. ~ **the better/less/more/worse** *etc* tanto melhor/menos/mais/pior *etc*. ~ **(the) men** todos os homens. ~ **of us** todos nós. ~ **but** quase, todos menos. ~ **in** (*colloq: exhausted*) estafado. ~**-in** *a* tudo incluído. ~ **out** a fundo, (*P*) completamente. ~**-out** *a* (*effort*) máximo. ~ **over** (*in one's body*) todo; (*finished*) acabado; (*in all parts of*) por todo. ~ **right** bem; (*as a response*) está bem. ~ **round** em tudo; (*for all*) para todos. ~**-round** *a* geral. ~ **the same** apesar de tudo. **it's** ~ **the same to me** (para mim) tanto faz

allay /ə'leɪ/ *vt* acalmar

allegation /ælɪ'geɪʃn/ *n* alegação *f*

allege /ə'ledʒ/ *vt* alegar. ~**dly** /-ɪdlɪ/ *adv* segundo dizem, alegadamente

allegiance /ə'li:dʒəns/ *n* fidelidade *f*, lealdade *f*

allegor|y /'ælɪgərɪ/ *n* alegoria *f*. ~**ical** /-'gɒrɪkl/ *a* alegórico

allerg|y /'ælədʒɪ/ *n* alergia *f*. ~**ic** /ə'lɜ:dʒɪk/ *a* alérgico

alleviate /ə'li:vɪeɪt/ *vt* aliviar

alley /'ælɪ/ *n* (*pl* -eys) (*street*) viela *f*; (*for bowling*) pista *f*

alliance /ə'laɪəns/ *n* aliança *f*

allied /'ælaɪd/ *a* aliado

alligator /'ælɪgeɪtə(r)/ *n* jacaré *m*

allocat|e /'æləkeɪt/ *vt* (*share out*) distribuir; (*assign*) destinar. ~**ion** /-'keɪʃn/ *n* atribuição *f*

allot /ə'lɒt/ *vt* (*pt* **allotted**) atribuir. **~ment** *n* atribuição *f*; (*share*) distribuição *f*; (*land*) horta *f* alugada
allow /ə'laʊ/ *vt* permitir; (*grant*) conceder, dar; (*reckon on*) contar com; (*agree*) admitir, reconhecer. **~ sb to** (+ *inf*) permitir a alg (+ *inf or que* + *subj*). **~ for** levar em conta
allowance /ə'laʊəns/ *n* (*for employees*) ajudas *fpl* de custo; (*monthly, for wife, child*) benefício *m*; (*tax*) desconto *m*. **make ~s for** (*person*) levar em consideração, ser indulgente para com; (*take into account*) atender a, levar em consideração
alloy /ə'lɔɪ/ *n* liga *f*
allude /ə'lu:d/ *vi* **~ to** aludir a
allure /ə'lʊə(r)/ *vt* seduzir, atrair
allusion /ə'lu:ʒn/ *n* alusão *f*
ally[1] /'ælaɪ/ *n* (*pl* **-lies**) aliado *m*
ally[2] /ə'laɪ/ *vt* aliar. **~ oneself with/ to** aliar-se com/a
almanac /'ɔ:lmənæk/ *n* almanaque *m*
almighty /ɔ:l'maɪtɪ/ *a* todo-poderoso; (*colloq*) grande, formidável
almond /'a:mənd/ *n* amêndoa *f*. **~ paste** maçapão *m*
almost /'ɔ:lməʊst/ *adv* quase
alone /ə'ləʊn/ *a* & *adv* só. **leave ~** (*abstain from interfering with*) deixar em paz. **let ~** (*without considering*) sem *or* para não falar de
along /ə'lɒŋ/ *prep* ao longo de □ *adv* (*onward*) para diante. **all ~** durante todo o tempo. **~ with** com. **move ~, please** ande, por favor
alongside /əlɒŋ'saɪd/ *adv* (*naut*) atracado. **come ~** acostar □ *prep* ao lado de
aloof /ə'lu:f/ *adv* à parte □ *a* distante. **~ness** *n* reserva *f*
aloud /ə'laʊd/ *adv* em voz alta
alphabet /'ælfəbet/ *n* alfabeto *m*. **~ical** /-'betɪkl/ *a* alfabético
alpine /'ælpaɪn/ *a* alpino, alpestre
Alps /ælps/ *npl* **the ~** os Alpes *mpl*
already /ɔ:l'redɪ/ *adv* já
also /'ɔl:səʊ/ *adv* também
altar /'ɔ:ltə(r)/ *n* altar *m*
alter /'ɔ:ltə(r)/ *vt/i* alterar(-se), modificar(-se). **~ation** /-'reɪʃn/ *n* alteração *f*; (*to garment*) modificação *f*
alternate[1] /ɔ:l'tɜ:nət/ *a* alternado. **~ly** *adv* alternadamente
alternat|e[2] /'ɔ:ltəneɪt/ *vt/i* alternar (-se). **~ing current** (*elect*) corrente *f* alterna. **~or** *n* (*elect*) alternador *m*
alternative /ɔ:l'tɜ:nətɪv/ *a* alternativo □ *n* alternativa *f*. **~ly** *adv* em alternativa. **or ~ly** ou então
although /ɔ:l'ðəʊ/ *conj* embora, conquanto
altitude /'æltɪtju:d/ *n* altitude *f*
altogether /ɔ:ltə'geðə(r)/ *adv* (*completely*) completamente; (*in total*) ao todo; (*on the whole*) de modo geral
aluminium /ælјʊ'mɪnɪəm/ (*Amer* **aluminum** /ə'lu:mɪnəm/) *n* alumínio *m*
always /'ɔ:lweɪz/ *adv* sempre
am /æm/ *see* **be**
a.m. /eɪ'em/ *adv* da manhã
amalgamate /ə'mælgəmeɪt/ *vt/i* amalgamar(-se); (*comm*) fundir
amass /ə'mæs/ *vt* amontoar, juntar
amateur /'æmətə(r)/ *n* & *a* amador (*m*). **~ish** *a* (*pej*) de amador, (*P*) amadoristico
amaz|e /ə'meɪz/ *vt* assombrar, espantar. **~ed** *a* assombrado. **~ement** *n* assombro *m*. **~ingly** *adv* espantosamente
Amazon /'æməzən/ *n* **the ~** o Amazonas
ambassador /æm'bæsədə(r)/ *n* embaixador *m*
amber /'æmbə(r)/ *n* âmbar *m*; (*traffic light*) luz *f* amarela
ambigu|ous /æm'bɪgjʊəs/ *a* ambíguo. **~ity** /-'gju:ətɪ/ *n* ambigüidade *f*, (*P*) ambiguidade *f*
ambiti|on /æm'bɪʃn/ *n* ambição *f*. **~ous** *a* ambicioso
ambivalen|t /æm'bɪvələnt/ *a* ambivalente. **~ce** *n* ambivalência *f*
amble /'æmbl/ *vi* caminhar sem pressa
ambulance /'æmbjʊləns/ *n* ambulância *f*
ambush /'æmbʊʃ/ *n* emboscada *f* □ *vt* fazer uma emboscada para, (*P*) fazer uma emboscada a
amenable /ə'mi:nəbl/ *a* **~ to** (*responsive*) sensível a
amend /ə'mend/ *vt* emendar, corrigir. **~ment** *n* (*to rule*) emenda *f*. **~s** *n* **make ~s for** reparar, compensar
amenities /ə'mi:nətɪz/ *npl* (*pleasant features*) atrativos *mpl*, (*P*) atractivos *mpl*; (*facilities*) confortos *mpl*, comodidades *fpl*
America /ə'merɪkə/ *n* América *f*. **~n** *a* & *n* americano (*m*). **~nism** /-nɪzəm/ *n* americanismo *m*. **~nize** *vt* americanizar
amiable /'eɪmɪəbl/ *a* amável
amicable /'æmɪkəbl/ *a* amigável, amigo
amid(st) /'əmɪd(st)/ *prep* entre, no meio de
amiss /ə'mɪs/ *a* & *adv* mal. **sth ~** qq coisa que não está bem. **take sth ~** levar qq coisa a mal
ammonia /ə'məʊnɪə/ *n* amoníaco *m*
ammunition /æmjʊ'nɪʃn/ *n* munições *fpl*
amnesia /æm'ni:zɪə/ *n* amnésia *f*

amnesty /'æmnəstɪ/ *n* anistia *f*, (*P*) amnistia *f*
amok /ə'mɒk/ *adv* run ~ enlouquecer; (*crowd*) correr desordenadamente
among(st) /ə'mʌŋ(st)/ *prep* entre, no meio de. ~ **ourselves** (aqui) entre nós
amoral /eɪ'mɒrəl/ *a* amoral
amorous /'æmərəs/ *a* amoroso
amount /ə'maʊnt/ *n* quantidade *f*; (*total*) montante *m*; (*sum of money*) quantia *f* □ *vi* ~ **to** elevar-se a; (*fig*) equivaler a
amp /æmp/ *n* (*colloq*) ampère *m*
amphibi|an /æm'fɪbɪən/ *n* anfíbio *m*. ~**ous** *a* anfíbio
ampl|e /'æmpl/ *a* (-er, -est) (*large, roomy*) amplo; (*enough*) suficiente, bastante. ~**y** *adv* amplamente
amplif|y /'æmplɪfaɪ/ *vt* ampliar, amplificar. ~**ier** *n* amplificador *m*
amputat|e /'æmpjʊteɪt/ *vt* amputar. ~**ion** /-'teɪʃn/ *n* amputação *f*
amus|e /ə'mju:z/ *vt* divertir. ~**ement** *n* divertimento *m*. ~**ing** *a* divertido
an /ən, æn/ *see* a
anachronism /ə'nækrənɪzəm/ *n* anacronismo *m*
anaem|ia /ə'ni:mɪə/ *n* anemia *f*. ~**ic** *a* anêmico, (*P*) anémico
anaesthetic /ænɪs'θetɪk/ *n* anestético *m*, (*P*) anestésico *m*. **give an** ~ **to** anestesiar
anaesthetist /ə'ni:sθətɪst/ *n* anestesista *mf*
anagram /'ænəgræm/ *n* anagrama *m*
analog(ue) /'ænəlɒg/ *a* análogo
analogy /ə'nælədʒɪ/ *n* analogia *f*
analys|e /'ænəlaɪz/ *vt* analisar. ~**t** /-ɪst/ *n* analista *mf*
analysis /ə'næləsɪs/ *n* (*pl* -yses) /-əsi:z/ análise *f*
analytic(al) /ænə'lɪtɪk(l)/ *a* analítico
anarch|y /'ænəkɪ/ *n* anarquia *f*. ~**ist** *n* anarquista *mf*
anatom|y /ə'nætəmɪ/ *n* anatomia *f*. ~**ical** /ænə'tɒmɪkl/ *a* anatômico, (*P*) anatómico
ancest|or /'ænsestə(r)/ *n* antepassado *m*. ~**ral** /-'sestrəl/ *a* ancestral (*pl* -ais)
ancestry /'ænsestrɪ/ *n* ascendência *f*, estirpe *f*
anchor /'æŋkə(r)/ *n* âncora *f* □ *vt/i* ancorar. ~**age** /-rɪdʒ/ *n* ancoradouro *m*
anchovy /'æntʃəvɪ/ *n* enchova *f*, (*P*) anchova *f*
ancient /'eɪnʃənt/ *a* antigo
ancillary /æn'sɪlərɪ/ *a* ancilar, (*P*) subordinado
and /ənd/; *emphatic* /ænd/ *conj* e. **go** ~ **see** vá ver. **better** ~ **better/less** ~ **less** *etc* cada vez melhor/menos *etc*
anecdote /'ænɪkdəʊt/ *n* anedota *f*
angel /'eɪndʒl/ *n* anjo *m*. ~**ic** /æn'dʒelɪk/ *a* angélico, angelical
anger /'æŋgə(r)/ *n* cólera *f*, zanga *f* □ *vt* irritar
angle[1] /'æŋgl/ *n* ângulo *m*
angle[2] /'æŋgl/ *vi* (*fish*) pescar (à linha). ~ **for** (*fig: compliments, information*) andar à procura de. ~**r** /-ə(r)/ *n* pescador *m*
anglicism /'æŋglɪsɪzəm/ *n* anglicismo *m*
Anglo- /'æŋgləʊ/ *pref* anglo-
Anglo-Saxon /'æŋgləʊ'sæksn/ *a* & *n* anglo-saxão (*m*)
angr|y /'æŋgrɪ/ *a* (-ier, -iest) zangado. **get** ~**y** zangar-se (**with** com). ~**ily** *adv* furiosamente
anguish /'æŋgwɪʃ/ *n* angústia *f*
angular /'æŋgjʊlə(r)/ *a* angular; (*features*) anguloso
animal /'ænɪml/ *a* & *n* animal (*m*)
animate[1] /'ænɪmət/ *a* animado
animat|e[2] /'ænɪmeɪt/ *vt* animar. ~**ion** /-'meɪʃn/ *n* animação *f*. ~**ed cartoon** filme *m* de bonecos animados, (*P*) de desenhos animados
animosity /ænɪ'mɒsətɪ/ *n* animosidade *f*
aniseed /'ænɪsi:d/ *n* semente *f* de anis
ankle /'æŋkl/ *n* tornozelo *m*. ~ **sock** meia *f* soquete
annex /ə'neks/ *vt* anexar. ~**ation** /ænek'seɪʃn/ *n* anexação *f*
annexe /'æneks/ *n* anexo *m*
annihilate /ə'naɪəleɪt/ *vt* aniquilar
anniversary /ænɪ'vɜ:sərɪ/ *n* aniversário *m*
announce /ə'naʊns/ *vt* anunciar. ~**ment** *n* anúncio *m*. ~**r** /-ə(r)/ *n* (*radio, TV*) locutor *m*
annoy /ə'nɔɪ/ *vt* irritar, aborrecer. ~**ance** *n* aborrecimento *m*. ~**ed** *a* aborrecido (**with** com). **get** ~**ed** aborrecer-se. ~**ing** *a* irritante
annual /'ænjʊəl/ *a* anual □ *n* (*bot*) planta *f* anual; (*book*) anuário *m*. ~**ly** *adv* anualmente
annuity /ə'nju:ətɪ/ *n* anuidade *f*
annul /ə'nʌl/ *vt* (*pt* **annulled**) anular. ~**ment** *n* anulação *f*
anomal|y /ə'nɒməlɪ/ *n* anomalia *f*. ~**ous** *a* anômalo, (*P*) anómalo
anonym|ous /ə'nɒnɪməs/ *a* anônimo, (*P*) anónimo. ~**ity** /ænə'nɪmətɪ/ *n* anonimato *m*
anorak /'ænəræk/ *n* anoraque *m*, anorak *m*
another /ə'nʌðə(r)/ *a* & *pron* (um) outro. ~ **ten minutes** mais dez minutos. **to one** ~ um ao outro, uns aos outros
answer /'a:nsə(r)/ *n* resposta *f*; (*solution*) solução *f* □ *vt* responder a;

(*prayer*) atender a □ *vi* responder. ~ the door atender à porta. ~ back retrucar, (*P*) responder torto. ~ for responder por. ~able *a* responsável (for por; to perante). ~ing machine *n* secretária *f* eletrónica

ant /ænt/ *n* formiga *f*

antagonis|m /æn'tægənɪzəm/ *n* antagonismo *m*. ~t *n* antagonista *mf*. ~tic /-'nɪstɪk/ *a* antagônico, (*P*) antagónico, hostil

antagonize /æn'tægənaɪz/ *vt* antagonizar, hostilizar

Antarctic /æn'ta:ktɪk/ *n* Antártico, (*P*) Antárctico *m* □ *a* antártico, (*P*) antárctico

ante- /'æntɪ/ *pref* ante-

antecedent /æntɪ'si:dnt/ *a* & *n* antecedente (*m*)

antelope /'æntɪləʊp/ *n* antílope *m*

antenatal /æntɪ'neɪtl/ *a* pré-natal

antenna /æn'tenə/ *n* (*pl* -ae /-i:/) antena *f*

anthem /'ænθəm/ *n* cântico *m*. national ~ hino *m* nacional

anthology /æn'θɒlədʒɪ/ *n* antologia *f*

anthropolog|y /ænθrə'pɒlədʒɪ/ *n* antropologia *f*. ~ist *n* antropólogo *m*

anti- /æntɪ/ *pref* anti-. ~-aircraft /-eəkra:ft/ *a* antiaéreo

antibiotic /æntɪbaɪ'ɒtɪk/ *n* antibiótico *m*

antibody /'æntɪbɒdɪ/ *n* anticorpo *m*

anticipat|e /æn'tɪsɪpeɪt/ *vt* (*foresee, expect*) prever; (*forestall*) antecipar-se a. ~ion /-'peɪʃn/ *n* antecipação *f*; (*expectation*) expectativa *f*. in ~ion of na previsão *or* expectativa de

anticlimax /æntɪ'klaɪmæks/ *n* anticlímax *m*; (*let-down*) decepção *f*. it was an ~ não correspondeu à expectativa

anticlockwise /æntɪ'klɒkwaɪz/ *adv* & *a* no sentido contrário ao dos ponteiros dum relógio

antics /'æntɪks/ *npl* (*of clown*) palhaçadas *fpl*; (*behaviour*) comportamento *m* bizarro

anticyclone /,æntɪ'saɪkləʊn/ *n* anticiclone *m*

antidote /'æntɪdəʊt/ *n* antídoto *m*

antifreeze /'æntɪfri:z/ *n* anticongelante *m*

antihistamine /æntɪ'hɪstəmi:n/ *a* & *n* anti-histamínico (*m*)

antipathy /æn'tɪpəθɪ/ *n* antipatia *f*

antiquated /'æntɪkweɪtɪd/ *a* antiquado

antique /æn'ti:k/ *a* antigo □ *n* antiguidade *f*. ~ dealer antiquário *m*. ~ shop loja *f* de antiguidades, (*P*) antiquário *m*

antiquity /æn'tɪkwətɪ/ *n* antiguidade *f*

antiseptic /æntɪ'septɪk/ *a* & *n* antiséptico (*m*)

antisocial /æntɪ'səʊʃl/ *a* anti-social; (*unsociable*) insociável

antithesis /æn'tɪθəsɪs/ *n* (*pl* -eses /-si:z/ antítese *f*.

antlers /'æntləz/ *npl* chifres *mpl*, esgalhos *mpl*

antonym /'æntənɪm/ *n* antônimo *m*, (*P*) antónimo *m*

anus /'eɪnəs/ *n* ânus *m*

anvil /'ænvɪl/ *n* bigorna *f*

anxiety /æŋ'zaɪətɪ/ *n* ansiedade *f*; (*eagerness*) ânsia *f*

anxious /'æŋkʃəs/ *a* (*worried, eager*) ansioso (to de, por). ~ly *adv* ansiosamente; (*eagerly*) impacientemente

any /'enɪ/ *a* & *pron* qualquer, quaisquer; (*in neg and interr sentences*) algum, alguns; (*in neg sentences*) nenhum, nenhuns; (*every*) todo. at ~ moment a qualquer momento. at ~ rate de qualquer modo, em todo o caso. in ~ case em todo o caso. have you ~ money/friends? você tem (algum) dinheiro/(alguns) amigos? I don't have ~ time não tenho nenhum tempo *or* tempo nenhum *or* tempo algum. has she ~? ela tem algum? she doesn't have ~ ela não tem nenhum □ *adv* (*at all*) de modo algum *or* nenhum; (*a little*) um pouco. ~ the less/the worse *etc* menos/pior *etc*

anybody /'enɪbɒdɪ/ *pron* qualquer pessoa; (*somebody*) alguém; (*after negative*) ninguém. he didn't see ~ ele não viu ninguém

anyhow /'enɪhaʊ/ *adv* (*no matter how*) de qualquer modo; (*badly*) de qualquer maneira, ao acaso; (*in any case*) em todo o caso. you can try, ~ em todo o caso, você pode tentar

anyone /'enɪwʌn/ *pron* = anybody

anything /'enɪθɪŋ/ *pron* (*something*) alguma coisa; (*no matter what*) qualquer coisa; (*after negative*) nada. he didn't say ~ não disse nada. it is ~ but cheap é tudo menos barato. ~ you do tudo o que você fizer

anyway /'enɪweɪ/ *adv* de qualquer modo; (*in any case*) em todo o caso

anywhere /'enɪweə(r)/ *adv* (*somewhere*) em qualquer parte; (*after negative*) em parte alguma/nenhuma. ~ else em qualquer outro lado. ~ you go onde quer que você vá. he doesn't go ~ ele não vai a lado nenhum

apart /ə'pa:t/ *adv* à parte; (*separated*) separado; (*into pieces*) aos bocados. ~ from à parte, além de. ten metres ~ a dez metros de distância entre si. come ~ desfazer-se. keep ~ manter separado. take ~ desmontar

apartment /ə'pa:tmənt/ *n* (*Amer*) apartamento *m*. ~**s** aposentos *mpl*
apath|y /'æpəθɪ/ *n* apatia *f*. ~**etic** /-'θetɪk/ *a* apático
ape /eɪp/ *n* macaco *m* □ *vt* macaquear
aperitif /ə'perətɪf/ *n* aperitivo *m*
aperture /'æpətʃə(r)/ *n* abertura *f*
apex /'eɪpeks/ *n* ápice *m*, cume *m*
apiece /ə'pi:s/ *adv* cada, por cabeça
apologetic /əpɒlə'dʒetɪk/ *a* (*tone etc*) apologético, de desculpas. **be** ~ desculpar-se. ~**ally** /-əlɪ/ *adv* desculpando-se
apologize /ə'pɒlədʒaɪz/ *vi* desculpar-se (**for** de, por; **to** junto de, perante), pedir desculpa (**for**, por; **to**, a)
apology /ə'pɒlədʒɪ/ *n* desculpa *f*; (*defence of belief*) apologia *f*
apostle /ə'pɒsl/ *n* apóstolo *m*
apostrophe /ə'pɒstrəfɪ/ *n* apóstrofe *f*
appal /ə'pɔ:l/ *vt* (*pt* **appalled**) estarrecer. ~**ling** *a* estarrecedor
apparatus /æpə'reɪtəs/ *n* aparelho *m*
apparent /ə'pærənt/ *a* aparente. ~**ly** *adv* aparentemente
apparition /æpə'rɪʃn/ *n* aparição *f*
appeal /ə'pi:l/ *vi* (*jur*) apelar (**to** para); (*attract*) atrair (**to** a); (*for funds*) angariar □ *n* apelo *m*; (*attractiveness*) atrativo *m*, (*P*) atractivo *m*; (*for funds*) angariação *f*. ~ **to sb for sth** pedir uma coisa a alg. ~**ing** *a* (*attractive*) atraente
appear /ə'pɪə(r)/ *vi* aparecer; (*seem*) parecer; (*in court, theatre*) apresentar-se. ~**ance** *n* aparição *f*; (*aspect*) aparência *f*; (*in court*) comparecimento *m*, (*P*) comparência *f*
appease /ə'pi:z/ *vt* apaziguar
appendage /ə'pendɪdʒ/ *n* apêndice *m*
appendicitis /əpendɪ'saɪtɪs/ *n* apendicite *f*
appendix /ə'pendɪks/ *n* (*pl* **-ices** /-si:z/) (*of book*) apêndice *m*; (*pl* **-ixes** /-ksɪz/) (*anat*) apêndice *m*
appetite /'æpɪtaɪt/ *n* apetite *m*
appetizer /'æpɪtaɪzə(r)/ *n* (*snack*) tira-gosto *m*; (*drink*) aperitivo *m*
appetizing /'æpɪtaɪzɪŋ/ *a* apetitoso
applau|d /ə'plɔ:d/ *vt/i* aplaudir. ~**se** *n* aplauso(s) *m*(*pl*)
apple /'æpl/ *n* maçã *f*. ~ **tree** macieira *f*
appliance /ə'plaɪəns/ *n* aparelho *m*, instrumento *m*, utensílio *m*. **household** ~**s** utensílios *mpl* domésticos
applicable /'æplɪkəbl/ *a* aplicável
applicant /'æplɪkənt/ *n* candidato *m* (**for** a)
application /æplɪ'keɪʃn/ *n* aplicação *f*; (*request*) pedido *m*; (*form*) formulário *m*; (*for job*) candidatura *f*
appl|y /ə'plaɪ/ *vt* aplicar □ *vi* ~**y to** (*refer*) aplicar-se a; (*ask*) dirigir-se a. ~**y for** (*job, grant*) candidatar-se a. ~**y o.s. to** aplicar-se a. ~**ied** *a* aplicado
appoint /ə'pɔɪnt/ *vt* (*to post*) nomear; (*time, date*) marcar. **well-**~**ed** *a* bem equipado, bem provido. ~**ment** *n* nomeação *f*; (*meeting*) entrevista *f*; (*with friends*) encontro *m*; (*with doctor etc*) consulta *f*, (*P*) marcação *f*; (*job*) posto *m*
apprais|e /ə'preɪz/ *vt* avaliar. ~**al** *n* avaliação *f*
appreciable /ə'pri:ʃəbl/ *a* apreciável
appreciat|e /ə'pri:ʃɪeɪt/ *vt* (*value*) apreciar; (*understand*) compreender; (*be grateful for*) estar/ficar grato por □ *vi* encarecer. ~**ion** /-'eɪʃn/ *n* apreciação *f*; (*rise in value*) encarecimento *m*; (*gratitude*) reconhecimento *m*. ~**ive** /ə'pri:ʃɪətɪv/ *a* apreciador; (*grateful*) reconhecido
apprehen|d /æprɪ'hend/ *vt* (*seize, understand*) apreender; (*dread*) recear. ~**sion** *n* apreensão *f*
apprehensive /æprɪ'hensɪv/ *a* apreensivo
apprentice /ə'prentɪs/ *n* aprendiz, -a *mf* □ *vt* pôr como aprendiz (**to** de). ~**ship** *n* aprendizagem *f*
approach /ə'prəʊtʃ/ *vt* aproximar; (*with request or offer*) abordar □ *vi* aproximar-se □ *n* aproximação *f*. ~ **to** (*problem*) abordagem *f* de; (*place*) acesso *m* a; (*person*) diligência junto de. ~**able** *a* acessível
appropriate[1] /ə'prəʊprɪət/ *a* apropriado, próprio. ~**ly** *adv* apropriadamente, a propósito
appropriate[2] /ə'prəʊprɪeɪt/ *vt* apropriar-se de
approval /ə'pru:vl/ *n* aprovação *f*. **on** ~ (*comm*) sob condição, à aprovação
approv|e /ə'pru:v/ *vt/i* aprovar. ~**e of** aprovar. ~**ingly** *adv* com ar de aprovação
approximate[1] /ə'prɒksɪmət/ *a* aproximado. ~**ly** *adv* aproximadamente
approximat|e[2] /ə'prɒksɪmeɪt/ *vt/i* aproximar(-se) de. ~**ion** /-'meɪʃn/ *n* aproximação *f*
apricot /'eɪprɪkɒt/ *n* damasco *m*
April /'eɪprəl/ *n* Abril *m*. ~ **Fool's Day** o primeiro de Abril, o dia das mentiras. **make an** ~ **fool of** pregar uma mentira em, (*P*) pregar uma mentira a
apron /'eɪprən/ *n* avental *m*
apt /æpt/ *a* apto; (*pupil*) dotado. **be** ~ **to** ser propenso a. ~**ly** *adv* apropriadamente
aptitude /'æptɪtju:d/ *n* aptidão *f*, (*P*) aptitude *f*
aqualung /'ækwəlʌŋ/ *n* escafandro autônomo, (*P*) autónomo *m*

aquarium /ə'kweərɪəm/ *n* (*pl* **-ums**) aquário *m*
Aquarius /ə'kwɛərɪəs/ *n* (*astr*) Aquário *m*
aquatic /ə'kwætɪk/ *a* aquático; (*sport*) náutico, aquático
aqueduct /'ækwɪdʌkt/ *n* aqueduto *m*
Arab /'ærəb/ *a* & *n* árabe (*mf*). **~ic** *a* & *n* (*lang*) árabe (*m*), arábico (*m*). **a~ic numerals** algarismos *mpl* árabes *or* arábicos
Arabian /ə'reɪbɪən/ *a* árabe
arable /'ærəbl/ *a* arável
arbitrary /'a:bɪtrərɪ/ *a* arbitrário
arbitrat|e /'a:bɪtreɪt/ *vi* arbitrar. **~ion** /-'treɪʃn/ *n* arbitragem *f*. **~or** *n* árbitro *m*
arc /a:k/ *n* arco *m*. **~ lamp** lâmpada *f* de arco. **~ welding** soldadura *f* a arco
arcade /a:'keɪd/ *n* (*shop*) arcada *f*. **amusement ~** fliperama *m*
arch /a:tʃ/ *n* arco *m*; (*vault*) abóbada *f* □ *vt/i* arquear(-se)
arch- /a:tʃ/ *pref* arqui-.
archaeolog|y /a:kɪ'ɒlədʒɪ/ *n* arqueologia *f*. **~ical** /-ə'lɒdʒɪkl/ *a* arqueológico. **~ist** *n* arqueólogo *m*
archaic /a:'keɪɪk/ *a* arcaico
archbishop /a:tʃ'bɪʃəp/ *n* arcebispo *m*
arch-enemy /a:tʃ'enəmɪ/ *n* inimigo *m* número um
archer /'a:tʃə(r)/ *n* arqueiro *m*. **~y** *n* tiro *m* ao arco
archetype /'a:kɪtaɪp/ *n* arquétipo *m*
architect /'a:kɪtekt/ *n* arquiteto *m*, (*P*) arquitecto *m*
architectur|e /'a:kɪtektʃə(r)/ *n* arquitetura *f*, (*P*) arquitectura *f*. **~al** /-'tektʃərəl/ *a* arquitetônico, (*P*) arquitectónico
archiv|es /'a:kaɪvz/ *npl* arquivo *m*. **~ist** /-ɪvɪst/ *n* arquivista *mf*
archway /'a:tʃweɪ/ *n* arcada *f*
Arctic /'a:ktɪk/ *n* ártico *m*, (*P*) árctico *m* □ *a* ártico, (*P*) árctico. **~ weather** tempo *m* glacial
ardent /'a:dnt/ *a* ardente. **~ly** *adv* ardentemente
ardour /'a:də(r)/ *n* ardor *m*
arduous /'a:djʊəs/ *a* árduo
are /ə(r)/; *emphatic* /a:(r)/ *see* **be**
area /'eərɪə/ *n* área *f*
arena /ə'ri:nə/ *n* arena *f*
aren't /a:nt/ = **are not**
Argentin|a /a:dʒən'ti:nə/ *n* Argentina *f*. **~ian** /-'tɪnɪən/ *a* & *n* argentino (*m*)
argu|e /'a:gju:/ *vi* discutir; (*reason*) argumentar, arguir □ *vt* (*debate*) discutir. **~e that** alegar que. **~able** *a* alegável. **it's ~able that** pode-se sustentar que
argument /'a:gjʊmənt/ *n* (*dispute*) disputa *f*; (*reasoning*) argumento *m*. **~ative** /-'mentətɪv/ *a* que gosta de discutir, argumentativo
arid /'ærɪd/ *a* árido
Aries /'eəri:z/ *n* (*astr*) Áries *m*, Carneiro *m*
arise /ə'raɪz/ *vi* (*pt* **arose**, *pp* **arisen**) surgir. **~ from** resultar de
aristocracy /ærɪ'stɒkrəsɪ/ *n* aristocracia *f*
aristocrat /'ærɪstəkræt/ *n* aristocrata *mf*. **~ic** /-'krætɪk/ *a* aristocrático
arithmetic /ə'rɪθmətɪk/ *n* aritmética *f*
ark /a:k/ *n* **Noah's ~** arca *f* de Noé
arm[1] /a:m/ *n* braço *m*. **~ in ~** de braço dado
arm[2] /a:m/ *vt* armar □ *n* (*mil*) arma *f*. **~ed robbery** assalto *m* à mão armada
armament /'a:məmənt/ *n* armamento *m*
armchair /'a:mtʃeə(r)/ *n* cadeira *f* de braços, poltrona *f*
armistice /'a:mɪstɪs/ *n* armistício *m*
armour /'a:mə(r)/ *n* armadura *f*; (*on tanks etc*) blindagem *f*. **~ed** *a* blindado
armoury /'a:mərɪ/ *n* arsenal *m*
armpit /'a:mpɪt/ *n* axila *f*, sovaco *m*
arms /a:mz/ *npl* armas *fpl*. **coat of ~** brasão *m*
army /'a:mɪ/ *n* exército *m*
aroma /ə'rəʊmə/ *n* aroma *m*. **~tic** /ærə'mætɪk/ *a* aromático
arose /ə'rəʊz/ *see* **arise**
around /ə'raʊnd/ *adv* em redor, em volta; (*here and there*) por aí □ *prep* em redor de, em torno de, em volta de; (*approximately*) aproximadamente. **~ here** por aqui
arouse /ə'raʊz/ *vt* despertar; (*excite*) excitar
arrange /ə'reɪndʒ/ *vt* arranjar; (*time, date*) combinar. **~ to do sth** combinar fazer alg coisa. **~ment** *n* arranjo *m*; (*agreement*) acordo *m*. **make ~ments (for)** (*plans*) tomar disposições (para); (*preparations*) fazer preparativos (para)
array /ə'reɪ/ *vt* revestir □ *n* **an ~ of** (*display*) um leque de, uma série de
arrears /ə'rɪəz/ *npl* dívidas *fpl* em atraso, atrasos *mpl*. **in ~** em atraso
arrest /ə'rest/ *vt* (*by law*) deter, prender; (*process, movement*) deter □ *n* captura *f*. **under ~** sob prisão
arrival /ə'raɪvl/ *n* chegada *f*. **new ~** recém-chegado *m*
arrive /ə'raɪv/ *vi* chegar
arrogan|t /'ærəgənt/ *a* arrogante. **~ce** *n* arrogância *f*. **~tly** *adv* com arrogância

arrow /'ærəʊ/ *n* flecha *f*, seta *f*
arsenal /'a:sənl/ *n* arsenal *m*
arsenic /'a:snɪk/ *n* arsênico *m*, (*P*) arsénico *m*
arson /'a:sn/ *n* fogo *m* posto. **~ist** *n* incendiário *m*
art[1] /a:t/ *n* arte *f*. **the ~s** (*univ*) letras *fpl*. **fine ~s** belas-artes *fpl*. **~ gallery** museu *m* (de arte); (*private*) galeria *f* de arte
artery /'a:tərɪ/ *n* artéria *f*
artful /'a:tfl/ *a* manhoso. **~ness** *n* manha *f*
arthritis /a:'θraɪtɪs/ *n* artrite *f*
artichoke /'a:tɪtʃəʊk/ *n* alcachofra *f*. **Jerusalem ~** topinambo *m*
article /'a:tɪkl/ *n* artigo *m*. **~d** *a* (*jur*) em estágio, (*P*) a estagiar
articulate[1] /a:'tɪkjʊlət/ *a* que se exprime com clareza; (*speech*) bem articulado
articulat|e[2] /a:'tɪkjʊleɪt/ *vt/i* articular. **~ed lorry** camião *m* articulado. **~ion** /-'leɪʃn/ *n* articulação *f*
artifice /'a:tɪfɪs/ *n* artifício *m*
artificial /a:tɪ'fɪʃl/ *a* artificial
artillery /a:'tɪlərɪ/ *n* artilharia *f*
artisan /a:tɪ'zæn/ *n* artífice *mf*, artesão *m*, artesã *f*
artist /'a:tɪst/ *n* artista *mf*. **~ic** /-'tɪstɪk/ *a* artístico. **~ry** *n* arte *f*
artiste /a:'ti:st/ *n* artista *mf*
artless /'a:tlɪs/ *a* ingênuo, (*P*) ingénuo, simples
as /əz/; *emphatic* /æz/ *adv & conj* como; (*while*) enquanto; (*when*) quando. **~ a gift** de presente. **~ tall as** tão alto quanto, (*P*) tão alto como □ *pron* que. **I ate the same ~ he** comi o mesmo que ele. **~ for, ~ to** quanto a. **~ from** a partir de. **~ if** como se. **~ much** tanto, tantos. **~ many** quanto, quantos. **~ soon as** logo que. **~ well** (*also*) também. **~ well as** (*in addition to*) assim como
asbestos /æz'bestəs/ *n* asbesto *m*, amianto *m*
ascend /ə'send/ *vt/i* subir. **~ the throne** ascender *or* subir ao trono
ascent /ə'sent/ *n* ascensão *f*; (*slope*) subida *f*, rampa *f*
ascertain /æsə'teɪn/ *vt* certificar-se de. **~ that** certificar-se de que
ascribe /ə'skraɪb/ *vt* atribuir
ash[1] /æʃ/ *n* **~(-tree)** freixo *m*
ash[2] /æʃ/ *n* cinza *f*. **A~ Wednesday** Quarta-feira *f* de Cinzas. **~en** *a* pálido
ashamed /ə'ʃeɪmd/ *a* **be ~** ter vergonha, ficar envergonhado (of de, por)
ashore /ə'ʃɔ:(r)/ *adv* em terra. **go ~** desembarcar
ashtray /'æʃtreɪ/ *n* cinzeiro *m*
Asia /'eɪʃə/ *n* ásia *f*. **~n** *a & n* asiático (*m*)
aside /ə'saɪd/ *adv* de lado, de parte □ *n* (*theat*) aparte *m*. **~ from** (*Amer*) à parte
ask /a:sk/ *vt/i* pedir; (*a question*) perguntar; (*invite*) convidar. **~ sb sth** pedir uma coisa a alguém. **~ about** informar-se de. **~ after sb** pedir notícias de alg, perguntar por alg. **~ for** pedir. **~ sb in** mandar entrar alg. **~ sb to do sth** pedir alguém para fazer alguma coisa
askew /ə'skju:/ *adv & a* de través, de esguelha
asleep /ə'sli:p/ *adv & a* adormecido; (*numb*) dormente. **fall ~** adormecer
asparagus /ə'spærəgəs/ *n* (*plant*) aspargo *m*, (*P*) espargo *m*; (*culin*) aspargos *mpl*, (*P*) espargo *m*
aspect /'æspekt/ *n* aspecto *m*; (*direction*) exposição *f*
aspersions /ə'spɜ:ʃnz/ *npl* **cast ~ on** caluniar
asphalt /'æsfælt/ *n* asfalto *m* □ *vt* asfaltar
asphyxiat|e /əs'fɪksɪeɪt/ *vt/i* asfixiar. **~ion** /-'eɪʃn/ *n* asfixia *f*
aspir|e /əs'paɪə(r)/ *vi* **~e to** aspirar a. **~ation** /æspə'reɪʃn/ *n* aspiração *f*
aspirin /'æsprɪn/ *n* aspirina *f*
ass /æs/ *n* burro *m*. **make an ~ of o.s.** fazer papel de palhaço, (*P*) fazer figura de parvo
assail /ə'seɪl/ *vt* assaltar, agredir. **~ant** *n* assaltante *mf*, agressor *m*
assassin /ə'sæsɪn/ *n* assassino *m*
assassinat|e /ə'sæsɪneɪt/ *vt* assassinar. **~ion** /-'eɪʃn/ *n* assassinato *m*
assault /ə'sɔ:lt/ *n* assalto *m* □ *vt* assaltar, atacar
assemble /ə'sembl/ *vt* (*people*) reunir; (*fit together*) montar □ *vi* reunir-se
assembly /ə'semblɪ/ *n* assembléia *f*, (*P*) assembleia *f*. **~ line** linha *f* de montagem
assent /ə'sent/ *n* assentimento *m* □ *vi* **~ to** consentir em
assert /ə'sɜ:t/ *vt* afirmar; (*one's rights*) reivindicar. **~ o.s.** impor-se. **~ion** /-ʃn/ *n* asserção *f*. **~ive** *a* dogmático, peremptório. **~iveness** *n* assertividade *f*, (*P*) firmeza *f*
assess /ə'ses/ avaliar; (*payment*) estabelecer o montante de. **~ment** *n* avaliação *f*. **~or** *n* (*valuer*) avaliador *m*
asset /'æset/ *n* (*advantage*) vantagem *f*. **~s** (*comm*) ativo *m*, (*P*) activo *m*; (*possessions*) bens *mpl*
assiduous /ə'sɪdjʊəs/ *a* assíduo
assign /ə'saɪn/ *vt* atribuir, destinar;

(*jur*) transmitir. ~ sb to designar alg para

assignation /æsɪg'neɪʃn/ *n* combinação *f* (de hora e local) de encontro

assignment /ə'saɪnmənt/ *n* tarefa *f*, missão *f*; (*jur*) transmissão *f*

assimilat|e /ə'sɪmɪleɪt/ *vt/i* assimilar(-se). **~ion** /-'eɪʃn/ *n* assimilação *f*

assist /ə'sɪst/ *vt/i* ajudar. **~ance** *n* ajuda *f*, assistência *f*

assistant /ə'sɪstənt/ *n* (*helper*) assistente *mf*, auxiliar *mf*; (*in shop*) ajudante *mf*, empregado *m* □ *a* adjunto

associat|e[1] /ə'səʊʃɪeɪt/ *vt* associar □ *vi* **~e with** conviver com. **~ion** /-'eɪʃn/ *n* associação *f*

associate[2] /ə'səʊʃɪət/ *a* & *n* associado (*m*)

assort|ed /ə'sɔːtɪd/ *a* variados; (*foods*) sortidos. **~ment** *n* sortimento *m*, (*P*) sortido *m*

assume /ə'sjuːm/ *vt* assumir; (*presume*) supor, presumir

assumption /ə'sʌmpʃn/ *n* suposição *f*

assurance /ə'ʃʊərəns/ *n* certeza *f*, garantia *f*; (*insurance*) seguro *m*; (*self-confidence*) segurança *f*, confiança *f*

assure /ə'ʃʊə(r)/ *vt* assegurar. **~d** *a* certo, garantido. **rest ~d that** ficar certo que

asterisk /'æstərɪsk/ *n* asterisco *m*

asthma /'æsmə/ *n* asma *f*. **~tic** /-'mætɪk/ *a* & *n* asmático (*m*)

astonish /ə'stɒnɪʃ/ *vt* espantar. **~ingly** *adv* espantosamente. **~ment** *n* espanto *m*

astound /ə'staʊnd/ *vt* assombrar

astray /ə'streɪ/ *adv* & *a* **go ~** perder-se, extraviar-se. **lead ~** desencaminhar

astride /ə'straɪd/ *adv* & *prep* escarranchado (em)

astringent /ə'strɪndʒənt/ *a* & *n* adstringente (*m*)

astrolog|y /ə'strɒlədʒɪ/ *n* astrologia *f*. **~er** *n* astrólogo *m*

astronaut /'æstrənɔːt/ *n* astronauta *mf*

astronom|y /ə'strɒnəmɪ/ *n* astronomia *f*. **~er** *n* astrônomo *m*, (*P*) astrónomo *m*. **~ical** /æstrə'nɒmɪkl/ *a* astronômico, (*P*) astronómico

astute /ə'stjuːt/ *a* astuto, astucioso. **~ness** *n* astúcia *f*

asylum /ə'saɪləm/ *n* asilo *m*

at /ət/; *emphatic* /æt/ *prep* a, em. **~ home** em casa. **~ night** à noite. **~ once** imediatamente; (*simultaneously*) ao mesmo tempo. **~ school** na escola. **~ sea** no mar. **~ the door** na porta. **~ times** às vezes. **angry/surprised ~** zangado/surpreendido com. **not ~ all** de nada. **no wind ~ all** nenhum vento

ate /et/ *see* eat

atheis|t /'eɪθɪɪst/ *n* ateu *m*. **~m** /-zəm/ *n* ateísmo *m*

athlet|e /'æθliːt/ *n* atleta *mf*. **~ic** /-'letɪk/ *a* atlético. **~ics** /-'letɪks/ *n*(*pl*) atletismo *m*

Atlantic /ət'læntɪk/ *a* atlântico □ *n* **~ (Ocean)** Atlântico *m*

atlas /'ætləs/ *n* atlas *m*

atmospher|e /'ætməsfɪə(r)/ *n* atmosfera *f*. **~ic** /-'ferɪk/ *a* atmosférico

atom /'ætəm/ *n* átomo *m*. **~ic** /ə'tɒmɪk/ *a* atômico, (*P*) atómico. **~(ic) bomb** bomba *f* atômica, (*P*) atómica

atomize /'ætəmaɪz/ *vt* atomizar, vaparizar, pulverizar. **~r** /-ə(r)/ *n* pulverizador *m*, vaporizador *m*

atone /ə'təʊn/ *vi* **~ for** expiar. **~ment** *n* expiação *f*

atrocious /ə'trəʊʃəs/ *a* atroz

atrocity /ə'trɒsətɪ/ *n* atrocidade *f*

atrophy /'ætrəfɪ/ *n* atrofia *f* □ *vt/i* atrofiar(-se)

attach /ə'tætʃ/ *vt/i* (*affix*) ligar(-se), prender(-se); (*join*) juntar(-se). **~ed** *a* (*document*) junto, anexo. **be ~ed to** (*like*) estar apegado a. **~ment** *n* ligação *f*; (*affection*) apego *m*; (*accessory*) acessório *m*

attaché /ə'tæʃeɪ/ *n* (*pol*) adido *m*. **~ case** pasta *f*

attack /ə'tæk/ *n* ataque *m* □ *vt/i* atacar. **~er** *n* atacante *mf*

attain /ə'teɪn/ *vt* atingir. **~able** *a* atingível. **~ment** *n* consecução *f*. **~ments** *npl* conhecimentos *mpl*, talentos *mpl* adquiridos

attempt /ə'tempt/ *vt* tentar □ *n* tentativa *f*

attend /ə'tend/ *vt/i* atender (to a); (*escort*) acompanhar; (*look after*) tratar; (*meeting*) comparecer a; (*school*) freqüentar, (*P*) frequentar. **~ance** *n* comparecimento *m*; (*times present*) freqüência *f*, (*P*) frequência *f*; (*people*) assistência *f*

attendant /ə'tendənt/ *a* concomitante, que acompanha □ *n* empregado *m*; (*servant*) servidor *m*

attention /ə'tenʃn/ *n* atenção *f*. **~!** (*mil*) sentido! **pay ~** prestar atenção (to a)

attentive /ə'tentɪv/ *a* atento; (*considerate*) atencioso

attest /ə'test/ *vt/i* **~ (to)** atestar. **~ a signature** reconhecer uma assinatura. **~ation** /ætə'steɪʃn/ *n* atestação *f*, prova *f*

attic /'ætɪk/ *n* sótão *m*, águafurtada *f*

attitude /'ætɪtjuːd/ *n* atitude *f*

attorney /əˈtɜ:nɪ/ *n* (*pl* -eys) procurador *m*; (*Amer*) advogado *m*
attract /əˈtrækt/ *vt* atrair. ~**ion** /-ʃn/ *n* atração *f*, (*P*) atracção *f*; (*charm*) atrativo *m*, (*P*) atractivo *m*
attractive /əˈtræktɪv/ *a* atraente. ~**ly** *adv* atraentemente, agradavelmente
attribute[1] /əˈtrɪbju:t/ *vt* ~ to atribuir a
attribute[2] /ˈætrɪbju:t/ *n* atributo *m*
attrition /əˈtrɪʃn/ *n* war of ~ guerra *f* de desgaste
aubergine /ˈəʊbəʒi:n/ *n* berinjela *f*
auburn /ˈɔ:bən/ *a* cor de acaju, castanho-avermelhado
auction /ˈɔ:kʃn/ *n* leilão *m* □ *vt* leiloar. ~**eer** /-əˈnɪə(r)/ *n* leiloeiro *m*, (*P*) pregoeiro *m*
audaci|ous /ɔ:ˈdeɪʃəs/ *a* audacioso, audaz. ~**ty** /-æsətɪ/ *n* audácia *f*
audible /ˈɔ:dəbl/ *a* audível
audience /ˈɔ:dɪəns/ *n* auditório *m*; (*theat, radio; interview*) audiência *f*
audiovisual /ɔ:dɪəʊˈvɪʒʊəl/ *a* audiovisual
audit /ˈɔ:dɪt/ *n* auditoria *f* □ *vt* fazer uma auditoria
audition /ɔ:ˈdɪʃn/ *n* audição *f* □ *vt* dar/fazer uma audição
auditor /ˈɔ:dɪtə(r)/ *n* perito-contador *m*, (*P*) perito-contabilista *m*
auditorium /ɔ:dɪˈtɔ:rɪəm/ *n* auditório *m*
augment /ɔ:gˈment/ *vt/i* aumentar (-se)
augur /ˈɔ:gə(r)/ *vi* ~ well/ill ser de bom ou mau agouro
August /ˈɔ:gəst/ *n* Agosto *m*
aunt /a:nt/ *n* tia *f*
au pair /əʊˈpeə(r)/ *n* au pair *f*
aura /ˈɔ:rə/ *n* aura *f*, emanação *f*
auspices /ˈɔ:spɪsɪz/ *npl* **under the** ~ **of** sob os auspícios *or* o patrocínio de
auspicious /ɔ:ˈspɪʃəs/ *a* auspicioso
auster|e /ɔ:ˈstɪə(r)/ *a* austero. ~**ity** /-erətɪ/ *n* austeridade *f*
Australia /ɒˈstreɪlɪə/ *n* Austrália *f*. ~**n** *a* & *n* australiano (*m*)
Austria /ˈɔstrɪə/ *n* áustria *f*. ~**n** *a* & *n* austríaco (*m*)
authentic /ɔ:ˈθentɪk/ *a* autêntico. ~**ity** /-ənˈtɪsətɪ/ *n* autenticidade *f*
authenticate /ɔ:ˈθentɪkeɪt/ *vt* autenticar
author /ˈɔ:θə(r)/ *n* autor *m*, autora *f*. ~**ship** *n* (*origin*) autoria *f*
authoritarian /ɔ:θɒrɪˈteərɪən/ *a* autoritário
authorit|y /ɔ:ˈθɒrətɪ/ *n* autoridade *f*; (*permission*) autorização *f*. ~**ative** /-ɪtətɪv/ *a* (*trusted*) autorizado; (*manner*) autoritário
authoriz|e /ˈɔ:θəraɪz/ *vt* autorizar. ~**ation** /-ˈzeɪʃn/ *n* autorização *f*
autistic /ɔ:ˈtɪstɪk/ *a* autista, autístico
autobiography /ɔ:təˈbaɪɒgrəfɪ/ *n* autobiografia *f*
autocrat /ˈɔ:təkræt/ *n* autocrata *mf*. ~**ic** /-ˈkrætɪk/ *a* autocrático
autograph /ˈɔ:təgra:f/ *n* autógrafo *m* □ *vt* autografar
automat|e /ˈɔ:təmeɪt/ *vt* automatizar. ~**ion** /ɔ:təˈmeɪʃn/ *n* automação *f*
automatic /ɔ:təˈmætɪk/ *a* automático □ *n* (*car*) automático *m*. ~**ally** /-klɪ/ *adv* automaticamente
automobile /ˈɔ:təməbi:l/ *n* (*Amer*) automóvel *m*
autonom|y /ɔ:ˈtɒnəmɪ/ *n* autonomia *f*. ~**ous** *a* autônomo, (*P*) autónomo
autopsy /ˈɔ:tɒpsɪ/ *n* autópsia *f*
autumn /ˈɔ:təm/ *n* outono *m*. ~**al** /-ˈtʌmnəl/ *a* outonal
auxiliary /ɔ:gˈzɪlɪərɪ/ *a* & *n* auxiliar (*mf*). ~ **verb** verbo *m* auxiliar
avail /əˈveɪl/ *vt* ~ o.s. of servir-se de □ *vi* (*be of use*) valer □ *n* **of no** ~ inútil. **to no** ~ sem resultado, em vão
availab|le /əˈveɪləbl/ *a* disponível. ~**ility** /-ˈbɪlətɪ/ *n* disponibilidade *f*
avalanche /ˈævəla:nʃ/ *n* avalanche *f*
avaric|e /ˈævərɪs/ *n* avareza *f*. ~**ious** /-ˈrɪʃəs/ *a* avarento
avenge /əˈvendʒ/ *vt* vingar
avenue /ˈævənju:/ *n* avenida *f*; (*fig: line of approach*) via *f*
average /ˈævərɪdʒ/ *n* média *f* □ *a* médio □ *vt* tirar a média de; (*produce, do*) fazer em média □ *vi* ~ **out at** dar de média, dar uma média de. **on** ~ em média
avers|e /əˈvɜ:s/ *a* **be** ~**e to** ser avesso a. ~**ion** /-ʃn/ *n* aversão *f*, repugnância *f*
avert /əˈvɜ:t/ *vt* (*turn away*) desviar; (*ward off*) evitar
aviary /ˈeɪvɪərɪ/ *n* aviário *m*
aviation /eɪvɪˈeɪʃn/ *n* aviação *f*
avid /ˈævɪd/ *a* ávido
avocado /ævəˈka:dəʊ/ *n* (*pl* -s) abacate *m*
avoid /əˈvɔɪd/ *vt* evitar. ~**able** *a* que se pode evitar, evitável. ~**ance** *n* evitação *f*
await /əˈweɪt/ *vt* aguardar
awake /əˈweɪk/ *vt/i* (*pt* **awoke**, *pp* **awoken**) acordar □ *a* **be** ~ estar acordado
awaken /əˈweɪkən/ *vt/i* despertar. ~**ing** *n* despertar *m*
award /əˈwɔ:d/ *vt* atribuir, conferir; (*jur*) adjudicar □ *n* recompensa *f*, prêmio *m*, (*P*) prémio *m*; (*scholarship*) bolsa *f*
aware /əˈweə(r)/ *a* ciente, cônscio. **be** ~ **of** estar consciente de *or* ter con-

sciência de. **become ~ of** tomar consciência de. **make sb ~ of** sensibilizar alg para. **~ness** *n* consciência *f*

away /ə'weɪ/ *adv* (*at a distance*) longe; (*to a distance*) para longe; (*absent*) fora; (*persistently*) sem parar; (*entirely*) completamente. **eight miles ~** a oito milhas (de distância). **four days ~** daí a quatro dias □ *a & n* **~ (match)** jogo *m* fora de casa

awe /ɔ:/ *n* assombro *m*, admiração *f* reverente, terror *m* respeitoso. **~some** *a* assombroso. **~struck** *a* assombrado, aterrado

awful /'ɔ:fl/ *a* terrível. **~ly** *adv* muito, terrivelmente

awhile /ə'waɪl/ *adv* por algum tempo

awkward /'ɔ:kwəd/ *a* difícil; (*clumsy, difficult to use*) desajeitado, maljeitoso; (*inconvenient*) inconveniente; (*embarrassing*) embaraçoso; (*embarrassed*) embaraçado. **an ~ customer** (*colloq*) um preguês perigoso *or* intratável

awning /'ɔ:nɪŋ/ *n* toldo *m*

awoke, awoken /ə'wəʊk, ə'wəʊkən/ *see* **awake**

awry /ə'raɪ/ *adv* torto. **go ~** dar errado. **be ~** estar torto

axe /æks/ *n* machado *m* □ *vt* (*pres p* **axing**) (*reduce*) cortar; (*dismiss*) despedir

axiom /'æksɪəm/ *n* axioma *m*

axis /'æksɪs/ *n* (*pl* **axes** /-i:z/) eixo *m*

axle /'æksl/ *n* eixo (de roda) *m*

Azores /ə'zɔ:z/ *n* Açores *mpl*

B

BA *abbr see* **Bachelor of Arts**

babble /'bæbl/ *vi* balbuciar; (*baby*) palrar; (*stream*) murmurar □ *n* balbucio *m*; (*of baby*) palrice *f*; (*of stream*) murmúrio *m*

baboon /bə'bu:n/ *n* babuíno *m*

baby /'beɪbɪ/ *n* bebê *m*, (*P*) bebé *m*. **~ carriage** (*Amer*) carrinho *m* de bebê, (*P*) bebé. **~-sit** *vi* tomar conta de crianças. **~-sitter** *n* baby-sitter *mf*, babá *f*

babyish /'beɪbɪɪʃ/ *a* infantil

bachelor /'bætʃələ(r)/ *n* solteiro *m*. **B~ of Arts/Science** Bacharel *m* em Letras/Ciencias

back /bæk/ *n* (*of person, hand, chair*) costas *fpl*; (*of animal*) dorso *m*; (*of car, train*) parte *f* traseira; (*of house, room*) fundo *m*; (*of coin*) reverso *m*; (*of page*) verso *m*; (*football*) beque *m*; zagueiro *m*, (*P*) defesa *m* □ *a* traseiro, posterior; (*taxes*) em atraso □ *adv* atrás, para trás; (*returned*) de volta □ *vt* (*support*) apoiar; (*horse*) apostar em; (*car*) (fazer) recuar □ *vi* recuar. **at the ~ of beyond** em casa do diabo, no fim do mundo. **~-bencher** *n* (*pol*) deputado *m* sem pasta. **~ down** desistir (**from** de). **~ number** número *m* atrasado. **~ out** (*of an undertaking etc*) fugir (ao combinado *etc*). **~ up** (*auto*) fazer marcha à ré, (*P*) atrás; (*comput*) tirar um back-up de. **~-up** *n* apoio *m*; (*comput*) back-up *m*; (*Amer*: *traffic-jam*) engarrafamento *m* □ *a* de reserva; (*comput*) back-up

backache /'bækeɪk/ *n* dor *f* nas costas

backbiting /'bækbaɪtɪŋ/ *n* maledicência *f*

backbone /'bækbəʊn/ *n* espinha *f* dorsal

backdate /bæk'deɪt/ *vt* antedatar

backer /'bækə(r)/ *n* (*of horse*) apostador *m*; (*of cause*) partidário *m*, apoiante *mf*; (*comm*) patrocinador *m*, financiador *m*

backfire /bæk'faɪə(r)/ *vi* (*auto*) dar explosões no tubo de escape; (*fig*) sair o tiro pela culatra

background /'bækgraʊnd/ *n* (*of picture*) fundo *m*, segundo-plano *m*; (*context*) contexto *m*; (*environment*) meio *m*; (*experience*) formação *f*

backhand /'bækhænd/ *n* (*tennis*) esquerda *f*. **~ed** *a* com as costas da mão. **~ed compliment** cumprimento *m* ambéguo. **~er** /-'hændə(r)/ *n* (*sl: bribe*) suborno *m*, (*P*) luvas *fpl* (*colloq*)

backing /'bækɪŋ/ *n* apoio *m*; (*comm*) patrocínio *m*

backlash /'bæklæʃ/ *n* (*fig*) reação *f* violenta, repercussões *fpl*

backlog /'bæklɒg/ *n* acúmulo *m* (de trabalho *etc*)

backside /'bæksaɪd/ *n* (*colloq: buttocks*) traseiro *m*

backstage /bæk'steɪdʒ/ *a & adv* por detrás dos bastidores

backstroke /'bækstrəʊk/ *n* nado *m* de costas

backtrack /'bæktræk/ *vi* (*fig*) voltar atrás

backward /'bækwəd/ *a* retrógrado; (*retarded*) atrasado; (*step, look, etc*) para trás

backwards /'bækwədz/ *adv* para trás; (*walk*) para trás; (*fall*) de costas, para trás; (*in reverse order*) de trás para diante, às avessas. **go ~ and forwards** ir e vir, andar para trás e para a frente. **know sth ~** saber alg coisa de trás para a frente

backwater /'bækwɔ:tə(r)/ *n* (*pej: place*) lugar *m* atrasado

bacon /'beɪkən/ *n* toucinho *m* defumado; (*in rashers*) bacon *m*

bacteria /bæk'tɪərɪə/ *npl* bactérias *fpl*. **~l** *a* bacteriano

bad /bæd/ *a* (**worse, worst**) mau; (*accident*) grave; (*food*) estragado; (*ill*) doente. **feel ~** sentir-se mal. **~ language** palavrões *mpl*. **~-mannered** *a* mal educado. **~-tempered** *a* mal humorado. **~ly** *adv* mal; (*seriously*) gravemente. **want ~ly** (*desire*) desejar imensamente, ter grande vontade de; (*need*) precisar muito de

badge /bædʒ/ *n* emblema *m*; (*policeman's*) crachá *m*, (*P*) distintivo *m*

badger /'bædʒə(r)/ *n* texugo *m* □ *vt* atormentar; (*pester*) importunar

badminton /'bædmmtən/ *n* badminton *m*

baffle /'bæfl/ *vt* atrapalhar, desconcertar

bag /bæg/ *n* saco *m*; (*handbag*) bolsa *f*, carteira *f*. **~s** (*luggage*) malas *fpl* □ *vt* (*pt* **bagged**) ensacar; (*colloq: take*) embolsar

baggage /'bægɪdʒ/ *n* bagagem *f*

baggy /'bægɪ/ *a* (*clothes*) muito largo, bufante

bagpipes /'bægpaɪps/ *npl* gaita *f* de foles

Bahamas /bə'ha:məz/ *npl* **the ~** as Bahamas *fpl*

bail[1] /beɪl/ *n* fiança *f* □ *vt* pôr em liberdade sob fiança. **be out on ~** estar solto sob fiança

bail[2] /beɪl/ *vt* **~ (out)** (*naut*) esgotar, tirar água de

bailiff /'beɪlɪf/ *n* (*officer*) oficial *m* de diligências; (*of estate*) feitor *m*

bait /beɪt/ *n* isca *f* □ *vt* pôr isca; (*fig*) atormentar (com insultos), atazanar

bak|e /beɪk/ *vt/i* cozer (no forno); (*bread, cakes, etc*) assar; (*in the sun*) torrar. **~er** *n* padeiro *m*; (*of cakes*) doceiro *m*. **~ing** *n* cozedura *f*; (*batch*) fornada *f*. **~ing-powder** *n* fermento *m* em pó. **~ing tin** forma *f*

bakery /'beɪkərɪ/ *n* padaria *f*; (*cakes*) confeitaria *f*

balance /'bæləns/ *n* equilíbrio *m*; (*scales*) balança *f*; (*sum*) saldo *m*; (*comm*) balanço *m*. **~ of power** equilíbrio *m* político. **~ of trade** balança *f* comercial. **~-sheet** *n* balanço *m* □ *vt* equilibrar; (*weigh up*) pesar; (*budget*) equilibrar □ *vi* equilibrar-se. **~d** *a* equilibrado

balcony /'bælkənɪ/ *n* balcão *m*; (*in a house*) varanda *f*

bald /bɔ:ld/ *a* (**-er, -est**) calvo, careca; (*tyre*) careca. **~ing** *a* **be ~ing** ficar calvo. **~ly** *adv* a nu e cru, (*P*) secamente. **~ness** *n* calvície *f*

bale[1] /beɪl/ *n* (*of straw*) fardo *m*; (*of cotton*) balote *m* □ *vt* enfardar

bale[2] /beɪl/ *vi* **~ out** saltar em pára-quedas

balk /bɔ:k/ *vt* frustrar, contrariar □ *vi* **~ at** assustar-se com, recuar perante

ball[1] /bɔ:l/ *n* bola *f*. **~-bearing** *n* rolamento *m* de esferas. **~-cock** *n* válvula *f* de depósito de água. **~-point** *n* esferográfica *f*

ball[2] /bɔ:l/ *n* (*dance*) baile *m*

ballad /'bæləd/ *n* balada *f*

ballast /'bæləst/ *n* lastro *m*

ballerina /bælə'ri:nə/ *n* bailarina *f*

ballet /'bæleɪ/ *n* balé *m*, (*P*) ballet *m*, bailado *m*

balloon /bə'lu:n/ *n* balão *m*

ballot /'bælət/ *n* escrutínio *m*. **~ (-paper)** *n* cédula *f* eleitoral, (*P*) boletim *m* de voto. **~-box** *n* urna *f* □ *vi* (*pt* **balloted**) (*pol*) votar □ *vt* (*members*) consultar por voto secreto

ballroom /'bɔ:lru:m/ *n* salão *m* de baile

balm /ba:m/ *n* bálsamo *m*. **~y** *a* balsâmico; (*mild*) suave

balustrade /bælə'streɪd/ *n* balaustrada *f*

bamboo /bæm'bu:/ *n* bambu *m*

ban /bæn/ *vt* (*pt* **banned**) banir. **~ from** proibir de □ *n* proibição *f*

banal /bə'na:l/ *a* banal. **~ity** /-ælətɪ/ *n* banalidade *f*

banana /bə'na:nə/ *n* banana *f*

band /bænd/ *n* (*for fastening*) cinta *f*, faixa *f*; (*strip*) tira *f*, banda *f*; (*mus: mil*) banda *f*; (*mus: dance, jazz*) conjunto *m*; (*group*) bando *m* □ *vi* **~ together** juntar-se

bandage /'bændɪdʒ/ *n* atadura *f*, (*P*) ligadura *f* □ *vt* ligar

bandit /'bændɪt/ *n* bandido *m*

bandstand /'bændstænd/ *n* coreto *m*

bandwagon /'bændwægən/ *n* **climb on the ~** (*fig*) apanhar o trem

bandy /'bændɪ/ *vt* trocar. **~ a story about** espalhar uma história

bandy-legged /'bændɪlegd/ *a* cambaio, de pernas tortas

bang /bæŋ/ *n* (*blow*) pancada *f*; (*loud noise*) estouro *m*, estrondo *m*; (*of gun*) detonação *f* □ *vt/i* (*hit, shut*) bater □ *vi* explodir □ *int* pum. **~ in the middle** jogar no meio. **shut the door with a ~** bater (com) a porta

banger /'bæŋə(r)/ *n* (*firework*) bomba *f*; (*sl: sausage*) salsicha *f*. **(old) ~** (*sl: car*) calhambeque *m* (*colloq*)

bangle /'bæŋgl/ *n* pulseira *f*, bracelete *m*

banish /'bænɪʃ/ *vt* banir, desterrar

banisters /'bænɪstəz/ *npl* corrimão *m*

banjo /'bændʒəʊ/ *pl* (**-os**) banjo *m*

bank[1] /bæŋk/ *n* (*of river*) margem *f*; (*of earth*) talude *m*; (*of sand*) banco *m*

□ *vt* amontoar □ *vi* (*aviat*) inclinar-se numa curva

bank[2] /bæŋk/ *n* (*comm*) banco *m* □ *vt* depositar no banco. ~ **account** conta *f* bancária. ~ **holiday** feriado *m* nacional. ~ **on** contar com. ~ **rate** taxa *f* bancária. ~ **with** ter conta em

bank|er /'bæŋkə(r)/ *n* banqueiro *m*. ~**ing** /-ɪŋ/ *n* operações *fpl* bancárias; (*career*) carreira *f* bancária, banca *f*

banknote /'bæŋknəʊt/ *n* nota *f* de banco

bankrupt /'bæŋkrʌpt/ *a* & *n* falido (*m*). **go** ~ falir □ *vt* levar à falência. ~**cy** *n* falência *f*, bancarrota *f*

banner /'bænə(r)/ *n* bandeira *f*, estandarte *m*

banns /bænz/ *npl* proclamas *mpl*, (*P*) banhos *mpl*

banquet /'bæŋkwɪt/ *n* banquete *m*

banter /'bæntə(r)/ *n* gracejo *m*, brincadeira *f* □ *vi* gracejar, brincar

baptism /'bæptɪzəm/ *n* batismo *m*, (*P*) baptismo *m*

Baptist /'bæptɪst/ *n* batista *mf*, (*P*) baptista *mf*

baptize /bæp'taɪz/ *vt* batizar, (*P*) baptizar

bar /ba:(r)/ *n* (*of chocolate*) tablette *f*, barra *f*; (*of metal, soap, sand etc*) barra *f*; (*of door, window*) tranca *f*; (*in pub*) bar *m*; (*counter*) balcão *m*, bar *m*; (*mus*) barra *f* de compasso; (*fig: obstacle*) barreira *f*; (*in lawcourt*) teia *f*. **the B**~ a advocacia *f* □ *vt* (*pt* **barred**) (*obstruct*) barrar; (*prohibit*) proibir (**from** de); (*exclude*) excluir; (*door, window*) trancar □ *prep* salvo, exceto, (*P*) excepto ~ **none** sem exceção, (*P*) excepção. ~ **code** código *m* de barra. **behind** ~**s** na cadeia

Barbados /ba:'beɪdɒs/ *n* Barbados *mpl*

barbarian /ba:'beərɪən/ *n* bárbaro *m*

barbari|c /ba:'bærɪk/ *a* bárbaro. ~**ty** /-ətɪ/ *n* barbaridade *f*

barbarous /'ba:bərəs/ *a* bárbaro

barbecue /'ba:bɪkju:/ *n* (*grill*) churrasqueira *f*, (*occasion, food*) churrasco *m* □ *vt* assar

barbed /ba:bd/ *a* ~ **wire** arame *m* farpado

barber /'ba:bə(r)/ *n* barbeiro *m*

barbiturate /ba:'bɪtjʊrət/ *n* barbitúrico *m*

bare /beə(r)/ *a* (-**er**, -**est**) nu; (*room*) vazio; (*mere*) mero □ *vt* pôr à mostra, pôr a nu, descobrir

bareback /'beəbæk/ *adv* em pêlo

barefaced /'beəfeɪst/ *a* descarado

barefoot /'beə(r)fʊt/ *adv* descalço

barely /'beəlɪ/ *adv* apenas, mal

bargain /'ba:gɪn/ *n* (*deal*) negócio *m*; (*good buy*) pechincha *f* □ *vi* negociar; (*haggle*) regatear. ~ **esperar for**

barge /ba:dʒ/ *n* barcaça *f* □ *vi* ~ **in** interromper (despropositadamente); (*into room*) irromper

bark[1] /ba:k/ *n* (*of tree*) casca *f*

bark[2] /ba:k/ *n* (*of dog*) latido *m* □ *vi* latir. **his** ~ **is worse than his bite** cão que ladra não morde

barley /'ba:lɪ/ *n* cevada *f*. ~ **sugar** *n* açúcar *m* de cevada. ~ **water** *n* água *f* de cevada

barmaid /'ba:meɪd/ *n* empregada *f* de bar

barman /'ba:mən/ *n* (*pl* -**men**) barman *m*, empregado *m* de bar

barmy /'ba:mɪ/ *a* (*sl*) maluco

barn /ba:n/ *n* celeiro *m*

barometer /bə'rɒmɪtə(r)/ *n* barômetro *m*, (*P*) barómetro *m*

baron /'bærən/ *n* barão *m*. ~**ess** *n* baronesa *f*

baroque /bə'rɒk/ *a* & *n* barroco (*m*)

barracks /'bærəks/ *n* quartel *m*, caserna *f*

barrage /'bæra:ʒ/ *n* barragem *f*; (*fig*) enxurrada *f*; (*mil*) fogo *m* de barragem

barrel /'bærəl/ *n* (*of oil, wine*) barril *m*; (*of gun*) cano *m*. ~-**organ** *n* realejo *m*

barren /'bærən/ *a* estéril; (*soil*) árido, estéril

barricade /bærɪ'keɪd/ *n* barricada *f* □ *vt* barricar

barrier /'bærɪə(r)/ *n* barreira *f*; (*hindrance*) entrave *m*, barreira *f*

barring /'ba:rɪŋ/ *prep* salvo, exceto, (*P*) excepto

barrister /'bærɪstə(r)/ *n* advogado *m*

barrow /'bærəʊ/ *n* carrinho *m* de mão

barter /'ba:tə(r)/ *n* troca *f* □ *vt* trocar

base/beɪs/ *n* base *f* □ *vt* basear (**on** em) □ *a* baixo, ignóbil. ~**less** *a* infundado

baseball /'beɪsbɔ:l/ *n* beisebol *m*

basement /'beɪsmənt/ *n* porão *m*, (*P*) cave *f*

bash /bæʃ/ *vt* bater com violência □ *n* pancada *f* forte. **have a** ~ **at** (*sl*) experimentar

bashful /'bæʃfl/ *a* tímido

basic /'beɪsɪk/ *a* básico, elementar, fundamental. ~**ally** *adv* basicamente, no fundo

basil /'bæzl/ *n* mangericão *m*

basin /'beɪsn/ *n* bacia *f*, (*for food*) tigela *f*, (*naut*) ante-doca *f*, (*for washing*) pia *f*

basis /'beɪsɪs/ *n* (*pl* **bases** /-si:z/) base *f*

bask /ba:sk/ *vi* ~ **in the sun** apanhar sol

basket /'ba:skɪt/ *n* cesto *m*

basketball /'ba:skɪtbɔ:l/ *n* basquete(-bol) *m*
Basque /ba:sk/ *a* & *n* basco (*m*)
bass[1] /bæs/ *n* (*pl* bass) (*fish*) perca *f*
bass[2] /beɪs/ *a* (*mus*) grave □ *n* (*pl* basses) (*mus*) baixo *m*
bassoon /bə'su:n/ *n* fagote *m*
bastard /'ba:stəd/ *n* (*illegitimate child*) bastardo *m*; (*sl: pej*) safado (*sl*) *m*; (*colloq: not pej*) cara (*colloq*) *m*
baste /beɪst/ *vt* (*culin*) regar (com molho)
bastion /'bæstɪən/ *n* bastião *m*, baluarte *m*
bat[1] /bæt/ *n* (*cricket*) pá *f*; (*baseball*) bastão *m*; (*table tennis*) rafuete *f* □ *vt/i* (*pt* **batted**) bater (em). **without ~ting an eyelid** sem pestanejar
bat[2] /bæt/ *n* (*zool*) morcego *m*
batch /bætʃ/ *n* (*loaves*) fornada *f*; (*people*) monte *m*; (*goods*) remessa *f*; (*papers, letters etc*) batelada *f*, monte *m*
bated /'beɪtɪd/ *a* **with ~ breath** com a respiração em suspenso, com a respiração suspensa
bath /ba:θ/ *n* (*pl* -s /ba:ðz/) banho *m*; (*tub*) banheira *f*. **~s** (*washing*) banho *m* público; (*swimming*) piscina *f* □ *vt* dar banho a □ *vi* tomar banho
bathe /beɪð/ *vt* dar banho em; (*wound*) limpar □ *vi* tomar banho (de mar) □ *n* banho *m* (de mar). **~r** /-ə(r)/ *n* banhista *mf*
bathing /'beɪðɪŋ/ *n* banho *m* de mar. **~-costume/-suit** *n* traje *m* de banho, (*P*) fato *m* de banho
bathrobe /'ba:θrəʊb/ *n* (*Amer*) roupão *m*
bathroom /'ba:θru:m/ *n* banheiro *m*, (*P*) casa *f* de banho
baton /'bætən/ *n* (*mus*) batuta *f*; (*policeman's*) cassetete *m*; (*mil*) bastão *m*
battalion /bə'tælɪən/ *n* batalhão *m*
batter /'bætə(r)/ *vt* bater, espancar, maltratar □ *n* (*culin: for cakes*) massa *f* de bolos; (*culin: for frying*) massa *f* de empanar. **~ed** *a* (*car, pan*) amassado; (*child, wife*) maltratado, espancado. **~ing** *n* **take a ~ing** levar pancada *or* uma surra
battery /'bætərɪ/ *n* (*mil, auto*) bateria *f*; (*electr*) pilha *f*
battle /'bætl/ *n* batalha *f*; (*fig*) luta *f* □ *vi* combater, batalhar, lutar
battlefield /'bætlfi:ld/ *n* campo *m* de batalha
battlements /'bætlmənts/ *npl* ameias *fpl*
battleship /'bætlʃɪp/ *n* couraçado *m*
baulk /bɔ:lk/ *vt/i* = **balk**
bawdy /'bɔ:dɪ/ *a* (-ier, -iest) obsceno, indecente
bawl /bɔ:l/ *vt/i* berrar
bay[1] /beɪ/ *n* (*bot*) loureiro *m*
bay[2] /beɪ/ *n* (*geog*) baía *f*. **~ window** janela *f* saliente
bay[3] /beɪ/ *n* (*bark*) latido *m* □ *vi* latir. **at ~** (*animal; fig*) cercado, (*P*) em apuros. **keep at ~** manter à distância
bayonet /'beɪənɪt/ *n* baioneta *f*
bazaar /bə'za:(r)/ *n* bazar *m*
BC *abbr* (*before Christ*) a C
be /bi:/ *vi* (*pres* **am, are, is**; *pt* **was, were**; *pp* **been**) (*permanent quality/place*) ser; (*temporary place/state*) estar; (*become*) ficar. **~ hot/right** *etc* ter calor/razão *etc*. **he's 30** (*age*) ele tem 30 anos. **it's fine/cold** *etc* (*weather*) faz bom tempo/frio *etc*. **how are you?** (*health*) como está? **I'm a doctor — are you?** eu sou médico — é mesmo? **it's pretty, isn't it?** é bonito, não é? **he is to come** (*must*) ele deve vir. **how much is it?** (*cost*) quanto é? **~ reading eating** *etc* estar lendo/comendo *etc*. **the money was found** o dinheiro foi encontrado. **have been to** ter ido a, ter estado em
beach /bi:tʃ/ *n* praia *f*
beacon /'bi:kən/ *n* farol *m*; (*marker*) baliza *f*
bead /bi:d/ *n* conta *f*. **~ of sweat** gota *f* de suor
beak /bi:k/ *n* bico *m*
beaker /'bi:kə(r)/ *n* copo *m* de plástico com bico; (*in lab*) proveta *f*
beam /bi:m/ *n* (*of wood*) trave *f*, viga *f*; (*of light*) raio *m*; (*of torch*) feixe *m* de luz □ *vt/i* (*radiate*) irradiar; (*fig*) sorrir radiante. **~ing** *a* radiante
bean /bi:n/ *n* feijão *m*. **broad ~** fava *f*. **coffee ~s** café *m* em grão. **runner ~** feijão *m* verde
bear[1] /beə(r)/ *n* urso *m*
bear[2] /beə(r)/ *vt/i* (*pt* **bore**, *pp* **borne**) sustentar, suportar; (*endure*) agüentar, (*P*) aguentar, suportar; (*child*) dar à luz. **~ in mind** ter em mente, lembrar. **~ left** virar à esquerda. **~ on** relacionar-se com, ter a ver com. **~ out** confirmar. **~ up!** coragem! **~able** *a* tolerável, suportável. **~er** *n* portador *m*
beard /bɪəd/ *n* barba *f*. **~ed** *a* barbado, com barba
bearing /'beərɪŋ/ *n* (*manner*) porte *m*; (*relevance*) relação *f*; (*naut*) marcação *f*. **get one's ~s** orientar-se
beast /bi:st/ *n* (*animal, person*) besta *f*, animal *m*; (*in fables*) fera *f*. **~ of burden** besta *f* de carga
beat /bi:t/ *vt/i* (*pt* **beat**, *pp* **beaten**) bater □ *n* (*med*) batimento *m*; (*mus*) compasso *m*, ritmo *m*; (*of drum*) toque *m*; (*of policeman*) ronda *f*, (*P*) giro *m*. **~ about the bush** estar com rodeios. **~ a retreat** bater em retirada. **~ it**

(*sl: go away*) pôr-se a andar. **it ~s me** (*colloq*) não consigo entender. **~ up** espancar. **~er** *n* (*culin*) batedeira *f*. **~ing** *n* sova *f*

beautician /bju:ˈtɪʃn/ *n* esteticista *mf*

beautiful /ˈbju:tɪfl/ *a* belo, lindo. **~ly** *adv* lindamente

beautify /ˈbju:tɪfaɪ/ *vt* embelezar

beauty /ˈbju:tɪ/ *n* beleza *f*. **~ parlour** instituto *m* de beleza. **~ spot** sinal *m* no rosto, mosca *f*; (*place*) local *m* pitoresco

beaver /ˈbi:və(r)/ *n* castor *m*

became /bɪˈkeɪm/ *see* **become**

because /bɪˈkɒz/ *conj* porque □ *adv* **~ of** por causa de

beckon /ˈbekən/ *vt/i* **~ (to)** fazer sinal (para)

become /bɪˈkʌm/ *vt/i* (*pt* **became**, *pp* **become**) tornar-se; (*befit*) ficar bem a. **what has ~ of her?** que é feito dela?

becoming /bɪˈkʌmɪŋ/ *a* que fica bem, apropriado

bed /bed/ *n* cama *f*; (*layer*) camada *f*; (*of sea*) fundo *m*; (*of river*) leito *m*; (*of flowers*) canteiro *m* □ *vt/i* (*pt* **bedded**) **~ down** ir deitar-se. **~ in** plantar. **~ and breakfast (b & b)** quarto *m* com café da manhã. **~-sit(ter)** *n* (*colloq*) mixto *m* de quarto e sala. **go to ~** ir para cama. **in ~** na cama. **~ding** *n* roupa *f* de cama

bedclothes /ˈbedkləʊðz/ *n* roupa *f* de cama

bedlam /ˈbedləm/ *n* confusão *f*, balbúrdia *f*

bedraggled /bɪˈdrægld/ *a* (*wet*) molhado; (*untidy*) desarrumado; (*dishevelled*) desgrenhado

bedridden /ˈbedrɪdn/ *a* preso ao leito, doente de cama

bedroom /ˈbedru:m/ *n* quarto *m* de dormir

bedside /ˈbedsaɪd/ *n* cabeceira *f*. **~ manner** (*doctor's*) modos *mpl* que inspiram confiança

bedspread /ˈbedspred/ *n* colcha *f*

bedtime /ˈbedtaɪm/ *n* hora *f* de deitar, hora *f* de ir para a cama

bee /bi:/ *n* abelha *f*. **make a ~-line for** ir direto a

beech /bi:tʃ/ *n* faia *f*

beef /bi:f/ *n* carne *f* de vaca

beefburger /ˈbi:fbɜ:gə(r)/ *n* hambúrguer *m*

beehive /ˈbi:haɪv/ *n* colméia *f*

been /bi:n/ *see* **be**

beer /bɪə(r)/ *n* cerveja *f*

beet /bi:t/ *n* beterraba *f*

beetle /ˈbi:tl/ *n* escaravelho *m*

beetroot /ˈbi:tru:t/ *n* (raiz de) beterraba *f*

before /bɪˈfɔ:(r)/ *prep* (*time*) antes de; (*place*) em frente de □ *adv* antes; (*already*) já □ *conj* antes que. **~ leaving** antes de partir. **~ he leaves** antes que ele parta, antes de ele partir

beforehand /bɪˈfɔ:hænd/ *adv* de antemão, antecipadamente

befriend /bɪˈfrend/ *vt* tornar-se amigo de; (*be helpful to*) auxiliar

beg /beg/ *vt/i* (*pt* **begged**) mendigar; (*entreat*) suplicar. **~ sb's pardon** pedir desculpa a alg. **~ the question** fazer uma petição de princípio. **it's going ~ging** está sobrando

began /bɪˈgæn/ *see* **begin**

beggar /ˈbegə(r)/ *n* mendigo *m*, pedinte *mf*; (*colloq: person*) cara (*colloq*) *m*

begin /bɪˈgɪn/ *vt/i* (*pt* **began**, *pp* **begun**, *pres p* **beginning**) começar, principiar. **~ner** *n* principiante *mf*. **~ning** *n* começo *m*, princípio *m*

begrudge /bɪˈgrʌdʒ/ *vt* ter inveja de; (*give*) dar de má vontade. **~ doing** fazer de má vontade *or* a contragosto

beguile /bɪˈgaɪl/ *vt* enganar

begun /bɪˈgʌn/ *see* **begin**

behalf /bɪˈha:f/ *n* **on ~ of** em nome de; (*in the interest of*) em favor de

behave /bɪˈheɪv/ *vi* portar-se. **~ (o.s.)** portar-se bem

behaviour /bɪˈheɪvjə(r)/ *n* conduta *f*, comportamento *m*

behead /bɪˈhed/ *vt* decapitar

behind /bɪˈhaɪnd/ *prep* atrás de □ *adv* atrás; (*late*) com atraso □ *n* (*colloq: buttocks*) traseiro (*colloq*) *m*. **~ the times** antiquado, retrógrado. **leave ~** deixar para trás

behold /bɪˈhəʊld/ *vt* (*pt* **beheld**) (*old use*) ver

beholden /bɪˈhəʊldən/ *a* em dívida (**to** para com)

beige /beɪʒ/ *a* & *n* bege (*m*), (*P*) beige (*m*)

being /ˈbi:ɪŋ/ *n* ser *m*. **bring into ~** criar. **come into ~** nascer, originar-se

belated /bɪˈleɪtɪd/ *a* tardio, atrasado

belch /beltʃ/ *vi* arrotar □ *vt* **~ out** (*smoke*) vomitar, lançar □ *n* arroto *m*

belfry /ˈbelfrɪ/ *n* campanário *m*

Belgi|um /ˈbeldʒəm/ *n* Bélgica *f*. **~an** *a* & *n* belga (*mf*)

belief /bɪˈli:f/ *n* crença *f*; (*trust*) confiança *f*; (*opinion*) convicção *f*

believ|e /bɪˈli:v/ *vt/i* acreditar. **~e in** acreditar em. **~able** *a* crível. **~er** /-ə(r)/ *n* crente *mf*

belittle /bɪˈlɪtl/ *vt* depreciar

bell /bel/ *n* sino *m*; (*small*) sineta *f*; (*on door, of phone*) campainha *f*; (*on cat, toy*) guizo *m*

belligerent /bɪˈlɪdʒərənt/ *a* & *n* beligerante (*mf*)

bellow /'beləʊ/ *vt/i* berrar, bramir. ~ out rugir
bellows /'beləʊz/ *npl* fole *m*
belly /'belɪ/ *n* barriga *f*, ventre *m*. ~-ache *n* dor *f* de barriga
bellyful /'belɪfʊl/ *n* have a ~ estar com a barriga cheia
belong /bɪ'lɒŋ/ *vi* ~ (to) pertencer (a); (*club*) ser sócio (de)
belongings /bɪ'lɒŋɪŋz/ *npl* pertences *mpl*. personal ~ objetos *mpl* de uso pessoal
beloved /bɪ'lʌvɪd/ *a* & *n* amado (*m*)
below /bɪ'ləʊ/ *prep* abaixo de, debaixo de □ *adv* abaixo, em baixo; (*on page*) abaixo
belt /belt/ *n* cinto *m*; (*techn*) correia *f*; (*fig*) zona *f* □ *vt* (*sl: hit*) zurzir □ *vi* (*sl: rush*) safar-se
bemused /bɪ'mju:zd/ *a* estonteado, confuso; (*thoughtful*) pensativo
bench /bentʃ/ *n* banco *m*; (*seat, working-table*) bancada *f*. the ~ (*jur*) os magistrados (no tribunal)
bend /bend/ *vt/i* (*pt* & *pp* bent) curvar(-se); (*arm, leg*) dobrar; (*road, river*) fazer uma curva, virar □ *n* curva *f*. ~ over debruçar-se *or* inclinar-se sobre
beneath /bɪ'ni:θ/ *prep* abaixo de, debaixo de; (*fig*) abaixo de □ *adv* debaixo, em baixo
benediction /benɪ'dɪkʃn/ *n* benção *f*
benefactor /'benɪfæktə(r)/ *n* benfeitor *m*
beneficial /benɪ'fɪʃl/ *a* benéfico, proveitoso
benefit /'benɪfɪt/ *n* (*advantage, performance*) benefício *m*; (*profit*) proveito *m*; (*allowance*) subsídio *m* □ *vt/i* (*pt* benefited, *pres p* benefiting) (*be useful to*) beneficiar (by de); (*do good to*) beneficiar, fazer bem a; (*receive benefit*) lucrar, ganhar (by, from com)
beneficiary /benɪ'fɪʃərɪ/ *n* beneficiário *m*
benevolen|t /bɪ'nevələnt/ *a* benevolente. ~ce *n* benevolência *f*
benign /bɪ'naɪn/ *a* (*incl med*) benigno
bent /bent/ *see* bend □ *n* (for para) (*skill*) aptidão *f*, jeito *m*; (*liking*) queda *f* □ *a* curvado; (*twisted*) torcido; (*sl: dishonest*) desonesto. ~ on decidido a
bequeath /bɪ'kwi:ð/ *vt* legar
bequest /bɪ'kwest/ *n* legado *m*
bereave|d /bɪ'ri:vd/ *a* the ~d wife/*etc* a esposa/*etc* do falecido. the ~d family a familia enlutada. ~ment *n* luto *m*
bereft /bɪ'reft/ *a* ~ of privado de
beret /'bereɪ/ *n* boina *f*
Bermuda /bə'mju:də/ *n* Bermudas *fpl*
berry /'berɪ/ *n* baga *f*
berserk /bə'sɜ:k/ *a* go ~ ficar louco de raiva, perder a cabeça
berth /bɜ:θ/ *n* (*in ship*) beliche *m*; (*in train*) couchette *f*; (*anchorage*) ancoradouro *m* □ *vi* atracar. give a wide ~ to passar ao largo, (*P*) de largo
beside /bɪ'saɪd/ *prep* ao lado de, junto de. ~ o.s. fora de si. be ~ the point não ter nada a ver com o assunto, não vir ao caso
besides /bɪ'saɪdz/ *prep* além de; (*except*) fora, salvo □ *adv* além disso
besiege /bɪ'si:dʒ/ *vt* sitiar, cercar. ~ with assediar
best /best/ *a* & *n* (the) ~ (o/a) melhor (*mf*) □ *adv* melhor. ~ man padrinho *m* de casamento. at (the) ~ na melhor das hipóteses. do one's ~ fazer o (melhor) que se pode. make the ~ of tirar o melhor partido de. the ~ part of a maior parte de. to the ~ of my knowledge que eu saiba
bestow /bɪ'stəʊ/ *vt* conferir. ~ praise fazer *or* tecer elogios
best-seller /best'selə(r)/ *n* best-seller *m*
bet /bet/ *n* aposta *f* □ *vt/i* (*pt* bet *or* betted) apostar (on em)
betray /bɪ'treɪ/ *vt* trair. ~al *n* traição *f*
better /'betə(r)/ *a* & *adv* melhor □ *vt* melhorar □ *n* our ~s os nossos superiores *mpl*. all the ~ tanto melhor. ~ off (*richer*) mais rico. he's ~ off at home é melhor para ele ficar em casa. I'd ~ go é melhor ir-me embora. the ~ part of it a maior parte disso. get ~ melhorar. get the ~ of sb levar a melhor em relação a alg
betting-shop /'betɪŋʃɒp/ *n* agência *f* de apostas
between /bɪ'twi:n/ *prep* entre □ *adv* in ~ no meio, no intervalo. ~ you and me aqui entre nós
beverage /'bevərɪdʒ/ *n* bebida *f*
beware /bɪ'weə(r)/ *vi* acautelar-se (of com), tomar cuidado (of com)
bewilder /bɪ'wɪldə(r)/ *vt* desorientar. ~ment *n* desorientação *f*, confusão *f*
bewitch /bɪ'wɪtʃ/ *vt* encantar, cativar
beyond /bɪ'jɒnd/ *prep* além de; (*doubt, reach*) fora de □ *adv* além. it's ~ me isso ultrapassame. he lives ~ his means ele vive acima dos seus meios
bias /'baɪəs/ *n* parcialidade *f*; (*pej: prejudice*) preconceito *m*; (*sewing*) viés *m* □ *vt* (*pt* biased) influenciar. ~ed *a* parcial. ~ed against de prevenção contra, (*P*) de pé atrás contra
bib /bɪb/ *n* babeiro *m*, babette *m*
Bible /'baɪbl/ *n* Bíblia *f*
biblical /'bɪblɪkl/ *a* bíblico

bibliography /bɪblɪ'ɒgrəfɪ/ *n* bibliografia *f*

bicarbonate /baɪ'kaːbənət/ *n* ~ of soda bicarbonato *m* de soda

biceps /'baɪseps/ *n* bíceps *m*

bicker /'bɪkə(r)/ *vi* questionar, discutir

bicycle /'baɪsɪkl/ *n* bicicleta *f* □ *vi* andar de bicicleta

bid /bɪd/ *n* oferta *f*, lançe *m*; (*attempt*) tentativa *f* □ *vt/i* (*pt* **bid**, *pres p* **bidding**) fazer uma oferta, lançar, oferecer como lançe. **~der** *n* licitante *mf*. **the highest ~der** quem dá *or* oferece mais

bide /baɪd/ *vt* **~ one's time** esperar pelo bom momento

bidet /'biːdeɪ/ *n* bidê *m*, (*P*) bidé *m*

biennial /baɪ'enɪəl/ *a* bienal

bifocals /baɪ'fəʊklz/ *npl* óculos *mpl* bifocais

big /bɪg/ *a* (**bigger, biggest**) grande; (*sl: generous*) generoso □ *adv* (*colloq*) em grande. **~-headed** *a* pretensioso, convencido. **~ shot** (*sl*) manda-chuva *m*. **talk ~** gabar-se (*colloq*). **think ~** (*colloq*) ter grandes planos

bigam|y /'bɪgəmɪ/ *n* bigamia *f*. **~ist** *n* bígamo *m*. **~ous** *a* bígamo

bigot /'bɪgət/ *n* fanático *m*, intolerante *mf*. **~ed** *a* fanático, intolerante. **~ry** *n* fanatismo *m*, intolerância *f*

bigwig /'bɪgwɪg/ *n* (*colloq*) mandachuva *m*

bike /baɪk/ *n* (*colloq*) bicicleta *f*

bikini /bɪ'kiːnɪ/ *n* (*pl* **-is**) biquíni *m*

bilberry /'bɪlbərɪ/ *n* arando *m*

bile /baɪl/ *n* bílis *f*

bilingual /baɪ'lɪŋgwəl/ *a* bilíngüe

bilious /'bɪlɪəs/ *a* bilioso

bill[1] /bɪl/ *n* (*invoice*) fatura *f*, (*P*) factura *f*; (*in restaurant*) conta *f*; (*pol*) projeto *m*, (*P*) projecto *m* de lei; (*Amer: banknote*) nota *f* de banco; (*poster*) cartaz *m* □ *vt* faturar, (*P*) facturar; (*theatre*) anunciar, pôr no programa. **~ of exchange** letra *f* de câmbio. **~ sb for** apresentar a alg a conta de

bill[2] /bɪl/ *n* (*of bird*) bico *m*

billiards /'bɪlɪədz/ *n* bilhar *m*

billion /'bɪlɪən/ *n* (10^9) mil milhões; (10^{12}) um milhão de milhões

bin /bɪn/ *n* (*for storage*) caixa *f*, lata *f*; (*for rubbish*) lata *f* do lixo, (*P*) caixote *m*

bind /baɪnd/ *vt* (*pt* **bound**) (*tie*) atar; (*book*) encadernar; (*jur*) obrigar; (*cover the edge of*) debruar □ *n* (*sl: bore*) chatice *f* (*sl*). **be ~ing on** ser obrigatório para

binding /'baɪndɪŋ/ *n* encadernação *f*; (*braid*) debrum *m*

binge /bɪndʒ/ *n* (*sl*) **go on a ~** cair na farra; (*overeat*) empanturrar-se

bingo /'bɪŋgəʊ/ *n* bingo *m* □ *int* acertei!

binoculars /bɪ'nɒkjʊləz/ *npl* binóculo *m*

biochemistry /baɪəʊ'kemɪstrɪ/ *n* bioquímica *f*

biodegradable /baɪəʊdɪ'greɪdəbl/ *a* biodegradável

biograph|y /baɪ'ɒgrəfɪ/ *n* biografia *f*. **~er** *n* biógrafo *m*

biolog|y /baɪ'ɒlədʒɪ/ *n* biologia *f*. **~ical** /-ə'lɒdʒɪkl/ *a* biológico. **~ist** *n* biólogo *m*

biopsy /'baɪɒpsɪ/ *n* biópsia *f*

birch /bɜːtʃ/ *n* (*tree*) bétula *f*; (*whip*) vara *f* de vidoeiro

bird /bɜːd/ *n* ave *f*, pássaro *m*; (*sl: girl*) garota *f* (*colloq*). **~ sanctuary** refúgio *m* ornitológico. **~-watcher** *n* ornitófilo *m*

Biro /'baɪərəʊ/ *n* (*pl* **-os**) (caneta) esferográfica *f*, Bic *f*

birth /bɜːθ/ *n* nascimento *m*. **~ certificate** certidão *f* de nascimento. **~ control/rate** controle *m*/índice *m* de natalidade. **~-place** *n* lugar *m* de nascimento. **give ~ to** dar à luz

birthday /'bɜːθdeɪ/ *n* aniversário *m*, (*P*) dia *m* de anos. **his ~ is on 9 July** ele faz anos no dia 9 de julho

birthmark /'bɜːθmaːk/ *n* sinal *m*

biscuit /'bɪskɪt/ *n* biscoito *m*, bolacha *f*

bisect /baɪ'sekt/ *vt* dividir ao meio

bishop /'bɪʃəp/ *n* bispo *m*

bit[1] /bɪt/ *n* (*small piece, short time*) pedaço *m*, bocado *m*; (*of bridle*) freio *m*; (*of tool*) broca *f*. **a ~** um pouco

bit[2] /bɪt/ *see* **bite**

bitch /bɪtʃ/ *n* cadela *f*; (*sl: woman*) peste *f* (*fig*), cadela *f* (*sl*) □ *vt/i* (*colloq: criticize*) malhar, (*P*) cortar (em) (*colloq*); (*colloq: grumble*) resmungar. **~y** *a* (*colloq*) maldoso

bite /baɪt/ *vt/i* (*pt* **bit**, *pp* **bitten**) morder; (*insect*) picar □ *n* mordida *f*; (*sting*) picada *f*. **have a ~ (to eat)** comer qualquer coisa

biting /'baɪtɪŋ/ *a* cortante

bitter /'bɪtə(r)/ *a* amargo; (*weather*) glacial. **~ly** *adv* amargamente. **it's ~ly cold** está um frio de rachar. **~ness** *n* amargura *f*; (*resentment*) ressentimento *m*

bizarre /bɪ'zaː(r)/ *a* bizarro

black /blæk/ *a* (**-er, -est**) negro, preto □ *n* negro *m*, preto *m*. **a B~** (*person*) um preto, um negro □ *vt* enegrecer; (*goods*) boicotar. **~ and blue** coberto de nódoas negras. **~ coffee** café *m* (sem leite). **~ eye** olho *m* negro. **~ ice** gelo *m* negro sobre o asfalto. **~ market** mercado *m* negro. **~ spot** *n* (*place*) local *m* perigoso, ponto *m* negro

blackberry /'blækbərɪ/ *n* amora *f* silvestre
blackbird /'blækbɜ:d/ *n* melro *m*
blackboard /'blækbɔ:d/ *n* quadro *m* preto
blackcurrant /'blækkʌrənt/ *n* groselha *f* negra
blacken /'blækən/ *vt/i* escurecer. ~ **sb's name** difamar, denegrir
blackleg /'blækleg/ *n* fura-greves *m*
blacklist /'blæklɪst/ *n* lista *f* negra □ *vt* pôr na lista negra
blackmail /'blækmeɪl/ *n* chantagem *f* □ *vt* fazer chantagem. ~**er** *n* chantagista *mf*
blackout /'blækaʊt/ *n* (*wartime*) blecaute *m*; (*med*) desmaio *m*; (*electr*) falta *f* de corrente; (*theatr*) apagar *m* de luzes
blacksmith /'blæksmɪθ/ *n* ferreiro *m*
bladder /'blædə(r)/ *n* bexiga *f*
blade /bleɪd/ *n* lâmina *f*; (*of oar, propeller*) pá *f*; (*of grass*) ervinha *f*, folhinha *f* de erva
blame /bleɪm/ *vt* culpar □ *n* culpa *f*. **be to** ~ ser o culpado. ~**less** *a* irrepreensível; (*innocent*) inocente
bland /blænd/ *a* (-er, -est) (*of manner*) suave; (*mild*) brando; (*insipid*) insípido
blank /blæŋk/ *a* (*space, cheque*) em branco; (*look*) vago; (*wall*) nu □ *n* espaço *m* em branco; (*cartridge*) cartucho *m* sem bala
blanket /'blæŋkɪt/ *n* cobertor *m*; (*fig*) manto *m* □ *vt* (*pt* **blanketed**) cobrir com cobertor; (*cover thickly*) encobrir, recobrir. **wet** ~ desmancha-prazeres *mf*
blare /bleə(r)/ *vt/i* ressoar, atroar □ *n* clangor *m*; (*of horn*) buzinar *m*
blasé /'bla:zeɪ/ *a* blasé
blaspheme /blæs'fi:m/ *vt/i* blasfemar
blasphem|y /'blæsfəmɪ/ *n* blasfêmia *f*, (*P*) blasfémia *f*. ~**ous** *a* blasfemo
blast /bla:st/ *n* (*gust*) rajada *f*; (*sound*) som *m*; (*explosion*) explosão *f* □ *vt* dinamitar. ~! droga! ~**ed** *a* maldito. ~**-furnace** *n* alto forno *m*. ~**-off** *n* (*of missile*) lançamento *m*, início *m* de combustão
blatant /'bleɪtnt/ *a* flagrante; (*shameless*) descarado
blaze /bleɪz/ *n* chamas *fpl*; (*light*) clarão *m*; (*outburst*) explosão *f* □ *vi* arder; (*shine*) resplandecer, brilhar. ~ **a trail** abrir o caminho, ser pioneiro
blazer /'bleɪzə(r)/ *n* blazer *m*
bleach /bli:tʃ/ *n* descolorante, descorante *m*; (*household*) água *f* sanitária □ *vt/i* branquear; (*hair*) oxigenar
bleak /bli:k/ *a* (-er, -est) (*place*) desolado; (*chilly*) frio; (*fig*) desanimador
bleary-eyed /'blɪərɪaɪd/ *a* com olhos injetados
bleat /bli:t/ *n* balido *m* □ *vi* balir
bleed /bli:d/ *vt/i* (*pt* **bled**) sangrar
bleep /bli:p/ *n* bip *m*. ~**er** *n* bip *m*
blemish /'blemɪʃ/ *n* defeito *m*; (*on reputation*) mancha *f* □ *vt* manchar
blend /blend/ *vt/i* misturar(-se); (*go well together*) combinar-se □ *n* mistura *f*. ~**er** *n* (*culin*) liquidificador *m*
bless /bles/ *vt* abençoar. **be** ~**ed with** ter a felicidade de ter. ~**ing** *n* benção *f*; (*thing one is glad of*) felicidade *f*. **it's a** ~**ing in disguise** há males que vêm para bem
blessed /'blesɪd/ *a* bem-aventurado; (*colloq: cursed*) maldito
blew /blu:/ *see* **blow**
blight /blaɪt/ *n* doença *f* de plantas; (*fig*) influência *f* maligna □ *vt* arruinar, frustrar
blind /blaɪnd/ *a* cego □ *vt* cegar □ *n* (*on window*) persiana *f*; (*deception*) ardil *m*. ~ **alley** (*incl fig*) beco *m* sem saída. ~ **man/woman** cego *m*/cega *f*. **be** ~ **to** não ver. **turn a** ~ **eye to** fingir não ver, fechar os olhos a. ~**ly** *adv* às cegas. ~**ness** *n* cegueira *f*
blindfold /'blaɪndfəʊld/ *a* & *adv* de olhos vendados □ *n* venda *f* □ *vt* vendar os olhos a
blink /blɪŋk/ *vi* piscar
blinkers /'blɪŋkəz/ *npl* antolhos *mpl*
bliss /blɪs/ *n* felicidade *f*, beatitude *f*. ~**ful** *a* felicíssimo. ~**fully** *adv* maravilhosamente
blister /'blɪstə(r)/ *n* bolha *f*, empola *f* □ *vi* empolar
blizzard /'blɪzəd/ *n* tempestade *f* de neve, nevasca *f*
bloated /'bləʊtɪd/ *a* inchado
bloater /'bləʊtə(r)/ *n* arenque *m* salgado e defumado
blob /blɒb/ *n* pingo *m* grosso; (*stain*) mancha *f*
bloc /blɒk/ *n* bloco *m*
block /blɒk/ *n* bloco *m*; (*buildings*) quarteirão *m*; (*in pipe*) entupimento *m*. ~ (**of flats**) prédio *m* (de andares) □ *vt* bloquear, obstruir; (*pipe*) entupir. ~ **letters** maiúsculas *fpl*. ~**age** *n* obstrução *f*
blockade /blɒ'keɪd/ *n* bloqueio *m* □ *vt* bloquear
bloke /bləʊk/ *n* (*colloq*) sujeito *m* (*colloq*), cara *m* (*colloq*)
blond /blɒnd/ *a* & *n* louro (*m*)
blonde /blɒnd/ *a* & *n* loura (*f*)
blood /blʌd/ *n* sangue *m* □ *a* (*bank, donor, transfusion, etc*) de sangue; (*poisoning*) do sangue; (*group, vessel*) sangüíneo. ~**-curdling** *a* horrendo. ~ **pressure** tensão *f* arterial. ~ **test**

exame *m* de sangue. ~**less** *a* (*fig*) pacífico
bloodhound /'blʌdhaʊnd/ *n* sabujo *m*
bloodshed /'blʌdʃed/ *n* derramamento *m* de sangue, carnificina *f*
bloodshot /'blʌdʃɒt/ *a* injetado *or* (*P*) injectado de sangue
bloodstream /'blʌdstri:m/ *n* sangue *m*, fluxo *m* sangüíneo
bloodthirsty /'blʌdθɜ:stɪ/ *a* sanguinário
bloody /'blʌdɪ/ *a* (-ier, -iest) ensangüentado; (*with much bloodshed*) sangrento; (*sl*) grande, maldito □ *adv* (*sl*) pra burro. ~**-minded** *a* (*colloq*) do contra (*colloq*), chato (*sl*)
bloom /blu:m/ *n* flor *f*; (*beauty*) frescura *f*, viço *m* □ *vi* florir; (*fig*) vicejar. **in ~** em flor
blossom /'blɒsəm/ *n* flor *f*. **in ~** em flor □ *vi* (*flower*) florir, desabrochar; (*develop, flourish*) florescer, desabrochar
blot /blɒt/ *n* mancha *f* □ *vt* (*pt* **blotted**) manchar; (*dry*) secar. **~ out** apagar; (*hide*) tapar, toldar. ~**ter**, ~**ting-paper** *n* (papel) mata-borrão *m*
blotch /blɒtʃ/ *n* mancha *f*. ~**y** *a* manchado
blouse /blaʊz/ *n* blusa *f*; (*in uniform*) blusão *m*
blow[1] /bləʊ/ *vt/i* (*pt* **blew**, *pp* **blown**) soprar; (*fuse*) fundir-se, queimar; (*sl: squander*) esbanjar; (*trumpet etc*) tocar. **~ a whistle** apitar. **~ away** *or* **off** *vt* levar, soprar □ *vi* roar, ir pelos ares (fora). ~**-dry** *vt* (*hair*) fazer um brushing □ *n* brushing *m*. **~ one's nose** assoar o nariz. **~ out** (*candle*) apagar, soprar. ~**-out** *n* (*colloq: of tyre*) rebentar *m*; (*colloq: large meal*) comilança *f* (*colloq*). **~ over** passar. **~ up** *vt* (*explode*) explodir; (*tyre*) encher; (*photograph*) ampliar □ *vi* (*explode*) explodir
blow[2] /bləʊ/ *n* pancada *f*; (*slap*) bofetada *f*; (*punch*) murro *m*; (*fig*) golpe *m*
blowlamp /'bləʊlæmp/ *n* maçarico *m*
blown /bləʊn/ *see* **blow**[1]
bludgeon /'blʌdʒən/ *n* moca *f* □ *vt* malhar em. **~ to death** matar à pancada
blue /blu:/ *a* (-er, -est) azul; (*indecent*) indecente □ *n* azul *m*. **come out of the ~** ser inesperado. ~**s** *n* (*mus*) blues. **have the ~s** estar deprimido (*colloq*)
bluebell /'blu:bel/ *n* jacinto *m* dos bosques
bluebottle /'blu:bɒtl/ *n* mosca *f* varejeira
blueprint /'blu:prɪnt/ *n* cópia *f* fotográfica de planta; (*fig*) projeto *m*, (*P*) projecto *m*
bluff /blʌf/ *vi* blefar, (*P*) fazer bluff □ *vt* enganar (fingindo), blefar □ *n* blefe *m*, (*P*) bluff *m*
blunder /'blʌndə(r)/ *vi* cometer um erro crasso; (*move*) avançar às cegas *or* tateando □ *n* erro *m* crasso, (*P*) bronca *f*
blunt /blʌnt/ *a* (-er, -est) embotado; (*person*) direto, (*P*) directo □ *vt* embotar. ~**ly** *adv* sem rodeios. ~**ness**- *n* franqueza *f* rude
blur /blɜ:(r)/ *n* mancha *f* □ *vt* (*pt* **blurred**) (*smear*) manchar; (*make indistinct*) toldar
blurb /blɜ:b/ *n* contracapa *f*, sinopse *f* de um livro
blurt /blɜ:t/ *vt* **~ out** deixar escapar
blush /blʌʃ/ *vi* corar □ *n* rubor *m*, vermelhidão *f*
bluster /'blʌstə(r)/ *vi* (*wind*) soprar em rajadas; (*swagger*) andar com ar fanfarrão. ~**y** *a* borrascoso
boar /bɔ:(r)/ *n* varrão *m*. **wild ~** javali *m*
board /bɔ:d/ *n* tábua *f*; (*for notices*) quadro *m*, (*P*) placard *m*; (*food*) pensão *f*; (*admin*) conselho *m* □ *vt/i* cobrir com tábuas; (*aircraft, ship, train*) embarcar (em); (*bus, train*) subir (em). **full ~** pensão *f* completa. **half ~** meia-pensão *f*. **on ~** a bordo. **~ up** entaipar. **~ with** ser pensionista em casa de. ~**er** *n* pensionista *mf*; (*at school*) interno *m*. ~**ing-card** *n* cartão *m* de embarque. ~**ing-house** *n* pensão *f*. ~**ing-school** *n* internato *m*
boast /bəʊst/ *vi* gabar-se □ *vt* orgulhar-se de □ *n* gabarolice *f*. ~**er** *n* gabola *mf*. ~**ful** *a* vaidoso. ~**fully** *adv* com vaidade, gabando-se
boat /bəʊt/ *n* barco *m*. **in the same ~** nas mesmas circunstâncias. ~**ing** *n* passear de barco
bob /bɒb/ *vt/i* (*pt* **bobbed**) (*curtsy*) inclinar-se; (*hair*) cortar pelos ombros, (*P*) cortar à Joãozinho. **~ (up and down)** andar para cima e para baixo
bobbin /'bɒbɪn/ *n* bobina *f*; (*sewing-machine*) canela *f*, bobina *f*
bob-sleigh /'bɒbsleɪ/ *n* trenó *m*
bode /bəʊd/ *vi* **~ well/ill** ser de bom/ mau agouro
bodice /'bɒdɪs/ *n* corpete *m*
bodily /'bɒdɪlɪ/ *a* corporal, físico. □ *adv* (*in person*) fisicamente, em pessoa; (*lift*) em peso
body /'bɒdɪ/ *n* corpo *m*; (*organization*) organismo *m*. ~**(work)** *n* (*of car*) carroçaria *f*. **in a ~** em massa. **the main ~ of** o grosso de. ~**-building** *n* body building *m*

bodyguard /ˈbɒdɪgaːd/ *n* guarda-costas *m*; (*escort*) escolta *f*

bog /bɒg/ *n* pântano *m* □ *vt* **get ~ged down** atolar-se; (*fig*) ficar emperrado

boggle /ˈbɒgl/ *vi* **the mind ~s** não da para imaginar

bogus /ˈbəʊgəs/ *a* falso

boil[1] /bɔɪl/ *n* (*med*) furúnculo *m*

boil[2] /bɔɪl/ *vt/i* ferver. **come to the ~** ferver. **~ down to** resumir-se a. **~ over** transbordar. **~ing hot** fervendo. **~ing point** ponto *m* de ebulição

boiler /ˈbɔɪlə(r)/ *n* caldeira *f*. **~ suit** macacão *m*, (*P*) fato *m* de macaco

boisterous /ˈbɔɪstərəs/ *a* turbulento; (*noisy and cheerful*) animado

bold /bəʊld/ *a* (-er, -est) ousado; (*of colours*) vivo. **~ness** *n* ousadia *f*

Bolivia /bəˈlɪvɪə/ *n* Bolívia *f*. **~n** *a* & *n* boliviano (*m*)

bollard /ˈbɒləd/ *n* (*ship*) abita *f*; (*road*) poste *m*

bolster /ˈbəʊlstə(r)/ *n* travesseiro *m* □ *vt* sustentar; ajudar. **~ one's spirits** levantar o moral

bolt /bəʊlt/ *n* (*on door etc*) ferrolho *m*; (*for nut*) parafuso *m*; (*lightning*) relâmpago *m* □ *vt* aferrolhar; (*food*) engolir □ *vi* fugir, disparar. **~ upright** reto como um fuso

bomb /bɒm/ *n* bomba *f* □ *vt* bombardear. **~er** *n* (*aircraft*) bombardeiro *m*; (*person*) bombista *mf*

bombard /bɒmˈbaːd/ *vt* bombardear. **~ment** *n* bombardeamento *m*

bombastic /bɒmˈbæstɪk/ *a* bombástico

bombshell /ˈbɒmʃel/ *n* granada *f*; (*fig*) bomba *f*

bond /bɒnd/ *n* (*agreement*) compromisso *m*; (*link*) laço *m*, vínculo *m*; (*comm*) obrigação *f*. **in ~** em depósito na alfândega

bondage /ˈbɒndɪdʒ/ *n* escravidão *f*, servidão *f*

bone /bəʊn/ *n* osso *m*; (*of fish*) espinha *f* □ *vt* desossar. **~-dry** *a* completamente seco, ressecado. **~ idle** preguiçoso

bonfire /ˈbɒnfaɪə(r)/ *n* fogueira *f*

bonnet /ˈbɒnɪt/ *n* chapéu *m*; (*auto*) capô *m* do motor, (*P*) capot *m*

bonus /ˈbəʊnəs/ *n* bônus *m*, (*P*) bónus *m*

bony /ˈbəʊnɪ/ *a* (-ier, -iest) ossudo; (*meat, fish*) cheio de ossos/de espinhas

boo /buː/ *int* fora □ *vt/i* vaiar □ *n* vaia *f*

boob /buːb/ *n* (*sl: mistake*) asneira *f*, disparate *m* □ *vi* (*sl*) fazer asneira(s)

booby /ˈbuːbɪ/ *n* **~ prize** prêmio *m* de consolação. **~ trap** bomba *f* armadilhada

book /bʊk/ *n* livro *m*. **~s** (*comm*) contas *fpl*, escrita *f* □ *vt* (*enter*) averbar, registrar; (*comm*) escriturar; (*reserve*) marcar, reservar. **~ of matches** carteira *f* de fósforos. **~ of tickets** (*bus, tube*) caderneta *f* de módulos. **be fully ~ed** ter a lotação esgotada. **~ing office** bilheteria *f*, (*P*) bilheteira *f*

bookcase /ˈbʊkkeɪs/ *n* estante *f*

bookkeep|er /ˈbʊkkiːpə(r)/ *n* guarda-livros *m*. **~ing** *n* contabilidade *f*, escrituração *f*

booklet /ˈbʊklɪt/ *n* brochura *f*

bookmaker /ˈbʊkmeɪkə(r)/ *n* book (maker) *m*

bookmark /ˈbʊkmaːk/ *n* marca *f* de livro, marcador *m* de página

bookseller /ˈbʊkselə(r)/ *n* livreiro *m*

bookshop /ˈbʊkʃɒp/ *n* livraria *f*

bookstall /ˈbʊkstɔːl/ *n* quiosque *m*

boom /buːm/ *vi* ribombar; (*of trade*) prosperar □ *n* (*sound*) ribombo *m*; (*comm*) boom *m*, prosperidade *f*

boon /buːn/ *n* benção *f*, vantagem *f*

boost /buːst/ *vt* desenvolver, promover; (*morale*) levantar; (*price*) aumentar □ *n* força *f* (*colloq*). **~er** *n* (*med*) dose suplementar *f*; (*vaccine*) revacinação *f*, (*P*) reforço *m*

boot /buːt/ *n* bota *f*; (*auto*) portamala *f* □ *vt* **~ (up)** (*comput*) **to ~** (*in addition*) ainda por cima

booth /buːð/ *n* barraca *f*; (*telephone, voting*) cabine *f*

booty /ˈbuːtɪ/ *n* saque *m*, pilhagem *f*

booze /buːz/ *vi* (*colloq*) embebedar-se (*colloq*), encharcar-se (*colloq*) □ *n* (*colloq*) pinga *f* (*colloq*)

border /ˈbɔːdə(r)/ *n* borda *f*, margem *f*; (*frontier*) fronteira *f*; (*garden bed*) canteiro *m* □ *vi* **~ on** confinar com; (*be almost the same as*) atingir as raias de

borderline /ˈbɔːdəlaɪn/ *n* linha *f* divisória. **~ case** caso *m* limite

bore[1] /bɔː(r)/ *see* **bear**[2]

bore[2] /bɔː(r)/ *vt/i* (*techn*) furar, perfurar □ *n* (*of gun barrel*) calibre *m*

bore[3] /bɔː(r)/ *vt* aborrecer, entediar □ *n* maçante *m*; (*thing*) chatice *f*. **be ~d** aborrecer-se, maçar-se. **~dom** *n* tédio *m*. **boring** *a* tedioso, maçante

born /bɔːn/ *a* nascido. **be ~** nascer

borne /bɔːn/ *see* **bear**[2]

borough /ˈbʌrə/ *n* município *m*

borrow /ˈbɒrəʊ/ *vt* pedir emprestado (from a)

bosom /ˈbʊzəm/ *n* peito *m*; (*woman's; fig: midst*) seio *m*. **~ friend** amigo *m* íntimo

boss /bɒs/ *n* (*colloq*) patrão *m*, patroa *f*, manda-chuva (*colloq*) *m* □ *vt* mandar. **~ sb about** (*colloq*) mandar em alg

bossy /'bɒsɪ/ *a* mandão, autoritário
botan|y /'bɒtənɪ/ *n* botânica *f*. **~ical** /bə'tænɪkl/ *a* botânico. **~ist** /-ɪst/ *n* botânico *m*
botch /bɒtʃ/ *vt* atamancar; (*spoil*) estragar, escangalhar
both /bəʊθ/ *a* & *pron* ambos, os dois □ *adv* **~ ... and** não só ... mas também, tanto ... como. **~ of us** nós dois. **~ the books** ambos os livros
bother /'bɒðə(r)/ *vt/i* incomodar(-se) □ *n* (*inconvenience*) incômodo *m*, (*P*) incómodo *m*, trabalho *m*; (*effort*) custo *m*, trabalho *m*; (*worry*) preocupação *f*. **don't ~** não se incomode. **I can't be ~ed** não posso me dar o trabalho
bottle /'bɒtl/ *n* garrafa *f*; (*small*) frasco *m*; (*for baby*) mamadeira *f*, (*P*) biberão *m* □ *vt* engarrafar. **~-opener** *n* sacarolhas *m*. **~ up** reprimir
bottleneck /'bɒtlnek/ *n* (*obstruction*) entrave *m*; (*traffic-jam*) engarrafamento *m*
bottom /'bɒtəm/ *n* fundo *m*; (*of hill*) sopé *m*; (*buttocks*) traseiro *m* □ *a* inferior; (*last*) último. **from top to ~** de alto a baixo. **~less** *a* sem fundo
bough /baʊ/ *n* ramo *m*
bought /bɔ:t/ *see* **buy**
boulder /'bəʊldə(r)/ *n* pedregulho *m*
bounce /baʊns/ *vi* saltar; (*of person*) pular, dar pulos; (*sl: of cheque*) ser devolvido □ *vt* fazer saltar □ *n* (*of ball*) salto *m*, (*P*) ressalto *m*
bound[1] /baʊnd/ *vi* pular; (*move by jumping*) ir aos pulos □ *n* pulo *m*
bound[2] /baʊnd/ *see* **bind** □ *a* **be ~ for** ir com destino a, ir para. **be ~ to** (*obliged*) ser obrigado a; (*certain*) haver de. **she's ~ to like it** ela há de gostar disso
boundary /'baʊndrɪ/ *n* limite *m*
bound|s /baʊndz/ *npl* limites *mpl*. **out of ~s** interdito. **~ed by** limitado por. **~less** *a* sem limites
bouquet /bʊ'keɪ/ *n* ramo *m* de flores; (*wine*) aroma *m*
bout /baʊt/ *n* período *m*; (*med*) ataque *m*; (*boxing*) combate *m*
boutique /bu:'ti:k/ *n* boutique *f*
bow[1] /bəʊ/ *n* (*weapon, mus*) arco *m*; (*knot*) laço *m*. **~-legged** *a* de pernas tortas. **~-tie** *n* gravata borboleta *f*, (*P*) laço *m*
bow[2] /baʊ/ *n* vênia *f*, (*P*) vénia *f* □ *vt/i* inclinar(-se), curvar-se
bow[3] /baʊ/ *n* (*naut*) proa *f*
bowels /'baʊəlz/ *npl* intestinos *mpl*; (*fig*) entranhas *fpl*
bowl[1] /bəʊl/ *n* (*basin*) bacia *f*; (*for food*) tigela *f*; (*of pipe*) fornilho *m*
bowl[2] /bəʊl/ *n* (*ball*) boliche *m*, (*P*) bola *f* de madeira. **~s** *npl* boliche *m*, (*P*) jogo *m* com bolas de madeira □ *vt* (*cricket*) lançar. **~ over** siderar, varar. **~ing** *n* boliche *m*, (*P*) bowling *m*. **~ing-alley** *n* pista *f*
bowler[1] /'bəʊlə(r)/ *n* (*cricket*) lançador *m*
bowler[2] /'bəʊlə(r)/ *n* **~ (hat)** (chapéu de) coco *m*
box[1] /bɒks/ *n* caixa *f*; (*theatr*) camarote *m* □ *vt* pôr dentro duma caixa. **~ in** fechar. **~ office** *n* bilheteria *f*, (*P*) bilheteira *f*. **Boxing Day** feriado *m* no primeiro dia útil depois do Natal
box[2] /bɒks/ *vt/i* (*sport*) lutar boxe. **~ the ears of** esbofetear. **~er** *n* pugilista *m*, boxeur *m*. **~ing** *n* boxe *m*, pugilismo *m*
boy /bɔɪ/ *n* rapaz *m*. **~friend** *n* namorado *m*. **~hood** *n* infância *f*. **~ish** *a* de menino
boycott /'bɔɪkɒt/ *vt* boicotar □ *n* boicote *m*
bra /bra:/ *n* soutien *m*
brace /breɪs/ *n* braçadeira *f*; (*dental*) aparelho *m*; (*tool*) berbequim *m*; (*of birds*) par *m*. **~s** *npl* (*for trousers*) suspensórios *mpl* □ *vt* apoiar, firmar. **~ o.s.** concentrar as energias, fazer força; (*for blow*) preparar-se
bracelet /'breɪslɪt/ *n* bracelete *m*, pulseira *f*
bracing /'breɪsɪŋ/ *a* tonificante, estimulante
bracken /'brækən/ *n* (*bot*) samambaia *f*, (*P*) feto *m*
bracket /'brækɪt/ *n* suporte *m*; (*group*) grupo *m* □ *vt* (*pt* **bracketed**) pôr entre parênteses; (*put together*) pôr em pé de igualdade, agrupar. **age/income ~** faixa *f* etária/salarial. **round ~s** parênteses *mpl*. **square ~s** parênteses *mpl*, colchetes *mpl*
brag /bræg/ *vi* (*pt* **bragged**) gabar-se (**about** de)
braid /breɪd/ *n* galão *m*; (*of hair*) trança *f*
Braille /breɪl/ *n* braile *m*
brain /breɪn/ *n* cérebro *m*, miolos *mpl* (*colloq*); (*fig*) inteligência *f*. **~s** (*culin*) miolos *mpl*. **~-child** *n* invenção *f*. **~less** *a* estúpido
brainwash /'breɪnwɒʃ/ *vt* fazer uma lavagem cerebral
brainwave /'breɪnweɪv/ *n* idéia *f*, (*P*) ideia *f* genial
brainy /'breɪnɪ/ *a* (-ier, -iest) inteligente, esperto
braise /breɪz/ *vt* (*culin*) estufar
brake /breɪk/ *n* travão *m* □ *vt/i* travar. **~ light** farol *m* do freio
bran /bræn/ *n* (*husks*) farelo *m*
branch /bra:ntʃ/ *n* ramo *m*; (*of road*) ramificação *f*; (*of railway line*) ramal

m; (*comm*) sucursal *f*; (*of bank*) balcão *m* □ *vi* ~ (**off**) bifurcar-se, ramificar-se

brand /brænd/ *n* marca *f* □ *vt* marcar. ~ **name** marca *f* de fábrica. ~**-new** *a* novo em folha. ~ **sb as** tachar alg de, (*P*) rotular alg de

brandish /'brændɪʃ/ *vt* brandir

brandy /'brændɪ/ *n* aguardente *f*, conhaque *m*

brass /bra:s/ *n* latão *m*. **the** ~ (*mus*) os metais *mpl* □ *a* de cobre, de latão. **get down to** ~ **tacks** tratar das coisas sérias. **top** ~ (*sl*) os chefões (*colloq*)

brassière /'bræsɪə(r)/ *n* soutien *m*

brat /bræt/ *n* (*pej*) fedelho *m*

bravado /brə'va:dəʊ/ *n* bravata *f*

brave /breɪv/ *a* (-er, -est) bravo, valente □ *vt* arrostar. ~**ry** /-ərɪ/ *n* bravura *f*

brawl /brɔ:l/ *n* briga *f*, rixa *f*, desordem *f* □ *vi* brigar

brawn /brɔ:n/ *n* força *f* muscular, músculo *m*. ~**y** *a* musculoso

bray /breɪ/ *n* zurro *m* □ *vi* zurrar

brazen /'breɪzn/ *a* descarado

brazier /'breɪzɪə(r)/ *n* braseiro *m*

Brazil /brə'zɪl/ *n* Brasil *m*. ~**ian** *a* & *n* brasileiro (*m*). ~ **nut** castanha *f* do Pará

breach /bri:tʃ/ *n* quebra *f*; (*gap*) brecha *f* □ *vt* abrir uma brecha em. ~ **of contract** quebra *f* de contrato. ~ **of the peace** perturbação *f* da ordem pública. ~ **of trust** abuso *m* de confiança

bread /bred/ *n* pão *m*. ~**-winner** *n* ganha-pão *m*

breadcrumbs /'bredkrʌmz/ *npl* migalhas *fpl*; (*culin*) farinha *f* de rosca

breadline /'bredlam/ *n* **on the** ~ na miséria

breadth /bredθ/ *n* largura *f*; (*of mind, view*) abertura *f*

break /breɪk/ *vt* (*pt* **broke**, *pp* **broken**) partir, quebrar; (*vow, silence, etc*) quebrar; (*law*) transgredir; (*journey*) interromper; (*news*) dar; (*a record*) bater □ *vi* partir-se, quebrar-se; (*voice, weather*) mudar □ *n* quebra *f*, ruptura *f*; (*interval*) intervalo *m*; (*colloq: opportunity*) oportunidade *f*, chance *f*. ~ **one's arm/leg**quebrar o braço/a perma ~ **down** *vt* analisar □ *vi* (*of person*) ir-se abaixo; (*of machine*) avariar-se. ~ **in** forçar uma entrada. ~ **off** *vt* quebrar □ *vi* desligar-se. ~ **out** rebentar. ~ **up** *vt/i* terminar *vi* (*of schools*) entrar em férias. ~**able** *a* quebrável. ~**age** *n* quebra *f*

breakdown /'breɪkdaʊn/ *n* (*techn*) avaria *f*, pane *f*; (*med*) esgotamento *m* nervoso; (*of figures*) análise *f* □ *a* (*auto*) de pronto-socorro. ~ **van** pronto-socorro *m*

breaker /'breɪkə(r)/ *n* vaga *f* de rebentação

breakfast /'brekfəst/ *n* café *m* da manhã

breakthrough /'breɪkθru:/ *n* descoberta *f* decisiva, avanço *m*

breakwater /'breɪkwɔ:tə(r)/ *n* quebra-mar *m*

breast /brest/ *n* peito *m*. ~**-feed** *vt* (*pt* **-fed**) amamentar. ~**-stroke** *n* estilo *m* bruços

breath /breθ/ *n* respiração *f*. **bad** ~ mau hálito *m*. **out of** ~ sem fôlego. **under one's** ~ num murmúrio, baixo. ~**less** *a* ofegante

breathalyser /'breθəlaɪzə(r)/ *n* aparelho *m* para medir o nível de álcool no sangue, bafômetro *m* (*colloq*)

breath|e /bri:ð/ *vt/i* respirar. ~**e in** inspirar. ~ **out** expirar. ~**ing** *n* respiração *f*. ~**ing-space** *n* pausa *f*

breather /'bri:ðə(r)/ *n* pausa *f* de descanso, momento *m* para respirar

breathtaking /'breθteɪkɪŋ/ *a* assombroso, arrebatador

bred /bred/ *see* **breed**

breed /bri:d/ *vt* (*pt* **bred**) criar □ *vi* reproduzir-se □ *n* raça *f*. ~**er** *n* criador *m*. ~**ing** *n* criação *f*; (*fig*) educação *f*

breez|e /bri:z/ *n* brisa *f*. ~**y** *a* fresco

brevity /'brevətɪ/ *n* brevidade *f*

brew /bru:/ *vt* (*beer*) fabricar; (*tea*) fazer; (*fig*) armar, tramar □ *vi* fermentar; (*tea*) preparar; (*fig*) armar-se, preparar-se □ *n* decocção *f*; (*tea*) infusão *f*. ~**er** *n* cervejeiro *m*. ~**ery** *n* cervejaria *f*

bribe /braɪb/ *n* suborno *m*, (*P*) peita *f* □ *vt* subornar. ~**ry** /-ərɪ/ *n* suborno *m*, corrupção *f*

brick /brɪk/ *n* tijolo *m*

bricklayer /'brɪkleɪə(r)/ *n* pedreiro *m*

bridal /'braɪdl/ *a* nupcial

bride /braɪd/ *n* noiva *f*

bridegroom /'braɪdgrʊm/ *n* noivo *m*

bridesmaid /'braɪdzmeɪd/ *n* dama *f* de honra, (*P*) honor

bridge[1] /brɪdʒ/ *n* ponte *f*; (*of nose*) cana *f* □ *vt* ~ **a gap** preencher uma lacuna

bridge[2] /brɪdʒ/ *n* (*cards*) bridge *m*

bridle /'braɪdl/ *n* cabeçada *f*, freio *m* □ *vt* refrear. ~**-path** *n* atalho *m*, carreiro *m*

brief[1] /bri:f/ *a* (-er, -est) breve. ~**s** *npl* (*men's*) cueca *f*, (*P*) slip *m*; (*women's*) calcinhas *fpl*, (*P*) cuecas *fpl*. ~**ly** *adv* brevemente

brief[2] /bri:f/ *n* (*jur*) sumário *m*; (*case*) causa *f*; (*instructions*) instruções *fpl* □ *vt* dar instruções a

briefcase /'bri:fkeɪs/ *n* pasta *f*

brigad|e /brɪ'geɪd/ *n* brigada *f*. **~ier** /-ə'dɪə(r)/ *n* brigadeiro *m*

bright /braɪt/ *a* (-er, -est) brilhante; (*of colour*) vivo; (*of light*) forte; (*room*) claro; (*cheerful*) alegre; (*clever*) inteligente. **~ness** *n* (*sheen*) brilho *m*; (*clarity*) claridade *f*; (*intelligence*) inteligência *f*

brighten /'braɪtn/ *vt* alegrar □ *vi* (*of weather*) clarear; (*of face*) animar-se, iluminar-se

brillian|t /'brɪljənt/ *a* brilhante. **~ce** *n* brilho *m*

brim /brɪm/ *n* borda *f*; (*of hat*) aba *f* □ *vi* (*pt* **brimmed**) **~ over** transbordar, cair por fora

brine /braɪn/ *n* salmoura *f*

bring /brɪŋ/ *vt* (*pt* **brought**) trazer. **~ about** causar. **~ back** trazer (de volta); (*call to mind*) relembrar. **~ down** trazer para baixo; (*bird, plane*) abater; (*prices*) baixar. **~ forward** adiantar, apresentar. **~ it off** ser bem sucedido (em alg coisa). **~ out** (*take out*) tirar; (*show*) revelar; (*book*) publicar. **~ round** *or* **to** reanimar, fazer voltar a si. **~ to bear** (*pressure etc*) exercer. **~ up** educar; (*med*) vomitar; (*question*) levantar

brink /brɪŋk/ *n* beira *f*, borda *f*

brisk /brɪsk/ *a* (-er, -est) (*pace, movement*) vivo, rápido; (*business, demand*) grande

bristl|e /'brɪsl/ *n* pêlo *m*. **~y** *a* eriçado

Britain /'brɪtən/ *n* Grã-Bretanha *f*

British /'brɪtɪʃ/ *a* britânico. **the ~** o povo *m* britânico, os britânicos *mpl*

brittle /'brɪtl/ *a* frágil

broach /brəʊtʃ/ *vt* abordar, entabular, encetar

broad /brɔ:d/ *a* (-er, -est) largo; (*daylight*) pleno. **~ bean** fava *f*. **~-minded** *a* tolerante, liberal. **~ly** *adv* de modo geral

broadcast /'brɔ:dka:st/ *vt/i* (*pt* **broadcast**) transmitir, fazer uma transmissão; (*person*) cantar, falar *etc* na rádio *or* na TV □ *n* emissão *f*. **~ing** *a* & *n* (de) rádiodifusão (*f*)

broaden /'brɔ:dn/ *vt/i* alargar(-se)

broccoli /'brɒkəlɪ/ *n inv* brócolis *mpl*, (*P*) brócolos *mpl*

brochure /'brəʊʃə(r)/ *n* brochura *f*

broke /brəʊk/ *see* **break** □ *a* (*sl*) depenado (*sl*), liso (*sl*), (*P*) teso (*sl*)

broken /'brəʊkən/ *see* **break** □ *a* **~ English** inglês *m* estropeado. **~-hearted** *a* com o coração despedaçado

broker /'brəʊkə(r)/ *n* corretor *m*, broker *m*

bronchitis /brɒŋ'kaɪtɪs/ *n* bronquite *f*

bronze /brɒnz/ *n* bronze *m*

brooch /brəʊtʃ/ *n* broche *m*

brood /bru:d/ *n* ninhada *f* □ *vi* chocar; (*fig*) cismar. **~y** *a* (*hen*) choca; (*fig*) sorumbático, melancólico

brook /brʊk/ *n* regato *m*, ribeiro *m*

broom /bru:m/ *n* vassoura *f*; (*bot*) giesta *f*

broth /brɒθ/ *n* caldo *m*

brothel /'brɒθl/ *n* bordel *m*

brother /'brʌðə(r)/ *n* irmão *m*. **~-in-law** *n* (*pl* **~s-in-law**) cunhado *m*. **~hood** *n* irmandade *f*, fraternidade *f*. **~ly** *a* fraternal

brought /brɔ:t/ *see* **bring**

brow /braʊ/ *n* (*forehead*) testa *f*; (*of hill*) cume *m*; (*eyebrow*) sobrancelha *f*

browbeat /'braʊbi:t/ *vt* (*pt* **-beat**, *pp* **-beaten**) intimidar

brown /braʊn/ *a* (-er, -est) castanho □ *n* castanho *m* □ *vt/i* acastanhar; (*in the sun*) bronzear, tostar; (*meat*) alourar

browse /braʊz/ *vi* (*through book*) folhear; (*of animal*) pastar; (*in a shop*) olhar sem comprar

bruise /bru:z/ *n* hematoma *m*, contusão *f* □ *vt* causar um hematoma. **~d** *a* coberto de hematomas, contuso; (*fruit*) machucado

brunette /bru:'net/ *n* morena *f*

brunt /brʌnt/ *n* **the ~ of** o maior peso de, o pior de

brush /brʌʃ/ *n* escova *f*; (*painter's*) pincel *m*; (*skirmish*) escaramuça *f*. **~ against** roçar. **~ aside** não fazer caso de. **~ off** (*colloq: reject*) mandar passear (*colloq*). **~ up (on)** aperfeiçoar

brusque /bru:sk/ *a* brusco

Brussels /'brʌslz/ *n* Bruxelas *f*. **~ sprouts** couve-de-Bruxelas *f*

brutal /'bru:tl/ *a* brutal. **~ity** /'tælətɪ/ *n* brutalidade *f*

brute /bru:t/ *n* & *a* (*animal, person*) bruto (*m*). **by ~ force** por força bruta

B Sc *abbr see* **Bachelor of Science**

bubb|le /'bʌbl/ *n* bolha *f*; (*of soap*) bola *f* de sabão □ *vi* borbulhar. **~le gum** *n* chiclete *m*, (*P*) pastilha *f* elástica. **~le over** transbordar. **~ly** *a* efervescente

buck[1] /bʌk/ *n* macho *m* □ *vi* dar galões, (*P*) corcovear. **~ up** *vt/i* (*sl*) animar(-se); (*sl: rush*) apressar-se, despachar-se

buck[2] /bʌk/ *n* (*Amer sl*) dólar *m*

buck[3] /bʌk/ *n* **pass the ~** (*sl*) fazer o jogo do empurra

bucket /'bʌkɪt/ *n* balde *m*

buckle /'bʌkl/ *n* fivela *f* □ *vt/i* afivelar(-se); (*bend*) torcer(-se), vergar. **~ down to** empenhar-se

bud /bʌd/ *n* botão *m*, rebento *m* □ *vi* (*pt* **budded**) rebentar. **in ~** em botão

Buddhis|t /ˈbʊdɪst/ *a* & *n* budista (*mf*). ~**m** /-zəm/ *n* budismo *m*
budding /ˈbʌdɪŋ/ *a* nascente, em botão, incipiente
budge /bʌdʒ/ *vt/i* mexer(-se)
budgerigar /ˈbʌdʒərɪga:(r)/ *n* periquito *m*
budget /ˈbʌdʒɪt/ *n* orçamento *m* □ *vi* (*pt* **budgeted**) ~ **for** prever no orçamento *m*
buff /bʌf/ *n* (*colour*) côr *f* de camurça; (*colloq*) fanático *m*, entusiasta *mf* □ *vt* polir
buffalo /ˈbʌfələʊ/ *n* (*pl* **-oes**) búfalo *m*; (*Amer*) bisão *m*
buffer /ˈbʌfə(r)/ *n* pára-choque *m*
buffet[1] /ˈbʊfeɪ/ *n* (*meal, counter*) bufê *m*, (*P*) bufete *m*
buffet[2] /ˈbʌfɪt/ *vt* (*pt* **buffeted**) esbofetear; (*by wind, rain; fig*) fustigar
buffoon /bəˈfu:n/ *n* palhaço *m*
bug /bʌg/ *n* (*insect*) bicho *m*; (*bed-bug*) percevejo *m*; (*sl: germ*) virus *m*; (*sl: device*) microfone *m* de escuta; (*sl: defect*) defeito *m* □ *vt* (*pt* **bugged**) grampear; (*Amer sl: annoy*) chatear (*sl*)
bugbear /ˈbʌgbeə(r)/ *n* papão *m*
buggy /ˈbʌgɪ/ *n* (*for baby*) carrinho *m*
bugle /ˈbju:gl/ *n* clarim *m*, corneta *f*
build /bɪld/ *vt/i* (*pt* **built**) construir, edificar □ *n* físico *m*, compleição *f*. ~ **up** *vt/i* criar; (*increase*) aumentar; (*accumulate*) acumular(-se). ~**-up** *n* acumulação *f*; (*fig*) publicidade *f*. ~**er** *n* construtor *m*, empreiteiro *m*; (*workman*) operário *m*
building /ˈbɪldɪŋ/ *n* edifício *m*, prédio *m*. ~ **site** canteiro *m* de obras. ~ **society** sociedade *f* de investimentos imobiliários
built /bɪlt/ *see* **build**. ~**-in** *a* incorporado. ~**-in wardrobe** armário *m* embutido na parede. ~**-up** *a* urbanizado
bulb /bʌlb/ *n* bolbo *m*; (*electr*) lâmpada *f*. ~**ous** *a* bolboso
Bulgaria /bʌlˈgeərɪə/ *n* Bulgária *f*. ~**n** *a* & *n* búlgaro (*m*)
bulg|e /bʌldʒ/ *n* bojo *m*, saliência *f* □ *vi* inchar; (*jut out*) fazer uma saliência. ~**ing** *a* inchado; (*pocket etc*) cheio
bulk /bʌlk/ *n* quantidade *f*, volume *m*. **in** ~ por grosso; (*loose*) a granel. **the** ~ **of** a maior parte de. ~**y** *a* volumoso
bull /bʊl/ *n* touro *m*. ~**'s-eye** *n* (*of target*) centro *m* do alvo, mosca *f*
bulldog /ˈbʊldɒg/ *n* buldogue *m*
bulldoze /ˈbʊldəʊz/ *vt* terraplanar. ~**r** /-ə(r)/ *n* bulldozer *m*
bullet /ˈbʊlɪt/ *n* bala *f*. ~**-proof** *a* à prova de balas; (*vehicle*) blindado
bulletin /ˈbʊlətɪn/ *n* boletim *m*
bullfight /ˈbʊlfaɪt/ *n* tourada *f*, corrida *f* de touros. ~**er** *n* toureiro *m*. ~**ing** *n* tauromaquia *f*
bullring /ˈbʊlrɪŋ/ *n* arena *f*, (*P*) praça *f* de touros
bully /ˈbʊlɪ/ *n* mandão *m*, pessoa *f* prepotente; (*schol*) terror *m*, o mau □ *vt* intimidar; (*treat badly*) atormentar; (*coerce*) forçar (**into** a)
bum[1] /bʌm/ *n* (*sl: buttocks*) traseiro *m*, bunda *f* (*sl*)
bum[2] /bʌm/ *n* (*Amer sl*) vagabundo *m*
bump /bʌmp/ *n* choque *m*, embate *m*; (*swelling*) inchaço *m*; (*on head*) galo *m* □ *vt/i* bater, chocar. ~ **into** bater em, chocar com; (*meet*) esbarrar com, encontrar. ~**y** *a* (*surface*) irregular; (*ride*) aos solavancos
bumper /ˈbʌmpə(r)/ *n* pára-choques *m inv* □ *a* excepcional
bun /bʌn/ *n* pãozinho *m* doce com passas; (*hair*) coque *m*
bunch /bʌntʃ/ *n* (*of flowers*) ramo *m*; (*of keys*) molho *m*; (*of people*) grupo *m*; (*of grapes*) cacho *m*
bundle /ˈbʌndl/ *n* molho *m* □ *vt* atar num molho; (*push*) despachar
bung /bʌŋ/ *n* batoque *m*, rolha *f* □ *vt* rolhar; (*sl: throw*) atirar, deitar. ~ **up** entupir
bungalow /ˈbʌŋgələʊ/ *n* chalé *m*; (*outside Europe*) bungalô *m*, (*P*) bungalow *m*
bungle /ˈbʌŋgl/ *vt* fazer mal feito, estragar
bunion /ˈbʌnjən/ *n* (*med*) joanete *m*
bunk /bʌŋk/ *n* (*in train*) couchette *f*; (*in ship*) beliche *m*. ~**-beds** *npl* beliches *mpl*
bunker /ˈbʌŋkə(r)/ *n* (*mil*) abrigo *m*, casamata *f*, bunker *m*; (*golf*) obstáculo *m* em cova de areia
buoy /bɔɪ/ *n* bóia *f* □ *vt* ~ **up** animar
buoyan|t /ˈbɔɪənt/ *a* flutuante; (*fig*) alegre. ~**cy** *n* (*fig*) alegria *f*, exuberância *f*
burden /ˈbɜ:dn/ *n* fardo *m* □ *vt* collegar, sobrecarregar. ~**some** *a* pesado
bureau /ˈbjʊərəʊ/ *n* (*pl* **-eaux**) /-əʊz/ (*desk*) secretária *f*; (*office*) seção *f*, (*P*) secção *f*
bureaucracy /bjʊəˈrɒkrəsɪ/ *n* burocracia *f*
bureaucrat /ˈbjʊərəkræt/ *n* burocrata *mf*. ~**ic** /-ˈkrætɪk/ *a* burocrático
burger /ˈbɜ:gə(r)/ *n* hambúrguer *m*
burglar /ˈbɜ:glə(r)/ *n* ladrão *m*, assaltante *mf*. ~ **alarm** *n* alarme *m* contra ladrões. ~**ize** *vt* (*Amer*) assaltar. ~**y** *n* assalto *m*
burgle /ˈbɜ:gl/ *vt* assaltar
burial /ˈberɪəl/ *n* enterro *m*
burlesque /bɜ:ˈlesk/ *n* paródia *f*
burly /ˈbɜ:lɪ/ *a* (**-ier, -iest**) robusto e corpulento, forte

Burm|a /'bɜ:mə/ *n* Birmânia *f*. **~ese** /-'mi:z/ *a* & *n* birmanês (*m*)

burn /bɜ:n/ *vt* (*pt* **burned** *or* **burnt**) queimar □ *vi* queimar(-se), arder □ *n* queimadura *f*. **~ down** reduzir a cinzas. **~er** *n* (*of stove*) bico *m* de gás. **~ing** *a* (*thirst, desire*) ardente; (*topic*) candente

burnish /'bɜ:nɪʃ/ *vt* polir, brunir

burnt /bɜ:nt/ *see* **burn**

burp /bɜ:p/ *n* (*colloq*) arroto *m* □ *vi* (*colloq*) arrotar

burrow /'bʌrəʊ/ *n* toca *f* □ *vi* cavar, fazer uma toca

burst /bɜ:st/ *vt/i* (*pt* **burst**) arrebentar □ *n* estouro *m*, rebentar *m*; (*of anger, laughter*) explosão *f*; (*of firing*) rajada *f*; (*of energy*) acesso *m*. **~ into** (*flames, room, etc*) irromper em. **~ into tears** desatar num choro, desfazer-se em lágrimas. **~ out laughing** desatar a rir

bury /'berɪ/ *vt* sepultar, enterrar; (*hide*) esconder; (*engross, thrust*) mergulhar

bus /bʌs/ *n* (*pl* **buses**) ônibus *m*, (*P*) autocarro *m*. **~-stop** *n* paragem *f*

bush /bʊʃ/ *n* arbusto *m*; (*land*) mato *m*. **~y** *a* espesso

business /'bɪznɪs/ *n* (*trade, shop, affair*) negócio *m*; (*task*) função *f*; (*occupation*) ocupação *f*. **have no ~ to** não ter o direito de. **it's no ~ of yours** não é da sua conta. **mind your own ~** cuide da sua vida. **that's my ~** isso é meu problema. **~like** *a* eficiente, sistemático. **~man** *n* homem *m* de negócios, comerciante *m*

busker /'bʌskə(r)/ *n* músico *m* ambulante

bust[1] /bʌst/ *n* busto *m*

bust[2] /bʌst/ *vt/i* (*pt* **busted** *or* **bust**) (*sl*) = **burst, break** □ *a* falido. **~-up** *n* (*sl*) discussão *f*, (*P*) bulha *f*. **go ~** (*sl*) falir

bustl|e /'bʌsl/ *vi* andar numa azáfama; (*hurry*) apressar-se □ *n* azáfama *f*. **~ing** *a* animado, movimentado

bus|y /'bɪzɪ/ *a* (-ier, -iest) ocupado; (*street*) movimentado; (*day*) atarefado □ *vt* **~y o.s. with** ocupar-se com. **~ily** *adv* ativamente, atarefadamente

busybody /'bɪzɪbɒdɪ/ *n* intrometido *m*, pessoa *f* abelhuda

but /bʌt/ *conj* mas □ *prep* exceto, (*p*) excepto, senão □ *adv* apenas, só. **all ~** todos menos; (*nearly*) quaze, por pouco não. **~ for** sem, se não fosse. **last ~ one/two** penúltimo/antepenúltimo. **nobody ~** ninguém a não ser

butcher /'bʊtʃə(r)/ *n* açougueiro *m*, (*P*) homem *m* do talho; (*fig*) carrasco *m* □ *vt* chacinar. **the ~'s** açougue *m*, (*P*) talho *m*. **~y** *n* chacina *f*

butler /'bʌtlə(r)/ *n* mordomo *m*

butt /bʌt/ *n* (*of gun*) coronha *f*; (*of cigarette*) ponta *f*; (*target*) alvo *m* de troça, de ridículo *etc*; (*cask*) barril *m* □ *vt/i* dar cabeçada em. **~ in** interromper

butter /'bʌtə(r)/ *n* manteiga *f* □ *vt* pôr manteiga em. **~-bean** *n* feijão *m* branco

buttercup /'bʌtəkʌp/ *n* botão-de-ouro *m*

butterfly /'bʌtəflaɪ/ *n* borboleta *f*

buttock /'bʌtək/ *n* nádega *f*

button /'bʌtn/ *n* botão *m* □ *vt/i* abotoar(-se)

buttonhole /'bʌtnhəʊl/ *n* casa *f* de botão; (*in lapel*) botoeira *f* □ *vt* (*fig*) obrigar a ouvir

buttress /'bʌtrɪs/ *n* contraforte *m*; (*fig*) esteio *m* □ *vt* sustentar

buxom /'bʌksəm/ *a* roliço, rechonchudo

buy /baɪ/ *vt* (*pt* **bought**) comprar (from a); (*sl*: *believe*) engolir (*colloq*) □ *n* compra *f*. **~er** *n* comprador *m*

buzz /bʌz/ *n* zumbido *m* □ *vi* zumbir. **~ off** (*sl*) pôr-se a andar. **~er** *n* campainha *f*

by /baɪ/ *prep* (*near*) junto de, perto de; (*along, past, means*) por; (*according to*) conforme; (*before*) antes de. **~ land/sea/air** por terra/mar/ar. **~ bike/car** *etc* de bicicleta/carro *etc*. **~ day/night** de dia/noite. **~ the kilo** por quilo. **~ now** a esta hora. **~ accident/mistake** sem querer. **~ oneself** sozinho □ *adv* (*near*) perto. **~ and ~** muito em breve. **~ and large** no conjunto. **~-election** *n* eleição *f* suplementar. **~-law** *n* regulamento *m*. **~-product** *n* derivado *m*

bye(-bye) /'baɪ(baɪ)/ *int* (*colloq*) adeus, adeusinho

bygone /'baɪgɒn/ *a* passado. **let ~s be ~s** o que passou, passou

bypass /'baɪpa:s/ *n* (estrada) secundária *f*, desvio *m*; (*med*) by-pass *m*, ponte *f* de safema □ *vt* fazer um desvio; (*fig*) contornar

bystander /'baɪstændə(r)/ *n* circumstante *mf*, espectador *m*

byte /baɪt/ *n*

C

cab /kæb/ *n* táxi *m*; (*of lorry, train*) cabina *f*, cabine *f*

cabaret /'kæbəreɪ/ *n* variedades *fpl*, cabaré *m*

cabbage /'kæbɪdʒ/ *n* couve *f*, repolho *m*

cabin /'kæbɪn/ *n* cabana *f*, (*in plane*) cabina *f*, (*in ship*) camarote *m*

cabinet /'kæbɪnɪt/ *n* armário *m*. **C~** (*pol*) gabinete *m*
cable /'keɪbl/ *n* cabo *m*. **~-car** *n* funicular *m*, teleférico *m*. **~ railway** funicular *m*. **~ television** televisão *f* a cabo
cache /kæʃ/ *n* (esconderijo *m* de) tesouro *m*, armas *fpl*, provisões *f pl*
cackle /'kækl/ *n* cacarejo *m* □ *vi* cacarejar
cactus /'kæktəs/ *n* (*pl* **~es** *or* **cacti** /-taɪ/) cacto *m*
caddie /'kædɪ/ *n* (*golf*) caddie *m*
caddy /'kædɪ/ *n* lata *f* para o chá
cadet /kə'det/ *n* cadete *m*
cadge /kædʒ/ *vt/i* filar, (*P*) cravar
Caesarean /sɪ'zeərɪən/ *a* **~ (section)** cesariana *f*
café /'kæfeɪ/ *n* café *m*
cafeteria /kæfɪ'tɪərɪə/ *n* cafeteria *f*, restaurante *m* self-service
caffeine /'kæfi:n/ *n* cafeína *f*
cage /keɪdʒ/ *n* gaiola *f*
cagey /'keɪdʒɪ/ *a* (*colloq: secretive*) misterioso, reservado
cajole /kə'dʒəʊl/ *vt* **~ sb into doing sth** convencer alguém (com lábia ou lisonjas) a fazer alg coisa
cake /keɪk/ *n* bolo *m*. **~d** *a* empastado. **his shoes were ~d with mud** tinha os sapatos cobertos de lama. **a piece of ~** (*sl*) canja *f* (*sl*)
calamity /kə'læmətɪ/ *n* calamidade *f*
calcium /'kælsɪəm/ *n* cálcio *m*
calculat|e /'kælkjʊleɪt/ *vt/i* calcular; (*Amer: suppose*) supor. **~ed** *a* (*action*) deliberado, calculado. **~ing** *a* calculista. **~ion** /-'leɪʃn/ *n* cálculo *m*. **~or** *n* calculador *m*, (*P*) maquina *f* de calcular
calendar /'kælɪndə(r)/ *n* calendário *m*
calf[1] /ka:f/ *n* (*pl* **calves**) (*young cow or bull*) vitelo *m*, bezerro *m*; (*of other animals*) cria *f*
calf[2] /ka:f/ *n* (*pl* **calves**) (*of leg*) barriga *f* da perna
calibrat|e /'kælɪbreɪt/ *vt* calibrar. **~ion** /-breɪʃn/ *n* calibragem *f*
calibre /'kælɪbə(r)/ *n* calibre *m*
calico /'kælɪkəʊ/ *n* pano *m* de algodão; (*printed*) chita *f*, algodão *m*
call /kɔ:l/ *vt/i* chamar; (*summon*) convocar; (*phone*) telefonar. **~ (in** *or* **round)** (*visit*) passar por casa de □ *n* chamada *f*; (*bird's cry*) canto *m*; (*shout*) brado *m*, grito *m*. **be ~ed** (*named*) chamar-se. **be on ~** estar de serviço. **~ back** (*phone*) tornar a telefonar; (*visit*) voltar. **~ for** (*demand*) pedir, requerer; (*fetch*) ir buscar. **~ off** cancelar. **~ on** (*visit*) visitar, fazer uma visita a. **~ out (to)** chamar. **~ up** (*mil*) mobilizar, recrutar; (*phone*) telefonar. **~-box** *n* cabina *f* telefônica, (*P*) telefónica. **~er** *n* visitante *f*, visita *f*; (*phone*) chamador *m*, (*P*) pessoa *f* que faz a chamada. **~ing** *n* vocação *f*
callous /'kæləs/ *a* insensível. **~ly** *adv* sem piedade.
callow /'kæləʊ/ *a* (-er, -est) inexperiente, verde
calm /ka:m/ *a* (-er, -est) calmo □ *n* calma *f* □ *vt/i* **~ (down)** acalmar (-se). **~ness** *n* calma *f*
calorie /'kælərɪ/ *n* caloria *f*
camber /'kæmbə(r)/ *n* (*of road*) abaulamento *m*
camcorder /'kæmkɔ:də(r)/ *n* câmera *f* de filmar
came /keɪm/ *see* **come**
camel /'kæml/ *n* camelo *m*
camera /'kæmərə/ *n* máquina *f* fotográfica; (*cine, TV*) câmera *f*. **~man** *n* (*pl* **-men**) operador *m*
camouflage /'kæməfla:ʒ/ *n* camuflagem *f* □ *vt* camuflar
camp[1] /kæmp/ *n* acampamento *m* □ *vi* acampar. **~-bed** *n* cama *f* de campanha. **~er** *n* campista *mf*; (*car*) auto-caravana *f*. **~ing** *n* campismo *m*
camp[2] /kæmp/ *a* afetado, efeminado
campaign /kæm'peɪn/ *n* campanha *f* □ *vi* fazer campanha
campsite /'kæmpsaɪt/ *n* área *f* de camping, (*P*) parque *m* de campismo
campus /'kæmpəs/ *n* (*pl* **-puses** /-pəsɪz/) campus *m*, (*P*) cidade *f* universitária
can[1] /kæn/ *n* vasilha *f* de lata; (*for food*) lata *f* (de conserva) □ *vt* (*pt* **canned**) enlatar. **~ned music** música *f* em fita para locais públicos. **~-opener** *n* abridor *m* de latas, (*P*) abrelatas *m*
can[2] /kæn/ *v aux* (*be able to*) poder, ser capaz de; (*know how to*) saber. **I ~not/~'t go** não posso ir
Canad|a /'kænədə/ *n* Canadá *m*. **~ian** /kə'neɪdɪən/ *a* & *n* canadense (*mf*), (*P*) canadiano (*m*)
canal /kə'næl/ *n* canal *m*
canary /kə'neərɪ/ *n* canário *m*. **C~ Islands** *npl* as (Ilhas) Canárias
cancel /'kænsl/ *vt* (*pt* **cancelled**) cancelar; (*cross out*) riscar; (*stamps*) inutilizar. **~ out** *vi* (*fig*) neutralizar-se mutuamente. **~lation** /-'leɪʃn/ *n* cancelamento *m*
cancer /'kænsə(r)/ *n* câncer *m*, cancro *m*. **C~** (*astrol*) Caranguejo *m*, Câncer *m*. **~ous** *a* canceroso
candid /'kændɪd/ *a* franco. **~ly** *adv* francamente
candida|te /'kændɪdeɪt/ *n* candidato *m*. **~cy** /-əsɪ/ *n* candidatura *f*
candle /'kændl/ *n* vela *f*; (*in church*) vela *f*, círio *m*. **~-light** *n* luz *f* de velas

candlestick /'kændlstɪk/ *n* castiçal *m*
candour /'kændə(r)/ *n* franqueza *f*, candura *f*
candy /'kændɪ/ *n* bala *f*, (*P*) açúcar cândi; (*Amer: sweet, sweets*) doce(s) *m* (*pl*). **~-floss** *n* algodão-doce *m*
cane /keɪn/ *n* cana *f*; (*walking-stick*) bengala *f*; (*for baskets*) verga *f*; (*school: for punishment*) vergasta *f* □ *vt* vergastar
canine /'keɪnaɪn/ *a* & *n* canino (*m*)
canister /'kænɪstə(r)/ *n* lata *f*
cannabis /'kænəbɪs/ *n* cânhamo *m*, maconha *f*
cannibal /'kænɪbl/ *n* canibal *mf*. **~ism** /-zəm/ *n* canibalismo *m*
cannon /'kænən/ *n inv* canhão *m*. **~-ball** *n* bala *f* de canhão
cannot /'kænət/ = **can not**
canny /'kænɪ/ *a* (-ier, -iest) astuto, manhoso
canoe /kə'nu:/ *n* canoa *f* □ *vi* andar de canoa. **~ing** *n* (*sport*) canoagem *f*. **~ist** *n* canoeiro *m*, (*P*) canoísta *mf*
canon /'kænən/ *n* cônego *m*, (*P*) cónego *m*; (*rule*) cânone *m*
canonize /'kænənaɪz/ *vt* canonizar
canopy /'kænəpɪ/ *n* dossel *m*; (*over doorway*) toldo *m*, marquise *f*; (*fig*) abóbada *f*
can't /ka:nt/ = **can not**
cantankerous /kæn'tæŋkərəs/ *a* irascível, intratável
canteen /kæn'ti:n/ *n* cantina *f*; (*flask*) cantil *m*; (*for cutlery*) estojo *m*
canter /'kæntə(r)/ *n* meio galope *m*, cânter *m* □ *vi* andar a meio galope
canton /'kæntɒn/ *n* cantão *m*
canvas /'kænvəs/ *n* lona *f*; (*for painting or tapestry*) tela *f*
canvass /'kænvəs/ *vt/i* angariar votos *or* fregueses
canyon /'kænjən/ *n* canhão *m*, (*P*) desfiladeiro *m*
cap /kæp/ *n* (*with peak*) boné *m*; (*without peak*) barrete *m*; (*of nurse*) touca *f*; (*of bottle, pen, tube, etc*) tampa *f*; (*mech*) tampa *f*, tampão *m* □ *vt* (*pt* **capped**) (*bottle, pen, tube, etc*) tapar, tampar; (*rates*) impôr um limite a; (*outdo*) suplantar; (*sport*) selecionar, (*P*) seleccionar. **~ped with** encimado de, coroado de
capab|le /'keɪpəbl/ *a* (*person*) capaz (of de); (*things, situations*) suscetível, (*P*) susceptível (of de). **~ility** /-'bɪlətɪ/ *n* capacidade *f*. **~ly** *adv* capazmente
capacity /kə'pæsətɪ/ *n* capacidade *f*. **in one's ~ as** na (sua) qualidade de
cape[1] /keɪp/ *n* (*cloak*) capa *f*
cape[2] /keɪp/ *n* (*geog*) cabo *m*
caper[1] /'keɪpə(r)/ *vi* andar aos pinotes
caper[2] /'keɪpə(r)/ *n* (*culin*) alcaparra *f*
capillary /kə'pɪlərɪ/ *n* (*pl* -ies) vaso *m* capilar
capital /'kæpɪtl/ *a* capital □ *n* (*town*) capital *f*; (*money*) capital *m*. **~ (letter)** maiúscula *f*. **~ punishment** pena *f* de morte
capitalis|t /'kæpɪtəlɪst/ *a* & *n* capitalista (*mf*). **~m** /-zəm/ *n* capitalismo *m*
capitalize /'kæpɪtəlaɪz/ *vi* capitalizar; (*finance*) financiar; (*writing*) escrever com maiúscula. **~ on** tirar partido de
capitulat|e /kə'pɪtʃʊleɪt/ *vi* capitular. **~ion** /'leɪʃn/ *n* capitulação *f*
capricious /kə'prɪʃəs/ *a* caprichoso
Capricorn /'kæprɪkɔ:n/ *n* (*astrol*) Capricórnio *m*
capsicum /'kæpsɪkəm/ *n* pimento *m*
capsize /kæp'saɪz/ *vt/i* virar(-se)
capsule /'kæpsju:l/ *n* cápsula *f*
captain /'kæptɪn/ *n* capitão *m*; (*navy*) capitão-de-mar-e-guerra *m* □ *vt* capitanear, comandar
caption /'kæpʃn/ *n* legenda *f*; (*heading*) título *m*
captivate /'kæptɪveɪt/ *vt* cativar
captiv|e /'kæptɪv/ *a* & *n* cativo (*m*), prisioneiro (*m*). **~ity** /-'tɪvətɪ/ *n* cativeiro *m*
captor /'kæptə(r)/ *n* captor *m*
capture /'kæptʃə(r)/ *vt* capturar; (*attention*) prender □ *n* captura *f*
car /ka:(r)/ *n* carro *m*. **~ ferry** barca *f* para carros. **~-park** *n* (parque *m* de) estacionamento (*m*). **~ phone** telefone *m* de carro. **~-wash** *n* estação *f* de lavagem
carafe /kə'ræf/ *n* garrafa *f* para água ou vinho
caramel /'kærəmel/ *n* caramelo *m*.
carat /'kærət/ *n* quilate *m*
caravan /'kærəvæn/ *n* caravana *f*, reboque *m*
caraway /'kærəweɪ/ *n* **~ seed** cariz *f*
carbohydrate /ka:bəʊ'haɪdreɪt/ *n* hidrato *m* de carbono
carbon /'ka:bən/ *n* carbono *m*. **~ copy** cópia *f* em papel carbono, (*P*) químico. **~ monoxide** óxido *m* de carbono. **~ paper** papel *m* carbono, (*P*) químico
carburettor /ka:bjʊ'retə(r)/ *n* carburador *m*
carcass /'ka:kəs/ *n* carcaça *f*
card /ka:d/ *n* cartão *m*; (*postcard*) postal *m*; (*playing-card*) carta *f*. **~-game(s)** *n*(*pl*) jogo(s) *m*(*pl*) de cartas. **~ index** *n* fichário *m*, (*P*) ficheiro *m*
cardboard /'ka:dbɔ:d/ *n* cartão *m*, papelão *m*
cardiac /'ka:dɪæk/ *a* cardíaco
cardigan /'ka:dɪgən/ *n* casaco *m* de lã

cardinal /'ka:dɪnl/ *a* cardeal, principal. ~ **number** numeral *m* cardinal □ *n* (*relig*) cardeal *m*
care /keə(r)/ *n* cuidado *m*; (*concern*) interesse *m* □ *vi* ~ **about** (*be interested*) estar interessado por; (*be worried*) estar preocupado com. ~ **for** (*like*) gostar de; (*look after*) tomar conta de. **take** ~ tomar cuidado. **take** ~ **of** cuidar de; (*deal with*) tratar de. **he couldn't** ~ less ele está pouco ligando, ele não dá a menor (*colloq*)
career /kə'rɪə(r)/ *n* carreira *f* □ *vi* ir a toda a velocidade, ir numa carreira
carefree /'keəfri:/ *a* despreocupado
careful /'keəfl/ *a* cuidadoso; (*cautious*) cauteloso. ~! cuidado! ~**ly** *adv* cuidadosamente; (*cautiously*) cautelosamente
careless /'keəlɪs/ *a* descuidado (**about** com). ~**ly** *adv* descuidadamente. ~**ness** *n* descuido *m*, negligência *f*
caress /kə'res/ *n* carícia *f* □ *vt* acariciar
caretaker /'keəteɪkə(r)/ *n* zelador *m* duma casa vizia; (*janitor*) zelador *m*, (*P*) porteiro *m*
cargo /'ka:gəʊ/ *n* (*pl* **-oes**) carregamento *m*, carga *f*
Caribbean /kærɪ'bi:ən/ *a* caraíba. **the** ~ as Caraíbas *fpl*
caricature /'kærɪkətjʊə(r)/ *n* caricatura *f* □ *vt* caricaturar
caring /'keərɪŋ/ *a* carinhoso, afetuoso, (*P*) afectuoso
carnage /'ka:nɪdʒ/ *n* carnificina *f*
carnation /ka:'neɪʃn/ *n* cravo *m*
carnival /'ka:nɪvl/ *n* carnaval *m*
carol /'kærəl/ *n* cântico *m* *or* canto *m* de Natal
carp[1] /ka:p/ *n inv* carpa *f*
carp[2] /ka:p/ *vi* ~ **(at)** criticar
carpent|er /'ka:pɪntə(r)/ *n* carpinteiro *m*. ~**ry** *n* carpintaria *f*
carpet /'ka:pɪt/ *n* tapete *m* □ *vt* (*pt* **carpeted**) atapetar. **with fitted** ~**s** (estar) atapetado. **be on the** ~ (*colloq*) ser chamado à ordem. ~-**sweeper** *n* limpador *m* de tapetes
carport /'ka:pɔ:t/ *n* abrigo *m*, (*P*) telheiro *m* para automóveis
carriage /'kærɪdʒ/ *n* carruagem *f*; (*of goods*) frete *m*, transporte *m*; (*cost, bearing*) porte *m*
carriageway /'kærɪdʒweɪ/ *n* faixa *f* de rodagem, pista *f*
carrier /'kærɪə(r)/ *n* transportador *m*; (*company*) transportadora *f*; (*med*) portador *m*. ~ **(bag)** saco *m* de plástico
carrot /'kærət/ *n* cenoura *f*
carry /'kærɪ/ *vt/i* levar; (*goods*) transportar; (*involve*) acarretar; (*have for sale*) ter à venda. **be carried away** entusiasmar-se, deixar-se levar. ~-**cot** *n* moisés *m*. ~ **off** levar à força; (*prize*) incluir. ~ **it off** sair-se bem (de). ~ **on** continuar; (*colloq: flirt*) flertar; (*colloq: behave*) portar-se (mal). ~ **out** executar; (*duty*) cumprir. ~ **through** levar a cabo
cart /ka:t/ *n* carroça *f*; carro *m* □ *vt* acarretar; (*colloq*) carregar com
cartilage /'ka:tɪlɪdʒ/ *n* cartilagem *f*
carton /'ka:tn/ *n* embalagem *f* de cartão *or* de plástico; (*of yogurt*) embalagem *f*, pote *m*; (*of milk*) pacote *m*
cartoon /ka:'tu:n/ *n* desenho *m* humorístico, caricatura *f*; (*strip*) estória *f* em quadrinhos, (*P*) banda *f* desenhada; (*film*) desenhos *mpl* animados. ~**ist** *n* caricaturista *mf*; (*of strip, film*) desenhador *m*
cartridge /'ka:trɪdʒ/ *n* cartucho *m*
carv|e /ka:v/ *vt* esculpir, talhar; (*meat*) trinchar. ~**ing** *n* obra *f* de talha; (*on tree-trunk*) incisão *f*. ~**ing knife** faca *f* de trinchar, trinchante *m*
cascade /kæs'keɪd/ *n* cascata *f* □ *vi* cair em cascata
case[1] /keɪs/ *n* caso *m*; (*jur*) causa *f*, processo *m*; (*phil*) argumentos *mpl*. **in any** ~ em todo caso. **in** ~ **(of)** no caso (de). **in that** ~ nesse caso
case[2] /keɪs/ *n* caixa *f*; (*crate*) caixa *f*, caixote *m*; (*for camera, jewels, spectacles, etc*) estojo *m*; (*suitcase*) mala *f*; (*for cigarettes*) cigarreira *f*
cash /kæʃ/ *n* dinheiro *m*, numerário *m*, cash *m* □ *vt* (*obtain money for*) cobrar, receber; (*give money for*) pagar. **be short of** ~ ter pouco dinheiro. ~ **a cheque** (*receive/give*) cobrar/descontar um cheque. ~ **in** receber. ~ **in (on)** aproveitar-se de. **in** ~ em dinheiro. **pay** ~ pagar em dinheiro. ~ **desk** caixa *f*. ~ **dispenser** caixa *f* electrônica. ~-**flow** *n* cash-flow *m*. ~ **register** caixa *f* registradora, (*P*) registradora *f*
cashew /kæ'ʃu:/ *n* caju *m*
cashier /kæ'ʃɪə(r)/ *n* caixa *mf*
cashmere /kæʃ'mɪə(r)/ *n* caxemira *f*
casino /kə'si:nəʊ/ *n* (*pl* **-os**) casino *m*
cask /ka:sk/ *n* casco *m*, barril *m*
casket /'ka:skɪt/ *n* pequeno cofre *m*; (*Amer: coffin*) caixão *m*
casserole /'kæsərəʊl/ *n* caçarola *f*; (*stew*) estufado *m*
cassette /kə'set/ *n* cassette *f*. ~ **player** gravador *m*. ~ **recorder** *n*
cast /ka:st/ *vt* (*pt* **cast**) lançar, arremessar; (*shed*) despojar-se de; (*vote*) dar; (*metal*) fundir; (*shadow*) projetar, (*P*) projectar □ *n* (*theatr*) elenco *m*; (*mould*) molde *m*; (*med*) aparelho

m de gesso. ~ **iron** *n* ferro *m* fundido. ~**-iron** *a* de ferro fundido; (*fig*) muito forte. ~**-offs** *npl* roupa *f* velha

castanets /kæstə'nets/ *npl* castanholas *fpl*

castaway /'ka:stəweɪ/ *n* náufrago *m*

caste /ka:st/ *n* casta *f*

castigate /'kæstɪgeɪt/ *vt* castigar

castle /'ka:sl/ *n* castelo *m*; (*chess*) torre *f*

castor /'ka:stə(r)/ *n* roda *f* de pé de móvel. ~ **sugar** açúcar *m* em pó

castrat|e /kæ'streɪt/ *vt* castrar. ~**ion** /-ʃn/ *n* castração *f*

casual /'kæʒʊəl/ *a* (*chance: meeting*) casual; (*careless, unmethodical*) descuidado; (*informal*) informal. ~ **clothes** roupa *f* prática *or* de lazer. ~ **work** trabalho *m* ocasional. ~**ly** *adv* casualmente; (*carelessly*) sem cuidado

casualty /'kæʒʊəltɪ/ *n* (*dead*) morto *m*; (*death*) morte *f*; (*injured*) ferido *m*; (*victim*) vítima *f*; (*mil*) baixa *f*

cat /kæt/ *n* gato *m*. ~**'s-eyes** *npl* (*P*) reflectores *mpl*

Catalonia /kætə'ləʊnɪə/ *n* Catalunha *f*

catalogue /'kætəlɒg/ *n* catálogo *m* □ *vt* catalogar

catalyst /'kætəlɪst/ *n* catalisador *m*

catapult /'kætəpʌlt/ *n* (*child's*) atiradeira *f*, (*P*) fisga *f* □ *vt* catapultar

cataract /'kætərækt/ *f* (*waterfall & med*) catarata *f*

catarrh /kə'ta:(r)/ *n* catarro *m*

catastroph|e /kə'tæstrəfɪ/ *n* catástrofe *f*. ~**ic** /kætəs'trɒfɪk/ *a* catastrófico

catch /kætʃ/ *vt* (*pt* **caught**) apanhar; (*grasp*) agarrar; (*hear*) perceber □ *vi* prender-se (**in** em); (*get stuck*) ficar preso □ *n* apanha *f*; (*of fish*) pesca *f*; (*trick*) ratoeira *f*; (*snag*) problema *m*; (*on door*) trinco *m*; (*fastener*) fecho *m*. ~ **fire** pegar fogo, (*P*) incendiar-se. ~ **on** (*colloq*) pegar, tornar-se popular. ~ **sb's eye** atrair a atenção de alg. ~ **sight of** avistar. ~ **up (with)** pôr-se a par (com); (*work*) pôr em dia. ~**-phrase** *n* clichê *m*

catching /'kætʃɪŋ/ *a* contagioso, infeccioso

catchment /'kætʃmənt/ *n* ~ **area** (*geog*) bacia *f* de captação; (*fig: of school, hospital*) área *f*

catchy /'kætʃɪ/ *a* (*tune*) que pega fácil

categorical /kætɪ'gɒrɪkl/ *a* categórico

category /'kætɪgərɪ/ *n* categoria *f*

cater /'keɪtə(r)/ *vi* fornecer comida (para clubes, casamentos, etc). ~ **for** (*pander to*) satisfazer; (*consumers*) dirigir-se a. ~**er** *n* fornecedor *m*. ~**ing** *n* catering *m*

caterpillar /'kætəpɪlə(r)/ *n* lagarta *f*

cathedral /kə'θi:drəl/ *n* catedral *f*

catholic /'kæθəlɪk/ *a* universal; (*eclectic*) eclético, (*P*) ecléctico. **C**~ *a* & *n* católico (*m*). **C**~**ism** /kə'θɒlɪsɪzəm/ *n* catolicismo *m*

cattle /'kætl/ *npl* gado *m*

catty /'kætɪ/ *a* (dissimuladamente) maldoso, com perfídia

caught /kɔ:t/ *see* **catch**

cauldron /'kɔ:ldrən/ *n* caldeirão *m*

cauliflower /'kɒlɪflaʊə(r)/ *n* couve-flor *f*

cause /kɔ:z/ *n* causa *f* □ *vt* causar. ~ **sth to grow/move** *etc* fazer crescer/mexer *etc* alg coisa

causeway /'kɔ:zweɪ/ *n* estrada *f* elevada, caminho *m* elevado

caustic /'kɔ:stɪk/ *a* cáustico

cauti|on /'kɔ:ʃn/ *n* cautela *f*; (*warning*) aviso *m* □ *vt* avisar. ~**ous** /'kɔ:ʃəs/ *a* cauteloso. ~**ously** *adv* cautelosamente

cavalry /'kævəlrɪ/ *n* cavalaria *f*

cave /keɪv/ *n* caverna *f*, gruta *f* □ *vi* ~ **in** desabar, dar de si

caveman /'keɪvmæn/ *n* (*pl* **-men**) troglodita *m*, homen *m* das cavernas; (*fig*) (tipo) primário *m*

cavern /'kævən/ *n* caverna *f*. ~**ous** *a* cavernoso

caviare /'kævɪa:(r)/ *n* caviar *m*

caving /'keɪvɪŋ/ *n* espeleologia *f*

cavity /'kævətɪ/ *n* cavidade *f*

cavort /kə'vɔ:t/ *vi* curvetear; (*person*) andar aos pinotes

CD /si:'di/ *see* **compact disc**

cease /si:s/ *vt/i* cessar. ~**-fire** *n* cessar-fogo *m*. ~**less** *a* incessante

cedar /'si:də(r)/ *n* cedro *m*

cedilla /sɪ'dɪlə/ *n* cedilha *f*

ceiling /'si:lɪŋ/ *n* (*lit & fig*) teto *m*, (*P*) tecto *m*

celebrat|e /'selɪbreɪt/ *vt/i* celebrar, festejar. ~**ion** /'breɪʃn/ *n* celebração *f*, festejo *m*

celebrated /'selɪbreɪtɪd/ *a* célebre

celebrity /sɪ'lebrətɪ/ *n* celebridade *f*

celery /'selərɪ/ *n* aipo *m*

celiba|te /'selɪbət/ *a* celibatário. ~**cy** *n* celibato *m*

cell /sel/ *n* (*of prison, convent*) cela *f*; (*biol, pol, electr*) célula *f*

cellar /'selə(r)/ *n* porão *m*, cave *f*; (*for wine*) adega *f*, cave *f*

cell|o /'tʃeləʊ/ *n* (*pl* **-os**) violoncelo *m*. ~**ist** *n* violoncelista *mf*

Cellophane /'seləfeɪn/ *n* (*p*) celofane *m*

cellular /'seljʊlə(r)/ *a* celular

Celt /kelt/ *n* celta *mf*. ~**ic** *a* celta, céltico

cement /sɪ'ment/ *n* cimento *m* □ *vt* cimentar. ~**-mixer** *n* betoneira *f*

cemetery /'semətrɪ/ *n* cemitério *m*
censor /'sensə(r)/ *n* censor *m* □ *vt* censurar. **~ship** *n* censura *f*
censure /'senʃə(r)/ *n* censura *f*, crítica *f* □ *vt* censurar, criticar
census /'sensəs/ *n* recenseamento *m*, censo *m*
cent /sent/ *n* cêntimo *m*
centenary /sen'ti:nərɪ/ *n* centenário *m*
centigrade /'sentɪgreɪd/ *a* centígrado
centilitre /'sentɪli:tə(r)/ *n* centilitro *m*
centimetre /'sentɪmi:tə(r)/ *n* centímetro *m*
centipede /'sentɪpi:d/ *n* centopéia *f*, (*P*) centopeia *f*
central /'sentrəl/ *a* central. **~ heating** aquecimento *m* central. **~ize** *vt* centralizar. **~ly** *adv* no centro
centre /'sentə(r)/ *n* centro *m* □ *vt* (*pt* **centred**) centrar □ *vi* **~ on** concentrar-se em, fixar-se em
centrifugal /sen'trɪfjʊgl/ *a* centrífugo
century /'sentʃərɪ/ *n* século *m*
ceramic /sɪ'ræmɪk/ *a* (*object*) em cerâmica. **~s** *n* cerâmica *f*
cereal /'sɪərɪəl/ *n* cereal *m*
cerebral /'serɪbrəl/ *a* cerebral
ceremonial /serɪ'məʊnɪəl/ *a* de cerimônia □ *n* cerimonial *m*
ceremon|y /'serɪmənɪ/ *n* cerimônia *f*, (*P*) cerimónia *f*. **~ious** /-'məʊnɪəs/ *a* cerimonioso
certain /'sɜ:tn/ *a* certo. **be ~** ter a certeza. **for ~** com certeza, ao certo. **make ~** confirmar, verificar. **~ly** *adv* com certeza, certamente. **~ty** *n* certeza *f*
certificate /sə'tɪfɪkət/ *n* certificado *m*; (*birth, marriage*) certidão *f*; (*health*) atestado *m*
certif|y /'sɜ:tɪfaɪ/ *vt/i* certificar. **~ied** *a* (*as insane*) declarado
cervical /sɜ:'vaɪkl/ *a* cervical; (*of cervix*) do útero
cesspit, cesspool /'sespɪt, 'sespu:l/ *ns* fossa *f* sanitária
chafe /tʃeɪf/ *vt/i* esfregar; (*make/become sore*) esfolar/ficar esfolado; (*fig*) irritar(-se)
chaff /tʃa:f/ *vt* brincar com □ *n* brincadeira *f*; (*husk*) casca *f*
chaffinch /'tʃæfɪntʃ/ *n* tentilhão *m*
chagrin /'ʃægrɪn/ *n* decepção *f*, desgosto *m*, aborrecimento *m*
chain /tʃeɪn/ *n* corrente *f*, cadeia *f*; (*series*) cadeia *f* □ *vt* acorrentar. **~ reaction** reação *f*, (*P*) reacção *f* em cadeia. **~-smoke** *vi* fumar cigarros um atrás do outro. **~ store** loja *f* pertencente a uma cadeia
chair /tʃeə(r)/ *n* cadeira *f*; (*position of chairman*) presidência *f*; (*univ*) cátedra *f* □ *vt* presidir
chairman /'tʃeəmən/ *n* (*pl* **-men**) presidente *mf*
chalet /'ʃæleɪ/ *n* chalé *m*
chalk /tʃɔ:k/ *n* greda *f*, cal *f*; (*for writing*) giz *m* □ *vt* traçar com giz
challeng|e /'tʃælɪndʒ/ *n* desafio *m*; (*by sentry*) interpelação *f* □ *vt* desafiar; (*question truth of*) contestar. **~er** *n* (*sport*) pretendente *mf* (ao título). **~ing** *a* estimulante, que constitui um desafio
chamber /'tʃeɪmbə(r)/ *n* (*old use*) aposento *m*. **~-maid** *n* arrumadeira *f*. **~ music** música *f* de câmara. **C~ of Commerce** Câmara *f* de Comércio
chamois /'ʃæmɪ/ *n* **~(-leather)** camurça *f*
champagne /ʃæm'peɪn/ *n* champanhe *m*
champion /'tʃæmpɪən/ *n* campeão *m*, campeã *f* □ *vt* defender. **~ship** *n* campeonato *m*
chance /tʃa:ns/ *n* acaso *m*; (*luck*) sorte *f*; (*opportunity*) oportunidade *f*, chance *f*; (*likelihood*) hipótese *f*, probabilidade *f*; (*risk*) risco *m* □ *a* casual, fortuito □ *vi* calhar □ *vt* arriscar. **by ~** por acaso
chancellor /'tʃa:nsələ(r)/ *n* chanceler *m*. **C~ of the Exchequer** Ministro *m* das Finanças
chancy /'tʃa:nsɪ/ *a* arriscado
chandelier /ʃændə'lɪə(r)/ *n* lustre *m*
change /tʃeɪndʒ/ *vt* mudar; (*exchange*) trocar (for por); (*clothes, house, trains, etc*) mudar de □ *vi* mudar; (*clothes*) mudar-se, mudar de roupa □ *n* mudança *f*; (*money*) troco *m*. **a ~ of clothes** uma muda de roupa. **~ hands** (*ownership*) mudar de dono. **~ into** (*a butterfly etc*) transformar-se em; (*evening dress etc*) pôr. **~ one's mind** mudar de idéia. **~ over** passar, mudar (to para). **~-over** *n* mudança *f*. **~able** *a* variável
channel /'tʃænl/ *n* canal *m* □ *vt* (*pt* **channelled**) canalizar. **the C~ Islands** as Ilhas do Canal da Mancha. **the (English) C~** o Canal da Mancha
chant /tʃa:nt/ *n* cântico *m*; (*of crowd etc*) *vt/i* cantar, entoar
chao|s /'keɪɒs/ *n* caos *m*. **~tic** /-'ɒtɪk/ *a* caótico
chap /tʃæp/ *n* (*colloq*) sujeito *m*, (*B*) cara *m*, (*P*) tipo *m*
chapel /'tʃæpl/ *n* capela *f*
chaperon /'ʃæpərəʊn/ *n* pau-de-cabeleira *m*, chaperon *m* □ *vt* servir de pau-de-cabeleira *or* de chaperon
chaplain /'tʃæplɪn/ *n* capelão *m*. **~cy** *n* capelania *f*
chapter /'tʃæptə(r)/ *n* capítulo *m*
char /tʃa:(r)/ *vt* (*pt* **charred**) carbonizar

character /'kærəktə(r)/ *n* caráter *m*, (*P*) carácter *m*; (*in novel, play*) personagem *m*; (*reputation*) fama *f*; (*eccentric person*) excêntrico *m*; (*letter*) caractere *m*, (*P*) carácter *m*. **~ize** *vt* caracterizar

characteristic /kærəktə'rɪstɪk/ *a* característico □ *n* característica *f*. **~ally** *adv* tipicamente

charade /ʃə'ra:d/ *n* charada *f*

charcoal /'tʃa:kəʊl/ *n* carvão *m* de lenha

charge /tʃa:dʒ/ *n* preço *m*; (*electr, mil*) carga *f*; (*jur*) acusação *f*; (*task, custody*) cargo *m* □ *vt/i* (*price*) cobrar; (*enemy*) atacar; (*jur*) incriminar. **be in ~ of** ter a cargo. **take ~ of** encarregar-se de

chariot /'tʃærɪət/ *n* carro *m* de guerra *or* triunfal

charisma /kə'rɪzmə/ *n* carisma *m*. **~tic** /kærɪz'mætɪk/ *a* carismático

charit|y /'tʃærətɪ/ *n* caridade *f*; (*society*) instituição *f* de caridade. **~able** *a* caridoso

charlatan /'ʃa:lətən/ *n* charlatão *m*

charm /tʃa:m/ *n* encanto *m*, charme *m*; (*spell*) feitiço *m*; (*talisman*) amuleto *m* □ *vt* encantar. **~ing** *a* encantador

chart /tʃa:t/ *n* (*naut*) carta *f*; (*table*) mapa *m*, gráfico *m*, tabela *f* □ *vt* fazer o mapa de

charter /'tʃa:tə(r)/ *n* carta *f*. **~ (flight)** (voo) charter *m* □ *vt* fretar. **~ed accountant** *n* perito *m* contador, (*P*) perito *m* de contabilidade

charwoman /'tʃa:wʊmən/ *n* (*pl* **-women**) faxineira *f*, (*P*) mulher *f* a dias

chase /tʃeɪs/ *vt* perseguir □ *vi* (*colloq*) correr (**after** atrás de) □ *n* caça *f*, perseguição *f*. **~ away** *or* **off** afugentar, expulsar

chasm /'kæzm/ *n* abismo *m*

chassis /'ʃæsɪ/ *n* chassi *m*

chaste /tʃeɪst/ *a* casto

chastise /tʃæs'taɪz/ *vt* castigar

chastity /'tʃæstətɪ/ *n* castidade *f*

chat /tʃæt/ *n* conversa *f* □ *vi* (*pt* **chatted**) conversar, cavaquear. **have a ~** bater um papo, (*P*) dar dois dedos de conversa. **~ty** *a* conversador

chatter /'tʃætə(r)/ *vi* tagarelar. **his teeth are ~ing** seus dentes estão tiritando □ *n* tagarelice *f*

chauffeur /'ʃəʊfə(r)/ *n* motorista *m*, chofer (particular) *m*, chauffeur *m*

chauvinis|t /'ʃəʊvɪnɪst/ *n* chauvinista *mf*. **male ~t** (*pej*) machista *m*. **~m** /-zəm/ *n* chauvinismo *m*

cheap /tʃi:p/ *a* (**-er, -est**) barato; (*fare, rate*) reduzido. **~(ly)** *adv* barato. **~ness** *n* barateza *f*

cheapen /'tʃi:pən/ *vt* depreciar

cheat /tʃi:t/ *vt* enganar, trapacear □ *vi* (*at games*) roubar, (*P*) fazer batota; (*in exams*) copiar □ *n* intrujão *m*; (*at games*) trapaceiro *m*, (*P*) batoteiro *m*

check[1] /tʃek/ *vt/i* (*examine*) verificar; (*tickets*) revisar; (*restrain*) controlar, refrear □ *n* verificação *f*; (*tickets*) controle *m*; (*curb*) freio *m*; (*chess*) xeque *m*; (*Amer: bill*) conta *f*; (*Amer: cheque*) cheque *m*. **~ in** assinar o registro; (*at airport*) fazer o check-in. **~-in** *n* check-in *m*. **~ out** pagar a conta. **~-out** *n* caixa *f*. **~-up** *n* exame *m* médico, check-up *m*

check[2] /tʃek/ *n* (*pattern*) xadrez *m*. **~ed** *a* de xadrez

checkmate /'tʃekmeɪt/ *n* xeque-mate *m*

cheek /tʃi:k/ *n* face *f*; (*fig*) descaramento *m*. **~y** *a* descarado

cheer /tʃɪə(r)/ *n* alegria *f*; (*shout*) viva *m* □ *vt/i* aclamar, aplaudir. **~s!** à sua, (*P*) vossa (saúde)!; (*thank you*) obrigadinho. **~ (up)** animar(-se). **~ful** *a* bem disposto; alegre

cheerio /tʃɪərɪ'əʊ/ *int* (*colloq*) até logo, (*P*) adeusinho

cheese /tʃi:z/ *n* queijo *m*

cheetah /'tʃi:tə/ *n* chita *f*, lobo-tigre *m*

chef /ʃef/ *n* cozinheiro-chefe *m*

chemical /'kemɪkl/ *a* químico □ *n* produto *m* químico

chemist /'kemɪst/ *n* farmacêutico *m*; (*scientist*) químico *m*. **~'s (shop)** *n* farmácia *f*. **~ry** *n* química *f*

cheque /tʃek/ *n* cheque *m*. **~-book** *n* talão *m* de cheques. **~-card** *n* cartão *m* de banco

cherish /'tʃerɪʃ/ *vt* estimar, querer; (*hope*) acalentar

cherry /'tʃerɪ/ *n* cereja *f*. **~-tree** *n* cerejeira *f*

chess /tʃes/ *n* jogo *m* de xadrez. **~-board** *n* tabuleiro *m* de xadrez

chest /tʃest/ *n* peito *m*; (*for money, jewels*) cofre *m*. **~ of drawers** cômoda *f*, (*P*) cómoda *f*

chestnut /'tʃesnʌt/ *n* castanha *f*. **~-tree** *n* castanheiro *m*

chew /tʃu:/ *vt* mastigar. **~ing-gum** *n* chiclete *m*, (*P*) pastilha *f* elástica

chic /ʃi:k/ *a* chique

chick /tʃɪk/ *n* pinto *m*

chicken /'tʃɪkɪn/ *n* galinha *f* □ *vi* **~ out** (*sl*) acovardar-se. **~-pox** *n* catapora *f*, (*P*) varicela *f*

chicory /'tʃɪkərɪ/ *n* (*for coffee*) chicória *f*; (*for salad*) endívia *f*

chief /tʃi:f/ *n* chefe *m* □ *a* principal. **~ly** *adv* principalmente

chilblain /'tʃɪlbleɪn/ *n* frieira *f*

child /tʃaɪld/ *n* (*pl* **children** /'tʃɪldrən/) criança *f*; (*son*) filho *m*;

(*daughter*) filha *f*. ~**hood** *n* infância *f*, meninice *f*. ~**ish** *a* infantil; (*immature*) acriançado, pueril. ~**less** *a* sem filhos. ~**like** *a* infantil. ~**-minder** *n* babá *f* que cuida de crianças em sua propria casa
childbirth /ˈtʃaɪldbɜ:θ/ *n* parto *m*
Chile /ˈtʃɪlɪ/ *n* Chile *m*. ~**an** *a* & *n* chileno (*m*)
chill /tʃɪl/ *n* frio *m*; (*med*) resfriado *m*, (*P*) constipação *f* □ *vt/i* arrefecer; (*culin*) refrigerar. ~**y** *a* frio. **be** *or* **feel** ~**y** ter frio
chilli /ˈtʃɪlɪ/ *n* (*pl* **-ies**) malagueta *f*
chime /tʃaɪm/ *n* carrilhão *m*; (*sound*) música *m* de carrilhão □ *vt/i* tocar
chimney /ˈtʃɪmnɪ/ *n* (*pl* **-eys**) chaminé *f*. ~**-sweep** *n* limpador *m* de chaminés, (*P*) limpa-chaminés *m*
chimpanzee /tʃɪmpænˈzi:/ *n* chimpanzé *m*
chin /tʃɪn/ *n* queixo *m*
china /ˈtʃaɪnə/ *n* porcelana *f*; (*crockery*) louça *f*
Chin|a /ˈtʃaɪnə/ *n* China *f*. ~**ese** /-ˈni:z/ *a* & *n* chinês (*m*)
chink[1] /tʃɪŋk/ *n* (*crack*) fenda *f*, fresta *f*
chink[2] /tʃɪŋk/ *n* tinir *m* □ *vt/i* (fazer) tinir
chip /tʃɪp/ *n* (*broken piece*) bocado *m*; (*culin*) batata *f* frita em palitos; (*gambling*) ficha *f*; (*electronic*) chip *m*, circuito *m* integrado □ *vt/i* (*pt* **chipped**) lascar(-se)
chipboard /ˈtʃɪpbɔ:d/ *n* compensado *m* (de madeira)
chiropodist /kɪˈrɒpədɪst/ *n* calista *mf*
chirp /tʃɜ:p/ *n* pipilar *m*; (*of cricket*) cricri *m* □ *vi* pipilar; (*cricket*) cantar, fazer cricri
chisel /ˈtʃɪzl/ *n* cinzel *m*, escopro *m* □ *vt* (*pt* **chiselled**) talhar
chivalr|y /ˈʃɪvlrɪ/ *n* cavalheirismo *m*. ~**ous** *a* cavalheiresco
chive /tʃaɪv/ *n* cebolinho *m*
chlorine /ˈklɔ:ri:n/ *n* cloro *m*
chocolate /ˈtʃɒklɪt/ *n* chocolate *m*
choice /tʃɔɪs/ *n* escolha *f* □ *a* escolhido, seleto, (*P*) seleccionado
choir /ˈkwaɪə(r)/ *n* coro *m*
choirboy /ˈkwaɪəbɔɪ/ *n* menino *m* de coro, corista *m*, (*P*) coralista *m*
choke /tʃəʊk/ *vt/i* sufocar; (*on food*) engasgar(-se) □ *n* (*auto*) afogador *m*, (*P*) botão *m* do ar (*colloq*)
cholesterol /kəˈlestərɒl/ *n* colesterol *m*
choose /tʃu:z/ *vt/i* (*pt* **chose**, *pp* **chosen**) escolher; (*prefer*) preferir. ~ **to do** decidir fazer
choosy /ˈtʃu:zɪ/ *a* (*colloq*) exigente, difícil de contentar
chop /tʃɒp/ *vt/i* (*pt* **chopped**) cortar □ *n* (*wood*) machadada *f*; (*culin*) costeleta *f*. ~ **down** abater. ~**per** *n* cutelo *m*; (*sl: helicopter*) helicóptero *m*
choppy /ˈtʃɒpɪ/ *a* (*sea*) picado
chopstick /ˈtʃɒpstɪk/ *n* fachi *m*, pauzinho *m*
choral /ˈkɔ:rəl/ *a* coral
chord /kɔ:d/ *n* (*mus*) acorde *m*
chore /tʃɔ:(r)/ *n* trabalho *m*; (*unpleasant task*) tarefa *f* maçante. **household** ~**s** afazeres *mpl* domésticos
choreograph|er /kɒrɪˈɒgrəfə(r)/ *n* coreógrafo *m*. ~**y** *n* coreografia *f*
chortle /ˈtʃɔ:tl/ *n* risada *f* □ *vi* rir alto
chorus /ˈkɔ:rəs/ *n* coro *m*; (*of song*) refrão *m*, estribilho *m*
chose, chosen /tʃəʊz, ˈtʃəʊzn/ *see* choose
Christ /kraɪst/ *n* Cristo *m*
christen /ˈkrɪsn/ *vt* batizar, (*P*) baptizar. ~**ing** *n* batismo *m*, (*P*) baptismo *m*
Christian /ˈkrɪstʃən/ *a* & *n* cristão (*m*). ~ **name** nome *m* de batismo, (*P*) baptismo. ~**ity** /-stɪˈænətɪ/ *n* cristandade *f*
Christmas /ˈkrɪsməs/ *n* Natal *m* □ *a* do Natal. ~ **card** cartão *m* de Boas Festas. ~ **Day/Eve** dia *m*/véspera *f* de Natal. ~ **tree** árvore *f* de Natal
chrome /krəʊm/ *n* cromo *m*
chromosome /ˈkrəʊməsəʊm/ *n* cromossoma *m*
chronic /ˈkrɒnɪk/ *a* crônico, (*P*) crónico
chronicle /ˈkrɒnɪkl/ *n* crônica *f*
chronological /krɒnəˈlɒdʒɪkl/ *a* cronológico
chrysanthemum /krɪˈsænθəməm/ *n* crisântemo *m*
chubby /ˈtʃʌbɪ/ *a* (**-ier**, **-iest**) gorducho, rechonchudo
chuck /tʃʌk/ *vt* (*colloq*) deitar, atirar. ~ **out** (*person*) expulsar; (*thing*) jogar fora, (*P*) deitar fora
chuckle /ˈtʃʌkl/ *n* riso *m* abafado □ *vi* rir sozinho
chum /tʃʌm/ *n* (*colloq*) amigo *m* íntimo, camarada *mf*. ~**my** *a* amigável
chunk /tʃʌŋk/ *n* (grande) bocado *m*, naco *m*
church /tʃɜ:tʃ/ *n* igreja *f*
churchyard /ˈtʃɜ:tʃja:d/ *n* cemitério *m*
churlish /ˈtʃɜ:lɪʃ/ *a* grosseiro, indelicado
churn /tʃɜ:n/ *n* batedeira *f*; (*milk-can*) vasilha *f* de leite □ *vt* bater. ~ **out** produzir em série
chute /ʃu:t/ *n* calha *f*; (*for rubbish*) conduta *f* de lixo
chutney /ˈtʃʌtnɪ/ *n* (*pl*-**eys**) chutney *m*
cider /ˈsaɪdə(r)/ *n* sidra *f*, (*P*) cidra *f*
cigar /sɪˈga:(r)/ *n* charuto *m*

cigarette /sɪgə'ret/ *n* cigarro *m*. **~-case** *n* cigarreira *f*
cinder /'sɪndə(r)/ *n* brasa *f*. **burnt to a ~** estorricado
cinema /'sɪnəmə/ *n* cinema *m*
cinnamon /'sɪnəmən/ *n* canela *f*
cipher /'saɪfə(r)/ *n* cifra *f*
circle /'sɛ:kl/ *n* círculo *m*; (*theat*) balcão *m* □ *vt* dar a volta a □ *vi* descrever círculos, voltear
circuit /'sɜ:kɪt/ *n* circuito *m*
circuitous /sɜ:'kju:ɪtəs/ *a* indireto, tortuoso
circular /'sɜ:kjʊlə(r)/ *a* circular
circulat|e /'sɜ:kjʊleɪt/ *vt/i* (fazer) circular. **~ion** /-'leɪʃn/ *n* circulação *f*; (*sales of newspaper*) tiragem *f*
circumcis|e /'sɜ:kəmsaɪz/ *vt* circuncidar. **~ion** /-'sɪʒn/ *n* circuncisão *f*
circumference /sə'kʌmfərəns/ *n* circunferência *f*
circumflex /'sɜ:kəmfleks/ *n* circunflexo *m*
circumstance /'sɜ:kəmstəns/ *n* circunstância *f*. **~s** (*means*) situação *f* econômica, (*P*) económica
circus /'sɜ:kəs/ *n* circo *m*
cistern /'sɪstən/ *n* reservatório *m*; (*of WC*) autoclismo *m*
cit|e /saɪt/ *vt* citar. **~ation** /-'teɪʃn/ *n* citação *f*
citizen /'sɪtɪzn/ *n* cidadão *m*, cidadã *f*; (*of town*) habitante *mf*. **~ship** *n* cidadania *f*
citrus /'sɪtrəs/ *n* **~ fruit** citrino *m*
city /'sɪtɪ/ *n* cidade *f*
civic /'sɪvɪk/ *a* cívico
civil /'sɪvl/ *a* civil; (*rights*) cívico; (*polite*) delicado. **~ servant** funcionário *m* público. **C~ Service** Administração *f* Pública. **~ war** guerra *f* civil. **~ity** /-'vɪlətɪ/ *n* civilidade *f*, cortesia *f*
civilian /sɪ'vɪlɪən/ *a* & *n* civil (*mf*), paisano *m*
civiliz|e /'sɪvəlaɪz/ *vt* civilizar. **~ation** /-'zeɪʃn/ *n* civilização *f*
claim /kleɪm/ *vt* reclamar; (*assert*) pretender □ *vi* (*from insurance*) reclamar □ *n* reivindicação *f*; (*assertion*) afirmação *f*; (*right*) direito *m*; (*from insurance*) reclamação *f*
clairvoyant /kleə'vɔɪənt/ *n* vidente *mf* □ *a* clarividente
clam /klæm/ *n* molusco *m*
clamber /'klæmbə(r)/ *vi* trepar
clammy /'klæmɪ/ *a* (-ier, -iest) úmido, (*P*) húmido e pegajoso
clamour /'klæmə(r)/ *n* clamor *m*, vociferação *f* □ *vi* **~ for** exigir aos gritos
clamp /klæmp/ *n* grampo *m*; (*for car*) bloqueador *m* □ *vt* prender com grampo; (*a car*) bloquear. **~ down on** apertar, suprimir; (*colloq*) cair em cima de (*colloq*)
clan /klæn/ *n* clã *m*
clandestine /klæn'destɪn/ *a* clandestino
clang /klæŋ/ *n* tinir *m*
clap /klæp/ *vt/i* (*pt* **clapped**) aplaudir; (*put*) meter □ *n* aplauso *m*; (*of thunder*) ribombo *m*. **~ one's hands** bater palmas
claptrap /'klæptræp/ *n* parlapatice *f*
claret /'klærət/ *n* clarete *m*
clarif|y /'klærɪfaɪ/ *vt* esclarecer. **~ication** /-ɪ'keɪʃn/ *n* esclarecimento *m*
clarinet /klærɪ'net/ *n* clarinete *m*
clarity /'klærətɪ/ *n* claridade *f*
clash /klæʃ/ *n* choque *m*; (*sound*) estridor *m*; (*fig*) conflito *m* □ *vt/i* entrechocar(-se); (*of colours*) destoar
clasp /kla:sp/ *n* (*fastener*) fecho *m*; (*hold, grip*) aperto *m* de mão □ *vt* apertar, serrar
class /kla:s/ *n* classe *f* □ *vt* classificar
classic /'klæsɪk/ *a* & *n* clássico (*m*). **~s** *npl* letras *fpl* clássicas, (*P*) estudos *mpl* clássicos. **~al** *a* clássico
classif|y /-'klæsɪfaɪ/ *vt* classificar. **~ication** /-ɪ'keɪʃn/ *n* classificação *f*. **~ied advertisement** (anúncio *m*) classificado (*m*)
classroom /'kla:sru:m/ *n* sala *f* de aulas
clatter /'klætə(r)/ *n* estardalhaço *m* □ *vi* fazer barulho
clause /klɔ:z/ *n* cláusula *f*; (*gram*) oração *f*
claustrophob|ia /klɔ:strə'fəʊbɪə/ *n* claustrofobia *f*. **~ic** *a* claustrofóbico
claw /klɔ:/ *n* garra *f*; (*of lobster*) tenaz *f*, pinça *f* □ *vt* (*seize*) agarrar; (*scratch*) arranhar; (*tear*) rasgar
clay /kleɪ/ *n* argila *f*, barro *m*
clean /kli:n/ *a* (-er, -est) limpo □ *adv* completamente □ *vt* limpar □ *vi* **~ up** fazer a limpeza. **~-shaven** *a* de cara rapada. **~er** *n* faxineira *f*, (*P*) mulher *f* da limpeza; (*of clothes*) empregado *m* da tinturaria. **~ly** *adv* com limpeza, como deve ser
cleans|e /klenz/ *vt* limpar; (*fig*) purificar. **~ing cream** creme *m* de limpeza
clear /klɪə(r)/ *a* (-er, -est) claro; (*glass*) transparente; (*without obstacles*) livre; (*profit*) líquido; (*sky*) limpo □ *adv* claramente □ *vt* (*snow, one's name, etc*) limpar; (*the table*) tirar; (*jump*) transpor; (*debt*) saldar; (*jur*) absolver; (*through customs*) despachar □ *vi* (*fog*) dissipar-se; (*sky*) limpar. **~ of** (*away from*) afastado de. **~ off** *or* **out** (*sl*) sair andando, zarpar. **~ out** (*clean*) fazer a

limpeza. ~ **up** (*tidy*) arrumar; (*mystery*) desvendar; (*of weather*) clarear, limpar. ~**ly** *adv* claramente
clearance /ˈklɪərəns/ *n* autorização *f*; (*for ship*) despacho *m*; (*space*) espaço *m* livre. ~ **sale** liquidação *f*, saldos *mpl*
clearing /ˈklɪərɪŋ/ *n* clareira *f*
clearway /ˈklɪəweɪ/ *n* rodovia *f* de estacionamento proibido
cleavage /ˈkli:vɪdʒ/ *n* divisão *f*; (*between breasts*) rego *m* (*of dress*) decote *m*
cleaver /ˈkli:və(r)/ *n* cutelo *m*
clef /klef/ *n* (*mus*) clave *f*
cleft /kleft/ *n* fenda *f*
clench /klentʃ/ *vt* (*teeth, fists*) cerrar; (*grasp*) agarrar
clergy /ˈklɜ:dʒɪ/ *n* clero *m*. ~**man** *n* (*pl* **-men**) clérigo *m*, sacerdote *m*
cleric /ˈklerɪk/ *n* clérigo *m*. ~**al** *a* (*relig*) clerical; (*of clerks*) de escritório
clerk /kla:k/ *n* auxiliar *m* de escritório
clever /ˈklevə(r)/ *a* (-er, -est) esperto, inteligente; (*skilful*) hábil, habilidoso. ~**ly** *adv* inteligentemente; (*skilfully*) habilmente, habilidosamente. ~**ness** *n* esperteza *f*, inteligência *f*
cliché /ˈkli:ʃeɪ/ *n* chavão *m*, lugar-comum *m*, clichê *m*
click /klɪk/ *n* estalido *m*, clique *m* □ *vi* dar um estalido
client /ˈklaɪənt/ *n* cliente *mf*
clientele /kli:ənˈtel/ *n* clientela *f*
cliff /klɪf/ *n* penhasco *m*. ~**s** *npl* falésia *f*
climat|e /ˈklaɪmɪt/ *n* clima *m*. ~**ic** /ˈmætɪk/ *a* climático
climax /ˈklaɪmæks/ *n* clímax *m*, ponto *m* culminante
climb /klaɪm/ *vt* (*stairs*) subir; (*tree, wall*) subir em, trepar em; (*mountain*) escalar □ *vi* subir, trepar □ *n* subida *f*; (*mountain*) escalada *f*. ~ **down** descer; (*fig*) dar a mão à palmatória (*fig*). ~**er** *n* (*sport*) alpinista *mf*; (*plant*) trepadeira *f*
clinch /klɪntʃ/ *vt* (*deal*) fechar; (*argument*) resolver
cling /klɪŋ/ *vi* (*pt* **clung**) ~ (to) agarrar-se (a); (*stick*) colar-se (a)
clinic /ˈklɪnɪk/ *n* clínica *f*
clinical /ˈklɪnɪkl/ *a* clínico
clink /klɪŋk/ *n* tinido *m* □ *vt/i* (fazer) tilintar
clip[1] /klɪp/ *m* (*for paper*) clipe *m*; (*for hair*) grampo *m*, (*P*) gancho *m*; (*for tube*) braçadeira *f* □ *vt* (*pt* **clipped**) prender
clip[2] /klɪp/ *vt* (*pt* **clipped**) cortar; (*trim*) aparar □ *n* tosquia *f*; (*colloq: blow*) murro *m*. ~**ping** *n* recorte *m*
clique /kli:k/ *n* panelinha *f*, facção *f*, conventículo *m*
cloak /kləʊk/ *n* capa *f*, manto *m*
cloakroom /ˈkləʊkru:m/ *n* vestiário *m*; (*toilet*) toalete *m*, (*P*) lavabo *m*
clock /klɒk/ *n* relógio *m* □ *vi* ~**in/out** marcar o ponto (à entrada/à saída). ~ **up** (*colloq: miles etc*) fazer
clockwise /ˈklɒkwaɪz/ *a* & *adv* no sentido dos ponteiros do relógio
clockwork /ˈklɒkwɜ:k/ *n* mecanismo *m*. **go like** ~ ir às mil maravilhas
clog /klɒg/ *n* tamanco *m*, soco *m* □ *vt/i* (*pt* **clogged**) entupir(-se)
cloister /ˈklɔɪstə(r)/ *n* claustro *m*
close[1] /kləʊs/ *a* (-er, -est) próximo (to de); (*link, collaboration*) estreito; (*friend*) íntimo; (*weather*) abafado □ *adv* perto. ~ **at hand**, ~ **by** muito perto. ~ **together** (*crowded*) espremido. **have a** ~ **shave** (*fig*) escapar por um triz. ~**-up** *n* grande plano *m*. ~**ly** *adv* de perto. ~**ness** *n* proximidade *f*
close[2] /kləʊz/ *vt/i* fechar(-se); (*end*) terminar; (*of shop etc*) fechar □ *n* fim *m*. ~**d shop** organização *f* que só admite trabalhadores sindicalizados
closet /ˈklɒzɪt/ *n* (*Amer*) armário *m*
closure /ˈkləʊʒə(r)/ *n* encerramento *m*
clot /klɒt/ *n* coágulo *m* □ *vi* (*pt* **clotted**) coagular
cloth /klɒθ/ *n* pano *m*; (*tablecloth*) toalha *f* de mesa
cloth|e /kləʊð/ *vt* vestir. ~**ing** *n* vestuário *m*, roupa *f*
clothes /kləʊðz/ *npl* roupa *f*, vestuário *m*. ~**-line** *n* varal *m* para roupa
cloud /klaʊd/ *n* núvem *f* □ *vt/i* toldar (-se). ~**y** *a* nublado, toldado; (*liquid*) turvo
clout /klaʊt/ *n* cascudo *m*, (*P*) carolo *m*; (*colloq: power*) poder *m* efectivo □ *vt* (*colloq*) bater
clove /kləʊv/ *n* cravo *m*. ~ **of garlic** dente *m* de alho
clover /ˈkləʊvə(r)/ *n* trevo *m*
clown /klaʊn/ *n* palhaço *m* □ *vi* fazer palhaçadas
club /klʌb/ *n* clube *m*; (*weapon*) cacete *m*. ~**s** (*cards*) paus *mpl* □ *vt/i* (*pt* **clubbed**) dar bordoadas *or* cacetadas (em). ~ **together** (*share costs*) cotizar-se
cluck /klʌk/ *vi* cacarejar
clue /klu:/ *n* indício *m*, pista *f*; (*in crossword*) definição *f*. **not have a** ~ (*colloq*) não fazer a menor idéia
clump /klʌmp/ *n* maciço *m*, tufo *m*
clumsy /ˈklʌmzɪ/ *a* (-ier, -iest) desajeitado
clung /klʌŋ/ *see* cling

cluster /ˈklʌstə(r)/ *n* (pequeno) grupo *m*; (*bot*) cacho *m* □ *vt/i* agrupar(-se)
clutch /klʌtʃ/ *vt* agarrar (em), apertar □ *vi* agarrar-se (at a) □ *n* (*auto*) embreagem *f*, (*P*) embraiagem *f*. ~**es** *npl* garras *fpl*
clutter /ˈklʌtə(r)/ *n* barafunda *f*, desordem *f* □ *vt* atravancar
coach /kəʊtʃ/ *n* ônibus *m*, (*P*) camioneta *f*; (*of train*) carruagem *f*; (*sport*) treinador *m* □ *vt* (*tutor*) dar aulas a; (*sport*) treinar
coagulate /kəʊˈægjʊleɪt/ *vt/i* coagular(-se)
coal /kəʊl/ *n* carvão *m*
coalfield /ˈkəʊlfiːld/ *n* região *f* carbonífera
coalition /kəʊəˈlɪʃn/ *n* coligação *f*
coarse /kɔːs/ *a* (-er, -est) grosseiro
coast /kəʊst/ *n* costa *f* □ *vi* costear; (*cycle*) descer em roda-livre; (*car*) ir em ponto morto. ~**al** *a* costeiro
coastguard /ˈkəʊstgaːd/ *n* polícia *f* marítima
coastline /ˈkəʊstlaɪn/ *n* litoral *m*
coat /kəʊt/ *n* casaco *m*; (*of animal*) pêlo *m*; (*of paint*) camada *f*, demão *f* □ *vt* cobrir. ~ **of arms** brasão *m*. ~**ing** *n* camada *f*
coax /kəʊks/ *vt* levar com afagos ou lisonjas, convencer
cobble /ˈkɒbl/ *n* ~(**-stone**) *n* pedra *f* de calçada
cobweb /ˈkɒbweb/ *n* teia *f* de aranha
cocaine /kəʊˈkeɪn/ *n* cocaína *f*
cock /kɒk/ *n* (*male bird*) macho *m*; (*rooster*) galo *m* □ *vt* (*gun*) engatilhar; (*ears*) fitar. ~**-eyed** *a* (*sl: askew*) de esguelha
cockerel /ˈkɒkərəl/ *n* frango *m*, galo *m* novo
cockle /ˈkɒkl/ *n* berbigão *m*
cockney /ˈkɒknɪ/ *n* (*pl* -eys) (*person*) londrino *m*; (*dialect*) dialeto *m* do leste de Londres
cockpit /ˈkɒkpɪt/ *n* cabine *f*
cockroach /ˈkɒkrəʊtʃ/ *n* barata *f*
cocktail /ˈkɒkteɪl/ *n* cocktail *m*, coquetel *m*. **fruit** ~ salada *f* de fruta
cocky /ˈkɒkɪ/ *a* (-ier, -iest) convencido (*colloq*)
cocoa /ˈkəʊkəʊ/ *n* cacau *m*
coconut /ˈkəʊkənʌt/ *n* coco *m*
cocoon /kəˈkuːn/ *n* casulo *m*
cod /kɒd/ *n* (*pl invar*) bacalhau *m*. ~**-liver oil** óleo *m* de fígado de bacalhau
code /kəʊd/ *n* código *m* □ *vt* codificar
coeducational /kəʊedʒʊˈkeɪʃənl/ *a* misto
coerc|e /kəʊˈɜːs/ *vt* coagir. ~**ion** /-ʃn/ *n* coação *f*, (*P*) coacção *f*
coexist /kəʊɪgˈzɪst/ *vi* coexistir. ~**ence** *n* coexistência *f*
coffee /ˈkɒfɪ/ *n* café *m*. ~ **bar** café *m*. ~**-pot** *n* cafeteira *f*. ~**-table** *n* mesa *f* baixa
coffin /ˈkɒfɪn/ *n* caixão *m*
cog /kɒg/ *n* dente *m* de roda. **a ~ in the machine** (*fig*) uma rodinha numa engrenagem
cogent /ˈkəʊdʒənt/ *a* convincente; (*relevant*) pertinente
cognac /ˈkɒnjæk/ *n* conhaque *m*
cohabit /kəʊˈhæbɪt/ *vi* coabitar
coherent /kəˈhɪərənt/ *a* coerente
coil /kɔɪl/ *vt/i* enrolar(-se) □ *n* rolo *m*; (*electr*) bobina *f*; (*one ring*) espiral *f*; (*contraceptive*) dispositivo *m* intra-uterino, DIU
coin /kɔɪn/ *n* moeda *f* □ *vt* cunhar
coincide /kəʊɪnˈsaɪd/ *vi* coincidir
coinciden|ce /kəʊˈɪnsɪdəns/ *n* coincidência *f*. ~**tal** /ˈdentl/ *a* que acontece por coincidência
colander /ˈkʌləndə(r)/ *n* peneira *f*, (*P*) coador *m*
cold /kəʊld/ *a* (-er, -est) frio □ *n* frio *m*; (*med*) resfriado *m*, constipação *f*. **be** *or* **feel** ~ estar com frio. **it's** ~ está frio. ~**-blooded** *a* (*person*) insensível; (*deed*) a sangue frio. ~ **cream** creme *m* para a pele. ~**ness** *n* frio *m*; (*of feeling*) frieza *f*
coleslaw /ˈkəʊlslɔː/ *n* salada *f* de repolho cru
colic /ˈkɒlɪk/ *n* cólica(s) *f* (*pl*)
collaborat|e /kəˈlæbəreɪt/ *vi* colaborar. ~**ion** /-ˈreɪʃn/ *n* colaboração *f*. ~**or** *n* colaborador *m*
collapse /kəˈlæps/ *vi* desabar; (*med*) ter um colapso □ *n* colapso *m*
collapsible /kəˈlæpsəbl/ *a* desmontável, dobrável
collar /ˈkɒlə(r)/ *n* gola *f*; (*of shirt*) colarinho *m*; (*of dog*) coleira *f* □ *vt* (*colloq*) pôr a mão a. ~**-bone** *n* clavícula *f*
colleague /ˈkɒliːg/ *n* colega *mf*
collect /kəˈlekt/ *vt* (*gather*) juntar; (*fetch*) ir/vir buscar; (*money, rent*) cobrar; (*as hobby*) colecionar, (*P*) coleccionar □ *vi* juntar-se. **call ~** (*Amer*) chamar a cobrar. ~**ion** /-ʃn/ *n* coleção *f*, (*P*) colecção *f*; (*in church*) coleta *f*, (*P*) colecta *f*; (*of mail*) tiragem *f*, coleta *f*, (*P*) abertura *f*. ~**or** *n* (*as hobby*) colecionador *m*, (*P*) coleccionador *m*
collective /kəˈlektɪv/ *a* coletivo, (*P*) colectivo
college /ˈkɒlɪdʒ/ *n* colégio *m*
collide /kəˈlaɪd/ *vi* colidir
colliery /ˈkɒlɪərɪ/ *n* mina *f* de carvão
collision /kəˈlɪʒn/ *n* colisão *f*, choque *m*; (*fig*) conflito *m*
colloquial /kəˈləʊkwɪəl/ *a* coloquial. ~**ism** *n* expressão *f* coloquial
collusion /kəˈluːʒn/ *n* conluio *m*
colon /ˈkəʊlən/ *n* (*gram*) dois pontos *mpl*; (*anat*) cólon *m*

colonel /'kɜ:nl/ *n* coronel *m*
colonize /'kɒlənaɪz/ *vt* colonizar
colon|y /'kɒlənɪ/ *n* colônia *f*, (*P*) colónia *f*. **~ial** /kə'ləʊnɪəl/ *a* & *n* colonial (*mf*)
colossal /kə'lɒsl/ *a* colossal
colour /'kʌlə(r)/ *n* cor *f* □ *a* (*photo, TV, etc*) a cores; (*film*) colorido □ *vt* colorir, dar cor a □ *vi* (*blush*) corar. **~-blind** *a* daltônico, (*P*) daltónico. **~ful** *a* colorido. **~ing** *n* (*of skin*) cor *f*; (*in food*) corante *m*. **~less** *a* descolorido
coloured /'kʌləd/ *a* (*pencil, person*) de cor □ *n* pessoa *f* de cor
column /'kɒləm/ *n* coluna *f*
columnist /'kɒləmnɪst/ *n* colunista *mf*
coma /'kəʊmə/ *n* coma *m*
comb /kəʊm/ *n* pente *m* □ *vt* pentear; (*search*) vasculhar. **~ one's hair** pentear-se
combat /'kɒmbæt/ *n* combate *m* □ *vt* (*pt* **combated**) combater
combination /kɒmbɪ'neɪʃn/ *n* combinação *f*
combine /kəm'baɪn/ *vt/i* combinar (-se), juntar(-se), reunir(-se)
combustion /kəm'bʌstʃən/ *n* combustão *f*
come /kʌm/ *vi* (*pt* **came**, *pp* **come**) vir; (*arrive*) chegar; (*occur*) suceder. **~ about** acontecer. **~ across** encontrar, dar com. **~ away** *or* **off** soltar-se. **~ back** voltar. **~-back** *n* regresso *m*; (*retort*) réplica *f*. **~ by** obter. **~ down** descer; (*price*) baixar. **~-down** *n* humilhação *f*. **~ from** vir de. **~ in** entrar. **~ into** (*money*) herdar. **~ off** (*succeed*) ter êxito; (*fare*) sair-se. **~ on!** vamos! **~ out** sair. **~ round** (*after fainting*) voltar a si; (*be converted*) deixar-se convencer. **~ to** (*amount to*) montar a. **~ up** subir; (*seeds*) despontar; (*fig*) surgir. **~ up with** (*idea*) vir com, propor. **~-uppance** *n* castigo *m* merecido
comedian /kə'mi:dɪən/ *n* comediante *mf*
comedy /'kɒmədɪ/ *n* comédia *f*
comet /'kɒmɪt/ *n* cometa *m*
comfort /'kʌmfət/ *n* conforto *m* □ *vt* confortar, consolar. **~able** *a* confortável
comic /'kɒmɪk/ *a* cômico, (*P*) cómico □ *n* cômico *m*, (*P*) cómico *m*; (*periodical*) estórias *fpl* em quadrinhos, (*P*) revista *f* de banda desenhada. **~ strip** estória *f* em quadrinhos, (*p*) banda *f* desenhada. **~al** *a* cômico, (*P*) cómico
coming /'kʌmɪŋ/ *n* vinda *f* □ *a* próximo. **~s and goings** idas e vindas *fpl*
comma /'kɒmə/ *n* vírgula *f*
command /kə'ma:nd/ *n* (*mil*) comando *m*; (*order*) ordem *f*; (*mastery*) domínio *m* □ *vt* comandar; (*respect*) inspirar, impor. **~er** *n* comandante *m*. **~ing** *a* imponente
commandeer /kɒmən'dɪə(r)/ *vt* requisitar
commandment /kə'ma:ndmənt/ *n* mandamento *m*
commemorat|e /kə'meməreɪt/ *vt* comemorar. **~ion** /'-reɪʃn/ *n* comemoração *f*. **~ive** *a* comemorativo
commence /kə'mens/ *vt/i* começar. **~ment** *n* começo *m*
commend /kə'mend/ *vt* louvar; (*entrust*) confiar. **~able** *a* louvável. **~ation** /kɒmen'deɪʃn/ *n* louvor *m*
comment /'kɒment/ *n* comentário *m* □ *vi* comentar. **~ on** comentar, fazer comentários
commentary /'kɒməntrɪ/ *n* comentário *m*; (*radio, TV*) relato *m*
commentat|e /'kɒmənteɪt/ *vi* fazer um relato. **~or** *n* (*radio, TV*) comentarista *mf*, (*P*) comentador *m*
commerce /'kɒmɜ:s/ *n* comércio *m*
commercial /kə'mɜ:ʃl/ *a* comercial □ *n* publicidade (comercial) *f*. **~ize** *vt* comercializar
commiserat|e /kə'mɪzəreɪt/ *vi* **~ with** compadecer-se de. **~ion** /-'reɪʃn/ *n* comiseração *f*, pesar *m*
commission /kə'mɪʃn/ *n* comissão *f*; (*order for work*) encomenda *f* □ *vt* encomendar; (*mil*) nomear. **~ to do** encarregar de fazer. **out of ~** fora de serviço ativo, (*P*) activo. **~er** *n* comissário *m*; (*police*) chefe *m*
commit /kə'mɪt/ *vt* (*pt* **committed**) cometer; (*entrust*) confiar. **~ o.s.** comprometer-se, empenhar-se. **~ suicide** suicidar-se. **~ to memory** decorar. **~ment** *n* compromisso *m*
committee /kə'mɪtɪ/ *n* comissão *f*, comitê *m*, (*P*) comité *m*
commodity /kə'mɒdətɪ/ *n* artigo *m*, mercadoria *f*
common /'kɒmən/ *a* (-er, -est) comum; (*usual*) usual, corrente; (*pej: ill-bred*) ordinario □ *n* prado *m* público, (*P*) baldio *m*. **~ law** direito *m* consuetudinário. **C~ Market** Mercado *m* Comum. **~-room** *n* sala *f* dos professores. **~ sense** bom senso *m*, senso *m* comum. **House of C~s** Câmara *f* dos Comuns. **in ~** em comum. **~ly** *adv* mais comum
commoner /'kɒmənə(r)/ *n* plebeu *m*
commonplace /'kɒmənpleɪs/ *a* banal □ *n* lugar-comum *m*
commotion /kə'məʊʃn/ *n* agitação *f*, confusão *f*, barulheira *f*
communal /'kɒmjʊnl/ *a* (*of a commune*) comunal; (*shared*) comum

commune /ˈkɒmjuːn/ *n* comuna *f*

communicat|e /kəˈmjuːnɪkeɪt/ *vt/i* comunicar. **~ion** /-ˈkeɪʃn/ *n* comunicação *f*. **~ion cord** sinal *m* de alarme. **~ive** /-ətɪv/ *a* comunicativo

communion /kəˈmjuːnɪən/ *n* comunhão *f*

communis|t /ˈkɒmjʊnɪst/ *n* comunista *mf* □ *a* comunista. **~m** /-zəm/ *n* comunismo *m*

community /kəˈmjuːnətɪ/ *n* comunidade *f*. **~ centre** centro *m* comunitário

commute /kəˈmjuːt/ *vi* viajar diariamente para o trabalho. **~r** /-ə(r)/ *n* pessoa *f* que viaja diariamente para o trabalho

compact[1] /kəmˈpækt/ *a* compacto. **~ disc** /ˈkɒmpækt/ cd *m*

compact[2] /ˈkɒmpækt/ *n* estojo *m* de pó-de-arroz, (*P*) caixa *f*

companion /kəmˈpænɪən/ *n* companheiro *m*. **~ship** *n* companhia *f*, convívio *m*

company /ˈkʌmpənɪ/ *n* companhia *f*; (*guests*) visitas *fpl*. **keep sb ~** fazer companhia a alg

comparable /ˈkɒmpərəbl/ *a* comparável

compar|e /kəmˈpeə(r)/ *vt/i* comparar(-se) (**to, with** com). **~ative** /ˈpærətɪv/ *a* comparativo; (*comfort etc*) relativo

comparison /kəmˈpærɪsn/ *n* comparação *f*

compartment /kəmˈpaːtmənt/ *n* compartimento *m*

compass /ˈkʌmpəs/ *n* bússola *f*. **~es** compasso *m*

compassion /kəmˈpæʃn/ *n* compaixão *f*. **~ate** *a* compassivo

compatib|le /kəmˈpætəbl/ *a* compatível. **~ility** /-ˈbɪlətɪ/ *n* compatibilidade *f*

compel /kəmˈpel/ *vt* (*pt* **compelled**) compelir, forçar. **~ling** *a* irresistível, convincente

compensat|e /ˈkɒmpənseɪt/ *vt/i* compensar. **~ion** /ˈseɪʃn/ *n* compensação *f*; (*financial*) indenização *f*, (*P*) indemnização *f*

compete /kəmˈpiːt/ *vi* competir. **~ with** rivalizar com

competen|t /ˈkɒmpɪtənt/ *a* competente. **~ce** *n* competência *f*

competition /kɒmpəˈtɪʃn/ *n* competição *f*; (*comm*) concorrência *f*

competitive /kəmˈpetɪtɪv/ *a* (*sport, prices*) competitivo. **~ examination** concurso *m*

competitor /kəmˈpetɪtə(r)/ *n* competidor *m*, concorrente *mf*

compile /kəmˈpaɪl/ *vt* compilar, coligir. **~r** /-ə(r)/ *n* compilador *m*

complacen|t /kəmˈpleɪsnt/ *a* satisfeito consigo mesmo, (*P*) complacente. **~cy** *n* (auto-)satisfação *f*, (*P*) complacência *f*

complain /kəmˈpleɪn/ *vi* queixar-se (**about, of** de)

complaint /kəmˈpleɪnt/ *n* queixa *f*; (*in shop*) reclamação *f*; (*med*) doença *f*, achaque *m*

complement /ˈkɒmplɪmənt/ *n* complemento *m* □ *vt* completar, complementar. **~ary** /-ˈmentrɪ/ *a* complementar

complet|e /kəmˈpliːt/ *a* completo; (*finished*) acabado; (*downright*) perfeito □ *vt* completar; (*a form*) preencher. **~ely** *adv* completamente. **~ion** /-ʃn/ *n* conclusão *f*, feitura *f*, realização *f*

complex /ˈkɒmpleks/ *a* complexo □ *n* complexo *m*. **~ity** /kəmˈpleksətɪ/ *n* complexidade *f*

complexion /kəmˈplekʃn/ *n* cor *f* da tez; (*fig*) caráter *m*, (*P*) carácter *m*, aspecto *m*

compliance /kəmˈplaɪəns/ *n* docilidade *f*; (*agreement*) conformidade *f*. **in ~ with** em conformidade com

complicat|e /ˈkɒmplɪkeɪt/ *vt* complicar. **~ed** *a* complicado. **~ion** /-ˈkeɪʃn/ *n* complicação *f*

compliment /ˈkɒmplɪmənt/ *n* cumprimento *m* □ *vt* /ˈkɒmplɪment/ cumprimentar

complimentary /kɒmplɪˈmentrɪ/ *a* amável, elogioso. **~ copy** oferta *f*. **~ ticket** bilhete *m* grátis

comply /kəmˈplaɪ/ *vi* **~ with** agir em conformidade com

component /kəmˈpəʊnənt/ *n* componente *m*; (*of machine*) peça *f* □ *a* componente, constituinte

compose /kəmˈpəʊz/ *vt* compor. **~ o.s.** acalmar-se, dominar-se. **~d** *a* calmo, senhor de si. **~r** /-ə(r)/ *n* compositor *m*

composition /kɒmpəˈzɪʃn/ *n* composição *f*

compost /ˈkɒmpɒst/ *n* húmus *m*, adubo *m*

composure /kəmˈpəʊʒə(r)/ *n* calma *f*, domínio *m* de si mesmo

compound /ˈkɒmpaʊnd/ *n* composto *m*; (*enclosure*) cercado *m*, recinto *m* □ *a* composto. **~ fracture** fratura *f*, (*P*) fractura *f* exposta

comprehen|d /kɒmprɪˈhend/ *vt* compreender. **~sion** *n* compreensão *f*

comprehensive /kɒmprɪˈhensɪv/ *a* compreensivo, vasto; (*insurance*) contra todos os riscos. **~ school** escola *f* de ensino secundário técnico e acadêmico, (*P*) académico

compress /kəm'pres/ *vt* comprimir. ~**ion** /-ʃn/ *n* compressão *f*
comprise /kəm'praɪz/ *vt* compreender, abranger
compromise /'kɒmprəmaɪz/ *n* compromisso *m* □ *vt* comprometer □ *vi* chegar a um meio-termo
compulsion /kəm'pʌlʃn/ *n* (*constraint*) coação *f*; (*psych*) desejo *m* irresistível
compulsive /kəm'pʌlsɪv/ *a* (*psych*) compulsivo; (*liar, smoker etc*) inveterado
compulsory /kəm'pʌlsərɪ/ *a* obrigatório, compulsório
computer /kəm'pju:tə(r)/ *n* computador *m*. ~ **science** informática *f*. ~**ize** *vt* computerizar
comrade /'kɒmreɪd/ *n* camarada *mf*. ~**ship** *n* camaradagem *f*
con[1] /kɒn/ *vt* (*pt* **conned**) (*sl*) enganar □ *n* (*sl*) intrujice *f*, vigarice *f*, burla *f*. ~ **man** (*sl*) intrujão *m*, vigarista *m*, burlão *m*
con[2] /kɒn/ *see* **pro**
concave /'kɒŋkeɪv/ *a* côncavo
conceal /kən'si:l/ *vt* ocultar, esconder. ~**ment** *n* encobrimento *m*
concede /kən'si:d/ *vt* conceder, admitir; (*in a game etc*) ceder
conceit /kən'si:t/ *n* presunção *f*. ~**ed** *a* presunçoso, presumido, cheio de si
conceivabl|e /kən'si:vəbl/ *a* concebível. ~**y** *adv* possivelmente
conceive /kən'si:v/ *vt/i* conceber
concentrat|e /'kɒnsntreɪt/ *vt/i* concentrar(-se). ~**ion** /-'treɪʃn/ *n* concentração *f*
concept /'kɒnsept/ *n* conceito *m*
conception /kən'sepʃn/ *n* concepção *f*
concern /kən'sɜ:n/ *n* (*worry*) preocupação *f*; (*business*) negócio *m* □ *vt* dizer respeito a, respeitar. ~ **o.s. with, be** ~**ed with** interessar-se por, ocupar-se de; (*regard*) dizer respeito a. **it's no** ~ **of mine** não me diz respeito. ~**ing** *prep* sobre, respeitante a
concerned /kən'sɜ:nd/ *a* inquieto, preocupado (**about** com)
concert /'kɒnsət/ *n* concerto *m*
concerted /kən'sɜ:tɪd/ *a* concertado
concession /kən'seʃn/ *n* concessão *f*
concise /kən'saɪs/ *a* conciso. ~**ly** *adv* concisamente
conclu|de /kən'klu:d/ *vt* concluir □ *vi* terminar. ~**ding** *a* final. ~**sion** *n* conclusão *f*
conclusive /kən'klu:sɪv/ *a* conclusivo. ~**ly** *adv* de forma conclusiva
concoct /kən'kɒkt/ *vt* preparar por mistura; (*fig: invent*) fabricar. ~**ion** /-ʃn/ *n* mistura *f*; (*fig*) invenção *f*, mentira *f*
concrete /'kɒŋkri:t/ *n* concreto *m*, (*P*) cimento *m* □ *a* concreto □ *vt* concretar, (*P*) cimentar
concur /kən'kɜ:(r)/ *vi* (*pt* **concurred**) concordar; (*of circumstances*) concorrer
concussion /kən'kʌʃn/ *n* comoção *f* cerebral
condemn /kən'dem/ *vt* condenar. ~**ation** /kɒndem'neɪʃn/ *n* condenação *f*
condens|e /kən'dens/ *vt/i* condensar (-se). ~**ation** /kɒnden'seɪʃn/ *n* condensação *f*
condescend /kɒndɪ'send/ *vi* condescender; (*lower o.s.*) rebaixar-se
condition /kən'dɪʃn/ *n* condição *f* □ *vt* condicionar. **on** ~ **that** com a condição de que. ~**al** *a* condicional. ~**er** *n* (*for hair*) condicionador *m*, creme *m* rinse
condolences /kən'dəʊlənsɪz/ *npl* condolências *fpl*, pêsames *mpl*, sentimentos *mpl*
condom /'kɒndəm/ *n* preservativo *m*
condone /kən'dəʊn/ *vt* desculpar, fechar os olhos a
conducive /kən'dju:sɪv/ *a* **be** ~ **to** contribuir para, ser propício a
conduct[1] /kən'dʌkt/ *vt* conduzir, dirigir; (*orchestra*) reger
conduct[2] /'kɒndʌkt/ *n* conduta *f*
conductor /kən'dʌktə(r)/ *n* maestro *m*; (*electr; of bus*) condutor *m*
cone /kəʊn/ *n* cone *m*; (*bot*) pinha *f*; (*for ice-cream*) casquinha *f*, (*P*) cone *m*
confectioner /kən'fekʃnə(r)/ *n* confeiteiro *m*, (*P*) pasteleiro *m*. ~**y** *n* confeitaria *f*, (*P*) pastelaria *f*
confederation /kənfedə'reɪʃn/ *n* confederação *f*
confer /kən'fɜ:(r)/ (*pt* **conferred**) *vt* conferir, outorgar □ *vi* conferenciar
conference /'kɒnfərəns/ *n* conferência *f*. **in** ~ em reunião *f*
confess /kən'fes/ *vt/i* confessar; (*relig*) confessar(-se). ~**ion** /-ʃn/ *n* confissão *f*. ~**ional** *n* confessionário *m*. ~**or** *n* confessor *m*
confetti /kən'fetɪ/ *n* confetes *mpl*, (*P*) confetti *mpl*
confide /kən'faɪd/ *vt* confiar □ *vi* ~ **in** confiar em
confiden|t /'kɒnfɪdənt/ *a* confiante, confiado. ~**ce** *n* confiança *f*; (*boldness*) confiança *f* em si; (*secret*) confidência *f*. ~**ce trick** vigarice *f*. **in** ~**ce** em confidência
confidential /kɒnfɪ'denʃl/ *a* confidencial
confine /kən'faɪn/ *vt* fechar; (*limit*) limitar (**to** a). ~**ment** *n* detenção *f*; (*med*) parto *m*

confirm /kən'fɜ:m/ *vt* confirmar. ~**ation** /kɒnfə'meɪʃn/ *n* confirmação *f*. ~**ed** *a* (*bachelor*) inveterado
confiscat|e /'kɒnfɪskeɪt/ *vt* confiscar. ~**ion** /-'keɪʃn/ *n* confiscação *f*
conflict[1] /'kɒnflɪkt/ *n* conflito *m*
conflict[2] /kən'flɪkt/ *vi* estar em contradição. ~**ing** *a* contraditório
conform /kən'fɔ:m/ *vt/i* conformar (-se)
confound /kən'faʊnd/ *vt* confundir. ~**ed** *a* (*colloq*) maldito
confront /kən'frʌnt/ *vt* confrontar, defrontar, enfrentar. ~ **with** confrontar-se com. ~**ation** /kɒnfrʌn'teɪʃn/ *n* confrontação *f*
confus|e /kən'fju:z/ *vt* confundir. ~**ed** *a* confuso. ~**ing** *a* que faz confusão. ~**ion** /-ʒn/ *n* confusão *f*
congeal /kən'dʒi:l/ *vt/i* congelar, solidificar
congenial /kən'dʒi:nɪəl/ *a* (*agreeable*) simpático
congenital /kən'dʒenɪtl/ *a* congênito, (*P*) congénito
congest|ed /kən'dʒestɪd/ *a* congestionado. ~**ion** /-tʃn/ *n* (*traffic*) congestionamento *m*; (*med*) congestão *f*
congratulat|e /kən'grætjʊleɪt/ *vt* felicitar, dar os parabéns (**on** por). ~**ions** /-'leɪʃnz/ *npl* felicitações *fpl*, parabéns *mpl*
congregat|e /'kɒŋgrɪgeɪt/ *vi* reunir-se. ~**ion** /-'geɪʃn/ *n* (*in church*) congregação *f*, fiéis *mpl*
congress /'kɒŋgres/ *n* congresso *m*. **C~** (*Amer*) Congresso *m*
conjecture /kən'dʒektʃə(r)/ *n* conjetura *f*, (*P*) conjectura *f* □ *vt/i* conjeturar, (*P*) conjecturar
conjugal /'kɒndʒʊgl/ *a* conjugal
conjugat|e /'kɒndʒʊgeɪt/ *vt* conjugar. ~**ion** /-'geɪʃn/ *n* conjugação *f*
conjunction /kən'dʒʌŋkʃn/ *n* conjunção *f*
conjur|e /'kʌndʒə(r)/ *vi* fazer truques mágicos □ *vt* ~**e up** fazer aparecer. ~**or** *n* mágico *m*, prestidigitador *m*
connect /kə'nekt/ *vt/i* ligar(-se); (*of train*) fazer ligação. ~**ed** *a* ligado. **be** ~**ed with** estar relacionado com
connection /kə'nekʃn/ *n* relação *f*; (*rail; phone call*) ligação *f*; (*electr*) contacto *m*
connoisseur /kɒnə'sɜ:(r)/ *n* conhecedor *m*, apreciador *m*
connotation /kɒnə'teɪʃn/ *n* conotação *f*
conquer /'kɒŋkə(r)/ *vt* vencer; (*country*) conquistar. ~**or** *n* conquistador *m*
conquest /'kɒŋkwest/ *n* conquista *f*
conscience /'kɒnʃəns/ *n* consciência *f*
conscientious /kɒnʃɪ'enʃəs/ *a* consciencioso
conscious /'kɒnʃəs/ *a* consciente. ~**ly** *adv* conscientemente. ~**ness** *n* consciência *f*
conscript[1] /kən'skrɪpt/ *vt* recrutar. ~**ion** /-ʃn/ *n* serviço *m* militar obrigatório
conscript[2] /'kɒnskrɪpt/ *n* recruta *m*
consecrate /'kɒnsɪkreɪt/ *vt* consagrar
consecutive /kən'sekjʊtɪv/ *a* consecutivo, seguido
consensus /kən'sensəs/ *n* consenso *m*
consent /kən'sent/ *vi* consentir (**to** em) □ *n* consentimento *m*
consequence /'kɒnsɪkwəns/ *n* conseqüência *f*, (*P*) consequência *f*
consequent /'kɒnsɪkwənt/ *a* resultante (**on, upon** de). ~**ly** *adv* por conseqüência, (*P*) consequência, por consequinte
conservation /kɒnsə'veɪʃn/ *n* conservação *f*
conservative /kən'sɜ:vətɪv/ *a* conservador; (*estimate*) moderado. **C~** *a & n* conservador (*m*)
conservatory /kən'sɜ:vətrɪ/ *n* (*greenhouse*) estufa *f*; (*house extension*) jardim *m* de inverno
conserve /kən'sɜ:v/ *vt* conservar
consider /kən'sɪdə(r)/ *vt* considerar; (*allow for*) levar em consideração. ~**ation** /'reɪʃn/ *n* consideração *f*. ~**ing** *prep* em vista de, tendo em conta
considerabl|e /kən'sɪdərəbl/ *a* considerável; (*much*) muito. ~**y** *adv* consideravelmente
considerate /kən'sɪdərət/ *a* atencioso, delicado
consign /kən'saɪn/ *vt* consignar. ~**ment** *n* consignação *f*
consist /kən'sɪst/ *vi* consistir (**of, in,** em)
consisten|t /kən'sɪstənt/ *a* (*unchanging*) constante; (*not contradictory*) coerente. ~**t with** conforme com. ~**cy** *n* consistência *f*; (*fig*) coerência *f*. ~**tly** *adv* regularmente
consol|e /kən'səʊl/ *vt* consolar. ~**ation** /kɒnsə'leɪʃn/ *n* consolação *f*. ~**ation prize** prêmio *m* de consolação
consolidat|e /kən'sɒlɪdeɪt/ *vt/i* consolidar(-se). ~**ion** /-'deɪʃn/ *n* consolidação *f*
consonant /'kɒnsənənt/ *n* consoante *f*
consortium /kən'sɔ:tɪəm/ *n* (*pl* -tia) consórcio *m*
conspicuous /kən'spɪkjʊəs/ *a* conspícuo, visível; (*striking*) notável. **make o.s.** ~ fazer-se notar, chamar a atenção

conspira|cy /kən'spɪrəsɪ/ *n* conspiração *f*. ~**tor** *n* conspirador *m*
conspire /kən'spaɪə(r)/ *vi* conspirar
constable /'kʌnstəbl/ *n* polícia *m*
constant /'kɒnstənt/ *a* constante. ~**ly** *adv* constantemente
constellation /kɒnstə'leɪʃn/ *n* constelação *f*
consternation /kɒnstə'neɪʃn/ *n* consternação *f*
constipation /kɒnstɪ'peɪʃn/ *n* prisão *f* de ventre
constituency /kən'stɪtjʊənsɪ/ *n* (*pl* -cies) círculo *m* eleitoral
constituent /kən'stɪtjʊənt/ *a* & *n* constituinte (*m*)
constitut|e /'kɒnstɪtju:t/ *vt* constituir. ~**ion** /-'tju:ʃn/ *n* constituição *f*. ~**ional** /-'tju:ʃənl/ *a* constitucional
constrain /kən'streɪn/ *vt* constranger
constraint /kən'streɪnt/ *n* constrangimento *m*
constrict /kən'strɪkt/ *vt* constringir, apertar. ~**ion** /-ʃn/ *n* constrição *f*
construct /kən'strʌkt/ *vt* construir. ~**ion** /-ʃn/ *n* construção *f*. **under** ~**ion** em construção
constructive /kən'strʌktɪv/ *a* construtivo
consul /'kɒnsl/ *n* cônsul *m*
consulate /'kɒnsjʊlət/ *n* consulado *m*
consult /kən'sʌlt/ *vt* consultar. ~**ation** /kɒnsl'teɪʃn/ *n* consulta *f*
consultant /kən'sʌltənt/ *n* consultor *m*; (*med*) especialista *mf*
consume /kən'sju:m/ *vt* consumir. ~**r** /-ə(r)/ *n* consumidor *m*
consumption /kən'sʌmpʃn/ *n* consumo *m*
contact /'kɒntækt/ *n* contacto *m*; (*person*) relação *f*. ~ **lenses** lentes *fpl* de contacto □ *vt* contactar
contagious /kən'teɪdʒəs/ *a* contagioso
contain /kən'teɪn/ *vt* conter. ~ **o.s.** conter-se. ~**er** *n* recipiente *m*; (*for transport*) contentor *m*
contaminat|e /kən'tæmɪneɪt/ *vt* contaminar. ~**ion** /-'neɪʃn/ *n* contaminação *f*
contemplat|e /'kɒntempleɪt/ *vt* contemplar; (*intend*) ter em vista; (*consider*) esperar, pensar em. ~**ion** /-'pleɪʃn/ *n* contemplação *f*
contemporary /kən'temprərɪ/ *a* & *n* contemporâneo (*m*)
contempt /kən'tempt/ *n* desprezo *m*. ~**ible** *a* desprezível. ~**uous** /-tʃʊəs/ *a* desdenhoso
contend /kən'tend/ *vt* afirmar, sustentar □ *vi* ~ **with** lutar contra. ~**er** *n* adversário *m*, contendor *m*
content[1] /kən'tent/ *a* satisfeito, contente □ *vt* contentar. ~**ed** *a* satisfeito, contente. ~**ment** *n* contentamento *m*, satisfação *f*
content[2] /'kɒntent/ *n* conteúdo *m*. (**table of**) ~**s** índice *m*
contention /kən'tenʃn/ *n* disputa *f*, contenda *f*; (*assertion*) argumento *m*
contest[1] /'kɒntest/ *n* competição *f*; (*struggle*) luta *f*
contest[2] /kən'test/ *vt* contestar; (*compete for*) disputar. ~**ant** *n* concorrente *mf*
context /'kɒntekst/ *n* contexto *m*
continent /'kɒntɪnənt/ *n* continente *m*. **the C**~ a Europa (continental) *f*. ~**al** /-'nentl/ *a* continental; (*of mainland Europe*) europeu ~**al breakfast** café *m* da manhã europeu, (*P*) pequeno almoço *m* europeu. ~**al quilt** edredom *m*, (*P*) edredão *m*
contingen|t /kən'tɪndʒənt/ *a* & *n* contingente (*m*). ~**cy** *n* contingência *f*. ~**cy plan** plano *m* de emergência
continual /kən'tɪnjʊəl/ *a* contínuo. ~**ly** *adv* continuamente
continu|e /kən'tɪnju:/ *vt/i* continuar. ~**ation** /-tɪnjʊ'eɪʃn/ *n* continuação *f*.
continuity /kɒntɪ'nju:ətɪ/ *n* continuidade *f*
continuous /kən'tɪnjʊəs/ *a* contínuo. ~**ly** *adv* continuamente
contort /kən'tɔ:t/ *vt* contorcer; (*fig*) distorcer. ~**ion** /-ʃn/ *n* contorção *f*
contour /'kɒntʊə(r)/ *n* contorno *m*
contraband /'kɒntrəbænd/ *n* contrabando *m*
contraception /kɒntrə'sepʃn/ *n* contracepção *f*
contraceptive /kɒntrə'septɪv/ *a* & *n* contraceptivo (*m*)
contract[1] /'kɒntrækt/ *n* contrato *m*
contract[2] /kən'trækt/ *vt/i* contrair (-se); (*make a contract*) contratar. ~**ion** /-ʃn/ *n* contração *f*, (*P*) contracção *f*
contractor /kən'træktə(r)/ *n* empreiteiro *m*; (*firm*) firma *f* empreiteira de serviços, (*P*) recrutadora *f* de mão de obra temporária
contradict /kɒntrə'dɪkt/ *vt* contradizer. ~**ion** /-ʃn/ *n* contradição *f*. ~**ory** *a* contraditório
contraflow /'kɒntrəfləʊ/ *n* fluxo *m* em sentido contrário
contrary[1] /'kɒntrərɪ/ *a* & *n* (*opposite*) contrário (*m*) □ *adv* ~ **to** contrariamente a. **on the** ~ ao *ou* pelo contrário
contrary[2] /kən'treərɪ/ *a* (*perverse*) do contra, embirrento
contrast[1] /'kɒntra:st/ *n* contraste *m*
contrast[2] /kən'tra:st/ *vt/i* contrastar. ~**ing** *a* contrastante
contraven|e /kɒntrə'vi:n/ *vt* infringir. ~**tion** /'-venʃn/ *n* contravenção *f*

contribut|e /kən'trɪbju:t/ *vt/i* contribuir (to para); (*to newspaper etc*) colaborar (to em). **~ion** /kɒntrɪ'bju:ʃn/ *n* contribuição *f*. **~or** /-'trɪbju:tə(r)/ *n* contribuinte *mf*; (*to newspaper*) colaborador *m*

contrivance /kən'traɪvəns/ *n* (*invention*) engenho *m*; (*device*) engenhoca *f*; (*trick*) maquinação *f*

contrive /kən'traɪv/ *vt* imaginar, inventar. **~ to do** conseguir fazer

control /kən'trəʊl/ *vt* (*pt* **controlled**) (*check, restrain*) controlar; (*firm etc*) dirigir □ *n* controle *m*; (*management*) direção *f*, (*P*) direcção *f*. **~s** (*of car, plane*) comandos *mpl*; (*knobs*) botões *mpl*. **be in ~ of** dirigir. **under ~** sob controle

controversial /kɒntrə'vɜ:ʃl/ *a* controverso, discutível

controversy /'kɒntrəvɜ:sɪ/ *n* controvérsia *f*

convalesce /kɒnvə'les/ *vi* convalescer. **~nce** *n* convalescença *f*. **~nt** /-nt/ *a* & *n* convalescente (*mf*). **~nt home** casa *f* de repouso

convene /kən'vi:n/ *vt* convocar □ *vi* reunir-se

convenience /kən'vi:nɪəns/ *n* conveniência *f*. **~s** (*appliances*) comodidades *fpl*; (*lavatory*) privada *f*, (*P*) casa *f* de banho. **at your ~** quando (e como) lhe convier. **~ foods** alimentos *mpl* semiprontos

convenient /kən'vi:nɪənt/ *a* conveniente. **be ~ for** convir a. **~ly** *adv* sem inconveniente; (*situated*) bem; (*arrive*) a propósito

convent /'kɒnvənt/ *n* convento *m*. **~ school** colégio *m* de freiras

convention /kən'venʃn/ *n* convenção *f*; (*custom*) uso *m*, costume *m*. **~al** *a* convencional

converge /kən'vɜ:dʒ/ *vi* convergir

conversant /kən'vɜ:snt/ *a* **be ~ with** conhecer; (*fact*) saber; (*machinery*) estar familiarizado com

conversation /kɒnvə'seɪʃn/ *n* conversa *f*. **~al** *a* de conversa, coloquial

converse[1] /kən'vɜ:s/ *vi* conversar

converse[2] /'kɒnvɜ:s/ *a* & *n* inverso (*m*). **~ly** /kən'vɜ:slɪ/ *adv* ao invés, inversamente

conver|t[1] /kən'vɜ:t/ *vt* converter; (*house*) transformar. **~sion** /-ʃn/ *n* conversão *f*; (*house*) transformação *f*. **~tible** *a* convertível, conversível □ *n* (*auto*) conversível *m*

convert[2] /'kɒnvɜ:t/ *n* convertido *m*, converso *m*

convex /'kɒnveks/ *a* convexo

convey /kən'veɪ/ *vt* transmitir; (*goods*) transportar; (*idea, feeling*) comunicar. **~ance** *n* transporte *m*. **~or belt** tapete *m* rolante, correia *f* transportadora

convict[1] /kən'vɪkt/ *vt* declarar culpado. **~ion** /-ʃn/ *n* condenação *f*; (*opinion*) convicção *f*

convict[2] /'kɒnvɪkt/ *n* condenado *m*

convinc|e /kən'vɪns/ *vt* convencer. **~ing** *a* convincente

convoluted /kɒnvə'lu:tɪd/ *a* retorcido; (*fig*) complicado; (*bot*) convoluto

convoy /'kɒnvɔɪ/ *n* escolta *f*

convuls|e /kən'vʌls/ *vt* convulsionar; (*fig*) abalar. **be ~ed with laughter** torcer-se de riso. **~ion** /-ʃn/ *n* convulsão *f*

coo /ku:/ *vi* (*pt* **cooed**) arrulhar □ *n* arrulho *m*

cook /kʊk/ *vt/i* cozinhar □ *n* cozinheira *f*, cozinheiro *m*. **~ up** (*colloq*) cozinhar (*fig*), fabricar

cooker /'kʊkə(r)/ *n* fogão *m*

cookery /'kʊkərɪ/ *n* cozinha *f*. **~ book** livro *m* de culinária

cookie /'kʊkɪ/ *n* (*Amer*) biscoito *m*

cool /ku:l/ *a* (-er, -est) fresco; (*calm*) calmo; (*unfriendly*) frio □ *n* frescura *f*; (*sl: composure*) sangue-frio *m* □ *vt/i* arrefecer. **~-box** *n* geladeira *f* portátil. **in the ~** no fresco. **~ly** /'ku:llɪ/ *adv* calmamente; (*fig*) friamente. **~ness** *n* frescura *f*; (*fig*) frieza *f*

coop /ku:p/ *n* galinheiro *m* □ *vt* **~ up** engaislar, fechar

co-operat|e /kəʊ'ɒpəreɪt/ *vi* cooperar. **~ion** /-'reɪʃn/ *n* cooperação *f*

cooperative /kəʊ'ɒpərətɪv/ *a* cooperativo □ *n* cooperativa *f*

coordinat|e /kəʊ'ɔ:dɪneɪt/ *vt* coordenar. **~ion** /-'neɪʃn/ *n* coordenação *f*

cop /kɒp/ *n* (*sl*) porco *m* (*sl*), (*P*) xui *m* (*sl*)

cope /kəʊp/ *vi* aguentar-se, arranjar-se. **~ with** poder com, dar conta de

copious /'kəʊpɪəs/ *a* copioso

copper[1] /'kɒpə(r)/ *n* cobre *m* □ *a* de cobre

copper[2] /'kɒpə(r)/ *n* (*sl*) porco *m* (*sl*), (*P*) xui *m* (*sl*)

coppice /'kɒpɪs/, **copse** /kɒps/ *ns* mata *f* de corte

copulat|e /'kɒpjʊleɪt/ *vi* copular. **~ion** /-'leɪʃn/ *n* cópula *f*

copy /'kɒpɪ/ *n* cópia *f*; (*of book*) exemplar *m*; (*of newspaper*) número *m* □ *vt/i* copiar

copyright /'kɒpɪraɪt/ *n* direitos *mpl* autorais

coral /'kɒrəl/ *n* coral *m*

cord /kɔ:d/ *n* cordão *m*; (*electr*) fio *m*

cordial /'kɔ:dɪəl/ *a* & *n* cordial (*m*)

cordon /'kɔ:dn/ *n* cordão *m* □ *vt* **~ off** fechar (com um cordão de isolamento)

corduroy /'kɔ:dərɔɪ/ *n* veludo *m* cotelé

core /kɔ:(r)/ *n* âmago *m*; (*of apple, pear*) coração *m*
cork /kɔ:k/ *n* cortiça *f*; (*for bottle*) rolha *f* □ *vt* rolhar
corkscrew /'kɔ:kskru:/ *n* sacarolhas *m*
corn[1] /kɔ:n/ *n* trigo *m*; (*Amer: maize*) milho *m*; (*seed*) grão *m*. ~ **on the cob** espiga *f* de milho
corn[2] /kɔ:n/ *n* (*hard skin*) calo *m*
corned /kɔ:nd/ *a* ~ **beef** carne *f* de vaca enlatada
corner /'kɔ:nə(r)/ *n* canto *m*; (*of street*) esquina *f*; (*bend in road*) curva *f* □ *vt* encurralar; (*market*) monopolizar □ *vi* dar uma curva, virar
cornet /'kɔ:nɪt/ *n* (*mus*) cornetim *m*; (*for ice-cream*) casquinha *f*, (*P*) cone *m*
cornflakes /'kɔ:nfleɪks/ *npl* cornflakes *mpl*, cereais *mpl*
cornflour /'kɔ:nflaʊə(r)/ *n* fécula *f* de milho, maisena *f*
Corn|wall /'kɔ:nwəl/ *n* Cornualha *f*. ~**ish** *a* da Cornualha
corny /'kɔ:nɪ/ *a* (*colloq*) batido, (*P*) estafado
coronary /'kɒrənrɪ/ *n* ~ (**thrombosis**) infarto *m*, enfarte *m*
coronation /kɒrə'neɪʃn/ *n* coroação *f*
coroner /'kɒrənə(r)/ *n* magistrado *m* que investiga os casos de morte suspeita
corporal[1] /'kɔ:pərəl/ *n* (*mil*) cabo *m*
corporal[2] /'kɔ:pərəl/ *a* ~ **punishment** castigo *m* corporal
corporate /'kɔ:pərət/ *a* coletivo, (*P*) colectivo; (*body*) corporativo
corporation /kɔ:pə'reɪʃn/ *n* corporação *f*; (*of town*) municipalidade *f*
corps /kɔ:(r)/ *n* (*pl* **corps** /kɔ:z/) corpo *m*
corpse /kɔ:ps/ *n* cadáver *m*
corpuscle /'kɔ:pʌsl/ *n* corpúsculo *m*
correct /kə'rekt/ *a* correto, (*P*) correcto. **the** ~ **time** a hora certa. **you are** ~ você tem razão □ *vt* corrigir. ~**ion** /-ʃn/ *n* correção *f*, (*P*) correcção *f*, emenda *f*
correlat|e /'kɒrəleɪt/ *vt/i* correlacionar(-se). ~**ion** /-'leɪʃn/ *n* correlação *f*
correspond /kɒrɪ'spɒnd/ *vi* corresponder (**to, with**, a); (*write letters*) corresponder-se (**with**, com). ~**ence** *n* correspondência *f*. ~**ent** *n* correspondente *mf*. ~**ing** *a* correspondente
corridor /'kɒrɪdɔ:(r)/ *n* corredor *m*
corroborate /kə'rɒbəreɪt/ *vt* corroborar
corro|de /kə'rəʊd/ *vt/i* corroer(-se). ~**sion** *n* corrosão *f*
corrugated /'kɒrəgeɪtɪd/ *a* corrugado. ~ **cardboard** cartão *m* canelado. ~ **iron** chapa *f* ondulada
corrupt /kə'rʌpt/ *a* corrupto □ *vt* corromper. ~**ion** /-ʃn/ *n* corrupção *f*
corset /'kɔ:sɪt/ *n* espartilho *m*; (*elasticated*) cinta *f* elástica
Corsica /'kɔ:sɪkə/ *n* Córsega *f*
cosmetic /kɒz'metɪk/ *n* cosmético *m* □ *a* cosmético; (*fig*) superficial
cosmonaut /'kɒzmənɔ:t/ *n* cosmonauta *mf*
cosmopolitan /kɒzmə'pɒlɪtən/ *a* & *n* cosmopolita (*mf*)
cosset /'kɒsɪt/ *vt* (*pt* **cosseted**) proteger
cost /kɒst/ *vt* (*pt* **cost**) custar; (*pt* **costed**) fixar o preço de □ *n* custo *m*. ~**s** (*jur*) custos *mpl*. **at all** ~**s** custe o que custar. **to one's** ~ à sua custa. ~ **of living** custo *m* de vida
costly /'kɒstlɪ/ *a* (-ier, -iest) *a* caro; (*valuable*) precioso
costume /'kɒstju:m/ *n* traje *m*
cos|y /'kəʊzɪ/ *a* (-ier, -iest) confortável, íntimo □ *n* abafador *m* (do bule do chá). ~**iness** *n* conforto *m*
cot /kɒt/ *n* cama *f* de bêbê, berço *m*
cottage /'kɒtɪdʒ/ *n* pequena casa *f* de campo. ~ **cheese** requeijão *m*, ricota *f*. ~ **industry** artesanato *m*. ~ **pie** empada *f* de carne picada
cotton /'kɒtn/ *n* algodão *m*; (*thread*) fio *m*, linha *f*. ~ **wool** algodão *m* hidrófilo
couch /kaʊtʃ/ *n* divã *m*
couchette /ku:'ʃet/ *n* couchette *f*
cough /kɒf/ *vi* tossir □ *n* tosse *f*
could /kʊd, kəd/ *pt of* **can**[2]
couldn't /'kʊdnt/ = **could not**
council /'kaʊnsl/ *n* conselho *m*. ~ **house** casa *f* de bairro popular
councillor /'kaʊnsələ(r)/ *n* vereador *m*
counsel /'kaʊnsl/ *n* conselho *m*; (*pl invar*) (*jur*) advogado *m*. ~**lor** *n* conselheiro *m*
count[1] /kaʊnt/ *vt/i* contar □ *n* conta *f*. ~**-down** *n* (*rocket*) contagem *f* regressiva. ~ **on** contar com
count[2] /kaʊnt/ *n* (*nobleman*) conde *m*
counter[1] /'kaʊntə(r)/ *n* (*in shop*) balcão *m*; (*in game*) ficha *f*, (*P*) tento *m*
counter[2] /'kaʊntə(r)/ *adv* ~ **to** contrário a; (*in the opposite direction*) em sentido contrário a □ *a* oposto □ *vt* opor; (*blow*) aparar □ *vi* ripostar
counter- /'kaʊntə(r)/ *pref* contra-
counteract /kaʊntər'ækt/ *vt* neutralizar, frustrar
counter-attack /'kaʊntərətæk/ *n* contra-ataque *m* □ *vt/i* contra-atacar
counterbalance /'kaʊntəbæləns/ *n* contrapeso *m* □ *vt* contrabalançar

counterfeit /'kaʊntəfɪt/ *a* falsificado, falso □ *n* falsificação *f* □ *vt* falsificar
counterfoil /'kaʊntəfɔɪl/ *n* talão *m*, canhoto *m*
counterpart /'kaʊntəpa:t/ *n* equivalente *m*; (*person*) homólogo *m*
counter-productive /'kaʊntəprədʌktɪv/ *a* contraproducente
countersign /'kaʊntəsaɪn/ *vt* subscrever documento já assinado; (*cheque*) contrassinar
countess /'kaʊntɪs/ *n* condessa *f*
countless /'kaʊntlɪs/ *a* sem conta, incontável, inúmero
country /'kʌntrɪ/ *n* país *m*; (*homeland*) pátria *f*; (*countryside*) campo *m*
countryside /'kʌntrɪsaɪd/ *n* campo *m*
county /'kaʊntɪ/ *n* condado *m*
coup /ku:/ *n* ~ (**d'état**) golpe *m* (de estado)
couple /'kʌpl/ *n* par *m*, casal *m* □ *vt/i* unir(-se), ligar(-se); (*techn*) acoplar. **a** ~ **of** um par de
coupon /'ku:pɒn/ *n* cupão *m*
courage /'kʌrɪdʒ/ *n* coragem *f*. ~**ous** /kə'reɪdʒəs/ *a* corajoso
courgette /kʊə'ʒet/ *n* abobrinha *f*
courier /'kʊrɪə(r)/ *n* correio *m*; (*for tourists*) guia *mf*; (*for parcels, mail*) estafeta *m*
course /kɔ:s/ *n* curso *m*; (*series*) série *f*; (*culin*) prato *m*; (*for golf*) campo *m*; (*fig*) caminho *m*. **in due** ~ na altura devida, oportunamente. **in the** ~ **of** durante. **of** ~ está claro, com certeza
court /kɔ:t/ *n* (*of monarch*) corte *f*; (*courtyard*) pátio *m*; (*tennis*) court *m*, quadra *f*, (*P*) campo *m*; (*jur*) tribunal *m* □ *vt* cortejar; (*danger*) provocar. ~ **martial** (*pl* **courts martial**) conselho *m* de guerra
courteous /'kɜ:tɪəs/ *a* cortês, delicado
courtesy /'kɜ:təsɪ/ *n* cortesia *f*
courtship /'kɔ:tʃɪp/ *n* namoro *m*, corte *f*
courtyard /'kɔ:tja:d/ *n* pátio *m*
cousin /'kʌzn/ *n* primo *m*. **first/second** ~ primo *m* em primeiro/segundo grau
cove /kəʊv/ *n* angra *f*, enseada *f*
covenant /'kʌvənənt/ *n* convenção *f*, convénio *m*; (*jur*) contrato *m*; (*relig*) aliança *f*
cover /'kʌvə(r)/ *vt* cobrir □ *n* cobertura *f*; (*for bed*) colcha *f*; (*for book, furniture*) capa *f*; (*lid*) tampa *f*; (*shelter*) abrigo *m*. ~ **charge** serviço *m*. ~ **up** tapar; (*fig*) encobrir. ~**-up** *n* (*fig*) encobrimento *m*. **take** ~ abrigar-se. **under separate** ~ em separado. ~**ing** *n* cobertura *f*. ~**ing letter** carta *f* (que acompanha um documento)
coverage /'kʌvərɪdʒ/ *n* (*of events*) reportagem *f*, cobertura *f*
covet /'kʌvɪt/ *vt* cobiçar
cow /kaʊ/ *n* vaca *f*
coward /'kaʊəd/ *n* covarde *mf*. ~**ly** *a* covarde
cowardice /'kaʊədɪs/ *n* covardia *f*
cowboy /'kaʊbɔɪ/ *n* cowboy *m*, vaqueiro *m*
cower /'kaʊə(r)/ *vi* encolher-se (de medo)
cowshed /'kaʊʃed/ *n* estábulo *m*
coy /kɔɪ/ *a* (**-er, -est**) (falsamente) tímido
crab /kræb/ *n* caranguejo *m*
crack /kræk/ *n* fenda *f*; (*in glass*) rachadura *f*; (*noise*) estalo *m*; (*sl: joke*) piada *f*; (*drug*) crack *m* □ *a* (*colloq*) de élite □ *vt/i* estalar; (*nut*) quebrar; (*joke*) contar; (*problem*) resolver; (*voice*) mudar. ~ **down on** (*colloq*) cair em cima de, arrochar. **get** ~**ing** (*colloq*) pôr mãos à obra
cracker /'krækə(r)/ *n* busca-pé *m*, bomba *f* de estalo; (*culin*) bolacha *f* de água e sal
crackers /'krækəz/ *a* (*sl*) desmiolado, maluco
crackle /'krækl/ *vi* crepitar □ *n* crepitação *f*
crackpot /'krækpɒt/ *n* (*sl*) desmiolado, maluco
cradle /'kreɪdl/ *n* berço *m* □ *vt* embalar
craft[1] /kra:ft/ *n* ofício *m*; (*technique*) arte *f*; (*cunning*) manha *f*, astúcia *f*
craft[2] /kra:ft/ *n* (*invar*) (*boat*) embarcação *f*
craftsman /'kra:ftsmən/ *n* (*pl* **-men**) artífice *mf*. ~**ship** *n* arte *f*
crafty /'kra:ftɪ/ *a* (**-ier, -iest**) manhoso, astucioso
crag /kræg/ *n* penhasco *m*. ~**gy** *a* escarpado, íngreme
cram /kræm/ *vt* (*pt* **crammed**) ~ (**for an exam**) decorar, (*P*) empinar. ~ **into/with** entulhar com
cramp /kræmp/ *n* cãimbra *f* □ *vt* restringir, tolher. ~**ed** *a* apertado
crane /kreɪn/ *n* grua *f*; (*bird*) grou *m* □ *vt* (*neck*) esticar
crank[1] /kræŋk/ *n* (*techn*) manivela *f*. ~**shaft** *n* (*techn*) cambota *f*
crank[2] /kræŋk/ *n* excêntrico *m*. ~**y** *a* excêntrico
crash /kræʃ/ *n* acidente *m*; (*noise*) estrondo *m*; (*comm*) falência *f*; (*financial*) colapso *m*, crash *m* □ *vt/i* (*fall/strike*) cair/bater com estrondo; (*two cars*) chocar, bater; (*comm*) abrir falência; (*plane*) cair □ *a* (*course, programme*) intensivo. ~**-helmet** *n* capacete *m*. ~**-land** *vi* fazer uma aterrissagem forçada

crate /kreɪt/ *n* engradado *m*
crater /'kreɪtə(r)/ *n* cratera *f*
crav|e /kreɪv/ *vt/i* **~e (for)** ansiar por. **~ing** *n* desejo *m* irresistível, ânsia *f*
crawl /krɔ:l/ *vi* rastejar; (*of baby*) engatinhar, (*P*) andar de gatas; (*of car*) mover-se lentamente □ *n* rastejo *m*; (*swimming*) crawl *m*. **be ~ing with** fervilhar de, estar cheio de
crayfish /'kreɪfɪʃ/ *n* (*pl invar*) lagostim *m*
crayon /'kreɪən/ *n* crayon *m*, lápis *m* de pastel
craze /kreɪz/ *n* moda *f*, febre *f*
craz|y /'kreɪzɪ/ *a* (-ier, -iest) doido, louco (**about** por). **~iness** *n* loucura *f*
creak /kri:k/ *n* rangido *m* □ *vi* ranger
cream /kri:m/ *n* (*milk fat; fig*) nata *f*; (*cosmetic; culin*) creme *m* □ *a* creme *invar* □ *vt* desnatar. **~ cheese** queijo-creme *m*. **~y** *a* cremoso
crease /kri:s/ *n* vinco *m* □ *vt/i* amarrotar(-se)
creat|e /kri:'eɪt/ *vt* criar. **~ion** /-ʃn/ *n* criação *f*. **~ive** *a* criador. **~or** *n* criador *m*
creature /'kri:tʃə(r)/ *n* criatura *f*
crèche /kreɪʃ/ *n* creche *f*
credentials /krɪ'denʃlz/ *npl* credenciais *fpl*; (*of competence etc*) referências *fpl*
credib|le /'kredəbl/ *a* crível, verosímil, (*P*) verossímil. **~ility** /-'bɪlətɪ/ *n* credibilidade *f*
credit /'kredɪt/ *n* crédito *m*; (*honour*) honra *f*. **~s** (*cinema*) créditos *mpl* □ *vt* (*pt* **credited**) acreditar em; (*comm*) creditar. **~ card** cartão *m* de crédito. **~ sb with** atribuir a alg. **~or** *n* credor *m*
creditable /'kredɪtəbl/ *a* louvável, honroso
credulous /'kredjʊləs/ *a* crédulo
creed /kri:d/ *n* credo *m*
creek /kri:k/ *n* enseada *f* estreita. **be up the ~** (*sl*) estar frito (*sl*)
creep /kri:p/ *vi* (*pt* **crept**) rastejar; (*move stealthily*) mover-se furtivamente □ *n* (*sl*) cara *m* nojento. **give sb the ~s** dar arrepios a alg. **~er** *n* (planta *f*) trepadeira (*f*). **~y** *a* arrepiante
cremat|e /krɪ'meɪt/ *vt* cremar. **~ion** /-ʃn/ *n* cremação *f*
crematorium /kremə'tɔ:rɪəm/ *n* (*pl* -ia) crematório *m*
crêpe /kreɪp/ *n* crepe *m*. **~ paper** papel *m* crepom, (*P*) plissado
crept /krept/ *see* **creep**
crescent /'kresnt/ *n* crescente *m*; (*street*) rua *f* em semicírculo
cress /kres/ *n* agrião *m*
crest /krest/ *n* (*of bird, hill*) crista *f*; (*on coat of arms*) timbre *m*
Crete /kri:t/ *n* Creta *f*
crevasse /krɪ'væs/ *n* fenda *f* (em geleira)
crevice /'krevɪs/ *n* racha *f*, fenda *f*
crew[1] /kru:/ *see* **crow**
crew[2] /kru:/ *n* tripulação *f*; (*gang*) bando *m*. **~-cut** *n* corte *m* à escovinha. **~-neck** *n* gola *f* redonda e un pouco subida
crib[1] /krɪb/ *n* berço *m*; (*Christmas*) presépio *m*
crib[2] /krɪb/ *vt/i* (*pt* **cribbed**) (*colloq*) colar (*sl*), (*P*) cabular (*sl*) □ *n* cópia *f*, plágio *m*; (*translation*) burro *m* (*sl*)
cricket[1] /'krɪkɪt/ *n* críquete *m*. **~er** *n* jogador *m* de críquete
cricket[2] /'krɪkɪt/ *n* (*insect*) grilo *m*
crime /kraɪm/ *n* crime *m*; (*minor*) delito *m*; (*collectively*) criminalidade *f*
criminal /'krɪmɪnl/ *a & n* criminoso (*m*)
crimp /krɪmp/ *vt* preguear; (*hair*) frisar
crimson /'krɪmzn/ *a & n* carmesim (*m*)
cring|e /krɪndʒ/ *vi* encolher-se. **~ing** *a* servil
crinkle /'krɪŋkl/ *vt/i* enrugar(-se) □ *n* vinco *m*, ruga *f*
cripple /'krɪpl/ *n* aleijado *m*, coxo *m* □ *vt* estropiar; (*fig*) paralisar
crisis /'kraɪsɪs/ *n* (*pl* **crises** /-si:z/) crise *f*
crisp /krɪsp/ *a* (-er, est) (*culin*) crocante; (*air*) fresco; (*manners, reply*) decidido. **~s** *npl* batatas *fpl* fritas redondas
criterion /kraɪ'tɪərɪən/ *n* (*pl* -ia) critério *m*
critic /'krɪtɪk/ *n* crítico *m*. **~al** *a* crítico. **~ally** *adv* de forma crítica; (*ill*) gravemente
criticism /'krɪtɪsɪzəm/ *n* crítica *f*
criticize /'krɪtɪsaɪz/ *vt/i* criticar
croak /krəʊk/ *n* (*frog*) coaxar *m*; (*raven*) crocitar *m*, crocito *m* □ *vi* (*frog*) coaxar; (*raven*) crocitar
crochet /'krəʊʃeɪ/ *n* crochê *m* □ *vt* fazer em crochê
crockery /'krɒkərɪ/ *n* louça *f*
crocodile /'krɒkədaɪl/ *n* crocodilo *m*
crocus /'krəʊkəs/ *n* (*pl* -**uses** /-sɪz/) croco *m*
crony /'krəʊnɪ/ *n* camarada *mf*, amigão *m*, parceiro *m*
crook /krʊk/ *n* (*colloq: criminal*) vigarista *mf*; (*stick*) cajado *m*
crooked /'krʊkɪd/ *a* torcido; (*winding*) tortuoso; (*askew*) torto; (*colloq: dishonest*) desonesto. **~ly** *adv* de través
crop /krɒp/ *n* colheita *f*; (*fig*) quantidade *f*; (*haircut*) corte *m* rente □ *vt* (*pt*

cropped) cortar □ *vi* ~ up aparecer, surgir

croquet /'krəʊkeɪ/ *n* croquet *m*, croqué *m*

cross /krɒs/ *n* cruz *f* □ *vt/i* cruzar; (*cheque*) cruzar, (*P*) barrar; (*oppose*) contrariar; (*of paths*) cruzar-se □ *a* zangado. ~ **off** *or* **out** riscar. ~ **o.s.** benzer-se. ~ **sb's mind** passar pela cabeça *or* pelo espírito de alg, ocorrer a alg. **talk at** ~ **purposes** falar sem se entender. ~**-country** *a & adv* a corta-mato. ~**-examine** *vt* fazer o contra-interrogatório (de testemunhas). ~**-eyed** *a* vesgo, estrábico. ~**-fire** *n* fogo *m* cruzado. ~**-reference** *n* nota *f* remissiva. ~**-section** *n* corte *m* transversal; (*fig*) grupo *m or* sector *m* representativo. ~**ly** *adv* irritadamente

crossbar /'krɒsba:(r)/ *n* barra *f* transversal *f*; (*of bicycle*) travessão *m*

crossing /'krɒsɪŋ/ *n* cruzamento *m*; (*by boat*) travessia *f*; (*on road*) passagem *f*

crossroads /'krɒsrəʊdz/ *n* encruzilhada *f*, cruzamento *m*

crossword /'krɒswɜ:d/ *n* palavras *fpl* cruzadas

crotch /krɒtʃ/ *n* entrepernas *fpl*

crotchet /'krɒtʃɪt/ *n* (*mus*) semínima *f*

crouch /kraʊtʃ/ *vi* agachar-se

crow /krəʊ/ *n* corvo *m* □ *vi* (*cock*) (*pt* **crew**) cantar; (*fig*) rejubilar-se (over com). **as the** ~ **flies** em linha reta, (*P*) recta

crowbar /'krəʊba:(r)/ *n* alavanca *f*, pé-de-cabra *m*

crowd /kraʊd/ *n* multidão *f* □ *vi* afluir □ *vt* encher. ~ **into** apinhar-se em. ~**ed** *a* cheio, apinhado

crown /kraʊn/ *n* coroa *f*; (*of hill*) topo *m*, cume *m* □ *vt* coroar; (*tooth*) pôr uma coroa em

crucial /'kru:ʃl/ *a* crucial

crucifix /'kru:sɪfɪks/ *n* crucifixo *m*

crucif|y /'kru:sɪfaɪ/ *vt* crucificar. ~**ixion** /-'fɪkʃn/ *n* crucificação *f*

crude /kru:d/ *a* (-er, -est) (*raw*) bruto; (*rough, vulgar*) grosseiro. ~ **oil** petróleo *m* bruto

cruel /krʊəl/ *a* (**crueller, cruellest**) cruel. ~**ty** *n* crueldade *f*

cruis|e /kru:z/ *n* cruzeiro *m* □ *vi* cruzar; (*of tourists*) fazer um cruzeiro; (*of car*) ir a velocidade de cruzeiro. ~**er** *n* cruzador *m*. ~**ing speed** velocidade *f* de cruzeiro

crumb /krʌm/ *n* migalha *f*, farelo *m*

crumble /'krʌmbl/ *vt/i* desfazer(-se); (*bread*) esmigalhar(-se); (*collapse*) desmoronar-se

crumple /'krʌmpl/ *vt/i* amarrotar (-se)

crunch /krʌntʃ/ *vt* trincar; (*under one's feet*) fazer ranger

crusade /kru:'seɪd/ *n* cruzada *f*. ~**r** /-ə(r)/ *n* cruzado *m*; (*fig*) militante *mf*

crush /krʌʃ/ *vt* esmagar; (*clothes, papers*) amassar, amarrotar □ *n* aperto *m*. **a** ~ **on** (*sl*) uma paixonite, (*P*) paixoneta por.

crust /krʌst/ *n* côdea *f*, crosta *f*. ~**y** *a* crocante

crutch /krʌtʃ/ *n* muleta *f*; (*crotch*) entrepernas *fpl*

crux /krʌks/ *n* (*pl* **cruxes**) o ponto crucial

cry /kraɪ/ *n* grito *m* □ *vi* (*weep*) chorar; (*call out*) gritar. **a far** ~ **from** muito diferente de.

crying /'kraɪɪŋ/ *a* **a** ~ **shame** uma grande vergonha

crypt /krɪpt/ *n* cripta *f*

cryptic /'krɪptɪk/ *a* críptico, enigmático

crystal /'krɪstl/ *n* cristal *m*. ~**lize** *vt/i* cristalizar(-se)

cub /kʌb/ *n* cria *f*, filhote *m*. **C**~ (**Scout**) lobito *m*

Cuba /'kju:bə/ *n* Cuba *f*. ~**n** *a & n* cubano (*m*)

cubby-hole /'kʌbɪhəʊl/ *n* cochicho *m*; (*snug place*) cantinho *m*

cub|e /kju:b/ *n* cubo *m*. ~**ic** *a* cúbico

cubicle /'kju:bɪkl/ *n* cubículo *m*, compartimento *m*; (*at swimming-pool*) cabine *f*

cuckoo /'kʊku:/ *n* cuco *m*

cucumber /'kju:kʌmbə(r)/ *n* pepino *m*

cuddl|e /'kʌdl/ *vt/i* abraçar com carinho; (*nestle*) aninhar(-se) □ *n* abracinho *m*, festinha *f*. ~**y** *a* fofo, aconchegante

cudgel /'kʌdʒl/ *n* cacete *m*, moca *f* □ *vt* (*pt* **cudgelled**) dar cacetadas em

cue[1] /kju:/ *n* (*theat*) deixa *f*; (*hint*) sugestão *f*, sinal *m*

cue[2] /kju:/ *n* (*billiards*) taco *m*

cuff /kʌf/ *n* punho *m*; (*blow*) sopapo *m* □ *vt* dar um sopapo. ~**-link** *n* botão *m* de punho. **off the** ~ de improviso

cul-de-sac /'kʌldəsæk/ *n* (*pl* **culs-de-sac**) beco *m* sem saída

culinary /'kʌlɪnərɪ/ *a* culinário

cull /kʌl/ *vt* (*select*) escolher; (*kill*) abater seletivamente, (*P*) selectivamente □ *n* abate *m*

culminat|e /'kʌlmɪneɪt/ *vi* ~**e in** acabar em. ~**ion** /-'neɪʃn/ *n* auge *m*, ponto *m* culminante

culprit /'kʌlprɪt/ *n* culpado *m*

cult /kʌlt/ *n* culto *m*

cultivat|e /'kʌltɪveɪt/ *vt* cultivar. ~**ion** /-'veɪʃn/ *n* cultivo *m*, cultivação *f*

cultural /ˈkʌltʃərəl/ *a* cultural
culture /ˈkʌltʃə(r)/ *n* cultura *f*. ~**d** *a* culto
cumbersome /ˈkʌmbəsəm/ *a* (*unwieldy*) pesado, incômodo, (*P*) incómodo
cumulative /ˈkjuːmjʊlətɪv/ *a* cumulativo
cunning /ˈkʌnɪŋ/ *a* astuto, manhoso □ *n* astúcia *f*, manha *f*
cup /kʌp/ *n* xícara *f*, (*P*) chávena *f*; (*prize*) taça *f*. **C~ Final** Final de Campeonato *f*
cupboard /ˈkʌbəd/ *n* armário *m*
cupful /ˈkʌpfʊl/ *n* xícara *f* cheia, (*P*) chávena *f* (cheia)
curable /ˈkjʊərəbl/ *a* curável
curator /kjʊəˈreɪtə(r)/ *n* (*museum*) conservador *m*; (*jur*) curador *m*
curb /kɜːb/ *n* freio *m* □ *vt* refrear; (*price increase etc*) sustar
curdle /ˈkɜːdl/ *vt/i* coalhar
cure /kjʊə(r)/ *vt* curar □ *n* cura *f*
curfew /ˈkɜːfjuː/ *n* toque *m* de recolher
curio /ˈkjʊərɪəʊ/ *n* (*pl* -os) curiosidade *f*
curi|ous /ˈkjʊərɪəs/ *a* curioso. ~**osity** /-ˈɒsətɪ/ *n* curiosidade *f*
curl /kɜːl/ *vt/i* encaracolar(-se) □ *n* caracol *m*. ~ **up** enroscar(-se)
curler /ˈkɜːlə(r)/ *n* rolo *m*
curly /ˈkɜːlɪ/ *a* (-ier, -iest) encaracolado, crespo
currant /ˈkʌrənt/ *n* passa *f* de Corinto
currency /ˈkʌrənsɪ/ *n* moeda *f* corrente; (*general use*) circulação *f*. **foreign** ~ moeda *f* estrangeita
current /ˈkʌrənt/ *a* (*common*) corrente; (*event, price, etc*) atual, (*P*) actual □ *n* corrente *f*. ~ **account** conta *f* corrente. ~ **affairs** atualidades *fpl*, (*P*) actualidades *fpl*. ~**ly** *adv* atualmente, (*P*) actualmente
curriculum /kəˈrɪkjʊləm/ *n* (*pl* -la) currículo *m*, programa *m* de estudos. ~ **vitae** *n* curriculum vitae *m*
curry[1] /ˈkʌrɪ/ *n* caril *m*
curry[2] /ˈkʌrɪ/ *vt* ~ **favour with** procurar agradar a
curse /kɜːs/ *n* maldição *f*, praga *f*; (*bad language*) palavrão *m* □ *vt* amaldiçoar, praguejar contra □ *vi* praguejar; (*swear*) dizer palavrões
cursor /ˈkɜːsə(r)/ *n* cursor *m*
cursory /ˈkɜːsərɪ/ *a* apressado, superficial. **a** ~ **look** uma olhada superficial
curt /kɜːt/ *a* brusco
curtail /kɜːˈteɪl/ *vt* abreviar; (*expenses etc*) reduzir
curtain /ˈkɜːtn/ *n* cortina *f*; (*theat*) pano *m*
curtsy /ˈkɜːtsɪ/ *n* reverência *f* □ *vi* fazer uma reverência
curve /kɜːv/ *n* curva *f* □ *vt/i* curvar (-se); (*of road*) fazer uma curva
cushion /ˈkʊʃn/ *n* almofada *f* □ *vt* (*a blow*) amortecer; (*fig*) proteger
cushy /ˈkʊʃɪ/ *a* (-ier, -iest) (*colloq*) fácil, agradável. ~ **job** sinecura *f*, boca *f* (*fig*)
custard /ˈkʌstəd/ *n* creme *m*
custodian /kʌˈstəʊdɪən/ *n* guarda *m*
custody /ˈkʌstədɪ/ *n* (*safe keeping*) custódia *f*; (*jur*) detenção *f*; (*of child*) tutela *f*
custom /ˈkʌstəm/ *n* costume *m*; (*comm*) freguesia *f*, clientela *f*. ~**ary** *a* habitual
customer /ˈkʌstəmə(r)/ *n* freguês *m*, cliente *mf*
customs /ˈkʌstəmz/ *npl* alfândega *f* □ *a* alfandegário. ~ **clearance** desembaraço *m* alfandegário. ~ **officer** funcionário *m* da alfândega
cut /kʌt/ *vt/i* (*pt* **cut**, *pres p* **cutting**) cortar; (*prices etc*) reduzir □ *n* corte *m*, golpe *m*; (*of clothes, hair*) corte *m*; (*piece*) pedaço *m*; (*prices etc*) redução *f*, corte *m*; (*sl: share*) comissão *f*, (*P*) talhada *f* (*sl*). ~ **back** *or* **down (on)** reduzir. ~**-back** *n* corte *m*. ~ **in** intrometer-se; (*auto*) cortar. ~ **off** cortar; (*fig*) isolar. ~ **out** recortar; (*leave out*) suprimir. ~**-out** *n* figura *f* para recortar. ~**-price** *a* a preço(s) reduzido(s). ~ **short** encurtar, (*P*) atalhar
cute /kjuːt/ *a* (-er, -est) (*colloq: clever*) esperto; (*attractive*) bonito, (*P*) giro (*colloq*)
cuticle /ˈkjuːtɪkl/ *n* cutícula *f*
cutlery /ˈkʌtlərɪ/ *n* talheres *mpl*
cutlet /ˈkʌtlɪt/ *n* costeleta *f*
cutting /ˈkʌtɪŋ/ *a* cortante □ *n* (*from newspaper*) recorte *m*; (*plant*) estaca *f*. ~ **edge** gume *m*
CV *abbr see* **curriculum vitae**
cyanide /ˈsaɪənaɪd/ *n* cianeto *m*
cycl|e /ˈsaɪkl/ *n* ciclo *m*; (*bicycle*) bicicleta *f* □ *vi* andar de bicicleta. ~**ing** *n* ciclismo *m*. ~**ist** *n* ciclista *mf*
cyclone /ˈsaɪkləʊn/ *n* ciclone *m*
cylind|er /ˈsɪlɪndə(r)/ *n* cilindro *m*. ~**rical** /-ˈlɪndrɪkl/ *a* cilíndrico
cymbals /ˈsɪmblz/ *npl* (*mus*) pratos *mpl*
cynic /ˈsɪnɪk/ *n* cínico *m*. ~**al** *a* cínico. ~**ism** /-sɪzəm/ *n* cinismo *m*
Cypr|us /ˈsaɪprəs/ *n* Chipre *m*. ~**iot** /ˈsɪprɪət/ *a* & *n* cipriota (*mf*)
cyst /sɪst/ *n* quisto *m*
Czech /tʃek/ *a* & *n* tcheco (*m*), (*P*) checo (*m*)

D

dab /dæb/ *vt* (*pt* **dabbed**) aplicar levemente □ *n* **a ~ of** uma aplicaçãozinha de. **~ sth on** aplicar qq coisa em gestos leves

dabble /'dæbl/ *vi* **~ in** interessar-se por, fazer um pouco de (como amador). **~r** /-ə(r)/ *n* amador *m*

dad /dæd/ *n* (*colloq*) paizinho *m*. **~dy** *n* (*children's use*) papai *m*, (*P*) papá *m*. **~dy-long-legs** *n* pernilongo *m*

daffodil /'dæfədɪl/ *n* narciso *m*

daft /dɑ:ft/ *a* (-er, -est) doido, maluco

dagger /'dægə(r)/ *n* punhal *m*. **at ~s drawn** prestes a lutar (with com)

daily /'deɪlɪ/ *a* diário, quotidiano □ *adv* diariamente, todos os dias □ *n* (*newspaper*) diário *m*; (*colloq: charwoman*) faxineira *f*, (*P*) mulher *f* a dias

dainty /'deɪntɪ/ *a* (-ier, -iest) delicado; (*pretty, neat*) gracioso

dairy /'deərɪ/ *n* leiteria *f*. **~ products** laticínios *mpl*

daisy /'deɪzɪ/ *n* margarida *f*

dam /dæm/ *n* barragem *f*, represa *f* □ *vt* (*pt* **dammed**) represar

damag|e /'dæmɪdʒ/ *n* estrago(s) *mpl*. **~es** (*jur*) perdas *fpl* e danos *mpl* □ *vt* estragar, danificar; (*fig*) prejudicar. **~ing** *a* prejudicial

dame /deɪm/ *n* (*old use*) dama *f*; (*Amer sl*) mulher *f*

damn /dæm/ *vt* (*relig*) condenar aõ inferno; (*swear at*) amaldiçoar, maldizer; (*fig: condemn*) condenar □ *int* raios!, bolas! □ *n* **not care a ~** (*colloq*) estar pouco ligando (*colloq*), (*P*) estar-se marimbando (*colloq*) □ *a* (*colloq*) do diabo, danado □ *adv* (*colloq*) muitíssimo. **I'll be ~ed if** que um raio me atinja se. **~ation** /-'neɪʃn/ *n* danação *f*, condenação *f*. **~ing** *a* comprometedor, condenatório

damp /dæmp/ *n* umidade *f*, (*P*) humidade *f* □ *a* (-er, -est) úmido, (*P*) húmido □ *vt* umedecer, (*P*) humedecer. **~en** *vt* = **damp**. **~ness** *n* umidade *f*, (*P*) humidade *f*

dance /dɑ:ns/ *vt/i* dançar □ *n* dança *f*. **~ hall** sala *f* de baile. **~r** /-ə(r)/ *n* dançarino *m*; (*professional*) bailarino *m*

dandelion /'dændɪlaɪən/ *n* dente-de-leão *m*

dandruff /'dændrʌf/ *n* caspa *f*

Dane /deɪn/ *n* dinamarquês *m*

danger /'deɪndʒə(r)/ *n* perigo *m*. **be in ~ of** correr o risco de. **~ous** *a* perigoso

dangle /'dæŋgl/ *vi* oscilar, pender □ *vt* ter *or* trazer dependurado; (*hold*) balançar; (*fig: hopes, etc*) acenar com

Danish /'deɪnɪʃ/ *a* dinamarquês □ *n* (*lang*) dinamarquês *m*

dank /dæŋk/ *a* (-er, -est) frio e úmido, (*P*) húmido

dare /deə(r)/ *vt* **~ to do** ousar fazer. **~ sb to do** desafiar alg a fazer □ *n* desafio *m*. **I ~ say** creio

daredevil /'deədevl/ *n* louco *m*, temerário *m*

daring /'deərɪŋ/ *a* audacioso □ *n* audácia *f*

dark /dɑ:k/ *a* (-er, -est) escuro, sombrio; (*gloomy*) sombrio; (*of colour*) escuro; (*of skin*) moreno □ *n* escuridão *f*, escuro *m*; (*nightfall*) anoitecer *m*, cair *m* da noite. **~ horse** concorrente *mf* que é uma incógnita. **~-room** *n* câmara *f* escura. **be in the ~ about** (*fig*) ignorar. **~ness** *n* escuridão *f*

darken /'dɑ:kən/ *vt/i* escurecer

darling /'dɑ:lɪŋ/ *a* & *n* querido (*m*)

darn /dɑ:n/ *vt* serzir, remendar

dart /dɑ:t/ *n* dardo *m*, flecha *f*. **~s** (*game*) jogo *m* de dardos □ *vi* lançar-se

dartboard /'dɑ:tbɔ:d/ *n* alvo *m*

dash /dæʃ/ *vi* precipitar-se □ *vt* arremessar; (*hopes*) destruir □ *n* corrida *f*; (*stroke*) travessão *m*; (*Morse*) traço *m*. **a ~ of** um pouco de. **~ off** partir a toda a velocidade; (*letter*) escrever às pressas

dashboard /'dæʃbɔ:d/ *n* painel *m* de instrumentos, quadro *m* de bordo

data /'deɪtə/ *npl* dados *mpl*. **~ capture** aquisição *f* de informações, recolha *f* de dados. **~base** *n* base *f* de dados. **~ processing** processamento *m or* tratamento *m* de dados

date[1] /deɪt/ *n* data *f*; (*colloq*) encontro *m* marcado □ *vt/i* datar; (*colloq*) andar com. **out of ~** desatualizado, (*P*) desactualizado. **to ~** até a data. **up to ~** (*style*) moderno; (*information etc*) em dia. **~d** *a* antiquado

date[2] /deɪt/ *n* (*fruit*) tâmara *f*

daub /dɔ:b/ *vt* borrar, pintar toscamente

daughter /'dɔ:tə(r)/ *n* filha *f*. **~-in-law** *n* (*pl* **~s-in-law**) nora *f*

daunt /dɔ:nt/ *vt* assustar, intimidar, desencorajar

dawdle /'dɔ:dl/ *vi* perder tempo

dawn /dɔ:n/ *n* madrugada *f* □ *vi* madrugar, amanhecer. **~ on** (*fig*) fazer-se luz no espírito de, começar a perceber

day /deɪ/ *n* dia *m*; (*period*) época *f*, tempo *m*. **~-dream** *n* devaneio *m* □ *vi* devanear. **the ~ before** a véspera

daybreak /'deɪbreɪk/ *n* romper *m* do dia, aurora *f*, amanhecer *m*

daylight /ˈdeɪlaɪt/ *n* luz *f* do dia. ~ **robbery** roubar descaradamente
daytime /ˈdeɪtaɪm/ *n* dia *m*, dia *m* claro
daze /deɪz/ *vt* aturdir □ *n* **in a** ~ aturdido
dazzle /ˈdæzl/ *vt* deslumbrar; (*with headlights*) ofuscar
dead /ded/ *a* morto; (*numb*) dormente □ *adv* completamente, de todo □ *n* **in the** ~ **of the night** a horas mortas, na calada da noite. **the** ~ os mortos. **in the** ~ **centre** bem no meio. **stop** ~ estacar. ~ **beat** *a* (*colloq*) morto de cansaço. ~ **end** beco *m* sem saída. ~**-pan** *a* inexpressivo
deaden /ˈdedn/ *vt* (*sound, blow*) amortecer; (*pain*) aliviar
deadline /ˈdedlaɪn/ *n* prazo *m* final
deadlock /ˈdedlɒk/ *n* impasse *m*
deadly /ˈdedlɪ/ *a* (-ier, -iest) mortal; (*weapon*) mortífero
deaf /def/ *a* (-er, -est) surdo. **turn a** ~ **ear** fingir que não ouve. ~ **mute** surdo-mudo *m*. ~**ness** *n* surdez *f*
deafen /ˈdefn/ *vt* ensurdecer. ~**ing** *a* ensurdecedor
deal /di:l/ *vt* (*pt* **dealt**) distribuir; (*a blow, cards*) dar □ *vi* negociar □ *n* negócio *m*; (*cards*) vez de dar *f*. **a great** ~ muito (of de). ~ **in** negociar em. ~ **with** (*person*) tratar (com); (*affair*) tratar de. ~**er** *n* comerciante *m*; (*agent*) concessionário *m*; representante *m*
dealings /ˈdi:lɪŋz/ *npl* relações *fpl*; (*comm*) negócios *mpl*
dealt /delt/ *see* **deal**
dean /di:n/ *n* decano *m*
dear /dɪə(r)/ *a* (-er, -est) (*cherished*) caro, querido; (*expensive*) caro □ *n* amor *m* □ *adv* caro □ *int* **oh** ~! meu Deus! ~**ly** *adv* (*very much*) muito; (*pay*) caro
dearth /dɜ:θ/ *n* escassez *f*
death /deθ/ *n* morte *f*. ~ **certificate** certidão *f* de óbito. ~ **penalty** pena *f* de morte. ~ **rate** taxa *f* de mortalidade. ~**-trap** *n* lugar *m* perigoso, ratoeira *f*. ~**ly** *a* de morte, mortal
debase /dɪˈbeɪs/ *vt* degradar
debat|e /dɪˈbeɪt/ *n* debate *m* □ *vt* debater. ~**able** *a* discutível
debauchery /dɪˈbɔ:tʃərɪ/ *n* deboche *m*, devassidão *f*
debility /dɪˈbɪlətɪ/ *n* debilidade *f*
debit /ˈdebɪt/ *n* débito *m* □ *vt* (*pt* **debited**) debitar
debris /ˈdeɪbri:/ *n* destroços *mpl*
debt /det/ *n* dívida *f*. **in** ~ endividado. ~**or** *n* devedor *m*
debunk /di:ˈbʌŋk/ *vt* (*colloq*) desmitificar
début /ˈdeɪbju:/ *n* (*of actor, play etc*) estréia *f*
decade /ˈdekeɪd/ *n* década *f*
decaden|t /ˈdekədənt/ *a* decadente. ~**ce** *n* decadência *f*
decaffeinated /di:ˈkæfi:neɪtɪd/ *a* sem cafeína
decanter /dɪˈkæntə(r)/ *n* garrafa *f* para vinho, de vidro ou cristal
decapitate /dɪˈkæpɪteɪt/ *vt* decapitar
decay /dɪˈkeɪ/ *vi* apodrecer, estragar-se; (*food; fig*) deteriorar-se; (*building*) degradar-se □ *n* apodrecimento *m*; (*of tooth*) cárie *f*; (*fig*) declínio *m*, decadência *f*
deceased /dɪˈsi:st/ *a* & *n* falecido (*m*), defunto (*m*)
deceit /dɪˈsi:t/ *n* engano *m*. ~**ful** *a* enganador
deceive /dɪˈsi:v/ *vt* enganar, iludir
December /dɪˈsembə(r)/ *n* dezembro *m*
decen|t /ˈdi:snt/ *a* decente; (*colloq: good*) (bastante) bom; (*colloq: likeable*) simpático. ~**cy** *n* decência *f*
decentralize /di:ˈsentrəlaɪz/ *vt* descentralizar
decept|ive /dɪˈseptɪv/ *a* enganador, ilusório. ~**ion** /-ʃn/ *n* engano *m*
decibel /ˈdesɪbel/ *n* decibel *m*
decide /dɪˈsaɪd/ *vt/i* decidir. ~ **on** decidir-se por. ~ **to do** decidir fazer. ~**d** /-ɪd/ *a* decidido; (*clear*) definido, nítido. ~**dly** /-ɪdlɪ/ *adv* decididamente
decimal /ˈdesɪml/ *a* decimal □ *n* (fração *f*, (*P*) fracção *f*) decimal *m*. ~ **point** vírgula *f* decimal
decipher /dɪˈsaɪfə(r)/ *vt* decifrar
decision /dɪˈsɪʒn/ *n* decisão *f*
decisive /dɪˈsaɪsɪv/ *a* decisivo; (*manner*) decidido. ~**ly** *adv* decisivamente
deck /dek/ *n* convés *m*; (*of cards*) baralho *m*. ~**-chair** *n* espreguiçadeira *f*
declar|e /dɪˈkleə(r)/ *vt* declarar. ~**ation** /dekləˈreɪʃn/ *n* declaração *f*
decline /dɪˈklaɪn/ *vt* (*refuse*) declinar, recusar delicadamente; (*gram*) declinar □ *vi* (*deteriorate*) declinar; (*fall*) baixar □ *n* declínio *m*; (*fall*) abaixamento *m*
decode /di:ˈkəʊd/ *vt* descodificar
decompos|e /di:kəmˈpəʊz/ *vt/i* decompor(-se). ~**ition** /-ɒmpəˈzɪʃn/ *n* decomposição *f*
décor /ˈdeɪkɔ:(r)/ *n* decoração *f*
decorat|e /ˈdekəreɪt/ *vt* decorar, enfeitar; (*paint*) pintar; (*paper*) pôr papel em. ~**ion** /-ˈreɪʃn/ *n* decoração *f*; (*medal etc*) condecoração *f*. ~**ive** /-ətɪv/ *a* decorativo
decorum /dɪˈkɔ:rəm/ *n* decoro *m*
decoy[1] /ˈdi:kɔɪ/ *n* chamariz *m*, engodo *m*; (*trap*) armadilha *f*

decoy[2] /dɪ'kɔɪ/ *vt* atrair, apanhar
decrease[1] /di:'kri:s/ *vt/i* diminuir
decrease[2] /'di:kri:s/ *n* diminuição *f*
decree /dɪ'kri:/ *n* decreto *m*; (*jur*) decisão *f* judicial □ *vt* decretar
decrepit /dɪ'krepɪt/ *a* decrépito
dedicat|e /'dedɪkeɪt/ *vt* dedicar. **~ed** *a* dedicado. **~ion** /-'keɪʃn/ *n* dedicação *f*; (*in book*) dedicatória *f*
deduce /dɪ'dju:s/ *vt* deduzir
deduct /dɪ'dʌkt/ *vt* deduzir; (*from pay*) descontar
deduction /dɪ'dʌkʃn/ *n* dedução *f*; (*from pay*) desconto *m*
deed /di:d/ *n* ato *m*; (*jur*) contrato *m*
deem /di:m/ *vt* julgar, considerar
deep /di:p/ *a* (-er, -est) profundo □ *adv* profundamente. **~-freeze** *n* congelador *m* □ *vt* congelar. **take a ~ breath** respirar fundo. **~ly** *adv* profundamente
deepen /'di:pən/ *vt/i* aprofundar(-se); (*mystery, night*) adensar-se
deer /dɪə(r)/ *n* (*pl invar*) veado *m*
deface /dɪ'feɪs/ *vt* danificar, degradar
defamation /defə'meɪʃn/ *n* difamação *f*
default /dɪ'fɔ:lt/ *vi* faltar □ *n* **by ~** à revelia. **win by ~** (*sport*) ganhar por não comparecimento, (*P*) comparência □ *a* (*comput*) default *m*
defeat /dɪ'fi:t/ *vt* derrotar; (*thwart*) malograr □ *n* derrota *f*; (*of plan, etc*) malogro *m*
defect[1] /'di:fekt/ *n* defeito *m*. **~ive** /dɪ'fektɪv/ *a* defeituoso
defect[2] /dɪ'fekt/ *vi* desertar. **~ion** *n* defecção *m*. **~or** *n* trânsfuga *mf*, dissidente *mf*; (*political*) asilado *m* político
defence /dɪ'fens/ *n* defesa *f*. **~less** *a* indefeso
defend /dɪ'fend/ *vt* defender. **~ant** *n* (*jur*) réu *m*, acusado *m*. **~er** *n* advogado *m* de defesa, defensor *m*
defensive /dɪ'fensɪv/ *a* defensivo □ *n* **on the ~** na defensiva *f*; (*person, sport*) na retranca *f* (*colloq*)
defer /dɪ'fɜ:(r)/ *vt* (*pt* **deferred**) adiar, diferir □ *vi* **~ to** ceder, deferir
deferen|ce /'defərəns/ *n* deferência *f*. **~tial** /-'renʃl/ *a* deferente
defian|ce /dɪ'faɪəns/ *n* desafio *m*. **in ~ of** sem respeito por. **~t** *a* de desafio. **~tly** *adv* com ar de desafio
deficien|t /dɪ'fɪʃnt/ *a* deficiente. **be ~t in** ter falta de. **~cy** *n* deficiência *f*
deficit /'defɪsɪt/ *n* déficit *m*
define /dɪ'faɪn/ *vt* definir
definite /'defɪnɪt/ *a* definido; (*clear*) categórico, claro; (*certain*) certo. **~ly** *adv* decididamente; (*clearly*) claramente
definition /defɪ'nɪʃn/ *n* definição *f*
definitive /dɪ'fɪnətɪv/ *a* definitivo
deflat|e /dɪ'fleɪt/ *vt* esvaziar; (*person*) desemproar, desinchar. **~ion** /-ʃn/ *n* esvaziamento *m*; (*econ*) deflação *f*
deflect /dɪ'flekt/ *vt/i* desviar(-se)
deform /dɪ'fɔ:m/ *vt* deformar. **~ed** *a* deformado, disforme. **~ity** *n* deformidade *f*
defraud /dɪ'frɔ:d/ *vt* defraudar
defrost /di:'frɒst/ *vt* descongelar
deft /deft/ *a* (-er, -est) hábil
defunct /dɪ'fʌŋkt/ *a* (*law etc*) caduco, extinto
defuse /di:'fju:z/ *vt* (*a bomb*) desativar, (*P*) desactivar; (*a situation*) acalmar
defy /dɪ'faɪ/ *vt* desafiar; (*attempts*) resistir a; (*the law*) desobedecer a; (*public opinion*) opor-se a
degenerate /dɪ'dʒenəreɪt/ *vi* degenerar (into em)
degrad|e /dɪ'greɪd/ *vt* degradar. **~ation** /degrə'deɪʃn/ *n* degradação *f*
degree /dɪ'gri:/ *n* grau *m*; (*univ*) diploma *m*. **to a ~** ao mais alto grau, muito
dehydrate /di:'haɪdreɪt/ *vt/i* desidratar(-se)
de-ice /di:'aɪs/ *vt* descongelar, degelar; (*windscreen*) tirar o gelo de
deign /deɪn/ *vt* **~ to do** dignar-se (a) fazer
deity /'di:ɪtɪ/ *n* divindade *f*
dejected /dɪ'dʒektɪd/ *a* abatido
delay /dɪ'leɪ/ *vt* atrasar; (*postpone*) retardar □ *vi* atrasar-se □ *n* atraso *m*, demora *f*
delegate[1] /'delɪgət/ *n* delegado *m*
delegat|e[2] /'delɪgeɪt/ *vt* delegar. **~ion** /-'geɪʃn/ *n* delegação *f*
delet|e /dɪ'li:t/ *vt* riscar. **~ion** /-ʃn/ *n* rasura *f*
deliberate[1] /dɪ'lɪbərət/ *a* deliberado; (*steps etc*) compassado. **~ly** *adv* deliberadamente, de propósito
deliberat|e[2] /dɪ'lɪbəreɪt/ *vt/i* deliberar. **~ion** /-'reɪʃn/ *n* deliberação *f*
delica|te /'delɪkət/ *a* delicado. **~cy** *n* delicadeza *f*; (*food*) guloseima *f*, iguaria *f*, (*P*) acepipe *m*
delicatessen /delɪkə'tesn/ *n* (*shop*) mercearias *fpl* finas
delicious /dɪ'lɪʃəs/ *a* delicioso
delight /dɪ'laɪt/ *n* grande prazer *m*, delícia *f*; (*thing*) delícia *f*, encanto *m* □ *vt* deliciar □ *vi* **~ in** deliciar-se com. **~ed** *a* deliciado, encantado. **~ful** *a* delicioso, encantador
delinquen|t /dɪ'lɪŋkwənt/ *a & n* delinqüente *mf*, (*P*) delinquente *mf*. **~cy** *n* delinqüência *f*, (*P*) delinquência *f*
deliri|ous /dɪ'lɪrɪəs/ *a* delirante. **be ~ous** delirar. **~um** /-əm/ *n* delírio *m*
deliver /dɪ'lɪvə(r)/ *vt* entregar;

(*letters*) distribuir; (*free*) libertar; (*med*) fazer o parto. **~ance** *n* libertação *f*. **~y** *n* entrega *f*; (*letters*) distribuição *f*; (*med*) parto *m*

delu|de /dɪ'lu:d/ *vt* enganar. **~de o.s.** ter ilusões. **~sion** /-ʒn/ *n* ilusão *f*

deluge /'delju:dʒ/ *n* dilúvio *m* □ *vt* inundar

de luxe /dɪ'lʌks/ *a* de luxo

delve /delv/ *vi* **~ into** pesquisar, rebuscar

demand /dɪ'ma:nd/ *vt* exigir; (*ask to be told*) perguntar □ *n* exigência *f*; (*comm*) procura *f*; (*claim*) reivindicação *f*. **in ~** procurado. **~ing** *a* exigente; (*work*) puxado, custoso

demean /dɪ'mi:n/ *vt* **~ o.s.** rebaixar-se

demeanour /dɪ'mi:nə(r)/ *n* comportamento *m*, conduta *f*

demented /dɪ'mentɪd/ *a* louco, demente. **become ~** enlouquecer

demo /'deməʊ/ *n* (*pl* -os) (*colloq*) manifestação *f*, (*P*) manif *f*

democracy /dɪ'mɒkrəsɪ/ *n* democracia *f*

democrat /'deməkræt/ *n* democrata *mf*. **~ic** /'krætɪk/ *a* democrático

demoli|sh /dɪ'mɒlɪʃ/ *vt* demolir. **~tion** /demə'lɪʃn/ *n* demolição *f*

demon /'di:mən/ *n* demônio *m*

demonstrat|e /'demənstreɪt/ *vt* demonstrar □ *vi* (*pol*) fazer uma manifestação, manifestar-se. **~ion** /-'streɪʃn/ *n* demonstração *f*; (*pol*) manifestação *f*. **~or** *n* (*pol*) manifestante *mf*

demonstrative /dɪ'mɒnstrətɪv/ *a* demonstrativo

demoralize /dɪ'mɒrəlaɪz/ *vt* desmoralizar

demote /dɪ'məʊt/ *vt* fazer baixar de posto, rebaixar

demure /dɪ'mjʊə(r)/ *a* recatado, modesto

den /den/ *n* antro *m*, covil *m*; (*room*) cantinho *m*, recanto *m*

denial /dɪ'naɪəl/ *n* negação *f*; (*refusal*) recusa *f*; (*statement*) desmentido *m*

denigrate /'denɪgreɪt/ *vt* denegrir

denim /'denɪm/ *n* brim *m*. **~s** (*jeans*) blue-jeans *mpl*

Denmark /'denma:k/ *n* Dinamarca *f*

denomination /dɪnɒmɪ'neɪʃn/ *n* denominação *f*; (*relig*) confissão *f*, seita *f*; (*money*) valor *m*

denote /dɪ'nəʊt/ *vt* denotar

denounce /dɪ'naʊns/ *vt* denunciar

dens|e /dens/ *a* (-er, -est) denso; (*colloq: person*) obtuso. **~ely** *adv* (*packed etc*) muito. **~ity** *n* densidade *f*

dent /dent/ *n* mossa *f*, depressão *f* □ *vt* dentear

dental /'dentl/ *a* dentário, dental

dentist /'dentɪst/ *n* dentista *mf*. **~ry** *n* odontologia *f*

denture /'dentʃə(r)/ *n* dentadura *f* (postiça)

denunciation /dɪnʌnsɪ'eɪʃn/ *n* denúncia *f*

deny /dɪ'naɪ/ *vt* negar; (*rumour*) desmentir; (*disown*) renegar; (*refuse*) recusar

deodorant /di:'əʊdərənt/ *n* & *a* desodorante (*m*), (*P*) desodorizante (*m*)

depart /dɪ'pa:t/ *vi* partir. **~ from** (*deviate*) afastar-se de, desviar-se de

department /dɪ'pa:tmənt/ *n* departamento *m*; (*in shop, office*) seção *f*, (*P*) secção *f*; (*government*) repartição *f*. **~ store** loja *f* de departamentos, (*P*) grande armazém *m*

departure /dɪ'pa:tʃə(r)/ *n* partida *f*. **a ~ from** (*custom, diet etc*) uma mudança de. **a new ~** uma nova orientação

depend /dɪ'pend/ *vi* **~ on** depender de; (*trust*) contar com. **~able** *a* de confiança. **~ence** *n* dependência *f*. **~ent (on)** *a* dependente (de)

dependant /dɪ'pendənt/ *n* dependente *mf*

depict /dɪ'pɪkt/ *vt* descrever; (*in pictures*) representar

deplete /dɪ'pli:t/ *vt* reduzir; (*use up*) esgotar

deplor|e /dɪ'plɔ:(r)/ *vt* deplorar. **~able** *a* deplorável

deport /dɪ'pɔ:t/ *vt* deportar. **~ation** /di:pɔ:'teɪʃn/ *n* deportação *f*

depose /dɪ'pəʊz/ *vt* depor

deposit /dɪ'pɒzɪt/ *vt* (*pt* **deposited**) depositar □ *n* depósito *m*. **~ account** conta *f* de depósito a prazo. **~or** *n* depositante *mf*

depot /'depəʊ/ *n* (*mil*) depósito *m*; (*buses*) garagem *f*; (*Amer: station*) rodoviária *f*, estação *f* de trem, (*P*) de comboio

deprav|e /dɪ'preɪv/ *vt* depravar. **~ity** /-'prævətɪ/ *n* depravação *f*

depreciat|e /dɪ'pri:ʃɪeɪt/ *vt/i* depreciar(-se). **~ion** /'eɪʃn/ *n* depreciação *f*

depress /dɪ'pres/ *vt* deprimir; (*press down*) carregar em. **~ion** /-ʃn/ *n* depressão *f*

deprivation /deprɪ'veɪʃn/ *n* privação *f*

deprive /dɪ'praɪv/ *vt* **~ of** privar de. **~d** *a* privado; (*underprivileged*) deserdado (da sorte), destituído; (*child*) carente

depth /depθ/ *n* profundidade *f*. **be out of one's ~** perder pé, (*P*) não ter pé; (*fig*) ficar desnorteado, estar perdido. **in the ~(s) of** no mais fundo de, nas profundezas de

deputation /depjʊ'teɪʃn/ *n* delegação *f*

deputy /'depjʊtɪ/ *n* (*pl* -ies) delegado *m* □ *a* adjunto. ~ **chairman** vice-presidente *m*

derail /dɪ'reɪl/ *vt* descarrilhar. **be** ~**ed** descarrilhar. ~**ment** *n* descarrilhamento *m*

deranged /dɪ'reɪndʒd/ *a* (*mind*) transtornado, louco

derelict /'derəlɪkt/ *a* abandonado

deri|de /dɪ'raɪd/ *vt* escarnecer de. ~**sion** /-'rɪʒn/ *n* escárnio *m*. ~**sive** *a* escarninho. ~**sory** *a* escarninho; (*offer etc*) irrisório

derivative /dɪ'rɪvətɪv/ *a* derivado; (*work*) pouco original □ *n* derivado *m*

deriv|e /dɪ'raɪv/ *vt* ~**e from** tirar de □ *vi* ~**e from** derivar de. ~**ation** /derɪ'veɪʃn/ *n* derivação *f*

derogatory /dɪ'rɒgətrɪ/ *a* pejorativo; (*remark*) depreciativo

derv /dɜ:v/ *n* gasóleo *m*

descend /dɪ'send/ *vt/i* descer, descender. **be** ~**ed from** descender de. ~**ant** *n* descendente *mf*

descent /dɪ'sent/ *n* descida *f*; (*lineage*) descendência *f*, origem *f*

descri|be /dɪs'kraɪb/ *vt* descrever. ~**ption** /-'krɪpʃn/ *n* descrição *f*; ~**ptive** /-'krɪptɪv/ *a* descritivo

desecrat|e /'desɪkreɪt/ *vt* profanar. ~**ion** /-'kreɪʃn/ *n* profanação *f*

desert[1] /'dezət/ *a* & *n* deserto (*m*). ~ **island** ilha *f* deserta

desert[2] /dɪ'zɜ:t/ *vt/i* desertar. ~**ed** *a* abandonado. ~**er** *n* desertor *m*. ~**ion** /-ʃn/ *n* deserção *f*

deserv|e /dɪ'zɜ:v/ *vt* merecer. ~**edly** /dɪ'zɜ:vɪdlɪ/ *adv* merecidamente, a justo título. ~**ing** *a* (*person*) merecedor; (*action*) meritório

design /dɪ'zaɪn/ *n* desenho *m*; (*artistic*) design *m*; (*style of dress*) modelo *m*; (*pattern*) padrão *m*, motivo *m* □ *vt* desenhar; (*devise*) conceber. ~**er** *n* desenhador *m*; (*of dresses*) costureiro *m*; (*of machine*) inventor *m*

designat|e /'dezɪgneɪt/ *vt* designar. ~**ion** /'-neɪʃn/ *n* designação *f*

desir|e /dɪ'zaɪə(r)/ *n* desejo *m* □ *vt* desejar. ~**able** *a* desejável, atraente

desk /desk/ *n* secretária *f*; (*of pupil*) carteira *f*; (*in hotel*) recepção *f*; (*in bank*) caixa *f*

desolat|e /'desələt/ *a* desolado. ~**ion** /-'leɪʃn/ *n* desolação *f*

despair /dɪ'speə(r)/ *n* desespero *m* □ *vi* desesperar (of de)

desperate /'despərət/ *a* desesperado; (*criminal*) capaz de tudo. **be** ~ **for** ter uma vontade doida de. ~**ly** *adv* desesperadamente

desperation /despə'reɪʃn/ *n* desespero *m*

despicable /dɪ'spɪkəbl/ *a* desprezível

despise /dɪ'spaɪz/ *vt* desprezar

despite /dɪ'spaɪt/ *prep* apesar de, a despeito de, mau grado

desponden|t /dɪ'spɒndənt/ *a* desanimado. ~**cy** *n* desânimo *m*

despot /'despɒt/ *n* déspota *mf*

dessert /dɪ'zɜ:t/ *n* sobremesa *f*. ~-**spoon** *n* colher *f* de sobremesa

destination /destɪ'neɪʃn/ *n* destino *m*, destinação *f*

destine /'destɪn/ *vt* destinar

destiny /'destɪnɪ/ *n* destino *m*

destitute /'destɪtju:t/ *a* destituído, indigente

destr|oy /dɪ'strɔɪ/ *vt* destruir. ~**uction** /-'strʌkʃn/ *n* destruição *f*. ~**uctive** *a* destrutivo, destruidor

detach /dɪ'tætʃ/ *vt* separar, arrancar. ~**able** *a* separável; (*lining etc*) solto. ~**ed** *a* separado; (*impartial*) imparcial; (*unemotional*) desprendido. ~**ed house** casa *f* sem parede-meia com outra

detachment /dɪ'tætʃmənt/ *n* separação *f*; (*indifference*) desprendimento *m*; (*mil*) destacamento *m*; (*impartiality*) imparcialidade *f*

detail /'di:teɪl/ *n* pormenor *m*, detalhe *m* □ *vt* detalhar; (*troops*) destacar. ~**ed** *a* detalhado

detain /dɪ'teɪn/ *vt* reter; (*in prison*) deter. ~**ee** /di:teɪ'ni:/ *n* detido *m*

detect /dɪ'tekt/ *vt* detectar. ~**ion** /-ʃn/ *n* detecção *f*. ~**or** *n* detector *m*

detective /dɪ'tektɪv/ *n* detective *m*. ~ **story** romance *m* policial

detention /dɪ'tenʃn/ *n* detenção *f*. **be given a** ~ (*school*) ficar de castigo na escola

deter /dɪ'tɜ:(r)/ *vt* (*pt* **deterred**) dissuadir; (*hinder*) impedir

detergent /dɪ'tɜ:dʒənt/ *a* & *n* detergente (*m*)

deteriorat|e /dɪ'tɪərɪəreɪt/ *vi* deteriorar(-se). ~**ion** /-'reɪʃn/ *n* deterioração *f*

determin|e /dɪ'tɜ:mɪn/ *vt* determinar. ~**e to do** decidir fazer. ~**ation** /-'neɪʃn/ *n* determinação *f*. ~**ed** *a* determinado. ~**ed to do** decidido a fazer

deterrent /dɪ'terənt/ *n* dissuasivo *m*

detest /dɪ'test/ *vt* detestar. ~**able** *a* detestável

detonat|e /'detəneɪt/ *vt/i* detonar. ~**ion** /-'neɪʃn/ *n* detonação *f*. ~**or** *n* espoleta *f*, detonador *m*

detour /'di:tʊə(r)/ *n* desvio *m*

detract /dɪ'trækt/ *vi* ~ **from** depreciar, menosprezar

detriment /'detrɪmənt/ *n* detrimento *m*. ~**al** /-'mentl/ *a* prejudicial

devalu|e /di:ˈvælju:/ *vt* desvalorizar. **~ation** /-ˈeɪʃn/ *n* desvalorização *f*
devastat|e /ˈdevəsteɪt/ *vi* devastar; (*fig: overwhelm*) arrasar. **~ing** *a* devastador; (*criticism*) de arrasar
develop /dɪˈveləp/ *vt/i* (*pt* **developed**) desenvolver(-se); (*get*) contrair; (*build on*) urbanizar; (*film*) revelar. **~ into** tornar-se. **~ing country** país *m* subdesenvolvido. **~ment** *n* desenvolvimento *m*; (*film*) revelação *f*; (*of land*) urbanização *f*
deviat|e /ˈdi:vɪeɪt/ *vi* desviar-se. **~ion** /-ˈeɪʃn/ *n* desvio *m*
device /dɪˈvaɪs/ *n* dispositivo *m*; (*scheme*) processo *m*. **left to one's own ~s** entregue a si mesmo
devil /ˈdevl/ *n* diabo *m*
devious /ˈdi:vɪəs/ *a* tortuoso; (*fig: means*) escuso; (*fig: person*) pouco franco
devise /dɪˈvaɪz/ *vt* imaginar, inventar
devoid /dɪˈvɔɪd/ *a* **~ of** desprovido de, destituído de
devot|e /dɪˈvəʊt/ *vt* dedicar, devotar. **~ed** *a* dedicado, devotado. **~ion** /-ʃn/ *n* devoção *f*
devotee /devəˈti:/ *n* **~ of** adepto *m* de, entusiasta *mf* de
devour /dɪˈvaʊə(r)/ *vt* devorar
devout /dɪˈvaʊt/ *a* devota; (*prayer*) fervoroso
dew /dju:/ *n* orvalho *m*
dext|erity /dekˈsterətɪ/ *n* destreza *f*, jeito *m*. **~rous** /ˈdekstrəs/ *a* destro, hábil
diabet|es /daɪəˈbi:tiz/ *n* diabetes *f*. **~ic** /-ˈbetɪk/ *a* & *n* diabético (*m*)
diabolical /daɪəˈbɒlɪkl/ *a* diabólico
diagnose /ˈdaɪəgnəʊz/ *vt* diagnosticar
diagnosis /daɪəgˈnəʊsɪs/ *n* (*pl* **-oses** /-si:z/) diagnóstico *m*
diagonal /daɪˈægənl/ *a* & *n* diagonal (*f*)
diagram /ˈdaɪəgræm/ *n* diagrama *m*, esquema *m*
dial /ˈdaɪəl/ *n* mostrador *m* □ *vt* (*pt* **dialled**) (*number*) marcar, discar. **~ling code** código *m* de discagem. **~ling tone** sinal *m* de discar
dialect /ˈdaɪəlekt/ *n* dialeto *m*, (*P*) dialecto *m*
dialogue /ˈdaɪəlɒg/ *n* diálogo *m*
diameter /daɪˈæmɪtə(r)/ *n* diâmetro *m*
diamond /ˈdaɪəmənd/ *n* diamante *m*, brilhante *m*; (*shape*) losango *m*. **~s** (*cards*) ouros *mpl*
diaper /ˈdaɪəpə(r)/ *n* (*Amer*) fralda *f*
diaphragm /ˈdaɪəfræm/ *n* diafragma *m*
diarrhoea /daɪəˈrɪə/ *n* diarréia *f*, (*P*) diarreia *f*
diary /ˈdaɪərɪ/ *n* agenda *f*; (*record*) diário *m*
dice /daɪs/ *n* (*pl invar*) dado *m*
dictat|e /dɪkˈteɪt/ *vt/i* ditar. **~ion** /-ʃn/ *n* ditado *m*
dictator /dɪkˈteɪtə(r)/ *n* ditador *m*. **~ship** *n* ditadura *f*
diction /ˈdɪkʃn/ *n* dicção *f*
dictionary /ˈdɪkʃənrɪ/ *n* dicionário *m*
did /dɪd/ *see* **do**
diddle /ˈdɪdl/ *vt* (*colloq*) trapacear, enganar
didn't /ˈdɪdnt/ = **did not**
die /daɪ/ *vi* (*pres p* **dying**) morrer. **be dying to** estar doido para. **~ down** diminuir, baixar. **~ out** desaparecer, extinguir-se
diesel /ˈdi:zl/ *n* diesel *m*. **~ engine** motor *m* diesel
diet /ˈdaɪət/ *n* dieta *f* □ *vi* fazer dieta, estar de dieta
differ /ˈdɪfə(r)/ *vi* diferir; (*disagree*) discordar
differen|t /ˈdɪfrənt/ *a* diferente. **~ce** *n* diferença *f*; (*disagreement*) desacordo *m*. **~ly** *adv* diferentemente
differentiate /dɪfəˈrenʃɪeɪt/ *vt/i* diferençar(-se), diferenciar(-se)
difficult /ˈdɪfɪkəlt/ *a* difícil. **~y** *n* dificuldade *f*
diffiden|t /ˈdɪfɪdənt/ *a* acanhado, inseguro. **~ce** *n* acanhamento *m*, insegurança *f*
diffuse[1] /dɪˈfju:s/ *a* difuso
diffus|e[2] /dɪˈfju:z/ *vt* difundir. **~ion** /-ʒn/ *n* difusão *f*
dig /dɪg/ *vt/i* (*pt* **dug**, *pres p* **digging**) cavar; (*thrust*) espetar □ *n* (*with elbow*) cotovelada *f*; (*with finger*) cutucada *f*, (*P*) espetadela *f*; (*remark*) ferroada *f*; (*archaeol*) excavação *f*. **~s** (*colloq*) quarto *m* alugado. **~ up** desenterrar
digest /dɪˈdʒest/ *vt/i* digerir. **~ible** *a* digerível, digestível. **~ion** /-ʃn/ *n* digestão *f*
digestive /dɪˈdʒestɪv/ *a* digestivo
digit /ˈdɪdʒɪt/ *n* dígito *m*
digital /ˈdɪdʒɪtl/ *a* digital. **~ clock** relógio *m* digital
dignif|y /ˈdɪgnɪfaɪ/ *vt* dignificar. **~ied** *a* digno
dignitary /ˈdɪgnɪtərɪ/ *n* dignitário *m*
dignity /ˈdɪgnətɪ/ *n* dignidade *f*
digress /daɪˈgres/ *vi* digressar, divagar. **~ from** desviar-se de. **~ion** /-ʃn/ *n* digressão *f*
dike /daɪk/ *n* dique *m*
dilapidated /dɪˈlæpɪdeɪtɪd/ *a* (*house*) arruinado, degradado; (*car*) estragado
dilat|e /daɪˈleɪt/ *vt/i* dilatar(-se). **~ion** /-ʃn/ *n* dilatação *f*
dilemma /dɪˈlemə/ *n* dilema *m*
diligen|t /ˈdɪlɪdʒənt/ *a* diligente, aplicado. **~ce** *n* diligência *f*, aplicação *f*

dilute /daɪ'lju:t/ *vt* diluir □ *a* diluído
dim /dɪm/ *a* (**dimmer**, **dimmest**) (*weak*) fraco; (*dark*) sombrio; (*indistinct*) vago; (*colloq: stupid*) burro (*colloq*) □ *vt/i* (*pt* **dimmed**) (*light*) baixar. **~ly** *adv* (*shine*) fracamente; (*remember*) vagamente
dime /daɪm/ *n* (*Amer*) moeda *f* de dez centavos
dimension /daɪ'menʃn/ *n* dimensão *f*
diminish /dɪ'mɪnɪʃ/ *vt/i* diminuir
diminutive /dɪ'mɪnjʊtɪv/ *a* diminuto □ *n* diminutivo *m*
dimple /'dɪmpl/ *n* covinha *f*
din /dɪn/ *n* barulheira *f*, (*P*) chinfrim *m*
dine /daɪn/ *vi* jantar. **~r** /-ə(r)/ *n* (*person*) comensal *m*; (*rail*) vagão-restaurante *m*; (*Amer: restaurant*) lanchonete *f*
dinghy /'dɪŋgɪ/ *n* (*pl* **-ghies**) bote *m*; (*inflatable*) bote *m* de borracha, (*P*) barco *m* de borracha
dingy /'dɪndʒɪ/ *a* (**-ier**, **-iest**) com ar sujo, esquálido
dining-room /'daɪnɪŋru:m/ *n* sala *f* de jantar
dinner /'dɪnə(r)/ *n* jantar *m*; (*lunch*) almoço *m*. **~-jacket** *n* smoking *m*
dinosaur /'daɪnəsɔ:(r)/ *n* dinossauro *m*
dip /dɪp/ *vt/i* (*pt* **dipped**) mergulhar; (*lower*) baixar □ *n* mergulho *m*; (*bathe*) banho *m* rápido, mergulho *m*; (*slope*) descida *f*; (*culin*) molho *m*. **~ into** (*book*) folhear. **~ one's headlights** baixar para médios
diphtheria /dɪf'θɪərɪə/ *n* difteria *f*
diphthong /'dɪfθɒŋ/ *n* ditongo *m*
diploma /dɪ'pləʊmə/ *n* diploma *m*
diplomacy /dɪ'pləʊməsɪ/ *n* diplomacia *f*
diplomat /'dɪpləmæt/ *n* diplomata *mf*. **~ic** /-'mætɪk/ *a* diplomático
dire /daɪə(r)/ *a* (**-er**, **-est**) terrível; (*need, poverty*) extremo
direct /dɪ'rekt/ *a* direto, (*P*) directo □ *adv* diretamente, (*P*) directamente □ *vt* dirigir. **~ sb to** indicar a alg o caminho para
direction /dɪ'rekʃn/ *n* direção *f*, (*P*) direcção *f*, sentido *m*. **~s** instruções *fpl*. **~s for use** modo *m* de emprego
directly /dɪ'rektlɪ/ *adv* diretamente, (*P*) directamente; (*at once*) imediatamente, logo
director /dɪ'rektə(r)/ *n* diretor *m*, (*P*) director *m*
directory /dɪ'rektərɪ/ *n* (**telephone**) **~** lista *f* telefônica, (*P*) telefónica
dirt /dɜ:t/ *n* sujeira *f*. **~ cheap** (*colloq*) baratíssimo
dirty /'dɜ:tɪ/ *a* (**-ier**, **-iest**) sujo; (*word*) obsceno □ *vt/i* sujar(-se). **~ trick** golpe *m* baixo, (*P*) boa partida *f*

disability /dɪsə'bɪlətɪ/ *n* deficiência *f*
disable /dɪs'eɪbl/ *vt* incapacitar. **~d** *a* inválido, deficiente
disadvantage /dɪsəd'va:ntɪdʒ/ *n* desvantagem *f*
disagree /dɪsə'gri:/ *vi* discordar (**with** de). **~ with** (*food, climate*) não fazer bem. **~ment** *n* desacordo *m*; (*quarrel*) desintendimento *m*
disagreeable /dɪsə'gri:əbl/ *a* desagradável
disappear /dɪsə'pɪə(r)/ *vi* desaparecer. **~ance** *n* desaparecimento *m*
disappoint /dɪsə'pɔɪnt/ *vt* desapontar, decepcionar. **~ment** *n* desapontamento *m*, decepção *f*
disapprov|e /dɪsə'pru:v/ *vi* **~e** (**of**) desaprovar. **~al** *n* desaprovação *f*
disarm /dɪ'sa:m/ *vt/i* desarmar. **~ament** *n* desarmamento *m*
disast|er /dɪ'za:stə(r)/ *n* desastre *m*. **~rous** *a* desastroso
disband /dɪs'bænd/ *vt/i* debandar; (*troops*) dispersar
disbelief /dɪsbɪ'li:f/ *n* incredulidade *f*
disc /dɪsk/ *n* disco *m*. **~ jockey** disc(o) jockey *m*
discard /dɪs'ka:d/ *vt* pôr de lado, descartar(-se) de; (*old clothes etc*) desfazer-se de
discern /dɪ'sɜ:n/ *vt* discernir. **~ible** *a* perceptível. **~ing** *a* perspicaz. **~ment** *n* discernimento *m*, perspicácia *f*
discharge[1] /dɪs'tʃa:dʒ/ *vt* descarregar; (*dismiss*) despedir, mandar embora; (*duty*) cumprir; (*liquid*) vazar, (*P*) deitar; (*patient*) dar alta a; (*prisoner*) absolver, pôr em liberdade; (*pus*) purgar, (*P*) deitar
discharge[2] /'dɪstʃa:dʒ/ *n* descarga *f*; (*dismissal*) despedimento *m*; (*of patient*) alta *f*; (*of prisoner*) absolvição *f*; (*med*) secreção *f*
disciple /dɪ'saɪpl/ *n* discípulo *m*
disciplin|e /'dɪsɪplɪn/ *n* disciplina *f* □ *vt* disciplinar; (*punish*) castigar. **~ary** *a* disciplinar
disclaim /dɪs'kleɪm/ *vt* (*jur*) repudiar; (*deny*) negar. **~er** *n* desmentido *m*
disclos|e /dɪs'kləʊz/ *vt* revelar. **~ure** /-ʒə(r)/ *n* revelação *f*
disco /'dɪskəʊ/ *n* (*pl* **-os**) (*colloq*) discoteca *f*
discolour /dɪs'kʌlə(r)/ *vt/i* descolorir(-se); (*in sunlight*) desbotar(-se)
discomfort /dɪs'kʌmfət/ *n* malestar *m*; (*lack of comfort*) desconforto *m*
disconcert /dɪskən'sɜ:t/ *vt* desconcertar. **~ing** *a* desconcertante
disconnect /dɪskə'nekt/ *vt* desligar
discontent /dɪskən'tent/ *n* descontentamento *m*. **~ed** *a* descontente

discontinue /dɪskən'tɪnju:/ *vt* descontinuar, suspender
discord /'dɪskɔ:d/ *n* discórdia *f*. **~ant** /-'skɔ:dənt/ *a* discordante
discothèque /'dɪskətek/ *n* discoteca *f*
discount[1] /'dɪskaʊnt/ *n* desconto *m*
discount[2] /dɪs'kaʊnt/ *vt* descontar; (*disregard*) dar o desconto a
discourage /dɪs'kʌrɪdʒ/ *vt* desencorajar
discourte|ous /dɪs'kɜ:tɪəs/ *a* indelicado. **~sy** /-sɪ/ *n* indelicadeza *f*
discover /dɪs'kʌvə(r)/ *vt* descobrir. **~y** *n* descoberta *f*; (*of island etc*) descobrimento *m*
discredit /dɪs'kredɪt/ *vt* (*pt* **discredited**) desacreditar □ *n* descrédito *m*
discreet /dɪ'skri:t/ *a* discreto
discrepancy /dɪ'skrepənsɪ/ *n* discrepância *f*
discretion /dɪ'skreʃn/ *n* discrição *f*; (*prudence*) prudência *f*
discriminat|e /dɪs'krɪmɪneɪt/ *vt/i* discriminar. **~e against** tomar partido contra, fazer discriminação contra. **~ing** *a* discriminador; (*having good taste*) com discernimento. **~ion** /-'neɪʃn/ *n* discernimento *m*; (*bias*) discriminação *f*
discus /'dɪskəs/ *n* disco *m*
discuss /dɪ'skʌs/ *vt* discutir. **~ion** /-ʃn/ *n* discussão *f*
disdain /dɪs'deɪn/ *n* desdém *m* □ *vt* desdenhar. **~ful** *a* desdenhoso
disease /dɪ'zi:z/ *n* doença *f*. **~d** *a* (*plant*) atacado por doença; (*person, animal*) doente
disembark /dɪsɪm'ba:k/ *vt/i* desembarcar
disembodied /dɪsɪm'bɒdɪd/ *a* desencarnado
disenchant /dɪsɪn'tʃa:nt/ *vt* desencantar. **~ment** *n* desencantamento *m*
disengage /dɪsɪn'geɪdʒ/ *vt* desprender, soltar; (*mech*) desengatar
disentangle /dɪsɪn'tæŋgl/ *vt* desembaraçar, desenredar
disfavour /dɪs'feɪvə(r)/ *n* desfavor *m*, desgraça *f*
disfigure /dɪs'fɪgə(r)/ *vt* desfigurar
disgrace /dɪs'greɪs/ *n* vergonha *f*; (*disfavour*) desgraça *f* □ *vt* desonrar. **~ful** *a* vergonhoso
disgruntled /dɪs'grʌntld/ *a* descontente
disguise /dɪs'gaɪz/ *vt* disfarçar □ *n* disfarce *m*. **in ~** disfarçado
disgust /dɪs'gʌst/ *n* repugnância *f* □ *vt* repugnar. **~ing** *a* repugnante
dish /dɪʃ/ *n* prato *m* □ *vt* **~ out** (*colloq*) distribuir. **~ up** servir. **the ~es** (*crockery*) a louça *f*
dishcloth /'dɪʃklɒθ/ *n* pano *m* de prato
dishearten /dɪs'ha:tn/ *vt* desencorajar, desalentar
dishevelled /dɪ'ʃevld/ *a* desgrenhado
dishonest /dɪs'ɒnɪst/ *a* desonesto. **~y** *n* desonestidade *f*
dishonour /dɪs'ɒnə(r)/ *n* desonra *f* □ *vt* desonrar. **~able** *a* desonroso
dishwasher /'dɪʃwɒʃə(r)/ *n* lavadora *f* de pratos, (*P*) máquina *f* de lavar a louça
disillusion /dɪsɪ'lu:ʒn/ *vt* desiludir. **~ment** *n* desilusão *f*
disinfect /dɪsɪn'fekt/ *vt* desinfetar, (*P*) desinfectar. **~ant** *n* desinfetante *m*, (*P*) desinfectante *m*
disinherit /dɪsɪn'herɪt/ *vt* deserdar
disintegrate /dɪs'ɪntɪgreɪt/ *vt/i* desintegrar(-se)
disinterested /dɪs'ɪntrəstɪd/ *a* desinteressado
disjointed /dɪs'dʒɔɪntɪd/ *a* (*talk*) descosido, desconexo
disk /dɪsk/ *n* (*comput*) disco *m*; (*Amer*) = disc. **~ drive** unidade *f* de disco
dislike /dɪs'laɪk/ *n* aversão *f*, antipatia *f* □ *vt* não gostar de, antipatizar com
dislocat|e /'dɪsləkeɪt/ *vt* (*limb*) deslocar. **~ion** /-'keɪʃn/ *n* deslocação *f*
dislodge /dɪs'lɒdʒ/ *vt* desalojar
disloyal /dɪs'lɔɪəl/ *a* desleal. **~ty** *n* deslealdade *f*
dismal /'dɪzməl/ *a* tristonho
dismantle /dɪs'mæntl/ *vt* desmantelar
dismay /dɪs'meɪ/ *n* consternação *f* □ *vt* consternar
dismiss /dɪs'mɪs/ *vt* despedir; (*from mind*) afastar, pôr de lado. **~al** *n* despedimento *m*
dismount /dɪs'maʊnt/ *vi* desmontar
disobedien|t /dɪsə'bi:dɪənt/ *a* desobediente. **~ce** *n* desobediência *f*
disobey /dɪsə'beɪ/ *vt/i* desobedecer (a)
disorder /dɪs'ɔ:də(r)/ *n* desordem *f*; (*med*) perturbações *fpl*, disfunção *f*. **~ly** *a* desordenado; (*riotous*) desordeiro
disorganize /dɪs'ɔ:gənaɪz/ *vt* desorganizar
disorientate /dɪs'ɔ:rɪənteɪt/ *vt* desorientar
disown /dɪs'əʊn/ *vt* repudiar
disparaging /dɪ'spærɪdʒɪŋ/ *a* depreciativo
disparity /dɪ'spærətɪ/ *n* disparidade *f*
dispatch /dɪ'spætʃ/ *vt* despachar □ *n* despacho *m*
dispel /dɪs'pel/ *vt* (*pt* **dispelled**) dissipar
dispensary /dɪ'spensərɪ/ *n* dispensário *m*, farmácia *f*
dispense /dɪ'spens/ *vt* dispensar □ *vi*

~ with dispensar, passar sem. ~r /-ə(r)/ *n* (*container*) distribuidor *m*
dispers|e /dɪ'spɜ:s/ *vt/i* dispersar (-se). ~al *n* dispersão *f*
dispirited /dɪ'spɪrɪtɪd/ *a* desanimado
displace /dɪ'spleɪs/ *vt* deslocar; (*take the place of*) substituir. ~d person deslocado *m* de guerra
display /dɪ'spleɪ/ *vt* exibir, mostrar; (*feeling*) manifestar, dar mostras de □ *n* exposição *f*; (*of computer*) apresentação *f* visual; (*comm*) objetos *mpl* expostos
displeas|e /dɪs'pli:z/ *vt* desagradar a. ~ed with descontente com. ~ure /'pleʒə(r)/ *n* desagrado *m*
disposable /dɪ'spəʊzəbl/ *a* descartável
dispos|e /dɪ'spəʊz/ *vt* dispor □ *vi* ~e of desfazer-se de. well ~ed towards bem disposto para com. ~al *n* (*of waste*) eliminação *f*. at sb's ~al à disposição de alg
disposition /dɪspə'zɪʃn/ *n* disposição *f*; (*character*) índole *f*
disproportionate /dɪsprə'pɔ:ʃənət/ *a* desproporcionado
disprove /dɪs'pru:v/ *vt* refutar
dispute /dɪ'spju:t/ *vt* contestar; (*fight for, quarrel*) disputar □ *n* disputa *f*; (*industrial, pol*) conflito *m*. in ~ em questão
disqualif|y /dɪs'kwɒlɪfaɪ/ *vt* tornar inapto; (*sport*) desqualificar. ~y from driving apreender a carteira de motorista. ~ication /-ɪ'keɪʃn/ *n* desqualificação *f*
disregard /dɪsrɪ'gɑ:d/ *vt* não fazer caso de □ *n* indiferença *f* (for por)
disrepair /dɪsrɪ'peə(r)/ *n* mau estado *m*, abandono *m*, degradação *f*
disreputable /dɪs'repjʊtəbl/ *a* pouco recomendável; (*in appearance*) com mau aspecto; (*in reputation*) vergonhoso, de má fama
disrepute /dɪsrɪ'pju:t/ *n* descrédito *m*
disrespect /dɪsrɪ'spekt/ *n* falta *f* de respeito. ~ful *a* desrespeitoso, irreverente
disrupt /dɪs'rʌpt/ *vt* perturbar; (*plans*) transtornar; (*break up*) dividir. ~ion /-ʃn/ *n* perturbação *f*. ~ive *a* perturbador
dissatisf|ied /dɪ'sætɪsfaɪd/ *a* descontente. ~action /dɪsætɪs'fækʃn/ *n* descontentamento *m*
dissect /dɪ'sekt/ *vt* dissecar. ~ion /-ʃn/ *n* dissecação *f*
dissent /dɪ'sent/ *vi* dissentir, discordar □ *n* dissensão *f*, desacordo *m*
dissertation /dɪsə'teɪʃn/ *n* dissertação *f*
disservice /dɪs'sɜ:vɪs/ *n* do sb a ~ prejudicar alg
dissident /'dɪsɪdənt/ *a* & *n* dissidente (*mf*)
dissimilar /dɪ'sɪmɪlə(r)/ *a* diferente
dissipate /'dɪsɪpeɪt/ *vt* dissipar; (*efforts, time*) desperdiçar. ~d *a* dissoluto
dissociate /dɪ'səʊʃɪeɪt/ *vt* dissociar, desassociar
dissolution /dɪsə'lu:ʃn/ *n* dissolução *f*
dissolve /dɪ'zɒlv/ *vt/i* dissolver(-se)
dissuade /dɪ'sweɪd/ *vt* dissuadir
distance /'dɪstəns/ *n* distância *f*. from a ~ de longe. in the ~ ao longe, à distância
distant /'dɪstənt/ *a* distante; (*relative*) afastado
distaste /dɪs'teɪst/ *n* aversão *f*. ~ful *a* desagradável
distemper /dɪ'stempə(r)/ *n* pintura *f* a têmpera; (*animal disease*) cinomose *f* □ *vt* pintar a têmpera
distend /dɪ'stend/ *vt/i* distender(-se)
distil /dɪ'stɪl/ *vt* (*pt* distilled) destilar. ~lation /'leɪʃn/ *n* destilação *f*
distillery /dɪ'stɪlərɪ/ *n* destilaria *f*
distinct /dɪ'stɪŋkt/ *a* distinto; (*marked*) claro, nítido. ~ion /-ʃn/ *n* distinção *f*. ~ive *a* distintivo, característico. ~ly *adv* distintamente; (*markedly*) claramente
distinguish /dɪ'stɪŋgwɪʃ/ *vt/i* distinguir. ~ed *a* distinto
distort /dɪ'stɔ:t/ *vt* distorcer; (*misrepresent*) deturpar. ~ion /-ʃn/ *n* distorção *f*; (*misrepresentation*) deturpação *f*
distract /dɪ'strækt/ *vt* distrair. ~ed *a* (*distraught*) desesperado, fora de si. ~ing *a* enlouquecedor. ~ion /-ʃn/ *n* distração *f*, (*P*) distracção *f*
distraught /dɪ'strɔ:t/ *a* desesperado, fora de si
distress /dɪ'stres/ *n* (*physical*) dor *f*; (*anguish*) aflição *f*; (*poverty*) miséria *f*; (*danger*) perigo *m* □ *vt* afligir. ~ing *a* aflitivo, doloroso
distribut|e /dɪ'strɪbju:t/ *vt* distribuir. ~ion /-'bju:ʃn/ *n* distribuição *f*. ~or *n* distribuidor *m*
district /'dɪstrɪkt/ *n* região *f*; (*of town*) zona *f*
distrust /dɪs'trʌst/ *n* desconfiança *f* □ *vt* desconfiar de
disturb /dɪ'stɜ:b/ *vt* perturbar; (*move*) desarrumar; (*bother*) incomodar. ~ance *n* (*noise, disorder*) distúrbio *m*. ~ed *a* perturbado. ~ing *a* perturbador
disused /dɪs'ju:zd/ *a* fora de uso, desusado, em desuso
ditch /dɪtʃ/ *n* fosso *m* □ *vt* (*sl: abandon*) abandonar, largar
dither /'dɪðə(r)/ *vi* hesitar

ditto /'dɪtəʊ/ *adv* idem
div|e /daɪv/ *vi* mergulhar; (*rush*) precipitar-se □ *n* mergulho *m*; (*of plane*) picada *f*; (*sl: place*) espelunca *f*. **~er** *n* mergulhador *m*. **~ing-board** *n* prancha *f* de saltos. **~ing-suit** *n* escafandro *m*
diverge /daɪ'vɜ:dʒ/ *vi* divergir
divergent /daɪ'vɜ:dʒənt/ *a* divergente
diverse /daɪ'vɜ:s/ *a* diverso
diversify /daɪ'vɜ:sɪfaɪ/ *vt* diversificar
diversity /daɪ'vɜ:sətɪ/ *n* diversidade *f*
diver|t /daɪ'vɜ:t/ *vt* desviar; (*entertain*) divertir. **~sion** /-ʃn/ *n* diversão *f*; (*traffic*) desvio *m*
divide /dɪ'vaɪd/ *vt/i* dividir(-se). **~ in two** (*branch, river, road*) bifurcar-se
dividend /'dɪvɪdend/ *n* dividendo *m*
divine /dɪ'vaɪn/ *a* divino
divinity /dɪ'vɪnətɪ/ *n* divindade *f*; (*theology*) teologia *f*
division /dɪ'vɪʒn/ *n* divisão *f*
divorce /dɪ'vɔ:s/ *n* divórcio *m* □ *vt/i* divorciar(-se) de. **~d** *a* divorciado
divorcee /dɪvɔ:'si:/ *n* divorciado *m*
divulge /daɪ'vʌldʒ/ *vt* divulgar
DIY *abbr see* **do-it-yourself**
dizz|y /'dɪzɪ/ *a* (-ier, -iest) tonto. **be** *or* **feel ~y** ter tonturas, sentir-se tonto. **~iness** *n* tontura *f*, vertigem *f*
do /du:/ *vt/i* (*3 sing pres* **does**, *pt* **did**, *pp* **done**) fazer; (*be suitable*) servir; (*be enough*) bastar (a); (*sl: swindle*) enganar, levar (*colloq*). **how ~ you ~?** como vai? **well done** muito bem!, (*P*) bravo!; (*culin*) bem passado. **done for** (*colloq*) liquidado (*colloq*), (*P*) anumado (*colloq*) □ *v aux* **~ you see?** vê?; **I ~ not smoke** não fumo. **don't you?, doesn't he?** *etc* não é? □ *n* (*pl* **dos** *or* **do's**) festa *f*. **~-it-yourself** *a* faça-você-mesmo. **~ away with** eliminar, suprimir. **~ in** (*sl*) matar, liquidar (*colloq*). **~ out** limpar. **~ up** (*fasten*) fechar; (*house*) renovar. **I could ~ with a cup of tea** apetecia-me uma xícara de chá. **it could ~ with a wash** precisa de uma lavagem
docile /'dəʊsaɪl/ *a* dócil
dock[1] /dɒk/ *n* doca *f* □ *vt* levar à doca □ *vi* entrar na doca. **~er** *n* estivador *m*
dock[2] /dɒk/ *n* (*jur*) banco *m* dos réus
dockyard /'dɒkja:d/ *n* estaleiro *m*
doctor /'dɒktə(r)/ *n* médico *m*, doutor *m*; (*univ*) doutor *m* □ *vt* (*cat*) capar; (*fig*) adulterar, falsificar
doctorate /'dɒktərət/ *n* doutorado *m*, (*P*) doutoramento *m*
doctrine /'dɒktrɪn/ *n* doutrina *f*
document /'dɒkjʊmənt/ *n* documento *m* □ *vt* documentar. **~ary** /-'mentrɪ/ *a* documental □ *n* documentário *m*
dodge /dɒdʒ/ *vt/i* esquivar(-se), furtar(-se) a □ *n* (*colloq*) truque *m*
dodgy /'dɒdʒɪ/ *a* (-ier, -iest) (*colloq*) delicado, difícil, embaraçoso
does /dʌz/ *see* **do**
doesn't /'dʌznt/ = **does not**
dog /dɒg/ *n* cão *m* □ *vt* (*pt* **dogged**) ir no encalço de, perseguir. **~-eared** *a* com os cantos dobrados
dogged /'dɒgɪd/ *a* obstinado, persistente
dogma /'dɒgmə/ *n* dogma *m*. **~tic** /-'mætɪk/ *a* dogmático
dogsbody /'dɒgzbɒdɪ/ *n* (*colloq*) pau-para-toda-obra *m* (*colloq*), factótum *m*
doldrums /'dɒldrəmz/ *npl* **be in the ~** estar com a neura; (*business*) estar parado
dole /dəʊl/ *vt* **~ out** distribuir □ *n* (*colloq*) auxílio *m* desemprego. **on the ~** (*colloq*) desempregado (titular de auxílio)
doleful /'dəʊlfl/ *a* tristonho, melancólico
doll /dɒl/ *n* boneca *f* □ *vt/i* **~ up** (*colloq*) embonecar(-se)
dollar /'dɒlə(r)/ *n* dólar *m*
dolphin /'dɒlfɪn/ *n* golfinho *m*
domain /dəʊ'meɪn/ *n* domínio *m*
dome /dəʊm/ *n* cúpula *f*; (*vault*) abóbada *f*
domestic /də'mestɪk/ *a* (*of home, animal, flights*) doméstico; (*trade*) interno; (*news*) nacional. **~ated** /-keɪtɪd/ *a* (*animal*) domesticado; (*person*) que gosta de trabalhos caseiros
dominant /'dɒmɪnənt/ *a* dominante
dominat|e /'dɒmɪneɪt/ *vt/i* dominar. **~ion** /-'neɪʃn/ *n* dominação *f*, domínio *m*
domineer /dɒmɪ'nɪə(r)/ *vi* **~ over** mandar (em), ser autocrático (para com). **~ing** *a* mandão, autocrático
dominion /də'mɪnjən/ *n* domínio *m*
domino /'dɒmɪnəʊ/ *n* (*pl* **-oes**) dominó *m*
donat|e /dəʊ'neɪt/ *vt* fazer doação de, doar, dar. **~ion** /-ʃn/ *n* donativo *m*
done /dʌn/ *see* **do**
donkey /'dɒŋkɪ/ *n* burro *m*
donor /'dəʊnə(r)/ *n* (*of blood*) doador *m*, (*P*) dador *m*
don't /dəʊnt/ = **do not**
doodle /'du:dl/ *vi* rabiscar
doom /du:m/ *n* ruína *f*; (*fate*) destino *m*. **be ~ed to** ser/estar condenado a. **~ed (to failure)** condenado ao fracasso
door /dɔ:(r)/ *n* porta *f*
doorman /'dɔ:mən/ *n* (*pl* **-men**) porteiro *m*
doormat /'dɔ:mæt/ *n* capacho *m*
doorstep /'dɔ:step/ *n* degrau *m* da porta

doorway /'dɔ:weɪ/ *n* vão *m* da porta, (*P*) entrada *f*

dope /dəʊp/ *n* (*colloq*) droga *f*; (*sl: idiot*) imbecil *mf* □ *vt* dopar, drogar

dormant /'dɔ:mənt/ *a* dormente; (*inactive*) inativo, (*P*) inactivo; (*latent*) latente

dormitory /'dɔ:mɪtrɪ/ *n* dormitório *m*; (*Amer univ*) residência *f*

dormouse /'dɔ:maʊs/ *n* (*pl* **-mice**) arganaz *m*

dos|e /dəʊs/ *n* dose *f* □ *vt* medicar. **~age** *n* dosagem *f*; (*on label*) posologia *f*

doss /dɒs/ *vi* ~ **(down)** dormir sem conforto. **~-house** *n* pensão *f* miserável, asilo *m* noturno, (*P*) nocturno. **~er** *n* vagabundo *m*

dot /dɒt/ *n* ponto *m*. **on the ~** no momento preciso □ *vt* **be ~ted with** estar semeado de. **~ted line** linha *f* pontilhada

dote /dəʊt/ *vi* ~ **on** ser louco por, adorar

double /'dʌbl/ *a* duplo; (*room, bed*) de casal □ *adv* duas vezes mais □ *n* dobro *m*. **~s** (*tennis*) dupla *f*, (*P*) pares *mpl* □ *vt/i* dobrar, duplicar; (*fold*) dobrar em dois. **at the ~** a passo acelerado. **~-bass** *n* contrabaixo *m*. **~ chin** papada *f*. **~-cross** *vt* enganar. **~-dealing** *n* jogo *m* duplo. **~-decker** *n* ônibus *m*, (*P*) autocarro *m* de dois andares. **~ Dutch** algaraviada *f*, fala *f* incompreensível. **~ glazing** (janela *f* de) vidro (*m*) duplo. **doubly** *adv* duplamente

doubt /daʊt/ *n* dúvida *f* □ *vt* duvidar de. **~ if** *or* **that** duvidar que. **~ful** *a* duvidoso; (*hesitant*) que tem dúvidas. **~less** *adv* sem dúvida, indubitavelmente

dough /dəʊ/ *n* massa *f*

doughnut /'dəʊnʌt/ *n* sonho *n*, (*P*) bola *f* de Berlim

dove /dʌv/ *n* pomba *f*

dowdy /'daʊdɪ/ *a* (-ier, -iest) sem graça, sem gosto

down[1] /daʊn/ *n* (*feathers, hair*) penugem *f*

down[2] /daʊn/ *adv* (*to lower place*) abaixo, para baixo; (*in lower place*) em baixo. **be ~** (*level, price*) descer; (*sun*) estar posto □ *prep* por (+*n*) (*n*+) abaixo. **~ the hill/street** *etc* pelo monte/pela rua *etc* abaixo □ *vt* (*colloq: knock down*) jogar abaixo; (*colloq: drink*) esvaziar. **come** *or* **go ~** descer. **~-and-out** *n* marginal *m*. **~-hearted** *a* desencorajado, desanimado. **~-to-earth** *a* terra-a-terra *invar*. **~ under** na Austrália. **~ with** abaixo

downcast /'daʊnka:st/ *a* abatido, deprimido, desmoralizado

downfall /'daʊnfɔ:l/ *n* queda *f*, ruína *f*

downhill /daʊn'hɪl/ *adv* **go ~** descer; (*fig*) ir abaixo □ *a* /'daʊnhɪl/ a descer, descendente

downpour /'daʊnpɔ:(r)/ *n* aguaceiro *m* forte, (*P*) chuvada *f*

downright /'daʊnraɪt/ *a* franco; (*utter*) autêntico, verdadeiro □ *adv* positivamente

downstairs /daʊn'steəz/ *adv* (*at/to*) em/para baixo, no/para o andar de baixo □ *a* /'daʊnsteəz/ (*flat etc*) de baixo, do andar de baixo

downstream /'daʊnstri:m/ *adv* rio abaixo

downtown /'daʊntaʊn/ *a & adv* (de, em, para) o centro da cidade. **~ Boston** o centro de Boston

downtrodden /'daʊntrɒdn/ *a* espezinhado, oprimido

downward /'daʊnwəd/ *a* descendente. **~(s)** *adv* para baixo

dowry /'daʊərɪ/ *n* dote *m*

doze /dəʊz/ *vi* dormitar. **~ off** cochilar □ *n* soneca *f*, cochilo *m*

dozen /'dʌzn/ *n* dúzia *f*. **~s of** (*colloq*) dezenas de, dúzias de

Dr *abbr* (*Doctor*) Dr

drab /dræb/ *a* insípido; (*of colour*) morto, apagado

draft[1] /dra:ft/ *n* rascunho *m*; (*comm*) ordem *f* de pagamento □ *vt* fazer o rascunho de; (*draw up*) redigir. **the ~** (*Amer: mil*) recrutamento *m*

draft[2] /dra:ft/ *n* (*Amer*) = **draught**

drag /dræg/ *vt/i* (*pt* **dragged**) arrastar(-se); (*river*) dragar; (*pull away*) arrancar □ *n* (*colloq: task*) chatice *f* (*sl*); (*colloq: person*) estorvo *m*; (*sl: clothes*) travesti *m*

dragon /'drægən/ *n* dragão *m*

dragonfly /'drægənflaɪ/ *n* libélula *f*

drain /dreɪn/ *vt* drenar; (*vegetables*) escorrer; (*glass, tank*) esvaziar; (*use up*) esgotar □ *vi* ~ **(off)** escoar-se □ *n* cano *m*. **~s** *npl* (*sewers*) esgotos *mpl*. **~age** *n* drenagem *f*. **~(-pipe)** cano *m* de esgoto. **~ing-board** *n* escorredouro *m*

drama /'dra:mə/ *n* arte *f* dramática; (*play, event*) drama *m*. **~tic** /drə'mætɪk/ *a* dramático. **~tist** /'dræmətɪst/ *n* dramaturgo *m*. **~tize** /'dræmətaɪz/ *vt* dramatizar

drank /dræŋk/ *see* **drink**

drape /dreɪp/ *vt* ~ **round/over** dispor (tecido) em pregas à volta de *or* sobre. **~s** *npl* (*Amer*) cortinas *fpl*

drastic /'dræstɪk/ *a* drástico, violento

draught /dra:ft/ *n* corrente *f* de ar; (*naut*) calado *m*. **~s** (*game*) (jogo *m* das) damas *fpl*. **~ beer** chope *m*, (*P*) cerveja *f* à caneca, imperial *f* (*colloq*). ~y *a* com correntes de ar, ventoso

draughtsman /ˈdra:ftsmən/ *n* (*pl* **-men**) desenhista *m*, (*P*) desenhador *m*

draw /drɔ:/ *vt* (*pt* **drew**, *pp* **drawn**) puxar; (*attract*) atrair; (*picture*) desenhar; (*in lottery*) tirar à sorte; (*line*) traçar; (*open curtains*) abrir; (*close curtains*) fechar □ *vi* desenhar; (*sport*) empatar; (*come*) vir □ *n* (*sport*) empate *m*; (*lottery*) sorteio *m*. ~ **back** recuar. ~ **in** (*of days*) diminuir. ~ **near** aproximar-se. ~ **out** (*money*) levantar. ~ **up** deter-se, parar; (*document*) redigir; (*chair*) aproximar, chegar

drawback /ˈdrɔ:bæk/ *n* inconveniente *m*, desvantagem *f*

drawer /drɔ:(r)/ *n* gaveta *f*

drawing /ˈdrɔ:ɪŋ/ *n* desenho *m*. ~-**board** *n* prancheta *f*. ~-**pin** *n* percevejo *m*

drawl /drɔ:l/ *n* fala *f* arrastada

drawn /drɔ:n/ *see* **draw**

dread /dred/ *n* terror *m* □ *vt* temer

dreadful /ˈdredfl/ *a* medonho, terrível. ~**ly** *adv* terrivelmente

dream /dri:m/ *n* sonho *m* □ *vt/i* (*pt* **dreamed** *or* **dreamt**) sonhar (**of** com) □ *a* (*ideal*) dos seus sonhos. ~ **up** imaginar. ~**er** *n* sonhador *m*. ~**y** *a* sonhador; (*music*) romântico

dreary /ˈdrɪərɪ/ *a* (**-ier**, **-iest**) tristonho; (*boring*) aborrecido

dredge /dredʒ/ *n* draga *f* □ *vt/i* dragar. ~**r** /-ə(r)/ *n* draga *f*; (*for sugar*) polvilhador *m*

dregs /dregz/ *npl* depósito *m*, sedimento *m*; (*fig*) escória *f*

drench /drentʃ/ *vt* encharcar

dress /dres/ *n* vestido *m*; (*clothing*) roupa *f* □ *vt/i* vestir(-se); (*food*) temperar; (*wound*) fazer curativo, (*P*) pensar, (*P*) tratar. ~ **rehearsal** ensaio *m* geral. ~ **up as** fantasiar-se de. **get** ~**ed** vestir-se

dresser /ˈdresə(r)/ *n* (*furniture*) guarda-louça *m*

dressing /ˈdresɪŋ/ *n* (*sauce*) tempero *m*; (*bandage*) curativo *m*, (*P*) penso *m*. ~-**gown** *n* roupão *m*. ~-**room** *n* (*sport*) vestiário *m*; (*theat*) camarim *m*. ~-**table** *n* toucador *m*

dressmak|er /ˈdresmeɪkə(r)/ *n* costureira *f*, modista *f*. ~**ing** *n* costura *f*

dressy /ˈdresɪ/ *a* (**-ier**, **-iest**) elegante, chique *invar*

drew /dru:/ *see* **draw**

dribble /ˈdrɪbl/ *vi* pingar; (*person*) babar-se; (*football*) driblar

dried /draɪd/ *a* (*fruit etc*) seco

drier /ˈdraɪə(r)/ *n* secador *m*

drift /drɪft/ *vi* ir à deriva; (*pile up*) amontoar-se □ *n* força *f* da corrente; (*pile*) monte *m*; (*of events*) rumo *m*; (*meaning*) sentido *m*. ~**er** *n* pessoa *f* sem rumo

drill /drɪl/ *n* (*tool*) broca *f*; (*training*) exercício *m*, treino *m*; (*routine procedure*) exercícios *mpl* □ *vt* furar, perfurar; (*train*) treinar; (*tooth*) abrir □ *vi* treinar-se

drink /drɪŋk/ *vt/i* (*pt* **drank**, *pp* **drunk**) beber □ *n* bebida *f*. **a** ~ **of water** um copo de água. ~**able** *a* potável; (*palatable*) bebível. ~**er** *n* bebedor *m*. ~**ing water** água *f* potável

drip /drɪp/ *vi* (*pt* **dripped**) pingar □ *n* pingar *m*; (*sl: person*) banana *mf* (*colloq*). ~-**dry** *vt* deixar escorrer □ *a* que não precisa passar

dripping /ˈdrɪpɪŋ/ *n* gordura *f* do assado

drive /draɪv/ *vt* (*pt* **drove**, *pp* **driven** /ˈdrɪvn/) empurrar, impelir, levar; (*car, animal*) dirigir, conduzir, (*P*) guiar; (*machine*) acionar, (*P*) accionar □ *vi* dirigir, conduzir, (*P*) guiar □ *n* passeio *m* de carro; (*private road*) entrada *f* para veículos; (*fig*) energia *f*; (*psych*) drive *m*, compulsão *f*, impulso *m*; (*campaign*) campanha *f*. ~ **at** chegar a. ~ **away** (*car*) partir. ~ **in** (*force in*) enterrar. ~-**in** *n* (*bank, cinema etc*) banco *m*, cinema *m etc* em que se é atendido no carro, drive-in *m*. ~ **mad** (fazer) enlouquecer, pôr fora de si

drivel /ˈdrɪvl/ *n* baboseira *f*, bobagem *f*

driver /ˈdraɪvə(r)/ *n* condutor *m*; (*of taxi, bus*) chofer *m*, motorista *mf*

driving /ˈdraɪvɪŋ/ *n* condução *f*. ~-**licence** *n* carteira *f* de motorista, (*P*) carta *f* de condução. ~ **school** auto-escola *f*, (*P*) escola *f* de condução. ~ **test** exame *m* de motorista, (*P*) de condução

drizzle /ˈdrɪzl/ *n* chuvisco *m* □ *vi* chuviscar

drone /drəʊn/ *n* zumbido *m*; (*male bee*) zangão *m* □ *vi* zumbir; (*fig*) falar monotonamente

drool /dru:l/ *vi* babar(-se)

droop /dru:p/ *vi* pender, curvar-se

drop /drɒp/ *n* gota *f*; (*fall*) queda *f*; (*distance*) altura *f* de queda □ *vt/i* (*pt* **dropped**) (deixar) cair; (*fall, lower*) baixar. ~ (**off**) (*person from car*) deixar, largar. ~ **a line** escrever duas linhas (**to** a). ~ **in** passar por (**on** em casa de). ~ **off** (*doze*) adormecer. ~ **out** (*withdraw*) retirar-se; (*of student*) abandonar. ~-**out** *n* marginal *mf*, marginalizado *m*

droppings /ˈdrɒpɪŋz/ *npl* excrementos *mpl* de animal; (*of birds*) cocô *m* (*colloq*), porcaria *f* (*colloq*)

dross /drɒs/ *n* escória *f*; (*refuse*) lixo *m*

drought /draʊt/ *n* seca *f*

drove /drəʊv/ *see* **drive**

drown /draʊn/ *vt/i* afogar(-se)

drowsy /'draʊzɪ/ *a* sonolento. **be** *or* **feel** ~ ter vontade de dormir

drudge /drʌdʒ/ *n* mouro *m* de trabalho. ~**ry** /-ərɪ/ *n* trabalho *m* penoso e monótono, estafa *f*

drug /drʌg/ *n* droga *f*; (*med*) medicamento *m*, remédio *m* □ *vt* (*pt* **drugged**) drogar. ~ **addict** drogado *m*, tóxico-dependente *m*

drugstore /'drʌgstɔ:(r)/ *n* (*Amer*) farmácia *f* que vende também sorvetes etc

drum /drʌm/ *n* (*mus*) tambor *m*; (*for oil*) barril *m*, tambor *m*. ~**s** (*mus*) bateria *f* □ *vi* (*pt* **drummed**) tocar tambor; (*with one's fingers*) tamborilar □ *vt* ~ **into sb** fazer entrar na cabeça de alg. ~ **up** (*support*) conseguir obter; (*business*) criar. ~**mer** *n* tambor *m*; (*in pop group etc*) baterista *m*, (*P*) bateria *m*

drunk /drʌŋk/ *see* **drink** □ *a* embriagado, bêbedo. **get** ~ embebedar-se, embriagar-se □ *n* bêbedo *m*. ~**ard** *n* alcoólico *m*, bêbedo *m*. ~**en** *a* embriagado, bêbedo; (*habitually*) bêbedo

dry /draɪ/ *a* (**drier, driest**) seco; (*day*) sem chuva □ *vt/i* secar. **be** *or* **feel** ~ ter sede. ~**-clean** *vt* limpar a seco. ~**-cleaner's** *n* (loja de) lavagem *f* a seco, lavanderia *f*. ~ **up** (*dishes*) secar a louça *f*; (*of supplies*) esgotar-se. ~**ness** *n* secura *f*

dual /'dju:əl/ *a* duplo. ~ **carriageway** estrada *f* dividida por faixa central. ~**-purpose** *a* com fim duplo

dub /dʌb/ *vt* (*pt* **dubbed**) (*film*) dobrar; (*nickname*) apelidar de

dubious /'dju:bɪəs/ *a* duvidoso; (*character, compliment*) dúbio. **feel** ~ **about** ter dúvidas quanto a

duchess /'dʌtʃɪs/ *n* duquesa *f*

duck /dʌk/ *n* pato *m* □ *vi* abaixar-se rapidamente □ *vt* (*head*) baixar; (*person*) batizar, pregar uma amona em. ~**ling** *n* patinho *m*

duct /dʌkt/ *n* canal *m*, tubo *m*

dud /dʌd/ *a* (*sl: thing*) que não presta ou não funciona; (*sl: coin*) falso; (*sl: cheque*) sem fundos, (*P*) careca (*sl*)

due /dju:/ *a* devido; (*expected*) esperado □ *adv* ~ **east**/*etc* exatamente, (*P*) exactamente a leste/*etc* □ *n* devido *m*. ~**s** direitos *mpl*; (*of club*) cota *f*. ~ **to** devido a, por causa de. **in** ~ **course** no tempo devido

duel /'dju:əl/ *n* duelo *m*

duet /dju:'et/ *n* dueto *m*

duffel /'dʌfl/ *a* ~ **bag** saco *m* de lona. ~**-coat** *n* casaco *m* de tecido de lã

dug /dʌg/ *see* **dig**

duke /dju:k/ *n* duque *m*

dull /dʌl/ *a* (**-er, -est**) (*boring*) enfadonho; (*colour*) morto; (*mirror*) embaçado; (*weather*) encoberto; (*sound*) surdo; (*stupid*) burro

duly /'dju:lɪ/ *adv* devidamente; (*in due time*) no tempo devido

dumb /dʌm/ *a* (**-er, -est**) mudo; (*colloq: stupid*) bronco, burro

dumbfound /dʌm'faʊnd/ *vt* pasmar

dummy /'dʌmɪ/ *n* imitação *f*, coisa *f* simulada; (*of tailor*) manequim *m*; (*of baby*) chupeta *f*

dump /dʌmp/ *vt* (*rubbish*) jogar fora; (*put down*) deixar cair; (*colloq: abandon*) largar □ *n* monte *m* de lixo; (*tip*) lixeira *f*; (*mil*) depósito *m*; (*colloq*) buraco *m*

dunce /dʌns/ *n* burro *m*. ~**'s cap** orelhas *fpl* de burro

dune /dju:n/ *n* duna *f*

dung /dʌŋ/ *n* esterco *m*; (*manure*) estrume *m*

dungarees /dʌŋgə'ri:z/ *npl* macacão *m*, (*P*) fato *m* de macaco

dungeon /'dʌndʒən/ *n* calabouço *m*, masmorra *f*

dupe /dju:p/ *vt* enganar □ *n* trouxa *m*

duplicate[1] /'dju:plɪkət/ *n* duplicado *m* □ *a* idêntico

duplicate[2] /'dju:plɪkeɪt/ *vt* duplicar, fazer em duplicado; (*on machine*) fotocopiar

duplicity /dju:'plɪsətɪ/ *n* duplicidade *f*

durable /'djʊərəbl/ *a* resistente; (*enduring*) duradouro, durável

duration /djʊ'reɪʃn/ *n* duração *f*

duress /djʊ'res/ *n* **under** ~ sob coação *f*, (*P*) coacção *f*

during /'djʊərɪŋ/ *prep* durante

dusk /dʌsk/ *n* crepúsculo *m*, anoitecer *m*

dusky /'dʌskɪ/ *a* (**-ier, -iest**) escuro, sombrio

dust /dʌst/ *n* pó *m*, poeira *f* □ *vt* limpar o pó de; (*sprinkle*) polvilhar. ~**-jacket** *n* sobrecapa *f* de livro

dustbin /'dʌstbɪn/ *n* lata *f* do lixo, (*P*) caixote *m*

duster /'dʌstə(r)/ *n* pano *m* do pó

dustman /'dʌstmən/ *n* (*pl* **-men**) lixeiro *m*, (*P*) homem *m* do lixo

dusty /'dʌstɪ/ *a* (**-ier, -iest**) poeirento, empoeirado

Dutch /dʌtʃ/ *a* holandês □ *n* (*lang*) holandês *m*. ~**man** *n* holandês *m*. ~**woman** *n* holandesa *f*. **go** ~ pagar cada um a sua despesa

dutiful /'dju:tɪfl/ *a* cumpridor; (*showing respect*) respeitador

dut|y /'dju:tɪ/ *n* dever *m*; (*tax*) impostos *mpl*. **~ies** (*of official etc*) funções *fpl*. **off ~y** de folga. **on ~y** de serviço. **~y-free** *a* isento de impostos. **~y-free shop** free shop *m*
duvet /'dju:veɪ/ *n* edredom *m*, (*P*) edredão *m* de penas
dwarf /dwɔ:f/ *n* (*pl* -fs) anão *m*
dwell /dwel/ *vi* (*pt* **dwelt**) morar. **~ on** alongar-se sobre. **~er** *n* habitante. **~ing** *n* habitação *f*
dwindle /'dwɪndl/ *vi* diminuir, reduzir-se
dye /daɪ/ *vt* (*pres p* **dyeing**) tingir □ *n* tinta *f*
dying /'daɪɪŋ/ *see* **die**
dynamic /daɪ'næmɪk/ *a* dinâmico
dynamite /'daɪnəmaɪt/ *n* dinamite *f* □ *vt* dinamitar
dynamo /'daɪnəməʊ/ *n* (*pl* -os) dínamo *m*
dynasty /'dɪnəstɪ/ *n* dinastia *f*
dysentery /'dɪsəntrɪ/ *n* disenteria *f*
dyslex|ia /dɪs'leksɪə/ *n* dislexia *f*. **~ic** *a* disléxico

E

each /i:tʃ/ *a & pron* cada. **~ one** cada um. **~ other** um ao outro, uns aos outros. **they like ~ other** gostam um do outro/uns dos outros. **know/love/*etc* ~ other** conhecer-se/amar-se/*etc*
eager /'i:gə(r)/ *a* ansioso (to por), desejoso (for de); (*supporter*) entusiástico. **be ~ to** ter vontade de. **~ly** *adv* com impaciência, ansiosamente; (*keenly*) com entusiasmo. **~ness** *n* ansiedade *f*, desejo *m*; (*keenness*) entusiasmo *m*
eagle /'i:gl/ *n* águia *f*
ear /ɪə(r)/ *n* ouvido *m*; (*external part*) orelha *f*. **~-drum** *n* tímpano *m*. **~-ring** *n* brinco *m*
earache /'ɪəreɪk/ *n* dor *f* de ouvidos
earl /3:l/ *n* conde *m*
early /'3:lɪ/ (-ier, -iest) *adv* cedo □ *a* primeiro; (*hour*) matinal; (*fruit*) temporão; (*retirement*) antecipado. **have an ~ dinner** jantar cedo. **in ~ summer** no princípio do verão
earmark /'ɪəma:k/ *vt* destinar, reservar (for para)
earn /3:n/ *vt* ganhar; (*deserve*) merecer
earnest /'3:nɪst/ *a* sério. **in ~** a sério
earnings /'3:nɪŋz/ *npl* salário *m*; (*profits*) ganhos *mpl*, lucros *mpl*
earshot /'ɪəʃɒt/ *n* **within ~** ao alcance da voz
earth /3:θ/ *n* terra *f* □ *vt* (*electr*) ligar à terra. **why on ~?** por que diabo?, por que cargas d'água? **~ly** *a* terrestre, terreno
earthenware /'3:θənweə(r)/ *n* louça *f* de barro, faiança *f*
earthquake /'3:θkweɪk/ *n* tremor *m* de terra, terremoto *m*
earthy /'3:θɪ/ *a* terroso, térreo; (*coarse*) grosseiro
earwig /'ɪəwɪg/ *n* lacrainha *f*, (*P*) bicha-cadela *f*
ease /i:z/ *n* facilidade *f*; (*comfort*) bem-estar *m* □ *vt/i* (*from pain, anxiety*) acalmar(-se); (*slow down*) afrouxar; (*slide*) deslizar. **at ~** à vontade; (*mil*) descansar. **ill at ~** pouco à vontade. **with ~** facilmente. **~ in/out** fazer entrar/sair com cuidado
easel /'i:zl/ *n* cavalete *m*
east /i:st/ *n* este *m*, leste *m*, pas-cente *m*, oriente *m*. **the E~** o Oriente □ *a* este, (de) leste, oriental □ *adv* a/para leste. **~ of** para o leste de **~erly** *a* oriental, leste, a/de leste **~ward** *a*, **~ward(s)** *adv* para leste
Easter /'i:stə(r)/ *n* Páscoa *f*. **~ egg** ovo *m* de Páscoa
eastern /'i:stən/ *a* oriental, leste
easy /'i:zɪ/ *a* (-ier, -iest) fácil; (*relaxed*) natural, descontraído. **take it ~** levar as coisas com calma. **~ chair** poltrona *f*. **~-going** *a* bonacheirão. **easily** *adv* facilmente
eat /i:t/ *vt/i* (*pt* **ate**, *pp* **eaten**) comer. **~ into** corroer. **~able** *a* comestível
eaves /i:vz/ *npl* beiral *m*
eavesdrop /'i:vzdrɒp/ *vi* (*pt* **-dropped**) escutar por detrás da porta
ebb /eb/ *n* vazante *f*, baixa-mar *m* □ *vi* vazar; (*fig*) declinar
EC /i:'si:/ *n* (*abbr of European Community*) CE *f*
eccentric /ɪk'sentrɪk/ *a & n* excêntrico (*m*). **~ity** /eksen'trɪsətɪ/ *n* excentricidade *f*
ecclesiastical /ɪkli:zɪ'æstɪkl/ *a* eclesiástico
echo /'ekəʊ/ *n* (*pl* -oes) eco *m* □ *vt/i* (*pt* **echoed**, *pres p* **echoing**) ecoar; (*fig*) repetir
eclipse /ɪ'klɪps/ *n* eclipse *m* □ *vt* eclipsar
ecolog|y /i:'kɒlədʒɪ/ *n* ecologia *f*. **~ical** /i:kə'lɒdʒɪkl/ *a* ecológico
economic /i:kə'nɒmɪk/ *a* econômico, (*P*) económico; (*profitable*) rentável. **~al** *a* econômico, (*P*) económico. **~s** *n* economia *f* política
economist /ɪ'kɒnəmɪst/ *n* economista *mf*
econom|y /ɪ'kɒnəmɪ/ *n* economia *f*. **~ize** *vt/i* economizar
ecstasy /'ekstəsɪ/ *n* êxtase *m*
ecstatic /ɪk'stætɪk/ *a* extático, extasiado

ecu /'eɪkju:/ *n* unidade *f* monetária européia
eczema /'ɛksɪmə/ *n* eczema *m*
edge /edʒ/ *n* borda *f*, beira *f*; (*of town*) periferia *f*, limite *m*; (*of knife*) fio *m* □ *vt* debruar □ *vi* (*move*) avançar pouco a pouco
edging /'edʒɪŋ/ *n* borda *f*, (*P*) bordadura *f*
edgy /'edʒɪ/ *a* irritadiço, nervoso
edible /'edɪbl/ *a* comestível
edict /'i:dɪkt/ *n* édito *m*
edifice /'edɪfɪs/ *n* edifício *m*
edit /'edɪt/ *vt* (*pt* **edited**) (*newspaper*) dirigir; (*text*) editar
edition /ɪ'dɪʃn/ *n* edição *f*
editor /'edɪtə(r)/ *n* (*of newspaper*) diretor *m*, (*P*) director *m*, editor *m* responsável; (*of text*) organizador *m* de texto. **the ~ (in chief)** redator-chefe *m*, (*P*) redactor-chefe *m*. **~ial** /edɪ'tɔ:rɪəl/ *a* & *n* editorial (*m*)
educat|e /'edʒʊkeɪt/ *vt* instruir; (*mind, public*) educar. **~ed** *a* instruído; educado. **~ion** /-'keɪʃn/ *n* educação *f*; (*schooling*) ensino *m*. **~ional** /'keɪʃənl/ *a* educativo, pedagógico
EEC /i:i:'si:/ *n* (*abbr of European Economic Community*) CEE *f*
eel /i:l/ *n* enguia *f*
eerie /'ɪərɪ/ *a* (-ier, -iest) arrepiante, misterioso
effect /ɪ'fekt/ *n* efeito *m* □ *vt* efetuar, (*P*) efectuar. **come into ~** entrar em vigor. **in ~** na realidade. **take ~** ter efeito
effective /ɪ'fektɪv/ *a* eficaz, eficiente; (*striking*) sensacional; (*actual*) efetivo, (*P*) efectivo. **~ly** *adv* (*efficiently*) eficazmente; (*strikingly*) de forma sensacional; (*actually*) efetivamente, (*P*) efectivamente. **~ness** *n* eficácia *f*
effeminate /ɪ'femɪnət/ *a* efeminado, afeminado
effervescent /efə'vesnt/ *a* efervescente
efficien|t /ɪ'fɪʃnt/ *a* eficiente, eficaz. **~cy** *n* eficiência *f*. **~tly** *adv* eficientemente
effigy /'efɪdʒɪ/ *n* efígie *f*
effort /'efət/ *n* esforço *m*. **~less** *a* fácil, sem esforço
effrontery /ɪ'frʌntərɪ/ *n* desfaçatez *f*
effusive /ɪ'fju:sɪv/ *a* efusivo, expansivo
e.g. /i:'dʒi:/ *abbr* por ex
egg[1] /eg/ *n* ovo *m*. **~-cup** *n* copinho *m* para ovo quente, oveiro *m*. **~-plant** *n* beringela *f*
egg[2] /eg/ *vt* **~ on** (*colloq*) incitar
eggshell /'egʃel/ *n* casca *f* de ovo
ego /'egəʊ/ *n* (*pl* -os) ego *m*, eu *m*. **~ism** *n* egoísmo *m*. **~ist** *n* egoísta *mf*. **~tism** *n* egotismo *m*. **~tist** *n* egotista *mf*
Egypt /'i:dʒɪpt/ *n* Egito *m*. **~ian** /ɪ'dʒɪpʃn/ *a* & *n* egípcio (*m*)
eh /eɪ/ *int* (*colloq*) hã?
eiderdown /'aɪdədaʊn/ *n* edredão *m*, edredom *m*
eight /eɪt/ *a* & *n* oito (*m*). **eighth** /eɪtθ/ *a* & *n* oitavo (*m*)
eighteen /eɪ'ti:n/ *a* & *n* dezoito (*m*). **~th** *a* & *n* décimo-oitavo (*m*)
eight|y /'eɪtɪ/ *a* & *n* oitenta (*m*). **~ieth** *a* & *n* octogésimo (*m*)
either /'aɪðə(r)/ *a* & *pron* um e outro; (*with negative*) nem um nem outro; (*each*) cada □ *adv* também não □ *conj* ~ ... **or** ou ... ou; (*with negative*) nem ... nem
ejaculate /ɪ'dʒækjʊleɪt/ *vt/i* ejacular; (*exclaim*) exclamar
eject /ɪ'dʒekt/ *vt* expelir; (*expel*) expulsar, despejar
elaborate[1] /ɪ'læbərət/ *a* elaborado, rebuscado, minucioso
elaborate[2] /ɪ'læbəreɪt/ *vt* elaborar □ *vi* entrar em pormenores. **~ on** estender-se sobre
elapse /ɪ'læps/ *vi* decorrer
elastic /ɪ'læstɪk/ *a* & *n* elástico (*m*). **~ band** elástico *m*
elat|ed /ɪ'leɪtɪd/ *a* radiante, exultante. **~ion** *n* exultação *f*
elbow /'elbəʊ/ *n* cotovelo *m*
elder[1] /'eldə(r)/ *a* mais velho. **~s** *npl* pessoas *fpl* mais velhas
elder[2] /'eldə(r)/ *n* (*tree*) sabugueiro *m*
elderly /'eldəlɪ/ *a* idoso. **the ~** as pessoas de idade
eldest /'eldɪst/ *a* & *n* o mais velho (*m*)
elect /ɪ'lekt/ *vt* eleger □ *a* eleito. **~ion** /-kʃn/ *n* eleição *f*
electric /ɪ'lektrɪk/ *a* elétrico, (*P*) eléctrico. **~al** *a* elétrico, (*P*) eléctrico
electrician /ɪlek'trɪʃn/ *n* eletricista *m*, (*P*) electricista *m*
electricity /ɪlek'trɪsətɪ/ *n* eletricidade *f*, (*P*) electricidade *f*
electrify /ɪ'lektrɪfaɪ/ *vt* eletrificar, (*P*) electrificar; (*fig: excite*) eletrizar, (*P*) electrizar
electrocute /ɪ'lektrəkju:t/ *vt* eletrocutar, (*P*) electrocutar
electronic /ɪlek'trɒnɪk/ *a* eletrônico, (*P*) electrónico. **~s** *n* eletrônica *f*, (*P*) electrónica *f*
elegan|t /'elɪgənt/ *a* elegante. **~ce** *n* elegância *f*. **~tly** *adv* elegantemente, com elegância
element /'elɪmənt/ *n* elemento *m*; (*of heater etc*) resistência *f*. **~ary** /-'mentrɪ/ *a* elementar; (*school*) primário
elephant /'elɪfənt/ *n* elefante *m*
elevat|e /'elɪveɪt/ *vt* elevar. **~ion** /'veɪʃn/ *n* elevação *f*
elevator /'elɪveɪtə(r)/ *n* (*Amer: lift*) elevador *m*, ascensor *m*

eleven /ɪ'levn/ *a & n* onze (*m*). **~th** *a & n* décimo primeiro (*m*). **at the ~th hour** à última hora

elf /elf/ *n* (*pl* **elves**) elfo *m*, duende *m*

elicit /ɪ'lɪsɪt/ *vt* extrair, obter

eligible /'elɪdʒəbl/ *a* (*for office*) idôneo, (*P*) idóneo (**for** para); (*desirable*) aceitável. **be ~ for** (*entitled to*) ter direito a

eliminat|e /ɪ'lɪmɪneɪt/ *vt* eliminar. **~ion** /-'neɪʃn/ *n* eliminação *f*

élite /eɪ'li:t/ *n* elite *f*

ellip|se /ɪ'lɪps/ *n* elipse *f*. **~tical** *a* elíptico

elm /elm/ *n* olmo *m*, ulmeiro *m*

elocution /elə'kju:ʃn/ *n* elocução *f*

elongate /'i:lɒŋgeɪt/ *vt* alongar

elope /ɪ'ləʊp/ *vi* fugir. **~ment** *n* fuga *f* (de amantes), (*P*) (de amorosos)

eloquen|t /'eləkwənt/ *a* eloqüente, (*P*) eloquente. **~ce** *n* eloqüência *f*, (*P*) eloquência *f*

else /els/ *adv* mais. **everybody ~** todos os outros. **nobody ~** mais ninguém. **nothing ~** nada mais. **or ~** ou então, senão. **somewhere ~** noutro lado qualquer. **~where** *adv* noutro lado

elude /ɪ'lu:d/ *vt* escapar a; (*a question*) evadir

elusive /ɪ'lu:sɪv/ *a* (*person*) esquivo, difícil de apanhar; (*answer*) evasivo

emaciated /ɪ'meɪʃɪeɪtɪd/ *a* emaciado, macilento

emancipat|e /ɪ'mænsɪpeɪt/ *vt* emancipar. **~ion** /-'peɪʃn/ *n* emancipação *f*

embalm /ɪm'ba:m/ *vt* embalsamar

embankment /ɪm'bæŋkmənt/ *n* (*of river*) dique *m*; (*of railway*) terrapleno *m*, talude *m*, (*P*) aterro *m*

embargo /ɪm'ba:gəʊ/ *n* (*pl* **-oes**) embargo *m*

embark /ɪm'ba:k/ *vt/i* embarcar. **~ on** (*business etc*) embarcar em, meter-se em (*colloq*); (*journey*) começar

embarrass /ɪm'bærəs/ *vt* embaraçar, confundir. **~ment** *n* embaraço *m*, atrapalhação *f*

embassy /'embəsɪ/ *n* embaixada *f*

embellish /ɪm'belɪʃ/ *vt* embelezar, enfeitar. **~ment** *n* embelezamento *m*, enfeite *m*

embezzle /ɪm'bezl/ *vt* desviar (fundos). **~ment** *n* desfalque *m*

embitter /ɪm'bɪtə(r)/ *vt* (*person*) amargurar; (*situation*) azedar

emblem /'embləm/ *n* emblema *m*

embod|y /ɪm'bɒdɪ/ *vt* encarnar; (*include*) incorporar, incluir. **~iment** *n* personificação *f*

emboss /ɪm'bɒs/ *vt* (*metal*) gravar em relevo; (*paper*) gofrar

embrace /ɪm'breɪs/ *vt/i* abraçar(-se); (*offer, opportunity*) acolher □ *n* abraço *m*

embroider /ɪm'brɔɪdə(r)/ *vt* bordar. **~y** *n* bordado *m*

embryo /'embrɪəʊ/ *n* (*pl* **-os**) embrião *m*. **~nic** /-'ɒnɪk/ *a* embrionário

emerald /'emərəld/ *n* esmeralda *f*

emerge /ɪ'mɜ:dʒ/ *vi* emergir, surgir

emergency /ɪ'mɜ:dʒənsɪ/ *n* emergência *f*; (*urgent case*) urgência *f*. **~ exit** saída *f* de emergência. **in an ~** em caso de urgência

emigrant /'emɪgrənt/ *n* emigrante *mf*

emigrat|e /'emɪgreɪt/ *vi* emigrar. **~ion** /'greɪʃn/ *n* emigração *f*

eminen|t /'emɪnənt/ *a* eminente. **~tly** *adv* eminentemente

emi|t /ɪ'mɪt/ *vt* (*pt* **emitted**) emitir. **~ssion** /-ʃn/ *n* emissão *f*

emotion /ɪ'məʊʃn/ *n* emoção *f*. **~al** *a* (*person, shock*) emotivo; (*speech, scene*) emocionante

emperor /'empərə(r)/ *n* imperador *m*

emphasis /'emfəsɪs/ *n* ênfase *f*. **lay ~ on** pôr em relevo

emphasize /'emfəsaɪz/ *vt* enfatizar, sublinhar; (*syllable, word*) acentuar

emphatic /ɪm'fætɪk/ *a* enfático; (*manner*) enérgico. **~ally** *adv* enfaticamente

empire /'empaɪə(r)/ *n* império *m*

employ /ɪm'plɔɪ/ *vt* empregar. **~ee** /emplɔɪ'i:/ *n* empregado *m*. **~er** *n* patrão *m*. **~ment** *n* emprego *m*. **~ment agency** agência *f* de empregos

empower /ɪm'paʊə(r)/ *vt* autorizar (**to do** a fazer)

empress /'emprɪs/ *n* imperatriz *f*

empt|y /'emptɪ/ *a* vazio; (*promise*) falso □ *vt/i* esvaziar(-se). **on an ~y stomach** com o estômago vazio, em jejum. **~ies** *npl* garrafas *fpl* vazias. **~iness** *n* vazio *m*

emulate /'emjʊleɪt/ *vt* imitar, rivalizar com, emular com

emulsion /ɪ'mʌlʃn/ *n* emulsão *f*

enable /ɪ'neɪbl/ *vt* **~ sb to do** permitir a alg fazer

enact /ɪ'nækt/ *vt* (*jur*) decretar; (*theat*) representar

enamel /ɪ'næml/ *n* esmalte *m* □ *vt* (*pt* **enamelled**) esmaltar

enamoured /ɪ'næməd/ *a* **~ of** enamorado de, apaixonado por

encase /ɪn'keɪs/ *vt* encerrar (**in** em); (*cover*) revestir (**in** de)

enchant /ɪn'tʃa:nt/ *vt* encantar. **~ing** *a* encantador. **~ment** *n* encantamento *m*

encircle /ɪn'sɜ:kl/ *vt* cercar, rodear

enclose /ɪn'kləʊz/ *vt* (*land*) cercar; (*with letter*) enviar incluso/junto. **~d** *a* (*space*) fechado; (*with letter*) anexo, incluso, junto

enclosure /ɪn'kləʊʒə(r)/ *n* cercado *m*, recinto *m*; (*with letter*) documento *m* anexo
encompass /ɪn'kʌmpəs/ *vt* abranger
encore /ɒŋ'kɔ:(r)/ *int & n* bis (*m*)
encounter /ɪn'kaʊntə(r)/ *vt* encontrar, deparar com □ *n* encontro *m*
encourage /ɪn'kʌrɪdʒ/ *vt* encorajar. **~ment** *n* encorajamento *m*
encroach /ɪn'krəʊtʃ/ *vi* **~ on** (*land*) invadir; (*time*) abusar de
encumb|er /ɪn'kʌmbə(r)/ *vt* estorvar; (*burden*) sobrecarregar. **~rance** *n* estorvo *m*, empecilho *m*; (*burden*) ônus *m*, (*P*) ónus *m*, encargo *m*
encycloped|ia /ɪnsaɪklə'pi:dɪə/ *n* enciclopédia *f*. **~ic** *a* enciclopédico
end /end/ *n* fim *m*; (*farthest part*) extremo *m*, ponta *f* □ *vt/i* acabar, terminar. **~ up** (*arrive finally*) ir parar (in a/em). **~ up doing** acabar por fazer. **in the ~** por fim. **no ~ of** (*colloq*) muito, enorme, imenso. **on ~** (*upright*) em pé; (*consecutive*) a fio, de seguida
endanger /ɪn'deɪndʒə(r)/ *vt* pôr em perigo
endear|ing /ɪn'dɪərɪŋ/ *a* cativante. **~ment** *n* palavra *f* meiga; (*act*) carinho *m*
endeavour /ɪn'devə(r)/ *n* esforço *m* □ *vi* esforçar-se (to por)
ending /'endɪŋ/ *n* fim *m*; (*of word*) terminação *f*
endless /'endlɪs/ *a* interminável; (*times*) sem conta; (*patience*) infinito
endorse /ɪn'dɔ:s/ *vt* (*document*) endossar; (*action*) aprovar. **~ment** *n* (*auto*) averbamento *m*
endow /ɪn'daʊ/ *vt* doar. **~ment** *n* doação *f*
endur|e /ɪn'djʊə(r)/ *vt* suportar □ *vi* durar. **~able** *a* suportável. **~ance** *n* resistência *f*
enemy /'enəmɪ/ *n & a* inimigo (*m*)
energetic /enə'dʒetɪk/ *a* enérgico
energy /'enədʒɪ/ *n* energia *f*
enforce /ɪn'fɔ:s/ *vt* aplicar
engage /ɪn'geɪdʒ/ *vt* (*staff*) contratar; (*mech*) engrenar □ *vi* **~ in** envolver-se em, lançar-se em. **~d** *a* noivo; (*busy*) ocupado. **~ment** *n* noivado *m*; (*undertaking, appointment*) compromisso *m*; (*mil*) combate *m*
engender /ɪn'dʒendə(r)/ *vt* engendrar, produzir, causar
engine /'endʒɪn/ *n* motor *m*; (*of train*) locomotiva *f*
engineer /endʒɪ'nɪə(r)/ *n* engenheiro *m* □ *vt* engenhar. **~ing** *n* engenharia *f*
England /'ɪŋglənd/ *n* Inglaterra *f*
English /'ɪŋglɪʃ/ *a* inglês □ *n* (*lang*) inglês *m*. **the ~** os ingleses *mpl*. **~man** *n* inglês *m*. **~-speaking** *a* de lingua inglesa *f*. **~woman** *n* inglesa *f*
engrav|e /ɪn'greɪv/ *vt* gravar. **~-ing** *n* gravura *f*
engrossed /ɪn'grəʊst/ *a* absorto (in em)
engulf /ɪn'gʌlf/ *vt* engolfar, tragar
enhance /ɪn'ha:ns/ *vt* aumentar; (*heighten*) realçar
enigma /ɪ'nɪgmə/ *n* enigma *m*. **~tic** /enɪg'mætɪk/ *a* enigmático
enjoy /ɪn'dʒɔɪ/ *vt* gostar de; (*benefit from*) gozar de. **~ o.s.** divertir-se. **~able** *a* agradável. **~ment** *n* prazer *m*
enlarge /ɪn'la:dʒ/ *vt/i* aumentar. **~ upon** alargar-se sobre. **~ment** *n* ampliação *f*
enlighten /ɪn'laɪtn/ *vt* esclarecer. **~ment** *n* esclarecimento *m*, elucidação *f*
enlist /ɪn'lɪst/ *vt* recrutar; (*fig*) aliciar, granjear □ *vi* alistar-se
enliven /ɪn'laɪvn/ *vt* animar
enmity /'enmətɪ/ *n* inimizade *f*
enormous /ɪ'nɔ:məs/ *a* enorme
enough /ɪ'nʌf/ *a, adv & n* bastante (*m*), suficiente (*m*) □ *int* basta!, chega! **have ~ of** estar farto de
enquir|e /ɪn'kwaɪə(r)/ *vt/i* perguntar, indagar. **~e about** informar-se de, pedir informações sobre. **~y** *n* pedido *m* de informações
enrage /ɪn'reɪdʒ/ *vt* enfurecer, enraivecer
enrich /ɪn'rɪtʃ/ *vt* enriquecer
enrol /ɪn'rəʊl/ *vt/i* (*pt* **enrolled**) inscrever(-se); (*schol*) matricular(-se). **~ment** *n* inscrição *f*; (*schol*) matrícula *f*
ensemble /ɒn'sɒmbl/ *n* conjunto *m*
ensign /'ensən/ *n* pavilhão *m*; (*officer*) guarda-marinha *m*
ensu|e /ɪn'sju:/ *vi* seguir-se. **~ing** *a* decorrente
ensure /ɪn'ʃʊə(r)/ *vt* assegurar. **~ that** assegurar-se de que
entail /ɪn'teɪl/ *vt* acarretar
entangle /ɪn'tæŋgl/ *vt* emaranhar, enredar
enter /'entə(r)/ *vt* (*room, club etc*) entrar em; (*register*) registar; (*data*) entrar com □ *vi* entrar (into em). **~ for** inscrever-se em
enterprise /'entəpraɪz/ *n* empresa *f*, empreendimento *m*; (*fig*) iniciativa *f*
enterprising /'entəpraɪzɪŋ/ *a* empreendedor
entertain /entə'teɪn/ *vt* entreter; (*guests*) receber; (*ideas*) alimentar, nutrir. **~er** *n* artista *mf*. **~ment** *n* entretenimento *m*; (*performance*) espetáculo *m*, (*P*) espectáculo *m*

enthral /ɪn'θrɔ:l/ *vt* (*pt* **enthralled**) fascinar
enthuse /ɪn'θju:z/ *vi* ~ **over** entusiasmar-se por
enthusias|m /ɪn'θju:zɪæzm/ *n* entusiasmo *m*. **~t** *n* entusiasta *mf*. **~tic** /-'æstɪk/ *a* entusiástico. **~tically** /-'æstɪkəlɪ/ *adv* entusiasticamente
entice /ɪn'taɪs/ *vt* atrair. ~ **to do** induzir a fazer. **~ment** *n* tentação *f*, engodo *m*
entire /ɪn'taɪə(r)/ *a* inteiro. **~ly** *adv* inteiramente
entirety /ɪn'taɪərətɪ/ *n* **in its ~** por inteiro, na (sua) totalidade
entitle /ɪn'taɪtl/ *vt* dar direito. **~d** *a* (*book*) intitulado. **be ~d to sth** ter direito a alg coisa. **~ment** *n* direito *m*
entity /'entətɪ/ *n* entidade *f*
entrance /'entrəns/ *n* entrada *f* (**to** para); (*right to enter*) admissão *f*
entrant /'entrənt/ *n* (*sport*) concorrente *mf*; (*in exam*) candidato *m*
entreat /ɪn'tri:t/ *vt* rogar, suplicar. **~y** *n* rogo *m*, súplica *f*
entrench /ɪn'trentʃ/ *vt* (*mil*) entrincheirar; (*fig*) fincar
entrust /ɪn'trʌst/ *vt* confiar
entry /'entrɪ/ *n* entrada *f*; (*on list*) item *m*; (*in dictionary*) verbete *m*. ~ **form** ficha *f* de inscrição, (*P*) boletim *m* de inscrição. **no ~** entrada proibida
enumerate /ɪ'nju:məreɪt/ *vt* enumerar
envelop /ɪn'veləp/ *vt* (*pt* **enveloped**) envolver
envelope /'envələʊp/ *n* envelope *m*, sobrescrito *m*
enviable /'envɪəbl/ *a* invejável
envious /'envɪəs/ *a* invejoso. **be ~ of** ter inveja de. **~ly** *adv* invejosamente, com inveja
environment /ɪn'vaɪərənmənt/ *n* meio *m*; (*ecological*) meio-ambiente *m*. **~al** /-'mentl/ *a* do meio; (*ecological*) do ambiente
envisage /ɪn'vɪzɪdʒ/ *vt* encarar; (*foresee*) prever
envoy /'envɔɪ/ *n* enviado *m*
envy /'envɪ/ *n* inveja *f* □ *vt* invejar, ter inveja de
enzyme /'enzaɪm/ *n* enzima *f*
epic /'epɪk/ *n* epopéia *f* □ *a* épico
epidemic /epɪ'demɪk/ *n* epidemia *f*
epilep|sy /'epɪlepsɪ/ *n* epilepsia *f*. **~tic** /'leptɪk/ *a* & *n* epiléptico (*m*)
episode /'epɪsəʊd/ *n* episódio *m*
epitaph /'epɪta:f/ *n* epitáfio *m*
epithet /'epɪθet/ *n* epíteto *m*
epitom|e /ɪ'pɪtəmɪ/ *n* (*summary*) epítome *m*; (*embodiment*) modelo *m*. **~ize** *vt* (*fig*) representar, encarnar; (*summarize*) resumir
epoch /'i:pɒk/ *n* época *f*. **~-making** *a* que marca uma época
equal /'i:kwəl/ *a* & *n* igual (*m*) □ *vt* (*pt* **equalled**) igualar, ser igual a. ~ **to** (*task*) à altura de. **~ity** /i:'kwɒlətɪ/ *n* igualdade *f*. **~ly** *adv* igualmente; (*similarly*) de igual modo
equalize /'i:kwəlaɪz/ *vt/i* igualar; (*sport*) empatar
equanimity /ekwə'nɪmətɪ/ *n* equanimidade *f*, serenidade *f*
equate /ɪ'kweɪt/ *vt* equacionar (**with** com); (*treat as equal*) equiparar (**with** a)
equation /ɪ'kweɪʒn/ *n* equação *f*
equator /ɪ'kweɪtə(r)/ *n* equador *m*. **~ial** /ekwə'tɔ:rɪəl/ *a* equatorial
equilibrium /i:kwɪ'lɪbrɪəm/ *n* equilíbrio *m*
equip /ɪ'kwɪp/ *vt* (*pt* **equipped**) equipar (**with** com), munir (**with** de). **~ment** *n* equipamento *m*
equitable /'ekwɪtəbl/ *a* eqüitativo, (*P*) equitativo
equity /'ekwətɪ/ *n* eqüidade *f*, (*P*) equidade *f*
equivalent /ɪ'kwɪvələnt/ *a* & *n* eqüivalente (*m*), (*P*) equivalente (*m*)
equivocal /ɪ'kwɪvəkl/ *a* equívoco
era /'ɪərə/ *n* era *f*, época *f*
eradicate /ɪ'rædɪkeɪt/ *vt* erradicar, suprimir
erase /ɪ'reɪz/ *vt* apagar. **~r** /-ə(r)/ *n* borracha *f* (de apagar)
erect /ɪ'rekt/ *a* ereto, (*P*) erecto □ *vt* erigir. **~ion** /-ʃn/ *n* ereção *f*, (*P*) erecção *f*; (*building*) construção *f*, edifício *m*
ero|de /ɪ'rəʊd/ *vt* corroer. **~sion** /ɪ'rəʊʒn/ *n* erosão *f*
erotic /ɪ'rɒtɪk/ *a* erótico
err /ɜ:(r)/ *vi* (*pt* **erred**) errar
errand /'erənd/ *n* recado *m*
erratic /ɪ'rætɪk/ *a* errático, irregular; (*person*) variável, imprevisível
erroneous /ɪ'rəʊnɪəs/ *a* errôneo, (*P*) erróneo, errado
error /'erə(r)/ *n* erro *m*
erudit|e /'eru:daɪt/ *a* erudito. **~ion** /-'dɪʃn/ *n* erudição *f*
erupt /ɪ'rʌpt/ *vi* (*war, fire*) irromper; (*volcano*) entrar em erupção. **~ion** /-ʃn/ *n* erupção *f*
escalat|e /'eskəleɪt/ *vt/i* intensificar (-se); (*of prices*) subir em espiral. **~ion** /'leɪʃn/ *n* escalada *f*
escalator /'eskəleɪtə(r)/ *n* escada *f* rolante
escapade /eskə'peɪd/ *n* peripécia *f*
escape /ɪ'skeɪp/ *vi* escapar-se □ *vt* escapar a □ *n* fuga *f*; (*of prisoner*) evasão *f*, fuga *f*. ~ **from sb** escapar de alguém. ~ **to** fugir para. **have a lucky** *or* **narrow ~** escapar por um tris

escapism /ɪ'skeɪpɪzəm/ *n* escapismo *m*

escort[1] /'eskɔ:t/ *n* escolta *f*; (*of woman*) cavalheiro *m*, acompanhante *m*

escort[2] /ɪ'skɔ:t/ *vt* escoltar; (*accompany*) acompanhar

escudo /es'kjudəʊ/ *n* (*pl* -os) escudo *m*

Eskimo /'eskɪməʊ/ *n* (*pl* -os) esquimó *mf*

especial /ɪ'speʃl/ *a* especial. **~ly** *adv* especialmente

espionage /'espɪəna:ʒ/ *n* espionagem *f*

espouse /ɪ'spaʊz/ *vt* (*a cause etc*) abraçar

espresso /e'spressəʊ/ *n* (*pl* -os) (*coffee*) expresso *m*

essay /'eseɪ/ *n* ensaio *m*; (*schol*) redação *f*, (*P*) redacção *f*

essence /'esns/ *n* essência *f*

essential /ɪ'senʃl/ *a* essencial □ *n* **the ~s** o essencial *m*. **~ly** *adv* essencialmente

establish /ɪ'stæblɪʃ/ *vt* estabelecer; (*business, state*) fundar; (*prove*) provar, apurar. **~ment** *n* estabelecimento *m*; (*institution*) instituição *f*. **the E~ment** o Establishment *m*, a classe *f* dirigente

estate /ɪ'steɪt/ *n* propriedade *f*; (*possessions*) bens *mpl*; (*inheritance*) herança *f*. **~ agent** agente *m* imobiliário. (**housing**) **~** conjunto *m* habitacional. **~ car** perua *f*

esteem /ɪ'sti:m/ *vt* estimar □ *n* estima *f*

estimate[1] /'estɪmət/ *n* cálculo *m*, avaliação *f*; (*comm*) orçamento *m*, estimativa *f*

estimat|e[2] /'estɪmeɪt/ *vt* calcular, estimar. **~ion** /-'meɪʃn/ *n* opinião *f*

estuary /'estʃʊərɪ/ *n* estuário *m*

etc *abbr* = et cetera /ɪt'setərə/ etc

etching /'etʃɪŋ/ *n* água-forte *f*

eternal /ɪ'tɜ:nl/ *a* eterno

eternity /ɪ'tɜ:nətɪ/ *n* eternidade *f*

ethic /'eθɪk/ *n* ética *f*. **~s** ética *f*. **~al** *a* ético

ethnic /'eθnɪk/ *a* étnico

etiquette /'etɪket/ *n* etiqueta *f*

etymology /etɪ'mɒlədʒɪ/ *n* etimologia *f*

eulogy /'ju:lədʒɪ/ *n* elogio *m*

euphemism /'ju:fəmɪzəm/ *n* eufemismo *m*

euphoria /ju'fɔ:rɪə/ *n* euforia *f*

Europe /'jʊərəp/ *n* Europa *f*. **~an** /-'pɪən/ *a* & *n* europeu (*m*)

euthanasia /ju:θə'neɪzɪə/ *n* eutanásia *f*

evacuat|e /ɪ'vækjʊeɪt/ *vt* evacuar. **~ion** /-'eɪʃn/ *n* evacuação *f*

evade /ɪ'veɪd/ *vt* evadir, esquivarse a

evaluate /ɪ'væljʊeɪt/ *vt* avaliar

evangelical /i:væn'dʒelɪkl/ *a* evangélico

evaporat|e /ɪ'væpəreɪt/ *vt/i* evaporar(-se). **~ed milk** leite *m* evaporado. **~ion** /-'reɪʃn/ *n* evaporação *f*

evasion /ɪ'veɪʒn/ *n* evasão *f*

evasive /ɪ'veɪsɪv/ *a* evasivo

eve /i:v/ *n* véspera *f*

even /'i:vn/ *a* regular; (*surface*) liso, plano; (*amounts*) igual; (*number*) par □ *vt/i* **~ up** igualar(-se), acertar □ *adv* mesmo. **~ better** ainda melhor. **get ~ with** ajustar contas com. **~ly** *adv* uniformemente; (*amounts*) em partes iguais

evening /'i:vnɪŋ/ *n* entardecer *m*, anoitecer *m*; (*whole evening*) serão *m*. **~ class** aula *f* à noite (*para adultos*). **~ dress** traje *m* de cerimônia, (*P*) trajo *m* de cerimónia *or* de rigor; (*woman's*) vestido *m* de noite

event /ɪ'vent/ *n* acontecimento *m*. **in the ~ of** no caso de. **~ful** *a* movimentado, memorável

eventual /ɪ'ventʃʊəl/ *a* final. **~ity** /-'ælətɪ/ *n* eventualidade *f*. **~ly** *adv* por fim; (*in future*) eventualmente

ever /'evə(r)/ *adv* jamais; (*at all times*) sempre. **do you ~ go?** você já foi alguma vez?, vais alguma vez? **the best I ~ saw** o melhor que já vi. **~ since** *adv* desde então □ *prep* desde □ *conj* desde que. **~ so** (*colloq*) muitíssimo, tão. **hardly ~** quase nunca

evergreen /'evəgri:n/ *n* sempre-verde *f*, planta *f* de folhas persistentes □ *a* persistente

everlasting /'evəla:stɪŋ/ *a* eterno

every /'evrɪ/ *a* cada. **~ now and then** de vez em quando, volta e meia. **~ one** cada um. **~ other day** dia sim dia não, de dois em dois dias. **~ three days** de três em três dias

everybody /'evrɪbɒdɪ/ *pron* todo mundo, todos

everyday /'evrɪdeɪ/ *a* cotidiano, (*P*) quotidiano, diário; (*common*) do dia a dia, vulgar

everyone /'evrɪwʌn/ *pron* todo mundo, todos

everything /'evrɪθɪŋ/ *pron* tudo

everywhere /'evrɪweə(r)/ *adv* (*position*) em todo lugar, em toda parte; (*direction*) a todo lugar, a toda parte

evict /ɪ'vɪkt/ *vt* expulsar, despejar. **~ion** /-ʃn/ *n* despejo *m*

evidence /'evɪdəns/ *n* evidência *f*; (*proof*) prova *f*; (*testimony*) testemunho *m*, depoimento *m*. **~ of** sinal de. **give ~** testemunhar. **in ~** em evidência

evident /'evɪdənt/ *a* evidente. **~ly** *adv* evidentemente

evil /'i:vl/ *a* mau □ *n* mal *m*
evo|ke /ɪ'vəʊk/ *vt* evocar. **~cative** /ɪ'vɒkətɪv/ *a* evocativo
evolution /i:və'lu:ʃn/ *n* evolução *f*
evolve /ɪ'vɒlv/ *vi* evolucionar, evoluir □ *vt* desenvolver, produzir
ex- /eks/ *pref* ex-
exacerbate /ɪg'zæsəbeɪt/ *vt* exacerbar
exact /ɪg'zækt/ *a* exato, (*P*) exacto □ *vt* exigir (**from** de). **~ing** *a* exigente; (*task*) difícil. **~ly** *adv* exatamente, (*P*) exactamente
exaggerat|e /ɪg'zædʒəreɪt/ *vt/i* exagerar. **~ion** /-'reɪʃn/ *n* exagero *m*
exam /ɪg'zæm/ *n* (*colloq*) exame *m*
examination /ɪgzæmɪ'neɪʃn/ *n* exame *m*; (*jur*) interrogatório *m*
examine /ɪg'zæmɪn/ *vt* examinar; (*witness etc*) interrogar. **~r** /-ə(r)/ *n* examinador *m*
example /ɪg'za:mpl/ *n* exemplo *m*. **for ~** por exemplo. **make an ~ of** castigar para servir de exemplo
exasperat|e /ɪg'zæspəreɪt/ *vt* exasperar. **~ion** /-'reɪʃn/ *n* exaspero *m*
excavat|e /'ekskəveɪt/ *vt* escavar; (*uncover*) desenterrar. **~ion** /-'veɪʃn/ *n* escavação *f*
exceed /ɪk'si:d/ *vt* exceder; (*speed limit*) ultrapassar, exceder
excel /ɪk'sel/ *vi* (*pt* **excelled**) distinguir-se □ *vt* superar, ultrapassar
excellen|t /'eksələnt/ *a* excelente. **~ce** *n* excelência *f*. **~tly** *adv* excelentemente
except /ɪk'sept/ *prep* exceto, (*P*) excepto, fora □ *vt* excetuar, (*P*) exceptuar. **~ for** a não ser, menos, salvo. **~ing** *prep* à exceção de, (*P*) à excepção de. **~ion** /-ʃn/ *n* exceção *f*, (*P*) excepção *f*. **take ~ion to** (*object to*) achar inaceitável; (*be offended by*) achar ofensivo
exceptional /ɪk'sepʃənl/ *a* excepcional. **~ly** *adv* excepcionalmente
excerpt /'eksɜ:pt/ *n* trecho *m*, excerto *m*
excess[1] /ɪk'ses/ *n* excesso *m*
excess[2] /'ekses/ *a* excedente, em excesso. **~ fare** excesso *m*, suplemento *m*. **~ luggage** excesso *m* de peso
excessive /ɪk'sesɪv/ *a* excessivo. **~ly** *adv* excessivamente
exchange /ɪks'tʃeɪndʒ/ *vt* trocar □ *n* troca *f*; (*of currency*) câmbio *m*. (**telephone**) **~** central *f* telefônica, (*P*) telefónica. **~ rate** taxa *f* de câmbio
excise /'eksaɪz/ *n* imposto *m* (indireto, (*P*) indirecto)
excit|e /ɪk'saɪt/ *vt* excitar; (*rouse*) despertar; (*enthuse*) entusiasmar. **~able** *a* excitável. **~ed** *a* excitado. **get ~ed** excitar-se, entusiasmar-se. **~ement** *n* excitação *f*. **~ing** *a* excitante, emocionante
exclaim /ɪk'skleɪm/ *vi* exclamar
exclamation /ekskləˈmeɪʃn/ *n* exclamação *f*. **~ mark** ponto *m* de exclamação
exclu|de /ɪk'sklu:d/ *vt* excluir. **~ding** *prep* excluído. **~sion** /ɪk'sklu:ʒn/ *n* exclusão *f*
exclusive /ɪk'sklu:sɪv/ *a* (*rights etc*) exclusivo; (*club etc*) seleto, (*P*) selecto; (*news item*) (em) exclusivo. **~ of** sem incluir. **~ly** *adv* exclusivamente
excruciating /ɪk'skru:ʃɪeɪtɪŋ/ *a* excruciante, atroz
excursion /ɪk'skɜ:ʃn/ *n* excursão *f*
excus|e[1] /ɪk'skju:z/ *vt* desculpar. **~e me!** desculpe!, com licença! **~e from** (*exempt*) dispensar de. **~able** *a* desculpável
excuse[2] /ɪk'skju:s/ *n* desculpa *f*
ex-directory /eksdɪ'rektərɪ/ *a* que não vem no anuário, (*P*) na lista
execute /'eksɪkju:t/ *vt* executar
execution /eksɪ'kju:ʃn/ *n* execução *f*
executive /ɪg'zekjʊtɪv/ *a & n* executivo (*m*)
exemplary /ɪg'zemplərɪ/ *a* exemplar
exemplify /ɪg'zemplɪfaɪ/ *vt* exemplificar, ilustrar
exempt /ɪg'zempt/ *a* isento (**from** de) □ *vt* dispensar, eximir. **~ion** /-ʃn/ *n* isenção *f*
exercise /'eksəsaɪz/ *n* exercício *m* □ *vt* (*powers, restraint etc*) exercer; (*dog*) levar para passear □ *vi* fazer exercício. **~ book** caderno *m*
exert /ɪg'zɜ:t/ *vt* empregar, exercer. **~ o.s.** esforçar-se, fazer um esforço. **~ion** /-ʃn/ *n* esforço *m*
exhaust /ɪg'zɔ:st/ *vt* esgotar □ *n* (*auto*) (tubo de) escape *m*. **~ed** *a* esgotado, exausto. **~ion** /-stʃən/ *n* esgotamento *m*, exaustão *f*
exhaustive /ɪg'zɔ:stɪv/ *a* exaustivo, completo
exhibit /ɪg'zɪbɪt/ *vt* exibir, mostrar; (*thing, collection*) expor □ *n* objeto *m*, (*P*) objecto *m* exposto
exhibition /eksɪ'bɪʃn/ *n* exposição *f*; (*act of showing*) demonstração *f*
exhilarat|e /ɪg'zɪləreɪt/ *vt* regozijar; (*invigorate*) animar, estimular. **~ion** /-'reɪʃn/ *n* animação *f*, alegria *f*
exhort /ɪg'zɔ:t/ *vt* exortar
exile /'eksaɪl/ *n* exílio *m*; (*person*) exilado *m* □ *vt* exilar, desterrar
exist /ɪg'zɪst/ *vi* existir. **~ence** *n* existência *f*. **be in ~ence** existir
exit /'eksɪt/ *n* saída *f*
exonerate /ɪg'zɒnəreɪt/ *vt* exonerar
exorbitant /ɪg'zɔ:bɪtənt/ *a* exorbitante
exorcize /'eksɔ:saɪz/ *vt* esconjurar, exorcisar
exotic /ɪg'zɒtɪk/ *a* exótico

expan|d /ɪk'spænd/ *vt/i* expandir(-se); (*extend*) estender(-se), alargar(-se); (*gas, liquid, metal*) dilatar(-se). **~sion** /ɪk'spænʃn/ *n* expansão *f*; (*extension*) alargamento *m*; (*of gas etc*) dilatação *f*

expanse /ɪk'spæns/ *n* extensão *f*

expatriate /eks'pætrɪət/ *a & n* expatriado (*m*)

expect /ɪk'spekt/ *vt* esperar; (*suppose*) crer, supor; (*require*) contar com, esperar; (*baby*) esperar. **~ to do** contar fazer. **~ation** /ekspek'teɪʃn/ *n* expectativa *f*

expectan|t /ɪk'spektənt/ *a* **~t mother** gestante *f*. **~cy** *n* expectativa *f*

expedient /ɪk'spi:dɪənt/ *a* oportuno □ *n* expediente *m*

expedition /ekspɪ'dɪʃn/ *n* expedição *f*

expel /ɪk'spel/ *vt* (*pt* **expelled**) expulsar; (*gas, poison etc*) expelir

expend /ɪk'spend/ *vt* despender. **~able** *a* descartável

expenditure /ɪk'spendɪtʃə(r)/ *n* despesa *f*, gasto *m*

expense /ɪk'spens/ *n* despesa *f*; (*cost*) custo *m*. **at sb's ~** à custa de alg. **at the ~ of** (*fig*) à custa de

expensive /ɪk'spensɪv/ *a* caro, dispendioso; (*tastes, habits*) de luxo

experience /ɪk'spɪərɪəns/ *n* experiência *f* □ *vt* experimentar; (*feel*) sentir. **~d** *a* experiente

experiment /ɪk'sperɪmənt/ *n* experiência *f* □ *vi* /ɪk'sperɪment/ fazer uma experiência. **~al** /-'mentl/ *a* experimental

expert /'ekspɜ:t/ *a & n* perito (*m*). **~ly** *adv* com perícia, habilmente

expertise /ekspɜ:'ti:z/ *n* perícia *f*, competência *f*

expir|e /ɪk'spaɪə(r)/ *vi* expirar. **~y** *n* fim *m* de prazo, expiração *f*

expl|ain /ɪk'spleɪn/ *vt* explicar. **~anation** /eksplə'neɪʃn/ *n* explicação *f*. **~anatory** /ɪk'splænətrɪ/ *a* explicativo

expletive /ɪk'spli:tɪv/ *n* imprecação *f*, praga *f*

explicit /ɪk'splɪsɪt/ *a* explícito

explo|de /ɪk'spləʊd/ *vt/i* (fazer) explodir. **~sion** /ɪk'spləʊʒn/ *n* explosão *f*. **~sive** *a & n* explosivo (*m*)

exploit[1] /'eksplɔɪt/ *n* façanha *f*

exploit[2] /ɪk'splɔɪt/ *vt* explorar. **~ation** /eksplɔɪ'teɪʃn/ *n* exploração *f*

exploratory /ɪk'splɒrətrɪ/ *a* exploratório; (*talks*) preliminar

explor|e /ɪk'splɔ:(r)/ *vt* explorar; (*fig*) examinar. **~ation** /eksplə'reɪʃn/ *n* exploração *f*. **~er** *n* explorador *m*

exponent /ɪk'spəʊnənt/ *n* (*person*) expoente *mf*; (*math*) expoente *m*

export[1] /ɪk'spɔ:t/ *vt* exportar. **~er** *n* exportador *m*

export[2] /'ekspɔ:t/ *n* exportação *f*. **~s** *npl* exportações *fpl*

expos|e /ɪk'spəʊz/ *vt* expor; (*disclose*) revelar; (*unmask*) desmascarar. **~ure** /-ʒə(r)/ *n* exposição *f*; (*cold*) frio *m*

expound /ɪk'spaʊnd/ *vt* explanar, expor

express[1] /ɪk'spres/ *a* expresso, categórico □ *adv* (por) expresso □ *n* (*train*) rápido *m*, expresso *m*. **~ly** *adv* expressamente

express[2] /ɪk'spres/ *vt* exprimir. **~ion** /-ʃn/ *n* expressão *f*. **~ive** *a* expressivo

expulsion /ɪk'spʌlʃn/ *n* expulsão *f*

exquisite /'ekskwɪzɪt/ *a* requintado

extempore /ek'stempərɪ/ *a* improvisado □ *adv* de improviso, sem preparação prévia

exten|d /ɪk'stend/ *vt* (*stretch*) estender; (*enlarge*) aumentar, ampliar; (*prolong*) prolongar; (*grant*) oferecer □ *vi* (*stretch*) estender-se; (*in time*) prolongar-se. **~sion** /ɪk'stenʃn/ *n* (*incl phone*) extensão *f*; (*of deadline*) prorrogação *f*; (*building*) anexo *m*

extensive /ɪk'stensɪv/ *a* extenso; (*damage, study*) vasto. **~ly** *adv* muito

extent /ɪk'stent/ *n* extensão *f*; (*degree*) medida *f*. **to some ~** até certo ponto, em certa medida. **to such an ~ that** a tal ponto que

exterior /ɪk'stɪərɪə(r)/ *a & n* exterior (*m*)

exterminat|e /ɪk'stɜ:mɪneɪt/ *vt* exterminar. **~ion** /'neɪʃn/ *n* exterminação *f*, extermínio *m*

external /ɪk'stɜ:nl/ *a* externo. **~ly** *adv* exteriormente

extinct /ɪk'stɪŋkt/ *a* extinto. **~ion** /-ʃn/ *n* extinção *f*

extinguish /ɪk'stɪŋgwɪʃ/ *vt* extinguir, apagar. **~er** *n* extintor *m*

extol /ɪk'stəʊl/ *vt* (*pt* **extolled**) exaltar, elogiar, louvar

extort /ɪk'stɔ:t/ *vt* extorquir (**from** a). **~ion** /-ʃn/ *n* extorsão *f*

extortionate /ɪk'stɔ:ʃənət/ *a* exorbitante

extra /'ekstrə/ *a* extra, adicional □ *adv* extra, excepcionalmente. **~ strong** extra-forte □ *n* extra *m*; (*cine, theat*) extra *mf*, figurante *mf*. **~ time** (*football*) prorrogação *f*

extra- /'ekstrə/ *pref* extra-

extract[1] /ɪk'strækt/ *vt* extrair; (*promise, tooth*) arrancar; (*fig*) obter. **~ion** /-ʃn/ *n* extração *f*, (*P*) extracção *f*; (*descent*) origem *f*

extract[2] /'ekstrækt/ *n* extrato *m*, (*P*) extracto *m*

extradit|e /'ekstrədaɪt/ *vt* extraditar. **~ion** /-'dɪʃn/ *n* extradição *f*

extramarital /ekstrə'mærɪtl/ *a* extraconjugal, extramatrimonial
extraordinary /ɪk'strɔ:dnrɪ/ *a* extraordinário
extravagan|t /ɪk'strævəgənt/ *a* extravagante; (*wasteful*) esbanjador. **~ce** *n* extravagância *f*; (*wastefulness*) esbanjamento *m*
extrem|e /ɪk'stri:m/ *a* & *n* extremo (*m*). **~ely** *adv* extremamente. **~ist** *n* extremista *mf*
extremity /ɪk'stremətɪ/ *n* extremidade *f*
extricate /'ekstrɪkeɪt/ *vt* desembaraçar, livrar
extrovert /'ekstrəvɜ:t/ *n* extrovertido *m*
exuberan|t /ɪg'zju:bərənt/ *a* exuberante. **~ce** *n* exuberância *f*
exude /ɪg'zju:d/ *vt* (*charm etc*) destilar, ressumar, (*P*) transpirar
exult /ɪg'zʌlt/ *vi* exultar
eye /aɪ/ *n* olho *m* □ *vt* (*pt* **eyed**, *pres p* **eyeing**) olhar. **keep an ~ on** vigiar. **see ~ to ~** concordar inteiramente. **~-opener** *n* revelação *f*. **~-shadow** *n* sombra *f*
eyeball /'aɪbɔ:l/ *n* globo *m* ocular
eyebrow /'aɪbraʊ/ *n* sobrancelha *f*
eyelash /'aɪlæʃ/ *n* pestana *f*
eyelid /'aɪlɪd/ *n* pálpebra *f*
eyesight /'aɪsaɪt/ *n* vista *f*
eyesore /'aɪsɔ:(r)/ *n* monstruosidade *f*, horror *m*
eyewitness /'aɪwɪtnɪs/ *n* testemunha *f* ocular

F

fable /'feɪbl/ *n* fábula *f*
fabric /'fæbrɪk/ *n* tecido *m*; (*structure*) edifício *m*
fabricat|e /'fæbrɪkeɪt/ *vt* fabricar; (*invent*) urdir, inventar. **~ion** /-'keɪʃn/ *n* fabrico *m*; (*invention*) invenção *f*
fabulous /'fæbjʊləs/ *a* fabuloso
façade /fə'sa:d/ *n* fachada *f*
face /feɪs/ *n* face *f*, cara *f*, rosto *m*; (*expression*) face *f*; (*grimace*) careta *f*; (*of clock*) mostrador *m* □ *vt* (*look towards*) encarar; (*confront*) enfrentar □ *vi* (*be opposite*) estar de frente para. **~ up to** enfrentar. **~ to face** cara a cara, frente a frente. **in the ~ of** em vista de. **on the ~ of it** a julgar pelas aparências. **pull ~s** fazer caretas. **~-cloth** *n* toalha *f* de rosto, (*P*) toalhete *m* de rosto. **~-lift** *n* cirurgia *f* plástica do rosto. **~-pack** *n* máscara de beleza *f*
faceless /'feɪslɪs/ *a* (*fig*) anônimo, (*P*) anónimo
facet /'fæsɪt/ *n* faceta *f*
facetious /fə'si:ʃəs/ *a* faceto; (*pej*) engraçadinho (*colloq pej*)
facial /'feɪʃl/ *a* facial
facile /'fæsaɪl/ *a* fácil; (*superficial*) superficial
facilitate /fə'sɪlɪteɪt/ *vt* facilitar
facilit|y /fə'sɪlətɪ/ *n* facilidade *f*. **~ies** (*means*) facilidades *fpl*; (*installations*) instalações *fpl*
facing /'feɪsɪŋ/ *n* revestimento *m*
facsimile /fæk'sɪməlɪ/ *n* fac-símile *m*
fact /fækt/ *n* fato *m*, (*P*) facto *m*. **in ~, as a matter of ~** na realidade
faction /'fækʃn/ *n* facção *f*
factor /'fæktə(r)/ *n* fator *m*, (*P*) factor *m*
factory /'fæktərɪ/ *n* fábrica *f*
factual /'fæktʃʊəl/ *a* concreto, real
faculty /'fækltɪ/ *n* faculdade *f*
fad /fæd/ *n* capricho *m*, mania *f*; (*craze*) moda *f*
fade /feɪd/ *vt/i* (*colour*) desbotar; (*sound*) diminuir; (*disappear*) apagar(-se)
fag /fæg/ *n* (*colloq: chore*) estafa *f*; (*sl: cigarette*) cigarro *m*. **~ged** *a* estafado
fail /feɪl/ *vt/i* falhar; (*in an examination*) reprovar; (*omit, neglect*) deixar de; (*comm*) falir □ *n* **without ~** sem falta
failing /'feɪlɪŋ/ *n* deficiência *f* □ *prep* na falta de, à falta de
failure /'feɪljə(r)/ *n* fracasso *m*, (*P*) falhanço *m*; (*of engine*) falha *f*; (*of electricity*) falta *f*; (*person*) fracassado *m*.
faint /feɪnt/ *a* (-er, -est) (*indistinct*) apagado; (*weak*) fraco; (*giddy*) tonto □ *vi* desmaiar □ *n* desmaio *m*. **~-hearted** *a* tímido. **~ly** *adv* vagamente. **~ness** *n* debilidade *f*; (*indistinctness*) apagado *m*
fair[1] /feə(r)/ *n* feira *f*. **~-ground** *n* parque *m* de diversões, (*P*) largo *m* de feira
fair[2] /feə(r)/ *a* (-er, -est) (*of hair*) louro; (*weather*) bom; (*moderate quality*) razoável; (*just*) justo. **~ play** jogo *m* limpo, fair-play *m*. **~ly** *adv* razoavelmente. **~ness** *n* justiça *f*
fairy /'feərɪ/ *n* fada *f*. **~ story, ~ tale** conto *m* de fadas
faith /feɪθ/ *n* fé *f*; (*religion*) religião *f*; (*loyalty*) lealdade *f*. **in good ~** de boa fé, (*P*) à boa fé. **~-healer** *n* curandeiro *m*
faithful /'feɪθfl/ *a* fiel. **~ly** *adv* fielmente. **yours ~ly** atenciosamente. **~ness** *n* fidelidade *f*
fake /feɪk/ *n* (*thing*) imitação *f*; (*person*) impostor *m* □ *a* falsificado □ *vt* falsificar; (*pretend*) simular, fingir
falcon /'fɔlkən/ *n* falcão *m*
fall /fɔ:l/ *vi* (*pt* **fell**, *pp* **fallen**) cair □ *n* quedas *f*; (*Amer: autumn*) outono *m*.

~s *npl* (*waterfall*) queda-d'água *f*. ~ **back** bater em retirada. ~ **back on** recorrer a. ~ **behind** atrasar-se (**with** em). ~ **down** *or* **off** cair. ~ **flat** falhar, não resultar. ~ **flat on one's face** estatelar-se. ~ **for** (*a trick*) cair em, deixar-se levar por; (*colloq: a person*) apaixonar-se por, ficar caído por (*colloq*). ~ **in** (*roof*) ruir; (*mil*) alinhar-se, pôr-se em forma. ~ **out** brigar, (*P*) zangar-se (**with** com). ~**-out** *n* poeira *f* radioativa, (*P*) radioactiva. ~ **through** (*of plans*) falhar

fallac|y /'fæləsɪ/ *n* falácia *f*, engano *m*. ~**ious** /fə'leɪʃəs/ *a* errôneo

fallen /'fɔːlən/ *see* **fall**

fallible /'fæləbl/ *a* falível

fallow /'fæləʊ/ *a* (*of ground*) de pousio; (*uncultivated*) inculto

false /fɔːls/ *a* falso. ~ **teeth**. ~**ly** *adv* falsamente. ~**ness** *n* falsidade *f*

falsehood /'fɔːlshʊd/ *n* falsidade *f*, mentira *f*

falsify /'fɔːlsɪfaɪ/ *vt* (*pt* **-fied**) falsificar; (*a story*) deturpar

falter /'fɔːltə(r)/ *vi* vacilar; (*of the voice*) hesitar

fame /feɪm/ *n* fama *f*. ~**d** *a* afamado

familiar /fə'mɪlɪə(r)/ *a* familiar; (*intimate*) íntimo. **be** ~ **with** estar familiarizado com

familiarity /fəmɪlɪ'ærɪtɪ/ *n* familiaridade *f*

familiarize /fə'mɪlɪəraɪz/ *vt* familiarizar (**with/to** com); (*make well known*) tornar conhecido

family /'fæməlɪ/ *n* família *f*. ~ **doctor** médico *m* da familia. ~ **tree** árvore *f* genealógica

famine /'fæmɪn/ *n* fome *f*

famished /'fæmɪʃt/ *a* esfomeado, faminto. **be** ~ (*colloq*) estar morrendo de fome, (*P*) estar a morrer de fome

famous /'feɪməs/ *a* famoso

fan[1] /fæn/ *n* (*in the hand*) leque *m*; (*mechanical*) ventilador *m*, (*P*) ventoínha *f* □ *vt* (*pt* **fanned**) abanar; (*a fire; fig*) atiçar □ *vi* ~ **out** abrir-se em leque. ~ **belt** correia *f* da ventoínhas

fan[2] /fæn/ *n* (*colloq*) fã *mf*. ~ **mail** correio *m* de fãs

fanatic /fə'nætɪk/ *n* fanático *m*. ~**al** *a* fanático. ~**ism** /-sɪzəm/ *n* fanatismo *m*

fanciful /'fænsɪfl/ *a* fantasioso, fantasista

fancy /'fænsɪ/ *n* fantasia *f*; (*liking*) gosto *m* □ *a* extravagante, fantástico; (*of buttons etc*) de fantasia; (*of prices*) exorbitante □ *vt* imaginar; (*colloq: like*) gostar de; (*colloq: want*) apetecer. **it took my** ~ gostei disso, (*P*) deu-me no gosto. **a passing** ~ um entusiasmo passageiro. ~ **dress** traje *m* fantasia, (*P*) trajo *m* de fantasia

fanfare /'fænfeə(r)/ *n* fanfarra *f*

fang /fæŋ/ *n* presa *f*, dente *m* canino

fantastic /fæn'tæstɪk/ *a* fantástico

fantas|y /'fæntəsɪ/ *n* fantasia *f*. ~**ize** *vt* fantasiar, imaginar

far /fɑː(r)/ *adv* longe; (*much, very*) muito □ *a* distante, longínquo; (*end, side*) outro. ~ **away**, ~ **off** ao longe. **as** ~ **as** (*up to*) até. **as** ~ **as I know** tanto quanto saiba. **the F**~ **East** o Extremo-Oriente *m*. ~**-away** *a* distante, longínquo. ~**-fetched** *a* forçado; (*unconvincing*) pouco plausível. ~**-reaching** *a* de grande alcance

farc|e /fɑːs/ *n* farsa *f*. ~**ical** *a* de farsa; ridículo

fare /feə(r)/ *n* preço *m* da passagem; (*in taxi*) tarifa *f*, preço *m* da corrida; (*passenger*) passageiro *m*; (*food*) comida *f* □ *vi* (*get on*) dar-se

farewell /feə'wel/ *int* & *n* adeus (*m*)

farm /fɑːm/ *n* quinta *f*, fazenda *f* □ *vt* cultivar □ *vi* ser fazendeiro, (*P*) lavrador. ~ **out** (*of work*) delegar a tarefeiros. ~**-hand** *n* trabalhador *m* rural. ~**er** *n* fazendeiro *m*, (*P*) lavrador *m*. ~**ing** *n* agricultura *f*, lavoura *f*

farmhouse /'fɑːmhaʊs/ *n* casa *f* da fazenda, (*P*) quinta

farmyard /'fɑːmjɑːd/ *n* quintal de fazenda *m*, (*P*) pátio *m* de quinta

farth|er /'fɑːðə(r)/ *adv* mais longe □ *a* mais distante. ~**est** *adv* mais longe □ *a* o mais distante

fascinat|e /'fæsɪneɪt/ *vt* fascinar. ~**ion** /-'neɪʃn/ *n* fascínio *m*, fascinação *f*

fascis|t /'fæʃɪst/ *n* fascista *mf*. ~**m** /-zəm/ *n* fascismo *m*

fashion /'fæʃn/ *n* moda *f*; (*manner*) maneira *f* □ *vt* amoldar, (*P*) moldar. ~**able** *a* na moda, (*P*) à moda. ~**ably** *adv* na moda, (*P*) à moda

fast[1] /fɑːst/ *a* (**-er, -est**) rápido; (*colour*) fixo, que não desbota □ *adv* depressa; (*firmly*) firmemente. **be** ~ (*of clock*) adiantar-se, estar adiantado. ~ **asleep** profundamente adormecido, ferrado no sono. ~ **food** *n* fast-food *f*

fast[2] /fɑːst/ *vi* jejuar □ *n* jejum *m*

fasten /'fɑːsn/ *vt/i* prender; (*door, window*) fechar(-se); (*seat-belt*) apertar. ~**er**, ~**ing** *ns* fecho *m*

fastidious /fə'stɪdɪəs/ *a* exigente

fat /fæt/ *n* gordura *f* □ *a* (**fatter, fattest**) gordo. ~**ness** *n* gordura *f*

fatal /'feɪtl/ *a* fatal. ~ **injuries** ferimentos *mpl* mortais. ~**ity** /fə'tælətɪ/ *n* fatalidade *f*. ~**ly** *adv* fatalmente, mortalmente

fate /feɪt/ *n* (*destiny*) destino *m*; (*one's lot*) destino *m*, sorte *f*. **~ful** *a* fatídico
fated /'feɪtɪd/ *a* predestinado; (*doomed*) condenado (to, a)
father /'fa:ðə(r)/ *n* pai *m* □ *vt* gerar. **~-in-law** *n* (*pl* **~s-in-law**) sogro *m*. **~ly** *a* paternal
fathom /'fæðəm/ *n* braça *f* □ *vt* **~ (out)** (*comprehend*) compreender
fatigue /fə'ti:g/ *n* fadiga *f* □ *vt* fatigar
fatten /'fætn/ *vt/i* engordar. **~ing** *a* que engorda
fatty /'fætɪ/ *a* (-ier, -iest) gorduroso; (*tissue*) adiposo
fault /fɔ:lt/ *n* defeito *m*, falha *f*; (*blame*) falta *f*, culpa *f*; (*geol*) falha *f*. **at ~** culpado. **it's your ~** é culpa sua. **~less** *a* impecável. **~y** *a* defeituoso
favour /'feɪvə(r)/ *n* favor *m* □ *vt* favorecer; (*prefer*) preferir. **do sb a ~** fazer um favor a alg. **~able** *a* favorável. **~ably** *adv* favoravelmente
favourit|e /'feɪvərɪt/ *a* & *n* favorito (*m*). **~ism** /-ɪzəm/ *n* favoritismo *m*
fawn[1] /fɔ:n/ *n* cervo *m* novo □ *a* (*colour*) castanho claro
fawn[2] /fɔ:n/ *vi* **~ on** adular, bajular
fax /fæks/ *n* fax *m*, fac-símile *m* □ *vt* mandar um fax. **~ machine** fax *m*
fear /fɪə(r)/ *n* medo *m*, receio *m*, temor *m*; (*likelihood*) perigo *m* □ *vt* recear, ter medo de. **for ~ of/that** com medo de/que. **~ful** *a* (*terrible*) medonho; (*timid*) medroso, receoso. **~less** *a* destemido, intrépido
feasib|le /'fi:zəbl/ *a* factível, praticável; (*likely*) plausível. **~ility** /-'bɪlətɪ/ *n* possibilidade *f*; (*plausibility*) plausibilidade *f*
feast /fi:st/ *n* festim *m*; (*relig; fig*) festa *f* □ *vt/i* festejar; (*eat and drink*) banquetear-se. **~ on** regalar-se com
feat /fi:t/ *n* feito *m*, façanha *f*
feather /'feðə(r)/ *n* pena *f*, pluma *f*
feature /'fi:tʃə(r)/ *n* feição *f*, traço *m*; (*quality*) característica *f*; (*film*) longa metragem *f*; (*article*) artigo *m* em destaque □ *vt* representar; (*film*) ter como protagonista □ *vi* figurar
February /'februərɪ/ *n* Fevereiro *m*
fed /fed/ *see* **feed** □ *a* **be ~ up** estar farto (*colloq*) (**with** de)
federa|l /'fedərəl/ *a* federal. **~tion** /-'reɪʃn/ *n* federação *f*
fee /fi:/ *n* preço *m*. **~(s)** (*of doctor, lawyer etc*) honorários *mpl*; (*member's subscription*) quota *f*; (*univ*) (*P*) propinas *fpl*. (errolment/registration) matricula *f* **school ~s** mensalidades *fpl* escolares, (*P*) mensalidades *fpl*
feeble /'fi:bl/ *a* (-er, -est) débil, fraco. **~-minded** *a* débil mental, (*P*) deficiente
feed /fi:d/ *vt* (*pt* **fed**) alimentar, dar de comer a; (*suckle*) alimentar; (*supply*) alimentar, abostecer □ *vi* alimentar-se □ *n* comida *f*; (*breast-feeding*) mamada *f*; (*mech*) alimentação *f*
feedback /'fi:dbæk/ *n* reação *f*, (*P*) reacção *f*; (*electr*) regeneração *f*
feel /fi:l/ *vt* (*pt* **felt**) sentir; (*touch*) apalpar, tatear □ *vi* (*tired, lonely etc*) sentir-se. **~ hot/thirsty** ter calor/sede. **~ as if** ter a impressão (de) que. **~ like** ter vontade de
feeler /'fi:lə(r)/ *n* antena *f*
feeling /'fi:lɪŋ/ *n* sentimento *m*; (*physical*) sensação *f*
feet /fi:t/ *see* **foot**
feign /feɪn/ *vt* fingir
feline /'fi:laɪn/ *a* felino
fell[1] /fel/ *vt* abater, derrubar
fell[2] /fel/ *see* **fall**
fellow /'feləʊ/ *n* companheiro *m*, camarada *m*; (*of society, college*) membro *m*; (*colloq*) cara *m*, (*P*) tipo *m* (*colloq*). **~-traveller** *n* companheiro *m* de viagem. **~-ship** *n* companheirismo *m*, camaradagem *f*; (*group*) associação *f*
felt[1] /felt/ *n* feltro *m*
felt[2] /felt/ *see* **feel**
female /'fi:meɪl/ *a* (*animal etc*) fêmea *f*; (*voice, sex etc*) feminino □ *n* mulher *f*; (*animal*) fêmea *f*
feminin|e /'femənɪn/ *a* & *n* feminino (*m*). **~ity** /-'nɪnətɪ/ *n* feminilidade *f*
feminist /'femmɪst/ *n* feminista *mf*
fenc|e /fens/ *n* tapume *m*, cerca *f* □ *vt* cercar □ *vi* esgrimir. **~er** *n* esgrimista *mf*. **~ing** *n* esgrima *f*; (*fences*) tapume *m*
fend /fend/ *vi* **~ for o.s.** defender-se, virar-se (*colloq*), governar-se □ *vt* **~ off** defender-se de
fender /'fendə(r)/ *n* guarda-fogo *m*; (*Amer: mudguard*) pára-lama *m*, guarda-lama *m*, (*P*) pára-choques *m*
fennel /'fenl/ *n* (*herb*) funcho *m*, erva-doce *f*
ferment[1] /fə'ment/ *vt/i* fermentar; (*excite*) excitar. **~ation** /fɜ:men'teɪʃn/ *n* fermentação *f*
ferment[2] /'fɜ:ment/ *n* fermento *m*; (*fig*) efervescência *f*
fern /fɜ:n/ *n* feto *m*
feroc|ious /fə'rəʊʃəs/ *a* feroz. **~ity** /-'rɒsətɪ/ *n* ferocidade *f*
ferret /'ferɪt/ *n* furão *m* □ *vi* (*pt* **ferreted**) caçar com furões □ *vt* **~ out** desenterrar
ferry /'ferɪ/ *n* barco *m* de travessia, ferry(-boat) *m* □ *vt* transportar
fertil|e /'fɜ:taɪl/ *a* fértil, fecundo. **~ity** /fə'tɪlətɪ/ *n* fertilidade *f*, fecundidade *f*. **~ize** /-əlaɪz/ *vt* fertilizar, fecundar
fertilizer /'fɜ:təlaɪzə(r)/ *n* adubo *m*, fertilizante *m*

fervent /'fɜ:vənt/ *a* fervoroso
fervour /'fɜ:və(r)/ *n* fervor *m*, ardor *m*
fester /'festə(r)/ *vt/i* infectar; (*fig*) envenenar
festival /'festɪvl/ *n* festival *m*; (*relig*) festa *f*
festiv|e /'festɪv/ *a* festivo. **~e season** periodo *m* das festas. **~ity** /fes'tɪvətɪ/ *n* festividade *f*, regozijo *m*. **~ities** festas *fpl*, festividades *fpl*
festoon /fe'stu:n/ *vt* engrinaldar
fetch /fetʃ/ *vt* (*go for*) ir buscar; (*bring*) trazer; (*be sold for*) vender-se por, render
fetching /'fetʃɪŋ/ *a* atraente
fête /feɪt/ *n* festa *f or* feira *f* de caridade ao ar livre □ *vt* festejar
fetish /'fetɪʃ/ *n* fetiche *m*, ídolo *m*; (*obsession*) mania *f*
fetter /'fetə(r)/ *vt* agrilhoar. **~s** *npl* ferros *mpl*, grilhões *mpl*, grilhetas *fpl*
feud /fju:d/ *n* discórdia *f*, inimizade *f*. **~al** *a* feudal
fever /'fi:və(r)/ *n* febre *f*. **~ish** *a* febril
few /fju:/ *a* & *n* poucos (*mpl*). **~ books** poucos livros. **they are ~** são poucos. **a ~** *a* & *n* alguns (*mpl*). **a good ~, quite a ~** bastantes. **~er** *a* & *n* menos (de). **they were ~er** eram menos numerosos. **~est** *a* & *n* o menor número (de)
fiancé /fɪ'anseɪ/ *n* noivo *m*. **~e** *n* noiva *f*
fiasco /fɪ'æskəʊ/ *n* (*pl* **-os**) fiasco *m*
fib /fɪb/ *n* lorota *f*, cascata *f*, peta *f*, (*P*) mentira *f* □ *vi* (*pt* **fibbed**)
fibre /'faɪbə(r)/ *n* fibra *f*
fibreglass /'faɪbəgla:s/ *n* fibra *f* de vidro
fickle /'fɪkl/ *a* leviano, inconstante
fiction /'fɪkʃn/ *n* ficção *f*. **(works of) ~** romances *mpl*, obras *fpl* de ficção. **~al** *a* de ficção, fictício
fictitious /fɪk'tɪʃəs/ *a* fictício
fiddle /'fɪdl/ *n* (*colloq*) violino *m*; (*sl: swindle*) trapaça *f* □ *vi* (*sl*) trapacear (*sl*) □ *vt* (*sl: falsify*) falsificar, cozinhar (*sl*). **~ with** (*colloq*) brincar com, remexer em, (*P*) estar a brincar com, estar a (re)mexer em. **~r** /-ə(r)/ *n* (*colloq*) violinista *m/f*
fidelity /fɪ'delətɪ/ *n* fidelidade *f*
fidget /'fɪdʒɪt/ *vi* (*pt* **fidgeted**) estar irrequieto, remexer-se. **~ with** remexer em. **~y** *a* irrequieto; (*impatient*) impaciente
field /fi:ld/ *n* campo *m* □ *vt/i* (*cricket*) (estar pronto para) apanhar ou interceptar a bola. **~-day** *n* grande dia *m*. **~-glasses** *npl* binóculo *m*. **F~ Marshal** marechal-de-campo *m*
fieldwork /'fi:ldwɜ:k/ *n* trabalho *m* de campo; (*mil*) fortificação *f* de campanha
fiend /fi:nd/ *n* diabo *m*, demônio *m*, (*P*) demónio *m*. **~ish** *a* diabólico
fierce /fɪəs/ *a* (**-er, -est**) feroz; (*storm, attack*) violento; (*heat*) intenso, abrasador. **~ness** *n* ferocidade *f*; (*of storm, attack*) violência *f*; (*of heat*) intensidade *f*
fiery /'faɪərɪ/ *a* (**-ier, -iest**) ardente; (*temper, speech*) inflamado
fifteen /fɪf'ti:n/ *a* & *n* quinze (*m*). **~th** *a* & *n* décimo quinto (*m*)
fifth /fɪfθ/ *a* & *n* quinto (*m*)
fift|y /'fɪftɪ/ *a* & *n* cinqüenta (*m*), (*P*) cinquenta (*m*). **~y-~y** *a* meias. **~ieth** *a* & *n* qüinquagésimo (*m*), (*P*) quinquagésimo (*m*)
fig /fɪg/ *n* figo *m*. **~-tree** *n* figueira *f*
fight /faɪt/ *vi* (*pt* **fought**) lutar, combater □ *vt* lutar contra, combater □ *n* luta *f*; (*quarrel, brawl*) briga *f*. **~ over sth** lutar por alg coisa. **~ shy of** esquivar-se de, fugir de. **~er** *n* lutador *m*; (*mil*) combatente *mf*; (*plane*) caça *m*. **~ing** *n* combate *m*
figment /'fɪgmənt/ *n* **~ of the imagination** fruto *m or* produto *m* da imaginação
figurative /'fɪgjərətɪv/ *a* figurado. **~ly** *adv* em sentido figurado
figure /'fɪgə(r)/ *n* (*number*) algarismo *m*; (*diagram, body*) figura *f*. **~s** *npl* (*arithmetic*) contas *fpl*, aritmética *f* □ *vt* imaginar, supor □ *vi* (*appear*) figurar (**in** em). **~ of speech** figura *f* de retórica. **~ out** compreender. **~-head** *n* figura *f* de proa; (*pej: person*) testa-de-ferro *m*, chefe *m* nominal
filament /'fɪləmənt/ *n* filamento *m*
fil|e[1] /faɪl/ *n* (*tool*) lixa *f*, lima *f* □ *vt* lixar, limar. **~ings** *npl* limalha *f*
fil|e[2] /faɪl/ *n* fichário *m*, (*P*) dossier *m*; (*box, drawer*) fichário *m*, (*P*) ficheiro *m*; (*comput*) arquivo *m* (*line*) fila *f* □ *vt* arquivar □ *vi* **~e (past)** desfilar, marchar em fila. **~e in/out** entrar/sair em fila. **(in) single ~e** (em) fila indiana. **~ing cabinet** fichário *m*, (*P*) ficheiro *m*
fill /fɪl/ *vt/i* encher(-se); (*vacancy*) preencher □ *n* **eat one's ~** comer o que quiser. **have one's ~** estar farto. **~ in** (*form*) preencher. **~ out** (*get fat*) engordar. **~ up** encher até cima; (*auto*) encher o tanque
fillet /'fɪlɪt/ *n* (*meat, fish*) filé *m*, (*P*) filete *m* □ *vt* (*pt* **filleted**) (*meat, fish*) cortar em filés, (*P*) filetes
filling /'fɪlɪŋ/ *n* recheio *m*; (*of tooth*) obturação *f*, (*P*) chumbo *m*. **~ station** posto *m* de gasolina
film /fɪlm/ *n* filme *m* □ *vt/i* filmar. **~ star** estrela *f or* vedete *f or* (*P*) vedeta *f* de cinema, astro *m*
filter /'fɪltə(r)/ *n* filtro *m* □ *vt/i* filtrar

(-se). ~ **coffee** café *m* filtro. ~**-tip** *n* cigarro *m* com filtro

filth /fɪlθ/ *n* imundície *f*; (*fig*) obscenidade *f*. ~**y** *a* imundo; (*fig*) obsceno

fin /fɪn/ *n* barbatana *f*

final /'faɪnl/ *a* final; (*conclusive*) decisivo □ *n* (*sport*) final *f*. ~**s** *npl* (*exams*) finais *fpl*. ~**ist** *n* finalista *mf*. ~**ly** *adv* finalmente, por fim; (*once and for all*) definitivamente

finale /fɪ'nɑ:lɪ/ *n* final *m*

finalize /'faɪnəlaɪz/ *vt* finalizar

financ|e /'faɪnæns/ *n* finança(s) *f* (*pl*) □ *a* financeiro □ *vt* financiar. ~**ier** /-'nænsɪə(r)/ *n* financeiro *m*

financial /faɪ'nænʃl/ *a* financeiro. ~**ly** *adv* financeiramente

find /faɪnd/ *vt* (*pt* **found**) (*sth lost*) achar, encontrar; (*think*) achar; (*discover*) descobrir; (*jur*) declarar □ *n* achado *m*. ~ **out** *vt* apurar, descobrir □ *vi* informar-se (**about** sobre)

fine[1] /faɪn/ *n* multa *f* □ *vt* multar

fine[2] /faɪn/ *a* (-**er**, -**est**) fino; (*splendid*) belo, lindo □ *adv* (muito) bem; (*small*) fino, fininho. ~ **arts** belas artes *fpl*. ~ **weather** bom tempo. ~**ly** *adv* lindamente; (*cut*) fininho, aos bocadinhos

finesse /fɪ'nes/ *n* finura *f*, sutileza *f*

finger /'fɪŋgə(r)/ *n* dedo *m* □ *vt* apalpar. ~**-mark** *n* dedada *f*. ~**-nail** *n* unha *f*

fingerprint /'fɪŋgəprɪnt/ *n* impressão *f* digital

fingertip /'fɪŋgətɪp/ *n* ponta *f* do dedo

finicky /'fɪnɪkɪ/ *a* meticuloso, miudinho

finish /'fɪnɪʃ/ *vt/i* acabar, terminar □ *n* fim *m*; (*of race*) chegada *f*; (*on wood, clothes*) acabamento *m*. ~ **doing** acabar de fazer. ~ **up doing** acabar por fazer. ~ **up in** ir parar a, acabar em

finite /'faɪnaɪt/ *a* finito

Fin|land /'fɪnlənd/ *n* Finlândia *f*. ~**n** *n* finlandês *m*. ~**nish** *a* & *n* (*lang*) finlandês (*m*)

fir /fɜ:(r)/ *n* abeto *m*

fire /'faɪə(r)/ *n* fogo *m*; (*conflagration*) incêndio *m*; (*heater*) aquecedor *m* □ *vt* (*bullet, gun, etc*) disparar; (*dismiss*) despedir; (*fig: stimulate*) inflamar □ *vi* atirar, fazer fogo (**at** sobre). **on** ~ em chamas. **set** ~ **to** pôr fogo em. ~**-alarm** *n* alarme *m* de incêndio. ~ **brigade** bombeiros *mpl*. ~**-engine** *n* carro *m* de bombeiro, (*P*) da bomba. ~**-escape** *n* saída *f* de incêndio. ~ **extinguisher** *n* extintor *m* de incêndio. ~ **station** quartel *m* dos bombeiros

firearm /'faɪərɑ:m/ *n* arma *f* de fogo

fireman /'faɪəmən/ *n* (*pl* -**men**) bombeiro *m*

fireplace /'faɪəpleɪs/ *n* chaminé *f*, lareira *f*

firewood /'faɪəwʊd/ *n* lenha *f*

firework /'faɪəwɜ:k/ *n* fogo *m* de artifício

firing-squad /'faɪərɪŋskwɒd/ *n* pelotão *m* de execução

firm[1] /fɜ:m/ *n* firma *f* comercial

firm[2] /fɜ:m/ *a* (-**er**, -**est**) firme; (*belief*) firme, inabalável. ~**ly** *adv* firmemente. ~**ness** *n* firmeza *f*

first /fɜ:st/ *a* & *n* primeiro (*m*); (*auto*) primeira (*f*) □ *adv* primeiro, em primeiro lugar. **at** ~ a princípio, no início. ~ **of all** antes de mais nada. **for the** ~ **time** pela primeira vez. ~ **aid** primeiros socorros *mpl*. ~**-class** *a* de primeira classe. ~ **name** nome de batismo *m*, (*P*) baptismo *m*. ~**-rate** *a* excelente. ~**ly** *adv* primeiramente, em primeiro lugar

fiscal /'fɪskl/ *a* fiscal

fish /fɪʃ/ *n* (*pl usually invar*) peixe *m* □ *vt/i* pescar. ~ **out** (*colloq*) tirar. ~**ing** *n* pesca *f*. **go** ~**ing** ir pescar, (*P*) ir à pesca. ~**ing-rod** *n* vara *f* de pescar. ~**y** *a* de peixe; (*fig: dubious*) suspeito

fisherman /'fɪʃəmən/ *n* (*pl* -**men**) pescador *m*

fishmonger /'fɪʃmʌŋgə(r)/ *n* dono *m*/empregado *m* de peixaria. ~**'s (shop)** peixaria *f*

fission /'fɪʃn/ *n* fissão *f*, cisão *f*

fist /fɪst/ *n* punho *m*, mão *f* fechada, (*P*) punho *m*

fit[1] /fɪt/ *n* acesso *m*, ataque *m*; (*of generosity*) rasgo *m*

fit[2] /fɪt/ *a* (**fitter, fittest**) de boa saúde, em forma; (*proper*) próprio; (*good enough*) em condições; (*able*) capaz □ *vt/i* (*pt* **fitted**) (*clothes*) assentar, ficar bem (a); (*into space*) (*match*) ajustar (-se) (a); (*install*) instalar □ *n* **be a good** ~ assentar bem. **be a tight** ~ estar justo. ~ **out** equipar. ~**ted carpet** carpete *m*, (*P*) alcatifa *f*. ~**ness** *n* saúde *f*, (*P*) condição *f* física

fitful /'fɪtfl/ *a* intermitente

fitment /'fɪtmənt/ *n* móvel *m* de parede

fitting /'fɪtɪŋ/ *a* apropriado □ *n* (*clothes*) prova *f*. ~**s** (*fixtures*) instalações *fpl*; (*fitments*) mobiliário *m*. ~ **room** cabine *f*

five /faɪv/ *a* & *n* cinco (*m*)

fix /fɪks/ *vt* fixar; (*mend, prepare*) arranjar □ *n* **in a** ~ em apuros, (*P*) numa alhada. ~ **sb up with sth** conseguir alg coisa para alguém. ~**ed** *a* fixo

fixation /fɪk'seɪʃn/ *n* fixação *f*; (*obsession*) obsessão *f*

fixture /'fɪkstʃə(r)/ *n* equipamento *m*,

instalação *f*; (*sport*) (data *f* marcada para) competição *f*

fizz /fɪz/ *vi* efervescer, borbulhar □ *n* efervescência *f*. **~y** *a* gasoso

fizzle /'fɪzl/ *vi* **~ out** (*plan etc*) acabar em nada *or* (*P*) em águas de bacalhau (*colloq*)

flab /flæb/ *n* (*colloq*) gordura *f*, banha *f* (*colloq*). **~by** *a* flácido

flabbergasted /'flæbəga:stɪd/ *a* (*colloq*) espantado, pasmado (*colloq*)

flag[1] /flæg/ *n* bandeira *f* □ *vt* (*pt* **flagged**) fazer sinal. **~ down** fazer sinal para parar. **~-pole** *n* mastro *m* (de bandeira)

flag[2] /flæg/ *vi* (*pt* **flagged**) (*droop*) cair, pender, tombar; (*of person*) esmorecer

flagrant /'fleɪgrənt/ *a* flagrante

flagstone /'flægstəʊn/ *n* laje *f*

flair /fleə(r)/ *n* jeito *m*, habilidade *f*

flak|e /fleɪk/ *n* floco *m*; (*paint*) lasca *f* □ *vi* descamar-se, lascar-se. **~y** *a* (*paint*) descamado, lascado

flamboyant /flæm'bɔɪənt/ *a* flamejante; (*showy*) flamante, vistoso; (*of manner*) extravagante

flame /fleɪm/ *n* chama *f*, labareda *f* □ *vi* flamejar. **burst into ~s** incendiar-se

flamingo /flə'mɪŋgəʊ/ *n* (*pl* -os) flamingo *m*

flammable /'flæməbl/ *a* inflamável

flan /flæn/ *n* torta *f*, (*P*) tarte *f*

flank /flæŋk/ *n* flanco *m* □ *vt* flanquear

flannel /'flænl/ *n* flanela *f*; (*for face*) toalha *f*, (*P*) toalhete *m* de rosto

flap /flæp/ *vi* (*pt* **flapped**) bater □ *vt* **~ its wings** bater as asas □ *n* (*of table, pocket*) aba *f*; (*sl: panic*) pânico *m*

flare /fleə(r)/ *vi* **~ up** irromper em chamas; (*of war*) rebentar; (*fig: of person*) enfurecer-se □ *n* chamejar *m*; (*dazzling light*) clarão *m*; (*signal*) foguete *m* de sinalização. **~d** *a* (*skirt*) évasé

flash /flæʃ/ *vi* brilhar subitamente; (*on and off*) piscar; (*auto*) fazer sinal com o pisca-pisca □ *vt* fazer brilhar; (*send*) lançar, dardejar; (*flaunt*) fazer alarde de, ostentar □ *n* clarão *m*, lampejo *m*; (*photo*) flash *m*. **~ past** passar como uma bala, (*P*) passar como um bólide

flashback /'flæʃbæk/ *n* cena *f* retrospectiva, flashback *m*

flashlight /'flæʃlaɪt/ *n* lanterna *f* elétrica, (*P*) eléctrica

flashy /'flæʃɪ/ *a* espalhafatoso, que dá na vista

flask /fla:sk/ *n* frasco *m*; (*vacuum flask*) garrafa *f* térmica, (*P*) garrafa *f* termos

flat /flæt/ *a* (**flatter**, **flattest**) plano, chato; (*tyre*) arriado, vazio; (*battery*) fraco; (*refusal*) categórico; (*fare, rate*) fixo; (*monotonous*) monótono; (*mus*) bemol; (*out of tune*) desafinado □ *n* apartamento *m*; (*colloq: tyre*) furo *m* no preu; (*mus*) bemol *m*. **~ out** (*drive*); (*work*) a dar tudo por tudo. **~ly** *adv* categoricamente

flatter /'flætə(r)/ *vt* lisonjear, adular. **~er** *n* lisonjeiro *m*, adulador *m*. **~ing** *a* lisonjeiro, adulador. **~y** *n* lisonja *f*

flatulence /'flætjʊləns/ *n* flatulência *f*

flaunt /flɔ:nt/ *vt/i* pavonear(-se), ostentar

flavour /'fleɪvə(r)/ *n* sabor *m* (**of** a) □ *vt* dar sabor a, temperar. **~ing** *n* aroma *m* sintético; (*seasoning*) tempero *m*

flaw /flɔ:/ *n* falha *f*, imperfeição *f*. **~ed** *a* imperfeito. **~less** *a* perfeito

flea /fli:/ *n* pulga *f*

fled /fled/ *see* **flee**

fledged /fledʒd/ *a* **fully-~** (*fig*) treinado, experiente

flee /fli:/ *vi* (*pt* **fled**) fugir □ *vt* fugir de

fleece /fli:s/ *n* lã *f* de carneiro, velo *m* □ *vt* (*fig*) esfolar, roubar

fleet /fli:t/ *n* (*of warships*) esquadra *f*; (*of merchant ships, vehicles*) frota *f*

fleeting /'fli:tɪŋ/ *a* curto, fugaz

Flemish /'flemɪʃ/ *a* & *n* (*lang*) flamengo (*m*)

flesh /fleʃ/ *n* carne *f*; (*of fruit*) polpa *f*. **~y** *a* carnudo

flew /flu:/ *see* **fly**[2]

flex[1] /fleks/ *vt* flexionar

flex[2] /fleks/ *n* (*electr*) fio *f* flexível

flexib|le /'fleksəbl/ *a* flexível. **~ility** /-'bɪlətɪ/ *n* flexibilidade *f*

flexitime /'fleksɪtaɪm/ *n* horário *m* flexível

flick /flɪk/ *n* (*light blow*) safanão *m*; (*with fingertip*) piparote *m* □ *vt* dar um safanão em; (*with fingertip*) dar um piparote a. **~-knife** *n* navalha *f* de ponta e mola. **~ through** folhear

flicker /'flɪkə(r)/ *vi* vacilar, oscilar, tremular □ *n* oscilação *f*, tremular *m*; (*light*) luz *f* oscilante

flier /'flaɪə(r)/ *n* = flyer

flies /flaɪz/ *npl* (*of trousers*) braguilha *f*

flight[1] /flaɪt/ *n* (*flying*) voo *m*. **~ of stairs** lance *m*, (*P*) lanço *m* de escada. **~-deck** *n* cabine *f*, (*P*) cabina *f*

flight[2] /flaɪt/ *n* (*fleeing*) fuga *f*. **put to ~** pôr em fuga. **take ~** pôr-se em fuga

flimsy /'flɪmzɪ/ *a* (-ier, -iest) (*material*) fino; (*object*) frágil; (*excuse etc*) fraco, esfarrapado

flinch /flmtʃ/ *vi* (*wince*) retrair-se; (*draw back*) recuar; (*hesitate*) hesitar

fling /flɪŋ/ *vt/i* (*pt* **flung**) atirar(-se), arremessar(-se); (*rush*) precipitar-se

flint /flɪnt/ *n* sílex *m*; (*for lighter*) pedra *f*

flip /flɪp/ *vt* (*pt* **flipped**) fazer girar com o dedo e o polegar □ *n* pancadinha *f*. ~ **through** folhear

flippant /'flɪpənt/ *a* irreverente, petulante

flipper /'flɪpə(r)/ *n* (*of seal*) nadadeira *f*; (*of swimmer*) pé-de-pato *m*

flirt /flɜ:t/ *vt* namoriscar, flertar, (*P*) flartar □ *n* namorador *m*, namoradeira *f*. ~**ation** /-'teɪʃn/ *n* namorico *m*, flerte *m*, (*P*) flirt *m*. ~**atious** *a* namorador *m*, namoradeira *f*

flit /flɪt/ *vi* (*pt* **flitted**) esvoaçar

float /fləʊt/ *vt/i* (fazer) flutuar; (*company*) lançar □ *n* bóia *f*; (*low cart*) carro *m* de alegórico

flock /flɒk/ *n* (*of sheep; congregation*) rebanho *m*; (*of birds*) bando *m*; (*crowd*) multidão *f* □ *vi* afluir, juntar-se

flog /flɒg/ *vt* (*pt* **flogged**) açoitar; (*sl: sell*) vender

flood /flʌd/ *n* inundação *f*, cheia *f*; (*of tears*) dilúvio *m* □ *vt* inundar, alagar □ *vi* estar inundado; (*river*) transbordar; (*fig: people*) afluir

floodlight /'flʌdlaɪt/ *n* projetor *m*, (*P*) projector *m*, holofote *m* □ *vt* (*pt* **floodlit**) iluminar

floor /flɔ:(r)/ *n* chão *m*, soalho *m*; (*for dancing*) pista *f*; (*storey*) andar *m* □ *vt* assoalhar; (*baffle*) desconcertar, embatucar

flop /flɒp/ *vi* (*pt* **flopped**) (*drop*) (deixar-se) cair; (*move helplessly*) debater-se; (*sl: fail*) ser um fiasco □ *n* (*sl*) fiasco *m*. ~**py** *a* mole, tombado. ~**py (disk)** disquete *m*

floral /'flɒ:rəl/ *a* floral

florid /'flɒrɪd/ *a* florido

florist /'flɒrɪst/ *n* florista *mf*

flounce /flaʊns/ *n* babado *m*, debrum *m*

flounder /'flaʊndə(r)/ *vi* esbracejar, debater-se; (*fig*) meter os pés pelas mãos

flour /'flaʊə(r)/ *n* farinha *f*. ~**y** *a* farinhento

flourish /'flʌrɪʃ/ *vi* florescer, prosperar □ *vt* brandir □ *n* floreado *m*; (*movement*) gesto *m* elegante. ~**ing** *a* próspero

flout /flaʊt/ *vt* escarnecer (de)

flow /fləʊ/ *vi* correr, fluir; (*traffic*) mover-se; (*hang loosely*) flutuar; (*gush*) jorrar □ *n* corrente *f*; (*of tide; fig*) enchente *f*. ~ **into** (*of river*) desaguar em. ~ **chart** organograma *m*, (*P*) organigrama *m*

flower /'flaʊə(r)/ *n* flor *f* □ *vi* florir, florescer. ~**-bed** *n* canteiro *m*. ~**ed** *a* de flores, (*P*) florido, às flores. ~**y** *a* florido

flown /fləʊn/ *see* **fly**[2]

flu /flu:/ *n* (*colloq*) gripe *f*

fluctuat|e /'flʌktʃʊeɪt/ *vi* flutuar, oscilar. ~**ion** /-'eɪʃn/ *n* flutuação *f*, oscilação *f*

flue /flu:/ *n* cano *m* de chaminé

fluen|t /'flu:ənt/ *a* fluente. **be** ~**t (in a language)** falar correntemente (uma língua). ~**cy** *n* fluência *f*. ~**tly** *adv* fluentemente

fluff /flʌf/ *n* cotão *m*; (*down*) penugem *f* □ *vt* (*colloq: bungle*) estender-se em (*sl*), executar mal. ~**y** *a* penugento, fofo

fluid /'flu:ɪd/ *a* & *n* fluido (*m*)

fluke /flu:k/ *n* bambúrrio (*colloq*) *m*, golpe *m* de sorte

flung /flʌŋ/ *see* **fling**

flunk /flʌŋk/ *vt/i* (*Amer colloq*) levar pau (*colloq*), (*P*) chumbar (*colloq*)

fluorescent /flʊə'resnt/ *a* fluorescente

fluoride /'flʊəraɪd/ *n* flúor *m*, fluor *m*

flurry /'flʌrɪ/ *n* rajada *f*, rabanada *f*, lufada *f*; (*fig*) atrapalhação *f*, agitação *f*

flush[1] /flʌʃ/ *vi* corar, ruborizar-se □ *vt* lavar com água, (*P*) lavar a jorros de água □ *n* rubor *m*, vermelhidão *f*; (*fig*) excitação *f*; (*of water*) jorro *m* □ *a* ~ **with** ao nível de, rente a. ~ **the toilet** dar descarga

flush[2] /flʌʃ/ *vt* ~ **out** desalojar

fluster /'flʌstə(r)/ *vt* atarantar, perturbar, enervar

flute /flu:t/ *n* flauta *f*

flutter /'flʌtə(r)/ *vi* esvoaçar; (*wings*) bater; (*heart*) palpitar □ *vt* bater. ~ **one's eyelashes** pestanejar □ *n* (*of wings*) batimento *m*; (*fig*) agitação *f*

flux /flʌks/ *n* **in a state of** ~ em mudança *f* contínua

fly[1] /flaɪ/ *n* mosca *f*

fly[2] /flaɪ/ *vi* (*pt* **flew**, *pp* **flown**) voar; (*passengers*) ir de/viajar de avião; (*rush*) correr □ *vt* pilotar; (*passengers, goods*) transportar por avião; (*flag*) hastear, (*P*) arvorar □ *n* (*of trousers*) braguilha *f*

flyer /'flaɪə(r)/ *n* aviador *m*; (*Amer: circular*) prospecto *m*

flying /'flaɪɪŋ/ *a* voador. **with** ~ **colours** com grande êxito, esplendidamente. ~ **saucer** disco *m* voador. ~ **start** bom arranque *m*. ~ **visit** visita *f* de médico

flyleaf /'flaɪli:f/ *n* (*pl* **-leaves**) guarda *f*, folha *f* em branco

flyover /'flaɪəʊvə(r)/ *n* viaduto *m*

foal /fəʊl/ *n* potro *m*

foam /fəʊm/ *n* espuma *f* □ *vi* espumar. ~ (rubber) *n* espuma *f* de borracha

fob /fɒb/ *vt* (*pt* fobbed) ~ off iludir, entreter com artifícios. ~ off on impingir a

focus /'fəʊkəs/ *n* (*pl* -cuses *or* -ci /-saɪ/) foco *m* □ *vt/i* (*pt* focused) focar; (*fig*) concentrar(-se). in ~ focado, em foco. out of ~ desfocado

fodder /'fɒdə(r)/ *n* forragem *f*

foetus /'fi:təs/ *n* (*pl* -tuses) feto *m*

fog /fɒg/ *n* nevoeiro *m* □ *vt/i* (*pt* fogged) enevoar(-se). ~-horn *n* sereia *f* de nevoeiro. ~gy *a* enevoado, brumoso. it is ~gy está nevoento

foible /'fɔɪbl/ *n* fraqueza *f*, ponto *m* fraco

foil[1] /fɔɪl/ *n* papel *m* de alumínio; (*fig*) contraste *m*

foil[2] /fɔɪl/ *vt* frustrar

foist /fɔɪst/ *vt* impingir (on a)

fold /fəʊld/ *vt/i* dobrar(-se); (*arms*) cruzar; (*colloq: fail*) falir □ *n* dobra *f*. ~er *n* pasta *f*; (*leaflet*) prospecto *m* (desdobrável). ~ing *a* dobrável, dobradiço

foliage /'fəʊlɪɪdʒ/ *n* folhagem *f*

folk /fəʊk/ *n* povo *m*. ~s (*family, people*) gente *f* (*colloq*) □ *a* folclórico, popular. ~lore *n* folclore *m*

follow /'fɒləʊ/ *vt/i* seguir. it ~s that quer dizer que. ~ suit (*cards*) servir o naipe jogado; (*fig*) seguir o exemplo, fazer o mesmo. ~ up (*letter etc*) dar seguimento a. ~er *n* partidário *m*, seguidor *m*. ~ing *n* partidários *mpl* □ *a* seguinte □ *prep* em seguimento a

folly /'fɒlɪ/ *n* loucura *f*

fond /fɒnd/ *a* (-er -est) carinhoso; (*hope*) caro. be ~ of gostar de, ser amigo de. ~ness *n* (*for people*) afeição *f*; (*for thing*) gosto *m*

fondle /'fɒndl/ *vt* acariciar

font /fɒnt/ *n* pia *f* batismal, (*P*) baptismal

food /fu:d/ *n* alimentação *f*, comida *f*; (*nutrient*) alimento *m* □ *a* alimentar. ~ poisoning envenenamento *m* alimentar

fool /fu:l/ *n* idiota *mf*, parvo *m* □ *vt* enganar □ *vi* ~ around andar sem fazer nada

foolhardy /'fu:lha:dɪ/ *a* imprudente, atrevido

foolish /'fu:lɪʃ/ *a* idiota, parvo. ~ly *adv* parvamente. ~ness *n* idiotice *f*, parvoice *f*

foolproof /'fu:lpru:f/ *a* infalível

foot /fʊt/ *n* (*pl* feet) (*of person, bed, stairs*) pé *m*; (*of animal*) pata *f*; (*measure*) pé *m* (= 30,48 cm) □ *vt* ~ the bill pagar a conta. on ~ a pé. on or to one's feet de pé. put one's ~ in it fazer uma gafe. to be under sb's feet atrapalhar alg. ~-bridge *n* passarela *f*

football /'fʊtbɔ:l/ *n* bola *f* de futebol; (*game*) futebol *m*. ~ pools loteria *f* esportiva, (*P*) totobola *m*. ~er *n* futebolista *mf*, jogador *m* de futebol

foothills /'fʊthɪlz/ *npl* contrafortes *mpl*

foothold /'fʊthəʊld/ *n* ponto *m* de apoio

footing /'fʊtɪŋ/ *n*: firm ~ stor. on an equal ~ em pé de igualdade

footlights /'fʊtlaɪts/ *npl* ribalta *f*

footnote /'fʊtnəʊt/ *n* nota *f* de rodapé

footpath /'fʊtpa:θ/ *n* (*pavement*) calçada *f*, (*P*) passeio *m*; (*in open country*) atalho *m*, caminho *m*

footprint /'fʊtprɪnt/ *n* pegada *f*

footstep /'fʊtstep/ *n* passo *m*

footwear /'fʊtweə(r)/ *n* calçado *m*

for /fə(r)/; *emphatic* /fɔ:(r)/ *prep* para; (*in favour of; in place of*) por; (*during*) durante □ *conj* porque, visto que. a liking ~ gosto por. he has been away ~ two years há dois anos que ele está fora. ~ ever para sempre

forage /'fɒrɪdʒ/ *vi* forragear; (*rummage*) remexer à procura (de) □ *n* forragem *f*

forbade /fə'bæd/ *see* forbid

forbear /fɔ:'beə(r)/ *vt/i* (*pt* forbore, *pp* forborne) abster-se (from de). ~ance *n* paciência *f*, tolerância *f*

forbid /fə'bɪd/ *vt* (*pt* forbade, *pp* forbidden) proibir. you are ~den to smoke você está proibido de fumar, (*P*) estás proibido de fumar. ~ding *a* severo, intimidante

force /fɔ:s/ *n* força *f* □ *vt* forçar. ~ into fazer entrar à força. ~ on impor a. come into ~ entrar em vigor. the ~s as Forças Armadas. ~d *a* forçado. ~ful *a* enérgico

force-feed /'fɔ:sfi:d/ *vt* (*pt* -fed) alimentar à força

forceps /'fɔ:seps/ *n* (*pl invar*) fórceps *m*

forcibl|e /'fɔ:səbl/ *a* convincente; (*done by force*) à força. ~y *adv* à força

ford /fɔ:d/ *n* vau *m* □ *vt* passar a vau, vadear

fore /fɔ:(r)/ *a* dianteiro □ *n* to the ~ em evidência

forearm /'fɔ:ra:m/ *n* antebraço *m*

foreboding /fɔ:'bəʊdɪŋ/ *n* pressentimento *m*

forecast /'fɔ:ka:st/ *vt* (*pt* forecast) prever □ *n* previsão *f*. weather ~ boletim *m* meteorológico, previsão *f* do tempo

forecourt /'fɔ:kɔ:t/ *n* pátio *m* de entrada; (*of garage*) área *f* das bombas de gasolina

forefinger /'fɔ:fɪŋgə(r)/ *n* (dedo) indicador *m*
forefront /'fɔ:frʌnt/ *n* vanguarda *f*
foregone /'fɔ:gɒn/ *a* ~ **conclusion** resultado *m* previsto
foreground /'fɔ:graʊnd/ *n* primeiro plano *m*
forehead /'fɒrɪd/ *n* testa *f*
foreign /'fɒrən/ *a* estrangeiro; (*trade*) externo; (*travel*) ao/no estrangeiro. **F~ Office** Ministério *m* dos Negócios Estrangeiros. **~er** *n* estrangeiro *m*.
foreman /'fɔ:mən/ *n* (*pl* **foremen**) contramestre *m*; (*of jury*) primeiro jurado *m*
foremost /'fɔ:məʊst/ *a* principal, primeiro □ *adv* **first and** ~ antes de mais nada, em primeiro lugar
forename /'fɔ:neɪm/ *n*
forensic /fə'rensɪk/ *a* forense. ~ **medicine** medicina *f* legal
forerunner /'fɔ:rʌnə(r)/ *n* precursor *m*
foresee /fɔ:'si:/ *vt* (*pt* **-saw**, *pp* **-seen**) prever. **~able** *a* previsível
foreshadow /fɔ:'ʃædəʊ/ *vt* prefigurar, pressagiar
foresight /'fɔ:saɪt/ *n* previsão *f*, previdência *f*
forest /'fɒrɪst/ *n* floresta *f*
forestall /fɔ:'stɔ:l/ *vt* (*do first*) antecipar-se a; (*prevent*) prevenir; (*anticipate*) antecipar
forestry /'fɒrɪstrɪ/ *n* silvicultura *f*
foretell /fɔ:'tel/ *vt* (*pt* **foretold**) predizer, profetizar
forever /fə'revə(r)/ *adv* (*endlessly*) constantemente
foreword /'fɔ:wɜ:d/ *n* prefácio *m*
forfeit /'fɔ:fɪt/ *n* penalidade *f*, preço *m*; (*in game*) prenda *f* □ *vt* perder
forgave /fə'geɪv/ *see* **forgive**
forge[1] /fɔ:dʒ/ *vi* ~ **ahead** tomar a dianteira, avançar
forge[2] /fɔ:dʒ/ *n* forja *f* □ *vt* (*metal, friendship*) forjar; (*counterfeit*) falsificar, forjar. **~r** /-ə(r)/ *n* falsificador *m*, forjador *m*. **~ry** /-ərɪ/ *n* falsificação *f*
forget /fə'get/ *vt/i* (*pt* **forgot**, *pp* **forgotten**) esquecer. ~ **o.s.** portar-se com menos dignidade, esquecer-se de quem é. **~-me-not** *n* miosótis *m*. **~ful** *a* esquecido. **~fulness** *n* esquecimento *m*
forgive /fə'gɪv/ *vt* (*pt* **forgave**, *pp* **forgiven**) perdoar (**sb for sth** alg coisa a alg). **~ness** *n* perdão *m*
forgo /fɔ:'gəʊ/ *vt* (*pt* **forwent**, *pp* **forgone**) renunciar a
fork /fɔ:k/ *n* garfo *m*; (*for digging etc*) forquilha *f*; (*in road*) bifurcação *f* □ *vi* bifurcar. ~ **out** (*sl*) desembolsar. **~-lift truck** empilhadeira *f*. **~ed** *a* bifurcado; (*lightning*) em zigzag
forlorn /fə'lɔ:n/ *a* abandonado, desolado
form /fɔ:m/ *n* forma *f*; (*document*) impresso *m*, formulário *m*; (*schol*) classe *f* □ *vt/i* formar(-se)
formal /'fɔ:ml/ *a* formal; (*dress*) de cerimônia, (*P*) cerimónia. **~ity** /-'mælətɪ/ *n* formalidade *f*. **~ly** *adv* formalmente
format /'fɔ:mæt/ *n* formato *m* □ *vt* (*pl* **formatted**) (*disk*) formatar
formation /fɔ:'meɪʃn/ *n* formação *f*
former /'fɔ:mə(r)/ *a* antigo; (*first of two*) primeiro. **the** ~ aquele. **~ly** *adv* antigamente
formidable /'fɔ:mɪdəbl/ *a* formidável, tremendo
formula /'fɔ:mjʊlə/ *n* (*pl* **-ae** /-i:/*or* **-as**) fórmula *f*
formulate /'fɔ:mjʊleɪt/ *vt* formular
forsake /fə'seɪk/ *vt* (*pt* **forsook**, *pp* **forsaken**) abandonar
fort /fɔ:t/ *n* (*mil*) forte *m*
forth /fɔ:θ/ *adv* adiante, para a frente. **and so** ~ e assim por diante, etcetera. **go back and** ~ andar de trás para diante.
forthcoming /fɔ:θ'kʌmɪŋ/ *a* que está para vir, próximo; (*communicative*) comunicativo, receptivo; (*book*) no prelo
forthright /'fɔ:θraɪt/ *a* franco, direto, (*P*) directo
fortif|y /'fɔ:tɪfaɪ/ *vt* fortificar. **~ication** /-ɪ'keɪʃn/ *n* fortificação *f*
fortitude /'fɔ:tɪtju:d/ *n* fortitude *f*, fortaleza *f*
fortnight /'fɔ:tnaɪt/ *n* quinze dias *mpl*, (*P*) quinzena *f*. **~ly** *a* quinzenal □ *adv* de quinze em quinze dias
fortress /'fɔ:trɪs/ *n* fortaleza *f*
fortuitous /fɔ:'tju:ɪtəs/ *a* fortuito, acidental
fortunate /'fɔ:tʃənət/ *a* feliz, afortunado. **be** ~ ter sorte. **~ly** *adv* felizmente
fortune /'fɔ:tʃən/ *n* sorte *f*; (*wealth*) fortuna *f*. **have the good** ~ **to** ter a sorte de. **~-teller** *n* cartomante *mf*
fort|y /'fɔ:tɪ/ *a* & *n* quarenta (*m*). **~ieth** *a* &*n* quadragésimo (*m*)
forum /'fɔ:rəm/ *n* fórum *m*, foro *m*
forward /'fɔ:wəd/ *a* (*in front*) dianteiro; (*towards the front*) para a frente; (*advanced*) adiantado; (*pert*) atrevido □ *n* (*sport*) atacante *m*, (*P*) avançado *m* □ *adv* ~(s) para a frente, para diante □ *vt* (*letter*) remeter; (*goods*) expedir; (*fig: help*) favorecer. **come** ~ apresentar-se. **go** ~ avançar. **~ness** *n* adiantamento *m*; (*pertness*) atrevimento *m*
fossil /'fɒsl/ *a* & *n* fóssil (*m*)
foster /'fɒstə(r)/ *vt* fomentar; (*child*)

criar. ~-child *n* filho *m* adotivo, (*P*) adoptivo. ~-mother *n* mãe *f* adotiva, (*P*) adoptiva

fought /fɔ:t/ *see* fight

foul /faʊl/ *a* (-er, -est) infecto; (*language*) obsceno; (*weather*) mau □ *n* (*football*) falta *f* □ *vt* sujar, emporcalhar. ~-**mouthed** *a* de linguagem obscena. ~ **play** jogo *m* desleal; (*crime*) crime *m*

found[1] /faʊnd/ *see* find

found[2] /faʊnd/ *vt* fundar. ~**ation** /-'deɪʃn/ *n* fundação *f*; (*basis*) fundamento *m*. ~**ations** *npl* (*of building*) alicerces *mpl*

founder[1] /'faʊndə(r)/ *n* fundador *m*

founder[2] /'faʊndə(r)/ *vi* afundar-se

foundry /'faʊndrɪ/ *n* fundição *f*

fountain /'faʊntɪn/ *n* fonte *f*. ~-**pen** *n* caneta-tinteiro *f*, (*P*) caneta *f* de tinta permanente

four /fɔ:(r)/ *a* & *n* quatro (*m*). ~**fold** *a* quádruplo □ *adv* quadruplamente. ~**th** *a* & *n* quarto (*m*)

foursome /'fɔ:səm/ *n* grupo *m* de quatro pessoas

fourteen /fɔ:'ti:n/ *a* & *n* catorze (*m*). ~**th** *a* & *n* décimo quarto (*m*)

fowl /faʊl/ *n* ave *f* de capoeira

fox /fɒks/ *n* raposa *f* □ *vt* (*colloq*) mistificar, enganar. **be** ~**ed** ficar perplexo

foyer /'fɔɪeɪ/ *n* foyer *m*

fraction /'frækʃn/ *n* fração *f*, (*P*) fracção *f*; (*small bit*) bocadinho *m*, partícula *f*

fracture /'fræktʃə(r)/ *n* fratura *f*, (*P*) fractura *f* □ *vt/i* fraturar(-se), (*P*) fracturar(-se)

fragile /'frædʒaɪl/ *a* frágil

fragment /'frægmənt/ *n* fragmento *m*. ~**ary** /'frægməntrɪ/ *a* fragmentário

fragran|t /'freɪgrənt/ *a* fragrante, perfumado. ~**ce** *n* fragrância *f*, perfume *m*

frail /freɪl/ *a* (-er, -est) frágil

frame /freɪm/ *n* (*techn; of spectacles*) armação *f*; (*of picture*) moldura *f*; (*of window*) caixilho *m*; (*body*) corpo *m*, (*P*) estrutura *f* □ *vt* colocar a armação em; (*picture*) emoldurar; (*fig*) formular; (*sl*) incriminar falsamente, tramar. ~ **of mind** estado *m* de espírito

framework /'freɪmwɜ:k/ *n* estrutura *f*; (*context*) quadro *m*, esquema *m*

France /frɑ:ns/ *n* França *f*

franchise /'fræntʃaɪz/ *n* (*pol*) direito *m* de voto; (*comm*) concessão *f*, franchise *f*

frank[1] /fræŋk/ *a* franco. ~**ly** *adv* francamente. ~**ness** *n* franqueza *f*

frank[2] /fræŋk/ *vt* franquear

frantic /'fræntɪk/ *a* frenético

fraternal /frə'tɜ:nl/ *a* fraternal

fraternize /'frætənaɪz/ *vi* confraternizar

fraud /frɔ:d/ *n* fraude *f*; (*person*) impostor *m*. ~**ulent** /'frɔ:djʊlənt/ *a* fraudulento

fraught /frɔ:t/ *a* ~ **with** cheio de

fray[1] /freɪ/ *n* rixa *f*

fray[2] /freɪ/ *vt/i* desfiar(-se), puir, esgarçar(-se)

freak /fri:k/ *n* aberração *f*, anomalia *f* □ *a* anormal. ~ **of nature** aborto *m* da natureza. ~**ish** *a* anormal

freckle /'frekl/ *n* sarda *f*. ~**d** *a* sardento

free /fri:/ *a* (**freer, freest**) livre; (*gratis*) grátis; (*lavish*) liberal □ *vt* (*pt* **freed**) libertar (**from** de); (*rid*) livrar (**of** de). ~ **of charge** grátis, de graça. **a** ~ **hand** carta *f* branca. ~**lance** *a* independente, free-lance. ~-**range** *a* (*egg*) de galinha criada em galinheiro. ~**ly** *adv* livremente

freedom /'fri:dəm/ *n* liberdade *f*

freez|e /fri:z/ *vt/i* (*pt* **froze**, *pp* **frozen**) gelar; (*culin; finance*) congelar (-se) □ *n* gelo *m*; (*culin; finance*) congelamento *m*. ~**er** *n* congelador *m*. ~**ing** *a* gélido, glacial. **below** ~**ing** abaixo de zero

freight /freɪt/ *n* frete *m*

French /frentʃ/ *a* francês □ *n* (*lang*) francês *m*. **the** ~ os franceses. ~**man** *n* francês *m*. ~-**speaking** *a* francófono. ~ **window** porta *f* envidraçada. ~**woman** *n* francesa *f*

frenz|y /'frenzɪ/ *n* frenesi *m*. ~**ied** *a* frenético

frequen|t[1] /'fri:kwənt/ *a* freqüente, (*P*) frequente. ~**cy** *n* freqüência *f*, (*P*) frequência *f*. ~**tly** *adv* freqüentemente, (*P*) frequentemente

frequent[2] /frɪ'kwent/ *vt* freqüentar, (*P*) frequentar

fresh /freʃ/ *a* (-er, -est) fresco; (*different, additional*) novo; (*colloq: cheeky*) descarado, atrevido. ~**ly** *adv* recentemente. ~**ness** *n* frescura *f*

freshen /'freʃn/ *vt/i* refrescar. ~ **up** refrescar-se

fret /fret/ *vt/i* (*pt* **fretted**) ralar(-se). ~**ful** *a* rabugento

friar /'fraɪə(r)/ *n* frade *m*; (*before name*) frei *m*

friction /'frɪkʃn/ *n* fricção *f*

Friday /'fraɪdɪ/ *n* sexta-feira *f*. **Good** ~ sexta-feira *f* santa

fridge /frɪdʒ/ *n* (*colloq*) geladeira *f*, (*P*) frigorífico *m*

fried /fraɪd/ *see* fry □ *a* frito

friend /frend/ *n* amigo *m*. ~**ship** *n* amizade *f*

friendl|y /'frendlɪ/ *a* (-ier, -iest)

amigável, amigo, simpático. **~iness** *n* simpatia *f*, gentileza *f*
frieze /fri:z/ *n* friso *m*
frigate /'frɪgət/ *n* fragata *f*
fright /fraɪt/ *n* medo *m*, susto *m*. **give sb a ~** pregar um susto em alguém. **~ful** *a* medonho, assustador
frighten /'fraɪtn/ *vt* assustar. **~ off** afugentar. **~ed** *a* assustado. **be ~ed (of)** ter medo (de)
frigid /'frɪdʒɪd/ *a* frígido. **~ity** /-'dʒɪdətɪ/ *n* frigidez *f*, frieza *f*; (*psych*) frigidez *f*
frill /frɪl/ *n* babado *m*, (*P*) folho *m*
fringe /frɪndʒ/ *n* franja *f*; (*of area*) borda *f*; (*of society*) margem *f*. **~ benefits** (*work*) regalias *fpl* extras. **~ theatre** teatro *m* alternativo, teatro *m* de vanguarda
frisk /frɪsk/ *vi* pular, brincar □ *vt* revistar
fritter[1] /'frɪtə(r)/ *n* bolinho *m* frito, (*P*) frito *m*
fritter[2] /'frɪtə(r)/ *vt* **~ away** desperdiçar
frivol|ous /'frɪvələs/ *a* frívolo. **~ity** /-'vɒlətɪ/ *n* frivolidade *f*
fro /frəʊ/ *see* **to and fro**
frock /frɒk/ *n* vestido *m*
frog /frɒg/ *n* rã *f*
frogman /'frɒgmən/ *n* (*pl* **-men**) homem-rã *m*
frolic /'frɒlɪk/ *vi* (*pt* **frolicked**) brincar, fazer travessuras □ *n* brincadeira *f*, travessura *f*
from /frəm/; *emphatic* /frɒm/ *prep* de; (*with time, prices etc*) de, a partir de; (*according to*) por, a julgar por
front /frʌnt/ *n* (*meteo, mil, pol; of car, train*) frente *f*; (*of shirt*) peitilho *m*; (*of building; fig*) fachada *f*; (*promenade*) calçada *f* à beiramar □ *a* da frente; (*first*) primeiro. **in ~ (of)** em frente (de). **~ door** porta *f* da rua. **~-wheel drive** tração *f*, (*P*) tracção *f* dianteira. **~age** *n* frontaria *f*. **~al** *a* frontal
frontier /'frʌntɪə(r)/ *n* fronteira *f*
frost /frɒst/ *n* gelo *m*, temperatura *f* abaixo de zero; (*on ground, plants etc*) geada *f* □ *vt/i* cobrir(-se) de geada. **~-bite** *n* queimadura *f* de frio. **~-bitten** *a* queimado pelo frio. **~ed** *a* (*glass*) fosco. **~y** *a* glacial
froth /frɒθ/ *n* espuma *f* □ *vi* espumar, fazer espuma. **~y** *a* espumoso
frown /fraʊn/ *vi* franzir as sobrancelhas □ *n* franzir *m* de sobrancelhas. **~ on** desaprovar
froze, frozen /frəʊz, 'frəʊzn/ *see* **freeze**
frugal /'fru:gl/ *a* poupado; (*meal*) frugal. **~ly** *adv* frugalmente
fruit /fru:t/ *n* fruto *m*; (*collectively*) fruta *f*. **~ machine** caça-níqueis *ms/pl*. **~ salad** salada *f* de frutas. **~y** *a* que tem gosto *or* cheiro de fruta
fruit|ful /'fru:tfl/ *a* frutífero, produtivo. **~less** *a* infrutífero
fruition /fru:'ɪʃn/ *n* **come to ~** realizar-se
frustrat|e /frʌ'streɪt/ *vt* frustrar. **~ion** /-ʃn/ *n* frustração *f*
fry /fraɪ/ *vt/i* (*pt* **fried**) fritar. **~ing-pan** *n* frigideira *f*
fudge /fʌdʒ/ *n* (*culin*) doce *m* de leite, (*P*) doce *m* acaramelado □ *vt/i* **~ (the issue)** lançar a confusão
fuel /'fju:əl/ *n* combustível *m*; (*for car*) carburante *m* □ *vt* (*pt* **fuelled**) abastecer de combustível; (*fig*) atear.
fugitive /'fju:dʒətɪv/ *a* & *n* fugitivo (*m*)
fulfil /fʊl'fɪl/ *vt* (*pt* **fulfilled**) cumprir, realizar; (*condition*) satisfazer. **~ o.s.** realizar-se. **~ling** *a* satisfatório. **~ment** *n* realização *f*, (*of condition*) satisfação *f*
full /fʊl/ *a* (**-er, -est**) cheio; (*meal*) completo; (*price*) total, por inteiro; (*skirt*) rodado □ *adv* **in ~** integralmente. **at ~ speed** a toda velocidade. **to the ~** ao máximo. **be ~ up** (*colloq: after eating*) estar cheio (*colloq*). **~ moon** lua *f* cheia. **~-scale** *a* em grande. **~-size** *a* em tamanho natural. **~ stop** ponto *m* final. **~-time** *a* & *adv* a tempo integral, full-time. **~y** *adv* completamente
fulsome /'fʊlsəm/ *a* excessivo
fumble /'fʌmbl/ *vi* tatear, (*P*) tactear; (*in the dark*) andar tateando. **~ with** estar atrapalhado com, andar às voltas com
fume /fju:m/ *vi* defumar, (*P*) deitar fumo, fumegar; (*with anger*) ferver. **~s** *npl* gases *mpl*
fumigate /'fju:mɪgeɪt/ *vt* fumigar
fun /fʌn/ *n* divertimento *m*. **for ~** de brincadeira. **make ~ of** zombar de, fazer troça de. **~-fair** *n* parque *m* de diversões, (*P*) feira *f* de diversões, (*P*) feira *f* popular
function /'fʌŋkʃn/ *n* função *f* □ *vi* funcionar. **~al** *a* funcional
fund /fʌnd/ *n* fundos *mpl* □ *vt* financiar
fundamental /fʌndə'mentl/ *a* fundamental
funeral /'fju:nərəl/ *n* enterro *m*, funeral *m* □ *a* fúnebre
fungus /'fʌŋgəs/ *n* (*pl* **-gi** /-gaɪ/) fungo *m*
funnel /'fʌnl/ *n* funil *m*; (*of ship*) chaminé *f*
funn|y /'fʌnɪ/ *a* (**-ier, -iest**) engraçado, divertido; (*odd*) esquisito. **~ily** *adv* comicamente; (*oddly*) estranhamente. **~ily enough** por incrível que pareça

fur /fɜ:(r)/ *n* pêlo *m*; (*for clothing*) pele *f*; (*in kettle*) depósito *m*, crosta *f*. ~ **coat** casaco *m* de pele
furious /'fjʊərɪəs/ *a* furioso. ~**ly** *adv* furiosamente
furnace /'fɜ:nɪs/ *n* fornalha *f*
furnish /'fɜ:nɪʃ/ *vt* mobiliar, (*P*) mobilar; (*supply*) prover (**with** de). ~**ings** *npl* mobiliário *m* e equipamento *m*
furniture /'fɜ:nɪtʃə(r)/ *n* mobília *f*
furrow /'fʌrəʊ/ *n* sulco *m*; (*wrinkle*) ruga *f* □ *vt* sulcar; (*wrinkle*) enrugar
furry /'fɜ:rɪ/ *a* (**-ier, -iest**) peludo; (*toy*) de pelúcia
furth|er /'fɜ:ðə(r)/ *a* mais distante; (*additional*) adicional, suplementar □ *adv* mais longe; (*more*) mais □ *vt* promover. ~**er education** ensino *m* supletivo, cursos *mpl* livres, (*P*) educação *f* superior. ~**est** *a* o mais distante □ *adv* mais longe
furthermore /fɜ:ðə'mɔ:(r)/ *adv* além disso
furtive /'fɜ:tɪv/ *a* furtivo
fury /'fjʊərɪ/ *n* fúria *f*, furor *m*
fuse[1] /fju:z/ *vt/i* fundir(-se); (*fig*) amalgamar □ *n* fusível *m*. **the lights** ~**d** os fusíveis queimaram
fuse[2] /fju:z/ *n* (*of bomb*) espoleta *f*
fuselage /'fju:zəla:ʒ/ *n* fuselagem *f*
fusion /'fju:ʒn/ *n* fusão *f*
fuss /fʌs/ *n* história(s) *f*(*pl*), escarcéu *m* □ *vi* preocupar-se com ninharias. **make a** ~ **of** ligar demasiado para, criar caso com, fazer um espalhafato com. ~**y** *a* exigente, complicado
futile /'fju:taɪl/ *a* fútil
future /'fju:tʃə(r)/ *a* & *n* futuro (*m*). **in** ~ no futuro, de agora em diante
futuristic /fju:tʃə'rɪstɪk/ *a* futurista, futurístico
fuzz /fʌz/ *n* penugem *f*; (*hair*) cabelo *m* frisado
fuzzy /'fʌzɪ/ *a* (*hair*) frisado; (*photo*) pouco nítido, desfocado

G

gab /gæb/ *n* (*colloq*) **have the gift of the** ~ ter o dom da palavra
gabble /'gæbl/ *vt/i* tagarelar, falar, ler muito depressa □ *n* tagarelice *f*, algaravia *f*
gable /'geɪbl/ *n* empena *f*, oitão *m*
gad /gæd/ *vi* (*pt* **gadded**) ~ **about** (*colloq*) badalar
gadget /'gædʒɪt/ *n* pequeno utensílio *m*; (*fitting*) dispositivo *m*; (*device*) engenhoca *f* (*colloq*)
Gaelic /'geɪlɪk/ *n* galês *m*
gaffe /gæf/ *n* gafe *f*
gag /gæg/ *n* mordaça *f*; (*joke*) gag *m*, piada *f* □ *vt* (*pt* **gagged**) amordaçar
gaiety /'geɪətɪ/ *n* alegria *f*
gaily /'geɪlɪ/ *adv* alegremente
gain /geɪn/ *vt* ganhar □ *vi* (*of clock*) adiantar-se. ~ **weight** aumentar de peso. ~ **on** (*get closer to*) aproximar-se de □ *n* ganho *m*; (*increase*) aumento *m*. ~**ful** *a* lucrativo, proveitoso
gait /geɪt/ *n* (modo de) andar *m*
gala /'ga:lə/ *n* gala *m*; (*sport*) festival *m*
galaxy /'gæləksɪ/ *n* galáxia *f*
gale /geɪl/ *n* vento *m* forte
gall /gɔ:l/ *n* bílis *f*; (*fig*) fel *m*; (*sl: impudence*) descaramento *m*, desplante *m*, (*P*) lata *f* (*sl*). ~**-bladder** *n* vesícula *f* biliar. ~**-stone** *n* cálculo *m* biliar
gallant /'gælənt/ *a* galhardo, valente; (*chivalrous*) galante, cortês. ~**ry** *n* galhardia *f*, valentia *f*; (*chivalry*) galanteria *f*, cortesia *f*
gallery /'gælərɪ/ *n* galeria *f*
galley /'gælɪ/ *n* (*pl* **-eys**) galera *f*; (*ship's kitchen*) cozinha *f*
gallivant /gælɪ'vænt/ *vi* (*colloq*) vadiar, (*P*) andar na paródia
gallon /'gælən/ *n* galão *m* (= *4,546 litros; Amer = 3.785 litros*)
gallop /'gæləp/ *n* galope *m* □ *vi* (*pt* **galloped**) galopar
gallows /'gæləʊz/ *npl* forca *f*
galore /gə'lɔ:(r)/ *adv* a beça, em abundância
galvanize /'gælvənaɪz/ *vt* galvanizar
gambit /'gæmbɪt/ *n* gambito *m*
gambl|e /'gæmbl/ *vt/i* jogar □ *n* jogo (de azar) *m*; (*fig*) risco *m*. ~**e on** apostar em. ~**er** *n* jogador *m*. ~**ing** *n* jogo *m* (de azar)
game /geɪm/ *n* jogo *m*; (*football*) desafio *m*; (*animals*) caça *f* □ *a* bravo. ~ **for** pronto para
gamekeeper /'geɪmki:pə(r)/ *n* guarda-florestal *m*
gammon /'gæmən/ *n* presunto *m* defumado
gamut /'gæmət/ *n* gama *f*
gang /gæng/ *n* bando *m*, gang *m*; (*of workmen*) turma *f*, (*P*) grupo *m* □ *vi* ~ **up** ligar-se (**on** contra)
gangling /'gæŋglɪŋ/ *a* desengonçado
gangrene /'gæŋgri:n/ *n* gangrena *f*
gangster /'gæŋstə(r)/ *n* gângster *m*, bandido *m*
gangway /'gæŋweɪ/ *n* passagem *f*; (*aisle*) coxia *f*; (*on ship*) portaló *m*; (*from ship to shore*) passadiço *m*
gaol /dʒeɪl/ *n* & *vt* = **jail**
gap /gæp/ *n* abertura *f*, brecha *f*; (*in time*) intervalo *m*; (*deficiency*) lacuna *f*
gap|e /geɪp/ *vi* ficar boquiaberto *or* embasbacado. ~**ing** *a* escancarado
garage /'gæra:ʒ/ *n* garagem *f*; (*service station*) posto *m* de gasolina, (*P*)

estação *f* de serviço □ *vt* pôr na garagem
garbage /'ga:bɪdʒ/ *n* lixo *m*. ~ **can** (*Amer*) lata *f* do lixo, (*P*) caixote *m* do lixo
garble /'ga:bl/ *vt* deturpar
garden /'ga:dn/ *n* jardim *m* □ *vi* jardinar. ~**er** *n* jardineiro *m*. ~**ing** *n* jardinagem *f*
gargle /'ga:gl/ *vi* gargarejar □ *n* gargarejo *m*
gargoyle /'ga:gɔɪl/ *n* gárgula *f*
garish /'geərɪʃ/ *a* berrante, espalhafatoso
garland /'ga:lənd/ *n* grinalda *f*
garlic /'ga:lɪk/ *n* alho *m*
garment /'ga:mənt/ *n* peça *f* de vestuário, roupa *f*
garnish /'ga:nɪʃ/ *vt* enfeitar, guarnecer □ *n* guarnição *f*
garrison /'gærɪsn/ *n* guarnição *f* □ *vt* guarnecer
garrulous /'gærələs/ *a* tagarela
garter /'ga:tə(r)/ *n* liga *f*. ~**-belt** *n* (*Amer*) cinta *f* de ligas
gas /gæs/ *n* (*pl* **gases**) gás *m*; (*med*) anestésico *m*; (*Amer colloq: petrol*) gasolina *f* □ *vt* (*pt* **gassed**) asfixiar; (*mil*) gasear □ *vi* (*colloq*) fazer conversa fiada. ~ **fire** aquecedor *m* a gás. ~ **mask** máscara *f* anti-gás. ~ **meter** medidor *m* do gás
gash /gæʃ/ *n* corte *m*, lanho *m* □ *vt* cortar
gasket /'gæskɪt/ *n* junta *f*
gasoline /'gæsəli:n/ *n* (*Amer*) gasolina *f*
gasp /ga:sp/ *vi* arfar, arquejar; (*fig: with rage, surprise*) ficar sem ar □ *n* arquejo *m*
gassy /'gæsɪ/ *a* gasoso; (*full of gas*) cheio de gás
gastric /'gæstrɪk/ *a* gástrico
gastronomy /gæ'strɒnəmɪ/ *n* gastronomia *f*
gate /geɪt/ *n* portão *m*; (*of wood*) cancela *f*; (*barrier*) barreira *f*; (*airport*) porta *f*
gateau /'gætəʊ/ *n* (*pl* ~**x** /-təʊz/) bolo *m* grande com creme
gatecrash /'geɪtkræʃ/ *vt/i* entrar (numa festa) sem convite
gateway /'geɪtweɪ/ *n* (porta de) entrada *f*
gather /'gæðə(r)/ *vt* reunir, juntar; (*pick up, collect*) apanhar; (*amass, pile up*) acumular, juntar; (*conclude*) deduzir; (*cloth*) franzir □ *vi* reunir-se; (*pile up*) acumular-se. ~ **speed** ganhar velocidade. ~**ing** *n* reunião *f*
gaudy /'gɔ:dɪ/ *a* (-ier, -iest) (*bright*) berrante; (*showy*) espalhafatoso
gauge /geɪdʒ/ *n* medida *f* padrão; (*device*) indicador *m*; (*railway*) bitola *f* □ *vt* medir, avaliar
gaunt /gɔ:nt/ *a* emagrecido, macilento; (*grim*) lúgubre, desolado
gauntlet /'gɔ:ntlɪt/ *n* **run the ~ of** (*fig*) expor-se a. **throw down the ~** lançar um desafio, (*P*) atirar a luva
gauze /gɔ:z/ *n* gaze *f*
gave /geɪv/ *see* give
gawky /'gɔ:kɪ/ *a* (-ier, -iest) desajeitado
gay /geɪ/ *a* (-er, -est) alegre; (*colloq: homosexual*) homosexual, gay
gaze /geɪz/ *vi* ~ (**at**) olhar fixamente (para) □ *n* contemplação *f*
gazelle /gə'zel/ *n* gazela *f*
GB *abbr of* **Great Britain**
gear /gɪə(r)/ *n* equipamento *m*; (*techn*) engrenagem *f*; (*auto*) velocidade *f* □ *vt* equipar; (*adapt*) adaptar. **in ~** engrenado. **out of ~** em ponto morto. ~**-lever** *n* alavanca *f* de mudanças
gearbox /'gɪəbɒks/ *n* caixa *f* de mudança, caixa *f* de transmissão, (*P*) caixa *f* de velocidades
geese /gi:s/ *see* **goose**
gel /dʒel/ *n* geléia *f*, (*P*) geleia *f*
gelatine /'dʒeləti:n/ *n* gelatina *f*
gelignite /'dʒelɪgnaɪt/ *n* gelignite *f*
gem /dʒem/ *n* gema *f*, pedra *f* preciosa
Gemini /'dʒemɪnaɪ/ *n* (*astr*) Gêmeos *mpl*, (*P*) Gémeos *mpl*
gender /'dʒendə(r)/ *n* gênero *m*, (*P*) género *m*
gene /dʒi:n/ *n* gene *m*
genealogy /dʒi:nɪ'ælədʒɪ/ *n* genealogia *f*
general /'dʒenrəl/ *a* geral □ *n* general *m*. ~ **election** eleições *fpl* legislativas. ~ **practitioner** *n* clínico-geral *m*, (*P*) médico *m* de família. **in ~** em geral. ~**ly** *adv* geralmente
generaliz|e /'dʒenrəlaɪz/ *vt/i* generalizar. ~**ation** /-'zeɪʃn/ *n* generalização *f*
generate /'dʒenəreɪt/ *vt* gerar, produzir
generation /dʒenə'reɪʃn/ *n* geração *f*
generator /'dʒenəreɪtə(r)/ *n* gerador *m*
gener|ous /'dʒenərəs/ *a* generoso; (*plentiful*) abundante. ~**osity** /-'rɒsətɪ/ *n* generosidade *f*
genetic /dʒɪ'netɪk/ *a* genético. ~**s** *n* genética *f*
genial /'dʒi:nɪəl/ *a* agradável
genital /'dʒenɪtl/ *a* genital. ~**s** *npl* órgãos *mpl* genitais
genius /'dʒi:nɪəs/ *n* (*pl* **-uses**) gênio *m*, (*P*) génio *m*
genocide /'dʒenəsaɪd/ *n* genocídio *m*
gent /dʒent/ *n* **the G~s** (*colloq*) banheiros *mpl* de homens, (*P*) lavabos *mpl* para homens

genteel /dʒen'ti:l/ *a* elegante, fino, refinado

gentl|e /'dʒentl/ *a* (~er, ~est) brando, suave. **~eness** *n* brandura *f*, suavidade *f*. **~y** *adv* brandamente, suavemente

gentleman /'dʒentlmən/ *n* (*pl* -men) senhor *m*; (*well-bred*) cavalheiro *m*

genuine /'dʒenjʊɪn/ *a* genuíno, verdadeiro; (*belief*) sincero

geograph|y /dʒɪ'ɒgrəfɪ/ *n* geografia *f*. **~er** *n* geógrafo *m*. **~ical** /dʒɪə'græfɪkl/ *a* geográfico

geolog|y /dʒɪ'ɒlədʒɪ/ *n* geologia *f*. **~ical** /dʒɪə'lɒdʒɪkl/ *a* geológico. **~ist** *n* geólogo *m*

geometr|y /dʒɪ'ɒmətrɪ/ *n* geometria *f*. **~ic(al)** /dʒɪə'metrɪk(l)/ *a* geométrico

geranium /dʒə'reɪnɪəm/ *n* gerânio *m*

geriatric /dʒerɪ'ætrɪk/ *a* geriátrico

germ /dʒɜ:m/ *n* germe *m*, micróbio *m*

German /'dʒɜ:mən/ *a* & *n* alemão (*m*), alemã (*f*); (*lang*) alemão (*m*). **~ measles** rubéola *f*. **~ic** /dʒə'mænɪk/ *a* germânico. **~y** *n* Alemanha *f*

germinate /'dʒɜ:mɪneɪt/ *vi* germinar

gestation /dʒe'steɪʃn/ *n* gestação *f*

gesticulate /dʒe'stɪkjʊleɪt/ *vi* gesticular

gesture /'dʒestʃə(r)/ *n* gesto *m*

get /get/ *vt* (*pt* **got**, *pres p* **getting**) (*have*) ter; (*receive*) receber; (*catch*) apanhar; (*earn, win*) ganhar; (*fetch*) ir buscar; (*find*) achar; (*colloq: understand*) entender. **~ sb to do sth** fazer com que alguém faça alg coisa □ *vi* ir, chegar; (*become*) ficar. **~ married/ready** casar-se/aprontar-se. **~ about** andar dum lado para o outro. **~ across** atravessar. **~ along** *or* **by** (*manage*) ir indo. **~ along** *or* **on with** entender-se com. **~ at** (*reach*) chegar a; (*attack*) atacar; (*imply*) insinuar. **~ away** ir-se embora; (*escape*) fugir. **~ back** *vi* voltar □ *vt* recuperar. **~ by** (*pass*) passar, escapar; (*manage*) aguentar-se. **~ down** descer. **~ in** entrar. **~ off** *vi* descer; (*leave*) partir; (*jur*) ser absolvido □ *vt* (*remove*) tirar. **~ on** (*succeed*) fazer progressos, ir; (*be on good terms*) dar-se bem. **~ out** sair. **~ out of** (*fig*) fugir de. **~ over** (*illness*) restabelecer-se de. **~ round** (*person*) convencer; (*rule*) contornar. **~ up** *vi* levantar-se □ *vt* (*mount*) montar. **~-up** *n* (*colloq*) apresentação *f*

getaway /'getəweɪ/ *n* fuga *f*

geyser /'gi:zə(r)/ *n* aquecedor *m*; (*geol*) gêiser *m*, (*P*) géiser *m*

Ghana /'ga:nə/ *n* Gana *m*

ghastly /'ga:stlɪ/ *a* (-ier, -iest) horrível; (*pale*) lívido

gherkin /'gɜ:kɪn/ *n* pepino *m* pequeno para conservas, cornichão *m*

ghetto /'getəʊ/ *n* (*pl* -os) gueto *m*, ghetto *m*

ghost /gəʊst/ *n* fantasma *m*, espectro *m*. **~ly** *a* fantasmagórico, espectral

giant /'dʒaɪənt/ *a* & *n* gigante (*m*)

gibberish /'dʒɪbərɪʃ/ *n* algaravia *f*, linguagem *f* incompreensível

gibe /dʒaɪb/ *n* zombaria *f* □ *vi* ~ (at) zombar (de)

giblets /'dʒɪblɪts/ *npl* miúdos *mpl*, miudezas *fpl*

giddy /'gɪdɪ/ *a* (-ier, -iest) estonteante, vertiginoso. **be** *or* **feel ~** ter tonturas *or* vertigens

gift /gɪft/ *n* presente *m*, dádiva *f*; (*ability*) dom *m*, dote *m*. **~-wrap** *vt* (*pt* **-wrapped**) fazer um embrulho de presente

gifted /'gɪftɪd/ *a* dotado

gig /gɪg/ *n* (*colloq*) show *m*, sessão *f* de jazz etc

gigantic /dʒaɪ'gæntɪk/ *a* gigantesco

giggle /'gɪgl/ *vi* dar risadinhas nervosas □ *n* risinho *m* nervoso

gild /gɪld/ *vt* dourar

gills /gɪlz/ *npl* guelras *fpl*

gilt /gɪlt/ *a* & *n* dourado (*m*). **~-edged** *a* de toda a confiança

gimmick /'gɪmɪk/ *n* truque *m*, artifício *m*

gin /dʒɪn/ *n* gin *m*, genebra *f*

ginger /'dʒɪndʒə(r)/ *n* gengibre *m* □ *a* louro-avermelhado, ruivo. **~ ale**, **~ beer** cerveja *f* de gengibre, (*P*) ginger ale *m*

gingerbread /'dʒɪndʒəbred/ *n* pão *m* de gengibre

gingerly /'dʒɪndʒəlɪ/ *adv* cautelosamente

gipsy /'dʒɪpsɪ/ *n* = gypsy

giraffe /dʒɪ'ra:f/ *n* girafa *f*

girder /'gɜ:də(r)/ *n* trave *f*, viga *f*

girdle /'gɜ:dl/ *n* cinto *m*; (*corset*) cinta *f* □ *vt* rodear

girl /gɜ:l/ *n* (*child*) menina *f*; (*young woman*) moça *f*, (*P*) rapariga *f*. **~-friend** *n* amiga *f*; (*of boy*) namorada *f*. **~hood** *n* (*of child*) meninice *f*; (*youth*) juventude *f*

giro /'dʒaɪrəʊ/ *n* sistema *m* de transferência de crédito entre bancos; (*cheque*) cheque *m* pago pelo governo a desempregados ou doentes

girth /gɜ:θ/ *n* circumferência *f*, perímetro *m*

gist /dʒɪst/ *n* essencial *m*

give /gɪv/ *vt/i* (*pt* **gave**, *pp* **given**) dar; (*bend, yield*) ceder. **~ away** dar; (*secret*) revelar, trair. **~ back** devolver. **~ in** dar-se por vencido, render-se. **~ off** emitir. **~ out** *vt* anunciar □ *vi* esgotar-se. **~ up** *vt/i* desistir (de),

renunciar (a). ~ **o.s. up** entregar-se. ~ **way** ceder; (*traffic*) dar prioridade; (*collapse*) dar de si
given /'gɪvn/ *see* **give** □ *a* dado. ~ **name** nome *m* de batismo, (*P*) baptismo
glacier /'glæsɪə(r)/ *n* glaciar *m*, geleira *f*
glad /glæd/ *a* contente. ~**ly** *adv* com (todo o) prazer
gladden /'glædn/ *vt* alegrar
glam|our /'glæmə(r)/ *n* fascinação *f*, encanto *m*. ~**orize** *vt* tornar fascinante. ~**orous** *a* fascinante, sedutor
glance /glɑ:ns/ *n* relance *m*, olhar *m* □ *vi* ~ **at** dar uma olhada a. **at first** ~ à primeira vista
gland /glænd/ *n* glândula *f*
glar|e /gleə(r)/ *vi* brilhar intensamente, faiscar □ *n* luz *f* crua; (*fig*) olhar *m* feroz. ~**e at** olhar ferozmente para. ~**ing** *a* brilhante; (*obvious*) flagrante
glass /glɑ:s/ *n* vidro *m*; (*vessel, its contents*) copo *m*; (*mirror*) espelho *m*. ~**es** óculos *mpl*. ~**y** *a* vítreo
glaze /gleɪz/ *vt* (*door etc*) envidraçar; (*pottery*) vidrar □ *n* vidrado *m*
gleam /gli:m/ *n* raio *m* de luz frouxa; (*fig*) vislumbre *m* □ *vi* luzir, brilhar
glean /gli:n/ *vt* catar
glee /gli:/ *n* alegria *f*. ~**ful** *a* cheio de alegria
glib /glɪb/ *a* que tem a palavra fácil, verboso. ~**ly** *adv* fluentemente, sem hesitação. ~**ness** *n* verbosidade *f*
glide /glaɪd/ *vi* deslizar; (*bird, plane*) planar. ~**r** /-ə(r)/ *n* planador *m*
glimmer /'glɪmə(r)/ *n* luz *f* trêmula □ *vi* tremular
glimpse /glɪmps/ *n* vislumbre *m*. **catch a** ~ **of** entrever, ver de relance
glint /glɪnt/ *n* brilho *m*, reflexo *m* □ *vi* brilhar, cintilar
glisten /'glɪsn/ *vi* reluzir
glitter /'glɪtə(r)/ *vi* luzir, resplandecer □ *n* esplendor *m*, cintilação *f*
gloat /gləʊt/ *vi* ~ **over** ter um prazer maligno em, exultar com
global /'gləʊbl/ *a* global
globe /gləʊb/ *n* globo *m*
gloom /glu:m/ *n* obscuridade *f*; (*fig*) tristeza *f*. ~**y** *a* sombrio; (*sad*) triste; (*pessimistic*) pessimista
glorif|y /'glɔ:rɪfaɪ/ *vt* glorificar. **a** ~**ied waitress**/*etc* pouco mais que uma garçonete/*etc*
glorious /'glɔ:rɪəs/ *a* glorioso
glory /'glɔ:rɪ/ *n* glória *f*; (*beauty*) esplendor *m* □ *vi* ~ **in** orgulhar-se de
gloss /glɒs/ *n* brilho *m* □ *a* brilhante □ *vt* ~ **over** minimizar, encobrir. ~**y** *a* brilhante
glossary /'glɒsərɪ/ *n* (*pl* **-ries**) glossário *m*
glove /glʌv/ *n* luva *f*. ~ **compartment** porta-luvas *m*. ~**d** *a* enluvado
glow /gləʊ/ *vi* arder; (*person*) resplandecer; (*eyes*) brilhar □ *n* brasa *f*. ~**ing** *a* (*fig*) entusiástico
glucose /'glu:kəʊs/ *n* glucose *f*
glue /glu:/ *n* cola *f* □ *vt* (*pres p* **gluing**) colar
glum /glʌm/ *a* (**glummer, glummest**) sorumbático; (*dejected*) abatido
glut /glʌt/ *n* superabundância *f*
glutton /'glʌtn/ *n* glutão *m*. ~**ous** *a* glutão. ~**y** *n* gula *f*
gnarled /nɑ:ld/ *a* nodoso
gnash /næʃ/ *vt* ~ **one's teeth** ranger os dentes
gnat /næt/ *n* mosquito *m*
gnaw /nɔ:/ *vt/i* roer
gnome /nəʊm/ *n* gnomo *m*
go /gəʊ/ *vi* (*pt* **went**, *pp* **gone**) ir; (*leave*) ir, ir-se; (*mech*) andar, funcionar; (*become*) ficar; (*be sold*) vender-se; (*vanish*) ir-se, desaparecer □ *n* (*pl* **goes**) (*energy*) dinamismo *m*; (*try*) tentativa *f*; (*success*) sucesso *m*; (*turn*) vez *f*. ~ **riding** ir andar *or* montar a cavalo. ~ **shopping** ir às compras. **be** ~**ing to do** ir fazer. ~ **ahead** ir para diante. ~ **away** ir-se embora. ~ **back** voltar atrás (**on** com). ~ **bad** estragar-se. ~ **by** (*pass*) passar. ~ **down** descer; (*sun*) pôr-se; (*ship*) afundar-se. ~ **for** ir buscar; (*like*) gostar de; (*sl: attack*) atirar-se a, ir-se a (*colloq*). ~ **in** entrar. ~ **in for** (*exam*) apresentar-se a. ~ **off** ir-se; (*explode*) rebentar; (*sound*) soar; (*decay*) estragar-se. ~ **on** continuar; (*happen*) acontecer. ~ **out** sair; (*light*) apagar-se. ~ **over** *or* **through** verificar, examinar. ~ **round** (*be enough*) chegar. ~ **under** ir abaixo. ~ **up** subir. ~ **without** passar sem. **on the** ~ em grande atividade, (*P*) actividade. ~**-ahead** *n* luz *f* verde □ *a* dinâmico, empreendedor. ~**-between** *n* intermediário *m*. ~**-kart** *n* kart *m*. ~**-slow** *n* operação *f* tartaruga, (*P*) greve *f* de zelo
goad /gəʊd/ *vt* aguilhoar, espicaçar
goal /gəʊl/ *n* meta *f*; (*area*) baliza *f*; (*score*) gol *m*, (*P*) golo *m*. ~**-post** *n* trave *f*
goalkeeper /'gəʊlki:pə(r)/ *n* goleiro *m*, (*P*) guarda-redes *m*
goat /gəʊt/ *n* cabra *f*
gobble /'gɒbl/ *vt* comer com sofreguidão, devorar
goblet /'gɒblɪt/ *n* taça *f*, cálice *m*
goblin /'gɒblɪn/ *n* duende *m*
God /gɒd/ *n* Deus *m*. ~**-forsaken** *a* miserável, abandonado

god /gɒd/ *n* deus *m*. **~-daughter** *n* afilhada *f*. **~dess** *n* deusa *f*. **~father** *n* padrinho *m*. **~ly** *a* devoto. **~mother** *n* madrinha *f*. **~son** *n* afilhado *m*

godsend /'gɒdsend/ *n* achado *m*, dádiva *f* do céu

goggles /'gɒglz/ *npl* óculos *mpl* de proteção, (*P*) protecção

going /'gəʊɪŋ/ *n* **it is slow/hard ~** é demorado/difícil □ *a* (*price, rate*) corrente, atual, (*P*) actual. **~s-on** *npl* acontecimentos *mpl* estranhos

gold /gəʊld/ *n* ouro *m* □ *a* de/em ouro. **~-mine** *n* mina *f* de ouro

golden /'gəʊldən/ *a* de ouro; (*like gold*) dourado; (*opportunity*) único. **~ wedding** bodas *fpl* de ouro

goldfish /'gəʊldfɪʃ/ *n* peixe *m* dourado/vermelho

goldsmith /'gəʊldsmɪθ/ *n* ourives *m inv*

golf /gɒlf/ *n* golfe *m*. **~ club** clube *m* de golfe, associação *f* de golfe; (*stick*) taco *m*. **~-course** *n* campo *m* de golfe. **~er** *n* jogador *m* de golfe

gone /gɒn/ *see* **go** □ *a* ido, passado. **~ six o'clock** depois das seis

gong /gɒŋ/ *n* gongo *m*

good /gʊd/ *a* (**better, best**) bom □ *n* bem *m*. **as ~ as** praticamente. **for ~** para sempre. **it is no ~** não adianta. **it is no ~ shouting/***etc* não adianta gritar/*etc*. **~ afternoon** *int* boa(s) tarde(s). **~ evening/night** *int* boa(s) noite(s). **G~ Friday** Sexta-feira *f* Santa. **~-looking** *a* bonito. **~ morning** *int* bom dia. **~ name** bom nome *m*

goodbye /gʊd'baɪ/ *int & n* adeus (*m*)

goodness /'gʊdnɪs/ *n* bondade *f*. **my ~ness!** meu Deus!

goods /gʊdz/ *npl* (*comm*) mercadorias *fpl*. **~ train** trem *m* de carga, (*P*) comboio *m* de mercadorias

goodwill /gʊd'wɪl/ *n* boa vontade *f*

goose /gu:s/ *n* (*pl* **geese**) ganso *m*. **~-flesh, ~-pimples** *ns* pele *f* de galinha

gooseberry /'gʊzbərɪ/ *n* (*fruit*) groselha *f*; (*bush*) groselheira *f*

gore[1] /gɔ:(r)/ *n* sangue *m* coagulado

gore[2] /gɔ:(r)/ *vt* perfurar

gorge /gɔ:dʒ/ *n* desfiladeiro *m*, garganta *f* □ *vt* **~ o.s.** empanturrar-se

gorgeous /'gɔ:dʒəs/ *a* magnífico, maravilhoso

gorilla /gə'rɪlə/ *n* gorila *m*

gormless /'gɔ:mlɪs/ *a* (*sl*) estúpido

gorse /gɔ:s/ *n* giesta *f*, tojo *m*, urze *f*

gory /'gɔ:rɪ/ *a* (-ier, -iest) sangrento

gosh /gɒʃ/ *int* puxa!, (*P*) caramba!

gospel /'gɒspl/ *n* evangelho *m*

gossip /'gɒsɪp/ *n* bisbilhotice *f*, fofoca *f*; (*person*) bisbilhoteiro *m*, fofoqueiro *m* □ *vi* (*pt* **gossiped**) bisbilhotar. **~y** *a* bisbilhoteiro, fofoqueiro

got /gɒt/ *see* **get**. **have ~** ter. **have ~ to do** ter de *or* que fazer

Gothic /'gɒθɪk/ *a* gótico

gouge /gaʊdʒ/ *vt* **~ out** arrancar

gourmet /'gʊəmeɪ/ *n* gastrônomo *m*, (*P*) gastrónomo *m*, gourmet *m*

gout /gaʊt/ *n* gota *f*

govern /'gʌvn/ *vt/i* governar. **~ess** *n* preceptora *f*. **~or** *n* governador *m*; (*of school, hospital etc*) diretor *m*, (*P*) director *m*

government /'gʌvənmənt/ *n* governo *m*. **~al** /-'mentl/ *a* governamental

gown /gaʊn/ *n* vestido *m*; (*of judge, teacher*) toga *f*

GP *abbr see* **general practitioner**

grab /græb/ *vt* (*pt* **grabbed**) agarrar, apanhar

grace /greɪs/ *n* graça *f* □ *vt* honrar; (*adorn*) ornar. **say ~** dar graças. **~ful** *a* gracioso

gracious /'greɪʃəs/ *a* gracioso; (*kind*) amável, afável

grade /greɪd/ *n* categoria *f*; (*of goods*) classe *f*, qualidade *f*; (*on scale*) grau *m*; (*school mark*) nota *f* □ *vt* classificar

gradient /'greɪdɪənt/ *n* gradiente *m*, declive *m*

gradual /'grædʒʊəl/ *a* gradual, progressivo. **~ly** *adv* gradualmente

graduate[1] /'grædʒʊət/ *n* diplomado *m*, graduado *m*, licenciado *m*

graduat|e[2] /'grædʒʊeɪt/ *vt/i* formar (-se). **~ion** /-'eɪʃn/ *n* colação *f* de grau, (*P*) formatura *f*

graffiti /grə'fi:ti:/ *npl* graffiti *mpl*

graft /gra:ft/ *n* (*med, bot*) enxerto *m*; (*work*) batalha *f* □ *vt* enxertar; (*work*) batalhar

grain /greɪn/ *n* grão *m*; (*collectively*) cereais *mpl*; (*in wood*) veio *m*. **against the ~** (*fig*) contra a maneira de ser

gram /græm/ *n* grama *m*

gramm|ar /'græmə(r)/ *n* gramática *f*. **~atical** /grə'mætɪkl/ *a* gramatical

grand /grænd/ *a* (-er, -est) grandioso, magnífico; (*duke, master*) grão. **~ piano** piano *m* de cauda.

grand|child /'grændtʃaɪld/ *n* (*pl* **-children**) neto *m*. **~daughter** *n* neta *f*. **~father** *n* avô *m*. **~mother** *n* avó *f*. **~parents** *npl* avós *mpl*. **~son** *n* neto *m*

grandeur /'grændʒə(r)/ *n* grandeza *f*

grandiose /'grændɪəʊs/ *a* grandioso

grandstand /'grændstænd/ *n* tribuna *f* principal

granite /'grænɪt/ *n* granito *m*

grant /gra:nt/ *vt* conceder; (*a request*) ceder a; (*admit*) admitir (**that** que) □ *n* subsídio *m*; (*univ*) bolsa *f*. **take for**

~ed ter como coisa garantida, contar com

grape /greɪp/ *n* uva *f*

grapefruit /'greɪpfru:t/ *n inv* grapefruit *m*, toronja *f*

graph /gra:f/ *n* gráfico *m*

graphic /'græfɪk/ *a* gráfico; (*fig*) vívido. ~s *npl* (*comput*) gráficos *mpl*

grapple /'græpl/ *vi* ~ **with** estar engalfinhado com; (*fig*) estar às voltas com

grasp /gra:sp/ *vt* agarrar; (*understand*) compreender □ *n* domínio *m*; (*reach*) alcance *m*; (*fig: understanding*) compreensão *f*

grasping /'gra:spɪŋ/ *a* ganancioso

grass /gra:s/ *n* erva *f*; (*lawn*) grama *f*, (*P*) relva *f*; (*pasture*) pastagem *f*; (*sl: informer*) delator *m* □ *vt* cobrir com grama; (*sl: betray*) delatar. ~ **roots** (*pol*) bases *fpl*. ~**y** *a* coberto de erva

grasshopper /'gra:shɒpə(r)/ *n* gafanhoto *m*

grate[1] /greɪt/ *n* (*fireplace*) lareira *f*; (*frame*) grelha *f*

grate[2] /greɪt/ *vt* ralar □ *vi* ranger. ~ **one's teeth** ranger os dentes. ~**r** /-ə(r)/ *n* ralador *m*

grateful /'greɪtfl/ *a* grato, agradecido. ~**ly** *adv* com reconhecimento, com gratidão

gratify /'grætɪfaɪ/ *vt* (*pt* -fied) contentar, satisfazer. ~**ing** *a* gratificante

grating /'greɪtɪŋ/ *n* grade *f*

gratis /'greɪtɪs/ *a & adv* grátis (*invar*), de graça

gratitude /'grætɪtju:d/ *n* gratidão *f*, reconhecimento *m*

gratuitous /grə'tju:ɪtəs/ *a* gratuito; (*uncalled-for*) sem motivo

gratuity /grə'tju:ətɪ/ *n* gratificação *f*, gorjeta *f*

grave[1] /greɪv/ *n* cova *f*, sepultura *f*, túmulo *m*

grave[2] /greɪv/ *a* (-er, -est) grave, sério. ~**ly** *adv* gravemente

grave[3] /gra:v/ *a* ~ **accent** acento *m* grave

gravel /'grævl/ *n* cascalho *m* miúdo, saibro *m*

gravestone /'greɪvstəʊn/ *n* lápide *f*, campa *f*

graveyard /'greɪvja:d/ *n* cemitério *m*

gravity /'grævətɪ/ *n* gravidade *f*

gravy /'greɪvɪ/ *n* molho *m* (de carne)

graze[1] /greɪz/ *vt/i* pastar

graze[2] /greɪz/ *vt* roçar; (*scrape*) esfolar □ *n* esfoladura *f*, (*P*) esfoladela *f*

greas|e /gri:s/ *n* gordura *f* □ *vt* engordurar; (*culin*) untar; (*mech*) lubrificar. ~**e-proof paper** papel *m* vegetal. ~**y** *a* gorduroso

great /greɪt/ *a* (-er, -est) grande; (*colloq: splendid*) esplêndido. **G~ Britain** Grã-Bretanha *f*. ~**-grandfather** *n* bisavô *m*. ~**-grandmother** *f* bisavó *f*. ~**ly** *adv* grandemente, muito. ~**ness** *n* grandeza *f*

Great Britain /greɪt'brɪtən/ *n* Grã-Bretanha *f*

Greece /gri:s/ *n* Grécia *f*

greed /gri:d/ *n* cobiça *f*, ganância *f*; (*for food*) gula *f*. ~**y** *a* cobiçoso, ganancioso; (*for food*) guloso

Greek /gri:k/ *a & n* grego (*m*)

green /gri:n/ *a* (-er, -est) verde □ *n* verde *m*; (*grass*) gramado *m*, (*P*) relvado *m*. ~**s** hortaliças *fpl*. ~ **belt** zona *f* verde, paisagem *f* protegida. ~ **light** luz *f* verde. ~**ery** *n* verdura *f*

greengrocer /'gri:ngrəʊsə(r)/ *n* quitandeiro *m*, (*P*) vendedor *m* de hortaliças

greenhouse /'gri:nhaʊs/ *n* estufa *f*. ~ **effect** efeito estufa

Greenland /'gri:nlənd/ *n* Groenlândia *f*

greet /gri:t/ *vt* acolher. ~**ing** *n* saudação *f*; (*welcome*) acolhimento *m*. ~**ings** *npl* cumprimentos *mpl*; (*Christmas etc*) votos *mpl*, desejos *mpl*

gregarious /grɪ'geərɪəs/ *a* gregário; (*person*) sociável

grenade /grɪ'neɪd/ *n* granada *f*

grew /gru:/ *see* **grow**

grey /greɪ/ *a* (-er, -est) cinzento; (*of hair*) grisalho □ *n* cinzento *m*

greyhound /'greɪhaʊnd/ *n* galgo *m*

grid /grɪd/ *n* (*grating*) gradeamento *m*, grade *f*; (*electr*) rede *f*

grief /gri:f/ *n* dor *f*. **come to** ~ acabar mal

grievance /'gri:vns/ *n* razão *f* de queixa

grieve /gri:v/ *vt* sofrer, afligir □ *vi* sofrer. ~ **for** chorar por

grill /grɪl/ *n* grelha *f*; (*food*) grelhado *m*; (*place*) grill *m* □ *vt* grelhar; (*question*) submeter a interrogatório cerrado, apertar com perguntas □ *vi* grelhar

grille /grɪl/ *n* grade *f*; (*of car*) grelha *f*

grim /grɪm/ *a* (**grimmer, grimmest**) sinistro; (*without mercy*) implacável

grimace /grɪ'meɪs/ *n* careta *f* □ *vi* fazer careta(s)

grim|e /graɪm/ *n* sujeira *f*. ~**y** *a* encardido, sujo

grin /grɪn/ *vi* (*pt* **grinned**) sorrir abertamente, dar um sorriso largo □ *n* sorriso *m* aberto

grind /graɪnd/ *vt* (*pt* **ground**) triturar; (*coffee*) moer; (*sharpen*) amolar, afiar. ~ **one's teeth** ranger os dentes. ~ **to a halt** parar freando lentamente

grip /grɪp/ *vt* (*pt* **gripped**) agarrar;

(*interest*) prender □ *n* (*of hands*) aperto *m*; (*control*) controle *m*, domínio *m*. **come to ~s with** arcar com. **~ping** *a* apaixonante

grisly /ˈgrɪzlɪ/ *a* (-ier, -iest) macabro, horrível

gristle /ˈgrɪsl/ *n* cartilagem *f*

grit /grɪt/ *n* areia *f*, grão *m* de areia; (*fig: pluck*) coragem *f*, fortaleza *f* □ *vt* (*pt* **gritted**) (*road*) jogar areia em; (*teeth*) cerrar

groan /grəʊn/ *vi* gemer □ *n* gemido *m*

grocer /ˈgrəʊsə(r)/ *n* dono/a *m/f* de mercearia. **~ies** *npl* artigos *mpl* de mercearia. **~y** *n* (*shop*) mercearia *f*

groggy /ˈgrɒgɪ/ *a* (-ier, -iest) grogue, fraco das pernas

groin /grɔɪn/ *n* virilha *f*

groom /gru:m/ *n* noivo *m*; (*for horses*) moço *m* de estrebaria □ *vt* (*horse*) tratar de; (*fig*) preparar

groove /gru:v/ *n* ranhura *f*; (*for door, window*) calha *f*; (*in record*) estria *f*; (*fig*) rotina *f*

grope /grəʊp/ *vi* tatear. **~ for** procurar às cegas

gross /grəʊs/ *a* (-er, -est) (*vulgar*) grosseiro; (*flagrant*) flagrante; (*of error*) crasso; (*of weight, figure etc*) bruto □ *n* (*pl invar*) grosa *f*. **~ly** *adv* grosseiramente; (*very*) extremamente

grotesque /grəʊˈtesk/ *a* grotesco

grotty /ˈgrɒtɪ/ *a* (*sl*) sórdido

grouch /graʊtʃ/ *vi* (*colloq*) ralhar. **~y** *a* (*colloq*) rabugento

ground[1] /graʊnd/ *n* chão *m*, solo *m*; (*area*) terreno *m*; (*reason*) razão *f*, motivo *m*. **~s** jardins *mpl*; (*of coffee*) borra(s) *f* (*pl*) □ *vt/i* (*naut*) encalhar; (*plane*) reter em terra. **~ floor** térreo *m*, (*P*) rés-do-chão *m*. **~less** *a* infundado, sem fundamento

ground[2] /graʊnd/ *see* **grind**

grounding /ˈgraʊndɪŋ/ *n* bases *fpl*, conhecimentos *mpl* básicos

groundsheet /ˈgraʊndʃi:t/ *n* impermeável *m* para o chão

groundwork /ˈgraʊndwɜ:k/ *n* trabalhos *mpl* de base *or* preliminares

group /gru:p/ *n* grupo *m* □ *vt/i* agrupar(-se)

grouse[1] /graʊs/ *n* (*pl invar*) galo *m* silvestre

grouse[2] /graʊs/ *vi* (*colloq: grumble*) resmungar; (*colloq: complain*) queixar-se

grovel /ˈgrɒvl/ *vi* (*pt* **grovelled**) humilhar-se; (*fig*) rebaixar-se

grow /grəʊ/ *vi* (*pt* **grew**, *pp* **grown**) crescer; (*become*) tornar-se □ *vt* cultivar. **~ old** envelhecer. **~ up** crescer, tornar-se adulto. **~er** *n* cultivador *m*, produtor *m*. **~ing** *a* crescente

growl /graʊl/ *vi* rosnar □ *n* rosnadela *f*

grown /grəʊn/ *see* **grow** □ *a* **~ man** homem feito. **~-up** *a* adulto □ (*increase*) aumento *m*; (*med*) tumor *m*

grub /grʌb/ *n* larva *f*; (*sl: food*) papança *f* (*collog*) (*B*) bóia (*sl*) *f*, (*P*) alimento *m*

grubby /ˈgrʌbɪ/ *a* (-ier, -iest) sujo, porco

grudge /grʌdʒ/ *vt* dar/reconhecer de má vontade □ *n* má vontade *f*. **~ doing** fazer de má vontade. **~ sb sth** dar alg a alguém má vontade. **have a ~ against** ter ressentimento contra. **grudgingly** *adv* relutantemente

gruelling /ˈgru:əlɪŋ/ *a* estafante, extenuante

gruesome /ˈgru:səm/ *a* macabro

gruff /grʌf/ *a* (-er, -est) carrancudo, rude

grumble /ˈgrʌmbl/ *vi* resmungar (at contra, por)

grumpy /ˈgrʌmpɪ/ *a* (-ier, -iest) mal-humorado, rabugento

grunt /grʌnt/ *vi* grunhir □ *n* grunhido *m*

guarantee /gærənˈti:/ *n* garantia *f* □ *vt* garantir

guard /ga:d/ *vt* guardar, proteger □ *vi* **~ against** precaver-se contra □ *n* guarda *f*; (*person*) guarda *m*; (*on train*) condutor *m*. **~ian** *n* guardião *m*, defensor *m*; (*of orphan*) tutor *m*

guarded /ˈga:dɪd/ *a* cauteloso, circunspeto, (*P*) circunspecto

guerrilla /gəˈrɪlə/ *n* guerrilheiro *m*, (*P*) guerrilha *m*. **~ warfare** guerrilha *f*, guerra *f* de guerrilhas

guess /ges/ *vt/i* adivinhar; (*suppose*) supor □ *n* suposição *f*, conjetura *f*, (*P*) conjectura *f*

guesswork /ˈgeswɜ:k/ *n* suposição *f*, conjetura(s) *f* (*pl*), (*P*) conjectura(s) *f* (*pl*)

guest /gest/ *n* convidado *m*; (*in hotel*) hóspede *mf*. **~-house** *n* pensão *f*

guffaw /gəˈfɔ:/ *n* gargalhada *f* □ *vi* rir à(s) gargalhada(s)

guidance /ˈgaɪdns/ *n* orientação *f*, direção *f*, (*P*) direcção *f*

guide /gaɪd/ *n* guia *mf* □ *vt* guiar. **~d missile** míssil *m* guiado; (*remote-control*) míssil *m* teleguiado. **~-dog** *n* cão *m* de cego, cão-guia *m*. **~-lines** *npl* diretrizes *fpl*, (*P*) directrizes *fpl*

Guide /gaɪd/ *n* Guia *f*

guidebook /ˈgaɪdbʊk/ *n* guia *m* (turístico)

guild /gɪld/ *n* corporação *f*

guile /gaɪl/ *n* astúcia *f*, manha *f*

guilt /gɪlt/ *n* culpa *f*. **~y** *a* culpado

guinea-pig /ˈgɪnɪpɪg/ *n* cobaia *f*, porquinho-da-India *m*
guitar /gɪˈtɑ:(r)/ *n* guitarra *f*, violão *m*, (*P*) viola *f*. **~ist** *n* guitarrista *mf*, tocador *m* de violão, (*P*) de viola
gulf /gʌlf/ *n* golfo *m*; (*hollow*) abismo *m*
gull /gʌl/ *n* gaivota *f*
gullible /ˈgʌləbl/ *a* crédulo
gully /ˈgʌlɪ/ *n* barranco *m*; (*drain*) sarjeta *f*
gulp /gʌlp/ *vt* engolir, devorar □ *vi* engolir em seco □ *n* trago *m*
gum[1] /gʌm/ *n* (*anat*) gengiva *f*
gum[2] /gʌm/ *n* goma *f*; (*chewing-gum*) chiclete *m*, goma *f* elástica, (*P*) pastilha *f* □ *vt* (*pt* **gummed**) colar
gumboot /ˈgʌmbu:t/ *n* bota *f* de borracha
gumption /ˈgʌmpʃn/ *n* (*colloq*) iniciativa *f* e bom senso *m*, cabeça *f*, juizo *m*
gun /gʌn/ *n* (*pistol*) pistola *f*; (*rifle*) espingarda *f*; (*cannon*) canhão *m* □ *vt* (*pt* **gunned**) ~ **down** abater a tiro
gunfire /ˈgʌnfaɪə(r)/ *n* tiroteio *m*
gunman /ˈgʌnmən/ *n* (*pl* **-men**) bandido *m* armado
gunpowder /ˈgʌnpaʊdə(r)/ *n* pólvora *f*
gunshot /ˈgʌnʃɒt/ *n* tiro *m*
gurgle /ˈgɜ:gl/ *n* gorgolejo *m* □ *vi* gorgolejar
gush /gʌʃ/ *vi* jorrar □ *n* jorro *m*. **~ing** *a* efusivo, derretido
gust /gʌst/ *n* (*of wind*) rajada *f*; (*of smoke*) nuvem *f*. **~y** *a* ventoso
gusto /ˈgʌstəʊ/ *n* gosto *m*, entusiasmo *m*
gut /gʌt/ *n* tripa *f*. **~s** (*belly*) barriga *f*; (*colloq: courage*) coragem *f* □ *vt* (*pt* **gutted**) estripar; (*fish*) limpar; (*fire*) destruir o interior de
gutter /ˈgʌtə(r)/ *n* calha *f*, canaleta *f*; (*in street*) sarjeta *f*, valeta *f*
guy /gaɪ/ *n* (*sl*: *man*) cara *m*, (*P*) tipo *m* (*colloq*)
guzzle /ˈgʌzl/ *vt*/*i* comer/beber com sofreguidão, encher-se (de)
gym /dʒɪm/ *n* (*colloq: gymnasium*) ginásio *m*; (*colloq: gymnastics*) ginástica *f*. **~-slip** *n* uniforme *m* escolar
gym|nasium /dʒɪmˈneɪzɪəm/ *n* ginásio *m*. **~nast** /ˈdʒɪmnæst/ *n* ginasta *mf*. **~nastics** /-ˈnæstɪks/ *npl* ginástica *f*
gynaecolog|y /gaɪnɪˈkɒlədʒɪ/ *n* ginecologia *f*. **~ist** *n* ginecologista *mf*
gypsy /ˈdʒɪpsɪ/ *n* cigano *m*
gyrate /dʒaɪˈreɪt/ *vi* girar

H

haberdashery /ˈhæbədæʃərɪ/ *n* armarinho *m*, (*P*) retrosaria *f*
habit /ˈhæbɪt/ *n* hábito *m*, costume *m*; (*costume*) hábito *m*. **be in/get into the ~ of** ter/apanhar o hábito de
habit|able /ˈhæbɪtəbl/ *a* habitável. **~ation** /-ˈteɪʃn/ *n* habitação *f*
habitat /ˈhæbɪtæt/ *n* habitat *m*
habitual /həˈbɪtʃʊəl/ *a* habitual, costumeiro; (*smoker, liar*) inveterado. **~ly** *adv* habitualmente
hack[1] /hæk/ *n* (*horse*) cavalo *m* de aluguel; (*writer*) escrevinhador (*pej*) *m*
hack[2] /hæk/ *vt* cortar, despedaçar. **~ to pieces** cortar em pedaços
hackneyed /ˈhæknɪd/ *a* banal, batido
had /hæd/ *see* **have**
haddock /ˈhædək/ *n invar* hadoque *m*, eglefim *m*. **smoked ~** hadoque *m* fumado
haemorrhage /ˈhemərɪdʒ/ *n* hemorragia *f*
haemorrhoids /ˈhemərɔɪdz/ *npl* hemorróidas *fpl*
haggard /ˈhægəd/ *a* desfigurado, com o rosto desfeito, magro e macilento
haggle /ˈhægl/ *vi* ~ **(over)** regatear
hail[1] /heɪl/ *vt* saudar; (*taxi*) fazer sinal para, chamar □ *vi* ~ **from** vir de
hail[2] /heɪl/ *n* granizo *m*, (*P*) saraiva *f*, (*P*) chuva de pedra *f* □ *vi* chover granizo, (*P*) saraivar
hailstone /ˈheɪlstəʊn/ *n* pedra *f* de granizo
hair /heə(r)/ *n* (*on head*) cabelo(s) *m*(*pl*); (*on body*) pêlos *mpl*; (*single strand*) cabelo *m*; (*of animal*) pêlo *m*. **~-do** *n* (*colloq*) penteado *m*. **~-dryer** *n* secador *m* de cabelo. **~-raising** *a* horripilante, de pôr os cabelos em pé. **~-style** *n* estilo *m* de penteado
hairbrush /ˈheəbrʌʃ/ *n* escova *f* para o cabelo
haircut /ˈheəkʌt/ *n* corte *m* de cabelo
hairdresser /ˈheədresə(r)/ *n* cabeleireiro *m*, cabeleireira *f*
hairpin /ˈheəpɪn/ *n* grampo *m*, (*P*) gancho *m* para o cabelo. **~ bend** curva *f* fechada, quase em W
hairy /ˈheərɪ/ *a* (-ier, -iest) peludo, cabeludo; (*sl: terrifying*) de pôr os cabelos em pé, horripilante
hake /heɪk/ *n* (*pl invar*) abrótea *f*
half /hɑ:f/ *n* (*pl* **halves** /hɑ:vz/) metade *f*, meio *m* □ *a* meio □ *adv* ao meio. **~ a dozen** meia dúzia. **~ an hour** meia hora. **~-caste** *n* mestiço *m*. **~-hearted** *a* sem grande

entusiasmo. ~-**term** *n* férias *fpl* no meio do trimestre. ~-**time** *n* meio-tempo *m*. ~-**way** *a* & *adv* a meio caminho. ~-**wit** *n* idiota *mf*. **go halves** dividir as despesas

halibut /'hælɪbət/ *n* (*pl invar*) halibute *m*

hall /hɔ:l/ *n* sala *f*; (*entrance*) vestíbulo *m*, entrada *f*; (*mansion*) solar *m*. ~ **of residence** residência *f* de estudantes

hallmark /'hɔ:lma:k/ *n* (*on gold etc*) marca *f* do contraste; (*fig*) cunho *m*, selo *m*

hallo /hə'ləʊ/ *int* & *n* (*greeting, surprise*) olá; (*on phone*) está

hallow /'hæləʊ/ *vt* consagrar, santificar

Halloween /hæləʊ'i:n/ *n* véspera *f* do Dia de Todos os Santos

hallucination /həlu:sɪ'neɪʃn/ *n* alucinação *f*

halo /'heɪləʊ/ *n* (*pl* -**oes**) halo *m*, auréola *f*

halt /hɔ:lt/ *n* parada *f*, (*P*) paragem *f* □ *vt* deter, fazer parar □ *vi* fazer alto, parar

halve /ha:v/ *vt* dividir ao meio; (*time etc*) reduzir à metade

ham /hæm/ *n* presunto *m*

hamburger /'hæmbɜ:gə(r)/ *n* hambúrguer *m*, (*P*) hamburgo *m*

hamlet /'hæmlɪt/ *n* aldeola *f*, lugarejo *m*

hammer /'hæmə(r)/ *n* martelo *m* □ *vt/i* martelar; (*fig*) bater com força

hammock /'hæmək/ *n* rede *f* (de dormir)

hamper[1] /'hæmpə(r)/ *n* cesto *m*, (*P*) cabaz *m*

hamper[2] /'hæmpə(r)/ *vt* dificultar, atrapalhar

hamster /'hæmstə(r)/ *n* hamster *m*

hand /hænd/ *n* mão *f*; (*of clock*) ponteiro *m*; (*writing*) letra *f*; (*worker*) trabalhador *m*; (*cards*) mão *f*; (*measure*) palmo *m*. (**helping**) ~ ajuda *f*, mão *f* □ *vt* dar, entregar. **at** ~ à mão. ~-**baggage** *n* bagagem *f* de mão. ~ **in** *or* **over** entregar. ~ **out** distribuir. ~-**out** *n* impresso *m*, folheto *m*; (*money*) esmola *f*, donativo *m*. **on the one** ~... **on the other** ~ por um lado ... por outro. **out of** ~ incontrolável. **to** ~ à mão

handbag /'hændbæg/ *n* carteira *f*, bolsa de mão *f*, mala de mão *f*

handbook /'hændbʊk/ *n* manual *m*

handbrake /'hændbreɪk/ *n* freio *m* de mão, (*P*) travão *m* de mão

handcuffs /'hændkʌfs/ *npl* algemas *fpl*

handful /'hændfʊl/ *n* mão-cheia *f*, punhado *m*; (*a few*) punhado *m*; (*difficult task*) mão-de-obra *f*. **she's a** ~ (*colloq*) ela é danada

handicap /'hændɪkæp/ *n* (*in competition*) handicap *m*; (*disadvantage*) desvantagem *f* □ *vt* (*pt* **handicapped**) prejudicar. ~**ped** *a* deficiente. **mentally** ~**ped** deficiente mental

handicraft /'hændɪkra:ft/ *n* artesanato *m*, trabalho *m* manual

handiwork /'hændɪwɜ:k/ *n* obra *f*, trabalho *m*

handkerchief /'hæŋkətʃɪf/ *n* lenço *m*

handle /'hændl/ *n* (*of door etc*) maçaneta *f*, puxador *m*; (*of cup etc*) asa *f*; (*of implement*) cabo *m*; (*of pan etc*) alça *f*, (*P*) pega *f* □ *vt* (*touch*) manusear, tocar; (*operate with hands*) manejar; (*deal in*) negociar em; (*deal with*) tratar de; (*person*) lidar com. **fly off the** ~ (*colloq*) perder as estribeiras

handlebar /'hændlba:(r)/ *n* guidão *m*, (*P*) guidador *m*

handmade /'hændmeɪd/ *a* feito à mão

handshake /'hændʃeɪk/ *n* aperto *m* de mão

handsome /'hænsəm/ *a* bonito; (*fig*) generoso

handwriting /'hændraɪtɪŋ/ *n* letra *f*, caligrafia *f*

handy /'hændɪ/ *a* (-**ier**, -**iest**) *a* (*convenient, useful*) útil, prático; (*person*) jeitoso; (*near*) à mão

handyman /'hændɪmæn/ *n* (*pl* -**men**) faz-tudo *m*

hang /hæŋ/ *vt* (*pt* **hung**) pendurar, suspender; (*head*) baixar; (*pt* **hanged**) (*criminal*) enforcar □ *vi* estar dependurado, pender; (*criminal*) ser enforcado. **get the** ~ **of** (*colloq*) pegar o jeito de, (*P*) apanhar. ~ **about** andar por aí. ~ **back** hesitar. ~-**gliding** *n* asa *f* delta. ~ **on** (*wait*) aguardar. ~ **on to** (*hold tightly*) agarrar-se a. ~ **out** (*sl: live*) morar. ~ **up** (*phone*) desligar. ~-**up** *n* (*sl*) complexo *m*

hangar /'hæŋə(r)/ *n* hangar *m*

hanger /'hæŋə(r)/ *n* (*for clothes*) cabide *m*. ~-**on** *n* parasita *mf*

hangover /'hæŋəʊvə(r)/ *n* (*from drinking*) ressaca *f*

hanker /'hæŋkə(r)/ *vi* ~ **after** ansiar por, suspirar por

haphazard /hæp'hæzəd/ *a* ~ **ly** *adv* ao acaso, à sorte

happen /'hæpən/ *vi* acontecer, suceder. **he** ~**s to be out** por acaso ele não está. ~**ing** *n* acontecimento *m*

happ|y /'hæpɪ/ *a* (-**ier**, -**iest**) feliz. **be** ~**y with** estar contente com. ~**y-go-lucky** *a* despreocupado. ~**ily** *adv* com satisfação; (*fortunately*) felizmente. she smiled ~ily ela sorriu feliz. ~iness *n* felicidade *f*

harass /'hærəs/ *vt* amofinar, atormentar, perseguir. ~**ment** *n* amofinação *f*, perseguição *f*. **sexual ~ment** assédio *m* sexual

harbour /'ha:bə(r)/ *n* porto *m*; (*shelter*) abrigo *m* □ *vt* abrigar, dar asilo a; (*fig: in the mind*) ocultar, obrigar

hard /ha:d/ *a* (-er, -est) duro; (*difficult*) difícil □ *adv* muito, intensamente; (*look*) fixamente; (*pull*) com força; (*think*) a fundo, a sério. ~**back** *n* livro *m* encadernado ~-**boiled egg** ovo *m* cozido. ~ **by** muito perto. ~ **disk** disco *m* rígido. ~-**headed** *a* realista, prático. ~ **of hearing** meio surdo. ~ **shoulder** acostamento *m*, (*P*) berma *f* alcatroada. ~ **up** (*colloq*) sem dinheiro, teso (*sl*), liso (*sl*). ~ **water** água *f* dura

hardboard /'ha:dbɔ:d/ *n* madeira *f* compensada, madeira *f* prensada, (*P*) tabopan *m*

harden /'ha:dn/ *vt/i* endurecer. ~**ed** *a* (*callous*) calejado; (*robust*) enrijado

hardly /'ha:dlɪ/ *adv* mal, dificilmente, a custo. ~ **ever** quase nunca

hardship /'ha:dʃɪp/ *n* provação *f*, adversidade *f*; (*suffering*) sofrimento *m*; (*financial*) privação *f*

hardware /'ha:dweə(r)/ *n* ferragens *fpl*; (*comput*) hardware *m*

hardy /'ha:dɪ/ *a* (-ier, -iest) resistente

hare /heə(r)/ *n* lebre *f*

hark /ha:k/ *vi* ~ **back to** voltar a, recordar

harm /ha:m/ *n* mal *m* □ *vt* prejudicar, fazer mal a. ~**ful** *a* prejudicial, nocivo. ~**less** *a* inofensivo. **out of ~'s way** a salvo. **there's no ~ in** não há mal em

harmonica /ha:'mɒnɪkə/ *n* gaita *f* de boca, (*P*) beiços

harmon|y /'ha:mənɪ/ *n* harmonia *f*. ~**ious** /-'məʊnɪəs/ *a* harmonioso. ~**ize** *vt/i* harmonizar(-se)

harness /'ha:nɪs/ *n* arreios *mpl* □ *vt* arrear; (*fig: use*) aproveitar, utilizar

harp /ha:p/ *n* harpa *f* □ *vi* ~ **on (about)** repisar. ~**ist** *n* harpista *mf*

harpoon /ha:'pu:n/ *n* arpão *m*

harpsichord /'ha:psɪkɔ:d/ *n* cravo *m*

harrowing /'hærəʊɪŋ/ *a* dilacerante, lancinante

harsh /ha:ʃ/ *a* (-er, -est) duro, severo; (*texture, voice*) áspero; (*light*) cru; (*colour*) gritante; (*climate*) rigoroso. ~**ly** *adv* duramente. ~**ness** *n* dureza *f*

harvest /'ha:vɪst/ *n* colheita *f*, ceifa *f* □ *vt* colher, ceifar

has /hæz/ *see* have

hash /hæʃ/ *n* picadinho *m*, carne *f* cozida; (*fig: jumble*) bagunça *f*. **make a ~ of** fazer uma bagunça

hashish /'hæʃɪʃ/ *n* haxixe *m*

hassle /'hæsl/ *n* (*colloq: quarrel*) discussão *f*; (*colloq: struggle*) dificuldade *f* □ *vt* (*colloq*) aborrecer

haste /heɪst/ *n* pressa *f*. **make ~** apressar-se

hasten /'heɪsn/ *vt/i* apressar(-se)

hast|y /'heɪstɪ/ *a* (-ier, -iest) apressado; (*too quick*) precipitado. ~**ily** *adv* às pressas, precipitadamente

hat /hæt/ *n* chapéu *m*

hatch[1] /hætʃ/ *n* (*for food*) postigo *m*; (*naut*) escotilha *f*

hatch[2] /hætʃ/ *vt/i* chocar; (*a plot etc*) tramar, urdir

hatchback /'hætʃbæk/ *n* carro *m* de três ou cinco portas

hatchet /'hætʃɪt/ *n* machadinha *f*

hate /heɪt/ *n* ódio *m* □ *vt* odiar, detestar. ~**ful** *a* odioso, detestável

hatred /'heɪtrɪd/ *n* ódio *m*

haughty /'hɔ:tɪ/ *a* (-ier, -iest) altivo, soberbo, arrogante

haul /hɔ:l/ *vt* arrastar, puxar; (*goods*) transportar em camião □ *n* (*booty*) presa *f*; (*fish caught*) apanha *f*; (*distance*) percurso *m*. ~**age** *n* transporte *m* de cargas. ~**ier** *n* (*firm*) transportadora *f* rodoviária; (*person*) fretador *m*

haunt /hɔ:nt/ *vt* rondar, freqüentar, (*P*) frequentar; (*ghost*) assombrar; (*thought*) obcecar □ *n* lugar *m* favorito. ~**ed house** casa *f* mal-assombrada

have /hæv/ *vt* (*3 sing pres* **has**, *pt* **had**) ter; (*bath etc*) tomar; (*meal*) fazer; (*walk*) dar □ *v aux* ter. ~ **done** ter feito. ~ **it out (with)** pôr a coisa em pratos limpos, pedir uma explicação (para). ~ **sth done** mandar fazer alg coisa

haven /'heɪvn/ *n* porto *m*; (*refuge*) refúgio *m*

haversack /'hævəsæk/ *n* mochila *f*

havoc /'hævək/ *n* estragos *mpl*. **play ~ with** causar estragos em

hawk[1] /hɔ:k/ *n* falcão *m*

hawk[2] /hɔ:k/ *vt* vender de porta em porta. ~**er** *n* vendedor *m* ambulante

hawthorn /'hɔ:θɔ:n/ *n* pirilteiro *m*, estrepeiro *m*

hay /heɪ/ *n* feno *m*. ~ **fever** febre *f* do feno

haystack /'heɪstæk/ *n* palheiro *m*, (*P*) meda *f* de feno

haywire /'heɪwaɪə(r)/ *a* **go ~** (*colloq*) ficar transtornado

hazard /'hæzəd/ *n* risco *m* □ *vt* arriscar. ~ **warning lights** pisca-alerta *m*. ~**ous** *a* arriscado

haze /heɪz/ *n* bruma *f*, neblina *f*, cerração *f*
hazel /ˈheɪzl/ *n* aveleira *f*. ~**-nut** *n* avelã *f*
hazy /ˈheɪzɪ/ *a* (-ier, -iest) brumoso, encoberto; (*fig: vague*) vago
he /hi:/ *pron* ele □ *n* macho *m*
head /hed/ *n* cabeça *f*; (*chief*) chefe *m*; (*of beer*) espuma *f* □ *a* principal □ *vt* encabeçar, estar à frente de □ *vi* ~ **for** dirigir-se para. ~**-dress** *n* toucador *m*. ~ **first** de cabeça. ~**-on** *a* frontal □ *adv* de frente. ~**s or tails?** cara ou coroa? ~ **waiter** chefe de garçons *m*, (*P*) dos criados. ~**er** *n* (*football*) cabeçada *f*
headache /ˈhedeɪk/ *n* dor *f* de cabeça
heading /ˈhedɪŋ/ *n* cabeçalho *m*, título *m*; (*subject category*) rubrica *f*
headlamp /ˈhedlæmp/ *n* farol *m*
headland /ˈhedlənd/ *n* promontório *m*
headlight /ˈhedlaɪt/ *n* farol *m*
headline /ˈhedlaɪn/ *n* título *m*, cabeçalho *m*
headlong /ˈhedlɒŋ/ *a* de cabeça; (*rash*) precipitado □ *adv* de cabeça; (*rashly*) precipitadamente
head|master /hedˈma:stə(r)/ *n* diretor *m*, (*P*) director *m*. ~**mistress** *n* diretora *f*, (*P*) directora *f*
headphone /ˈhedfəʊn/ *n* fone *m* de cabeça, (*P*) auscultador *m*
headquarters /hedˈkwɔ:təz/ *npl* sede *f*; (*mil*) quartel *m* general
headrest /ˈhedrest/ *n* apoio *m* para a cabeça
headroom /ˈhedru:m/ *n* (*auto*) espaço *m* para a cabeça; (*bridge*) limite *m* de altura, altura *f* máxima
headstrong /ˈhedstrɒŋ/ *a* teimoso
headway /ˈhedweɪ/ *n* progresso *m*. **make** ~ fazer progressos
heady /ˈhedɪ/ *a* (-ier, -iest) empolgante
heal /hi:l/ *vt/i* curar(-se), sarar; (*wound*) cicatrizar
health /helθ/ *n* saúde *f*. ~ **centre** posto *m* de saúde. ~ **foods** alimentos *mpl* naturais. ~**y** *a* saudável, sadio
heap /hi:p/ *n* monte *m*, pilha *f* □ *vt* amontoar, empilhar. ~**s of money** (*colloq*) dinheiro aos montes (*colloq*)
hear /hɪə(r)/ *vt/i* (*pt* **heard** /hɜ:d/) ouvir. ~, **hear!** apoiado! ~ **from** ter notícias de. ~ **of** *or* **about** ouvir falar de. **I won't** ~ **of it** nem quero ouvir falar nisso. ~**ing** *n* ouvido *m*, audição *f*; (*jur*) audiência *f*. ~**ing-aid** *n* aparelho *m* de audição
hearsay /ˈhɪəseɪ/ *n* boato *m*. **it's only** ~ é só por ouvir dizer
hearse /hɜ:s/ *n* carro *m* funerário
heart /ha:t/ *n* coração *m*. ~**s** (*cards*) copas *fpl*. **at** ~ no fundo. **by** ~ de cor. ~ **attack** ataque *m* de coração. ~**-beat** *n* pulsação *f*, batida *f*. ~**-breaking** *a* de cortar o coração. ~**-broken** *a* com o coração partido, desfeito. ~**-to-heart** *a* com o coração nas mãos. **lose** ~ perder a coragem, desanimar
heartburn /ˈha:tbɜ:n/ *n* azia *f*
hearten /ˈha:tn/ *vt* animar, encorajar
heartfelt /ˈha:tfelt/ *a* sincero, sentido
hearth /ha:θ/ *n* lareira *f*
heartless /ˈha:tlɪs/ *a* insensível, desalmado, cruel
heart|y /ˈha:tɪ/ *a* (-ier, -iest) caloroso; (*meal*) abundante. ~**ily** *adv* calorosamente; (*eat, laugh*) com vontade
heat /hi:t/ *n* calor *m*; (*fig*) ardor *m*; (*contest*) eliminatória *f* □ *vt/i* aquecer. ~**stroke** *n* insolação *f*. ~**wave** *n* onda *f* de calor. ~**er** *n* aquecedor *m*. ~**ing** *n* aquecimento *m*
heated /ˈhi:tɪd/ *a* (*fig*) acalorado, aceso
heathen /ˈhi:ðn/ *n* pagão *m*, pagã *f*
heather /ˈheðə(r)/ *n* urze *f*
heave /hi:v/ *vt/i* (*lift*) içar; (*a sigh*) soltar; (*retch*) ter náuseas; (*colloq: throw*) atirar
heaven /ˈhevn/ *n* céu *m*. ~**ly** *a* celestial; (*colloq*) divino
heav|y /ˈhevɪ/ *a* (-ier, -iest) pesado; (*blow, rain*) forte; (*cold, drinker*) grande; (*traffic*) intenso. ~**ily** *adv* pesadamente; (*drink, smoke etc*) inveterado
heavyweight /ˈhevɪweɪt/ *n* (*boxing*) peso-pesado *m*
Hebrew /ˈhi:bru:/ *a* hebreu, hebraico □ *n* (*lang*) hebreu *m*
heckle /ˈhekl/ *vt* interromper, interpelar
hectic /ˈhektɪk/ *a* muito agitado, febril
hedge /hedʒ/ *n* sebe *f* □ *vt* cercar □ *vi* (*in answering*) usar de evasivas. ~ **one's bets** (*fig*) resguardar-se
hedgehog /ˈhedʒhɒg/ *n* ouriço-cacheiro *m*
heed /hi:d/ *vt* prestar atenção a, escutar □ *n* **pay** ~ **to** prestar atenção a, dar ouvidos a. ~**less** *a* ~**less of** indiferente a, sem prestar atenção a
heel /hi:l/ *n* calcanhar *m*; (*of shoe*) salto *m*; (*sl*) canalha *m*
hefty /ˈheftɪ/ *a* (-ier, -iest) robusto e corpulento
height /haɪt/ *n* altura *f*; (*of mountain, plane*) altitude *f*; (*fig*) auge *m*, cúmulo *m*
heighten /ˈhaɪtn/ *vt/i* aumentar, elevar(-se)
heir /eə(r)/ *n* herdeiro *m*. ~**ess** *n* herdeira *f*

heirloom /'eəlu:m/ *n* peça *f* de família, (*P*) relíquia *f* de família
held /held/ *see* **hold**[1]
helicopter /'helıkɒptə(r)/ *n* helicóptero *m*
hell /hel/ *n* inferno *m*. **for the ~ of it** só por gozo. **~-bent** *a* decidido a todo o custo (**on** a). **~ish** *a* infernal
hello /hə'ləʊ/ *int & n* = **hallo**
helm /helm/ *n* leme *m*
helmet /'helmıt/ *n* capacete *m*
help /help/ *vt/i* ajudar □ *n* ajuda *f*. **home ~** empregada *f*, faxineira *f*, (*P*) mulher *f* a dias. **~ o.s. to** servir-se de. **he cannot ~ laughing** ele não pode conter o riso. **it can't be ~ed** não há remédio. **~er** *n* ajudante *mf*. **~ful** *a* útil; (*serviceable*) de grande ajuda. **~less** *a* impotente
helping /'helpıŋ/ *n* porção *f*, dose *f*
hem /hem/ *n* bainha *f* □ *vt* (*pt* **hemmed**) fazer a bainha. **~ in** cercar, encurralar
hemisphere /'hemısfıə(r)/ *n* hemisfério *m*
hemp /hemp/ *n* cânhamo *m*
hen /hen/ *n* galinha *f*
hence /hens/ *adv* (*from now*) a partir desta altura; (*for this reason*) daí, por isso. **a week ~** daqui a uma semana. **~forth** *adv* de agora em diante, doravante
henpecked /'henpekt/ *a* mandado, (*P*) dominado pela mulher
her /hɜ:(r)/ *pron* a (a ela); (*after prep*) ela. (**to**) **~** lhe. **I know ~** conheço-a □ *a* seu(s), sua(s); dela
herald /'herəld/ *vt* anunciar
heraldry /'herəldrı/ *n* heráldica *f*
herb /hɜ:b/ *n* erva *f* culinária *or* medicinal
herd /hɜ:d/ *n* manada *f*; (*of pigs*) vara *f* □ *vi* **~ together** juntar-se em rebanho
here /hıə(r)/ *adv* aqui □ *int* tome; aqui está. **to/from ~** para aqui/daqui
hereafter /hıər'a:ftə(r)/ *adv* de/para o futuro, daqui em diante □ *n* **the ~** a vida de além-túmulo, (*P*) a vida futura
hereby /hıə'baı/ *adv* (*jur*) pelo presente ato ou decreto, etc, (*P*) pelo presente acto ou decreto, etc
hereditary /hı'redıtrı/ *a* hereditário
heredity /hı'redətı/ *n* hereditariedade *f*
here|sy /'herəsı/ *n* heresia *f*. **~tic** *n* herege *mf*. **~tical** /hı'retıkl/ *a* herético
heritage /'herıtıdʒ/ *n* herança *f*, patrimônio *m*, (*P*) património *m*
hermit /'hɜ:mıt/ *n* eremita *m*
hernia /'hɜ:nıə/ *n* hérnia *f*
hero /'hıərəʊ/ *n* (*pl* **-oes**) herói *m*
heroic /hı'rəʊık/ *a* heróico
heroin /'herəʊın/ *n* heroína *f*
heroine /'herəʊın/ *n* heroína *f*
heroism /'herəʊızəm/ *n* heroísmo *m*
heron /'herən/ *n* garça *f*
herring /'herıŋ/ *n* arenque *m*
hers /hɜ:z/ *poss pron* o(s) seu(s), a(s) sua(s), o(s) dela, a(s) dela. **it is ~** é (o) dela *or* o seu
herself /hɜ:'self/ *pron* ela mesma; (*reflexive*) se. **by ~** sozinha. **for ~** para si mesma. **to ~** a/para si mesma. **Mary ~ said so** foi a própria Maria que o disse
hesitant /'hezıtənt/ *a* hesitante
hesitat|e /'hezıteıt/ *vt* hesitar. **~ion** /-'teıʃn/ *n* hesitação *f*
heterosexual /hetərəʊ'seksjʊəl/ *a & n* heterossexual (*mf*)
hexagon /'heksəgən/ *n* hexágono *m*. **~al** /-'ægənl/ *a* hexagonal
hey /heı/ *int* eh, olá
heyday /'heıdeı/ *n* auge *m*, apogeu *m*
hi /haı/ *int* olá, viva
hibernat|e /'haıbəneıt/ *vi* hibernar. **~ion** /-'neıʃn/ *n* hibernação *f*
hiccup /'hıkʌp/ *n* soluço *m* □ *vi* soluçar, estar com soluços
hide[1] /haıd/ *vt/i* (*pt* **hid**, *pp* **hidden**) esconder(-se) (**from** de). **~-and-seek** *n* (*game*) esconde-esconde *m*. **~-out** *n* (*colloq*) esconderijo *m*
hide[2] /haıd/ *n* pele *f*, couro *m*
hideous /'hıdıəs/ *a* horrendo, medonho
hiding /'haıdıŋ/ *n* (*colloq*: *thrashing*) sova *f*, surra *f*. **go into ~** esconder-se. **~-place** *n* esconderijo *m*
hierarchy /'haıəra:kı/ *n* hierarquia *f*
hi-fi /haı'faı/ *a & n* (de) alta fidelidade (*f*)
high /haı/ *a* (**-er**, **-est**) alto; (*price, number*) elevado; (*voice, pitch*) agudo □ *n* alta *f* □ *adv* alto. **two metres ~** com dois metros de altura. **~ chair** cadeira *f* alta para crianças. **~-handed** *a* autoritário, prepotente. **~ jump** salto *m* em altura. **~-rise building** edifício *m* alto, (*P*) torre *f*. **~ school** escola *f* secundária. **in the ~ season** em plena estação. **~-speed** *a* ultra-rápido. **~-spirited** *a* animado, vivo. **~ spot** (*sl*) ponto *m* culminante. **~ street** rua *f* principal. **~ tide** maré *f* alta. **~er education** ensino *m* superior
highbrow /'haıbraʊ/ *a & n* (*colloq*) intelectual (*m*)
highlight /'haılaıt/ *n* (*fig*) ponto *m* alto □ *vt* salientar, pôr em relevo, realçar
highly /'haılı/ *adv* altamente, extremamente. **~-strung** *a* muito sensível, nervoso, tenso. **speak ~ of** falar bem de

Highness /'haɪnɪs/ *n* Alteza *f*
highway /'haɪweɪ/ *n* estrada *f*, rodovia *f*. **H~ Code** Código *m* Nacional de Trânsito
hijack /'haɪdʒæk/ *vt* seqüestrar, (*P*) sequestrar □ *n* seqüestro *m*, (*P*) sequestro *m*. **~er** *n* (*of plane*) pirata *m* (do ar)
hike /haɪk/ *n* caminhada no campo *f* □ *vi* fazer uma caminhada. **~r** /-ə(r)/ *n* excursionista *mf*, caminhante *mf*
hilarious /hɪ'leərɪəs/ *a* divertido, desopilante
hill /hɪl/ *n* colina *f*, monte *m*; (*slope*) ladeira *f*, subida *f*. **~y** *a* acidentado
hillside /'hɪlsaɪd/ *n* encosta *f*, vertente *f*
hilt /hɪlt/ *n* punho *m*. **to the ~** completamente, inteiramente
him /hɪm/ *pron* o (a ele); (*after prep*) ele. **(to) ~** lhe. **I know ~** conheço-o
himself /hɪm'self/ *pron* ele mesmo; (*reflexive*) se. **by ~** sozinho. **for ~** para si mesmo. **to ~** a/para si mesmo. **Peter ~ saw it** foi o próprio Pedro que o viu
hind /haɪnd/ *a* traseiro, posterior
hind|er /'hɪndə(r)/ *vt* empatar, estorvar; (*prevent*) impedir. **~rance** *n* estorvo *m*
hindsight /'haɪndsaɪt/ *n* **with ~** em retrospecto
Hindu /hɪn'du:/ *n* & *a* hindu (*mf*). **~ism** /-ɪzəm/ *n* hinduísmo *m*
hinge /hɪndʒ/ *n* dobradiça *f* □ *vi* **~ on** depender de
hint /hɪnt/ *n* insinuação *f*, indireta *f*, (*P*) indirecta *f*; (*advice*) sugestão *f*, dica *f* (*colloq*) □ *vt* dar a entender, insinuar □ *vi* **~ at** fazer alusão a
hip /hɪp/ *n* quadril *m*
hippie /'hɪpɪ/ *n* hippie *mf*
hippopotamus /hɪpə'pɒtəməs/ *n* (*pl* **-muses**) hipopótamo *m*
hire /'haɪə(r)/ *vt* alugar; (*person*) contratar □ *n* aluguel *m*, (*P*) aluguer *m*. **~-purchase** *n* compra *f* a prestações, (*P*) crediário *m*
hirsute /'hɜ:sju:t/ *a* hirsuto
his /hɪz/ *a* seu(s), sua(s), dele □ *poss pron* o(s) seu(s), a(s) sua(s), o(s) dele, a(s) dele. **it is ~** é (o) dele *or* o seu
Hispanic /hɪs'pænɪk/ *a* hispânico
hiss /hɪs/ *n* silvo *m*; (*for disapproval*) assobio *m*, vaia *f* □ *vt/i* sibilar; (*for disapproval*) assobiar, vaiar
historian /hɪ'stɔ:rɪən/ *n* historiador *m*
histor|y /'hɪstərɪ/ *n* história *f*. **~ic(al)** /hɪ'stɒrɪk(l)/ *a* histórico
hit /hɪt/ *vt* (*pt* **hit**, *pres p* **hitting**) atingir, bater em; (*knock against, collide with*) chocar com, ir de encontro a; (*strike a target*) acertar em; (*find*) descobrir; (*affect*) atingir □ *vi* **~ on** dar com □ *n* pancada *f*; (*fig: success*) sucesso *m*. **~ it off** dar-se bem (**with** com). **~-and-run** *a* (*driver*) que foge depois do desastre. **~-or-miss** *a* ao acaso
hitch /hɪtʃ/ *vt* atar, prender; (*to a hook*) enganchar □ *n* sacão *m*; (*snag*) problema *m*. **~ a lift**, **~-hike** viajar de carona, (*P*) boleia. **~-hiker** *n* o que viaja de carona, boleia. **~ up** puxar para cima
hive /haɪv/ *n* colméia *f* □ *vt* **~ off** separar e tornar independente
hoard /hɔ:d/ *vt* juntar, açambarcar □ *n* provisão *f*; (*of valuables*) tesouro *m*
hoarding /'hɔ:dɪŋ/ *n* tapume *m*, outdoor *m*
hoarse /hɔ:s/ *a* (**-er**, **-est**) rouco. **~ness** *n* rouquidão *f*
hoax /həʊks/ *n* (*malicious*) logro *m*, embuste *m*; (*humorous*) trote *m* □ *vt* (*malicious*) engancer, lograr; passar um trote, pregar uma peça
hob /hɒb/ *n* placa *f* de aquecimento (do fogão)
hobble /'hɒbl/ *vi* coxear □ *vt* pear
hobby /'hɒbɪ/ *n* passatempo *m* favorito. **~-horse** *n* (*fig*) tópico *m* favorito
hock /hɒk/ *n* vinho *m* branco do Reno
hockey /'hɒkɪ/ *n* hóquei *m*
hoe /həʊ/ *n* enxada *f* □ *vt* trabalhar com enxada
hog /hɒg/ *n* porco *m*; (*greedy person*) glutão *m* □ *vt* (*pt* **hogged**) (*colloq*) açambarcar
hoist /hɔɪst/ *vt* içar □ *n* guindaste *m*, (*P*) monta-cargas *m*
hold[1] /həʊld/ *vt* (*pt* **held**) segurar; (*contain*) levar; (*possess*) ter, possuir; (*occupy*) ocupar; (*keep, maintain*) conservar, manter; (*affirm*) manter □ *vi* (*of rope etc*) agüentar(-se), (*P*) aguentar(-se) □ *n* (*influence*) domínio *m*. **get ~ of** pôr as mãos em; (*fig*) apanhar. **~ back** reter. **~ on** (*colloq*) esperar. **~ on to** guardar; (*cling to*) agarrar-se a. **~ one's breath** suster a respiração. **~ one's tongue** calar-se. **~ the line** não desligar. **~ out** resistir. **~ up** (*support*) sustentar; (*delay*) demorar; (*rob*) assaltar. **~-up** *n* atraso *m*; (*auto*) engarrafamento *m*; (*robbery*) assalto *m*. **~ with** agüentar, (*P*) aguentar. **~er** *n* detentor *m*; (*of post, title etc*) titular *mf*; (*for object*) suporte *m*
hold[2] /həʊld/ *n* (*of ship, plane*) porão *m*
holdall /'həʊldɔ:l/ *n* saco *m* de viagem
holding /'həʊldɪŋ/ *n* (*land*) propriedade *f*; (*comm*) ações *fpl*, (*P*) acções *fpl*, valores *mpl*, holding *m*

hole /həʊl/ *n* buraco *m* □ *vt* abrir buraco(s) em, esburacar
holiday /ˈhɒlədeɪ/ *n* férias *fpl*; (*day off; public*) feriado *m* □ *vi* passar férias. **~-maker** *n* pessoa *f* em férias; (*in summer*) veranista *mf*, (*P*) veraneante *mf*
holiness /ˈhəʊlmɪs/ *n* santidade *f*
Holland /ˈhɒlənd/ *n* Holanda *f*
hollow /ˈhɒləʊ/ *a* oco, vazio; (*fig*) falso; (*cheeks*) fundo; (*sound*) surdo □ *n* (*in the ground*) cavidade *f*; (*in the hand*) cova *f*
holly /ˈhɒlɪ/ *n* azevinho *m*
holster /ˈhəʊlstə(r)/ *n* coldre *m*
holy /ˈhəʊlɪ/ *a* (-ier, -iest) santo, sagrado; (*water*) benta. **H~ Ghost, H~ Spirit** Espírito *m* Santo
homage /ˈhɒmɪdʒ/ *n* homenagem *f*. **pay ~ to** prestar homenagem a
home /həʊm/ *n* casa *f*, lar *m*; (*institution*) lar *m*, asilo *m*; (*country*) país *m* natal □ *a* caseiro, doméstico; (*of family*) de família; (*pol*) nacional, interno; (*football match*) em casa □ *adv* (at) **~** en casa. **come/go ~** vir/ir para casa. **make oneself at ~** não fazer cerimônia, (*P*) cerimónia. **~-made** *a* caseiro. **H~ Office** Ministério *m* do Interior. **~ town** cidade *f or* terra *f* natal. **~ truth** dura verdade *f*, verdade(s) *f* (*pl*) amarga(s). **~less** *a* sem casa, desabrigado
homeland /ˈhəʊmlænd/ *n* pátria *f*
homely /ˈhəʊmlɪ/ *a* (-ier, -iest) (*simple*) simples; (*Amer: ugly*) sem graça
homesick /ˈhəʊmsɪk/ *a* **be ~** ter saudades
homeward /ˈhəʊmwəd/ *a* (*journey*) de regresso
homework /ˈhəʊmwɜːk/ *n* trabalho *m* de casa, dever *m* de casa
homicide /ˈhɒmɪsaɪd/ *n* homicídio *m*; (*person*) homicida *mf*
homoeopath|y /həʊmɪˈɒpəθɪ/ *n* homeopatia *f*. **~ic** *a* homeopático
homosexual /hɒməˈsekʃʊəl/ *a* & *n* homossexual (*mf*)
honest /ˈɒnɪst/ *a* honesto; (*frank*) franco. **~ly** *adv* honestamente; (*frankly*) francamente. **~y** *n* honestidade *f*
honey /ˈhʌnɪ/ *n* mel *m*; (*colloq: darling*) querido *m*, querida *f*, meu bem *m*
honeycomb /ˈhʌnɪkəʊm/ *n* favo *m* de mel
honeymoon /ˈhʌnɪmuːn/ *n* lua de mel *f*
honorary /ˈɒnərərɪ/ *a* honorário
honour /ˈɒnə(r)/ *n* honra *f* □ *vt* honrar. **~able** *a* honrado, honroso
hood /hʊd/ *n* capuz *m*; (*car roof*) capota *f*, (*P*) tejadilho *m*; (*Amer: bonnet*) capô *m*, (*P*) capot *m*
hoodwink /ˈhʊdwɪŋk/ *vt* enganar
hoof /huːf/ *n* (*pl* -fs) casco *m*
hook /hʊk/ *n* gancho *m*; (*on garment*) colchete *m*; (*for fishing*) anzol *m* □ *vt* enganchar; (*fish*) apanhar, pescar. **off the ~** livre de dificuldades; (*phone*) desligado
hooked /hʊkt/ *a* **be ~ on** (*sl*) ter o vício de, estar viciado em
hookey /ˈhʊkɪ/ *n* **play ~** (*Amer sl*) fazer gazeta
hooligan /ˈhuːlɪgən/ *n* desordeiro *m*
hoop /huːp/ *n* arco *m*; (*of cask*) cinta *f*
hooray /huːˈreɪ/ *int* & *n* = **hurrah**
hoot /huːt/ *n* (*of owl*) pio *m* de mocho; (*of horn*) buzinada *f*; (*jeer*) apupo *m* □ *vi* (*of owl*) piar; (*of horn*) buzinar; (*jeer*) apupar. **~er** *n* buzina *f*; (*of factory*) sereia *f*
Hoover /ˈhuːvə(r)/ *n* aspirador de pó *m*, (*P*) aspirador *m* □ *vt* passar o aspirador
hop[1] /hɒp/ *vi* (*pt* **hopped**) saltar num pé só, (*P*) ao pé coxinho □ *n* salto *m*. **~ in** (*colloq*) subir, saltar (*colloq*). **~ it** (*sl*) pôr-se a andar (*colloq*). **~ out** (*colloq*) descer, saltar (*colloq*)
hop[2] /hɒp/ *n* (*plant*) lúpulo *m*. **~s** espigas *fpl* de lúpulo
hope /həʊp/ *n* esperança *f* □ *vt/i* esperar. **~ for** esperar (ter). **~ful** *a* esperançoso; (*promising*) promissor. **be ~ful (that)** ter esperança (que), confiar (em que). **~fully** *adv* esperançosamente; (*it is hoped that*) é de esperar que. **~less** *a* desesperado, sem esperança; (*incompetent*) incapaz
horde /hɔːd/ *n* horda *f*
horizon /həˈraɪzn/ *n* horizonte *m*
horizontal /hɒrɪˈzɒntl/ *a* horizontal
hormone /ˈhɔːməʊn/ *n* hormônio *m*, (*P*) hormona *f*
horn /hɔːn/ *n* chifre *m*, corno *m*; (*of car*) buzina *f*; (*mus*) trompa *f*. **~y** *a* caloso, calejado
hornet /ˈhɔːnɪt/ *n* vespão *m*
horoscope /ˈhɒrəskəʊp/ *n* horóscopo *m*, (*P*) horoscópio *m*
horrible /ˈhɒrəbl/ *a* horrível, horroroso
horrid /ˈhɒrɪd/ *a* horrível, horripilante
horrific /həˈrɪfɪk/ *a* horrífico
horr|or /ˈhɒrə(r)/ *n* horror *m* □ *a* (*film etc*) de terror. **~ify** *vt* horrorizar, horripilar
horse /hɔːs/ *n* cavalo *m*. **~-chestnut** *n* castanha *f* da India. **~-racing** *n* corrida *f* de cavalos, hipismo *m*. **~-radish** *n* rábano *m*
horseback /ˈhɔːsbæk/ *n* **on ~** a cavalo

horseplay /'hɔ:spleɪ/ *n* brincadeira *f* grosseira, abrutalhada *f*
horsepower /'hɔ:spaʊə(r)/ *n* cavalo-vapor *m*
horseshoe /'hɔ:sʃu:/ *n* ferradura *f*
horticultur|e /'hɔ:tɪkʌltʃə(r)/ *n* horticultura *f*. **~al** /-'kʌltʃərəl/ *a* hortícola
hose /həʊz/ *n* **~(-pipe)** mangueira *f* □ *vt* regar com a mangueira
hospice /'hɒspɪs/ *n* hospício *m*; (*for travellers*) hospedaria *f*
hospit|able /hə'spɪtəbl/ *a* hospitaleiro. **~ality** /-'tælətɪ/ *n* hospitalidade *f*
hospital /'hɒspɪtl/ *n* hospital *m*
host[1] /həʊst/ *n* anfitrião *m*, dono *m* da casa. **~ess** *n* anfitriã *f*, dona *f* da casa
host[2] /həʊst/ *n* **a ~ of** uma multidão de, um grande número de
host[3] /həʊst/ *n* (*relig*) hóstia *f*
hostage /'hɒstɪdʒ/ *n* refém *m*
hostel /'hɒstl/ *n* residência *f* de estudantes *etc*
hostil|e /'hɒstaɪl/ *a* hostil. **~ity** /hɒ'stɪlətɪ/ *n* hostilidade *f*
hot /hɒt/ *a* (**hotter, hottest**) quente; (*culin*) picante. **be** *or* **feel ~** estar com *or* ter calor. **it is ~** está *or* faz calor □ *vt/i* (*pt* **hotted**) **~ up** (*colloq*) aquecer. **~ dog** cachorro-quente *m*. **~ line** linha direta *f*, (*P*) directa esp entre chefes de estado. **~-water bottle** saco *m* de água quente
hotbed /'hɒtbed/ *n* (*fig*) foco *m*
hotchpotch /'hɒtʃpɒtʃ/ *n* misturada *f*, (*P*) salgalhada *f*
hotel /həʊ'tel/ *n* hotel *m*. **~ier** /-ɪə(r)/ *n* hoteleiro *m*
hound /haʊnd/ *n* cão *m* de caça e de corrida, sabujo *m* □ *vt* acossar, perseguir
hour /'aʊə(r)/ *n* hora *f*. **~ly** *adv* de hora em hora □ *a* de hora em hora. **~ly pay** retribuição *f* horária. **paid ~ly** pago por hora
house[1] /haʊs/ *n* (*pl* **~s** /'haʊzɪz/) *n* casa *f*; (*pol*) câmara *f*. **on the ~** por conta da casa. **~-warming** *n* inauguração *f* da casa
house[2] /haʊz/ *vt* alojar; (*store*) arrecadar, guardar
houseboat /'haʊsbəʊt/ *n* casa *f* flutuante
household /'haʊshəʊld/ *n* família *f*, agregado *m* familiar. **~er** *n* ocupante *mf*; (*owner*) proprietário *m*
housekeep|er /'haʊski:pə(r)/ *n* governanta *f*. **~ing** *n* (*work*) tarefas *fpl* domésticas
housewife /'haʊswaɪf/ *n* (*pl* **-wives**) dona *f* de casa
housework /'haʊswɜ:k/ *n* tarefas *fpl* domésticas
housing /'haʊzɪŋ/ *n* alojamento *m*. **~ estate** zona *f* residencial
hovel /'hɒvl/ *n* casebre *m*, tugúrio *m*
hover /'hɒvə(r)/ *vi* pairar; (*linger*) deixar-se ficar, demorar-se
hovercraft /'hɒvəkra:ft/ *n invar* aerobarco *m*, hovercraft *m*
how /haʊ/ *adv* como. **~ long/old is...?** que comprimento/idade tem...? **~ far?** a que distância? **~ many?** quantos? **~ much?** quanto? **~ often?** com que freqüência, (*P*) frequência? **~ pretty it is** como é lindo. **~ about a walk?** e se fôssemos dar uma volta? **~ are you?** como vai? **~ do you do?** muito prazer! **and ~!** oh se é!
however /haʊ'evə(r)/ *adv* de qualquer maneira; (*though*) contudo, no entanto, todavia. **~ small it may be** por menor que seja
howl /haʊl/ *n* uivo *m* □ *vi* uivar
HP *abbr see* **hire-purchase**
hp *abbr see* **horsepower**
hub /hʌb/ *n* cubo *m* da roda; (*fig*) centro *m*. **~-cap** *n* calota *f*, (*P*) tampão *m* da roda
hubbub /'hʌbʌb/ *n* chinfrim *m*
huddle /'hʌdl/ *vt/i* apinhar(-se). **~ together** aconchegar-se
hue[1] /hju:/ *n* matiz *f*, tom *m*
hue[2] /hju:/ *n* **~ and cry** clamor *m*, alarido *m*
huff /hʌf/ *n* **in a ~** com raiva, zangado
hug /hʌg/ *vt* (*pt* **hugged**) abraçar, apertar nos braços; (*keep close to*) chegar-se a □ *n* abraço *m*
huge /hju:dʒ/ *a* enorme
hulk /hʌlk/ *n* casco (esp de navio desmantelado) *m*. **~ing** *a* (*colloq*) desajeitadão (*colloq*)
hull /hʌl/ *n* (*of ship*) casco *m*
hullo /hə'ləʊ/ *int* & *n* = **hallo**
hum /hʌm/ *vt/i* (*pt* **hummed**) cantar com a boca fechada; (*of insect, engine*) zumbir □ *n* zumbido *m*
human /'hju:mən/ *a* humano □ *n* **~ (being)** ser *m* humano
humane /hju:'meɪn/ *a* humano, compassivo
humanitarian /hju:mænɪ'teərɪən/ *a* humanitário
humanity /hju:'mænətɪ/ *n* humanidade *f*
humbl|e /'hʌmbl/ *a* (**-er, -est**) humilde □ *vt* humilhar. **~y** *adv* humildemente
humdrum /'hʌmdrʌm/ *a* monótono, rotineiro
humid /'hju:mɪd/ *a* úmido, (*P*) húmido. **~ity** /-'mɪdətɪ/ *n* umidade *f*, (*P*) humidade *f*
humiliat|e /hju:'mɪlɪeɪt/ *vt* humilhar. **~ion** /-'eɪʃn/ *n* humilhação *f*

humility /hju:'mɪlətɪ/ *n* humildade *f*
humorist /'hju:mərɪst/ *n* humorista *mf*
hum|our /'hju:mə(r)/ *n* humor *m* □ *vt* fazer a vontade de. **~orous** *a* humorístico; (*person*) divertido, espirituoso
hump /hʌmp/ *n* corcova *f*; (*of the back*) corcunda *f* □ *vt* corcovar, arquear. **the ~** (*sl*) a neura (*colloq*)
hunch[1] /hʌntʃ/ *vt* curvar. **~ed up** curvado
hunch[2] /hʌntʃ/ *n* (*colloq*) palpite *m*
hunchback /'hʌntʃbæk/ *n* corcunda *mf*
hundred /'hʌndrəd/ *a* cem □ *n* centena *f*, cento *m*. **~s of** centenas de. **~fold** *a* cêntuplo □ *adv* cem vezes mais. **~th** *a* & *n* centésimo (*m*)
hundredweight /'hʌndrədweɪt/ *n* quintal *m* (= *50,8 kg*; *Amer 45,36 kg*)
hung /hʌŋ/ *see* **hang**
Hungar|y /'hʌŋgərɪ/ *n* Hungria *f*. **~ian** /-'geərɪən/ *a* & *n* húngaro (*m*)
hunger /'hʌŋgə(r)/ *n* fome *f* □ *vi* **~ for** ter fome de; (*fig*) desejar vivamente, ansiar por
hungr|y /'hʌŋgrɪ/ *a* (**ier**, **-iest**) esfomeado, faminto. **be ~y** ter fome, estar com fome. **~ily** *adv* avidamente
hunk /hʌŋk/ *n* grande naco *m*
hunt /hʌnt/ *vt/i* caçar □ *n* caça *f*. **~ for** andar à caça de, andar à procura de. **~er** *n* caçador *m*. **~ing** *n* caça *f*, caçada *f*
hurdle /'hɜ:dl/ *n* obstáculo *m*
hurl /hɜ:l/ *vt* arremessar, lançar com força
hurrah, hurray /hʊ'ra:, hʊ'reɪ/ *int* & *n* hurra (*m*), viva (*m*)
hurricane /'hʌrɪkən/ *n* furacão *m*
hurried /'hʌrɪd/ *a* apressado. **~ly** *adv* apressadamente, às pressas
hurry /'hʌrɪ/ *vt/i* apressar(-se), despachar(-se) □ *n* pressa *f*. **be in a ~** estar com *or* ter pressa. **do sth in a ~** fazer alg coisa às pressas. **~up!** ande logo
hurt /hɜ:t/ *vt* (*pt* **hurt**) fazer mal a; (*injure, offend*) magoar, ferir □ *vi* doer □ *a* magoado, ferido □ *n* mal *m*; (*feelings*) mágoa *f*. **~ful** *a* prejudicial; (*remark etc*) que magoa
hurtle /'hɜ:tl/ *vi* despenhar-se; (*move rapidly*) precipitar-se □ *vt* arremessar
husband /'hʌzbənd/ *n* marido *m*, esposo *m*
hush /hʌʃ/ *vt* (fazer) calar. **~!** silêncio! □ *vi* calar-se □ *n* silêncio *m*. **~-hush** *a* (*colloq*) muito em segredo. **~ up** abafar, encobrir
husk /hʌsk/ *n* casca *f*
husky /'hʌskɪ/ *a* (**-ier**, **-iest**) (*hoarse*) rouco, enrouquecido; (*burly*) corpulento □ *n* cão *m* esquimó
hustle /'hʌsl/ *vt* empurrar, dar encontrões a □ *n* empurrão *m*. **~ and bustle** grande movimento *m*
hut /hʌt/ *n* cabana *f*, barraca *f* de madeira
hutch /hʌtʃ/ *n* coelheira *f*
hyacinth /'haɪəsɪnθ/ *n* jacinto *m*
hybrid /'haɪbrɪd/ *a* & *n* híbrido (*m*)
hydrant /'haɪdrənt/ *n* hidrante *m*
hydraulic /haɪ'drɔ:lɪk/ *a* hidráulico
hydroelectric /haɪdrəʊɪ'lektrɪk/ *a* hidrelétrico, (*P*) hidroelectrico
hydrofoil /'haɪdrəʊfɔɪl/ *n*
hydrogen /'haɪdrədʒən/ *n* hidrogênio *m*, (*P*) hidrogénio *m*
hyena /haɪ'i:nə/ *n* hiena *f*
hygiene /'haɪdʒi:n/ *n* higiene *f*
hygienic /haɪ'dʒi:nɪk/ *a* higiênico, (*P*) higiénico
hymn /hɪm/ *n* hino *m*, cântico *m*
hyper- /'haɪpə(r)/ *pref* hiper-
hypermarket /'haɪpəma:kɪt/ *n* hipermercado *m*
hyphen /'haɪfn/ *n* hífen *m*, traço-de-união *m*. **~ate** *vt* unir com hífen
hypno|sis /hɪp'nəʊsɪs/ *n* hipnose *f*. **~tic** /-'nɒtɪk/ *a* hipnótico
hypnot|ize /'hɪpnətaɪz/ *vt* hipnotizar. **~ism** /-ɪzəm/ *n* hipnotismo *m*
hypochondriac /haɪpə'kɒndrɪæk/ *n* hipocondríaco *m*
hypocrisy /hɪ'pɒkrəsɪ/ *n* hipocrisia *f*
hypocrit|e /'hɪpəkrɪt/ *n* hipócrita *mf*. **~ical** /-'krɪtɪkl/ *a* hipócrita
hypodermic /haɪpə'dɜ:mɪk/ *a* hipodérmico □ *n* seringa *f*
hypothe|sis /haɪ'pɒθəsɪs/ *n* (*pl* **-theses** /-si:z/) hipótese *f*. **~tical** /-ə'θetɪkl/ *a* hipotético
hyster|ia /hɪ'stɪərɪə/ *n* histeria *f*. **~ical** /hɪ'sterɪkl/ *a* histérico

I

I /aɪ/ *pron* eu
Iberian /aɪ'bi:rɪən/ *a* ibérico □ *n* íbero *m*
ice /aɪs/ *n* gelo *m* □ *vt/i* gelar; (*cake*) cobrir com glacê □ *vi* **~ up** gelar. **~-box** *n* (*Amer*) geladeira *f*, (*P*) frigorífico *m*. **~(-cream)** *n* sorvete *m*, (*P*) gelado *m*. **~-cube** *n* cubo *m* *or* pedra *f* de gelo. **~ hockey** hóquei *m* sobre o gelo. **~ lolly** picolé *m*. **~-pack** *n* saco *m* de gelo. **~-rink** *n* rimque *m* de patinação, (*P*) patinagem *f* no gelo. **~ skating** *n* patinação *f*, (*P*) patinagem *f* no gelo
iceberg /'aɪsbɜ:g/ *n* iceberg *m*; (*fig*) pedaço *m* de gelo
Iceland /'aɪslənd/ *n* Islândia *f*. **~er** *n* islandês *m*. **~ic** /-'lændɪk/ *a* & *n* islandês (*m*)
icicle /'aɪsɪkl/ *n* pingente *m* de gelo

icing /ˈaɪsɪŋ/ *n* (*culin*) cobertura *f* de açúcar, glacê *m*
icy /ˈaɪsɪ/ *a* (**-ier, -iest**) gelado, gélido, glacial; (*road*) com gelo
idea /aɪˈdɪə/ *n* idéia *f*, (*P*) ideia *f*
ideal /aɪˈdɪəl/ *a* & *n* ideal (*m*). **~ize** *vt* idealizar. **~ly** *adv* idealmente
idealis|t /aɪˈdɪəlɪst/ *n* idealista *mf*. **~m** /-zəm/ *n* idealismo *m*. **~tic** /-ˈlɪstɪk/ *a* idealista
identical /aɪˈdentɪkl/ *a* idêntico
identif|y /aɪˈdentɪfaɪ/ *vt* identificar □ *vi* **~y with** identificar-se com. **~ication** /-ɪˈkeɪʃn/ *n* identificação *f*; (*papers*) documentos *mpl* de identificação
identity /aɪˈdentətɪ/ *n* identidade *f*. **~ card** carteira *f* de identidade
ideolog|y /aɪdɪˈɒlədʒɪ/ *n* ideologia *f*. **~ical** *a* /-ɪəˈlɒdʒɪkl/ *a* ideológico
idiom /ˈɪdɪəm/ *n* idioma *m*; (*phrase*) expressão *f* idiomática. **~atic** /-ˈmætɪk/ *a* idiomático
idiosyncrasy /ɪdɪəˈsɪŋkrəsɪ/ *n* idiossincrasia *f*, peculiaridade *f*
idiot /ˈɪdɪət/ *n* idiota *mf*. **~ic** /-ˈɒtɪk/ *a* idiota
idl|e /ˈaɪdl/ *a* (**-er, -est**) (*not active; lazy*) ocioso; (*unemployed*) sem trabalho; (*of machines*) parado; (*fig: useless*) inútil □ *vt/i* (*of engine*) estar em ponto morto, *P* estar no ralenti. **~eness** *n* ociosidade *f*. **~y** *adv* ociosamente
idol /ˈaɪdl/ *n* ídolo *m*. **~ize** *vt* idolatrar
idyllic /ɪˈdɪlɪk/ *a* idílico
i.e. *abbr* isto é, quer dizer
if /ɪf/ *conj* se
igloo /ˈɪglu:/ *n* iglu *m*
ignite /ɪgˈnaɪt/ *vt/i* inflamar(-se), acender; (*catch fire*) pegar fogo; (*set fire to*) atear fogo a, (*P*) deitar fogo a
ignition /ɪgˈnɪʃn/ *n* (*auto*) ignição *f*. **~ (key)** chave *f* de ignição
ignoran|t /ˈɪgnərənt/ *a* ignorante. **~ce** *n* ignorância *f*. **be ~t of** ignorar
ignore /ɪgˈnɔ:(r)/ *vt* não fazer caso de, passar por cima de; (*person in the street etc*) fingir não ver
ill /ɪl/ *a* (*sick*) doente; (*bad*) mau □ *adv* mal □ *n* mal *m*. **~-advised** *a* pouco aconselhável. **~ at ease** pouco à vontade. **~-bred** *a* mal educado. **~-fated** *a* malfadado. **~-treat** *vt* maltratar. **~ will** má vontade *f*, animosidade *f*
illegal /ɪˈli:gl/ *a* ilegal
illegible /ɪˈledʒəbl/ *a* ilegível
illegitima|te /ɪlɪˈdʒɪtɪmət/ *a* ilegítimo. **~cy** *n* ilegitimidade *f*
illitera|te /ɪˈlɪtərət/ *a* analfabeto; (*uneducated*) iletrado. **~cy** *n* analfabetismo *m*
illness /ˈɪlnɪs/ *n* doença *f*
illogical /ɪˈlɒdʒɪkl/ *a* ilógico
illuminat|e /ɪˈlu:mɪneɪt/ *vt* iluminar; (*explain*) esclarecer. **~ion** /-ˈneɪʃn/ *n* iluminação *f*. **~ions** *npl* luminárias *fpl*
illusion /ɪˈlu:ʒn/ *n* ilusão *f*
illusory /ɪˈlu:sərɪ/ *a* ilusório
illustrat|e /ˈɪləstreɪt/ *vt* ilustrar. **~ion** /-ˈstreɪʃn/ *n* ilustração *f*. **~ive** /-ətɪv/ *a* ilustrativo
illustrious /ɪˈlʌstrɪəs/ *a* ilustre
image /ˈɪmɪdʒ/ *n* imagem *f*. **(public) ~** imagem *f* pública
imaginary /ɪˈmædʒɪnərɪ/ *a* imaginário
imaginat|ion /ɪmædʒɪˈneɪʃn/ *n* imaginação *f*. **~ive** /ɪˈmædʒɪnətɪv/ *a* imaginativo
imagin|e /ɪˈmædʒɪn/ *vt* imaginar. **~able** *a* imaginável
imbalance /ɪmˈbæləns/ *n* desequilíbrio *m*
imbecile /ˈɪmbəsi:l/ *a* & *n* imbecil (*mf*)
imbue /ɪmˈbju:/ *vt* imbuir, impregnar
imitat|e /ˈɪmɪteɪt/ *vt* imitar. **~ion** /-ˈteɪʃn/ *n* imitação *f*
immaculate /ɪˈmækjʊlət/ *a* imaculado; (*impeccable*) impecável
immaterial /ɪməˈtɪərɪəl/ *a* (*of no importance*) irrelevante. **that's ~ to me** para mim tanto faz
immature /ɪməˈtjʊə(r)/ *a* imaturo
immediate /ɪˈmi:dɪət/ *a* imediato. **~ly** *adv* imediatamente □ *conj* logo que, assim que
immens|e /ɪˈmens/ *a* imenso. **~ely** /-slɪ/ *adv* imensamente. **~ity** *n* imensidade *f*
immers|e /ɪˈmɜ:s/ *vt* mergulhar, imergir. **be ~ed in** (*fig*) estar imerso em. **~ion** /-ʃn/ *n* imersão *f*. **~ion heater** aquecedor *m* de água elétrico, (*P*) eléctrico
immigr|ate /ˈɪmɪgreɪt/ *vi* imigrar. **~ant** *n* & *a* imigrante (*mf*), imigrado (*m*). **~ation** /-ˈgreɪʃn/ *n* imigração *f*
imminen|t /ˈɪmɪnənt/ *a* iminente. **~ce** *n* iminência *f*
immobil|e /ɪˈməʊbaɪl/ *a* imóvel. **~ize** /-əlaɪz/ *vt* imobilizar
immoderate /ɪˈmɒdərət/ *a* imoderado, descomedido
immoral /ɪˈmɒrəl/ *a* imoral. **~ity** /ɪməˈrælətɪ/ *n* imoralidade *f*
immortal /ɪˈmɔ:tl/ *a* imortal. **~ity** /-ˈtælətɪ/ *n* imortalidade *f*. **~ize** *vt* imortalizar
immun|e /ɪˈmju:n/ *a* imune, imunizado (**from, to** contra). **~ity** *n* imunidade *f*
imp /ɪmp/ *n* diabrete *m*
impact /ˈɪmpækt/ *n* impacto *m*

impair /ɪm'peə(r)/ *vt* deteriorar; (*damage*) prejudicar
impale /ɪm'peɪl/ *vt* empalar
impart /ɪm'pa:t/ *vt* comunicar, transmitir (to a)
impartial /ɪm'pa:ʃl/ *a* imparcial. **~ity** /-ʃɪ'ælətɪ/ *n* imparcialidade *f*
impassable /ɪm'pa:səbl/ *a* (*road, river*) impraticável, intransitável; (*barrier etc*) intransponível
impasse /'æmpa:s/ *n* impasse *m*
impatien|t /ɪm'peɪʃənt/ *a* impaciente. **~ce** *n* impaciência *f*. **~tly** *adv* impacientemente
impeach /ɪm'pi:tʃ/ *vt* incriminar, acusar
impeccable /ɪm'pekəbl/ *a* impecável
impede /ɪm'pi:d/ *vt* impedir, estorvar
impediment /ɪm'pedɪmənt/ *n* impedimento *m*, obstáculo *m*. **(speech) ~** defeito *m* (na fala)
impel /ɪm'pel/ *vt* (*pt* **impelled**) impelir, forçar (to do a fazer)
impending /ɪm'pendɪŋ/ *a* iminente
impenetrable /ɪm'penɪtrəbl/ *a* impenetrável
imperative /ɪm'perətɪv/ *a* imperativo; (*need etc*) imperioso □ *n* imperativo *m*
imperceptible /ɪmpə'septəbl/ *a* imperceptível
imperfect /ɪm'pɜ:fɪkt/ *a* imperfeito. **~ion** /-ə'fekʃn/ *n* imperfeição *f*
imperial /ɪm'pɪərɪəl/ *a* imperial; (*of measures*) legal (*na GB*). **~ism** /-lɪzəm/ *n* imperialismo *m*
imperious /ɪm'pɪərɪəs/ *a* imperioso
impersonal /ɪm'pɜ:sənl/ *a* impessoal
impersonat|e /ɪm'pɜ:səneɪt/ *vt* fazer-se passar por; (*theat*) fazer *or* representar (o papel) de. **~ion** /'neɪʃn/ *n* imitação *f*
impertinen|t /ɪm'pɜ:tɪnənt/ *a* impertinente. **~ce** *n* impertinência *f*. **~tly** *adv* com impertinência
impervious /ɪm'pɜ:vɪəs/ *a* **~ to** (*water*) impermeável a; (*fig*) insensível a
impetuous /ɪm'petʃʊəs/ *a* impetuoso
impetus /'ɪmpɪtəs/ *n* ímpeto *m*
impinge /ɪm'pɪndʒ/ *vi* **~ on** afetar, *P* afectar; (*encroach*) infringir
impish /'ɪmpɪʃ/ *a* travesso, malicioso
implacable /ɪm'plækəbl/ *a* implacável
implant /ɪm'pla:nt/ *vt* implantar
implement[1] /'ɪmplɪmənt/ *n* instrumento *m*, utensílio *m*
implement[2] /'ɪmplɪment/ *vt* implementar, executar
implicat|e /'ɪmplɪkeɪt/ *vt* implicar. **~ion** /-'keɪʃn/ *n* implicação *f*
implicit /ɪm'plɪsɪt/ *a* implícito; (*unquestioning*) absoluto, incondicional
implore /ɪm'plɔ:(r)/ *vt* implorar, suplicar, rogar
imply /ɪm'plaɪ/ *vt* implicar; (*hint*) sugerir, dar a entender, insinuar
impolite /ɪmpə'laɪt/ *a* indelicado, incorreto, (*P*) incorrecto
import[1] /ɪm'pɔ:t/ *vt* importar. **~ation** /-'teɪʃn/ *n* importação *f*. **~er** *n* importador *m*
import[2] /'ɪmpɔ:t/ *n* importação *f*; (*meaning*) significado *m*; (*importance*) importância *f*
importan|t /ɪm'pɔ:tnt/ *a* importante. **~ce** *n* importância *f*
impos|e /ɪm'pəʊz/ *vt* impôr; (*inflict*) infligir □ *vi* **~e on** abusar de. **~ition** /-ə'zɪʃn/ *n* imposição *f*; (*unfair burden*) abuso *m*
imposing /ɪm'pəʊzɪŋ/ *a* imponente
impossib|le /ɪm'pɒsəbl/ *a* impossível. **~ility** /-'bɪlətɪ/ *n* impossibilidade *f*
impostor /ɪm'pɒstə(r)/ *n* impostor *m*
impoten|t /'ɪmpətənt/ *a* impotente. **~ce** *n* impotência *f*
impound /ɪm'paʊnd/ *vt* apreender, confiscar
impoverish /ɪm'pɒvərɪʃ/ *vt* empobrecer
impracticable /ɪm'præktɪkəbl/ *a* impraticável
impractical /ɪm'præktɪkl/ *a* pouco prático
imprecise /ɪmprɪ'saɪs/ *a* impreciso
impregnable /ɪm'pregnəbl/ *a* inexpugnável; (*fig*) inabalável, irrefutável
impregnate /'ɪmpregneɪt/ *vt* impregnar (with de)
impresario /ɪmprɪ'sa:rɪəʊ/ *n* (*pl* -os) empresário *m*
impress /ɪm'pres/ *vt* impressionar, causar impressão a; (*imprint*) imprimir. **~ on s.o.** inculcar algo em alguém
impression /ɪm'preʃn/ *n* impressão *f*. **~able** *a* impressionável. **~ist** *n* impressionista *mf*
impressive /ɪm'presɪv/ *a* impressionante, imponente
imprint[1] /'ɪmprɪnt/ *n* impressão *f*, marca *f*
imprint[2] /ɪm'prɪnt/ *vt* imprimir
imprison /ɪm'prɪzn/ *vt* prender, aprisionar. **~ment** *n* aprisionamento *m*, prisão *f*
improbab|le /ɪm'prɒbəbl/ *a* improvável. **~ility** /-'bɪlətɪ/ *n* improbabilidade *f*
impromptu /ɪm'prɒmptju:/ *a & adv* de improviso □ *n* impromptu *m*
improper /ɪm'prɒpə(r)/ *a* impróprio; (*indecent*) indecente, pouco decente; (*wrong*) incorreto, (*P*) incorrecto
improve /ɪm'pru:v/ *vt/i* melhorar. **~ on** aperfeiçoar. **~ment** *n* melhoria *f*;

(*in house etc*) melhoramento *m*; (*in health*) melhoras *fpl*

improvis|e /'ɪmprəvaɪz/ *vt/i* improvisar. **~ation** /-'zeɪʃn/ *n* improvisação *f*

imprudent /ɪm'pru:dnt/ *a* imprudente

impuden|t /'ɪmpjʊdənt/ *a* descarado, insolente. **~ce** *n* descaramento *m*, insolência *f*

impulse /'ɪmpʌls/ *n* impulso *m*

impulsive /ɪm'pʌlsɪv/ *a* impulsivo

impur|e /ɪm'pjʊə(r)/ *a* impuro. **~ity** *n* impureza *f*

in /ɪn/ *prep* em, dentro de □ *adv* dentro; (*at home*) em casa; (*in fashion*) na moda. **~ Lisbon/English** em Lisboa/inglês. **~ winter** no inverno. **~ an hour** (*at end of, within*) numa hora. **~ the rain** na chuva. **~ doing** ao fazer. **~ the evening** à tardinha. **the best ~** o melhor em. **we are ~ for** vamos ter. **~-laws** *npl* (*colloq*) sogros *mpl*. **~-patient** *n* doente *m* internado. **the ~s and outs** meandros *mpl*

inability /ɪnə'bɪlətɪ/ *n* incapacidade *f* (to do para fazer)

inaccessible /ɪnæk'sesəbl/ *a* inacessível

inaccura|te /ɪn'ækjərət/ *a* inexato, (*P*) inexacto. **~cy** *n* inexatidão *f*, (*P*) inexactidão *f*, falta *f* de rigor

inaction /ɪn'ækʃn/ *n* inação *f*, (*P*) inacção *f*

inactiv|e /ɪn'æktɪv/ *a* inativo, (*P*) inactivo. **~ity** /-'tɪvətɪ/ *n* inação *f*, (*P*) inacção *f*

inadequa|te /ɪn'ædɪkwət/ *a* inadequado, impróprio; (*insufficient*) insuficiente. **~cy** *n* inadequação *f*; (*insufficiency*) insuficiência *f*

inadmissible /ɪnəd'mɪsəbl/ *a* inadmissível

inadvertently /ɪnəd'vɜ:təntlɪ/ *adv* inadvertidamente; (*unintentionally*) sem querer, sem ser por mal

inadvisable /ɪnəd'vaɪzəbl/ *a* desaconselhável, não aconselhável

inane /ɪ'neɪn/ *a* tolo, oco

inanimate /ɪn'ænɪmət/ *a* inanimado

inappropriate /ɪnə'prəʊprɪət/ *a* impróprio, inadequado

inarticulate /ɪnɑ:'tɪkjʊlət/ *a* inarticulado; (*of person*) incapaz de se exprimir claramente

inattentive /ɪnə'tentɪv/ *a* desatento

inaugural /ɪ'nɔ:gjʊrəl/ *a* inaugural

inaugurat|e /ɪ'nɔ:gjʊreɪt/ *vt* inaugurar. **~ion** /-'reɪʃn/ *n* inauguração *f*

inauspicious /ɪnɔ:'spɪʃəs/ *a* pouco auspicioso

inborn /ɪn'bɔ:n/ *a* inato

inbred /ɪn'bred/ *a* inato, congênito, (*P*) congénito

incalculable /ɪn'kælkjʊləbl/ *a* incalculável

incapable /ɪn'keɪpəbl/ *a* incapaz

incapacit|y /ɪnkə'pæsətɪ/ *n* incapacidade *f*. **~ate** *vt* incapacitar

incarnat|e /ɪn'kɑ:neɪt/ *a* encarnado. **the devil ~e** o diabo em pessoa. **~ion** /-'neɪʃn/ *n* encarnação *f*

incendiary /ɪn'sendɪərɪ/ *a* incendiário □ *n* bomba *f* incendiária

incense[1] /'ɪnsens/ *n* incenso *m*

incense[2] /ɪn'sens/ *vt* exasperar, enfurecer

incentive /ɪn'sentɪv/ *n* incentivo, estímulo

incessant /ɪn'sesənt/ *a* incessante. **~ly** *adv* incessantemente, sem cessar

incest /'ɪnsest/ *n* incesto *m*. **~uous** /ɪn'sestjʊəs/ *a* incestuoso

inch /ɪntʃ/ *n* polegada *f* (= *2.54 cm*) □ *vt/i* avançar palmo a palmo *or* pouco a pouco. **within an ~ of** a um passo de

incidence /'ɪnsɪdəns/ *n* incidência *f*; (*rate*) percentagem *f*

incident /'ɪnsɪdənt/ *n* incidente *m*

incidental /ɪnsɪ'dentl/ *a* incidental, acessório; (*casual*) acidental; (*expenses*) eventuais; (*music*) de cena, incidental. **~ly** *adv* incidentalmente; (*by the way*) a propósito

incinerat|e /ɪn'sɪnəreɪt/ *vt* incinerar. **~or** *n* incinerador *m*

incision /ɪn'sɪʒn/ *n* incisão *f*

incisive /ɪn'saɪsɪv/ *a* incisivo

incite /ɪn'saɪt/ *vt* incitar, instigar. **~ment** *n* incitamento *m*

inclination /ɪnklɪ'neɪʃn/ *n* inclinação *f*, tendência *f*

incline[1] /ɪn'klaɪn/ *vt/i* inclinar(-se). **be ~d to** inclinar-se para; (*have tendency*) ter tendência para

incline[2] /'ɪnklaɪn/ *n* inclinação *f*, declive *m*

inclu|de /ɪn'klu:d/ *vt* incluir; (*in letter*) enviar junto *or* em anexo. **~ding** *prep* inclusive. **~sion** *n* inclusão *f*

inclusive /ɪn'klu:sɪv/ *a* & *adv* inclusive. **be ~ of** incluir

incognito /ɪnkɒg'ni:təʊ/ *a* & *adv* incógnito

incoherent /ɪnkə'hɪərənt/ *a* incoerente

income /'ɪŋkʌm/ *n* rendimento *m*. **~ tax** imposto sobre a renda, (*P*) sobre o rendimento

incoming /'ɪnkʌmɪŋ/ *a* (*tide*) enchente; (*tenant etc*) novo

incomparable /ɪn'kɒmpərəbl/ *a* incomparável

incompatible /ɪnkəm'pætəbl/ *a* incompatível

incompeten|t /ɪn'kɒmpɪtənt/ *a* incompetente. **~ce** *n* incompetência *f*

incomplete /ɪnkəm'pli:t/ *a* incompleto

incomprehensible /ɪnkɒmprɪ'hensəbl/ *a* incompreensível

inconceivable /ɪnkən'si:vəbl/ *a* inconcebível

inconclusive /ɪnkən'klu:sɪv/ *a* inconcludente

incongruous /ɪn'kɒŋgrʊəs/ *a* incongruente; (*absurd*) absurdo

inconsequential /ɪnkɒnsɪ'kwenʃl/ *a* sem importância

inconsiderate /ɪnkən'sɪdərət/ *a* impensado, inconsiderado; (*lacking in regard*) pouco atencioso, sem consideração (pelos sentimentos *etc* de outrem)

inconsisten|t /ɪnkən'sɪstənt/ *a* incoerente; (*at variance*) contraditório. **~t with** incompatível com. **~cy** *n* incoerência *f*. **~cies** *npl* contradições *fpl*

inconspicuous /ɪnkən'spɪkjʊəs/ *a* que não dá nas vistas, que não chama a atenção

incontinen|t /ɪn'kɒntɪnənt/ *a* incontinente. **~ce** *n* incontinência *f*

inconvenien|t /ɪnkən'vi:nɪənt/ *a* inconveniente, incômodo. **~ce** *n* inconveniência *f*; (*drawback*) inconveniente *m* □ *vt* incomodar

incorporate /ɪn'kɔ:pəreɪt/ *vt* incorporar; (*include*) incluir

incorrect /ɪnkə'rekt/ *a* incorreto, (*P*) incorrecto

incorrigible /ɪn'kɒrɪdʒəbl/ *a* incorrigível

increas|e[1] /ɪn'kri:s/ *vt/i* aumentar. **~ing** *a* crescente. **~ingly** *adv* cada vez mais

increase[2] /'ɪnkri:s/ *n* aumento *m*. **on the ~** aumentando, crescendo

incredible /ɪn'kredəbl/ *a* incrível

incredulous /ɪn'kredjʊləs/ *a* incrédulo

increment /'ɪŋkrəmənt/ *n* incremento *m*, aumento *m*

incriminat|e /ɪn'krɪmɪneɪt/ *vt* incriminar. **~ing** *a* comprometedor

incubat|e /'ɪnkjʊbeɪt/ *vt* incubar. **~ion** /-'beɪʃn/ *n* incubação *f*. **~or** *n* incubadora *f*

inculcate /'ɪnkʌlkeɪt/ *vt* inculcar

incumbent /ɪn'kʌmbənt/ *n* (*pol, relig*) titular *mf* □ *a* **be ~ on** incumbir a, caber a

incur /ɪn'kɜ:r/ *vt* (*pt* **incurred**) (*displeasure, expense etc*) incorrer em; (*debts*) contrair

incurable /ɪn'kjʊərəbl/ *a* incurável, que não tem cura

indebted /ɪn'detɪd/ *a* **~ to s.o.** em dívida (para) com alg (**for** por)

indecen|t /ɪn'di:snt/ *a* indecente. **~t assault** atentado *m* contra o pudor. **~cy** *n* indecência *f*

indecision /ɪndɪ'sɪʒn/ *n* indecisão *f*

indecisive /ɪndɪ'saɪsɪv/ *a* inconcludente, não decisivo; (*hesitating*) indeciso

indeed /ɪn'di:d/ *adv* realmente, deveras, mesmo; (*in fact*) de fato, (*P*) facto. **very much ~** muitíssimo

indefinite /ɪn'defɪnət/ *a* indefinido; (*time*) indeterminado. **~ly** *adv* indefinidamente

indelible /ɪn'deləbl/ *a* indelével

indemnify /ɪn'demnɪfaɪ/ *vt* indenizar, (*P*) indemnizar (**for** de); (*safeguard*) garantir (**against** contra)

indemnity /ɪn'demnətɪ/ *n* (*legal exemption*) isenção *f*; (*compensation*) indenização *f*, (*P*) indemnização *f*; (*safeguard*) garantia *f*

indent /ɪn'dent/ *vt* (*notch*) recortar; (*typ*) entrar. **~ation** /-'teɪʃn/ *n* recorte *m*; (*typ*) entrada *f*

independen|t /ɪndɪ'pendənt/ *a* independente. **~ce** *n* independência *f*. **~tly** *adv* independentemente

indescribable /ɪndɪ'skraɪbəbl/ *a* indescritível

indestructible /ɪndɪ'strʌktəbl/ *a* indestrutível

indeterminate /ɪndɪ'tɜ:mɪnət/ *a* indeterminado

index /'ɪndeks/ *n* (*pl* **indexes**) *n* (*in book*) índice *m*; (*in library*) catálogo *m* □ *vt* indexar. **~ card** ficha *f* (de fichário). **~ finger** index *m*, (dedo) indicador *m*. **~-linked** *a* ligado ao índice de inflação

India /'ɪndɪə/ *n* Índia *f*. **~n** *a* & *n* (*of India*) indiano (*m*); (*American*) índio (*m*)

indicat|e /'ɪndɪkeɪt/ *vt* indicar. **~ion** /-'keɪʃn/ *n* indicação *f*. **~or** *n* indicador *m*; (*auto*) pisca-pisca *m*; (*board*) quadro *m*

indicative /ɪn'dɪkətɪv/ *a* & *n* indicativo (*m*)

indict /ɪn'daɪt/ *vt* acusar. **~ment** *n* acusação *f*

indifferen|t /ɪn'dɪfrənt/ *a* indiferente; (*not good*) medíocre. **~ce** *n* indiferença *f*

indigenous /ɪn'dɪdʒɪnəs/ *a* indígena, natural, nativo (**to** de)

indigest|ion /ɪndɪ'dʒestʃən/ *n* indigestão *f*. **~ible** /-təbl/ *a* indigesto

indign|ant /ɪn'dɪgnənt/ *a* indignado. **~ation** /-'neɪʃn/ *n* indignação *f*

indirect /ɪndɪ'rekt/ *a* indireto, (*P*) indirecto. **~ly** *adv* indiretamente, (*P*) indirectamente

indiscr|eet /ɪndɪ'skri:t/ *a* indiscreto; (*not wary*) imprudente. **~etion**

/-'eʃn/ *n* indiscrição *f*; (*action, remark etc*) deslize *m*

indiscriminate /ɪndɪ'skrɪmɪnət/ *a* que tem falta de discernimento; (*random*) indiscriminado. **~ly** *adv* sem discernimento; (*at random*) indiscriminadamente, ao acaso

indispensable /ɪndɪ'spensəbl/ *a* indispensável

indispos|ed /ɪndɪ'spəʊzd/ *a* indisposto. **~ition** /-ə'zɪʃn/ *n* indisposição *f*

indisputable /ɪndɪ'spju:təbl/ *a* indisputável, incontestável

indistinct /ɪndɪ'stɪŋkt/ *a* indistinto

indistinguishable /ɪndɪ'stɪŋgwɪʃəbl/ *a* indistinguível, imperceptível; (*identical*) indiferenciável

individual /ɪndɪ'vɪdʒʊəl/ *a* individual □ *n* indivíduo *m*. **~ity** /-'æləti/ *n* individualidade *f*. **~ly** *adv* individualmente

indivisible /ɪndɪ'vɪzəbl/ *a* indivisível

indoctrinat|e /ɪn'dɒktrɪmeɪt/ *vt* (en) doutrinar. **~ion** /-'neɪʃn/ *n* (en) doutrinação *f*

indolen|t /'ɪndələnt/ *a* indolente. **~ce** *n* indolência *f*

indoor /'ɪndɔ:(r)/ *a* (de) interior, interno; (*under cover*) coberto; (*games*) de salão. **~s** /ɪn'dɔ:z/ *adv* dentro de casa, no interior

induce /ɪn'dju:s/ *vt* induzir, levar; (*cause*) causar, provocar. **~ment** *n* incentivo *m*, encorajamento *m*

indulge /ɪn'dʌldʒ/ *vt* satisfazer; (*spoil*) fazer a(s) vontade(s) de □ *vi* **~ in** entregar-se a

indulgen|t /ɪn'dʌldʒənt/ *a* indulgente. **~ce** *n* (*leniency*) indulgência *f*; (*desire*) satisfação *f*

industrial /ɪn'dʌstrɪəl/ *a* industrial; (*unrest etc*) trabalhista; (*action*) reivindicativo. **~ estate** zona *f* industrial. **~ist** *n* industrial *m*. **~ized** *a* industrializado

industrious /ɪn'dʌstrɪəs/ *a* trabalhador, aplicado

industry /'ɪndəstrɪ/ *n* indústria *f*; (*zeal*) aplicação *f*, diligência *f*, zelo *m*

inebriated /ɪ'ni:brɪeɪtɪd/ *a* embriagado, ébrio

inedible /ɪ'nedɪbl/ *a* não comestível

ineffective /ɪnɪ'fektɪv/ *a* ineficaz; (*person*) ineficiente, incapaz

ineffectual /ɪnɪ'fektʃʊəl/ *a* ineficaz, improfícuo

inefficien|t /ɪnɪ'fɪʃnt/ *a* ineficiente. **~cy** *n* ineficiência *f*

ineligible /ɪn'elɪdʒəbl/ *a* inelegível; (*undesirable*) indesejável. **be ~ for** não ter direito a

inept /ɪ'nept/ *a* inepto

inequality /ɪnɪ'kwɒlətɪ/ *n* desigualdade *f*

inert /ɪ'nɜ:t/ *a* inerte. **~ia** /-ʃə/ *n* inércia *f*

inevitable /ɪn'evɪtəbl/ *a* inevitável, fatal

inexcusable /ɪnɪk'skju:zəbl/ *a* indesculpável, imperdoável

inexhaustible /ɪnɪg'zɔ:stəbl/ *a* inesgotável, inexaurível

inexorable /ɪn'eksərəbl/ *a* inexorável

inexpensive /ɪnɪk'spensɪv/ *a* barato, em conta

inexperience /ɪnɪk'spɪərɪəns/ *n* inexperiência *f*, falta de experiência *f*. **~d** *a* inexperiente

inexplicable /ɪn'eksplɪkəbl/ *a* inexplicável

inextricable /ɪn'ekstrɪkəbl/ *a* inextricável

infallib|le /ɪn'fæləbl/ *a* infalível. **~ility** /-'bɪlətɪ/ *n* infalibilidade *f*

infam|ous /'ɪnfəməs/ *a* infame. **~y** *n* infâmia *f*

infan|t /'ɪnfənt/ *n* bebê *m*, (*P*) bebé *m*; (*child*) criança *f*. **~cy** *n* infância *f*; (*babyhood*) primeira infância *f*

infantile /'ɪnfəntaɪl/ *a* infantil

infantry /'ɪnfəntrɪ/ *n* infantaria *f*

infatuat|ed /ɪn'fætʃʊeɪtɪd/ *a* **~ed with** cego *or* perdido por. **~ion** /-'eɪʃn/ *n* cegueira *f*, paixão *f*

infect /ɪn'fekt/ *vt* infectar. **~ s.o. with** contagiar *or* contaminar alg com. **~ion** /-ʃn/ *n* infecção *f*, contágio *m*. **~ious** /-ʃəs/ *a* infeccioso, contagioso

infer /ɪn'fɜ:(r)/ *vt* (*pt* **inferred**) inferir, deduzir. **~ence** /'ɪnfərəns/ *n* inferência *f*

inferior /ɪn'fɪərɪə(r)/ *a* inferior; (*work etc*) de qualidade inferior □ *n* inferior *mf*; (*in rank*) subalterno *m*. **~ity** /-'ɒrətɪ/ *n* inferioridade *f*

infernal /ɪn'fɜ:nl/ *a* infernal

infertil|e /ɪn'fɜ:taɪl/ *a* infértil, estéril. **~ity** /-ə'tɪlətɪ/ *n* infertilidade *f*, esterilidade *f*

infest /ɪn'fest/ *vt* infestar (**with** de). **~ation** *n* infestação *f*

infidelity /ɪnfɪ'delətɪ/ *n* infidelidade *f*

infiltrat|e /'ɪnfɪltreɪt/ *vt/i* infiltrar (-se). **~ion** /-'treɪʃn/ *n* infiltração *f*

infinite /'ɪnfɪnət/ *a* & *n* infinito (*m*). **~ly** *adv* infinitamente

infinitesimal /ɪnfɪnɪ'tesɪml/ *a* infinitesimal, infinitésimo

infinitive /ɪn'fɪnətɪv/ *n* infinitivo *m*

infinity /ɪn'fɪnətɪ/ *n* infinidade *f*, infinito *m*

infirm /ɪn'fɜ:m/ *a* débil, fraco. **~ity** *n* (*illness*) enfermidade *f*; (*weakness*) fraqueza *f*

inflam|e /ɪn'fleɪm/ *vt* inflamar. **~mable** /-æməbl/ *a* inflamável. **~mation** /-ə'meɪʃn/ *n* inflamação *f*

inflate /ɪn'fleɪt/ *vt* (*balloon etc*) encher de ar; (*prices*) causar inflação de
inflation /ɪn'fleɪʃn/ *n* inflação *f*. **~ary** *a* inflacionário
inflection /ɪn'flekʃn/ *n* inflexão *f*; (*gram*) flexão *f*, desinência *f*
inflexible /ɪn'fleksəbl/ *a* inflexível
inflict /ɪn'flɪkt/ *vt* infligir, impor (**on** a)
influence /'ɪnflʊəns/ *n* influência *f* □ *vt* influenciar, influir sobre
influential /ɪnflʊ'enʃl/ *a* influente
influenza /ɪnflʊ'enzə/ *n* gripe *f*
influx /'ɪnflʌks/ *n* afluência *f*, influxo *m*
inform /ɪn'fɔ:m/ *vt* informar. **~ against** *or* **on** denunciar. **keep ~ed** manter ao corrente *or* a par. **~ant** *n* informante *mf*. **~er** *n* delator *m*, denunciante *mf*
informal /ɪn'fɔ:ml/ *a* informal; (*simple*) simples, sem cerimônia, (*P*) cerimónia; (*unofficial*) oficioso; (*colloquial*) familiar; (*dress*) de passeio, à vontade; (*dinner, gathering*) íntimo. **~ity** /-'mælətɪ/ *n* informalidade *f*; (*simplicity*) simplicidade *f*; (*intimacy*) intimidade *f*. **~ly** *adv* informalmente, sem cerimônia, (*P*) cerimónia, à vontade
information /ɪnfə'meɪʃn/ *n* informação*f*; (*facts, data*) informações *fpl*. **~ technology** tecnologia *f* da informação
informative /ɪn'fɔ:mətɪv/ *a* informativo
infra-red /ɪnfrə'red/ *a* infravermelho
infrequent /ɪn'fri:kwənt/ *a* pouco freqüente, (*P*) frequente. **~ly** *adv* raramente
infringe /ɪn'frɪndʒ/ *vt* infringir. **~ on** transgredir; (*rights*) violar. **~ment** *n* infração *f*, (*P*) infracção *f*; (*rights*) violação *f*
infuriat|e /ɪn'fjʊərɪeɪt/ *vt* enfurecer, enraivecer. **~ing** *a* enfurecedor, de enfurecer, de dar raiva
infus|e /ɪn'fju:z/ *vt* infundir, incutir; (*herbs, tea*) pôr de infusão. **~ion** /-ʒn/ *n* infusão *f*
ingen|ious /ɪn'dʒi:nɪəs/ *a* engenhoso, bem pensado. **~uity** /-ɪ'nju:ətɪ/ *n* engenho *m*, habilidade *f*, imaginação *f*
ingenuous /ɪn'dʒenjʊəs/ *a* cândido, ingênuo, (*P*) ingénuo
ingot /'ɪŋgət/ *n* barra *f*, lingote *m*
ingrained /ɪn'greɪnd/ *a* arraigado, enraizado; (*dirt*) entranhado
ingratiate /ɪn'greɪʃɪeɪt/ *vt* **~ o.s. with** insinuar-se junto de, cair nas *or* ganhar as boas graças de
ingratitude /ɪn'grætɪtju:d/ *n* ingratidão *f*
ingredient /ɪn'gri:dɪənt/ *n* ingrediente *m*
inhabit /ɪn'hæbɪt/ *vt* habitar. **~able** *a* habitável. **~ant** *n* habitante *mf*
inhale /ɪn'heɪl/ *vt* inalar, aspirar. **~r** /-ə(r)/ *n* inalador *m*
inherent /ɪn'hɪərənt/ *a* inerente. **~ly** *adv* inerentemente, em si
inherit /ɪn'herɪt/ *vt* herdar (**from** de). **~ance** *n* herança *f*
inhibit /ɪn'hɪbɪt/ *vt* inibir; (*prevent*) impedir. **be ~ed** ser (um) inibido. **~ion** /-'bɪʃn/ *n* inibição *f*
inhospitable /ɪn'hɒspɪtəbl/ *a* inóspito; (*of person*) inospitaleiro, pouco/nada hospitaleiro
inhuman /ɪn'hju:mən/ *a* desumano. **~ity** /-'mænətɪ/ *n* desumanidade *f*
inhumane /ɪnhju:'meɪn/ *a* inumano, cruel
inimitable /ɪ'nɪmɪtəbl/ *a* inimitável
iniquitous /ɪ'nɪkwɪtəs/ *a* iníquo
initial /ɪ'nɪʃl/ *a* & *n* inicial (*f*) □ *vt* (*pt* **initialled**) assinar com as iniciais, rubricar. **~ly** *adv* inicialmente
initiat|e /ɪ'nɪʃɪeɪt/ *vt* iniciar (**into** em); (*scheme*) lançar. **~ion** /-'eɪʃn/ *n* iniciação *f*; (*start*) início *m*
initiative /ɪ'nɪʃətɪv/ *n* iniciativa *f*
inject /ɪn'dʒekt/ *vt* injetar, (*P*) injectar; (*fig*) insuflar. **~ion** /-ʃn/ *n* injeção *f*, (*P*) injecção *f*
injure /'ɪndʒə(r)/ *vt* (*harm*) fazer mal a, prejudicar, lesar; (*hurt*) ferir
injury /'ɪndʒərɪ/ *n* ferimento *m*, lesão *f*; (*wrong*) mal *m*
injustice /ɪn'dʒʌstɪs/ *n* injustiça *f*
ink /ɪŋk/ *n* tinta *f*. **~-well** *n* tinteiro *m*. **~y** *a* sujo de tinta
inkling /'ɪŋklɪŋ/ *n* idéia *f*, (*P*) ideia *f*, suspeita *f*
inlaid /ɪn'leɪd/ *see* **inlay**[1]
inland /'ɪnlənd/ *a* interior □ *adv* /ɪn'lænd/ no interior, para o interior. **the I~ Revenue** o Fisco, a Receita Federal
inlay[1] /ɪn'leɪ/ *vt* (*pt* **inlaid**) embutir, incrustar
inlay[2] /'ɪnleɪ/ *n* incrustação *f*, obturação *f*
inlet /'ɪnlet/ *n* braço *m* de mar, enseada *f*; (*techn*) admissão *f*
inmate /'ɪnmeɪt/ *n* residente *mf*; (*in hospital*) internado *m*; (*in prison*) presidiário *m*
inn /ɪn/ *n* estalagem *f*
innards /'ɪnədz/ *npl* (*colloq*) tripas (*colloq*) *fpl*
innate /ɪ'neɪt/ *a* inato
inner /'ɪnə(r)/ *a* interior, interno; (*fig*) íntimo. **~ city** centro *m* da cidade. **~most** *a* mais profundo, mais íntimo. **~ tube** *n* câmara *f* de ar

innings /'ɪnɪŋz/ *n* (*cricket*) vez *f* de bater; (*pol*) período *m* no poder
innocen|t /'ɪnəsnt/ *a* & *n* inocente (*mf*). **~ce** *n* inocência *f*
innocuous /ɪ'nɒkjʊəs/ *a* inócuo, inofensivo
innovat|e /'ɪnəveɪt/ *vi* inovar. **~ion** /-'veɪʃn/ *n* inovação *f*. **~or** *n* inovador *m*
innuendo /ɪnju:'endəʊ/ *n* (*pl* -oes) insinuação *f*, indireta *f*, (*P*) indirecta *f*
innumerable /ɪ'nju:mərəbl/ *a* inumerável
inoculat|e /ɪ'nɒkjʊleɪt/ *vt* inocular. **~ion** /-'leɪʃn/ *n* inoculação *f*, vacina *f*
inoffensive /ɪnə'fensɪv/ *a* inofensivo
inoperative /ɪn'ɒpərətɪv/ *a* inoperante, ineficaz
inopportune /ɪn'ɒpətju:n/ *a* inoportuno
inordinate /ɪ'nɔ:dɪnət/ *a* excessivo, desmedido. **~ly** *adv* excessivamente, desmedidamente
input /'ɪnpʊt/ *n* (*data*) dados *mpl*; (*electr: power*) energia *f*; (*computer process*) entrada *f*, dados *mpl*
inquest /'ɪnkwest/ *n* inquérito *m*
inquir|e /ɪn'kwaɪə(r)/ *vi* informar-se □ *vt* perguntar, indagar, inquirir. **~e about** procurar informações sobre, indagar. **~e into** inquirir, indagar. **~ing** *a* (*look*) interrogativo; (*mind*) inquisitivo. **~y** *n* (*question*) pergunta *f*; (*jur*) inquérito *m*; (*investigation*) investigação *f*
inquisition /ɪnkwɪ'zɪʃn/ *n* inquisição *f*
inquisitive /ɪn'kwɪzətɪv/ *a* curioso, inquisitivo; (*prying*) intrometido, bisbilhoteiro
insan|e /ɪn'seɪn/ *a* louco, doido. **~ity** /ɪn'sænətɪ/ *n* loucura *f*, demência *f*
insanitary /ɪn'sænɪtrɪ/ *a* insalubre, anti-higiênico, (*P*) anti-higiénico
insatiable /ɪn'seɪʃəbl/ *a* insaciável
inscri|be /ɪn'skraɪb/ *vt* inscrever; (*book*) dedicar. **~ption** /-ɪpʃn/ *n* inscrição *f*; (*in book*) dedicatória *f*
inscrutable /ɪn'skru:təbl/ *a* impenetrável, misterioso
insect /'ɪnsekt/ *n* inseto *m*, (*P*) insecto *m*
insecur|e /ɪnsɪ'kjʊə(r)/ *a* (*not firm*) inseguro, mal seguro; (*unsafe; psych*) inseguro. **~ity** *n* insegurança *f*, falta *f* de segurança
insensible /ɪn'sensəbl/ *a* insensível; (*unconscious*) inconsciente
insensitive /ɪn'sensətɪv/ *a* insensível
inseparable /ɪn'seprəbl/ *a* inseparável
insert[1] /ɪn'sɜ:t/ *vt* inserir; (*key*) meter, colocar; (*add*) pôr, inserir. **~ion** /-ʃn/ *n* inserção *f*
insert[2] /'ɪnsɜ:t/ *n* coisa *f* inserida
inside /ɪn'saɪd/ *n* interior *m*. **~s** (*colloq*) tripas *fpl* (*colloq*) □ *a* interior, interno □ *adv* no interior, dentro, por dentro □ *prep* dentro de; (*of time*) em menos de. **~ out** de dentro para fora, do avesso; (*thoroughly*) por dentro e por fora, a fundo
insidious /ɪn'sɪdɪəs/ *a* insidioso
insight /'ɪnsaɪt/ *n* penetração *f*, perspicácia *f*; (*glimpse*) vislumbre *m*
insignificant /ɪnsɪg'nɪfɪkənt/ *a* insignificante
insincer|e /ɪnsɪn'sɪə(r)/ *a* insincero. **~ity** /-'serətɪ/ *n* insinceridade *f*, falta *f* de sinceridade
insinuat|e /ɪn'sɪnjʊeɪt/ *vt* insinuar. **~ion** /-'eɪʃn/ *n* (*act*) insinuação *f*; (*hint*) indireta *f*, (*P*) indirecta *f*, insinuação *f*
insipid /ɪn'sɪpɪd/ *a* insípido, sem sabor
insist /ɪn'sɪst/ *vt/i* **~ (on/that)** insistir (em/em que)
insisten|t /ɪn'sɪstənt/ *a* insistente. **~ce** *n* insistência *f*. **~tly** *adv* insistentemente
insolen|t /'ɪnsələnt/ *a* insolente. **~ce** *n* insolência *f*
insoluble /ɪn'sɒljʊbl/ *a* insolúvel
insolvent /ɪn'sɒlvənt/ *a* insolvente
insomnia /ɪn'sɒmnɪə/ *n* insônia *f*, (*P*) insónia *f*
inspect /ɪn'spekt/ *vt* inspecionar, (*P*) inspeccionar, examinar; (*tickets*) fiscalizar; (*passport*) controlar; (*troops*) passar revista a. **~ion** /-ʃn/ *n* inspeção *f*, (*P*) inspecção *f*, exame *m*; (*ticket*) fiscalização *f*; (*troops*) revista *f*. **~or** *n* inspetor *m*, (*P*) inspector *m*; (*on train*) fiscal *m*
inspir|e /ɪn'spaɪə(r)/ *vt* inspirar. **~ation** /-ə'reɪʃn/ *n* inspiração *f*
instability /ɪnstə'bɪlətɪ/ *n* instabilidade *f*
install /ɪn'stɔ:l/ *vt* instalar; (*heater etc*) montar, instalar. **~ation** /-ə'leɪʃn/ *n* instalação *f*
instalment /ɪn'stɔ:lmənt/ *n* prestação *f*; (*of serial*) episódio *m*
instance /'ɪnstəns/ *n* exemplo *m*, caso *m*. **for ~** por exemplo. **in the first ~** em primeiro lugar
instant /'ɪnstənt/ *a* imediato; (*food*) instantâneo □ *n* instante *m*. **~ly** *adv* imediatamente, logo
instantaneous /ɪnstən'teɪmɪəs/ *a* instantâneo
instead /ɪn'sted/ *adv* em vez disso, em lugar disso. **~ of** em vez de, em lugar de
instigat|e /'ɪnstɪgeɪt/ *vt* instigar, incitar. **~ion** /-'geɪʃn/ *n* instigação *f*. **~or** *n* instigador *m*

instil /ɪn'stɪl/ *vt* (*pt* **instilled**) instilar, insuflar
instinct /'ɪnstɪŋkt/ *n* instinto *m*. **~ive** /ɪn'stɪŋktɪv/ *a* instintivo
institut|e /'ɪnstɪtju:t/ *n* instituto *m* □ *vt* instituir; (*legal proceedings*) intentar; (*inquiry*) ordenar. **~ion** /-'tju:ʃn/ *n* instituição *f*; (*school*) estabelecimento *m* de ensino; (*hospital*) estabelecimento *m* hospitalar
instruct /ɪn'strʌkt/ *vt* instruir; (*order*) mandar, ordenar; (*a solicitor etc*) dar instruções a. **~ s.o. in sth** ensinar alg coisa a alguém. **~ion** /-ʃn/ *n* instrução *f*. **~ions** /-ʃnz/ *npl* instruções *fpl*, modo *m* de emprego; (*orders*) ordens *fpl*. **~ive** *a* instrutivo. **~or** *n* instrutor *m*
instrument /'ɪnstrʊmənt/ *n* instrumento *m*. **~ panel** painel *m* de instrumentos
instrumental /ɪnstrʊ'mentl/ *a* instrumental. **be ~ in** ter um papel decisivo em. **~ist** *n* instrumentalista *mf*
insubordinat|e /ɪnsə'bɔ:dɪnət/ *a* insubordinado. **~ion** /-'neɪʃn/ *n* insubordinação *f*
insufferable /ɪn'sʌfrəbl/ *a* intolerável, insuportável
insufficient /ɪnsə'fɪʃnt/ *a* insuficiente
insular /'ɪnsjʊlə(r)/ *a* insular; (*fig: narrow-minded*) bitolado, limitado, (*P*) tacanho
insulat|e /'ɪnsjʊleɪt/ *vt* isolar. **~ing tape** fita *f* isolante. **~ion** /-'leɪʃn/ *n* isolamento *m*
insulin /'ɪnsjʊlɪn/ *n* insulina *f*
insult[1] /ɪn'sʌlt/ *vt* insultar, injuriar. **~ing** *a* insultante, injurioso
insult[2] /'ɪnsʌlt/ *n* insulto *m*, injúria *f*
insur|e /ɪn'ʃʊə(r)/ *vt* segurar, pôr no seguro; (*Amer*) = **ensure**. **~ance** *n* seguro *m*. **~ance policy** apólice *f* de seguro
insurmountable /ɪnsə'maʊntəbl/ *a* insuperável
intact /ɪn'tækt/ *a* intato, (*P*) intacto
intake /'ɪnteɪk/ *n* admissão *f*; (*techn*) admissão *f*, entrada *f*; (*of food*) ingestão *f*
intangible /ɪn'tændʒəbl/ *a* intangível
integral /'ɪntɪgrəl/ *a* integral. **be an ~ part of** ser parte integrante de
integrat|e /'ɪntɪgreɪt/ *vt/i* integrar (-se). **~ed circuit** circuito *m* integrado. **~ion** /'greɪʃn/ *n* integração *f*
integrity /ɪn'tegrətɪ/ *n* integridade *f*
intellect /'ɪntəlekt/ *n* intelecto *m*, inteligência *f*. **~ual** /-'lektʃʊəl/ *a* & *n* intelectual (*mf*)
intelligen|t /ɪn'telɪdʒənt/ *a* inteligente. **~ce** *n* inteligência *f*; (*mil*) informações *fpl*. **~tly** *adv* inteligentemente
intelligible /ɪn'telɪdʒəbl/ *a* inteligível
intend /ɪn'tend/ *vt* tencionar; (*destine*) reservar, destinar. **~ed** *a* intencional, propositado
intens|e /ɪn'tens/ *a* intenso; (*person*) emotivo. **~ely** *adv* intensamente; (*very*) extremamente. **~ity** *n* intensidade *f*
intensif|y /ɪn'tensɪfaɪ/ *vt* intensificar. **~ication** /-ɪ'keɪʃn/ *n* intensificação *f*
intensive /ɪn'tensɪv/ *a* intensivo. **~ care** tratamento *m* intensivo
intent /ɪn'tent/ *n* intento *m*, desígnio *m*, propósito *m* □ *a* atento, concentrado. **~ on** absorto em; (*intending to*) decidido a. **~ly** *adv* atentamente
intention /ɪn'tenʃn/ *n* intenção *f*. **~al** *a* intencional. **~ally** *adv* de propósito
inter /ɪn'tɜ:(r)/ *vt* (*pt* **interred**) enterrar
inter- /'ɪntə(r)/ *pref* inter-
interact /ɪntə'rækt/ *vi* agir uns sobre os outros. **~ion** /-ʃn/ *n* interação *f*, (*P*) interacção *f*
intercede /ɪntə'si:d/ *vi* interceder
intercept /ɪntə'sept/ *vt* interceptar
interchange[1] /ɪntə'tʃeɪndʒ/ *vt* permutar, trocar. **~able** *a* permutável
interchange[2] /'ɪntətʃeɪndʒ/ *n* permuta *f*, intercâmbio *m*; (*road junction*) trevo *m* de trânsito, (*P*) nó *m*
intercom /'ɪntəkɒm/ *n* interfone *m*, (*P*) intercomunicador *m*
interconnected /ɪntəkə'nektɪd/ *a* (*facts, events etc*) ligado, relacionado
intercourse /'ɪntəkɔ:s/ *n* (*sexual*) relações *fpl* sexuais
interest /'ɪntrəst/ *n* interesse *m*; (*legal share*) título *m*; (*in finance*) juro(s) *m*(*pl*). **rate of ~** taxa *f* de juros □ *vt* interessar. **~ed** *a* interessado. **be ~ed in** interessar-se por. **~ing** *a* interessante
interface /'ɪntəfeɪs/ *n* interface *f*
interfer|e /ɪntə'fɪə(r)/ *vi* interferir, intrometer-se (**in** em); (*meddle, hinder*) interferir (**with** com); (*tamper*) mexer indevidamente (**with** em). **~ence** *n* interferência *f*
interim /'ɪntərɪm/ *n* **in the ~** nesse/neste ínterim *m*, (*P*) interim *m* □ *a* interino, provisório
interior /ɪn'tɪərɪə(r)/ *a* & *n* interior (*m*)
interjection /ɪntə'dʒekʃn/ *n* interjeição *f*
interlock /ɪntə'lɒk/ *vt/i* entrelaçar; (*pieces of puzzle etc*) encaixar(-se); (*mech: wheels*) engrenar, engatar
interloper /'ɪntələʊpə(r)/ *n* intruso *m*

intermarr|iage /ɪntə'mærɪdʒ/ *n* casamento *m* entre membros de diferentes famílias, raças etc; (*between near relations*) casamento *m* consangüineo, (*P*) consanguíneo. ~**y** *vi* ligar-se por casamento

intermediary /ɪntə'mi:dɪərɪ/ *a* & *n* intermediário (*m*)

intermediate /ɪntə'mi:dɪət/ *a* intermédio, intermediário

interminable /ɪn'tɜ:mɪnəbl/ *a* interminável, infindável

intermission /ɪntə'mɪʃn/ *n* intervalo *m*

intermittent /ɪntə'mɪtnt/ *a* intermitente. ~**ly** *adv* intermitentemente

intern /ɪn'tɜ:n/ *vt* internar. ~**ee** /-'ni:/ *n* internado *m*. ~**ment** *n* internamento *m*

internal /ɪn'tɜ:nl/ *a* interno, interior. ~**ly** *adv* internamente, interiormente

international /ɪntə'næʃnəl/ *a* & *n* internacional (*mf*)

interpolate /ɪn'tɜ:pəleɪt/ *vt* interpolar

interpret /ɪn'tɜ:prɪt/ *vt/i* interpretar. ~**ation** /-'teɪʃn/ *n* interpretação *f*. ~**er** *n* intérprete *mf*

interrelated /ɪntərɪ'leɪtɪd/ *a* inter-relacionado, correlacionado

interrogat|e /ɪn'terəgeɪt/ *vt* interrogar. ~**ion** /'geɪʃn/ *n* interrogação *f*; (*of police etc*) interrogatório *m*

interrogative /ɪntə'rɒgətɪv/ *a* interrogativo □ *n* (*pronoun*) pronome *m* interrogativo

interrupt /ɪntə'rʌpt/ *vt* interromper. ~**ion** /-ʃn/ *n* interrupção *f*

intersect /ɪntə'sekt/ *vt/i* intersectar (-se); (*roads*) cruzar-se. ~**ion** /-ʃn/ *n* intersecção *f*; (*crossroads*) cruzamento *m*

intersperse /ɪntə'spɜ:s/ *vt* entremear, intercalar; (*scatter*) espalhar

interval /'ɪntəvl/ *n* intervalo *m*. **at ~s** a intervalos

interven|e /ɪntə'vi:n/ *vi* (*interfere*) intervir; (*of time*) passar-se, decorrer; (*occur*) sobrevir, intervir. ~**tion** /-'venʃn/ *n* intervenção *f*

interview /'ɪntəvju:/ *n* entrevista *f* □ *vt* entrevistar. ~**ee** *n* entrevistado *m*. ~**er** *n* entrevistador *m*

intestin|e /ɪn'testɪn/ *n* intestino *m*. ~**al** *a* intestinal

intima|te[1] /'ɪntɪmət/ *a* íntimo; (*detailed*) profundo. ~**cy** *n* intimidade *f*. ~**tely** *adv* intimamente

intimate[2] /'ɪntɪmeɪt/ *vt* (*announce*) dar a conhecer, fazer saber; (*imply*) dar a entender

intimidat|e /ɪn'tɪmɪdeɪt/ *vt* intimidar. ~**ion** /-'deɪʃn/ *n* intimidação *f*

into /'ɪntə/; *emphatic* /'ɪntʊ/ *prep* para dentro de. **divide ~ three** dividir em tres. **~ pieces** aos bocados. **translate ~** traduzir para

intolerable /ɪn'tɒlərəbl/ *a* intolerável, insuportável

intoleran|t /ɪn'tɒlərənt/ *a* intolerante. ~**ce** *n* intolerância *f*

intonation /ɪntə'neɪʃn/ *n* entonação *f*, entoação *f*, inflexão *f*

intoxicat|ed /ɪn'tɒksɪkeɪtɪd/ *a* embriagado, etilizado. ~**ion** /'keɪʃn/ *n* embriaguez *f*

intra- /ɪntrə/ *pref* intra-

intractable /ɪn'træktəbl/ *a* intratável, difícil

intransigent /ɪn'trænsɪdʒənt/ *a* intransigente

intransitive /ɪn'trænsətɪv/ *a* (*verb*) intransitivo

intravenous /ɪntrə'vi:nəs/ *a* intravenoso

intrepid /ɪn'trepɪd/ *a* intrépido, arrojado

intrica|te /'ɪntrɪkət/ *a* intrincado, complexo. ~**cy** *n* complexidade *f*

intrigu|e /ɪn'tri:g/ *vt/i* intrigar □ *n* intriga *f*. ~**ing** *a* intrigante, curioso

intrinsic /ɪn'trɪnsɪk/ *a* intrínseco. ~**ally** /-klɪ/ *adv* intrinsecamente

introduce /ɪntrə'dju:s/ *vt* (*programme, question*) apresentar; (*bring in, insert*) introduzir; (*initiate*) iniciar. **~ sb to sb** (*person*) apresentar alg a alguém

introduct|ion /ɪntrə'dʌkʃn/ *n* introdução *f*; (*of/to person*) apresentação *f*. ~**ory** /-tərɪ/ *a* introdutório, de introdução; (*letter, words*) de apresentação

introspective /ɪntrə'spektɪv/ *a* introspectivo

introvert /'ɪntrəvɜ:t/ *n* & *a* introvertido (*m*)

intru|de /ɪn'tru:d/ *vi* intrometer-se, ser a mais. ~**der** *n* intruso *m*. ~**sion** *n* intrusão *f*. ~**sive** *a* intruso

intuit|ion /ɪntju:'ɪʃn/ *n* intuição *f*. ~**ive** /ɪn'tju:ɪtɪv/ *a* intuitivo

inundate /'ɪnʌndeɪt/ *vt* inundar (**with** de)

invade /ɪn'veɪd/ *vt* invadir. ~**r** /-ə(r)/ *n* invasor *m*

invalid[1] /'ɪnvəlɪd/ *n* inválido *m*

invalid[2] /ɪn'vælɪd/ *a* inválido. ~**ate** *vt* invalidar

invaluable /ɪn'væljʊəbl/ *a* inestimável

invariabl|e /ɪn'veərɪəbl/ *a* invariável. ~**y** *adv* invariavelmente

invasion /ɪn'veɪʒn/ *n* invasão *f*

invective /ɪn'vektɪv/ *n* invectiva *f*

invent /ɪn'vent/ *vt* inventar. **~ion** *n* invenção *f*. **~ive** *a* inventivo. **~or** *n* inventor *m*

inventory /'ɪnvəntrɪ/ *n* inventário *m*

inverse /ɪn'vɜ:s/ *a* & *n* inverso (*m*). **~ly** *adv* inversamente

inver|t /ɪn'vɜ:t/ *vt* inverter. **~ted commas** aspas *fpl*. **~sion** *n* inversão *f*

invest /ɪn'vest/ *vt* investir; (*time, effort*) dedicar □ *vi* fazer um investimento. **~ in** (*colloq: buy*) gastar dinheiro em. **~ment** *n* investimento *m*. **~or** *n* investidor *m*, financiador *m*

investigat|e /ɪn'vestɪgeɪt/ *vt* investigar. **~ion** /-'geɪʃn/ *n* investigação *f*. **under ~ion** em estudo. **~or** *n* investigador *m*

inveterate /ɪn'vetərət/ *a* inveterado

invidious /ɪn'vɪdɪəs/ *a* antipático, odioso

invigorate /ɪn'vɪgəreɪt/ *vt* revigorar; (*encourage*) estimular

invincible /ɪn'vɪnsəbl/ *a* invencível

invisible /ɪn'vɪzəbl/ *a* invisível

invit|e /ɪn'vaɪt/ *vt* convidar; (*bring on*) pedir, provocar. **~ation** /ɪnvɪ'teɪʃn/ *n* convite *m*. **~ing** *a* (*tempting*) tentador; (*pleasant*) acolhedor, convidativo

invoice /'ɪnvɔɪs/ *n* fatura *f*, (*P*) factura *f* □ *vt* faturar, (*P*) facturar

invoke /ɪn'vəʊk/ *vt* invocar

involuntary /ɪn'vɒləntrɪ/ *a* involuntário

involve /ɪn'vɒlv/ *vt* implicar, envolver. **~d** *a* (*complex*) complicado; (*at stake*) em jogo; (*emotionally*) envolvido. **~d in** implicado em. **~ment** *n* envolvimento *m*, participação *f*

invulnerable /ɪn'vʌlnərəbl/ *a* invulnerável

inward /'ɪnwəd/ *a* interior; (*thought etc*) íntimo. **~(s)** *adv* para dentro, para o interior. **~ly** *adv* interiormente, intimamente

iodine /'aɪədi:n/ *n* iodo *m*; (*antiseptic*) tintura *f* de iodo

IOU /aɪəʊ'ju:/ *n abbr* vale *m*

IQ /aɪ'kju:/ *abbr* (*intelligence quotient*) Q I *m*

Iran /ɪ'ra:n/ *n* Irã *m*. **~ian** /ɪ'remɪən/ *a* & *n* iraniano (*m*)

Iraq /ɪ'ra:k/ *n* Iraque *m*. **~i** *a* & *n* iraquiano (*m*)

irascible /ɪ'ræsəbl/ *a* irascível

irate /aɪ'reɪt/ *a* irado, enraivecido

Ireland /'aɪələnd/ *n* Irlanda *f*

iris /'aɪərɪs/ *n* (*anat, bot*) íris *f*

Irish /'aɪərɪʃ/ *a* & *n* (*language*) irlandês (*m*). **~man** *n* irlandês *m*. **~woman** *n* irlandesa *f*

irk /ɜ:k/ *vt* aborrecer,ncomodar. **~some** *a* aborrecido

iron /'aɪən/ *n* ferro *m*; (*appliance*) ferro *m* de engomar □ *a* de ferro □ *vt* passar a ferro. **~ out** fazer desaparecer; (*fig*) aplanar, resolver. **~ing** *n* do **the ~ing** passar a roupa. **~ing-board** *n* tábua *f* de passar roupa, (*P*) tábua *f* de engomar

ironic(al) /aɪ'rɒnɪk(l)/ *a* irônico, (*P*) irónico

ironmonger /'aɪənmʌŋgə(r)/ *n* ferreiro *m*, (*P*) ferrageiro *m*. **~'s** *n* (*shop*) loja *f* de ferragens

irony /'aɪərənɪ/ *n* ironia *f*

irrational /ɪ'ræʃənl/ *a* irracional; (*person*) ilógico, que não raciocina

irreconcilable /ɪrekən'saɪləbl/ *a* irreconciliável

irrefutable /ɪrɪ'fju:təbl/ *a* irrefutável

irregular /ɪ'regjʊlə(r)/ *a* irregular. **~ity** /-'lærətɪ/ *n* irregularidade *f*

irrelevant /ɪ'reləvənt/ *a* irrelevante, que não é pertinente

irreparable /ɪ'repərəbl/ *a* irreparável, irremediável

irreplaceable /ɪrɪ'pleɪsəbl/ *a* insubstituível

irresistible /ɪrɪ'zɪstəbl/ *a* irresistível

irresolute /ɪ'rezəlu:t/ *a* irresoluto

irrespective /ɪrɪ'spektɪv/ *a* **~ of** sem levar em conta, independente de

irresponsible /ɪrɪ'spɒnsəbl/ *a* irresponsável

irretrievable /ɪrɪ'tri:vəbl/ *a* irreparável

irreverent /ɪ'revərənt/ *a* irreverente

irreversible /ɪrɪ'vɜ:səbl/ *a* irreversível; (*decision*) irrevogável

irrigat|e /'ɪrɪgeɪt/ *vt* irrigar. **~ion** /-'geɪʃn/ *n* irrigação *f*

irritable /'ɪrɪtəbl/ *a* irritável, irascível

irritat|e /'ɪrɪteɪt/ *vt* irritar. **~ion** /-'teɪʃn/ *n* irritação *f*

is /ɪz/ *see* **be**

Islam /'ɪzla:m/ *n* Islã *m*. **~ic** /ɪz'læmɪk/ *a* islâmico

island /'aɪlənd/ *n* ilha *f*. **traffic ~** abrigo *m* de pedestres, (*P*) placa *f* de refugio

isolat|e /'aɪsəleɪt/ *vt* isolar. **~ion** /-'leɪʃn/ *n* isolamento *m*

Israel /'ɪzreɪl/ *n* Israel *m*. **~i** /ɪz'reɪlɪ/ *a* & *n* israelense (*mf*), (*P*) israelita (*mf*)

issue /'ɪʃu:/ *n* questão *f*; (*outcome*) resultado *m*; (*of magazine etc*) número *m*; (*of stamps, money etc*) emissão *f* □ *vt* distribuir, dar; (*stamps, money etc*) emitir; (*orders*) dar □ *vi* **~ from** sair de. **at ~** em questão. **take ~ with** entrar em discussão com, discutir com

it /ɪt/ *pron* (*subject*) ele, ela; (*object*) o, a; (*non-specific*) isto, isso, aquilo. ~ **is cold** está *or* faz frio. ~ **is the 6th of May** hoje é seis de maio. **that's** ~ é isso. **take** ~ leva isso. **who is** ~? quem é?

italic /ɪ'tælɪk/ *a* itálico. ~**s** *npl* itálico *m*

Ital|y /'ɪtəlɪ/ *n* Itália *f*. ~**ian** /ɪ'tælɪən/ *a* & *n* (*person, lang*) italiano (*m*)

itch /ɪtʃ/ coceira *f*, (*P*) comichão *f*; (*fig: desire*) desejo *m* ardente □ *vi* coçar, sentir comichão, comichar. **my arm** ~**es** estou com coceira no braço. **I am** ~**ing to** estou morto por (*colloq*). ~**y** *a* que dá coceira

item /'aɪtəm/ *n* item *m*, artigo *m*; (*on programme*) número *m*; (*on agenda*) ponto *m*. **news** ~ notícia *f*. ~**ize** /-aɪz/ *vt* discriminar, especificar

itinerant /aɪ'tɪnərənt/ *a* itinerante; (*musician, actor*) ambulante

itinerary /aɪ'tɪnərərɪ/ *n* itinerário *m*

its /ɪts/ *a* seu, sua, seus, suas

it's /ɪts/ = **it is, it has**

itself /ɪt'self/ *pron* ele mesmo, ele próprio, ela mesma, ela própria; (*reflexive*) se; (*after prep*) si mesmo, si próprio, si mesma, si própria. **by** ~ sozinho, por si

ivory /'aɪvərɪ/ *n* marfim *m*

ivy /'aɪvɪ/ *n* hera *f*

J

jab /dʒæb/ *vt* (*pt* **jabbed**) espetar □ *n* espetadela *f*; (*colloq: injection*) picada *f*

jabber /'dʒæbə(r)/ *vi* tagarelar; (*indistinctly*) falar confusamente □ *n* tagarelice *f*; (*indistinct speech*) algaravia *f*; (*indistinct voices*) algaraviada *f*

jack /dʒæk/ *n* (*techn*) macaco *m*; (*cards*) valete *m* □ *vt* ~ **up** levantar com macaco. **the Union J**~ a bandeira *f* inglesa

jackal /'dʒækl/ *n* chacal *m*

jackdaw /'dʒækdɔ:/ *n* gralha *f*

jacket /'dʒækɪt/ *n* casaco (curto) *m*; (*of book*) sobrecapa *f*; (*of potato*) casca *f*

jack-knife /'dʒæknaɪf/ *vi* (*lorry*) perder o controle

jackpot /'dʒækpɒt/ *n* sorte *f* grande. **hit the** ~ ganhar a sorte grande

Jacuzzi /dʒə'ku:zi:/ *n* (*P*) jacuzzi *m*, banheira *f* de hidromassagem

jade /dʒeɪd/ *n* (*stone*) jade *m*

jaded /'dʒeɪdɪd/ *a* (*tired*) estafado; (*bored*) enfastiado

jagged /'dʒægɪd/ *a* recortado, denteado; (*sharp*) pontiagudo

jail /dʒeɪl/ *n* prisão *f* □ *vt* prender, colocar na cadeia. ~**er** *n* carcereiro *m*

jam[1] /dʒæm/ *n* geléia *f*, compota *f*

jam[2] /dʒæm/ *vt/i* (*pt* **jammed**) (*wedge*) entalar; (*become wedged*) entalar-se; (*crowd*) apinhar(-se); (*mech*) bloquear; (*radio*) provocar interferências em □ *n* (*crush*) aperto *m*; (*traffic*) engarrafamento *m*; (*colloq: difficulty*) apuro *m*, aperto *m*. ~ **one's brakes on** (*colloq*) pôr o pé no freio, (*P*) no travão subitamente, apertar o freio subitamente. ~**-packed** *a* (*colloq*) abarrotado (**with** de)

Jamaica /dʒə'meɪkə/ *n* Jamaica *f*

jangle /'dʒæŋgl/ *n* som *m* estridente □ *vi* retinir

janitor /'dʒænɪtə(r)/ *n* porteiro *m*; (*caretaker*) zelador *m*

January /'dʒænjʊərɪ/ *n* Janeiro *m*

Japan /dʒə'pæn/ *n* Japão *m*. ~**ese** /dʒæpə'ni:z/ *a* & *n* japonês (*m*)

jar[1] /dʒa:(r)/ *n* pote *m*. **jam-**~ *n* frasco *m* de geléia

jar[2] /dʒa:(r)/ *vt/i* (*pt* **jarred**) ressoar, bater ruidosamente (**against** contra); (*of colours*) destoar; (*disagree*) discorder (**with** de) □ *n* (*shock*) choque *m*. ~**ring** *a* dissonante

jargon /'dʒa:gən/ *n* jargão *m*, gíria *f* profissional

jaundice /'dʒɔ:ndɪs/ *n* icterícia *f*. ~**d** *a* (*fig*) invejoso, despeitado

jaunt /dʒɔ:nt/ *n* (*trip*) passeata *f*

jaunty /'dʒɔ:ntɪ/ *a* (**-ier, -iest**) (*cheerful*) alegre, jovial; (*sprightly*) desenvolto

javelin /'dʒævlɪn/ *n* dardo *m*

jaw /dʒɔ:/ *n* maxilar *m*, mandíbula *f*

jay /dʒeɪ/ *n* gaio *m*. ~**-walker** *n* pedestre *m* imprudente, (*P*) peão *m* indisciplinado

jazz /dʒæz/ *n* jazz *m* □ *vt* ~ **up** animar. ~**y** *a* (*colloq*) espalhafatoso

jealous /'dʒeləs/ *a* ciumento; (*envious*) invejoso. ~**y** *n* ciúme *m*; (*envy*) inveja *f*

jeans /dʒi:nz/ *npl* (blue-)jeans *mpl*, calça *f* de zuarte, (*P*) calças *fpl* de ganga

jeep /dʒi:p/ *n* jipe *m*

jeer /dʒɪə(r)/ *vt/i* ~ **at** (*laugh*) fazer troça de; (*scorn*) escarnecer de; (*boo*) vaiar □ *n* (*mockery*) troça *f*; (*booing*) vaia *f*

jell /dʒel/ *vi* tomar consistência, gelatinizar-se

jelly /'dʒelɪ/ *n* gelatina *f*.

jellyfish /'dʒelɪfɪʃ/ *n* água-viva *f*

jeopard|y /'dʒepədɪ/ *n* perigo *m*. ~**ize** *vt* comprometer, pôr em perigo

jerk /dʒɜ:k/ *n* solavanco *m*, (*P*) sacão *m*; (*sl: fool*) idiota *mf* □ *vt/i* sacudir; (*move*) mover-se aos solavancos, (*P*) mover(-se) aos sacões. ~y *a* sacudido

jersey /'dʒɜ:zɪ/ *n* (*pl* -eys) camisola *f*, pulôver *m*, suéter *m*; (*fabric*) jérsei *m*

jest /dʒest/ *n* gracejo *m*, graça *f* □ *vi* gracejar, brincar

Jesus /'dʒi:zəs/ *n* Jesus *m*

jet[1] /dʒet/ *n* azeviche *m*. ~-black *a* negro de azeviche

jet[2] /dʒet/ *n* jato *m*, (*P*) jacto *m*; (*plane*) (avião a) jato *m*, (*P*) jacto *m*. ~ lag cansaço *m* provocado pela diferença de fuso horário. ~-propelled *a* de propulsão a jato, (*P*) jacto

jettison /'dʒetɪsn/ *vt* alijar; (*discard*) desfazer-se de; (*fig*) abandonar

jetty /'dʒetɪ/ *n* (*breakwater*) quebra-mar *m*; (*landing-stage*) desembarcadouro *m*, cais *m*

Jew /dʒu:/ *n* judeu *m*

jewel /'dʒu:əl/ *n* jóia *f*. ~ler *n* joalheiro *m*. ~ler's (shop) joalheria *f*. ~lery *n* jóias *fpl*

Jewish /'dʒu:ɪʃ/ *a* judeu

jib /dʒɪb/ *vi* (*pt* jibbed) recusar-se a avançar; (*of a horse*) empacar. ~ at (*fig*) opor-se a, ter relutância em □ *n* (*sail*) bujarrona *f*

jig /dʒɪg/ *n* jiga *f*

jiggle /'dʒɪgl/ *vt* (*rock*) balançar; (*jerk*) sacolejar

jigsaw /'dʒɪgsɔ:/ *n* ~(-puzzle) puzzle *m*, quebra-cabeça *m*, (*P*) quebra-cabeças *m*

jilt /dʒɪlt/ *vt* deixar, abandonar, dar um fora em (*colloq*), (*P*) mandar passear (*colloq*)

jingle /'dʒɪŋgl/ *vt/i* tilintar, tinir □ *n* tilintar *m*, tinido *m*; (*advertising etc*) música *f* de anúncio

jinx /dʒɪŋks/ *n* (*colloq*) pessoa *f* or coisa *f* azarenta; (*fig: spell*) azar *m*

jitter|s /'dʒɪtəz/ *npl* the ~s (*colloq*) nervos *mpl*. ~y /-ərɪ/ *a* be ~y (*colloq*) estar nervoso, ter os nervos a flor da pele (*colloq*)

job /dʒɒb/ *n* trabalho *m*; (*post*) emprego *m*. have a ~ doing ter dificuldade em fazer. it is a good ~ that felizmente que. ~less *a* desempregado

jobcentre /'dʒɔbsentə(r)/ *n* posto *m* de desemprego

jockey /'dʒɒkɪ/ *n* (*pl* -eys) jóquei *m*

jocular /'dʒɒkjʊlə(r)/ *a* jocoso, galhofeiro, brincalhão

jog /dʒɒg/ *vt* (*pt* jogged) dar um leve empurrão em, tocar em; (*memory*) refrescar □ *vi* (*sport*) fazer jogging. ~ging *n* jogging *m*

join /dʒɔɪn/ *vt* juntar, unir; (*become member*) fazer-se sócio de, entrar para. ~ sb juntar-se a alg □ *vi* (*of roads*) juntar-se, entroncar-se; (*of rivers*) confluir □ *n* junção *f*, junta *f*. ~ in *vt/i* participar (em). ~ up alistar-se

joiner /'dʒɔɪnə(r)/ *n* marceneiro *m*

joint /dʒɔɪnt/ *a* comum, conjunto; (*effort*) conjunto □ *n* junta *f*, junção *f*; (*anat*) articulação *f*; (*culin*) quarto *m*; (*roast meat*) carne *f* assada; (*sl: place*) espelunca *f*. ~ author co-autor *m*. ~ly *adv* conjuntamente

joist /dʒɔɪst/ *n* trave *f*, barrote *m*

jok|e /dʒəʊk/ *n* piada *f*, gracejo *m* □ *vi* gracejar. ~er *n* brincalhão *m*; (*cards*) curinga *f* de baralho, (*P*) diabo *m*. ~ingly *adv* brincadeira

joll|y /'dʒɒlɪ/ *a* (-ier, -iest) alegre, bem disposto □ *adv* (*colloq*) muito. ~ity *n* festança *f*, pândega *f*

jolt /dʒəʊlt/ *vt* sacudir, sacolejar □ *vi* ir aos solavancos □ *n* solavanco *m*; (*shock*) choque *m*, sobressalto *m*

jostle /'dʒɒsl/ *vt* dar um encontrão *or* encontrões em, empurrar □ *vi* empurrar, acotovelar-se

jot /dʒɒt/ *n* (not a) ~ nada □ *vt* (*pt* jotted) ~ (down) apontar, tomar nota de. ~ter *n* (*pad*) bloco *m* de notas

journal /'dʒɜ:nl/ *n* diário *m*; (*newspaper*) jornal *m*; (*periodical*) periódico *m*, revista *f*. ~ism *n* jornalismo *m*. ~ist *n* jornalista *mf*

journey /'dʒɜ:nɪ/ *n* (*pl* -eys) viagem *f*; (*distance*) trajeto *m*, (*P*) trajecto *m* □ *vi* viajar

jovial /'dʒəʊvɪəl/ *a* jovial

joy /dʒɔɪ/ *n* alegria *f*. ~-ride *n* passeio *m* em carro roubado. ~ful, ~ous *adjs* alegre

jubil|ant /'dʒu:bɪlənt/ *a* cheio de alegria, jubiloso. ~ation /'leɪʃn/ *n* júbilo *m*, regozijo *m*

jubilee /'dʒu:bɪli:/ *n* jubileu *m*

Judaism /'dʒu:deɪɪzəm/ *n* judaísmo *m*

judder /'dʒʌdə(r)/ *vi* trepidar, vibrar □ *n* trepidação *f*, vibração *f*

judge /dʒʌdʒ/ *n* juiz *m* □ *vt* julgar. ~ment *n* (*judging*) julgamento *m*, juízo *m*; (*opinion*) juízo *m*; (*decision*) julgamento *m*

judic|iary /dʒu:'dɪʃərɪ/ *n* magistratura *f*; (*system*) judiciário *m*. ~ial *a* judiciário

judicious /dʒu:'dɪʃəs/ *a* judicioso

judo /'dʒu:dəʊ/ *n* judô *m*, (*P*) judo *m*

jug /dʒʌg/ *n* (*tall*) jarro *m*; (*round*) botija *f*, milk-~ *n* leiteira *f*

juggernaut /'dʒʌgənɔ:t/ *n* (*lorry*) jamanta *f*, (*P*) camião *m* TIR

juggle /'dʒʌgl/ *vt/i* fazer malabarismos (with com). ~r /-ə(r)/ *n* malabarista *mf*

juic|e /dʒu:s/ *n* suco *m*, (*P*) sumo *m*. ~y *a* suculento; (*colloq: story etc*) picante

juke-box /'dʒu:kbɒks/ *n* juke-box *m*, (*P*) máquina *f* de música
July /dʒu:'laɪ/ *n* julho *m*
jumble /'dʒʌmbl/ *vt* misturar □ *n* mistura *f*. ~ **sale** venda *f* de caridade de objetos usados
jumbo /'dʒʌmbəʊ/ *a* ~ **jet** (avião) jumbo *m*
jump /dʒʌmp/ *vt/i* saltar; (*start*) sobressaltar(-se); (*of prices etc*) subir repentinamente □ *n* salto *m*; (*start*) sobressalto *m*; (*of prices*) alta *f*. ~ **at** aceitar imediatamente. ~ **the gun** agir prematuramente. ~ **the queue** furar a fila. ~ **to conclusions** tirar conclusões apressadas
jumper /'dʒʌmpə(r)/ *n* pulôver *m*, suéter *m*, (*P*) camisada *f* de lã
jumpy /'dʒʌmpɪ/ *a* nervoso
junction /'dʒʌŋkʃn/ *n* junção *f*; (*of roads etc*) entroncamento *m*
June /dʒu:n/ *n* junho *m*
jungle /'dʒʌŋgl/ *n* selva *f*, floresta *f*
junior /'dʒu:nɪə(r)/ *a* júnior; (*in age*) mais novo (**to** que); (*in rank*) subalterno; (*school*) primária □ *n* o mais novo *m*; (*sport*) júnior *mf*. ~ **to** (*in rank*) abaixo de
junk /dʒʌŋk/ *n* ferro-velho *m*, velharias *fpl*; (*rubbish*) lixo *m*. ~ **food** comida *f* sem valor nutritivo. ~ **mail** material *m* impresso, enviado por correio, sem ter sido solicitado. ~ **shop** loja *f* de ferro-velho, bricabraque *m*
junkie /'dʒʌŋkɪ/ *n* (*sl*) drogado *m*
jurisdiction /dʒʊərɪs'dɪkʃn/ *n* jurisdição *f*
juror /'dʒʊərə(r)/ *n* jurado *m*
jury /'dʒʊərɪ/ *n* júri *m*
just /dʒʌst/ *a* justo □ *adv* justamente, exatamente, (*P*) exactamente; (*only*) só. **he has ~ left** ele acabou de sair. ~ **listen!** escuta só! ~ **as** assim como; (*with time*) assim que. ~ **as tall as** exatamente, (*P*) exactamente tão alto quanto. ~ **as well that** ainda bem que. ~ **before** um momento antes (de). ~**ly** *adv* com justiça, justamente
justice /'dʒʌstɪs/ *n* justiça *f*. **J~ of the Peace** juiz *m* de paz
justifiabl|e /'dʒʌstɪfaɪəbl/ *a* justificável. ~**y** *adv* com razão, justificadamente
justif|y /'dʒʌstɪfaɪ/ *vt* justificar. ~**ication** /-ɪ'keɪʃn/ *n* justificação *f*
jut /dʒʌt/ *vi* (*pt* **jutted**) ~ **out** fazer saliência, sobressair
juvenile /'dʒu:vənaɪl/ *a* (*youthful*) juvenil; (*childish*) pueril; (*delinquent*) jovem; (*court*) de menores □ *n* jovem *mf*
juxtapose /dʒʌkstə'pəʊz/ *vt* justapor

K

kaleidoscope /kə'laɪdəskəʊp/ *n* caleidoscópio *m*
kangaroo /kæŋgə'ru:/ *n* canguru *m*
karate /kə'ra:tɪ/ *n* klaratê *m*
kebab /kə'bæb/ *n* churrasquinho *m*, espetinho *m*
keel /ki:l/ *n* quilha *f* □ *vi* ~ **over** virar-se
keen /ki:n/ *a* (-er, -est) (*sharp*) agudo; (*eager*) entusiástico; (*of appetite*) devorador; (*of intelligence*) vivo; (*of wind*) cortante. ~**ly** *adv* vivamente; (*eagerly*) com entusiasmo. ~**ness** *n* vivacidade *f*; (*enthusiasm*) entusiasmo *m*
keep /ki:p/ (*pt* **kept**) *vt* guardar; (*family*) sustentar; (*animals*) ter, criar; (*celebrate*) festejar; (*conceal*) esconder; (*delay*) demorar; (*prevent*) impedir (**from** de); (*promise*) cumprir; (*shop*) ter □ *vi* manter-se, conservar-se; (*remain*) ficar. ~ (**on**) continuar (**doing** fazendo) □ *n* sustento *m*; (*of castle*) torre *f* de menagem. ~ **back** *vt* (*withhold*) reter □ *vi* manter-se afastado. ~ **in/out** impedir de entrar/de sair. ~ **up** conservar. ~ **up** (**with**) acompanhar. ~**er** *n* guarda *mf*
keeping /'ki:pɪŋ/ *n* guarda *f*, cuidado *m*. **in ~ with** em harmonia com, (*P*) de harmonia com
keepsake /'ki:pseɪk/ *n* (*thing*) lembrança *f*, recordação *f*
keg /keg/ *n* barril *m* pequeno
kennel /'kenl/ *n* casota *f* (de cão). ~**s** *npl* canil *m*
kept /kept/ *see* **keep**
kerb /kɜ:b/ *n* meio fio *m*, (*P*) borda *f* do passeio
kernel /'kɜ:nl/ *n* (*of nut*) miolo *m*
kerosene /'kerəsi:n/ *n* (*paraffin*) querosene *m*, (*P*) petróleo *m*; (*aviation fuel*) gasolina *f*
ketchup /'ketʃəp/ *n* molho *m* de tomate, ketchup *m*
kettle /'ketl/ *n* chaleira *f*
key /ki:/ *n* chave *f*; (*of piano etc*) tecla *f*; (*mus*) clave *f* □ *a* chave. ~**-ring** *n* chaveiro *m*, porta-chaves *m invar* □ *vt* ~ **in** digitar, bater. ~**ed up** tenso
keyboard /'ki:bɔ:d/ *n* teclado *m*
keyhole /'ki:həʊl/ *n* buraco *m* da fechadura
khaki /'ka:kɪ/ *a* & *n* cáqui (*invar m*), (*P*) caqui (*invar m*)
kick /kɪk/ *vt/i* dar um pontapé *or* pontapés (a, em); (*ball*) chutar (em); (*of horse*) dar um coice *or* coices, escoicear □ *n* pontapé *m*; (*of gun, horse*) coice *m*; (*colloq: thrill*) excitação *f*,

prazer *m*. ~-**off** *n* chute *m* inicial, kick-off *m*. ~ **out** (*colloq*) pôr na rua. ~ **up** (*colloq: fuss, racket*) fazer

kid /kɪd/ *n* (*goat*) cabrito *m*; (*sl: child*) garoto *m*; (*leather*) pelica *f* □ *vt/i* (*pt* **kidded**) (*colloq*) brincar (com)

kidnap /ˈkɪdnæp/ *vt* (*pt* **kidnapped**) raptar. ~**ping** *n* rapto *m*

kidney /ˈkɪdnɪ/ *n* rim *m*

kill /kɪl/ *vt* matar; (*fig: put an end to*) acabar com □ *n* matança *f*. ~**er** *n* assassino *m*. ~**ing** *n* matança *f*, massacre *m*; (*of game*) caçada *f* □ *a* (*colloq: funny*) de morrer de rir; (*colloq: exhausting*) de morte

killjoy /ˈkɪldʒɔɪ/ *n* desmancha-prazeres *mf*

kiln /kɪln/ *n* forno *m*

kilo /ˈki:ləʊ/ *n* (*pl* -os) quilo *m*

kilogram /ˈkɪləgræm/ *n* quilograma *m*

kilometre /ˈkɪləmi:tə(r)/ *n* quilômetro *m*, (*P*) quilómetro *m*

kilowatt /ˈkɪləwɒt/ *n* quilowatt *m*, (*P*) quilovate *m*

kilt /kɪlt/ *n* kilt *m*, saiote *m* escocês

kin /kɪn/ *n* família *f*, parentes *mpl*. **next of** ~ os parentes mais próximos

kind[1] /kaɪnd/ *n* espécie *f*, gênero *m*, (*P*) género *m*, natureza *f*. **in** ~ em gêneros, (*P*) géneros; (*fig: in the same form*) na mesma moeda. ~ **of** (*colloq: somewhat*) de certo modo, um pouco

kind[2] /kaɪnd/ *a* (-er, -est) (*good*) bom; (*friendly*) gentil, amável. ~-**hearted** *a* bom, bondoso. ~**ness** *n* bondade *f*

kindergarten /ˈkɪndəgɑ:tn/ *n* jardim de infância *m*, (*P*) infantil

kindle /ˈkɪndl/ *vt/i* acender(-se), atear(-se)

kindly /ˈkaɪndlɪ/ *a* (-ier, -iest) benévolo, bondoso □ *adv* bondosamente, gentilmente, com simpatia. ~ **wait** tenha a bondade de esperar

kindred /ˈkɪndrɪd/ *a* aparentado; (*fig: connected*) afim. ~ **spirit** espírito *m* congênere, alma *f* gêmea

kinetic /kɪˈnetɪk/ *a* cinético

king /kɪŋ/ *n* rei *m*. ~-**size(d)** *a* de tamanho grande

kingdom /ˈkɪŋdəm/ *n* reino *m*

kingfisher /ˈkɪŋfɪʃə(r)/ *n* pica-peixe *m*, martim-pescador *m*

kink /kɪŋk/ *n* (*in rope*) volta *f*, nó *m*; (*fig*) perversão *f*. ~**y** *a* (*colloq*) excêntrico, pervertido; (*of hair*) encarapinhado

kiosk /ˈki:ɒsk/ *n* quiosque *m*. **telephone** ~ cabine telefônica, (*P*) telefónica

kip /kɪp/ *n* (*sl*) sono *m* □ *vi* (*pt* **kipped**) (*sl*) dormir

kipper /ˈkɪpə(r)/ *n* arenque *m* defumado

kiss /kɪs/ *n* beijo *m* □ *vt/i* beijar(-se)

kit /kɪt/ *n* equipamento *m*; (*set of tools*) ferramenta *f*; (*for assembly*) kit *m* □ *vt* (*pt* **kitted**) ~ **out** equipar

kitbag /ˈkɪtbæg/ *n* mochila *f* (de soldado etc); saco *m* de viagem

kitchen /ˈkɪtʃɪn/ *n* cozinha *f*. ~ **garden** horta *f*. ~ **sink** pia *f*, (*P*) lava-louças *m*

kite /kaɪt/ *n* (*toy*) pipa *f*, (*P*) papagaio *m* de papel

kith /kɪθ/ *n* ~ **and kin** parentes e amigos *mpl*

kitten /ˈkɪtn/ *n* gatinho *m*

kitty /ˈkɪtɪ/ *n* (*fund*) fundo *m* comum, vaquinha *f*; (*cards*) bolo *m*

knack /næk/ *n* jeito *m*

knapsack /ˈnæpsæk/ *n* mochila *f*

knead /ni:d/ *vt* amassar

knee /ni:/ *n* joelho *m*

kneecap /ˈni:kæp/ *n* rótula *f*

kneel /ni:l/ *vi* (*pt* **knelt**) ~ **(down)** ajoelhar(-se)

knelt /nelt/ *see* **kneel**

knew /nju:/ *see* **know**

knickers /ˈnɪkəz/ *npl* calcinhas (de senhora) *fpl*

knife /naɪf/ *n* (*pl* **knives**) faca *f* □ *vt* esfaquear, apunhalar

knight /naɪt/ *n* cavaleiro *m*; (*chess*) cavalo *m*. ~**hood** *n* grau *m* de cavaleiro

knit /nɪt/ *vt* (*pt* **knitted** *or* **knit**) tricotar □ *vi* tricotar, fazer tricô; (*fig: unite*) unir-se; (*of bones*) soldar-se. ~ **one's brow** franzir as sobrancelhas. ~**ting** *n* malha *f*, tricô *m*

knitwear /ˈnɪtweə(r)/ *n* roupa *f* de malha, malhas *fpl*

knob /nɒb/ *n* (*of door*) maçaneta *f*; (*of drawer*) puxador *m*; (*of radio, TV etc*) botão *m*; (*of butter*) noz *f*. ~**bly** *a* nodoso

knock /nɒk/ *vt/i* bater (em); (*sl: criticize*) desancar (em). ~ **about** *vt* tratar mal □ *vi* (*wander*) andar a esmo. ~ **down** (*chair, pedestrian*) deitar no chão, derrubar; (*demolish*) jogar abaixo; (*colloq: reduce*) baixar, reduzir; (*at auction*) adjudicar (to a). ~-**down** *a* (*price*) muito baixo. ~-**kneed** *a* de pernas de tesoura. ~ **off** *vt* (*colloq: complete quickly*) despachar; (*sl: steal*) roubar □ *vi* (*colloq*) parar de trabalhar, fechar a loja (*colloq*). ~ **out** pôr fora de combate, eliminar; (*stun*) assombrar. ~-**out** *n* (*boxing*) nocaute *m*, KO *m*. ~ **over** entornar. ~ **up** (*meal etc*) arranjar às pressas. ~**er** *n* aldrava *f*

knot /nɒt/ *n* nó *m* □ *vt* (*pt* **knotted**) atar com nó, dar nó *or* nós em

knotty /ˈnɒtɪ/ *a* (-ier, -iest) nodoso, cheio de nós; (*difficult*) complicado, espinhoso

know /nəʊ/ *vt/i* (*pt* **knew**, *pp* **known**) saber (that que); (*person, place*) conhecer □ *n* **in the ~** (*colloq*) por dentro. **~ about** (*cars etc*) saber sobre, saber de. **~-all** *n* sabe-tudo *m* (*colloq*). **~-how** *n* know-how *m*, conhecimentos *mpl* técnicos, culturais etc. **~ of** ter conhecimento de, ter ouvido falar de. **~ingly** *adv* com ar conhecedor; (*consciously*) conscientemente

knowledge /'nɒlɪdʒ/ *n* conhecimento *m*; (*learning*) saber *m*. **~able** *a* conhecedor, entendido, versado

known /nəʊn/ *see* **know** □ *a* conhecido

knuckle /'nʌkl/ *n* nó *m* dos dedos □ *vi* **~ under** ceder, submeter-se

Koran /kə'ra:n/ *n* Alcorão *m*, Corão *m*

Korea /kə'rɪə/ *n* Coréia *f*

kosher /'kəʊʃə(r)/ *a* aprovado pela lei judaica; (*colloq*) como deve ser

kowtow /kaʊ'taʊ/ *vi* prosternar-se (to diante de); (*act obsequiously*) bajular

L

lab /læb/ *n* (*colloq*) laboratório *m*

label /'leɪbl/ *n* (*on bottle etc*) rótulo *m*; (*on clothes, luggage*) etiqueta *f* □ *vt* (*pt* **labelled**) rotular; etiquetar, pôr etiqueta em

laboratory /lə'bɒrətrɪ/ *n* laboratório *m*

laborious /lə'bɔ:rɪəs/ *a* laborioso, trabalhoso

labour /'leɪbə(r)/ *n* trabalho *m*, labuta *f*; (*workers*) mão-de-obra *f* □ *vi* trabalhar; (*try hard*) esforçar-se □ *vt* alongar-se sobre, insistir em. **in ~** em trabalho de parto. **~ed** *a* (*writing*) laborioso, sem espontaneidade; (*breathing, movement*) difícil. **~-saving** *a* que poupa trabalho

Labour /'leɪbə(r)/ *n* (*party*) Partido *m* Trabalhista, os trabalhistas □ *a* trabalhista

labourer /'leɪbərə(r)/ *n* trabalhador *m*; (*on farm*) trabalhador *m* rural

labyrinth /'læbərɪnθ/ *n* labirinto *m*

lace /leɪs/ *n* renda *f*; (*of shoe*) cordão *m* de sapato, (*P*) atacador *m* □ *vt* atar; (*drink*) juntar um pouco (de aguardente, rum etc)

lacerate /'læsəreɪt/ *vt* lacerar, rasgar

lack /læk/ *n* falta *f* □ *vt* faltar (a), não ter. **be ~ing** faltar. **be ~ing in** carecer de

lackadaisical /lækə'deɪzɪkl/ *a* lânguido, apático, desinteressado

laconic /lə'kɒnɪk/ *a* lacônico, (*P*) lacónico

lacquer /'lækə(r)/ *n* laca *f*

lad /læd/ *n* rapaz *m*, moço *m*

ladder /'lædə(r)/ *n* escada de mão *f*, (*P*) escadote *m*; (*in stocking*) fio *m* corrido, (*P*) malha *f* caída □ *vi* deixar correr um fio, (*P*) cair uma malha □ *vt* fazer malhas em

laden /'leɪdn/ *a* carregado (with de)

ladle /'leɪdl/ *n* concha (de sopa) *f*

lady /'leɪdɪ/ *n* senhora *f*; (*title*) Lady *f*. **~-in-waiting** *n* dama *f* de companhia, (*P*) dama *f* de honor. **young ~** jovem *f*. **~like** *a* senhoril, elegante. **Ladies** *n* (*toilets*) toalete *m* das Senhoras

ladybird /'leɪdɪbɜ:d/ *n* joaninha *f*

lag[1] /læg/ *vi* (*pt* **lagged**) atrasar-se, ficar para trás □ *n* atraso *m*

lag[2] /læg/ *vt* (*pt* **lagged**) (*pipes etc*) revestir com isolante térmico

lager /'la:gə(r)/ *n* cerveja *f* leve e clara, "loura" *f* (*sl*)

lagoon /lə'gu:n/ *n* lagoa *f*

laid /leɪd/ *see* **lay**[2]

lain /leɪn/ *see* **lie**[2]

lair /leə(r)/ *n* toca *f*, covil *m*

laity /'leɪətɪ/ *n* leigos *mpl*

lake /leɪk/ *n* lago *m*

lamb /læm/ *n* cordeiro *m*, carneiro *m*; (*meat*) carneiro *m*

lambswool /'læmzwʊl/ *n* lã *f*

lame /leɪm/ *a* (-er, -est) coxo; (*fig: unconvincing*) fraco. **~ness** *n* claudicação *f*, coxeadura *f*

lament /lə'ment/ *n* lamento *m*, lamentação *f* □ *vt/i* lamentar(-se) (de). **~able** *a* lamentável

laminated /'læmɪneɪtɪd/ *a* laminado

lamp /læmp/ *n* lâmpada *f*

lamppost /'læmppəʊst/ *n* poste *m* (do candeeiro) (de iluminação pública)

lampshade /'læmpʃeɪd/ *n* abajur *m*, quebra-luz *m*

lance /la:ns/ *n* lança *f* □ *vt* lancetar

lancet /'lan:sɪt/ *n* bisturi *m*, (*P*) lanceta *f*

land /lænd/ *n* terra *f*; (*country*) país *m*; (*plot*) terreno *m*; (*property*) terras *fpl* □ *a* de terra, terrestre; (*policy etc*) agrário □ *vt/i* desembarcar; (*aviat*) aterrissar, (*P*) aterrar; (*fall*) ir parar (on em); (*colloq: obtain*) arranjar; (*a blow*) aplicar, mandar. **~-locked** *a* rodeado de terra

landing /'lændɪŋ/ *n* desembarque *m*; (*aviat*) aterrissagem *f*, (*P*) aterragem *f*; (*top of stairs*) patamar *m*. **~-stage** *n* cais *m* flutuante

land|lady /'lændleɪdɪ/ *n* (*of rented house*) senhoria *f*, proprietária *f*; (*who lets rooms*) dona *f* da casa; (*of boarding-house*) dona *f* da pensão; (*of inn etc*) proprietária *f*, estalajadeira *f*. **~lord** *n* (*of rented house*) senhorio *m*, proprietário *m*; (*of inn etc*) proprietário *m*, estalajadeiro *m*

landmark /'lændmaːk/ *n* (*conspicuous feature*) ponto *m* de referência; (*fig*) marco *m*

landscape /'lændskeɪp/ *n* paisagem *f* □ *vt* projetar, (*P*) projectar paisagisticamente

landslide /'lændslaɪd/ *n* desabamento *m or* desmoronamento *m* de terras; (*fig: pol*) vitoria *f* esmagadora

lane /leɪn/ *n* senda *f*, caminho *m*; (*in country*) estrada *f* pequena; (*in town*) viela *f*, ruela *f*; (*of road*) faixa *f*, pista *f*; (*of traffic*) fila *f*; (*aviat*) corredor *m*; (*naut*) rota *f*

language /'læŋgwɪdʒ/ *n* língua *f*; (*speech, style*) linguagem *f*. **bad ~** linguagem *f* grosseira. **~ lab** laboratório *m* de línguas

languid /'læŋgwɪd/ *a* lânguido

languish /'læŋgwɪʃ/ *vi* elanguescer

lank /læŋk/ *a* (*of hair*) escorrido, liso

lanky /'læŋkɪ/ *a* (**-ier, -iest**) desengonçado, escanifrado

lantern /'læntən/ *n* lanterna *f*

lap[1] /læp/ *n* colo *m*; (*sport*) volta *f* completa. **~-dog** *n* cãozinho *m* de estimação

lap[2] /læp/ *vt* **~ up** beber lambendo □ *vi* marulhar

lapel /lə'pel/ *n* lapela *f*

lapse /læps/ *vi* decair, degenerar-se; (*expire*) caducar □ *n* lapso *m*; (*jur*) prescrição *f*. **~ into** (*thought*) mergulhar em; (*bad habit*) adquirir

larceny /'laːsənɪ/ *n* furto *m*

lard /laːd/ *n* banha de porco *f*

larder /'laːdə(r)/ *n* despensa *f*

large /laːdʒ/ *a* (**-er, -est**) grande. **at ~** à solta, em liberdade. **by and ~** em geral. **~ly** *adv* largamente, em grande parte. **~ness** *n* grandeza *f*

lark[1] /laːk/ *n* (*bird*) cotovia *f*

lark[2] /laːk/ *n* (*colloq*) pândega *f*, brincadeira *f* □ *vi* **~ about** (*colloq*) fazer travessuras, brincar

larva /'laːvə/ *n* (*pl* **-vae** /-viː/) larva *f*

laryngitis /lærɪn'dʒaɪtɪs/ *n* laringite *f*

larynx /'lærɪŋks/ *n* laringe *f*

lascivious /lə'sɪvɪəs/ *a* lascivo, sensual

laser /'leɪzə(r)/ *n* laser *m*. **~ printer** impressora *f* a laser

lash /læʃ/ *vt* chicotear, açoitar; (*rain*) fustigar □ *n* chicote *m*; (*stroke*) chicotada *f*; (*eyelash*) pestana *f*, cílio *m*. **~ out** atacar, atirar-se a; (*colloq: spend*) esbanjar dinheiro em algo

lashings /'læʃɪŋz/ *npl* **~ of** (*sl*) montes de (*colloq*)

lasso /læ'suː/ *n* (*pl* **-os**) laço *m* □ *vt* laçar

last[1] /laːst/ *a* último □ *adv* no fim, em último lugar; (*most recently*) a última vez □ *n* último *m*. **at (long) ~** por fim, finalmente. **~-minute** *a* de última hora. **~ night** ontem à noite, a noite passada. **the ~ straw** a gota d'água. **to the ~** até o fim. **~ly** *adv* finalmente, em último lugar

last[2] /laːst/ *vt/i* durar, continuar. **~ing** *a* duradouro, durável

latch /lætʃ/ *n* trinco *m*

late /leɪt/ *a* (**-er, -est**) atrasado; (*recent*) recente; (*former*) antigo, ex-, anterior; (*hour, fruit etc*) tardio; (*deceased*) falecido □ *adv* tarde. **in ~ July** no fim de julho. **of ~** ultimamente. **at the ~st** o mais tardar. **~ness** *n* atraso *m*

lately /'leɪtlɪ/ *adv* nos últimos tempos, ultimamente

latent /'leɪtnt/ *a* latente

lateral /'lætərəl/ *a* lateral

lathe /leɪð/ *n* torno *m*

lather /'laːðə(r)/ *n* espuma *f* de sabão □ *vt* ensaboar □ *vi* fazer espuma

Latin /'lætɪn/ *n* (*lang*) latim *m* □ *a* latino. **~ America** *n* América *f* Latina. **~ American** *a* & *n* latino-americano (*m*)

latitude /'lætɪtjuːd/ *n* latitude *f*

latter /'lætə(r)/ *a* último, mais recente □ *n* **the ~** este, esta. **~ly** *adv* recentemente

lattice /'lætɪs/ *n* treliça *f*, (*P*) gradeamento *m* de ripas

laudable /'lɔːdəbl/ *a* louvável

laugh /laːf/ *vi* rir (**at** de). **~ off** disfarçar com uma piada □ *n* riso *m*. **~able** *a* irrisório, ridículo. **~ing-stock** *n* objeto *m*, (*P*) objecto *m* de troça

laughter /'laːftə(r)/ *n* riso *m*, risada *f*

launch[1] /lɔːntʃ/ *vt* lançar □ *n* lançamento *m*. **~ into** lançar-se *or* meter-se em. **~ing pad** plataforma *f* de lançamento

launch[2] /lɔːntʃ/ *n* (*boat*) lancha *f*

launder /'lɔːndə(r)/ *vt* lavar e passar

launderette /lɔːn'dret/ *n* lavanderia *f* automática

laundry /'lɔːndrɪ/ *n* lavanderia *f*; (*clothes*) roupa *f*. **do the ~** lavar a roupa

laurel /'lɒrəl/ *n* loureiro *m*, louro *m*

lava /'laːvə/ *n* lava *f*

lavatory /'lɒvətrɪ/ *n* privada *f*, (*P*) retrete *f*; (*room*) toalete *m*, (*P*) lavabo *m*

lavender /'lævəndə(r)/ *n* alfazema *f*, lavanda *f*

lavish /'lævɪʃ/ *a* pródigo; (*plentiful*) copioso, generoso; (*lush*) suntuoso □ *vt* ser pródigoem, encher de. **~ly** *adv* prodigamente; copiosamente; suntuosamente

law /lɔː/ *n* lei *f*; (*profession, study*) direito *m*. **~-abiding** *a* cumpridor da lei, respeitador da lei. ~ **and order** ordem *f* pública. ~**-breaker** *n* transgressor *m* da lei. ~**ful** *a* legal, legítimo. ~**fully** *adv* legalmente. ~**less** *a* sem lei; (*act*) ilegal; (*person*) rebelde

lawcourt /'lɔ:kɔ:t/ *n* tribunal *m*

lawn /lɔ:n/ *n* gramado *m*, (*P*) relvado *m*. ~**-mower** *n* cortador *m* de grama, (*P*) máquina *f* de cortar a relva

lawsuit /'lɔ:su:t/ *n* processo *m*, ação *f*, (*P*) acção *f* judicial

lawyer /'lɔ:jə(r)/ *n* advogado *m*

lax /læks/ *a* negligente; (*discipline*) frouxo; (*morals*) relaxado. ~**ity** *n* negligência *f*; (*of discipline*) frouxidão *f*; (*of morals*) relaxamento *m*

laxative /'læksətɪv/ *n* laxante *m*, laxativo *m*

lay[1] /leɪ/ *a* leigo. ~ **opinion** opinião *f* de um leigo

lay[2] /leɪ/ *vt* (*pt* **laid**) pôr, colocar; (*trap*) preparar, pôr; (*eggs, table, siege*) pôr; (*plan*) fazer □ *vi* pôr (ovos). ~ **aside** pôr de lado. ~ **down** pousar; (*condition, law, rule*) impôr; (*arms*) depor; (*one's life*) oferecer; (*policy*) ditar. ~ **hold of** agarrar(-se a). ~ **off** *vt* (*worker*) suspender do trabalho □ *vi* (*colloq*) parar, desistir. ~**-off** *n* suspensão *f* temporária. ~ **on** (*gas, water etc*) instalar, ligar; (*entertainment etc*) organizar, providenciar; (*food*) servir. ~ **out** (*design*) traçar, planejar; (*spread out*) estender, espalhar; (*money*) gastar. ~ **up** *vt* (*store*) juntar; (*ship, car*) pôr fora de serviço

lay[3] /leɪ/ *see* **lie**

layabout /'leɪəbaʊt/ *n* (*sl*) vadio *m*

lay-by /'leɪbaɪ/ *n* acostamento *m*, (*P*) berma *f*

layer /'leɪə(r)/ *n* camada *f*

layman /'leɪmən/ *n* (*pl* **-men**) leigo *m*

layout /'leɪaʊt/ *n* disposição *f*; (*typ*) composição *f*

laze /leɪz/ *vi* descansar, vadiar

laz|y /'leɪzɪ/ *a* (-ier, -iest) preguiçoso. ~**iness** *n* preguiça *f*. ~**y-bones** *n* (*colloq*) vadio *m*, vagabundo *m*

lead[1] /li:d/ *vt/i* (*pt* **led**) conduzir, guiar, levar; (*team etc*) chefiar, liderar; (*life*) levar; (*choir, band etc*) dirigir □ *n* (*distance*) avanço *m*; (*first place*) dianteira *f*; (*clue*) indício *m*, pista *f*; (*leash*) coleira *f*; (*electr*) cabo *m*; (*theatr*) papel *m* principal; (*example*) exemplo *m*. **in the** ~ na frente. ~ **away** levar. ~ **on** (*fig*) encorajar. ~ **the way** ir na frente. ~ **up to** conduzir a

lead[2] /led/ *n* chumbo *m*; (*of pencil*) grafite *f*. ~**en** *a* de chumbo; (*of colour*) plúmbeo

leader /'li:də(r)/ *n* chefe *m*, líder *m*; (*of country, club, union etc*) dirigente *mf*; (*pol*) líder; (*of orchestra*) regente *mf*, maestro *m*; (*in newspaper*) editorial *m*. ~**ship** *n* direção *f*, (*P*) direcção *f*, liderança *f*

leading /'li:dɪŋ/ *a* principal. ~ **article** artigo *m* de fundo, editorial *m*

leaf /li:f/ *n* (*pl* **leaves**) folha *f*; (*flap of table*) aba *f* □ *vi* ~ **through** folhear. ~**y** *a* frondoso

leaflet /'li:flɪt/ *n* prospecto *m*, folheto *m* informativo

league /li:g/ *n* liga *f*; (*sport*) campeonato *m* da Liga. **in** ~ **with** de coligação com, em conluio com

leak /li:k/ *n* (*escape*) fuga *f*; (*hole*) buraco *m* □ *vt/i* (*roof, container*) pingar; (*eletr gas*) ter um escapamento, (*P*) ter uma fuga; (*naut*) fazer água. ~ **(out)** (*fig: divulge*) divulgar; (*fig: become known*) transpirar, divulgar-se. ~**age** *n* vazamento *m*. ~**y** *a* que tem um vazamento

lean[1] /li:n/ *a* (-er, -est) magro. ~**ness** *n* magreza *f*

lean[2] /li:n/ *vt/i* (*pt* **leaned** *or* **leant** /lent/) encostar(-se), apoiar-se (on em); (*be slanting*) inclinar(-se). ~ **back/forward** *or* **over** inclinar-se para trás/para a frente. ~ **on** (*colloq*) pressionar. ~ **to** *n* alpendre *m*

leaning /'li:nɪŋ/ *a* inclinado □ *n* inclinação *f*

leap /li:p/ *vt* (*pt* **leaped** *or* **leapt**/ lept/) galgar, saltar por cima de □ *vi* saltar □ *n* salto *m*, pulo *m*. ~**-frog** *n* eixo-badeixo *m*, (*P*) jogo *m* do eixo. ~ **year** ano *m* bissexto

learn /lɜ:n/ *vt/i* (*pt* **learned** *or* **learnt**) aprender; (*be told*) vir a saber, ouvir dizer. ~**er** *n* principiante *mf*, aprendiz *m*

learn|ed /'lɜ:nɪd/ *a* erudito. ~**ing** *n* saber *m*, erudição *f*

lease /li:s/ *n* arrendamento *m*, aluguel *m*, (*P*) aluguer *m* □ *vt* arrendar, (*P*) alugar

leash /li:ʃ/ *n* coleira *f*

least /li:st/ *a* o menor □ *n* o mínino *m*, o menos *m* □ *adv* o menos. **at** ~ pelo menos. **not in the** ~ de maneira alguma

leather /'leðə(r)/ *n* couro *m*, cabedal *m*

leave /li:v/ *vt/i* (*pt* **left**) deixar; (*depart from*) sair/partir (de), ir-se (de) □ *n* licença *f*, permissão *f*. **be left (over)** restar, sobrar. ~ **alone** deixar em paz, não tocar. ~ **out** omitir. ~ **of absence** licença *f*. **on** ~ (*mil*) de licença. **take one's** ~ despedir-se (of de)

leavings /'li:vɪŋz/ *npl* restos *mpl*

Leban|on /'lebənən/ *n* Líbano *m*. ~**ese** /'ni:z/ *a* & *n* libanês (*m*)
lecherous /'letʃərəs/ *a* lascivo
lectern /'lektən/ *n* estante *f* (de coro de igreja)
lecture /'lektʃə(r)/ *n* conferência *f*; (*univ*) aula *f* teórica; (*fig*) sermão *m* □ *vi* dar uma conferência; (*univ*) dar aula(s) □ *vt* pregar um sermão a alg (*colloq*). ~**r** /-ə(r)/ *n* conferente *mf*, conferencista *mf*; (*univ*) professor *m*
led /led/ *see* **lead**[1]
ledge /ledʒ/ *n* rebordo *m*, saliência *f*; (*of window*) peitoril *m*
ledger /'ledʒə(r)/ *n* livro-mestre *m*, razão *m*
leech /li:tʃ/ *n* sanguessuga *f*
leek /li:k/ *n* alho-poró *m*, (*P*) alho-porro *m*
leer /lɪə(r)/ *vi* ~ **(at)** olhar de modo malicioso *or* manhoso (para) □ *n* olhar *m* malicioso *or* manhoso
leeway /'li:weɪ/ *n* (*naut*) deriva *f*; (*fig*) liberdade *f* de ação, (*P*) acção, margem *f* (*colloq*)
left[1] /left/ *see* **leave**. ~ **luggage (office)** depósito *m* de bagagens. ~**-overs** *npl* restos *mpl*, sobras *fpl*
left[2] /left/ *a* esquerdo; (*pol*) de esquerda □ *n* esquerda *f* □ *adv* à/para à esquerda. ~**-hand** *a* da esquerda; (*position*) à esquerda. ~**-handed** *a* canhoto. ~**-wing** *a* (*pol*) de esquerda
leg /leg/ *n* perna *f*; (*of table*) pé *m*, perna *f*; (*of journey*) etapa *f*. **pull sb's** ~ brincar or mexer com alg. **stretch one's** ~**s** esticar as pernas. ~**-room** *n* espaço *m* para as pernas
legacy /'legəsɪ/ *n* legado *m*
legal /'li:gl/ *a* legal; (*affairs etc*) jurídico. ~ **adviser** advogado *m*. ~**ity** /li:'gælətɪ/ *n* legalidade *f*. ~**ly** *adv* legalmente
legalize /'li:gəlaɪz/ *vt* legalizar
legend /'ledʒənd/ *n* lenda *f*. ~**ary** /'ledʒəndrɪ/ *a* lendário
leggings /'legɪŋz/ *npl* perneiras *fpl*; (*women's*) legging *m*
legib|le /'ledʒəbl/ *a* legível. ~**ility** /-'bɪlətɪ/ *n* legibilidade *f*
legion /'li:dʒən/ *n* legião *f*
legislat|e /'ledʒɪsleɪt/ *vi* legislar. ~**ion** /-'leɪʃn/ *n* legislação *f*
legislat|ive /'ledʒɪslətɪv/ *a* legislativo. ~**ure** /-eɪtʃə(r)/ *n* corpo *m* legislativo
legitima|te /lɪ'dʒɪtɪmət/ *a* legítimo. ~**cy** *n* legitimidade *f*
leisure /'leʒə(r)/ *n* lazer *m*, tempo livre *m*. **at one's** ~ ao bel prazer, (*P*) a seu belo prazer. ~ **centre** centro *m* de lazer. ~**ly** *a* pausado, compassado □ *adv* sem pressa, devagar
lemon /'lemən/ *n* limão *m*
lemonade /lemə'neɪd/ *n* limonada *f*
lend /lend/ *vt* (*pt* **lent**) emprestar; (*contribute*) dar. ~ **a hand to** (*help*) ajudar. ~ **itself to** prestar-se a. ~**er** *n* pessoa *f* que empresta. ~**ing** *n* empréstimo *m*
length /leŋθ/ *n* comprimento *m*; (*in time*) período *m*; (*of cloth*) corte *m*. **at** ~ extensamente; (*at last*) por fim, finalmente. ~**y** *a* longo, demorado
lengthen /'leŋθən/ *vt/i* alongar(-se)
lengthways /'leŋθweɪz/ *adv* ao comprido, em comprimento, longitudinalmente
lenien|t /'li:nɪənt/ *a* indulgente, clemente. ~**cy** *n* indulgência *f*, clemência *f*
lens /lenz/ *n* (*of spectacles*) lente *f*; (*photo*) objetiva *f*, (*P*) objectiva *f*
lent /lent/ *see* **lend**
Lent /lent/ *n* Quaresma *f*
lentil /'lentl/ *n* lentilha *f*
Leo /'li:əʊ/ *n* (*astr*) Leão *m*
leopard /'lepəd/ *n* leopardo *m*
leotard /'li:əʊta:d/ *n* collant(s) *m* (*pl*), (*P*) maillot *m* de ginástica ou dança
leper /'lepə(r)/ *n* leproso *m*
leprosy /'leprəsɪ/ *n* lepra *f*
lesbian /'lezbɪən/ *a* lésbico □ *n* lésbica *f*
less /les/ *a* (*in number*) menor **(than** que); (*in quantity*) menos **(than** que) □ *n*, *adv* & *prep* menos. ~ **and** ~ cada vez menos
lessen /'lesn/ *vt/i* diminuir
lesser /'lesə(r)/ *a* menor. **to a** ~ **degree** em menor grau
lesson /'lesn/ *n* lição *f*
let /let/ *vt* (*pt* **let**, *pres p* **letting**) deixar, permitir; (*lease*) alugar, arrendar □ *v aux* ~**'s go** vamos. ~ **him do it** que o faça ele. ~ **me know** diga-me, avise-me □ *n* aluguel *m*, (*P*) aluguer *m*. ~ **alone** deixar em paz; (*not to mention*) sem falar em, para não falar em. ~ **down** baixar; (*deflate*) esvaziar; (*disappoint*) desapontar; (*fail to help*) deixar na mão. ~**-down** *n* desapontamento *m*. ~ **go** *vt/i* soltar. ~ **in** deixar entrar. ~ **o.s. in for** (*task, trouble*) meter-se em. ~ **off** (*gun*) disparar; (*firework*) soltar, (*P*) deitar; (*excuse*) desculpar. ~ **on** (*colloq*) *vt* revelar **(that** que) □ *vi* descoser-se (*colloq*), (*P*) descair-se (*colloq*). ~ **out** deixar sair. ~ **through** deixar passar. ~ **up** (*colloq*) abrandar, diminuir. ~**up** *n* (*colloq*) pausa *f*, trégua *f*
lethal /'li:θl/ *a* fatal, mortal
letharg|y /'leθədʒɪ/ *n* letargia *f*, apatia *f*. ~**ic** /lɪ'θa:dʒɪk/ *a* letárgico, apático
letter /'letə(r)/ *n* (*symbol*) letra *f*; (*message*) carta *f*. ~**-bomb** *n* carta-bomba *f*. ~**-box** *n* caixa *f* do correio. ~**ing** *n* letras *fpl*

lettuce /'letɪs/ *n* alface *f*
leukaemia /lu:'ki:mɪə/ *n* leucemia *f*
level /'levl/ *a* plano; (*on surface*) horizontal; (*in height*) no mesmo nível (with que); (*spoonful etc*) raso □ *n* nível *m* □ *vt* (*pt* **levelled**) nivelar; (*gun, missile*) apontar; (*accusation*) dirigir. **on the ~** (*colloq*) franco, sincero. **~ crossing** passagem *f* de nível. **~-headed** *a* equilibrado, sensato
lever /'li:və(r)/ *n* alavanca *f* □ *vt* **~ up** levantar com alavanca
leverage /'li:vərɪdʒ/ *n* influência *f*
levity /'levətɪ/ *n* frivolidade *f*, leviandade *f*
levy /'levɪ/ *vt* (*tax*) cobrar □ *n* imposto *m*
lewd /lu:d/ *a* (-er, -est) libidinoso, obsceno
liabilit|y /laɪə'bɪlətɪ/ *n* responsabilidade *f*; (*colloq: handicap*) desvantagem *f*. **~ies** dívidas *fpl*
liable /'laɪəbl/ *a* **~ to do** suscetível, (*P*) susceptível de fazer; **~ to** (*illness etc*) suscetível, (*P*) susceptível a; (*fine*) sujeito a. **~ for** responsável por
liaise /lɪ'eɪz/ *vi* (*colloq*) servir de intermediário (**between** entre), fazer a ligação (**with** com)
liaison /lɪ'eɪzn/ *n* ligação *f*
liar /'laɪə(r)/ *n* mentiroso *m*
libel /'laɪbl/ *n* difamação *f* □ *vt* (*pt* **libelled**) difamar
liberal /'lɪbərəl/ *a* liberal. **~ly** *adv* liberalmente
Liberal /'lɪbərəl/ *a* & *n* liberal (*mf*)
liberat|e /'lɪbəreɪt/ *vt* libertar. **~ion** /-'reɪʃn/ *n* libertação *f*; (*of women*) emancipação *f*
libert|y /'lɪbətɪ/ *n* liberdade *f*. **at ~y to** livre de. **take ~ies** tomar liberdades
libido /lɪ'bi:dəʊ/ *n* (*pl* -os) libido *m*
Libra /'li:brə/ *n* (*astr*) Balança *f*, Libra *f*
librar|y /'laɪbrərɪ/ *n* biblioteca *f*. **~ian** /-'breərɪən/ *n* bibliotecário *m*
Libya /'lɪbɪə/ *n* Líbia *f*. **~n** *a* & *n* líbio (*m*)
lice /laɪs/ *n see* **louse**
licence /'laɪsns/ *n* licença *f*; d (*for TV*) taxa *f*; (*for driving*) carteira *f*, (*P*) carta *f*; (*behaviour*) libertinagem *f*
license /'laɪsns/ *vt* dar licença para, autorizar □ *n* (*Amer*) = **licence**. **~ plate** placa *f* do carro, (*P*) placa *f* de matrícula
licentious /laɪ'senʃəs/ *a* licencioso
lichen /'laɪkən/ *n* líquen *m*
lick /lɪk/ *vt* lamber; (*sl: defeat*) bater (*colloq*), dar uma surra em (*colloq*) □ *n* lambidela *f*. **a ~ of paint** uma mão de pintura
lid /lɪd/ *n* tampa *f*
lido /'li:dəʊ/ *n* (*pl* ~os) piscina *f* pública ao ar livre
lie[1] /laɪ/ *n* mentira *f* □ *vi* (*pt* **lied**, *pres p* **lying**) mentir. **give the ~ to** desmentir
lie[2] /laɪ/ *vi* (*pt* **lay**, *pp* **lain**, *pres p* **lying**) estar deitado; (*remain*) ficar; (*be situated*) estar, encontrar-se; (*in grave, on ground*) jazer. **~ down** descansar. **~ in, have a ~-in** dormir até tarde. **~ low** (*colloq: hide*) andar escondido
lieu /lu:/ *n* **in ~ of** em vez de
lieutenant /lef'tenənt/ *n* (*army*) tenente *m*; (*navy*) 1° tenente *m*
life /laɪf/ *n* (*pl* **lives**) vida *f*. **~ cycle** ciclo *m* vital. **~ expectancy** probabilidade *f* de vida. **~-guard** *n* salva-vidas *m*. **~ insurance** seguro *m* de vida. **~-jacket** *n* colete *m* salva-vidas. **~-size(d)** *a* (de) tamanho natural *invar*
lifebelt /'laɪfbelt/ *n* cinto *m* salva-vidas, (*P*) cinto *m* de salvação
lifeboat /'laɪfbəʊt/ *n* barco *m* salva-vidas
lifebuoy /'laɪfbɔɪ/ *n* bóia *f* salva-vidas, (*P*) bóia *f* de salvação
lifeless /'laɪflɪs/ *a* sem vida
lifelike /'laɪflaɪk/ *a* natural, real; (*of portrait*) muito parecido
lifelong /'laɪflɒŋ/ *a* de toda a vida, perpétuo
lifestyle /'laɪfstaɪl/ *n* estilo *m* de vida
lifetime /'laɪftaɪm/ *n* vida *f*. **the chance of a ~** uma oportunidade única
lift /lɪft/ *vt/i* levantar(-se), erguer(-se); (*colloq: steal*) roubar, surripiar (*colloq*); (*of fog*) levantar, dispersar-se □ *n* ascensor *m*, elevador *m*. **give a ~ to** dar carona, (*P*) boleia a (*colloq*). **~-off** *n* decolagem *f*, (*P*) descolagem *f*
ligament /'lɪgəmənt/ *n* ligamento *m*
light[1] /laɪt/ *n* luz *f*; (*lamp*) lâmpada *f*; (*on vehicle*) farol *m*; (*spark*) lume *m* □ *a* claro □ *vt* (*pt* **lit** *or* **lighted**) (*ignite*) acender; (*illuminate*) iluminar. **bring to ~** trazer à luz, revelar. **come to ~** vir à luz. **~ up** iluminar(-se), acender(-se). **~-year** *n* ano-luz *m*
light[2] /laɪt/ *a* & *adv* (-er, -est) leve. **~-headed** *a* (*dizzy*) estonteado, tonto; (*frivolous*) leviano. **~-hearted** *a* alegre, despreocupado. **~ly** *adv* de leve, levemente, ligeiramente. **~ness** *n* leveza *f*
lighten[1] /'laɪtn/ *vt/i* iluminar(-se); (*make brighter*) clarear
lighten[2] /'laɪtn/ *vt/i* (*load etc*) aligeirar(-se), tornar mais leve
lighter /'laɪtə(r)/ *n* isqueiro *m*
lighthouse /'laɪthaʊs/ *n* farol *m*

lighting /'laɪtɪŋ/ *n* iluminação *f*
lightning /'laɪtnɪŋ/ *n* relâmpago *m*; (*thunderbolt*) raio *m* □ *a* muito rápido. **like ~** como um relâmpago
lightweight /'laɪtweɪt/ *a* leve
like[1] /laɪk/ *a* semelhante (a), parecido (com) □ *prep* como □ *conj* (*colloq*) como □ *n* igual *m*, coisa *f* parecida. **~-minded** *a* da mesma opinião. **the ~s of you** gente como você(s).
like[2] /laɪk/ *vt* gostar (de). **~s** *npl* gostos *mpl*. **I would ~** gostaria (de), queria. **if you ~** se quiser. **would you ~?** gostaria?, queria? **~able** *a* simpático
like|ly /'laɪklɪ/ *a* (-ier, -iest) provável □ *adv* provavelmente. **he is ~ly to come** é provável que ele venha. **not ~ly!** (*colloq*) nem morto, nem por sonhos. **~lihood** *n* probabilidade *f*
liken /'laɪkn/ *vt* comparar (**to** com)
likeness /'laɪknɪs/ *n* semelhança *f*
likewise /'laɪkwaɪz/ *adv* também; (*in the same way*) da mesma maneira
liking /'laɪkɪŋ/ *n* gosto *m*, inclinação *f*; (*for person*) afeição *f*. **take a ~ to** (*thing*) tomar gosto por; (*person*) simpatizar com
lilac /'laɪlək/ *n* lilás *m* □ *a* lilás *invar*
lily /'lɪlɪ/ *n* lírio *m*, lis *m*. **~ of the valley** lírio *m* do vale
limb /lɪm/ *n* membro *m*
limber /'lɪmbə(r)/ *vi* **~ up** fazer exercícios para desenferrujar (*colloq*)
lime[1] /laɪm/ *n* cal *f*
lime[2] /laɪm/ *n* (*fruit*) limão *m*
lime[3] /laɪm/ *n* **~(-tree)** tília *f*
limelight /'laɪmlaɪt/ *n* **be in the ~** estar em evidência
limerick /'lɪmərɪk/ *n* poema *m* humorístico (*de cinco versos*)
limit /'lɪmɪt/ *n* limite *m* □ *vt* limitar. **~ation** /-'teɪʃn/ *n* limitação *f*. **~ed company** sociedade *f* anônima, (*P*) anónima de responsabilidade limitada
limousine /'lɪməzi:n/ *n* limusine *f*
limp[1] /lɪmp/ *vi* mancar, coxear □ *n* **have a ~** coxear
limp[2] /lɪmp/ *a* (-er, -est) mole, frouxo
line[1] /laɪn/ *n* linha *f*; (*string*) fio *m*; (*rope*) corda *f*; (*row*) fila *f*; (*of poem*) verso *m*; (*wrinkle*) ruga *f*; (*of business*) ramo *m*; (*of goods*) linha *f*; (*Amer: queue*) fila *f*, (*P*) bicha *f* □ *vt* marcar com linhas; (*streets etc*) ladear, enfileirar-se ao longo de. **~d paper** papel *m* pautado. **in ~ with** de acordo com. **~ up** alinhar(-se), enfileirar(-se); (*in queue*) pôr(-se) em fila, (*P*) bicha. **~-up** *n* (*players*) formação *f*
line[2] /laɪn/ *vt* (*garment*) forrar (**with** de)
lineage /'lɪnɪɪdʒ/ *n* linhagem *f*
linear /'lɪnɪə(r)/ *a* linear
linen /'lɪnɪn/ *n* (*sheets etc*) roupa *f* (branca) de cama; (*material*) linho *m*
liner /'laɪnə(r)/ *n* navio *m* de linha regular, (*P*) paquete *m*
linesman /'laɪnzmən/ *n* (*football, tennis*) juiz *m* de linha
linger /'lɪŋgə(r)/ *vi* demorar-se, deixar-se ficar; (*of smells etc*) persistir
lingerie /'lænʒərɪ/ *n* roupa *f* de baixo (de senhora), lingerie *f*
linguist /'lɪŋgwɪst/ *n* lingüista *mf*, (*P*) linguista *mf*
linguistic /lɪŋ'gwɪstɪk/ *a* lingüístico, (*P*) linguístico. **~s** *n* lingüística *f*, (*P*) linguística *f*
lining /'laɪnɪŋ/ *n* forro *m*
link /lɪŋk/ *n* laço *m*; (*of chain; fig*) elo *m* □ *vt* unir, ligar; (*relate*) ligar; (*arm*) enfiar. **~ up** (*of roads*) juntar-se (**with** a). **~age** *n* ligação *f*
lino, linoleum /'laɪnəʊ, lɪ'nəʊlɪəm/ *n* linóleo *m*
lint /lɪnt/ *n* (*med*) curativo *m* de fibra de algodão; (*fluff*) cotão *m*
lion /'laɪən/ *n* leão *m*. **~ess** *n* leoa *f*
lip /lɪp/ *n* lábio *m*, beiço *m*; (*edge*) borda *f*; (*of jug etc*) bico *m*. **~-read** *vt/i* entender pelos movimentos dos lábios. **pay ~- service to** fingir pena, admiração etc
lipstick /'lɪpstɪk/ *n* batom *m*, (*P*) bâton *m*
liquefy /'lɪkwɪfaɪ/ *vt/i* liquefazer(-se)
liqueur /lɪ'kjʊə(r)/ *n* licor *m*
liquid /'lɪkwɪd/ *n* & *a* líquido (*m*). **~ize** *vt* liqüidificar, (*P*) liquidificar. **~izer** *n* liqüidificador *m*, (*P*) liquidificador *m*
liquidat|e /'lɪkwɪdeɪt/ *vt* liquidar. **~ion** /-'deɪʃn/ *n* liquidação *f*
liquor /'lɪkə(r)/ *n* bebida *f* alcoólica
liquorice /'lɪkərɪs/ *n* alcaçuz *m*
Lisbon /'lɪzbən/ *n* Lisboa *f*
lisp /lɪsp/ *n* ceceio *m* □ *vi* cecear
list[1] /lɪst/ *n* lista *f* □ *vt* fazer uma lista de; (*enter*) pôr na lista
list[2] /lɪst/ *vi* (*of ship*) adernar □ *n* adernamento *m*
listen /'lɪsn/ *vi* escutar, prestar atenção. **~ to, ~ in (to)** escutar, pôr-se à escuta. **~er** *n* ouvinte *mf*
listless /'lɪstlɪs/ *a* sem energia, apático
lit /lɪt/ *see* **light**[1]
literal /'lɪtərəl/ *a* literal. **~ly** *adv* literalmente
litera|te /'lɪtərət/ *a* alfabetizado. **~cy** *n* alfabetização *f*, instrução *f*
literature /'lɪtrətʃə(r)/ *n* literatura *f*; (*colloq: leaflets etc*) folhetos *mpl*
lithe /laɪð/ *a* ágil, flexível
litigation /lɪtɪ'geɪʃn/ *n* litígio *m*
litre /'li:tə(r)/ *n* litro *m*
litter /'lɪtə(r)/ *n* lixo *m*; (*animals*) ninhada *f* □ *vt* cobrir de lixo. **~ed**

with coberto de. ~-**bin** *n* lata *f*, (*P*) caixote *m* do lixo
little /'lɪtl/ *a* pequeno; (*not much*) pouco □ *n* pouco *m* □ *adv* pouco, mal, nem. **a ~** um pouco (de). **he ~ knows** ele mal/nem sabe. **~ by ~** pouco a pouco
liturgy /'lɪtədʒɪ/ *n* liturgia *f*
live[1] /laɪv/ *a* vivo; (*wire*) eletrizado; (*broadcast*) em direto, (*P*) directo, ao vivo
live[2] /lɪv/ *vt/i* viver; (*reside*) habitar, morar, viver. **~ down** fazer esquecer. **~ it up** cair na farra. **~ on** viver de; (*continue*) continuar a viver. **~ up to** mostrar-se à altura de; (*fulfil*) cumprir
livelihood /'laɪvlɪhʊd/ *n* modo *m* de vida
livel|y /'laɪvlɪ/ *a* (**-ier, -iest**) vivo, animado. **~iness** *n* vivacidade *f*, animação *f*
liven /'laɪvn/ *vt/i* **~ up** animar(-se)
liver /'lɪvə(r)/ *n* fígado *m*
livery /'lɪvərɪ/ *n* libré *f*
livestock /'laɪvstɒk/ *n* gado *m*
livid /'lɪvɪd/ *a* lívido; (*colloq: furious*) furioso
living /'lɪvɪŋ/ *a* vivo □ *n* vida *f*; (*livelihood*) modo de vida *m*, sustento *m*. **earn** *or* **make a ~** ganhar a vida. **standard of ~** nível *m* de vida. **~-room** *n* sala *f* de estar
lizard /'lɪzəd/ *n* lagarto *m*
llama /'la:mə/ *n* lama *m*
load /ləʊd/ *n* carga *f*; (*of lorry, ship*) carga *f*, carregamento *m*; (*weight, strain*) peso *m*. **~s of** (*colloq*) montes de (*colloq*) □ *vt* carregar. **~ed** *a* (*dice*) viciado; (*sl: rich*) cheio da nota
loaf[1] /ləʊf/ *n* (*pl* **loaves**) pão *m*
loaf[2] /ləʊf/ *vi* vadiar. **~er** *n* preguiçoso *m*, vagabundo *m*
loan /ləʊn/ *n* empréstimo *m* □ *vt* emprestar. **on ~** emprestado
loath /ləʊθ/ *a* sem vontade de, pouco disposto a, relutante em
loath|e /ləʊð/ *vt* detestar. **~ing** *n* repugnância *f*, aversão *f*. **~some** *a* repugnante
lobby /'lɒbɪ/ *n* entrada *f*, vestíbulo *m*; (*pol*) lobby *m*, grupo *m* de pressão □ *vt* fazer pressão sobre
lobe /ləʊb/ *n* lóbulo *m*
lobster /'lɒbstə(r)/ *n* lagosta *f*
local /'ləʊkl/ *a* local; (*shops etc*) do bairro □ *n* pessoa *f* do lugar; (*colloq: pub*) taberna *f*/pub *m* do bairro. **~ government** administração *f* municipal. **~ly** *adv* localmente; (*nearby*) na vizinhança
locale /ləʊ'ka:l/ *n* local *m*
locality /ləʊ'kælətɪ/ *n* localidade *f*; (*position*) lugar *m*
localized /'ləʊkəlaɪzd/ *a* localizado
locat|e /ləʊ'keɪt/ *vt* localizar; (*situate*) situar. **~ion** /-ʃn/ *n* localização *f*. **on ~ion** (*cinema*) em external, (*P*) no exterior
lock[1] /lɒk/ *n* (*hair*) mecha *f* de cabelo
lock[2] /lɒk/ *n* (*on door etc*) fecho *m*, fechadura *f*; (*on canal*) comporta *f* □ *vt/i* fechar à chave; (*auto: wheels*) imobilizar(-se). **~ in** fechar à chave, encerrar. **~ out** fechar a porta para, deixar na rua. **~-out** *n* lockout *m*. **~ up** fechar a casa. **under ~ and key** a sete chaves
locker /'lɒkə(r)/ *n* compartimento *m* com chave
locket /'lɒkɪt/ *n* medalhão *m*
locksmith /'lɒksmɪθ/ *n* serralheiro *m*, chaveiro *m*
locomotion /ləʊkə'məʊʃn/ *n* locomoção *f*
locomotive /'ləʊkəməʊtɪv/ *n* locomotiva *f*
locum /'ləʊkəm/ *n* (*med*) substituto *m*
locust /'ləʊkəst/ *n* gafanhoto *m*
lodge /lɒdʒ/ *n* casa *f* do guarda numa propriedade; (*of porter*) portaria *f* □ *vt* alojar; (*money*) depositar. **~ a complaint** apresentar uma queixa □ *vi* estar alojado (**with** em casa de); (*become fixed*) alojar-se. **~r** /-ə(r)/ *n* hóspede *mf*
lodgings /'lɒdʒɪŋz/ *n* quarto *m* mobiliado; (*flat*) apartamento *m*
loft /lɒft/ *n* sótão *m*
lofty /'lɒftɪ/ *a* (**-ier, -iest**) elevado; (*haughty*) altivo
log /lɒg/ *n* tronco *m*, toro *m*. **~(-book)** *n* (*naut*) diário *m* de bordo; (*aviat*) diario *m* de vôo. **sleep like a ~** dormir como uma pedra □ *vt* (*pt* **logged**) (*naut/aviat*) lançar no diário de bordo. **~ off** acabar de usar. **~ on** começar a usar
loggerheads /'lɒgəhedz/ *npl* **at ~** às turras (**with** com)
logic /'lɒdʒɪk/ *a* lógico. **~al** *a* lógico. **~ally** *adv* logicamente
logistics /lə'dʒɪstɪks/ *n* logística *f*
logo /'ləʊgəʊ/ *n* (*pl* **-os**) (*colloq*) emblema *m*, logotipo *m*, (*P*) logótipo *m*
loin /lɔɪn/ *n* (*culin*) lombo *m*, alcatra *f*
loiter /'lɔɪtə(r)/ *vi* andar vagarosamente; (*stand about*) rondar
loll /lɒl/ *vi* refestelar-se
loll|ipop /'lɒlɪpɒp/ *n* pirulito *m*, (*P*) chupa-chupa *m*. **~y** *n* (*colloq*) pirulito *m*, (*P*) chupa-chupa *m*; (*sl: money*) grana *f*
London /'lʌndən/ *n* Londres
lone /ləʊn/ *a* solitário. **~r** /-ə(r)/ *n* solitário *m*. **~some** *a* solitário
lonely /'ləʊnlɪ/ *a* (**-ier, -iest**) solitário; (*person*) só, solitário

long[1] /lɒŋ/ *a* (-er, -est) longo, comprido □ *adv* muito tempo, longamente. **how ~ is...?** (*in size*) qual é o comprimento de...? **how ~?** (*in time*) quanto tempo? **he will not be ~** ele não vai demorar. **a ~ time** muito tempo. **a ~ way** longe. **as** *or* **so ~ as** contanto que, desde que. **~ ago** há muito tempo. **before ~** (*future*) daqui a pouco, dentro em pouco; (*past*) pouco (tempo) depois. **in the ~ run** no fim de contas. **~ before** muito (tempo) antes. **~-distance** *a* (*flight*) de longa distância; (*phone call*) interurbano. **~ face** cara *f* triste. **~ jump** salto *m* em distância. **~-playing record** LP *m*. **~-range** *a* de longo alcance; (*forecast*) a longo prazo. **~-sighted** *a* que emxerga mal a distância. **~-standing** *a* de longa data. **~-suffering** *a* com paciência exemplar/de santo. **~-term** *a* a longo prazo. **~ wave** ondas *fpl* longas. **~-winded** *a* prolixo. **so ~!** (*colloq*) até logo!

long[2] /lɒŋ/ *vi* **~ for** ansiar por, ter grande desejo de. **~ to** desejar. **~ing** *n* desejo *m* ardente

longevity /lɒn'dʒevətɪ/ *n* longevidade *f*, vida *f* longa

longhand /'lɒŋhænd/ *n* escrita *f* à mão

longitude /'lɒndʒɪtju:d/ *n* longitude *f*

loo /lu:/ *n* (*colloq*) banheiro *m*, (*P*) casa *f* de banho

look /lʊk/ *vt/i* olhar; (*seem*) parecer □ *n* olhar *m*; (*appearance*) ar *m*, aspecto *m*. **(good) ~s** beleza *f*. **~ after** tomar conta de, olhar por. **~ at** olhar para. **~ down on** desprezar. **~ for** procurar. **~ forward to** aguardar com impaciência. **~ in on** visitar. **~ into** examinar, investigar. **~ like** parecer-se com, ter ar de. **~ on** (*as spectator*) ver, assistir; (*regard as*) considerar. **~ out** ter cautela. **~ out for** procurar; (*watch*) estar à espreita de. **~-out** *n* (*mil*) posto *m* de observação; (*watcher*) vigia *m*. **~ round** olhar em redor. **~ up** (*word*) procurar; (*visit*) ir ver. **~ up to** respeitar

loom[1] /lu:m/ *n* tear *m*

loom[2] /lu:m/ *vi* surgir indistintamente; (*fig*) ameaçar

loony /'lu:nɪ/ *n* & *a* (*sl*) maluco (*m*), doido (*m*)

loop /lu:p/ *n* laçada *f*; (*curve*) volta *f*, arco *m*; (*aviat*) loop *m* □ *vt* dar uma laçada

loophole /'lu:phəʊl/ *n* (*in rule*) saída *f*, furo *m*

loose /lu:s/ *a* (-er, -est) (*knot etc*) frouxo; (*page etc*) solto; (*clothes*) folgado; (*not packed*) a granel; (*inexact*) vago; (*morals*) dissoluto, imoral. **at a ~ end** sem saber o que fazer, sem ocupação definida. **break ~** soltar-se. **~ly** *adv* sem apertar; (*roughly*) vagamente

loosen /'lu:sn/ *vt* (*slacken*) soltar, desapertar; (*untie*) desfazer, desatar

loot /lu:t/ *n* saque *m* □ *vt* pilhar, saquear. **~er** *n* assaltante *mf*. **~ing** *n* pilhagem *f*, saque *m*

lop /lɒp/ *vt* (*pt* **lopped**) **~ off** cortar, podar

lop-sided /lɒp'saɪdɪd/ *a* torto, inclinado para um lado

lord /lɔ:d/ *n* senhor *m*; (*title*) lord *m*. **the L~** o Senhor. **the L~'s Prayer** o Pai-Nosso. **(good) L~!** meu Deus! **~ly** *a* magnífico, nobre; (*haughty*) altivo, arrogante

lorry /'lɒrɪ/ *n* camião *m*, caminhão *m*

lose /lu:z/ *vt/i* (*pt* **lost**) perder. **get lost** perder-se. **get lost** (*sl*) vai passear! (*colloq*). **~r** /-ə(r)/ *n* perdedor *m*

loss /lɒs/ *n* perda *f*. **be at a ~** estar perplexo. **at a ~ for words** sem saber o que dizer

lost /lɒst/ *see* **lose** □ *a* perdido. **~ property** objetos *mpl*, (*P*) objectos *mpl* perdidos (e achados)

lot[1] /lɒt/ *n* sorte *f*; (*at auction, land*) lote *m*. **draw ~s** tirar à sorte

lot[2] /lɒt/ *n* **the ~** tudo; (*people*) todos *mpl*. **a ~ (of)**, **~s (of)** (*colloq*) uma porção (de) (*colloq*). **quite a ~ (of)** (*colloq*) uma boa porção (de) (*colloq*)

lotion /'ləʊʃn/ *n* loção *f*

lottery /'lɒtərɪ/ *n* loteria *f*, (*P*) lotaria *f*

loud /laʊd/ *a* (-er, -est) alto, barulhento, ruidoso; (*of colours*) berrante □ *adv* alto. **~hailer** *n* megafone *m*. **out ~** em voz alta. **~ly** *adv* alto

loudspeaker /laʊd'spi:kə(r)/ *n* alto-falante *m*

lounge /laʊndʒ/ *vi* recostar-se preguiçosamente □ *n* sala *f*, salão *m*

louse /laʊs/ *n* (*pl* **lice**) piolho *m*

lousy /'laʊzɪ/ *a* (-ier, -iest) piolhento; (*sl: very bad*) péssimo

lout /laʊt/ *n* pessoa *f* grosseira, arruaceiro *m*

lovable /'lʌvəbl/ *a* amoroso, adorável

love /lʌv/ *n* amor *m*; (*tennis*) zero *m*, nada *m* □ *vt* amar, estar apaixonado por; (*like greatly*) gostar muito de. **in ~** apaixonado (**with** por). **~ affair** aventura *f* amorosa. **she sends you her ~** ela lhe manda lembranças

lovely /'lʌvlɪ/ *a* (-ier, -iest) lindo; (*colloq: delightful*) encantador, delicioso

lover /'lʌvə(r)/ *n* namorado *m*, apaixonado *m*; (*illicit*) amante *m*; (*devotee*) admirador *m*, apreciador *m*

lovesick /'lʌvsɪk/ *a* perdido de amor

loving /'lʌvɪŋ/ *a* amoroso, terno, extremoso

low /ləʊ/ *a* (-er, -est) baixo □ *adv* baixo □ *n* baixa *f*; (*low pressure*) área de baixa pressão *f*. **~-cut** *a* decotado. **~-down** *a* baixo, reles □ *n* (*colloq*) a verdade autêntica, (*P*) a verdade nua e crua. **~-fat** *a* de baixo teor de gordura. **~-key** *a* (*fig*) moderado, discreto

lower /ˈləʊə(r)/ *a* & *adv see* **low** □ *vt* baixar. **~ o.s.** (re)baixar-se (to a)

lowlands /ˈləʊləndz/ *npl* planície(s) *f* (*pl*)

lowly /ˈləʊlɪ/ *a* (-ier, -iest) humilde, modesto

loyal /ˈlɔɪəl/ *a* leal. **~ly** *adv* lealmente. **~ty** *n* lealdade *f*

lozenge /ˈlɒzɪndʒ/ *n* (*shape*) losango *m*; (*tablet*) pastilha *f*

LP *abbr see* **long-playing record**

lubric|ate /ˈlu:brɪkeɪt/ *vt* lubrificar. **~ant** *n* lubrificante *m*. **~ation** /-ˈkeɪ/ *n* lubrificação *f*

lucid /ˈlu:sɪd/ *a* lúcido. **~ity** /lu:ˈsɪdətɪ/ *n* lucidez *f*

luck /lʌk/ *n* sorte *f*. **bad ~** pouca sorte *f*. **for ~** para dar sorte. **good ~!**

luck|y /ˈlʌkɪ/ *a* (-ier, -iest) sortudo, com sorte; (*event etc*) feliz; (*number etc*) que dá sorte. **~ily** *adv* felizmente

lucrative /ˈlu:krətɪv/ *a* lucrativo, rentável

ludicrous /ˈlu:dɪkrəs/ *a* ridículo, absurdo

lug /lʌg/ *vt* (*pt* **lugged**) arrstar

luggage /ˈlʌgɪdʒ/ *n* bagagem *f*. **~-rack** *n* porta-bagagem *m*. **~-van** *n* furgão *m*

lukewarm /ˈlu:kwɔ:m/ *a* morno; (*fig*) sem entusiasmo, indiferente

lull /lʌl/ *vt* (*send to sleep*) embalar; (*suspicions*) acalmar □ *n* calmarica *f*, (*P*) acalmia *f*

lullaby /ˈlʌləbaɪ/ *n* canção *f* de embalar

lumbago /lʌmˈbeɪgəʊ/ *n* lumbago *m*

lumber /ˈlʌmbə(r)/ *n* trastes *mpl* velhos; (*wood*) madeira *f* cortada □ *vt* **~ sb with**

luminous /ˈlu:mɪnəs/ *a* luminoso

lump /lʌmp/ *n* bocado *m*; (*swelling*) caroço *m*; (*in the throat*) nó *m*; (*in liquid*) grumo *m*; (*of sugar*) torrão *m* □ *vt* **~ together** amontoar, juntar indiscriminadamente. **~ sum** quantia *f* total; (*payment*) pagamento *m* de uma vez. **~y** *a* grumoso, encaroçado

lunacy /ˈlu:nəsɪ/ *n* loucura *f*

lunar /ˈlu:nə(r)/ *a* lunar

lunatic /ˈlu:nətɪk/ *n* lunático *m*. **~ asylum** manicômio *m*, (*P*) manicómio *m*

lunch /lʌntʃ/ *n* almoço *m* □ *vi* almoçar. **~-time** *n* hora *f* do almoço

luncheon /ˈlʌntʃən/ *n* (*formal*) almoço *m*. **~ meat** carne *f* enlatada, (*P*) 'merenda' *f*. **~ voucher** senha *f* de almoço

lung /lʌŋ/ *n* pulmão *m*

lunge /lʌndʒ/ *n* mergulho *m*, movimento *m* súbito para a frente; (*thrust*) arremetida *f* □ *vi* mergulhar, arremessar-se (at para cima de, contra)

lurch[1] /lɜ:tʃ/ *n* **leave sb in the ~** deixar alg em apuros

lurch[2] /lɜ:tʃ/ *vi* ir aos ziguezagues, dar guinadas; (*stagger*) cambalear

lure /lʊə(r)/ *vt* atrair, tentar □ *n* chamariz *m*, engodo *m*. **the ~ of the sea** a atração, (*P*) atracção do mar

lurid /ˈlʊərɪd/ *a* berrante; (*fig: sensational*) sensacional; (*fig: shocking*) horrífico

lurk /lɜ:k/ *vi* esconder-se à espreita; (*prowl*) rondar; (*be latent*) estar latente

luscious /ˈlʌʃəs/ *a* apetitoso; (*voluptuous*) desejável

lush /lʌʃ/ *a* viçoso, luxuriante

Lusitanian /lusɪˈteɪmɪən/ *a* & *n* lusitano (*m*)

lust /lʌst/ *n* luxúria *f*, sensualidade *f*; (*fig*) cobiça *f*, desejo *m* ardente □ *vi* **~ after** cobiçar, desejar ardentemente. **~ful** *a* sensual

lustre /ˈlʌstə(r)/ *n* lustre *m*; (*fig*) prestígio *m*

lusty /ˈlʌstɪ/ *a* (-ier, -iest) robusto, vigoroso

lute /lu:t/ *n* alaúde *m*

Luxemburg /ˈlʌksəmbɜ:g/ *n* Luxemburgo *m*

luxuriant /lʌgˈʒʊərɪənt/ *a* luxuriante

luxurious /lʌgˈʒʊərɪəs/ *a* luxuoso

luxury /ˈlʌkʃərɪ/ *n* luxo *m* □ *a* de luxo

lying /ˈlaɪɪŋ/ *see* **lie**[1], **lie**[2]

lynch /lɪntʃ/ *vt* linchar

lynx /lɪŋks/ *n* lince *m*

lyre /ˈlaɪə(r)/ *n* lira *f*

lyric /ˈlɪrɪk/ *a* lírico. **~s** *npl* (*mus*) letra *f*. **~al** *a* lírico

M

MA *abbr see* **Master of Arts**

mac /mæk/ *n* (*colloq*) impermeável *m*, gabardine *f*

macabre /məˈkɑ:brə/ *a* macabro

macaroni /mækəˈrəʊnɪ/ *n* macarrão *m*

macaroon /mækəˈru:n/ *n* bolinho *m* seco de amêndoa ralada

mace[1] /meɪs/ *n* (*staff*) maça *f*

mace[2] /meɪs/ *n* (*spice*) macis *m*

machination /mækɪ'neɪʃn/ *n* maquinação *f*
machine /mə'ʃi:n/ *n* máquina *f* □ *vt* fazer à máquina; (*sewing*) coser à máquina. ~**-gun** *n* metralhadora *f*. ~**-readable** *a* em linguagem de máquina. ~ **tool** máquina-ferramenta *f*
machinery /mə'ʃi:nərɪ/ *n* maquinaria *f*; (*working parts; fig*) mecanismo *m*
machinist /mə'ʃi:nɪst/ *n* maquinista *m*
macho /'mætʃəʊ/ *a* machista
mackerel /'mækrəl/ *n* (*pl invar*) cavala *f*
mackintosh /'mækɪntɒʃ/ *n* impermeável *m*, gabardine *f*
mad /mæd/ *a* (**madder, maddest**) doido, louco; (*dog*) raivoso; (*colloq: angry*) furioso (*colloq*). **be** ~ **about** ser doido por. **like** ~ como (um) doido. ~**ly** *adv* loucamente; (*frantically*) enlouquecidamente. ~**ness** *n* loucura *f*
Madagascar /mædə'gæskə(r)/ *n* Madagáscar *m*
madam /'mædəm/ *n* senhora *f*. **no,** ~ não senhora
madden /'mædn/ *vt* endoidecer, enlouquecer. **it's** ~**ing** é de enlouquecer
made /meɪd/ *see* **make**. ~ **to measure** feito sob medida
Madeira /mə'dɪərə/ *n* Madeira *f*; (*wine*) Madeira *m*
madman /'mædmən/ *n* (*pl* **-men**) doido *m*
madrigal /'mædrɪgl/ *n* madrigal *m*
Mafia /'mæfɪə/ *n* Máfia *f*
magazine /mægə'zi:n/ *n* revista *f*, magazine *m*; (*of gun*) carregador *m*
magenta /mə'dʒentə/ *a* & *n* magenta (*m*), carmin (*m*)
maggot /'mægət/ *n* larva *f*. ~**y** *a* bichento
Magi /'meɪdʒaɪ/ *npl* **the** ~ os Reis *mpl* Magos
magic /'mædʒɪk/ *n* magia *f* □ *a* mágico. ~**al** *a* mágico
magician /mə'dʒɪʃn/ *n* (*conjuror*) prestidigitador *m*; (*wizard*) feiticeiro *m*
magistrate /'mædʒɪstreɪt/ *n* magistrado *m*
magnanim|ous /mæg'nænɪməs/ *a* magnânimo. ~**ity** /-ə'nɪmətɪ/ *n* magnanimidade *f*
magnate /'mægneɪt/ *n* magnata *m*
magnet /'mægnɪt/ *n* ímã *m*, (*P*) íman *m*. ~**ic** /-'netɪk/ *a* magnético. ~**ism** /-ɪzəm/ *n* magnetismo *m*. ~**ize** *vt* magnetizar
magnificen|t /mæg'nɪfɪsnt/ *a* magnífico. ~**ce** *n* magnificência *f*
magnif|y /'mægnɪfaɪ/ *vt* aumentar; (*sound*) ampliar, amplificar. ~**ication** /-ɪ'keɪʃn/ *n* aumento *m*, ampliação *f*. ~**ying glass** lupa *f*
magnitude /'mægnɪtju:d/ *n* magnitude *f*
magpie /'mægpaɪ/ *n* pega *f*
mahogany /mə'hɒgənɪ/ *n* mogno *m*
maid /meɪd/ *n* criada *f*, empregada *f*. **old** ~ solteirona *f*
maiden /'meɪdn/ *n* (*old use*) donzela *f* □ *a* (*aunt*) solteira; (*speech, voyage*) inaugural. ~ **name** nome *m* de solteira
mail[1] /meɪl/ *n* correio *m*; (*letters*) correio *m*, correspondência *f* □ *a* postal □ *vt* postar, pôr no correio; (*send by mail*) mandar pelo correio. ~**-bag** *n* mala *f* postal. ~**-box** *n* (*Amer*) caixa *f* do correio. ~**ing-list** *n* lista *f* de endereços. ~ **order** *n* encomenda *f* por correspondência, (*P*) por correio
mail[2] /meɪl/ *n* (*armour*) cota *f* de malha
mailman /'meɪlmæn/ *n* (*pl* **-men**) (*Amer*) carteiro *m*
maim /meɪm/ *vt* mutilar, aleijar
main[1] /meɪn/ *a* principal □ *n* **in the** ~ em geral, essencialmente. ~ **road** estrada *f* principal. ~**ly** *adv* principalmente, sobretudo
main[2] /meɪn/ *n* **(water/gas)** ~ cano *m* de água/gás. **the** ~**s** (*electr*) a rede *f* elétrica
mainland /'meɪnlənd/ *n* continente *m*
mainstay /'meɪnsteɪ/ *n* (*fig*) esteio *m*
mainstream /'meɪnstri:m/ *n* tendência *f* dominante, linha *f* principal
maintain /meɪn'teɪn/ *vt* manter, sustentar; (*rights*) defender, manter
maintenance /'meɪntənəns/ *n* (*care, continuation*) manutenção *f*; (*allowance*) pensão *f*
maisonette /meɪzə'net/ *n* dúplex *m*
maize /meɪz/ *n* milho *m*
majestic /mə'dʒestɪk/ *a* majestoso. ~**ally** *adv* majestosamente
majesty /'mædʒəstɪ/ *n* majestade *f*
major /'meɪdʒə(r)/ *a* maior; (*very important*) de vulto □ *n* major *m* □ *vi* ~ **in** (*Amer: univ*) especializar-se em. ~ **road** estrada *f* principal
Majorca /mə'dʒɔ:kə/ *n* Maiorca *f*
majority /mə'dʒɒrətɪ/ *n* maioria *f*; (*age*) maioridade *f* □ *a* majoritário, (*P*) maioritário. **the** ~ **of people** a maioria *or* a maior parte das pessoas
make /meɪk/ *vt/i* (*pt* **made**) fazer; (*decision*) tomar; (*destination*) chegar a; (*cause to*) fazer (+ *inf*) *or* (com) que (+ *subj*). **you** ~ **me angry** você me aborrece □ *n* (*brand*) marca *f*. **on the** ~ (*sl*) oportunista. **be made of** ser feito de. ~ **o.s. at home** estar à vontade/

como em sua casa. ~ **it** chegar; (*succeed*) triunfar. **I ~ it two o'clock** são duas pelo meu relógio. ~ **as if to** fazer *ou* fingir que. ~ **believe** fingir. **~-believe** *a* fingido □ *n* fantasia *f*. ~ **do with** arranjar-se com, contentar-se com. ~ **for** dirigir-se para; (*contribute to*) ajudar a. ~ **good** *vi* triunfar □ *vt* compensar; (*repair*) reparar. ~ **off** fugir (**with** com). ~ **out** avistar, distinguir; (*understand*) entender; (*claim*) pretender; (*a cheque*) passar, emitir. ~ **over** ceder, transferir. ~ **up** *vt* fazer, compor; (*story*) inventar; (*deficit*) suprir □ *vi* fazer as pazes. ~ **up (one's face)** maquilar-se, (*P*) maquilhar-se. **~-up** *n* maquilagem *f*, (*P*) maquilhagem *f*; (*of object*) composição *f*; (*psych*) maneira *f* de ser, natureza *f*. ~ **up for** compensar. ~ **up one's mind** decidir-se

maker /ˈmeɪkə(r)/ *n* fabricante *mf*

makeshift /ˈmeɪkʃɪft/ *n* solução *f* temporária □ *a* provisório

making /ˈmeɪkɪŋ/ *n* **be the ~ of** fazer, ser a causa do sucesso de. **in the ~** em formação. **he has the ~s of** ele tem as qualidades essenciais de

maladjusted /mæləˈdʒʌstɪd/ *a* desajustado, inadaptado

maladministration /mælədmɪnɪˈstreɪʃn/ *n* mau governo *m*, má gestão *f*

malaise /mæˈleɪz/ *n* mal-estar *m*

malaria /məˈleərɪə/ *n* malária *f*

Malay /məˈleɪ/ *a* & *n* malaio (*m*). **~sia** /-ʒə/ *n* Malásia *f*

male /meɪl/ *a* (*voice, sex*) masculino; (*biol, techn*) macho □ *n* (*human*) homem *m*, indivíduo *m* do sexo masculino; (*arrival*) macho *m*

malevolen|t /məˈlevələnt/ *a* malévolo. **~ce** *n* malevolência *f*, má vontade *f*

malform|ation /mælfɔːˈmeɪʃn/ *n* malformação *f*, deformidade *f*. **~ed** *a* deformado

malfunction /mælˈfʌŋkʃn/ *n* mau funcionamento *m* □ *vi* funcionar mal

malice /ˈmælɪs/ *n* maldade *f*, malícia *f*. **bear sb ~** guardar rancor a alg

malicious /məˈlɪʃəs/ *a* maldoso, malicioso. **~ly** *adv* maldosamente, maliciosamente

malign /məˈlaɪn/ *vt* caluniar, difamar

malignan|t /məˈlɪgnənt/ *a* (*tumour*) maligno; (*malevolent*) malévolo. **~cy** *n* malignidade *f*; malevolência *f*

malinger /məˈlɪŋgə(r)/ *vi* fingir-se doente. **~er** *n* pessoa *f* que se finge doente

mallet /ˈmælɪt/ *n* maço *m*

malnutrition /mælnjuːˈtrɪʃn/ *n* desnutrição *f*, subalimentação *f*

malpractice /mælˈpræktɪs/ *n* abuso *m*; (*incompetence*) incompetência *f* profissional, negligência *f*

malt /mɔːlt/ *n* malte *m*

Malt|a /ˈmɔːltə/ *n* Malta *f*. **~ese** /-ˈtiːz/ *a* & *n* maltês (*m*)

maltreat /mælˈtriːt/ *vt* maltratar. **~ment** *n* mau(s) trato(s) *m* (*pl*)

mammal /ˈmæml/ *n* mamífero *m*

mammoth /ˈmæməθ/ *n* mamute *m* □ *a* gigantesco, colossal

man /mæn/ *n* (*pl* **men**) homem *m*; (*in sports team*) jogador *m*; (*chess*) peça *f* □ *vt* (*pt* **manned**) prover de pessoal; (*mil*) guarnecer; (*naut*) guarnecer, equipar, tripular; (*be on duty at*) estar de serviço em. ~ **in the street** o homem da rua. **~-hour** *n* hora *f* de trabalho per capita, homem-hora *f*. **~-hunt** *n* caça *f* ao homem. **~-made** *a* artificial. ~ **to man** de homem para homem

manage /ˈmænɪdʒ/ *vt* (*household*) governar; (*tool*) manejar; (*boat, affair, crowd*) manobrar; (*shop*) dirigir, gerir. **I could ~ another drink** (*colloq*) até que tomaria mais um drinque (*colloq*) □ *vi* arranjar-se. ~ **to do** conseguir fazer. **~able** *a* manejável; (*easily controlled*) controlável. **~ment** *n* gerência *f*, direção *f*, (*P*) direcção *f*. **managing director** diretor *m*, (*P*) director *m* geral

manager /ˈmænɪdʒə(r)/ *n* diretor *m*, (*P*) director *m*; (*of bank, shop*) gerente *m*; (*of actor*) empresário *m*; (*sport*) treinador *m*. **~ess** /-ˈres/ *n* diretora *f*, (*P*) directora *f*; gerente *f*. **~ial** /-ˈdʒɪərɪəl/*a* diretivo, (*P*) directivo, administrativo. **~ial staff** gestores *mpl*

mandarin /ˈmændərɪn/ *n* mandarim *m*. ~ **(orange)** mandarina *f*, tangerina *f*

mandate /ˈmændeɪt/ *n* mandato *m*

mandatory /ˈmændətrɪ/ *a* obrigatório

mane /meɪn/ *n* crina *f*; (*of lion*) juba *f*

mangle[1] /ˈmæŋgl/ *n* calandra *f* □ *vt* espremer (com a calandra)

mangle[2] /ˈmæŋgl/ *vt* (*mutilate*) mutilar, estropiar

mango /ˈmæŋgəʊ/ *n* (*pl* -**oes**) manga *f*

manhandle /ˈmænhændl/ *vt* mover à força de braço; (*treat roughly*) tratar com brutalidade

manhole /ˈmænhəʊl/ *n* poço *m* de inspeção, (*P*) inspecção

manhood /ˈmænhʊd/ *n* idade adulta *f*; (*quality*) virilidade *f*

mania /ˈmeɪnɪə/ *n* mania *f*. **~c** /-ɪæk/ *n* maníaco *m*

manicur|e /ˈmænɪkjʊə(r)/ *n* manicure *f* □ *vt* fazer. **~ist** *n* manicure *m*

manifest /'mænɪfest/ *a* manifes to □ *vt* manifestar. **~ation** /-'steɪʃn/ *n* manifestação *f*

manifesto /mænɪ'festəʊ/ *n* (*pl* -os) manifesto *m*

manipulat|e /mə'nɪpjʊleɪt/ *vt* manipular. **~ion** /'leɪʃn/ *n* manipulação *f*

mankind /mæn'kaɪnd/ *n* humanidade *f*, gênero *m*, (*P*) género *m* humano

manly /'mænlɪ/ *a* viril, másculo

manner /'mænə(r)/ *n* maneira *f*, modo *m*; (*attitude*) modo(s) *m* (*pl*); (*kind*) espécie *f*. **~s** maneiras *fpl*. **bad ~s** má-criação *f*, falta *f* de educação. **good ~s** (boa) educação *f*. **~ed** *a* afetado.

mannerism /'mænərɪzəm/ *n* maneirismo *m*

manoeuvre /mə'nu:və(r)/ *n* manobra *f* □ *vt/i* manobrar

manor /'mænə(r)/ *n* solar *m*

manpower /'mænpaʊə(r)/ *n* mão-de-obra *f*

mansion /'mænʃn/ *n* mansão *f*

manslaughter /'mænslɔ:tə(r)/ *n* homicídio *m* involuntário

mantelpiece /'mæntlpi:s/ *n* (*shelf*) consolo *m* da lareira, (*P*) prateleira *f* da chaminé

manual /'mænjʊəl/ *a* manual □ *n* manual *m*

manufacture /mænjʊ'fæktʃə(r)/ *vt* fabricar □ *n* fabrico *m*, fabricação *f*. **~r** /-ə(r)/ *n* fabricante *mf*

manure /mə'njʊə(r)/ *n* estrume *m*

manuscript /'mænjʊskrɪpt/ *n* manuscrito *m*

many /'menɪ/ *a* (**more, most**) muitos □ *n* muitos; (*many people*) muita gente *f*. **a great ~** muitíssimos. **~ a man/tear/***etc* muitos homens/muitas lágrimas/*etc*. **you may take as ~ as you want** você pode levar quantos quiser. **~ of us/them/you** muitos de nós/deles/de vocês. **how ~?** quantos? **one too ~** um a mais

map /mæp/ *n* mapa *m* □ *vt* (*pt* **mapped**) fazer mapa de. **~ out** planear em pormenor; (*route*) traçar

maple /'meɪpl/ *n* bordo *m*

mar /ma:(r)/ *vt* (*pt* **marred**) estragar; (*beauty*) desfigurar

marathon /'mærəθən/ *n* maratona *f*

marble /'ma:bl/ *n* mármore *m*; (*for game*) bola *f* de gude, (*P*) berlinde *m*

March /ma:tʃ/ *n* março *m*

march /ma:tʃ/ *vi* marchar □ *vt* **~ off** fazer marchar, conduzir à força. **he was ~ed off to prison** fizeram-no marchar para a prisão □ *n* marcha *f*. **~-past** *n* desfile *m* em revista militar

mare /meə(r)/ *n* égua *f*

margarine /ma:dʒə'ri:n/ *n* margarina *f*

margin /'ma:dʒɪn/ *n* margem *f*. **~al** *a* marginal. **~al seat** (*pol*) lugar *m* ganho com pequena maioria. **~ally** *adv* por uma pequena margem, muito pouco

marigold /'mærɪgəʊld/ *n* cravo-de-defunto *m*, (*P*) malmequer *m*

marijuana /mærɪ'wa:nə/ *n* maconha *f*

marina /mə'ri:nə/ *n* marina *f*

marinade /mærɪ'neɪd/ *n* vinha d'alho, escalabeche *m* □ *vt* pôr na vinha d'alho

marine /mə'ri:n/ *a* marinho; (*of ship, trade etc*) marítimo □ *n* (*shipping*) marinha *f*; (*sailor*) fuzileiro *m* naval

marionette /mærɪə'net/ *n* fantoche *m*, marionete *f*

marital /'mærɪtl/ *a* marital, conjugal, matrimonial. **~ status** estado *m* civil

maritime /'mærɪtaɪm/ *a* marítimo

mark[1] /ma:k/ *n* (*currency*) marco *m*

mark[2] /ma:k/ *n* marca *f*; (*trace*) marca *f*, sinal *m*; (*stain*) mancha *f*; (*schol*) nota *f*; (*target*) alvo *m* □ *vt* marcar; (*exam etc*) marcar, classificar. **~ out** marcar. **~ out for** escolher para, designar para. **~ time** marcar passo. **make one's ~** ganhar nome. **~er** *n* marcador *m*. **~ing** *n* marcas *fpl*, marcação *f*

marked /ma:kt/ *a* marcado. **~ly** /-ɪdlɪ/ *adv* manifestamente, visivelmente

market /'ma:kɪt/ *n* mercado *m* □ *vt* vender; (*launch*) comercializar, lançar. **~ garden** horta *f* de legumes para venda. **~-place** *n* mercado *m*. **~ research** pesquisa *f* de mercado. **on the ~** à venda. **~ing** *n* marketing *m*

marksman /'ma:ksmən/ *n* (*pl* **-men**) atirador *m* especial

marmalade /'ma:məleɪd/ *n* compota *f* de laranja

maroon /mə'ru:n/ *a & n* bordô (*m*), (*P*) bordeaux (*m*)

marooned /mə'ru:nd/ *a* abandonado em ilha, costa deserta etc; (*fig: stranded*) encalhado (*fig*)

marquee /ma:'ki:/ *n* barraca *f ou* tenda *f* grande; (*Amer: awning*) toldo *m*

marriage /'mærɪdʒ/ *n* casamento *m*, matrimônio *m*, (*P*) matrimónio *m*. **~ certificate** certidão *f* de casamento. **~able** *a* casadouro

marrow /'mærəʊ/ *n* (*of bone*) tutano *m*, medula *f*; (*vegetable*) abóbora *f*. **chilled to the ~** gelado até os ossos

marr|y /'mærɪ/ *vt* casar(-se) com; (*give or unite in marriage*) casar □ *vi* casar-se. **~ied** *a* casado; (*life*) de casado, conjugal. **get ~ied** casar-se

Mars /ma:z/ *n* Marte *m*

marsh /ma:ʃ/ *n* pântano *m*. ~**y** *a* pantanoso

marshal /'ma:ʃl/ *n* (*mil*) marechal *m*; (*steward*) mestre *m* de cerimônias, (*P*) cerimónias □ *vt* (*pt* **marshalled**) dispor em ordem, ordenar; (*usher*) conduzir, escoltar

marshmallow /ma:ʃ'mæləʊ/ *n* marshmallow *m*

martial /'ma:ʃl/ *a* marcial. ~ **law** lei *f* marcial

martyr /'ma:tə(r)/ *n* mártir *mf* □ *vt* martirizar. ~**dom** *n* martírio *m*

marvel /'ma:vl/ *n* maravilha *f*, prodígio *m* □ *vi* (*pt* **marvelled**) (*feel wonder*) maravilhar-se (**at** com); (*be astonished*) pasmar (**at** com)

marvellous /'ma:vələs/ *a* maravilhoso

Marxis|t /'ma:ksɪst/ *a* & *n* marxista (*mf*). ~**m** /-zəm/ *n* marxismo *m*

marzipan /'ma:zɪpæn/ *n* maçapão *m*

mascara /mæ'ska:rə/ *n* rímel *m*

mascot /'mæskət/ *n* mascote *f*

masculin|e /'mæskjʊlm/ *a* masculino □ *n* masculino *m*. ~**ity** /'lmətɪ/ *n* masculinidade *f*

mash /mæʃ/ *n* (*pulp*) papa *f* □ *vt* esmagar. ~**ed potatoes** purê *m* de batata(s)

mask /ma:sk/ *n* máscara *f* □ *vt* mascarar

masochis|t /'mæsəkɪst/ *n* masoquista *mf*. ~**m** /-zəm/ *n* masoquismo *m*

mason /'meɪsn/ *n* maçom *m*; (*building*) pedreiro *m*. ~**ry** *n* maçonaria *f*; (*building*) alvenaria *f*

Mason /'meɪsn/ *n* Maçônico *m*, (*P*) Maçónico *m*. ~**ic** /mə'sɒnɪk/ *a* Maçônico, (*P*) Maçónico

masquerade /mæ:skə'reɪd/ *n* mascarada *f* □ *vi* ~ **as** mascarar-se de, disfarçar-se de

mass[1] /mæs/ *n* (*relig*) missa *f*

mass[2] /mæs/ *n* massa *f*; (*heap*) montão *m* □ *vt/i* aglomerar(-se), reunir(-se) em massa. ~**-produce** *vt* produzir em série. **the** ~**es** as massas, a grande massa

massacre /'mæsəkə(r)/ *n* massacre *m* □ *vt* massacrar

massage /'mæsa:ʒ/ *n* massagem *f* □ *vt* massagear, fazer massagens em, (*P*) dar massagens a

masseu|r /mæ'sɜ:(r)/ *n* massagista *m*. ~**se** /mæ'sɜ:z/ *n* massagista *f*

massive /'mæsɪv/ *a* (*heavy*) maciço; (*huge*) enorme

mast /ma:st/ *n* mastro *m*; (*for radio etc*) antena *f*

master /'ma:stə(r)/ *n* (*in school*) professor *m*, mestre *m*; (*expert*) mestre *m*; (*boss*) patrão *m*; (*owner*) dono *m*. **M**~ (*boy*) menino *m* □ *vt* dominar. ~**-key** *n* chave-mestra *f*. ~**-mind** *n* (*of scheme etc*) cérebro *m* □ *vt* planejar, dirigir. **M**~ **of Arts**/*etc* Licenciado *m* em Letras/*etc*. ~**-stroke** *n* golpe *m* de mestre. ~**y** *n* domínio *m* (**over** sobre); (*knowledge*) conhecimento *m*; (*skill*) perícia *f*

masterly /'ma:stəlɪ/ *a* magistral

masterpiece /'ma:stəpi:s/ *n* obra-prima *f*

masturbat|e /'mæstəbeɪt/ *vi* masturbar-se. ~**ion** /'beɪʃn/ *n* masturbação *f*

mat /mæt/ *n* tapete *m* pequeno; (*at door*) capacho *m*. (**table-**)~ *n* (*of cloth*) paninho *m* de mesa; (*for hot dishes*) descanso *m* para pratos

match[1] /mætʃ/ *n* fósforo *m*

match[2] /mætʃ/ *n* (*contest*) competição *f*, torneio *m*; (*game*) partida *f*; (*equal*) par *m*, parceiro *m*, igual *mf*; (*fig: marriage*) casamento *m*; (*marriage partner*) partido *m* □ *vt/i* (*set against*) contrapôr (**against** a); (*equal*) igualar; (*go with*) condizer; (*be alike*) ir com, emparceirar com. **her shoes** ~**ed her bag** os sapatos dela combinavam com a bolsa. ~**ing** *a* condizente, a condizer

matchbox /'mætʃbɒks/ *n* caixa *f* de fósforos

mat|e[1] /meɪt/ *n* companheiro *m*, camarada *mf*; (*of birds, animals*) macho *m*, fêmea *f*; (*assistant*) ajudante *mf* □ *vt/i* acasalar(-se) (**with** com). ~**ing season** *n* época *f* de cio

mate[2] /meɪt/ *n* (*chess*) mate *m*, xeque-mate *m*

material /mə'tɪərɪəl/ *n* material *m*; (*fabric*) tecido *m*; (*equipment*) apetrechos *mpl* □ *a* material; (*significant*) importante

materialis|m /mə'tɪərɪəlɪzəm/ *n* materialismo *m*. ~**tic** /'lɪstɪk/ *a* materialista

materialize /mə'tɪərɪəlaɪz/ *vi* realizar-se, concretizar-se; (*appear*) aparecer

maternal /mə'tɜ:nəl/ *a* maternal

maternity /mə'tɜ:nətɪ/ *n* maternidade *f* □ *a* (*clothes*) de grávida. ~ **hospital** maternidade *f*. ~ **leave** licença *f* de maternidade

mathematic|s /mæθə'mætɪks/ *n* matemática *f*. ~**al** *a* matemático. ~**ian** /-ə'tɪʃn/ *n* matemático *m*.

maths /mæθs/ *n* (*colloq*) matemática *f*

matinée /'mætɪneɪ/ *n* matinê *f*, (*P*) matinée *f*

matrimon|y /'mætrɪmənɪ/ *n* matrimônio *m*, (*P*) matrimónio *m*. ~**ial** /'məʊnɪəl/ *a* matrimonial, conjugal

matrix /'meɪtrɪks/ *n* (*pl* **matrices** /-si:z/) matriz *f*

matron /'meɪtrən/ *n* matrona *f*; (*in school*) inspetora *f*; (*former use: senior nursing officer*) enfermeira-chefe *f*. **~ly** *a* respeitável, muito digno
matt /mæt/ *a* fosco, sem brilho
matted /'mætɪd/ *a* emaranhado
matter /'mætə(r)/ *n* (*substance*) matéria *f*; (*affair*) assunto *m*, caso *m*, questão *f*; (*pus*) pus *m* □ *vi* importar. **as a ~ of fact** na verdade. **it does not ~** não importa. **~-of-fact** *a* prosaico, terra-a-terra. **no ~ what happens** não importa o que acontecer. **what is the ~?** o que é que há? **what is the ~ with you?** o que é que você tem?
mattress /'mætrɪs/ *n* colchão *m*
matur|e /mə'tjʊə(r)/ *a* maduro, amadurecido □ *vt/i* amadurecer; (*comm*) vencer-se. **~ity** *n* madureza *f*, maturidade *f*; (*comm*) vencimento *m*
maul /mɔ:l/ *vt* maltratar, atacar
Mauritius /mə'rɪʃəs/ *n* Ilha *f* Maurícia
mausoleum /mɔ:sə'lɪəm/ *n* mausoléu *m*
mauve /məʊv/ *a* & *n* lilás (*m*)
maxim /'mæksɪm/ *n* máxima *f*
maxim|um /'mæksɪməm/ *a* & *n* (*pl* **-ima**) máximo (*m*). **~ize** *vt* aumentar ao máximo, maximizar
may /meɪ/ *v aux* (*pt* **might**) poder. **he ~/might come** talvez venha/viesse. **you might have** podia ter. **you ~ leave** pode ir. **~ I smoke?** posso fumar?, dá licença que eu fume? **~ he be happy** que ele seja feliz. **I ~** *or* **might as well go** talvez seja *or* fosse melhor eu ir
May /meɪ/ *n* maio *n*. **~ Day** o primeiro de maio
maybe /'meɪbi:/ *adv* talvez
mayhem /'meɪhem/ *n* (*disorder*) distúrbios *mpl* violentos; (*havoc*) estragos *mpl*
mayonnaise /meɪə'neɪz/ *n* maionese *f*
mayor /meə(r)/ *n* prefeito *m*. **~ess** *n* prefeita *f*; (*mayor's wife*) mulher *f* do prefeito
maze /meɪz/ *n* labirinto *m*
me /mi:/ *pron* me; (*after prep*) mim. **with ~** comigo. **he knows ~** ele me conhece. **it's ~** sou eu
meadow /'medəʊ/ *n* prado *m*, campina *f*
meagre /'mi:gə(r)/ *a* (*thin*) magro; (*scanty*) escasso
meal[1] /mi:l/ *n* refeição *f*
meal[2] /mi:l/ *n* (*grain*) farinha *f* grossa
mean[1] /mi:n/ *a* (**-er, -est**) mesquinho; (*unkind*) mau. **~ness** *n* mesquinhez *f*
mean[2] /mi:n/ *a* médio □ *n* média *f*. **Greenwich ~ time** tempo *m* médio de Greenwich
mean[3] /mi:n/ *vt* (*pt* **meant**) (*intend*) tencionar *or* ter (a) intenção (**to** de); (*signify*) querer dizer, significar; (*entail*) dar em resultado, resultar provavelmente em; (*refer to*) referir-se a. **be meant for** destinar-se a. **I didn't ~ it** desculpe, foi sem querer. **he ~s what he says** ele está falando sério
meander /mɪ'ændə(r)/ *vi* serpentear; (*wander*) perambular
meaning /'mi:nɪŋ/ *n* sentido *m*, significado *m*. **~ful** *a* significativo. **~less** *a* sem sentido
means /mi:nz/ *n* meio(s) *m*(*pl*) □ *npl* meios *mpl* pecuniários, recursos *mpl*. **by all ~** com certeza. **by ~ of** por meio de, através de. **by no ~** de modo nenhum
meant /ment/ see **mean**[3]
mean|time /'mi:ntaɪm/ *adv* (**in the**) **~time** entretanto. **~while** /-waɪl/ *adv* entretanto
measles /'mi:zlz/ *n* sarampo *m*. **German ~** rubéola *f*
measly /'mi:zlɪ/ *a* (*sl*) miserável, ínfimo
measurable /'meʒərəbl/ *a* mensurável
measure /'meʒə(r)/ *n* medida *f* □ *vt/i* medir. **made to ~** feito sob medida. **~ up to** mostrar-se à altura de. **~d** *a* medido, calculado. **~ment** *n* medida *f*
meat /mi:t/ *n* carne *f*. **~y** *a* carnudo; (*fig: substantial*) substancial
mechanic /mɪ'kænɪk/ *n* mecânico *m*
mechanic|al /mɪ'kænɪkl/ *a* mecânico. **~s** *n* mecânica *f*; *npl* mecanismo *m*
mechan|ism /'mekənɪzəm/ *n* mecanismo *m*. **~ize** *vt* mecanizar
medal /'medl/ *n* medalha *f*. **~list** *n* condecorado *m*. **be a gold ~list** ser medalha de ouro
medallion /mɪ'dælɪən/ *n* medalhão *m*
meddle /'medl/ *vi* (*interfere*) imiscuir-se, intrometer-se (**in** em); (*tinker*) mexer (**with** em). **~some** *a* intrometido, abelhudo
media /'mi:dɪə/ *see* **medium** □ *npl* **the ~** a média, os meios de comunicação social *or* de massa
mediat|e /'mi:dɪeɪt/ *vi* servir de intermediário, mediar. **~ion** /-'eɪʃn/ *n* mediação *f*. **~or** *n* mediador *m*, intermediário *m*
medical /'medɪkl/ *a* médico □ *n* (*colloq: examination*) exame *m* médico
medicat|ed /'medɪkeɪtɪd/ *a* medicinal. **~ion** /-'keɪʃn/ *n* medicamentação *f*
medicinal /mɪ'dɪsɪnl/ *a* medicinal
medicine /'medsn/ *n* medicina *f*; (*substance*) remédio *m*, medicamento *m*
medieval /medɪ'i:vl/ *a* medieval
mediocr|e /mi:dɪ'əʊkə(r)/ *a* medíocre. **~ity** /-'ɒkrətɪ/ *n* mediocridade *f*

meditat|e /'medɪteɪt/ *vt/i* meditar. **~ion** /-'teɪʃn/ *n* meditação *f*

Mediterranean /medɪtə'reɪmɪən/ *a* mediterrâneo □ *n* **the ~** o Mediterrâneo

medium /'mi:dɪəm/ *n* (*pl* **media**) meio *m*; (*pl* **mediums**) (*person*) médium *mf* □ *a* médio. **~ wave** (*radio*) onda *f* média. **the happy ~** o meio-termo

medley /'medlɪ/ *n* (*pl* **-eys**) miscelânea *f*

meek /mi:k/ *a* (**-er, -est**) manso, submisso, sofrido

meet /mi:t/ *vt* (*pt* **met**) encontrar; (*intentionally*) encontrar-se com, ir ter com; (*at station etc*) ir esperar, ir buscar; (*make the acquaintance of*) conhecer; (*conform with*) ir ao encontro de, satisfazer; (*opponent, obligation etc*) fazer face a; (*bill, expenses*) pagar □ *vi* encontrar-se; (*get acquainted*) familiarizar-se; (*in session*) reunir-se. **~ with** encontrar; (*accident, misfortune*) sofrer, ter

meeting /'mi:tɪŋ/ *n* reunião *f*, encontro *m*; (*between two people*) encontro *m*. **~-place** *n* ponto *m* de encontro

megalomania /megələʊ'meɪnɪə/ *n* megalomania *f*, mania *f* de grandezas

megaphone /'megəfəʊn/ *n* megafone *m*, porta-voz *m*

melancholy /'melənkɒlɪ/ *n* melancolia *f* □ *a* melancólico

mellow /'meləʊ/ *a* (**-er, -est**) (*fruit, person*) amadurecido, maduro; (*sound, colour*) quente, suave □ *vt/i* amadurecer; (*soften*) suavizar

melodious /mɪ'ləʊdɪəs/ *a* melodioso

melodrama /'melədra:mə/ *n* melodrama *m*. **~tic** /-ə'mætɪk/ *a* melodramático

melod|y /'melədɪ/ *n* melodia *f*. **~ic** /mɪ'lɒdɪk/ *a* melódico

melon /'melən/ *n* melão *m*

melt /melt/ *vt/i* (*metals*) fundir(-se); (*butter, snow etc*) derreter (-se); (*fade away*) desvanecer (-se). **~ing-pot** *n* cadinho *m*

member /'membə(r)/ *n* membro *m*; (*of club etc*) sócio *m*. **M~ of Parliament** deputado *m*. **~ship** *n* qualidade *f* de sócio; (*members*) número *m* de sócios; (*fee*) cota *f*. **~ship card** carteira *f*, (*P*) cartão *m* de sócio

membrane /'membreɪn/ *n* membrana *f*

memento /mɪ'mentəʊ/ *n* (*pl* **-oes**) lembrança *f*, recordação *f*

memo /'meməʊ/ *n* (*pl* **-os**) (*colloq*) nota *f*, apontamento *m*, lembrete *m*

memoir /'memwa:(r)/ *n* (*record, essay*) memória *f*, memorial *m*; **~s** *npl* (*autobiography*) memórias *fpl*

memorable /'memərəbl/ *a* memorável

memorandum /memə'rændəm/ *n* (*pl* **-da** *or* **-dums**) nota *f*, lembrete *m*; (*diplomatic*) memorando *m*

memorial /mɪ'mɔ:rɪəl/ *n* monumento *m* comemorativo □ *a* comemorativo

memorize /'meməraɪz/ *vt* decorar, memorizar, aprender de cor

memory /'memərɪ/ *n* memória *f*. **from ~** de memória, de cor. **in ~ of** em memória de

men /men/ *see* **man**

menac|e /'menəs/ *n* ameaça *f*; (*nuisance*) praga *f*, chaga *f* □ *vt* ameaçar. **~ingly** *adv* ameaçadoramente, de modo ameaçador

menagerie /mɪ'nædʒərɪ/ *n* coleção *f*, (*P*) colecção *f* de animais ferozes em jaulas

mend /mend/ *vt* consertar, reparar; (*darn*) remendar □ *n* conserto *m*; (*darn*) remendo *m*. **~ one's ways** corrigir-se, emendar-se. **on the ~** melhorando

menial /'mi:nɪəl/ *a* humilde

meningitis /menɪn'dʒaɪtɪs/ *n* meningite *f*

menopause /'menəpɔ:z/ *n* menopausa *f*

menstruation /menstrʊ'eɪʃn/ *n* menstruação *f*

mental /'mentl/ *a* mental; (*hospital*) de doentes mentais, psiquiátrico

mentality /men'tælətɪ/ *n* mentalidade *f*

mention /'menʃn/ *vt* mencionar □ *n* menção *f*. **don't ~ it!** não tem de quê, de nada

menu /'menju:/ *n* (*pl* **-us**) menu *m*, (*P*) ementa *f*

mercenary /'mɜ:snərɪ/ *a* & *n* mercenário (*m*)

merchandise /'mɜ:tʃəndaɪz/ *n* mercadorias *fpl* □ *vt/i* negociar

merchant /'mɜ:tʃənt/ *n* mercador *m* □ *a* (*ship, navy*) mercante. **~ bank** banco *m* comercial

merciful /'mɜ:sɪfl/ *a* misericordioso

merciless /'mɜ:sɪlɪs/ *a* impiedoso, sem dó

mercury /'mɜ:kjʊrɪ/ *n* mercúrio *m*

mercy /'mɜ:sɪ/ *n* piedade *f*, misericórdia *f*. **at the ~ of** à mercê de

mere /mɪə(r)/ *a* mero, simples. **~ly** *adv* meramente, simplesmente, apenas

merge /mɜ:dʒ/ *vt/i* fundir(-se), amalgamar(-se); (*comm: companies*) fundir(-se). **~r** /-ə(r)/ *n* fusão *f*

meringue /mə'ræŋ/ *n* merengue *m*, suspiro *m*

merit /'merɪt/ *n* mérito *m* □ *vt* (*pt* **merited**) merecer

mermaid /ˈmɜːmeɪd/ *n* sereia *f*
merriment /ˈmerɪmənt/ *n* divertimento *m*, alegria *f*, folguedo *m*
merry /ˈmerɪ/ *a* (-ier, -iest) alegre, divertido. **~ Christmas** Feliz Natal. **~-go-round** *n* carrossel *m*. **~-making** *n* festa *f*, divertimento *m*. **merrily** *adv* alegremente
mesh /meʃ/ *n* malha *f*. **~es** *npl* (*network; fig*) malhas *fpl*.
mesmerize /ˈmezməraɪz/ *vt* hipnotizar
mess /mes/ *n* (*disorder*) desordem *f*, trapalhada *f*; (*trouble*) embrulhada *f*, trapalhada *f*; (*dirt*) porcaria *f*; (*mil: place*) cantina *f*; (*mil: food*) rancho *m* □ *vt* **~ up** (*make untidy*) desarrumar; (*make dirty*) sujar; (*confuse*) atrapalhar, estragar □ *vi* **~ about** perder tempo; (*behave foolishly*) fazer asneiras. **~ about with** (*tinker with*) entreter-se com, andar às voltas com. **make a ~ of** estragar
message /ˈmesɪdʒ/ *n* mensagem *f*; (*informal*) recado *m*
messenger /ˈmesɪndʒə(r)/ *n* mensageiro *m*
Messiah /mɪˈsaɪə/ *n* Messias *m*
messy /ˈmesɪ/ *a* (-ier, -iest) desarrumado, bagunçado; (*dirty*) sujo, porco
met /met/ *see* **meet**
metabolism /mɪˈtæbəlɪzm/ *n* metabolismo *m*
metal /ˈmetl/ *n* metal *m* □ *a* de metal. **~lic** /mɪˈtælɪk/ *a* metálico; (*paint, colour*) metalizado
metamorphosis /metəˈmɔːfəsɪs/ *n* (*pl* **-phoses** /-siːz/) metamorfose *f*
metaphor /ˈmetəfə(r)/ *n* metáfora *f*. **~ical** /ˈfɒrɪkl/ *a* metafórico
meteor /ˈmiːtɪə(r)/ *n* meteoro *m*
meteorolog|y /miːtɪəˈrɒlədʒɪ/ *n* meteorologia *f*. **~ical** /-əˈlɒdʒɪkl/ *a* meteorológico
meter[1] /ˈmiːtə(r)/ *n* contador *m*
meter[2] /ˈmiːtə(r)/ *n* (*Amer*) = **metre**
method /ˈmeθəd/ *n* método *m*
methodical /mɪˈθɒdɪkl/ *a* metódico
Methodist /ˈmeθədɪst/ *n* metodista *mf*
methylated /ˈmeθɪleɪtɪd/ *a* **~ spirit** álcool *m* metílico
meticulous /mɪˈtɪkjʊləs/ *a* meticuloso
metre /ˈmiːtə(r)/ *n* metro *m*
metric /ˈmetrɪk/ *a* métrico. **~ation** /-ˈkeɪʃn/ *n* conversão *f* para o sistema métrico
metropol|is /məˈtrɒpəlɪs/ *n* metrópole *f*. **~itan** /metrəˈpɒlɪtən/ *a* metropolitano
mettle /ˈmetl/ *n* têmpera *f*, caráter *m*, (*P*) carácter *m*; (*spirit*) brio *m*
mew /mjuː/ *n* miado *m* □ *vi* miar
Mexic|o /ˈmeksɪkəʊ/ *n* México *m*. **~an** *a* & *n* mexicano (*m*)
miaow /miːˈaʊ/ *n* & *vi* = **mew**
mice /maɪs/ *see* **mouse**
mickey /ˈmɪkɪ/ *n* **take the ~ out of** (*sl*) fazer troça de, gozar (*colloq*)
micro- /ˈmaɪkrəʊ/ *pref* micro-
microbe /ˈmaɪkrəʊb/ *n* micróbio *m*
microchip /ˈmaɪkrəʊtʃɪp/ *n* microchip *m*
microcomputer /ˈmaɪkrəʊkəmpjuːtə(r)/ *n* microcomputador *m*
microfilm /ˈmaɪkrəʊfɪlm/ *n* microfilme *m*
microlight /ˈmaɪkrəʊlaɪt/ *n* (*aviat*) ultraleve *m*
microphone /ˈmaɪkrəfəʊn/ *n* microfone *m*
microprocessor /maɪkrəʊˈprəʊsesə(r)/ *n* microprocessador *m*
microscop|e /ˈmaɪkrəskəʊp/ *n* microscópio *m*. **~ic** /ˈskɒpɪk/ *a* microscópico
microwave /ˈmaɪkrəʊweɪv/ *n* micro-onda *f*. **~ oven** forno *m* de microondas
mid /mɪd/ *a* meio. **in ~-air** no ar, em pleno vôo. **in ~-March** em meados de março
midday /mɪdˈdeɪ/ *n* meio-dia *m*
middle /ˈmɪdl/ *a* médio, meio; (*quality*) médio, mediano □ *n* meio *m*. **in the ~ of** no meio de. **~-aged** *a* de meia idade. **M~ Ages** Idade *f* Média. **~ class** classe *f* média. **~-class** *a* burguês. **M~ East** Médio Oriente *m*. **~ name** segundo nome *m*
middleman /ˈmɪdlmæn/ *n* (*pl* **-men**) intermediário *m*
midge /mɪdʒ/ *n* mosquito *m*
midget /ˈmɪdʒɪt/ *n* anão *m* □ *a* minúsculo
Midlands /ˈmɪdləndz/ *npl* região *f* do centro da Inglaterra
midnight /ˈmɪdnaɪt/ *n* meia-noite *f*
midriff /ˈmɪdrɪf/ *n* diafragma *m*; (*abdomen*) ventre *m*
midst /mɪdst/ *n* **in the ~ of** no meio de
midsummer /mɪdˈsʌmə(r)/ *n* pleno verão *m*; (*solstice*) solstício *m* do verão
midway /mɪdˈweɪ/ *adv* a meio caminho
midwife /ˈmɪdwaɪf/ *n* (*pl* **-wives**) parteira *f*
might[1] /maɪt/ *n* potência *f*; (*strength*) força *f*. **~y** *a* poderoso; (*fig: great*) imenso □ *adv* (*colloq*) muito
might[2] /maɪt/ *see* **may**
migraine /ˈmiːgreɪn/ *n* enxaqueca *f*
migrant /ˈmaɪgrənt/ *a* migratório □ *n* (*person*) migrante *mf*, emigrante *mf*
migrat|e /maɪˈgreɪt/ *vi* migrar. **~ion** /-ʃn/ *n* migração *f*
mike /maɪk/ *n* (*colloq*) microfone *m*

mild /maɪld/ *a* (-er, -est) brando, manso; (*illness, taste*) leve; (*climate*) temperado; (*weather*) ameno. **~ly** *adv* brandamente, mansamente. **to put it ~ly** para não dizer coisa pior. **~ness** *n* brandura *f*

mildew /ˈmɪldju:/ *n* bolor *m*, mofo *m*; (*in plants*) míldio *m*

mile /maɪl/ *n* milha *f* (= *1.6 km*). **~s too big/***etc* (*colloq*) grande demais. **~age** *n* (*loosely*) quilometragem *f*

milestone /ˈmaɪlstəʊn/ *n* marco *m* miliário; (*fig*) data *f or* acontecimento *m* importante

militant /ˈmɪlɪtənt/ *a* & *n* militante (*mf*)

military /ˈmɪlɪtrɪ/ *a* militar

militate /ˈmɪlɪteɪt/ *vi* militar. **~ against** militar contra

milk /mɪlk/ *n* leite *m* □ *a* (*product*) lácteo □ *vt* ordenhar; (*fig: exploit*) explorar. **~-shake** *n* milk-shake *m*, leite *m* batido. **~y** *a* (*like milk*) leitoso; (*tea etc*) com muito leite. **M~ Way** Via *f* Láctea

milkman /ˈmɪlkmən/ *n* (*pl* -men) leiteiro *m*

mill /mɪl/ *n* moinho *m*; (*factory*) fábrica *f* □ *vt* moer □ *vi* **~ around** aglomerar-se; (*crowd*) apinhar-se, (*P*) agitar-se. **~er** *n* moleiro *m*. **pepper-~** *n* moedor *m* de pimenta

millennium /mɪˈlenɪəm/ *n* (*pl* -iums *or* -ia) milênio *m*, (*P*) milénio *m*

millet /ˈmɪlɪt/ *n* painço *m*, milhete *m*

milli- /ˈmɪlɪ/ *pref* mili-

milligram /ˈmɪlɪgræm/ *n* miligrama *m*

millilitre /ˈmɪlɪli:tə(r)/ *n* mililitro *m*

millimetre /ˈmɪlɪmi:tə(r)/ *n* milímetro *m*

million /ˈmɪlɪən/ *n* milhão *m*. **a ~ pounds** um milhão de libras. **~aire** /-ˈneə(r)/ *n* milionário *m*

millstone /ˈmɪlstəʊn/ *n* mó *f*. **a ~ round one's neck** um peso nos ombros

mime /maɪm/ *n* mímica *f*; (*actor*) mímico *m* □ *vt/i* exprimir por mímica, mimar

mimic /ˈmɪmɪk/ *vt* (*pt* **mimicked**) imitar □ *n* imitador *m*, parodiante *mf*. **~ry** *n* imitação *f*.

mince /mɪns/ *vt* picar □ *n* carne *f* moída, (*P*) carne *f* picada. **~-pie** *n* pastel *m* recheado com massa de passas, amêndoas, especiarias etc. **~r** *n* máquina *f* de moer

mincemeat /ˈmɪnsmi:t/ *n* massa *f* de passas, amêndoas, especiarias etc usada para recheio. **make ~ of** (*colloq*) arrasar, aniquilar

mind *n* espírito *m*, mente *f*; (*intellect*) intelecto *m*; (*sanity*) razão *f* □ *vt* (*look after*) tomar conta de, tratar de; (*heed*) prestar atenção a; (*object to*) importar-se com, incomodar-se com. **do you ~ if I smoke?** você se incomoda que eu fume? **do you ~ helping me?** quer fazer o favor de me ajudar? **never ~** não se importe, não tem importância. **to be out of one's ~** estar fora de si. **have a good ~ to** estar disposto a. **make up one's ~** decidir-se. **presence of ~** presença *f* de espírito. **to my ~** a meu ver. **~ful of** atento a, consciente de. **~less** *a* insensato

minder /ˈmaɪndə(r)/ *n* pessoa *f* que toma conta *mf*; (*bodyguard*) guarda-costa *mf*, (*P*) guarda-costas *mf*

mine[1] /maɪn/ *poss pron* o(s) meu(s), a(s) minha(s). **it is ~** é (o) meu *or* (a) minha

min|e[2] /maɪn/ *n* mina *f* □ *vt* escavar, explorar; (*extract*) extrair; (*mil*) minar. **~er** *n* mineiro *m*. **~ing** *n* exploração *f* mineira □ *a* mineiro

minefield /ˈmaɪnfi:ld/ *n* campo *m* minado

mineral /ˈmɪnərəl/ *n* mineral *m*; (*soft drink*) bebida *f* gasosa. **~ water** água *f* mineral

minesweeper /ˈmaɪnswi:pə(r)/ *n* caça-minas *m*

mingle /ˈmɪŋgl/ *vt/i* misturar(-se) (**with** com)

mingy /ˈmɪndʒɪ/ *a* (-ier, -iest) (*colloq*) sovina, unha(s)-de-fome (*colloq*)

mini- /ˈmɪnɪ/ *pref* mini-

miniature /ˈmɪnɪtʃə(r)/ *n* miniatura *f* □ *a* miniatural

minibus /ˈmɪnɪbʌs/ *n* (*public*) microônibus *m*, (*P*) autocarro *m* pequeno

minim /ˈmɪnɪm/ *n* (*mus*) mínima *f*

minim|um /ˈmɪnɪməm/ *a* & *n* (*pl* -ma) mínimo (*m*). **~al** *a* mínimo. **~ize** *vt* minimizar, dar pouca importância a

miniskirt /ˈmɪnɪskɜ:t/ *n* minissaia *f*

minist|er /ˈmɪnɪstə(r)/ *n* ministro *m*; (*relig*) pastor *m*. **~erial** /-ˈstɪərɪəl/ *a* ministerial. **~ry** *n* ministério *m*

mink /mɪŋk/ *n* (*fur*) marta *f*, visão *m*

minor /ˈmaɪnə(r)/ *a* & *n* menor (*mf*)

minority /maɪˈnɒrətɪ/ *n* minoria *f* □ *a* minoritário

mint[1] /mɪnt/ *n* **the M~** a Casa da Moeda. **a ~** uma fortuna □ *vt* cunhar. **in ~ condition** em perfeito estado, como novo, impecável

mint[2] /mɪnt/ *n* (*plant*) hortelã *f*; (*sweet*) pastilha *f* de hortelã

minus /ˈmaɪnəs/ *prep* menos; (*colloq: without*) sem □ *n* menos *m*

minute[1] /ˈmɪnɪt/ *n* minuto *m*. **~s** (*of meeting*) ata *f*, (*P*) acta *f*

minute[2] /maɪ'nju:t/ *a* diminuto, minúsculo; (*detailed*) minucioso
mirac|le /'mɪrəkl/ *n* milagre *m*. **~ulous** /mɪ'rækjʊləs/ *a* milagroso, miraculoso
mirage /'mɪra:ʒ/ *n* miragem *f*
mire /maɪə(r)/ *n* lodo *m*, lama *f*
mirror /'mɪrə(r)/ *n* espelho *m*; (*in car*) retrovisor *m* □ *vt* refletir, (*P*) reflectir, espelhar
mirth /mɜ:θ/ *n* alegria *f*, hilaridade *f*
misadventure /mɪsəd'ventʃə(r)/ *n* desgraça *f*. **death by ~** morte *f* acidental
misanthropist /mɪs'ænθrəpɪst/ *n* misantropo *m*
misapprehension /mɪsæprɪ'henʃn/ *n* mal-entendido *m*
misbehav|e /mɪsbɪ'heɪv/ *vi* portar-se mal, proceder mal. **~iour** /-'heɪvɪə(r)/ *n* mau comportamento *m*, má conduta *f*
miscalculat|e /mɪs'kælkjʊleɪt/ *vi* calcular mal, enganar-se. **~ion** /-'leɪʃn/ *n* erro *m* de cálculo
miscarr|y /mɪs'kærɪ/ *vi* abortar, ter um aborto; (*fail*) falhar, malograr-se. **~iage** /-ɪdʒ/ *n* aborto *m*. **~iage of justice** erro *m* judiciário
miscellaneous /mɪsə'leɪnɪəs/ *a* variado, diverso
mischief /'mɪstʃɪf/ *n* (*of children*) diabrura *f*, travessura *f*; (*harm*) mal *m*, dano *m*. **get into ~** fazer disparates. **make ~** criar *or* semear discórdias
mischievous /'mɪstʃɪvəs/ *a* endiabrado, travesso
misconception /mɪskən'sepʃn/ *n* idéia *f* errada, falso conceito *m*
misconduct /mɪs'kɒndʌkt/ *n* conduta *f* imprópria
misconstrue /mɪskən'stru:/ *vt* interpretar mal
misdeed /mɪs'di:d/ *n* má ação *f*, (*P*) acção *f*; (*crime*) crime *m*
misdemeanour /mɪsdɪ'mi:nə(r)/ *n* delito *m*
miser /'maɪzə(r)/ *n* avarento *m*, sovina *mf*. **~ly** *a* avarento, sovina
miserable /'mɪzrəbl/ *a* infeliz; (*wretched, mean*) desgraçado, miserável
misery /'mɪzərɪ/ *n* infelicidade *f*
misfire /mɪs'faɪə(r)/ *vi* (*plan, gun, engine*) falhar
misfit /'mɪsfɪt/ *n* inadaptado *m*
misfortune /mɪs'fɔ:tʃən/ *n* desgraça *f*, infelicidade *f*, pouca sorte *f*
misgiving(s) /mɪs'gɪvɪŋ(z)/ *n*(*pl*) dúvida(s) *f*(*pl*), receio(s) *m*(*pl*)
misguided /mɪs'gaɪdɪd/ *a* (*mistaken*) desencaminhado; (*misled*) mal aconselhado, enganado
mishap /'mɪshæp/ *n* contratempo *m*, desastre *m*
misinform /mɪsɪn'fɔ:m/ *vt* informar mal
misinterpret /mɪsɪn'tɜ:prɪt/ *vt* interpretar mal
misjudge /mɪs'dʒʌdʒ/ *vt* julgar mal
mislay /mɪs'leɪ/ *vt* (*pt* **mislaid**) perder, extraviar
mislead /mɪs'li:d/ *vt* (*pt* **misled**) induzir em erro, enganar. **~ing** *a* enganador
mismanage /mɪs'mænɪdʒ/ *vt* dirigir mal. **~ment** *n* má gestão *f*, desgoverno *m*
misnomer /mɪs'nəʊmə(r)/ *n* termo *m* impróprio
misogynist /mɪ'sɒdʒɪnɪst/ *n* misógino *m*
misprint /'mɪsprɪnt/ *n* erro *m* tipográfico
mispronounce /mɪsprə'naʊns/ *vt* pronunciar mal
misquote /mɪs'kwəʊt/ *vt* citar incorretamente
misread /mɪs'ri:d/ *vt* (*pt* **misread** /-'red/) ler *or* interpretar mal
misrepresent /mɪsreprɪ'zent/ *vt* deturpar, desvirtuar
miss /mɪs/ *vt/i* (*chance, bus etc*) perder; (*target*) errar, falhar; (*notice the loss of*) dar pela falta de; (*regret the absence of*) sentir a falta de, ter saudades de. **he ~es her/Portugal/*etc*** ele sente a falta *or* tem saudades dela/de Portugal/*etc* □ *n* falha *f*. **it was a near ~** foi *or* escapou por um triz. **~ out** omitir. **~ the point** não compreender
Miss /mɪs/ *n* (*pl* **Misses**) Senhorita *f*, (*P*) Senhora *f*
misshapen /mɪs'ʃeɪpn/ *a* disforme
missile /'mɪsaɪl/ *n* míssil *m*; (*object thrown*) projétil *m*, (*P*) projéctil *m*
missing /'mɪsɪŋ/ *a* que falta; (*lost*) perdido; (*person*) desaparecido. **a book with a page ~** um livro com uma página a menos
mission /'mɪʃn/ *n* missão *f*
missionary /'mɪʃənrɪ/ *n* missionário *m*
misspell /mɪs'spel/ *vt* (*pt* **misspelt** *or* **misspelled**) escrever mal
mist /mɪst/ *n* neblina *f*, névoa *f*, bruma *f*; (*fig*) névoa *f* □ *vt/i* enevoar(-se); (*window*) embaçar(-se)
mistake /mɪ'steɪk/ *n* engano *m*, erro *m* □ *vt* (*pt* **mistook**, *pp* **mistaken**) compreender mal; (*choose wrongly*) enganar-se em. **~ for** confundir com, tomar por. **~n** /-ən/ *a* errado. **be ~n** enganar-se. **~nly** /-ənlɪ/ *adv* por engano
mistletoe /'mɪsltəʊ/ *n* visco *m*
mistreat /mɪs'tri:t/ *vt* maltratar. **~ment** *n* mau trato *m*

mistress /'mɪstrɪs/ *n* senhora *f*, dona *f*; (*teacher*) professora *f*; (*lover*) amante *f*
mistrust /mɪs'trʌst/ *vt* desconfiar de, duvidar de □ *n* desconfiança *f*
misty /'mɪstɪ/ *a* (**-ier, -iest**) enevoado, brumoso; (*window*) embaçado; (*indistinct*) indistinto
misunderstand /mɪsʌndə'stænd/ *vt* (*pt* **-stood**) compreender mal. **~ing** *n* mal-entendido *m*
misuse[1] /mɪs'ju:z/ *vt* empregar mal; (*power etc*) abusar de
misuse[2] /mɪs'ju:s/ *n* mau uso *m*; (*abuse*) abuso *m*; (*of funds*) desvio *m*
mitigat|e /'mɪtɪgeɪt/ *vt* atenuar, mitigar. **~ing circumstances** circunstâncias *fpl* atenuantes
mitten /'mɪtn/ *n* luva *f* com uma única divisão entre o polegar e os dedos
mix /mɪks/ *vt/i* misturar(-se) □ *n* mistura *f*. **~ up** misturar bem; (*fig: confuse*) confundir. **~-up** *n* trapalhada *f*, confusão *f*. **~ with** associar-se com. **~er** *n* (*culin*) batedeira *f*
mixed /mɪkst/ *a* (*school etc*) misto; (*assorted*) sortido. **be ~ up** (*colloq*) estar confuso
mixture /'mɪkstʃə(r)/ *n* mistura *f*. **cough ~** xarope *m* para a tosse
moan /məʊn/ *n* gemido *m* □ *vi* gemer; (*complain*) queixar-se, lastimar-se (**about** de). **~er** *n* pessoa *f* lamurienta
moat /məʊt/ *n* fosso *m*
mob /mɒb/ *n* multidão *f*; (*tumultuous*) turba *f*; (*sl: gang*) bando *m* □ *vt* (*pt* **mobbed**) cercar, assediar
mobil|e /'məʊbaɪl/ *a* móvel. **~e home** caravana *f*, trailer *m*. **~ity** /-'bɪlətɪ/ *n* mobilidade *f*
mobiliz|e /'məʊbɪlaɪz/ *vt/i* mobilizar. **~ation** /-'zeɪʃn/ *n* mobilização *f*
moccasin /'mɒkəsɪn/ *n* mocassim *m*
mock /mɒk/ *vt/i* zombar de, gozar □ *a* falso. **~-up** *n* modelo *m*, maqueta *f*
mockery /'mɒkərɪ/ *n* troça *f*, gozação *f*. **a ~ of** uma gozação de
mode /məʊd/ *n* modo *m*; (*fashion*) moda *f*
model /'mɒdl/ *n* modelo *m* □ *a* modelo; (*exemplary*) exemplar; (*toy*) em miniatura □ *vt* (*pt* **modelled**) modelar; (*clothes*) apresentar □ *vi* ser *or* trabalhar como modelo
modem /'məʊdem/ *n* modem *m*
moderate[1] /'mɒdərət/ *a* & *n* moderado (*m*). **~ly** *adv* moderadamente. **~ly good** sofrível
moderat|e[2] /'mɒdəreɪt/ *vt/i* moderar (-se). **~ion** /-'reɪʃn/ *n* moderação *f*. **in ~ion** com moderação
modern /'mɒdn/ *a* moderno. **~ languages** línguas *fpl* vivas. **~ize** *vt* modernizar
modest /'mɒdɪst/ *a* modesto. **~y** *n* modéstia *f*. **~ly** *adv* modestamente
modicum /'mɒdɪkəm/ *n* **a ~ of** um pouco de
modif|y /'mɒdɪfaɪ/ *vt* modificar. **~ication** /-ɪ'keɪʃn/ *n* modificação *f*
modulat|e /'mɒdjʊleɪt/ *vt/i* modular. **~ion** /-'leɪʃn/ *n* modulação *f*
module /'mɒdju:l/ *n* módulo *m*
mohair /'məʊheə(r)/ *n* mohair *m*
moist /mɔɪst/ *a* (**-er, -est**) úmido, (*P*) húmido. **~ure** /'mɔɪstʃə(r)/ *n* umidade *f*, (*P*) humidade *f*. **~urizer** /-tʃəraɪzə(r)/ *n* creme *m* hidratante
moisten /'mɔɪsn/ *vt/i* umedecer, (*P*) humedecer
molasses /mə'læsɪz/ *n* melaço *m*
mole[1] /məʊl/ *n* (*on skin*) sinal na pele *m*
mole[2] /məʊl/ *n* (*animal*) toupeira *f*
molecule /'mɒlɪkju:l/ *n* molécula *f*
molest /mə'lest/ *vt* meter-se com, molestar
mollusc /'mɒləsk/ *n* molusco *m*
mollycoddle /'mɒlɪkɒdl/ *vt* mimar
molten /'məʊltən/ *a* fundido
moment /'məʊmənt/ *n* momento *m*
momentar|y /'məʊməntrɪ/ *a* momentâneo. **~ily** /'məʊməntrəlɪ/ *adv* momentâneamente
momentous /mə'mentəs/ *a* grave, importante
momentum /mə'mentəm/ *n* ímpeto *m*, velocidade *f* adquirida
Monaco /'mɒnəkəʊ/ *n* Mônaco *m*
monarch /'mɒnək/ *n* monarca *mf*. **~y** *n* monarquia *f*
monast|ery /'mɒnəstrɪ/ *n* mosteiro *m*, convento *m*. **~ic** /mə'næstɪk/ *a* monástico
Monday /'mʌndɪ/ *n* segunda-feira *f*
monetary /'mʌnɪtrɪ/ *a* monetário
money /'mʌnɪ/ *n* dinheiro *m*. **~-box** *n* cofre *m*. **~-lender** *n* agiota *mf*. **~ order** vale *m* postal
mongrel /'mʌŋgrəl/ *n* (cão) vira-lata *m*, (*P*) rafeiro *m*
monitor /'mɒnɪtə(r)/ *n* chefe *m* de turma; (*techn*) monitor *m* □ *vt* controlar; (*a broadcast*) monitorar (a transmissão)
monk /mʌŋk/ *n* monge *m*, frade *m*
monkey /'mʌŋkɪ/ *n* (*pl* **-eys**) macaco *m*. **~-nut** *n* amendoim *m*. **~-wrench** *n* chave *f* inglesa
mono /'mɒnəʊ/ *n* (*pl* **-os**) gravação *f* mono □ *a* mono *invar*
monocle /'mɒnəkl/ *n* monóculo *m*
monogram /'mɒnəgræm/ *n* monograma *m*
monologue /'mɒnəlɒg/ *n* monólogo *m*
monopol|y /mə'nɒpəlɪ/ *n* monopólio *m*. **~ize** *vt* monopolizar
monosyllab|le /'mɒnəsɪləbl/ *n*

monossílabo *m*. **~ic** /-'læbɪk/ *a* monossilábico
monotone /'mɒnətəʊn/ *n* tom *m* uniforme
monoton|ous /mə'nɒtənəs/ *a* monótono. **~y** *n* monotonia *f*
monsoon /mɒn'su:n/ *n* monção *f*
monst|er /'mɒnstə(r)/ *n* monstro *m*. **~rous** *a* monstruoso
monstrosity /mɒn'strɒsətɪ/ *n* monstruosidade *f*
month /mʌnθ/ *n* mês *m*
monthly /'mʌnθlɪ/ *a* mensal □ *adv* mensalmente □ *n* (*periodical*) revista *f* mensal
monument /'mɒnjʊmənt/ *n* monumento *m*. **~al** /-'mentl/ *a* monumental
moo /mu:/ *n* mugido *m* □ *vi* mugir
mood /mu:d/ *n* humor *m*, disposição *f*. **in a good/bad ~** de bom/mau humor. **~y** *a* de humor instável; (*sullen*) carrancudo
moon /mu:n/ *n* lua *f*
moon|light /'mu:nlaɪt/ *n* luar *m*. **~lit** *a* iluminado pela lua, enluarado
moonlighting /'mu:nlaɪtɪŋ/ *n* (*colloq*) segundo emprego *m*, esp à noite
moor[1] /mʊə(r)/ *n* charneca *f*
moor[2] /mʊə(r)/ *vt* amarrar, atracar. **~ings** *npl* amarras *fpl*; (*place*) amarradouro *m*, fundeadouro *m*
moose /mu:s/ *n* (*pl invar*) alce *m*
moot /mu:t/ *a* discutível □ *vt* levantar
mop /mɒp/ *n* esfregão *m* □ *vt* (*pt* **mopped**) **~ (up)** limpar. **~ of hair** trunfa *f*
mope /məʊp/ *vi* estar *or* andar abatido e triste
moped /'məʊped/ *n* (bicicleta) motorizada *f*
moral /'mɒrəl/ *a* moral □ *n* moral *f*. **~s** moral *f*, bons costumes *mpl*. **~ize** *vi* moralizar. **~ly** *adv* moralmente
morale /mə'ra:l/ *n* moral *m*
morality /mə'rælətɪ/ *n* moralidade *f*
morass /mə'ræs/ *n* pântano *m*
morbid /'mɔ:bɪd/ *a* mórbido
more /mɔ:(r)/ *a* & *adv* mais **(than** (do) **que)** □ *n* mais *m*. **(some) ~ tea/pens/***etc* mais chá/canetas/*etc*. **there is no ~ bread** não há mais pão. **~ or less** mais ou menos
moreover /mɔ:'rəʊvə(r)/ *adv* além disso, de mais a mais
morgue /mɔ:g/ *n* morgue *f*, necrotério *m*
moribund /'mɒrɪbʌnd/ *a* moribundo, agonizante
morning /'mɔ:nɪŋ/ *n* manhã *f*. **in the ~** de manhã
Morocc|o /mə'rɒkəʊ/ *n* Marrocos *m*. **~an** *a* & *n* marroquino (*m*)
moron /'mɔ:rɒn/ *n* idiota *mf*
morose /mə'rəʊs/ *a* taciturno e insociável, carrancudo
morphine /'mɔ:fi:n/ *n* morfina *f*
Morse /mɔ:s/ *n* **~ (code)** (alfabeto) Morse *m*
morsel /'mɔ:sl/ *n* bocado *m* (esp de comida)
mortal /'mɔ:tl/ *a* & *n* mortal (*mf*). **~ity** /mɔ:'tælətɪ/ *n* mortalidade *f*
mortar /'mɔ:tə(r)/ *n* argamassa *f*; (*bowl*) almofariz *m*; (*mil*) morteiro *m*
mortgage /'mɔ:gɪdʒ/ *n* hipoteca *f* □ *vt* hipotecar
mortify /'mɔ:tɪfaɪ/ *vt* mortificar
mortuary /'mɔ:tʃərɪ/ *n* casa *f* mortuária
mosaic /məʊ'zeɪɪk/ *n* mosaico *m*
Moscow /'mɔskəʊ/ *n* Moscou *m*, (*P*) Moscovo *m*
mosque /mɒsk/ *n* mesquita *f*
mosquito /mə'ski:təʊ/ *n* (*pl* **-oes**) mosquito *m*
moss /mɒs/ *n* musgo *m*. **~y** *a* musgoso
most /məʊst/ *a* o mais, o maior; (*majority*) a maioria de, a maior parte de □ *n* mais *m*; (*majority*) a maioria, a maior parte, o máximo □ *adv* o mais; (*very*) muito. **at ~** no máximo. **for the ~ part** na maior parte, na grande maioria. **make the ~ of** aproveitar ao máximo, tirar o melhor partido de. **~ly** *adv* sobretudo
motel /məʊ'tel/ *n* motel *m*
moth /mɒθ/ *n* mariposa *f*, (*P*) borboleta *f* nocturna. **(clothes-)~** *n* traça *f*. **~-ball** *n* bola *f* de naftalina. **~-eaten** *a* roído por traças
mother /'mʌðə(r)/ *n* mãe *f* □ *vt* tratar como a um filho. **~hood** *n* maternidade *f*. **~-in-law** *n* (*pl* **~s-in-law**) sogra *f*. **~-of-pearl** *n* madrepérola *f*. **M~'s Day** o Dia das Mães. **~-to-be** *n* futura mãe *f*. **~ly** *a* maternal
motif /məʊ'ti:f/ *n* tema *m*
motion /'məʊʃn/ *n* movimento *m*; (*proposal*) moção *f* □ *vt/i* **~ (to) sb to** fazer sinal a alg para. **~less** *a* imóvel
motivat|e /'məʊtɪveɪt/ *vt* motivar. **~ion** /-'veɪʃn/ *n* motivação *f*
motive /'məʊtɪv/ *n* motivo *m*
motor /'məʊtə(r)/ *n* motor *m*; (*car*) automóvel *m* □ *a* (*anat*) motor; (*boat*) a motor □ *vi* ir de automóvel. **~ bike** (*colloq*) moto *f* (*colloq*). **~ car** carro *m*. **~ cycle** motocicleta *f*. **~ cyclist** motociclista *mf*. **~ vehicle** veículo *m* automóvel. **~ing** *n* automobilismo *m*. **~ized** *a* motorizado
motorist /'məʊtərɪst/ *n* motorista *mf*, automobilista *mf*
motorway /'məʊtəweɪ/ *n* autoestrada *f*

mottled /'mɒtld/ *a* sarapintado, pintalgado

motto /'mɒtəʊ/ *n* (*pl* **-oes**) divisa *f*, lema *m*

mould[1] /məʊld/ *n* (*container*) forma *f*, molde *m*; (*culin*) forma *f* □ *vt* moldar. **~ing** *n* (*archit*) moldura *f*

mould[2] /məʊld/ *n* (*fungi*) bolor *m*, mofo *m*. **~y** *a* bolorento

moult /məʊlt/ *vi* estar na muda

mound /maʊnd/ *n* monte *m* de terra *or* de pedras; (*small hill*) montículo *m*

mount /maʊnt/ *vt/i* montar □ *n* (*support*) suporte *m*; (*for gem etc*) engaste *m*. **~ up** aumentar, subir

mountain /'maʊntɪn/ *n* montanha *f*. **~ bike** mountain bike *f*. **~ous** *a* montanhoso

mountaineer /maʊntɪ'nɪə(r)/ *n* alpinista *mf*. **~ing** *n* alpinismo *m*

mourn /mɔ:n/ *vt/i* **~ (for)** chorar (a morte de). **~ (over)** sofrer (por). **~er** *n* pessoa *f* que acompanha o enterro. **~ing** *n* luto *m*. **in ~ing** de luto

mournful /'mɔ:nfl/ *a* triste; (*sorrowful*) pesaroso

mouse /maʊs/ *n* (*pl* **mice**) camundongo *m*

mousetrap /'maʊstræp/ *n* ratoeira *f*

mousse /mu:s/ *n* mousse *f*

moustache /mə'sta:ʃ/ *n* bigode *m*

mouth[1] /maʊθ/ *n* boca *f*. **~-organ** *n* gaita *f* de boca, (*P*) beiços

mouth[2] /maʊð/ *vt/i* declamar; (*silently*) articular sem som

mouthful /'maʊθfʊl/ *n* bocado *m*

mouthpiece /'maʊθpi:s/ *n* (*mus*) bocal *m*, boquilha *f*; (*fig: person*) porta-voz *mf*

mouthwash /'maʊθwɒʃ/ *n* líquido *m* para bochecho

movable /'mu:vəbl/ *a* móvel

move /mu:v/ *vt/i* mover(-se), mexer (-se), deslocar(-se); (*emotionally*) comover; (*incite*) convencer, levar a; (*act*) agir; (*propose*) propor; (*depart*) ir, partir; (*go forward*) avançar. **~ (out)** mudar-se, sair □ *n* movimento *m*; (*in game*) jogada *f*; (*player's turn*) vez *f*; (*house change*) mudança *f*. **~ back** recuar. **~ forward** avançar. **~ in** mudar-se para. **~ on!** circulem! **~ over, please** chegue-se para lá, por favor. **on the ~** em marcha

movement /'mu:vmənt/ *n* movimento *m*

movie /'mu:vɪ/ *n* (*Amer*) filme *m*. **the ~s** o cinema

moving /'mu:vɪŋ/ *a* (*touching*) comovente; (*movable*) móvil; (*in motion*) em movimento

mow /məʊ/ *vt* (*pp* **mowed** *or* **mown**) ceifar; (*lawn*) cortar a grama, (*P*) relva. **~ down** ceifar. **~er** *n* (*for lawn*) máquina *f* de cortar a grama, (*P*) relva

MP *abbr see* **Member of Parliament**

Mr /'mɪstə(r)/ *n* (*pl* **Messrs**) Senhor *m*. **~ Smith** o Sr Smith

Mrs /'mɪsɪz/ *n* Senhora *f*. **~ Smith** a Sra Smith. **Mr and ~ Smith** o Sr Smith e a mulher

Ms /mɪz/ *n* Senhora D *f*

much /mʌtʃ/ (**more, most**) *a, adv & n* muito (*m*). **very ~** muito, muitíssimo. **you may have as ~ as you need** você pode levar o que precisar. **~ of it** muito *or* grande parte dele. **so ~ the better/worse** tanto melhor/pior. **how ~?** quanto? **not ~** não muito. **too ~** demasiado, demais. **he's not ~ of a gardener** não é lá grande jardineiro

muck /mʌk/ *n* estrume *m*; (*colloq: dirt*) porcaria *f* □ *vi* **~ about** (*sl*) entreter-se, perder tempo. **~ in** (*sl*) ajudar, dar uma mão □ *vt* **~ up** (*sl*) estragar. **~y** *a* sujo

mucus /'mju:kəs/ *n* muco *m*

mud /mʌd/ *n* lama *f*. **~dy** *a* lamacento, enlameado

muddle /'mʌdl/ *vt* baralhar, atrapalhar, confundir □ *vi* **~ through** sair-se bem, desenrascar-se (*sl*) □ *n* desordem *f*; (*mix-up*) confusão *f*, trapalhada *f*

mudguard /'mʌdga:d/ *n* para-lama *m*

muff /mʌf/ *n* (*for hands*) regalo *m*

muffle /'mʌfl/ *vt* abafar. **~ (up)** agasalhar(-se). **~d sounds** sons *mpl* abafados. **~r** /-ə(r)/ *n* cachecol *m*

mug /mʌg/ *n* caneca *f*; (*sl: face*) cara *f*; (*sl: fool*) trouxa *mf* (*colloq*) □ *vt* (*pt* **mugged**) assaltar, agredir. **~ger** *n* assaltante *mf*. **~ging** *n* assalto *m*

muggy /'mʌgɪ/ *a* abafado

mule /mju:l/ *n* mulo *m*; (*female*) mula *f*

mull /mʌl/ *vt* **~ over** ruminar; (*fig*) matutar em

multi- /'mʌltɪ/ *pref* mult(i)-

multicoloured /'mʌltɪkʌləd/ *a* multicolor

multinational /mʌltɪ'næʃnəl/ *a & n* multinacional (*f*)

multiple /'mʌltɪpl/ *a & n* múltiplo (*m*)

multipl|y /'mʌltɪplaɪ/ *vt/i* multiplicar(-se). **~ication** /-ɪ'keɪʃn/ *n* multiplicação *f*

multi-storey /mʌltɪ'stɔ:rɪ/ *a* (*car park*) em vários níveis

multitude /'mʌltɪtju:d/ *n* multidão *f*

mum[1] /mʌm/ *a* **keep ~** (*colloq*) ficar calado

mum[2] /mʌm/ (*B*) mamãe *f* (*colloq*) *n* (*colloq*) (*P*) mamã

mumble /'mʌmbl/ *vt/i* resmungar, resmonear

mummy[1] /'mʌmɪ/ *n* (*body*) múmia *f*
mummy[2] /'mʌmɪ/ *n* (*esp child's lang*) mamã (*B*) mamãe *f* (*colloq*) mãezinha *f* (*colloq*), (*P*)
mumps /mʌmps/ *n* parotidite *f*, papeira *f*
munch /mʌntʃ/ *vt* mastigar
mundane /mʌn'deɪn/ *a* banal; (*worldly*) mundano
municipal /mju:'nɪsɪpl/ *a* municipal. **~ity** /-'pælətɪ/ *n* municipalidade *f*
munitions /mju:'nɪʃnz/ *npl* munições *fpl*
mural /'mjʊərəl/ *a* & *n* mural (*m*)
murder /'mɜ:də(r)/ *n* assassínio *m*, assassinato *m* □ *vt* assassinar. **~er** *n* assassino *m*, assassina *f*. **~ous** *a* assassino, sanguinário; (*of weapon*) mortífero
murky /'mɜ:kɪ/ *a* (**-ier**, **-iest**) escuro, sombrio
murmur /'mɜ:mə(r)/ *n* murmúrio *m* □ *vt/i* murmurar
muscle /'mʌsl/ *n* músculo *m* □ *vi* **~ in** (*colloq*) impor-se, intrometer-se
muscular /'mʌskjʊlə(r)/ *a* muscular; (*brawny*) musculoso
muse /mju:z/ *vi* meditar, cismar
museum /mju:'zɪəm/ *n* museu *m*
mush /mʌʃ/ *n* papa *f* de farinha de milho. **~y** *a* mole; (*sentimental*) piegas *inv*
mushroom /'mʌʃrʊm/ *n* cogumelo *m* □ *vi* pulular, multiplicar-se com rapidez
music /'mju:zɪk/ *n* música *f*. **~al** *a* musical □ *n* (*show*) comédia *f* musical, musical *m*. **~al box** *n* caixa *f* de música. **~-stand** *n* estante *f* de música
musician /mju:'zɪʃn/ *n* músico *m*
musk /mʌsk/ *n* almíscar *m*
Muslim /'mʊzlɪm/ *a* & *n* muçulmano (*m*)
muslin /'mʌzlɪn/ *n* musselina *f*
mussel /'mʌsl/ *n* mexilhão *m*
must /mʌst/ *v aux* dever. **you ~ go** é necessário que você parta. **he ~ be old** ele deve ser velho. **I ~ have done it** eu devo tê-lo feito □ *n* **be a ~** (*colloq*) ser imprescindível
mustard /'mʌstəd/ *n* mostarda *f*
muster /'mʌstə(r)/ *vt/i* juntar(-se), reunir(-se). **pass ~** ser aceitável
musty /'mʌstɪ/ *a* (**-ier**, **-iest**) mofado, bolorento
mutation /mju:'teɪʃn/ *n* mutação *f*
mute /mju:t/ *a* & *n* mudo (*m*)
muted /'mju:tɪd/ *a* (*sound*) em surdina; (*colour*) suave
mutilat|e /'mju:tɪleɪt/ *vt* mutilar. **~ion** /-'leɪʃn/ *n* mutilação *f*
mutin|y /'mju:tɪnɪ/ *n* motim *f* □ *vi* amotinar-se. **~ous** *a* amotinado
mutter /'mʌtə(r)/ *vt/i* resmungar
mutton /'mʌtn/ *n* (carne de) carneiro *m*
mutual /'mju:tʃʊəl/ *a* mútuo; (*colloq: common*) comum. **~ly** *adv* mutuamente
muzzle /'mʌzl/ *n* focinho *m*; (*device*) focinheira *f*; (*of gun*) boca *f* □ *vt* amordaçar; (*dog*) pôr focinheira em
my /maɪ/ *a* meu(s), minha(s)
myself /maɪ'self/ *pron* eu mesmo, eu próprio; (*reflexive*) me; (*after prep*) mim (próprio, mesmo). **by ~** sozinho
mysterious /mɪ'stɪərɪəs/ *a* misterioso
mystery /'mɪstərɪ/ *n* mistério *m*
mystic /'mɪstɪk/ *a* & *n* místico (*m*). **~al** *a* místico. **~ism** /-sɪzəm/ *n* misticismo *m*
mystify /'mɪstɪfaɪ/ *vt* deixar perplexo
mystique /mɪ'sti:k/ *n* mística *f*
myth /mɪθ/ *n* mito *m*. **~ical** *a* mítico
mytholog|y /mɪ'θɒlədʒɪ/ *n* mitologia *f*. **~ical** /mɪθə'lɒdʒɪkl/ *a* mitológico

N

nab /næb/ *vt* (*pt* **nabbed**) (*sl*) apanhar em flagrante, apanhar com a boca na botija (*colloq*), pilhar
nag /næg/ *vt/i* (*pt* **nagged**) implicar (com), criticar constantemente; (*pester*) apoquentar
nagging /'nægɪŋ/ *a* implicante; (*pain*) constante, contínuo
nail /neɪl/ *n* prego *m*; (*of finger, toe*) unha *f* □ *vt* pregar. **~-brush** *n* escova *f* de unhas. **~-file** *n* lixa *f* de unhas. **~ polish** esmalte *m*, (*P*) verniz *m* para as unhas. **hit the ~ on the head** acertar em cheio. **on the ~** sem demora
naïve /naɪ'i:v/ *a* ingênuo, (*P*) ingénuo
naked /'neɪkɪd/ *a* nu. **to the ~ eye** a olho nu, à vista desarmada **~ness** *f* nudez *f*
name /neɪm/ *n* nome *m*; (*fig*) reputação *f*, fama *f* □ *vt* (*mention; appoint*) nomear; (*give a name to*) chamar, dar o nome de; (*a date*) marcar. **be ~d after** ter o nome de. **~less** *a* sem nome, anônimo, (*P*) anónimo
namely /'neɪmlɪ/ *adv* a saber
namesake /'neɪmseɪk/ *n* homônimo *m* (*P*) homónimo *m*
nanny /'nænɪ/ *n* ama *f*, babá *f*
nap[1] /næp/ *n* soneca *f* □ *vi* (*pt* **napped**) dormitar, tirar um cochilo. **catch ~ping** apanhar desprevenido
nap[2] /næp/ *n* (*of material*) felpa *f*
nape /neɪp/ *n* nuca *f*
napkin /'næpkɪn/ *n* guardanapo *m*; (*for baby*) fralda *f*

nappy /'næpɪ/ *n* fralda *f*. **~-rash** *n* assadura *f*
narcotic /na:'kɒtɪk/ *a* & *n* narcótico (*m*)
narrat|e /nə'reɪt/ *vt* narrar. **~ion** /-ʃn/ *n* narrativa *f*. **~or** *n* narrador *m*
narrative /'nærətɪv/ *n* narrativa *f* □ *a* narrativo
narrow /'nærəʊ/ *a* (-er, -est) estreito; (*fig*) restrito □ *vt/i* estreitar(-se); (*limit*) limitar(-se). **~ly** *adv* (*only just*) por pouco; (*closely, carefully*) de perto, com cuidado. **~-minded** *a* bitolado, de visão limitada. **~ness** *n* estreiteza *f*
nasal /'neɪzl/ *a* nasal
nast|y /'na:stɪ/ *a* (-ier, -iest) (*malicious, of weather*) mau; (*unpleasant*) desagradável, intragável; (*rude*) grosseiro. **~ily** *adv* maldosamente; (*unpleasantly*) desagradavelmente. **~iness** *f* (*malice*) maldade *f*; (*rudeness*) grosseria *f*
nation /'neɪʃn/ *n* nação *f*. **~-wide** *a* em todo o país, em escala *or* a nível nacional
national /'næʃnəl/ *a* nacional □ *n* natural *mf*. **~ anthem** hino *m* nacional. **~ism** *n* nacionalismo *m*. **~ize** *vt* nacionalizar. **~ly** *adv* em escala nacional
nationality /næʃə'nælətɪ/ *n* nacionalidade *f*
native /'neɪtɪv/ *n* natural *mf*, nativo *m* □ *a* nativo; (*country*) natal; (*inborn*) inato. **be a ~ of** ser natural de. **~ language** língua *f* materna. **~ speaker of Portuguese** pessoa *f* de língua portuguesa, falante *m* nativo de Português
Nativity /nə'tɪvətɪ/ *n* **the ~** a Natividade *f*
natter /'nætə(r)/ *vi* fazer conversa fiada, falar à toa, tagarelar
natural /'nætʃrəl/ *a* natural. **~ history** história *f* natural. **~ist** *n* naturalista *mf*. **~ly** *adv* naturalmente; (*by nature*) por natureza
naturaliz|e /'nætʃrəlaɪz/ *vt/i* naturalizar(-se); (*animal, plant*) aclimatar (-se). **~ation** /-'zeɪʃn/ *n* naturalização *f*
nature /'neɪtʃə(r)/ *n* natureza *f*; (*kind*) gênero *m*, (*P*) género *m*; (*of person*) índole *f*
naughty /'nɔ:tɪ/ *a* (-ier, -iest) (*child*) levado; (*indecent*) picante
nause|a /'nɔ:sɪə/ *n* náusea *f*. **~ate** /'nɔ:sɪeɪt/ *vt* nausear. **~ating, ~ous** *a* nauseabundo, repugnante
nautical /'nɔ:tɪkl/ *a* náutico. **~ mile** milha *f* marítima
naval /'neɪvl/ *a* naval; (*officer*) de marinha
nave /neɪv/ *n* nave *f*
navel /'neɪvl/ *n* umbigo *m*
navigable /'nævɪgəbl/ *a* navegável
navigat|e /'nævɪgeɪt/ *vt* (*sea etc*) navegar; (*ship*) pilotar □ *vi* navegar. **~ion** /-'geɪʃn/ *n* navegação *f*. **~or** *n* navegador *m*
navy /'neɪvɪ/ *n* marinha *f* de guerra. **~ (blue)** azul-marinho *m invar*
near /nɪə(r)/ *adv* perto, quaze □ *prep* perto de □ *a* próximo □ *vt* aproximar-se de, chegar-se a. **draw ~** aproximar(-se) (**to** de). **~ by** *adv* perto, próximo. **N~ East** Oriente *m* Próximo. **~ to** perto de. **~ness** *n* proximidade *f*
nearby /'nɪəbaɪ/ *a* & *adv* próximo, perto
nearly /'nɪəlɪ/ *adv* quase, por pouco. **not ~ as pretty**/*etc* as longe de ser tão bonita/*etc* como
neat /ni:t/ *a* (-er, -est) (bem) cuidado; (*room*) bem arrumado; (*spirits*) puro, sem gelo. **~ly** *adv* (*with care*) com cuidado; (*cleverly*) habilmente. **~ness** *n* aspecto *m* cuidado
nebulous /'nebjʊləs/ *a* nebuloso; (*vague*) vago, confuso
necessar|y /'nesəsərɪ/ *a* necessário. **~ily** *adv* necessariamente
necessitate /nɪ'sesɪteɪt/ *vt* exigir, obrigar a, tornar necessário
necessity /nɪ'sesətɪ/ *n* necessidade *f*; (*thing*) coisa *f* indispensável, artigo *m* de primeira necessidade
neck /nek/ *n* pescoço *m*; (*of dress*) gola *f*. **~ and neck** emparelhados
necklace /'neklɪs/ *n* colar *m*
neckline /'neklaɪn/ *n* decote *m*
nectarine /'nektərɪn/ *n* pêssego *m*
née /neɪ/ *a* em solteira. **Ann Jones ~ Drewe** Ann Jones cujo nome de solteira era Drewe
need /ni:d/ *n* necessidade *f* □ *vt* precisar de, necessitar de. **you ~ not come** não temde *or* não precisa vir. **~less** *a* inútil, desnecessário. **~lessly** *adv* inutilmente, sem necessidade
needle /'ni:dl/ *a* agulha *f* □ *vt* (*colloq: provoke*) provocar
needlework /'ni:dlwɜ:k/ *n* costura *f*; (*embroidery*) bordado *m*
needy /'ni:dɪ/ *a* (-ier, -iest) necessitado, carenciado
negation /nɪ'geɪʃn/ *n* negação *f*
negative /'negətɪv/ *a* negativo □ *n* negativa *f*, negação *f*; (*photo*) negativo *m*. **in the ~** (*answer*) na negativa; (*gram*) na forma negativa. **~ly** *adv* negativamente
neglect /nɪ'glekt/ *vt* descuidar; (*opportunity*) desprezar; (*family*) não cuidar de, abandonar; (*duty*) não cumprir □ *n* falta *f* de cuidado(s), descuido *m*. **(state of) ~** abandono

m. ~ to (*omit to*) esquecer-se de. **~ful** *a* negligente

negligen|t /'neglɪdʒənt/ *a* negligente. **~ce** *n* negligência *f*, desleixo *m*

negligible /'neglɪdʒəbl/ *a* insignificante, ínfimo

negotiable /nɪ'gəʊʃəbl/ *a* negociável

negotiat|e /nɪ'gəʊʃɪeɪt/ *vt/i* negociar; (*obstacle*) transpor; (*difficulty*) vencer. **~ion** /-sɪ'eɪʃn/ *n* negociação *f*. **~or** *n* negociador *m*

Negro /'ni:grəʊ/ *a* & *n* (*pl* **~oes**) negro (*m*), preto (*m*)

neigh /neɪ/ *n* relincho *m* □ *vi* relinchar

neighbour /'neɪbə(r)/ *n* vizinho *m*. **~hood** *n* vizinhança *f*. **~ing** *a* vizinho. **~ly** *a* de boa vizinhança

neither /'naɪðə(r)/ *a* & *pron* nenhum(a) (de dois *ou* duas), nem um nem outro, nem uma nem outra □ *adv* tampouco, também não □ *conj* nem. **~ big nor small** nem grande nem pequeno. **~ am I** nem eu

neon /'ni:ɒn/ *n* néon *m* □ *a* (*lamp etc*) de néon

nephew /'nevju:/ *n* sobrinho *m*

nerve /nɜ:v/ *n* nervo *m*; (*fig: courage*) coragem *f*; (*colloq: impudence*) descaramento *m*, (*P*) lata *f* (*colloq*). **get on sb's nerves** irritar, dar nos nervos de alg. **~-racking** *a* de arrasar os nervos, enervante

nervous /'nɜ:vəs/ *a* nervoso. **be** *or* **feel ~** (*afraid*) ter receio/um certo medo. **~ breakdown** esgotamento *m* nervoso. **~ly** *adv* nervosamente. **~ness** *n* nervosismo *m*; (*fear*) receio *m*

nest /nest/ *n* ninho *m* □ *vi* aninhar-se, fazer *or* ter ninho. **~-egg** *n* pé-de-meia *m*

nestle /'nesl/ *vi* aninhar-se

net[1] /net/ *n* rede *f* □ *vt* (*pt* **netted**) apanhar na rede. **~ting** *n* rede *f*. **wire ~ting** rede *f* de arame

net[2] /net/ *a* (*weight etc*) líquido

Netherlands /'neðələndz/ *npl* **the ~** os Países Baixos

nettle /'netl/ *n* urtiga *f*

network /'netwɜ:k/ *n* rede *f*, cadeia *f*

neuro|sis /njʊə'rəʊsɪs/ *n* (*pl* **-oses** /-si:z/) neurose *f*. **~tic** /-'rɒtɪk/ *a* & *n* neurótico (*m*)

neuter /'nju:tə(r)/ *a* & *n* neutro (*m*) □ *vt* castrar, capar

neutral /'nju:trəl/ *a* neutro. **~ (gear)** ponto *m* morto. **~ity** /-'trælətɪ/ *n* neutralidade *f*

never /'nevə(r)/ *adv* nunca; (*colloq: not*) não. **he ~ refuses** ele nunca recusa. **I ~ saw him** (*colloq*) nunca o vi. **~ mind** não faz mal, deixe para lá. **~-ending** *a* interminável

nevertheless /nevəðə'les/ *adv* & *conj* contudo, no entanto

new /nju:/ *a* (-er, -est) novo. **~-born** *a* recém-nascido. **~ moon** lua *f* nova. **~ year** ano *m* novo. **N~ Year's Day** dia *m* de Ano Novo. **N~ Year's Eve** véspera *f* de Ano Novo. **N~ Zealand** Nova Zelândia *f*. **N~ Zealander** neozelandês *m*. **~ness** *n* novidade *f*

newcomer /'nju:kʌmə(r)/ *n* recém-chegado *m*, (*P*) recém-vindo *m*

newfangled /nju:'fæŋgld/ *a* (*pej*) moderno

newly /'nju:lɪ/ *adv* há pouco, recentemente. **~-weds** *npl* recém-casados *mpl*

news /nju:z/ *n* notícia(s) *f*(*pl*); (*radio*) noticiário *m*, notícias *fpl*; (*TV*) telejornal *m*. **~-caster**, **~-reader** *n* locutor *m*. **~-flash** *n* notícia *f* de última hora

newsagent /'nju:zeɪdʒənt/ *n* jornaleiro *m*

newsletter /'nju:zletə(r)/ *n* boletim *m* informativo

newspaper /'nju:zpeɪpə(r)/ *n* jornal *m*

newsreel /'nju:zri:l/ *n* atualidades *fpl*, (*P*) actualidades *fpl*

newt /nju:t/ *n* tritão *m*

next /nekst/ *a* próximo; (*adjoining*) pegado, ao lado, contíguo; (*following*) seguinte □ *adv* a seguir □ *n* seguinte *mf*. **~-door** *a* do lado. **~ of kin** parente *m* mais próximo. **~ to** ao lado de. **~ to nothing** quase nada

nib /nɪb/ *n* bico *m*, (*P*) aparo *m*

nibble /'nɪbl/ *vt* mordiscar, dar dentadinhas em

nice /naɪs/ *a* (-er, -est) agradável, bom; (*kind*) simpático, gentil; (*pretty*) bonito; (*respectable*) bem educado, correto, (*P*) correcto; (*subtle*) fino, subtil. **~ly** *adv* agradavelmente; (*well*) bem

nicety /'naɪsətɪ/ *n* sutileza *f*, (*P*) subtileza *f*

niche /nɪtʃ/ *n* nicho *m*; (*fig*) bom lugar *m*

nick /nɪk/ *n* corte *m*, chanfradura *f*; (*sl: prison*) cadeia *f* □ *vt* dar um corte em; (*sl: steal*) roubar, limpar (*colloq*); (*sl: arrest*) apanhar, pôr a mão em (*colloq*). **in good ~** (*colloq*) em boa forma, em bom estado. **in the ~ of time** mesmo a tempo

nickel /'nɪkl/ *n* níquel *m*; (*Amer*) moeda *f* de cinco cêntimos

nickname /'nɪkneɪm/ *n* apelido *m*, (*P*) alcunha *f*; (*short form*) diminutivo *m* □ *vt* apelidar de

nicotine /'nɪkəti:n/ *n* nicotina *f*

niece /ni:s/ *n* sobrinha *f*

Nigeria /naɪ'dʒɪərɪə/ *n* Nigéria *f*. **~n** *a* & *n* nigeriano (*m*)

niggardly /'nɪgədlɪ/ *a* miserável
night /naɪt/ *n* noite *f* □ *a* de noite, noturno, (*P*) nocturno. **at ~** à/de noite. **by ~** de noite. **~-cap** *n* (*drink*) bebida *f* na hora de deitar. **~-club** *n* boate *f*, (*P*) boîte *f*. **~-dress, ~-gown** *ns* camisola *f* de dormir, (*P*) camisa *f* de noite. **~-life** *n* vida *f* noturna, (*P*) nocturna. **~-school** *n* escola *f* noturna, (*P*) nocturna. **~-time** *n* noite *f*. **~-watchman** *n* guarda-noturno *m*, (*P*) guarda-nocturno *m*
nightfall /'naɪtfɔ:l/ *n* anoitecer *m*
nightingale /'naɪtɪŋgeɪl/ *n* rouxinol *m*
nightly /'naɪtlɪ/ *a* noturno, (*P*) nocturno □ *adv* de noite, à noite, todas as noites
nightmare /'naɪtmeə(r)/ *n* pesadelo *m*
nil /nɪl/ *n* nada *m*; (*sport*) zero *m* □ *a* nulo
nimble /'nɪmbl/ *a* (-er, -est) ágil, ligeiro
nin|e /naɪn/ *a* & *n* nove (*m*). **~th** *a* & *n* nono (*m*)
nineteen /naɪn'ti:n/ *a* & *n* dezenove (*m*), (*P*) dezanove (*m*). **~th** *a* & *n* décimo nono (*m*)
ninet|y /'naɪntɪ/ *a* & *n* noventa (*m*). **~ieth** *a* & *n* nonagésimo (*m*)
nip /nɪp/ *vt/i* (*pt* **nipped**) apertar, beliscar; (*colloq*: *rush*) ir correndo, ir num pulo (*colloq*) □ *n* aperto *m*, beliscão *m*; (*drink*) gole *m*, trago *m*. **a ~ in the air** um frio cortante. **~ in the bud** cortar pela raiz
nipple /'nɪpl/ *n* mamilo *m*
nippy /'nɪpɪ/ *a* (-ier, -iest) (*colloq: quick*) rápido; (*colloq: chilly*) cortante
nitrogen /'naɪtrədʒən/ *n* azoto *m*, nitrogênio *m*, (*P*) nitrogénio *m*
nitwit /'nɪtwɪt/ *n* (*colloq*) imbecil *m*
no /nəʊ/ *a* nenhum □ *adv* não □ *n* (*pl* **noes**) não *m*. **~ entry** entrada *f* proibida. **~ money/time/** *etc* nenhum dinheiro/tempo/*etc*. **~ man's land** terra *f* de ninguém. **~ one** = **nobody**. **~ smoking** é proibido fumar. **~ way!** (*colloq*) de modo nenhum!
nob|le /'nəʊbl/ *a* (-er, -est) nobre. **~ility** /-'bɪlətɪ/ *n* nobreza *f*
nobleman /'nəʊblmən/ *n* (*pl* -**men**) nobre *m*, fidalgo *m*
nobody /'nəʊbɒdɪ/ *pron* ninguém □ *n* nulidade *f*. **he knows ~** ele não conhece ninguém. **~ is there** não tem ninguém lá
nocturnal /nɒk'tɜ:nl/ *a* noturno, (*P*) nocturno
nod /nɒd/ *vt/i* (*pt* **nodded**) **~ (one's head)** acenar (com) a cabeça; **~ (off)** cabecear □ *n* aceno *m* com a cabeça (para dizer que sim *or* para cumprimentar)
noise /nɔɪz/ *n* ruído *m*, barulho *m*. **~less** *a* silencioso
nois|y /'nɔɪzɪ/ *a* (-ier, -iest) ruidoso, barulhento. **~ily** *adv* ruidosamente
nomad /'nəʊmæd/ *n* nômade *mf*, (*P*) nómade *mf*. **~ic** /'mædɪk/ *a* nômade, (*P*) nómade
nominal /'nɒmɪnl/ *a* nominal; (*fee, sum*) simbólico
nominat|e /'nɒmɪneɪt/ *vt* (*appoint*) nomear; (*put forward*) propor. **~ion** /-'neɪʃn/ *n* nomeação *f*
non- /nɒn/ *pref* não, sem, in-, a-, anti-, des-. **~-skid** *a* antiderrapante. **~-stick** *a* não-aderente
nonchalant /'nɒnʃələnt/ *a* indiferente, desinteressado
non-commissioned /nɒnkə'mɪʃnd/ *a* **~ officer** sargento *m*, cabo *m*
non-committal /nɒnkə'mɪtl/ *a* evasivo
nondescript /'nɒndɪskrɪpt/ *a* insignificante, medíocre, indefinível
none /nʌn/ *pron* (*person*) nenhum, ninguém; (*thing*) nenhum, nada. **~ of us** nenhum de nós. **I have ~** não tenho nenhum. **~ of that!** nada disso! □ *adv* **~ too** não muito. **he is ~ the happier** nem por isso ele é mais feliz. **~ the less** contudo, no entanto, apesar disso
nonentity /nɒ'nentətɪ/ *n* nulidade *f*, zero *m* à esquerda, João Ninguém *m*
non-existent /nɒnɪg'zɪstənt/ *a* inexistente
nonplussed /nɒn'plʌst/ *a* perplexo, pasmado
nonsens|e /'nɒnsns/ *n* absurdo *m*, disparate *m*. **~ical** /-'sensɪkl/ *a* absurdo, disparatado
non-smoker /nɒn'sməʊkə(r)/ *n* não-fumante *m*, (*P*) não-fumador *m*
non-stop /nɒn'stɒp/ *a* ininterrupto, contínuo; (*train*) direto, (*P*) directo; (*flight*) sem escala □ *adv* sem parar
noodles /'nu:dlz/ *npl* talharim *m*, (*P*) macarronete *m*
nook /nʊk/ *n* (re)canto *m*
noon /nu:n/ *n* meio-dia *m*
noose /nu:s/ *n* laço *m* corrediço
nor /nɔ:(r)/ *conj* & *adv* nem, também não. **~ do I** nem eu
norm /nɔ:m/ *n* norma *f*
normal /'nɔ:ml/ *a* & *n* normal (*m*). **above/below ~** acima/abaixo do normal. **~ity** /nɔ:'mælətɪ/ *n* normalidade *f*. **~ly** *adv* normalmente
north /nɔ:θ/ *n* norte *m* □ *a* norte, do norte; (*of country, people etc*) setentrional □ *adv* a, ao/para o norte. **N~ America** América *f* do Norte. **N~ American** *a* & *n* norte-americano

(*m*). ~**-east** *n* nordeste *m*. ~**erly** /'nɔ:ðəlɪ/ *a* do norte. ~**ward** *a* ao norte. ~**ward(s)** *adv* para o norte. ~**-west** *n* noroeste *m*

northern /'nɔ:ðən/ *a* do norte

Norw|ay /'nɔ:weɪ/ *n* Noruega *f*. ~**egian** /nɔ:'wi:dʒən/ *a* & *n* norueguês (*m*)

nose /nəʊz/ *n* nariz *m*; (*of animal*) focinho *m* □ *vi* ~ **about** farejar. **pay through the** ~ pagar um preço exorbitante

nosebleed /'nəʊzbli:d/ *n* hemorragia *f* nasal *or* pelo nariz

nosedive /'nəʊzdaɪv/ *n* vôo *m* picado

nostalg|ia /nɒ'stældʒə/ *n* nostalgia *f*. ~**ic** *a* nostálgico

nostril /'nɒstrəl/ *n* narina *f*; (*of horse*) venta *f* (*usually pl*)

nosy /'nəʊzɪ/ *a* (-ier, -iest) (*colloq*) bisbilhoteiro

not /nɒt/ *adv* não. ~ **at all** nada, de modo nenhum; (*reply to thanks*) de nada. **he is** ~ **at all bored** ele não está nem um pouco entediado. ~ **yet** ainda não. **I suppose** ~ creio que não

notable /'nəʊtəbl/ *a* notável □ *n* notabilidade *f*

notably /'nəʊtəblɪ/ *adv* notavelmente; (*particularly*) especialmente

notch /nɒtʃ/ *n* corte *m* em V □ *vt* marcar com cortes. ~ **up** (*score etc*) marcar

note /nəʊt/ *n* nota *f*; (*banknote*) nota (de banco) *f*; (*short letter*) bilhete *m* □ *vt* notar

notebook /'nəʊtbʊk/ *n* livrinho *m* de notas, (*P*) bloco-notas *m*

noted /'nəʊtɪd/ *a* conhecido, famoso

notepaper /'nəʊtpeɪpə(r)/ *n* papel *m* de carta

noteworthy /'nəʊtwɜ:ðɪ/ *a* notável

nothing /'nʌθɪŋ/ *n* nada *m*; (*person*) nulidade *f*, zero *m* □ *adv* nada, de modo algum *or* nenhum, de maneira alguma *or* nenhuma. **he eats** ~ ele não come nada. ~ **big**/*etc* nada (de) grande/*etc*. ~ **else** nada mais. ~ **much** pouca coisa. **for** ~ (*free*) de graça; (*in vain*) em vão

notice /'nəʊtɪs/ *n* anúncio *m*, notícia *f*; (*in street, on wall*) letreiro *m*; (*warning*) aviso *m*; (*attention*) atenção *f*. **(advance)** ~ pré-aviso *m* □ *vt* notar, reparar. **at short** ~ num prazo curto. **a week's** ~ o prazo de uma semana. ~**-board** *n* quadro *m* para afixar anúncios etc. **hand in one's** ~ pedir demissão. **take** ~ reparar (of em). **take no** ~ não fazer caso (of de)

noticeabl|e /'nəʊtɪsəbl/ *a* visível. ~**y** *adv* visivelmente

notif|y /'nəʊtɪfaɪ/ *vt* participar, notificar. ~**ication** /-ɪ'keɪʃn/ *n* participação *f*, notificação *f*

notion /'nəʊʃn/ *n* noção *f*

notor|ious /nəʊ'tɔ:rɪəs/ *a* notório. ~**iety** /-ə'raɪətɪ/ *n* fama *f*

notwithstanding /nɒtwɪθ'stændɪŋ/ *prep* apesar de, não obstante □ *adv* mesmo assim, ainda assim □ *conj* embora, conquanto, apesar de que

nougat /'nu:ga:/ *n* nugá *m*, torrone *m*

nought /nɔ:t/ *n* zero *m*

noun /naʊn/ *n* substantivo *m*, nome *m*

nourish /'nʌrɪʃ/ *vt* alimentar, nutrir. ~**ing** *a* alimentício, nutritivo. ~**ment** *n* alimento *m*, sustento *m*

novel /'nɒvl/ *n* romance *m* □ *a* novo, original. ~**ist** *n* romancista *mf*. ~**ty** *n* novidade *f*

November /nəʊ'vembə(r)/ *n* novembro *m*

novice /'nɒvɪs/ *n* (*beginner*) noviço *m*, novato *m*; (*relig*) noviço *m*

now /naʊ/ *adv* agora □ *conj* ~ **(that)** agora que. **by** ~ a estas horas, por esta altura. **from** ~ **on** de agora em diante. ~ **and again**, ~ **and then** de vez em quando. **right** ~ já

nowadays /'naʊədeɪz/ *adv* hoje em dia, presentemente, atualmente, (*P*) actualmente

nowhere /'nəʊweə(r)/ *adv* (*position*) em lugar nenhum, em lado nenhum; (*direction*) a lado nenhum, a parte alguma *or* nenhuma

nozzle /'nɒzl/ *n* bico *m*, bocal *m*; (*of hose*) agulheta *f*

nuance /'nju:a:ns/ *n* nuance *f*, matiz *m*

nuclear /'nju:klɪə(r)/ *a* nuclear

nucleus /'nju:klɪəs/ *n* (*pl* -lei /-lɪaɪ/) núcleo *m*

nud|e /nju:d/ *a* & *n* nu (*m*). **in the** ~**e** nu. ~**ity** *n* nudez *f*

nudge /nʌdʒ/ *vt* tocar com o cotovelo, cutucar □ *n* ligeira cotovelada *f*, cutucada *f*

nudis|t /'nju:dɪst/ *n* nudista *mf*. ~**m** /-zəm/ *n* nudismo *m*

nuisance /'nju:sns/ *n* aborrecimento *m*, chatice *f* (*sl*); (*person*) chato *m* (*sl*)

null /nʌl/ *a* nulo. ~ **and void** (*jur*) írrito e nulo. ~**ify** *vt* anular, invalidar

numb /nʌm/ *a* entorpecido, dormente □ *vt* entorpecer, adormecer

number /'nʌmbə(r)/ *n* número *m*; (*numeral*) algarismo *m* □ *vt* numerar; (*amount to*) ser em número de; (*count*) contar, incluir. ~**-plate** *n* chapa (do carro) *f*

numeral /'nju:mərəl/ *n* número *m*, algarismo *m*

numerate /'nju:mərət/ *a* que tem conhecimentos básicos de matemática

numerical /nju:'merɪkl/ *a* numérico
numerous /'nju:mərəs/ *a* numeroso
nun /nʌn/ *n* freira *f*, religiosa *f*
nurs|e /nɜ:s/ *n* enfermeira *f*, enfermeiro *m*; (*nanny*) ama(-seca) *f*, babá *f* □ *vt* cuidar de, tratar de; (*hopes etc*) alimentar, acalentar. **~ing** *n* enfermagem *f*. **~ing home** clínica *f* de repouso
nursery /'nɜ:sərɪ/ *n* quarto *m* de crianças; (*for plants*) viveiro *m*. (**day**) **~** creche *f*. **~ rhyme** poema *m or* canção *f* infantil. **~ school** jardim *m* de infância
nurture /'nɜ:tʃə(r)/ *vt* educar
nut /nʌt/ *n* (*bot*) noz *f*; (*techn*) porca *f* de parafuso
nutcrackers /'nʌtkrækəz/ *npl* quebra-nozes *m invar*
nutmeg /'nʌtmeg/ *n* noz-moscada *f*
nutrient /'nju:trɪənt/ *n* substância *f* nutritiva, nutriente *m*
nutrit|ion /nju:'trɪʃn/ *n* nutrição *f*. **~ious** *a* nutritivo
nutshell /'nʌtʃel/ *n* casca *f* de noz. **in a ~** em poucas palavras
nuzzle /'nʌzl/ *vt* esfregar com o focinho
nylon /'naɪlɒn/ *n* nylon *m*. **~s** meias *fpl* de nylon

O

oaf /əʊf/ *n* (*pl* **oafs**) imbecil *m*, idiota *m*
oak /əʊk/ *n* carvalho *m*
OAP *abbr see* **old-age pensioner**
oar /ɔ:(r)/ *n* remo *m*
oasis /əʊ'eɪsɪs/ *n* (*pl* **oases** /-si:z/) oásis *m*
oath /əʊθ/ *n* juramento *m*; (*swear-word*) praga *f*
oatmeal /'əʊtmi:l/ *n* farinha *f* de aveia; (*porridge*) papa *f* de aveia
oats /əʊts/ *npl* aveia *f*
obedien|t /ə'bi:dɪənt/ *a* obediente. **~ce** *n* obediência *f*. **~tly** *adv* obedientemente
obes|e /əʊ'bi:s/ *a* obeso. **~ity** *n* obesidade *f*
obey /ə'beɪ/ *vt/i* obedecer (a)
obituary /ə'bɪtʃʊərɪ/ *n* necrológio *m*, (*P*) necrologia *f*
object[1] /'ɒbdʒɪkt/ *n* objeto *m*, (*P*) objecto *m*; (*aim*) objetivo *m*, (*P*) objectivo *m*; (*gram*) complemento *m*
object[2] /əb'dʒekt/ *vt/i* objetar, (*P*) objectar (que). **~ to** opor-se a, discordar de. **~ion** /-ʃn/ *n* objeção *f*, (*P*) objecção *f*
objectionable /əb'dʒekʃnəbl/ *a* censurável; (*unpleasant*) desagradável
objectiv|e /əb'dʒektɪv/ *a* objetivo, (*P*) objectivo. **~ity** /-'tɪvətɪ/ *n* objetividade *f*, (*P*) objectividade *f*
obligation /ɒblɪ'geɪʃn/ *n* obrigação *f*. **be under an ~ to sb** dever favores a alg
obligatory /ə'blɪgətrɪ/ *a* obrigatório
oblig|e /ə'blaɪdʒ/ *vt* obrigar; (*do a favour*) fazer um favor a, obsequiar. **~ed** *a* obrigado (to a). **~ed to sb** em dívida (para) com alg. **~ing** *a* prestável, amável. **~ingly** *adv* amavelmente
oblique /ə'bli:k/ *a* oblíquo
obliterat|e /ə'blɪtəreɪt/ *vt* obliterar. **~ion** /-'reɪʃn/ *n* obliteração *f*
oblivion /ə'blɪvɪən/ *n* esquecimento *m*
oblivious /ə'blɪvɪəs/ *a* esquecido, sem consciência (**of/to** de)
oblong /'ɒblɒŋ/ *a* oblongo □ *n* retângulo *m*, (*P*) rectângulo *m*
obnoxious /əb'nɒkʃəs/ *a* ofensivo, detestável
oboe /'əʊbəʊ/ *n* oboé *m*
obscen|e /əb'si:n/ *a* obsceno. **~ity** /-'enətɪ/ *n* obscenidade *f*
obscur|e /əb'skjʊə(r)/ *a* obscuro □ *vt* obscurecer; (*conceal*) encobrir. **~ity** *n* obscuridade *f*
obsequious /əb'si:kwɪəs/ *a* demasiado obsequioso, subserviente
observan|t /əb'zɜ:vənt/ *a* observador. **~ce** *n* observância *f*, cumprimento *m*
observatory /əb'zɜ:vətrɪ/ *n* observatório *m*
observ|e /əb'zɜ:v/ *vt* observar. **~ation** /ɒbzə'veɪʃn/ *n* observação *f*. **keep under ~ation** vigiar. **~er** *n* observador *m*
obsess /əb'ses/ *vt* obcecar. **~ion** /-ʃn/ *n* obsessão *f*. **~ive** *a* obsessivo
obsolete /'ɒbsəli:t/ *a* obsoleto, antiguado
obstacle /'ɒbstəkl/ *n* obstáculo *m*
obstetric|s /əb'stetrɪks/ *n* obstetrícia *f*. **~ian** /ɒbstɪ'trɪʃn/ *n* obstetra *mf*
obstina|te /'ɒbstɪnət/ *a* obstinado. **~cy** *n* obstinação *f*
obstruct /əb'strʌkt/ *vt* obstruir, bloquear; (*hinder*) estorvar, obstruir. **~ion** /-ʃn/ *n* obstrução *f*; (*thing*) obstáculo *m*
obtain /əb'teɪn/ *vt* obter □ *vi* prevalecer, estar em vigor. **~able** *a* que se pode obter
obtrusive /əb'tru:sɪv/ *a* importuno; (*thing*) demasiadamente em evidência, que dá muito na vista (*colloq*)
obvious /'ɒbvɪəs/ *a* óbvio, evidente. **~ly** *adv* obviamente
occasion /ə'keɪʒn/ *n* ocasião *f*; (*event*) acontecimento *m* □ *vt* ocasionar. **on ~** de vez em quando, ocasionalmente
occasional /ə'keɪʒənl/ *a* ocasional.

~ly *adv* de vez em quando, ocasionalmente
occult /ɒ'kʌlt/ *a* oculto
occupation /ɒkjʊ'peɪʃn/ *n* ocupação *f*. **~al** *a* profissional; (*therapy*) ocupacional
occup|y /'ɒkjʊpaɪ/ *vt* ocupar. **~ant**, **~ier** *ns* ocupante *mf*
occur /ə'kɜ:(r)/ *vi* (*pt* **occurred**) ocorrer, acontecer, dar-se; (*arise*) apresentar-se, aparecer. **~ to sb** ocorrer a alg
occurrence /ə'kʌrəns/ *n* acontecimento *m*, ocorrência *f*
ocean /'əʊʃn/ *n* oceano *m*
o'clock /ə'klɒk/ *adv* **it is one ~** é uma hora. **it is six ~** são seis horas
octagon /'ɒktəgən/ *n* octógono *m*. **~al** /-'tægənl/ *a* octogonal
octave /'ɒktɪv/ *n* oitava *f*
October /ɒk'təʊbə(r)/ *n* outubro *m*
octopus /'ɒktəpəs/ *n* (*pl* **-puses**) polvo *m*
odd /ɒd/ *a* (**-er**, **-est**) estranho, singular; (*number*) ímpar; (*left over*) de sobra; (*not of set*) desemparelhado; (*occasional*) ocasional. **~ jobs** (*paid*) biscates *mpl*; (*in garden etc*) trabalhos *mpl* diversos. **twenty ~** vinte e tantos. **~ity** *n* singularidade *f*; (*thing*) curiosidade *f*. **~ly** *adv* de modo estranho
oddment /'ɒdmənt/ *n* resto *m*, artigo *m* avulso
odds /ɒdz/ *npl* probabilidades *fpl*; (*in betting*) ganhos *mpl* líquidos. **at ~** em desacordo; (*quarrelling*) de mal, brigado. **it makes no ~** não faz diferença. **~ and ends** artigos *mpl* avulsos, coisas *fpl* pequenas
odious /'əʊdɪəs/ *a* odioso
odour /'əʊdə(r)/ *n* odor *m*. **~less** *a* inodoro
of /əv/; *emphatic* /ɒv/ *prep* de. **a friend ~ mine** um amigo meu. **the fifth ~ June** (no dia) cinco de junho. **take six ~ them** leve seis deles
off /ɒf/ *adv* embora, fora; (*switched off*) apagado, desligado; (*taken off*) tirado, desligado; (*cancelled*) cancelado; (*food*) estragado □ *prep* (fora) de; (*distant from*) a alguma distância de. **be ~** (*depart*) ir-se embora, partir. **be well ~** ser abastado. **be better/worse ~** estar em melhor/pior situação. **a day ~** um dia de folga. **20% ~** redução de 20%. **on the ~ chance that** no caso de. **~ colour** indisposto, adoentado. **~-licence** *n* loja *f* de bebidas alcoólicas. **~-load** *vt* descarregar. **~-putting** *a* desconcertante. **~-stage** *adv* fora de cena. **~-white** *a* branco-sujo
offal /'ɒfl/ *n* miudezas *fpl*, fressura *f*
offence /ə'fens/ *n* (*feeling*) ofensa *f*; (*crime*) delito *m*, transgressão *f*. **give ~ to** ofender. **take ~** ofender-se (at com)
offend /ə'fend/ *vt* ofender. **be ~ed** ofender-se (at com). **~er** *n* delinqüente *mf*, (*P*) delinquente *mf*
offensive /ə'fensɪv/ *a* ofensivo; (*disgusting*) repugnante □ *n* ofensiva *f*
offer /'ɒfə(r)/ *vt* (*pt* **offered**) oferecer □ *n* oferta *f*. **on ~** em promoção. **~ing** *n* oferenda *f*
offhand /ɒf'hænd/ *a* espontâneo; (*curt*) seco □ *adv* de improviso, sem pensar
office /'ɒfɪs/ *n* escritório *m*; (*post*) cargo *m*; (*branch*) filial *f*. **~ hours** horas *fpl* de expediente. **in ~** no poder. **take ~** assumir o cargo
officer /'ɒfɪsə(r)/ *n* oficial *m*; (*policeman*) agente *m*
official /ə'fɪʃl/ *a* oficial □ *n* funcionário *m*. **~ly** *adv* oficialmente
officiate /ə'fɪʃɪeɪt/ *vi* (*relig*) oficiar. **~ as** presidir, exercer as funções de
officious /ə'fɪʃəs/ *a* intrometido
offing /'ɒfɪŋ/ *n* **in the ~** (*fig*) em perspectiva
offset /'ɒfset/ *vt* (*pt* **-set**, *pres p* **-setting**) compensar, contrabalançar
offshoot /'ɔfʃu:t/ *n* rebento *m*; (*fig*) efeito *m* secundário
offshore /'ɒfʃɔ:(r)/ *a* ao largo da costa
offside /ɒf'saɪd/ *a* & *adv* offside, em impedimento, (*P*) fora de jogo
offspring /'ɒfsprɪŋ/ *n* (*pl invar*) descendência *f*, prole *f*
often /'ɒfn/ *adv* muitas vezes, freqüentemente, (*P*) frequentemente. **every so ~** de vez em quando. **how ~?** quantas vezes?
oh /əʊ/ *int* oh, ah
oil /ɔɪl/ *n* óleo *m*; (*petroleum*) petróleo *m* □ *vt* lubrificar. **~-painting** *n* pintura *f* a óleo. **~ rig** plataforma *f* de poço de petróleo. **~ well** poço *m* de petróleo. **~y** *a* oleoso; (*food*) gorduroso
oilfield /'ɔɪlfi:ld/ *n* campo *m* petrolífero
oilskins /'ɔɪlskɪnz/ *npl* roupa *f* de oleado
ointment /'ɔɪntmənt/ *n* pomada *f*
OK /əʊ'keɪ/ *a* & *adv* (*colloq*) (está) bem, (está) certo, (está) legal
old /əʊld/ *a* (**-er**, **-est**) velho; (*person*) velho, idoso; (*former*) antigo. **how ~ is he?** que idade tem ele? **he is eight years ~** ele tem oito anos (de idade). **of ~** (d)antes, antigamente. **~ age** velhice *f*. **~-age pensioner** reformado *m*, aposentado *m*, pessoa *f* de terceira idade. **~ boy** antigo aluno *m*. **~-fashioned** *a* fora de moda. **~ girl** antiga aluna *f*. **~ maid** solteirona *f*.

~ man homem *m* idoso, velho *m*. ~ -time *a* antigo. ~ woman mulher *f* idosa, velha *f*

olive /'ɒlɪv/ *n* azeitona *f* □ *a* de azeitona. ~ oil azeite *m*

Olympic /ə'lɪmpɪk/ *a* olímpico. ~s *npl* Olimpíadas *fpl*. ~ Games Jogos *mpl* Olímpicos

omelette /'ɒmlɪt/ *n* omelete *f*

omen /'əʊmən/ *n* agouro *m*, presságio *m*

ominous /'ɒmɪnəs/ *a* agourento; (*fig: threatening*) ameaçador

omi|t /ə'mɪt/ *vt* (*pt* omitted) omitir. ~ssion /-ʃn/ *n* omissão *f*

on /ɒn/ *prep* sobre, em cima de, de, em □ *adv* para diante, para a frente; (*switched on*) aceso, ligado; (*tap*) aberto; (*machine*) em funcionamento; (*put on*) posto; (*happening*) em curso. ~ arrival na chegada, ao chegar. ~ foot *etc* a pé *etc*. ~ doing ao fazer. ~ time na hora, dentro do horário. ~ Tuesday na terça-feira. ~ Tuesdays às terças-feiras. walk/*etc* ~ continuar a andar/*etc*. be ~ at (*film, TV*) estar levando *or* passando. ~ and off de vez em quando. ~ and ~ sem parar

once /wʌns/ *adv* uma vez; (*formerly*) noutro(s) tempo(s) □ *conj* uma vez que, desde que. all at ~ de repente; (*simultaneously*) todos ao mesmo tempo. just this ~ só esta vez. ~ (and) for all duma vez para sempre. ~ upon a time era uma vez. ~-over *n* (*colloq*) vista *f* de olhos

oncoming /'ɒnkʌmɪŋ/ *a* que se aproxima, próximo. the ~ traffic o trânsito que vem do sentido oposto, (*P*) no sentido contrário

one /wʌn/ *a* um(a); (*sole*) único □ *n* um(a) *mf* □ *pron* um(a) *mf*; (*impersonal*) se. ~ by ~ um a um. a big/red/*etc* ~ um grande/vermelho/*etc*. this/that ~ este/esse. ~ another um ao outro, uns aos outros. ~-sided *a* parcial. ~-way *a* (*street*) mão única; (*ticket*) simples

oneself /wʌn'self/ *pron* si, si mesmo/próprio; (*reflexive*) se. by ~ sozinho

onion /'ʌnɪən/ *n* cebola *f*

onlooker /'ɒnlʊkə(r)/ *n* espectador *m*, circunstante *mf*

only /'əʊnlɪ/ *a* único □ *adv* apenas, só, somente □ *conj* só que. an ~ child um filho único. he ~ has six ele só tem seis. not ~ ... but also não só ... mas também. ~ too muito, mais que

onset /'ɒnset/ *n* começo *m*; (*attack*) ataque *m*

onslaught /'ɒnslɔ:t/ *n* ataque *m* violento, assalto *m*

onward(s) /'ɒnwəd(z)/ *adv* para a frente/diante

ooze /u:z/ *vt/i* escorrer, verter

opal /'əʊpl/ *n* opala *f*

opaque /əʊ'peɪk/ *a* opaco, tosco

open /'əʊpən/ *a* aberto; (*view*) aberto, amplo; (*free to all*) aberto ao público; (*attempt*) franco □ *vt/i* abrir(-se); (*of shop, play*) abrir. in the ~ air ao ar livre. keep ~ house receber muito, abrir a porta para todos. ~ on to dar para. ~ out *or* up abrir(-se). ~-heart *a* (*of surgery*) de coração aberto. ~-minded *a* imparcial. ~-plan *a* sem divisórias. ~ secret segredo *m* de polichinelo. ~ sea mar *m* alto. ~ness *n* abertura *f*; (*frankness*) franqueza *f*

opener /'əʊpənə(r)/ *n* (*tins*) abridor *m* de latas; (*bottles*) saca-rolhas *m invar*

opening /'əʊpənɪŋ/ *n* abertura *f*; (*beginning*) começo *m*; (*opportunity*) oportunidade *f*; (*job*) vaga *f*

openly /'əʊpənlɪ/ *adv* abertamente

opera /'ɒprə/ *n* ópera *f*. ~-glasses *npl* binóculo (de teatro) *m*, (*P*) binóculos *mpl*. ~tic /ɒpə'rætɪk/ *a* de ópera

operat|e /'ɒpəreɪt/ *vt/i* operar; (*techn*) (pôr a) funcionar. ~e on (*med*) operar. ~ing-theatre *n* (*med*) anfiteatro *m*, sala *f* de operações. ~ion /-'reɪʃn/ *n* operação *f*. in ~ion em vigor; (*techn*) em funcionamento. ~ional /'reɪʃənl/ *a* operacional. ~or *n* operador *m*; (*telephonist*) telefonista *mf*

operative /'ɒpərətɪv/ *a* (*surgical*) operatório; (*law etc*) em vigor

opinion /ə'pɪnɪən/ *n* opinião *f*, parecer *m*. in my ~ a meu ver. ~ poll *n* sondagem (de opinião) *f*. ~ated /-eɪtɪd/ *a* dogmático

opium /'əʊpɪəm/ *n* ópio *m*

Oporto /ə'pɔ:təʊ/ *n* Porto *m*

opponent /ə'pəʊnənt/ *n* adversário *m*, antagonista *mf*, oponente *mf*

opportune /'ɒpətju:n/ *a* oportuno

opportunity /ɒpə'tju:nətɪ/ *n* oportunidade *f*

oppos|e /ə'pəʊz/ *vt* opor-se a. ~ed to oposto a. ~ing *a* oposto

opposite /'ɒpəzɪt/ *a* & *n* oposto (*m*), contrário (*m*) □ *adv* em frente □ *prep* ~ (to) em frente de

opposition /ɒpə'zɪʃn/ *n* oposição *f*

oppress /ə'pres/ *vt* oprimir. ~ion /-ʃn/ *n* opressão *f*. ~ive *a* opressivo. ~or *n* opressor *m*

opt /ɒpt/ *vi* ~ for optar por. ~ out recusar-se a participar (of de). ~ to do escolher fazer

optical /'ɒptɪkl/ *a* óptico. ~ illusion ilusão *f* óptica

optician /ɒp'tɪʃn/ *n* oculista *mf*

optimis|t /'ɒptɪmɪst/ *n* otimista *mf*, (*P*) optimista *mf*. **~m** /-zəm/ *n* otimismo *m*, (*P*) optimismo *m*. **~tic** /-'mɪstɪk/ *a* otimista, (*P*) optimista. **~tically** /-'mɪstɪklɪ/ *adv* com otimismo, (*P*) optimismo

optimum /'ɒptɪməm/ *a* & *n* (*pl* -ima) ótimo (*m*), (*P*) óptimo (*m*)

option /'ɒpʃn/ *n* escolha *f*, opção *f*. **have no ~ (but)** não ter outro remédio (senão)

optional /'ɒpʃənl/ *a* opcional, facultativo

opulen|t /'ɒpjʊlənt/ *a* opulento. **~ce** *n* opulência *f*

or /ɔ:(r)/ *conj* ou; (*with negative*) nem. **~ else** senão

oracle /'ɒrəkl/ *n* oráculo *m*

oral /'ɔ:rəl/ *a* oral

orange /'ɒrɪndʒ/ *n* laranja *f*; (*colour*) laranja *m*, cor *f* de laranja □ *a* de laranja; (*colour*) alaranjado, cor de laranja

orator /'ɒrətə(r)/ *n* orador *m*. **~y** *n* oratória *f*

orbit /'ɔ:bɪt/ *n* órbita *f* □ *vt* (*pt* **orbited**) gravitar em torno de

orchard /'ɔ:tʃəd/ *n* pomar *m*

orchestra /'ɔ:kɪstrə/ *n* orquestra *f*. **~l** /'kestrəl/ *a* orquestral

orchestrate /'ɔ:kɪstreɪt/ *vt* orquestrar

orchid /'ɔ:kɪd/ *n* orquídea *f*

ordain /ɔ:'deɪn/ *vt* decretar; (*relig*) ordenar

ordeal /ɔ:'di:l/ *n* prova *f*, provação *f*

order /'ɔ:də(r)/ *n* ordem *f*, (*comm*) encomenda *f*, pedido *m* □ *vt* ordenar; (*goods etc*) encomendar. **in ~ that** para que. **in ~ to** para

orderly /'ɔ:dəlɪ/ *a* ordenado, em ordem; (*not unruly*) ordeiro □ *n* (*mil*) ordenança *f*; (*med*) servente *m* de hospital

ordinary /'ɔ:dnrɪ/ *a* normal, ordinário, vulgar. **out of the ~** fora do comum

ordination /ɔ:dɪ'neɪʃn/ *n* (*relig*) ordenação *f*

ore /ɔ:(r)/ *n* minério *m*

organ /'ɔ:gən/ *n* órgão *m*. **~ist** *n* organista *mf*

organic /ɔ:'gænɪk/ *a* orgânico

organism /'ɔ:gənɪzəm/ *n* organismo *m*

organiz|e /'ɔ:gənaɪz/ *vt* organizar. **~ation** /-'zeɪʃn/ *n* organização *f*. **~er** *n* organizador *m*

orgasm /'ɔ:gæzəm/ *n* orgasmo *m*

orgy /'ɔ:dʒɪ/ *n* orgia *f*

Orient /'ɔ:rɪənt/ *n* **the ~** o Oriente *m*. **~al** /-'entl/ *a* & *n* oriental (*mf*)

orientat|e /'ɔ:rɪənteɪt/ *vt* orientar. **~ion** /-'teɪʃn/ *n* orientação *f*

orifice /'ɒrɪfɪs/ *n* orifício *m*

origin /'ɒrɪdʒɪn/ *n* origem *f*

original /ə'rɪdʒənl/ *a* original; (*not copied*) original. **~ity** /-'nælətɪ/ *n* originalidade *f*. **~ly** *adv* originalmente; (*in the beginning*) originariamente

originat|e /ə'rɪdʒəneɪt/ *vt/i* originar (-se). **~e from** provir de. **~or** *n* iniciador *m*, criador *m*, autor *m*

ornament /'ɔ:nəmənt/ *n* ornamento *m*; (*object*) peça *f* decorativa. **~al** /-'mentl/ *a* ornamental. **~ation** /-en'teɪʃn/ *n* ornamentação *f*

ornate /ɔ:'neɪt/ *a* florido, floreado

ornitholog|y /ɔ:nɪ'θɒlədʒɪ/ *n* ornitologia *f*. **~ist** *n* ornitólogo *m*

orphan /'ɔ:fn/ *n* órfã(o) *f*(*m*) □ *vt* deixar órfão. **~age** *n* orfanato *m*

orthodox /'ɔ:θədɒks/ *a* ortodoxo

orthopaedic /ɔ:θə'pi:dɪk/ *a* ortopédico

oscillate /'ɒsɪleɪt/ *vi* oscilar, vacilar

ostensibl|e /ɒs'tensəbl/ *a* aparente, pretenso. **~y** *adv* aparentemente, pretensamente

ostentati|on /ɒsten'teɪʃn/ *n* ostentação *f*. **~ous** /-'teɪʃəs/ *a* ostentoso, ostensivo

osteopath /'ɒstɪəpæθ/ *n* osteopata *mf*

ostracize /'ɒstrəsaɪz/ *vt* pôr de lado, marginalizar

ostrich /'ɒstrɪtʃ/ *n* avestruz *mf*

other /'ʌðə(r)/ *a*, *n* & *pron* outro (*m*) □ *adv* **~ than** diferente de, senão. **(some) ~s** outros. **the ~ day** no outro dia. **the ~ one** o outro

otherwise /'ʌðəwaɪz/ *adv* de outro modo □ *conj* senão, caso contrário

otter /'ɒtə(r)/ *n* lontra *f*

ouch /aʊtʃ/ *int* ai!, ui!

ought /ɔ:t/ *v aux* (*pt* **ought**) dever. **you ~ to stay** você devia ficar. **he ~ to succeed** ele deve vencer. **I ~ to have done it** eu devia tê-lo feito

ounce /aʊns/ *n* onça *f* (*= 28,35g*)

our /'aʊə(r)/ *a* nosso(s), nossa(s)

ours /'aʊəz/ *poss pron* o(s) nosso(s), a(s) nossa(s)

ourselves /aʊə'selvz/ *pron* nós mesmos/próprios; (*reflexive*) nos. **by ~** sozinhos

oust /aʊst/ *vt* expulsar, obrigar a sair

out /aʊt/ *adv* fora; (*of light, fire*) apagado; (*in blossom*) aberto, desabrochado; (*of tide*) baixo. **be ~** não estar em casa, estar fora (de casa); (*wrong*) enganar-se. **be ~ to** estar resolvido a. **run/***etc* **~** sair correndo/*etc*. **~-and-~** *a* completo, rematado. **~ of** fora de; (*without*) sem. **~ of pity/***etc* por pena/*etc*. **made ~ of** feito de *or* em. **take ~ of** tirar de. **5 ~ of 6** 5 (de) entre 6. **~ of date** fora de moda; (*not valid*) fora do prazo. **~ of doors** ao ar livre. **~ of one's mind** doido. **~ of**

order quebrado. ~ of place deslocado. ~ of the way afastado. ~-patient *n* doente *mf* de consulta externa

outboard /'aʊtbɔ:d/ *a* ~ motor motor *m* de popa

outbreak /'aʊtbreɪk/ *n* (*of flu etc*) surto *m*, epidemia *f*; (*of war*) deflagração *f*

outburst /'aʊtbɜ:st/ *n* explosão *f*

outcast /'aʊtka:st/ *n* pária *m*

outcome /'aʊtkʌm/ *n* resultado *m*

outcry /'aʊtkraɪ/ *n* clamor *m*; (*protest*) protesto *m*

outdated /aʊt'deɪtɪd/ *a* fora da moda, ultrapassado

outdo /aʊt'du:/ *vt* (*pt* -did, *pp* -done) ultrapassar, superar

outdoor /'aʊtdɔ:(r)/ *a* ao ar livre. ~s /-'dɔ:z/ *adv* fora de casa, ao ar livre

outer /'aʊtə(r)/ *a* exterior. ~ space espaço (cósmico) *m*

outfit /'aʊtfɪt/ *n* equipamento *m*; (*clothes*) roupa *f*

outgoing /'aʊtgəʊɪŋ/ *a* que vai sair; (*of minister etc*) demissionário; (*fig*) sociável. ~s *npl* despesas *fpl*

outgrow /aʊt'grəʊ/ *vt* (*pt* -grew, *pp* -grown) crescer mais do que; (*clothes*) já não caber em

outhouse /'aʊthaʊs/ *n* anexo *m*, dependência *f*

outing /'aʊtɪŋ/ *n* saída *f*, passeio *m*

outlandish /aʊt'lændɪʃ/ *a* exótico, estranho

outlaw /'aʊtlɔ:/ *n* fora-da-lei *mf*, bandido *m* □ *vt* banir, proscrever

outlay /'aʊtleɪ/ *n* despesa(s) *f*(*pl*)

outlet /'aʊtlet/ *n* saída *f*, escoadouro *m*; (*for goods*) mercado *m*, saída *f*; (*for feelings*) escape *m*, vazão *m*; (*electr*) tomada *f*

outline /'aʊtlaɪn/ *n* contorno *m*; (*summary*) plano *m* geral, esquema *m*, esboço *m* □ *vt* contornar; (*summarize*) descrever em linhas gerais

outlive /aʊt'lɪv/ *vt* sobreviver a

outlook /'aʊtlʊk/ *n* (*view*) vista *f*; (*mental attitude*) visão *f*; (*future prospects*) perspectiva(s) *f*(*pl*)

outlying /'aʊtlaɪɪŋ/ *a* afastado, remoto

outnumber /aʊt'nʌmbə(r)/ *vt* ultrapassar em número

outpost /'aʊtpəʊst/ *n* posto *m* avançado

output /'aʊtpʊt/ *n* rendimento *m*; (*of computer*) saída *f*, output *m*

outrage /'aʊtreɪdʒ/ *n* atrocidade *f*, crime *m*; (*scandal*) escândalo *m* □ *vt* ultrajar

outrageous /aʊt'reɪdʒəs/ *a* (*shocking*) escandaloso; (*very cruel*) atroz

outright /'aʊtraɪt/ *adv* completamente; (*at once*) imediatamente; (*frankly*) abertamente □ *a* completo; (*refusal*) claro

outset /'aʊtset/ *n* início *m*, começo *m*, princípio *m*

outside[1] /aʊt'saɪd/ *n* exterior *m* □ *adv* (lá) (por) fora □ *prep* (para) fora de, além de; (*in front of*) diante de. at the ~ no máximo

outside[2] /'aʊtsaɪd/ *a* exterior

outsider /aʊt'saɪdə(r)/ *n* estranho *m*; (*in race*) cavalo *m* com poucas probabilidades, azarão *m*

outsize /'aʊtsaɪz/ *a* tamanho extra *invar*

outskirts /'aʊtskɜ:ts/ *npl* arredores *mpl*, subúrbios *mpl*

outspoken /aʊt'spəʊkn/ *a* franco

outstanding /aʊt'stændɪŋ/ *a* saliente, proeminente; (*debt*) por saldar; (*very good*) notável, destacado

outstretched /aʊt'stretʃt/ *a* (*arm*) estendido, esticado

outstrip /aʊt'strɪp/ *vt* (*pt* -stripped) ultrapassar, passar à frente de

outward /'aʊtwəd/ *a* para o exterior; (*sign etc*) exterior; (*journey*) de ida. ~ly *adv* exteriormente. ~s *adv* para o exterior

outwit /aʊt'wɪt/ *vt* (*pt* -witted) ser mais esperto que, enganar

oval /'əʊvl/ *n* & *a* oval (*m*)

ovary /'əʊvərɪ/ *n* ovário *m*

ovation /əʊ'veɪʃn/ *n* ovação *f*

oven /'ʌvn/ *n* forno *m*

over /'əʊvə(r)/ *prep* sobre, acima de, por cima de; (*across*) de para o/do outro lado de; (*during*) durante, em; (*more than*) mais de □ *adv* por cima; (*too*) demais, demasiadamente; (*ended*) acabado. the film is ~ o filme já acabou. jump/*etc* ~ saltar/*etc* por cima. he has some ~ ele tem uns de sobra. all ~ the country em/por todo o país. all ~ the table por toda a mesa. ~ and above (*besides, in addition to*) (para) além de. ~ and ~ repetidas vezes. ~ there ali, lá, acolá

over- /'əʊvə(r)/ *pref* sobre-, super-; (*excessively*) demais, demasiado

overall[1] /'əʊvərɔ:l/ *n* bata *f*. ~s macacão *m*, (*P*) fato-macaco *m*

overall[2] /'əʊvərɔ:l/ *a* global; (*length etc*) total □ *adv* globalmente

overawe /əʊvər'ɔ:/ *vt* intimidar

overbalance /əʊvə'bæləns/ *vt*/*i* (fazer) perder o equilíbrio

overbearing /əʊvə'beərɪŋ/ *a* autoritário, despótico; (*arrogant*) arrogante

overboard /'əʊvəbɔ:d/ *adv* (pela) borda fora

overcast /əʊvə'ka:st/ *a* encoberto, nublado

overcharge /əʊvə'tʃa:dʒ/ *vt* ~ sb (for) cobrar demais a alg (por)

overcoat /'əʊvəkəʊt/ *n* casacão *m*; (*for men*) sobretudo *m*
overcome /əʊvə'kʌm/ *vt* (*pt* **-came**, *pp* **-come**) superar, vencer. ~ **by** sucumbindo a, dominado *or* vencido por
overcrowded /əʊvə'kraʊdɪd/ *a* apinhado, superlotado; (*country*) superpovoado
overdo /əʊvə'du:/ *vt* (*pt* **-did**, *pp* **-done**) exagerar, levar longe demais. ~**ne** (*culin*) cozinhado demais
overdose /'əʊvədəʊs/ *n* dose *f* excessiva
overdraft /'əʊvədra:ft/ *n* saldo *m* negativo
overdraw /əʊvə'drɔ:/ *vt* (*pt* **-drew**, *pp* **-drawn**) sacar a descoberto
overdue /əʊvə'dju:/ *a* em atraso, atrasado; (*belated*) tardio
overestimate /əʊvər'estɪmeɪt/ *vt* sobreestimar, atribuir valor excessivo a
overexpose /əʊvərɪk'spəʊz/ *vt* expor demais
overflow[1] /əʊvə'fləʊ/ *vt/i* extravasar, transbordar (**with** de)
overflow[2] /'əʊvəfləʊ/ *n* (*outlet*) descarga *f*; (*excess*) excesso *m*
overgrown /əʊvə'grəʊn/ *a* que cresceu demais; (*garden etc*) invadido pela vegetação
overhang /əʊvə'hæŋ/ *vt* (*pt* **-hung**) estar sobranceiro a, pairar sobre □ *vi* projetar-se, (*P*) projectar-se para fora □ *n* saliência *f*
overhaul[1] /əʊvə'hɔ:l/ *vt* fazer uma revisão em
overhaul[2] /'əʊvəhɔ:l/ *n* revisão *f*
overhead[1] /əʊvə'hed/ *adv* em *or* por cima, ao *or* no alto
overhead[2] /'əʊvəhed/ *a* aéreo. ~**s** *npl* despesas *fpl* gerais
overhear /əʊvə'hɪə(r)/ *vt* (*pt* **-heard**) (*eavesdrop*) ouvir sem conhecimento do falante; (*hear by chance*) ouvir por acaso
overjoyed /əʊvə'dʒɔɪd/ *a* radiante, felicíssimo
overlap /əʊvə'læp/ *vt/i* (*pt* **-lapped**) sobrepor(-se) parcialmente; (*fig*) coincidir
overleaf /əʊvə'li:f/ *adv* no verso
overload /əʊvə'ləʊd/ *vt* sobrecarregar
overlook /əʊvə'lʊk/ *vt* deixar passar; (*of window*) dar para; (*of building*) dominar
overnight /əʊvə'naɪt/ *adv* durante a noite; (*fig*) dum dia para o outro □ *a* (*train*) da noite; (*stay, journey, etc*) noite, noturno; (*fig*) súbito
overpass /əʊvə'pa:s/ *n* passagem *f* superior
overpay /əʊvə'peɪ/ *vt* (*pt* **-paid**) pagar em excesso
overpower /əʊvə'paʊə(r)/ *vt* dominar, subjugar; (*fig*) esmagar. ~**ing** *a* esmagador; (*heat*) sufocante, insuportável
overpriced /əʊvə'praɪst/ *a* muito caro
overrate /əʊvə'reɪt/ *vt* sobreestimar, exagerar o valor de
overrid|e /əʊvə'raɪd/ *vt* (*pt* **-rode**, *pp* **-ridden**) prevalecer sobre, passar por cima de. ~**ing** *a* primordial, preponderante; (*importance*) maior
overripe /'əʊvəraɪp/ *a* demasiado maduro
overrule /əʊvə'ru:l/ *vt* anular, rejeitar; (*claim*) indeferir
overrun /əʊvə'rʌn/ *vt* (*pt* **-ran**, *pp* **-run**, *pres p* **-running**) invadir; (*a limit*) exceder, ultrapassar
overseas /əʊvə'si:z/ *a* ultramarino; (*abroad*) estrangeiro □ *adv* no ultramar, no estrangeiro
oversee /əʊvə'si:/ *vt* (*pt* **-saw** *pp* **-seen**) supervisionar. ~**r** /'əʊvəsɪə(r)/ *n* capataz *m*
overshadow /əʊvə'ʃædəʊ/ *vt* (*fig*) eclipsar, ofuscar
oversight /'əʊvəsaɪt/ *n* lapso *m*
oversleep /əʊvə'sli:p/ *vi* (*pt* **-slept**) acordar tarde, dormir demais
overt /'əʊvɜ:t/ *a* manifesto, claro, patente
overtake /əʊvə'teɪk/ *vt/i* (*pt* **-took**, *pp* **-taken**) ultrapassar
overthrow /əʊvə'θrəʊ/ *vt* (*pt* **-threw**, *pp* **-thrown**) derrubar □ *n* /'əʊvəθrəʊ/ (*pol*) derrubada *f*
overtime /'əʊvətaɪm/ *n* horas *fpl* extras
overtones /'əʊvətəʊnz/ *npl* (*fig*) tom *m*, implicação *f*
overture /'əʊvətjʊə(r)/ *n* (*mus*) abertura *f*; (*fig*) proposta *f*, abordagem *f*
overturn /əʊvə'tɜ:n/ *vt/i* virar(-se); (*car, plane*) capotar, virar-se
overweight /əʊvə'weɪt/ *a* **be** ~ ter excesso de peso
overwhelm /əʊvə'welm/ *vt* oprimir; (*defeat*) esmagar; (*amaze*) assoberbar. ~**ing** *a* esmagador; (*urge*) irresistível
overwork /əʊvə'wɜ:k/ *vt/i* sobrecarregar(-se) com trabalho □ *n* excesso *m* de trabalho
overwrought /əʊvə'rɔ:t/ *a* muito agitado, superexcitado
ow|e /əʊ/ *vt* dever. ~**ing** *a* devido. ~**ing to** devido a
owl /aʊl/ *n* coruja *f*
own[1] /əʊn/ *a* próprio. **a house**/*etc* **of one's** ~ uma casa/*etc* própria. **get one's** ~ **back** (*colloq*) ir à forra, (*P*) desforrarse. **hold one's** ~ agüentar-se, (*P*) aguentar-se. **on one's** ~ sozinho

own[2] /əʊn/ *vt* possuir. ~ **up (to)** (*colloq*) confessar. ~**er** *n* proprietário *m*, dono *m*. ~**ership** *n* posse *f*, propriedade *f*
ox /ɒks/ *n* (*pl* **oxen**) boi *m*
oxygen /'ɒksɪdʒən/ *n* oxigênio *m*, (*P*) oxigénio *m*
oyster /'ɔɪstə(r)/ *n* ostra *f*
ozone /'əʊzəʊn/ *n* ozônio *m*, (*P*) ozono *m*. ~ **layer** camada *f* de ozônio, (*P*) ozono *m*

P

pace /peɪs/ *n* passo *m*; (*fig*) ritmo *m* □ *vt* percorrer passo a passo □ *vi* ~ **up and down** andar de um lado para o outro. **keep** ~ **with** acompanhar, manter-se a par de
pacemaker /'peɪsmeɪkə(r)/ *n* (*med*) marcapasso *m*, (*P*) pacemaker *m*
Pacific /pə'sɪfɪk/ *a* pacífico □ *n* ~ (**Ocean**) (Oceano) Pacífico *m*
pacifist /'pæsɪfɪst/ *n* pacifista *mf*
pacify /'pæsɪfaɪ/ *vt* pacificar, apaziguar
pack /pæk/ *n* pacote *m*; (*mil*) mochila *f*; (*of hounds*) matilha *f*; (*of lies*) porção *f*; (*of cards*) baralho *m* □ *vt* empacotar; (*suitcase*) fazer; (*box, room*) encher; (*press down*) atulhar, encher até não caber mais □ *vi* fazer as malas. ~ **into** (*cram*) apinhar em, comprimir em. **send** ~**ing** pôr a andar, mandar passear. ~**ed** *a* apinhado. ~**ed lunch** merenda *f*
package /'pækɪdʒ/ *n* pacote *m*, embrulho *m* □ *vt* embalar. ~ **deal** pacote *m* de propostas. ~ **holiday** pacote *m* turístico, (*P*) viagem *f* organizada
packet /'pækɪt/ *n* pacote *m*; (*of cigarettes*) maço *m*
pact /pækt/ *n* pacto *m*
pad /pæd/ *n* (*in clothing*) chumaço *m*; (*for writing*) bloco *m* de papel/de notas; (*for ink*) almofada (de carimbo) *f*. (**launching**) ~ rampa *f* de lançamento □ *vt* (*pt* **padded**) enchumaçar, acolchoar; (*fig: essay etc*) encher linguiça. ~**ding** *n* chumaço *m*; (*fig*) linguiça *f*
paddle[1] /'pædl/ *n* remo *m* de canoa. ~**-steamer** *n* vapor *m* movido a rodas
paddl|e[2] /'pædl/ *vi* chapinhar, molhar os pés. ~**ing pool** piscina *f* de plástico para crianças
paddock /'pædək/ *n* cercado *m*; (*at racecourse*) paddock *m*
padlock /'pædlɒk/ *n* cadeado *m* □ *vt* fechar com cadeado
paediatrician /pi:dɪə'trɪʃn/ *n* pediatra *mf*
pagan /'peɪgən/ *a* & *n* pagão (*m*), pagã (*f*)
page[1] /peɪdʒ/ *n* (*of book etc*) página *f*
page[2] /peɪdʒ/ *vt* mandar chamar
pageant /'pædʒənt/ *n* espetáculo *m*, (*P*) espectáculo *m* (histórico); (*procession*) cortejo *m*. ~**ry** *n* pompa *f*
pagoda /pə'gəʊdə/ *n* pagode *m*
paid /peɪd/ *see* **pay** □ *a* **put** ~ **to** (*colloq: end*) pôr fim a
pail /peɪl/ *n* balde *m*
pain /peɪn/ *n* dor *f*. ~**s** esforços *mpl* □ *vt* magoar. **be in** ~ sofrer, ter dores. ~**-killer** *n* analgésico *m*. **take** ~**s to** esforçar-se por. ~**ful** *a* doloroso; (*grievous, laborious*) penoso. ~**less** *a* sem dor, indolor
painstaking /'peɪnzteɪkɪŋ/ *a* cuidadoso, esmerado, meticuloso
paint /peɪnt/ *n* tinta *f*. ~**s** (*in box*) tintas *fpl* □ *vt/i* pintar. ~**er** *n* pintor *m*. ~**ing** *n* pintura *f*
paintbrush /'peɪntbrʌʃ/ *n* pincel *m*
pair /peə(r)/ *n* par *m*. **a** ~ **of scissors** uma tesoura. **a** ~ **of trousers** um par de calças. **in** ~**s** aos pares □ *vi* ~ **off** formar pares
Pakistan /pa:kɪ'sta:n/ *n* Paquistão *m*. ~**i** *a* & *n* paquistanês (*m*)
pal /pæl/ *n* (*colloq*) colega *mf*, amigo *m*
palace /'pælɪs/ *n* palácio *m*
palat|e /'pælət/ *n* palato *m*. ~**able** *a* saboroso, gostoso; (*fig*) agradável
palatial /pə'leɪʃl/ *a* suntuoso, (*P*) sumptuoso
pale /peɪl/ *a* (**-er**, **-est**) pálido; (*colour*) claro □ *vi* empalidecer. ~**ness** *n* palidez *f*
Palestin|e /'pælɪstaɪn/ *n* Palestina *f*. ~**ian** /-'stɪnɪən/ *a* & *n* palestino (*m*)
palette /'pælɪt/ *n* paleta *f*. ~**-knife** *n* espátula *f*
pall /pɔ:l/ *vi* tornar-se enfadonho, perder o interesse (**on** para)
pallid /'pælɪd/ *a* pálido
palm /pa:m/ *n* (*of hand*) palma *f*; (*tree*) palmeira *f* □ *vt* ~ **off** impingir (**on** a). **P**~ **Sunday** Domingo *m* de Ramos
palpable /'pælpəbl/ *a* palpável
palpitat|e /'pælpɪteɪt/ *vi* palpitar. ~**ion** /-'teɪʃn/ *n* palpitação *f*
paltry /'pɔ:ltrɪ/ *a* (**-ier**, **-iest**) irrisório
pamper /'pæmpə(r)/ *vt* mimar, paparicar
pamphlet /'pæmflɪt/ *n* panfleto *m*, folheto *m*
pan /pæn/ *n* panela *f*; (*for frying*) frigideira *f* □ *vt* (*pt* **panned**) (*colloq*) criticar severamente
panacea /pænə'sɪə/ *n* panacéia *f*
panache /pæ'næʃ/ *n* brio *m*, estilo *m*, panache *m*
pancake /'pænkeɪk/ *n* crepe *m*, panqueca *f*

pancreas /'pæŋkrɪəs/ *n* pâncreas *m*
panda /'pændə/ *n* panda *m*
pandemonium /pændɪ'məʊnɪəm/ *n* pandemônio *m*, (*P*) pandemónio *m*, caos *m*
pander /'pændə(r)/ *vi* ~ **to** prestar-se a servir, ir ao encontro de, fazer concessões a
pane /peɪn/ *n* vidraça *f*
panel /'pænl/ *n* painel *m*; (*jury*) júri *m*; (*speakers*) convidados *mpl*. (**instrument**) ~ painel *m* de instrumentos, (*P*) de bordo. ~**led** *a* apainelado. ~**ling** *n* apainelamento *m*. ~**list** *n* convidado *m*
pang /pæŋ/ *n* pontada *f*, dor *f* aguda e súbita. ~**s** (*of hunger*) ataques *mpl* de fome. ~**s of conscience** remorsos *mpl*
panic /'pænɪk/ *n* pânico *m* □ *vt/i* (*pt* **panicked**) desorientar(-se), (fazer) entrar em pânico. ~**-stricken** *a* tomado de pânico
panoram|a /pænə'ra:mə/ *n* panorama *m*. ~**ic** /-'ræmɪk/ *a* panorâmico
pansy /'pænzɪ/ *n* amor-perfeito *m*
pant /pænt/ *vi* ofegar, arquejar
panther /'pænθə(r)/ *n* pantera *f*
panties /'pæntɪz/ *npl* (*colloq*) calcinhas *fpl*
pantomime /'pæntəmaɪm/ *n* pantomima *f*
pantry /'pæntrɪ/ *n* despensa *f*
pants /pænts/ *npl* (*colloq: underwear*) cuecas *fpl*; (*colloq: trousers*) calças *fpl*
papal /'peɪpl/ *a* papal
paper /'peɪpə(r)/ *n* papel *m*; (*newspaper*) jornal *m*; (*exam*) prova *f* escrita; (*essay*) comunicação *f*. ~**s** *npl* (*for identification*) documentos *mpl* □ *vt* forrar com papel. **on** ~ por escrito. ~**-clip** *n* clipe *m*
paperback /'peɪpəbæk/ *a* & *n* ~ (**book**) livro *m* de capa mole
paperweight /'peɪpəweɪt/ *n* pesa-papéis *m invar*, (*P*) pisa-papéis *m invar*
paperwork /'peɪpəwɜ:k/ *n* trabalho *m* de secretária; (*pej*) papelada *f*
paprika /'pæprɪkə/ *n* páprica *f*, pimentão *m* doce
par /pa:(r)/ *n* **be below** ~ estar abaixo do padrão desejado. **on a** ~ **with** em igualdade com
parable /'pærəbl/ *n* parábola *f*
parachut|e /'pærəʃu:t/ *n* pára-quedas *m invar* □ *vi* descer de pára-quedas. ~**ist** *n* pára-quedista *mf*
parade /pə'reɪd/ *n* (*mil*) parada *f* militar; (*procession*) procissão *f* □ *vi* desfilar □ *vt* alardear, exibir
paradise /'pærədaɪs/ *n* paraíso *m*
paradox /'pærədɒks/ *n* paradoxo *m*. ~**ical** /-'dɒksɪkl/ *a* paradoxal
paraffin /'pærəfɪn/ *n* querosene *m*, (*P*) petróleo *m*
paragon /'pærəgən/ *n* modelo *m* de perfeição
paragraph /'pærəgra:f/ *n* parágrafo *m*
parallel /'pærəlel/ *a* & *n* paralelo (*m*) □ *vt* (*pt* **parelleled**) comparar(-se) a
paralyse /'pærəlaɪz/ *vt* paralisar
paraly|sis /pə'ræləsɪs/ *n* paralisia *f*. ~**tic** /-'lɪtɪk/ *a* & *n* paralítico (*m*)
parameter /pə'ræmɪtə(r)/ *n* parâmetro *m*
paramount /'pærəmaʊnt/ *a* supremo, primordial
parapet /'pærəpɪt/ *n* parapeito *m*
paraphernalia /pærəfə'neɪlɪə/ *n* equipamento *m*, tralha *f* (*colloq*)
paraphrase /'pærəfreɪz/ *n* paráfrase *f* □ *vt* parafrasear
paraplegic /pærə'pli:dʒɪk/ *n* paraplégico *m*
parasite /'pærəsaɪt/ *n* parasita *mf*
parasol /'pærəsɒl/ *n* sombrinha *f*; (*on table*) pára-sol *m*, guarda-sol *m*
parcel /'pa:sl/ *n* embrulho *m*; (*for post*) encomenda *f*
parch /pa:tʃ/ *vt* ressecar. **be** ~**ed** estar com muita sede
parchment /'pa:tʃmənt/ *n* pergaminho *m*
pardon /'pa:dn/ *n* perdão *m*; (*jur*) perdão *m*, indulto *m* □ *vt* (*pt* **pardoned**) perdoar. **I beg your** ~ perdão, desculpe. (**I beg your**) ~? como?
pare /peə(r)/ *vt* aparar, cortar; (*peel*) descascar
parent /'peərənt/ *n* pai *m*, mãe *f*. ~**s** *npl* pais *mpl*. ~**al** /pə'rentl/ *a* dos pais, paterno, materno
parenthesis /pə'renθəsɪs/ *n* (*pl* **-theses**) /-si:z/ parêntese *m*, parêntesis *m*
Paris /'pærɪs/ *n* Paris *m*
parish /'pærɪʃ/ *n* paróquia *f*; (*municipal*) freguesia *f*. ~**ioner** /pə'rɪʃənə(r)/ *n* paroquiano *m*
parity /'pærətɪ/ *n* paridade *f*
park /pa:k/ *n* parque *m* □ *vt* estacionar. ~**ing** *n* estacionamento *m*. **no** ~**ing** estacionamento proibido. ~**ing-meter** *n* parquímetro *m*
parliament /'pa:ləmənt/ *n* parlamento *m*, assembléia *f*. ~**ary** /-'mentrɪ/ *a* parlamentar
parochial /pə'rəʊkɪəl/ *a* paroquial; (*fig*) provinciano, tacanho
parody /'pærədɪ/ *n* paródia *f* □ *vt* parodiar
parole /pə'rəʊl/ *n* **on** ~ em liberdade condicional □ *vt* pôr em liberdade condicional
parquet /'pa:keɪ/ *n* parquê *m*, parquete *m*

parrot /'pærət/ *n* papagaio *m*

parry /'pærɪ/ *vt* (a)parar □ *n* parada *f*

parsimonious /pa:sɪ'məʊnɪəs/ *a* parco; (*mean*) avarento

parsley /'pa:slɪ/ *n* salsa *f*

parsnip /'pa:snɪp/ *n* cherovia *f*, pastinaga *f*

parson /'pa:sn/ *n* pároco *m*, pastor *m*

part /pa:t/ *n* parte *f*; (*of serial*) episódio *m*; (*of machine*) peça *f*; (*theatre*) papel *m*; (*side in dispute*) partido *m* □ *a* parcial □ *adv* em parte □ *vt/i* separar (-se) (from de). **in ~** em parte. **on the ~ of** da parte de. **~-exchange** *n* troca *f* parcial. **~ of speech** categoria *f* gramatical. **~-time** *a & adv* a tempo parcial, part-time. **take ~ in** tomar parte em. **these ~s** estas partes

partial /'pa:ʃl/ *a* (*incomplete, biased*) parcial. **be ~ to** gostar de. **~ity** /-ɪ'ælətɪ/ *n* parcialidade *f*; (*liking*) predileção *f*, (*P*) predilecção *f* (for por). **~ly** *adv* parcialmente

particip|ate /pa:'tɪsɪpeɪt/ *vi* participar (in em). **~ant** *n* /-ənt/ participante *mf*. **~ation** /-'peɪʃn/ *n* participação *f*

participle /'pa:tɪsɪpl/ *n* particípio *m*

particle /'pa:tɪkl/ *n* partícula *f*; (*of dust*) grão *m*; (*fig*) mínimo *m*

particular /pə'tɪkjʊlə(r)/ *a* especial, particular; (*fussy*) exigente; (*careful*) escrupuloso. **~s** *npl* pormenores *mpl*. **in ~** *adv* em especial, particularmente. **~ly** *adv* particularmente

parting /'pa:tɪŋ/ *n* separação *f*; (*in hair*) risca *f* □ *a* de despedida

partisan /pa:tɪ'zæn/ *n* partidário *m*; (*mil*) guerrilheiro *m*

partition /pa:'tɪʃn/ *n* (*of room*) tabique *m*, divisória *f*; (*pol: division*) partilha *f*, divisão *f* □ *vt* dividir, repartir. **~ off** dividir por meio de tabique

partly /'pa:tlɪ/ *adv* em parte

partner /'pa:tnə(r)/ *n* sócio *m*; (*cards, sport*) parceiro *m*; (*dancing*) par *m*. **~ship** *n* associação *f*; (*comm*) sociedade *f*

partridge /'pa:trɪdʒ/ *n* perdiz *f*

party /'pa:tɪ/ *n* festa *f*, reunião *f*; (*group*) grupo *m*; (*pol*) partido *m*; (*jur*) parte *f*. **~ line** (*telephone*) linha *f* coletiva, (*P*) colectiva

pass /pa:s/ *vt/i* (*pt* **passed**) passar; (*overtake*) ultrapassar; (*exam*) passar; (*approve*) passar; (*law*) aprovar. **~ (by)** passar por □ *n* (*permit, sport*) passe *m*; (*geog*) desfiladeiro *m*, garganta *f*; (*in exam*) aprovação *f*. **make a ~ at** (*colloq*) atirar-se para (*colloq*). **~ away** falecer. **~ out** *or* **round** distribuir. **~ out** (*colloq: faint*) perder os sentidos, desmaiar. **~ over** (*disregard, overlook*) passar por cima de. **~ up** (*colloq: forgo*) deixar perder

passable /'pa:səbl/ *a* passável; (*road*) transitável

passage /'pæsɪdʒ/ *n* passagem *f*; (*voyage*) travessia *f*; (*corridor*) corredor *m*, passagem *f*

passenger /'pæsɪndʒə(r)/ *n* passageiro *m*

passer-by /pa:sə'baɪ/ *n* (*pl* **passers-by**) transeunte *mf*

passion /'pæʃn/ *n* paixão *f*. **~ate** *a* apaixonado, exaltado

passive /'pæsɪv/ *a* passivo. **~ness** *n* passividade *f*

Passover /'pa:səʊvə(r)/ *n* Páscoa *f* dos judeus

passport /'pa:spɔ:t/ *n* passaporte *m*

password /'pa:swɜ:d/ *n* senha *f*

past /pa:st/ *a* passado; (*former*) antigo □ *n* passado □ *prep* para além de; (*in time*) mais de; (*in front of*) diante de □ *adv* em frente. **be ~ it** já não ser capaz. **it's five ~ eleven** são onze e cinco. **these ~ months** estes últimos meses

pasta /'pæstə/ *n* prato *m* de massa(s)

paste /peɪst/ *n* cola *f*; (*culin*) massa(s) *f*(*pl*); (*dough*) massa *f*; (*jewellery*) strass *m* □ *vt* colar

pastel /'pæstl/ *n* pastel *m* □ *a* pastel *invar*

pasteurize /'pæstʃəraɪz/ *vt* pasteurizar

pastille /'pæstɪl/ *n* pastilha *f*

pastime /'pa:staɪm/ *n* passatempo *m*

pastoral /'pa:stərəl/ *a & n* pastoral (*f*)

pastry /'peɪstrɪ/ *n* massa *f* (de pastelaria); (*tart*) pastel *m*

pasture /'pa:stʃə(r)/ *n* pastagem *f*

pasty[1] /'pæstɪ/ *n* empadinha *f*

pasty[2] /'peɪstɪ/ *a* pastoso

pat /pæt/ *vt* (*pt* **patted**) (*hit gently*) dar pancadinhas em; (*caress*) fazer festinhas a □ *n* pancadinha *f*; (*caress*) festinha *f* □ *adv* a propósito; (*readily*) prontamente □ *a* preparado, pronto

patch /pætʃ/ *n* remendo *m*; (*over eye*) tapa-ôlho *m*; (*spot*) mancha *f*; (*small area*) pedaço *m*; (*of vegetables*) canteiro *m*, (*P*) leira *f* □ *vt* **~ up** remendar. **~ up a quarrel** fazer as pazes. **bad ~** mau bocado *m*. **not be a ~ on** não chegar aos pés de. **~-work** *n* obra *f* de retalhos. **~y** *a* desigual

pâté /'pæteɪ/ *n* patê *m*

patent /'peɪtnt/ *a & n* patente (*f*) □ *vt* patentear. **~ leather** verniz *m*, polimento *m*. **~ly** *adv* claramente

paternal /pə'tɜ:nl/ *a* paternal; (*relative*) paterno

paternity /pə'tɜ:nətɪ/ *n* paternidade *f*

path /pa:θ/ *n* (*pl* -s /pa:ðz/) caminho *m*, trilha *f*; (*in park*) aléia *f*; (*of rocket*) trajetória *f*, (*P*) trajectória *f*
pathetic /pəˈθetɪk/ *a* patético; (*colloq: contemptible*) desgraçado (*colloq*)
patholog|y /pəˈθɒlədʒɪ/ *n* patologia *f*. **~ist** *n* patologista *mf*
pathos /ˈpeɪθɒs/ *n* patos *m*, patético *m*
patience /ˈpeɪʃns/ *n* paciência *f*
patient /ˈpeɪʃnt/ *a* paciente □ *n* doente *mf*, paciente *mf*. **~ly** *adv* pacientemente
patio /ˈpætɪəʊ/ *n* (*pl* -os) pátio *m*
patriot /ˈpætrɪət/ *n* patriota *mf*. **~ic** /-ˈɒtɪk/ *a* patriótico. **~ism** /-ɪzəm/ *n* patriotismo *m*
patrol /pəˈtrəʊl/ *n* patrulha *f* □ *vt/i* patrulhar. **~ car** carro *m* de patrulha
patron /ˈpeɪtrən/ *n* (*of the arts etc*) patrocinador *m*, protetor *m*, (*P*) protector *m*; (*of charity*) benfeitor *m*; (*customer*) freguês *m*, cliente *mf*. **~ saint** padroeiro *m*, patrono *m*
patron|age /ˈpætrənɪdʒ/ *n* freguesia *f*, clientela *f*; (*support*) patrocínio *m*. **~ize** *vt* ser cliente de; (*support*) patrocinar; (*condescend*) tratar com ares de superioridade
patter[1] /ˈpætə(r)/ *n* (*of rain*) tamborilar *m*, rufo *m*. **~ of steps** som *m* leve de passos miúdos, corridinha *f* leve
patter[2] /ˈpætə(r)/ *n* (*of class, profession*) gíria *f*, jargão *m*; (*chatter*) conversa *f* fiada
pattern /ˈpætn/ *n* padrão *m*; (*for sewing*) molde *m*; (*example*) modelo *m*
paunch /pɔ:ntʃ/ *n* pança *f*
pause /pɔ:z/ *n* pausa *f* □ *vi* pausar, fazer (uma) pausa
pav|e /peɪv/ *vt* pavimentar. **~e the way** preparar o caminho (for para). **~ing-stone** *n* paralelepípedo *m*, laje *f*
pavement /ˈpeɪvmənt/ *n* passeio *m*
pavilion /pəˈvɪlɪən/ *n* pavilhão *m*
paw /pɔ:/ *n* pata *f* □ *vt* dar patadas em; (*horse*) escarvar; (*colloq: person*) pôr as patas em cima de
pawn[1] /pɔ:n/ *n* (*chess*) peão *m*; (*fig*) joguete *m*
pawn[2] /pɔ:n/ *vt* empenhar. **~-shop** casa *f* de penhores, prego *m* (*colloq*)
pawnbroker /ˈpɔ:nbrəʊkə(r)/ *n* penhorista *mf*, dono *m* de casa de penhores, agiota *mf*
pay /peɪ/ *vt/i* (*pt* **paid**) pagar; (*interest*) render; (*visit, compliment*) fazer □ *n* pagamento *m*; (*wages*) vencimento *m*, ordenado *m*, salário *m*. **in the ~ of** em pagamento de. **~ attention** prestar atenção. **~ back** restituir. **~ for** pagar. **~ homage** prestar homenagem. **~ in** depositar. **~-slip** *n* contracheque *m*, (*P*) folha *f* de pagamento
payable /ˈpeɪəbl/ *a* pagável
payment /ˈpeɪmənt/ *n* pagamento *m*; (*fig: reward*) recompensa *f*
payroll /ˈpeɪrəʊl/ *n* folha *f* de pagamentos. **be on the ~** fazer parte da folha de pagamento de uma firma
pea /pi:/ *n* ervilha *f*
peace /pi:s/ *n* paz *f*. **disturb the ~** perturbar a ordem pública. **~able** *a* pacífico
peaceful /ˈpi:sfl/ *a* pacífico; (*calm*) calmo, sereno
peacemaker /ˈpi:smeɪkə(r)/ *n* mediador *m*, pacificador *m*
peach /pi:tʃ/ *n* pêssego *m*
peacock /ˈpi:kɒk/ *n* pavão *m*
peak /pi:k/ *n* pico *m*, cume *m*, cimo *m*; (*of cap*) pala *f*; (*maximum*) máximo *m*. **~ hours** horas *fpl* de ponta; (*electr*) horas *fpl* de carga máxima. **~ed cap** boné *m* de pala
peaky /ˈpi:ki/ *a* com ar doentio
peal /pi:l/ *n* (*of bells*) repique *m*; (*of laughter*) gargalhada *f*, risada *f*
peanut /ˈpi:nʌt/ *n* amendoim *m*. **~s** (*sl: small sum*) uma bagatela *f*
pear /peə(r)/ *n* pera
pearl /pɜ:l/ *n* pérola *f*. **~y** *a* nacarado
peasant /ˈpeznt/ *n* camponês *m*, aldeão *m*
peat /pi:t/ *n* turfa *f*
pebble /ˈpebl/ *n* seixo *m*, calhau *m*
peck /pek/ *vt/i* bicar; (*attack*) dar bicadas (em) □ *n* bicada *f*; (*colloq: kiss*) beijo *m* seco. **~ing order** hierarquia *f*, ordem *f* de importância
peckish /ˈpekɪʃ/ *a* **be ~** (*colloq*) ter vontade de comer
peculiar /pɪˈkju:lɪə(r)/ *a* bizarro, singular; (*special*) peculiar (to a), característico (to de). **~ity** /-ˈærətɪ/ *n* singularidade *f*; (*feature*) peculiaridade *f*
pedal /ˈpedl/ *n* pedal *m* □ *vi* (*pt* **pedalled**) pedalar
pedantic /pɪˈdæntɪk/ *a* pedante
peddle /ˈpedl/ *vt* vender de porta em porta; (*drugs*) fazer tráfico de
pedestal /ˈpedɪstl/ *n* pedestal *m*
pedestrian /pɪˈdestrɪən/ *n* pedestre *mf*, (*P*) peão *m* □ *a* pedestre; (*fig*) prosaico. **~ crossing** faixa *f* para pedestres, (*P*) passadeira *f*
pedigree /ˈpedɪgri:/ *n* estirpe *f*, linhagem *f*; (*of animal*) raça *f* □ *a* de raça
pedlar /ˈpedlə(r)/ *n* vendedor *m* ambulante
peek /pi:k/ *vi* espreitar □ *n* espreitadela *f*
peel /pi:l/ *n* casca *f* □ *vt* descascar □ *vi* (*skin*) pelar; (*paint*) escamar-se, descascar; (*wallpaper*) descolar-se. **~ings** *npl* cascas *fpl*
peep /pi:p/ *vi* espreitar □ *n* espreita-

dela *f*. ~**-hole** *n* vigia *f*; (*in door*) olho *m* mágico

peer[1] /pɪə(r)/ *vi* ~ **at/into** (*searchingly*) perscrutar; (*with difficulty*) esforçar-se por ver

peer[2] /pɪə(r)/ *n* (*equal, noble*) par *m*. ~**age** *n* pariato *m*

peeved /pi:vd/ *a* (*sl*) irritado, chateado (*sl*)

peevish /'pi:vɪʃ/ *a* irritável

peg /peg/ *n* cavilha *f*; (*for washing*) pregador *m* de roupa, (*P*) mola *f*; (*for coats etc*) cabide *m*; (*for tent*) □ *vt* (*pt* **pegged**) prender com estacas. **off the** ~ prêt-à-porter

pejorative /pɪ'dʒɒrətɪv/ *a* pejorativo

pelican /'pelɪkən/ *n* pelicano *m*. ~ **crossing** passagem *f* com sinais manobrados pelos pedestres

pellet /'pelɪt/ *n* bolinha *f*; (*for gun*) grão *m* de chumbo

pelt[1] /pelt/ *n* pele *f*

pelt[2] /pelt/ *vt* bombardear (**with** com) □ *vi* chover a cântaros; (*run fast*) correr em disparada

pelvis /'pelvɪs/ *n* (*anat*) pélvis *m*, bacia *f*

pen[1] /pen/ *n* (*enclosure*) cercado *m*. **play-**~ *n* cercado *m*, (*P*) pargue *m* □ *vt* (*pt* **penned**) encurralar

pen[2] /pen/ *n* caneta *f* □ *vt* (*pt* **penned**) escrever. ~**-friend** *n* correspondente *mf*. ~**-name** *n* pseudônimo *m*, (*P*) pseudónimo *m*

penal /'pi:nl/ *a* penal. ~**ize** *vt* impôr uma penalidadea; (*sport*) penalizar

penalty /'penltɪ/ *n* pena *f*; (*fine*) multa *f*; (*sport*) penalidade *f*. ~ **kick** pênalti *m*, (*P*) grande penalidade *f*

penance /'penəns/ *n* penitência *f*

pence /pens/ *see* **penny**

pencil /'pensl/ *n* lápis *m* □ *vt* (*pt* **pencilled**) escrever *or* desenhar a lápis. ~**-sharpener** *n* apontador *m*, (*P*) apara-lápis *m invar*

pendant /'pendənt/ *n* berloque *m*

pending /'pendɪŋ/ *a* pendente □ *prep* (*during*) durante; (*until*) até

pendulum /'pendjʊləm/ *n* pêndulo *m*

penetrat|e /'penɪtreɪt/ *vt/i* penetrar (em). ~**ing** *a* penetrante. ~**ion** /-'treɪʃn/ *n* penetração *f*

penguin /'peŋgwɪn/ *n* pingüim *m*, (*P*) pinguin *m*

penicillin /penɪ'sɪlɪn/ *n* penicilina *f*

peninsula /pə'nɪnsjʊlə/ *n* península *f*

penis /'pi:nɪs/ *n* pênis *m*, (*P*) pénis *m*

peniten|t /'penɪtənt/ *a* & *n* penitente (*mf*). ~**ce** *n* /-əns/ contrição *f*, penitência *f*

penitentiary /penɪ'tenʃərɪ/ *n* (*Amer*) penitenciária *f*, cadeia *f*

penknife /'pennaɪf/ *n* (*pl* **-knives**) canivete *m*

penniless /'penɪlɪs/ *a* sem vintém, sem um tostão

penny /'penɪ/ *n* (*pl* **pennies** *or* **pence**) pêni *m*, (*P*) péni *m*; (*fig*) centavo *m*, vintém *m*

pension /'penʃn/ *n* pensão *f*; (*in retirement*) aposentadoria *f*, (*P*) reforma *f* □ *vt* ~ **off** reformar, aposentar. ~**er** *n* (**old-age**) ~**er** reformado *m*

pensive /'pensɪv/ *a* pensativo

Pentecost /'pentɪkɒst/ *n* Pentecostes *m*

penthouse /'penthaʊs/ *n* cobertura *f*, (*P*) apartamento de luxo (no último andar)

pent-up /'pentʌp/ *a* reprimido

penultimate /pen'ʌltɪmət/ *a* penúltimo

people /'pi:pl/ *npl* pessoas *fpl* □ *n* gente *f*, povo *m* □ *vt* povoar. **the Portuguese** ~ os portugueses *mpl*. ~ **say** dizem, diz-se

pep /pep/ *n* vigor *m* □ *vt* ~ **up** animar. ~ **talk** discurso *m* de encorajamento

pepper /'pepə(r)/ *n* pimenta *f*; (*vegetable*) pimentão *m*, (*P*) pimento *m* □ *vt* apimentar. ~**y** *a* apimentado, picante

peppermint /'pepəmɪnt/ *n* hortelã-pimenta *f*; (*sweet*) bala *f*, (*P*) pastilha *f* de hortelã-pimenta

per /pɜ:(r)/ *prep* por. ~ **annum** por ano. ~ **cent** por cento. ~ **kilo**/*etc* o quilo/*etc*

perceive /pə'si:v/ *vt* perceber; (*notice*) aperceber-se de

percentage /pə'sentɪdʒ/ *n* percentagem *f*

perceptible /pə'septəbl/ *a* perceptível

percept|ion /pə'sepʃn/ *n* percepção *f*. ~**ive** /-tɪv/ *a* perceptivo, penetrante, perspicaz

perch[1] /pɜ:tʃ/ *n* poleiro *m* □ *vi* empoleirar-se, pousar

perch[2] /pɜ:tʃ/ *n* (*fish*) perca *f*

percolat|e /'pɜ:kəleɪt/ *vt/i* filtrar(-se), passar. ~**or** *n* máquina *f* de café com filtro, cafeteira *f*

percussion /pə'kʌʃn/ *n* percussão *f*

peremptory /pə'remptərɪ/ *a* peremptório, decisivo

perennial /pə'renɪəl/ *a* perene; (*plant*) perene

perfect[1] /'pɜ:fɪkt/ *a* perfeito. ~**ly** *adv* perfeitamente

perfect[2] /pə'fekt/ *vt* aperfeiçoar. ~**ion** /-ʃn/ *n* perfeição *f*. ~**ionist** *n* perfeccionista *mf*

perforat|e /'pɜ:fəreɪt/ *vt* perfurar. ~**ion** /'reɪʃn/ *n* perfuração *f*; (*line of holes*) pontilhado *m*, picotado *m*

perform /pə'fɔ:m/ *vt* (*a task; mus*) executar; (*a function; theat*) desempenhar □ *vi* representar; (*function*) funcionar. ~**ance** *n* (*of task; mus*)

execução *f*; (*of function; theat*) desempenho *m*; (*of car*) performance *f*, comportamento *m*, rendimento *m*; (*colloq: fuss*) drama *m*, cena *f*. **~er** *n* artista *mf*
perfume /'pɜ:fju:m/ *n* perfume *m*
perfunctory /pə'fʌŋktərɪ/ *a* superficial, negligente
perhaps /pə'hæps/ *adv* talvez
peril /'perəl/ *n* perigo *m*. **~ous** *a* perigoso
perimeter /pə'rɪmɪtə(r)/ *n* perímetro *m*
period /'pɪərɪəd/ *n* período *m*, época *f*; (*era*) época *f*; (*lesson*) hora *f* de aula, período *m* letivo, (*P*) lectivo; (*med*) período *m*; (*full stop*) ponto (final) *m* □ *a* (*of novel*) de costumes; (*of furniture*) de estilo. **~ic** /-'ɒdɪk/ *a* periódico. **~ical** /-'ɒdɪkl/ *n* periódico *m*. **~ically** /-'ɒdɪklɪ/ *adv* periodicamente
peripher|y /pə'rɪfərɪ/ *n* periferia *f*. **~al** *a* periférico; (*fig*) marginal, à margem
perish /'perɪʃ/ *vi* morrer, perecer; (*rot*) estragar-se, deteriorar-se. **~able** *a* (*of goods*) deteriorável
perjur|e /'pɜ:dʒə(r)/ *vpr* **~e o.s.** jurar falso, perjurar. **~y** *n* perjúrio *m*
perk[1] /pɜ:k/ *vt/i* **~ up** (*colloq*) arrebitar(-se). **~y** *a* (*colloq*) vivo, animado
perk[2] /pɜ:k/ *n* (*colloq*) regalia *f*, extra *m*
perm /pɜ:m/ *n* permanente *f* □ *vt* **have one's hair ~ed** fazer uma permanente
permanen|t /'pɜ:mənənt/ *a* permanente. **~ce** *n* permanência *f*. **~tly** *adv* permanentemente, a título permanente
permeable /'pɜ:mɪəbl/ *a* permeável
permeate /'pɜ:mɪeɪt/ *vt/i* permear, penetrar
permissible /pə'mɪsəbl/ *a* permissível, admissível
permission /pə'mɪʃn/ *n* permissão *f*, licença *f*
permissive /pə'mɪsɪv/ *a* permissivo. **~ society** sociedade *f* permissiva. **~ness** *n* permissividade *f*
permit[1] /pə'mɪt/ *vt* (*pt* **permitted**) permitir, consentir (**sb to** a alguém que)
permit[2] /'pɜ:mɪt/ *n* licença *f*; (*pass*) passe *m*
permutation /pɜ:mju:'teɪʃn/ *n* permutação *f*
pernicious /pə'nɪʃəs/ *a* pernicioso, prejudicial
perpendicular /pɜ:pən'dɪkjʊlə(r)/ *a* & *n* perpendicular (*f*)
perpetrat|e /'pɜ:pɪtreɪt/ *vt* perpetrar. **~or** *n* autor *m*
perpetual /pə'petʃʊəl/ *a* perpétuo
perpetuate /pə'petʃʊeɪt/ *vt* perpetuar
perplex /pə'pleks/ *vt* deixar perplexo. **~ed** *a* perplexo. **~ing** *a* confuso. **~ity** *n* perplexidade *f*
persecut|e /'pɜ:sɪkju:t/ *vt* perseguir. **~ion** *n* /-'kju:ʃn/ *n* perseguição *f*
persever|e /pɜ:sɪ'vɪə(r)/ *vi* perseverar. **~ance** *n* perseverança *f*
Persian /'pɜ:ʃn/ *a* & *n* (*lang*) persa (*m*)
persist /pə'sɪst/ *vi* persistir (**in doing** em fazer). **~ence** *n* persistência *f*. **~ent** *a* persistente; (*obstinate*) teimoso; (*continual*) contínuo, constante. **~ently** *adv* persistentemente
person /'pɜ:sn/ *n* pessoa *f*. **in ~** em pessoa
personal /'pɜ:sənl/ *a* pessoal; (*secretary*) particular. **~ stereo** estereo *m* pessoal. **~ly** *adv* pessoalmente
personality /pɜ:sə'nælətɪ/ *n* personalidade *f*; (*on TV*) vedete *f*
personify /pə'sɒnɪfaɪ/ *vt* personificar
personnel /pɜ:sə'nel/ *n* pessoal *m*
perspective /pə'spektɪv/ *n* perspectiva *f*
perspir|e /pə'spaɪə(r)/ *vi* transpirar. **~ation** /-ə'reɪʃn/ *n* transpiração *f*
persua|de /pə'sweɪd/ *vt* persuadir (**to** a). **~sion** /-'sweɪʒn/ *n* persuasão *f*; (*belief*) crença *f*, convicção *f*. **~sive** /-'sweɪsɪv/ *a* persuasivo
pert /pɜ:t/ *a* (*saucy*) atrevido, descarado; (*lively*) vivo
pertain /pə'teɪn/ *vi* **~ to** pertencer a; (*be relevant*) ser pertinente a, (*P*) ser próprio de
pertinent /'pɜ:tɪnənt/ *a* pertinente
perturb /pə'tɜ:b/ *vt* perturbar, transtornar
Peru /pə'ru:/ *n* Peru *m*. **~vian** *a* & *n* peruano (*m*), (*P*) peruviano (*m*)
peruse /pə'ru:z/ *vt* ler com atenção
perva|de /pə'veɪd/ *vt* espalhar-se por, invadir. **~sive** *a* penetrante
pervers|e /pə'vɜ:s/ *a* que insiste no erro; (*wicked*) perverso; (*wayward*) caprichoso. **~ity** *n* obstinação *f*; (*wickedness*) perversidade *f*; (*waywardness*) capricho *m*, birra *f*
perver|t[1] /pə'vɜ:t/ *vt* perverter. **~sion** *n* perversão *f*
pervert[2] /'pɜ:vɜ:t/ *n* pervertido *m*
peseta /pə'seɪtə/ *n* peseta *f*
pessimis|t /'pesmɪst/ *n* pessimista *mf*. **~m** /-zəm/ *n* pessimismo *m*. **~tic** /-'mɪstɪk/ *a* pessimista
pest /pest/ *n* inseto *m*, (*P*) insecto *m* nocivo; (*animal*) animal *m* daninho; (*person*) peste *f*
pester /'pestə(r)/ *vt* incomodar (*colloq*)
pesticide /'pestɪsaɪd/ *n* pesticida *m*

pet /pet/ *n* animal *m* de estimação; (*favourite*) preferido *m*, querido *m* □ *a* (*rabbit etc*) de estimação □ *vt* (*pt* **petted**) acariciar. ~ **name** nome *m* usado em família

petal /'petl/ *n* pétala *f*

peter /'pi:tə(r)/ *vi* ~ **out** extinguir-se, acabar pouco a pouco, morrer (*fig*)

petition /pɪ'tɪʃn/ *n* petição *f* □ *vt* requerer

petrify /'petrɪfaɪ/ *vt* petrificar

petrol /'petrəl/ *n* gasolina *f*. ~ **pump** bomba *f* de gasolina. ~ **station** posto *m* de gasolina. ~ **tank** tanque *m* de gasolina

petroleum /pɪ'trəʊlɪəm/ *n* petróleo *m*

petticoat /'petɪkəʊt/ *n* combinação *f*, anágua *f*

petty /'petɪ/ *a* (-ier, -iest) pequeno, insignificante; (*mean*) mesquinho. ~ **cash** fundo *m* para pequenas despesas, caixa *f* pequena

petulan|t /'petjʊlənt/ *a* irritável. ~**ce** *n* irritabilidade *f*

pew /pju:/ *n* banco (de igreja) *m*

pewter /'pju:tə(r)/ *n* estanho *m*

phallic /'fælɪk/ *a* fálico

phantom /'fæntəm/ *n* fantasma *m*

pharmaceutical /fa:mə'sju:tɪkl/ *a* farmacêutico

pharmac|y /'fa:məsɪ/ *n* farmácia *f*. ~**ist** *n* farmacêutico *m*

phase /feɪz/ *n* fase *f* □ *vt* ~ **in/out** introduzir/retirar progressivamente

PhD *abbr of* **Doctor of Philosophy** *n* doutorado *m*

pheasant /'feznt/ *n* faisão *m*

phenomen|on /fɪ'nɒmɪnən/ *n* (*pl* -**ena**) fenômeno *m*, (*P*) fenómeno *m*. ~**al** *a* fenomenal

philanthrop|ist /fɪ'lænθrəpɪst/ *n* filantropo *m*. ~**ic** /-ən'θrɒpɪk/ *a* filantrópico

Philippines /'fɪlɪpi:nz/ *npl* **the** ~ as Filipinas *fpl*

philistine /'fɪlɪstaɪn/ *n* filisteu *m*

philosoph|y /fɪ'lɒsəfɪ/ *n* filosofia *f*. ~**er** *n* filósofo *m*. ~**ical** /-ə'sɒfɪkl/ *a* filosófico

phlegm /flem/ *n* (*med*) catarro *m*, fleuma *f*

phobia /'fəʊbɪə/ *n* fobia *f*

phone /fəʊn/ *n* (*colloq*) telefone *m* □ *vt/i* (*colloq*) telefonar (para). **on the** ~ no telefone. ~ **back** voltar a telefonar, ligar de volta. ~ **book** lista *f* telefônica, (*P*) telefónica. ~ **box** cabine *f* telefônica, (*P*) telefónica. ~ **call** chamada *f*, telefonema *m*. ~**-in** *n* programa *m* de rádio ou tv com participação dos ouvintes

phonecard /'fəʊnka:d/ *n* cartão *m* para uso em telefone público

phonetic /fə'netɪk/ *a* fonetico. ~**s** *n* fonética *f*

phoney /'fəʊnɪ/ *a* (-ier, -iest) (*sl*) falso, fingido □ *n* (*sl: person*) fingido *m*; (*sl: thing*) falso *m*, (*P*) falsificação *f*

phosphate /'fɒsfeɪt/ *n* fosfato *m*

phosphorus /'fɒsfərəs/ *n* fósforo *m*

photo /'fəʊtəʊ/ *n* (*pl* -**os**) (*colloq*) retrato *m*, foto *f*

photocop|y /'fəʊtəʊkɒpɪ/ *n* fotocópia *f* □ *vt* fotocopiar. ~**ier** *n* fotocopiadora *f*

photogenic /fəʊtəʊ'dʒenɪk/ *a* fotogênico, (*P*) fotogénico

photograph /'fəʊtəgra:f/ *n* fotografia *f* □ *vt* fotografar. ~**er** /fə'tɒgrəfə(r)/ *n* fotógrafo *m*. ~**ic** /-'græfɪk/ *a* fotográfico. ~**y** /fə'tɒgrəfɪ/ *n* fotografia *f*

phrase /freɪz/ *n* expressão *f*, frase *f*; (*gram*) locução *f*, frase *f* elíptica □ *vt* exprimir. ~**-book** *n* livro *m* de expressões idiomáticas

physical /'fɪzɪkl/ *a* físico

physician /fɪ'zɪʃn/ *n* médico *m*

physicist /'fɪzɪsɪst/ *n* físico *m*

physics /'fɪzɪks/ *n* física *f*

physiology /fɪzɪ'ɒlədʒɪ/ *n* fisiologia *f*

physiotherap|y /fɪzɪəʊ'θerəpɪ/ *n* fisioterapia *f*. ~**ist** *n* fisioterapeuta *mf*

physique /fɪ'zi:k/ *n* físico *m*

pian|o /pɪ'ænəʊ/ *n* (*pl* -**os**) piano *m*. ~**ist** /'pɪənɪst/ *n* pianista *mf*

pick[1] /pɪk/ *n* (*tool*) picareta *f*

pick[2] /pɪk/ *vt* escolher; (*flowers, fruit etc*) colher; (*lock*) forçar; (*teeth*) palitar □ *n* escolha *f*; (*best*) o/a melhor. ~ **a quarrel with** puxar uma briga com. ~ **holes in an argument** descobrir os pontos fracos dum argumento. ~ **sb's pocket** bater a carteira de alg. ~ **off** tirar, arrancar. ~ **on** implicar com. ~ **out** escolher; (*identify*) identificar, reconhecer. ~ **up** *vt* apanhar; (*speed*) ganhar. **take one's** ~ escolher livremente

pickaxe /'pɪkæks/ *n* picareta *f*

picket /'pɪkɪt/ *n* piquete *m*; (*single striker*) grevista *mf* de piquete □ *vt* (*pt* **picketed**) colocar um piquete em □ *vi* fazer piquete

pickings /'pɪkɪŋz/ *npl* restos *mpl*

pickle /'pɪkl/ *n* vinagre *m*. ~**s** picles *mpl*, (*P*) pickles *mpl* □ *vt* conservar em vinagre. **in a** ~ (*colloq*) numa encrenca (*colloq*)

pickpocket /'pɪkpɒkɪt/ *n* batedor *m* de carteiras, (*P*) carteirista *m*

picnic /'pɪknɪk/ *n* piquenique *m* □ *vi* (*pt* **picnicked**) piquenicar, (*P*) fazer um piquenique

pictorial /pɪk'tɔ:rɪəl/ *a* ilustrado

picture /'pɪktʃə(r)/ *n* imagem *f*; (*illustration*) estampa *f*, ilustração *f*; (*painting*) quadro *m*, pintura *f*;

(*photo*) fotografia *f*, retrato *m*; (*drawing*) desenho *m*; (*fig*) descrição *f*, quadro *m* □ *vt* imaginar; (*describe*) pintar, descrever. **the ~s** o cinema

picturesque /pɪktʃə'resk/ *a* pitoresco

pidgin /'pɪdʒɪn/ *a* ~ **English** inglês *m* estropiado

pie /paɪ/ *n* torta *f*, (*P*) tarte *f*; (*of meat*) empada *f*

piece /pi:s/ *n* pedaço *m*, bocado *m*; (*of machine, in game*) peça *f*; (*of currency*) moeda *f* □ *vt* ~ **together** juntar, montar. **a ~ of advice/furniture/***etc* um conselho/um móvel/*etc*. **~-work** *n* trabalho *m* por, (*P*) a peça *or* por, (*P*) a tarefa. **take to ~s** desmontar

piecemeal /'pi:smi:l/ *a* aos poucos, pouco a pouco

pier /pɪə(r)/ *n* molhe *m*

pierc|e /pɪəs/ *vt* furar, penetrar. **~ing** *a* penetrante; (*of scream, pain*) lancinante

piety /'paɪətɪ/ *n* piedade *f*, devoção *f*

pig /pɪg/ *n* porco *m*. **~-headed** *a* cabeçudo, teimoso

pigeon /'pɪdʒɪn/ *n* pombo *m*. **~-hole** *n* escaninho *m*

piggy /'pɪgɪ/ *a* como um porco. **~-back** *adv* nas costas. **~ bank** cofre *m* de criança

pigment /'pɪgmənt/ *n* pigmento *m*. **~ation** /-'teɪʃn/ *n* pigmentação *f*

pigsty /'pɪgstaɪ/ *n* pocilga *f*, chiqueiro *m*

pigtail /'pɪgteɪl/ *n* trança *f*

pike /paɪk/ *n* (*pl invar*) (*fish*) lúcio *m*

pilchard /'pɪltʃəd/ *n* peixe *m* pequeno da família do arenque, sardinha *f* européia

pile /paɪl/ *n* pilha *f*; (*of carpet*) pêlo *m* □ *vt/i* amontoar(-se), empilhar(-se) (**into** em). **a ~ of** (*colloq*) um monte de (*colloq*). **~ up** acumular(-se). **~-up** *n* choque *m* em cadeia

piles /paɪlz/ *npl* hemorróidas *fpl*

pilfer /'pɪlfə(r)/ *vt* furtar. **~age** *n* furto *m* (de coisas pequenas *or* em pequenas quantidades)

pilgrim /'pɪlgrɪm/ *n* peregrino *m*, romeiro *m*. **~age** *n* peregrinação *f*, romaria *f*

pill /pɪl/ *n* pílula *f*, comprimido *m*

pillage /'pɪlɪdʒ/ *n* pilhagem *f*, saque *m* □ *vt* pilhar, saquear

pillar /'pɪlə(r)/ *n* pilar *m*. **~-box** *n* marco *m* do correio

pillion /'pɪlɪən/ *n* assento *m* traseiro de motorizada. **ride ~** ir no assento de trás

pillow /'pɪləʊ/ *n* travesseiro *m*

pillowcase /'pɪləʊkeɪs/ *n* fronha *f*

pilot /'paɪlət/ *n* piloto *m* □ *vt* (*pt* **piloted**) pilotar. **~-light** *n* piloto *m*; (*electr*) lâmpada *f* testemunho; (*gas*) piloto *m*

pimento /pɪ'mentəʊ/ *n* (*pl* **-os**) pimentão *m* vermelho

pimple /'pɪmpl/ *n* borbulha *f*, espinha *f*

pin /pɪn/ *n* alfinete *m*; (*techn*) cavilha *f* □ *vt* (*pt* **pinned**) pregar *or* prender com alfinete(s); (*hold down*) prender, segurar. **have ~s and needles** estar com cãibra. **~ sb down** (*fig*) obrigar alg a definir-se, apertar alg (*fig*). **~-point** *vt* localizar com precisão. **~-stripe** *a* de listras finas. **~ up** pregar. **~-up** *n* (*colloq*) pin-up *f*

pinafore /'pɪnəfɔ:(r)/ *n* avental *m*. **~ dress** veste *f*

pincers /'pɪnsəz/ *npl* (*tool*) torquês *f*, (*P*) alicate *m*; (*med*) pinça *f*; (*zool*) pinça(s) *f*(*pl*), tenaz(es) *f* (*pl*)

pinch /pɪntʃ/ *vt* apertar; (*sl: steal*) surripiar (*colloq*) □ *n* aperto *m*; (*tweak*) beliscão *m*; (*small amount*) pitada *f*. **at a ~** em caso de necessidade

pine[1] /paɪn/ *n* (*tree*) pinheiro *m*; (*wood*) pinho *m*

pine[2] /paɪn/ *vi* ~ **away** definhar, consumir-se. **~ for** suspirar por

pineapple /'paɪnæpl/ *n* abacaxi *m*, (*P*) ananás *m*

ping-pong /'pɪŋpɒŋ/ *n* pingue-pongue *m*

pink /pɪŋk/ *a* & *n* rosa (*m*)

pinnacle /'pɪnəkl/ *n* pináculo *m*

pint /paɪnt/ *n* quartilho *m* (= *0,57l*; *Amer = 0,47l*)

pioneer /paɪə'nɪə(r)/ *n* pioneiro *m* □ *vt* ser o pioneiro em, preparar o caminho para

pious /'paɪəs/ *a* piedoso, devoto

pip /pɪp/ *n* (*seed*) pevide *f*

pipe /paɪp/ *n* cano *m*, tubo *m*; (*of smoker*) cachimbo *m* □ *vt* encanar, canalizer **~ down** calar a boca

pipeline /'paɪplaɪn/ *n* (*for oil*) oleoduto *m*; (*for gas*) gaseoduto *m*, (*P*) gasoduto *m*. **in the ~** (*fig*) encaminhado

piping /'paɪpɪŋ/ *n* tubagem *f*. **~ hot** muito quente

piquant /'pi:kənt/ *a* picante

pira|te /'paɪərət/ *n* pirata *m*. **~cy** *n* pirataria *f*

Pisces /'paɪsi:z/ *n* (*astr*) Peixe *m*, (*P*) Pisces *m*

pistol /'pɪstl/ *n* pistola *f*

piston /'pɪstən/ *n* êmbolo *m*, pistão *m*

pit /pɪt/ *n* (*hole*) cova *f*, fosso *m*; (*mine*) poço *m*; (*quarry*) pedreira *f* □ *vt* (*pt* **pitted**) picar, esburacar; (*fig*) opor. **~ o.s. against** (*struggle*) medir-se com

pitch[1] /pɪtʃ/ *n* breu *m*. **~-black** *a* escuro como breu

pitch² /pɪtʃ/ *vt* (*throw*) lançar; (*tent*) armar □ *vi* cair □ *n* (*slope*) declive *m*; (*of sound*) som *m*; (*of voice*) altura *f*; (*sport*) campo *m*

pitchfork /ˈpɪtʃfɔːk/ *n* forcado *m*

pitfall /ˈpɪtfɔːl/ *n* (*fig*) cilada *f*, perigo *m* inesperado

pith /pɪθ/ *n* (*of orange*) parte *f* branca da casca, mesocarpo *m*; (*fig: essential part*) cerne *m*, âmago *m*

pithy /ˈpɪθɪ/ *a* (**-ier, -iest**) preciso, conciso

piti|ful /ˈpɪtɪfl/ *a* lastimoso; (*contemptible*) miserável. **~less** *a* impiedoso

pittance /ˈpɪtns/ *n* salário *m* miserável, miséria *f*

pity /ˈpɪtɪ/ *n* dó *m*, pena *f*, piedade *f* □ *vt* compadecer-se de. **it's a ~** é uma pena. **take ~ on** ter pena de. **what a ~!** que pena!

pivot /ˈpɪvət/ *n* eixo *m* □ *vt* (*pt* **pivoted**) girar em torno de

placard /ˈplækaːd/ *n* (*poster*) cartaz *m*

placate /pləˈkeɪt/ *vt* apaziguar, aplacar

place /pleɪs/ *n* lugar *m*, sítio *m*; (*house*) casa *f*; (*seat, rank etc*) lugar *m* □ *vt* colocar, pôr. **~ an order** fazer uma encomenda. **at/to my ~** em a *or* na minha casa. **~-mat** *n* pano *m* de mesa individual, (*P*) napperon *m* à americana

placid /ˈplæsɪd/ *a* plácido

plagiar|ize /ˈpleɪdʒəraɪz/ *vt* plagiar. **~ism** *n* plágio *m*

plague /pleɪɡ/ *n* peste *f*; (*of insects*) praga *f* □ *vt* atormentar, atazanar

plaice /pleɪs/ *n* (*pl invar*) solha *f*

plain /pleɪn/ *a* (**-er, -est**) claro; (*candid*) franco; (*simple*) simples; (*not pretty*) sem beleza; (*not patterned*) liso □ *adv* com franqueza □ *n* planície *f*. **in ~ clothes** à paisana. **~ly** *adv* claramente; (*candidly*) francamente

plaintiff /ˈpleɪntɪf/ *n* queixoso *m*

plaintive /ˈpleɪntɪv/ *a* queixoso

plait /plæt/ *vt* entrançar □ *n* trança *f*

plan /plæn/ *n* plano *m*, projeto *m*, (*P*) projecto *m*; (*of a house, city etc*) plano *m*, planta *f* □ *vt* (*pt* **planned**) planear, planejar □ *vi* fazer planos. **~ to do** ter a intenção de fazer

plane¹ /pleɪn/ *n* (*level*) plano *m*; (*aeroplane*) avião *m* □ *a* plano

plane² /pleɪn/ *n* (*tool*) plaina *f* □ *vt* aplainar

planet /ˈplænɪt/ *n* planeta *m*

plank /plæŋk/ *n* prancha *f*

planning /ˈplænɪŋ/ *n* planeamento *m*, planejamento *m*. **~ permission** permissão *f* para construir

plant /plaːnt/ *n* planta *f*; (*techn*) aparelhagem *f*; (*factory*) fábrica *f* □ *vt* plantar. **~ a bomb** colocar uma bomba. **~ation** /-ˈteɪʃn/ *n* plantação *f*

plaque /plaːk/ *n* placa *f*; (*on teeth*) tártaro *m*, pedra *f*

plaster /ˈplaːstə(r)/ *n* reboco *m*; (*adhesive*) esparadrapo *m*, band-aid *m* □ *vt* rebocar; (*cover*) cobrir (**with** com, de). **in ~** engessado. **~ of Paris** gesso *m*. **~er** *n* rebocador *m*, caiador *m*

plastic /ˈplæstɪk/ *a* plástico □ *n* plástica *f*. **~ surgery** cirurgia *f* plástica

plate /pleɪt/ *n* prato *m*; (*in book*) gravura *f* □ *vt* revestir de metal

plateau /ˈplætəʊ/ *n* (*pl* **-eaux** /-əʊz/) planalto *m*, platô *m*

platform /ˈplætfɔːm/ *n* estrado *m*; (*for speaking*) tribuna *f*; (*rail*) plataforma *f*, cais *m*; (*fig*) programa *m* de partido político. **~ ticket** bilhete *m* de gare

platinum /ˈplætɪnəm/ *n* platina *f*

platitude /ˈplætɪtjuːd/ *n* banalidade *f*, lugar-comum *m*

platonic /pləˈtɒnɪk/ *a* platônico, (*P*) platónico

plausible /ˈplɔːzəbl/ *a* plausível; (*person*) convincente

play /pleɪ/ *vt/i* (*for amusement*) brincar; (*instrument*) tocar; (*cards, game*) jogar; (*opponent*) jogar contra; (*match*) disputar □ *n* jogo *m*; (*theatre*) peça *f*; (*movement*) folga *f*, margem *f*. **~ down** minimizar. **~ on** (*take advantage of*) aproveitar-se de. **~ safe** jogar pelo seguro. **~ up** (*colloq*) dar problemas (a). **~-group** *n* jardim *m* de infância, (*P*) jardim *m* infantil. **~-pen** *n* cercado *m* para crianças

playboy /ˈpleɪbɔɪ/ *n* play-boy *m*

player /ˈpleɪə(r)/ *n* jogador *m*; (*theat*) artista *mf*; (*mus*) artista *mf*, executante *mf*, instrumentista *mf*

playful /ˈpleɪfl/ *a* brincalhão *m*

playground /ˈpleɪɡraʊnd/ *n* pátio *m* de recreio

playing /ˈpleɪɪŋ/ *n* atuação *f*, (*P*) actuação *f*. **~-card** *n* carta *f* de jogar. **~-field** *n* campo *m* de jogos

playwright /ˈpleɪraɪt/ *n* dramaturgo *m*

plc *abbr* (*of public limited company*) SARL

plea /pliː/ *n* súplica *f*; (*reason*) pretexto *m*, desculpa *f*; (*jur*) alegação *f* da defesa

plead /pliːd/ *vt/i* pleitear; (*as excuse*) alegar. **~ guilty** confessar-se culpado. **~ with** implorar a

pleasant /ˈpleznt/ *a* agradável

pleas|e /pliːz/ *vt/i* agradar (a), dar prazer (a) □ *adv* por favor, (*P*) se faz favor. **they ~e themselves, they do as they ~e** eles fazem como bem

entendem. ~ed *a* contente, satisfeito (with com). ~ing *a* agradável
pleasur|e /'pleʒə(r)/ *n* prazer *m*. ~able *a* agradável
pleat /pli:t/ *n* prega *f* □ *vt* preguear
pledge /pledʒ/ *n* penhor *m*, garantia *f*; (*fig*) promessa *f* □ *vt* prometer; (*pawn*) empenhar
plentiful /'plentɪfl/ *a* abundante
plenty /'plentɪ/ *n* abundância *f*, fartura *f*. ~ (of) muito (de); (*enough*) bastante (de)
pliable /'plaɪəbl/ *a* flexível
pliers /'plaɪəz/ *npl* alicate *m*
plight /plaɪt/ *n* triste situação *f*
plimsoll /'plɪmsəl/ *n* alpargata *f*, tênis *m*, (*P*) ténis *m*
plinth /plɪnθ/ *n* plinto *m*
plod /plɒd/ *vi* (*pt* **plodded**) caminhar lentamente; (*work*) trabalhar, marrar (*sl*). ~der *n* trabalhador *m* lento mas perseverante. ~ding *a* lento
plonk /plɒŋk/ *n* (*sl*) vinho *m* ordinário, (*P*) carrascão *m*
plot /plɒt/ *n* complô *m*, conspiração *f*; (*of novel etc*) trama *f*; (*of land*) lote *m* □ *vt/i* (*pt* **plotted**) conspirar; (*mark out*) traçar
plough /plaʊ/ *n* arado *m* □ *vt/i* arar. ~ **back** reinvestir. ~ **into** colidir. ~ **through** abrir caminho por
ploy /plɔɪ/ *n* (*colloq*) estratagema *m*
pluck /plʌk/ *vt* apanhar; (*bird*) depenar; (*eyebrows*) depilar; (*mus*) tanger □ *n* coragem *f*. ~ **up courage** ganhar coragem. ~y *a* corajoso
plug /plʌg/ *n* tampão *m*; (*electr*) tomada *f*, (*P*) ficha *f* □ *vt* (*pt* **plugged**) tapar com tampão; (*colloq: publicize*) fazer grande propaganda de □ *vi* ~ **away** (*colloq*) trabalhar com afinco. ~ **in** (*electr*) ligar. ~-**hole** *n* buraco *m* do cano
plum /plʌm/ *n* ameixa *f*
plumb /plʌm/ *adv* exatamente, (*P*) exactamente, mesmo □ *vt* sondar. ~-**line** *n* fio *m* de prumo
plumb|er /'plʌmə(r)/ *n* bombeiro *m*, encanador *m*, (*P*) canalizador *m*. ~ing *n* encanamento *m*, (*P*) canalização *f*
plummet /'plʌmɪt/ *vi* (*pt* **plummeted**) despencar
plump /plʌmp/ *a* (-er, -est) rechonchudo, roliço □ *vi* ~ **for** optar por. ~ness *n* gordura *f*
plunder /'plʌndə(r)/ *vt* pilhar, saquear □ *n* pilhagem *f*, saque *m*; (*goods*) despojo *m*
plunge /plʌndʒ/ *vt/i* mergulhar, atirar(-se), afundar(-se) □ *n* mergulho *m*. **take the** ~ (*fig*) decidir-se, dar o salto (*fig*)
plunger /'plʌndʒə(r)/ *n* (*of pump*) êmbolo *m*, pistão *m*; (*for sink etc*) desentupidor *m*
pluperfect /plu:'pɜ:fɪkt/ *n* mais-que-perfeito *m*
plural /'plʊərəl/ *a* plural; (*noun*) no plural □ *n* plural *m*
plus /plʌs/ *prep* mais □ *a* positivo □ *n* sinal +; (*fig*) qualidade *f* positiva
plush /plʌʃ/ *n* pelúcia *f* □ *a* de pelúcia; (*colloq*) de luxo
ply /plaɪ/ *vt* (*tool*) manejar; (*trade*) exercer □ *vi* (*ship, bus*) fazer carreira entre dois lugares. ~ **sb with drink** encher alguém de bebidas
plywood /'plaɪwʊd/ *n* madeira *f* compensada
p.m. /pi:'em/ *adv* da tarde, da noite
pneumatic /nju:'mætɪk/ *a* pneumático. ~ **drill** broca *f* pneumática
pneumonia /nju:'məʊnɪə/ *n* pneumonia *f*
PO *abbr see* **Post Office**
poach /pəʊtʃ/ *vt/i* (*steal*) caçar/pescar em propriedade alheia; (*culin*) fazer pochê, (*P*) escalfar. ~**ed eggs** ovos *mpl* pochês, (*P*) ovos *mpl* escalfados
pocket /'pɒkɪt/ *n* bolso *m*, algibeira *f* □ *a* de algibeira □ *vt* meter no bolso. ~-**book** *n* (*notebook*) livro *m* de apontamentos; (*Amer: handbag*) carteira *f*. ~-**money** *n* (*monthly*) mesada *f*; (*weekly*) semanada *f*, dinheiro *m* para pequenas despesas
pod /pɒd/ *n* vagem *f*
poem /'pəʊɪm/ *n* poema *m*
poet /'pəʊɪt/ *n* poeta *m*, poetisa *f*. ~ic /-'etɪk/ *a* poético
poetry /'pəʊɪtrɪ/ *n* poesia *f*
poignant /'pɔɪnjənt/ *a* pungente, doloroso
point /pɔɪnt/ *n* ponto *m*; (*tip*) ponta *f*; (*decimal point*) vírgula *f*; (*meaning*) sentido *m*, razão *m*; (*electr*) tomada *f*. ~s (*rail*) agulhas *fpl* □ *vt/i* (*aim*) apontar (at para); (*show*) apontar, indicar (at/to para). **on the** ~ **of** prestes a, quase a. ~-**blank** *a* & *adv* à queima-roupa; (*fig*) categórico. ~ **of view** ponto *m* de vista. ~ **out** apontar, fazer ver. **that is a good** ~ (*remark*) é uma boa observação. **to the** ~ a propósito. **what is the** ~? de que adianta?
pointed /'pɔɪntɪd/ *a* ponteagudo; (*of remark*) intencional, contundente
pointer /'pɔɪntə(r)/ *n* ponteiro *m*; (*colloq: hint*) sugestão *f*
pointless /'pɔɪntlɪs/ *a* inútil, sem sentido
poise /pɔɪz/ *n* equilíbrio *m*; (*carriage*) porte *m*; (*fig: self-possession*) presença *f*, segurança *f*. ~d *a* equilibrado; (*person*) seguro de si

poison /ˈpɔɪzn/ *n* veneno *m*, peçonha *f* □ *vt* envenenar. **blood-~ing** *n* envenenamento *m* do sangue. **food-~ing** *n* intoxicação *f* alimentar. **~ous** *a* venenoso

poke /pəʊk/ *vt/i* espetar; (*with elbow*) acotovelar; (*fire*) atiçar □ *n* espetadela *f*; (*with elbow*) cotovelada *f*. **~ about** esgaravatar, remexer, procurar. **~ fun at** fazer troça/pouco de. **~ out** (*head*) enfiar

poker[1] /ˈpəʊkə(r)/ *n* atiçador *m*

poker[2] /ˈpəʊkə(r)/ *n* (*cards*) pôquer *m*, (*P*) póquer *m*

poky /ˈpəʊkɪ/ *a* (-ier, -iest) acanhado, apertado

Poland /ˈpəʊlənd/ *n* Polônia *f*, (*P*) Polónia *f*

polar /ˈpəʊlə(r)/ *a* polar. **~ bear** urso *m* branco

polarize /ˈpəʊləraɪz/ *vt* polarizar

pole[1] /pəʊl/ *n* vara *f*; (*for flag*) mastro *m*; (*post*) poste *m*

pole[2] /pəʊl/ *n* (*geog*) pólo *m*

Pole /pəʊl/ *n* polaco *m*

polemic /pəˈlemɪk/ *n* polêmica *f*, (*P*) polémica *f*

police /pəˈli:s/ *n* polícia *f* □ *vt* policiar. **~ state** estado *m* policial. **~ station** distrito *m*, delegacia *f*, (*P*) esquadra *f* de polícia

police|man /pəˈli:smən/ *n* (*pl* -men) policial *m*, (*P*) polícia *m*, guarda *m*, agente *m* de polícia. **~-woman** (*pl* -women) *n* polícia *f* feminina, (*P*) mulher-polícia *f*

policy[1] /ˈpɒlɪsɪ/ *n* (*plan of action*) política *f*

policy[2] /ˈpɒlɪsɪ/ *n* (*insurance*) apólice *f* de seguro

polio /ˈpəʊlɪəʊ/ *n* polio *f*

polish /ˈpɒlɪʃ/ *vt* polir, dar lustro em; (*shoes*) engraxar; (*floor*) encerar □ *n* (*for shoes*) graxa *f*; (*for floor*) cera *f*; (*for nails*) esmalte *m*, (*P*) verniz *m*; (*shine*) polimento *m*; (*fig*) requinte *m*. **~ off** acabar (rapidamente). **~ up** (*language*) aperfeiçoar. **~ed** *a* requintado, elegante

Polish /ˈpəʊlɪʃ/ *a* & *n* polonês (*m*), (*P*) polaco (*m*)

polite /pəˈlaɪt/ *a* polido, educado, delicado. **~ly** *adv* delicadamente. **~ness** *n* delicadeza *f*, cortesia *f*

political /pəˈlɪtɪkl/ *a* político

politician /pɒlɪˈtɪʃn/ *n* político *m*

politics /ˈpɒlətɪks/ *n* política *f*

polka /ˈpɒlkə/ *n* polca *f*. **~ dots** bolas *fpl*

poll /pəʊl/ *n* votação *f*; (*survey*) sondagem *f*, pesquisa *f* □ *vt* (*votes*) obter. **go to the ~s** votar, ir às urnas. **~ing-booth** *n* cabine *f* de voto

pollen /ˈpɒlən/ *n* pólen *m*

pollut|e /pəˈlu:t/ *vt* poluir. **~ion** /-ʃn/ *n* poluição *f*

polo /ˈpəʊləʊ/ *n* pólo *m*. **~ neck** gola *f* rolê

polyester /pɒlɪˈestə/ *n* poliéster *m*

polytechnic /pɒlɪˈteknɪk/ *n* politécnica *f*

polythene /ˈpɒlɪθi:n/ *n* politeno *m*. **~ bag** *n* saco *m* de plástico

pomegranate /ˈpɒmɪgrænɪt/ *n* romã *f*

pomp /pɒmp/ *n* pompa *f*

pompon /ˈpɒmpɒn/ *n* pompom *m*

pomp|ous /ˈpɒmpəs/ *a* pomposo. **~osity** /-ˈpɒsətɪ/ *n* imponência *f*

pond /pɒnd/ *n* lagoa *f*, lago *m*; (*artificial*) tanque *m*, lago *m*

ponder /ˈpɒndə(r)/ *vt/i* ponderar, meditar (**over** sobre)

pong /pɒŋ/ *n* (*sl*) pivete *m* □ *vi* (*sl*) cheirar mal, tresandar

pony /ˈpəʊnɪ/ *n* pônei *m*, (*P*) pónei *m*. **~-tail** *n* rabo *m* de cavalo. **~-trekking** *n* passeio *m* de pônei, (*P*) pónei

poodle /ˈpu:dl/ *n* cão *m* de água, caniche *m*

pool[1] /pu:l/ *n* (*puddle*) charco *m*, poça *f*; (*for swimming*) piscina *f*

pool[2] /pu:l/ *n* (*fund*) fundo *m* comum; (*econ, comm*) pool *m*; (*game*) forma *f* de bilhar. **~s** loteca *f*, (*P*) totobola *m* □ *vt* pôr num fundo comum

poor /pʊə(r)/ *a* (-er, -est) pobre; (*not good*) medíocre. **~ly** *adv* mal □ *a* doente

pop[1] /pɒp/ *n* estalido *m*, ruído *m* seco □ *vt/i* (*pt* **popped**) dar um estalido, estalar; (*of cork*) saltar. **~ in/out/off** entrar/sair/ir-se embora. **~ up** aparecer de repente, saltar

pop[2] /pɒp/ *n* música *f* pop □ *a* pop *invar*

popcorn /ˈpɒpkɔ:n/ *n* pipoca *f*

pope /pəʊp/ *n* papa *m*

poplar /ˈpɒplə(r)/ *n* choupo *m*, álamo *m*

poppy /ˈpɒpɪ/ *n* papoula *f*

popular /ˈpɒpjʊlə(r)/ *a* popular; (*in fashion*) em voga, na moda. **be ~ with** ser popular entre. **~ity** /-ˈlærətɪ/ *n* popularidade *f*. **~ize** *vt* popularizar, vulgarizar

populat|e /ˈpɒpjʊleɪt/ *vt* povoar. **~ion** /-ˈleɪʃn/ *n* população *f*

populous /ˈpɒpjʊləs/ *a* populoso

porcelain /ˈpɔ:slɪn/ *n* porcelana *f*

porch /pɔ:tʃ/ *n* alpendre *m*; (*Amer*) varanda *f*

porcupine /ˈpɔ:kjʊpaɪn/ *n* porco-espinho *m*

pore[1] /pɔ:(r)/ *n* poro *m*

pore[2] /pɔ:(r)/ *vi* **~ over** examinar, estudar

pork /pɔ:k/ *n* carne *f* de porco

pornograph|y /pɔ:'nɒgrəfɪ/ *n* pornografia *f*. **~ic** /-ə'græfɪk/ *a* pornográfico

porous /'pɔ:rəs/ *a* poroso

porpoise /'pɔ:pəs/ *n* toninha *f*, (*P*) golfinho *m*

porridge /'pɒrɪdʒ/ *n* (papa *f* de) flocos *mpl* de aveia

port[1] /pɔ:t/ *n* (*harbour*) porto *m*

port[2] /pɔ:t/ *n* (*wine*) (vinho do) Porto *m*

portable /'pɔ:təbl/ *a* portátil

porter[1] /'pɔ:tə(r)/ *n* (*carrier*) carregador *m*

porter[2] /'pɔ:tə(r)/ *n* (*doorkeeper*) porteiro *m*

portfolio /pɔ:t'fəʊlɪəʊ/ *n* (*pl* -os) (*case, post*) pasta *f*; (*securities*) carteira *f* de investimentos

porthole /'pɔ:thəʊl/ *n* vigia *f*

portion /'pɔ:ʃn/ *n* (*share, helping*) porção *f*; (*part*) parte *f*

portly /'pɔ:tlɪ/ *a* (-ier, -iest) corpulento e digno

portrait /'pɔ:trɪt/ *n* retrato *m*

portray /pɔ:'treɪ/ *vt* retratar, pintar; (*fig*) descrever. **~al** *n* retrato *m*

Portug|al /'pɔ:tjʊgl/ *n* Portugal *m*. **~uese** /-'gi:z/ *a* & *n invar* português (*m*)

pose /pəʊz/ *vt/i* (fazer) posar; (*question*) fazer □ *n* pose *f*, postura *f*. **~ as** fazer-se passar por

poser /'pəʊzə(r)/ *n* quebra-cabeças *m*

posh /pɒʃ/ *a* (*sl*) chique *invar*

position /pə'zɪʃn/ *n* posição *f*; (*job*) lugar *m*, colocação *f*; (*state*) situação *f* □ *vt* colocar

positive /'pɒzətɪv/ *a* positivo; (*definite*) categórico, definitivo; (*colloq: downright*) autêntico. **she's ~ that** ela tem certeza que. **~ly** *adv* positivamente; (*absolutely*) completamente

possess /pə'zes/ *vt* possuir. **~ion** /-ʃn/ *n* posse *f*; (*thing possessed*) possessão *f*. **~or** *n* possuidor *m*

possessive /pə'zesɪv/ *a* possessivo

possib|le /'pɒsəbl/ *a* possível. **~ility** /-'bɪlətɪ/ *n* possibilidade *f*

possibly /'pɒsəblɪ/ *adv* possivelmente, talvez. **if I ~ can** se me fôr possível. **I cannot ~ leave** estou impossibilitado de partir

post[1] /pəʊst/ *n* (*pole*) poste *m* □ *vt* (*notice*) afixar, pregar

post[2] /pəʊst/ *n* (*station, job*) posto *m* □ *vt* colocar; (*appoint*) colocar

post[3] /pəʊst/ *n* (*mail*) correio *m* □ *a* postal □ *vt* mandar pelo correio. **keep ~ed** manter informado. **~-code** *n* código *m* postal. **P~ Office** agência *f* dos correios, (*P*) estação *f* dos correios; (*corporation*) Departamento *m* dos Correios e Telégrafos, (*P*) Correios, Telégrafos e Telefones *mpl* (CTT)

post- /pəʊst/ *pref* pós-

postage /'pəʊstɪdʒ/ *n* porte *m*

postal /'pəʊstl/ *a* postal. **~ order** vale *m* postal

postcard /'pəʊstka:d/ *n* cartão-postal *m*, (*P*) (bilhete) postal *m*

poster /'pəʊstə(r)/ *n* cartaz *m*

posterity /pɒ'sterətɪ/ *n* posteridade *f*

postgraduate /pəʊst'grædʒʊet/ *n* pós-graduado *m*

posthumous /'pɒstjʊməs/ *a* póstumo. **~ly** *adv* a título póstumo

postman /'pəʊstmən/ *n* (*pl* **-men**) carteiro *m*

postmark /'pəʊstma:k/ *n* carimbo *m* do correio

post-mortem /pəʊst'mɔ:təm/ *n* autópsia *f*

postpone /pə'spəʊn/ *vt* adiar. **~ment** *n* adiamento *m*

postscript /'pəʊsskrɪpt/ *n* post scriptum *m*

postulate /'pɒstjʊleɪt/ *vt* postular

posture /'pɒstʃə(r)/ *n* postura *f*, posição *f* □ *vi* posar

post-war /'pəʊstwɔ:(r)/ *a* de após-guerra

posy /'pəʊzɪ/ *n* raminho *m* de flores

pot /pɒt/ *n* pote *m*; (*for cooking*) panela *f*; (*for plants*) vaso *m*; (*sl: marijuana*) maconha *f* □ *vt* (*pt* **potted**) **~ (up)** plantar em vaso. **go to ~** (*sl: business*) arruinar, degringolar (*colloq*); (*sl: person*) estar arruinado *or* liquidado. **~-belly** *n* pança *f*, barriga *f*. **take ~ luck** aceitar o que houver. **take a ~-shot** dar um tiro de perto (**at** em); (*at random*) dar um tiro a esmo (**at** em)

potato /pə'teɪtəʊ/ *n* (*pl* **-oes**) batata *f*

poten|t /'pəʊtnt/ *a* potente, poderoso; (*drink*) forte. **~cy** *n* potência *f*

potential /pə'tenʃl/ *a* & *n* potencial (*m*). **~ly** *adv* potencialmente

pothol|e /'pɒthəʊl/ *n* caverna *f*, caldeirão *m*; (*in road*) buraco *m*. **~ing** *n* espeleologia *f*

potion /'pəʊʃn/ *n* poção *f*

potted /'pɒtɪd/ *a* (*of plant*) de vaso; (*preserved*) de conserva

potter[1] /'pɒtə(r)/ *n* oleiro *m*, ceramista *mf*. **~y** *n* olaria *f*, cerâmica *f*

potter[2] /'pɒtə(r)/ *vi* entreter-se com isto ou aquilo

potty[1] /'pɒtɪ/ *a* (-ier, -iest) (*sl*) doido, pirado (*sl*), (*P*) chanfrado (*colloq*)

potty[2] /'pɒtɪ/ *n* (-ties) (*colloq*) penico *m* de criança

pouch /paʊtʃ/ *n* bolsa *f*; (*for tobacco*) tabaqueira *f*

poultice /'pəʊltɪs/ *n* cataplasma *f*

poultry /'pəʊltrɪ/ *n* aves *fpl* domésticas

pounce /paʊns/ *vi* atirar-se (**on** sobre, para cima de) □ *n* salto *m*

pound[1] /paʊnd/ *n* (*weight*) libra *f* (= *453 g*); (*money*) libra *f*

pound[2] /paʊnd/ *n* (*for dogs*) canil municipal *m*; (*for cars*) parque de viaturas rebocadas *m*

pound[3] /paʊnd/ *vt/i* (*crush*) esmagar, pisar; (*of heart*) bater com força; (*bombard*) bombardear; (*on piano etc*) martelar

pour /pɔ:(r)/ *vt* deitar □ *vi* correr; (*rain*) chover torrencialmente. **~ in/out** (*of people*) afluir/sair em massa. **~ off** *or* **out** esvaziar, vazar. **~ing rain** chuva *f* torrencial

pout /paʊt/ *vt/i* **~ (one's lips)** (*sulk*) fazer beicinho; (*in annoyance*) ficar de trombas □ *n* beicinho *m*

poverty /'pɒvətɪ/ *n* pobreza *f*, miséria *f*. **~-stricken** *a* pobre

powder /'paʊdə(r)/ *n* pó *m*; (*for face*) pó-de-arroz *m* □ *vt* polvilhar; (*face*) empoar. **~ed** *a* em pó. **~-room** *n* toalete *m*, toucador *m*. **~y** *a* como pó

power /'paʊə(r)/ *n* poder *m*; (*maths, mech*) potência *f*; (*energy*) energia *f*; (*electr*) corrente *f*. **~ cut** corte *m* de energia, blecaute *m*. **~ station** central *f* elétrica, (*P*) eléctrica. **~ed by** movido a; (*jet etc*) de propulsão. **~ful** *a* poderoso; (*mech*) potente. **~less** *a* impotente

practicable /'præktɪkəbl/ *a* viável

practical /'præktɪkl/ *a* prático. **~ joke** brincadeira *f* de mau gosto

practically /'præktɪklɪ/ *adv* praticamente

practice /'præktɪs/ *n* prática *f*; (*of law etc*) exercício *m*; (*sport*) treino *m*; (*clients*) clientela *f*. **in ~** (*in fact*) na prática; (*well-trained*) em forma. **out of ~** destreinado, sem prática. **put into ~** pôr em prática

practis|e /'præktɪs/ *vt/i* (*skill, sport*) praticar, exercitar-se em; (*profession*) exercer; (*put into practice*) pôr em prática. **~ed** *a* experimentado, experiente. **~ing** *a* (*Catholic etc*) praticante

practitioner /præk'tɪʃənə(r)/ *n* praticante *mf*. **general ~** médico *m* de clínica geral *or* de família

pragmatic /præg'mætɪk/ *a* pragmático

prairie /'preərɪ/ *n* pradaria *f*

praise /preɪz/ *vt* louvar, elogiar □ *n* elogio(s) *m(pl)*, louvor(es) *m(pl)*

praiseworthy /'preɪzwɜ:ðɪ/ *a* louvável, digno de louvor

pram /præm/ *n* carrinho *m* de bebê, (*P*) bebé

prance /prɑ:ns/ *vi* (*of horse*) curvetear, empinar-se; (*of person*) pavonear-se

prank /præŋk/ *n* brincadeira *f* de mau gosto

prattle /'prætl/ *vi* tagarelar

prawn /prɔ:n/ *n* camarão *m* grande, (*P*) gamba *f*

pray /preɪ/ *vi* rezar, orar

prayer /preə(r)/ *n* oração *f*. **the Lord's P~** o Padre-Nosso. **~-book** *n* missal *m*

pre- /pri:/ *pref* pré-

preach /pri:tʃ/ *vt/i* pregar (**at, to** a). **~er** *n* pregador *m*

preamble /pri:'æmbl/ *n* preâmbulo *m*

prearrange /pri:ə'reɪndʒ/ *vt* combinar *or* arranjar de antemão

precarious /prɪ'keərɪəs/ *a* precário; (*of position*) instável, inseguro

precaution /prɪ'kɔ:ʃn/ *n* precaução *f*. **~ary** *a* de precaução

preced|e /prɪ'si:d/ *vt* preceder. **~ing** *a* precedente

precedent /'presɪdənt/ *n* precedente *m*

precinct /'pri:sɪŋkt/ *n* precinto *m*; (*Amer: district*) circunscrição *f*. **(pedestrian) ~** área *f* de pedestres, (*P*) zona *f* para peões

precious /'preʃəs/ *a* precioso

precipice /'presɪpɪs/ *n* precipício *m*

precipitat|e /prɪ'sɪpɪteɪt/ *vt* precipitar □ *a* /-ɪtət/ precipitado. **~ion** /-'teɪʃn/ *n* precipitação *f*

precis|e /prɪ'saɪs/ *a* preciso; (*careful*) meticuloso. **~ely** *adv* precisamente. **~ion** /-'sɪʒn/ *n* precisão *f*

preclude /prɪ'klu:d/ *vt* evitar, excluir, impedir

precocious /prɪ'kəʊʃəs/ *a* precoce

preconc|eived /pri:kən'si:vd/ *a* preconcebido. **~eption** /pri:kən'sepʃn/ *n* idéia *f* preconcebida

precursor /pri:'kɜ:sə(r)/ *n* precursor *m*

predator /'predətə(r)/ *n* animal *m* de rapina, predador *m*. **~y** *a* predatório

predecessor /'pri:dɪsesə(r)/ *n* predecessor *m*

predicament /prɪ'dɪkəmənt/ *n* situação *f* difícil

predict /prɪ'dɪkt/ *vt* predizer, prognosticar. **~able** *a* previsível. **~ion** /-ʃn/ *n* predição *f*, prognóstico *m*

predominant /prɪ'dɒmɪnənt/ *a* predominante, preponderante. **~ly** *adv* predominantemente, preponderantemente

predominate /prɪ'dɒmɪneɪt/ *vi* predominar

pre-eminent /pri:'emɪnənt/ *a* preeminente, superior

pre-empt /pri:'empt/ *vt* adquirir por

preempção. **~ive** *a* antecipado; (*mil*) preventivo
preen /pri:n/ *vt* alisar. **~ o.s.** enfeitar-se
prefab /'pri:fæb/ *n* (*colloq*) casa *f* pré-fabricada. **~ricated** /-'fæbrɪkeɪtɪd/ *a* pré-fabricado
preface /'prefɪs/ *n* prefácio *m*
prefect /'pri:fekt/ *n* aluno *m* autorizado a disciplinar outros; (*official*) prefeito *m*
prefer /prɪ'fɜ:(r)/ *vt* (*pt* **preferred**) preferir. **~able** /'prefrəbl/ *a* preferível
preferen|ce /'prefrəns/ *n* preferência *f*. **~tial** /-ə'renʃl/ *a* preferencial, privilegiado
prefix /'pri:fɪks/ *n* (*pl* **-ixes**) prefixo *m*
pregnan|t /'pregnənt/ *a* (*woman*) grávida; (*animal*) prenhe. **~cy** *n* gravidez *f*
prehistoric /pri:hɪ'stɒrɪk/ *a* pré-histórico
prejudice /'predʒʊdɪs/ *n* preconceito *m*, idéia *f* preconcebida, prejuízo *m*; (*harm*) prejuízo *m* □ *vt* influenciar. **~d** *a* com preconceitos
preliminar|y /prɪ'lɪmɪnərɪ/ *a* preliminar. **~ies** *npl* preliminares *mpl*, preâmbulos *mpl*
prelude /'prelju:d/ *n* prelúdio *m*
premarital /pri:'mærɪtl/ *a* antes do casamento, pré-marital
premature /'premətjʊə(r)/ *a* prematuro
premeditated /pri:'medɪteɪtɪd/ *a* premeditado
premier /'premɪə(r)/ *a* primeiro □ *n* (*pol*) primeiro-ministro *m*
premises /'premɪsɪz/ *npl* local *m*, edifício *m*. **on the ~** neste estabelecimento, no local
premium /'pri:mɪəm/ *n* prêmio *m*, (*P*) prémio *m*. **at a ~** a peso de ouro
premonition /pri:mə'nɪʃn/ *n* pressentimento *m*
preoccup|ation /pri:ɒkjʊ'peɪʃn/ *n* preocupação *f*. **~ied** /-'ɒkjʊpaɪd/ *a* preocupado
preparation /prepə'reɪʃn/ *n* preparação *f*. **~s** preparativos *mpl*
preparatory /prɪ'pærətrɪ/ *a* preparatório. **~ school** escola *f* primária particular
prepare /prɪ'peə(r)/ *vt/i* preparar(-se) (**for** para). **~d to** pronto a, preparado para
preposition /prepə'zɪʃn/ *n* preposição *f*
preposterous /prɪ'pɒstərəs/ *a* absurdo, disparatado, ridículo
prerequisite /pri:'rekwɪzɪt/ *n* condição *f* prévia
prerogative /prɪ'rɒgətɪv/ *n* prerrogativa *f*
Presbyterian /prezbɪ'tɪərɪən/ *a* & *n* presbiteriano (*m*)
prescri|be /prɪ'skraɪb/ *vt* prescrever; (*med*) receitar, prescrever. **~ption** /-ɪpʃn/ *n* prescrição *f*; (*med*) receita *f*
presence /'prezns/ *n* presença *f*. **~ of mind** presença *f* de espírito
present[1] /'preznt/ *a* & *n* presente (*mf*). **at ~** no momento, presentemente
present[2] /'preznt/ *n* (*gift*) presente *m*
present[3] /prɪ'zent/ *vt* apresentar; (*film etc*) dar. **~ sb with** oferecer a alg. **~able** *a* apresentável. **~ation** /prezn'teɪʃn/ *n* apresentação *f*. **~er** *n* apresentador *m*
presently /'prezntlɪ/ *adv* dentro em pouco, daqui a pouco; (*Amer: now*) neste momento
preservative /prɪ'zɜ:vətɪv/ *n* preservativo *m*
preserv|e /prɪ'zɜ:v/ *vt* preservar; (*maintain; culin*) conservar □ *n* reserva *f*; (*fig*) área *f*, terreno *m*; (*jam*) compota *f*. **~ation** /prezə'veɪʃn/ *n* conservação *f*
preside /prɪ'zaɪd/ *vi* presidir (**over** a)
presiden|t /'prezɪdənt/ *n* presidente *mf*. **~cy** *n* presidência *f*. **~tial** /-'denʃl/ *a* presidencial
press /pres/ *vt/i* carregar (**on** em); (*squeeze*) espremer; (*urge*) pressionar; (*iron*) passar a ferro □ *n* imprensa *f*; (*mech*) prensa *f*; (*for wine*) lagar *m*. **be ~ed for** estar apertado com falta de. **~ on (with)** continuar (com), prosseguir (com). **~ conference** entrevista *f* coletiva. **~-stud** *n* mola *f*, botão *m* de pressão
pressing /'presɪŋ/ *a* premente, urgente
pressure /'preʃə(r)/ *n* pressão *f* □ *vt* fazer pressão sobre. **~-cooker** *n* panela *f* de pressão. **~ group** grupo *m* de pressão
pressurize /'preʃəraɪz/ *vt* pressionar, fazer pressão sobre
prestige /pre'sti:ʒ/ *n* prestígio *m*
prestigious /pre'stɪdʒəs/ *a* prestigioso
presumably /prɪ'zju:məblɪ/ *adv* provavelmente
presum|e /prɪ'zju:m/ *vt* presumir. **~e to** tomar a liberdade de, atrever-se a. **~ption** /-'zʌmpʃn/ *n* presunção *f*
presumptuous /prɪ'zʌmptʃʊəs/ *a* presunçoso
pretence /prɪ'tens/ *n* fingimento *m*; (*claim*) pretensão *f*; (*pretext*) desculpa *f*, pretexto *m*
pretend /prɪ'tend/ *vt/i* fingir (**to do** fazer). **~ to** (*lay claim to*) ter pretensões a, ser pretendente a; (*profess to have*) pretender ter

pretentious /prɪ'tenʃəs/ *a* pretencioso
pretext /'pri:tekst/ *n* pretexto *m*
pretty /'prɪtɪ/ *a* (-ier, -iest) bonito, lindo □ *adv* bastante
prevail /prɪ'veɪl/ *vi* prevalecer. ~ **on sb to** convencer alguéma. ~**ing** *a* dominante
prevalen|t /'prevələnt/ *a* geral, dominante. ~**ce** *n* frequência *f*
prevent /prɪ'vent/ *vt* impedir (**from doing** de fazer). ~**able** *a* que se pode evitar, evitável. ~**ion** /-ʃn/ *n* prevenção *f*. ~**ive** *a* preventivo
preview /'pri:vju:/ *n* pré-estréia *f*, (*P*) ante-estréia *f*
previous /'pri:vɪəs/ *a* precedente, anterior. ~ **to** antes de. ~**ly** *adv* antes, anteriormente
pre-war /pri:'wɔ:(r)/ *a* do pré-guerra, (*P*) de antes da guerra
prey /preɪ/ *n* presa *f* □ *vi* ~ **on** dar caça a; (*worry*) preocupar, atormentar. **bird of** ~ ave *f* de rapina, predador *m*
price /praɪs/ *n* preço *m* □ *vt* marcar o preço de. ~**less** *a* inestimável; (*colloq: amusing*) impagável
prick /prɪk/ *vt* picar, furar □ *n* picada *f*. ~ **up one's ears** arrebitar a(s) orelha(s)
prickl|e /'prɪkl/ *n* pico *m*, espinho *m*; (*sensation*) picada *f*. ~**y** *a* espinhoso, que pica; (*person*) irritável
pride /praɪd/ *n* orgulho *m* □ *vpr* ~ **o.s. on** orgulhar-se de
priest /pri:st/ *n* padre *m*, sacerdote *m*. ~**hood** *n* sacerdócio *m*; (*clergy*) clero *m*
prim /prɪm/ *a* (**primmer, primmest**) formal, cheio de nove-horas; (*prudish*) pudico
primary /'praɪmərɪ/ *a* primário; (*chief, first*) primeiro. ~ **school** escola *f* primária
prime[1] /praɪm/ *a* primeiro, principal; (*first-rate*) de primeira qualidade. **P**~ **Minister** Primeiro-Ministro *m*. ~ **number** número *m* primo
prime[2] /praɪm/ *vt* aprontar, aprestar; (*with facts*) preparar; (*surface*) preparar, aparelhar. ~**r** /-ə(r)/ *n* (*paint*) aparelho *m*
primeval /praɪ'mi:vl/ *a* primitivo
primitive /'prɪmɪtɪv/ *a* primitivo
primrose /'prɪmrəʊz/ *n* primavera *f*, prímula *f*
prince /prɪns/ *n* príncipe *m*
princess /prɪn'ses/ *n* princesa *f*
principal /'prɪnsəpl/ *a* principal □ *n* (*schol*) diretor *m*, (*P*) director *m*. ~**ly** *adv* principalmente
principle /'prɪnsəpl/ *n* princípio *m*. **in/on** ~ em/por princípio
print /prɪnt/ *vt* imprimir; (*write*) escrever em letra de imprensa □ *n* marca *f*, impressão *f*; (*letters*) letra *f* de imprensa; (*photo*) prova (fotográfica) *f*; (*engraving*) gravura *f*. **out of** ~ esgotado. ~**-out** *n* cópia *f* impressa. ~**ed matter** impressos *mpl*
print|er /'prɪntə(r)/ *n* tipógrafo *m*; (*comput*) impressora *f*. ~**ing** *n* impressão *f*, tipografia *f*
prior /'praɪə(r)/ *a* anterior, precedente. ~ **to** antes de
priority /praɪ'ɒrətɪ/ *n* prioridade *f*
prise /praɪz/ *vt* forçar (com alavanca). ~ **open** arrombar
prison /'prɪzn/ *n* prisão *f*. ~**er** *n* prisioneiro *m*
pristine /'prɪsti:n/ *a* primitivo; (*condition*) perfeito, como novo
privacy /'prɪvəsɪ/ *n* privacidade *f*, intimidade *f*; (*solitude*) isolamento *m*
private /'praɪvət/ *a* privado; (*confidential*) confidencial; (*lesson, life, house etc*) particular; (*ceremony*) íntimo □ *n* soldado *m* raso. **in** ~ em particular; (*of ceremony*) na intimidade. ~**ly** *adv* particularmente; (*inwardly*) no fundo, interiormente
privet /'prɪvɪt/ *n* (*bot*) alfena *f*, ligustro *m*
privilege /'prɪvəlɪdʒ/ *n* privilégio *m*. ~**d** *a* privilegiado. **be** ~**d to** ter o privilégio de
prize /praɪz/ *n* prêmio *m*, (*P*) prémio *m* □ *a* premiado; (*fool etc*) perfeito □ *vt* ter em grande apreço, apreciar muito. ~**-giving** *n* distribuição *f* de prêmios, (*P*) prémios. ~**-winner** *n* premiado *m*, vencedor *m*
pro[1] /prəʊ/ *n* **the** ~**s and cons** os prós e os contras
pro- /prəʊ/ *pref* (*acting for*) pro-; (*favouring*) pró-
probab|le /'prɒbəbl/ *a* provável. ~**ility** /-'bɪlətɪ/ *n* probabilidade *f*. ~**ly** *adv* provavelmente
probation /prə'beɪʃn/ *n* (*testing*) estágio *m*, tirocínio *m*; (*jur*) liberdade *f* condicional. ~**ary** *a* probatório
probe /prəʊb/ *n* (*med*) sonda *f*; (*fig: investigation*) inquérito *m* □ *vt/i* ~ (**into**) sondar, investigar
problem /'prɒbləm/ *n* problema *m* □ *a* difícil. ~**atic** /-'mætɪk/ *a* problemático
procedure /prə'si:dʒə(r)/ *n* procedimento *m*, processo *m*, norma *f*
proceed /prə'si:d/ *vi* prosseguir, ir para diante, avançar. ~ **to do** passar a fazer. ~ **with sth** continuar *or* avançar com alguma coisa. ~**ing** *n* procedimento *m*
proceedings /prə'si:dɪŋz/ *npl* (*jur*) processo *m*; (*report*) ata *f*, (*P*) acta *f*

proceeds /'prəʊsi:dz/ *npl* produto *m*, luco *m*, proventos *mpl*

process /'prəʊses/ *n* processo *m* □ *vt* tratar; (*photo*) revelar. **in ~** em curso. **in the ~ of doing** sendo feito

procession /prə'seʃn/ *n* procissão *f*, cortejo *m*

procl|aim /prə'kleɪm/ *vt* proclamar. **~amation** /prɒklə'meɪʃn/ *n* proclamação *f*

procure /prə'kjʊə(r)/ *vt* obter

prod /prɒd/ *vt/i* (*pt* **prodded**) (*push*) empurrar; (*poke*) espetar; (*fig: urge*) incitar □ *n* espetadela *f*; (*fig*) incitamento *m*

prodigal /'prɒdɪgl/ *a* pródigo

prodigious /prə'dɪdʒəs/ *a* prodigioso

prodigy /'prɒdɪdʒɪ/ *n* prodígio *m*

produc|e[1] /prə'dju:s/ *vt/i* produzir; (*bring out*) tirar, extrair; (*show*) apresentar, mostrar; (*cause*) causar, provocar; (*theat*) pôr em cena. **~er** *n* produtor *m*. **~tion** /-'dʌkʃn/ *n* produção *f*; (*theat*) encenação *f*

produce[2] /'prɒdju:s/ *n* produtos (agrícolas) *mpl*

product /'prɒdʌkt/ *n* produto *m*

productiv|e /prə'dʌktɪv/ *a* produtivo. **~ity** /prɒdʌk'tɪvətɪ/ *n* produtividade *f*

profan|e /prə'feɪn/ *a* profano; (*blasphemous*) blasfemo. **~ity** /-'fænətɪ/ *n* profanidade *f*

profess /prə'fes/ *vt* professar. **~ to do** alegar fazer

profession /prə'feʃn/ *n* profissão *f*. **~al** *a* profissional; (*well done*) de profissional; (*person*) que exerce uma profissão liberal □ *n* profissional *mf*

professor /prə'fesə(r)/ *n* professor (universitário) *m*

proficien|t /prə'fɪʃnt/ *a* proficiente, competente. **~cy** *n* proficiência *f*, competência *f*

profile /'prəʊfaɪl/ *n* perfil *m*

profit /'prɒfɪt/ *n* proveito *m*; (*money*) lucro *m* □ *vi* (*pt* **profited**) **~ by** aproveitar-se de; **~ from** tirar proveito de. **~able** *a* proveitoso; (*of business*) lucrativo, rentável

profound /prə'faʊnd/ *a* profundo. **~ly** *adv* profundamente

profus|e /prə'fju:s/ *a* profuso. **~ely** *adv* profusamente, em abundância. **~ion** /-ʒn/ *n* profusão *f*

program /'prəʊgræm/ *n* (**computer**) **~** programa *m* □ *vt* (*pt* **programmed**) programar. **~mer** *n* programador *m*

programme /'prəʊgræm/ *n* programa *m*

progress[1] /'prəʊgres/ *n* progresso *m*. **in ~** em curso, em andamento

progress[2] /prə'gres/ *vi* progredir. **~ion** /-ʃn/ *n* progressão *f*

progressive /prə'gresɪv/ *a* progressivo; (*reforming*) progressista. **~ly** *adv* progressivamente

prohibit /prə'hɪbɪt/ *vt* proibir (**sb from doing** alg de fazer)

project[1] /prə'dʒekt/ *vt* projetar, (*P*) projectar □ *vi* ressaltar, sobressair. **~ion** /-ʃn/ *n* projeção *f*, (*P*) projecção *f*; (*protruding*) saliência *f*, ressalto *m*

project[2] /'prɒdʒekt/ *n* projeto *m*, (*P*) projecto *m*

projectile /prə'dʒektaɪl/ *n* projétil *m*, (*P*) projéctil *m*

projector /prə'dʒektə(r)/ *n* projetor *m*, (*P*) projector *m*

proletari|at /prəʊlɪ'teərɪət/ *n* proletariado *m*. **~an** *a* & *n* proletário (*m*)

proliferat|e /prə'lɪfəreɪt/ *vi* proliferar. **~ion** /-'reɪʃn/ *n* proliferação *f*

prolific /prə'lɪfɪk/ *a* prolífico

prologue /'prəʊlɒg/ *n* prólogo *m*

prolong /prə'lɒŋ/ *vt* prolongar

promenade /prɒmə'na:d/ *n* passeio *m* □ *vt/i* passear

prominen|t /'prɒmɪnənt/ *a* (*projecting; important*) proeminente; (*conspicuous*) bem à vista, conspícuo. **~ce** *n* proeminência *f*. **~tly** *adv* bem à vista

promiscu|ous /prə'mɪskjʊəs/ *a* promíscuo, de costumes livres. **~ity** /prɒmɪs'kju:ətɪ/ *n* promiscuidade *f*, liberdade *f* de costumes

promis|e /'prɒmɪs/ *n* promessa *f* □ *vt/i* prometer. **~ing** *a* prometedor, promissor

promot|e /prə'məʊt/ *vt* promover. **~ion** /-'məʊʃn/ *n* promoção *f*

prompt /prɒmpt/ *a* pronto, rápido, imediato; (*punctual*) pontual □ *adv* em ponto □ *vt* levar; (*theat*) soprar, servir de ponto para. **~er** *n* ponto *m*. **~ly** *adv* prontamente; pontualmente. **~ness** *n* prontidão *f*

prone /prəʊn/ *a* deitado (de bruços). **~ to** propenso a

prong /prɒŋ/ *n* (*of fork*) dente *m*

pronoun /'prəʊnaʊn/ *n* pronome *m*

pron|ounce /prə'naʊns/ *vt* pronunciar; (*declare*) declarar. **~ounced** *a* pronunciado. **~ouncement** *n* declaração *f*. **~unciation** /-ʌnsɪ'eɪʃn/ *n* pronúncia *f*

proof /pru:f/ *n* prova *f*; (*of liquor*) teor *m* alcóolico, graduação *f* □ *a* **~ against** à prova de

prop[1] /prɒp/ *n* suporte *m*; (*lit & fig*) apoio *m*, esteio *m* □ *vt* (*pt* **propped**) sustentar, suportar, apoiar. **~ against** apoiar contra

prop[2] /prɒp/ *n* (*colloq: theat*) acessório *m*, (*P*) adereço *m*
propaganda /prɒpə'gændə/ *n* propaganda *f*
propagat|e /'prɒpəgeɪt/ *vt/i* propagar(-se). **~ion** /-'geɪʃn/ *n* propagação *f*
propel /prə'pel/ *vt* (*pt* **propelled**) propulsionar, impelir
propeller /prə'pelə(r)/ *n* hélice *f*
proper /'prɒpə(r)/ *a* correto, (*P*) correcto; (*seemly*) conveniente; (*real*) propriamente dito; (*colloq: thorough*) belo. **~ noun** substantivo *m* próprio. **~ly** *adv* corretamente, (*P*) correctamente; (*rightly*) com razão, acertadamente; (*accurately*) propriamente
property /'prɒpətɪ/ *n* (*house*) imóvel *m*; (*land, quality*) propriedade *f*; (*possessions*) bens *mpl*
prophecy /'prɒfəsɪ/ *n* profecia *f*
prophesy /'prɒfɪsaɪ/ *vt/i* profetizar. **~ that** predizer que
prophet /'prɒfɪt/ *n* profeta *m*. **~ic** /prə'fetɪk/ *a* profético
proportion /prə'pɔ:ʃn/ *n* proporção *f*. **~al, ~ate** *adjs* proporcional
proposal /prə'pəʊzl/ *n* proposta *f*; (*of marriage*) pedido *m* de casamento
propos|e /prə'pəʊz/ *vt* propor □ *vi* pedir em casamento. **~e to do** propor-se fazer. **~ition** /prɒpə'zɪʃn/ *n* proposição *f*; (*colloq: matter*) caso *m*, questão *f*
propound /prə'paʊnd/ *vt* propor
proprietor /prə'praɪətə(r)/ *n* proprietário *m*
propriety /prə'praɪətɪ/ *n* propriedade *f*, correção *f*, (*P*) correcção *f*
propulsion /prə'pʌlʃn/ *n* propulsão *f*
prosaic /prə'zeɪɪk/ *a* prosaico
prose /prəʊz/ *n* prosa *f*
prosecut|e /'prɒsɪkju:t/ *vt* (*jur*) processar. **~ion** /-'kju:ʃn/ *n* (*jur*) acusação *f*
prospect[1] /'prɒspekt/ *n* perspectiva *f*
prospect[2] /prə'spekt/ *vt/i* pesquisar, prospectar
prospective /prə'spektɪv/ *a* futuro; (*possible*) provável
prosper /'prɒspə(r)/ *vi* prosperar
prosper|ous /'prɒspərəs/ *a* próspero. **~ity** /-'sperətɪ/ *n* prosperidade *f*
prostitut|e /'prɒstɪtju:t/ *n* prostituta *f*. **~ion** /-'tju:ʃn/ *n* prostituição *f*
prostrate /'prɒstreɪt/ *a* prostrado
protect /prə'tekt/ *vt* proteger. **~ion** /-ʃn/ *n* proteção *f*, (*P*) protecção *f*. **~ive** *a* protetor, (*P*) protector. **~or** *n* protetor *m*, (*P*) protector *m*
protégé /'prɒtɪʒeɪ/ *n* protegido *m*. **~e** *n* protegida *f*
protein /'prəʊti:n/ *n* proteína *f*
protest[1] /'prəʊtest/ *n* protesto *m*
protest[2] /prə'test/ *vt/i* protestar. **~er** *n* (*pol*) manifestante *mf*
Protestant /'prɒtɪstənt/ *a* & *n* protestante (*mf*). **~ism** /-ɪzəm/ *n* protestantismo *m*
protocol /'prəʊtəkɒl/ *n* protocolo *m*
prototype /'prəʊtətaɪp/ *n* protótipo *m*
protract /prə'trækt/ *vt* prolongar, arrastar
protrud|e /prə'tru:d/ *vi* sobressair, sair do alinhamento. **~ing** *a* saliente
proud /praʊd/ *a* (er, -est) orgulhoso. **~ly** *adv* orgulhosamente
prove /pru:v/ *vt* provar, demonstrar □ *vi* **~ (to be) easy**/*etc* verificar-se ser fácil/*etc*. **~ o.s.** dar provas de si. **~n** /-n/ *a* provado
proverb /'prɒvɜ:b/ *n* provérbio *m*. **~ial** /prə'vɜ:bɪəl/ *a* proverbial
provid|e /prə'vaɪd/ *vt* prover, munir (**sb with sth** alg de alguma coisa) □ *vi* **~ for** providenciar para; (*person*) prover de, cuidar de; (*allow for*) levar em conta. **~ed, ~ing (that)** *conj* desde que, contanto que
providence /'prɒvɪdəns/ *n* providência *f*
province /'prɒvɪns/ *n* província *f*; (*fig*) competência *f*
provincial /prə'vɪnʃl/ *a* provincial; (*rustic*) provinciano
provision /prə'vɪʒn/ *n* provisão *f*; (*stipulation*) disposição *f*. **~s** (*pl* (*food*) provisões *fpl*
provisional /prə'vɪʒənl/ *a* provisório. **~ly** *adv* provisoriamente
proviso /prə'vaɪzəʊ/ *n* (*pl* -os) condição *f*
provo|ke /prə'vəʊk/ *vt* provocar. **~cation** /prɒvə'keɪʃn/ *n* provocação *f*. **~cative** /-'vɒkətɪv/ *a* provocante
prowess /'praʊɪs/ *n* proeza *f*, façanha *f*
prowl /praʊl/ *vi* rondar □ *n* **be on the ~** andar à espreita. **~er** *n* pessoa *f* que anda à espreita
proximity /prɒk'sɪmətɪ/ *n* proximidade *f*
proxy /'prɒksɪ/ *n* **by ~** por procuração
prude /pru:d/ *n* puritano *m*, pudico *m*
pruden|t /'pru:dnt/ *a* prudente. **~ce** *n* prudência *f*
prune[1] /pru:n/ *n* ameixa *f* seca
prune[2] /pru:n/ *vt* podar
pry /praɪ/ *vi* bisbilhotar. **~ into** meter o nariz em, intrometer-se em
psalm /sa:m/ *n* salmo *m*
pseudo- /'sju:dəʊ/ *pref* pseudo-
pseudonym /'sju:dənɪm/ *n* pseudônimo *m*, (*P*) pseudónimo *m*
psychiatr|y /saɪ'kaɪətrɪ/ *n* psiquiatria *f*. **~ic** /-ɪ'ætrɪk/ *a* psiquiátrico. **~ist** *n* psiquiatra *mf*

psychic /'saɪkɪk/ *a* psíquico; (*person*) com capacidade de telepatia
psychoanalys|e /saɪkəʊ'ænəlaɪz/ *vt* psicanalisar. **~t** /-ɪst/ *n* psicanalista *mf*
psychoanalysis /saɪkəʊə'næləsɪs/ *n* psicanálise *f*
psycholog|y /saɪ'kɒlədʒɪ/ *n* psicologia *f*. **~ical** /-ə'lɒdʒɪkl/ *a* psicológico. **~ist** *n* psicólogo *m*
psychopath /'saɪkəʊpæθ/ *n* psicopata *mf*
pub /pʌb/ *n* pub *m*
puberty /'pju:bətɪ/ *n* puberdade *f*
public /'pʌblɪk/ *a* público; (*holiday*) feriado. **in ~** em público. **~ house** pub *m*. **~ relations** relações *fpl* públicas. **~ school** escola *f* particular; (*Amer*) escola *f* oficial. **~-spirited** *a* de espírito cívico, patriótico. **~ly** *adv* publicamente
publication /pʌblɪ'keɪʃn/ *n* publicação *f*
publicity /pʌ'blɪsətɪ/ *n* publicidade *f*
publicize /'pʌblɪsaɪz/ *vt* fazer publicidade de
publish /'pʌblɪʃ/ *vt* publicar. **~er** *n* editor *m*. **~ing** *n* publicação *f*. **~ing house** editora *f*
pucker /'pʌkə(r)/ *vt/i* franzir
pudding /'pʊdɪŋ/ *n* pudim *m*; (*dessert*) doce *m*
puddle /'pʌdl/ *n* poça *f* de água, charco *m*
puerile /'pjʊəraɪl/ *a* pueril
puff /pʌf/ *n* baforada *f* □ *vt/i* lançar baforadas; (*breathe hard*) arquejar, ofegar. **~ at** (*cigar etc*) dar baforadas em. **~ out** (*swell*) inchar(-se). **~-pastry** *n* massa *f* folhada
puffy /'pʌfɪ/ *a* inchado
pugnacious /pʌg'neɪʃəs/ *a* belicoso, combativo
pull /pʊl/ *vt/i* puxar; (*muscle*) distender □ *n* puxão *m*; (*fig: influence*) influência *f*, empenho *m*. **give a ~** dar um puxão. **~ a face** fazer uma careta. **~ one's weight** (*fig*) fazer a sua quota-parte. **~ sb's leg** brincar com alguém, meter-se com alguém. **~ away** *or* **out** (*auto*) arrancar. **~ down** puxar para baixo; (*building*) demolir. **~ in** (*auto*) encostar-se. **~ off** tirar; (*fig*) sair-se bem em, conseguir alcançar. **~ out** partir; (*extract*) arrancar, tirar. **~ through** sair-se bem. **~ o.s. together** recompor-se, refazer-se. **~ up** puxar para cima; (*uproot*) arrancar; (*auto*) parar
pulley /'pʊlɪ/ *n* roldana *f*
pullover /'pʊləʊvə(r)/ *n* pulôver *m*
pulp /pʌlp/ *n* polpa *f*; (*for paper*) pasta *f* de papel
pulpit /'pʊlpɪt/ *n* púlpito *m*
pulsat|e /pʌl'seɪt/ *vi* pulsar, bater, palpitar. **~ion** /-'seɪʃn/ *n* pulsação *f*
pulse /pʌls/ *n* pulso *m*. **feel sb's ~** tirar o pulso de alguém
pulverize /'pʌlvəraɪz/ *vt* (*grind, defeat*) pulverizar
pummel /'pʌml/ *vt* (*pt* **pummelled**) esmurrar
pump[1] /pʌmp/ *n* bomba *f* □ *vt/i* bombear; (*person*) arrancar *or* extrair informações de. **~ up** encher com bomba
pump[2] /pʌmp/ *n* (*shoe*) sapato *m*
pumpkin /'pʌmpkɪn/ *n* abóbora *f*
pun /pʌn/ *n* trocadilho *m*, jogo *m* de palavras
punch[1] /pʌntʃ/ *vt* esmurrar, dar um murro *or* soco; (*perforate*) furar, perfurar; (*a hole*) fazer □ *n* murro *m*, soco *m*; (*device*) furador *m*. **~-line** *n* remate *m*. **~-up** *n* (*colloq*) pancadaria *f*
punch[2] /pʌntʃ/ *n* (*drink*) ponche *m*
punctual /'pʌŋktʃʊəl/ *a* pontual. **~ity** /-'ælətɪ/ *n* pontualidade *f*
punctuat|e /'pʌŋktʃʊeɪt/ *vt* pontuar. **~ion** /-'eɪʃn/ *n* pontuação *f*
puncture /'pʌŋktʃə(r)/ *n* (*in tyre*) furo *m* □ *vt/i* furar
pundit /'pʌndɪt/ *n* autoridade *f*, sumidade *f*
pungent /'pʌndʒənt/ *a* acre, pungente
punish /'pʌnɪʃ/ *vt* punir, castigar. **~able** *a* punível. **~ment** *n* punição *f*, castigo *m*
punitive /'pju:nɪtɪv/ *a* (*expedition, measure etc*) punitivo; (*taxation etc*) penalizador
punt /pʌnt/ *n* (*boat*) chalana *f*
punter /'pʌntə(r)/ *n* (*gambler*) jogador *m*; (*colloq: customer*) freguês *m*
puny /'pju:nɪ/ *a* (-ier, -iest) fraco, débil
pup(py) /'pʌp(ɪ)/ *n* cachorro *m*, cachorrinho *m*
pupil /'pju:pl/ *n* aluno *m*; (*of eye*) pupila *f*
puppet /'pʌpɪt/ *n* (*lit* & *fig*) fantoche *m*, marionete *f*
purchase /'pɜ:tʃəs/ *vt* comprar (**from sb** de alg) □ *n* compra *f*. **~r** /-ə(r)/ *n* comprador *m*
pur|e /'pjʊə(r)/ *a* (-er, -est) puro. **~ely** *adv* puramente. **~ity** *n* pureza *f*
purgatory /'pɜ:gətrɪ/ *n* purgatório *m*
purge /pɜ:dʒ/ *vt* purgar; (*pol*) sanear □ *n* (*med*) purgante *m*; (*pol*) saneamento *m*
purif|y /'pjʊərɪfaɪ/ *vt* purificar. **~ication** /-ɪ'keɪʃn/ *n* purificação *f*
puritan /'pjʊərɪtən/ *n* puritano *m*. **~ical** /-'tænɪkl/ *a* puritano
purple /'pɜ:pl/ *a* roxo, purpúreo □ *n* roxo *m*, púrpura *f*

purport /pə'pɔ:t/ *vt* dizer-se, (*P*) dar a entender. ~ **to be** pretender ser
purpose /'pɜ:pəs/ *n* propósito *m*; (*determination*) firmeza *f*. **on** ~ de propósito. **to no** ~ em vão. ~**-built** *a* construído especialmente.
purposely /'pɜ:pəslɪ/ *adv* de propósito, propositadamente
purr /pɜ:r/ *n* ronrom *m* □ *vi* ronronar
purse /pɜ:s/ *n* carteira *f*; (*Amer*) bolsa *f* □ *vt* franzir
pursue /pə'sju:/ *vt* perseguir; (*go on with*) prosseguir; (*engage in*) entregar-se a, dedicar-se a. ~**r** /-ə(r)/ *n* perseguidor *m*
pursuit /pə'sju:t/ *n* perseguição *f*; (*fig*) atividade *f*, (*P*) actividade *f*
pus /pʌs/ *n* pus *m*
push /pʊʃ/ *vt/i* empurrar; (*button*) apertar; (*thrust*) enfiar; (*colloq: recommend*) insistir □ *n* empurrão *m*; (*effort*) esforço *m*; (*drive*) energia *f*. **be** ~**ed for** (*time etc*) estar com pouco. **be** ~**ing thirty**/*etc* (*colloq*) estar beirando os trinta/*etc*. **give the** ~ **to** (*sl*) dar o fora em alguém. ~ **s.o. around** fazer alguém de bobo. ~ **back** repelir. ~**-chair** *n* carrinho *m* (de criança). ~**er** *n* fornecedor *m* (de droga). ~ **off** (*sl*) dar o fora. ~ **on** continuar. ~**-over** *n* canja *f*, coisa *f* fácil. ~ **up** (*lift*) levantar; (*prices*) forçar o aumento de. ~**-up** *n* (*Amer*) flexão *f*. ~**y** *a* (*colloq*) agressivo, furão
put /pʊt/ *vt/i* (*pt* **put**, *pres p* **putting**) colocar, pôr; (*question*) fazer. ~ **the damage at a million** estimar os danos em um milhão. **I'd** ~ **it at a thousand** eu diria mil. ~ **sth tactfully** dizer alg coisa com tato. ~ **across** comunicar. ~ **away** guardar. ~ **back** repor; (*delay*) retardar, atrasar. ~ **by** pôr de lado. ~ **down** pôr em lugar baixo; (*write*) anotar; (*pay*) pagar; (*suppress*) sufocar, reprimir. ~ **forward** (*plan*) submeter. ~ **in** (*insert*) introduzir; (*fix*) instalar; (*submit*) submeter. ~ **in for** fazer um pedido, candidatar-se. ~ **off** (*postpone*) adiar; (*disconcert*) desanimar; (*displease*) desagradar. ~ **s.o. off sth** tirar o gosto de alguém por alg coisa. ~ **on** (*clothes*) pôr; (*radio*) ligar; (*light*) acender; (*speed, weight*) ganhar; (*accent*) adotar. ~ **out** pôr para fora; (*stretch*) esticar; (*extinguish*) extinguir, apagar; (*disconcert*) desconcertar; (*inconvenience*) incomodar. ~ **up** levantar; (*building*) erguer, construir; (*notice*) colocar; (*price*) aumentar; (*guest*) hospedar; (*offer*) oferecer. ~**-up job** embuste *m*. ~ **up with** suportar
putrefy /'pju:trɪfaɪ/ *vi* putrefazer-se, apodrecer
putty /'pʌtɪ/ *n* massa de vidraceiro *f*, betume *m*
puzzl|e /'pʌzl/ *n* puzzle *m*, quebra-cabeça *m* □ *vt* deixar perplexo, intrigar □ *vi* quebrar a cabeça. ~**ing** *a* intrigante
pygmy /'pɪgmɪ/ *n* pigmeu *m*
pyjamas /pə'dʒa:məz/ *npl* pijama *m*
pylon /'paɪlɒn/ *n* poste *m*
pyramid /'pɪrəmɪd/ *n* pirâmide *f*
python /'paɪθn/ *n* píton *m*

Q

quack[1] /kwæk/ *n* (*of duck*) grasnido *m* □ *vi* grasnar
quack[2] /kwæk/ *n* charlatão *m*
quadrangle /'kwɒdræŋgl/ *n* quadrângulo *m*; (*of college*) pátio *m* quadrangular
quadruped /'kwɒdrʊped/ *n* quadrúpede *m*
quadruple /'kwɒdrʊpl/ *a & n* quádruplo (*m*) □ *vt/i* /kwɒ'drʊpl/ quadruplicar. ~**ts** /-plɪts/ *npl* quadrigêmeos *mpl*, (*P*) quadrigémeos *mpl*
quagmire /'kwægmaɪə(r)/ *n* pântano *m*, lamaçal *m*
quail /kweɪl/ *n* codorniz *f*
quaint /kweɪnt/ *a* (-er, -est) pitoresco; (*whimsical*) estranho, bizarro
quake /kweɪk/ *vi* tremer □ *n* (*colloq*) tremor *m* de terra
Quaker /'kweɪkə(r)/ *n* quaker *mf*, quacre *m*
qualification /kwɒlɪfɪ'keɪʃn/ *n* qualificação *f*; (*accomplishment*) habilitação *f*; (*diploma*) diploma *m*, título *m*; (*condition*) requisito *m*, condição *f*; (*fig*) restrição *f*, reserva *f*
qualif|y /'kwɒlɪfaɪ/ *vt* qualificar; (*fig: moderate*) atenuar, moderar; (*fig: limit*) pôr ressalvas *or* restrições a □ *vi* (*fig: be entitled to*) ter os requisitos (**for** para); (*sport*) classificar-se. **he** ~**ied as a vet** ele formou-se em veterinária. ~**ied** *a* formado; (*able*) qualificado, habilitado; (*moderated*) atenuado; (*limited*) limitado
quality /'kwɒlətɪ/ *n* qualidade *f*
qualm /kwa:m/ *n* escrúpulo *m*
quandary /'kwɒndərɪ/ *n* dilema *m*
quantity /'kwɒntətɪ/ *n* quantidade *f*
quarantine /'kwɒrənti:n/ *n* quarentena *f*
quarrel /'kwɒrəl/ *n* zanga *f*, questão *f*, discussão *f* □ *vi* (*pt* **quarrelled**) zangar-se, questionar, discutir. ~**some** *a* conflituoso, brigão
quarry[1] /'kwɒrɪ/ *n* (*prey*) presa *f*, caça *f*

quarry[2] /ˈkwɒrɪ/ *n* (*excavation*) pedreira *f*
quarter /ˈkwɔ:tə(r)/ *n* quarto *m*; (*of year*) trimestre *m*; (*Amer: coin*) quarto *m* de dólar, 25 cêtimos *mpl*; (*district*) bairro *m*, quarteirão *m*. **~s** (*lodgings*) alojamento *m*, residência *f*; (*mil*) quartel *m* □ *vt* dividir em quarto; (*mil*) aquartelar. **from all ~s** de todos os lados. **~ of an hour** quarto *m* de hora. **(a) ~ past six** seis e quinze. **(a) ~ to seven** quinze para as sete. **~-final** *n* (*sport*) quarta *f* de final. **~ly** *a* trimestral □ *adv* trimestralmente
quartet /kwɔ:ˈtet/ *n* quarteto *m*
quartz /kwɔ:ts/ *n* quartzo *m* □ *a* (*watch etc*) de quartzo
quash /kwɒʃ/ *vt* reprimir; (*jur*) revogar
quaver /ˈkweɪvə(r)/ *vi* tremer, tremular □ *n* (*mus*) colcheia *f*
quay /ki:/ *n* cais *m*
queasy /ˈkwi:zɪ/ *a* delicado. **feel ~** estar enjoado
queen /kwi:n/ *n* rainha *f*; (*cards*) dama *f*
queer /kwɪə(r)/ *a* (-er, -est) estranho; (*slightly ill*) indisposto; (*sl: homosexual*) bicha, maricas (*sl*); (*dubious*) suspeito □ *n* (*sl*) bicha *m*, maricas *m* (*sl*)
quell /kwel/ *vt* reprimir, abafar, sufocar
quench /kwentʃ/ *vt* (*fire, flame*) apagar; (*thirst*) matar, saciar
query /ˈkwɪərɪ/ *n* questão *f* □ *vt* pôr em dúvida
quest /kwest/ *n* busca *f*, procura *f*. **in ~ of** em demanda de
question /ˈkwestʃən/ *n* pergunta *f*, interrogação *f*; (*problem, affair*) questão *f* □ *vt* perguntar, interrogar; (*doubt*) pôr em dúvida *or* em causa. **in ~** em questão *or* em causa. **out of the ~** fora de toda a questão. **there's no ~ of** nem pensar em. **without ~** sem dúvida. **~ mark** ponto *m* de interrogação. **~able** *a* discutível
questionnaire /kwestʃəˈneə(r)/ *n* questionário *m*
queue /kju:/ *n* fila *f*, (*P*) bicha *f* □ *vi* (*pres p* **queuing**) fazer fila, (*P*) fazer bicha
quibble /ˈkwɪbl/ *vi* tergiversar, usar de evasivas; (*raise petty objections*) discutir por coisas insignificantes
quick /kwɪk/ *a* (-er, -est) rápido □ *adv* depressa. **be ~** despachar-se. **have a ~ temper** exaltar-se facilmente. **~ly** *adv* rapidamente, depressa. **~ness** *n* rapidez *f*
quicken /ˈkwɪkən/ *vt/i* apressar(-se)
quicksand /ˈkwɪksænd/ *n* areia *f* movediça
quid /kwɪd/ *n invar* (*sl*) libra *f*
quiet /ˈkwaɪət/ *a* (-er, -est) quieto, sossegado, tranquilo □ *n* quietude *f*, sossego *m*, tranqüilidade *f*. **keep ~** calar-se. **on the ~** às escondidas, na calada. **~ly** *adv* sossegadamente, silenciosamente. **~ness** *n* sossego *m*, tranquilidade *f*, calma *f*
quieten /ˈkwaɪətn/ *vt/i* sossegar, acalmar(-se)
quilt /kwɪlt/ *n* coberta *f* acolchoada. **(continental) ~** edredão *m* de penas □ *vt* acolchoar
quince /kwɪns/ *n* marmelo *m*
quintet /kwɪnˈtet/ *n* quinteto *m*
quintuplets /kwɪnˈtju:plɪts/ *npl* quíntuplos *mpl*
quip /kwɪp/ *n* piada *f* □ *vt* contar piadas
quirk /kwɜ:k/ *n* mania *f*, singularidade *f*
quit /kwɪt/ *vt* (*pt* **quitted**) deixar □ *vi* ir-se embora; (*resign*) demitir-se. **~ doing** (*Amer*) parar de fazer
quite /kwaɪt/ *adv* completamente, absolutamente; (*rather*) bastante. **~ (so)!** isso mesmo!, exatamente! **~ a few** bastante, alguns/algumas. **~ a lot** bastante
quiver /ˈkwɪvə(r)/ *vi* tremer, estremecer □ *n* tremor *m*, estremecimento *m*
quiz /kwɪz/ *n* (*pl* **quizzes**) teste *m*; (*game*) concurso *m* □ *vt* (*pt* **quizzed**) interrogar
quizzical /ˈkwɪzɪkl/ *a* zombeteiro
quorum /ˈkwɔ:rəm/ *n* quorum *m*
quota /ˈkwəʊtə/ *n* cota *f*, quota *f*
quotation /kwəʊˈteɪʃn/ *n* citação *f*; (*estimate*) orçamento *m*. **~ marks** aspas *fpl*
quote /kwəʊt/ *vt* citar; (*estimate*) fazer um orçamento □ *n* (*colloq: passage*) citação *f*; (*colloq: estimate*) orçamento *m*

R

rabbi /ˈræbaɪ/ *n* rabino *m*
rabbit /ˈræbɪt/ *n* coelho *m*
rabble /ˈræbl/ *n* turba *f*. **the ~** a ralé, a gentalha, o povinho
rabid /ˈræbɪd/ *a* (*fig*) fanático, ferrenho; (*dog*) raivoso
rabies /ˈreɪbi:z/ *n* raiva *f*
race[1] /reɪs/ *n* corrida *f* □ *vt* (*horse*) fazer correr □ *vi* correr, dar uma corrida; (*rush*) ir em grande *or* a toda (a) velocidade. **~-track** *n* pista *f*
race[2] /reɪs/ *n* (*group*) raça *f* □ *a* racial
racecourse /ˈreɪskɔ:s/ *n* hipódromo *m*

racehorse /'reɪshɔ:s/ *n* cavalo *m* de corrida
racial /'reɪʃl/ *a* racial
racing /'reɪsɪŋ/ *n* corridas *fpl*. ~ **car** carro *m* de corridas
racis|t /'reɪsɪst/ *a* & *n* racista (*mf*). ~**m** /-zəm/ *n* racismo *m*
rack[1] /ræk/ *n* (*for luggage*) porta-bagagem *m*, bagageiro *m*; (*for plates*) escorredor *m* de prato □ *vt* ~ **one's brains** dar tratos à imaginação
rack[2] /ræk/ *n* **go to ~ and ruin** arruinar-se; (*of buildings etc*) cair em ruínas
racket[1] /'rækɪt/ *n* (*sport*) raquete *f*, (*P*) raqueta *f*
racket[2] /'rækɪt/ *n* (*din*) barulheira *f*; (*swindle*) roubalheira *f*; (*sl: business*) negociata *f* (*colloq*)
racy /'reɪsɪ/ *a* (**-ier, -iest**) vivo, vigoroso
radar /'reɪda:(r)/ *n* radar *m* □ *a* de radar
radian|t /'reɪdɪənt/ *a* radiante. ~**ce** *n* brilho *m*
radiator /'reɪdɪeɪtə(r)/ *n* radiador *m*
radical /'rædɪkl/ *a* & *n* radical (*m*)
radio /'reɪdɪəʊ/ *n* (*pl* **-os**) rádio *f*; (*set*) (aparelho de) rádio *m* □ *vt* transmitir pelo rádio. ~ **station** estação *f* de rádio, emissora *f*
radioactiv|e /reɪdɪəʊ'æktɪv/ *a* radioativo, (*P*) radioactivo. ~**ity** /'tɪvətɪ/ *n* radioatividade *f*, (*P*) radioactividade *f*
radiograph|er /reɪdɪ'ɒgrəfə(r)/ *n* radiologista *mf*. ~**y** *n* radiografia *f*
radish /'rædɪʃ/ *n* rabanete *m*
radius /'reɪdɪəs/ *n* (*pl* **-dii** /-dɪaɪ/) raio *m*
raffle /'ræfl/ *n* rifa *f* □ *vt* rifar
raft /ra:ft/ *n* jangada *f*
rafter /'ra:ftə(r)/ *n* trave *f*, viga *f*
rag[1] /ræg/ *n* farrapo *m*; (*for wiping*) trapo *m*; (*pej: newspaper*) jornaleco *m*. ~**s** *npl* farrapos *mpl*, andrajos *mpl*. **in ~s** maltrapilho. ~ **doll** boneca *f* de trapos
rag[2] /ræg/ *vt* (*pt* **ragged**) zombar de
rage /reɪdʒ/ *n* raiva *f*, fúria *f* □ *vi* estar furioso; (*of storm*) rugir; (*of battle*) estar acesa. **be all the ~** (*colloq*) fazer furor, estar na moda (*colloq*)
ragged /'rægɪd/ *a* (*clothes, person*) esfarrapado, roto; (*edge*) esfiapado, esgarçado
raid /reɪd/ *n* (*mil*) ataque *m*; (*by police*) batida *f*; (*by criminals*) assalto *m* □ *vt* fazer um ataque *or* uma batida *or* um assalto. ~**er** *n* atacante *m*, assaltante *m*
rail /reɪl/ *n* (*of stairs*) corrimão *m*; (*of ship*) amurada *f*; (*on balcony*) parapeito *m*; (*for train*) trilho *m*; (*for curtain*) varão *m*. **by ~** por estrada, (*P*) caminho de ferro
railings /'reɪlɪŋz/ *npl* grade *f*
railroad /'reɪlrəʊd/ *n* (*Amer*) = railway
railway /'reɪlweɪ/ *n* estrada *f*, (*P*) caminho *m* de ferro. ~ **line** linha *f* do trem. ~ **station** estação *f* ferroviária, (*P*) estação *f* de caminho de ferro
rain /reɪn/ *n* chuva *f* □ *vi* chover. ~ **forest** floresta *f* tropical. ~**-storm** *n* tempestade *f* com chuva. ~**-water** *n* água *f* da chuva
rainbow /'reɪnbəʊ/ *n* arco-íris *m*
raincoat /'reɪnkəʊt/ *n* impermeável *m*
raindrop /'reɪndrɒp/ *n* pingo *m* de chuva
rainfall /'reɪnfɔ:l/ *n* precipitação *f*, pluviosidade *f*
rainy /'reɪnɪ/ *a* (**-ier, -iest**) chuvoso
raise /reɪz/ *vt* levantar, erguer; (*breed*) criar; (*voice*) levantar; (*question*) fazer; (*price etc*) aumentar, subir; (*funds*) angariar; (*loan*) obter □ *n* (*Amer*) aumento *m*
raisin /'reɪzn/ *n* passa *f*
rake /reɪk/ *n* ancinho *m* □ *vt* juntar, alisar com ancinho; (*search*) revolver, remexer. ~ **in** (*money*) ganhar a rodos. ~**-off** *n* (*colloq*) percentagem *f* (*colloq*). ~ **up** desenterrar, ressuscitar
rally /'rælɪ/ *vt/i* reunir(-se); (*reassemble*) reagrupar(-se), reorganizar(-se); (*health*) restabelecer(-se); (*strength*) recuperar as forças □ *n* (*recovery*) recuperação *f*; (*meeting*) comício *m*, assembléia *f*; (*auto*) rally *m*, rali *m*
ram /ræm/ *n* (*sheep*) carneiro *m* □ *vt* (*pt* **rammed**) (*beat down*) calcar; (*push*) meter à força; (*crash into*) bater contra
rambl|e /'ræmbl/ *n* caminhada *f*, perambulação *f* □ *vi* perambular, vaguear. ~**e on** divagar. ~**er** *n* caminhante *mf*; (*plant*) trepadeira *f*. ~**ing** *a* (*speech*) desconexo
ramp /ræmp/ *n* rampa *f*
rampage /ræm'peɪdʒ/ *vi* causar distúrbios violentos
rampant /'ræmpənt/ *a* **be ~** vicejar, florescer; (*diseases etc*) grassar
rampart /'ræmpa:t/ *n* baluarte *m*; (*fig*) defesa *f*
ramshackle /'ræmʃækl/ *a* (*car*) desconjuntado; (*house*) caindo aos pedaços
ran /ræn/ *see* **run**
ranch /ra:ntʃ/ *n* rancho *m*, estância *f*. ~**er** *n* rancheiro *m*
rancid /'rænsɪd/ *a* rançoso
rancour /'ræŋkə(r)/ *n* rancor *m*

random /ˈrændəm/ *a* feito, tirado *etc* ao acaso □ *n* **at ~** ao acaso, a esmo, aleatoriamente
randy /ˈrændɪ/ *a* (-ier, -iest) lascivo, sensual
rang /ræŋ/ *see* ring
range /reɪndʒ/ *n* (*distance*) alcance *m*; (*scope*) âmbito *m*; (*variety*) gama *f*, variedade *f*; (*stove*) fogão *m*; (*of voice*) registro *m*, (*P*) registo *m*; (*of temperature*) variação *f* □ *vt* dispor, ordenar □ *vi* estender-se; (*vary*) variar. **~ of mountains** cordilheira *f*, serra *f*. **~r** *n* guarda *m* florestal
rank[1] /ræŋk/ *n* fila *f*, fileira *f*; (*mil*) posto *m*; (*social position*) classe *f*, categoria *f* □ *vt/i* **~ among** contar(-se) entre. **the ~ and file** a massa
rank[2] /ræŋk/ *a* (-er, -est) (*plants*) luxuriante; (*smell*) fétido; (*out-and-out*) total
ransack /ˈrænsæk/ *vt* (*search*) espionar, revistar, remexer; (*pillage*) pilhar, saquear
ransom /ˈrænsəm/ *n* resgate *m* □ *vt* resgatar. **hold to ~** prender como refém
rant /rænt/ *vi* usar linguagem bombástica
rap /ræp/ *n* pancadinha *f* seca □ *vt/i* (*pt* **rapped**) bater, dar uma pancada seca em
rape /reɪp/ *vt* violar, estuprar □ *n* violação *f*, estupro *m*
rapid /ˈræpɪd/ *a* rápido. **~ity** /rəˈpɪdətɪ/ *n* rapidez *f*
rapids /ˈræpɪdz/ *npl* rápidos *mpl*
rapist /ˈreɪpɪst/ *n* violador *m*, estuprador *m*
rapport /ræˈpɔ:(r)/ *n* bom relacionamento *m*
rapt /ræpt/ *a* absorto. **~ in** mergulhado em
raptur|e /ˈræptʃə(r)/ *n* êxtase *m*. **~ous** *a* extático; (*welcome etc*) entusiástico
rar|e[1] /reə(r)/ *a* (-er, -est) raro. **~ely** *adv* raramente, raras vezes. **~ity** *n* raridade *f*
rare[2] /reə(r)/ *a* (-er, -est) (*culin*) mal passado
rarefied /ˈreərɪfaɪd/ *a* rarefeito; (*refined*) requintado
raring /ˈreərɪŋ/ *a* **~ to** (*colloq*) impaciente por, louco por (*colloq*)
rascal /ˈra:skl/ *n* (*dishonest*) patife *m*; (*mischievous*) maroto *m*
rash[1] /ræʃ/ *n* erupção *f* cutânea, irritação *f* na pele (*colloq*)
rash[2] /ræʃ/ *a* (-er, -est) imprudente, precipitado. **~ly** *adv* imprudentemente, precipitadamente
rasher /ˈræʃə(r)/ *n* fatia *f* (de presunto *or* de bacon)
rasp /ra:sp/ *n* lixa *f* grossa, (*P*) lima *f* grossa
raspberry /ˈra:zbrɪ/ *n* framboesa *f*
rasping /ˈra:spɪŋ/ *a* áspero
rat /ræt/ *n* rato *m*, (*P*) ratazana *f*. **~ race** (*fig*) luta renhida para vencer na vida, arrivismo *m*
rate /reɪt/ *n* (*ratio*) razão *f*; (*speed*) velocidade *f*; (*price*) tarifa *f*; (*of exchange*) (taxa *m* de) câmbio *m*; (*of interest*) taxa *f*. **~s** (*taxes*) impostos *mpl* municipais, taxas *fpl* □ *vt* avaliar; (*fig: consider*) considerar. **at any ~** de qualquer modo, pelo menos. **at the ~ of** à razão de. **at this ~** desse jeito, desse modo
ratepayer /ˈreɪtpeɪə(r)/ *n* contribuinte *mf*
rather /ˈra:ðə(r)/ *adv* (*by preference*) antes; (*fairly*) muito, bastante; (*a little*) um pouco. **I would ~ go** preferia ir
ratif|y /ˈrætɪfaɪ/ *vt* ratificar. **~ication** /-ɪˈkeɪʃn/ *n* ratificação *f*
rating /ˈreɪtɪŋ/ *n* (*comm*) rating *m*, (*P*) valor *m*; (*sailor*) praça *f*, marinheiro *m*; (*radio, TV*) índice *m* de audiência
ratio /ˈreɪʃɪəʊ/ *n* (*pl* -os) proporção *f*
ration /ˈræʃn/ *n* ração *f* □ *vt* racionar
rational /ˈræʃnəl/ *a* racional; (*person*) sensato, razoável. **~ize** *vt* racionalizar
rattle /ˈrætl/ *vt/i* matraquear; (*of door, window*) bater; (*of bottles*) chocalhar; (*colloq*) agitar, mexer com os nervos de □ *n* (*baby's toy*) guizo *m*, chocalho *m*; (*of football fan*) matraca *f*; (*sound*) matraquear *m*, chocalhar *m*. **~ off** despejar (*colloq*)
rattlesnake /ˈrætlsneɪk/ *n* cobra *f* cascavel
raucous /ˈrɔ:kəs/ *a* áspero, rouco
ravage /ˈrævɪdʒ/ *vt* devastar, causar estragos a. **~s** *npl* devastação *f*, estragos *mpl*
rave /reɪv/ *vi* delirar; (*in anger*) urrar. **~ about** delirar (de entusiasmo) com
raven /ˈreɪvn/ *n* corvo *m*
ravenous /ˈrævənəs/ *a* esfomeado; (*greedy*) voraz
ravine /rəˈvi:n/ *n* ravina *f*, barranco *m*
raving /ˈreɪvɪŋ/ *a* **~ lunatic** doido *m* varrido □ *adv* **~ mad** loucamente
ravish /ˈrævɪʃ/ *vt* (*rape*) violar; (*enrapture*) arrebatar, encantar. **~ing** *a* arrebatador, encantador
raw /rɔ:/ *a* (-er, -est) cru; (*not processed*) bruto; (*wound*) em carne viva; (*weather*) frio e úmido, (*P*) húmido; (*immature*) inexperiente, verde. **~ deal** tratamento *m* injusto. **~ material** matéria-prima *f*
ray /reɪ/ *n* raio *m*

raze /reɪz/ *vt* arrasar

razor /'reɪzə(r)/ *n* navalha *f* de barba. **~-blade** *n* lâmina *f* de barbear

re /ri:/ *prep* a respeito de, em referência a, relativo a

re- /ri/ *pref* re-

reach /ri:tʃ/ *vt* chegar a atingir; (*contact*) contatar; (*pass*) passar □ *vi* estender-se, chegar □ *n* alcance *m*. **out of ~** fora de alcance. **~ for** estender a mão para agarrar. **within ~ of** ao alcance de; (*close to*) próximo de

react /rɪ'ækt/ *vi* reagir

reaction /rɪ'ækʃn/ *n* reação *f*, (*P*) reacção *f*. **~ary** *a* & *n* reacionário (*m*), (*P*) reaccionário (*m*)

reactor /rɪ'æktə(r)/ *n* reator *m*, (*P*) reactor *m*

read /ri:d/ *vt/i* (*pt* **read** /red/) ler; (*fig: interpret*) interpretar; (*study*) estudar; (*of instrument*) marcar, indicar □ *n* (*colloq*) leitura *f*. **~ about** ler um artigo sobre. **~ out** ler em voz alta. **~able** *a* agradável *or* fácil de ler; (*legible*) legível. **~er** *n* leitor *m*; (*book*) livro *m* de leitura. **~ing** *n* leitura *f*; (*of instrument*) registro *m*, (*P*) registo *m*

readily /'redɪlɪ/ *adv* de boa vontade, prontamente; (*easily*) facilmente

readiness /'redɪnɪs/ *n* prontidão *f*. **in ~** pronto (for para)

readjust /ri:ə'dʒʌst/ *vt* reajustar □ *vi* readaptar-se

ready /'redɪ/ *a* (-ier, -iest) pronto □ *n* **at the ~** pronto para disparar. **~-made** *a* pronto. **~ money** dinheiro *m* vivo, (*P*) dinheiro *m* de contado, pagamento *m* à vista. **~-to-wear** *a* prêt-à-porter

real /rɪəl/ *a* real, verdadeiro; (*genuine*) autêntico □ *adv* (*Amer: colloq*) realmente. **~ estate** bens *mpl* imobiliários

realis|t /'rɪəlɪst/ *n* realista *mf*. **~m** /-zəm/ *n* realismo *m*. **~tic** /'lɪstɪk/ *a* realista. **~tically** /'lɪstɪkəlɪ/ *adv* realisticamente

reality /rɪ'ælətɪ/ *n* realidade *f*

realiz|e /'rɪəlaɪz/ *vt* dar-se conta de, aperceber-se de, perceber; (*fulfil; turn into cash*) realizar. **~ation** /-'zeɪʃn/ *n* consciência *f*, noção *f*; (*fulfilment*) realização *f*

really /'rɪəlɪ/ *adv* realmente, na verdade

realm /relm/ *n* reino *m*; (*fig*) domínio *m*, esfera *f*

reap /ri:p/ *vt* (*cut*) ceifar; (*gather; fig*) colher

reappear /ri:ə'pɪə(r)/ *vi* reaparecer. **~ance** *n* reaparição *f*

rear[1] /rɪə(r)/ *n* traseira *f*, retaguarda *f* □ *a* traseiro, de trás, posterior. **bring up the ~** ir na retaguarda, fechar a marcha. **~-view mirror** espelho *m* retrovisor

rear[2] /rɪə(r)/ *vt* levantar, erguer; (*children, cattle*) criar □ *vi* (*of horse etc*) empinar-se. **~ one's head** levantar a cabeça

rearrange /ri:ə'reɪndʒ/ *vt* arranjar doutro modo, reorganizar

reason /'ri:zn/ *n* razão *f* □ *vt/i* raciocinar, argumentar. **~ with sb** procurar convencer alguém. **within ~** razoável. **~ing** *n* raciocínio *m*

reasonable /'ri:znəbl/ *a* razoável

reassur|e /ri:ə'ʃʊə(r)/ *vt* tranqüilizar, sossegar. **~ance** *n* garantia *f*. **~ing** *a* animador, reconfortante

rebate /'ri:beɪt/ *n* (*refund*) reimbolso *m*; (*discount*) desconto *m*, abatimento *m*

rebel[1] /'rebl/ *n* rebelde *mf*

rebel[2] /rɪ'bel/ *vi* (*pt* **rebelled**) rebelar-se, revoltar-se, sublevar-se. **~lion** *n* rebelião *f*, revolta *f*. **~lious** *a* rebelde

rebound[1] /rɪ'baʊnd/ *vi* repercutir, ressoar; (*fig: backfire*) recair (**on** sobre)

rebound[2] /'ri:baʊnd/ *n* ricochete *m*

rebuff /rɪ'bʌf/ *vt* receber mal, repelir (*colloq*) □ *n* rejeição *f*

rebuild /ri:'bɪld/ *vt* (*pt* **rebuilt**) reconstruir

rebuke /rɪ'bju:k/ *vt* repreender □ *n* reprimenda *f*

recall /rɪ'kɔ:l/ *vt* chamar, mandar regressar; (*remember*) lembrar-se de □ *n* (*summons*) ordem *f* de regresso

recant /rɪ'kænt/ *vi* retratar-se, (*P*) retractar-se

recap /'ri:kæp/ *vt/i* (*pt* **recapped**) (*colloq*) recapitular □ *n* recapitulação *f*

recapitulat|e /ri:kə'pɪtʃʊleɪt/ *vt/i* recapitular. **~ion** /-'leɪʃn/ *n* recapitulação *f*

reced|e /rɪ'si:d/ *vi* recuar, retroceder. **his hair is ~ing** ele está ficando com entradas. **~ing** *a* (*forehead, chin*) recuado, voltado para dentro

receipt /rɪ'si:t/ *n* recibo *m*; (*receiving*) recepção *f*. **~s** (*comm*) receitas *fpl*

receive /rɪ'si:v/ *vt* receber. **~r** /-ə(r)/ *n* (*of stolen goods*) receptador *m*; (*phone*) fone *m*, (*P*) auscultador *m*; (*radio/TV*) receptor *m*. (**official**) **~r** síndico *m* de massa falida

recent /'ri:snt/ *a* recente. **~ly** *adv* recentemente

receptacle /rɪ'septəkl/ *n* recipiente *m*, receptáculo *m*

reception /rɪ'sepʃn/ *n* recepção *f*; (*welcome*) acolhimento *m*. **~ist** *n* recepcionista *mf*

receptive /rɪ'septɪv/ *a* receptivo

recess /rɪ'ses/ *n* recesso *m*; (*of legisla-*

ture) recesso *m*; (*Amer: schol*) recreio *m*

recession /rɪ'seʃn/ *n* recessão *f*, depressão *f*

recharge /ri:'tʃa:dʒ/ *vt* tornar a carregar, recarregar

recipe /'resəpɪ/ *n* (*culin*) receita *f*

recipient /rɪ'sɪpɪənt/ *n* recipiente *mf*; (*of letter*) destinatário *m*

reciprocal /rɪ'sɪprəkl/ *a* recíproco

reciprocate /rɪ'sɪprəkəɪt/ *vt/i* reciprocar(-se), retribuir, fazer o mesmo

recital /rɪ'saɪtl/ *n* (*music etc*) recital *m*

recite /rɪ'saɪt/ *vt* recitar; (*list*) enumerar

reckless /'reklɪs/ *a* inconsciente, imprudente, estouvado

reckon /'rekən/ *vt/i* calcular; (*judge*) considerar; (*think*) supor, pensar. ~ **on** contar com, depender de. ~ **with** contar com, levar em conta. ~**ing** *n* conta(s) *f* (*pl*)

reclaim /rɪ'kleɪm/ *vt* (*demand*) reclamar; (*land*) recuperar

reclin|e /rɪ'klaɪn/ *vt/i* reclinar(-se). ~**ing** *a* (*person*) reclinado; (*chair*) reclinável

recluse /rɪ'klu:s/ *n* solitário *m*, recluso *m*

recognition /rekəg'nɪʃn/ *n* reconhecimento *m*. **beyond** ~ irreconhecível. **gain** ~ ganhar nome, ser reconhecido

recogniz|e /'rekəgnaɪz/ *vt* reconhecer. ~**able** /'rekəgnaɪzəbl/ *a* reconhecível

recoil /rɪ'kɔɪl/ *vi* recuar; (*gun*) dar coice □ *n* recuo *m*; (*gun*) coice *m*. ~ **from doing** recusar-se a fazer

recollect /rekə'lekt/ *vt* recordar-se de. ~**ion** /-ʃn/ *n* recordação *f*

recommend /rekə'mend/ *vt* recomendar. ~**ation** /-'deɪʃn/ *n* recomendação *f*

recompense /'rekəmpens/ *vt* recompensar □ *n* recompensa *f*

reconcil|e /'rekənsaɪl/ *vt* (*people*) reconciliar; (*facts*) conciliar. ~**e o.s. to** resignar-se a, conformar-se com. ~**iation** /-sɪlɪ'eɪʃn/ *n* reconciliação *f*

reconnaissance /rɪ'kɒnɪsns/ *n* reconhecimento *m*

reconnoitre /rekə'nɔɪtə(r)/ *vt/i* (*pres p* -tring) (*mil*) reconhecer, fazer um reconhecimento (de)

reconsider /ri:kən'sɪdə(r)/ *vt* reconsiderar

reconstruct /ri:kən'strʌkt/ *vt* reconstruir. ~**ion** /-ʃn/ *n* reconstrução *f*

record[1] /rɪ'kɔ:d/ *vt* registar; (*disc, tape etc*) gravar. ~ **that** referir/relatar que. ~**ing** *n* (*disc, tape etc*) gravação *f*

record[2] /'rekɔ:d/ *n* (*register*) registro *m*, (*P*) registo *m*; (*mention*) menção *f*, nota *f*; (*file*) arquivo *m*; (*mus*) disco *m*; (*sport*) record(e) *m* □ *a* record(e) *invar*. **have a (criminal)** ~ ter cadastro. **off the** ~ (*unofficial*) oficioso; (*secret*) confidencial. ~**-player** *n* toca-discos *m invar*, (*P*) gira-discos *m invar*

recorder /rɪ'kɔ:də(r)/ *n* (*mus*) flauta *f* de ponta; (*techn*) instrumento *m* registrador

recount /rɪ'kaʊnt/ *vt* narrar em pormenor, relatar

re-count /'ri:kaʊnt/ *n* (*pol*) nova contagem *f*

recoup /rɪ'ku:p/ *vt* compensar; (*recover*) recuperar

recourse /rɪ'kɔ:s/ *n* recurso *m*. **have** ~ **to** recorrer a

recover /rɪ'kʌvə(r)/ *vt* recuperar □ *vi* restabelecer-se. ~**y** *n* recuperação *f*; (*health*) recuperação *f*, restabelecimento *m*

recreation /rekrɪ'eɪʃn/ *n* recreação *f*, recreio *m*; (*pastime*) passatempo *m*. ~**al** *a* recreativo

recrimination /rɪkrɪmɪ'neɪʃn/ *n* recriminação *f*

recruit /rɪ'kru:t/ *n* recruta *m* □ *vt* recrutar. ~**ment** *n* recrutamento *m*

rectang|le /'rektæŋgl/ *n* retângulo *m*, (*P*) rectângulo *m*. ~**ular** /-'tæŋgjʊlə(r)/ *a* retangular, (*P*) rectangular

rectify /'rektɪfaɪ/ *vt* retificar, (*P*) rectificar

recuperate /rɪ'kju:pəreɪt/ *vt/i* recuperar(-se)

recur /rɪ'kɜ:(r)/ *vi* (*pt* **recurred**) repetir-se; (*come back*) voltar (to a)

recurren|t /rɪ'kʌrənt/ *a* freqüente, (*P*) frequente, repetido, periódico. ~**ce** *n* repetição *f*

recycle /ri:'saɪkl/ *vt* reciclar

red /red/ *a* (**redder, reddest**) encarnado, vermelho; (*hair*) ruivo □ *n* encarnado *m*, vermelho *m*. **in the** ~ em déficit. ~ **carpet** (*fig*) recepção *f* solene, tratamento *m* especial. **R**~ **Cross** Cruz *f* Vermelha. ~**-handed** *a* em flagrante (delito), com a boca na botija (*colloq*). ~ **herring** (*fig*) pista *f* falsa. ~**-hot** *a* escaldante, incandescente. ~ **light** luz *f* vermelha. ~ **tape** (*fig*) papelada *f*, burocracia *f*. ~ **wine** vinho *m* tinto

redden /'redn/ *vt/i* avermelhar(-se); (*blush*) corar, ruborizar-se

redecorate /ri:'dekəreɪt/ *vt* decorar/pintar de novo

red|eem /rɪ'di:m/ *vt* (*sins etc*) redimir; (*sth pawned*) tirar do prego (*colloq*); (*voucher etc*) resgatar. ~**emption** /rɪ'dempʃn/ *n* resgate *m*; (*of honour*) salvação *f*

redirect /ri:daɪ'rekt/ *vt* (*letter*) reendereçar

redness /'rednɪs/ *n* vermelhidão *f*, cor *f* vermelha
redo /ri:'du:/ *vt* (*pt* **-did**, *pp* **-done**) refazer
redress /rɪ'dres/ *vt* reparar; (*set right*) remediar, emendar. ~ **the balance** restabelecer o equilíbrio □ *n* reparação *f*
reduc|e /rɪ'dju:s/ *vt* reduzir; (*temperature etc*) baixar. **~tion** /rɪ'dʌkʃən/ *n* redução *f*
redundan|t /rɪ'dʌndənt/ *a* redundante, supérfluo; (*worker*) desempregado. **be made ~t** ficar desempregado. **~cy** *n* demissão *f* por excesso de pessoal
reed /ri:d/ *n* cana *f*, junco *m*; (*mus*) palheta *f*
reef /ri:f/ *n* recife *m*
reek /ri:k/ *n* mau cheiro *m* □ *vi* cheirar mal, tresandar. **he ~s of wine** ele está com cheiro de vinho
reel /ri:l/ *n* carretel *m*; (*spool*) bobina *f* □ *vi* cambalear, vacilar □ *vt* ~ **off** recitar (*colloq*)
refectory /rɪ'fektərɪ/ *n* refeitório *m*
refer /rɪ'fɜ:(r)/ *vt/i* (*pt* **referred**) ~ **to** referir-se a; (*concern*) aplicar-se a, dizer respeito a; (*consult*) consultar; (*direct*) remeter a
referee /refə'ri:/ *n* árbitro *m*; (*for job*) pessoa *f* que dá referências □ *vt* (*pt* **refereed**) arbitrar
reference /'refrəns/ *n* referência *f*; (*testimonial*) referências *fpl*. **in ~** *or* **with ~ to** com referência a. **~ book** livro *m* de consulta
referendum /refə'rendəm/ *n* (*pl* **-dums** *or* **-da**) referendo *m*, plebiscito *m*
refill[1] /ri:'fɪl/ *vt* encher de novo; (*pen etc*) pôr carga nova em
refill[2] /'ri:fɪl/ *n* (*pen etc*) carga *f* nova, (*P*) recarga *f*
refine /rɪ'faɪn/ *vt* refinar. **~d** *a* refinado; (*taste, manners etc*) requintado. **~ment** *n* (*taste, manners etc*) refinamento *m*, requinte *m*; (*tech*) refinação *f*. **~ry** /-ərɪ/ *n* refinaria *f*
reflect /rɪ'flekt/ *vt/i* refletir, (*P*) reflectir (**on/upon** em). **~ion** /-ʃn/ *n* reflexão *f*; (*image*) reflexo *m*. **~or** *n* refletor *m*, (*P*) reflector *m*
reflective /rɪ'flektɪv/ *a* refletor, (*P*) reflector; (*thoughtful*) refletido, (*P*) reflectido, ponderado
reflex /'ri:fleks/ *a* & *n* reflexo (*m*)
reflexive /rɪ'fleksɪv/ *a* (*gram*) reflexivo, (*P*) reflexo
reform /rɪ'fɔ:m/ *vt/i* reformar(-se) □ *n* reforma *f*. **~er** *n* reformador *m*
refract /rɪ'frækt/ *vt* refratar, (*P*) refractar
refrain[1] /rɪ'freɪn/ *n* refrão *m*, estribilho *m*
refrain[2] /rɪ'freɪn/ *vi* abster-se (**from** de)
refresh /rɪ'freʃ/ *vt* refrescar; (*of rest etc*) restaurar. ~ **one's memory** avivar *or* refrescar a memória. **~ing** *a* refrescante; (*of rest etc*) reparador. **~ments** *npl* refeição *f* leve; (*drinks*) refrescos *mpl*
refresher /rɪ'freʃə(r)/ *n* ~ **course** curso *m* de reciclagem
refrigerat|e /rɪ'frɪdʒəreɪt/ *vt* refrigerar. **~or** *n* frigorífico *m*, refrigerador *m*, geladeira *f*
refuel /ri:'fju:əl/ *vt/i* (*pt* **refuelled**) reabastecer(-se) (de combustível)
refuge /'refju:dʒ/ *n* refúgio *m*, asilo *m*. **take ~** refugiar-se
refugee /refjʊ'dʒi:/ *n* refugiado *m*
refund[1] /rɪ'fʌnd/ *vt* reembolsar
refund[2] /'ri:fʌnd/ *n* reembolso *m*
refus|e[1] /rɪ'fju:z/ *vt/i* recusar(-se). **~al** *n* recusa *f*. **first ~al** preferência *f*, primeira opção *f*
refuse[2] /'refju:s/ *n* refugo *m*, lixo *m*. **~-collector** *n* lixeiro *m*, (*P*) homem *m* do lixo
refute /rɪ'fju:t/ *vt* refutar
regain /rɪ'geɪn/ *vt* recobrar, recuperar
regal /'ri:gl/ *a* real, régio
regalia /rɪ'geɪlɪə/ *npl* insígnias *fpl*
regard /rɪ'ga:d/ *vt* considerar; (*gaze*) olhar □ *n* consideração *f*, estima *f*; (*gaze*) olhar *m*. **~s** cumprimentos *mpl*; (*less formally*) lembranças *fpl*, saudades *fpl*. **as ~s**, **~ing** *prep* no que diz respeito a, quanto a. **~less** *adv* apesar de tudo. **~less of** apesar de
regatta /rɪ'gætə/ *n* regata *f*
regenerate /rɪ'dʒenəreɪt/ *vt* regenerar
regen|t /'ri:dʒənt/ *n* regente *mf*. **~cy** *n* regência *f*
regime /reɪ'ʒi:m/ *n* regime *m*
regiment /'redʒɪmənt/ *n* regimento *m*. **~al** /-'mentl/ *a* de regimento, regimental. **~ation** /-en'teɪʃn/ *n* arregimentação *f*, disciplina *f* excessiva
region /'ri:dʒən/ *n* região *f*. **in the ~ of** por volta de. **~al** *a* regional
regist|er /'redʒɪstə(r)/ *n* registro *m*, (*P*) registo *m* □ *vt* (*record*) anotar; (*notice*) fixar, registar, prestar atenção a; (*birth, letter*) registrar, (*P*) registar; (*vehicle*) matricular; (*emotions etc*) exprimir □ *vi* inscrever-se. **~er office** registro *m*, (*P*) registo *m*. **~ration** /-'streɪʃn/ *n* registro *m*, (*P*) registo *m*; (*for course*) inscrição *f*, matrícula *f*. **~ration (number)** número *m* de placa
registrar /redʒɪ'stra:(r)/ *n* oficial *m* do registro, (*P*) registo civil; (*univ*) secretário *m*

regret /rɪ'gret/ *n* pena *f*, pesar *m*; (*repentance*) remorso *m*. **I have no ~s** não estou arrependido □ *vt* (*pt* **regretted**) lamentar, sentir (**to do** fazer); (*feel repentance*) arrepender-se de, lamentar. **~fully** *adv* com pena, pesarosamente. **~table** *a* lamentável. **~tably** *adv* infelizmente

regular /'regjʊlə(r)/ *a* regular; (*usual*) normal; (*colloq: thorough*) perfeito, verdadeiro, autêntico □ *n* (*colloq: client*) cliente *mf* habitual. **~ity** /-'lærətɪ/ *n* regularidade *f*. **~ly** *adv* regularmente

regulat|e /'regjʊleɪt/ *vt* regular. **~ion** /-'leɪʃn/ *n* regulação *f*; (*rule*) regulamento *m*, regra *f*

rehabilitat|e /ri:ə'bɪlɪteɪt/ *vt* reabilitar. **~ion** /-'teɪʃn/ *n* reabilitação *f*

rehash[1] /ri:'hæʃ/ *vt* apresentar sob nova forma, (*P*) cozinhar (*colloq*)

rehash[2] /'ri:hæʃ/ *n* (*fig*) apanhado *m*, (*P*) cozinhado *m* (*colloq*)

rehears|e /rɪ'hɜ:s/ *vt* ensaiar. **~al** *n* ensaio *m*. **dress ~al** ensaio *m* geral

reign /reɪn/ *n* reinado *m* □ *vi* reinar (**over** em)

reimburse /ri:ɪm'bɜ:s/ *vt* reembolsar. **~ment** *n* reembolso *m*

rein /reɪn/ *n* rédea *f*

reincarnation /ri:ɪnka:'neɪʃn/ *n* reencarnação *f*

reindeer /'reɪndɪə(r)/ *n invar* rena *f*

reinforce /ri:ɪn'fɔ:s/ *vt* reforçar. **~ment** *n* reforço *m*. **~ments** reforços *mpl*. **~d concrete** concreto *m* armado, (*P*) cimento *m or* betão *m* armado

reinstate /ri:ɪn'steɪt/ *vt* reintegrar

reiterate /ri:'ɪtəreɪt/ *vt* reiterar

reject[1] /rɪ'dʒekt/ *vt* rejeitar. **~ion** /-ʃn/ *n* rejeição *f*

reject[2] /'ri:dʒekt/ *n* (artigo de) refugo *m*

rejoic|e /rɪ'dʒɔɪs/ *vi* regozijar-se (**at/over** com). **~ing** *n* regozijo *m*

rejuvenate /ri:'dʒu:vəneɪt/ *vt* rejuvenescer

relapse /rɪ'læps/ *n* recaída *f* □ *vi* recair

relate /rɪ'leɪt/ *vt* relatar; (*associate*) relacionar □ *vi* **~ to** ter relação com, dizer respeito a; (*get on with*) entender-se com. **~d** *a* aparentado; (*ideas etc*) afim, relacionado

relation /rɪ'leɪʃn/ *n* relação *f*; (*person*) parente *mf*. **~ship** *n* parentesco *m*; (*link*) relação *f*; (*affair*) ligação *f*

relative /'relətɪv/ *n* parente *mf* □ *a* relativo. **~ly** *adv* relativamente

relax /rɪ'læks/ *vt/i* relaxar(-se); (*fig*) descontrair(-se). **~ation** /ri:læk'seɪʃn/ *n* relaxamento *m*; (*fig*) descontração *f*, (*P*) descontracção *f*; (*recreation*) distração *f*, (*P*) distracção *f* **~ing** *a* relaxante

relay[1] /'ri:leɪ/ *n* turma *f*, (*P*) turno *m*. **~ race** corrida *f* de revezamento, (*P*) estafetas

relay[2] /rɪ'leɪ/ *vt* (*message*) retransmitir

release /rɪ'li:s/ *vt* libertar, soltar; (*mech*) desengatar, soltar; (*bomb, film, record*) lançar; (*news*) dar, publicar; (*gas, smoke*) soltar □ *n* libertação *f*; (*mech*) desengate *m*; (*bomb, film, record*) lançamento *m*; (*news*) publicação *f*; (*gas, smoke*) emissão *f*. **new ~** estréia *f*

relegate /'relɪgeɪt/ *vt* relegar

relent /rɪ'lent/ *vi* ceder. **~less** *a* implacável, inexorável, inflexível

relevan|t /'reləvənt/ *a* relevante, pertinente, a propósito. **be ~ to** ter a ver com. **~ce** *n* pertinência *f*, relevância *f*

reliab|le /rɪ'laɪəbl/ *a* de confiança, com que se pode contar; (*source etc*) fidedigno; (*machine etc*) seguro, confiável. **~ility** /-'bɪlətɪ/ *n* confiabilidade *f*

reliance /rɪ'laɪəns/ *n* (*dependence*) segurança *f*; (*trust*) confiança *f*, fé *f* (**on** em)

relic /'relɪk/ *n* relíquia *f*. **~s** vestígios *mpl*, ruínas *fpl*

relief /rɪ'li:f/ *n* alívio *m*; (*assistance*) auxílio *m*, assistência *f*; (*outline, design*) relevo *m*. **~ road** estrada *f* alternativa

relieve /rɪ'li:v/ *vt* aliviar; (*help*) socorrer; (*take over from*) revezar, substituir; (*mil*) render

religion /rɪ'lɪdʒən/ *n* religião *f*

religious /rɪ'lɪdʒəs/ *a* religioso

relinquish /rɪ'lɪŋkwɪʃ/ *vt* abandonar, renunciar a

relish /'relɪʃ/ *n* prazer *m*, gosto *m*; (*culin*) molho *m* condimentado □ *vt* saborear, apreciar, gostar de

relocate /ri:ləʊ'keɪt/ *vt/i* transferir (-se), mudar(-se)

reluctan|t /rɪ'lʌktənt/ *a* relutante (**to** em), pouco inclinado (**to** a). **~ce** *n* relutância *f*. **~tly** *adv* a contragosto, relutantemente

rely /rɪ'laɪ/ *vi* **~ on** contar com; (*depend*) depender de

remain /rɪ'meɪn/ *vi* ficar, permanecer. **~s** *npl* restos *mpl*; (*ruins*) ruínas *fpl*. **~ing** *a* restante

remainder /rɪ'meɪndə(r)/ *n* restante *m*, remanescente *m*

remand /rɪ'ma:nd/ *vt* reconduzir à prisão para detenção provisória □ *n* **on ~** sob prisão preventiva

remark /rɪ'ma:k/ *n* observação *f*, comentário *m* □ *vt* observar, comentar □ *vi* ~ on fazer observações *or* comentários sobre. ~**able** *a* notável

remarr|y /ri:ˈmærɪ/ *vt/i* tornar a casar(-se) (com). ~**iage** *n* novo casamento *m*

remed|y /ˈremədɪ/ *n* remédio *m* □ *vt* remediar. ~**ial** /rɪˈmi:dɪəl/ *a* (*med*) corretivo, (*P*) correctivo

rememb|er /rɪˈmembə(r)/ *vt* lembrar-se de, recordar-se de. ~**rance** *n* lembrança *f*, recordação *f*

remind /rɪˈmaɪnd/ *vt* (fazer) lembrar (sb of sth alg coisa a alguém). ~ sb to do lembrar a alguém que faça. ~**er** *n* o que serve para fazer lembrar; (*note*) lembrete *m*

reminisce /remɪˈnɪs/ *vi* (re)lembrar (coisas passadas). ~**nces** *npl* reminiscências *fpl*

reminiscent /remɪˈnɪsnt/ *a* ~ of que faz lembrar, evocativo de

remiss /rɪˈmɪs/ *a* negligente, descuidado

remission /rɪˈmɪʃn/ *n* remissão *f*; (*jur*) comutação *f* (de pena)

remit /rɪˈmɪt/ *vt* (*pt* **remitted**) (*money*) remeter. ~**tance** *n* remessa *f* (de dinheiro)

remnant /ˈremnənt/ *n* resto *m*; (*trace*) vestígio *m*; (*of cloth*) retalho *m*

remorse /rɪˈmɔ:s/ *n* remorso *m*. ~**ful** *a* arrependido, com remorsos. ~**less** *a* implacável

remote /rɪˈməʊt/ *a* remoto, distante; (*person*) distante; (*slight*) vago, leve. ~ **control** comando *m* à distância, telecomando *m*. ~**ly** *adv* de longe; vagamente

remov|e /rɪˈmu:v/ *vt* tirar, remover; (*lead away*) levar; (*dismiss*) demitir; (*get rid of*) eliminar. ~**al** *n* remoção *f*; (*dismissal*) desmissão *f*; (*from house*) mudança *f*

remunerat|e /rɪˈmju:nəreɪt/ *vt* remunerar. ~**ion** /-ˈreɪʃn/ *n* remuneração *f*

rename /ri:ˈneɪm/ *vt* rebatizar, (*P*) rebaptizar

render /ˈrendə(r)/ *vt* retribuir; (*services*) prestar; (*mus*) interpretar; (*translate*) traduzir. ~**ing** *n* (*mus*) interpretação *f*; (*plaster*) reboco *m*

renegade /ˈrenɪgeɪd/ *n* renegado *m*

renew /rɪˈnju:/ *vt* renovar; (*resume*) retomar. ~**able** *a* renovável. ~**al** *n* renovação *f*; (*resumption*) reatamento *m*

renounce /rɪˈnaʊns/ *vt* renunciar a; (*disown*) renegar, repudiar

renovat|e /ˈrenəveɪt/ *vt* renovar. ~**ion** /-ˈveɪʃn/ *n* renovação *f*

renown /rɪˈnaʊn/ *n* renome *m*. ~**ed** *a* conceituado, célebre, de renome

rent /rent/ *n* aluguel *m*, (*P*) aluguer *m*, renda *f* □ *vt* alugar, arrendar. ~**al** *n* (*charge*) aluguel *m*, (*P*) aluguer *m*, renda *f*; (*act of renting*) aluguel *m*, (*P*) aluguer *m*

renunciation /rɪnʌnsɪˈeɪʃn/ *n* renúncia *f*

reopen /ri:ˈəʊpən/ *vt/i* reabrir(-se). ~**ing** *n* reabertura *f*

reorganize /ri:ˈɔ:gənaɪz/ *vt/i* reorganizar(-se)

rep /rep/ *n* (*colloq*) vendedor *m*, caixeiro-viajante *m*

repair /rɪˈpeə(r)/ *vt* reparar, consertar □ *n* reparo *m*, conserto *m*. **in good** ~ em bom estado (de conservação)

repartee /repa:ˈti:/ *n* resposta *f* pronta e espirituosa

repatriat|e /ri:ˈpætrɪeɪt/ *vt* repatriar. ~**ion** /ˈeɪʃn/ *n* repatriamento *m*

repay /ri:ˈpeɪ/ *vt* (*pt* **repaid**) pagar, devolver, reembolsar; (*reward*) recompensar. ~**ment** *n* pagamento *m*, reembolso *m*

repeal /rɪˈpi:l/ *vt* revogar □ *n* revogação *f*

repeat /rɪˈpi:t/ *vt/i* repetir(-se) □ *n* repetição *f*; (*broadcast*) retransmissão *f*. ~**edly** *adv* repetidas vezes, repetidamente

repel /rɪˈpel/ *vt* (*pt* **repelled**) repelir. ~**lent** *a* & *n* repelente (*m*)

repent /rɪˈpent/ *vi* arrepender-se (of de). ~**ance** *n* arrependimento *m*. ~**ant** *a* arrependido

repercussion /ri:pəˈkʌʃn/ *n* repercussão *f*

repertoire /ˈrepətwa:(r)/ *n* repertório *m*

repertory /ˈrepətrɪ/ *n* repertório *m*

repetit|ion /repɪˈtɪʃn/ *n* repetição *f*. ~**ious** /-ˈtɪʃəs/, ~**ive** /rɪˈpetətɪv/ *a* repetitivo

replace /rɪˈpleɪs/ *vt* colocar no mesmo lugar, repor; (*take the place of*) substituir. ~**ment** *n* reposição *f*; (*substitution*) substituição *f*; (*person*) substituto *m*

replenish /rɪˈplenɪʃ/ *vt* voltar a encher, reabastecer; (*renew*) renovar

replica /ˈreplɪkə/ *n* réplica *f*, cópia *f*, reprodução *f*

reply /rɪˈplaɪ/ *vt/i* responder, replicar □ *n* resposta *f*, réplica *f*

report /rɪˈpɔ:t/ *vt* relatar; (*notify*) informar; (*denounce*) denunciar, apresentar queixa de □ *vi* fazer um relatório. ~ **(on)** (*news item*) fazer uma reportagem (sobre). ~ **to** (*go*) apresentar-se a □ *n* (*in newspapers*) reportagem *f*; (*of company, doctor*) relatório *m*; (*schol*) boletim *m* escolar; (*sound*) detonação *f*; (*rumour*) rumores *mpl*. ~**edly** *adv* segundo consta. ~**er** *n* repórter *m*

repose /rɪ'pəʊz/ *n* repouso *m*
repossess /ri:pə'zes/ *vt* reapossar-se de, retomar de
represent /reprɪ'zent/ *vt* representar. **~ation** /-'teɪʃn/ *n* representação *f*
representative /reprɪ'zentətɪv/ *a* representativo □ *n* representante *mf*
repress /rɪ'pres/ *vt* reprimir. **~ion** /-ʃn/ *n* repressão *f*. **~ive** *a* repressor, repressivo
reprieve /rɪ'pri:v/ *n* suspensão *f* temporária; (*temporary relief*) tréguas *fpl* □ *vt* suspender temporariamente; (*fig*) dar tréguas a
reprimand /'reprɪma:nd/ *vt* repreender □ *n* repreensão *f*, reprimenda *f*
reprint /'ri:prɪnt/ *n* reimpressão *f*, reedição *f* □ *vt* /ri:'prɪnt/
reprisals /rɪ'praɪzlz/ *npl* represálias *fpl*
reproach /rɪ'prəʊtʃ/ *vt* censurar, repreender (**sb for sth** alguém por alg coisa, alg coisa a alguém) □ *n* censura *f*. **above ~** irrepreensível. **~ful** *a* repreensivo, reprovador. **~fully** *adv* reprovadoramente
reproduc|e /ri:prə'dju:s/ *vt/i* reproduzir(-se). **~tion** /-'dʌkʃn/ *n* reprodução *f*. **~tive** /-'dʌktɪv/ *a* reprodutivo, reprodutor
reptile /'reptaɪl/ *n* réptil *m*
republic /rɪ'pʌblɪk/ *n* república *f*. **~an** *a* & *n* republicano (*m*)
repudiate /rɪ'pju:dɪeɪt/ *vt* repudiar, rejeitar
repugnan|t /rɪ'pʌgnənt/ *a* repugnante. **~ce** *n* repugnância *f*
repuls|e /rɪ'pʌls/ *vt* repelir, repulsar. **~ion** /-ʃn/ *n* repulsa *f*. **~ive** *a* repulsivo, repelente, repugnante
reputable /'repjʊtəbl/ *a* respeitado, honrado; (*firm, make etc*) de renome, conceituado
reputation /repjʊ'teɪʃn/ *n* reputação *f*
repute /rɪ'pju:t/ *n* reputação *f*. **~d** /-ɪd/ *a* suposto, putativo. **~d to be** tido como, tido na conta de. **~dly** /-ɪdlɪ/ *adv* segundo consta, com fama de
request /rɪ'kwest/ *n* pedido *m* □ *vt* pedir, solicitar (**of, from** a)
requiem /'rekwɪəm/ *n* réquiem *m*; (*mass*) missa *f* de réquiem
require /rɪ'kwaɪə(r)/ *vt* requerer. **~d** *a* requerido; (*needed*) necessário, preciso. **~ment** *n* (*fig*) requisito *m*; (*need*) necessidade *f*; (*demand*) exigência *f*
requisite /'rekwɪzɪt/ *a* necessário □ *n* coisa necessária *f*, requisito *m*. **~s** (*for travel etc*) artigos *mpl*
requisition /rekwɪ'zɪʃn/ *n* requisição *f* □ *vt* requisitar
resale /'ri:seɪl/ *n* revenda *f*
rescue /'reskju:/ *vt* salvar, socorrer (**from** de) □ *n* salvamento *m*; (*help*) socorro *m*, ajuda *f*. **~r** /-ə(r)/ *n* salvador *m*
research /rɪ'sɜ:tʃ/ *n* pesquisa *f*, investigação *f* □ *vt/i* pesquisar, fazer investigação (**into** sobre). **~er** *n* investigador *m*
resembl|e /rɪ'zembl/ *vt* assemelhar-se a, parecer-se com. **~ance** *n* semelhança *f*, similaridade *f* (**to** com)
resent /rɪ'zent/ *vt* ressentir(-se de), ficar ressentido com. **~ful** *a* ressentido. **~ment** *n* ressentimento *m*
reservation /rezə'veɪʃn/ *n* (*booking*) reserva *f*; (*Amer*) reserva *f* (de índios)
reserve /rɪ'zɜ:v/ *vt* reservar □ *n* reserva *f*; (*sport*) suplente *mf*. **in ~** de reserva. **~d** *a* reservado
reservoir /'rezəvwa:(r)/ *n* (*lake, supply etc*) reservatório *m*; (*container*) depósito *m*
reshape /ri:'ʃeɪp/ *vt* remodelar
reshuffle /ri:'ʃʌfl/ *vt* (*pol*) remodelar □ *n* (*pol*) reforma *f* (do Ministério)
reside /rɪ'zaɪd/ *vi* residir
residen|t /'rezɪdənt/ *a* residente □ *n* morador *m*, habitante *mf*; (*foreigner*) residente *mf*; (*in hotel*) hóspede *mf*. **~ce** *n* residência *f*; (*of students*) residência *f*, lar *m*. **~ce permit** visto *m* de residência
residential /rezɪ'denʃl/ *a* residencial
residue /'rezɪdju:/ *n* resíduo *m*
resign /rɪ'zaɪn/ *vt* (*post*) demitir-se. **~ o.s. to** resignar-se a □ *vi* demitir-se de. **~ation** /rezɪg'neɪʃn/ *n* resignação *f*; (*from job*) demissão *f*. **~ed** *a* resignado
resilien|t /rɪ'zɪlɪənt/ *a* (*springy*) elástico; (*person*) resistente. **~ce** *n* elasticidade *f*; (*of person*) resistência *f*
resin /'rezɪn/ *n* resina *f*
resist /rɪ'zɪst/ *vt/i* resistir (a). **~ance** *n* resistência *f*. **~ant** *a* resistente
resolut|e /'rezəlu:t/ *a* resoluto. **~ion** /-'lu:ʃn/ *n* resolução *f*
resolve /rɪ'zɒlv/ *vt* resolver. **~ to do** resolver fazer □ *n* resolução *f*. **~d** *a* (*resolute*) resoluto; (*decided*) resolvido (**to** a)
resonan|t /'rezənənt/ *a* ressonante. **~ce** *n* ressonância *f*
resort /rɪ'zɔ:t/ *vi* **~ to** recorrer a, valer-se de □ *n* recurso *m*; (*place*) estância *f*, local *m* turístico. **as a last ~** em último recurso. **seaside ~** praia *f*, balneário *m*, (*P*) estância *f* balnear
resound /rɪ'zaʊnd/ *vi* reboar, ressoar (**with** com). **~ing** *a* ressoante; (*fig*) retumbante
resource /rɪ'sɔ:s/ *n* recurso *m*. **~s** recursos *mpl*, riquezas *fpl*. **~ful** *a*

expedito, engenhoso, desembaraçado. ~fulness *n* expediente *m*, engenho *m*

respect /rɪ'spekt/ *n* respeito *m* □ *vt* respeitar. with ~ to a respeito de, com respeito a, relativamente a. ~ful *a* respeitoso

respectab|le /rɪ'spektəbl/ *a* respeitável; (*passable*) passável, aceitável. ~ility /-'bɪlətɪ/ *n* res-peitabilidade *f*

respective /rɪ'spektɪv/ *a* respectivo. ~ly *adv* respectivamente

respiration /respə'reɪʃn/ *n* respiração *f*

respite /'respaɪt/ *n* pausa *f*, trégua *f*, folga *f*

respond /rɪ'spɒnd/ *vi* responder (to a); (*react*) reagir (to a)

response /rɪ'spɒns/ *n* resposta *f*; (*reaction*) reação *f*, (*P*) reacção *f*

responsib|le /rɪ'spɒnsəbl/ *a* responsável; (*job*) de responsabilidade. ~ility /-'bɪlətɪ/ *n* responsabilidade *f*

responsive /rɪ'spɒnsɪv/ *a* receptivo, que reage bem. ~ to sensível a

rest[1] /rest/ *vt/i* descansar, repousar; (*lean*) apoiar(-se) □ *n* descanso *m*, repouso *m*; (*support*) suporte *m*. ~-room *n* (*Amer*) banheiro *m*, (*P*) toaletes *mpl*

rest[2] /rest/ *vi* (*remain*) ficar □ *n* (*remainder*) resto *m* (of de). the ~ (of the) (*others*) os outros. it ~s with him cabe a ele

restaurant /'restrɒnt/ *n* restaurante *m*

restful /'restfl/ *a* sossegado, repousante, tranqüilo, (*P*) tranquilo

restitution /restɪ'tju:ʃn/ *n* restituição *f*; (*for injury*) indenização *f*, (*P*) indemnização *f*

restless /'restlɪs/ *a* agitado, desassossegado

restor|e /rɪ'stɔ:(r)/ *vt* restaurar; (*give back*) restituir, devolver. ~ation /restə'reɪʃn/ *n* restauração *f*

restrain /rɪ'streɪn/ *vt* conter, reprimir. ~ o.s. controlar-se. ~ sb from impedir alguém de. ~ed *a* comedido, reservado. ~t *n* controle *m*; (*moderation*) moderação *f*, comedimento *m*

restrict /rɪ'strɪkt/ *vt* restringir, limitar. ~ion /-ʃn/ *n* restrição *f*. ~ive *a* restritivo

result /rɪ'zʌlt/ *n* resultado *m* □ *vi* resultar (from de). ~ in resultar em

resum|e /rɪ'zju:m/ *vt/i* reatar, retomar; (*work, travel*) recomeçar. ~ption /rɪ'zʌmpʃn/ *n* reatamento *m*, retomada *f*; (*of work*) recomeço *m*

résumé /'rezju:meɪ/ *n* resumo *m*

resurgence /rɪ'sɜ:dʒəns/ *n* reaparecimento *m*, ressurgimento *m*

resurrect /rezə'rekt/ *vt* ressuscitar. ~ion /-ʃn/ *n* ressureição *f*

resuscitat|e /rɪ'sʌsɪteɪt/ *vt* ressuscitar, reanimar. ~ion /-'teɪʃn/ *n* reanimação *f*

retail /'ri:teɪl/ *n* retalho *m* □ *a* & *adv* a retalho □ *vt/i* vender(-se) a retalho. ~er *n* retalhista *mf*

retain /rɪ'teɪn/ *vt* reter; (*keep*) conservar, guardar

retaliat|e /rɪ'tælɪeɪt/ *vi* retaliar, exercer represálias, desforrar-se. ~ion /-'eɪʃn/ *n* retaliação *f*, represália *f*, desforra *f*

retarded /rɪ'ta:dɪd/ *a* retardado, atrasado

retch /retʃ/ *vi* fazer esforço para vomitar, estar com ânsias de vômito

retention /rɪ'tenʃn/ *n* retenção *f*

retentive /rɪ'tentɪv/ *a* retentivo. ~ memory boa memória *f*

reticen|t /'retɪsnt/ *a* reticente. ~ce *n* reticência *f*

retina /'retɪnə/ *n* retina *f*

retinue /'retɪnju:/ *n* séquito *m*, comitiva *f*

retire /rɪ'taɪə(r)/ *vi* reformar-se, aposentar-se; (*withdraw*) retirar-se; (*go to bed*) ir deitar-se □ *vt* reformar, aposentar. ~d *a* reformado, aposentado. ~ment *n* reforma *f*, aposentadoria *f*, (*P*) aposentação *f*

retiring /rɪ'taɪərɪŋ/ *a* reservado, retraído

retort /rɪ'tɔ:t/ *vt/i* retrucar, retorquir □ *n* réplica *f*

retrace /ri:'treɪs/ *vt* ~ one's steps refazer o mesmo caminho; (*fig*) recordar, recapitular

retract /rɪ'trækt/ *vt/i* retratar(-se); (*wheels*) recolher; (*claws*) encolher, recolher

retreat /rɪ'tri:t/ *vi* retirar-se; (*mil*) retirar, bater em retirada □ *n* retirada *f*; (*seclusion*) retiro *m*

retrial /ri:'traɪəl/ *n* novo julgamento *m*

retribution /retrɪ'bju:ʃn/ *n* castigo (merecido) *m*; (*vengeance*) vingança *f*

retriev|e /rɪ'tri:v/ *vt* ir buscar; (*rescue*) salvar; (*recover*) recuperar; (*put right*) reparar. ~al *n* recuperação *f*. information ~al (*comput*) acesso *m* à informação. ~er *n* (*dog*) perdigueiro *m*, (*P*) cobrador *m*

retrograde /'retrəgreɪd/ *a* retrógrado □ *vt* retroceder, recuar

retrospect /'retrəspekt/ *n* in ~ em retrospecto, (*P*) retrospectivamente. ~ive /-'spektɪv/ *a* retrospectivo; (*of law, payment*) retroativo, (*P*) retroactivo

return /rɪ'tɜ:n/ *vi* voltar, regressar, retornar (to, a) □ *vt* devolver; (*compli-*

ment, visit) retribuir; (*put back*) pôr de volta □ *n* volta *f*, regresso *m*, retorno *m*; (*profit*) lucro *m*, rendimento *m*; (*restitution*) devolução *f*. in ~ for em troca de. ~ journey viagem *f* de volta. ~ match (*sport*) desafio *m* de desforra. ~ ticket bilhete *m* de ida e volta. many happy ~s (of the day) muitos parabéns

reunion /ri:'ju:nɪən/ *n* reunião *f*

reunite /ri:ju:'naɪt/ *vt* reunir

rev /rev/ *n* (*colloq: auto*) rotação *f* □ *vt/i* (*pt* revved) ~ (up) (*colloq: auto*) acelerar (o motor)

reveal /rɪ'vi:l/ *vt* revelar; (*display*) expor. ~ing *a* revelador

revel /'revl/ *vi* (*pt* revelled) divertir-se. ~ in deleitar-se com. ~ry *n* festas *fpl*, festejos *mpl*

revelation /revə'leɪʃn/ *n* revelação *f*

revenge /rɪ'vendʒ/ *n* vingança *f*; (*sport*) desforra *f* □ *vt* vingar

revenue /'revənju:/ *n* receita *f*, rendimento *m*. Inland R~ Fisco *m*

reverberate /rɪ'vɜ:bəreɪt/ *vi* ecoar, repercutir

revere /rɪ'vɪə(r)/ *vt* reverenciar, venerar

reverend /'revərənd/ *a* reverendo. R~ Reverendo

reveren|t /'revərənt/ *a* reverente. ~ce *n* reverência *f*, veneração *f*

revers|e /rɪ'vɜ:s/ *a* contrário, inverso □ *n* contrário *m*; (*back*) reverso *m*; (*gear*) marcha *f* à ré, (*P*) atrás □ *vt* virar ao contrário; (*order*) inverter; (*turn inside out*) virar do avesso; (*decision*) anular □ *vi* (*auto*) fazer marcha à ré, (*P*) atrás. ~al *n* inversão *f*, mudança *f* em sentido contrário; (*of view etc*) mudança *f*

revert /rɪ'vɜ:t/ *vi* ~ to reverter a

review /rɪ'vju:/ *n* (*inspection; magazine*) revista *f*; (*of a situation*) revisão *f*; (*critique*) crítica *f* □ *vt* revistar, passar revista em; (*situation*) rever; (*book, film etc*) fazer a crítica de. ~er *n* crítico *m*

revis|e /rɪ'vaɪz/ *vt* rever; (*amend*) corrigir. ~ion /-ɪʒn/ *n* revisão *f*; (*amendment*) correção *f*

reviv|e /rɪ'vaɪv/ *vt/i* ressuscitar, reavivar; (*play*) reapresentar; (*person*) reanimar(-se). ~al *n* reflorescimento *m*, renascimento *m*

revoke /rɪ'vəʊk/ *vt* revogar, anular, invalidar

revolt /rɪ'vəʊlt/ *vt/i* revoltar(-se) □ *n* revolta *f*

revolting /rɪ'vəʊltɪŋ/ *a* (*disgusting*) repugnante

revolution /revə'lu:ʃn/ *n* revolução *f*. ~ary *a* & *n* revolucionário (*m*). ~ize *vt* revolucionar

revolv|e /rɪ'vɒlv/ *vi* girar. ~ing door porta *f* giratória

revolver /rɪ'vɒlvə(r)/ *n* revólver *m*

revulsion /rɪ'vʌlʃn/ *n* repugnância *f*, repulsa *f*

reward /rɪ'wɔ:d/ *n* prêmio *m*, (*P*) prémio *m*; (*for criminal, for lost/stolen property*) recompensa *f* □ *vt* recompensar. ~ing *a* compensador; (*task etc*) gratificante

rewind /ri:'waɪnd/ *vt* (*pt* rewound) rebobinar

rewrite /ri:'raɪt/ *vt* (*pt* rewrote, *pp* rewritten) reescrever

rhetoric /'retərɪk/ *n* retórica *f*. ~al /rɪ'tɒrɪkl/ *a* retórico; (*question*) pro forma

rheumati|c /ru:'mætɪk/ *a* reumático. ~sm /'ru:mətɪzm/ *n* reumatismo *m*

rhinoceros /raɪ'nɒsərəs/ *n* (*pl* -oses) rinoceronte *m*

rhubarb /'ru:ba:b/ *n* ruibarbo *m*

rhyme /raɪm/ *n* rima *f*; (*poem*) versos *mpl* □ *vt/i* (fazer) rimar

rhythm /'rɪðəm/ *n* ritmo *m*. ~ic(al) /'rɪðmɪk(l)/ *a* rítmico, compassado

rib /rɪb/ *n* costela *f*

ribbon /'rɪbən/ *n* fita *f*. in ~s em tiras

rice /raɪs/ *n* arroz *m*

rich /rɪtʃ/ *a* (-er, -est) rico; (*food*) rico em açucar e gordura. ~es *npl* riquezas *fpl*. ~ly *adv* ricamente. ~ness *n* riqueza *f*

rickety /'rɪkətɪ/ *a* (*shaky*) desconjuntado

ricochet /'rɪkəʃeɪ/ *n* ricochete *m* □ *vi* (*pt* ricocheted /-ʃeɪd/) fazer ricochete, ricochetear

rid /rɪd/ *vt* (*pt* rid, *pres p* ridding) desembaraçar (of de). get ~ of desembaraçar-se de, livrar-se de

riddance /'rɪdns/ *n* good ~! que alívio!, vai com Deus!

ridden /'rɪdn/ *see* ride

riddle[1] /'rɪdl/ *n* enigma *m*; (*puzzle*) charada *f*

riddle[2] /'rɪdl/ *vt* ~ with crivar de

ride /raɪd/ *vi* (*pt* rode, *pp* ridden) andar (de bicicleta, a cavalo, de carro) □ *vt* (*horse*) montar; (*bicycle*) andar de; (*distance*) percorrer □ *n* passeio *m or* volta *f* (de carro, a cavalo etc); (*distance*) percurso *m*. ~r /-ə(r)/ *n* cavaleiro *m*, amazona *f*; (*cyclist*) ciclista *mf*; (*in document*) aditamento *m*

ridge /rɪdʒ/ *n* aresta *f*; (*of hill*) cume *m*

ridicule /'rɪdɪkju:l/ *n* ridículo *m* □ *vt* ridicularizar

ridiculous /rɪ'dɪkjʊləs/ *a* ridículo

riding /'raɪdɪŋ/ *n* equitação *f*

rife /raɪf/ *a* be ~ estar espalhado; (*of illness*) grassar. ~ with cheio de

riff-raff /'rɪfræf/ *n* gentinha *f*, povinho *m*, ralé *f*
rifle /'raɪfl/ *n* espingarda *f* □ *vt* revistar e roubar, saquear
rift /rɪft/ *n* fenda *f*, brecha *f*; (*fig: dissension*) desacordo *m*, desavença *f*, desentendimento *m*
rig[1] /rɪg/ *vt* (*pt* **rigged**) equipar □ *n* (*for oil*) plataforma *f* de poço de petróleo. ~ **out** enfarpelar (*colloq*). ~**-out** *n* (*colloq*) roupa *f*, farpela *f* (*colloq*). ~ **up** arranjar
rig[2] /rɪg/ *vt* (*pt* **rigged**) (*pej*) manipular. ~**ged** *a* (*election*) fraudulento
right /raɪt/ *a* (*correct, moral*) certo, correto, (*P*) correcto; (*fair*) justo; (*not left*) direito; (*suitable*) certo, próprio □ *n* (*entitlement*) direito *m*; (*not left*) direita *f*; (*not evil*) o bem □ *vt* (*a wrong*) reparar; (*sth fallen*) endireitar □ *adv* (*not left*) à direita; (*directly*) direito; (*exactly*) mesmo, bem; (*completely*) completamente. **be** ~ (*person*) ter razão (to em). **be in the** ~ ter razão. **on the** ~ à direita. **put** ~ acertar, corrigir. ~ **of way** (*auto*) prioridade *f*. ~ **angle** *n* ângulo reto *m*, (*P*) recto. ~ **away** logo, imediatamente. ~**-hand** *a* à *or* de direita. ~**-handed** *a* (*person*) destro. ~**-wing** *a* (*pol*) de direita
righteous /'raɪtʃəs/ *a* justo, virtuoso
rightful /'raɪtfl/ *a* legítimo. ~**ly** *adv* legitimamente, legalmente
rightly /'raɪtlɪ/ *adv* devidamente, corretamente, (*P*) correctamente; (*with reason*) justificadamente
rigid /'rɪdʒɪd/ *a* rígido. ~**ity** /rɪ'dʒɪdətɪ/ *n* rigidez *f*
rigmarole /'rɪgmərəʊl/ *n* (*speech: procedure*) embrulhada *f*
rig|our /'rɪgə(r)/ *n* rigor *m*. ~**orous** *a* rigoroso
rile /raɪl/ *vt* (*colloq*) irritar, exasperar
rim /rɪm/ *n* borda *f*; (*of wheel*) aro *m*
rind /raɪnd/ *n* (*on cheese, fruit*) casca *f*; (*on bacon*) pele *f*
ring[1] /rɪŋ/ *n* (*on finger*) anel *m*; (*for napkin, key etc*) argola *f*; (*circle*) roda *f*, círculo *m*; (*boxing*) ringue *m*; (*arena*) arena *f*; (*of people*) quadrilha *f* □ *vt* rodear, cercar. ~ **road** *n* estrada *f* periférica *or* perimetral
ring[2] /rɪŋ/ *vt/i* (*pt* **rang**, *pp* **rung**) tocar; (*of words etc*) soar □ *n* toque *m*; (*colloq: phone call*) telefonadela *f* (*colloq*). ~ **the bell** tocar a campaínha. ~ **back** telefonar de volta. ~ **off** desligar. ~ **up** telefonar (a)
ringleader /'rɪŋli:də(r)/ *n* cabeça *m*, cérebro *m*
rink /rɪŋk/ *n* rinque *m* de patinação
rinse /rɪns/ *vt* passar uma água, enxaguar □ *n* enxaguadura *f*, (*P*) enxuagadela *f*; (*hair tint*) rinsagem *f*
riot /'raɪət/ *n* distúrbio *m*, motim *m*; (*of colours*) festival *m* □ *vi* fazer distúrbios *or* motins. **run** ~ desenfrear-se, descontrolar-se; (*of plants*) crescer em matagal. ~**er** *n* desordeiro *m*
riotous /'raɪətəs/ *a* desenfreado, turbulento, desordeiro
rip /rɪp/ *vt/i* (*pt* **ripped**) rasgar(-se) □ *n* rasgão *m*. ~ **off** (*sl: defraud*) defraudar, enrolar (*sl*). ~**-off** *n* (*sl*) roubalheira *f* (*colloq*)
ripe /raɪp/ *a* (-er, -est) maduro. ~**ness** *n* madureza *f*, (*P*) amadurecimento *m*
ripen /'raɪpən/ *vt/i* amadurecer
ripple /'rɪpl/ *n* ondulação *f* leve; (*sound*) murmúrio *m* □ *vt/i* encrespar(-se), agitar(-se), ondular
rise /raɪz/ *vi* (*pt* **rose**, *pp* **risen**) subir, elevar-se; (*stand up*) erguer-se, levantar-se; (*rebel*) sublevar-se; (*sun*) nascer; (*curtain, prices*) subir □ *n* (*increase*) aumento *m*; (*slope*) subida *f*, ladeira *f*; (*origin*) origem *f*. **give** ~ **to** originar, causar, dar origem a. ~**r** /-ə(r)/ *n* **early** ~**r** madrugador *m*
rising /'raɪzɪŋ/ *n* (*revolt*) insurreição *f* □ *a* (*sun*) nascente
risk /rɪsk/ *n* risco *m* □ *vt* arriscar. **at** ~ em risco, em perigo. **at one's own** ~ por sua conta e risco. ~ **doing** (*venture*) arriscar-se a fazer. ~**y** *a* arriscado
risqué /'ri:skeɪ/ *a* picante
rite /raɪt/ *n* rito *m*. **last** ~**s** últimos sacramentos *mpl*
ritual /'rɪtʃʊəl/ *a* & *n* ritual (*m*)
rival /'raɪvl/ *n* & *a* rival (*mf*); (*fig*) concorrente (*mf*), competidor (*m*) □ *vt* (*pt* **rivalled**) rivalizar com. ~**ry** *n* rivalidade *f*
river /'rɪvə(r)/ *n* rio *m* □ *a* fluvial
rivet /'rɪvɪt/ *n* rebite *m* □ *vt* (*pt* **riveted**) rebitar; (*fig*) prender, cravar. ~**ing** *a* fascinante
road /rəʊd/ *n* estrada *f*; (*in town*) rua *f*; (*small; fig*) caminho *m*. ~**-block** *n* barricada *f*. ~**-map** *n* mapa *m* das estradas. ~ **sign** *n* sinal *m*, placa *f* de sinalização. ~ **tax** imposto *m* de circulação. ~**-works** *npl* obras *fpl*
roadside /'rəʊdsaɪd/ *n* beira *f* da estrada
roadway /'reʊdweɪ/ *n* pista *f* de rolamento, (*P*) rodagem
roadworthy /'reʊdwɜ:ðɪ/ *a* em condições de ser utilizado na rua/estrada
roam /rəʊm/ *vi* errar, andar sem destino □ *vt* percorrer
roar /rɔ:(r)/ *n* berro *m*, rugido *m*; (*of thunder*) ribombo *m*, troar *m*; (*of sea,*

wind) bramido *m* □ *vt/i* berrar, rugir; (*of lion*) rugir; (*of thunder*) ribombar, troar; (*of sea, wind*) bramir. ~ with laughter rir às gargalhadas

roaring /'rɔ:rɪŋ/ *a* (*trade*) florescente; (*success*) enorme; (*fire*) com grandes chamas

roast /rəʊst/ *vt/i* assar □ *a* & *n* assado (*m*)

rob /rɒb/ *vt* (*pt* robbed) roubar (sb of sth alg coisa de alguém); (*bank*) assaltar; (*deprive*) privar (of de). ~ber *n* ladrão *m*. ~bery *n* roubo *m*; (*of bank*) assalto *m*

robe /rəʊb/ *n* veste *f* comprida e solta; (*dressing-gown*) robe *m*. ~s *npl* (*of judge etc*) toga *f*

robin /'rɒbɪn/ *n* papo-roxo *m*, (*P*) pintarroxo *m*

robot /'rəʊbɒt/ *n* robô *m*, (*P*) robot *m*, autômato *m*, (*P*) autómato *m*

robust /rəʊ'bʌst/ *a* robusto

rock[1] /rɒk/ *n* rocha *f*; (*boulder*) penhasco *m*, rochedo *m*; (*sweet*) pirulito *m*, (*P*) chupa-chupa *m* comprido. on the ~s (*colloq: of marriage*) em crise; (*colloq: of drinks*) com gelo. ~-bottom *n* ponto *m* mais baixo □ *a* (*of prices*) baixíssimo (*colloq*)

rock[2] /rɒk/ *vt/i* balouçar(-se); (*shake*) abanar, sacudir; (*child*) embalar □ *n* (*mus*) rock *m*. ~ing-chair *n* cadeira *f* de balanço, (*P*) cadeira *f* de balouço. ~ing-horse *n* cavalo *m* de balanço, (*P*) cavalo *m* de balouço

rocket /'rɒkɪt/ *n* foguete *m*

rocky /'rɒkɪ/ *a* (-ier, -iest) (*ground*) pedregoso; (*hill*) rochoso; (*colloq: unsteady*) instável; (*colloq: shaky*) tremido (*colloq*)

rod /rɒd/ *n* vara *f*, vareta *f*; (*mech*) haste *f*; (*for curtains*) bastão *m*, (*P*) varão *m*; (*for fishing*) vara (de pescar) *f*

rode /rəʊd/ *see* ride

rodent /'rəʊdnt/ *n* roedor *m*

rodeo /rəʊ'deɪəʊ/ *n* (*pl* -os) rode(i)o *m*

roe /rəʊ/ *n* ova(s) *f* (*pl*) de peixe

rogue /rəʊg/ *n* (*dishonest*) patife *m*, velhaco *m*; (*mischievous*) brincalhão *m*

role /rəʊl/ *n* papel *m*

roll /rəʊl/ *vt/i* (fazer) rolar; (*into ball or cylinder*) enrolar(-se) □ *n* rolo *m*; (*list*) rol *m*, lista *f*; (*bread*) pãozinho *m*; (*of ship*) balanço *m*; (*of drum*) rufar *m*; (*of thunder*) ribombo *m*. be ~ing in money (*colloq*) nadar em dinheiro (*colloq*). ~ over (*turn over*) virar-se ao contrário. ~ up *vi* (*colloq*) aparecer □ *vt* (*sleeves*) arregaçar; (*umbrella*) fechar. ~-call *n* chamada *f*. ~ing-pin *n* rolo *m* de pastel

roller /'rəʊlə(r)/ *n* cilindro *m*; (*wave*) vagalhão *m*; (*for hair*) rolo *m*. ~-blind *n* estore *m*. ~-coaster *n* montanha *f* russa. ~-skate *n* patim *m* de rodas

rolling /'rəʊlɪŋ/ *a* ondulante

Roman /'rəʊmən/ *a* & *n* romano (*m*). R~ Catholic *a* & *n* católico (*m*). ~ numerals algarismos *mpl* romanos

romance /rəʊ'mæns/ *n* (*love affair*) romance *m*; (*fig*) poesia *f*

Romania /rʊ'meɪnɪə/ *n* Romênia *f*, (*P*) Roménia *f*. ~n *a* & *n* romeno (*m*)

romantic /rəʊ'mæntɪk/ *a* romântico. ~ally *adv* romanticamente. ~ism *n* romantismo *m*. ~ize *vi* fazer romance □ *vt* romantizar

romp /rɒmp/ *vi* brincar animadamente □ *n* brincadeira *f* animada. ~ers *npl* macacão *m* de bebê, (*P*) fato *m* de bebé

roof /ru:f/ *n* (*pl* roofs) telhado *m*; (*of car*) teto *m*, (*P*) capota *f*; (*of mouth*) palato *m*, céu *m* da boca □ *vt* cobrir com telhado. hit the ~ (*colloq*) ficar furioso. ~ing *n* material *m* para telhados. ~-rack *n* porta-bagagem *m*. ~-top *n* cimo *m* do telhado

rook[1] /rʊk/ *n* (*bird*) gralha *f*

rook[2] /rʊk/ *n* (*chess*) torre *f*

room /rʊ:m/ *n* quarto *m*, divisão *f*; (*bedroom*) quarto *m* de dormir; (*large hall*) sala *f*; (*space*) espaço *m*, lugar *m*. ~s (*lodgings*) apartamento *m*, cômodos *mpl*. ~-mate *n* companheiro *m* de quarto. ~y *a* espaçoso; (*clothes*) amplo, largo

roost /ru:st/ *n* poleiro *m* □ *vi* empoleirar-se. ~er *n* (*Amer*) galo *m*

root[1] /ru:t/ *n* raiz *f*; (*fig*) origem *f* □ *vt/i* enraizar(-se), radicar(-se). ~ out extirpar, erradicar. take ~ criar raízes. ~less *a* sem raízes, desenraizado

root[2] /ru:t/ *vi* ~ about revolver, remexer. ~ for (*Amer sl*) torcer por

rope /rəʊp/ *n* corda *f* □ *vt* atar. know the ~s estar por dentro (do assunto). ~ in convencer a participar de

rosary /'rəʊzərɪ/ *n* rosário *m*

rose[1] /rəʊz/ *n* rosa *f*; (*nozzle*) ralo *m* (de regador). ~-bush *n* roseira *f*

rose[2] /rəʊz/ *see* rise

rosé /'rəʊzeɪ/ *n* rosé *m*

rosette /rəʊ'zet/ *n* roseta *f*

rosewood /'rəʊzwʊd/ *n* pau-rosa *m*

roster /'rɒstə(r)/ *n* lista (de serviço) *f*, escala *f* (de serviço)

rostrum /'rɒstrəm/ *n* tribuna *f*; (*for conductor*) estrado *m*; (*sport*) podium *m*

rosy /'rəʊzɪ/ *a* (-ier, -iest) rosado; (*fig*) risonho

rot /rɒt/ *vt/i* (*pt* rotted) apodrecer □ *n*

putrefação *f*, podridão *f*; (*sl*: *nonsense*) disparate *m*, asneiras *fpl*
rota /'rəʊtə/ *n* escala *f* de serviço
rotary /'rəʊtərɪ/ *a* rotativo, giratório
rotat|e /rəʊ'teɪt/ *vt/i* (fazer) girar, (fazer) revolver; (*change round*) alternar. **~ing** *a* rotativo. **~ion** /-ʃn/ *n* rotação *f*
rote /rəʊt/ *n* **by ~** de cor, maquinalmente
rotten /'rɒtn/ *a* podre; (*corrupt*) corrupto; (*colloq: bad*) mau, ruim. **~ eggs** ovos *mpl* podres. **feel ~** (*ill*) não se sentir nada bem
rotund /rəʊ'tʌnd/ *a* rotundo, redondo
rough /rʌf/ *a* (-er, -est) rude; (*to touch*) áspero, rugoso; (*of ground*) acidentado, irregular; (*violent*) violento; (*of sea*) agitado, encapelado; (*of weather*) tempestuoso; (*not perfect*) tosco, rudimentar; (*of estimate etc*) aproximado □ *n* (*ruffian*) rufia *m*, desordeiro *m* □ *adv* (*live*) ao relento; (*play*) bruto □ *vt* **~ it** viver de modo primitivo, não ter onde morar (*colloq*). **~ out** fazer um esboço preliminar de. **~-and-ready** *a* grosseiro mas eficiente. **~ paper** rascunho *m*, borrão *m*. **~ly** *adv* asperamente, rudemente; (*approximately*) aproximadamente. **~ness** *n* rudeza *f*, aspereza *f*; (*violence*) brutalidade *f*
roughage /'rʌfɪdʒ/ *n* alimentos *mpl* fibrosos
roulette /ru:'let/ *n* roleta *f*
round /raʊnd/ *a* (-er, -est) redondo □ *n* (*circle*) círculo *m*; (*slice*) fatia *f*; (*postman's*) entrega *f*; (*patrol*) ronda *f*; (*of drinks*) rodada *f*; (*competition*) partida *f*, rodada *f*; (*boxing*) round *m*; (*of talks*) ciclo *m*, série *f* □ *prep* & *adv* em volta (de), em torno (de) □ *vt* arredondar; (*cape, corner*) dobrar, virar. **come ~** (*into consciousness*) voltar a si. **go** *or* **come ~ to** (*a friend etc*) dar um pulo na casa de. **~ about** (*nearby*) por aí; (*fig*) mais ou menos. **~ of applause** salva *f* de palmas. **~ off** terminar. **~-shouldered** *a* curvado. **~ the clock** noite e dia sem parar. **~ trip** viagem *f* de ida e volta. **~ up** (*gather*) juntar; (*a figure*) arredondar. **~-up** *n* (*of cattle*) rodeio *m*; (*of suspects*) captura *f*
roundabout /'raʊndəbaʊt/ *n* carrossel *m*; (*for traffic*) rotatória *f*, (*P*) rotunda *f* □ *a* indireto, (*P*) indirecto
rous|e /raʊz/ *vt* acordar, despertar. **be ~ed** (*angry*) exaltar-se, inflamar-se, ser provocado. **~ing** *a* (*speech*) inflamado, exaltado; (*music*) vibrante; (*cheers*) frenético
rout /raʊt/ *n* derrota *f*; (*retreat*) debandada *f* □ *vt* derrotar; (*cause to retreat*) pôr em debandada
route /ru:t/ *n* percurso *m*, itinerário *m*; (*naut, aviat*) rota *f*
routine /ru:'ti:n/ *n* rotina *f*; (*theat*) número *m* □ *a* de rotina, rotineiro. **daily ~** rotina *f* diária
rov|e /rəʊv/ *vt/i* errar (por), vaguear (em/por). **~ing** *a* (*life*) errante
row[1] /rəʊ/ *n* fila *f*, fileira *f*; (*in knitting*) carreira *f*. **in a ~** (*consecutive*) em fila
row[2] /rəʊ/ *vt/i* remar. **~ing** *n* remo *m*. **~ing-boat** *n* barco *m* a remo
row[3] /raʊ/ *n* (*colloq: noise*) barulho *m*, bagunça *f*, banzé *m* (*colloq*); (*colloq: quarrel*) discussão *f*, briga *f*. **~ (with)** *vi* (*colloq*) brigar (com), discutir (com)
rowdy /'raʊdɪ/ *a* (-ier, -iest) desordeiro
royal /'rɔɪəl/ *a* real
royalty /'rɔɪəltɪ/ *n* família real *f*; (*payment*) direitos *mpl* (de autor, de patente, etc)
rub /rʌb/ *vt/i* (*pt* **rubbed**) esfregar; (*with ointment etc*) esfregar, friccionar □ *n* esfrega *f*; (*with ointment etc*) fricção *f*. **~ it in** repisar/insistir em. **~ off on** comunicar-se a, transmitir-se a. **~ out** (*with rubber*) apagar
rubber /'rʌbə(r)/ *n* borracha *f*. **~ band** elástico *m*. **~ stamp** carimbo *m*. **~-stamp** *vt* aprovar sem questionar. **~y** *a* semelhante à borracha
rubbish /'rʌbɪʃ/ *n* (*refuse*) lixo *m*; (*nonsense*) disparates *mpl*. **~ dump** *n* lixeira *f*. **~y** *a* sem valor
rubble /'rʌbl/ *n* entulho *m*
ruby /'ru:bɪ/ *n* rubi *m*
rucksack /'rʌksæk/ *n* mochila *f*
rudder /'rʌdə(r)/ *n* leme *m*
ruddy /'rʌdɪ/ *a* (-ier, -iest) avermelhado; (*of cheeks*) corado, vermelho; (*sl: damned*) maldito (*colloq*)
rude /ru:d/ *a* (-er, -est) mal-educado, malcriado, grosseiro. **~ly** *adv* grosseiramente, malcriadamente. **~ness** *n* má-educação *f*, má-criação *f*, grosseria *f*
rudiment /'ru:dɪmənt/ *n* rudimento *m*. **~ary** /-'mentrɪ/ *a* rudimentar
rueful /'ru:fl/ *a* contrito, pesaroso
ruffian /'rʌfɪən/ *n* desordeiro *m*
ruffle /'rʌfl/ *vt* (*feathers*) eriçar; (*hair*) despentear; (*clothes*) amarrotar; (*fig*) perturbar □ *n* (*frill*) franzido *m*, (*P*) folho *m*
rug /rʌg/ *n* tapete *m*; (*covering*) manta *f*
rugged /'rʌgɪd/ *a* rude, irregular; (*coast, landscape*) acidentado; (*character*) forte; (*features*) marcado

ruin /'ru:ɪn/ *n* ruína *f* □ *vt* arruinar; (*fig*) estragar. **~ous** *a* desastroso
rule /ru:l/ *n* regra *f*; (*regulation*) regulamento *m*; (*pol*) governo *m* □ *vt* governar; (*master*) dominar; (*jur*) decretar; (*decide*) decidir □ *vi* governar. **as a ~** regra geral, por via de regra. **~ out** excluir. **~d paper** papel *m* pautado. **~r** /-ə(r)/ *n* (*sovereign*) soberano *m*; (*leader*) governante *m*; (*measure*) régua *f*
ruling /'ru:lɪŋ/ *a* (*class*) dirigente; (*pol*) no poder □ *n* decisão *f*
rum /rʌm/ *n* rum *m*
rumble /'rʌmbl/ *vi* ribombar, ressoar; (*of stomach*) roncar □ *n* ribombo *m*, estrondo *m*
rummage /'rʌmɪdʒ/ *vt* revistar, remexer
rumour /'ru:mə(r)/ *n* boato *m*, rumor *m* □ *vt* **it is ~ed that** corre o boato de que, consta que
rump /rʌmp/ *n* (*of horse etc*) garupa *f*; (*of fowl*) mitra *f*. **~ steak** *n* bife *m* de alcatra
run /rʌn/ *vi* (*pt* ran, *pp* run, *pres p* running) correr; (*flow*) correr; (*pass*) passar; (*function*) andar, funcionar; (*melt*) derreter, pingar; (*bus etc*) circular; (*play*) estar em cartaz; (*colour*) desbotar; (*in election*) candidatar-se (for a) □ *vt* (*manage*) dirigir, gerir; (*a risk*) correr; (*a race*) participar em; (*water*) deixar correr; (*a car*) ter, manter □ *n* corrida *f*; (*excursion*) passeio *m*, ida *f*; (*rush*) corrida *f*, correria *f*; (*in cricket*) ponto *m*. **be on the ~** estar foragido. **have the ~ of** ter à sua disposição. **in the long ~** a longo prazo. **~ across** encontrar por acaso, dar com. **~ away** fugir. **~ down** descer correndo; (*of vehicle*) atropelar; (*belittle*) dizer mal de, denegrir. **be ~ down** estar exausto. **~ in** (*engine*) ligar. **~ into** (*meet*) encontrar por acaso; (*hit*) bater em, ir de encontro a. **~ off** *vt* (*copies*) tirar; (*water*) deixar correr □ *vi* fugir. **~-of-the-mill** *a* vulgar. **~ out** esgotar-se; (*lease*) expirar. **I ran out of sugar** o açúcar acabou. **~ over** (*of vehicle*) atropelar. **~ up** deixar acumular. **the ~-up to** o período que precede
runaway /'rʌnəweɪ/ *n* fugitivo *m* □ *a* fugitivo; (*horse*) desembestado; (*vehicle*) desarvorado; (*success*) grande
rung[1] /rʌŋ/ *n* (*of ladder*) degrace *m*
rung[2] /rʌŋ/ *see* ring[2]
runner /'rʌnə(r)/ *n* (*person*) corredor *m*; (*carpet*) passadeira *f*. **~ bean** feijão *m* verde. **~-up** *n* segundo classificado *m*
running /'rʌnɪŋ/ *n* corrida *f*; (*functioning*) funcionamento *m* □ *a* consecutivo, seguido; (*water*) corrente. **be in the ~** (*competitor*) ter probabilidades de êxito. **four days ~** quatro dias seguidos *or* a fio. **~ commentary** reportagem *f*, comentário *m*
runny /'rʌnɪ/ *a* derretido
runway /'rʌnweɪ/ *n* pista *f* de decolagem, (*P*) descolagem
rupture /'rʌptʃə(r)/ *n* ruptura *f*; (*med*) hérnia *f* □ *vt/i* romper(-se), rebentar
rural /'rʊərəl/ *a* rural
ruse /ru:z/ *n* ardil *m*, estratagema *m*, manha *f*
rush[1] /rʌʃ/ *n* (*plant*) junco *m*
rush[2] /rʌʃ/ *vi* (*move*) precipitar-se, (*be in a hurry*) apressar-se □ *vt* fazer, mandar *etc* a toda a pressa; (*person*) pressionar; (*mil*) tomar de assalto □ *n* tropel *m*; (*haste*) pressa *f*. **in a ~** às pressas. **~ hour** rush *m*, (*P*) hora *f* de ponta
rusk /rʌsk/ *n* bolacha *f*, biscoito *m*
russet /'rʌsɪt/ *a* castanho avermelhado □ *n* maçã *f* reineta
Russia /'rʌʃə/ *n* Rússia *f*. **~n** *a* & *n* russo (*m*)
rust /rʌst/ *n* (*on iron, plants*) ferrugem *f* □ *vt/i* enferrujar(-se). **~-proof** *a* inoxidável. **~y** *a* ferrugento, enferrujado; (*fig*) enferrujado
rustic /'rʌstɪk/ *a* rústico
rustle /'rʌsl/ *vt/i* restolhar, (fazer) farfalhar; (*Amer: steal*) roubar. **~ up** (*colloq: food etc*) arranjar
rut /rʌt/ *n* sulco *m*; (*fig*) rotina *f*. **in a ~** numa vida rotineira
ruthless /'ru:θlɪs/ *a* implacável
rye /raɪ/ *n* centeio *m*

S

sabbath /'sæbəθ/ *n* (*Jewish*) sábado *m*; (*Christian*) domingo *m*
sabbatical /sə'bætɪkl/ *n* (*univ*) período *m* de licença
sabot|age /'sæbəta:ʒ/ *n* sabotagem *f* □ *vt* sabotar. **~eur** /-'tɜ:(r)/ *n* sabotador *m*
sachet /'sæʃeɪ/ *n* saché *m*
sack /sæk/ *n* saco *m*, saca *f* □ *vt* (*colloq*) despedir. **get the ~** (*colloq*) ser despedido
sacrament /'sækrəmənt/ *n* sacramento *m*
sacred /'seɪkrɪd/ *a* sagrado
sacrifice /'sækrɪfaɪs/ *n* sacrifício *m*; (*fig*) sacrifício *m* □ *vt* sacrificar
sacrileg|e /'sækrɪlɪdʒ/ *n* sacrilégio *m*. **~ious** /-'lɪdʒəs/ *a* sacrílego
sad /sæd/ *a* (sadder, saddest) (*person*) triste; (*story, news*) triste. **~ly**

adv tristemente; (*unfortunately*) infelizmente. ~**ness** *n* tristeza *f*

sadden /'sædn/ *vt* entristecer

saddle /'sædl/ *n* sela *f* □ *vt* (*horse*) selar. ~ **sb with** sobrecarregar alguém com

sadis|m /'seɪdɪzəm/ *n* sadismo *m*. ~**t** /-ɪst/ *n* sádico *m*. ~**tic** /sə'dɪstɪk/ *a* sádico

safe /seɪf/ *a* (-er, -est) (*not dangerous*) seguro; (*out of danger*) fora de perigo; (*reliable*) confiável. ~ **from** salvo de risco de □ *n* cofre *m*, caixa-forte *f*. ~ **and sound** são e salvo. ~ **conduct** salvo-conduto *m*. ~ **keeping** custódia *f*, proteção *f*. **to be on the** ~ **side** por via das dúvidas. ~**ly** *adv* (*arrive etc*) em segurança; (*keep*) seguro

safeguard /'seɪfga:d/ *n* salvaguarda *f* □ *vt* salvaguardar

safety /'seɪftɪ/ *n* segurança *f*. ~**-belt** *n* cinto *m* de segurança. ~**-pin** *n* alfinete *m* de fralda. ~**-valve** *n* válvula *f* de segurança

sag /sæg/ *vi* (*pt* **sagged**) afrouxar

saga /'sa:gə/ *n* saga *f*

sage[1] /seɪdʒ/ *n* (*herb*) salva *f*

sage[2] /seɪdʒ/ *a* sensato, prudente □ *n* sábio *m*

Sagittarius /sædʒɪ'teərɪəs/ *n* (*astrol*) Sagitário *m*

said /sed/ *see* **say**

sail /seɪl/ *n* vela *f*; (*trip*) viagem *f* em barco à vela □ *vi* navegar; (*leave*) partir; (*sport*) velejar □ *vt* navegar. ~**ing** *n* navegação *f* à vela. ~**ing-boat** *n* barco *m* à vela

sailor /'seɪlə(r)/ *n* marinheiro *m*

saint /seɪnt/ *n* santo *m*. ~**ly** *a* santo, santificado

sake /seɪk/ *n* **for the** ~ **of** em consideração a. **for my/your/its own** ~ por mim/por isso

salad /'sæləd/ *n* salada *f*. ~ **dressing** *n* molho *m* para salada

salary /'sælərɪ/ *n* salário *m*

sale /seɪl/ *n* venda *f*; (*at reduced prices*) liquidação *f*. **for** ~ "vende-se". **on** ~ à venda. ~**s assistant**, (*Amer*) ~**s clerk** vendedor *m*. ~**s department** departamento *m* de vendas

sales|man /'seɪlzmən/ *n* (*pl* **-men**) (*in shop*) vendedor *m*; (*traveller*) caixeiro-viajante *m*. ~**woman** *n* (*pl* **-women**) (*in shop*) vendedora *f*; (*traveller*) caixeira-viajante *f*

saline /'seɪlaɪn/ *a* salino □ *n* salina *f*

saliva /sə'laɪvə/ *n* saliva *f*

sallow /'sæləʊ/ *a* (-er, -est) amarelado

salmon /'sæmən/ *n* (*pl invar*) salmão *m*

saloon /sə'lu:n/ *n* (*on ship*) salão *m*; (*bar*) botequim *m*. ~ **(car)** sedã *m*

salt /sɔ:lt/ *n* sal *m* □ *a* salgado □ *vt* (*season*) salgar; (*cure*) pôr em salmoura. ~**-cellar** *n* saleiro *m*. ~ **water** água *f* salgada, água *f* do mar. ~**y** *a* salgado

salutary /'sæljʊtrɪ/ *a* salutar

salute /sə'lu:t/ *n* saudação *f* □ *vt/i* saudar

salvage /'sælvɪdʒ/ *n* (*naut*) salvamento *m*; (*of waste*) reciclagem *f* □ *vt* salvar

salvation /sæl'veɪʃn/ *n* salvação *f*

same /seɪm/ *a* mesmo (as que) □ *pron* **the** ~ o mesmo □ *adv* **the** ~ o mesmo. **all the** ~ (*nevertheless*) mesmo assim, apesar de tudo. **at the** ~ **time** (*at once*) ao mesmo tempo

sample /'sa:mpl/ *n* amostra *f* □ *vt* experimentar, provar

sanatorium /sænə'tɔ:rɪəm/ *n* (*pl* -iums) sanatório *m*

sanctify /'sæŋktɪfaɪ/ *vt* santificar

sanctimonious /sæŋktɪ'məʊnɪəs/ *a* santarrão, carola

sanction /'sæŋkʃn/ *n* (*approval*) aprovação *f*; (*penalty*) pena *f*, sanção *f* □ *vt* sancionar

sanctity /'sæŋktɪtɪ/ *n* santidade *f*

sanctuary /'sæŋktʃʊərɪ/ *n* (*relig*) santuário *m*; (*refuge*) refúgio *m*; (*for animals*) reserva *f*

sand /sænd/ *n* areia *f*; (*beach*) praia *f* □ *vt* (*with sandpaper*) lixar

sandal /'sændl/ *n* sandália *f*

sandbag /'sændbæg/ *n* saco *m* de areia

sandbank /'sændbæŋk/ *n* banco *m* de areia

sandcastle /'sændka:sl/ *n* castelo *m* de areia

sandpaper /'sændpeɪpə(r)/ *n* lixa *f* □ *vt* lixar

sandpit /'sændpɪt/ *n* caixa *f* de areia

sandwich /'sænwɪdʒ/ *n* sanduíche *m*, (*P*) sandes *f invar* □ *vt* ~**ed between** encaixado entre. ~ **course** curso *m* profissionalizante envolvendo estudo teórico e estágio em local de trabalho

sandy /'sændɪ/ *a* (-ier, iest) arenoso; (*beach*) arenoso; (*hair*) ruivo

sane /seɪn/ *a* (-er, -est) (*not mad*) são *m*; (*sensible*) sensato, ajuizado

sang /sæŋ/ *see* **sing**

sanitary /'sænɪtrɪ/ *a* sanitário; (*system*) sanitário. ~ **towel**, (*Amer*) ~ **napkin** toalha *f* absorvente

sanitation /sænɪ'teɪʃn/ *n* condições *fpl* sanitárias, saneamento *m*

sanity /'sænɪtɪ/ *n* sanidade *f*

sank /sæŋk/ *see* **sink**

Santa Claus /'sæntəklɔ:z/ *n* Papai Noel *m*

sap /sæp/ *n* seiva *f* □ *vt* (*pt* **sapped**) esgotar, minar

sapphire /ˈsæfaɪə(r)/ *n* safira *f*
sarcas|m /ˈsaːrkæzəm/ *n* sarcasmo *m*. ~**tic** /saːrˈkæstɪk/ *a* sarcástico
sardine /saːˈdiːn/ *n* sardinha *f*
sardonic /saːˈdɒnɪk/ *a* sardônico
sash /sæʃ/ *n* (*around waist*) cinto *m*; (*over shoulder*) faixa *f*. ~**window** *n* janela *f* de guilhotina
sat /sæt/ *see* sit
satanic /səˈtænɪk/ *a* satânico
satchel /ˈsætʃl/ *n* sacola *f*
satellite /ˈsætəlaɪt/ *n* satélite *m*. ~ **dish** antena *f* de satélite. ~ **television** televisão *f* via satélite
satin /ˈsætɪn/ *n* cetim *m*
satir|e /ˈsætaɪə(r)/ *n* sátira *f*. ~**ical** /səˈtɪrɪkl/ *a* satirical. ~**ist** /ˈsætərɪst/ *n* satirista *mf*. ~**ize** *vt* satirizar
satisfact|ion /sætɪsˈfækʃn/ *n* satisfação *f*. ~**ory** /fæktərɪ/ *a* satisfatório
satisfy /ˈsætɪsfaɪ/ *vt* satisfazer; (*convince*) convencer; (*fulfil*) atender. ~**ing** *a* satisfatório
saturat|e /ˈsætʃəreɪt/ *vt* saturar; (*fig*) ~**ed** *a* (*wet*) encharcado; (*fat*) saturado. ~**ion** /ˈreɪʃn/ *n* saturação *f*
Saturday /ˈsætədɪ/ *n* sábado *m*
sauce /sɔːs/ *n* molho *m*; (*colloq: cheek*) atrevimento *m*
saucepan /ˈsɔːspən/ *n* panela *f*, (*P*) caçarola *f*
saucer /ˈsɔːsə(r)/ *n* pires *m invar*
saucy /ˈsɔːsɪ/ *a* (-ier, -iest) picante
Saudi Arabia /saʊdɪəˈreɪbɪə/ *n* Arábia *f* Saudita
sauna /ˈsɔːnə/ *n* sauna *f*
saunter /ˈsɔːntə(r)/ *vi* perambular
sausage /ˈsɒsɪdʒ/ *n* salsicha *f*, linguiça *f*; (*precooked*) salsicha *f*
savage /ˈsævɪdʒ/ *a* (*wild*) selvagem; (*fierce*) cruel; (*brutal*) brutal □ *n* selvagem *mf* □ *vt* atacar ferozmente. ~**ry** *n* selvageria *f*, ferocidade *f*
sav|e /seɪv/ *vt* (*rescue*) salvar; (*keep*) guardar; (*collect*) colecionar; (*money*) economizar; (*time*) ganhar; (*prevent*) evitar, impedir (from de) □ *n* (*sport*) salvamento *m* □ *prep* salvo, exceto. ~**er** *n* poupador *m*. ~**ing** *n* economia *f*, poupança *f*. ~**ings** *npl* economias *fpl*
saviour /ˈseɪvɪə(r)/ *n* salvador *m*
savour /ˈseɪvə(r)/ *n* sabor *m* □ *vt* saborear. ~**y** *a* (*tasty*) saboroso; (*not sweet*) salgado
saw[1] /sɔː/ *see* see[1]
saw[2] /sɔː/ *n* serra *f* □ *vt* (*pt* **sawed**, *pp* **sawn** *or* **sawed**) serrar
sawdust /ˈsɔːdʌst/ *n* serragem *f*
saxophone /ˈsæksəfəʊn/ *n* saxofone *m*
say /seɪ/ *vt/i* (*pt* **said** /sed/) □ *n* **have a** ~ (in) opinar sobre alg coisa. **have one's** ~ exprimir sua opinião. **I** ~! olhe! *or* escute! ~**ing** *n* ditado *m*, provérbio *m*
scab /skæb/ *n* casca *f*, crosta *f*; (*colloq: blackleg*) fura-greve *mf invar*
scaffold /ˈskæfəʊld/ *n* cadafalso *m*, andaime *m*. ~**ing** /-əldɪŋ/ *n* andaime *m*
scald /skɔːld/ *vt* escaldar, queimar □ *n* escaldadura *f*
scale[1] /skeɪl/ *n* (*of fish etc*) escama *f*
scale[2] /skeɪl/ *n* (*ratio, size*) escala *f*; (*mus*) escala *f*; (*of salaries, charges*) tabela *f*. **on a small/large/***etc* ~ numa pequena/grande/*etc* escala □ *vt* (*climb*) escalar. ~ **down** reduzir
scales /skeɪlz/ *npl* (*for weighing*) balança *f*
scallop /ˈskɒləp/ *n* (*culin*) concha *f* de vieira; (*shape*) concha *f* de vieira
scalp /skælp/ *n* couro *m* cabeludo □ *vt* escalpar
scalpel /ˈskælpl/ *n* bisturi *m*
scamper /ˈskæmpə(r)/ *vi* sair correndo
scampi /ˈskæmpɪ/ *npl* camarões *mpl* fritos
scan /skæn/ *vt* (*pt* **scanned**) (*intently*) perscrutar, esquadrinhar; (*quickly*) passar os olhos em; (*med*) examinar; (*radar*) explorar □ *n* (*med*) exame *m*
scandal /ˈskændl/ *n* (*disgrace*) escândalo *m*; (*gossip*) fofoca *f*. ~**ous** *a* escandaloso
Scandinavia /skændɪˈneɪvɪə/ *n* Escandinávia *f*. ~**n** *a* & *n* escandinavo (*m*)
scanty /ˈskæntɪ/ *a* (-ier, -iest) escasso; (*clothing*) sumário
scapegoat /ˈskeɪpgəʊt/ *n* bode *m* expiatório
scar /skaː(r)/ *n* cicatriz *f* □ *vt* (*pt* **scarred**) marcar; (*fig*) deixar marcas
scarc|e /skeəs/ *a* (-er, -est) escasso, raro. **make o.s.** ~**e** (*colloq*) sumir, dar o fora (*colloq*). ~**ity** *n* escassez *f*. ~**ely** *adv* mal, apenas
scare /skeə(r)/ *vt* assustar, apavorar. **be** ~**d** estar com medo (of de) □ *n* pavor *m*, pânico *m*. **bomb** ~ pânico *m* causado por suspeita de bomba num local
scarecrow /ˈskeəkrəʊ/ *n* espantalho *m*
scarf /skaːf/ *n* (*pl* **scarves**) (*oblong*) cachecol *m*; (*square*) lenço *m* de cabelo
scarlet /ˈskaːlət/ *a* escarlate *m*
scary /ˈskeərɪ/ *a* (-ier, -iest) (*colloq*) assustador, apavorante
scathing /ˈskeɪðɪŋ/ *a* mordaz
scatter /ˈskætə(r)/ *vt* (*strew*) espalhar; (*disperse*) dispersar □ *vi* espalhar-se
scavenge /ˈskævɪndʒ/ *vi* procurar

comida *etc* no lixo. ~r /-ə(r)/ *n* (*person*) que procura comida *etc* no lixo; (*animal*) que se alimenta de carniça
scenario /sɪ'nɑ:rɪəʊ/ *n* (*pl* -os) sinopse *f*, resumo *m* detalhado
scene /si:n/ *n* cena *f*; (*of event*) cenário *m*; (*sight*) vista *f*, panorama *m*. **behind the** ~s nos bastidores. **make a** ~ fazer um escândalo
scenery /'si:nərɪ/ *n* cenário *m*, paisagem *f*; (*theat*) cenário *m*
scenic /'si:nɪk/ *a* pitoresco, cênico
scent /sent/ *n* (*perfume*) perfume *m*, fragância *f*; (*trail*) rastro *m*, pista *f* □ *vt* (*discern*) sentir. ~**ed** *a* perfumado
sceptic /'skeptɪk/ *n* cético *m*. ~**al** *a* cético. ~**ism** /-sɪzəm/ *n* ceticismo *m*
schedule /'ʃedju:l/ *n* programa *m*; (*timetable*) horário *m* □ *vt* marcar, programar. **according to** ~ conforme planejado. **behind** ~ atrasado. **on** ~ (*train*) na hora; (*work*) em dia. ~**d flight** *n* vôo *m* regular
scheme /ski:m/ *n* esquema *m*; (*plan of work*) plano *m*; (*plot*) conspiração *f*, maquinação *f* □ *vi* planejar, (*P*) planear; (*pej*) intrigar, maquinar, tramar
schism /'sɪzəm/ *n* cisma *m*
schizophreni|a /skɪtsəʊ'fri:nɪə/ *n* esquizofrenia *f*. ~**c** /-'frenɪk/ *a* esquizofrênico, (*P*) esquizofrénico
scholar /'skɒlə(r)/ *n* erudito *m*, estudioso *m*, escolar *m*. ~**ly** *a* erudito. ~**ship** *n* erudição *f*, saber *m*; (*grant*) bolsa *f* de estudo
school /sku:l/ *n* escola *f*; (*of university*) escola *f*, faculdade *f* □ *a* (*age, year, holidays*) escolar □ *vt* ensinar; (*train*) treinar, adestrar. ~**ing** *n* instrução *f*; (*attendance*) escolaridade *f*
school|boy /'sku:lbɔɪ/ *n* aluno *m*. ~**girl** *n* aluna *f*
school|master /'sku:lmɑ:stə(r)/, ~**mistress**, ~**teacher** *ns* professor *m*, professora *f*
schooner /'sku:nə(r)/ *n* escuna *f*; (*glass*) copo *m* alto
sciatica /saɪ'ætɪkə/ *n* ciática *f*
scien|ce /'saɪəns/ *n* ciência *f*. ~**ce fiction** ficção *f* científica. ~**tific** /-'tɪfɪk/ *a* científico
scientist /'saɪəntɪst/ *n* cientista *mf*
scintillate /'sɪntɪleɪt/ *vi* cintilar; (*fig: person*) brilhar
scissors /'sɪzəz/ *npl* (pair of) ~ tesoura *f*
scoff[1] /skɒf/ *vi* ~ **at** zombar de, (*P*) troçar de
scoff[2] /skɒf/ *vt* (*sl: eat*) devorar, tragar
scold /skəʊld/ *vt* ralhar com. ~**ing** *n* reprensão *f*, (*P*) descompostura *f*
scone /skɒn/ *n* (*culin*) scone *m*, bolinho *m* para o chá
scoop /sku:p/ *n* (*for grain, sugar etc*) pá *f*; (*ladle*) concha *f*; (*news*) furo *m* □ *vt* ~ **out** (*hollow out*) escavar, tirar com concha *or* pá. ~ **up** (*lift*) apanhar
scoot /sku:t/ *vi* (*colloq*) fugir, mandar-se (*colloq*), (*P*) pôr-se a milhas (*colloq*)
scooter /'sku:tə(r)/ *n* (*child's*) patinete *f*, (*P*) trotinete *m*; (*motor cycle*) motoreta *f*, lambreta *f*
scope /skəʊp/ *n* âmbito *m*; (*fig: opportunity*) oportunidade *f*
scorch /skɔ:tʃ/ *vt/i* chamuscar(-se), queimar de leve. ~**ing** *a* (*colloq*) escaldante, abrasador
score /skɔ:(r)/ *n* (*sport*) contagem *f*, escore *m*; (*mus*) partitura *f* □ *vt* marcar com corte(s), riscar; (*a goal*) marcar; (*mus*) orquestrar □ *vi* marcar pontos; (*keep score*) fazer a contagem; (*football*) marcar um gol, (*P*) golo. **a** ~ (**of**) (*twenty*) uma vintena (de), vinte. ~**s** muitos, dezenas. **on that** ~ nesse respeito, quanto a isso. ~-**board** *n* marcador *m*. ~**r** /-ə(r)/ *n* (*score-keeper*) marcador *m*; (*of goals*) autor *m*
scorn /skɔ:n/ *n* desprezo *m* □ *vt* desprezar. ~**ful** *a* desdenhoso, escarninho. ~**fully** *adv* com desdém, desdenhosamente
Scorpio /'skɔ:pɪəʊ/ *n* (*astr*) Escorpião *m*
scorpion /'skɔ:pɪən/ *n* escorpião *m*
Scot /skɒt/ *n*, ~**tish** *a* escocês (*m*)
Scotch /skɒtʃ/ *a* escocês □ *n* uísque *m*
scotch /skɒtʃ/ *vt* pôr fim a, frustrar
scot-free /skɒt'fri:/ *a* impune □ *adv* impunemente
Scotland /'skɒtlənd/ *n* Escócia *f*
Scots /skɒts/ *a* escocês. ~**man** *n* escocês *m*. ~**woman** *n* escocesa *f*
scoundrel /'skaʊndrəl/ *n* patife *m*, canalha *m*
scour[1] /'skaʊə(r)/ *vt* (*clean*) esfregar, arear. ~**er** *n* esfregão *m* de palha de aço *or* de nylon
scour[2] /'skaʊə(r)/ *vt* (*search*) percorrer, esquadrinhar
scourge /skɜ:dʒ/ *n* açoite *m*; (*fig*) flagelo *m*
scout /skaʊt/ *n* (*mil*) explorador *m* □ *vi* ~ **about (for)** andar à procura de
Scout /skaʊt/ *n* escoteiro *m*, (*P*) escuteiro *m*. ~**ing** *n* escotismo *m*, (*P*) escutismo *m*
scowl /skaʊl/ *n* carranca *f*, ar *m* carrancudo □ *vi* fazer um ar carrancudo
scraggy /'skrægɪ/ *a* (-ier, -iest) descarnado, ossudo
scramble /'skræmbl/ *vi* trepar; (*crawl*) avançar de rastros, rastejar, arrastar-se □ *vt* (*eggs*) mexer □ *n* luta *f*, confusão *f*
scrap[1] /skræp/ *n* bocadinho *m*. ~s

npl restos *mpl* □ *vt* (*pt* **scrapped**) jogar fora, (*P*) deitar fora; (*plan etc*) abandonar, pôr de lado. **~-book** *n* álbum *m* de recortes. **~ heap** monte *m* de ferro-velho. **~-iron** *n* ferro *m* velho, sucata *f.* **~ merchant** sucateiro *m.* **~-paper** *n* papel *m* de rascunho. **~py** *a* fragmentário

scrap² /skræp/ *n* (*colloq: fight*) briga *f*, pancadaria *f* (*colloq*), rixa *f*

scrape /skreɪp/ *vt* raspar; (*graze*) esfolar, arranhar □ *vi* (*graze, rub*) roçar □ *n* (*act of scraping*) raspagem *f*; (*mark*) raspão *m*, esfoladura *f*; (*fig*) encrenca *f*, maus lençóis *mpl.* **~ through** escapar pela tangente, (*P*) à tangente; (*exam*) passar pela tangente, (*P*) à tangente. **~ together** conseguir juntar. **~r** /-ə(r)/ *n* raspadeira *f*

scratch /skrætʃ/ *vt/i* arranhar(-se); (*a line*) riscar; (*to relieve itching*) coçar(-se) □ *n* arranhão *m*; (*line*) risco *m*; (*wound with claw, nail*) unhada *f*. **start from ~** começar do princípio. **up to ~** à altura, ao nível requerido

scrawl /skrɔ:l/ *n* rabisco *m*, garrancho *m*, garatuja *f* □ *vt/i* rabiscar, fazer garranchos, garatujar

scrawny /'skrɔ:nɪ/ *a* (-**ier**, -**iest**) descarnado, ossudo, magricela

scream /skri:m/ *vt/i* gritar □ *n* grito *m* (agudo)

screech /skri:tʃ/ *vi* guinchar, gritar; (*of brakes*) chiar, guinchar □ *n* guincho *m*, grito *m* agudo

screen /skri:n/ *n* écran *m*, tela *f*; (*folding*) biombo *m*; (*fig: protection*) manto *m* (*fig*), capa *f* (*fig*) □ *vt* resguardar, tapar; (*film*) passar; (*candidates etc*) fazer a triagem de. **~ing** *n* (*med*) exame *m* médico

screw /skru:/ *n* parafuso *m* □ *vt* aparafusar, atarraxar. **~ up** (*eyes, face*) franzir; (*sl*: *ruin*) estragar. **~ up one's courage** cobrar coragem

screwdriver /'skru:draɪvə(r)/ *n* chave *f* de parafusos *or* de fenda

scribble /'skrɪbl/ *vt/i* rabiscar, garatujar □ *n* rabisco *m*, garatuja *f*

script /skrɪpt/ *n* escrita *f*; (*of film*) roteiro *m*, (*P*) guião *m.* **~-writer** *n* (*film*) roteirista *m*, (*P*) autor *m* do guião

Scriptures /'skrɪptʃəz/ *npl* **the ~** a Sagrada Escritura

scroll /skrəʊl/ *n* rolo *m* (de papel ou pergaminho); (*archit*) voluta *f* □ *vt/i* (*comput*) passar na tela

scrounge /skraʊndʒ/ *vt* (*colloq: cadge*) filar (*sl*), (*P*) cravar (*sl*) □ *vi* (*beg*) parasitar, viver às custas de alguém. **~r** /-ə(r)/ *n* parasita *mf*, filão *m* (*sl*), (*P*) crava *mf* (*sl*)

scrub¹ /skrʌb/ *n* (*land*) mato *m*

scrub² /skrʌb/ *vt/i* (*pt* **scrubbed**) esfregar, lavar com escova e sabão; (*colloq: cancel*) cancelar □ *n* esfrega *f*

scruff /skrʌf/ *n* **by the ~ of the neck** pelo cangote, (*P*) pelo cachaço

scruffy /'skrʌfɪ/ *a* (-**ier**, -**iest**) desmazelado, desleixado, mal ajambrado (*colloq*)

scrum /skrʌm/ *n* rixa *f*; (*Rugby*) placagem *f*

scruple /'skru:pl/ *n* escrúpulo *m*

scrupulous /'skru:pjʊləs/ *a* escrupuloso. **~ly** *adv* escrupulosamente. **~ly clean** impecavelmente limpo

scrutin|y /'skru:tɪnɪ/ *n* averiguação *f*, escrutínio *m*. **~ize** *vt* examinar em detalhes

scuff /skʌf/ *vt* (*scrape*) esfolar, safar □ *n* esfoladura *f*

scuffle /'skʌfl/ *n* tumulto *m*, briga *f*

sculpt /skʌlpt/ *vt/i* esculpir. **~or** *n* escultor *m*. **~ure** /-tʃə(r)/ *n* escultura *f* □ *vt/i* esculpir

scum /skʌm/ *n* (*on liquid*) espuma *f*; (*pej: people*) gentinha *f*, escumalha *f*, ralé *f*

scurf /skɜ:f/ *n* películas *fpl*; (*dandruff*) caspa *f*

scurrilous /'skʌrɪləs/ *a* injurioso, insultuoso

scurry /'skʌrɪ/ *vi* dar corridinhas; (*hurry*) apressar-se. **~ off** escapulir-se

scurvy /'skɜ:vɪ/ *n* escorbuto *m*

scuttle¹ /'skʌtl/ *n* (*bucket, box*) balde *m* para carvão

scuttle² /'skʌtl/ *vt* (*ship*) afundar abrindo rombos *or* as torneiras de fundo

scuttle³ /'skʌtl/ *vi* **~ away** *or* **off** fugir, escapulir-se

scythe /saɪð/ *n* gadanha *f*, foice *f* grande

sea /si:/ *n* mar *m* □ *a* do mar, marinho, marítimo. **at ~** no alto mar, ao largo. **all at ~** desnorteado. **by ~** por mar. **~bird** ave *f* marinha. **~-green** *a* verde-mar. **~ horse** cavalo-marinho *m*, hipocampo *m*. **~ level** nível *m* do mar. **~ lion** leão-marinho *m*. **~ shell** concha *f*. **~-shore** *n* litoral *m*; (*beach*) praia *f*. **~ water** água *f* do mar

seaboard /'si:bɔ:d/ *n* litoral *m*, costa *f*

seafarer /'si:feərə(r)/ *n* marinheiro *m*, navegante *m*

seafood /'si:fu:d/ *n* marisco(s) *m* (*pl*)

seagull /'si:gʌl/ *n* gaivota *f*

seal¹ /si:l/ *n* (*animal*) foca *f*

seal² /si:l/ *n* selo *m*, sinete *m* □ *vt* selar; (*with wax*) lacrar. **~ing-wax** *n* lacre *m*. **~ off** (*area*) vedar

seam /si:m/ *n* (*in cloth etc*) costura *f*; (*of mineral*) veio *m*, filão *m*. **~less** *a* sem costura

seaman /ˈsi:mən/ *n* (*pl* -men) marinheiro *m*, marítimo *m*
seamy /ˈsi:mɪ/ *a* ~ **side** lado *m* (do) avesso; (*fig*) lado *m* sórdido
seance /ˈseɪa:ns/ *n* sessão *f* espírita
seaplane /ˈsi:pleɪn/ *n* hidroavião *m*
seaport /ˈsi:pɔ:t/ *n* porto *m* de mar
search /sɜ:tʃ/ *vt/i* revistar, dar busca (a); (*one's heart, conscience etc*) examinar □ *n* revista *f*, busca *f*; (*quest*) procura *f*, busca *f*; (*official*) inquérito *m*. **in ~ of** à procura de. **~ for** procurar. **~-party** *n* equipe *f* de busca. **~-warrant** *n* mandado *m* de busca. **~ing** *a* (*of look*) penetrante; (*of test etc*) minucioso
searchlight /ˈsɜ:tʃlaɪt/ *n* holofote *m*
seasick /ˈsi:sɪk/ *a* enjoado. **~ness** *n* enjôo *m*, *P* enjoo *m*
seaside /ˈsi:saɪd/ *n* costa *f*, praia *f*, beira-mar *f*. **~ resort** *n* balneário *m*, praia *f*
season /ˈsi:zn/ *n* (*of year*) estação *f*; (*proper time*) época *f*; (*cricket, football etc*) temporada *f* □ *vt* temperar; (*wood*) secar. **in ~** na época. **~able** *a* próprio da estação. **~al** *a* sazonal. **~ed** *a* (*of people*) experimentado. **~ing** *n* tempero *m*. **~-ticket** *n* (*train etc*) passe *m*; (*theatre etc*) assinatura *f*
seat /si:t/ *n* assento *m*; (*place*) lugar *m*; (*of bicycle*) selim *m*; (*of chair*) assento *m*; (*of trousers*) fundilho *m* □ *vt* sentar; (*have seats for*) ter lugares sentados para. **be ~ed, take a ~** sentar-se. **~ of learning** centro *m* de cultura. **~-belt** *n* cinto *m* de segurança
seaweed /ˈsi:wi:d/ *n* alga *f* marinha
seaworthy /ˈsi:wɜ:ðɪ/ *a* navegável, em condições de navegabilidade
secateurs /ˈsekətɜ:z/ *npl* tesoura *f* de poda
seclu|de /sɪˈklu:d/ *vt* isolar. **~ded** *a* isolado, retirado. **~sion** /sɪˈklu:ʒn/ *n* isolamento *m*
second[1] /ˈsekənd/ *a* segundo □ *n* segundo *m*; (*in duel*) testemunha *f*. **~ (gear)** (*auto*) segunda *f* (velocidade). **the ~ of April** dois de Abril. **~s** (*goods*) artigos *mpl* de segunda *or* de refugo □ *adv* (*in race etc*) em segundo lugar □ *vt* secundar. **~-best** *a* escolhido em segundo lugar. **~-class** *a* de segunda classe. **~-hand** *a* de segunda mão □ *n* (*on clock*) ponteiro *m* dos segundos. **~-rate** *a* medíocre, de segunda ordem. **~ thoughts** dúvidas *fpl*. **on ~ thoughts** pensando melhor. **~ly** *adv* segundo, em segundo lugar
second[2] /sɪˈkɒnd/ *vt* (*transfer*) destacar (to para)
secondary /ˈsekəndrɪ/ *a* secundário. **~ school** escola *f* secundária
secrecy /ˈsi:krəsɪ/ *n* segredo *m*
secret /ˈsi:krɪt/ *a* secreto □ *n* segredo *m*. **in ~** em segredo. **~ agent** *n* agente *mf* secreto. **~ly** *adv* em segredo, secretamente
secretar|y /ˈsekrətrɪ/ *n* secretário *m*, secretária *f*. **S~y of State** ministro *m* de Estado, (*P*) Secretário *m* de Estado; (*Amer*) ministro *m* dos Negócios Estrangeiros. **~ial** /-ˈteərɪəl/ *a* (*work, course etc*) de secretária
secret|e /sɪˈkri:t/ *vt* segregar; (*hide*) esconder. **~ion** /-ʃn/ *n* secreção *f*
secretive /ˈsi:krətɪv/ *a* misterioso, reservado
sect /sekt/ *n* seita *f*. **~arian** /ˈteərɪən/ *a* sectário
section /ˈsekʃn/ *n* seção *f*, (*P*) secção *f*; (*of country, community etc*) setor *m*, (*P*) sector *m*; (*district of town*) zona *f*
sector /ˈsektə(r)/ *n* setor *m*, (*P*) sector *m*
secular /ˈsekjʊlə(r)/ *a* secular, leigo, *P* laico; (*art, music etc*) profano
secure /sɪˈkjʊə(r)/ *a* seguro, em segurança; (*firm*) seguro, sólido; (*in mind*) tranqüilo, *P* tranquilo □ *vt* prender bem *or* com segurança; (*obtain*) conseguir, arranjar; (*ensure*) assegurar; (*windows, doors*) fechar bem. **~ly** *adv* solidamente; (*safely*) em segurança
securit|y /sɪˈkjʊərətɪ/ *n* segurança *f*; (*for loan*) fiança *f*, caução *f*. **~ies** *npl* (*finance*) títulos *mpl*
sedate /sɪˈdeɪt/ *a* sereno, comedido □ *vt* (*med*) tratar com sedativos
sedation /sɪˈdeɪʃn/ *n* (*med*) sedação *f*. **under ~** sob o efeito de sedativos
sedative /ˈsedətɪv/ *n* (*med*) sedativo *m*
sedentary /ˈsedntrɪ/ *a* sedentário
sediment /ˈsedɪmənt/ *n* sedimento *m*, depósito *m*
seduce /sɪˈdju:s/ *vt* seduzir
seduct|ion /sɪˈdʌkʃn/ *n* sedução *f*. **~ive** /-tɪv/ *a* sedutor, aliciante
see[1] /si:/ *vt/i* (*pt* **saw**, *pp* **seen**) ver; (*escort*) acompanhar. **~ about** *or* **to** tratar de, encarregar-se de. **~ off** *vt* (*wave goodbye*) ir despedir-se de; (*chase*) **~ through** (*task*) levar a cabo; (*not be deceived by*) não se deixar enganar por. **~ (to it) that** assegurar que, tratar de fazer com que. **~ing that** visto que, uma vez que. **~ you later!** (*colloq*) até logo! (*colloq*)
see[2] /si:/ *n* sé *f*, bispado *m*
seed /si:d/ *n* semente *f*; (*fig: origin*) germe(n) *m*; (*tennis*) cabeça *f* de série; (*pip*) caroço *m*. **go to ~** produzir sementes; (*fig*) desmazelar-se (*colloq*).

~ling *n* planta *f* brotada a partir da semente
seedy /'si:dɪ/ *a* (-ier, -iest) (com um ar) gasto, surrado; (*colloq: unwell*) abatido, deprimido, em baixo astral (*colloq*)
seek /si:k/ *vt* (*pt* **sought**) procurar; (*help etc*) pedir
seem /si:m/ *vi* parecer. **~ingly** *adv* aparentemente, ao que parece
seemly /'si:mlɪ/ *adv* decente, conveniente, próprio
seen /si:n/ *see* **see**[1]
seep /si:p/ *vi* (*ooze*) filtrar-se; (*trickle*) pingar, escorrer, passar. **~age** *n* infiltração *f*
see-saw /'si:sɔ:/ *n* gangorra *f*, (*P*) balanço *m*
seethe /si:ð/ *vi* **~ with** (*anger*) ferver de; (*people*) fervilhar de
segment /'segmənt/ *n* segmento *m*; (*of orange*) gomo *m*
segregat|e /'segrɪgeɪt/ *vt* segregar, separar. **~ion** /-'geɪʃn/ *n* segregação *f*
seize /si:z/ *vt* agarrar, (*P*) deitar a mão a, apanhar; (*take possession by force*) apoderar-se de; (*by law*) apreender, confiscar, (*P*) apresar □ *vi* **~ on** (*opportunity*) aproveitar. **~ up** (*engine etc*) grimpar, emperrar. **be ~d with** (*fear, illness*) ter um ataque de
seizure /'si:ʒə(r)/ *n* (*med*) ataque *m*, crise *f*; (*law*) apreensão *f*, captura *f*
seldom /'seldəm/ *adv* raras vezes, raramente, raro
select /sɪ'lekt/ *vt* escolher, selecionar, (*P*) seleccionar □ *a* seleto, (*P*) selecto. **~ion** /-ʃn/ *n* seleção *f*, (*P*) selecção *f*; (*comm*) sortido *m*
selective /sɪ'lektɪv/ *a* seletivo, (*P*) selectivo
self /self/ *n* (*pl* **selves**) **the ~** o eu, o ego
self- /self/ *pref* **~-assurance** *n* segurança *f*. **~-assured** *a* seguro de si. **~-catering** *a* em que os hóspedes tem facilidades de cozinhar. **~-centred** *a* egocêntrico. **~-confidence** *n* autoconfiança *f*, confiança *f* em si mesmo. **~-confident** *a* que tem confiança em si mesmo. **~-conscious** *a* inibido, constrangido. **~-contained** *a* independente. **~-control** *n* autodomínio *m*. **~-controlled** *a* senhor de si. **~-defence** *n* legítima defesa *f*. **~-denial** *n* abnegação *f*. **~-employed** *a* autónomo. **~-esteem** *n* amor *m* próprio. **~-evident** *a* evidente. **~-indulgent** *a* que não resiste a tentações; (*for ease*) comodista. **~-interest** *n* interesse *m* pessoal. **~-portrait** *n* auto-retrato *m*. **~-possessed** *a* senhor de si. **~-reliant** *a* independente, seguro de si. **~-respect** *n* amor *m* próprio. **~-righteous** *a* que se tem em boa conta. **~-sacrifice** *n* abnegação *f*, sacrifício *m*. **~-satisfied** *a* cheio de si, convencido (*colloq*). **~-seeking** *a* egoísta. **~-service** *a* auto-serviço, self-service. **~-styled** *a* pretenso. **~-sufficient** *a* auto-suficiente. **~-willed** *a* voluntarioso
selfish /'selfɪʃ/ *a* egoísta; (*motive*) interesseiro. **~ness** *n* egoísmo *m*
selfless /'selflɪs/ *a* desinteressado
sell /sel/ *vt/i* (*pt* **sold**) vender(-se). **~-by date ~ off** liquidar. **be sold out** estar esgotado. **~-out** *n* (*show*) sucesso *m*; (*colloq: betrayal*) traição *f*. **~er** *n* vendedor *m*
Sellotape /'seləʊteɪp/ *n* fita *f* adesiva, (*P*) fitacola *f*
semantic /sɪ'mæntɪk/ *a* semântico. **~s** *n* semântica *f*
semblance /'sembləns/ *n* aparência *f*
semen /'si:mən/ *n* sêmen *m*, (*P*) sémen *m*, esperma *m*
semester /sɪ'mestə(r)/ *n* (*Amer: univ*) semestre *m*
semi- /'semɪ/ *pref* semi-, meio
semibreve /'semɪbri:v/ *n* (*mus*) semibreve *f*
semicirc|le /'semɪsɜ:kl/ *n* semicírculo *m*. **~ular** /-sɜ:kjʊlə(r)/ *a* semicircular
semicolon /semɪ'kəʊlən/ *n* ponto-e-vírgula *m*
semi-detached /semɪdɪ'tætʃt/ *a* **~ house** casa *f* geminada
semifinal /semɪ'faɪnl/ *n* semifinal *f*, (*P*) meiafinal *f*
seminar /'semɪna:(r)/ *n* seminário *m*
semiquaver /'semɪkweɪvə(r)/ *n* (*mus*) semicolcheia *f*
Semit|e /'si:maɪt/ *a* & *n* semita (*mf*). **~ic** /sɪ'mɪtɪk/ *a* & *n* (*lang*) semítico (*m*)
semitone /'semɪtəʊn/ *n* (*mus*) semitom *m*
semolina /semə'li:nə/ *n* sêmola *f*, (*P*) sémola *f*, semolina *f*
senat|e /'senɪt/ *n* senado *m*. **~or** /-ətə(r)/ *n* senador *m*
send /send/ *vt/i* (*pt* **sent**) enviar, mandar. **~ back** devolver. **~ for** (*person*) chamar, mandar vir; (*help*) pedir. **~ (away** *or* **off) for** encomendar, mandar vir (por carta). **~-off** *n* despedida *f*, bota-fora *m*. **~ up** (*colloq*) parodiar. **~er** *n* expedidor *m*, remetente *m*
senil|e /'si:naɪl/ *a* senil. **~ity** /sɪ'nɪlətɪ/ *n* senilidade *f*
senior /'si:nɪə(r)/ *a* mais velho, mais idoso (to que); (*in rank*) superior; (*in service*) mais antigo; (*after surname*) sênior, (*P*) sénior □ *n* pessoa *f* mais velha; (*schol*) finalista *mf*. **~ citizen**

pessoa *f* de idade *or* da terceira idade. ~ity /-'ɒrətɪ/ *n* (*in age*) idade *f*; (*in service*) antiguidade *f*

sensation /sen'seɪʃn/ *n* sensação *f*. ~al *a* sensacional. ~alism *n* sensacionalismo *m*

sense /sens/ *n* sentido *m*; (*wisdom*) bom senso *m*; (*sensation*) sensação *f*; (*mental impression*) sentimento *m*. ~s (*sanity*) razão *f* □ *vt* pressentir. make ~ fazer sentido. make ~ of compreender. ~less *a* disparatado, sem sentido; (*med*) sem sentidos, inconsciente

sensible /'sensəbl/ *a* sensato, razoável; (*clothes*) prático

sensitiv|e /'sensətɪv/ *a* sensível (to a); (*touchy*) susceptível. ~ity /-'tɪvətɪ/ *n* sensibilidade *f*

sensory /'sensərɪ/ *a* sensorial

sensual /'senʃʊəl/ *a* sensual. ~ity /-'ælətɪ/ *n* sensualidade *f*

sensuous /'senʃʊəs/ *a* sensual

sent /sent/ *see* send

sentence /'sentəns/ *n* frase *f*; (*jur: decision*) sentença *f*; (*punishment*) pena *f* □ *vt* ~ to condenar a

sentiment /'sentɪmənt/ *n* sentimento *m*; (*opinion*) modo *m* de ver

sentimental /sentɪ'mentl/ *a* sentimental. ~ity /-men'tælətɪ/ *n* sentimentalidade *f*, sentimentalismo *m*. ~ value valor *m* estimativo

sentry /'sentrɪ/ *n* sentinela *f*

separable /'sepərəbl/ *a* separável

separate[1] /-'seprət/ *a* separado, diferente. ~s *npl* (*clothes*) conjuntos *mpl*. ~ly *adv* separadamente, em separado

separat|e[2] /'sepəreɪt/ *vt/i* separar (-se). ~ion /-'reɪʃn/ *n* separação *f*

September /sep'tembə(r)/ *n* setembro *m*

septic /'septɪk/ *a* séptico, infectado

sequel /'si:kwəl/ *n* resultado *m*, seqüela *f*, (*P*) sequela *f*; (*of novel, film*) continuação *f*

sequence /'si:kwəns/ *n* seqüência *f*, (*P*) sequência *f*

sequin /'si:kwɪn/ *n* lantejoula *f*

serenade /serə'neɪd/ *n* serenata *f* □ *vt* fazer uma serenata para

seren|e /sɪ'ri:n/ *a* sereno. ~ity /-'enətɪ/ *n* serenidade *f*

sergeant /'sa:dʒənt/ *n* sargento *m*

serial /'sɪərɪəl/ *n* folhetim *m* □ *a* (*number*) de série. ~ize /-laɪz/ *vt* publicar em folhetim

series /'sɪərɪ:z/ *n invar* série *f*

serious /'sɪərɪəs/ *a* sério; (*very bad, critical*) grave, sério. ~ly *adv* seriamente, gravemente, a sério. take ~ly levar a sério. ~ness *n* seriedade *f*, gravidade *f*

sermon /'sɜ:mən/ *n* sermão *m*

serpent /'sɜ:pənt/ *n* serpente *f*

serrated /sɪ'reɪtɪd/ *a* (*edge*) serr(e)ado, com serrilha

serum /'sɪərəm/ *n* (*pl* -a) soro *m*

servant /'sɜ:vənt/ *n* criado *m*, criada *f*, empregado *m*, empregada *f*

serv|e /sɜ:v/ *vt/i* servir; (*a sentence*) cumprir; (*jur: a writ*) entregar; (*mil*) servir, prestar serviço; (*apprenticeship*) fazer □ *n* (*tennis*) saque *m*, (*P*) serviço *m*. ~e as/to servir de/para. ~e its purpose servir para o que é (*colloq*), servir os seus fins. it ~es you/him *etc* right é bem feito. ~ing *n* (*portion*) dose *f*, porção *f*

service /'sɜ:vɪs/ *n* serviço *m*; (*relig*) culto *m*; (*tennis*) saque *m* (*P*) serviço *m*; (*maintenance*) revisão *f*. ~s (*mil*) forças *fpl* armadas □ *vt* (*car etc*) fazer a revisão de. of ~ to útil a, de utilidade a. ~ area área *f* de serviço. ~ charge serviço *m*. ~ station posto *m* de gasolina

serviceable /'sɜ:vɪsəbl/ *a* (*of use, usable*) útil, prático; (*durable*) resistente; (*of person*) prestável

serviceman /'sɜ:vɪsmən/ *n* (*pl* -men) militar *m*

serviette /sɜ:vɪ'et/ *n* guardanapo *m*

servile /'sɜ:vaɪl/ *a* servil

session /'seʃn/ *n* sessão *f*; (*univ*) ano *m* acadêmico, (*P*) académico; (*Amer: univ*) semestre *m*. in ~ (*sitting*) em sessão, reunidos

set /set/ *vt* (*pt* set, *pres p* setting) pôr, colocar; (*put down*) pousar; (*limit etc*) fixar; (*watch, clock*) regular; (*example*) dar; (*exam, task*) marcar; (*in plaster*) engessar □ *vi* (*of sun*) pôr-se; (*of jelly*) endurecer, solidificar(-se) □ *n* (*of people*) circulo *m*, roda *f*; (*of books*) coleção *f*, (*P*) colecção *f*; (*of tools, chairs etc*) jogo *m*; (*TV, radio*) aparelho *m*; (*hair*) mise *f*; (*theat*) cenário *m*; (*tennis*) partida *f*, set *m* □ *a* fixo; (*habit*) inveterado; (*jelly*) duro, sólido; (*book*) do programa, (*P*) adoptado; (*meal*) a preço fixo. be ~ on doing estar decidido a fazer. ~ about *or* to começar a, pôr-se a. ~ back (*plans etc*) atrasar; (*sl: cost*) custar. ~-back *n* revés *m*, contratempo *m*, atraso *m* de vida (*colloq*). ~ fire to atear fogo a, (*P*) deitar fogo a. ~ free pôr em liberdade. ~ in (*rain etc*) pegar. ~ off *or* out partir, começar a viajar. ~ off (*mechanism*) pôr para funcionar, (*P*) pôr a funcionar; (*bomb*) explodir; (*by contrast*) realçar. ~ out (*state*) expor; (*arrange*) dispôr. ~ sail partir, içar as velas. ~ square esquadro *m*. ~ the table pôr a mesa. ~ theory teoria *f* de conjuntos. ~-to *n* briga *f*.

~ **up** (*establish*) fundar, estabelecer. **~-up** *n* (*system*) sistema *m*, organização *f*; (*situation*) situação *f*

settee /se'ti:/ *n* sofá *m*

setting /'setɪŋ/ *n* (*framework*) quadro *m*; (*of jewel*) engaste *m*; (*typ*) composição *f*; (*mus*) arranjo *m* musical

settle /'setl/ *vt* (*arrange*) resolver; (*date*) marcar; (*nerves*) acalmar; (*doubts*) esclarecer; (*new country*) colonizar, povoar; (*bill*) pagar □ *vi* assentar; (*in country*) estabelecer-se; (*in house, chair etc*) instalar-se; (*weather*) estabilizar-se. ~ **down** acalmar-se; (*become orderly*) assentar; (*sit, rest*) instalar-se. ~ **for** aceitar. ~ **up (with)** fazer contas (com); (*fig*) ajustar contas (com). **~r** /-ə(r)/ *n* colono *m*, colonizador *m*

settlement /'setlmənt/ *n* (*agreement*) acordo *m*; (*payment*) pagamento *m*; (*colony*) colônia *f*, (*P*) colónia *f*; (*colonization*) colonização *f*

seven /'sevn/ *a* & *n* sete (*m*). **~th** *a* & *n* sétimo (*m*)

seventeen /sevn'ti:n/ *a* & *n* dezessete (*m*), (*P*) dezassete (*m*). **~th** *a* & *n* décimo sétimo (*m*)

sevent|y /'sevntɪ/ *a* & *n* setenta (*m*). **~ieth** *a* & *n* septuagésimo (*m*)

sever /'sevə(r)/ *vt* cortar. **~ance** *n* corte *m*

several /'sevrəl/ *a* & *pron* vários, diversos

sever|e /sɪ'vɪə(r)/ *a* (-er, -est) severo; (*pain*) forte, violento; (*illness*) grave; (*winter*) rigoroso. **~ely** *adv* severamente; (*seriously*) gravemente. **~ity** /sɪ'verɪtɪ/ *n* severidade *f*; (*seriousness*) gravidade *f*

sew /səʊ/ *vt/i* (*pt* **sewed**, *pp* **sewn** *or* **sewed**) coser, costurar. **~ing** *n* costura *f*. **~ing-machine** *n* máquina *f* de costura

sewage /'sju:ɪdʒ/ *n* efluentes *mpl* dos esgotos, detritos *mpl*

sewer /'sju:ə(r)/ *n* cano *m* de esgoto

sewn /səʊn/ *see* **sew**

sex /seks/ *n* sexo *m* □ *a* sexual. **have** ~ ter relações. ~ **maniac** tarado *m* sexual. **~y** *a* sexy *invar*, que tem sex-appeal

sexist /'seksɪst/ *a* & *n* sexista *mf*

sexual /'sekʃʊəl/ *a* sexual. ~ **harassment** assédio *m* sexual. ~ **intercourse** relações *fpl* sexuais. **~ity** /'ælətɪ/ *n* sexualidade *f*

shabb|y /'ʃæbɪ/ *a* (-ier, -iest) (*clothes, object*) gasto, surrado; (*person*) maltrapilho, mal vestido; (*mean*) miserável. **~ily** *adv* miseravelmente

shack /ʃæk/ *n* cabana *f*, barraca *f*

shackles /'ʃæklz/ *npl* grilhões *mpl*, algemas *fpl*

shade /ʃeɪd/ *n* sombra *f*; (*of colour*) tom *m*, matiz *m*; (*of opinion*) matiz *m*; (*for lamp*) abat-jour *m*, quebra-luz *m*; (*Amer: blind*) estore *m* □ *vt* resguardar da luz; (*darken*) sombrear. **a ~ bigger/***etc* ligeiramente maior/*etc*. **in the ~** à sombra

shadow /'ʃædəʊ/ *n* sombra *f* □ *vt* cobrir de sombra; (*follow*) seguir, vigiar. **S~ Cabinet** gabinete *m* formado pelo partido da oposição. **~y** *a* ensombrado, sombreado; (*fig*) vago, indistinto

shady /'ʃeɪdɪ/ *a* (-ier, -iest) sombreiro, (*P*) que dá sombra; (*in shade*) à sombra; (*fig: dubious*) suspeito, duvidoso

shaft /ʃa:ft/ *n* (*of arrow, spear*) haste *f*; (*axle*) eixo *m*, veio *m*; (*of mine, lift*) poço *m*; (*of light*) raio *m*

shaggy /'ʃægɪ/ *a* (-ier, -iest) (*beard*) hirsuto; (*hair*) desgrenhado; (*animal*) peludo, felpudo

shake /ʃeɪk/ *vt* (*pt* **shook**, *pp* **shaken**) abanar, sacudir; (*bottle*) agitar; (*belief, house etc*) abalar □ *vi* estremecer, tremer □ *n* (*violent*) abanão *m*, safanão *m*; (*light*) sacudidela *f*. ~ **hands with** apertar a mão de. ~ **off** (*get rid of*) sacudir, livrar-se de. ~ **one's head** (*to say no*) fazer que não com a cabeça. ~ **up** agitar. **~-up** *n* (*upheaval*) reviravolta *f*

shaky /'ʃeɪkɪ/ *a* (-ier, -iest) (*hand, voice*) trêmulo, (*P*) trémulo; (*unsteady, unsafe*) pouco firme, inseguro; (*weak*) fraco

shall /ʃæl/; *unstressed* /ʃəl/ *v aux* **I/we ~ do** (*future*) farei/faremos. **I/you/he ~ do** (*command*) eu hei de/você há de/tu hás de/ele há de fazer

shallot /ʃə'lɒt/ *n* cebolinha *f*, (*P*) chalota *f*

shallow /'ʃæləʊ/ *a* (-er, -est) pouco fundo, raso; (*fig*) superficial

sham /ʃæm/ *n* fingimento *m*; (*jewel etc*) imitação *f*; (*person*) impostor *m*, fingido *m* □ *a* fingido; (*false*) falso □ *vt* (*pt* **shammed**) fingir

shambles /'ʃæmblz/ *npl* (*colloq: mess*) balbúrdia *f*, trapalhada *f*

shame /ʃeɪm/ *n* vergonha *f* □ *vt* (fazer) envergonhar. **it's a ~** é uma pena. **what a ~!** que pena! **~ful** *a* vergonhoso. **~less** *a* sem vergonha, descarado; (*immodest*) despudorado, desavergonhado

shamefaced /'ʃeɪmfeɪst/ *a* envergonhado

shampoo /ʃæm'pu:/ *n* xampu *m*, (*P*) champô *m*, shampoo *m* □ *vt* lavar com xampu, (*P*) champô *or* shampoo

shan't /ʃa:nt/ = **shall not**

shanty /'ʃæntɪ/ *n* barraca *f*. ~ **town** favela *f*, (*P*) bairro(s) *m*(*pl*) da lata

shape /ʃeɪp/ *n* forma *f* □ *vt* moldar □ *vi* ~ **(up)** andar bem, fazer progressos. **take** ~ concretizar-se, avançar. ~**less** *a* informe, sem forma; (*of body*) deselegante, disforme
shapely /ˈʃeɪplɪ/ *a* (-ier, -iest) (*leg, person*) bem feito, elegante
share /ʃeə(r)/ *n* parte *f*, porção *f*; (*comm*) ação *f*, (*P*) acção *f* □ *vt/i* partilhar (**with** com, **in** de)
shareholder /ˈʃeəhəʊldə(r)/ *n* acionista *mf*, (*P*) accionista *mf*
shark /ʃa:k/ *n* tubarão *m*
sharp /ʃa:p/ *a* (-er, -est) (*knife, pencil etc*) afiado; (*pin, point etc*) pontiagudo, aguçado; (*words, reply*) áspero; (*of bend*) fechado; (*acute*) agudo; (*sudden*) brusco; (*dishonest*) pouco honesto; (*well-defined*) nítido; (*brisk*) rápido, vigoroso; (*clever*) vivo □ *adv* (*stop*) de repente □ *n* (*mus*) sustenido *m*. **six o'clock** ~ seis horas em ponto. ~**ly** *adv* (*harshly*) rispidamente; (*suddenly*) de repente
sharpen /ˈʃa:pən/ *vt* aguçar; (*pencil*) fazer a ponta de, (*P*) afiar; (*knife etc*) afiar, amolar. ~**er** *n* afiadeira *f*; (*for pencil*) apontador *m*, (*P*) apára-lápis *m*, (*P*) afia-lápis *m*
shatter /ˈʃætə(r)/ *vt/i* despedaçar (-se), esmigalhar(-se); (*hopes*) destruir(-se); (*nerves*) abalar(-se). ~**ed** *a* (*upset*) passado; (*exhausted*) estourado (*colloq*)
shav|e /ʃeɪv/ *vt/i* barbear(-se), fazer a barba (de) □ *n* **have a** ~**e** barbear-se. **have a close** ~**e** (*fig*) escapar por um triz. ~**en** *a* raspado, barbeado. ~**er** *n* aparelho *m* de barbear, (*P*) máquina *f* de barbear. ~**ing-brush** *n* pincel *m* para a barba. ~**ing-cream** *n* creme *m* de barbear
shaving /ˈʃeɪvɪŋ/ *n* apara *f*
shawl /ʃɔ:l/ *n* xale *m*, (*P*) xaile *m*
she /ʃi:/ *pron* ela □ *n* fêmea *f*
sheaf /ʃi:f/ *n* (*pl* **sheaves**) feixe *m*; (*of papers*) maço *m*, molho *m*
shear /ʃɪə(r)/ *vt* (*pp* **shorn** *or* **sheared**) (*sheep etc*) tosquiar
shears /ʃɪəz/ *npl* tesoura *f* para jardim
sheath /ʃi:θ/ *n* (*pl* ~s /ʃi:ðz/) bainha *f*; (*condom*) preservativo *m*, camisa-de-Vênus *f*
sheathe /ʃi:ð/ *vt* embainhar
shed[1] /ʃed/ *n* (*hut*) casinhola *f*; (*for cows*) estábulo *m*
shed[2] /ʃed/ (*pt* **shed**, *pres p* **shedding**) perder, deixar cair; (*spread*) espalhar; (*blood, tears*) deitar, derramar. ~ **light on** lançar luz sobre
sheen /ʃi:n/ *n* brilho *m*, lustre *m*
sheep /ʃi:p/ *n* (*pl invar*) carneiro *m*, ovelha *f*. ~**-dog** *n* cão *m* de pastor
sheepish /ˈʃi:pɪʃ/ *a* encabulado. ~**ly** *adv* com um ar encabulado
sheepskin /ˈʃi:pskɪn/ *n* pele *f* de carneiro; (*leather*) carneira *f*
sheer /ʃɪə(r)/ *a* mero, simples; (*steep*) íngreme, a pique; (*fabric*) diáfano, transparente □ *adv* a pique, verticalmente
sheet /ʃi:t/ *n* lençol *m*; (*of glass, metal*) chapa *f*, placa *f*; (*of paper*) folha *f*
sheikh /ʃeɪk/ *n* xeque *m*, sheik *m*
shelf /ʃelf/ *n* (*pl* **shelves**) prateleira *f*
shell /ʃel/ *n* (*of egg, nut etc*) casca *f*; (*of mollusc*) concha *f*; (*of ship, tortoise*) casco *m*; (*of building*) estrutura *f*, armação *f*; (*of explosive*) cartucho *m* □ *vt* descascar; (*mil*) bombardear
shellfish /ˈʃelfɪʃ/ *n* (*pl invar*) crustáceo *m*; (*as food*) marisco *m*
shelter /ˈʃeltə(r)/ *n* abrigo *m*, refúgio *m* □ *vt* abrigar; (*protect*) proteger; (*harbour*) dar asilo a □ *vi* abrigar-se, refugiar-se. ~**ed** *a* (*life etc*) protegido; (*spot*) abrigado
shelve /ʃelv/ *vt* pôr em prateleiras; (*fit with shelves*) pôr prateleiras em; (*fig*) engavetar, pôr de lado
shelving /ˈʃelvɪŋ/ *n* (*shelves*) prateleiras *fpl*
shepherd /ˈʃepəd/ *n* pastor *m* □ *vt* guiar. ~**'s pie** empadão *m* de batata e carne moída
sheriff /ˈʃerɪf/ *n* xerife *m*
sherry /ˈʃerɪ/ *n* Xerez *m*
shield /ʃi:ld/ *n* (*armour, heraldry*) escudo *m*; (*screen*) anteparo *m* □ *vt* proteger (**from** contra, de)
shift /ʃɪft/ *vt/i* mudar de posição, deslocar(-se); (*exchange, alter*) mudar de □ *n* mudança *f*; (*workers; work*) turno *m*. **make** ~ arranjar-se
shiftless /ˈʃɪftlɪs/ *a* (*lazy*) molengão, preguiçoso
shifty /ˈʃɪftɪ/ *a* (-ier, -iest) velhaco, duvidoso
shimmer /ˈʃɪmə(r)/ *vi* luzir suavemente □ *n* luzir *m*
shin /ʃɪn/ *n* perna *f*. ~**-bone** *n* tíbia *f*, canela *f*. ~**-pad** *n* (*football*) caneleira *f*
shin|e /ʃaɪn/ *vt/i* (*pt* **shone**) (fazer) brilhar, (fazer) reluzir; (*shoes*) engraxar □ *n* lustro *m*. ~**e a torch (on)** iluminar com uma lanterna de mão. **the sun is** ~**ing** faz sol
shingle /ˈʃɪŋgl/ *n* (*pebbles*) seixos *mpl*
shingles /ˈʃɪŋglz/ *npl med* zona *f*, herpes-zóster *f*
shiny /ˈʃaɪnɪ/ *a* (-ier, -iest) brilhante; (*of coat, trousers*) lustroso
ship /ʃɪp/ *n* barco *m*, navio *m* □ *vt* (*pt* **shipped**) transportar; (*send*) mandar por via marítima; (*load*) embarcar. ~**ment** *n* (*goods*) carregamento *m*;

(*shipping*) embarque *m*. ~**per** *n* expedidor *m*. ~**ping** *n* navegação *f*; (*ships*) navios *mpl*

shipbuilding /'ʃɪpbɪldɪŋ/ *n* construção *f* naval

shipshape /'ʃɪpʃeɪp/ *adv* & *a* em (perfeita) ordem, impecável

shipwreck /'ʃɪprek/ *n* naufrágio *m*. ~**ed** *a* naufragado. **be** ~**ed** naufragar

shipyard /'ʃɪpja:d/ *n* estaleiro *m*

shirk /ʃɜ:k/ *vt* fugir a, furtar-se a, (*P*) baldar-se a (*sl*). ~**er** *n* parasita *mf*

shirt /ʃɜ:t/ *n* camisa *f*; (*of woman*) blusa *f*. **in** ~**-sleeves** em mangas de camisa

shiver /'ʃɪvə(r)/ *vi* arrepiar-se, tiritar □ *n* arrepio *m*

shoal /ʃəʊl/ *n* (*of fish*) cardume *m*

shock /ʃɒk/ choque *m*, embate *m*; (*electr*) choque *m* elétrico, (*P*) eléctrico; (*med*) choque *m* □ *a* de choque □ *vt* chocar. ~ **absorber** (*mech*) amortecedor *m*. ~**ing** *a* chocante; (*colloq: very bad*) horrível

shod /ʃɒd/ *see* **shoe**

shodd|y /'ʃɒdɪ/ *a* (-ier, -iest) mal feito, ordinário, de má qualidade. ~**ily** *adv* mal

shoe /ʃu:/ *n* sapato *m*; (*footwear*) calçado *m*; (*horse*) ferradura *f*; (*brake*) sapata *f*, (*P*) calço *m* (de travão) □ *vt* (*pt* **shod**, *pres p* **shoeing**) (*horse*) ferrar. ~ **polish** *n* pomada *f*, (*P*) graxa *f* para sapatos. ~**-shop** *n* sapataria *f*. **on a** ~**-string** (*colloq*) com/por muito pouco dinheiro, na pindaíba (*colloq*)

shoehorn /'ʃu:hɔ:n/ *n* calçadeira *f*

shoelace /'ʃu:leɪs/ *n* cordão *m* de sapato, (*P*) atacador *m*

shoemaker /'ʃu:meɪkə(r)/ *n* sapateiro *m*

shone /ʃɒn/ *see* **shine**

shoo /ʃu:/ *vt* enxotar □ *int* xô

shook /ʃuk/ *see* **shake**

shoot /ʃu:t/ *vt* (*pt* **shot**) (*gun*) disparar; (*glance, missile*) lançar; (*kill*) matar a tiro; (*wound*) ferir a tiro; (*execute*) executar, fuzilar; (*hunt*) caçar; (*film*) filmar, rodar □ *vi* disparar, atirar (at contra, sobre); (*bot*) rebentar; (*football*) rematar □ *n* (*bot*) rebento *m*. ~ **down** abater (a tiro). ~ **in/out** (*rush*) entrar/sair correndo *or* disparado. ~ **up** (*spurt*) jorrar; (*grow quickly*) crescer a olhos vistos, dar um pulo; (*prices*) subir em disparada. ~**ing** *n* (*shots*) tiroteio *m*. ~**ing-range** *n* carreira *f* de tiro. ~**ing star** estrela *f* cadente

shop /ʃɒp/ *n* loja *f*; (*workshop*) oficina *f* □ *vi* (*pt* **shopped**) fazer compras. ~ **around** procurar, ver o que há. ~ **assistant** empregado *m*, caixeiro *m*; vendedor *m*. ~**-floor** *n* (*workers*) trabalhadores *mpl*. ~**per** *n* comprador *m*. ~**-soiled**, (*Amer*) ~**-worn** *adjs* enxovalhado. ~ **steward** delegado *m* sindical. ~ **window** vitrina *f*, (*P*) montra *f*. **talk** ~ falar de coisas profissionais

shopkeeper /'ʃɒpki:pə(r)/ *n* lojista *mf*, comerciante *mf*

shoplift|er /'ʃɒplɪftə(r)/ *n* gatuno *m* de lojas. ~**ing** *n* furto *m* em lojas

shopping /'ʃɒpɪŋ/ *n* (*goods*) compras *fpl*. **go** ~ ir às compras. ~ **bag** sacola *f* de compras. ~ **centre** centro *m* comercial

shore /ʃɔ:(r)/ *n* (*of sea*) praia *f*, costa *f*; (*of lake*) margem *f*

shorn /ʃɔ:n/ *see* **shear** □ *a* tosquiado. ~ **of** despojado de

short /ʃɔ:t/ *a* (-er, -est) curto; (*person*) baixo; (*brief*) breve, curto; (*curt*) seco, brusco. **be** ~ **of** (*lack*) ter falta de □ *adv* (*abruptly*) bruscamente, de repente. **cut** ~ abreviar; (*interrupt*) interromper □ *n* (*electr*) curto-circuito *m*; (*film*) curta-metragem *f*, short *m*. ~**s** (*trousers*) calção *m*, (*P*) calções *mpl*, short *m*, (*P*) shorts *mpl*. **a** ~ **time** pouco tempo. **he is called Tom for** ~ o diminutivo dele é Tom. **in** ~ em suma. ~**-change** *vt* (*cheat*) enganar. ~ **circuit** (*electr*) curto-circuito *m* ~**-circuit** *vt/i* (*electr*) fazer *or* dar um curto-circuito (em). ~ **cut** atalho *m*. ~**-handed** *a* com falta de pessoal. ~ **list** pré-seleção *f*, (*P*) pré-selecção *f*. ~**-lived** *a* de pouca duração. ~**-sighted** *a* míope, (*P*) curto de vista. ~**-tempered** *a* irritadiço. ~ **story** conto *m*. ~ **wave** (*radio*) onda(s) *f*(*pl*) curta(s)

shortage /'ʃɔ:tɪdʒ/ *n* falta *f*, escassez *f*

shortbread /'ʃɔ:tbred/ *n* shortbread *m*, biscoito *m* de massa amanteigada

shortcoming /'ʃɔ:tkʌmɪŋ/ *n* falha *f*, imperfeição *f*

shorten /'ʃɔ:tn/ *vt/i* encurtar(-se), abreviar(-se), diminuir

shorthand /'ʃɔ:thænd/ *n* estenografia *f*. ~ **typist** estenodactilógrafa *f*

shortly /'ʃɔ:tlɪ/ *adv* (*soon*) em breve, dentro em pouco

shot /ʃɒt/ *see* **shoot** □ *n* (*firing, bullet*) tiro *m*; (*person*) atirador *m*; (*pellets*) chumbo *m*; (*photograph*) fotografia *f*; (*injection*) injeção *f*, (*P*) injecção *f*; (*in golf, billiards*) tacada *f*. **go like a** ~ ir disparado. **have a** ~ **(at sth)** experimentar (fazer alg coisa). ~**-gun** *n* espingarda *f*, caçadeira *f*

should /ʃʊd/; *unstressed* /ʃəd/ *v aux* **you** ~ **help me** você devia me ajudar. **I** ~ **have stayed** devia ter ficado. I ~ like to gostaria de *or* gostava de. if he ~ come se ele vier

shoulder /'ʃəʊldə(r)/ *n* ombro *m* □ *vt* (*responsibility*) tomar, assumir; (*burden*) carregar, arcar com. ~-**blade** *n* (*anat*) omoplata *f*. ~-**pad** *n* enchimento *m* de ombro, ombreira *f*

shout /ʃaʊt/ *n* grito *m*, brado *m*; (*very loud*) berro *m* □ *vt/i* gritar (**at** com); (*very loudly*) berrar (**at** com). ~ **down** fazer calar com gritos. ~**ing** *n* gritaria *f*, berraria *f*

shove /ʃʌv/ *n* empurrão *m* □ *vt/i* empurrar; (*colloq: put*) meter, enfiar. ~ **off** (*colloq: depart*) começar a andar (*colloq*), dar o fora (*colloq*), (*P*) cavar (*colloq*)

shovel /'ʃʌvl/ *n* pá *f*; (*machine*) escavadora *f* □ *vt* (*pt* **shovelled**) remover com pá

show /ʃəʊ/ *vt* (*pt* **showed**, *pp* **shown**) mostrar; (*of dial, needle*) marcar; (*put on display*) expor; (*film*) dar, passar □ *vi* ver-se, aparecer, estar à vista □ *n* mostra *f*, demonstração *f*, manifestação *f*; (*ostentation*) alarde *m*, espalhafato *m*; (*exhibition*) mostra *f*, exposição *f*; (*theatre, cinema*) espetáculo *m*, (*P*) espectáculo *m*, show *m*. **for** ~ para fazer vista. **on** ~ exposto, em exposição. ~-**down** *n* confrontação *f*. ~-**jumping** *n* concurso *m* hípico. ~ **in** mandar entrar. ~ **off** *vt* exibir, ostentar □ *vi* exibir-se, querer fazer figura. ~-**off** *n* exibicionista *mf*. ~ **out** acompanhar à porta. ~-**piece** *n* peça *f* digna de se expor. ~ **up** ser claramente visível, ver-se bem; (*colloq: arrive*) aparecer. ~**ing** *n* (*performance*) atuação *f*, performance *f*; (*cinema*) exibição *f*

shower /'ʃaʊə(r)/ *n* (*of rain*) aguaceiro *m*, chuvarada *f*; (*of blows etc*) saraivada *f*; (*in bathroom*) chuveiro *m*, ducha *f*, (*P*) duche *m* □ *vt* ~ **with** cumular de, encher de □ *vi* tomar um banho de chuveiro *or* uma ducha, (*P*) um duche. ~**y** *a* chuvoso

showerproof /'ʃaʊəpru:f/ *a* impermeável

shown /ʃəʊn/ *see* **show**

showroom /'ʃəʊrʊm/ *n* espaço *m* de exposição, show-room *m*; (*for cars*) stand *m*

showy /'ʃəʊɪ/ *a* (-**ier**, -**iest**) vistoso; (*too bright*) berrante; (*pej*) espalhafatoso

shrank /ʃræŋk/ *see* **shrink**

shred /ʃred/ *n* tira *f*, retalho *m*, farrapo *m*; (*fig*) mínimo *m*, sombra *f* □ *vt* (*pt* **shredded**) reduzir a tiras, estraçalhar; (*culin*) desfiar. ~**der** *n* trituradora *f*; (*for paper*) fragmentadora *f*

shrewd /ʃru:d/ *a* (-**er**, -**est**) astucioso, fino, perspicaz. ~**ness** *n* astúcia *f*, perspicácia *f*

shriek /ʃri:k/ *n* grito *m* agudo, guincho *m* □ *vt/i* gritar, guinchar

shrift /ʃrɪft/ *n* **give sb short** ~ tratar alguém com brusquidão, despachar alguém sem mais cerimônias, (*P*) cerimónias

shrill /ʃrɪl/ *a* estridente, agudo

shrimp /ʃrɪmp/ *n* camarão *m*

shrine /ʃraɪn/ *n* (*place*) santuário *m*; (*tomb*) túmulo *m*; (*casket*) relicário *m*

shrink /ʃrɪŋk/ *vt/i* (*pt* **shrank**, *pp* **shrunk**) encolher; (*recoil*) encolher-se. ~ **from** esquivar-se a, fugir a (+ *inf*)/de (+ *noun*), retrair-se de. ~**age** *n* encolhimento *m*; (*comm*) contração *f*

shrivel /'ʃrɪvl/ *vt/i* (*pt* **shrivelled**) encarquilhar(-se)

shroud /ʃraʊd/ *n* mortalha *f* □ *vt* (*veil*) encobrir, envolver

Shrove /ʃrəʊv/ *n* ~ **Tuesday** Terça-feira *f* gorda *or* de Carnaval

shrub /ʃrʌb/ *n* arbusto *m*. ~**bery** *n* arbustos *mpl*

shrug /ʃrʌg/ *vt* (*pt* **shrugged**) ~ **one's shoulders** encolher os ombros □ *n* encolher *m* de ombros. ~ **off** não dar importância a

shrunk /ʃrʌŋk/ *see* **shrink**. ~**en** *a* encolhido; (*person*) mirrado, chupado

shudder /'ʃʌdə(r)/ *vi* arrepiar-se, estremecer, tremer □ *n* arrepio *m*, tremor *m*, estremecimento *m*. **I** ~ **to think** tremo só de pensar

shuffle /'ʃʌfl/ *vt* (*feet*) arrastar; (*cards*) embaralhar □ *vi* arrastar os pés □ *n* marcha *f* arrastada

shun /ʃʌn/ *vt* (*pt* **shunned**) evitar, fugir de

shunt /ʃʌnt/ *vt/i* (*train*) mudar de linha, manobrar

shut /ʃʌt/ *vt* (*pt* **shut**, *pres p* **shutting**) fechar □ *vi* fechar-se; (*shop, bank etc*) encerrar, fechar. ~ **down** *or* **up** fechar. ~-**down** *n* encerramento *m*. ~ **in** *or* **up** trancar. ~ **up** *vi* (*colloq: stop talking*) calar-se □ *vt* (*colloq: silence*) mandar calar. ~ **up!** (*colloq*) cale-se!, cale a boca!

shutter /'ʃʌtə(r)/ *n* taipais *mpl*, (*P*) portada *f* de madeira; (*of laths*) persiana *f*; (*in shop*) taipais *mpl*; (*photo*) obturador *m*

shuttle /'ʃʌtl/ *n* (*of spaceship*) ônibus *m* espacial. ~ **service** (*plane*) ponte *f* aérea; (*bus*) navete *f*

shuttlecock /'ʃʌtlkɒk/ *n* volante *m*

shy /ʃaɪ/ *a* (-**er**, -**est**) tímido, acanhado, envergonhado □ *vi* (*horse*) espantar-se (**at** com); (*fig*) assustar-se (**at** *or* **away from** com). ~**ness** *n* timidez *f*, acanhamento *m*, vergonha *f*

Siamese /saɪə'mi:z/ *a* & *n* siamês (*m*). ~ **cat** gato *m* siamês
Sicily /'sɪsɪlɪ/ *n* Sicília *f*
sick /sɪk/ *a* doente; (*humour*) negro. **be** ~ (*vomit*) vomitar. **be** ~ **of** estar farto de. **feel** ~ estar enjoado. ~**-bay** *n* enfermaria *f*. ~**-leave** *n* licença *f* por doença ~**-room** *n* quarto *m* de doente
sicken /'sɪkn/ *vt* (*distress*) desesperar; (*disgust*) repugnar □ *vi* **be** ~**ing for** flu *etc* começar a pegar uma gripe (*colloq*)
sickle /'sɪkl/ *n* foice *f*
sickly /'sɪklɪ/ *a* (-ier, -iest) (*person*) doentio, achacado; (*smell*) enjoativo; (*pale*) pálido
sickness /'sɪknɪs/ *n* doença *f*; (*vomiting*) náusea *f*, vômito *m*, (*P*) vómito *m*
side /saɪd/ *n* lado *m*; (*of road, river*) beira *f*; (*of hill*) encosta *f*; (*sport*) equipe *f*, (*P*) equipa *f* □ *a* lateral □ *vi* ~ **with** tomar o partido de. **on the** ~ (*extra*) nas horas vagas; (*secretly*) pela calada. ~ **by** ~ lado a lado. ~**-car** *n* sidecar *m*. ~**-effect** *n* efeito *m* secundário. ~**-show** *n* espetáculo *m*, (*P*) espectáculo *m* suplementar. ~**-step** *vt* (*pt* -stepped) evitar. ~**-track** *vt* (fazer) desviar dum propósito
sideboard /'saɪdbɔ:d/ *n* aparador *m*
sideburns /'saɪdbɜ:nz/ *npl* suiças *fpl*, costeletas *fpl*, (*P*) patilhas *fpl*
sidelight /'saɪdlaɪt/ *n* (*auto*) luz *f* lateral, (*P*) farolim *m*
sideline /'saɪdlaɪn/ *n* atividade *f*, (*P*) actividade *f* secundária; (*sport*) linha *f* lateral
sidelong /'saɪdlɒŋ/ *adv* & *a* de lado
sidewalk /'saɪdwɔ:k/ *n* (*Amer*) passeio *m*
sideways /'saɪdweɪz/ *adv* & *a* de lado
siding /'saɪdɪŋ/ *n* desvio *m*, ramal *m*
sidle /'saɪdl/ *vi* ~ **up (to)** avançar furtivamente (para), chegar-se furtivamente (a)
siege /si:dʒ/ *n* cerco *m*
siesta /sɪ'estə/ *n* sesta *f*
sieve /sɪv/ *n* peneira *f*; (*for liquids*) coador *m* □ *vt* peneirar; (*liquids*) passar, coar
sift /sɪft/ *vt* peneirar; (*sprinkle*) polvilhar. ~ **through** examinar minuciosamente, esquadrinhar
sigh /saɪ/ *n* suspiro *m* □ *vt/i* suspirar
sight /saɪt/ *n* vista *f*; (*scene*) cena *f*; (*on gun*) mira *f* □ *vt* avistar, ver, divisar. **at** *or* **on** ~ à vista. **catch** ~ **of** avistar. **in** ~ à vista, visível. **lose** ~ **of** perder de vista. **out of** ~ longe dos olhos
sightsee|ing /'saɪtsi:ɪŋ/ *n* visita *f*, turismo *m*. **go** ~**ing** visitar lugares turísticos. ~**r** /'saɪtsi:ə(r)/ *n* turista *mf*
sign /saɪn/ *n* sinal *m*; (*symbol*) signo *m* □ *vt* (*in writing*) assinar □ *vi* (*make a sign*) fazer sinal. ~ **on** *or* **up** (*worker*) assinar contrato. ~**-board** *n* tabuleta *f*. ~ **language** *n* mímica *f*
signal /'sɪgnəl/ *n* sinal *m* □ *vi* (*pt* **signalled**) fazer signal □ *vt* comunicar (por sinais); (*person*) fazer sinal para. ~**-box** *n* cabine *f* de sinalização
signature /'sɪgnətʃə(r)/ *n* assinatura *f*. ~ **tune** indicativo *m* musical
signet-ring /'sɪgnɪtrɪŋ/ *n* anel *m* de sinete
significan|t /sɪg'nɪfɪkənt/ *a* importante; (*meaningful*) significativo. ~**ce** *n* importância *f*; (*meaning*) significado *m*. ~**tly** *adv* (*much*) sensivelmente
signify /'sɪgnɪfaɪ/ *vt* significar
signpost /'saɪnpəʊst/ *n* poste *m* de sinalização □ *vt* sinalizar
silence /'saɪləns/ *n* silêncio *m* □ *vt* silenciar, calar. ~**r** /-ə(r)/ *n* (*on gun*) silenciador *m*; (*on car*) silencioso *m*
silent /'saɪlənt/ *a* silencioso; (*not speaking*) calado; (*film*) mudo. ~**ly** *adv* silenciosamente
silhouette /sɪlu'et/ *n* silhueta *f* □ *vt* **be** ~**d against** estar em silhueta contra
silicon /'sɪlɪkən/ *n* silicone *m*. ~ **chip** circuito *m* integrado
silk /sɪlk/ *n* seda *f*. ~**en**, ~**y** *adjs* sedoso
sill /sɪl/ *n* (*of window*) parapeito *m*; (*of door*) soleira *f*, limiar *m*
sill|y /'sɪlɪ/ *a* (-ier, -iest) tolo, idiota. ~**iness** *n* tolice *f*, idiotice *f*
silo /'saɪləʊ/ *n* (*pl* -os) silo *m*
silt /sɪlt/ *n* aluvião *m*, sedimento *m*
silver /'sɪlvə(r)/ *n* prata *f*; (*silverware*) prataria *f*, pratas *fpl* □ *a* de prata. ~ **papel** papel *m* prateado. ~ **wedding** bodas *fpl* de prata. ~**y** *a* prateado; (*sound*) argentino
silversmith /'sɪlvəsmɪθ/ *n* ourives *m*
silverware /'sɪlvəweə(r)/ *n* prataria *f*, pratas *fpl*
similar /'sɪmɪlə(r)/ *a* ~ (to) semelhante (a), parecido (com). ~**ity** /-ə'lærətɪ/ *n* semelhança *f*. ~**ly** *adv* de igual modo, analogamente
simile /'sɪmɪlɪ/ *n* símile *m*, comparação *f*
simmer /'sɪmə(r)/ *vt/i* cozinhar em fogo brando; (*fig: smoulder*) ferver, fremir; ~ **down** acalmar(-se)
simpl|e /'sɪmpl/ *a* (-er, -est) simples. ~**e-minded** *a* simples; (*feeble-minded*) pobre de espírito, tolo. ~**icity** /-'plɪsətɪ/ *n* simplicidade *f*.

~y *adv* simplesmente; (*absolutely*) absolutamente, simplesmente

simpleton /'sɪmpltən/ *n* simplório *m*

simplif|y /'sɪmplɪfaɪ/ *vt* simplificar. **~ication** /-ɪ'keɪʃn/ *n* simplificação *f*

simulat|e /'sɪmjʊleɪt/ *vt* simular, imitar. **~ion** /-'leɪʃn/ *n* simulação *f*, imitação *f*

simultaneous /sɪml'teɪnɪəs/ *a* simultâneo, concomitante. **~ly** *adv* simultaneamente

sin /sɪn/ *n* pecado *m* □ *vi* (*pt* **sinned**) pecar

since /sɪns/ *prep* desde □ *adv* desde então □ *conj* desde que; (*because*) uma vez que, visto que. **~ then** desde então

sincer|e /sɪn'sɪə(r)/ *a* sincero. **~ely** *adv* sinceramente. **~ity** /-'serətɪ/ *n* sinceridade *f*

sinew /'sɪnju:/ *n* (*anat*) tendão *m*. **~s** músculos *mpl*. **~y** *a* forte, musculoso

sinful /'sɪnfl/ *a* (*wicked*) pecaminoso; (*shocking*) escandaloso

sing /sɪŋ/ *vt/i* (*pt* **sang**, *pp* **sung**) cantar. **~er** *n* cantor *m*

singe /sɪndʒ/ *vt* (*pres p* **singeing**) chamuscar

single /'sɪŋgl/ *a* único, só; (*unmarried*) solteiro; (*bed*) de solteiro; (*room*) individual; (*ticket*) de ida, simples □ *n* (*ticket*) bilhete *m* de ida *or* simples; (*record*) disco *m* de 45 r.p.m. **~s** (*tennis*) singulares *mpl* □ *vt* **~ out** escolher. **in ~ file** em fila indiana. **~-handed** *a* sem ajuda, sozinho. **~-minded** *a* decidido, aferrado à sua idéia, tenaz. **~ parent** pai *m* solteiro, mãe *f* solteira. **singly** *adv* um a um, um por um

singsong /'sɪŋsɒŋ/ *n* **have a ~** cantar em coro □ *a* (*voice*) monótono, monocórdico

singular /'sɪŋgjʊlə(r)/ *n* singular *m* □ *a* (*uncommon; gram*) singular; (*noun*) no singular. **~ly** *adv* singularmente

sinister /'sɪnɪstə(r)/ *a* sinistro

sink /sɪŋk/ *vt* (*pt* **sank**, *pp* **sunk**) (*ship*) afundar, ir a pique; (*well*) abrir; (*invest money*) empatar; (*lose money*) enterrar □ *vi* afundar-se; (*of ground*) ceder; (*of voice*) baixar □ *n* pia *f*, (*P*) lava-louça *m*. **~ in** (*fig*) ficar gravado, entrar (*colloq*). **~ or swim** ou vai ou racha

sinner /'sɪnə(r)/ *n* pecador *m*

sinuous /'sɪnjʊəs/ *a* sinuoso

sinus /'saɪnəs/ *n* (*pl* -**es**) (*anat*) seio (nasal) *m*. **~itis** /saɪnə'saɪtɪs/ *n* sinusite *f*

sip /sɪp/ *n* gole *m* □ *vt* (*pt* **sipped**) bebericar, beber aos golinhos

siphon /'saɪfn/ *n* sifão *m* □ *vt* **~ off** extrair por meio de sifão

sir /sɜ:(r)/ *n* senhor *m*. **S~** (*title*) Sir *m*. **Dear S~** Exmo Senhor. **excuse me, ~** desculpe, senhor. **no, ~** não, senhor

siren /'saɪərən/ *n* sereia *f*, sirene *f*

sirloin /'sɜ:lɔɪn/ *n* lombo *m* de vaca

sissy /'sɪsɪ/ *n* maricas *m*

sister /'sɪstə(r)/ *n* irmã *f*; (*nun*) irmã *f*, freira *f*; (*nurse*) enfermeira-chefe *f*. **~-in-law** (*pl* **~s-in-law**) cunhada *f*. **~ly** *a* fraterno, fraternal

sit /sɪt/ *vt/i* (*pt* **sat**, *pres p* **sitting**) sentar(-se); (*of committee etc*) reunir-se. **~ for an exam** fazer um exame, prestar uma prova. **be ~ting** estar sentado. **~ around** não fazer nada. **~ down** sentar-se. **~-in** *n* ocupação *f*. **~ting** *n* reunião *f*, sessão *f*; (*in restaurant*) serviço *m*. **~ting-room** *n* sala *f* de estar. **~ up** endireitar-se na cadeira; (*not go to bed*) passar a noite acordado

site /saɪt/ *n* local *m*. (**building**) **~** terreno *m* para construção, lote *m* □ *vt* localizar, situar

situat|e /'sɪtʃʊeɪt/ *vt* situar. **be ~ed** estar situado. **~ion** /-'eɪʃn/ *n* (*position, condition*) situação *f*; (*job*) emprego *m*, colocação *f*

six /sɪks/ *a* & *n* seis (*m*). **~th** *a* & *n* sexto (*m*)

sixteen /sɪk'sti:n/ *a* & *n* dezesseis *m*, (*P*) dezasseis (*m*). **~th** *a* & *n* décimo sexto (*m*)

sixt|y /'sɪkstɪ/ *a* & *n* sessenta (*m*). **~ieth** *a* & *n* sexagésimo (*m*)

size /saɪz/ *n* tamanho *m*; (*of person, garment etc*) tamanho *m*, medida *f*; (*of shoes*) número *m*; (*extent*) grandeza *f* □ *vt* **~ up** calcular o tamanho de; (*colloq: judge*) formar um juízo sobre, avaliar. **~able** *a* bastante grande, considerável

sizzle /'sɪzl/ *vi* chiar, rechinar

skate[1] /skeɪt/ *n* (*pl invar*) (*fish*) (ar)raia *f*

skat|e[2] /skeɪt/ *n* patim *m* □ *vi* patinar. **~er** *n* patinador *m*. **~ing** *n* patinação *f*. **~ing-rink** *n* rinque *m* de patinação

skateboard /'skeɪtbɔ:d/ *n* skate *m*

skelet|on /'skelɪtən/ *n* esqueleto *m*; (*framework*) armação *f*. **~on crew** *or* **staff** pessoal *m* reduzido. **~on key** chave *f* mestra. **~al** *a* esquelético

sketch /sketʃ/ *n* esboço *m*, croqui(s) *m*; (*theat*) sketch *m*, peça *f* curta e humorística; (*outline*) idéia *f* geral, esboço *m* □ *vt* esboçar, delinear □ *vi* fazer esboços. **~-book** *n* caderno *m* de desenho

sketchy /'sketʃɪ/ *a* (-**ier**, -**iest**) incompleto, esboçado

skewer /'skjʊə(r)/ *n* espeto *m*

ski /ski:/ *n* (*pl* -s) esqui *m* □ *vi* (*pt* **ski'd** *or* **skied**, *pres p* **skiing**) esquiar; (*go skiing*) fazer esqui. **~er** *n* esquiador *m*. **~ing** *n* esqui *m*

skid /skɪd/ *vi* (*pt* **skidded**) derrapar, patinar □ *n* derrapagem *f*

skilful /ˈskɪlfl/ *a* hábil, habilidoso. **~ly** *adv* habilmente, com perícia

skill /skɪl/ *n* habilidade *f*, jeito *m*; (*craft*) arte *f*. **~s** aptidões *fpl*. **~ed** *a* hábil, habilidoso; (*worker*) especializado

skim /skɪm/ *vt* (*pt* **skimmed**) tirar a espuma de; (*milk*) desnatar, tirar a nata de; (*pass or glide over*) deslizar sobre, roçar □ *vi* **~ through** ler por alto, passar os olhos por. **~med milk** leite *m* desnatado

skimp /skɪmp/ *vt* (*use too little*) poupar em □ *vi* ser poupado

skimpy /ˈskɪmpɪ/ *a* (-ier, -iest) (*clothes*) sumário; (*meal*) escasso, racionado (*fig*)

skin /skɪn/ *n* (*of person, animal*) pele *f*; (*of fruit*) casca *f* □ *vt* (*pt* **skinned**) (*animal*) esfolar, tirar a pele de; (*fruit*) descascar. **~-diving** *n* mergulho *m*, caça *f* submarina

skinny /ˈskɪnɪ/ *a* (-ier, -iest) magricela, escanzelado

skint /skɪnt/ *a* (*sl*) sem dinheiro, na última lona (*sl*), (*P*) nas lonas

skip[1] /skɪp/ *vi* (*pt* **skipped**) saltar, pular; (*jump about*) saltitar; (*with rope*) pular corda □ *vt* (*page*) saltar; (*class*) faltar a □ *n* salto *m*. **~ping rope** *n* corda *f* de pular

skip[2] /skɪp/ *n* (*container*) container *m* grande para entulho

skipper /ˈskɪpə(r)/ *n* capitão *m*

skirmish /ˈskɜ:mɪʃ/ *n* escaramuça *f*

skirt /skɜ:t/ *n* saia *f* □ *vt* contornar, ladear. **~ing-board** *n* rodapé *m*

skit /skɪt/ *n* (*theat*) paródia *f*, sketch *m* satírico

skittle /ˈskɪtl/ *n* pino *m*. **~s** *npl* boliche *m*, (*P*) jogo *m* de laranjinha

skive /skaɪv/ *vi* (*sl*) eximir-se de um dever, evitar trabalhar (*sl*)

skulk /skʌlk/ *vi* (*move*) rondar furtivamente; (*hide*) esconder-se

skull /skʌl/ *n* caveira *f*, crânio *m*

skunk /skʌŋk/ *n* (*animal*) gambá *m*

sky /skaɪ/ *n* céu *m*. **~-blue** *a* & *n* azul-celeste (*m*)

skylight /ˈskaɪlaɪt/ *n* clarabóia *f*

skyscraper /ˈskaɪskreɪpə(r)/ *n* arranha-céus *m invar*

slab /slæb/ *n* (*of marble*) placa *f*; (*of paving-stone*) laje *f*; (*of metal*) chapa *f*; (*of cake*) fatia *f* grossa

slack /slæk/ *a* (-er, -est) (*rope*) bambo, frouxo; (*person*) descuidado, negligente; (*business*) parado, fraco; (*period, season*) morto □ *n* **the ~** (*in rope*) a parte bamba □ *vt/i* (*be lazy*) estar com preguiça, fazer cera (*fig*)

slacken /ˈslækən/ *vt/i* (*speed, activity etc*) afrouxar, abrandar

slacks /slæks/ *npl* calças *fpl*

slag /slæg/ *n* escória *f*

slain /sleɪn/ *see* **slay**

slam /slæm/ *vt* (*pt* **slammed**) bater violentamente com; (*throw*) atirar; (*sl: criticize*) criticar, malhar □ *vi* (*door etc*) bater violentamente □ *n* (*noise*) bater *m*, pancada *f*

slander /ˈsla:ndə(r)/ *n* calúnia *f*, difamação *f* □ *vt* caluniar, difamar. **~ous** *a* calunioso, difamatório

slang /slæŋ/ *n* calão *m*, gíria *f*. **~y** *a* de calão

slant /sla:nt/ *vt/i* inclinar(-se); (*news*) apresentar de forma tendenciosa □ *n* inclinação *f*; (*bias*) tendência *f*; (*point of view*) ângulo *m*. **be ~ing** ser/estar inclinado *or* em declive

slap /slæp/ *vt* (*pt* **slapped**) (*strike*) bater, dar uma palmada em; (*on face*) esbofetear, dar uma bofetada em; (*put forcefully*) atirar com □ *n* palmada *f*, bofetada *f* □ *adv* em cheio. **~-up** *a* (*sl: excellent*) excelente

slapdash /ˈslæpdæʃ/ *a* descuidado; (*impetuous*) precipitado

slapstick /ˈslæpstɪk/ *n* farsa *f* com palhaçadas

slash /slæʃ/ *vt* (*cut*) retalhar, dar golpes em; (*sever*) cortar; (*a garment*) golpear; (*fig: reduce*) reduzir drasticamente, fazer um corte radical em □ *n* corte *m*, golpe *m*

slat /slæt/ *n* (*in blind*) ripa *f*, (*P*) lâmina *f*

slate /sleɪt/ *n* ardósia *f* □ *vt* (*colloq: criticize*) criticar severamente

slaughter /ˈslɔ:tə(r)/ *vt* chacinar, massacrar; (*animals*) abater □ *n* chacina *f*, massacre *m*, mortandade *f*; (*animals*) abate *m*

slaughterhouse /ˈslɔ:təhaʊs/ *n* matadouro *m*

slave /sleɪv/ *n* escravo *m* □ *vi* mourejar, trabalhar como um escravo. **~-driver** *n* (*fig*) o que obriga os outros a trabalharem como escravos, condutor *m* de escravos. **~ry** /-ərɪ/ *n* escravatura *f*

slavish /ˈsleɪvɪʃ/ *a* servil

slay /sleɪ/ *vt* (*pt* **slew**, *pp* **slain**) matar

sleazy /ˈsli:zɪ/ *a* (-ier, -iest) (*colloq*) esquálido, sórdido

sledge /sledʒ/ *n* trenó *m*. **~-hammer** *n* martelo *m* de forja, marreta *f*

sleek /sli:k/ *a* (-er, -est) liso, macio e lustroso

sleep /sli:p/ *n* sono *m* □ *vi* (*pt* **slept**) dormir □ *vt* ter lugar para, alojar. **go**

to ~ ir dormir, adormecer. **put to ~** (*kill*) mandar matar. **~ around** ser promíscuo. **~er** *n* aquele que dorme; (*rail: beam*) dormente *m*; (*berth*) couchette *f*. **~ing-bag** *n* saco *m* de dormir. **~ing-car** *n* carro-dormitório *m*, carruagemcama *f*, (*P*) vagon-lit *m*. **~less** *a* insone; (*night*) em claro, insone. **~-walker** *n* sonâmbulo *m*

sleep|y /'sli:pɪ/ *a* (-ier, -iest) sonolento. **be ~y** ter *or* estar com sono. **~ily** *adv* meio dormindo

sleet /sli:t/ *n* geada *f* miúda □ *vi* cair geada miúda

sleeve /sli:v/ *n* manga *f*; (*of record*) capa *f*. **up one's ~** de reserva, escondido. **~less** *a* sem mangas

sleigh /sleɪ/ *n* trenó *m*

sleight /slaɪt/ *n* **~ of hand** prestidigitação *f*, passe *m* de mágica

slender /'slendə(r)/ *a* esguio, esbelto; (*fig: scanty*) escasso. **~ness** *n* aspecto *m* esguio, esbelteza *f*, elegância *f*; (*scantiness*) escassez *f*

slept /slept/ *see* sleep

sleuth /slu:θ/ *n* (*colloq*) detective *m*

slew[1] /slu:/ *vi* (*turn*) virar-se

slew[2] /slu:/ *see* slay

slice /slaɪs/ *n* fatia *f* □ *vt* cortar em fatias; (*golf, tennis*) cortar

slick /slɪk/ *a* (*slippery*) escorregadio; (*cunning*) astuto, habilidoso; (*unctuous*) melífluo □ *n* (oil) **~** mancha *f* de óleo

slid|e /slaɪd/ *vt/i* (*pt* **slid**) escorregar, deslizar □ *n* escorregadela *f*, escorregão *m*; (*in playground*) escorrega *m*; (*for hair*) prendedor *m*, (*P*) travessa *f*; (*photo*) diapositivo *m*, slide *m*. **~e-rule** *n* régua *f* de cálculo. **~ing** *a* (*door, panel*) corrediço, de correr. **~ing scale** escala *f* móvel

slight /slaɪt/ *a* (-er, -est) (*slender, frail*) delgado, franzino; (*inconsiderable*) leve, ligeiro □ *vt* desconsiderar, desfeitear □ *n* desconsideração *f*, desfeita *f*. **the ~est** *a* o/a menor. **not in the ~est** em absoluto. **~ly** *adv* ligeiramente, um pouco

slim /slɪm/ *a* (**slimmer, slimmest**) magro, esbelto; (*chance*) pequeno, remoto □ *vi* (*pt* **slimmed**) emagrecer. **~ness** *n* magreza *f*, esbelteza *f*

slim|e /slaɪm/ *n* lodo *m*. **~y** *a* lodoso; (*slippery*) escorregadio; (*fig: servile*) servil, bajulador

sling /slɪŋ/ *n* (*weapon*) funda *f*; (*for arm*) tipóia *f* □ *vt* (*pt* **slung**) atirar, lançar

slip /slɪp/ *vt/i* (*pt* **slipped**) escorregar; (*move quietly*) mover-se de mansinho □ *n* escorregadela *f*, escorregão *m*; (*mistake*) engano *m*, lapso *m*; (*petticoat*) combinação *f*; (*of paper*) tira *f* de papel. **give the ~ to** livrar-se de, escapar(-se) de. **~ away** esgueirar-se. **~ by** passar sem se dar conta, passar despercebido. **~-cover** *n* (*Amer*) capa *f* para móveis. **~ into** (*go*) entrar de mansinho, enfiar-se em; (*clothes*) enfiar. **~ of the tongue** lapso *m*. **~ped disc** disco *m* deslocado. **~-road** *n* acesso *m* a autoestrada. **~ sb's mind** passar pela cabeça de alguém. **~ up** (*colloq*) cometer uma gafe. **~-up** *n* (*colloq*) gafe *f*

slipper /'slɪpə(r)/ *n* chinelo *m*

slippery /'slɪpərɪ/ *a* escorregadio; (*fig: person*) que não é de confiança, sem escrúpulos

slipshod /'slɪpʃɒd/ *a* (*person*) desleixado, desmazelado; (*work*) feito sem cuidado, desleixado

slit /slɪt/ *n* fenda *f*; (*cut*) corte *m*; (*tear*) rasgão *m* □ *vt* (*pt* **slit**, *pres p* **slitting**) fender; (*cut*) fazer um corte em, cortar

slither /'slɪðə(r)/ *vi* escorregar, resvalar

sliver /'slɪvə(r)/ *n* (*of cheese etc*) fatia *f*; (*splinter*) lasca *f*

slobber /'slɒbə(r)/ *vi* babar-se

slog /slɒg/ *vt* (*pt* **slogged**) (*hit*) bater com força □ *vi* (*walk*) caminhar com passos pesados e firmes; (*work*) trabalhar duro □ *n* (*work*) trabalheira *f*; (*walk, effort*) estafa *f*

slogan /'sləʊgən/ *n* slogan *m*, lema *m*, palavra *f* de ordem

slop /slɒp/ *vt/i* (*pt* **slopped**) transbordar, entornar. **~s** *npl* (*dirty water*) água(s) *f*(*pl*) suja(s); (*liquid refuse*) despejos *mpl*

slop|e /sləʊp/ *vt/i* inclinar(-se), formar declive □ *n* (*of mountain*) encosta *f*; (*of street*) rampa *f*, ladeira *f*. **~ing** *a* inclinado, em declive

sloppy /'slɒpɪ/ *a* (-ier, -iest) (*ground*) molhado, com poças de água; (*food*) aguado; (*clothes*) desleixado; (*work*) descuidado, feito de qualquer jeito *or* maneira (*colloq*); (*person*) desmazelado; (*maudlin*) piegas

slosh /slɒʃ/ *vt* entornar; (*colloq: splash*) esparrinhar; (*sl: hit*) bater em, dar (uma) sova em □ *vi* chapinhar

slot /slɒt/ *n* ranhura *f*; (*in timetable*) horário *m*; (*TV*) espaço *m*; (*aviat*) slot *m* □ *vt/i* (*pt* **slotted**) enfiar(-se), meter(-se), encaixar (-se). **~-machine** *n* (*for stamps, tickets etc*) distribuidor *m* automático; (*for gambling*) caça-níqueis *m*, (*P*) slot machine *f*

sloth /sləʊθ/ *n* preguiça *f*, indolência *f*; (*zool*) preguiça *f*

slouch /slaʊtʃ/ *vi* (*stand, move*) andar com as costas curvadas; (*sit*) sentar em má postura

slovenly /ˈslʌvnlɪ/ *a* desmazelado, desleixado

slow /sləʊ/ *a* (-er, -est) lento, vagaroso □ *adv* devagar, lentamente □ *vt/i* ~ (**up** *or* **down**) diminuir a velocidade, afrouxar; (*auto*) desacelerar. **be** ~ (*clock etc*) atrasar-se, estar atrasado. **in** ~ **motion** em câmara lenta. ~**ly** *adv* devagar, lentamente, vagarosamente

slow|coach /ˈsləʊkəʊtʃ/, (*Amer*) ~**poke** *ns* lesma *m/f*, pastelão *m* (*fig*)

sludge /slʌdʒ/ *n* lama *f*, lodo *m*

slug /slʌg/ *n* lesma *f*

sluggish /ˈslʌgɪʃ/ *a* (*slow*) lento, moroso; (*lazy*) indolente, preguiçoso

sluice /slu:s/ *n* (*gate*) comporta *f*; (*channel*) canal *m* □ *vt* lavar com jorros de água

slum /slʌm/ *n* favela *f*, (*P*) bairro *m* da lata; (*building*) cortiço *m*

slumber /ˈslʌmbə(r)/ *n* sono *m* □ *vi* dormir

slump /slʌmp/ *n* (*in prices*) baixa *f*, descida *f*; (*in demand*) quebra *f* na procura; (*econ*) depressão *f* □ *vi* (*fall limply*) cair, afundar-se; (*of price*) baixar bruscamente

slung /slʌŋ/ *see* **sling**

slur /slɜ:(r)/ *vt/i* (*pt* **slurred**) (*speech*) pronunciar indistintamente, mastigar □ *n* (*in speech*) som *m* indistinto; (*discredit*) nódoa *f*, estigma *m*

slush /slʌʃ/ *n* (*snow*) neve *f* meio derretida. ~ **fund** (*comm*) fundo *m* para subornos. ~**y** *a* (*road*) coberto de neve derretida, lamacento

slut /slʌt/ *n* (*dirty woman*) porca *f*, desmazelada *f*; (*immoral woman*) desavergonhada *f*

sly /slaɪ/ *a* (**slyer, slyest**) (*crafty*) manhoso; (*secretive*) sonso □ *n* **on the** ~ na calada. ~**ly** *adv* (*craftily*) astutamente; (*secretively*) sonsamente

smack[1] /smæk/ *n* palmada *f*; (*on face*) bofetada *f* □ *vt* dar uma palmada *or* tapa em; (*on the face*) esbofetear, dar uma bofetada em □ *adv* (*colloq*) em cheio, direto

smack[2] /smæk/ *vi* ~ **of sth** cheirar a alg coisa

small /smɔ:l/ *a* (-er, -est) pequeno □ *n* ~ **of the back** zona *f* dos rins □ *adv* (*cut etc*) em pedaços pequenos, aos bocadinhos. ~ **change** trocado *m*, dinheiro *m* miúdo. ~ **talk** conversa *f* fiada, bate-papo *m*. ~**ness** *n* pequenez *f*

smallholding /ˈsmɔ:lhəʊldɪŋ/ *n* pequena propriedade *f*

smallpox /ˈsmɔ:lpɒks/ *n* varíola *f*

smarmy /ˈsma:mɪ/ *a* (-ier, -iest) (*colloq*) bajulador, puxa-saco (*colloq*)

smart /sma:t/ *a* (-er, -est) elegante; (*clever*) esperto, vivo; (*brisk*) rápido □ *vi* (*sting*) arder, picar. ~**ly** *adv* elegantemente, com elegância; (*cleverly*) com esperteza, vivamente; (*briskly*) rapidamente. ~**ness** *n* elegância *f*

smarten /ˈsma:tn/ *vt/i* ~ (**up**) arranjar, dar um ar mais cuidado a. ~ (**o.s.**) **up** embelezar-se, arrumar-se, (*P*) pôr-se elegante/bonito; (*tidy*) arranjar-se

smash /smæʃ/ *vt/i* (*to pieces*) despedaçar(-se), espatifar(-se) (*colloq*); (*a record*) quebrar; (*opponent*) esmagar; (*ruin*) (fazer) falir; (*of vehicle*) espatifar(-se) □ *n* (*noise*) estrondo *m*; (*blow*) pancada *f* forte, golpe *m*; (*collision*) colisão *f*; (*tennis*) smash *m*

smashing /ˈsmæʃɪŋ/ *a* (*colloq*) formidável, estupendo (*colloq*)

smattering /ˈsmætərɪŋ/ *n* leves noções *fpl*

smear /smɪə(r)/ *vt* (*stain; discredit*) manchar; (*coat*) untar, besuntar □ *n* mancha *f*, nódoa *f*; (*med*) esfregaço *m*

smell /smel/ *n* cheiro *m*, odor *m*; (*sense*) cheiro *m*, olfato *m*, (*P*) olfacto *m* □ *vt/i* (*pt* **smelt** *or* **smelled**) ~ (**of**) cheirar (a). ~**y** *a* malcheiroso

smelt[1] /smelt/ *see* **smell**

smelt[2] /smelt/ *vt* (*ore*) fundir

smil|e /smaɪl/ *n* sorriso *m* □ *vi* sorrir. ~**ing** *a* sorridente, risonho

smirk /smɜ:k/ *n* sorriso *m* falso *or* afetado, (*P*) afectado

smithereens /smɪðəˈri:nz/ *npl* **to** *or* **in** ~ em pedaços *mpl*

smock /smɒk/ *n* guarda-pó *m*

smog /smɒg/ *n* mistura *f* de nevoeiro e fumaça, smog *m*

smoke /sməʊk/ *n* fumo *m*, fumaça *f* □ *vt* fumar; (*bacon etc*) fumar, defumar □ *vi* fumar, fumegar. ~**-screen** *n* (*lit & fig*) cortina *f* de fumaça. ~**less** *a* (*fuel*) sem fumo. ~**r** /-ə(r)/ *n* (*person*) fumante *mf*, (*P*) fumador *m*. **smoky** *a* (*air*) enfumaçado, fumacento

smooth /smu:ð/ *a* (-er, -est) liso; (*soft*) macio; (*movement*) regular, suave; (*manners*) lisonjeiro, conciliador, suave □ *vt* alisar. ~ **out** (*fig*) aplanar, remover. ~**ly** *adv* suavemente, facilmente

smother /ˈsmʌðə(r)/ *vt* (*stifle*) abafar, sufocar; (*cover, overwhelm*) cobrir (**with** de); (*suppress*) abafar, reprimir

smoulder /ˈsməʊldə(r)/ *vi* (*lit & fig*) arder, abrasar-se

smudge /smʌdʒ/ *n* mancha *f*, borrão *m* □ *vt/i* sujar(-se), manchar(-se), borrar(-se)

smug /smʌg/ *a* (**smugger, smuggest**) presunçoso, convencido (*colloq*). ~**ly** *adv* presunçosamente. ~**ness** *n* presunção *f*

smuggl|e /ˈsmʌgl/ *vt* contrabandear, fazer contrabando de. **~er** *n* contrabandista *mf*. **~ing** *n* contrabando *m*

smut /smʌt/ *n* fuligem *f*. **~ty** *a* cheio de fuligem; (*colloq: obscene*) indecente, sujo (*colloq*)

snack /snæk/ *n* refeição *f* ligeira. **~-bar** *n* lanchonete *f*, (*P*) snack(-bar) *m*

snag /snæg/ *n* (*obstacle*) obstáculo *m*; (*drawback*) problema *m*, contra *m*; (*in cloth*) rasgão *m*; (*in stocking*) fio *m* puxado

snail /sneɪl/ *n* caracol *m*. **at a ~'s pace** em passo de tartaruga

snake /sneɪk/ *n* serpente *f*, cobra *f*

snap /snæp/ *vt/i* (*pt* **snapped**) (*whip, fingers*) (fazer) estalar; (*break*) estalar(-se), partir(-se) com um estalo, rebentar; (*say*) dizer irritadamente □ *n* estalo *m*; (*photo*) instantâneo *m*; (*Amer: fastener*) mola *f* □ *a* súbito, repentino. **~ at** (*bite*) abocanhar, tentar morder; (*speak angrily*) retrucar asperamente. **~ up** (*buy*) comprar rapidamente

snappish /ˈsnæpɪʃ/ *a* irritadiço

snappy /ˈsnæpɪ/ *a* (-ier, -iest) (*colloq*) vivo, animado. **make it ~** (*colloq*) vai rápido!, apresse-se! (*colloq*)

snapshot /ˈsnæpʃɒt/ *n* instantâneo *m*

snare /sneə(r)/ *n* laço *m*, cilada *f*, armadilha *f*

snarl /sna:l/ *vi* rosnar □ *n* rosnadela *f*

snatch /snætʃ/ *vt* (*grab*) agarrar, apanhar; (*steal*) roubar. **~ from sb** arrancar de alguém □ *n* (*theft*) roubo *m*; (*bit*) bocado *m*, pedaço *m*

sneak /sni:k/ *vi* (*slink*) esgueirar-se furtivamente; (*sl: tell tales*) fazer queixa, delatar □ *vt* (*sl: steal*) rapinar (*colloq*) □ *n* (*sl*) dedo-duro *m*, queixinhas *mf* (*sl*). **~ing** *a* secreto. **~y** *a* sonso

sneer /snɪə(r)/ *n* sorriso *m* de desdém □ *vi* sorrir desdenhosamente

sneeze /sni:z/ *n* espirro *m* □ *vi* espirrar

snide /snaɪd/ *a* (*colloq*) sarcástico

sniff /snɪf/ *vi* fungar □ *vt/i* **~ (at)** (*smell*) cheirar; (*dog*) farejar. **~ at** (*fig: in contempt*) desprezar □ *n* fungadela *f*

snigger /ˈsnɪgə(r)/ *n* riso *m* abafado □ *vi* rir dissimuladamente

snip /snɪp/ *vt* (*pt* **snipped**) cortar com tesoura □ *n* pedaço *m*, retalho *m*; (*sl: bargain*) pechincha *f*

snipe /snaɪp/ *vi* dar tiros de emboscada. **~r** /-ə(r)/ *n* franco-atirador *m*

snivel /ˈsnɪvl/ *vi* (*pt* **snivelled**) choramingar, lamuriar-se

snob /snɒb/ *n* esnobe *mf*, (*P*) snob *mf*. **~bery** *n* esnobismo *m*, (*P*) snobismo *m*. **~bish** *a* esnobe, (*P*) snob

snooker /ˈsnu:kə(r)/ *n* snooker *m*, sinuca *f*

snoop /snu:p/ *vi* (*colloq*) bisbilhotar, meter o nariz em toda a parte. **~ on** espiar, espionar. **~er** *n* bisbilhoteiro *m*

snooty /ˈsnu:tɪ/ *a* (-ier, -iest) (*colloq*) convencido, arrogante (*colloq*)

snooze /snu:z/ *n* (*colloq*) soneca *f* (*colloq*) □ *vi* (*colloq*) tirar uma soneca

snore /snɔ:(r)/ *n* ronco *m* □ *vi* roncar

snorkel /ˈsnɔ:kl/ *n* tubo *m* de respiração, snorkel *m*

snort /snɔ:t/ *n* resfôlego *m* , bufido *m* □ *vi* resfolegar, bufar

snout /snaʊt/ *n* focinho *m*

snow /snəʊ/ *n* neve *f* □ *vi* nevar. **be ~ed under** (*fig: be overwhelmed*) estar sobrecarregado (*fig*). **~-bound** *a* bloqueado pela neve. **~-drift** *n* banco *m* de neve. **~-plough** *n* limpa-neve *m*. **~y** *a* nevado, coberto de neve

snowball /ˈsnəʊbɔ:l/ *n* bola *f* de neve □ *vi* atirar bolas de neve (em); (*fig*) acumular-se, ir num crescendo, aumentar rapidamente

snowdrop /ˈsnəʊdrɒp/ *n* (*bot*) fura-neve *m*

snowfall /ˈsnəʊfɔ:l/ *n* nevada *f*, (*P*) nevão *m*

snowflake /ˈsnəʊfleɪk/ *n* floco *m* de neve

snowman /ˈsnəʊmæn/ *n* (*pl* **-men**) boneco *m* de neve

snub /snʌb/ *vt* (*pt* **snubbed**) desdenhar, tratar com desdém □ *n* desdém *m*

snuff[1] /ˈsnʌf/ *n* rapé *m*

snuff[2] /snʌf/ *vt* **~ out** (*candles, hopes etc*) apagar, extinguir

snuffle /ˈsnʌfl/ *vi* fungar

snug /snʌg/ *a* (**snugger, snuggest**) (*cosy*) aconchegado; (*close-fitting*) justo

snuggle /ˈsnʌgl/ *vt/i* (*nestle*) aninhar-se, aconchegar-se; (*cuddle*) aconchegar

so /səʊ/ *adv* tão, de tal modo; (*thus*) assim, deste modo □ *conj* por isso, portanto, por consequinte. **~ am I** eu também. **~ does he** ele também. **that is ~** é isso. **I think ~** acho que sim. **five or ~** uns cinco. **~ as to** de modo a. **~ far** até agora, até aqui. **~ long!** (*colloq*) até já! (*colloq*). **~ many** tantos. **~ much** tanto. **~ that** para que, de modo que. **~-and-~** fulano *m*. **~-called** *a* pretenso, soidisant. **~-so** *a & adv* assim assim, mais ou menos

soak /səʊk/ *vt/i* molhar(-se), ensopar (-se), enchacar(-se). **leave to ~** pôr de molho. **~ in** *or* **up** *vt* absorver, embeber. **~ through** repassar. **~ing** *a* ensopado, encharcado

soap /səʊp/ *n* sabão *m*. (toilet) ~ sabonete *m* □ *vt* ensaboar. ~ **opera** (*radio*) novela *f* radiofônica, (*P*) radiofónica; (*TV*) telenovela *f*. ~ **flakes** flocos *mpl* de sabão. ~ **powder** sabão *m* em pó. ~**y** *a* ensaboado
soar /sɔ:(r)/ *vi* voar alto; (*go high*) elevar-se; (*hover*) pairar
sob /sɒb/ *n* soluço *m* □ *vi* (*pt* **sobbed**) soluçar
sober /'səʊbə(r)/ *a* (*not drunk, calm, of colour*) sóbrio; (*serious*) sério, grave □ *vt/i* ~ **up** (fazer) ficar sóbrio, (fazer) curar a bebedeira (*colloq*)
soccer /'sɒkə(r)/ *n* (*colloq*) futebol *m*
sociable /'səʊʃəbl/ *a* sociável
social /'səʊʃl/ *a* social; (*sociable*) sociável; (*gathering, life*) de sociedade □ *n* reunião *f* social. ~**ly** *adv* socialmente; (*meet*) em sociedade. ~ **security** previdência *f* social; (*for old age*) pensão *f*. ~ **worker** assistente *mf* social
socialis|t /'səʊʃəlɪst/ *n* socialista *mf*. ~**m** /-zəm/ *n* socialismo *m*
socialize /'səʊʃəlaɪz/ *vi* socializar-se, reunir-se em sociedade. ~ **with** freqüentar, (*P*) frequentar, conviver com
society /sə'saɪətɪ/ *n* sociedade *f*
sociolog|y /səʊsɪ'ɒlədʒɪ/ *n* sociologia *f*. ~**ical** /-ə'lɒdʒɪkl/ *a* sociológico. ~**ist** *n* sociólogo *m*
sock[1] /sɒk/ *n* meia *f* curta; (*men's*) meia *f* (curta), (*P*) peuga *f*; (*women's*) soquete *f*
sock[2] /sɒk/ *vt* (*sl: hit*) esmurrar, dar um murro em (*colloq*)
socket /'sɒkɪt/ *n* cavidade *f*; (*for lamp*) suporte *m*; (*electr*) tomada *f*; (*of tooth*) alvéolo *m*
soda /'səʊdə/ *n* soda *f*. (baking) ~ (*culin*) bicarbonato *m* de soda. ~ **(-water)** água *f* gasosa, soda *f* limonada, (*P*) água *f* gaseificada
sodden /'sɒdn/ *a* ensopado, empapado
sodium /'səʊdɪəm/ *n* sódio *m*
sofa /'səʊfə/ *n* sofá *m*
soft /sɒft/ *a* (-er, -est) (*not hard, feeble*) mole; (*not rough, not firm*) macio; (*gentle, not loud, not bright*) suave; (*tender-hearted*) sensível; (*fruit*) sem caroço; (*wood*) de coníferas; (*drink*) não alcoólico. ~**-boiled** *a* (*egg*) quente. ~ **spot** (*fig*) fraco *m*. ~**ly** *adv* docemente. ~**ness** *n* moleza *f*; (*to touch*) maciez *f*; (*gentleness*) suavidade *f*, brandura *f*
soften /'sɒfn/ *vt/i* amaciar, amolecer; (*tone down, lessen*) abrandar
software /'sɒftweə(r)/ *n* software *m*
soggy /'sɒgɪ/ *a* (-ier, -iest) ensopado, empapado
soil[1] /sɔɪl/ *n* solo *m*, terra *f*
soil[2] /sɔɪl/ *vt/i* sujar(-se). ~**ed** *a* sujo
solace /'sɒlɪs/ *n* consolo *m*; (*relief*) alívio *m*
solar /'səʊlə(r)/ *a* solar
sold /səʊld/ *see* **sell** □ *a* ~ **out** esgotado
solder /'səʊldə(r)/ *n* solda *f* □ *vt* soldar
soldier /'səʊldʒə(r)/ *n* soldado *m* □ *vi* ~ **on** (*colloq*) perseverar com afinco, batalhar (*colloq*)
sole[1] /səʊl/ *n* (*of foot*) planta *f*, sola *f* do pé; (*of shoe*) sola *f*
sole[2] /səʊl/ *n* (*fish*) solha *f*
sole[3] /səʊl/ *a* único. ~**ly** *adv* unicamente
solemn /'sɒləm/ *a* solene. ~**ity** /sə'lemnətɪ/ *n* solenidade *f*. ~**ly** *adv* solenemente
solicit /sə'lɪsɪt/ *vt* (*seek*) solicitar □ *vi* (*of prostitute*) aproximar-se de homens na rua
solicitor /sə'lɪsɪtə(r)/ *n* advogado *m*
solicitous /sə'lɪsɪtəs/ *a* solícito
solid /'sɒlɪd/ *a* sólido; (*not hollow*) maciço, cheio, compacto; (*gold etc*) maciço; (*meal*) substancial □ *n* sólido *m* ~**s** (*food*) alimentos *mpl* sólidos. ~**ity** /sə'lɪdətɪ/ *n* solidez *f*. ~**ly** *adv* solidamente
solidarity /sɒlɪ'dærətɪ/ *n* solidariedade *f*
solidify /sə'lɪdɪfaɪ/ *vt/i* solidificar(-se)
soliloquy /sə'lɪləkwɪ/ *n* monólogo *m*, solilóquio *m*
solitary /'sɒlɪtrɪ/ *a* solitário, só; (*only one*) um único. ~ **confinement** prisão *f* celular, solitária *f*
solitude /'sɒlɪtju:d/ *n* solidão *f*
solo /'səʊləʊ/ *n* (*pl* -os) solo *m* □ *a* solo. ~ **flight** vôo *m* solo. ~**ist** *n* solista *mf*
soluble /'sɒljʊbl/ *a* solúvel
solution /sə'lu:ʃn/ *n* solução *f*
solv|e /sɒlv/ *vt* resolver, solucionar. ~**able** *a* resolúvel, solúvel
solvent /'sɒlvənt/ *a* (dis)solvente; (*comm*) solvente □ *n* (dis)solvente *m*
sombre /'sɒmbə(r)/ *a* sombrio
some /sʌm/ *a* (*quantity*) algum(a); (*number*) alguns, algumas, uns, umas; (*unspecified, some or other*) um(a)... qualquer, uns... quaisquer, umas... quaisquer; (*a little*) um pouco de, algum; (*a certain*) um certo; (*contrasted with others*) uns, umas, alguns, algumas, certos, certas □ *pron* uns, umas, algum(a), alguns, algumas; (*a little*) um pouco, algum □ *adv* (*approximately*) uns, umas. **will you have** ~ **coffee**/*etc*? você quer café/*etc*? ~ **day** algum dia. ~ **of my friends** alguns dos meus amigos. ~ **people say...** algumas pessoas dizem... ~ **time ago** algum tempo atrás

somebody /'sʌmbədɪ/ *pron* alguém □ *n* **be a ~** ser alguém
somehow /'sʌmhaʊ/ *adv* (*in some way*) de algum modo, de alguma maneira; (*for some reason*) por alguma razão
someone /'sʌmwʌn/ *pron & n* = somebody
somersault /'sʌməsɔ:lt/ *n* cambalhota *f*; (*in the air*) salto *m* mortal □ *vi* dar uma cambalhota/um salto mortal
something /'sʌmθɪŋ/ *pron & n* uma/alguma/qualquer coisa *f*, algo. **~ good/***etc* uma coisa boa/*etc*, qualquer coisa de bom/*etc*. **~ like** um pouco como
sometime /'sʌmtaɪm/ *adv* a certa altura, um dia □ *a* (*former*) antigo. **~ last summer** a certa altura no verão passado. **I'll go ~** hei de ir um dia
sometimes /'sʌmtaɪmz/ *adv* às vezes, de vez em quando
somewhat /'sʌmwɒt/ *adv* um pouco, um tanto (ou quanto)
somewhere /'sʌmweə(r)/ *adv* (*position*) em algum lugar; (*direction*) para algum lugar
son /sʌn/ *n* filho *m*. **~-in-law** *n* (*pl* **~s-in-law**) genro *m*
sonar /'səʊna:(r)/ *n* sonar *m*
sonata /sə'na:tə/ *n* (*mus*) sonata *f*
song /sɒŋ/ *n* canção *f*. **~-bird** *n* ave *f* canora
sonic /'sɒnɪk/ *a* **~ boom** estrondo *m* sônico, (*P*) sónico
sonnet /'sɒnɪt/ *n* soneto *m*
soon /su:n/ *adv* (-er, -est) em breve, dentro em pouco, daqui a pouco; (*early*) cedo. **as ~ as possible** o mais rápido possível. **I would ~er stay** preferia ficar. **~ after** pouco depois. **~er or later** mais cedo ou mais tarde
soot /sʊt/ *n* fuligem *f*. **~y** *a* coberto de fuligem
sooth|e /su:ð/ *vt* acalmar, suavizar; (*pain*) aliviar. **~ing** *a* (*remedy*) calmante, suavizante; (*words*) confortante
sophisticated /sə'fɪstɪkeɪtɪd/ *a* sofisticado, refinado, requintado; (*machine etc*) sofisticado
soporific /sɒpə'rɪfɪk/ *a* soporífico
sopping /'sɒpɪŋ/ *a* encharcado, ensopado
soppy /'sɒpɪ/ *a* (-ier, -iest) (*colloq: sentimental*) piegas; (*colloq: silly*) bobo
soprano /sə'pra:nəʊ/ *n* (*pl* **~s**) & *adj* soprano (*mf*)
sorbet /'sɔ:beɪ/ *n* (*water-ice*) sorvete *m* feito sem leite
sorcerer /'sɔ:sərə(r)/ *n* feiticeiro *m*
sordid /'sɔ:dɪd/ *a* sórdido
sore /sɔ:(r)/ *a* (-er, -est) dolorido; (*vexed*) aborrecido (at, with com) □ *n* ferida *f*. **have a ~ throat** ter a garganta inflamada, ter dores de garganta
sorely /'sɔ:lɪ/ *adv* fortemente, seriamente
sorrow /'sɒrəʊ/ *n* dor *f*, mágoa *f*, pesar *m*. **~ful** *a* pesaroso, triste
sorry /'sɒrɪ/ *a* (-ier, -iest) (*state, sight etc*) triste. **be ~ to/that** (*regretful*) sentir muito/que, lamentar que; **be ~ about/for** (*repentant*) ter pena de, estar arrependido de. **feel ~ for** ter pena de. **~!** desculpe!, perdão!
sort /sɔ:t/ *n* gênero *m*, (*P*) género *m*, espécie *f*, qualidade *f*. **of ~s** (*colloq*) uma espécie de (*colloq, pej*). **out of ~s** indisposto □ *vt* separar por grupos; (*tidy*) arrumar. **~ out** (*problem*) resolver; (*arrange, separate*) separar, distribuir
soufflé /'su:fleɪ/ *n* (*culin*) suflê *m*, (*P*) soufflé *m*
sought /sɔ:t/ *see* **seek**
soul /səʊl/ *n* alma *f*. **the life and ~ of** (*fig*) a alma *f* de (*fig*)
soulful /'səʊlfl/ *a* emotivo, expressivo, cheio de sentimento
sound[1] /saʊnd/ *n* som *m*, barulho *m*, ruído *m* □ *vt/i* soar; (*seem*) dar a impressão de, parecer (as if que). **~ a horn** tocar uma buzina, buzinar. **~ barrier** barreira *f* de som. **~ like** parecer ser, soar como. **~-proof** *a* à prova de som □ *vt* fazer o isolamento sonoro de, isolar. **~-track** *n* (*of film*) trilha *f* sonora, (*P*) banda *f* sonora
sound[2] /saʊnd/ *a* (-er, -est) (*healthy*) saudável, sadio; (*sensible*) sensato, acertado; (*secure*) firme, sólido. **~ asleep** profundamente adormecido. **~ly** *adv* solidamente
sound[3] /saʊnd/ *vt* (*test*) sondar; (*med; views*) auscultar
soup /su:p/ *n* sopa *f*
sour /'saʊə(r)/ *a* (-er, -est) azedo □ *vt/i* azedar, envinagrar
source /sɔ:s/ *n* fonte *f*; (*of river*) nascente *f*
souse /saʊs/ *vt* (*throw water on*) atirar água em cima de; (*pickle*) pôr em vinagre; (*salt*) pôr em salmoura
south /saʊθ/ *n* sul *m* □ *a* sul, do sul; (*of country, people etc*) meridional □ *adv* a, ao/para o sul. **S~ Africa/America** África *f*/América *f* do Sul. **S~ African/American** *a & n* sul-africano (*m*)/sul-americano (*m*). **~-east** *n* sudeste *m*. **~erly** /'sʌðəlɪ/ *a* do sul, meridional. **~ward** *a* ao sul. **~ward(s)** *adv* para o sul. **~-west** *n* sudoeste *m*
southern /'sʌðən/ *a* do sul, meridional, austral

souvenir /su:və'nɪə(r)/ *n* recordação *f*, lembrança *f*
sovereign /'sɒvrɪn/ *n* & *a* soberano (*m*). **~ty** *n* soberania *f*
Soviet /'səʊvɪət/ *a* soviético. **the S~ Union** a União Soviética
sow[1] /səʊ/ *vt* (*pt* **sowed**, *pp* **sowed** *or* **sown**) semear
sow[2] /saʊ/ *n* (*zool*) porca *f*
soy /'sɔɪ/ *n* **~ sauce** molho *m* de soja
soya /'sɔɪə/ *n* soja *f*. **~-bean** semente *f* de soja
spa /spa:/ *n* termas *fpl*
space /speɪs/ *n* espaço *m*; (*room*) lugar *m*; (*period*) espaço *m*, período *m* □ *a* (*research etc*) espacial □ *vt* **~ out** espaçar
space|craft /'speɪskra:ft/ *n* (*pl invar*), **~ship** *n* nave espacial *f*
spacious /'speɪʃəs/ *a* espaçoso
spade /speɪd/ *n* (*gardener's*) pá *f* de ferro; (*child's*) pá *f*. **~s** (*cards*) espadas *fpl*
spadework /'speɪdwɜ:k/ *n* (*fig*) trabalho *m* preliminar
spaghetti /spə'getɪ/ *n* espaguete *m*, (*P*) esparguete *m*
Spain /speɪn/ *n* Espanha *f*
span[1] /spæn/ *n* (*of arch*) vão *m*; (*of wings*) envergadura *f*; (*of time*) espaço *m*, duração *f*; (*measure*) palmo *m* □ *vt* (*pt* **spanned**) (*extend across*) transpor; (*measure*) medir em palmos; (*in time*) abarcar, abranger, estender-se por
span[2] /spæn/ *see* **spick**
Spaniard /'spænɪəd/ *n* espanhol *m*
Spanish /'spænɪʃ/ *a* espanhol □ *n* (*lang*) espanhol *m*
spaniel /'spænɪəl/ *n* spaniel *m*, epagneul *m*
spank /spæŋk/ *vt* dar palmadas *or* chineladas no. **~ing** *n* (*with hand*) palmada *f*; (*with slipper*) chinelada *f*
spanner /'spænə(r)/ *n* (*tool*) chave *f* de porcas; (*adjustable*) chave *f* inglesa
spar /spa:(r)/ *vi* (*pt* **sparred**) jogar boxe, esp para treino; (*fig: argue*) discutir
spare /speə(r)/ *vt* (*not hurt; use with restraint*) poupar; (*afford to give*) dispensar, ceder □ *a* (*in reserve*) de reserva, de sobra; (*tyre*) sobressalente; (*bed*) extra; (*room*) de hóspedes □ *n* (*part*) sobressalente *m*. **~ time** horas *fpl* vagas. **have an hour to ~** dispôr de uma hora. **have no time to ~** não ter tempo a perder
sparing /'speərɪŋ/ *a* poupado. **be ~ of** poupar em, ser poupado com. **~ly** *adv* frugalmente
spark /spa:k/ *n* centelha *f*, faísca *f* □ *vt* lançar faíscas. **~ off** (*initiate*) desencadear, provocar. **~(ing)-plug** *n* vela *f* de ignição
sparkle /'spa:kl/ *vi* cintilar, brilhar □ *n* brilho *m*, cintilação *f*
sparkling /'spa:klɪŋ/ *a* (*wine*) espumante
sparrow /'spærəʊ/ *n* pardal *m*
sparse /spa:s/ *a* esparso; (*hair*) ralo. **~ly** *adv* (*furnished etc*) escassamente
spasm /'spæzəm/ *n* (*of muscle*) espasmo *m*; (*of coughing, anger etc*) ataque *m*, acesso *m*
spasmodic /spæz'mɒdɪk/ *a* espasmódico; (*at irregular intervals*) intermitente
spastic /'spæstɪk/ *n* deficiente *mf* motor
spat /spæt/ *see* **spit**[1]
spate /speɪt/ *n* (*in river*) enxurrada *f*, cheia *f*. **a ~ of** (*letters etc*) uma avalanche de
spatter /'spætə(r)/ *vt* salpicar (**with** de, com)
spawn /spɔ:n/ *n* ovas *fpl* □ *vi* desovar □ *vt* gerar em quantidade
speak /spi:k/ *vt/i* (*pt* **spoke**, *pp* **spoken**) falar (**to/with sb about sth** com alguém de/sobre alg coisa); (*say*) dizer. **~ out/up** falar abertamente; (*louder*) falar mais alto. **~ one's mind** dizer o que se pensa. **so to ~** por assim dizer. **English/Portuguese spoken** fala-se português/inglês
speaker /'spi:kə(r)/ *n* (*in public*) orador *m*; (*loudspeaker*) alto-falante *m*; (*of a language*) pessoa *f* de língua nativa
spear /spɪə(r)/ *n* lança *f*
spearhead /'spɪəhed/ *n* ponta *f* de lança □ *vt* (*lead*) estar à frente de, encabeçar
special /'speʃl/ *a* especial. **~ity** /-ɪ'ælətɪ/ *n* especialidade *f*. **~ly** *adv* especialmente. **~ty** *n* especialidade *f*
specialist /'speʃəlɪst/ *n* especialista *mf*
specialize /'speʃəlaɪz/ *vi* especializar-se (**in** em). **~d** *a* especializado
species /'spi:ʃɪz/ *n* (*pl invar*) espécie *f*
specific /spə'sɪfɪk/ *a* específico. **~ally** *adv* especificamente, explicitamente
specif|y /'spesɪfaɪ/ *vt* especificar. **~ication** /-ɪ'keɪʃn/ *n* especificação *f*. **~ications** *npl* (*of work etc*) caderno *m* de encargos
specimen /'spesɪmɪn/ *n* espécime(n) *m*, amostra *f*
speck /spek/ *n* (*stain*) mancha *f* pequena; (*dot*) pontinho *m*, pinta *f*; (*particle*) grão *m*
speckled /'spekld/ *a* salpicado, manchado

specs /speks/ *npl* (*colloq*) óculos *mpl*
spectacle /'spektəkl/ *n* espetáculo *m*, (*P*) espectáculo *m*. **(pair of) ~s** (par *m* de) óculos *mpl*
spectacular /spek'tækjʊlə(r)/ *a* espetacular, (*P*) espectacular
spectator /spek'teɪtə(r)/ *n* espectador *m*
spectre /'spektə(r)/ *n* espectro *m*, fantasma *m*
spectrum /'spektrəm/ *n* (*pl* **-tra**) espectro *m*; (*of ideas etc*) faixa *f*, gama *f*, leque *m*
speculat|e /'spekjʊleɪt/ *vi* especular, fazer especulações *or* conjeturas, (*P*) conjecturas (**about** sobre); (*comm*) especular, fazer especulação (**in** em). **~ion** /-'leɪʃn/ *n* especulação *f*, conjetura *f*, (*P*) conjectura *f*; (*comm*) especulação *f*. **~or** *n* especulador *m*
speech /spi:tʃ/ *n* (*faculty*) fala *f*; (*diction*) elocução *f*; (*dialect*) falar *m*; (*address*) discurso *m*. **~less** *a* mudo, sem fala (**with** com, de)
speed /spi:d/ *n* velocidade *f*, rapidez *f* □ *vt/i* (*pt* **sped** /sped/) (*move*) ir depressa *or* a grande velocidade; (*send*) despedir, mandar; (*pt* **speeded**) (*drive too fast*) ultrapassar o limite de velocidade. **~ limit** limite *m* de velocidade. **~ up** acelerar(-se). **~ing** *n* excesso *m* de velocidade
speedometer /spi:'dɒmɪtə(r)/ *n* velocímetro *m*, (*P*) conta-quilómetros *m inv*
speed|y /'spi:dɪ/ *a* (**-ier, -iest**) rápido; (*prompt*) pronto. **~ily** *adv* rapidamente; (*promptly*) prontamente
spell[1] /spel/ *n* (*magic*) sortilégio *m*
spell[2] /spel/ *vt/i* (*pt* **spelled** *or* **spelt**) escrever; (*fig: mean*) significar, ter como resultado. **~ out** soletrar; (*fig: explain*) explicar claramente. **~ing** *n* ortografia *f*
spell[3] /spel/ *n* (*short period*) período *m* curto, breve espaço *m* de tempo; (*turn*) turno *m*
spend /spend/ *vt* (*pt* **spent**) (*money, energy*) gastar (**on** em); (*time, holiday*) passar. **~er** *n* gastador *m*
spendthrift /'spendθrɪft/ *n* perdulário *m*, esbanjador *m*
spent /spent/ *see* **spend** □ *a* (*used*) gasto
sperm /spɜ:m/ *n* (*pl* **sperms** *or* **sperm**) (*semen*) esperma *m*, sêmen *m*, (*P*) sémen *m*; (*cell*) espermatozóide *m*
spew /spju:/ *vt/i* vomitar, lançar
sphere /sfɪə(r)/ *n* esfera *f*
spherical /'sferɪkl/ *a* esférico
spic|e /spaɪs/ *n* especiaria *f*, condimento *m*; (*fig*) picante *m* □ *vt* condimentar. **~y** *a* condimentado; (*fig*) picante
spick /spɪk/ *a* **~ and span** novo em folha, impecável
spider /'spaɪdə(r)/ *n* aranha *f*
spik|e /spaɪk/ *n* (*of metal etc*) bico *m*, espigão *m*, ponta *f*. **~y** *a* guarnecido de bicos *or* pontas
spill /spɪl/ *vt/i* (*pt* **spilled** *or* **spilt**) derramar(-se), entornar(-se), espalhar(-se). **~ over** transbordar, extravasar
spin /spɪn/ *vt/i* (*pt* **spun**, *pres p* **spinning**) (*wool, cotton*) fiar; (*web*) tecer; (*turn*) (fazer) girar, (fazer) rodopiar. **~ out** (*money, story*) fazer durar; (*time*) (fazer) parar □ *n* volta *f*; (*aviat*) parafuso *m*. **go for a ~** dar uma volta *or* um giro. **~-drier** *n* centrifugadora *f* para a roupa, secadora *f*. **~ning-wheel** *n* roda *f* de fiar. **~-off** *n* bônus *m*, (*P*) bónus *m* inesperado; (*by-product*) derivado *m*
spinach /'spɪnɪdʒ/ *n* (*plant*) espinafre *m*; (*as food*) espinafres *mpl*
spinal /'spaɪnl/ *a* vertebral. **~ cord** espina *f* dorsal
spindl|e /'spɪndl/ *n* roca *f*, fuso *m*; (*mech*) eixo *m*. **~y** *a* alto e magro; (*of plant*) espigado
spine /spaɪn/ *n* espinha *f*, coluna *f* vertebral; (*prickle*) espinho *m*, pico *m*; (*of book*) lombada *f*
spineless /'spaɪnlɪs/ *a* (*fig: cowardly*) covarde, sem fibra (*fig*)
spinster /'spɪnstə(r)/ *n* solteira *f*; (*pej*) solteirona *f*
spiral /'spaɪərəl/ *a* (em) espiral; (*staircase*) em caracol □ *n* espiral *f* □ *vi* (*pt* **spiralled**) subir em espiral
spire /'spaɪə(r)/ *n* agulha *f*, flecha *f*
spirit /'spɪrɪt/ *n* espírito *m*; (*boldness*) coragem *f*, brio *m*. **~s** (*morale*) moral *m*; (*drink*) bebidas *fpl* alcoólicas, (*P*) bebidas *fpl* espirituosas. **in high ~s** alegre □ *vt* **~ away** dar sumiço em, arrebatar. **~-level** *n* nível *m* de bolha de ar
spirited /'spɪrɪtɪd/ *a* fogoso; (*attack, defence*) vigoroso, enérgico
spiritual /'spɪrɪtʃʊəl/ *a* espiritual
spiritualism /'spɪrɪtʃʊəlɪzəm/ *n* espiritismo *m*
spit[1] /spɪt/ *vt/i* (*pt* **spat** *or* **spit**, *pres p* **spitting**) cuspir; (*of rain*) chuviscar; (*of cat*) bufar □ *n* cuspe *m*, (*P*) cuspo *m*. **the ~ting image of** o retrato vivo de, a cara chapada de (*colloq*)
spit[2] /spɪt/ *n* (*for meat*) espeto *m*; (*of land*) restinga *f*, (*P*) lingua *f* de terra
spite /spaɪt/ *n* má vontade *f*, despeito *m*, rancor *m* □ *vt* aborrecer, mortificar. **in ~ of** a despeito de, apesar de. **~ful** *a* rancoroso, maldoso. **~fully** *adv* rancorosamente, maldosamente

spittle /'spɪtl/ *n* cuspe *m*, (*P*) cuspo *m*, saliva *f*

splash /splæʃ/ *vt* salpicar, respingar □ *vi* esparrinhar, esparramar-se. ~ **(about)** chapinhar □ *n* (*act, mark*) salpico *m*; (*sound*) chape *m*; (*of colour*) mancha *f*. **make a** ~ (*striking display*) fazer um vistão, causar furor

spleen /spli:n/ *n* (*anat*) baço *m*. **vent one's** ~ **on sb** descarregar a neura em alguém (*colloq*)

splendid /'splendɪd/ *a* esplêndido, magnífico; (*excellent*) estupendo (*colloq*), ótimo, (*P*) óptimo

splendour /'splendə(r)/ *n* esplendor *m*

splint /splɪnt/ *n* (*med*) tala *f*

splinter /'splɪntə(r)/ *n* lasca *f*, estilhaço *m*; (*under the skin*) farpa *f*, lasca *f* □ *vi* estilhaçar-se, lascar-se. ~ **group** grupo *m* dissidente

split /splɪt/ *vt/i* (*pt* **split**, *pres p* **splitting**) rachar, fender(-se); (*divide, share*) dividir; (*tear*) romper(-se) □ *n* racha *f*, fenda *f*; (*share*) quinhão *m*, parte *f*; (*pol*) cisão *f*. ~ **on** (*sl: inform on*) denunciar. ~ **one's sides** rebentar de risa. ~ **up** (*of couple*) separar-se. **a** ~ **second** uma fração de segundo. ~**ting headache** dor *f* de cabeça forte

splurge /splɜ:dʒ/ *n* (*colloq*) espalhafato *m*, estardalhaço *m* □ *vi* (*colloq: spend*) gastar os tubos, (*P*) gastar à doida (*colloq*)

spool /spu:l/ *n* (*of sewing machine*) bobina *f*; (*for cotton thread*) carretel *m*, carrinho *m*; (*naut; fishing*) carretel *m*

splutter /'splʌtə(r)/ *vi* falar cuspindo; (*engine*) cuspir; (*fat*) crepitar

spoil /spɔɪl/ *vt* (*pt* **spoilt** *or* **spoiled**) estragar; (*pamper*) mimar □ *n* ~(s) (*plunder*) despojo(s) *m(pl)*, espólios *mpl*. ~**-sport** *n* desmancha-prazeres *mf invar*. ~**t** *a* (*pampered*) mimado, estragado com mimos

spoke[1] /spəʊk/ *n* raio *m*

spoke[2], **spoken** /spəʊk, 'spəʊkən/ *see* **speak**

spokes|man /'spəʊksmən/ *n* (*pl* **-men**) ~**woman** *n* (*pl* **-women**) porta-voz *mf*

sponge /spʌndʒ/ *n* esponja *f* □ *vt* (*clean*) lavar com esponja; (*wipe*) limpar com esponja □ *vi* ~ **on** (*colloq: cadge*) viver à custa de. ~ **bag** bolsa *f* de toalete. ~ **cake** pão-de-ló *m*. ~**r** /-ə(r)/ *n* parasita *mf* (*colloq*) (*sl*). **spongy** *a* esponjoso

sponsor /'spɒnsə(r)/ *n* patrocinador *m*; (*for membership*) (sócio) proponente *m* □ *vt* patrocinar; (*for membership*) propor. ~**ship** *n* patrocínio *m*

spontaneous /spɒn'teɪnɪəs/ *a* espontâneo

spoof /spu:f/ *n* (*colloq*) paródia *f*

spooky /'spu:kɪ/ *a* (**-ier**, **-iest**) (*colloq*) fantasmagórico, que dá arrepios

spool /spu:l/ *n* (*of sewing machine*) bobina *f*; (*for thread, line*) carretel *m*, (*P*) carrinho *m*

spoon /spu:n/ *n* colher *f*. ~**-feed** *vt* (*pt* **-fed**) alimentar de colher; (*fig: help*) dar na bandeja para (*fig*). ~**ful** *n* (*pl* ~**fuls**) colherada *f*

sporadic /spə'rædɪk/ *a* esporádico, acidental

sport /spɔ:t/ *n* esporte *m*, (*P*) desporto *m*. **(good)** ~ (*sl: person*) gente *f* fina, (*P*) bom tipo *m* (*colloq*), (*P*) tipo *m* bestial □ *vt* (*display*) exibir, ostentar. ~**s car/coat** carro *m*/casaco *m* esporte, (*P*) de desporto. ~**y** *a* (*colloq*) esportivo, (*P*) desportivo

sporting /'spɔ:tɪŋ/ *a* esportivo, (*P*) desportivo. **a** ~ **chance** uma certa possibilidade de sucesso, uma boa chance

sports|man /'spɔ:tsmən/ *n* (*pl* **-men**), ~**woman** (*pl* **-women**) desportista *mf*. ~**manship** *n* (*spirit*) espírito *m* esportivo, (*P*) desportivo; (*activity*) esportismo *m*, (*P*) desportismo *m*

spot /spɒt/ *n* (*mark, stain*) mancha *f*; (*in pattern*) pinta *f*, bola *f*; (*drop*) gota *f*; (*place*) lugar *m*, ponto *m*; (*pimple*) borbulha *f*, espinha *f*; (*TV*) spot *m* televisivo □ *vt* (*pt* **spotted**) manchar; (*colloq: detect*) descobrir, detectar (*colloq*). **a** ~ **of** (*colloq*) um pouco de. **be in a** ~ (*colloq*) estar numa encrenca (*colloq*), (*P*) estar metido numa alhada (*colloq*). **on the** ~ no local; (*there and then*) ali mesmo, logo ali. ~**-on** *a* (*colloq*) certo. ~ **check** inspeção *f*, (*P*) inspecção *f* de surpresa; (*of cars*) fiscalização *f* de surpresa. ~**ted** *a* manchado; (*with dots*) de pintas, de bolas; (*animal*) malhado. ~**ty** *a* (*with pimples*) com borbulhas

spotless /'spɒtlɪs/ *a* impecável, imaculado

spotlight /'spɒtlaɪt/ *n* foco *m*; (*cine, theat*) refletor *m*, holofote *m*

spouse /spaʊz/ *n* cônjuge *mf*, esposo *m*

spout /spaʊt/ *n* (*of vessel*) bico *m*; (*of liquid*) esguicho *m*, jorro *m*; (*pipe*) cano *m* □ *vi* jorrar, esguichar. **up the** ~ (*sl: ruined*) liquidado (*sl*)

sprain /spreɪn/ *n* entorse *f*, mau jeito *m* □ *vt* torcer, dar um mau jeito a

sprang /spræŋ/ *see* **spring**

sprawl /sprɔ:l/ *vi* (*sit*) estirar-se, esparramar-se; (*fall*) estatelar-se; (*town*) estender-se, espraiar-se

spray[1] /spreɪ/ *n* (*of flowers*) raminho *m*, ramalhete *m*

spray[2] /spreɪ/ *n* (*water*) borrifo *m*, salpico *m*; (*from sea*) borrifo *m* de espuma; (*device*) bomba *f*, aerossol *m*; (*for perfume*) vaporizador *m*, atomizador *m* □ *vt* aspergir, borrifar, pulverizar; (*with insecticide*) pulverizar. **~-gun** *n* (*for paint*) pistola *f*

spread /spred/ *vt/i* (*pt* **spread**) (*extend, stretch*) estender(-se); (*news, fear, illness etc*) alastrar(-se), espalhar(-se), propagar(-se); (*butter etc*) passar; (*wings*) abrir □ *n* (*expanse*) expansão *f*, extensão *f*; (*spreading*) propagação *f*; (*paste*) pasta *f* para passar pão; (*colloq: meal*) banquete *m*. **~-eagled** *a* de braços e pernas abertos. **~sheet** *n* (*comput*) folha *f* de cálculo

spree /spriː/ *n* **go on a ~** (*colloq*) cair na farra

sprig /sprɪg/ *n* raminho *m*

sprightly /ˈspraɪtlɪ/ *a* (-ier, -iest) vivo, animado

spring /sprɪŋ/ *vi* (*pt* **sprang**, *pp* **sprung**) (*arise*) nascer; (*jump*) saltar, pular □ *vt* (*produce suddenly*) sair-se com; (*a surprise*) fazer (on sb a alguém) □ *n* salto *m*, pulo *m*; (*device*) mola *f*; (*season*) primavera *f*; (*of water*) fonte *f*, nascente *f*. **~ from** vir de, originar, provir de. **~-clean** *vt* fazer limpeza geral. **~ onion** cebolinha *f*. **~ up** surgir

springboard /ˈsprɪŋbɔːd/ *n* trampolim *m*

springtime /ˈsprɪŋtaɪm/ *n* primavera *f*

springy /ˈsprɪŋɪ/ *a* (-ier, -iest) elástico

sprinkle /ˈsprɪŋkl/ *vt* (*with liquid*) borrifar, salpicar; (*with salt, flour*) polvilhar (with de). **~ sand**/*etc* espalhar areia/*etc*. **~r** /-ə(r)/ *n* (*in garden*) regador *m*; (*for fires*) sprinkler *m*

sprinkling /ˈsprɪŋklɪŋ/ *n* (*amount*) pequena quantidade *f*; (*number*) pequeno número *m*

sprint /sprɪnt/ *n* (*sport*) corrida *f* de pequena distância, sprint *m* □ *vi* correr em sprint *or* a toda a velocidade; (*sport*) correr

sprout /spraʊt/ *vt/i* brotar, germinar; (*put forth*) deitar □ *n* (*on plant etc*) broto *m*. **(Brussels) ~s** couves *f* de Bruxelas

spruce /spruːs/ *a* bem arrumado □ *vt* **~ o.s. up** arrumar(-se)

sprung /sprʌŋ/ *see* **spring** □ *a* (*mattress etc*) de molas

spry /spraɪ/ *a* (**spryer, spryest**) vivo, ativo, (*P*) activo; (*nimble*) ágil

spud /spʌd/ *n* (*sl*) batata *f*

spun /spʌn/ *see* **spin**

spur /spɜː(r)/ *n* (*of rider*) espora *f*; (*fig: stimulus*) aguilhão *m*; (*fig*) espora *f* (*fig*) □ *vt* (*pt* **spurred**) esporear, picar com esporas; (*fig: incite*) aguilhoar, esporear. **on the ~ of the moment** impulsivamente

spurious /ˈspjʊərɪəs/ *a* falso, espúrio

spurn /spɜːn/ *vt* desdenhar, desprezar, rejeitar

spurt /spɜːt/ *vi* jorrar, esguichar; (*fig: accelerate*) acelerar subitamente, dar um arranco súbito □ *n* jorro *m*, esguicho *m*; (*of energy, speed*) arranco *m*, surto *m*

spy /spaɪ/ *n* espião *m* □ *vt* (*make out*) avistar, descortinar □ *vi* **~ (on)** espiar, espionar. **~ out** descobrir. **~ing** *n* espionagem *f*

squabble /ˈskwɒbl/ *vi* discutir, brigar □ *n* briga *f*, disputa *f*

squad /skwɒd/ *n* (*mil*) pelotão *m*; (*team*) equipe *f*, (*P*) equipa *f*. **firing ~** pelotão *m* de fuzilamento. **flying ~** brigada *f* móvel

squadron /ˈskwɒdrən/ *n* (*mil*) esquadrão *m*; (*aviat*) esquadrilha *f*; (*naut*) esquadra *f*

squal|id /ˈskwɒlɪd/ *a* esquálido, sórdido. **~or** *n* sordidez *f*

squall /skwɔːl/ *n* borrasca *f*

squander /ˈskwɒndə(r)/ *vt* desperdiçar

square /skweə(r)/ *n* quadrado *m*; (*in town*) largo *m*, praça *f*; (*T-square*) régua-tê *f*; (*set-square*) esquadro *m* □ *a* (*of shape*) quadrado; (*metre, mile etc*) quadrado; (*honest*) direito, honesto; (*of meal*) abundante, substancial. **(all) ~** (*quits*) quite(s) □ *vt* (*math*) elevar ao quadrado; (*settle*) acertar □ *vi* (*agree*) concordar. **go back to ~ one** recomeçar tudo do princípio, voltar à estaca zero. **~ brackets** parênteses *mpl* retos, (*P*) rectos. **~ up to** enfrentar. **~ly** *adv* diretamente, (*P*) directamente; (*fairly*) honestamente

squash /skwɒʃ/ *vt* (*crush*) esmagar; (*squeeze*) espremer; (*crowd*) comprimir, apertar □ *n* (*game*) squash *m*; (*Amer: marrow*) abóbora *f*. **lemon ~** limonada *f*. **orange ~** laranjada *f*. **~y** *a* mole

squat /skwɒt/ *vi* (*pt* **squatted**) acocorar-se, agachar-se; (*be a squatter*) ser ocupante ilegal □ *a* (*dumpy*) atarracado. **~ter** *n* ocupante *mf* ilegal de casa vazia, posseiro *m*

squawk /skwɔːk/ *n* grasnido *m*, crocito *m* □ *vi* grasnar, crocitar

squeak /skwiːk/ *n* guincho *m*, chio *m*; (*of door, shoes etc*) rangido *m* □ *vi* guinchar, chiar; (*of door, shoes etc*) ranger. **~y** *a* (*shoe etc*) que range; (*voice*) esganiçado

squeal /skwiːl/ *vi* dar gritos agudos,

guinchar □ *n* grito *m* agudo, guincho *m*. ~ **(on)** (*sl: inform on*) delatar, (*P*) denunciar

squeamish /'skwi:mɪʃ/ *a* (*nauseated*) que enjoa à toa

squeeze /skwi:z/ *vt* (*lemon, sponge etc*) espremer; (*hand, arm*) apertar; (*extract*) arrancar, extorquir (**from** de) □ *vi* (*force one's way*) passar à força, meter-se por □ *n* aperto *m*, apertão *m*; (*hug*) abraço *m*; (*comm*) restrições *fpl* de crédito

squelch /skweltʃ/ *vi* chapinhar *or* fazer chape-chape na lama

squid /skwɪd/ *n* lula *f*

squiggle /'skwɪgl/ *n* rabisco *m*, floreado *m*

squint /skwɪnt/ *vi* ser estrábico *or* vesgo; (*with half-shut eyes*) franzir os olhos □ *n* (*med*) estrabismo *m*

squirm /skwɜ:m/ *vi* (re)torcer-se, contorcer-se

squirrel /'skwɪrəl/ *n* esquilo *m*

squirt /skwɜ:t/ *vt/i* esguichar □ *n* esguicho *m*

stab /stæb/ *vt* (*pt* **stabbed**) apunhalar; (*knife*) esfaquear □ *n* punhalada *f*; (*with knife*) facada *f*; (*of pain*) pontada *f*; (*colloq: attempt*) tentativa *f*

stabilize /'steɪbəlaɪz/ *vt* estabilizar

stab|le[1] /'steɪbl/ *a* (-er, -est) estável. **~ility** /stə'bɪlətɪ/ *n* estabilidade *f*

stable[2] /'steɪbl/ *n* cavalariça *f*, estrebaria *f*. **~-boy** *n* moço *m* de estrebaria

stack /stæk/ *n* pilha *f*, montão *m*; (*of hay etc*) meda *f* □ *vt* ~ **(up)** empilhar, amontoar

stadium /'steɪdɪəm/ *n* estádio *m*

staff /sta:f/ *n* pessoal *m*; (*in school*) professores *mpl*; (*mil*) estado-maior *m*; (*stick*) bordão *m*, cajado *m*; (*mus*) (*pl* **staves**) pauta *f* □ *vt* prover de pessoal

stag /stæg/ *n* veado (macho) *m*, cervo *m*. **~-party** *n* (*colloq*) reunião *f* masculina; (*before wedding*) despedida *f* de solteiro

stage /steɪdʒ/ *n* (*theatre*) palco *m*; (*phase*) fase *f*, ponto *m*; (*platform in hall*) estrado *m* □ *vt* encenar, pôr em cena; (*fig: organize*) organizar. **go on the ~** seguir a carreira teatral, ir para o teatro (*colloq*). **~ door** entrada *f* dos artistas. **~-fright** *n* nervosismo *m*

stagger /'stægə(r)/ *vi* vacilar, cambalear □ *vt* (*shock*) atordoar, chocar; (*holidays etc*) escalonar. **~ing** *a* atordoador, chocante

stagnant /'stægnənt/ *a* estagnado, parado

stagnat|e /stæg'neɪt/ *vi* estagnar. **~ion** /-ʃn/ *n* estagnação *f*

staid /steɪd/ *a* sério, sensato, estável

stain /steɪn/ *vt* manchar, pôr nódoa em; (*colour*) tingir, dar cor a □ *n* mancha *f*, nódoa *f*; (*colouring*) corante *m*. **~ed glass window** vitral *m*. **~less steel** aço *m* inoxidável

stair /steə(r)/ *n* degrau *m*. **~s** escada(s) *f*(*pl*)

stair|case /'steəkeɪs/, **~way** /-weɪ/ *ns* escada(s) *f*(*pl*), escadaria *f*

stake /steɪk/ *n* (*post*) estaca *f*, poste *m*; (*wager*) parada *f*, aposta *f* □ *vt* (*area*) demarcar, delimitar; (*wager*) jogar, apostar. **at ~** em jogo. **have a ~ in** ter interesse em. **~ a claim to** reivindicar

stale /steɪl/ *a* (-er, -est) estragado, velho; (*bread*) duro, mofado; (*smell*) rançoso; (*air*) viciado; (*news*) velho

stalemate /'steɪlmeɪt/ *n* (*chess*) empate *m*; (*fig: deadlock*) impasse *m*, beco-sem-saída *m*

stalk[1] /stɔ:k/ *n* (*of plant*) caule *m*

stalk[2] /stɔ:k/ *vi* andar com ar empertigado □ *vt* (*prey*) perseguir furtivamente, tocaiar

stall /stɔ:l/ *n* (*in stable*) baia *f*; (*in market*) tenda *f*, barraca *f*. **~s** (*theat*) poltronas *fpl* de orquestra; (*cinema*) platéia *f*, (*P*) plateia *f* □ *vt/i* (*auto*) enguiçar, (*P*) ir abaixo. ~ **(for time)** ganhar tempo

stalwart /'stɔ:lwət/ *a* forte, rijo; (*supporter*) fiel

stamina /'stæmɪnə/ *n* resistência *f*

stammer /'stæmə(r)/ *vt/i* gaguejar □ *n* gagueira *f*, (*P*) gaguez *f*

stamp /stæmp/ *vt/i* ~ **(one's foot)** bater com o pé (no chão), pisar com força □ *vt* estampar; (*letter*) estampilhar, selar; (*with rubber stamp*) carimbar. ~ **out** (*fire, rebellion etc*) esmagar; (*disease*) erradicar □ *n* estampa *f*; (*for postage*) selo *m*; (*fig: mark*) cunho *m*. **(rubber) ~** carimbo *m*. **~-collecting** *n* filatelia *f*

stampede /stæm'pi:d/ *n* (*scattering*) debandada *f*; (*of horses, cattle etc*) tresma/hada *f*, debandada *f*; (*fig: rush*) corrida *f* □ *vt/i* (fazer) debandar; (*horses, cattle etc*) tresmalhar

stance /stæns/ *n* posição *f*, postura *f*

stand /stænd/ *vi* (*pt* **stood**) estar em pé; (*keep upright position*) ficar em pé; (*rise*) levantar-se; (*be situated*) encontrar-se, ficar, situar-se; (*pol*) candidatar-se (**for** por) □ *vt* pôr (de pé), colocar; (*tolerate*) suportar, agüentar, (*P*) aguentar □ *n* posição *f*, (*support*) apoio *m*; (*mil*) resistência *f*, (*at fair*) stand *m*, pavilhão *m*; (*in street*) quiosque *m*; (*for spectators*) arquibancada *f*, (*P*) bancada *f*, (*Amer: witness-box*) banco *m* das testemunhas. ~ a chance ter uma possibilidade. ~ **back** recuar. ~ **by** *or* **around** estar parado sem fazer nada. ~ **by** (*be ready*) estar a postos; (*promise, person*) manter-se fiel a. ~ **down** desistir, retirar-se. ~ **for** representar, simbolizar; (*colloq: tolerate*) aturar. ~ **in for** substituir. ~ **out** (*be conspicuous*) sobressair. ~ **still** estar/ficar imóvel. ~ **still!** não se mexa!, quieto! ~ **to reason** ser lógico. ~ **up** levantar-se, pôr-se em *or* de pé. ~ **up for** defender, apoiar. ~ **up to** enfrentar. ~**-by** *a* (*for emergency*) de reserva; (*ticket*) de stand-by □ *n* (*at airport*) stand-by *m*. **on ~-by** (*mil*) de prontidão; (*med*) de plantão. **~-in** *n* substituto *m*, suplente *mf*. **~-offish** *a* (*colloq: aloof*) reservado, distante

standard /'stændəd/ *n* norma *f*, padrão *m*; (*level*) nível *m*; (*flag*) estandarte *m*, bandeira *f*. **~s** (*morals*) princípios *mpl* □ *a* regulamentar; (*average*) standard, normal. ~ **lamp** abajur *m* de pé. ~ **of living** padrão *m* de vida, (*P*) nível *m* de vida

standardize /'stændədaɪz/ *vt* padronizar

standing /'stændɪŋ/ *a* em pé, de pé *invar*; (*army, committee etc*) permanente □ *n* posição *f*; (*reputation*) prestígio *m*; (*duration*) duração *f*. ~ **order** (*at bank*) ordem *f* permanente. **~-room** *n* lugares *mpl* em pé

standpoint /'stændpɔɪnt/ *n* ponto *m* de vista

standstill /'stændstɪl/ *n* paralisação *f*. **at a** ~ parado, paralisado. **bring/come to a** ~ (fazer) parar, paralisar(-se), imobilizar (-se)

stank /stæŋk/ *see* **stink**

staple[1] /'steɪpl/ *n* (*for paper*) grampo *m*, (*P*) agrafo *m* □ *vt* (*paper*) grampear, (*P*) agrafar. **~r** /-ə(r)/ *n* grampeador *m*, (*P*) agrafador *m*

staple[2] /'steɪpl/ *a* principal, básico □ *n* (*comm*) artigo *m* básico

star /sta:(r)/ *n* estrela *f*; (*cinema*) estrela *f*, vedete *f*; (*celebrity*) celebridade *f* □ *vt* (*pt* **starred**) (*of film*) ter no papel principal, (*P*) ter como actor principal □ *vi* ~ **in** ser a vedete *or* ter o papel principal em. **~dom** *n* celebridade *f*, estrelato *m*

starch /sta:tʃ/ *n* amido *m*, fécula *f*; (*for clothes*) goma *f* □ *vt* pôr em goma, engomar. **~y** *a* (*of food*) farináceo, feculento; (*fig: of person*) rígido, formal

stare /steə(r)/ *vi* ~ **at** olhar fixamente □ *n* olhar *m* fixo

starfish /'sta:fɪʃ/ *n* (*pl invar*) estrela-do-mar *f*

stark /sta:k/ *a* (-er, -est) (*desolate*) árido, desolado; (*severe*) austero, severo; (*utter*) completo, rematado; (*fact etc*) brutal □ *adv* completamente. ~ **naked** nu em pêlo, (*P*) em pelota (*colloq*)

starling /'sta:lɪŋ/ *n* estorninho *m*

starlit /'sta:lɪt/ *a* estrelado

starry /'sta:rɪ/ *a* estrelado. **~-eyed** *a* (*colloq*) sonhador, idealista

start /sta:t/ *vt/i* começar; (*machine*) ligar, pôr em andamento; (*fashion etc*) lançar; (*leave*) partir; (*cause*) causar, provocar; (*jump*) sobressaltar-se, estremecer; (*of car*) arrancar, partir □ *n* começo *m*, início *m*; (*of race*) largada *f*, partida *f*; (*lead*) avanço *m*; (*jump*) sobressalto *m*, estremecimento *m*. **by fits and ~s** aosarrancos, intermitentemente. **for a** ~ para começar. **give sb a** sobressaltar alguém, pregar um susto a alguém. ~ **to do** começar a *or* pôr-se a fazer. **~er** *n* (*auto*) arranque *m*; (*competitor*) corredor *m*; (*culin*) entrada *f*. **~ing-point** *n* ponto *m* de partida

startl|e /'sta:tl/ *vt* (*make jump*) sobressaltar, pregar um susto a; (*shock*) alarmar, chocar. **~ing** *a* alarmante; (*surprising*) surpreendente

starv|e /sta:v/ *vi* (*suffer*) passar fome; (*die*) morrer de fome. **be ~ing** (*colloq: very hungry*) ter muita fome, morrer de fome (*colloq*) □ *vt* fazer passar fome a; (*deprive*) privar. **~ation** /-'veɪʃn/ *n* fome *f*

stash /stæʃ/ *vt* (*sl*) guardar, esconder, enfurnar (*colloq*)

state /steɪt/ *n* estado *m*, condição *f*; (*pomp*) pompa *f*, gala *f*; (*pol*) Estado *m* □ *a* de Estado, do Estado; (*school*) público; (*visit etc*) oficial □ *vt* afirmar (**that** que); (*views*) exprimir; (*fix*) marcar, fixar. **in a** ~ muito abalado

stateless /'steɪtlɪs/ *a* apátrida

stately /'steɪtlɪ/ *a* (-ier, -iest) majestoso. ~ **home** solar *m*, palácio *m*

statement /'steɪtmənt/ *n* declaração *f*; (*of account*) extrato *m*, (*P*) extracto *m* de conta

statesman /'steɪtsmən/ *n* (*pl* **-men**) homem *m* de estado, estadista *m*

static /'stætɪk/ *a* estático □ *n* (*radio, TV*) estática *f*, interferência *f*

station /'steɪʃn/ *n* (*position*) posto *m*; (*rail, bus, radio*) estação *f*; (*rank*) condição *f*, posição *f* social □ *vt* colocar. **~-wagon** *n* perua *f*, (*P*) carrinha *f*. **~ed at** *or* **in** (*mil*) estacionado em

stationary /'steɪʃnrɪ/ *a* estacionário, parado, imóvel; (*vehicle*) estacionado, parado

stationer /'steɪʃənə(r)/ *n* dono *m* de

papelaria. ~'s shop papelaria *f*. ~y *n* artigos *mpl* de papelaria; (*writing-paper*) papel *m* de carta
statistic /stə'tɪstɪk/ *n* dado *m* estatístico. ~s *n* (*as a science*) estatística *f*. ~al *a* estatístico
statue /'stætʃu:/ *n* estátua *f*
stature /'stætʃə(r)/ *n* estatura *f*
status /'steɪtəs/ *n* (*pl* -uses) situação *f*, posição *f*, categoria *f*; (*prestige*) prestígio *m*, importância *f*, status *m*. ~ quo status quo *m*. ~ symbol símbolo *m* de status
statut|e /'stætju:t/ *n* estatuto *m*, lei *f*. ~ory /-ʊtrɪ/ *a* estatutário, regulamentar; (*holiday*) legal
staunch /stɔ:ntʃ/ *a* (-er, -est) (*friend*) fiel, leal
stave /steɪv/ *n* (*mus*) pauta *f* □ *vt* ~ off (*keep off*) conjurar, evitar; (*delay*) adiar
stay /steɪ/ *vi* estar, ficar, permanecer; (*dwell temporarily*) ficar, alojar-se, hospedar-se; (*spend time*) demorar-se □ *vt* (*hunger*) enganar □ *n* estada *f*, visita *f*, permanência *f*. ~ behind ficar para trás. ~ in ficar em casa. ~ put (*colloq*) não se mexer (*colloq*). ~ up (late) deitar-se tarde. ~ing-power *n* resistência *f*
stead /sted/ *n* in my/your/*etc* ~ no meu/teu/*etc* lugar. stand in good ~ ser muito útil
steadfast /'stedfa:st/ *a* firme, constante
stead|y /'stedɪ/ *a* (-ier, -iest) (*stable*) estável, firme, seguro; (*regular*) regular, constante; (*hand, voice*) firme □ *vt* firmar, fixar, estabilizar; (*calm*) acalmar. go ~y with (*colloq*) namorar. ~ily *adv* firmemente; (*regularly*) regularmente, de modo constante
steak /steɪk/ *n* bife *m*
steal /sti:l/ *vt/i* (*pt* stole, *pp* stolen) roubar (from sb de alguém). ~ away/in/*etc* sair/entrar/*etc* furtivamente, esgueirar-se. ~ the show pôr os outros na sombra
stealth /stelθ/ *n* by ~ furtivamente, na calada, às escondidas. ~y *a* furtivo
steam /sti:m/ *n* vapor *m* de água; (*on window*) condensação *f* □ *vt* (*cook*) cozinhar a vapor. ~ up (*window*) embaciar. □ *vi* soltar vapor, fumegar; (*move*) avançar. ~-engine *n* máquina *f* a vapor; (*locomotive*) locomotiva *f* a vapor. ~ iron ferro *m* a vapor. ~y *a* (*heat*) úmido, (*P*) húmido
steamer /'sti:mə(r)/ *n* (*ship*) (barco a) vapor *m*; (*culin*) utensílio *m* para cozinhar a vapor
steamroller /'sti:mrəʊlə(r)/ *n* cilindro *m* a vapor, rolo *m* compressor
steel /sti:l/ *n* aço *m* □ *a* de aço □ *vpr* ~ o.s. endurecer-se, fortalecer-se. ~ industry siderurgia *f*
steep[1] /sti:p/ *vt* (*soak*) mergulhar, pôr de molho; (*permeate*) passar, impregnar. ~ed in (*fig: vice, misery etc*) mergulhado em; (*fig: knowledge, wisdom etc*) impregnado de, repassado de
steep[2] /sti:p/ *a* (-er, -est) íngreme, escarpado; (*colloq*) exagerado, exorbitante. rise ~ly (*slope*) subir a pique; (*price*) disparar
steeple /'sti:pl/ *n* campanário *m*, torre *f*
steeplechase /'sti:pltʃeɪs/ *n* (*race*) corrida *f* de obstáculos
steer /stɪə(r)/ *vt/i* guiar, conduzir, dirigir; (*ship*) governar; (*fig*) guiar, orientar. ~ clear of evitar passar perto de. ~ing *n* (*auto*) direção *f*, (*P*) direcção *f*. ~ing-wheel *n* (*auto*) volante *m*
stem[1] /stem/ *n* caule *m*, haste *f*; (*of glass*) pé *m*; (*of pipe*) boquilha *f*; (*of word*) radical *m* □ *vi* (*pt* stemmed) ~ from provir de, vir de
stem[2] /stem/ *vt* (*pt* stemmed) (*check*) conter; (*stop*) estancar
stench /stentʃ/ *n* mau cheiro *m*, fedor *m*
stencil /'stensl/ *n* estênsil *m*, (*P*) stencil *m* □ *vt* (*pt* stencilled) (*document*) policopiar
step /step/ *vi* (*pt* stepped) ir andar □ *vt* ~ up aumentar □ *n* passo *m*, passada *f*; (*of stair, train*) degrau *m*; (*action*) medida *f*, passo *m*. ~s (*ladder*) escada *f*. in ~ no mesmo passo, a passo certo; (*fig*) em conformidade (with com). ~ down (*resign*) demitir-se. ~ in (*intervene*) intervir. ~-ladder *n* escada *f* portátil. ~ping-stone *n* (*fig: means to an end*) ponte *f*, trampolim *m*
stepbrother /'stepbrʌðə(r)/ *n* meio-irmão *m*. ~daughter *n* nora *f*, (*P*) enteada *f*. ~father *n* padrasto *m*. ~mother *n* madrasta *f*. ~sister *n* meio-irmã *f*. ~son *n* genro *m*, (*P*) enteado *m*
stereo /'sterɪəʊ/ *n* (*pl* -os) estéreo *m*; (*record-player etc*) equipamento *m or* sistema *m* estéreo □ *a* estéreo *invar*. ~phonic /-ə'fɒnɪk/ *a* estereofônico, (*P*) estereofónico
stereotype /'sterɪətaɪp/ *n* estereótipo *m*. ~d *a* estereotipado
steril|e /'steraɪl/ *a* estéril. ~ity /stə'rɪlətɪ/ *n* esterilidade *f*
steriliz|e /'sterəlaɪz/ *vt* esterilizar. ~ation /-'zeɪʃn/ *n* esterilização *f*
sterling /'stɜ:lɪŋ/ *n* libra *f* esterlina □ *a* esterlino; (*silver*) de lei; (*fig*) excelente, de (primeira) qualidade

stern[1] /stɜ:n/ *a* (-er, -est) severo

stern[2] /stɜ:n/ *n* (*of ship*) popa *f*, ré *f*

stethoscope /'steθəskəʊp/ *n* estetoscópio *m*

stew /stju:/ *vt/i* estufar, guisar; (*fruit*) cozer □ *n* ensopado *m*. **~ed fruit** compota *f*

steward /'stjʊəd/ *n* (*of club etc*) ecônomo *m*, (*P*) ecónomo *m*, administrador *m*; (*on ship etc*) camareiro *m* (de bordo), (*P*) criado *m* (de bordo). **~ess** /-'des/ *n* aeromoça *f*, (*P*) hospedeira *f*

stick[1] /stɪk/ *n* pau *m*; (*for walking*) bengala *f*; (*of celery*) talo *m*

stick[2] /stɪk/ *vt* (*pt* **stuck**) (*glue*) colar; (*thrust*) cravar, espetar; (*colloq: put*) enfiar, meter; (*sl: endure*) agüentar, (*P*) aguentar, aturar, suportar □ *vi* (*adhere*) colar, aderir; (*remain*) ficar enfiado *or* metido; (*be jammed*) emperrar, ficar engatado. **~ in one's mind** ficar na memória. **be stuck with sb/sth** (*colloq*) não conseguir descartar-se de alguém/alg coisa (*colloq*). **~ out** *vt* (*head*) esticar; (*tongue etc*) mostrar □ *vi* (*protrude*) sobressair. **~ to** (*promise*) ser fiel a. **~-up** *n* (*sl*) assalto *m* à mão armada. **~ up for** (*colloq*) tomar o partido de, defender. **~ing-plaster** *n* esparadrapo *m*, (*P*) adesivo *m*

sticker /'stɪkə(r)/ *n* adesivo *m*, etiqueta *f* (adesiva)

stickler /'stɪklə(r)/ *n* **be a ~ for** fazer grande questão de, insistir em

sticky /'stɪkɪ/ *a* (-ier, -iest) pegajoso; (*label, tape*) adesivo; (*weather*) abafado, mormacento

stiff /stɪf/ *a* (-er, -est) teso, hirto, rígido; (*limb, joint; hard*) duro; (*unbending*) inflexível; (*price*) elevado, puxado (*colloq*); (*penalty*) severo; (*drink*) forte; (*manner*) reservado, formal. **be bored/scared ~** (*colloq*) estar muito aborrecido/com muito medo (*colloq*). **~ neck** torcicolo *m*. **~ness** *n* rigidez *f*

stiffen /'stɪfn/ *vt/i* (*harden*) endurecer; (*limb, joint*) emperrar

stifl|e /'staɪfl/ *vt/i* abafar, sufocar. **~ing** *a* sufocante

stigma /'stɪgmə/ *n* estigma *m*. **~tize** *vt* estigmatizar

stile /staɪl/ *n* degrau *m* para passar por cima de cerca

stiletto /stɪ'letəʊ/ *n* (*pl* -os) estilete *m*. **~ heel** *n* salto *m* alto fino

still[1] /stɪl/ *a* imóvel, quieto; (*quiet*) sossegado □ *n* silêncio *m*, sossego *m* □ *adv* ainda; (*nevertheless*) apesar disso, apesar de tudo. **keep ~!** fique quieto!, não se mexa! **~ life** natureza *f* morta. **~ness** *n* calma *f*

still[2] /stɪl/ *n* (*apparatus*) alambique *m*

stillborn /'stɪlbɔ:n/ *a* natimorto, (*P*) nado-morto

stilted /'stɪltɪd/ *a* afetado, (*P*) afectado

stilts /stɪlts/ *npl* pernas de pau *fpl*, (*P*) andas *fpl*

stimul|ate /'stɪmjʊleɪt/ *vt* estimular. **~ant** *n* estimulante *m*. **~ating** *a* estimulante. **~ation** /-'leɪʃn/ *n* estimulação *f*

stimulus /'stɪmjʊləs/ *n* (*pl* -li /-laɪ/) (*spur*) estímulo *m*

sting /stɪŋ/ *n* picada *f*; (*organ*) ferrão *m* □ *vt* (*pt* **stung**) picar □ *vi* picar, arder. **~ing nettle** urtiga *f*

stingy /'stɪndʒɪ/ *a* (-ier, -iest) pão-duro *m*, sovina (**with** com)

stink /stɪŋk/ *n* fedor *m*, catinga *f*, mau cheiro *m* □ *vi* (*pt* **stank** *or* **stunk**, *pp* **stunk**) **~ (of)** cheirar (a), tresandar (a) □ *vt* **~ out** (*room etc*) empestar. **~ing** *a* malcheiroso. **~ing rich** (*sl*) podre de rico (*colloq*)

stinker /'stɪŋkə(r)/ *n* (*sl: person*) cara *m* horroroso (*colloq*); (*sl: sth difficult*) osso *m* duro de moer

stint /stɪnt/ *vi* **~ on** poupar em, apertar em □ *n* (*work*) tarefa *f*, parte *f*, quinhão *m*

stipulat|e /'stɪpjʊleɪt/ *vt* estipular. **~ion** /-'leɪʃn/ *n* condição *f*, estipulação *f*

stir /stɜ:r/ *vt/i* (*pt* **stirred**) (*move*) mexer(-se), mover(-se); (*excite*) excitar; (*a liquid*) mexer □ *n* agitação *f*, rebuliço *m*. **~ up** (*trouble etc*) provocar, fomentar. **~ring** *a* excitante

stirrup /'stɪrəp/ *n* estribo *m*

stitch /stɪtʃ/ *n* (*in sewing; med*) ponto *m*; (*in knitting*) malha *f*, ponto *m*; (*pain*) pontada *f* □ *vt* coser. **in ~es** (*colloq*) às gargalhadas (*colloq*)

stoat /stəʊt/ *n* arminho *m*

stock /stɒk/ *n* (*comm*) estoque *m*, (*P*) stock *m*, provisão *f*; (*finance*) valores *mpl*, fundos *mpl*; (*family*) família *f*, estirpe *f*; (*culin*) caldo *m*; (*flower*) goivo *m* □ *a* (*goods*) corrente, comum; (*hackneyed*) estereotipado □ *vt* (*shop etc*) abastecer, fornecer; (*sell*) vender □ *vi* **~ up with** abastecer-se de. **in ~** em estoque. **out of ~** esgotado. **take ~** (*fig*) fazer um balanço. **~-car** *n* stock-car *m*. **~-cube** *n* cubo *m* de caldo. **~ market** Bolsa *f* (de Valores). **~-still** *a, adv* imóvel. **~-taking** *n* (*comm*) inventário *m*

stockbroker /'stɒkbrəʊkə(r)/ *n* corretor *m* da Bolsa

stocking /'stɒkɪŋ/ *n* meia *f*

stockist /'stɒkɪst/ *n* armazenista *m*

stockpile /'stɒkpaɪl/ *n* reservas *fpl* □ *vt* acumular reservas de, estocar

stocky /'stɒkɪ/ *a* (-ier, -iest) atarracado

stodg|e /stɒdʒ/ *n* (*colloq*) comida *f* pesada (*colloq*). **~y** *a* (*of food, book*) pesado, maçudo
stoic /'stəʊɪk/ *n* estóico *m*. **~al** *a* estoico. **~ism** /-sɪzəm/ *n* estoicismo *m*
stoke /stəʊk/ *vt* (*boiler, fire*) alimentar, carregar
stole[1] /stəʊl/ *n* (*garment*) estola *m*
stole[2], **stolen** /stəʊl, 'stəʊlən/ *see* **steal**
stomach /'stʌmək/ *n* estômago *m*; (*abdomen*) barriga *f*, ventre *m* □ *vt* (*put up with*) aturar. **~-ache** *n* dor *f* de estômago; (*abdomen*) dores *fpl* de barriga
ston|e /stəʊn/ *n* pedra *f*; (*pebble*) seixo *m*; (*in fruit*) caroço *m*; (*weight*) 6,348 kg; (*med*) cálculo *m*, pedra *f* □ *vt* apedrejar; (*fruit*) tirar o caroço de. **within a ~e's throw (of)** muito perto (de). **~e-cold** gelado. **~e-deaf** totalmente surdo. **~ed** *a* (*colloq: drunk*) bebão *m* (*colloq*); (*colloq: drugged*) drogado. **~y** *a* pedregoso. **~y-broke** *a* (*sl*) duro, liso (*sl*)
stonemason /'stəʊnmeɪsn/ *n* pedreiro *m*
stood /stʊd/ *see* **stand**
stooge /stu:dʒ/ *n* (*colloq: actor*) ajudante *mf*; (*colloq: puppet*) antoche *m*, (*P*) comparsa *mf*, parceiro *m*
stool /stu:l/ *n* banco *m*, tamborete *m*
stoop /stu:p/ *vi* (*bend*) curvar-se, baixar-se; (*condescend*) condescender, dignar-se. **~ to sth** rebaixar-se para (fazer) alg coisa □ *n* **walk with a ~** andar curvado
stop /stɒp/ *vt/i* (*pt* **stopped**) parar; (*prevent*) impedir (**from** de); (*hole, leak etc*) tapar, vedar; (*pain, noise etc*) parar; (*colloq: stay*) ficar □ *n* (*of bus*) parada *f*, (*P*) paragem *f*; (*full stop*) ponto *m* final. **put a ~ to** pôr fim a. **~ it!** acabe logo com isso! **~-over** *n* (*break in journey*) parada *f*, (*P*) paragem *f*; (*port of call*) escala *f*. **~press** *n* notícia *f* de última hora. **~-watch** *n* cronômetro *m*, (*P*) cronómetro *m*
stopgap /'stɒpgæp/ *n* substituto *m* provisório, tapa-buracos *mpl* (*colloq*) □ *a* temporário
stoppage /'stopɪdʒ/ *n* parada *f*, (*P*) paragem *f*; (*of work*) paralisação *f* de trabalho; (*of pay*) suspensão *f*
stopper /'stɒpə(r)/ *n* rolha *f*, tampa *f*
storage /'stɔ:rɪdʒ/ *n* (*of goods, food etc*) armazenagem *f*, armazenamento *m*. **in cold ~** em frigorífico
store /stɔ:(r)/ *n* reserva *f*, provisão *f*; (*warehouse*) armazém *m*, entreposto *m*; (*shop*) grande armazém *m*; (*Amer*) loja *f*; (*in computer*) memória *f* □ *vt* (*for future*) pôr de reserva, juntar, fazer provisão de; (*in warehouse*) armazenar. **be in ~** estar guardado. **have in ~ for** reservar para. **set ~ by** dar valor a. **~-room** *n* depósito *m*, almortarifado *m*, (*P*) armazém *m*
storey /'stɔ:rɪ/ *n* (*pl* **-eys**) andar *m*
stork /stɔ:k/ *n* cegonha *f*
storm /stɔ:m/ *n* tempestade *f* □ *vt* tomar de assalto □ *vi* enfurecer-se. **a ~ in a teacup** uma tempestade num copo de água. **~y** *a* tempestuoso
story /'stɔ:rɪ/ *n* estória *f*, (*P*) história *f*; (*in press*) artigo *m*, matéria *f*; (*Amer: storey*) andar *m*; (*colloq: lie*) cascata *f*, (*P*) peta *f*. **~-teller** *n* contador *m* de estórias, (*P*) histórias
stout /staʊt/ *a* (**-er, -est**) (*fat*) gordo, corpulento; (*strong, thick*) resistente, sólido, grosso; (*brave*) resoluto □ *n* cerveja *f* preta forte
stove /stəʊv/ *n* (*for cooking*) fogão *m* (de cozinha)
stow /stəʊ/ *vt* **~** (**away**) (*put away*) guardar, arrumar; (*hide*) esconder □ *vi* **~ away** viajar clandestinamente
stowaway /'stəʊəweɪ/ *n* passageiro *m* clandestino
straddle /'strædl/ *vt* (*sit*) escarranchar-se em, montar; (*stand*) pôr-se de pernas abertas sobre
straggle /'strægl/ *vi* (*lag behind*) desgarrar-se, ficar para trás; (*spread*) estender-se desordenadamente. **~r** /-ə(r)/ *n* retardatário *m*
straight /streɪt/ *a* (**-er, -est**) direito; (*tidy*) em ordem; (*frank*) franco, direto, (*P*) directo; (*of hair*) liso; (*of drink*) puro □ *adv* (*in straight line*) reto; (*directly*) direito, direto, (*P*) directo, diretamente, (*P*) directamente □ *n* linha *f* reta, (*P*) recta. **~ ahead** *or* **on** (sempre) em frente. **~ away** logo, imediatamente. **go ~** viver honestamente. **keep a ~ face** não se desmanchar, manter um ar sério
straighten /'streɪtn/ *vt* endireitar; (*tidy*) arrumar, pôr em ordem
straightforward /streɪt'fɔ:wəd/ *a* franco, sincero; (*easy*) simples
strain[1] /streɪn/ *n* (*breed*) raça *f*; (*streak*) tendência *f*, veia *f*
strain[2] /streɪn/ *vt* (*rope*) esticar, puxar; (*tire*) cansar; (*filter*) filtrar, passar; (*vegetables, tea etc*) coar; (*med*) distender, torcer; (*fig*) forçar, pôr à prova □ *vi* esforçar-se □ *n* tensão *f*; (*fig: effort*) esforço *m*; (*med*) distensão *f*. **~s** (*music*) melodias *fpl*. **~ one's ears** apurar o ouvido. **~ed** *a* forçado; (*relations*) tenso. **~er** *n* coador *m*, (*P*) passador *m*
strait /streɪt/ *n* estreito *m*. **~s** estreito *m*; (*fig*) apuros *mpl*, dificuldades *fpl*. **~-jacket** *n* camisa-de-força *f*. **~-laced** *a* severo, puritano

strand /strænd/ *n* (*thread*) fio *m*; (*lock of hair*) mecha *f*, madeixa *f*

stranded /'strændɪd/ *a* (*person*) em dificuldades, deixado para trás, abandonado

strange /streɪndʒ/ *a* (-er, -est) estranho. **~ly** *adv* estranhamente. **~ness** *n* estranheza *f*

stranger /'streɪndʒə(r)/ *n* estranho *m*, desconhecido *m*

strangle /'strængl/ *vt* estrangular, sufocar

stranglehold /'strænglhəʊld/ *n* **have a ~ on** ter domínio sobre

strangulation /strængjʊ'leɪʃn/ *n* estrangulamento *m*

strap /stræp/ *n* (*of leather etc*) correia *f*; (*of dress*) alça *f*; (*of watch*) pulseira *f* com correia □ *vt* (*pt* **strapped**) prender com correia

strapping /'stræpɪŋ/ *a* robusto, grande

strata /'streɪtə/ *see* **stratum**

stratagem /'strætədʒəm/ *n* estratagema *m*

strategic /strə'ti:dʒɪk/ *a* estratégico; (*of weapons*) de longo alcance

strategy /'strætədʒɪ/ *n* estratégia *f*

stratum /'stra:təm/ *n* (*pl* **strata**) estrato *m*, camada *f*

straw /strɔ:/ *n* palha *f*; (*for drinking*) canudo *m*, (*P*) palhinha *f*. **the last ~** a última gota *f*

strawberry /'strɔ:brɪ/ *n* (*fruit*) morango *m*; (*plant*) morangueiro *m*

stray /streɪ/ *vi* (*deviate from path etc*) extraviar-se, desencaminhar-se, afastar-se (**from** de); (*lose one's way*) perder-se; (*wander*) vagar, errar □ *a* perdido, extraviado; (*isolated*) isolado, raro, esporádico □ *n* animal *m* perdido *or* vadio

streak /stri:k/ *n* risca *f*, lista *f*; (*strain*) veia *f*; (*period*) período *m*. **~ of lightning** relâmpago *m* □ *vt* listrar, riscar □ *vi* ir como um raio. **~er** *n* (*colloq*) pessoa *f* que corre nua em lugares públicos. **~y** *a* listrado, riscado. **~y bacon** toucinho *m* entremeado com gordura

stream /stri:m/ *n* riacho *m*, córrego *m*, regato *m*; (*current*) corrente *f*; (*fig: flow*) jorro *m*, torrente *f*; (*schol*) nível *m*, grupo *m* □ *vi* correr; (*of banner, hair*) flutuar; (*sweat*) escorrer, pingar

streamer /'stri:mə(r)/ *n* (*of paper*) serpentina *f*; (*flag*) flâmula *f*, bandeirola *f*

streamline /'stri:mlaɪn/ *vt* dar forma aerodinâmica a; (*fig*) racionalizar. **~d** *a* (*shape*) aerodinâmico

street /stri:t/ *n* rua *f*. **the man in the ~** (*fig*) o homem da rua. **~ lamp** poste *m* de iluminação

streetcar /'stri:tka:(r)/ *n* (*Amer*) bonde *m*, (*P*) carro *m* eléctrico

strength /streŋθ/ *n* força *f*; (*of wall*) solidez *f*; (*of fabric etc*) resistência *f*. **on the ~ of** à base de, em virtude de

strengthen /'streŋθn/ *vt* fortificar, fortalecer, reforçar

strenuous /'strenjʊəs/ *a* enérgico; (*arduous*) árduo, estrênuo, (*P*) estrénuo; (*tiring*) fatigante, esgotante. **~ly** *adv* esforçadamente, energicamente

stress /stres/ *n* acento *m*; (*pressure*) pressão *f*, tensão *f*; (*med*) stress *m* □ *vt* acentuar, sublinhar; (*sound*) acentuar. **~ful** *a* estressante

stretch /stretʃ/ *vt* (*pull taut*) esticar; (*arm, leg, neck*) estender, esticar; (*clothes*) alargar; (*truth*) forçar, torcer □ *vi* estender-se; (*after sleep etc*) espreguiçar-se; (*of clothes*) alargar-se □ *n* extensão *f*, trecho *m*; (*period*) período *m*; (*of road*) troço *m* □ *a* (*of fabric*) com elasticidade. **at a ~** sem parar. **~ one's legs** esticar as pernas

stretcher /'stretʃə(r)/ *n* maca *f*, padiola *f*. **~-bearer** *n* padioleiro *m*, (*P*) maqueiro *m*

strew /stru:/ *vt* (*pt* **strewed**, *pp* **strewed** *or* **strewn**) (*scatter*) espalhar; (*cover*) juncar, cobrir

stricken /'strɪkən/ *a* **~ with** atacado *or* acometido de

strict /strɪkt/ *a* (-er, -est) estrito, rigoroso. **~ly** *adv* estritamente. **~ly speaking** a rigor. **~ness** *n* severidade *f*, rigor *m*

stride /straɪd/ *vi* (*pt* **strode**, *pp* **stridden**) caminhar a passos largos □ *n* passada *f*. **make great ~s** (*fig*) fazer grandes progressos. **take sth in one's ~** fazer alg coisa sem problemas

strident /'straɪdnt/ *a* estridente

strife /straɪf/ *n* conflito *m* , dissensão *f*, luta *f*

strike /straɪk/ *vt* (*pt* **struck**) bater (em); (*blow*) dar; (*match*) riscar, acender; (*gold etc*) descobrir; (*of clock*) soar, dar, bater (horas); (*of lightning*) atingir □ *vi* fazer greve; (*attack*) atacar □ *n* (*of workers*) greve *f*; (*mil*) ataque *m*; (*find*) descoberta *f*. **on ~** em greve. **~ a bargain** fechar negócio. **~ off** *or* **out** riscar. **~ up** (*mus*) começar a tocar; (*friendship*) travar

striker /'straɪkə(r)/ *n* grevista *mf*

striking /'straɪkɪŋ/ *a* notável, impressionante; (*attractive*) atraente

string /strɪŋ/ *n* corda *f*, fio *m*; (*of violin, racket etc*) corda *f*; (*of pearls*) fio *m*; (*of onions, garlic*) réstia *f*; (*of lies etc*) série *f*; (*row*) fila *f* □ *vt* (*pt* **strung**) (*thread*) enfiar. **pull ~s** usar pistolão, (*P*) puxar os cordelinhos. **~ out**

espaçar-se. ~ed *a* (*instrument*) de cordas. ~y *a* filamentoso, fibroso; (*meat*) com nervos

stringent /'strɪndʒənt/ *a* rigoroso, estrito

strip[1] /strɪp/ *vt/i* (*pt* **stripped**) (*undress*) despir(-se); (*machine*) desmontar; (*deprive*) despojar, privar. ~**per** *n* artista *mf* de striptease; (*solvent*) removedor *m*

strip[2] /strɪp/ *n* tira *f*; (*of land*) faixa *f*. **comic** ~ história *f* em quadrinhos, (*P*) banda *f* desenhada. ~ **light** tubo *m* de luz fluorescente

stripe /straɪp/ *n* risca *f*, lista *f*, barra *f*. ~**d** *a* listrado, com listras

strive /straɪv/ *vi* (*pt* **strove**, *pp* **striven**) esforçar-se (**to** por)

strode /strəʊd/ *see* **stride**

stroke[1] /strəʊk/ *n* golpe *m*; (*of pen*) penada *f*, (*P*) traço *m*; (*in swimming*) braçada *f*; (*in rowing*) remada *f*; (*med*) ataque *m*, congestão *f*. ~ **of genius** rasgo *m* de genialidade. ~ **of luck** golpe *m* de sorte

stroke[2] /strəʊk/ *vt* (*with hand*) acariciar, fazer festas em

stroll /strəʊl/ *vi* passear, dar uma volta □ *n* volta *f*, (*P*) giro *m*. ~ **in**/*etc* entrar/*etc* tranquilamente

strong /strɒŋ/ *a* (-**er**, -**est**) forte; (*shoes, fabric etc*) resistente. **be a hundred**/*etc* ~ ser em número de cem/*etc*. ~-**box** *n* cofre-forte *m*. ~ **language** linguagem *f* grosseira, palavrões *mpl*. ~-**minded** *a* resoluto, firme. ~-**room** *n* casa-forte *f*. ~**ly** *adv* (*greatly*) fortemente, grandemente; (*with energy*) com força; (*deeply*) profundamente

stronghold /'strɒŋhəʊld/ *n* fortaleza *f*; (*fig*) baluarte *m*, bastião *m*

strove /strəʊv/ *see* **strive**

struck /strʌk/ *see* **strike** □ *a* ~ **on** (*sl*) apaixonado por

structur|e /'strʌktʃə(r)/ *n* estrutura *f*; (*of building etc*) edifício *m*, construção *f*. ~**al** *a* estrutural, de estrutura, de construção

struggle /'strʌgl/ *vi* (*to get free*) debater-se; (*contend*) lutar; (*strive*) esforçar-se (**to**, **for** por) □ *n* luta *f*; (*effort*) esforço *m*. **have a** ~ **to** ter dificuldade em. ~ **to one's feet** levantar-se a custo

strum /strʌm/ *vt* (*pt* **strummed**) (*banjo etc*) dedilhar

strung /strʌŋ/ *see* **string**

strut /strʌt/ *n* (*support*) suporte *m*, escora *f* □ *vi* (*pt* **strutted**) (*walk*) pavonear-se

stub /stʌb/ *n* (*of pencil, cigarette*) ponta *f*; (*of tree*) cepo *m*, toco *m*; (*counterfoil*) talão *m*, canhoto *m* □ *vt* (*pt* **stubbed**) ~ **one's toe** dar uma topada. ~ **out** esmagar

stubble /'stʌbl/ *n* (*on chin*) barba *f* por fazer; (*of crop*) restolho *m*

stubborn /'stʌbən/ *a* teimoso, obstinado. ~**ly** *adv* obstinadamente, teimosamente. ~**ness** *n* teimosia *f*, obstinação *f*

stubby /'stʌbɪ/ *a* (-**ier**, -**iest**) (*finger*) curto e grosso; (*person*) atarracado

stuck /stʌk/ *see* **stick**[2] □ *a* emperrado. ~-**up** *a* (*colloq: snobbish*) convencido, esnobe

stud[1] /stʌd/ *n* tacha *f*; (*for collar*) botão *m* de colarinho □ *vt* (*pt* **studded**) enfeitar com tachas. ~**ded with** salpicado de

stud[2] /stʌd/ *n* (*horses*) haras *m*. ~ (-**farm**) *n* coudelaria *f*. ~(-**horse**) *n* garanhão *m*

student /'stju:dnt/ *n* (*univ*) estudante *mf*, aluno *m*; (*schol*) aluno *m* □ *a* (*life, residence*) universitário

studied /'stʌdɪd/ *a* estudado

studio /'stju:dɪəʊ/ *n* (*pl* -**os**) estúdio *m*. ~ **flat** estúdio *m*

studious /'stju:dɪəs/ *a* (*person*) estudioso; (*deliberate*) estudado. ~**ly** *adv* (*carefully*) cuidadosamente

study /'stʌdɪ/ *n* estudo *m*; (*office*) escritório *m* □ *vt/i* estudar

stuff /stʌf/ *n* substância *f*, matéria *f*; (*sl: things*) coisa(s) *f* (*pl*) □ *vt* encher; (*animal*) empalhar; (*cram*) apinhar, encher ao máximo; (*culin*) rechear; (*block up*) entupir; (*put*) enfiar, meter. ~**ing** *n* enchimento *m*; (*culin*) recheio *m*

stuffy /'stʌfɪ/ *a* (-**ier**, -**iest**) abafado, mal arejado; (*dull*) enfadonho

stumbl|e /'stʌmbl/ *vi* tropeçar. ~**e across** *or* **on** dar com, encontrar por acaso, topar com. ~**ing-block** *n* obstáculo *m*

stump /stʌmp/ *n* (*of tree*) cepo *m*, toco *m*; (*of limb*) coto *m*; (*of pencil, cigar*) ponta *f*

stumped /stʌmpt/ *a* (*colloq: baffled*) atrapalhado, perplexo

stun /stʌn/ *vt* (*pt* **stunned**) aturdir, estontear

stung /stʌŋ/ *see* **sting**

stunk /stʌŋk/ *see* **stink**

stunning /'stʌnɪŋ/ *a* atordoador; (*colloq: delightful*) fantástico, sensacional

stunt[1] /stʌnt/ *vt* (*growth*) atrofiar. ~**ed** *a* atrofiado

stunt[2] /stʌnt/ *n* (*feat*) façanha *f*, proeza *f*; (*trick*) truque *m*; (*aviat*) acrobacia *f* aérea. ~ **man** *n* dublê *m*, (*P*) duplo *m*

stupefy /'stju:pɪfaɪ/ *vt* estupefazer, (*P*) estupeficar

stupendous /stju:'pendəs/ *a* estupendo, assombroso, prodigioso
stupid /'stju:pɪd/ *a* estúpido, obtuso. **~ity** /-'pɪdətɪ/ *n* estupidez *f*. **~ly** *adv* estupidamente
stupor /'stju:pə(r)/ *n* estupor *m*, torpor *m*
sturdy /'stɜ:dɪ/ *a* (**-ier, -iest**) robusto, vigoroso, forte
stutter /'stʌtə(r)/ *vi* gaguejar □ *n* gagueira *f*, (*P*) gaguez *f*
sty /staɪ/ *n* (*pigsty*) pocilga *f*, chiqueiro *m*
stye /staɪ/ *n* (*on eye*) terçol *m*, terçolho *m*
styl|e /staɪl/ *n* estilo *m*; (*fashion*) moda *f*; (*kind*) gênero *m*, (*P*) género *m*, tipo *m*; (*pattern*) feitio *m*, modelo *m* □ *vt* (*design*) desenhar, criar. **in ~e** (*live*) em grande estilo; (*do things*) com classe. **~e sb's hair** fazer um penteado em alguém. **~ist** *n* (*of hair*) cabeleireiro *m*
stylish /'staɪlɪʃ/ *a* elegante, na moda
stylized /'staɪlaɪzd/ *a* estilizado
stylus /'staɪləs/ *n* (*pl* **-uses**) (*of record-player*) agulha *f*, safira *f*
suave /swa:v/ *a* polido, de fala mansa, (*P*) melífluo
sub- /sʌb/ *pref* sub-
subconscious /sʌb'kɒnʃəs/ *a* & *n* subconsciente (*m*)
subcontract /sʌbkən'trækt/ *vt* dar de subempreitada
subdivide /sʌbdɪ'vaɪd/ *vt* subdividir
subdue /səb'dju:/ *vt* (*enemy, feeling*) dominar, subjugar; (*sound, voice*) abrandar. **~d** *a* (*weak*) submisso; (*quiet*) recolhido; (*light*) velado
subject[1] /'sʌbdʒɪkt/ *a* (*state etc*) dominado □ *n* sujeito *m*; (*schol, univ*) disciplina *f*, matéria *f*; (*citizen*) súdito *m*. **~-matter** *n* conteúdo *m*, tema *m*, assunto *m*. **~ to** sujeito a
subject[2] /səb'dʒekt/ *vt* submeter. **~ion** /-kʃn/ *n* submissão *f*
subjective /sʌb'dʒektɪv/ *a* subjetivo, (*P*) subjectivo
subjunctive /səb'dʒʌŋktɪv/ *a* & *n* subjuntivo (*m*), (*P*) conjuntivo (*m*)
sublime /sə'blaɪm/ *a* sublime
submarine /sʌbmə'ri:n/ *n* submarino *m*
submerge /səb'mɜ:dʒ/ *vt* submergir □ *vi* submergir, mergulhar
submissive /səb'mɪsɪv/ *a* submisso
submi|t /səb'mɪt/ *vt/i* (*pt* **submitted**) submeter(-se) (to a); (*jur: argue*) alegar. **~ssion** /-'mɪʃn/ *n* submissão *f*
subnormal /sʌb'nɔ:ml/ *a* subnormal; (*temperature*) abaixo do normal
subordinate[1] /sə'bɔ:dɪnət/ *a* subordinado, subalterno; (*gram*) subordinado □ *n* subordinado *m*, subalterno *m*
subordinate[2] /sə'bɔ:dɪneɪt/ *vt* subordinar (to a)
subpoena /səb'pi:nə/ *n* (*pl* **-as**) (*jur*) citação *f*, intimação *f*
subscribe /səb'skraɪb/ *vt/i* subscrever, contribuir (to para). **~ to** (*theory, opinion*) subscrever, aceitar; (*newspaper*) assinar. **~r** /-ə(r)/ *n* subscritor *m*, assinante *m*
subscription /səb'skrɪpʃn/ *n* subscrição *f*; (*to newspaper*) assinatura *f*
subsequent /'sʌbsɪkwənt/ *a* subseqüente, (*P*) subsequente, posterior. **~ly** *adv* subsequentemente, a seguir, posteriormente
subservient /səb'sɜ:vɪənt/ *a* servil, subserviente
subside /səb'saɪd/ *vi* (*flood, noise etc*) baixar; (*land*) ceder, afundar; (*wind, storm, excitement*) abrandar. **~nce** /-əns/ *n* (*of land*) afundamento *m*
subsidiary /səb'sɪdɪərɪ/ *a* subsidiário □ *n* (*comm*) filial *f*, sucursal *f*
subsid|y /'sʌbsədɪ/ *n* subsídio *m*, subvenção *f*. **~ize** /-ɪdaɪz/ *vt* subsidiar, subvencionar
subsist /səb'sɪst/ *vi* subsistir. **~ on** viver de. **~ence** *n* subsistência *f*. **~ence allowance** ajudas *fpl* de custo
substance /'sʌbstəns/ *n* substância *f*
substandard /sʌb'stændəd/ *a* de qualidade inferior
substantial /səb'stænʃl/ *a* substancial. **~ly** *adv* substancialmente
substantiate /səb'stænʃɪeɪt/ *vt* comprovar, fundamentar
substitut|e /'sʌbstɪtju:t/ *n* (*person*) substituto *m*, suplente *mf* (for de); (*thing*) substituto *m* (for de) □ *vt* substituir (for por). **~ion** /'tju:ʃn/ *n* substituição *f*
subterfuge /'sʌbtəfju:dʒ/ *n* subterfúgio *m*
subtitle /'sʌbtaɪtl/ *n* subtitulo *m*
subtle /'sʌtl/ *a* (**-er, -est**) sutil, (*P*) subtil. **~ty** *n* sutileza *f*, (*P*) subtileza *f*
subtotal /'sʌbtəʊtl/ *n* soma *f* parcial
subtract /səb'trækt/ *vt* subtrair, diminuir. **~ion** /-kʃn/ *n* subtração *f*, diminuição *f*
suburb /'sʌbɜ:b/ *n* subúrbio *m*, arredores *mpl*. **~an** /sə'bɜ:bən/ *a* dos subúrbios, suburbano. **~ia** /sə'bɜ:bɪə/ *n* (*pej*) os arredores
subver|t /səb'vɜ:t/ *vt* subverter. **~sion** /-ʃn/ *n* subverção *f*. **~sive** /-sɪv/ *a* subversivo
subway /'sʌbweɪ/ *n* passagem *f* subterrânea; (*Amer: underground*) metropolitano *m*
succeed /sək'si:d/ *vi* ser bem sucedido, ter êxito. **~ in doing sth** conseguir fazer alg coisa □ *vt* (*follow*) suceder a. **~ing** *a* seguinte, sucessivo

success /sək'ses/ *n* sucesso *m*, êxito *m*

succession /sək'seʃn/ *n* sucessão *f*; (*series*) série *f*. **in ~** seguidos, consecutivos

successive /sək'sesɪv/ *a* sucessivo, consecutivo

successor /sək'sesə(r)/ *n* sucessor *m*

succinct /sək'sɪŋkt/ *a* sucinto

succulent /'sʌkjʊlənt/ *a* suculento

succumb /sə'kʌm/ *vi* sucumbir

such /sʌtʃ/ *a & pron* tal, semelhante, assim; (*so much*) tanto □ *adv* tanto. **~ a book/***etc* un tal livro/*etc or* um livro/*etc* assim. **~ books/***etc* tais livros/*etc or* livros/*etc* assim. **~ courage/** *etc* tanta coragem/*etc*. **~ a big house** uma casa tão grande. **as ~** como tal. **~ as** como, tal como. **there's no ~ thing** uma coisa dessa não existe. **~-and-such** *a & pron* tal e tal

suck /sʌk/ *vt* chupar; (*breast*) mamar. **~ in** *or* **up** (*absorb*) absorver, aspirar; (*engulf*) tragar. **~ up to** puxar o saco a (*colloq*). **~ one's thumb** chupar o dedo. **~er** *n* (*sl: greenhorn*) trouxa *mf* (*colloq*); (*bot*) broto *m*

suckle /'sʌkl/ *vt* amamentar, dar de mamar a

suction /'sʌkʃn/ *n* sucção *f*

sudden /'sʌdn/ *a* súbito, repentino. **all of a ~** de repente, de súbito. **~ly** *adv* subitamente, repentinamente. **~ness** *n* subitaneidade *f*, brusquidão *f*

suds /sʌdz/ *npl* espuma *f* de sabão; (*soapy water*) água *f* de sabão

sue /su:/ *vt* (*pres p* **suing**) processar

suede /sweɪd/ *n* camurça *f*

suet /'su:ɪt/ *n* sebo *m*

suffer /'sʌfə(r)/ *vt/i* sofrer; (*tolerate*) tolerar, suportar. **~er** *n* sofredor *m*, o que sofre; (*patient*) doente *mf*, vítima *f*. **~ing** *n* sufrimento *m*

suffice /sə'faɪs/ *vi* bastar, chegar, ser suficiente

sufficien|t /sə'fɪʃnt/ *a* suficiente, bastante. **~cy** *n* suficiência *f*, quantidade *f* suficiente. **~tly** *adv* suficientemente

suffix /'sʌfɪx/ *n* sufixo *m*

suffocat|e /'sʌfəkeɪt/ *vt/i* sufocar. **~ion** /'keɪʃn/ *n* sufocação *f*, asfixia *f*. **~ing** *a* sufocante, asfixiante

sugar /'ʃʊgə(r)/ *n* açucar *m* □ *vt* adoçar, pôr açúcar em. **~-bowl** *n* açucareiro *m*. **~-lump** *n* torrão *m* de açúcar, (*P*) quadradinho *m* de açúcar. **brown ~** açúcar *m* preto, (*P*) açúcar *m* amarelo. **~y** *a* açucarado; (*fig: too sweet*) delico-doce

suggest /sə'dʒest/ *vt* sugerir. **~ion** /-tʃn/ *n* sugestão *f*. **~ive** *a* sugestivo; (*improper*) brejeiro, picante. **be ~ive of** sugerir, fazer lembrar

suicid|e /'su:ɪsaɪd/ *n* suicídio *m*. **commit ~e** suicidar-se. **~al** /-'saɪdl/ *a* suicida

suit /su:t/ *n* terno *m*, (*P*) fato *m*; (*woman's*) costume *m*, (*P*) saia-casaco *m*; (*cards*) naipe *m* □ *vt* convir a; (*of garment, style*) ficar bem em; (*adapt*) adaptar. **follow ~** (*fig*) seguir o exemplo. **~ability** *n* (*of action*) conveniência *f*, oportunidade *f*; (*of candidate*) aptidão *f*. **~able** *a* conveniente, apropriado (**for** para). **~ably** *adv* convenientemente. **~ed** *a* **be ~ed to** ser feito para, servir para. **be well ~ed** (*matched*) combinar-se bem; (*of people*) ser o ideal

suitcase /'su:tkeɪs/ *n* mala *f* (de viagem)

suite /swi:t/ *n* (*of rooms; mus*) suíte *f*, (*P*) suite *f*; (*of furniture*) mobília *f*

suitor /'su:tə(r)/ *n* pretendente *m*

sulk /sʌlk/ *vi* amuar, ficar emburrado. **~y** *a* amuado, emburrado (*colloq*)

sullen /'sʌlən/ *a* carrancudo

sulphur /'sʌlfə(r)/ *n* enxofre *m*. **~ic** /-'fjʊərɪk/ *a* **~ic acid** ácido *m* sulfúrico

sultan /'sʌltən/ *n* sultão *m*

sultana /sʌl'ta:nə/ *n* (*fruit*) passa *f* branca, (*P*) sultana *f*

sultry /'sʌltrɪ/ *a* (-ier, -iest) abafado, opressivo; (*fig*) sensual

sum /sʌm/ *n* soma *f*; (*amount of money*) soma *f*, quantia *f*, importância *f*; (*in arithmetic*) conta *f* □ *vt* (*pt* **summed**) somar. **~ up** recapitular, resumir; (*assess*) avaliar, medir

summar|y /'sʌmərɪ/ *n* sumário *m*, resumo *m* □ *a* sumário. **~ize** *vt* resumir

summer /'sʌmə(r)/ *n* verão *m*, estio *m* □ *a* de verão. **~-time** *n* verão *m*, época *f* de verão. **~y** *a* estival, próprio de verão

summit /'sʌmɪt/ *n* cume *m*, cimo *m*. **~ conference** (*pol*) conferência *f* de cúpula, (*P*) reunião *f* de cimeira

summon /'sʌmən/ *vt* mandar chamar; (*to meeting*) convocar. **~ up** (*strength, courage etc*) chamar a si, fazer apelo a

summons /'sʌmənz/ *n* (*jur*) citação *f*, intimação *f* □ *vt* citar, intimar

sump /sʌmp/ *n* (*auto*) cárter *m*

sumptuous /'sʌmptʃʊəs/ *a* suntuoso, (*P*) sumptuoso, luxuoso

sun /sʌn/ *n* sol *m* □ *vt* (*pt* **sunned**) **~ o.s.** aquecer-se ao sol. **~glasses** *npl* óculos *mpl* de sol. **~-roof** *n* teto *m* solar. **~-tan** *n* bronzeado *m*. **~-tanned** *a* bronzeado. **~-tan oil** *n* óleo *m* de bronzear

sunbathe /'sʌnbeɪð/ *vi* tomar um banho de sol

sunburn /'sʌnbɜ:n/ *n* queimadura *f* de sol. **~t** *a* queimado pelo sol
Sunday /'sʌndɪ/ *n* domingo *m*. **~ school** catecismo *m*
sundial /'sʌndaɪəl/ *n* relógio *m* de sol
sundown /'sʌndaʊn/ *n* = sunset
sundr|y /'sʌndrɪ/ *a* vários, diversos. **~ies** *npl* artigos *mpl* diversos. **all and ~y** todo o mundo
sunflower /'sʌnflaʊə(r)/ *n* girassol *m*
sung /sʌŋ/ *see* sing
sunk /sʌŋk/ *see* sink
sunken /'sʌŋkən/ *a* (*ship etc*) afundado; (*eyes*) fundo
sunlight /'sʌnlaɪt/ *n* luz *f* do sol, sol *m*
sunny /'sʌnɪ/ *a* (-ier, -iest) (*room, day etc*) ensolarado
sunrise /'sʌnraɪz/ *n* nascer *m* do sol
sunset /'sʌnset/ *n* pôr *m* do sol
sunshade /'sʌnʃeɪd/ *n* (*awning*) toldo *m*; (*parasol*) pára-sol *m*, (*P*) guarda-sol *m*
sunshine /'sʌnʃaɪn/ *n* sol *m*, luz *f* do sol
sunstroke /'sʌnstrəʊk/ *n* (*med*) insolação *f*
super /'su:pə(r)/ *a* (*colloq: excellent*) formidável
superb /su:'pɜ:b/ *a* soberbo, esplêndido
supercilious /su:pə'sɪlɪəs/ *a* (*haughty*) altivo; (*disdainful*) desdenhoso
superficial /su:pə'fɪʃl/ *a* superficial. **~ity** /-ɪ'ælətɪ/ *n* superficialidade *f*. **~ly** *adv* superficialmente
superfluous /su'pɜ:flʊəs/ *a* supérfluo
superhuman /su:pə'hju:mən/ *a* sobre-humano
superimpose /su:pərɪm'pəʊz/ *vt* sobrepor (on a)
superintendent /su:pərɪn'tendənt/ *n* superintendente *m*; (*of police*) comissário *m*, chefe *m* de polícia
superior /su:'pɪərɪə(r)/ *a & n* superior (*m*). **~ity** /-'ɒrətɪ/ *n* superioridade *f*
superlative /su:'pɜ:lətɪv/ *a* supremo, superlativo □ *n* (*gram*) superlativo *m*
supermarket /'su:pəma:kɪt/ *n* supermercado *m*
supernatural /su:pə'nætʃrəl/ *a* sobrenatural
superpower /'su:pəpaʊə(r)/ *n* superpotência *f*
supersede /su:pə'si:d/ *vt* suplantar, substituir
supersonic /su:pə'sɒnɪk/ *a* supersônico, (*P*) supersónico
superstiti|on /su:pə'stɪʃn/ *n* superstição *f*. **~ous** *a* /-'stɪʃəs/ supersticioso
superstore /'su:pəstɔ:(r)/ *n* hipermercado *m*
supertanker /'su:pətæŋkə(r)/ *n* superpetroleiro *m*
supervis|e /'su:pəvaɪz/ *vt* supervisar, fiscalizar. **~ion** /-'vɪʒn/ *n* supervisão *f*. **~or** *n* supervisor *m*; (*shop*) chefe *mf* de seção; (*firm*) chefe *mf* de serviço. **~ory** /'su:pəvaɪzərɪ/ *a* de supervisão
supper /'sʌpə(r)/ *n* jantar *m*; (*late at night*) ceia *f*
supple /'sʌpl/ *a* flexível, maleável
supplement[1] /'sʌplɪmənt/ *n* suplemento *m*. **~ary** /-'mentrɪ/ *a* suplementar
supplement[2] /'sʌplɪment/ *vt* suplementar
supplier /sə'plaɪə(r)/ *n* fornecedor *m*
suppl|y /sə'plaɪ/ *vt* suprir, prover; (*comm*) fornecer, abastecer □ *n* provisão *f*; (*of goods, gas etc*) fornecimento *m*, abastecimento *m* □ *a* (*teacher*) substituto. **~ies** (*food*) víveres *mpl*; (*mil*) suprimentos *mpl*. **~y and demand** oferta e procura
support /sə'pɔ:t/ *vt* (*hold up, endure*) suportar; (*provide for*) sustentar, suster; (*back*) apoiar, patrocinar; (*sport*) torcer por □ *n* apoio *m*; (*techn*) suporte *m*. **~er** *n* partidário *m*; (*sport*) torcedor *m*
suppos|e /sə'pəʊz/ *vt/i* supor. **~e that** supondo que, na hipótese de que. **~ed** *a* suposto. **he's ~ed to do** ele deve fazer; (*believed to*) consta que ele faz. **~edly** /-ɪdlɪ/ *adv* segundo dizem; (*probably*) supostamente, em princípio. **~ing** *conj* se. **~ition** /sʌpə'zɪʃn/ *n* suposição *f*
suppress /sə'pres/ *vt* (*put an end to*) suprimir; (*restrain*) conter, reprimir; (*stifle*) abafar, sufocar; (*psych*) recalcar. **~ion** /-ʃn/ *n* supressão *f*; (*restraint*) repressão *f*; (*psych*) recalque *m*, (*P*) recalcamento *m*
suprem|e /su:'pri:m/ *a* supremo. **~acy** /-eməsɪ/ *n* supremacia *f*
surcharge /'sɜ:tʃa:dʒ/ *n* sobretaxa *f*; (*on stamp*) sobrecarga *f*
sure /ʃʊə(r)/ *a* (-er, -est) seguro, certo □ *adv* (*colloq: certainly*) deveras, não há dúvida que, de certeza. **be ~ about** *or* **of** ter a certeza de. **be ~ to** (*not fail*) não deixar de. **he is ~ to find out** ele vai descobrir com certeza. **make ~** assegurar. **~ly** *adv* com certeza, certamente
surety /'ʃʊərətɪ/ *n* (*person*) fiador *m*; (*thing*) garantia *f*
surf /sɜ:f/ *n* (*waves*) ressaca *f*, rebentação *f*. **~er** *n* surfista *mf*. **~ing** *n* surfe *m*, (*P*) surf *m*, jacaré-na-praia *m*
surface /'sɜ:fɪs/ *n* superfície *f* □ *a* superficial □ *vt/i* revestir; (*rise, become known*) emergir. **~ mail** via *f* marítima

surfboard /ˈsɜːbɔːd/ *n* prancha *f* de surfe, (*P*) surf
surfeit /ˈsɜːfɪt/ *n* excesso *m* (of de)
surge /sɜːdʒ/ *vi* (*waves*) ondular, encapelar-se; (*move forward*) avançar □ *n* (*wave*) onda *f*, vaga *f*; (*motion*) arremetida *f*
surgeon /ˈsɜːdʒən/ *n* cirurgião *m*
surg|ery /ˈsɜːdʒərɪ/ *n* cirurgia *f*; (*office*) consultório *m*; (*session*) consulta *f*; (*consulting hours*) horas *fpl* de consulta. **~ical** *a* cirúrgico
surly /ˈsɜːlɪ/ *a* (-ier, -iest) carrancudo, trombudo
surmise /səˈmaɪz/ *vt* imaginar, supor, calcular □ *n* conjetura *f*, (*P*) conjectura *f*; hipótese *f*
surmount /səˈmaʊnt/ *vt* sobrepujar, vencer, (*P*) superar
surname /ˈsɜːneɪm/ *n* sobrenome *m*, (*P*) apelido *m*
surpass /səˈpaːs/ *vt* superar, ultrapassar, exceder
surplus /ˈsɜːpləs/ *n* excedente *m*, excesso *m*; (*finance*) saldo *m* positivo □ *a* excedente, em excesso
surpris|e /səˈpraɪz/ *n* surpresa *f* □ *vt* surpreender. **~ed** *a* surpreendido, admirado (at com). **~ing** *a* surpreendente. **~ingly** *adv* surpreendentemente
surrender /səˈrendə(r)/ *vi* render-se □ *vt* (*hand over; mil*) entregar □ *n* (*mil*) rendição *f*; (*of rights*) renúncia *f*
surreptitious /sʌrepˈtɪʃəs/ *a* subreptício, furtivo
surrogate /ˈsʌrəgeɪt/ *n* delegado *m*. **~ mother** mãe *f* de aluguel, (*P*) aluguer
surround /səˈraʊnd/ *vt* rodear, cercar; (*mil etc*) cercar. **~ing** *a* circundante, vizinho. **~ings** *npl* arredores *mpl*; (*setting*) meio *m*, ambiente *m*
surveillance /sɜːˈveɪləns/ *n* vigilância *f*
survey[1] /səˈveɪ/ *vt* (*landscape etc*) observar; (*review*) passar em revista; (*inquire about*) pesquisar; (*land*) fazer o levantamento de; (*building*) vistoriar, inspecionar, (*P*) inspeccionar. **~or** *n* (*of buildings*) fiscal *m*; (*of land*) agrimensor *m*
survey[2] /ˈsɜːveɪ/ *n* (*inspection*) vistoria *f*, inspeção *f*, (*P*) inspecção *f*; (*general view*) panorâmica *f*; (*inquiry*) pesquisa *f*
survival /səˈvaɪvl/ *n* sobrevivência *f*; (*relic*) relíquia *f*, vestígio *m*
surviv|e /səˈvaɪv/ *vt/i* sobreviver (a). **~or** *n* sobrevivente *mf*
susceptib|le /səˈseptəbl/ *a* (*prone*) susceptível (to a); (*sensitive, impressionable*) susceptível, sensível. **~ility** /-ˈbɪlətɪ/ *n* susceptibilidade *f*
suspect[1] /səˈspekt/ *vt* suspeitar; (*doubt, distrust*) desconfiar de, suspeitar de
suspect[2] /ˈsʌspekt/ *a* & *n* suspeito (*m*)
suspen|d /səˈspend/ *vt* (*hang, stop*) suspender; (*from duty etc*) suspender. **~ded sentence** suspensão *f* de pena. **~sion** *n* suspensão *f*. **~sion bridge** ponte *f* suspensa *or* pênsil
suspender /səˈspendə(r)/ *n* (presilha de) liga *f*. **~ belt** *n* cintaliga *f*, (*P*) cinta *f* de ligas. **~s** (*Amer: braces*) suspensórios *mpl*
suspense /səˈspens/ *n* ansiedade *f*, incerteza *f*; (*in book etc*) suspense *m*, tensão *f*
suspicion /səˈspɪʃn/ *n* suspeita *f*; (*distrust*) desconfiança *f*; (*trace*) vestígio *m*, (*P*) traço *m*
suspicious /səsˈpɪʃəs/ *a* desconfiado; (*causing suspicion*) suspeito. **be ~ of** desconfiar de. **~ly** *adv* de modo suspeito
sustain /səˈsteɪn/ *vt* (*support*) suster, sustentar; (*suffer*) sofrer; (*keep up*) sustentar; (*jur: uphold*) sancionar; (*interest, effort*) manter. **~ed effort** esforço *m* contínuo
sustenance /ˈsʌstɪnəns/ *n* (*food*) alimento *m*, sustento *m*
swagger /ˈswægə(r)/ *vi* pavonear-se, andar com arrogância
swallow[1] /ˈswɒləʊ/ *vt/i* engolir. **~ up** (*absorb, engulf*) devorar, tragar
swallow[2] /ˈswɒləʊ/ *n* (*bird*) andorinha *f*
swam /swæm/ *see* swim
swamp /swɒmp/ *n* pântano *m*, brejo *m* □ *vt* (*flood, overwhelm*) inundar, submergir. **~y** *a* pantanoso
swan /swɒn/ *n* cisne *m*
swank /swæŋk/ *vi* (*colloq: show off*) gabar-se, mostrar-se (*colloq*)
swap /swɒp/ *vt/i* (*pt* **swapped**) (*colloq*) trocar (for por) □ *n* (*colloq*) troca *f*
swarm /swɔːm/ *n* (*of insects, people*) enxame *m* □ *vi* formigar. **~ into** *or* **round** invadir
swarthy /ˈswɔːðɪ/ *a* (-ier, -iest) moreno, trigueiro
swat /swɒt/ *vt* (*pt* **swatted**) (*fly etc*) esmagar, esborrachar
sway /sweɪ/ *vt/i* oscilar, balançar(-se); (*influence*) mover, influenciar □ *n* oscilação *f*, balanceio *m*; (*rule*) domínio *m*, poder *m*
swear /sweə(r)/ *vt/i* (*pt* **swore**, *pp* **sworn**) jurar; (*curse*) praguejar, rogar pragas (at contra). **~ by** jurar por; (*colloq: recommend*) ter grande fé em. **~-word** *n* palavrão *m*
sweat /swet/ *n* suor *m* □ *vi* suar. **~y** *a* suado

sweater /'swetə(r)/ *n* suéter *m*, (*P*) camisola *f*

sweatshirt /'swetʃɜ:t/ *n* suéter *m* de malha *or* algodão

swede /swi:d/ *n* couve-nabo *f*

Swed|e /swi:d/ *n* sueco *m*. **~en** *n* Suécia *f*. **~ish** *a* & *n* sueco (*m*)

sweep /swi:p/ *vt/i* (*pt* **swept**) varrer; (*go majestically*) avançar majestosamente; (*carry away*) arrastar; (*chimney*) limpar □ *n* (*with broom*) varredela *f*; (*curve*) curva *f*; (*movement*) gesto *m* largo. **(chimney-)~** limpa-chaminés *m*. **~ing** *a* (*gesture*) largo; (*action*) de grande alcance. **~ing statement** generalização *f* fácil

sweet /swi:t/ *a* (-er, -est) doce; (*colloq: charming*) doce, gracinha; (*colloq: pleasant*) agradável □ *n* doce *m*. **~ corn** milho *m*. **~ pea** ervilha-de-cheiro *f*. **~ shop** confeitaria *f*. **have a ~ tooth** gostar de doce. **~ly** *adv* docemente. **~ness** *n* doçura *f*

sweeten /'swi:tn/ *vt* adoçar; (*fig: mitigate*) suavizar. **~er** *n* (*for tea, coffee*) adoçante *m* (artificial); (*colloq: bribe*) agrado *m*

sweetheart /'swi:tha:t/ *n* namorado *m*, namorada *f*; (*term of endearment*) querido *m*, querida *f*, amor *m*

swell /swel/ *vt/i* (*pt* **swelled**, *pp* **swollen** *or* **swelled**) (*expand*) inchar; (*increase*) aumentar □ *n* (*of sea*) ondulação *f* □ *a* (*colloq: excellent*) excelente; (*colloq : smart*) chique. **~ing** *n* (*med*) inchação *f*, inchaço *m*

swelter /'sweltə(r)/ *vi* fazer um calor abrasador; (*person*) abafar (com calor)

swept /swept/ *see* **sweep**

swerve /swɜ:v/ *vi* desviar-se, dar uma guinada

swift /swɪft/ *a* (-er, -est) rápido, veloz. **~ly** *adv* rapidamente. **~ness** *n* rapidez *f*

swig /swɪg/ *vt* (*pt* **swigged**) (*colloq: drink*) emborcar, beber em longos tragos □ *n* (*colloq*) trago *m*, gole *m*

swill /swɪl/ *vt* passar por água □ *n* (*pig-food*) lavagem *f*, (*P*) lavadura *f*

swim /swɪm/ *vi* (*pt* **swam**, *pp* **swum**, *pres p* **swimming**) nadar; (*room, head*) rodar □ *vt* atravessar a nado; (*distance*) nadar □ *n* banho *m*. **~mer** *n* nadador *m*. **~ming** *n* natação *f*. **~ming-bath**, **~ming-pool** *ns* piscina *f*. **~ming-cap** *n* touca *f* de banho. **~ming-costume**, **~-suit** *ns* maiô *m*, (*P*) fato *m* de banho. **~ming-trunks** *npl* calção *m* de banho

swindle /'swɪndl/ *vt* trapacear, fraudar, (*P*) vigarizar □ *n* vigarice *f*. **~r** /-ə(r)/ *n* vigarista *mf*

swine /swaɪn/ *npl* (*pigs*) porcos *mpl* □ *n* (*pl invar*) (*colloq: person*) animal *m*, canalha *m* (*colloq*)

swing /swɪŋ/ *vt/i* (*pt* **swung**) balançar(-se); (*turn round*) girar □ *n* (*seat*) balanço *m*; (*of opinion*) reviravolta *f*; (*mus*) swing *m*; (*rhythm*) ritmo *m*. **in full ~** no máximo, em plena atividade, (*P*) actividade. **~ round** (*of person*) virar-se. **~-bridge/door** *ns* ponte *f*/porta *f* giratória

swipe /swaɪp/ *vt* (*colloq: hit*) bater em, dar uma pancada em (*colloq*); (*colloq: steal*) afanar, roubar (*colloq*) □ *n* (*colloq: hit*) pancada *f* (*colloq*)

swirl /swɜ:l/ *vi* rodopiar, redemoinhar □ *n* turbilhão *m*, redemoinho *m*

swish /swɪʃ/ *vt/i* sibilar, zunir, (fazer) cortar o ar; (*with brushing sound*) roçar □ *a* (*colloq*) chique

Swiss /swɪs/ *a* & *n* suíço (*m*)

switch /swɪtʃ/ *n* interruptor *m*; (*change*) mudança *f* □ *vt* (*transfer*) transferir; (*exchange*) trocar □ *vi* desviar-se. **~ off** desligar

switchboard /'swɪtʃbɔ:d/ *n* (*telephone*) PBX *m*, mesa *f* telefônica

Switzerland /'swɪtsələnd/ *n* Suíça *f*

swivel /'swɪvl/ *vt/i* (*pt* **swivelled**) (fazer) girar. **~ chair** cadeira *f* giratória

swollen /'swəʊlən/ *see* **swell** □ *a* inchado

swoop /swu:p/ *vi* (*bird*) lançar-se, cair (**down on** sobre); (*police*) dar uma batida policial, (*P*) rusga

sword /sɔ:d/ *n* espada *f*

swore /swɔ:(r)/ *see* **swear**

sworn /swɔ:n/ *see* **swear** □ *a* (*enemy*) jurado, declarado; (*ally*) fiel

swot /swɒt/ *vt/i* (*pt* **swotted**) (*colloq: study*) estudar muito, (*P*) marrar (*sl*) □ *n* (*colloq*) estudante *m* muito aplicado, (*P*) marrão *m* (*sl*)

swum /swʌm/ *see* **swim**

swung /swʌŋ/ *see* **swing**

sycamore /'sɪkəmɔ:(r)/ *n* (*maple*) sicômoro *m*, (*P*) sicómoro *m*; (*Amer: plane*) plátano *m*

syllable /'sɪləbl/ *n* sílaba *f*

syllabus /'sɪləbəs/ *n* (*pl* -uses) programa *m*

symbol /'sɪmbl/ *n* símbolo *m*. **~ic(al)** /-'bɒlɪk(l)/ *a* simbólico. **~ism** *n* simbolismo *m*

symbolize /'sɪmbəlaɪz/ *vt* simbolizar

symmetr|y /'sɪmətrɪ/ *n* simetria *f*. **~ical** /sɪ'metrɪkl/ *a* simétrico

sympathize /'sɪmpəθaɪz/ *vi* **~ with** ter pena de, condoer-se de; (*fig*) compartilhar os sentimentos de. **~r** *n* simpatizante *mf*

sympath|y /'sɪmpəθɪ/ *n* (*pity*) pena *f*, compaixão *f*; (*solidarity*) solidariedade *f*; (*condolences*) pêsames *mpl*, condolências *fpl*. **be in ~y with** estar

de acordo com. **~etic** /-ˈθetɪk/ *a* compreensivo, simpático; (*likeable*) simpático; (*showing pity*) compassivo. **~etically** /-ˈθetɪklɪ/ *adv* compassivamente; (*fig*) compreensivamente
symphon|y /ˈsɪmfənɪ/ *n* sinfonia *f* □ *a* sinfônico, (*P*) sinfónico. **~ic** /-ˈfɒnɪk/ *a* sinfônico, (*P*) sinfónico
symptom /ˈsɪmptəm/ *n* sintoma *m*. **~atic** /-ˈmætɪk/ *a* sintomático (of de)
synagogue /ˈsɪnəgɒg/ *n* sinagoga *f*
synchronize /ˈsɪŋkrənaɪz/ *vt* sincronizar
syndicate /ˈsɪndɪkət/ *n* sindicato *m*
syndrome /ˈsɪndrəʊm/ *n* (*med*) síndrome *m*, (*P*) sindroma *m*
synonym /ˈsɪnənɪm/ *n* sinônimo *m*, (*P*) sinónimo *m*. **~ous** /sɪˈnɒnɪməs/ *a* sinônimo, (*P*) sinónimo (with de)
synopsis /sɪˈnɒpsɪs/ *n* (*pl* **-opses** /-si:z/) sinopse *f*, resumo *m*
syntax /ˈsɪntæks/ *n* sintaxe *f*
synthesis /ˈsɪnθəsɪs/ *n* (*pl* **-theses** /-si:z/) síntese *f*
synthetic /sɪnˈθetɪk/ *a* sintético
syphilis /ˈsɪfɪlɪs/ *n* sífilis *f*
Syria /ˈsɪrɪə/ *n* Síria *f*. **~n** *a* & *n* sírio (*m*)
syringe /sɪˈrɪndʒ/ *n* seringa *f* □ *vt* seringar
syrup /ˈsɪrəp/ *n* (*liquid*) xarope *m*; (*treacle*) calda *f* de açúcar. **~y** *a* (*fig*) melado, enjoativo
system /ˈsɪstəm/ *n* sistema *m*; (*body*) organismo *m*; (*order*) método *m*. **~atic** /sɪstəˈmætɪk/ *a* sistemático

T

tab /tæb/ *n* (*flap*) lingueta *f*; (*for fastening, hanging*) aba *f*; (*label*) etiqueta *f*; (*loop*) argola *f*; (*Amer colloq: bill*) conta *f*. **keep ~s on** (*colloq*) vigiar
table /ˈteɪbl/ *n* mesa *f*; (*list*) tabela *f*, lista *f* □ *vt* (*submit*) apresentar; (*postpone*) adiar. **at ~** à mesa. **lay** *or* **set the ~** pôr a mesa. **~ of contents** índice *m* (das matérias). **turn the ~s** inverter as posições. **~-cloth** *n* toalha de mesa *f*. **~-mat** *n* descanso *m*. **~ tennis** pingue-pongue *m*
tablespoon /ˈteɪblspu:n/ *n* colher *f* grande de sopa. **~ful** *n* (*pl* **~fuls**) colher *f* de sopa cheia
tablet /ˈtæblɪt/ *n* (*of stone*) lápide *f*, placa *f*; (*drug*) comprimido *m*
tabloid /ˈtæblɔɪd/ *n* tablóide *m*. **~ journalism** (*pej*) jornalismo *m* sensacionalista, imprensa *f* marron
taboo /təˈbu:/ *n* & *a* tabu (*m*)
tacit /ˈtæsɪt/ *a* tácito
taciturn /ˈtæsɪtɜ:n/ *a* taciturno
tack /tæk/ *n* (*nail*) tacha *f*; (*stitch*) ponto *m* de alinhavo; (*naut*) amura *f*; (*fig: course of action*) rumo *m* □ *vt* (*nail*) pregar com tachas; (*stitch*) alinhavar □ *vi* (*naut*) bordejar. **~ on** (*add*) acrescentar, juntar
tackle /ˈtækl/ *n* equipamento *m*, apetrechos *mpl*; (*sport*) placagem *f* □ *vt* (*problem etc*) atacar; (*sport*) placar; (*a thief etc*) agarrar-se a
tacky /ˈtækɪ/ *a* (-ier, -iest) peganhento, pegajoso
tact /tækt/ *n* tato *m*, (*P*) tacto *m*. **~ful** *a* cheio de tato, (*P*) tacto, diplomático. **~fully** *adv* com tato, (*P*) tacto. **~less** *a* sem tato, (*P*) tacto. **~lessly** *adv* sem tato, (*P*) tacto
tactic /ˈtæktɪk/ *n* (*expedient*) tática *f*, (*P*) táctica *f*. **~s** *n(pl)* (*procedure*) tática *f*, (*P*) táctica *f*. **~al** *a* tático, (*P*) táctico
tadpole /ˈtædpəʊl/ *n* girino *m*
tag /tæg/ *n* (*label*) etiqueta *f*; (*on shoelace*) agulheta *f*; (*phrase*) chavão *m*, clichê *m* □ *vi* (*pt* **tagged**) etiquetar; (*add*) juntar □ *vi* **~ along** (*colloq*) andar atrás, seguir
Tagus /ˈteɪgʌs/ *n* Tejo *m*
tail /teɪl/ *n* cauda *f*, rabo *m*; (*of shirt*) fralda *f*. **~s!** (*tossing coin*) coroa! □ *vt* (*follow*) seguir, vigiar □ *vi* **~ away** *or* **off** diminuir, baixar. **~-back** *n* (*traffic*) fila *f*, (*P*) bicha *f*. **~-end** *n* parte *f* traseira, cauda *f*. **~-light** *n* (*auto*) farolete *m* traseiro, (*P*) farolim *m* da rectaguarda
tailor /ˈteɪlə(r)/ *n* alfaiate *m* □ *vt* (*garment*) fazer; (*fig: adapt*) adaptar. **~-made** *a* feito sob medida, (*P*) por medida. **~-made for** (*fig*) feito para, talhado para
tainted /ˈteɪntɪd/ *a* (*infected*) contaminado; (*decayed*) estragado; (*fig*) manchado
take /teɪk/ *vt/i* (*pt* **took**, *pp* **taken**) (*get hold of*) agarrar em, pegar em; (*capture*) tomar; (*a seat, a drink; train, bus etc*) tomar; (*carry*) levar (to a, para); (*contain, escort*) levar; (*tolerate*) suportar, agüentar, (*P*) aguentar; (*choice, exam*) fazer; (*photo*) tirar; (*require*) exigir. **be ~n by** *or* **with** ficar encantado com. **be ~n ill** adoecer. **it ~s time to** leva tempo para. **~ after** parecer-se a. **~-away** *n* (*meal*) comida *f* para levar, takeaway *m*; (*shop*) loja *f* que só vende comida para ser consumida em outro lugar. **~ away** levar. **~ away from sb/sth** tirar de alguém/de alg coisa. **~ back** aceitar de volta; (*return*) devolver; (*accompany*) acompanhar; (*statement*) retirar, retratar. **~ down** (*object*) tirar para baixo; (*notes*) tirar, tomar. **~ in** (*garment*) meter para

dentro; (*include*) incluir; (*cheat*) enganar, levar (*colloq*); (*grasp*) compreender; (*receive*) receber. ~ **it that** supor que. ~ **off** *vt* (*remove*) tirar; (*mimic*) imitar, macaquear □ *vi* (*aviat*) decolar, levantar vôo. ~**-off** *n* imitação *f*; (*aviat*) decolagem *f*, (*P*) descolagem *f*. ~ **on** (*task*) encarregar-se de; (*staff*) admitir, contratar. ~ **out** tirar; (*on an outing*) levar para sair. ~ **over** *vt* tomar conta de, assumir a direção, (*P*) direcção de □ *vi* tomar o poder. ~ **over from** (*relieve*) render, substituir; (*succeed*) suceder a. ~**-over** *n* (*pol*) tomada *f* de poder; (*comm*) take-over *m*. ~ **part** participar *or* tomar parte (in em). ~ **place** ocorrer, suceder. ~ **sides** tomar partido. ~ **sides with** tomar o partido de. ~ **to** gostar de, simpatizar com; (*activity*) tomar gosto por, entregar-se a. ~ **up** (*object*) apanhar, pegar em; (*hobby*) dedicar-se a; (*occupy*) ocupar, tomar

takings /'teɪkɪŋz/ *npl* receita *f*

talcum /'tælkəm/ *n* talco *m*. ~ **powder** pó *m* talco

tale /teɪl/ *n* conto *m*, história *f*

talent /'tælənt/ *n* talento *m*. ~**ed** *a* talentoso, bem dotado

talk /tɔ:k/ *vt/i* falar; (*chat*) conversar □ *n* conversa *f*; (*mode of speech*) fala *f*; (*lecture*) palestra *f*. **small** ~ conversa *f* banal. ~ **into doing** convencer a fazer. ~ **nonsense** dizer disparates. ~ **over** discutir. ~ **shop** falar de assuntos profissionais. ~ **to o.s.** falar sozinho, falar com os seus botões. **there's** ~ **of** fala-se de. ~**er** *n* conversador *m*. ~**ing-to** *n* (*colloq*) descompostura *f*

talkative /'tɔ:kətɪv/ *a* falador, conversador, tagarela

tall /tɔ:l/ *a* (-er, -est) alto. ~ **story** (*colloq*) história *f* do arco-da-velha

tallboy /'tɔ:lbɔɪ/ *n* cômoda *f*, (*P*) cómoda *f* alta

tally /'tælɪ/ *vi* corresponder (**with** a), conferir (**with** com)

tambourine /tæmbə'ri:n/ *n* tamborim *m*, pandeiro *m*

tame /teɪm/ *a* (-er, -est) manso; (*domesticated*) domesticado; (*dull*) insípido □ *vt* amansar, domesticar

tamper /'tæmpə(r)/ *vi* ~ **with** mexer indevidamente em; (*text*) alterar

tampon /'tæmpən/ *n* (*med*) tampão *m*; (*sanitary towel*) toalha *f* higiênica

tan /tæn/ *vt/i* (*pt* **tanned**) queimar, bronzear; (*hide*) curtir □ *n* bronzeado *m* □ *a* castanho amarelado

tandem /'tændəm/ *n* (*bicycle*) tandem *m*. **in** ~ em tandem, um atrás do outro

tang /tæŋ/ *n* (*taste*) sabor *m or* gosto *m* característico; (*smell*) cheiro *m* característico

tangent /'tændʒənt/ *n* tangente *f*

tangerine /tændʒə'ri:n/ *n* tangerina *f*

tangible /'tændʒəbl/ *a* tangível

tangle /'tæŋgl/ *vt* emaranhar, enredar □ *n* emaranhado *m*. **become** ~**d** emaranhar-se, enredar-se

tank /tæŋk/ *n* tanque *m*, reservatório *m*; (*for petrol*) tanque *m*, (*P*) depósito *m*; (*for fish*) aquário *m*; (*mil*) tanque *m*

tankard /'tæŋkəd/ *n* caneca *f* grande

tanker /'tæŋkə(r)/ *n* carro-tanque *m*, camião-cisterna *m*; (*ship*) petroleiro *m*

tantaliz|e /'tæntəlaɪz/ *vt* atormentar, tantalizar. ~**ing** *a* tentador

tantamount /'tæntəmaʊnt/ *a* **be** ~ **to** equivaler a

tantrum /'tæntrəm/ *n* chilique *m*, ataque *m* de mau gênio, (*P*) génio, birra *f*

tap[1] /tæp/ *n* (*for water etc*) torneira *f* □ *vt* (*pt* **tapped**) (*resources*) explorar; (*telephone*) gram-pear. **on** ~ (*colloq: available*) disponível

tap[2] /tæp/ *vt/i* (*pt* **tapped**) bater levemente. ~**-dance** *n* sapateado *m*

tape /teɪp/ *n* (*for dressmaking*) fita *f*; (*sticky*) fita *f* adesiva. (**magnetic**) ~ fita *f* (magnética) □ *vt* (*tie*) atar, prender; (*stick*) colar; (*record*) gravar. ~**-measure** *n* fita *f* métrica. ~ **recorder** gravador *m*

taper /'teɪpə(r)/ *n* vela *f* comprida e fina □ *vt/i* ~ (**off**) estreitar(-se), afilar(-se). ~**ed**, ~**ing** *adjs* (*fingers etc*) afilado; (*trousers*) afunilado

tapestry /'tæpɪstrɪ/ *n* tapeçaria *f*

tapioca /tæpɪ'əʊkə/ *n* tapioca *f*

tar /ta:(r)/ *n* alcatrão *m* □ *vt* (*pt* **tarred**) alcatroar

target /'ta:gɪt/ *n* alvo *m* □ *vt* ter como alvo

tariff /'tærɪf/ *n* tarifa *f*; (*on import*) direitos *mpl* aduaneiros

Tarmac /'ta:mæk/ *n* macadame (alcatroado) *m*; (*runway*) pista *f*

tarnish /'ta:nɪʃ/ *vt/i* (fazer) perder o brilho; (*stain*) manchar

tarpaulin /ta:'pɔ:lɪn/ *n* lona *f* impermeável (alcatroada *or* encerada)

tart[1] /ta:t/ *a* (-er, -est) ácido; (*fig: cutting*) mordaz, azedo

tart[2] /ta:t/ *n* (*culin*) torta *f* de fruta, (*P*) tarte *f*; (*sl: prostitute*) prostituta *f*, mulher *f* da vida (*sl*) □ *vt* ~ **up** (*colloq*) embonecar(-se)

tartan /'ta:tn/ *n* tecido *m* escocês □ *a* escocês

tartar /'ta:tə(r)/ *n* (*on teeth*) tártaro *m*, (*P*) pedra *f*. ~ **sauce** molho *m* tártaro

task /ta:sk/ *n* tarefa *f*, trabalho *m*.

take to ~ repreender, censurar. ~ force (*mil*) força-tarefa *f*
tassel /'tæsl/ *n* borla *f*
taste /teɪst/ *n* gosto *m*; (*fig: sample*) amostra *f* □ *vt* (*eat, enjoy*) saborear; (*try*) provar; (*perceive taste of*) sentir o gosto de □ *vi* ~ of *or* like ter o sabor de. have a ~ of (*experience*) provar. ~**ful** *a* de bom gosto. ~**fully** *adv* com bom gosto. ~**less** *a* insípido, insosso; (*fig: not in good taste*) sem gosto; (*fig: in bad taste*) de mau gosto
tasty /'teɪstɪ/ *a* (-ier, -iest) saboroso, gostoso
tat /tæt/ *see* tit[2]
tatter|s /'tætəz/ *npl* farrapos *mpl*. ~**ed** /-əd/ *a* esfarrapado
tattoo /tə'tu:/ *vt* tatuar □ *n* tatuagem *f*
tatty /'tætɪ/ *a* (-ier, -iest) (*colloq*) enxovalhado, em mau estado
taught /tɔ:t/ *see* teach
taunt /tɔ:nt/ *vt* escarnecer de, zombar de □ *n* escárnio *m*. ~**ing** *a* escarninho
Taurus /'tɔ:rəs/ *n* (*astr*) Touro *m*, (*P*) Taurus *m*
taut /tɔ:t/ *a* esticado, retesado; (*fig: of nerves*) tenso
tawdry /'tɔ:drɪ/ *a* (-ier, -iest) espalhafatoso e ordinário
tawny /'tɔ:nɪ/ *a* fulvo
tax /tæks/ *n* taxa *f*, imposto *m*; (*on income*) imposto *m* de renda, (*P*) sobre o rendimento □ *vt* taxar, lançar impostos sobre, tributar; (*fig: put to test*) pôr à prova. ~**-collector** *n* cobrador *m* de impostos. ~**-free** *a* isento de imposto. ~ **relief** isenção *f* de imposto. ~ **return** declaração *f* do imposto de renda, (*P*) sobre o rendimento. ~ **year** ano *m* fiscal. ~**able** *a* tributável, passível de imposto. ~**ation** /-'seɪʃn/ *n* impostos *mpl*, tributação *f*. ~**ing** *a* penoso, difícil
taxi /'tæksɪ/ *n* (*pl* -is) táxi *m* □ *vi* (*pt* taxied, *pres p* taxiing) (*aviat*) rolar na pista, taxiar. ~**-cab** *n* táxi *m*. ~**-driver** *n* motorista *mf* de táxi. ~ **rank**, (*Amer*) ~ **stand** ponto *m* de táxis, (*P*) praça *f* de táxis
taxpayer /'tækspeɪə(r)/ *n* contribuinte *mf*
tea /ti:/ *n* chá *m*. **high** ~ refeição *f* leve à noite. ~**-bag** *n* saquinho *m* de chá. ~**-break** *n* intervalo *m* para o chá. ~**-cosy** *n* abafador *m*. ~**-leaf** *n* folha *f* de chá. ~**-set** *n* serviço *m* de chá. ~**-shop** *n* salão *m* *or* casa *f* de chá. ~**-time** *n* hora *f* do chá. ~**-towel** *n* pano *m* de prato
teach /ti:tʃ/ *vt* (*pt* taught) ensinar, lecionar, (*P*) leccionar (**sb sth** alg coisa a alguém) □ *vi* ensinar, ser professor. ~**er** *n* professor *m*. ~**ing** *n* ensino *m*; (*doctrines*) ensinamento(s) *m* (*pl*) □ *a* pedagógico, de ensino; (*staff*) docente
teacup /'ti:kʌp/ *n* xícara *f* de chá, (*P*) chávena *f*
teak /ti:k/ *n* teca *f*
team /ti:m/ *n* equipe *f*, (*P*) equipa *f*; (*of oxen*) junta *f*; (*of horses*) parelha *f* □ *vi* ~ **up** juntar-se, associar-se (**with** a). ~**-work** *n* trabalho *m* de equipe, (*P*) equipa
teapot /'ti:pɒt/ *n* bule *m*
tear[1] /teə(r)/ *vt/i* (*pt* tore, *pp* torn) rasgar(-se); (*snatch*) arrancar, puxar; (*rush*) lançar-se, ir numa correria; (*fig*) dividir □ *n* rasgão *m*. ~ **o.s. away** arrancar-se (**from** de)
tear[2] /tɪə(r)/ *n* lágrima *f*. ~**-gas** *n* gases *mpl* lacrimogênios, (*P*) lacrimogénios
tearful /'tɪəfl/ *a* lacrimoso, choroso. ~**ly** *adv* choroso, com (as) lágrimas nos olhos
tease /ti:z/ *vt* implicar; (*make fun of*) caçoar de
teaspoon /'ti:spu:n/ *n* colher *f* de chá. ~**ful** *n* (*pl* -fuls) colher *f* de chá cheia
teat /ti:t/ *n* (*of bottle*) bico *m*; (*of animal*) teta *f*
technical /'teknɪkl/ *a* técnico. ~**ity** /-'kælətɪ/ *n* questão *f* de ordem técnica. ~**ly** *adv* tecnicamente
technician /tek'nɪʃn/ *n* técnico *m*
technique /tek'ni:k/ *n* técnica *f*
technolog|y /tek'nɒlədʒɪ/ *n* tecnologia *f*. ~**ical** /-ə'lɒdʒɪkl/ *a* tecnológico
teddy /'tedɪ/ *a* ~ (**bear**) ursinho *m* de pelúcia, (*P*) peluche
tedious /'ti:dɪəs/ *a* maçante
tedium /'ti:dɪəm/ *n* tédio *m*
tee /ti:/ *n* (*golf*) tee *m*
teem[1] /ti:m/ *vi* ~ (**with**) (*swarm*) pulular (de), fervilhar (de), abundar (em)
teem[2] /ti:m/ *vi* ~ (**with rain**) chover torrencialmente
teenage /'ti:neɪdʒ/ *a* juvenil, de/para adolescente. ~**r** /-ə(r)/ *n* jovem *mf*, adolescente *mf*
teens /ti:nz/ *npl* **in one's** ~ na adolescência, entre os 13 e os 19 anos
teeter /'ti:tə(r)/ *vi* cambalear, vacilar
teeth /ti:θ/ *see* tooth
teeth|e /ti:ð/ *vi* começar a ter dentes. ~**ing troubles** (*fig*) problemas *mpl* iniciais
teetotaller /ti:'təʊtlə(r)/ *n* abstêmio *m*, (*P*) abstémio *m*
telecommunications /telɪkəmju:nɪ'keɪʃnz/ *npl* telecomunicações *fpl*
telegram /'telɪgræm/ *n* telegrama *m*
telegraph /'telɪgra:f/ *n* telégrafo *m* □

a telegráfico. **~ic** /-'græfɪk/ *a* telegráfico
telepath|y /tɪ'lepəθɪ/ *n* telepatia *f*. **~ic** /telɪ'pæθɪk/ *a* telepático
telephone /'telɪfəʊn/ *n* telefone *m* □ *vt* (*person*) telefonar a; (*message*) telefonar □ *vi* telefonar. **~ book** lista *f* telefônica, (*P*) telefónica, guia *m* telefônico, (*P*) telefónico. **~ box, ~ booth** cabine *f* telefônica, (*P*) telefónica. **~ call** chamada *f*. **~ directory** lista *f* telefônica, (*P*) telefónica, guia *m* telefônico, (*P*) telefónico. **~ number** número *m* de telefone
telephonist /tɪ'lefənɪst/ *n* (*in exchange*) telefonista *mf*
telephoto /telɪ'fəʊtəʊ/ *n* **~ lens** teleobjetiva *f*, (*P*) teleobjectiva *f*
telescop|e /'telɪskəʊp/ *n* telescópio *m* □ *vt/i* encaixar(-se). **~ic** /-'skɒpɪk/ *a* telescópico
teletext /'telɪtekst/ *n* teletexto *m*
televise /'telɪvaɪz/ *vt* televisionar
television /'telɪvɪʒn/ *n* televisão *f*. **~ set** aparelho *m* de televisão, televisor *m*
telex /'teleks/ *n* telex *m* □ *vt* transmitir por telex, telexar
tell /tel/ *vt* (*pt* **told**) dizer (**sb sth** alg coisa a alguém); (*story*) contar; (*distinguish*) distinguir, diferençar □ *vi* (*know*) ver-se, saber. **I told you so** bem lhe disse. **~ of** falar de. **~ off** (*colloq: scold*) ralhar, dar uma bronca em. **~ on** (*have effect on*) afetar, (*P*) afectar; (*colloq: inform on*) fazer queixa de (*colloq*). **~-tale** *n* mexeriqueiro *m*, fofoqueiro *m* □ *a* (*revealing*) revelador. **tales** mexericar, fofocar
telly /'telɪ/ *n* (*colloq*) TV *f* (*colloq*)
temp /temp/ *n* (*colloq*) empregado *m* temporário
temper /'tempə(r)/ *n* humor *m*, disposição *f*; (*anger*) mau humor *m* □ *vt* temperar. **keep/lose one's ~** manter a calma/perder a calma *or* a cabeça, zangar-se
temperament /'temprəmənt/ *n* temperamento *m*. **~al** /'mentl/ *a* caprichoso
temperance /'tempərəns/ *n* (*in drinking*) moderação *f*, sobriedade *f*
temperate /'tempərət/ *a* moderado, comedido; (*climate*) temperado
temperature /'temprətʃə(r)/ *n* temperatura *f*. **have a ~** estar com *or* ter febre
tempest /'tempɪst/ *n* tempestade *f*, temporal *m*
tempestuous /tem'pestʃʊəs/ *a* tempestuoso
template /'templ(e)ɪt/ *n* molde *m*
temple[1] /'templ/ *n* templo *m*
temple[2] /'templ/ *n* (*anat*) têmpora *f*, fonte *f*
tempo /'tempəʊ/ *n* (*pl* -os) (*mus*) tempo *m*; (*pace*) ritmo *m*
temporar|y /'temprərɪ/ *a* temporário, provisório. **~ily** *adv* temporariamente, provisoriamente
tempt /tempt/ *vt* tentar. **~ sb to do** dar a alguém vontade de fazer, tentar alguém a fazer. **~ation** /-'teɪʃn/ *n* tentação *f*. **~ing** *a* tentador
ten /ten/ *a* & *n* dez (*m*)
tenac|ious /tɪ'neɪʃəs/ *a* tenaz. **~ity** /-æsətɪ/ *n* tenacidade *f*
tenant /'tenənt/ *n* inquilino *m*, locatário *m*
tend[1] /tend/ *vt* tomar conta de, cuidar de
tend[2] /tend/ *vi* **~ to** (*be apt to*) tender a, ter tendência para
tendency /'tendənsɪ/ *n* tendência *f*
tender[1] /'tendə(r)/ *a* (*soft, delicate*) terno; (*sore, painful*) sensível, dolorido; (*loving*) terno, meigo. **~-hearted** *a* compassivo. **~ly** *adv* (*lovingly*) ternamente, meigamente; (*delicately*) delicadamente. **~ness** *n* (*love*) ternura *f*, meiguice *f*
tender[2] /'tendə(r)/ *vt* (*money*) oferecer; (*apologies, resignation*) apresentar □ *vi* **~ (for)** apresentar orçamento (para) □ *n* (*comm*) orçamento *m*. **legal ~** (*money*) moeda *f* corrente
tendon /'tendən/ *n* tendão *m*
tenement /'tenəmənt/ *n* prédio *m* de apartamentos de renda moderada; (*Amer: slum*) prédio *m* pobre
tenet /'tenɪt/ *n* princípio *m*, dogma *m*
tennis /'tenɪs/ *n* tênis *m*, (*P*) ténis *m*. **~ court** quadra *f* de tênis, (*P*) court *m* de ténis
tenor /'tenə(r)/ *n* (*meaning*) teor *m*; (*mus*) tenor *m*
tense[1] /tens/ *n* (*gram*) tempo *m*
tense[2] /tens/ *a* (-er, -est) tenso □ *vt* (*muscles*) retesar
tension /'tenʃn/ *n* tensão *f*
tent /tent/ *n* tenda *f*, barraca *f*. **~-peg** *n* estaca *f*
tentacle /'tentəkl/ *n* tentáculo *m*
tentative /'tentətɪv/ *a* provisório; (*hesitant*) hesitante. **~ly** *adv* tentativamente, a título experimental; (*hesitantly*) hesitantemente
tenterhooks /'tentəhʊks/ *npl* **on ~** em suspense
tenth /tenθ/ *a* & *n* décimo (*m*)
tenuous /'tenjʊəs/ *a* tênue, (*P*) ténue
tepid /'tepɪd/ *a* tépido, morno
term /tɜ:m/ *n* (*word*) termo *m*; (*limit*) prazo *m*, termo *m*; (*schol etc*) período *m*, trimestre *m*; (*Amer*) semestre *m*; (*of imprisonment*) (duração de) pena *f*. **~s** (*conditions*) condições *fpl* □ *vt* designar, denominar, chamar. **on good/**

bad ~s de boas/más relações. **not on speaking** ~s de relações cortadas. **come to** ~s **with** chegar a um acordo com; (*become resigned to*) resignar-se a. ~ **of office** (*pol*) mandato *m*

terminal /'tɜ:mɪnl/ *a* terminal, final; (*illness*) fatal, mortal □ *n* (*oil, computer*) terminal *m*; (*rail*) estação *f* terminal; (*electr*) borne *m*. (**air**) ~ terminal *m* (de avião)

terminat|e /'tɜ:mɪneɪt/ *vt* terminar, pôr termo a □ *vi* terminar. ~**ion** /-'neɪʃn/ *n* término *m*, (*P*) terminação *f*, termo *m*

terminology /tɜ:mɪ'nɒlədʒɪ/ *n* terminologia *f*

terminus /'tɜ:mɪnəs/ *n* (*pl* -ni /-naɪ/) (*rail, coach*) estação *f* terminal

terrace /'terəs/ *n* terraço *m*; (*in cultivation*) socalco *m*; (*houses*) casas *fpl* em fileira contínua, lance *m* de casas. **the** ~s (*sport*) arquibancada *f*. ~**d house** casa *f* ladeada por outras casas

terrain /te'reɪn/ *n* terreno *m*

terribl|e /'terəbl/ *a* terrível. ~**y** *adv* terrivelmente; (*colloq: very*) extremamente, espantosamente

terrific /tə'rɪfɪk/ *a* terrífico, tremendo; (*colloq: excellent; great*) tremendo. ~**ally** *adv* (*colloq: very*) tremendamente (*colloq*); (*colloq: very well*) lindamente, maravilhosamente

terrif|y /'terɪfaɪ/ *vt* aterrar, aterrorizar. **be** ~**ied of** ter pavor de

territorial /terɪ'tɔ:rɪəl/ *a* territorial

territory /'terɪtərɪ/ *n* território *m*

terror /'terə(r)/ *n* terror *m*, pavor *m*

terroris|t /'terərɪst/ *n* terrorista *mf*. ~**m** /-zəm/ *n* terrorismo *m*

terrorize /'terəraɪz/ *vt* aterrorizar, aterrar

terse /tɜ:s/ *a* conciso, lapidar; (*curt*) lacônico, (*P*) lacónico

test /test/ *n* teste *m*, exame *m*, prova *f*; (*schol*) prova *f*, teste *m*; (*of goods*) controle *m*; (*of machine etc*) ensaio *m*; (*of strength*) prova *f* □ *vt* examinar; (*check*) controlar; (*try*) ensaiar; (*pupil*) interrogar. **put to the** ~ pôr à prova. ~ **match** jogo *m* internacional. ~**-tube** *n* proveta *f*. ~**-tube baby** bebê *m* de proveta

testament /'testəmənt/ *n* testamento *m*. **Old/New T**~ Antigo/Novo Testamento *m*

testicle /'testɪkl/ *n* testículo *m*

testify /'testɪfaɪ/ *vt/i* testificar, testemunhar, depôr

testimonial /testɪ'məʊnɪəl/ *n* carta *f* de recomendação

testimony /'testɪmənɪ/ *n* testemunho *m*

tetanus /'tetənəs/ *n* tétano *m*

tether /'teðə(r)/ *vt* prender com corda □ *n* **be at the end of one's** ~ não poder mais, estar nas últimas

text /tekst/ *n* texto *m*

textbook /'tekstbʊk/ *n* compêndio *m*, manual *m*, livro *m* de texto

textile /'tekstaɪl/ *n* & *a* têxtil (*m*)

texture /'tekstʃə(r)/ *n* (*of fabric*) textura *f*; (*of paper*) grão *m*

Thai /taɪ/ *a* & *n* tailandês (*m*). ~**land** *n* Tailândia *f*

Thames /temz/ *n* Tâmisa *m*

than /ðæn/; *unstressed* /ðən/ *conj* que, do que; (*with numbers*) de. **more/less** ~ **ten** mais/menos de dez

thank /θæŋk/ *vt* agradecer. ~ **you!** obrigado! ~s! (*colloq*) (*P*) obrigadinho! (*colloq*). ~s *npl* agradecimentos *mpl*. ~**s to** graças a. **T**~**sgiving (Day)** (*Amer*) Dia *m* de Ação, (*P*) Acção de Graças

thankful /'θæŋkfl/ *a* grato, agradecido, reconhecido (**for** por). ~**ly** *adv* com gratidão; (*happily*) felizmente

thankless /'θæŋklɪs/ *a* ingrato, mal agradecido

that /ðæt/; *unstressed* /ðət/ *a* & *pron* (*pl* **those**) esse/essa, esses/essas; (*more distant*) aquele/aquela, aqueles /aquelas; (*neuter*) isso *invar*; (*more distant*) aquilo *invar* □ *adv* tão, tanto, de tal modo □ *rel pron* que □ *conj* que. ~ **boy** esse/aquele rapaz. **what is** ~? o que é isso? **who is** ~? quem é? **is** ~ **you?** é você? **give me** ~ **(one)** dá-me esse. ~ **is (to say)** isto é, quer dizer. **after** ~ depois disso. **the day** ~ o dia em que. ~ **much** tanto assim, tanto como isto

thatch /θætʃ/ *n* colmo *m*. ~**ed** *a* de colmo. ~**ed cottage** casa *f* com telhado de colmo

thaw /θɔ:/ *vt/i* derreter(-se), degelar; (*food*) descongelar □ *n* degelo *m*, derretimento *m*

the /*before vowel* ðɪ/, *before consonant* ðə/, *stressed* ði:/ *a* o, a (*pl* os, as). **of** ~, **from** ~ do, da (*pl* dos, das). **at** ~, **to** ~ ao, à (*pl* aos, às), para o/a/os/as. **in** ~ no, na (*pl* nos, nas). **by** ~ **hour** a cada hora □ *adv* **all** ~ **better** tanto melhor. ~ **more**... ~ **more**... quanto mais... tanto mais...

theatre /'θɪətə(r)/ *n* teatro *m*

theatrical /θɪ'ætrɪkl/ *a* teatral

theft /θeft/ *n* roubo *m*

their /ðeə(r)/ *a* deles, delas, seu

theirs /ðeəz/ *poss pron* o(s) seu(s), a(s) sua(s), o(s) deles, a(s) delas. **it is** ~ é (o) deles/delas *or* o seu

them /ðem/; *unstressed* /ðəm/ *pron* os, as; (*after prep*) eles, elas. (**to**) ~ lhes

theme /θi:m/ *n* tema *m*

themselves /ðəm'selvz/ *pron* eles

mesmos/próprios, elas mesmas/ próprias; (*reflexive*) se; (*after prep*) si (mesmos, próprios). **by ~** sozinhos. **with ~** consigo

then /ðen/ *adv* (*at that time*) então, nessa altura; (*next*) depois, em seguida; (*in that case*) então, nesse caso; (*therefore*) então, portanto, por conseguinte □ *a* (de) então. **from ~ on** desde então

theolog|y /θɪ'ɒlədʒɪ/ *n* teologia *f*. **~ian** /θɪə'ləʊdʒən/ *n* teólogo *m*

theorem /'θɪərəm/ *n* teorema *m*

theor|y /'θɪərɪ/ *n* teoria *f*. **~etical** /'retɪkl/ *a* teórico

therapeutic /θerə'pju:tɪk/ *a* terapêutico

therap|y /'θerəpɪ/ *n* terapia *f*. **~ist** *n* terapeuta *mf*

there /ðeə(r)/ *adv* aí, ali, lá; (*over there*) lá, acolá □ *int* (*triumphant*) pronto, aí está; (*consoling*) então, vamos lá. **he goes ~** ele vai aí *or* lá. **~ he goes** aí vai ele. **~ is, ~ are** há. **~ you are** (*giving*) toma. **~ and then** logo ali. **~abouts** *adv* por aí. **~after** *adv* daí em diante, depois disso. **~by** *adv* desse modo

therefore /'ðeəfɔ:(r)/ *adv* por isso, portanto, por conseguinte

thermal /'θɜ:ml/ *a* térmico

thermometer /θə'mɒmɪtə(r)/ *n* termômetro *m*, (*P*) termómetro *m*

Thermos /'θɜ:məs/ *n* garrafa *f* térmica, (*P*) termo *m*

thermostat /'θɜ:məstæt/ *n* termostato *m*

thesaurus /θɪ'sɔ:rəs/ *n* (*pl* -ri /-raɪ/) dicionário *m* de sinônimos, (*P*) sinónimos

these /ði:z/ *see* **this**

thesis /'θi:sɪs/ *n* (*pl* **theses** /-si:z/) tese *f*

they /ðeɪ/ *pron* eles, elas. **~ say (that)...** diz-se *or* dizem que...

thick /θɪk/ *a* (-er, -est) espesso, grosso; (*colloq: stupid*) estúpido □ *adv* = **thickly** □ *n* **in the ~ of** no meio de. **~-skinned** *a* insensível. **~ly** *adv* espessamente; (*spread*) em camada espessa. **~ness** *n* espessura *f*, grossura *f*

thicken /'θɪkən/ *vt/i* engrossar, espessar(-se). **the plot ~s** o enredo complica-se

thickset /θɪk'set/ *a* (*person*) atarracado

thief /θi:f/ *n* (*pl* **thieves** /θi:vz/) ladrão *m*, gatuno *m*

thigh /θaɪ/ *n* coxa *f*

thimble /'θɪmbl/ *n* dedal *m*

thin /θɪn/ *a* (**thinner, thinnest**) (*slender*) estreito, fino, delgado; (*lean, not plump*) magro; (*sparse*) ralo, escasso; (*flimsy*) leve, fino; (*soup*) aguado; (*hair*) ralo □ *adv* = **thinly** □ *vt/i* (*pt* **thinned**) (*of liquid*) diluir(-se); (*of fog etc*) dissipar(-se); (*of hair*) rarear. **~ out** (*in quantity*) diminuir, reduzir; (*seedlings etc*) desbastar. **~ly** *adv* (*sparsely*) esparsamente. **~ness** *n* (*of board, wire etc*) finura *f*; (*of person*) magreza *f*

thing /θɪŋ/ *n* coisa *f*. **~s** (*belongings*) pertences *mpl*. **the best ~ is to** o melhor é. **for one ~** em primeiro lugar. **just the ~** exatamente o que era preciso. **poor ~** coitado

think /θɪŋk/ *vt/i* (*pt* **thought**) pensar (**about, of** em); (*carefully*) refletir, (*P*) reflectir (**about, of** em). **I ~ so** eu acho que sim. **~ better of it** (*change one's mind*) pensar melhor. **~ nothing of** achar natural. **~ of** (*hold opinion of*) pensar de, achar de. **~ over** pensar bem em. **~-tank** *n* comissão *f* de peritos. **~ up** inventar. **~er** *n* pensador *m*

third /θɜ:d/ *a* terceiro □ *n* terceiro *m*; (*fraction*) terço *m*. **~-party insurance** seguro *m* contra terceiros. **~-rate** *a* inferior, medíocre. **T~ World** Terceiro Mundo *m*. **~ly** *adv* em terceiro lugar

thirst /θɜ:st/ *n* sede *f*. **~y** *a* sequioso, sedento. **be ~y** estar com *or* ter sede. **~ily** *adv* sofregamente

thirteen /θɜ:'ti:n/ *a* & *n* treze (*m*). **~th** *a* & *n* décimo terceiro (*m*)

thirt|y /'θɜ:tɪ/ *a* & *n* trinta (*m*). **~ieth** *a* & *n* trigésimo (*m*)

this /ðɪs/ *a* & *pron* (*pl* **these**) este, esta □ *pron* isto *invar*. **~ one** este, esta. **these ones** estes, estas. **~ boy** este rapaz. **~ is** isto é. **after ~** depois disto. **like ~** assim. **~ is the man** este é o homem. **~ far** até aqui. **~ morning** esta manhã. **~ Wednesday** esta quarta-feira

thistle /'θɪsl/ *n* cardo *m*

thorn /θɔ:n/ *n* espinho *m*, pico *m*. **~y** *a* espinhoso; (*fig*) bicudo, espinhoso

thorough /'θʌrə/ *a* consciencioso; (*deep*) completo, profundo; (*cleaning, washing*) a fundo. **~ly** *adv* (*clean, study etc*) completo, a fundo; (*very*) perfeitamente, muito bem

thoroughbred /'θʌrəbred/ *n* (*horse etc*) puro-sangue *m invar*

thoroughfare /'θʌrəfeə(r)/ *n* artéria *f*. **no ~** passagem *f* proibida

those /ðəʊz/ *see* **that**

though /ðəʊ/ *conj* se bem que, embora, conquanto □ *adv* (*colloq*) contudo, no entanto

thought /θɔ:t/ *see* **think** □ *n* pensamento *m*; idéia *f*. **on second ~s** pensando bem

thoughtful /ˈθɔːtfl/ *a* pensativo; (*considerate*) atencioso, solícito. ~**ly** *adv* pensativamente; (*considerately*) com consideração, atenciosamente

thoughtless /ˈθɔːtlɪs/ *a* irrefletido, (*P*) irreflectido; (*inconsiderate*) pouco atencioso. ~**ly** *adv* sem pensar; (*inconsiderately*) sem consideração

thousand /ˈθaʊznd/ *a* & *n* mil (*m*). ~**s of** milhares de. ~**th** *a* & *n* milésimo (*m*)

thrash /θræʃ/ *vt* surrar, espancar; (*defeat*) dar uma surra *or* sova em. ~ **about** debater-se. ~ **out** debater a fundo, discutir bem

thread /θred/ *n* fio *m*; (*for sewing*) linha *f* de coser; (*of screw*) rosca *f* □ *vt* enfiar. ~ **one's way** abrir caminho, furar

threadbare /ˈθredbeə(r)/ *a* puído, surrado

threat /θret/ *n* ameaça *f*

threaten /ˈθretn/ *vt/i* ameaçar. ~**ingly** *adv* com ar ameaçador, ameaçadoramente

three /θriː/ *a* & *n* três (*m*)

thresh /θreʃ/ *vt* (*corn etc*) malhar, debulhar

threshold /ˈθreʃəʊld/ *n* limiar *m*, soleira *f*; (*fig*) limiar *m*

threw /θruː/ *see* **throw**

thrift /θrɪft/ *n* economia *f*, poupança *f*. ~**y** *a* econômico, (*P*) económico, poupado

thrill /θrɪl/ *n* arrepio *m* de emoção, frêmito *m*, (*P*) frémito *m* □ *vt* excitar(-se), emocionar(-se), (fazer) vibrar. **be** ~**ed** estar/ficar encantado. ~**ing** *a* excitante, emocionante

thriller /ˈθrɪlə(r)/ *n* livro *m or* filme *m* de suspense

thriv|e /θraɪv/ *vi* (*pt* **thrived** *or* **throve**, *pp* **thrived** *or* **thriven**) prosperar, florescer; (*grow strong*) crescer, dar-se bem (**on** com). ~**ing** *a* próspero

throat /θrəʊt/ *n* garganta *f*. **have a sore** ~ ter dores de garganta

throb /θrɒb/ *vi* (*pt* **throbbed**) (*wound, head*) latejar; (*heart*) palpitar, bater; (*engine; fig*) vibrar, trepidar □ *n* (*of pain*) latejo *m*, espasmo *m*; (*of heart*) palpitação *f*, batida *f*; (*of engine*) vibração *f*, trepidação *f*. ~**bing** *a* (*pain*) latejante

throes /θrəʊz/ *npl* **in the** ~ **of** (*fig*) às voltas com, no meio de

thrombosis /θrɒmˈbəʊsɪs/ *n* trombose *f*

throne /θrəʊn/ *n* trono *m*

throng /θrɒŋ/ *n* multidão *f* □ *vt/i* apinhar(-se); (*arrive*) afluir

throttle /ˈθrɒtl/ *n* (*auto*) válvula-borboleta *f*, estrangulador *m*, acelerador *m* de mão □ *vt* estrangular

through /θruː/ *prep* através de, por; (*during*) durante; (*by means or way of, out of*) por; (*by reason of*) por, por causa de □ *adv* através; (*entirely*) completamente, até o fim □ *a* (*train, traffic etc*) direto, (*P*) directo. **be** ~ ter acabado (**with** com); (*telephone*) estar ligado. **come** *or* **go** ~ (*cross, pierce*) atravessar. **get** ~ (*exam*) passar. **be wet** ~ estar ensopado *or* encharcado

throughout /θruːˈaʊt/ *prep* durante, por todo. ~ **the country** por todo o país afora. ~ **the day** durante todo a dia, pelo dia afora □ *adv* completamente; (*place*) por toda a parte; (*time*) durante todo o tempo

throw /θrəʊ/ *vt* (*pt* **threw**, *pp* **thrown**) atirar, jogar, lançar; (*colloq: baffle*) desconcertar □ *n* lançamento *m*; (*of dice*) lançe *m*. ~ **a party** (*colloq*) dar uma festa. ~ **away** jogar fora, (*P*) deitar fora. ~ **off** (*get rid of*) livrar-se de. ~ **out** (*person*) expulsar; (*reject*) rejeitar. ~ **over** (*desert*) abandonar, deixar. ~ **up** (*one's arms*) levantar; (*resign from*) abandonar; (*colloq: vomit*) vomitar

thrush /θrʌʃ/ *n* (*bird*) tordo *m*

thrust /θrʌst/ *vt* (*pt* **thrust**) arremeter, empurrar, impelir □ *n* empurrão *m*, arremetida *f*. ~ **into** (*put*) enfiar em, mergulhar em. ~ **upon** (*force on*) impôr a

thud /θʌd/ *n* som *m* surdo, baque *m*

thug /θʌg/ *n* bandido *m*, facínora *m*, malfeitor *m*

thumb /θʌm/ *n* polegar *m* □ *vt* (*book*) manusear. ~ **a lift** pedir carona, (*P*) boleia. **under sb's** ~ completamente dominado por alguém. ~**-index** *n* índice *m* de dedo

thumbtack /ˈθʌmtæk/ *n* (*Amer*) percevejo *m*

thump /θʌmp/ *vt/i* bater (em), dar pancadas (em); (*with fists*) dar murros (em); (*piano*) martelar (em); (*of heart*) bater com força □ *n* pancada *f*; (*thud*) baque *m*. ~**ing** *a* (*colloq*) enorme

thunder /ˈθʌndə(r)/ *n* trovão *m*, trovoada *f*; (*loud noise*) estrondo *m* □ *vi* (*weather, person*) trovejar. ~ **past** passar como um raio. ~**y** *a* (*weather*) tempestuoso

thunderbolt /ˈθʌndəbəʊlt/ *n* raio *m* e ribombo *m* de trovão; (*fig*) raio *m* fulminante (*fig*)

thunderstorm /ˈθʌndəstɔːm/ *n* tempestade *f* com trovoadas, temporal *m*

Thursday /ˈθɜːzdɪ/ *n* quinta-feira *f*

thus /ðʌs/ *adv* assim, desta maneira. ~ **far** até aqui

thwart /θwɔːt/ *vt* frustrar, contrariar

thyme /taɪm/ *n* tomilho *m*

tiara /tɪˈaːrə/ *n* tiara *f*, diadema *m*

tic /tɪk/ *n* tique *m*

tick[1] /tɪk/ *n* (*sound*) tique-taque *m*; (*mark*) sinal (V) *m*; (*colloq: moment*) instantinho *m* □ *vi* fazer tique-taque □ *vt* ~ (**off**) marcar com sinal (V). ~ **off** (*colloq: scold*) dar uma bronca em (*colloq*). ~ **over** (*engine, factory*) funcionar em marcha lenta, (*P*) no "ralenti"

tick[2] /tɪk/ *n* (*insect*) carrapato *m*

ticket /'tɪkɪt/ *n* bilhete *m*; (*label*) etiqueta *f*; (*for traffic offence*) aviso *m* de multa. ~**-collector** *n* (*railway*) guarda *m*. ~**-office** *n* bilheteira *f*

tickle /'tɪkl/ *vt* fazer cócegas; (*fig: amuse*) divertir □ *n* cócegas *fpl*, comichão *m*

ticklish /'tɪklɪʃ/ *a* coceguento, sensível a cócegas; (*fig*) delicado, melindroso

tidal /'taɪdl/ *a* de marés, que tem marés. ~ **wave** onda *f* gigantesca; (*fig*) onda *f* de sentimento popular

tiddly-winks /'tɪdlɪwɪŋks/ *n* (*game*) jogo *m* da pulga

tide /taɪd/ *n* maré *f*; (*of events*) marcha *f*, curso *m*. **high** ~ maré *f* cheia, preia-mar *f*. **low** ~ maré *f* baixa, baixa-mar *f* □ *vt* ~ **over** (*help temporarily*) agüentar, (*P*) aguentar

tid|y /'taɪdɪ/ *a* (-ier, -iest) (*room*) arrumado; (*appearance, work*) asseado, cuidado; (*methodical*) bem ordenado; (*colloq: amount*) belo (*colloq*) □ *vt* arrumar, arranjar. ~**ily** *adv* com cuidado. ~**iness** *n* arrumação *f*, ordem *f*

tie /taɪ/ *vt* (*pres p* **tying**) atar, amarrar, prender; (*link*) ligar, vincular; (*a knot*) dar, fazer □ *vi* (*sport*) empatar □ *n* fio *m*, cordel *m*; (*necktie*) gravata *f*; (*link*) laço *m*, vínculo *m*; (*sport*) empate *m*. ~ **in with** estar ligado com, relacionar-se com. ~ **up** amarrar, atar; (*animal*) prender; (*money*) imobilizar; (*occupy*) ocupar

tier /tɪə(r)/ *n* cada fila *f*, camada *f*, prateleira *f etc* colocada em cima de outra; (*in stadium*) bancada *f*; (*of cake*) andar *m*; (*of society*) camada *f*

tiff /tɪf/ *n* arrufo *m*

tiger /'taɪgə(r)/ *n* tigre *m*

tight /taɪt/ *a* (-er, -est) (*clothes*) apertado, justo; (*rope*) esticado, tenso; (*control*) rigoroso; (*knot, schedule, lid*) apertado; (*colloq: drunk*) embriagado (*colloq*) □ *adv* = **tightly**. **be in a** ~ **corner** (*fig*) estar em apuros *or* num aperto, (*P*) estar entalado (*colloq*). ~**-fisted** *a* sovina, pão-duro, (*P*) agarrado (*colloq*). ~**ly** *adv* bem; (*squeeze*) com força

tighten /'taɪtn/ *vt/i* (*rope*) esticar; (*bolt, control*) apertar. ~ **up on** apertar o cinto

tightrope /'taɪtrəʊp/ *n* corda *f* (de acrobacias). ~ **walker** funâmbulo *m*

tights /taɪts/ *npl* collants *mpl*, meias-colant *fpl*

tile /taɪl/ *n* (*on wall, floor*) ladrilho *m*, azulejo *m*; (*on roof*) telha *f* □ *vt* ladrilhar, pôr azulejos em; (*roof*) telhar, cobrir com telhas

till[1] /tɪl/ *vt* (*land*) cultivar

till[2] /tɪl/ *prep & conj* = **until**

till[3] /tɪl/ *n* caixa (registadora) *f*

tilt /tɪlt/ *vt/i* inclinar(-se), pender □ *n* (*slope*) inclinação *f*. (**at**) **full** ~ a toda a velocidade

timber /'tɪmbə(r)/ *n* madeira *f* (de construção); (*trees*) árvores *fpl*

time /taɪm/ *n* tempo *m*; (*moment*) momento *m*; (*epoch*) época *f*, tempo *m*; (*by clock*) horas *fpl*; (*occasion*) vez *f*; (*rhythm*) compasso *m*. ~**s** (*multiplying*) vezes □ *vt* escolher a hora para; (*measure*) marcar o tempo; (*sport*) cronometrar; (*regulate*) acertar. **at** ~**s** às vezes. **for the** ~ **being** por agora, por enquanto. **from** ~ **to** ~ de vez em quando. **have a good** ~ divertir-se. **have no** ~ **for** não ter paciência para. **in no** ~ num instante. **in** ~ a tempo; (*eventually*) com o tempo. **in two days** ~ daqui a dois dias. **on** ~ na hora, (*P*) a horas. **take your** ~ não se apresse. **what's the** ~? que horas são? ~ **bomb** bomba-relógio *f*. ~**-limit** *n* prazo *m*. ~ **off** tempo *m* livre. ~**-sharing** *n* time-sharing *m*. ~ **zone** fuso *m* horário

timeless /'taɪmlɪs/ *a* intemporal; (*unending*) eterno

timely /'taɪmlɪ/ *a* oportuno

timer /'taɪmə(r)/ *n* (*techn*) relógio *m*; (*with sand*) ampulheta *f*

timetable /'taɪmteɪbl/ *n* horário *m*

timid /'tɪmɪd/ *a* tímido; (*fearful*) assustadiço, medroso. ~**ly** *adv* timidamente

timing /'taɪmɪŋ/ *n* (*measuring*) cronometragem *f*; (*of artist*) ritmo *m*; (*moment*) cálculo *m* do tempo, timing *m*. **good/bad** ~ (*moment*) momento *m* bem/mal escolhido

tin /tɪn/ *n* estanho *m*; (*container*) lata *f* □ *vt* (*pt* **tinned**) estanhar; (*food*) enlatar. ~ **foil** papel *m* de alumínio. ~**-opener** *n* abridor *m* de latas, (*P*) abre-latas *m*. ~ **plate** lata *f*, folha(-de-Flandes) *f*. ~**ned foods** conservas *fpl*. ~**ny** *a* (*sound*) metálico

tinge /tɪndʒ/ *vt* ~ (**with**) tingir (de); (*fig*) dar um toque (de) □ *n* tom *m*, matiz *m*; (*fig*) toque *m*

tingle /'tɪŋgl/ *vi* (*sting*) arder; (*prickle*) picar □ *n* ardor *m*; (*prickle*) picadela *f*

tinker /'tɪŋkə(r)/ *n* latoeiro *m* ambulante □ *vi* ~ **(with)** mexer (em), tentar consertar
tinkle /'tɪŋkl/ *n* tinido *m*, tilintar *m* □ *vt/i* tilintar
tinsel /'tɪnsl/ *n* fio *m* prateado/dourado, enfeites *mpl* metálicos de Natal; (*fig*) falso brilho *m*, ouropel *m*
tint /tɪnt/ *n* tom *m*, matiz *m*; (*for hair*) tintura *f*, tinta *f* □ *vt* tingir, colorir
tiny /'taɪnɪ/ *a* (**-ier, -iest**) minúsculo, pequenino
tip[1] /tɪp/ *n* ponta *f*. **(have sth) on the ~ of one's tongue** ter alg coisa na ponta de língua
tip[2] /tɪp/ *vt/i* (*pt* **tipped**) (*tilt*) inclinar(-se); (*overturn*) virar(-se); (*pour*) colocar, (*P*) deitar; (*empty*) despejar(-se) □ *n* (*money*) gorjeta *f*; (*advice*) sugestão *f*, dica *f* (*colloq*); (*for rubbish*) lixeira *f*. ~ **off** avisar, prevenir. ~**-off** *n* (*warning*) aviso *m*; (*information*) informação *f*
tipsy /'tɪpsɪ/ *a* ligeiramente embriagado, alegre, tocado
tiptoe /'tɪptəʊ/ *n* **on ~** na ponta dos pés
tir|e[1] /'taɪə(r)/ *vt/i* cansar(-se) (**of** de). ~**eless** *a* incansável, infatigável. ~**ing** *a* fatigante, cansativo
tire[2] /'taɪə(r)/ *n* (*Amer*) pneu *m*
tired /taɪəd/ *a* cansado, fatigado. ~ **of** (*sick of*) farto de. ~ **out** morto de cansaço
tiresome /'taɪəsəm/ *a* maçador, aborrecido, chato (*sl*)
tissue /'tɪʃu:/ *n* tecido *m*; (*handkerchief*) lenço *m* de papel. ~**-paper** *n* papel *m* de seda
tit[1] /tɪt/ *n* (*bird*) chapim *m*, canário-da-terra *m*
tit[2] /tɪt/ *n* **give ~ for tat** pagar na mesma moeda
titbit /'tɪtbɪt/ *n* petisco *m*
titillate /'tɪtɪleɪt/ *vt* excitar, titilar, (*P*) dar gozo a
title /'taɪtl/ *n* título *m*. ~**-deed** *n* título *m* de propriedade. ~**-page** *n* página *f* de rosto, (*P*) frontispício *m*. ~**-role** *n* papel *m* principal
titter /'tɪtə(r)/ *vi* rir com riso abafado
to /tu:/; *unstressed* /tə/ *prep* a, para; (*as far as*) até; (*towards*) para; (*of attitude*) para (com) □ *adv* **push** *or* **pull ~** (*close*) fechar. ~ **Portugal** (*for a short time*) a Portugal; (*to stay*) para Portugal. ~ **the baker's** para o padeiro, (*P*) ao padeiro. ~ **do/sit/***etc* (*infinitive*) fazer/sentar-se/*etc*; (*expressing purpose*) para fazer/para se sentar/*etc*. **it's ten ~ six** são dez para as seis, faltam dez para as seis. **go ~ and fro** andar de um lado para outro. **husband/***etc***-~-be** *n* futuro marido *m*/*etc*. ~**-do** *n* (*fuss*) agitação *f*, alvoroço *m*
toad /təʊd/ *n* sapo *m*
toadstool /'təʊdstu:l/ *n* cogumelo *m* venenoso
toady /'təʊdɪ/ *n* lambe-botas *mf*, puxa-saco *m* □ *vi* puxar saco
toast /təʊst/ *n* fatia *f* de pão torrado, torrada *f*; (*drink*) brinde *m*, saúde *f* □ *vt* (*bread*) torrar; (*drink to*) brindar, beber à saúde de. ~**er** *n* torradeira *f*
tobacco /tə'bækəʊ/ *n* tabaco *m*
tobacconist /tə'bækənɪst/ *n* vendedor *m* de tabaco, homem *m* da tabacaria (*colloq*). ~**'s shop** tabacaria *f*
toboggan /tə'bɒgən/ *n* tobogã *m*, (*P*) toboggan *m*
today /tə'deɪ/ *n* & *adv* hoje (*m*)
toddler /'tɒdlə(r)/ *n* criança *f* que está aprendendo a andar
toe /təʊ/ *n* dedo *m* do pé; (*of shoe, stocking*) biqueira *f* □ *vt* ~ **the line** andar na linha. **on one's ~s** alerta, vigilante. ~**-hold** *n* apoio (precário) *m*. ~**nail** *n* unha *f* do dedo do pé
toffee /'tɒfɪ/ *n* puxa-puxa *m*, (*P*) caramelo *m*. ~**-apple** *n* maçã *f* caramelizada
together /tə'geðə(r)/ *adv* junto, juntamente, juntos; (*at the same time*) ao mesmo tempo. ~ **with** juntamente com. ~**ness** *n* camaradagem *f*, companheirismo *m*
toil /tɔɪl/ *vi* labutar □ *n* labuta *f*, labor *m*
toilet /'tɔɪlɪt/ *n* banheiro *m*, (*P*) casa *f* de banho; (*grooming*) toalete *f*. ~**-paper** *n* papel *m* higiênico, (*P*) higiénico. ~**-roll** *n* rolo *m* de papel higiênico, (*P*) higiénico. ~ **water** água-de-colônia *f*
toiletries /'tɔɪlɪtrɪz/ *npl* artigos *mpl* de toalete
token /'təʊkən/ *n* sinal *m*, prova *f*; (*voucher*) cheque *m*; (*coin*) ficha *f* □ *a* simbólico
told /təʊld/ *see* **tell** □ *a* **all ~** (*all in all*) ao todo
tolerabl|e /'tɒlərəbl/ *a* tolerável; (*not bad*) sofrível, razoável. ~**y** *adv* (*work, play*) razoavelmente
toleran|t /'tɒlərənt/ *a* tolerante (**of** para com). ~**ce** *n* tolerância *f*. ~**tly** *adv* com tolerância
tolerate /'tɒləreɪt/ *vt* tolerar
toll[1] /təʊl/ *n* pedágio *m*, (*P*) portagem *f*. **death ~** número *m* de mortos. **take its ~** (*of age*) fazer sentir o seu peso
toll[2] /təʊl/ *vt/i* (*of bell*) dobrar
tomato /tə'ma:təʊ/ *n* (*pl* **-oes**) tomate *m*
tomb /tu:m/ *n* túmulo *m*, sepultura *f*
tomboy /'tɒmbɔɪ/ *n* menina *f* levada (E masculinizada), (*P*) maria-rapaz *f*

tombstone /'tu:mstəʊn/ *n* lápide *f*, pedra *f* tumular
tome /təʊm/ *n* tomo *m*, volume *m*
tomfoolery /tɒm'fu:lərɪ/ *n* disparates *mpl*, imbecilidades *fpl*
tomorrow /tə'mɒrəʊ/ *n* & *adv* amanhã (*m*). ~ **morning/night** amanhã de manhã/à noite
ton /tʌn/ *n* tonelada *f* (= *1016 kg*). (**metric**) ~ tonelada *f* (= *1000 kg*). ~**s of** (*colloq*) montes de (*colloq*), (*P*) carradas de (*colloq*)
tone /təʊn/ *n* tom *m*; (*of radio, telephone etc*) sinal *m*; (*colour*) tom *m*, tonalidade *f*; (*med*) tonicidade *f* □ *vt* ~ **down** atenuar □ *vi* ~ **in** combinar-se, harmonizar-se (**with** com). ~ **up** (*muscles*) tonificar. ~**-deaf** *a* sem ouvido musical
tongs /tɒŋz/ *n* tenaz *f*; (*for sugar*) pinça *f*; (*for hair*) pinça *f*
tongue /tʌŋ/ *n* língua *f*. ~**-in-cheek** *a* & *adv* sem ser a sério, com ironia. ~**-tied** *a* calado. ~**-twister** *n* trava-língua *m*
tonic /'tɒnɪk/ *n* (*med*) tônico *m*, (*P*) tónico *m*; (*mus*) tônica *f*, (*P*) tónica *f* □ *a* tônico, (*P*) tónico
tonight /tə'naɪt/ *adv* & *n* hoje à noite, logo à noite, esta noite (*f*)
tonne /tʌn/ *n* (*metric*) tonelada *f*
tonsil /'tɒnsl/ *n* amígdala *f*
tonsillitis /tɒnsɪ'laɪtɪs/ *n* amigdalite *f*
too /tu:/ *adv* demasiado, demais; (*also*) também, igualmente; (*colloq: very*) muito. ~ **many** *a* demais, demasiados. ~ **much** *a* & *adv* demais, demasiado
took /tʊk/ *see* **take**
tool /tu:l/ *n* (*carpenter's, plumber's etc*) ferramenta *f*; (*gardener's*) utensílio *m*; (*fig: person*) joguete *m*. ~**-bag** *n* saco *m* de ferramenta
toot /tu:t/ *n* toque *m* de buzina □ *vt/i* ~ (**the horn**) buzinar, tocar a buzina
tooth /tu:θ/ *n* (*pl* **teeth**) dente *m*. ~**less** *a* desdentado
toothache /'tu:θeɪk/ *n* dor *f* de dentes
toothbrush /'tu:θbrʌʃ/ *n* escova *f* de dentes
toothpaste /'tu:θpeɪst/ *n* pasta *f* de dentes, dentifrício *m*
toothpick /'tu:θpɪk/ *n* palito *m*
top[1] /tɒp/ *n* (*highest point; upper part*) alto *m*, cimo *m*, topo *m*; (*of hill; fig*) cume *m*; (*upper surface*) cimo *m*, topo *m*; (*surface of table*) tampo *m*; (*lid*) tampa *f*; (*of bottle*) rolha *f*; (*of list*) cabeça *f* □ *a* (*shelf etc*) de cima, superior; (*in rank*) primeiro; (*best*) melhor; (*distinguished*) eminente; (*maximum*) máximo □ *vt* (*pt* **topped**) (*exceed*) ultrapassar, ir acima de. **from** ~ **to bottom** de alto a baixo. **on** ~ **of** em cima de; (*fig*) além de. **on** ~ **of that** ainda por cima. ~ **gear** (*auto*) a velocidade mais alta. ~ **hat** chapéu *m* alto. ~**-heavy** *a* mais pesado na parte de cima. ~ **secret** ultra-secreto. ~ **up** encher. ~**ped with** coberto de
top[2] /tɒp/ *n* (*toy*) pião *m*. **sleep like a** ~ dormir como uma pedra
topic /'tɒpɪk/ *n* tópico *m*, assunto *m*
topical /'tɒpɪkl/ *a* da atualidade, (*P*) actualidade, corrente
topless /'tɒplɪs/ *a* com o peito nu, topless
topple /'tɒpl/ *vt/i* (fazer) desabar, (fazer) tombar, (fazer) cair
torch /tɔ:tʃ/ *n* (*electric*) lanterna *f* elétrica, (*P*) eléctrica; (*flaming*) archote *m*, facho *m*
tore /tɔ:(r)/ *see* **tear**[1]
torment[1] /'tɔ:mənt/ *n* tormento *m*
torment[2] /tɔ:'ment/ *vt* atormentar, torturar; (*annoy*) aborrecer, chatear
torn /tɔ:n/ *see* **tear**[1]
tornado /tɔ:'neɪdəʊ/ *n* (*pl* **-oes**) tornado *m*
torpedo /tɔ:'pi:dəʊ/ *n* (*pl* **-oes**) torpedo *m* □ *vt* torpedear
torrent /'tɒrənt/ *n* torrente *f*. ~**ial** /tə'renʃl/ *a* torrencial
torrid /'tɒrɪd/ *a* (*climate etc*) tórrido; (*fig*) intenso, ardente
torso /'tɔ:səʊ/ *n* (*pl* **-os**) torso *m*
tortoise /'tɔ:təs/ *n* tartaruga *f*
tortoiseshell /'tɔ:təsʃel/ *n* (*for ornaments etc*) tartaruga *f*
tortuous /'tɔ:tʃʊəs/ *a* (*of path etc*) que dá muitas voltas, sinuoso; (*fig*) tortuoso, retorcido
torture /'tɔ:tʃə(r)/ *n* tortura *f*, suplício *m* □ *vt* torturar. ~**r** /-ə(r)/ *n* carrasco *m*, algoz *m*, torturador *m*
Tory /'tɔ:rɪ/ *a* & *n* (*colloq*) conservador (*m*), (*P*) tóri (*m*)
toss /tɒs/ *vt* atirar, jogar, (*P*) deitar; (*shake*) agitar, sacudir □ *vi* agitar-se, debater-se. ~ **a coin**, ~ **up** tirar cara ou coroa
tot[1] /tɒt/ *n* criancinha *f*; (*colloq: glass*) copinho *m*
tot[2] /tɒt/ *vt/i* (*pt* **totted**) ~ **up** (*colloq*) somar
total /'təʊtl/ *a* & *n* total (*m*) □ *vt* (*pt* **totalled**) (*find total of*) totalizar; (*amount to*) elevar-se a, montar a. ~**ity** /-'tælətɪ/ *n* totalidade *f*. ~**ly** *adv* totalmente
totalitarian /təʊtælɪ'teərɪən/ *a* totalitário
totter /'tɒtə(r)/ *vi* cambalear, andar aos tombos; (*of tower etc*) oscilar
touch /tʌtʃ/ *vt/i* tocar; (*of ends, gardens etc*) tocar-se; (*tamper with*) mexer em; (*affect*) comover □ *n* (*sense*) ta-to *m*, (*P*) tacto *m*; (*contact*) toque *m*; (*of*

colour) toque *m*, retoque *m*. **a ~ of** (*small amount*) um pouco de. **get in ~ with** entrar em contato, (*P*) contacto com. **lose ~** perder contato, (*P*) contacto. **~ down** (*aviat*) aterrissar, (*P*) aterrar. **~ off** disparar; (*cause*) dar início a, desencadear. **~ on** (*mention*) tocar em. **~ up** retocar. **~-and-go** *a* (*risky*) arriscado; (*uncertain*) duvidoso, incerto. **~-line** *n* linha *f* lateral

touching /ˈtʌtʃɪŋ/ *a* comovente, comovedor

touchy /ˈtʌtʃɪ/ *a* melindroso, suscetível, (*P*) susceptível, que se ofende facilmente

tough /tʌf/ *a* (-er, -est) (*hard, difficult; relentless*) duro; (*strong*) forte, resistente □ *n* **~** (guy) valentão *m*, durão *m* (*colloq*). **~ luck!** (*colloq*) pouca sorte! **~ness** *n* dureza *f*; (*strength*) força *f*, resistência *f*

toughen /ˈtʌfn/ *vt/i* (*person*) endurecer; (*strengthen*) reforçar

tour /tʊə(r)/ *n* viagem *f*; (*visit*) visita *f*; (*by team etc*) tournée *f* □ *vt* visitar. **on ~** em tournée

tourism /ˈtʊərɪzəm/ *n* turismo *m*

tourist /ˈtʊərɪst/ *n* turista *mf* □ *a* turístico. **~ office** agência *f* de turismo

tournament /ˈtʊərnəmənt/ *n* torneio *m*

tousle /ˈtaʊzl/ *vt* despentear, esguedelhar

tout /taʊt/ *vi* angariar clientes (for para) □ *vt* (*try to sell*) tentar revender □ *n* (*hotel etc*) angariador *m*; (*ticket*) cambista *m*, (*P*) revendedor *m*

tow /təʊ/ *vt* rebocar □ *n* reboque *m*. **on ~** a reboque. **~ away** (*vehicle*) rebocar. **~-path** *n* caminho *m* de sirga. **~-rope** *n* cabo *m* de reboque

toward(s) /təˈwɔ:d(z)/ *prep* para, em direção, (*P*) direcção a, na direção, (*P*) direcção de; (*of attitude*) para com; (*time*) por volta de

towel /ˈtaʊəl/ *n* toalha *f*; (*tea towel*) pano *m* de prato □ *vt* (*pt* towelled) esfregar com a toalha. **~-rail** *n* toalheiro *m*. **~ling** *n* atoalhado *m*, (*P*) pano *m* turco

tower /ˈtaʊə(r)/ *n* torre *f* □ *vi* **~ above** dominar. **~ block** prédio *m* alto. **~ing** *a* muito alto; (*fig: of rage etc*) violento

town /taʊn/ *n* cidade *f*. **go to ~** (*colloq*) perder a cabeça (*colloq*). **~ council** município *m*. **~ hall** câmara *f* municipal. **~ planning** urbanização *f*

toxic /ˈtɒksɪk/ *a* tóxico

toy /tɔɪ/ *n* brinquedo *m* □ *vi* **~ with** (*object*) brincar com; (*idea*) considerar, cogitar

trace /treɪs/ *n* traço *m*, rastro *m*, sinal *m*; (*small quantity*) traço *m*, vestígio *m* □ *vt* seguir *or* encontrar a pista de; (*draw*) traçar; (*with tracing-paper*) decalcar

tracing /ˈtreɪsɪŋ/ *n* decalque *m*, desenho *m*. **~-paper** *n* papel *m* vegetal

track /træk/ *n* (*of person etc*) rastro *m*, pista *f*; (*race-track, of tape*) pista *f*; (*record*) faixa *f*; (*path*) trilho *m*, carreiro *m*; (*rail*) via *f* □ *vt* seguir a pista *or* a trajetória, (*P*) trajectória de. **keep ~ of** manter-se em contato com; (*keep oneself informed*) seguir. **~ down** (*find*) encontrar, descobrir; (*hunt*) seguir a pista de. **~ suit** conjunto *m* de jogging, (*P*) fato *m* de treino

tract /trækt/ *n* (*land*) extensão *f*; (*anat*) aparelho *m*

tractor /ˈtræktə(r)/ *n* trator *m*, (*P*) tractor *m*

trade /treɪd/ *n* comércio *m*; (*job*) ofício *m*, profissão *f*; (*swap*) troca *f* □ *vt/i* comerciar (em), negociar (em) □ *vt* (*swap*) trocar. **~ in** (*used article*) trocar. **~-in** *n* troca *f*. **~ mark** marca *f* de fábrica. **~ on** (*exploit*) tirar partido de, abusar de. **~ union** sindicato *m*. **~r** /-ə(r)/ *n* negociante *mf*, comerciante *mf*

tradesman /ˈtreɪdzmən/ *n* (*pl* **-men**) comerciante *m*

trading /ˈtreɪdɪŋ/ *n* comércio *m*. **~ estate** zona *f* industrial

tradition /trəˈdɪʃn/ *n* tradição *f*. **~al** *a* tradicional

traffic /ˈtræfɪk/ *n* (*trade*) tráfego *m*, tráfico *m*; (*on road*) trânsito *m*, tráfego *m*; (*aviat*) tráfego *m* □ *vi* (*pt* **trafficked**) traficar (in em). **~ circle** (*Amer*) giratória *f*, (*P*) rotunda *f*. **~ island** ilha *f* de pedestres, (*P*) refúgio *m* para peões. **~ jam** engarrafamento *m*. **~-lights** *npl* sinal *m* luminoso, (*P*) semáforo *m*. **~ warden** guarda *mf* de trânsito. **~ker** *n* traficante *mf*

tragedy /ˈtrædʒədɪ/ *n* tragédia *f*

tragic /ˈtrædʒɪk/ *a* trágico

trail /treɪl/ *vt/i* arrastar(-se), rastejar; (*of plant, on ground*) rastejar; (*of plant, over wall*) trepar; (*track*) seguir □ *n* (*of powder, smoke etc*) esteira *f*, rastro *m*, (*P*) rasto *m*; (*track*) pista *f*; (*beaten path*) trilho *m*

trailer /ˈtreɪlə(r)/ *n* reboque *m*; (*Amer: caravan*) reboque *m*, caravana *f*, trailer *m*; (*film*) trailer *m*, apresentação *f* de filme

train /treɪn/ *n* (*rail*) trem *m*, (*P*) comboio *m*; (*procession*) fila *f*; (*of dress*) cauda *f*; (*retinue*) comitiva *f* □ *vt* (*instruct, develop*) educar, formar, treinar; (*plant*) guiar; (*sportsman, animal*) treinar; (*aim*) assestar, apontar □ *vi* estudar, treinar-se. ~**ed** *a* (*skilled*) qualificado; (*doctor etc*) diplomado. ~**er** *n* (*sport*) treinador *m*; (*shoe*) tênis *m*. ~**ing** *n* treino *m*

trainee /treɪ'ni:/ *n* estagiário *m*

trait /treɪ(t)/ *n* traço *m*, característica *f*

traitor /'treɪtə(r)/ *n* traidor *m*

tram /træm/ *n* bonde *m*, (*P*) (carro) eléctrico *m*

tramp /træmp/ *vi* marchar (com passo pesado) □ *vt* percorrer, palmilhar □ *n* som *m* de passos pesados; (*vagrant*) vagabundo *m*, andarilho *m*; (*hike*) longa caminhada *f*

trample /'træmpl/ *vt/i* ~ **(on)** pisar com força; (*fig*) menosprezar

trampoline /'træmpəli:n/ *n* (lona *f* usada como) trampolim *m*

trance /tra:ns/ *n* (*hypnotic*) transe *m*; (*ecstasy*) êxtase *m*, arrebatamento *m*; (*med*) estupor *m*

tranquil /'træŋkwɪl/ *a* tranqüilo, (*P*) tranquilo, sossegado. ~**lity** /-'kwɪlətɪ/ *n* tranqüilidade *f*, (*P*) tranquilidade *f*, sossego *m*

tranquillizer /'træŋkwɪlaɪzə(r)/ *n* (*drug*) tranqüilizante *m*, (*P*) tranquilizante *m*, calmante *m*

transact /træn'zækt/ *vt* (*business*) fazer, efetuar, (*P*) efectuar. ~**ion** /-kʃn/ *n* transação *f*, (*P*) transacção *f*

transcend /træn'send/ *vt* transcender. ~**ent** *a* transcendente

transcri|be /træn'skraɪb/ *vt* transcrever. ~**pt**, ~**ption** /-ɪpʃn/ *ns* transcrição *f*

transfer[1] /træns'fɜ:(r)/ *vt* (*pt* **transferred**) transferir; (*power, property*) transmitir □ *vi* mudar, ser transferido; (*change planes etc*) fazer transferência. ~ **the charges** (*telephone*) ligar a cobrar

transfer[2] /'trænsfɜ:(r)/ *n* transferência *f*; (*of power, property*) transmissão *f*; (*image*) decalcomania *f*

transfigure /træns'fɪgə(r)/ *vt* transfigurar

transform /træns'fɔ:m/ *vt* transformar. ~**ation** /-ə'meɪʃn/ *n* transformação *f*. ~**er** *n* (*electr*) transformador *m*

transfusion /træns'fju:ʒn/ *n* (*of blood*) transfusão *f*

transient /'trænzɪənt/ *a* transitório, transiente, efêmero, (*P*) efémero, passageiro

transistor /træn'zɪstə(r)/ *n* (*device, radio*) transistor *m*

transit /'trænsɪt/ *n* trânsito *m*. **in** ~ em trânsito

transition /træn'zɪʃn/ *n* transição *f*. ~**al** *a* transitório

transitive /'trænsətɪv/ *a* transitivo

transitory /'trænsɪtərɪ/ *a* transitório

translat|e /trænz'leɪt/ *vt* traduzir. ~**ion** /-ʃn/ *n* tradução *f*. ~**or** *n* tradutor *m*

translucent /trænz'lu:snt/ *a* translúcido

transmi|t /trænz'mɪt/ *vt* (*pt* **transmitted**) transmitir. ~**ssion** *n* transmissão *f*. ~**tter** *n* transmissor *m*

transparen|t /træns'pærənt/ *a* transparente. ~**cy** *n* transparência *f*; (*photo*) diapositivo *m*

transpire /træn'spaɪə(r)/ *vi* (*secret etc*) transpirar; (*happen*) suceder, acontecer

transplant[1] /træns'pla:nt/ *vt* transplantar

transplant[2] /'trænspla:nt/ *n* (*med*) transplantação *f*, transplante *m*

transport[1] /træn'spɔ:t/ *vt* (*carry, delight*) transportar. ~**ation** /'teɪʃn/ *n* transporte *m*

transport[2] /'trænspɔ:t/ *n* (*of goods, delight etc*) transporte *m*

transpose /træn'spəʊz/ *vt* transpor

transverse /'trænzvɜ:s/ *a* transversal

transvestite /trænz'vestaɪt/ *n* travesti *mf*

trap /træp/ *n* armadilha *f*, ratoeira *f*, cilada *f* □ *vt* (*pt* **trapped**) apanhar na armadilha; (*cut off*) prender, bloquear. ~**per** *n* caçador *m* de armadilha (esp de peles)

trapdoor /træp'dɔ:(r)/ *n* alçapão *m*

trapeze /trə'pi:z/ *n* trapézio *m*

trash /træʃ/ *n* (*worthless stuff*) porcaria *f*; (*refuse*) lixo *m*; (*nonsense*) disparates *mpl*. ~ **can** *n* (*Amer*) lata *f* do lixo, (*P*) caixote *m* do lixo. ~**y** *a* que não vale nada, porcaria

trauma /'trɔ:mə/ *n* trauma *m*, traumatismo *m*. ~**tic** /-'mætɪk/ *a* traumático

travel /'trævl/ *vi* (*pt* **travelled**) viajar; (*of vehicle, bullet, sound*) ir □ *vt* percorrer □ *n* viagem *f*. ~ **agent** agente *mf* de viagem. ~**ler** *n* viajante *mf*. ~**ler's cheque** cheque *m* de viagem. ~**ling** *n* viagem *f*, viagens *fpl*, viajar *m*

travesty /'trævəstɪ/ *n* paródia *f*, caricatura *f*

trawler /'trɔ:lə(r)/ *n* traineira *f*, (*P*) arrastão *m*

tray /treɪ/ *n* tabuleiro *m*, bandeja *f*

treacherous /'tretʃərəs/ *a* traiçoeiro

treachery /'tretʃərɪ/ *n* traição *f*, perfídia *f*, deslealdade *f*

treacle /'tri:kl/ *n* melaço *m*

tread /tred/ *vt/i* (*pt* **trod**, *pp* **trodden**) (*step*) pisar; (*walk*) andar, caminhar; (*walk along*) seguir □ *n* passo *m*, maneira *f* de andar; (*of tyre*) trilho *m*. ~ **sth into** (*carpet*) esmigalhar alg coisa sobre/em

treason /'tri:zn/ *n* traição *f*
treasure /'treʒə(r)/ *n* tesouro *m* □ *vt* ter o maior apreço por; (*store*) guardar bem guardado. **~r** *n* tesoureiro *m*
treasury /'treʒərɪ/ *n* (*building*) tesouraria *f*; (*department*) Ministério *m* das Finanças *or* da Fazenda; (*fig*) tesouro *m*
treat /tri:t/ *vt/i* tratar □ *n* (*pleasure*) prazer *m*, regalo *m*; (*present*) mimo *m*, gentileza *f*. **~ sb to sth** convidar alguém para alg coisa
treatise /'tri:tɪz/ *n* tratado *m*
treatment /'tri:tmənt/ *n* tratamento *m*
treaty /'tri:tɪ/ *n* (*pact*) tratado *m*
trebl|e /'trebl/ *a* triplo □ *vt/i* triplicar □ *n* (*mus: voice*) soprano *m*. **~y** *adv* triplamente
tree /tri:/ *n* árvore *f*
trek /trek/ *n* viagem *f* penosa; (*walk*) caminhada *f* □ *vi* (*pt* **trekked**) viajar penosamente; (*walk*) caminhar
trellis /'trelɪs/ *n* grade *f* para trepadeiras, treliça *f*
tremble /'trembl/ *vi* tremer
tremendous /trɪ'mendəs/ *a* (*fearful, huge*) tremendo; (*colloq: excellent*) fantástico, formidável
tremor /'tremə(r)/ *n* tremor *m*, estremecimento *m*. **(earth) ~** abalo (sísmico) *m*, tremor *m* de terra
trench /trentʃ/ *n* fossa *f*, vala *f*; (*mil*) trincheira *f*
trend /trend/ *n* tendência *f*; (*fashion*) moda *f*. **~y** *a* (*colloq*) na última moda, (*P*) na berra (*colloq*)
trepidation /trepɪ'deɪʃn/ *n* (*fear*) receio *m*, apreensão *f*
trespass /'trespəs/ *vi* entrar ilegalmente (**on** em). **no ~ing** entrada *f* proibida. **~er** *n* intruso *m*
trestle /'tresl/ *n* cavalete *m*, armação *f* de mesa. **~-table** *n* mesa *f* de cavaletes
trial /'traɪəl/ *n* (*jur*) julgamento *m*, processo *m*; (*test*) ensaio *m*, experiência *f*, prova *f*; (*ordeal*) provação *f*. **on ~** em julgamento. **~ and error** tentativas *fpl*
triang|le /'traɪæŋgl/ *n* triângulo *m*. **~ular** /-'æŋgjʊlə(r)/ *a* triangular
trib|e /traɪb/ *n* tribo *f*. **~al** *a* tribal
tribulation /trɪbjʊ'leɪʃn/ *n* tribulação *f*
tribunal /traɪ'bju:nl/ *n* tribunal *m*
tributary /'trɪbjʊtərɪ/ *n* afluente *m*, tributário *m*
tribute /'trɪbju:t/ *n* tributo *m*. **pay ~ to** prestar homenagem a, render tributo a
trick /trɪk/ *n* truque *m*; (*prank*) partida *f*; (*habit*) jeito *m* □ *vt* enganar. **do the ~** (*colloq: work*) dar resultado
trickery /'trɪkərɪ/ *n* trapaça *f*
trickle /'trɪkl/ *vi* pingar, gotejar, escorrer □ *n* fio *m* de água *etc*; (*fig: small number*) punhado *m*
tricky /'trɪkɪ/ *a* (*crafty*) manhoso; (*problem*) delicado, complicado
tricycle /'traɪsɪkl/ *n* triciclo *m*
trifle /'traɪfl/ *n* ninharia *f*, bagatela *f*; (*sweet*) sobremesa *f* feita de pão-de-ló e frutas e creme □ *vi* **~ with** brincar com. **a ~** um pouquinho, (*P*) um pouquinho
trifling /'traɪflɪŋ/ *a* insignificante
trigger /'trɪgə(r)/ *n* (*of gun*) gatilho *m* □ *vt* **~ (off)** (*initiate*) desencadear, despoletar
trill /trɪl/ *n* trinado *m*, gorjeio *m*
trilogy /'trɪlədʒɪ/ *n* trilogia *f*
trim /trɪm/ *a* (**trimmer, trimmest**) bem arranjado, bem cuidado; (*figure*) elegante, esbelto □ *vt* (*pt* **trimmed**) (*cut*) aparar; (*sails*) orientar, marear; (*ornament*) enfeitar, guarnecer (**with** com) □ *n* (*cut*) aparadela *f*, corte *m* leve; (*decoration*) enfeite *m*; (*on car*) acabamento(s) *m*(*pl*), estofado *m*. **in ~** em ordem; (*fit*) em boa forma. **~ming(s)** *n*(*pl*) (*dress*) enfeite *m*; (*culin*) guarnição *f*, acompanhamento *m*
Trinity /'trɪnətɪ/ *n* **the (Holy) ~** a Santíssima Trindade
trinket /'trɪŋkɪt/ *n* bugiganga *f*; (*jewel*) bijuteria *f*, berloque *m*
trio /'tri:əʊ/ *n* (*pl* **-os**) trio *m*
trip /trɪp/ *vi* (*pt* **tripped**) (*stumble*) tropeçar, dar um passo em falso; (*go or dance lightly*) andar/dançar com passos leves □ *vt* **~ (up)** fazer tropeçar, passar uma rasteira a □ *n* (*journey*) viagem *f*; (*outing*) passeio *m*, excursão *f*; (*stumble*) tropeção *m*, passo *m* em falso
tripe /traɪp/ *n* (*food*) dobrada *f*, tripas *fpl*; (*colloq: nonsense*) disparates *mpl*
triple /'trɪpl/ *a* triplo, tríplice □ *vt/i* triplicar. **~ts** /-plɪts/ *npl* trigêmeos *mpl*, (*P*) trigémeos *mpl*
triplicate /'trɪplɪkət/ *n* **in ~** em triplicata
tripod /'traɪpɒd/ *n* tripé *m*
trite /traɪt/ *a* banal, corriqueiro
triumph /'traɪəmf/ *n* triunfo *m* □ *vi* triunfar (**over** sobre); (*exult*) exultar, rejubilar-se. **~al** /-'ʌmfl/ *a* triunfal. **~ant** /-'ʌmfənt/ *a* triunfante. **~antly** /-'ʌmfəntlɪ/ *adv* em triunfo, triunfantemente
trivial /'trɪvɪəl/ *a* insignificante
trod, trodden /trɒd, 'trɒdn/ *see* **tread**
trolley /'trɒlɪ/ *n* carrinho *m*. **(tea-)~** carrinho *m* de chá
trombone /trɒm'bəʊn/ *n* (*mus*) trombone *m*
troop /tru:p/ *n* bando *m*, grupo *m*. **~s**

(*mil*) tropas *fpl* □ *vi* ~ **in/out** entrar/ sair em bando *or* grupo. **~ing the colour** a saudação da bandeira. **~er** *n* soldado *m* de cavalaria

trophy /'trəʊfɪ/ *n* troféu *m*

tropic /'trɒpɪk/ *n* trópico *m*. **~s** trópicos *mpl*. **~al** *a* tropical

trot /trɒt/ *n* trote *m* □ *vi* (*pt* **trotted**) trotar; (*of person*) correr em passos curtos, ir num *or* a trote (*colloq*). **on the ~** (*colloq*) a seguir, a fio. **~ out** (*colloq: produce*) exibir; (*colloq: state*) desfiar

trouble /'trʌbl/ *n* (*difficulty*) dificuldade(s) *f*(*pl*), problema(s) *m*(*pl*); (*distress*) desgosto(s) *m*(*pl*), aborrecimento(s) *m*(*pl*); (*pains, effort*) cuidado *m*, trabalho *m*, maçada *f*; (*inconvenience*) transtorno *m*, incômodo *m*, (*P*) incómodo *m*; (*med*) doença *f*. **~(s)** (*unrest*) agitação *f*, conflito(s) *m*(*pl*) □ *vt/i* (*bother*) incomodar(-se), (*P*) maçar(-se); (*worry*) preocupar(-se); (*agitate*) perturbar. **be in ~** estar em apuros, estar em dificuldades. **get into ~** meter-se em encrenca/apuros. **it is not worth the ~** não vale a pena. **~-maker** *n* desordeiro *m*, provocador *m*. **~-shooter** *n* mediador *m*, negociador *m*. **~d** *a* agitado, perturbado; (*of sleep*) agitado; (*of water*) turvo

troublesome /'trʌblsəm/ *a* problemático, importuno, (*P*) maçador

trough /trɒf/ *n* (*drinking*) bebedouro *m*; (*feeding*) comedouro *m*. **~ (of low pressure)** depressão *f*, linha *f* de baixa pressão

trounce /traʊns/ *vt* (*defeat*) esmagar; (*thrash*) espancar

troupe /tru:p/ *n* (*theat*) companhia *f*, troupe *f*

trousers /'traʊzəz/ *npl* calça *f*, (*P*) calças *fpl*. **short ~** calções *mpl*

trousseau /'tru:səʊ/ *n* (*pl* -s /-əʊz/) (*of bride*) enxoval *m* de noiva

trout /traʊt/ *n* (*pl invar*) truta *f*

trowel /'traʊəl/ *n* (*garden*) colher *f* de jardineiro; (*for mortar*) trolha *f*

truan|t /'tru:ənt/ *n* absenteísta *mf*, (*P*) absentista *mf*; (*schol*) gazeteiro *m*. **play ~t** fazer gazeta. **~cy** *n* absenteísmo *m*, (*P*) absentismo *m*

truce /tru:s/ *n* trégua(s) *f*(*pl*), armistício *m*

truck /trʌk/ *n* (*lorry*) camião *m*; (*barrow*) carro *m* de bagageiro; (*wagon*) vagão *m* aberto. **~-driver** *n* motorista *mf* de camião, (*P*) camionista *mf*

truculent /'trʌkjʊlənt/ *a* agressivo, brigão

trudge /trʌdʒ/ *vi* caminhar com dificuldade, caminhar a custo, arrastar-se

true /tru:/ *a* (-er, -est) verdadeiro; (*accurate*) exato, (*P*) exacto; (*faithful*) fiel. **come ~** (*happen*) realizar-se, concretizar-se. **it is ~** é verdade

truffle /'trʌfl/ *n* trufa *f*

truism /'tru:ɪzəm/ *n* truísmo *m*, verdade *f* evidente, (*P*) verdade *f* do Amigo Banana (*colloq*)

truly /'tru:lɪ/ *adv* verdadeiramente; (*faithfully*) fielmente; (*truthfully*) sinceramente

trump /trʌmp/ *n* trunfo *m* □ *vt* jogar trunfo, trunfar. **~ up** forjar, inventar. **~ card** carta *f* de trunfo; (*colloq: valuable resource*) trunfo *m*

trumpet /'trʌmpɪt/ *n* trombeta *f*

truncheon /'trʌntʃən/ *n* cassetete *m*, (*P*) cassetête *m*

trundle /'trʌndl/ *vt/i* (fazer) rolar ruidosamente/pesadamente

trunk /trʌŋk/ *n* (*of tree, body*) tronco *m*; (*of elephant*) tromba *f*; (*box*) mala *f* grande; (*Amer, auto*) mala *f*. **~s** (*for swimming*) calção *m* de banho. **~ call** *n* chamada *f* interurbana. **~ road** *n* estrada *f* nacional

truss /trʌs/ *n* (*med*) funda *f* □ *vt* atar, amarrar

trust /trʌst/ *n* confiança *f*; (*association*) truste *m*, (*P*) trust *m*, consórcio *m*; (*foundation*) fundação *f*; (*responsibility*) responsabilidade *f*; (*jur*) fideicomisso *m* □ *vt* (*rely on*) ter confiança em, confiar em; (*hope*) esperar □ *vi* **~ in** *or* **to** confiar em. **in ~** em fideicomisso. **on ~** (*without proof*) sem verificação prévia; (*on credit*) a crédito. **~ sb with** confiar em alguém. **~ed** *a* (*friend etc*) de confiança, seguro. **~ful**, **~ing** *adjs* confiante. **~y** *a* fiel

trustee /trʌs'ti:/ *n* administrador *m*; (*jur*) fideicomissório *m*

trustworthy /'trʌstwɜ:ðɪ/ *a* (digno) de confiança

truth /tru:θ/ *n* (*pl* -s /tru:ðz/) verdade *f*. **~ful** *a* (*account etc*) verídico; (*person*) verdadeiro, que fala verdade. **~fully** *adv* sinceramente

try /traɪ/ *vt/i* (*pt* **tried**) tentar, experimentar; (*be a strain on*) cansar, pôr à prova; (*jur*) julgar □ *n* (*attempt*) tentativa *f*, experiência *f*; (*Rugby*) ensaio *m*. **~ for** (*post, scholarship*) candidatar-se a; (*record*) tentar alcançar. **~ on** (*clothes*) provar. **~ out** experimentar. **~ to do** tentar fazer. **~ing** *a* difícil

tsar /za:(r)/ *n* czar *m*

T-shirt /'ti:ʃɜ:t/ *n* T-shirt *f*, camiseta *f* de algodão de mangas curtas

tub /tʌb/ *n* selha *f*; (*colloq: bath*) tina *f*, banheira *f*

tuba /'tju:bə/ *n* (*mus*) tuba *f*

tubby /'tʌbɪ/ *a* (-ier, -iest) baixote e gorducho
tub|e /tju:b/ *n* tubo *m*; (*colloq: railway*) metrô *m*. **inner ~e** câmara *f* de ar. **~ing** *n* tubos *mpl*, tubagem *f*
tuber /'tju:bə(r)/ *n* tubérculo *m*
tuberculosis /tju:bɜ:kjʊ'ləʊsɪs/ *n* tuberculose *f*
tubular /'tju:bjʊlə(r)/ *a* tubular
tuck /tʌk/ *n* (*fold*) prega *f* cosida; (*for shortening or ornament*) refego *m* □ *vt/i* fazer pregas; (*put*) guardar, meter, enfiar; (*hide*) esconder. **~ in** *or* **into** (*colloq: eat*) atacar. **~ in** (*shirt*) meter as fraldas para dentro; (*blanket*) prender em; (*person*) cobrir bem, aconchegar. **~-shop** *n* (*schol*) loja *f* de balas, (*P*) pastelaria *f* (junto à escola)
Tuesday /'tju:zdɪ/ *n* terça-feira *f*
tuft /tʌft/ *n* tufo *m*
tug /tʌg/ *vt/i* (*pt* **tugged**) puxar com força; (*vessel*) rebocar □ *n* (*boat*) rebocador *m*; (*pull*) puxão *m*. **~ of war** cabo-de-guerra *m*, (*P*) jogo *m* da guerra
tuition /tju:'ɪʃn/ *n* ensino *m*
tulip /'tju:lɪp/ *n* tulipa *f*
tumble /'tʌmbl/ *vi* tombar, baquear, dar um trambolhão □ *n* tombo *m*, trambolhão *m*. **~-drier** *n* máquina *f* de secar (roupa)
tumbledown /'tʌmbldaʊn/ *a* em ruínas
tumbler /'tʌmblə(r)/ *n* copo *m*
tummy /'tʌmɪ/ *n* (*colloq: stomach*) estômago *m*; (*colloq: abdomen*) barriga *f*. **~-ache** *n* (*colloq*) dor *f* de barriga/de estômago
tumour /'tju:mə(r)/ *n* tumor *m*
tumult /'tju:mʌlt/ *n* tumulto *m*. **~uous** /'mʌltʃʊəs/ *a* tumultuado, barulhento, agitado
tuna /'tju:nə/ *n* (*pl invar*) atum *m*
tune /tju:n/ *n* melodia *f* □ *vt* (*engine*) regular; (*piano etc*) afinar □ *vi* **~ in (to)** (*radio, TV*) ligar (em), (*P*) sintonizar. **~ up** afinar. **be in ~/out of ~** (*instrument*) estar afinado/desafinado; (*singer*) cantar afinado/desafinado. **~ful** *a* melodioso, harmonioso. **~r** *n* afinador *m*; (*radio*) sintonizador *m*
tunic /'tju:nɪk/ *n* túnica *f*
Tunisia /tju:'nɪzɪə/ *n* Tunísia *f*. **~n** *a* & *n* tunisiano (*m*), (*P*) tunisino (*m*)
tunnel /'tʌnl/ *n* túnel *m* □ *vi* (*pt* **tunnelled**) abrir um túnel (into em)
turban /'tɜ:bən/ *n* turbante *m*
turbine /'tɜ:baɪn/ *n* turbina *f*
turbo- /'tɜ:bəʊ/ *pref* turbo-
turbot /'tɜ:bət/ *n* rodovalho *m*
turbulen|t /'tɜ:bjʊlənt/ *a* turbulento. **~ce** *n* turbulência *f*
tureen /tə'ri:n/ *n* terrina *f*
turf /tɜ:f/ *n* (*pl* **turfs** *or* **turves**) gramado *m*, (*P*) relva *f*, relvado *m* □ *vt* **~ out** (*colloq*) jogar fora, (*P*) deitar fora. **the ~** (*racing*) turfe *m*, hipismo *m*. **~ accountant** corretor *m* de apostas
turgid /'tɜ:dʒɪd/ *a* (*speech, style*) pomposo, empolado
Turk /tɜ:k/ *n* turco *m*. **~ey** *n* Turquia *f*. **~ish** *a* turco *m* □ *n* (*lang*) turco *m*
turkey /'tɜ:kɪ/ *n* peru *m*
turmoil /'tɜ:mɔɪl/ *n* agitação *f*, confusão *f*, desordem *f*. **in ~** em ebulição
turn /tɜ:n/ *vt/i* virar(-se), voltar(-se), girar; (*change*) transformar(-se) (into em); (*become*) ficar, tornar-se; (*corner*) virar, dobrar; (*page*) virar, voltar □ *n* volta *f*; (*in road*) curva *f*; (*of mind, events*) mudança *f*; (*occasion, opportunity*) vez *f*; (*colloq*) ataque *m*, crise *f*; (*colloq: shock*) susto *m*. **do a good ~** prestar (um) serviço. **in ~** por sua vez, sucessivamente. **speak out of ~** dizer o que não se deve, cometer uma indiscrição. **take ~s** revezar-se. **~ of the century** virada *f* do século. **~ against** virar-se *or* voltar-se contra. **~ away** *vi* virar-se *or* voltar-se para o outro lado □ *vt* (*avert*) desviar; (*reject*) recusar; (*send back*) mandar embora. **~ back** *vi* (*return*) devolver; (*vehicle*) dar meia volta, voltar para trás □ *vt* (*fold*) dobrar para trás. **~ down** recusar; (*fold*) dobrar para baixo; (*reduce*) baixar. **~ in** (*hand in*) entregar; (*colloq: go to bed*) deitar-se. **~ off** (*light etc*) apagar; (*tap*) fechar; (*road*) virar (para rua transversal). **~ on** (*light etc*) acender, ligar; (*tap*) abrir. **~ out** *vt* (*light*) apagar; (*empty*) esvaziar, despejar; (*pocket*) virar do avesso; (*produce*) produzir □ *vi* (*transpire*) vir a saber-se, descobrir-se; (*colloq: come*) aparecer. **~ round** virar-se, voltar-se. **~ up** *vi* aparecer, chegar; (*be found*) aparecer □ *vt* (*find*) desenterrar; (*increase*) aumentar; (*collar*) levantar. **~-out** *n* assistência *f*. **~-up** *n* (*of trousers*) dobra *f*
turning /'tɜ:nɪŋ/ *n* rua *f* transversal; (*corner*) esquina *f*. **~-point** *n* momento *m* decisivo
turnip /'tɜ:nɪp/ *n* nabo *m*
turnover /'tɜ:nəʊvə(r)/ *n* (*pie, tart*) pastel *m*, empada *f*; (*money*) faturamento *m*, (*P*) facturação *f*; (*of staff*) rotatividade *f*
turnpike /'tɜ:npaɪk/ *n* (*Amer*) auto-estrada *f* com pedágio, (*P*) portagem
turnstile /'tɜ:nstaɪl/ *n* (*gate*) torniquete *m*, borboleta *f*

turntable /'tɜ:nteɪbl/ *n* (*for record*) prato *m* do toca-disco, (*P*) giradiscos; (*record-player*) toca-disco *m*, (*P*) giradiscos *m*
turpentine /'tɜ:pəntaɪn/ *n* terebentina *f*, aguarrás *m*
turquoise /'tɜ:kwɔɪz/ *a* turquesa *invar*
turret /'tʌrɪt/ *n* torreão *m*, torrinha *f*
turtle /'tɜ:tl/ *n* tartaruga-do-mar *f*. **~-neck** *a* de gola alta
tusk /tʌsk/ *n* (*tooth*) presa *f*; (*elephant's*) defesa *f*, dente *m*
tussle /'tʌsl/ *n* luta *f*, briga *f*
tutor /'tju:tə(r)/ *n* professor *m* particular; (*univ*) professor *m* universitário
tutorial /tju:'tɔ:rɪəl/ *n* (*univ*) seminário *m*
TV /ti:'vi:/ *n* tevê *f*
twaddle /'twɒdl/ *n* disparates *mpl*
twang /twæŋ/ *n* (*mus*) som *m* duma corda esticada; (*in voice*) nasalação *f* □ *vt/i* (*mus*) (fazer) vibrar, dedilhar
tweet /twi:t/ *n* pio *m*, pipilo *m* □ *vi* pipilar
tweezers /'twi:zəz/ *npl* pinça *f*
twel|ve /twelv/ *a* & *n* doze (*m*). **~ (o'clock)** doze horas. **~fth** *a* & *n* décimo segundo (*m*). **T~fth Night** véspera *f* de Reis
twent|y /'twentɪ/ *a* & *n* vinte (*m*). **~ieth** *a* & *n* vigésimo (*m*)
twice /twaɪs/ *adv* duas vezes
twiddle /'twɪdl/ *vt/i* **~ (with)** (*fiddle with*) torcer, brincar (com). **~ one's thumbs** girar os polegares
twig /twɪg/ *n* galho *m*, graveto *m*
twilight /'twaɪlaɪt/ *n* crepúsculo *m* □ *a* crepuscular
twin /twɪn/ *n* & *a* gêmeo (*m*), (*P*) gémeo (*m*) □ *vt* (*pt* **twinned**) (*pair*) emparelhar, emparceirar. **~ beds** par *m* de camas de solteiro. **~ning** *n* emparelhamento *m*
twine /twaɪn/ *n* guita *f*, cordel *m* □ *vt/i* (*weave together*) entrançar; (*wind*) enroscar(-se)
twinge /twɪndʒ/ *n* dor *f* aguda e súbita, pontada *f*; (*fig*) pontada *f*, (*P*) ferroada *f*
twinkle /'twɪŋkl/ *vi* cintilar, brilhar □ *n* cintilação *f*, brilho *m*
twirl /twɜ:l/ *vt/i* (fazer) girar; (*moustache*) torcer
twist /twɪst/ *vt* torcer; (*weave together*) entrançar; (*roll*) enrolar; (*distort*) torcer, deturpar □ *vi* (*rope etc*) torcer-se, enrolar-se; (*road*) dar voltas *or* curvas, serpentear □ *n* (*act of twisting*) torcedura *f*, (*P*) torcedela *f*; (*of rope*) nó *m*; (*of events*) reviravolta *f*. **~ sb's arm** (*fig*) forçar alguém
twit /twɪt/ *n* (*colloq*) idiota *mf*
twitch /twɪtʃ/ *vt/i* contrair(-se) □ *n* (*tic*) tique *m*; (*jerk*) puxão *m*
two /tu:/ *a* & *n* dois (*m*). **in** *or* **of ~ minds** indeciso. **put ~ and ~ together** tirar conclusões. **~-faced** *a* de duas caras, hipócrita. **~-piece** *n* (*garment*) duas-peças *m invar*. **~-seater** *n* (*car*) carro *m* de dois lugares. **~-way** *a* (*of road*) mão dupla
twosome /'tu:səm/ *n* par *m*
tycoon /taɪ'ku:n/ *n* magnata *m*
tying /'taɪɪŋ/ *see* tie
type /taɪp/ *n* (*example, print*) tipo *m*; (*kind*) tipo *m*, gênero *m*, (*P*) género *m*; (*colloq: person*) cara *m*, (*P*) tipo *m* (*colloq*) □ *vt/i* (*write*) bater à máquina, datilografar, (*P*) dactilografar
typescript /'taɪpskrɪpt/ *n* texto *m* datilografado, (*P*) dactilografado
typewrit|er /'taɪpraɪtə(r)/ *n* máquina *f* de escrever. **~ten** /-ɪtn/ *a* batido à máquina, datilografado, (*P*) dactilografado
typhoid /'taɪfɔɪd/ *n* **~ (fever)** febre *f* tifóide
typhoon /taɪ'fu:n/ *n* tufão *m*
typical /'tɪpɪkl/ *a* típico. **~ly** *adv* tipicamente
typify /'tɪpɪfaɪ/ *vt* ser o (protó)tipo de, tipificar
typing /'taɪpɪŋ/ *n* datilografia *f*, (*P*) dactilografia *f*
typist /'taɪpɪst/ *n* datilógrafa *f*, (*P*) dactilógrafa *f*
tyrann|y /'tɪrənɪ/ *n* tirania *f*. **~ical** /tɪ'rænɪkl/ *a* tirânico
tyrant /'taɪərənt/ *n* tirano *m*
tyre /'taɪə(r)/ *n* pneu *m*

U

ubiquitous /ju:'bɪkwɪtəs/ *a* ubíquo, omnipresente
udder /'ʌdər/ *n* úbere *m*
UFO /'ju:fəʊ/ *n* OVNI *m*
ugl|y /'ʌglɪ/ *a* (-ier, -iest) feio. **~iness** *n* feiúra *f*, (*P*) fealdade *f*
UK *abbr see* **United Kingdom**
ulcer /'ʌlsə(r)/ *n* úlcera *f*
ulterior /ʌl'tɪərɪə(r)/ *a* ulterior. **~ motive** razão *f* inconfessada, segundas intenções *fpl*
ultimate /'ʌltɪmət/ *a* último, derradeiro; (*definitive*) definitivo; (*maximum*) supremo; (*basic*) fundamental. **~ly** *adv* finalmente
ultimatum /ʌltɪ'meɪtəm/ *n* (*pl* **-ums**) ultimato *m*
ultra- /'ʌltrə/ *pref* ultra-, super-
ultraviolet /ʌltrə'vaɪələt/ *a* ultravioleta
umbilical /ʌm'bɪlɪkl/ *a* **~ cord** cordão *m* umbilical

umbrage /'ʌmbrɪdʒ/ *n* **take ~ (at sth)** ofender-se *or* melindrar-se (com alg coisa)
umbrella /ʌm'brelə/ *n* guardachuva *m*
umpire /'ʌmpaɪə(r)/ *n* (*sport*) árbitro *m* □ *vt* arbitrar
umpteen /'ʌmpti:n/ *a* (*sl*) sem conta, montes de (*colloq*). **for the ~th time** (*sl*) pela centésima *or* enésima vez
UN *abbr* (*United Nations*) ONU *f*
un- /ʌn/ *pref* não, pouco
unable /ʌn'eɪbl/ *a* **be ~ to do** ser incapaz de/não poder fazer
unabridged /ʌnə'brɪdʒd/ *a* (*text*) integral
unacceptable /ʌnək'septəbl/ *a* inaceitável, inadmissível
unaccompanied /ʌnə'kʌmpənɪd/ *a* só, desacompanhado
unaccountable /ʌnə'kaʊntəbl/ *a* (*strange*) inexplicável; (*not responsible*) que não tem que dar contas
unaccustomed /ʌnə'kʌstəmd/ *a* desacostumado. **~ to** não acostumado *or* não habituado a
unadulterated /ʌnə'dʌltəreɪtɪd/ *a* (*pure, sheer*) puro
unaided /ʌn'eɪdɪd/ *a* sem ajuda, sozinho, por si só
unanim|ous /ju:'nænɪməs/ *a* unânime. **~ity** /-ə'nɪmətɪ/ *n* unanimidade *f*. **~ously** *adv* unânimemente, por unanimidade
unarmed /ʌn'a:md/ *a* desarmado, indefeso
unashamed /ʌnə'ʃeɪmd/ *a* desavergonhado, sem vergonha. **~ly** /-ɪdlɪ/ *adv* sem vergonha
unassuming /ʌnə'sju:mɪŋ/ *a* modesto, despretencioso
unattached /ʌnə'tætʃt/ *a* (*person*) livre
unattainable /ʌnə'teɪnəbl/ *a* inaccessível
unattended /ʌnə'tendɪd/ *a* (*person*) desacompanhado; (*car, luggage*) abandonado
unattractive /ʌnə'træktɪv/ *a* sem atrativos, (*P*) atractivos; (*offer*) de pouco interesse
unauthorized /ʌn'ɔ:θəraɪzd/ *a* não-autorizado, sem autorização
unavoidabl|e /ʌnə'vɔɪdəbl/ *a* inevitável. **~y** *adv* inevitavelmente
unaware /ʌnə'weə(r)/ *a* **be ~ of** desconhecer, ignorar, não ter consciência de. **~s** /-eəz/ *adv* (*unexpectedly*) inesperadamente. **catch sb ~s** apanhar alguém desprevenido
unbalanced /ʌn'bælənst/ *a* (*mind, person*) desequilibrado
unbearable /ʌn'beərəbl/ *a* insuportável
unbeat|able /ʌn'bi:təbl/ *a* imbatível. **~en** *a* não vencido, invicto; (*unsurpassed*) insuperado
unbeknown(st) /ʌnbɪ'nəʊn(st)/ *a* **~ to** (*colloq*) sem o conhecimento de
unbelievable /ʌnbɪ'lɪ:vəbl/ *a* inacreditável, incrível
unbend /ʌn'bend/ *vi* (*pt* **unbent**) (*relax*) descontrair. **~ing** *a* inflexível
unbiased /ʌn'baɪəst/ *a* imparcial
unblock /ʌn'blɒk/ *vt* desbloquear, desobstruir; (*pipe*) desentupir
unborn /'ʌnbɔ:n/ *a* por nascer; (*future*) vindouro, futuro
unbounded /ʌn'baʊndɪd/ *a* ilimitado
unbreakable /ʌn'breɪkəbl/ *a* inquebrável
unbridled /ʌn'braɪdld/ *a* desequilibrado, (*P*) desenfreado
unbroken /ʌn'brəʊkən/ *a* (*intact*) intato, (*P*) intacto, inteiro; (*continuous*) ininterrupto
unburden /ʌn'bɜ:dn/ *vpr* **~ o.s.** (*open one's heart*) desabafar (to com)
unbutton /ʌn'bʌtn/ *vt* desabotoar
uncalled-for /ʌn'kɔ:ldfɔ:(r)/ *a* injustificável, gratuito
uncanny /ʌn'kænɪ/ *a* (-ier, -iest) estranho, misterioso
unceasing /ʌn'si:sɪŋ/ *a* incessante
unceremonious /ʌnserɪ'məʊnɪəs/ *a* sem cerimônia, (*P*) cerimónia, brusco
uncertain /ʌn'sɜ:tn/ *a* incerto. **be ~ whether** não saber ao certo se, estar indeciso quanto a. **~ty** *n* incerteza *f*
unchang|ed /ʌn'tʃeɪndʒd/ *a* inalterado, sem modificação. **~ing** *a* inalterável, imutável
uncivilized /ʌn'sɪvɪlaɪzd/ *a* não civilizado, bárbaro
uncle /'ʌŋkl/ *n* tio *m*
uncomfortable /ʌn'kʌmfətəbl/ *a* (*thing*) desconfortável, incômodo, (*P*) incómodo; (*unpleasant*) desagradável. **feel** *or* **be ~** (*uneasy*) sentir-se *or* estar pouco à vontade
uncommon /ʌn'kɒmən/ *a* pouco vulgar, invulgar, fora do comum. **~ly** *adv* invulgarmente, excepcionalmente
uncompromising /ʌn'kɒmprəmaɪzɪŋ/ *a* intransigente
unconcerned /ʌnkən'sɜ:nd/ *a* (*indifferent*) indiferente (by a)
unconditional /ʌnkən'dɪʃənl/ *a* incondicional
unconscious /ʌn'kɒnʃəs/ *a* inconsciente (of de). **~ly** *adv* inconscientemente. **~ness** *n* inconsciência *f*
unconventional /ʌnkən'venʃənl/ *a* não convencional, fora do comum
uncooperative /ʌnkəʊ'ɒpərətɪv/ *a*

(*person*) pouco cooperativo, do contra (*colloq*)
uncork /ʌn'kɔ:k/ *vt* desarolhar, tirar a rolha de
uncouth /ʌn'ku:θ/ *a* rude, grosseiro
uncover /ʌn'kʌvə(r)/ *vt* descobrir, revelar
unctuous /'ʌŋktʃʊəs/ *a* untuoso, gorduroso; (*fig*) melífluo
undecided /ʌndɪ'saɪdɪd/ *a* (*irresolute*) indeciso; (*not settled*) por decidir, pendente
undeniable /ʌndɪ'naɪəbl/ *a* inegável, incontestável
under /'ʌndə(r)/ *prep* debaixo de, sob; (*less than*) com menos de; (*according to*) conforme, segundo □ *adv* por baixo, debaixo. ~ age menor de idade. ~ way em preparo
under- /'ʌndə(r)/ *pref* sub-
undercarriage /'ʌndəkærɪdʒ/ *n* (*aviat*) trem *m* de aterrissagem, (*P*) trem *m* de aterragem
underclothes /'ʌndəkləʊðz/ *npl see* underwear
undercoat /'ʌndəkəʊt/ *n* (*of paint*) primeira mão *f*, (*P*) primeira demão *f*
undercover /ʌndə'kʌvə(r)/ *a* (*agent, operation*) secreto
undercurrent /'ʌndəkʌrənt/ *n* corrente *f* subterrânea; (*fig*) filão *m* (*fig*), tendência *f* oculta
undercut /ʌndə'kʌt/ *vt* (*pt* **undercut**, *pres p* **undercutting**) (*comm*) vender a preços mais baixos que
underdeveloped /ʌndədɪ'veləpt/ *a* atrofiado; (*country*) subdesenvolvido
underdog /ʌndə'dɒg/ *n* desprotegido *m*, o mais fraco (*colloq*)
underdone /'ʌndədʌn/ *a* (*of meat*) mal passado
underestimate /ʌndə'restɪmeɪt/ *vt* subestimar, não dar o devido valor a
underfed /ʌndə'fed/ *a* subalimentado, subnutrido
underfoot /ʌndə'fʊt/ *adv* debaixo dos pés; (*on the ground*) no chão
undergo /ʌndə'gəʊ/ *vt* (*pt* **-went**, *pp* **-gone**) (*be subjected to*) sofrer; (*treatment*) ser submetido a
undergraduate /ʌndə'grædʒʊət/ *n* estudante *mf* universitário
underground[1] /ʌndə'graʊnd/ *adv* debaixo da terra; (*fig: secretly*) clandestinamente
underground[2] /'ʌndəgraʊnd/ *a* subterrâneo; (*fig: secret*) clandestino □ *n* (*rail*) metro(politano) *m*
undergrowth /'ʌndəgrəʊθ/ *n* mato *m*
underhand /'ʌndəhænd/ *a* (*deceitful*) sonso, dissimulado
under|lie /ʌndə'laɪ/ *vt* (*pt* **-lay**, *pp* **-lain**, *pres p* **-lying**) estar por baixo de. **~lying** *a* subjacente
underline /ʌndə'laɪn/ *vt* sublinhar
undermine /ʌndə'maɪn/ *vt* minar, solapar
underneath /ʌndə'ni:θ/ *prep* sob, debaixo de, por baixo de □ *adv* abaixo, em baixo, por baixo
underpaid /ʌndə'peɪd/ *a* mal pago
underpants /'ʌndəpænts/ *npl* (*man's*) cuecas *fpl*
underpass /'ʌndəpa:s/ *n* (*for cars, people*) passagem *f* inferior
underprivileged /ʌndə'prɪvɪlɪdʒd/ *a* desfavorecido
underrate /ʌndə'reɪt/ *vt* subestimar, depreciar
underside /'ʌndəsaɪd/ *n* lado *m* inferior, base *f*
underskirt /'ʌndəskɜ:t/ *n* anágua *f*
understand /ʌndə'stænd/ *vt/i* (*pt* **-stood**) compreender, entender. **~able** *a* compreensível. **~ing** *a* compreensivo □ *n* compreensão *f*; (*agreement*) acordo *m*, entendimento *m*
understatement /'ʌndəsteɪtmənt/ *n* versão *f* atenuada da verdade, litotes *f*
understudy /'ʌndəstʌdɪ/ *n* substituto *m*
undertak|e /ʌndə'teɪk/ *vt* (*pt* **-took**, *pp* **-taken**) empreender; (*responsibility*) assumir. **~e to** encarregar-se de. **~ing** *n* (*task*) empreendimento *m*; (*promise*) compromisso *m*
undertaker /'ʌndəteɪkə(r)/ *n* agente *m* funerário, papa-defuntos *m* (*colloq*)
undertone /'ʌndətəʊn/ *n* **in an ~** a meia voz
undervalue /ʌndə'vælju:/ *vt* avaliar por baixo, subestimar
underwater /ʌndə'wɔ:tə(r)/ *a* submarino □ *adv* debaixo de água
underwear /'ʌndəweə(r)/ *n* roupa *f* interior *or* de baixo
underweight /'ʌndəweɪt/ *a* **be ~** estar com o peso abaixo do normal, ter peso a menos
underwent /ʌndə'went/ *see* **undergo**
underworld /'ʌndəwɜ:ld/ *n* (*of crime*) submundo *m*, bas-fonds *mpl*
underwriter /'ʌndəraɪtə(r)/ *n* segurador *m*; (*marine*) underwriter *m*
undeserved /ʌndɪ'zɜ:vd/ *a* imerecido, injusto
undesirable /ʌndɪ'zaɪərəbl/ *a* indesejável, inconveniente
undies /'ʌndɪz/ *npl* (*colloq*) roupa *f* de baixo *or* interior
undignified /ʌn'dɪgnɪfaɪd/ *a* pouco digno, sem dignidade
undisputed /ʌndɪ'spju:tɪd/ *a* incontestado
undo /ʌn'du:/ *vt* (*pt* **-did**, *pp* **-done** /dʌn/) desfazer; (*knot*) desfazer, desatar; (*coat, button*) abrir. **leave ~ne**

não fazer, deixar por fazer. ~**ing** *n* desgraça *f*, ruína *f*
undoubted /ʌn'daʊtɪd/ *a* indubitável. ~**ly** *adv* indubitavelmente
undress /ʌn'dres/ *vt/i* despir(-se). get ~ed despir-se
undu|e /ʌn'dju:/ *a* excessivo, indevido. ~**ly** *adv* excessivamente, indevidamente
undulate /'ʌndjʊleɪt/ *vi* ondular
undying /ʌn'daɪɪŋ/ *a* eterno, perene
unearth /ʌn'ɜ:θ/ *vt* desenterrar; (*fig*) descobrir
unearthly /ʌn'ɜ:θlɪ/ *a* sobrenatural, misterioso. ~ **hour** (*colloq*) hora *f* absurda *or* inconveniente
uneasy /ʌn'i:zɪ/ *a* (*ill at ease*) pouco à vontade; (*worried*) preocupado
uneconomic /ʌni:kə'nɒmɪk/ *a* antieconômico. ~**al** *a* antiecoñomico
uneducated /ʌn'edʒʊkeɪtɪd/ *a* (*person*) inculto, sem instrução
unemploy|ed /ʌnɪm'plɔɪd/ *a* desempregado. ~**ment** *n* desemprego *m*. ~**ment benefit** auxílio-desemprego *m*
unending /ʌn'endɪŋ/ *a* interminável, sem fim
unequal /ʌn'i:kwəl/ *a* desigual. ~**led** *a* sem igual, inigualável
unequivocal /ʌnɪ'kwɪvəkl/ *a* inequívoco, claro
uneven /ʌn'i:vn/ *a* desigual, irregular
unexpected /ʌnɪk'spektɪd/ *a* inesperado. ~**ly** *a* inesperadamente
unfair /ʌn'feə(r)/ *a* injusto (to com). ~**ness** *n* injustiça *f*
unfaithful /ʌn'feɪθfl/ *a* infiel
unfamiliar /ʌnfə'mɪlɪə(r)/ *a* estranho, desconhecido. **be** ~ **with** desconhecer, não conhecer, não estar familiarizado com
unfashionable /ʌn'fæʃənəbl/ *a* fora de moda
unfasten /ʌn'fa:sn/ *vt* (*knot*) desatar, soltar; (*button*) abrir
unfavourable /ʌn'feɪvərəbl/ *a* desfavorável
unfeeling /ʌn'fi:lɪŋ/ *a* insensível
unfinished /ʌn'fɪnɪʃt/ *a* incompleto, inacabado
unfit /ʌn'fɪt/ *a* sem preparo físico, fora de forma; (*unsuitable*) impróprio (for para)
unfold /ʌn'fəʊld/ *vt* desdobrar; (*expose*) expor, revelar □ *vi* desenrolar-se
unforeseen /ʌnfɔ:'si:n/ *a* imprevisto, inesperado
unforgettable /ʌnfə'getəbl/ *a* inesquecível
unforgivable /ʌnfə'gɪvəbl/ *a* imperdoável, indesculpável
unfortunate /ʌn'fɔ:tʃənət/ *a* (*unlucky*) infeliz; (*regrettable*) lamentável. it was very ~ that foi uma pena que ~**ly** *adv* infelizmente
unfounded /ʌn'faʊndɪd/ *a* (*rumour etc*) infundado, sem fundamento
unfriendly /ʌn'frendlɪ/ *a* pouco amável, antipático, frio
unfurnished /ʌn'fɜ:nɪʃt/ *a* sem mobília
ungainly /ʌn'geɪnlɪ/ *a* desajeitado, desgracioso
ungodly /ʌn'gɒdlɪ/ *a* ímpio. ~ **hour** (*colloq*) hora *f* absurda, às altas horas (*colloq*)
ungrateful /ʌn'greɪtfl/ *a* ingrato
unhapp|y /ʌn'hæpɪ/ *a* (-ier, -iest) infeliz, triste; (*not pleased*) descontente, pouco contente (with com). ~**ily** *adv* infelizmente. ~**iness** *n* infelicidade *f*, tristeza *f*
unharmed /ʌn'ha:md/ *a* incólume, são e salvo, ileso
unhealthy /ʌn'helθɪ/ *a* (-ier, -iest) (*climate etc*) doentio, insalubre; (*person*) adoentado, com pouca saúde
unheard-of /ʌn'hɜ:dɒv/ *a* inaudito, sem precedentes
unhinge /ʌn'hɪndʒ/ *vt* (*person, mind*) desequilibrar
unholy /ʌn'həʊlɪ/ *a* (-ier, -iest) (*person, act etc*) ímpio; (*colloq: great*) incrível, espantoso
unhook /ʌn'hʊk/ *vt* desenganchar; (*dress*) desapertar
unhoped /ʌn'həʊpt/ *a* ~ **for** inesperado
unhurt /ʌn'hɜ:t/ *a* ileso, incólume
unicorn /'ju:nɪkɔ:n/ *n* unicórnio *m*
uniform /'ju:nɪfɔ:m/ *n* uniforme *m* □ *a* uniforme, sempre igual. ~**ity** /'fɔ:mətɪ/ *n* uniformidade *f*. ~**ly** *adv* uniformemente
unif|y /'ju:nɪfaɪ/ *vt* unificar. ~**ication** /-ɪ'keɪʃn/ *n* unificação *f*
unilateral /ju:nɪ'lætrəl/ *a* unilateral
unimaginable /ʌnɪ'mædʒɪnəbl/ *a* inimaginável
unimportant /ʌnɪm'pɔ:tnt/ *a* sem importância, insignificante
uninhabited /ʌnɪn'hæbɪtɪd/ *a* desabitado
unintentional /ʌnɪn'tenʃənl/ *a* involuntário, não propositado
uninterest|ed /ʌn'ɪntrəstɪd/ *a* desinteressado (in em), indiferente (in a). ~**ing** *a* desinteressante, sem interesse
union /'ju:nɪən/ *n* união *f*; (*trade union*) sindicato *m*. ~**ist** *n* sindicalista *mf*; (*pol*) unionista *mf*. **U**~ **Jack** bandeira *f* britânica
unique /ju:'ni:k/ *a* único, sem igual
unisex /'ju:nɪseks/ *a* unisexo
unison /'ju:nɪsn/ *n* **in** ~ em uníssono

unit /'ju:nɪt/ *n* unidade *f*; (*of furniture*) peça *f*, unidade *f*, (*P*) módulo *m*
unite /ju:'naɪt/ *vt/i* unir(-se). **U~d Kingdom** *n* Reino *m* Unido. **U~d Nations (Organization)** *n* Organização *f* das Nações Unidas. **U~ States (of America)** Estados *mpl* Unidos (da América)
unity /'ju:nətɪ/ *n* unidade *f*; (*fig: harmony*) união *f*
universal /ju:nɪ'vɜ:sl/ *a* universal
universe /'ju:nɪvɜ:s/ *n* universo *m*
university /ju:nɪ'vɜ:sətɪ/ *n* universidade *f* □ *a* universitário; (*student, teacher*) universitário, da universidade
unjust /ʌn'dʒʌst/ *a* injusto
unkempt /ʌn'kempt/ *a* desmazelado, desleixado; (*of hair*) despenteado, desgrenhado
unkind /ʌn'kaɪnd/ *a* desagradável, duro. **~ly** *adv* mal
unknowingly /ʌn'nəʊɪŋlɪ/ *adv* sem saber, inconscientemente
unknown /ʌn'nəʊn/ *a* desconhecido □ *n* the ~ o desconhecido
unleaded /ʌn'ledɪd/ *a* sem chumbo
unless /ʌn'les/ *conj* a não ser que, a menos que, salvo se, se não
unlike /ʌn'laɪk/ *a* diferente □ *prep* ao contrário de
unlikely /ʌn'laɪklɪ/ *a* improvável
unlimited /ʌn'lɪmɪtɪd/ *a* ilimitado
unload /ʌn'ləʊd/ *vt* descarregar
unlock /ʌn'lɒk/ *vt* abrir (com chave)
unluck|y /ʌn'lʌkɪ/ *a* (-ier, -iest) infeliz, sem sorte; (*number*) que dá azar. be **~y** ter pouca sorte. **~ily** *adv* infelizmente
unmarried /ʌn'mærɪd/ *a* solteiro, celibatário
unmask /ʌn'ma:sk/ *vt* desmascarar
unmistakable /ʌnmɪs'teɪkəbl/ *a* (*voice etc*) inconfundível; (*clear*) claro, inequívoco
unmitigated /ʌn'mɪtɪgeɪtɪd/ *a* (*absolute*) completo, absoluto
unmoved /ʌn'mu:vd/ *a* impassível; (*indifferent*) indiferente (by a), insensível (by a)
unnatural /ʌn'nætʃrəl/ *a* que não é natural; (*wicked*) desnaturado
unnecessary /ʌn'nesəserɪ/ *a* desnecessário; (*superfluous*) supérfluo, dispensável
unnerve /ʌn'nɜ:v/ *vt* desencorajar, desmoralizar, intimidar
unnoticed /ʌn'nəʊtɪst/ *a* go ~ passar despercebido
unobtrusive /ʌnəb'tru:sɪv/ *a* discreto
unofficial /ʌnə'fɪʃl/ *a* oficioso, que não é oficial; (*strike*) ilegal, inautorizado
unorthodox /ʌn'ɔ:θədɒks/ *a* pouco ortodoxo, não ortodoxo
unpack /ʌn'pæk/ *vt* (*suitcase etc*) desfazer; (*contents*) desembalar, desempacotar □ *vi* desfazer a mala
unpaid /ʌn'peɪd/ *a* não remunerado; (*bill*) a pagar
unpalatable /ʌn'pælətəbl/ *a* (*food, fact etc*) desagradável, intragável
unparalleled /ʌn'pærəleld/ *a* sem paralelo, incomparável
unpleasant /ʌn'pleznt/ *a* desagradável (to com); (*person*) antipático
unplug /ʌn'plʌg/ *vt* (*pt* -plugged) (*electr*) desligar a tomada, (*P*) tirar a ficha da tomada
unpopular /ʌn'pɒpjʊlə(r)/ *a* impopular
unprecedented /ʌn'presɪdentɪd/ *a* sem precedentes, inaudito, nunca visto
unpredictable /ʌnprə'dɪktəbl/ *a* imprevisível
unprepared /ʌnprɪ'peəd/ *a* sem preparação, improvisado; (*person*) desprevenido
unpretentious /ʌnprɪ'tenʃəs/ *a* despretencioso, sem pretensões
unprincipled /ʌn'prɪnsəpld/ *a* sem princípios, sem escrúpulos
unprofessional /ʌnprə'feʃənl/ *a* (*work*) de amador; (*conduct*) sem consciência profissional
unprofitable /ʌn'prɒfɪtəbl/ *a* não lucrativo
unqualified /ʌn'kwɒlɪfaɪd/ *a* sem habilitações; (*success etc*) total, absoluto. be ~ to não estar habilitado para
unquestionable /ʌn'kwestʃənəbl/ *a* incontestável, indiscutível
unravel /ʌn'rævl/ *vt* (*pt* **unravelled**) desenredar, desemaranhar; (*knitting*) desmanchar
unreal /ʌn'rɪəl/ *a* irreal
unreasonable /ʌn'ri:znəbl/ *a* pouco razoável, disparatado; (*excessive*) excessivo
unrecognizable /ʌn'rekəgnaɪzəbl/ *a* irreconhecível
unrelated /ʌnrɪ'leɪtɪd/ *a* (*facts*) desconexo, sem relação (to com); (*people*) não aparentado (to com)
unreliable /ʌnrɪ'laɪəbl/ *a* que não é de confiança
unremitting /ʌnrɪ'mɪtɪŋ/ *a* incessante, infatigável
unreservedly /ʌnrɪ'zɜ:vɪdlɪ/ *adv* sem reservas
unrest /ʌn'rest/ *n* agitação *f*, distúrbios *mpl*
unrivalled /ʌn'raɪvld/ *a* sem igual, incomparável
unroll /ʌn'rəʊl/ *vt* desenrolar
unruffled /ʌn'rʌfld/ *a* calmo, tranqüilo, imperturbável
unruly /ʌn'ru:lɪ/ *a* indisciplinado, turbulento

unsafe /ʌn'seɪf/ *a* (*dangerous*) que não é seguro, perigoso; (*person*) em perigo
unsaid /ʌn'sed/ *a* **leave ~** não mencionar, não dizer, deixar algo por dizer
unsatisfactory /ʌnsætɪs'fæktərɪ/ *a* insatisfatório, pouco satisfatório
unsavoury /ʌn'seɪvərɪ/ *a* desagradável, repugnante
unscathed /ʌn'skeɪðd/ *a* ileso, incólume
unscrew /ʌn'skru:/ *vt* desenroscar, desparafusar
unscrupulous /ʌn'skru:pjʊləs/ *a* sem escrúpulos, pouco escrupuloso, sem consciência
unseemly /ʌn'si:mlɪ/ *a* inconveniente, indecoroso, impróprio
unsettle /ʌn'setl/ *vt* perturbar, agitar. **~d** *a* perturbado; (*weather*) instável, variável; (*bill*) não saldado
unshakeable /ʌn'ʃeɪkəbl/ *a* (*person, belief etc*) inabalável
unshaven /ʌn'ʃeɪvn/ *a* com a barba por fazer, por barbear
unsightly /ʌn'saɪtlɪ/ *a* feio
unskilled /ʌn'skɪld/ *a* inexperiente; (*work, worker*) não especializado; (*labour*) mão-de-obra *f* não especializada
unsociable /ʌn'səʊʃəbl/ *a* insociável, misantropo
unsophisticated /ʌnsə'fɪstɪkeɪtɪd/ *a* insofisticado, simples
unsound /ʌn'saʊnd/ *a* pouco sólido. **of ~ mind** (*jur*) não estar em plena posse das suas faculdades mentais (*jur*)
unspeakable /ʌn'spi:kəbl/ *a* indescritível; (*bad*) inqualificável
unspecified /ʌn'spesɪfaɪd/ *a* não especificado, indeterminado
unstable /ʌn'steɪbl/ *a* instável
unsteady /ʌn'stedɪ/ *a* (*step*) vacilante, incerto; (*ladder*) instável; (*hand*) pouco firme
unstuck /ʌn'stʌk/ *a* (*not stuck*) descolado. **come ~** (*colloq: fail*) falhar
unsuccessful /ʌnsək'sesfl/ *a* (*candidate*) mal sucedido; (*attempt*) malogrado, fracassado. **be ~** não ter êxito. **~ly** *adv* em vão
unsuit|able /ʌn's(j)u:təbl/ *a* impróprio, pouco apropriado, inadequado (for para). **~ed** *a* inadequado (to para)
unsure /ʌn'ʃʊə(r)/ *a* incerto
unsuspecting /ʌnsə'spektɪŋ/ *a* sem desconfiar de nada, insuspeitado
untangle /ʌn'tæŋgl/ *vt* desemaranhar, desenredar
unthinkable /ʌn'θɪŋkəbl/ *a* impensável, inconcebível
untid|y /ʌn'taɪdɪ/ *a* (-ier, -iest) (*room, desk etc*) desarrumado; (*appearance*) desleixado, desmazelado; (*hair*) despenteado. **~ily** *adv* sem cuidado. **~iness** *n* desordem *f*; (*of appearance*) desmazelo *m*
untie /ʌn'taɪ/ *vt* (*knot, parcel*) desatar, desfazer; (*person*) desamarrar
until /ən'tɪl/ *prep* até. **not ~** não antes de □ *conj* até que
untimely /ʌn'taɪmlɪ/ *a* inoportuno, intempestivo; (*death*) prematuro
untold /ʌn'təʊld/ *a* incalculável
untoward /ʌntə'wɔ:d/ *a* inconveniente, desagradável
untrue /ʌn'tru:/ *a* falso
unused[1] /ʌn'ju:zd/ *a* (*new*) novo, por usar; (*not in use*) não utilizado
unused[2] /ʌn'ju:st/ *a* **~ to** não habituado a, não acostumado a
unusual /ʌn'ju:ʒʊəl/ *a* insólito, fora do comum. **~ly** *adv* excepcionalmente
unveil /ʌn'veɪl/ *vt* descobrir; (*statue, portrait etc*) desvelar
unwanted /ʌn'wɒntɪd/ *a* (*useless*) que já não serve; (*child*) indesejado
unwarranted /ʌn'wɒrəntɪd/ *a* injustificado
unwelcome /ʌn'welkəm/ *a* desagradável; (*guest*) indesejável
unwell /ʌn'wel/ *a* indisposto
unwieldy /ʌn'wi:ldɪ/ *a* difícil de manejar, pouco jeitoso
unwilling /ʌn'wɪlɪŋ/ *a* relutante (to em), pouco disposto (to a)
unwind /ʌn'waɪnd/ *vt/i* (*pt* **unwound** /ʌn'waʊnd/) desenrolar(-se); (*colloq: relax*) descontrair(-se)
unwise /ʌn'waɪz/ *a* imprudente, insensato
unwittingly /ʌn'wɪtɪŋlɪ/ *adv* sem querer
unworthy /ʌn'wɜ:ðɪ/ *a* indigno
unwrap /ʌn'ræp/ *vt* (*pt* **unwrapped**) desembrulhar, abrir, desfazer
unwritten /ʌn'rɪtn/ *a* (*agreement*) verbal, tácito
up /ʌp/ *adv* (*to higher place*) cima, para cima, para o alto; (*in higher place*) em cima, no alto; (*out of bed*) acordado, de pé; (*up and dressed*) pronto; (*finished*) acabado; (*sun*) alto □ *prep* no cimo de, em cima de, no alto de. **~ the street/river/*etc*** pela rua/pelo rio/*etc* acima □ *vt* (*pt* **upped**) (*increase*) aumentar. **be ~ against** defrontar, enfrentar. **be ~ in** (*colloq*) saber. **be ~ to** (*do*) estar fazendo; (*plot*) estar tramando; (*task*) estar à altura de. **feel ~ to doing** (*able*) sentir-se capaz de fazer. **it is ~ to you** depende de você. **come** *or* **go ~** subir. **have ~s and downs** (*fig*) ter (os

seus) altos e baixos. **walk ~ and down** andar dum lado para o outro *or* para a frente e para trás. **~-and-coming** *a* prometedor. **~-market** *a* requintado, fino

upbringing /'ʌpbrɪŋɪŋ/ *n* educação *f*

update /ʌp'deɪt/ *vt* atualizar, (*P*) actualizar

upheaval /ʌp'hi:vl/ *n* pandemônio *m*, (*P*) pandemónio *m*, revolução *f* (*fig*); (*social, political*) convulsão *f*

uphill /'ʌphɪl/ *a* ladeira acima, ascendente; (*fig: difficult*) árduo □ *adv* /ʌp'hɪl/ go ~ subir

uphold /ʌp'həʊld/ *vt* (*pt* **upheld**) sustentar, manter, apoiar

upholster /ʌp'həʊlstə(r)/ *vt* estofar. **~y** *n* estofados *mpl*, (*P*) estofo(s) *m* (*pl*)

upkeep /'ʌpki:p/ *n* manutenção *f*

upon /ə'pɒn/ *prep* sobre

upper /'ʌpə(r)/ *a* superior □ *n* (*of shoe*) gáspea *f*. **have the ~ hand** estar por cima, estar em posição de superioridade. **~ class** aristocracia *f*. **~most** *a* (*highest*) o mais alto, superior

upright /'ʌpraɪt/ *a* vertical; (*honourable*) honesto, honrado, (*P*) recto

uprising /'ʌpraɪzɪŋ/ *n* insurreição *f*, sublevação *f*, levantamento *m*

uproar /'ʌprɔ:(r)/ *n* tumulto *m*, alvoroço *m*

uproot /ʌp'ru:t/ *vt* desenraizar; (*fig*) erradicar, desarraigar

upset[1] /ʌp'set/ *vt* (*pt* **upset**, *pres p* **upsetting**) (*overturn*) entornar, virar; (*plan*) contrariar, transtornar; (*stomach*) desarranjar; (*person*) contrariar, transtornar, incomodar □ *a* aborrecido

upset[2] /'ʌpset/ *n* transtorno *m*; (*of stomach*) indisposição *f*; (*distress*) choque *m*

upshot /'ʌpʃɒt/ *n* resultado *m*

upside-down /ʌpsaɪd'daʊn/ *adv* (*lit & fig*) ao contrário, de pernas para o ar

upstairs /ʌp'steəz/ *adv* (*at/to*) em/para cima, no/para o andar de cima □ *a* /'ʌpsteəz/ (*flat etc*) de cima, do andar de cima

upstart /'ʌpsta:t/ *n* arrivista *mf*

upstream /ʌp'stri:m/ *adv* rio acima, contra a corrente

upsurge /'ʌpsɜ:dʒ/ *n* recrudescência *f*, recrudescimento *m*; (*of anger*) acesso *m*, ataque *m*

uptake /'ʌpteɪk/ *n* **be quick on the ~** pegar rapidamente as coisas; (*fig*) ser de compreensão rápida, ser vivo

up-to-date /'ʌptədeɪt/ *a* moderno, atualizado, (*P*) actualizado

upturn /'ʌptɜ:n/ *n* melhoria *f*

upward /'ʌpwəd/ *a* ascendente, voltado para cima. **~s** *adv* para cima

uranium /jʊ'reɪnɪəm/ *n* urânio *m*

urban /'ɜ:bən/ *a* urbano

urbane /ɜ:'beɪn/ *a* delicado, cortês, urbano

urge /ɜ:dʒ/ *vt* aconselhar vivamente (**to a**) □ *n* (*strong desire*) grande vontade *f*. **~ on** (*impel*) incitar

urgen|t /'ɜ:dʒənt/ *a* urgente. **be ~t** urgir. **~cy** *n* urgência *f*

urinal /jʊə'raɪnl/ *n* urinol *m*

urin|e /'jʊərɪn/ *n* urina *f*. **~ate** *vi* urinar

urn /ɜ:n/ *n* urna *f*; (*for tea, coffee*) espécie *f* de samovar

us /ʌs/; *unstressed* /əs/ *pron* nos; (*after preps*) nós. **with ~** conosco. **he knows ~** ele nos conhece

US *abbr* **United States**

USA *abbr* **United States of America**

usable /'ju:zəbl/ *a* utilizável

usage /'ju:zɪdʒ/ *n* uso *m*

use[1] /ju:z/ *vt* usar, utilizar, servir-se de; (*exploit*) servir-se de; (*consume*) gastar, usar, consumir. **~ up** esgotar, consumir. **~r** /-ə(r)/ *n* usuário *m*, (*P*) utente *mf*. **~r-friendly** *a* fácil de usar

use[2] /ju:s/ *n* uso *m*, emprego *m*. **in ~** em uso. **it is no ~ shouting/*etc*** não serve de nada *or* não adianta gritar/*etc*. **make ~ of** servir-se de. **of ~** útil

used[1] /ju:zd/ *a* (*second-hand*) usado

used[2] /ju:st/ *pt* **he ~ to** ele costumava, ele tinha por costume *or* hábito □ *a* **~ to** acostumado a, habituado a

use|ful /'ju:sfl/ *a* útil. **~less** *a* inútil; (*person*) incompetente

usher /'ʌʃə(r)/ *n* vagalume *m*, (*P*) arrumador *m* □ *vt* **~ in** mandar entrar. **~ette** *n* vagalume *m*, (*P*) arrumadora *f*

usual /'ju:ʒʊəl/ *a* usual, habitual, normal. **as ~** como de costume, como habitualmente. **at the ~ time** na hora de costume, (*P*) à(s) hora(s) de costume. **~ly** *adv* habitualmente, normalmente

USSR *abbr* URSS

usurp /ju:'zɜ:p/ *vt* usurpar

utensil /ju:'tensl/ *n* utensílio *m*

uterus /'ju:tərəs/ *n* útero *m*

utilitarian /ju:tɪlɪ'teərɪən/ *a* utilitário

utility /ju:'tɪlətɪ/ *n* utilidade *f*. (**public**) **~** serviço *m* público. **~ room** área *f* de serviço (para as máquinas de lavar a roupa e a louça)

utilize /'ju:tɪlaɪz/ *vt* utilizar

utmost /'ʌtməʊst/ *a* (*furthest, most intense*) extremo. **the ~ care/*etc*** (*greatest*) o maior cuidado/*etc* □ *n* **do one's ~** fazer todo o possível

utter[1] /'ʌtə(r)/ *a* completo, absoluto. **~ly** *adv* completamente
utter[2] /'ʌtə(r)/ *vt* proferir; (*sigh, shout*) dar. **~ance** *n* expressão *f*
U-turn /'ju:tɜ:n/ *n* retorno *m*

V

vacan|t /'veɪkənt/ *a* (*post, room, look*) vago; (*mind*) vazio; (*seat, space, time*) desocupado, livre. **~cy** *n* (*post*) vaga *f*; (*room in hotel*) vago *m*
vacate /və'keɪt/ *vt* vagar, deixar vago
vacation /və'keɪʃn/ *n* férias *fpl*
vaccinat|e /'væksɪneɪt/ *vt* vacinar. **~ion** /-'neɪʃn/ *n* vacinação *f*
vaccine /'væksi:n/ *n* vacina *f*
vacuum /'vækjʊəm/ *n* (*pl* **-cuums** *or* **-cua**) vácuo *m*, vazio *m*. **~ flask** garrafa *f* térmica, (*P*) termo(s) *m*. **~ cleaner** aspirador *m* de pó
vagina /və'dʒaɪnə/ *n* vagina *f*
vagrant /'veɪgrənt/ *n* vadio *m*, vagabundo *m*
vague /veɪg/ *a* (-er, -est) vago; (*outline*) impreciso. **be ~ about** ser vago acerca de, não precisar. **~ly** *adv* vagamente
vain /veɪn/ *a* (-er, -est) (*conceited*) vaidoso; (*useless*) vão, inútil; (*fruitless*) infrutífero. **in ~** em vão. **~ly** *adv* em vão
valentine /'væləntaɪn/ *n* (*card*) cartão *m* do dia de São Valentin
valet /'vælɪt, 'væleɪ/ *n* (*manservant*) criado *m* de quarto; (*of hotel*) camareiro *m* □ *vt* (*car*) lavar e limpar o interior
valiant /'vælɪənt/ *a* corajoso, valente
valid /'vælɪd/ *a* válido. **~ity** /və'lɪdətɪ/ *n* validade *f*
validate /'vælɪdeɪt/ *vt* validar, confirmar, ratificar
valley /'vælɪ/ *n* vale *m*
valuable /'væljʊəbl/ *a* (*object*) valioso, de valor; (*help, time etc*) precioso. **~s** *npl* objetos *mpl*, (*P*) objectos *mpl* de valor
valuation /væljʊ'eɪʃn/ *n* avaliação *f*
value /'vælju:/ *n* valor *m* □ *vt* avaliar; (*cherish*) dar valor a. **~ added tax** imposto *m* de valor adicional, (*P*) acrescentado. **~r** /-ə(r)/ *n* avaliador *m*
valve /vælv/ *n* (*anat, techn, of car tyre*) válvula *f*; (*of bicycle tyre*) pipo *m*; (*of radio*) lâmpada *f*, válvula *f*
vampire /'væmpaɪə(r)/ *n* vampiro *m*
van /væn/ *n* (*large*) camião *m*; (*small*) camionete *f*, comercial *m*; (*milkman's, baker's etc*) camionete *f*; (*rail*) bagageiro *m*, (*P*) furgão *m*
vandal /'vændl/ *n* vândalo *m*. **~ism** /-əlɪzəm/ *n* vandalismo *m*
vandalize /'vændəlaɪz/ *vt* destruir, estragar
vanguard /'vænga:d/ *n* vanguarda *f*
vanilla /və'nɪlə/ *n* baunilha *f*
vanish /'vænɪʃ/ *vi* desaparecer, sumir-se, desvanecer-se
vanity /'vænətɪ/ *n* vaidade *f*. **~ case** bolsa *f* de maquilagem
vantage-point /'va:ntɪdʒpɔɪnt/ *n* (bom) ponto *m* de observação
vapour /'veɪpə(r)/ *n* vapor *m*; (*mist*) bruma *f*
vari|able /'veərɪəbl/ *a* variável. **~ation** /-'eɪʃn/ *n* variação *f*. **~ed** /-ɪd/ *a* variado
variance /'veərɪəns/ *n* **at ~** em desacordo (with com)
variant /'veərɪənt/ *a* diverso, diferente □ *n* variante *f*
varicose /'værɪkəʊs/ *a* **~ veins** varizes *fpl*
variety /və'raɪətɪ/ *n* variedade *f*; (*entertainment*) variedades *fpl*
various /'veərɪəs/ *a* vários, diversos, variados
varnish /'va:nɪʃ/ *n* verniz *m* □ *vt* envernizar; (*nails*) pintar
vary /'veərɪ/ *vt/i* variar. **~ing** *a* variado
vase /va:z/ *n* vaso *m*, jarra *f*
vast /va:st/ *a* vasto, imenso. **~ly** *adv* imensamente, infinitamente. **~ness** *n* vastidão *f*, imensidão *f*, imensidade *f*
vat /væt/ *n* tonel *m*, dorna *f*, cuba *f*
VAT /vi:eɪ'ti:, væt/ *abbr* ICM *m*, (*P*) IVA *m*
vault[1] /vɔ:lt/ *n* (*roof*) abóbada *f*; (*in bank*) casa-forte *f*; (*tomb*) cripta *f*; (*cellar*) adega *f*
vault[2] /vɔ:lt/ *vt/i* saltar □ *n* salto *m*
vaunt /vɔ:nt/ *vt/i* gabar(-se), ufanar (-se) (de), vangloriar(-se)
VD *abbr see* **venereal disease**
VDU *abbr see* **visual display unit**
veal /vi:l/ *n* (*meat*) vitela *f*
veer /vɪə(r)/ *vi* virar, mudar de direção, (*P*) direcção
vegan /'vi:gən/ *a & n* vegetariano (*m*) estrito
vegetable /'vedʒɪtəbl/ *n* hortaliça *f*, legume *m* □ *a* vegetal
vegetarian /vedʒɪ'teərɪən/ *a & n* vegetariano (*m*)
vegetate /'vedʒɪteɪt/ *vi* vegetar
vegetation /vedʒɪ'teɪʃn/ *n* vegetação *f*
vehement /'vi:əmənt/ *a* veemente. **~ly** *adv* veementemente
vehicle /'vi:ɪkl/ *n* veículo *m*
veil /veɪl/ *n* véu *m* □ *vt* velar, cobrir com véu; (*fig*) esconder, disfarçar
vein /veɪn/ *n* (*in body; mood*) veia *f*; (*in rock*) veio *m*, filão *m*; (*of leaf*) nervura *f*

velocity /vɪ'lɒsətɪ/ *n* velocidade *f*
velvet /'velvɪt/ *n* veludo *m*. ~**y** *a* aveludado
vendetta /ven'detə/ *n* vendeta *f*
vending-machine /'vendɪŋməʃi:n/ *n* vendedora *f* automática, (*P*) máquina *f* de distribuição
vendor /'vendə(r)/ *n* vendedor *m*. **street** ~ vendedor *m* ambulante
veneer /və'nɪə(r)/ *n* folheado *m*; (*fig*) fachada *f*, máscara *f*
venerable /'venərəbl/ *a* venerável
venereal /və'nɪərɪəl/ *a* venéreo. ~ **disease** doença *f* venérea
venetian /və'ni:ʃn/ *a* ~ **blinds** persiana *f*
Venezuela /venɪz'weɪlə/ *n* Venezuela *f*. ~**n** *a* & *n* venezuelano (*m*)
vengeance /'vendʒəns/ *n* vingança. **with a** ~ furiosamente, em excesso, com mais força do que se pretende
venison /'venɪzn/ *n* carne *f* de veado
venom /'venəm/ *n* veneno *m*. ~**ous** /'venəməs/ *a* venenoso
vent[1] /vent/ *n* (*in coat*) abertura *f*
vent[2] /vent/ *n* (*hole*) orifício *m*, abertura *f*; (*for air*) respiradouro *m* □ *vt* (*anger*) descarregar (on para cima de). **give** ~ **to** (*fig*) desabafar, dar vazão a
ventilat|e /'ventɪleɪt/ *vt* ventilar. ~**ion** /-'leɪʃn/ *n* ventilação *f*. ~**or** *n* ventilador *m*
ventriloquist /ven'trɪləkwɪst/ *n* ventríloquo *m*
venture /'ventʃə(r)/ *n* emprendimento *m* arriscado, aventura *f* □ *vt/i* arriscar(-se)
venue /'venju:/ *n* porto *m* de encontro
veranda /və'rændə/ *n* varanda *f*
verb /vɜ:b/ *n* verbo *m*
verbal /'vɜ:bl/ *a* verbal; (*literal*) literal
verbatim /vɜ:'beɪtɪm/ *adv* literalmente, palavra por palavra
verbose /vɜ:'bəʊs/ *a* palavroso, prolixo
verdict /'vɜ:dɪkt/ *n* veredicto *m*; (*opinion*) opinião *f*
verge /vɜ:dʒ/ *n* beira *f*, borda *f* □ *vi* ~ **on** estar à beira de. **on the** ~ **of doing** prestes a fazer
verify /'verɪfaɪ/ *vt* verificar
veritable /'verɪtəbl/ *a* autêntico, verdadeiro
vermicelli /vɜ:mɪ'selɪ/ *n* aletria *f*
vermin /'vɜ:mɪn/ *n* animais *mpl* nocivos; (*lice, fleas etc*) parasitas *mpl*
vermouth /'vɜ:məθ/ *n* vermute *m*
vernacular /və'nækjʊlə(r)/ *n* vernáculo *m*; (*dialect*) dialeto *m*, (*P*) dialecto *m*
versatil|e /'vɜ:sətaɪl/ *a* versátil; (*tool*) que serve para vários fins. ~**ity** /-'tɪlətɪ/ *n* versatilidade *f*
verse /vɜ:s/ *n* (*poetry*) verso *m*, poesia *f*; (*stanza*) estrofe *f*; (*of Bible*) versículo *m*
versed /vɜ:st/ *a* ~ **in** versado em, conhecedor de
version /'vɜ:ʃn/ *n* versão *f*
versus /'vɜ:səs/ *prep* contra
vertebra /'vɜ:tɪbrə/ *n* (*pl* -brae /-bri:/) vértebra *f*
vertical /'vɜ:tɪkl/ *a* vertical. ~**ly** *adv* verticalmente
vertigo /'vɜ:tɪgəʊ/ *n* vertigem *f*
verve /vɜ:v/ *n* verve *f*, vivacidade *f*
very /'verɪ/ *adv* muito □ *a* (*actual*) mesmo, próprio; (*exact*) preciso, exato, (*P*) exacto. **the** ~ **day**/*etc* o próprio *or* o mesmo dia/*etc*. **at the** ~ **end** mesmo *or* precisamente no fim. **the** ~ **first**/**best**/*etc* (*emph*) o primeiro/melhor/*etc* de todos. ~ **much** muito. ~ **well** muito bem
vessel /'vesl/ *n* vaso *m*
vest[1] /vest/ *n* corpete *m*, (*P*) camisola *f* interior; (*Amer: waistcoat*) colete *m*
vest[2] /vest/ *vt* conferir (in a). ~**ed interests** interesses *mpl*
vestige /'vestɪdʒ/ *n* vestígio *m*
vestry /'vestrɪ/ *n* sacristia *f*
vet /vet/ *n* (*colloq*) veterinário *m* □ *vt* (*pt* **vetted**) (*candidate etc*) examinar atentamente, estudar
veteran /'vetərən/ *n* veterano *m*. (**war**) ~ veterano *m* de guerra
veterinary /'vetərmərɪ/ *a* veterinário. ~ **surgeon** veterinário *m*
veto /'vi:təʊ/ *n* (*pl* -oes) veto *m*; (*right*) direito *m* de veto □ *vt* vetar, opor o veto a
vex /veks/ *vt* aborrecer, irritar, contrariar. ~**ed question** questão *f* muito debatida, assunto *m* controverso
via /'vaɪə/ *prep* por, via
viab|le /'vaɪəbl/ *a* viável. ~**ility** /-'bɪlətɪ/ *n* viabilidade *f*
viaduct /'vaɪədʌkt/ *n* viaduto *m*
vibrant /'vaɪbrənt/ *a* vibrante
vibrat|e /vaɪ'breɪt/ *vt/i* (fazer) vibrar. ~**ion** /-ʃn/ *n* vibração *f*
vicar /'vɪkə(r)/ *n* (*Anglican*) pastor *m*; (*Catholic*) vigário *m*, pároco *m*. ~**age** *n* presbitério *m*
vicarious /vɪ'keərɪəs/ *a* vivido indiretamente, (*P*) indirectamente
vice[1] /vaɪs/ *n* (*depravity*) vício *m*
vice[2] /vaɪs/ *n* (*techn*) torno *m*
vice- /vaɪs/ *pref* vice-. ~**-chairman** vice-presidente *m*. ~**-chancellor** *n* vice-chanceler *m*; (*univ*) reitor *m*. ~**-consul** *n* vice-cônsul *m*. ~**-president** *n* vice-presidente *mf*
vice versa /'vaɪsɪ'vɜ:sə/ *adv* vice-versa
vicinity /vɪ'sɪnətɪ/ *n* vizinhança *f*,

cercania(s) *fpl*, arredores *mpl*. **in the ~ of** nos arredores de

vicious /'vɪʃəs/ *a* (*spiteful*) mau, maldoso; (*violent*) brutal, feroz. **~ circle** círculo *m* vicioso. **~ly** *adv* maldosamente; (*violently*) brutalmente, ferozmente

victim /'vɪktɪm/ *n* vítima *f*

victimiz|e /'vɪktɪmaɪz/ *vt* perseguir. **~ation** /-'zeɪʃn/ *n* perseguição *f*

victor /'vɪktə(r)/ *n* vencedor *m*

victor|y /'vɪktərɪ/ *n* vitória *f*. **~ious** /-'tɔːrɪəs/ *a* vitorioso

video /'vɪdɪəʊ/ *a* vídeo □ *n* (*pl* -os) (*colloq*) vídeo □ *vt* (*record*) gravar em vídeo. **~ cassette** video-cassete *f*. **~ recorder** videocassete *m*

vie /vaɪ/ *vi* (*pres p* **vying**) rivalizar, competir (with com)

view /vjuː/ *n* vista *f* □ *vt* ver; (*examine*) examinar; (*consider*) considerar, ver; (*a house*) visitar, ver. **in my ~** a meu ver, na minha opinião. **in ~ of** em vista de. **on ~** em exposição, à mostra; (*open to the public*) aberto ao público. **with a ~ to** com a intenção de, com o fim de. **~er** *n* (*TV*) telespectador *m*; (*for slides*) visor *m*

viewfinder /'vjuːfaɪndə(r)/ *n* visor *m*

viewpoint /'vjuːpɔɪnt/ *n* ponto *m* de vista

vigil /'vɪdʒɪl/ *n* vigília *f*; (*over corpse*) velório *m*; (*relig*) vigília *f*

vigilan|t /'vɪdʒɪlənt/ *a* vigilante. **~ce** *n* vigilância *f*. **~te** /vɪdʒɪ'læntɪ/ *n* vigilante *m*

vig|our /'vɪgə(r)/ *n* vigor *m*. **~orous** /'vɪgərəs/ *a* vigoroso

vile /vaɪl/ *a* (*base*) infame, vil; (*colloq: bad*) horroroso, péssimo

vilify /'vɪlɪfaɪ/ *vt* difamar

villa /'vɪlə/ *n* vivenda *f*, vila *f*; (*country residence*) casa *f* de campo

village /'vɪlɪdʒ/ *n* aldeia *f*, povoado *m*. **~r** *n* aldeão *m*, aldeã *f*

villain /'vɪlən/ *n* patife *m*, mau-caráter *m*. **~y** *n* infâmia *f*, vilania *f*

vindicat|e /'vɪndɪkeɪt/ *vt* vindicar, justificar. **~ion** /-'keɪʃn/ *n* justificação *f*

vindictive /vɪn'dɪktɪv/ *a* vingativo

vine /vaɪn/ *n* (*plant*) vinha *f*

vinegar /'vɪnɪgə(r)/ *n* vinagre *m*

vineyard /'vɪnjəd/ *n* vinha *f*, vinhedo *m*

vintage /'vɪntɪdʒ/ *n* (*year*) ano *m* de colheita de qualidade excepcional □ *a* (*wine*) de colheita excepcional e de um determinado ano; (*car*) de museu (*colloq*), fabricado entre 1917 e 1930

vinyl /'vaɪnɪl/ *n* vinil *m*

viola /vɪ'əʊlə/ *n* (*mus*) viola *f*, violeta *f*

violat|e /'vaɪəleɪt/ *vt* violar. **~ion** /-'leɪʃn/ *n* violação *f*

violen|t /'vaɪələnt/ *a* violento. **~ce** *n* violência *f*. **~tly** *adv* violentamente, com violência

violet /'vaɪələt/ *n* (*bot*) violeta *f*; (*colour*) violeta *m* □ *a* violeta

violin /vaɪə'lɪn/ *n* violino *m*. **~ist** *n* violinista *mf*

VIP /viːaɪ'piː/ *abbr* (*very important person*) VIP *m*, personalidade *f* importante

viper /'vaɪpə(r)/ *n* víbora *f*

virgin /'vɜːdʒɪn/ *a* & *n* virgem (*f*); **~ity** /və'dʒɪnətɪ/ *n* virgindade *f*

Virgo /'vɜːgəʊ/ *n* (*astr*) Virgem *f*, (*P*) virgo *m*

viril|e /'vɪraɪl/ *a* viril, varonil. **~ity** /vɪ'rɪlətɪ/ *n* virilidade *f*

virtual /'vɜːtʃʊəl/ *a* que é na prática embora não em teoria, verdadeiro. **a ~ failure/*etc*** praticamente um fracasso/*etc*. **~ly** *adv* praticamente

virtue /'vɜːtʃuː/ *n* (*goodness, chastity*) virtude *f*; (*merit*) mérito *m*. **by** *or* **in ~ of** por *or* em virtude de

virtuos|o /vɜːtʃʊ'əʊsəʊ/ *n* (*pl* -si /-siː/) virtuoso *m*, virtuose *mf*. **~ity** /-'ɒsətɪ/ *n* virtuosidade *f*, virtuosismo *m*

virtuous /'vɜːtʃʊəs/ *a* virtuoso

virulen|t /'vɪrʊlənt/ *a* virulento. **~ce** /-ləns/ *n* virulência *f*

virus /'vaɪərəs/ *n* (*pl* -es) vírus *m*; (*colloq: disease*) virose *f*

visa /'viːzə/ *n* visto *m*

viscount /'vaɪkaʊnt/ *n* visconde *m*. **~ess** /-ɪs/ *n* viscondessa *f*

viscous /'vɪskəs/ *a* viscoso

vise /vaɪs/ *n* (*Amer: vice*) torno *m*

visib|le /'vɪzəbl/ *a* visível. **~ility** /-'bɪlətɪ/ *n* visibilidade *f*. **~ly** *adv* visivelmente

vision /'vɪʒn/ *n* (*dream, insight*) visão *f*; (*seeing, sight*) vista *f*, visão *f*

visionary /'vɪʒənərɪ/ *a* visionário; (*plan, scheme etc*) fantasista, quimérico □ *n* visionário *m*

visit /'vɪzɪt/ *vt* (*pt* **visited**) (*person*) visitar, fazer uma visita a; (*place*) visitar □ *vi* estar de visita □ *n* (*tour, call*) visita *f*; (*stay*) estada *f*, visita *f*. **~or** *n* visitante *mf*; (*guest*) visita *f*

visor /'vaɪzə(r)/ *n* viseira *f*; (*in vehicle*) visor *m*

vista /'vɪstə/ *n* vista *f*, panorama *m*

visual /'vɪʒʊəl/ *a* visual. **~ display unit** terminal *m* de vídeo. **~ly** *adv* visualmente

visualize /'vɪʒʊəlaɪz/ *vt* visualizar; (*foresee*) imaginar, prever

vital /'vaɪtl/ *a* vital. **~ statistics** estatísticas *fpl* demográficas; (*colloq: woman*) medidas *fpl*

vitality /vaɪ'tælətɪ/ *n* vitalidade *f*

vitamin /'vɪtəmɪn/ *n* vitamina *f*

vivac|ious /vɪ'veɪʃəs/ *a* cheio de vida,

vivo, animado. ~ity /-'væsətɪ/ *n* vivacidade *f*, animação *f*
vivid /'vɪvɪd/ *a* vívido; (*imagination*) vivo. ~ly *adv* vividamente
vivisection /vɪvɪ'sekʃn/ *n* vivissecção *f*
vixen /'vɪksn/ *n* raposa *f* fêmea
vocabulary /və'kæbjʊlərɪ/ *n* vocabulário *m*
vocal /'vəʊkl/ *a* vocal; (*fig: person*) eloqüente, (*P*) eloquente. ~ **cords** cordas *fpl* vocais. ~**ist** *n* vocalista *mf*
vocation /və'keɪʃn/ *n* vocação *f*; (*trade*) profissão *f*. ~**al** *a* vocacional, profissional
vociferous /və'sɪfərəs/ *a* vociferante
vodka /'vɒdkə/ *n* vodka *m*
vogue /vəʊg/ *n* voga *f*, moda *f*, popularidade *f*. **in** ~ em voga, na moda
voice /vɔɪs/ *n* voz *f* □ *vt* (*express*) exprimir
void /vɔɪd/ *a* vazio; (*jur*) nulo, sem validade □ *n* vácuo *m*, vazio *m*. **make** ~ anular, invalidar. ~ **of** sem, destituído de
volatile /'vɒlətaɪl/ *a* (*substance*) volátil; (*fig: changeable*) instável
volcan|o /vɒl'keɪnəʊ/ *n* (*pl* -oes) vulcão *m*. ~**ic** /-ænɪk/ *a* vulcânico
volition /və'lɪʃn/ *n* **of one's own** ~ de sua própria vontade
volley /'vɒlɪ/ *n* (*of blows etc*) saraivada *f*; (*of gunfire*) salva *f*; (*tennis*) voleio *m*. ~**ball** *n* voleibol *m*, vôlei *m*
volt /vəʊlt/ *n* volt *m*. ~**age** *n* voltagem *f*
voluble /'vɒljʊbl/ *a* falante, loquaz
volume /'vɒlju:m/ *n* (*book, sound*) volume *m*; (*capacity*) capacidade *f*
voluntar|y /'vɒləntərɪ/ *a* voluntário; (*unpaid*) não-remunerado. ~**ily** /-trəlɪ/ *adv* voluntariamente
volunteer /vɒlən'tɪə(r)/ *n* voluntário *m* □ *vi* oferecer-se (**to do** para fazer); (*mil*) alistar-se como voluntário □ *vt* oferecer espontaneamente
voluptuous /və'lʌptʃʊəs/ *a* voluptuoso, sensual
vomit /'vɒmɪt/ *vt/i* (*pt* **vomited**) vomitar □ *n* vômito *m*, (*P*) vómito *m*
voodoo /'vu:du:/ *n* vodu *m*
voraci|ous /və'reɪʃəs/ *a* voraz. ~**ously** *adv* vorazmente. ~**ty** /və'ræsətɪ/ *n* voracidade *f*
vot|e /vəʊt/ *n* voto *m*; (*right*) direito *m* de voto □ *vt/i* votar. ~**er** *n* eleitor *m*. ~**ing** *n* votação *f*; (*poll*) escrutínio *m*
vouch /vaʊtʃ/ *vi* ~ **for** responder por, garantir
voucher /'vaʊtʃə(r)/ *n* (*for meal, transport*) vale *m*; (*receipt*) comprovante *m*
vow /vaʊ/ *n* voto *m* □ *vt* (*loyalty etc*) jurar (**to** a). ~ **to do** jurar fazer
vowel /'vaʊəl/ *n* vogal *f*
voyage /'vɔɪɪdʒ/ *n* viagem (por mar) *f*. ~**r** /-ə(r)/ *n* viajante *m*
vulgar /'vʌlgə(r)/ *a* ordinário, grosseiro; (*in common use*) vulgar. ~**ity** /-'gærətɪ/ *n* (*behaviour*) grosseria *f*, vulgaridade *f*
vulnerab|le /'vʌlnərəbl/ *a* vulnerável. ~**ility** /-'bɪlətɪ/ *n* vulnerabilidade *f*
vulture /'vʌltʃə(r)/ *n* abutre *m*, urubu *m*
vying /'vaɪɪŋ/ *see* vie

W

wad /wɒd/ *n* bucha *f*, tampão *m*; (*bundle*) maço *m*, rolo *m*
wadding /'wɒdɪŋ/ *n* enchimento *m*
waddle /'wɒdl/ *vi* bambolear-se, rebolar-se, gingar
wade /weɪd/ *vi* ~ **through** (*fig*) avançar a custo por; (*mud, water*) patinhar em
wafer /'weɪfə(r)/ *n* (*biscuit*) bolacha *f* de baunilha; (*relig*) hóstia *f*
waffle[1] /'wɒfl/ *n* (*colloq: talk*) lengalenga *f*, papo *m*, conversa *f*; (*colloq: writing*) □ *vi* (*colloq*) escrever muito sem dizer nada de importante
waffle[2] /'wɒfl/ *n* (*culin*) waffle *m*
waft /wɒft/ *vi* flutuar □ *vt* espalhar, levar suavemente
wag /wæg/ *vt/i* (*pt* **wagged**) abanar, agitar, sacudir
wage[1] /weɪdʒ/ *vt* (*campaign, war*) fazer
wage[2] /weɪdʒ/ *n* ~(s) (*weekly, daily*) salário *m*, ordenado *m*. ~**-claim** *n* pedido *m* de aumento de salário. ~**-earner** *n* trabalhador *m* assalariado. ~**-freeze** *n* congelamento *m* de salários
wager /'weɪdʒə(r)/ *n* (*bet*) aposta *f* □ *vt* apostar (**that** que)
waggle /'wægl/ *vt/i* abanar, agitar, sacudir
wagon /'wægən/ *n* (*horse-drawn*) carroça *f*; (*rail*) vagão *m* de mercadorias
waif /weɪf/ *n* criança *f* abandonada
wail /weɪl/ *vi* lamentar-se, gemer lamentosamente □ *n* lamentação *f*, gemido *m* lamentoso
waist /weɪst/ *n* cintura *f*. ~**line** *n* cintura *f*
waistcoat /'weɪskəʊt/ *n* colete *m*
wait /weɪt/ *vt/i* esperar □ *n* espera *f*. ~ **for** esperar. ~ **on** servir. **lie in** ~ **(for)** estar escondido à espera (de), armar uma emboscada (para). **keep sb** ~**ing** fazer alguém esperar. ~**ing-list** *n*

lista *f* de espera. ~ing-room *n* sala *f* de espera

wait|er /'weɪtə(r)/ *n* garçon *m*, (*P*) criado *m* (de mesa). ~ress *n* garçonete *f*, (*P*) criada *f* (de mesa)

waive /weɪv/ *vt* renunciar a, desistir de

wake[1] /weɪk/ *vt/i* (*pt* woke, *pp* woken) ~ (up) acordar, despertar □ *n* (*before burial*) velório *m*

wake[2] /weɪk/ *n* (*ship*) esteira (de espuma) *f*. in the ~ of (*following*) atrás de, em seguida a

waken /'weɪkən/ *vt/i* acordar, despertar

Wales /weɪlz/ *n* País *m* de Gales

walk /wɔ:k/ *vi* andar, caminhar; (*not ride*) ir a pé; (*stroll*) passear □ *vt* (*streets*) andar por, percorrer; (*distance*) andar, fazer a pé, percorrer; (*dog*) (levar para) passear □ *n* (*stroll*) passeio *m*, volta *f*; (*excursion*) caminhada *f*; (*gait*) passo *m*, maneira *f* de andar; (*pace*) passo *m*; (*path*) caminho *m*. it's a 5-minute ~ são 5 minutos a pé. ~ of life meio *m*, condição *f* social. ~ out (*go away*) sair; (*go on strike*) fazer greve. ~ out on abandonar. ~-over *n* vitória *f* fácil

walker /'wɔ:kə(r)/ *n* caminhante *mf*

walkie-talkie /wɔ:kɪ'tɔ:kɪ/ *n* walkie-talkie *m*

walking /'wɔ:kɪŋ/ *n* andar (a pé) *m*, marcha (a pé) *f* □ *a* (*colloq: dictionary*) vivo. ~-stick *n* bengala *f*

Walkman /'wɔ:kmæn/ *n* walkman *m*

wall /wɔ:l/ *n* parede *f*; (*around land*) muro *m*; (*of castle, town; fig*) muralha *f*; (*of stomach etc*) parede(s) *f* (*pl*) □ *vt* (*city*) fortificar; (*property*) murar. go to the ~ sucumbir, falir; (*firm*) ir à falência. up the ~ (*colloq*) fora de si

wallet /'wɒlɪt/ *n* carteira *f*

wallflower /'wɔ:lflaʊə(r)/ *n* (*bot*) goivo *m*. be a ~ (*fig*) tomar chá de cadeira, (*P*) levar banho de cadeira

wallop /'wɒləp/ *vt* (*pt* walloped) (*sl*) espancar (*colloq*) □ *n* (*sl*) pancada *f* forte

wallow /'wɒləʊ/ *vi* (*in mud*) chafurdar, atolar-se; (*fig*) regozijar-se

wallpaper /'wɔ:lpeɪpə(r)/ *n* papel *m* de parede □ *vt* forrar com papel de parede

walnut /'wɔ:lnʌt/ *n* (*nut*) noz *f*; (*tree*) nogueira *f*

walrus /'wɔ:lrəs/ *n* morsa *f*

waltz /wɔ:ls/ *n* valsa *f* □ *vi* valsar

wan /wɒn/ *a* pálido

wand /wɒnd/ *n* (*magic*) varinha *f* mágica *or* de condão

wander /'wɒndə(r)/ *vi* andar ao acaso, vagar, errar; (*river*) serpentear; (*mind, speech*) divagar; (*stray*) extraviar-se. ~er *n* vagabundo *m*, andarilho *m*. ~ing *a* errante

wane /weɪn/ *vi* diminuir, minguar; (*decline*) declinar □ *n* on the ~ em declínio; (*moon*) no quarto minguante

wangle /'wæŋgl/ *vt* (*colloq*) conseguir algo através de pistolão

want /wɒnt/ *vt* querer (to do fazer); (*need*) precisar (de); (*ask for*) exigir, requerer □ *vi* ~ for ter falta de □ *n* (*need*) necessidade *f*, precisão *f*; (*desire*) desejo *m*; (*lack*) falta *f*, carência *f*. for ~ of por falta de. I ~ you to go eu quero que você vá. ~ed *a* (*criminal*) procurado pela polícia; (*in ad*) precisa(m)-se

wanting /'wɒntɪŋ/ *a* falho, falto (in de). be found ~ não estar à altura

wanton /'wɒntən/ *a* (*playful*) travesso, brincalhão; (*cruelty, destruction etc*) gratuito; (*woman*) despudorado

war /wɔ:(r)/ *n* guerra *f*. at ~ em guerra. on the ~-path em pé de guerra

warble /'wɔ:bl/ *vt/i* gorjear

ward /wɔ:d/ *n* (*in hospital*) enfermaria *f*; (*jur: minor*) pupilo *m*; (*pol*) círculo *m* eleitoral □ *vt* ~ off (*a blow*) aparar; (*anger*) desviar; (*danger*) prevenir, evitar

warden /'wɔ:dn/ *n* (*of institution*) diretor *m*, (*P*) director *m*; (*of park*) guarda *m*

warder /'wɔ:də(r)/ *n* guarda (de prisão) *m*, carcereiro *m*

wardrobe /'wɔ:drəʊb/ *n* (*place*) armário *m*, guarda-roupa *m*, (*P*) guarda-fato *m*, (*P*) roupeiro *m*; (*clothes*) guarda-roupa *m*

warehouse /'weəhaʊs/ *n* (*pl* -s /-haʊzɪz/) armazém *m*, depósito *m* de mercadorias

wares /weəz/ *npl* (*goods*) mercadorias *fpl*, artigos *mpl*

warfare /'wɔ:feə(r)/ *n* guerra *f*

warhead /'wɔ:hed/ *n* ogiva (de combate) *f*

warlike /'wɔ:laɪk/ *a* marcial, guerreiro; (*bellicose*) belicoso

warm /wɔ:m/ *a* (-er, -est) quente; (*hearty*) caloroso, cordial. be *or* feel ~ estar com *or* ter *or* sentir calor □ *vt/i* ~ (up) aquecer(-se). ~-hearted *a* afetuoso, (*P*) afectuoso, com calor humano. ~ly *adv* (*heartily*) calorosamente. wrap up ~ly agasalhar-se bem. ~th *n* calor *m*

warn /wɔ:n/ *vt* avisar, prevenir. ~ sb off sth (*advise against*) pôr alguém de prevenção *or* de pé atrás com alg coisa; (*forbid*) proibir alg coisa a alguém. ~ing *n* aviso *m*. ~ing light lâmpada *f* de advertência. without ~ing sem aviso, sem prevenir

warp /wɔ:p/ *vt/i* (*wood etc*) empenar; (*fig: pervert*) torcer, deformar, desvirtuar. **~ed** *a* (*fig*) deturpado, pervertido

warrant /'wɒrənt/ *n* autorização *f*; (*for arrest*) mandato (de captura) *m*; (*comm*) título *m* de crédito, warrant *m* □ *vt* justificar; (*guarantee*) garantir

warranty /'wɒrəntɪ/ *n* garantia *f*

warring /'wɔ:rɪŋ/ *a* em guerra; (*rival*) contrário, antagônico, (*P*) antagónico

warrior /'wɒrɪə(r)/ *n* guerreiro *m*

warship /'wɔ:ʃɪp/ *n* navio *m* de guerra

wart /wɔ:t/ *n* verruga *f*

wartime /'wɔ:taɪm/ *n* **in ~** em tempo de guerra

wary /'weərɪ/ *a* (**-ier, -iest**) cauteloso, prudente

was /wɒz/; *unstressed* /wəz/ *see* be

wash /wɒʃ/ *vt/i* lavar(-se); (*flow over*) molhar, inundar □ *n* lavagem *f*; (*dirty clothes*) roupa *f* para lavar; (*of ship*) esteira *f*; (*of paint*) fina camada *f* de tinta. **have a ~** lavar-se. **~-basin** *n* pia *f*, (*P*) lavatório *m*. **~-cloth** *n* (*Amer: face-cloth*) toalha *f* de rosto. **~ one's hands of** lavar as mãos de. **~ out** (*cup etc*) lavar; (*stain*) tirar lavando. **~-out** *n* (*sl*) fiasco *m*. **~-room** *n* (*Amer*) banheiro *m*, (*P*) casa *f* de banho. **~ up** lavar a louça; (*Amer: wash oneself*) lavar-se. **~able** *a* lavável. **~ing** *n* (*dirty*) roupa *f* suja; (*clean*) roupa *f* lavada. **~ing-machine** *n* máquina *f* de lavar roupa. **~ing-powder** *n* detergente *m* em pó. **~ing-up** *n* lavagem *f* da louça

washed-out /wɒʃt'aʊt/ *a* (*faded*) desbotado; (*exhausted*) exausto

washer /'wɒʃə(r)/ *n* (*machine*) máquina *f* de lavar roupa, louça *f*, (*P*) loiça *f*; (*ring*) anilha *f*

wasp /wɒsp/ *n* vespa *f*

wastage /'weɪstɪdʒ/ *n* desperdício *m*, perda *f*. **natural ~** desgaste *m* natural

waste /weɪst/ *vt* desperdiçar, esbanjar; (*time*) perder □ *vi* **~ away** consumir-se □ *a* (*useless*) inútil; (*material*) de refugo □ *n* desperdício *m*, perda *f*; (*of time*) perda *f*; (*rubbish*) lixo *m*. **lay ~** assolar, desvastar. **~ (land)** (*desolate*) região *f* desolada, ermo *m*; (*unused*) (terreno) baldio *m*. **~-disposal unit** triturador *m* de lixo. **~ paper** papéis *mpl* velhos. **~-paper basket** cesto *m* de papéis

wasteful /'weɪstfl/ *a* dispendioso; (*person*) esbanjador, gastador, perdulário

watch /wɒtʃ/ *vt/i* ver bem, olhar com atenção, observar; (*game, TV*) ver; (*guard, spy on*) vigiar; (*be careful about*) tomar cuidado com □ *n* vigia *f*, vigilância *f*; (*naut*) quarto *m*; (*for telling time*) relógio *m*. **~-dog** *n* cão *m* de guarda. **~ out** (*look out*) estar à espreita (for de); (*take care*) acautelar-se. **~-strap** *n* correia *f*, pulseira *f* do relógio. **~-tower** *n* torre *f* de observação. **~ful** *a* atento, vigilante

watchmaker /'wɒtʃmeɪkə(r)/ *n* relojoeiro *m*

watchman /'wɒtʃmən/ *n* (*pl* **-men**) (*of building*) guarda *m*. **(night-)~** guarda-noturno *m*

watchword /'wɒtʃwɜ:d/ *n* lema *m*, divisa *f*

water /'wɔ:tə(r)/ *n* água *f* □ *vt* regar □ *vi* (*of eyes*) lacrimejar, chorar. **~ down** juntar água a, diluir; (*milk, wine*) aguar, batizar, (*P*) baptizar (*colloq*); (*fig: tone down*) suavizar. **~-closet** *n* WC *m*, banheiro *m*, (*P*) lavabos *mpl*. **~-colour** *n* aquarela *f*. **~-ice** *n* sorvete *m*. **~-lily** *n* nenúfar *m*. **~-main** *n* cano *m* principal da rede. **~-melon** *n* melancia *f*. **~-pistol** *n* pistola *f* de água. **~ polo** pólo *m* aquático. **~-skiing** *n* esqui *m* aquático. **~-wheel** *n* roda *f* hidráulica

watercress /'wɔ:təkres/ *n* agrião *m*

waterfall /'wɔ:təfɔ:l/ *n* queda *f* de água, cascata *f*

watering-can /'wɔ:tərɪŋkæn/ *n* regador *m*

waterlogged /'wɔ:təlɒgd/ *a* saturado de água; (*land*) empapado, alagado; (*vessel*) inundado, alagado

watermark /'wɔ:təma:k/ *n* (*in paper*) marca-d'água *f*, filigrana *f*

waterproof /'wɔ:təpru:f/ *a* impermeável; (*watch*) à prova d'água

watershed /'wɔ:təʃed/ *n* (*fig*) momento *m* decisivo; (*in affairs*) ponto *m* crítico

watertight /'wɔ:tətaɪt/ *a* à prova d'água, hermético; (*fig: argument etc*) inequívoco, irrefutável

waterway /'wɔ:təweɪ/ *n* via *f* navegável

waterworks /'wɔ:təwɜ:ks/ *n* (*place*) estação *f* hidráulica

watery /'wɔ:tərɪ/ *a* (*colour*) pálido; (*eyes*) lacrimoso; (*soup*) aguado; (*tea*) fraco

watt /wɒt/ *n* watt *m*

wav|e /weɪv/ *n* onda *f*; (*in hair; radio*) onda *f*; (*sign*) aceno *m* □ *vt* acenar com; (*sword*) brandir; (*hair*) ondular □ *vi* acenar (com a mão); (*hair etc*) ondular; (*flag*) tremular. **~eband** *n* faixa *f* de onda. **~e goodbye** dizer adeus. **~elength** *n* comprimento *m* de onda. **~y** *a* ondulado

waver /'weɪvə(r)/ *vi* vacilar; (*hesitate*) hesitar

wax[1] /wæks/ *n* cera *f* □ *vt* encerar; (*car*) polir. **~en, ~y** *adjs* de cera

wax[2] /wæks/ *vi* (*of moon*) aumentar, crescer

waxwork /'wækswɜ:k/ *n* (*dummy*) figura *f* de cera. **~s** *npl* (*exhibition*) museu *m* de figuras de cera

way /weɪ/ *n* (*road, path*) caminho *m*, estrada *f*, rua *f* (to para); (*distance*) percurso *m*; (*direction*) (P) direção *f*; (*manner*) modo *m*, maneira *f*; (*means*) meios *mpl*; (*respect*) respeito *m*. **~s** (*habits*) costumes *mpl* □ *adv* (*colloq*) consideravelmente, de longe. **be in the ~** atrapalhar. **be on one's** *or* **the ~** estar a caminho. **by the ~** a propósito. **by ~ of** por, via, através. **get one's own ~** conseguir o que quer. **give ~** (*yield*) ceder; (*collapse*) desabar; (*auto*) dar a preferência. **in a ~** de certo modo. **make one's ~** ir. **that ~** dessa maneira. **this ~** desta maneira. **~ in** entrada *f*. **~ out** saída *f*. **~-out** *a* (*colloq*) excêntrico

waylay /weɪ'leɪ/ *vt* (*pt* **-laid**) (*assail*) armar uma cilada para; (*stop*) interceptar

wayward /'weɪwəd/ *a* (*wilful*) teimoso; (*perverse*) caprichoso, difícil

WC /dʌb(ə)lju:'si:/ *n* WC *m*, banheiro *m*, (*P*) casa *f* de banho

we /wi:/ *pron* nós

weak /wi:k/ *a* (-er, -est) fraco; (*delicate*) frágil. **~en** *vt/i* enfraquecer; (*give way*) fraquejar. **~ly** *adv* fracamente. **~ness** *n* fraqueza *f*; (*fault*) ponto *m* fraco. **a ~ness for** (*liking*) um fraco por

weakling /'wi:klɪŋ/ *n* fraco *m*

wealth /welθ/ *n* riqueza *f*; (*riches, resources*) riquezas *fpl*; (*quantity*) abundância *f*

wealthy /'welθɪ/ *a* (-ier, -iest) rico

wean /wi:n/ *vt* (*baby*) desmamar; (*from habit etc*) desabituar

weapon /'wepən/ *n* arma *f*

wear /weə(r)/ *vt* (*pt* **wore**, *pp* **worn**) (*have on*) usar, trazer; (*put on*) pôr; (*expression*) ter; (*damage*) gastar. **~ black/red/***etc* vestir-se de preto/vermelho/*etc* □ *vi* (*last*) durar; (*become old, damaged etc*) gastar-se □ *n* (*use*) uso *m*; (*deterioration*) gasto *m*, uso *m*; (*endurance*) resistência *f*; (*clothing*) roupa *f*. **~ and tear** desgaste *m*. **~ down** gastar; (*person*) extenuar. **~ off** passar. **~ on** (*time*) passar lentamente. **~ out** gastar; (*tire*) cansar, esgotar

wear|y /'wɪərɪ/ *a* (-ier, -iest) fatigado, cansado; (*tiring*) fatigante, cansativo □ *vi* **~y of** cansar-se de. **~ily** *adv* com lassidão, cansadamente. **~iness** *n* fadiga *f*, cansaço *m*

weasel /'wi:zl/ *n* doninha *f*

weather /'weðə(r)/ *n* tempo *m* □ *a* meteorológico □ *vt* (*survive*) agüentar, (*P*) aguentar, resistir a. **under the ~** (*colloq: ill*) indisposto, achacado. **~-beaten** *a* curtido pelo tempo. **~ forecast** *n* boletim *m* meteorológico. **~-vane** *n* cata-vento *m*

weathercock /'weðəkɒk/ *n* (*lit & fig*) cata-vento *m*

weav|e[1] /wi:v/ *vt* (*pt* **wove**, *pp* **woven**) (*cloth etc*) tecer; (*plot*) urdir, criar □ *n* (*style*) tipo *m* de tecido. **~er** /-ə(r)/ *n* tecelão *m*, tecelã *f*. **~ing** *n* tecelagem *f*

weave[2] /wi:v/ *vi* (*move*) serpear; (*through traffic, obstacles*) ziguezaguear

web /web/ *n* (*of spider*) teia *f*; (*fabric*) tecido *m*; (*on foot*) membrana *f* interdigital. **~bed** *a* (*foot*) palmado. **~bing** *n* (*in chair*) tira *f* de tecido forte. **~-footed** *a* palmípede

wed /wed/ *vt/i* (*pt* **wedded**) casar(-se)

wedding /'wedɪŋ/ *n* casamento *m*. **~-cake** *n* bolo *m* de noiva. **~-ring** *n* aliança (de casamento) *f*

wedge /wedʒ/ *n* calço *m*, cunha *f*; (*cake*) fatia *f*; (*of lemon*) quarto *m*; (*under wheel etc*) calço *m*, cunha *f* □ *vt* calçar; (*push*) meter *or* enfiar à força; (*pack in*) entalar

Wednesday /'wenzdɪ/ *n* quartafeira *f*

weed /wi:d/ *n* erva *f* daninha □ *vt/i* arrancar as ervas, capinar. **~-killer** *n* herbicida *m*. **~ out** suprimir, arrancar. **~y** *a* (*fig: person*) fraco

week /wi:k/ *n* semana *f*. **a ~ today/tomorrow** de hoje/de amanhã a oito dias. **~ly** *a* semanal □ *a* & *n* (*periodical*) (jornal) semanário (*m*) □ *adv* semanalmente, todas as semanas

weekday /'wi:kdeɪ/ *n* dia *m* de semana

weekend /'wi:kend/ *n* fim-de-semana *m*

weep /wi:p/ *vt/i* (*pt* **wept**) chorar (**for sb** por alguém). **~ing willow** (salgueiro-)chorão *m*

weigh /weɪ/ *vt/i* pesar. **~ anchor** levantar âncora *or* ferro, zarpar. **~ down** (*weight*) sobrecarregar; (*bend*) envergar; (*fig*) acabrunhar. **~ up** (*colloq: examine*) pesar

weight /weɪt/ *n* peso *m*. **lose ~** emagrecer. **put on ~** engordar. **~less** *a* imponderável. **~-lifter** *n* halterofilista *m*. **~-lifting** *n* halterofilia *f*. **~y** *a* pesado; (*subject etc*) de peso; (*influential*) influente

weighting /'weɪtɪŋ/ *n* suplemento *m* salarial

weir /wɪə(r)/ *n* represa *f*, açude *m*

weird /wɪəd/ *a* (-er, -est) misterioso; (*strange*) estranho, bizarro

welcom|e /'welkəm/ *a* agradável; (*timely*) oportuno □ *int* (seja) benvindo! □ *n* acolhimento *m* □ *vt* acolher, receber; (*as greeting*) dar as boas vindas a. **be ~e** ser bem-vindo. **you're ~e!** (*after thank you*) não tem de quê!, de nada! **~e to do** livre para fazer. **~ing** *a* acolhedor

weld /weld/ *vt* soldar □ *n* solda *f*. **~er** *n* soldador *m*. **~ing** *n* soldagem *f*, soldadura *f*

welfare /'welfeə(r)/ *n* bem-estar *m*; (*aid*) assistência *f*, previdência *f* social. **W~ State** Estado-Providência *m*

well[1] /wel/ *n* (*for water, oil*) poço *m*; (*of stairs*) vão *m*; (*of lift*) poço *m*

well[2] /wel/ *adv* (**better, best**) bem □ *a* bem (*invar*) □ *int* bem! **as ~** também. **we may as ~ go** é melhor irnos andando. **as ~ as** tão bem como; (*in addition*) assim como. **be ~** (*healthy*) ir *or* passar bem. **do ~** (*succeed*) sair-se bem, ser bem sucedido. **very ~** muito bem. **~ done!** bravo!, muito bem! **~-behaved** *a* bem comportado, educado. **~-being** *n* bem-estar *m*. **~-bred** *a* (bem) educado. **~-done** *a* (*of meat*) bem passado. **~-dressed** *a* bem vestido. **~-heeled** *a* (*colloq: wealthy*) rico. **~-informed** *a* versado, bem informado. **~-known** *a* (bem-) conhecido. **~-meaning** *a* bem intencionado. **~-off** *a* rico, próspero. **~-read** *a* instruído. **~-spoken** *a* bem-falante. **~-timed** *a* oportuno. **~-to-do** *a* rico. **~-wisher** *n* admirador *m*, simpatizante *mf*

wellington /'welɪŋtən/ *n* (*boot*) bota *f* alta de borracha

Welsh /welʃ/ *a* galês □ *n* (*lang*) galês *m*. **~man** *n* galês *m*. **~woman** *n* galesa *f*

wend /wend/ *vt* **~ one's way** dirigir-se, seguir o seu caminho

went /went/ *see* **go**

wept /wept/ *see* **weep**

were /wɜ:(r)/; *unstressed* /wə(r)/ *see* **be**

west /west/ *n* oeste *m*. **the W~** (*pol*) o Oeste, o Ocidente □ *a* ocidental, do oeste □ *adv* ao oeste, para o oeste. **W~ Indian** *a* & *n* antilhano (*m*). **the W~ Indies** as Antilhas. **~erly** *a* ocidental, oeste. **~ward** *a* para o oeste. **~ward(s)** *adv* para o oeste

western /'westən/ *a* ocidental, do oeste; (*pol*) ocidental □ *n* (*film*) filme *m* de cowboys, bangue-bangue *m*

westernize /'westənaɪz/ *vt* ocidentalizar

wet /wet/ *a* (**wetter, wettest**) molhado; (*of weather*) chuvoso, de chuva; (*colloq: person*) fraco. **get ~** molhar-se □ *vt* (*pt* **wetted**) molhar. **~ blanket** (*colloq*) desmancha-prazeres *mf invar* (*colloq*). **~ paint** pintado de fresco. **~ suit** roupa *f* de mergulho

whack /wæk/ *vt* (*colloq*) bater em □ *n* (*colloq*) pancada *f*. **~ed** *a* (*colloq*) morto de cansaço, rebentado (*colloq*). **~ing** *a* (*sl*) enorme, de todo o tamanho

whale /weɪl/ *n* baleia *f*

wharf /wɔ:f/ *n* (*pl* **wharfs**) cais *m*

what /wɒt/ *a* (*interr, excl*) que. **~ time is it?** que horas são? **~ an idea!** que idéia! □ *pron* (*interr*) (o) quê, como, o que, qual, quais; (*object*) o que; (*after prep*) que; (*that which*) o que, aquilo que. **~?** (o) quê?, como? **~ is it?** o que é? **~ is your address?** qual é o seu endereço? **~ is your name?** como se chama? **~ can you see?** o que é que você pode ver? **this is ~ I write with** é com isto que escrevo. **that's ~ I need** é disso que eu preciso. **do ~ you want** faça o que *or* aquilo que quiser. **~ about me/him/***etc*? e eu/ele/*etc*? **~ about doing sth?** e se fizéssemos alg coisa? **~ for?** para quê?

whatever /wɒt'evə(r)/ *a* **~ book/***etc* qualquer livro/*etc* que seja □ *pron* (*no matter what*) qualquer que seja; (*anything that*) o que quer que, tudo o que. **nothing ~** absolutamente nada. **~ happens** aconteça o que acontecer. **do ~ you like** faça o que quiser

whatsoever /wɒtsəʊ'evə(r)/ *a* & *pron* = **whatever**

wheat /wi:t/ *n* trigo *m*

wheedle /'wi:dl/ *vt* convencer, persuadir, levar a

wheel /wi:l/ *n* roda *f* □ *vt* empurrar □ *vi* rodar, rolar. **at the ~** (*of vehicle*) ao volante; (*helm*) ao leme

wheelbarrow /'wi:lbærəʊ/ *n* carrinho *m* de mão

wheelchair /'wi:ltʃeə(r)/ *n* cadeira *f* de rodas

wheeze /wi:z/ *vi* respirar ruidosamente □ *n* respiração *f* difícil

when /wen/ *adv, conj* & *pron* quando. **the day/moment ~** o dia/momento em que

whenever /wen'evə(r)/ *conj* & *adv* (*at whatever time*) quando quer que, quando; (*every time that*) (de) cada vez que, sempre que

where /weə(r)/ *adv, conj* & *pron* onde, aonde; (*in which place*) em que, onde; (*whereas*) enquanto que, ao passo que. **~ is he going?** aonde é que ele vai? **~abouts** *adv* onde □ *n* paradeiro *m*.

~by *adv* pelo que. ~upon *adv* após o que, depois do que
whereas /weər'æz/ *conj* enquanto que, ao passo que
wherever /weər'evə(r)/ *conj* & *adv* onde quer que. ~ can it be? onde pode estar?
whet /wet/ *vt* (*pt* whetted) (*appetite, desire*) aguçar, despertar
whether /'weðə(r)/ *conj* se. not know ~ não saber se. ~ I go or not caso eu vá ou não
which /wɪtʃ/ *interr a & pron* qual, que ~ bag is yours? qual das malas é a sua? ~ is your coat? qual é o seu casaco? do you know ~ he's taken? sabe qual/quais é que ele levou? □ *rel pron* que, o qual; (*referring to whole sentence*) o que; (*after prep*) que, o qual, cujo. at ~ em qual/que. from ~ do qual/que. of ~ do qual/de que. to ~ para o qual/o que
whichever /wɪtʃ'evə(r)/ *a* ~ book/*etc* qualquer livro/*etc* que seja, seja que livro/*etc* for. take ~ book you wish leve o livro que quiser □ *pron* qualquer, quaisquer
whiff /wɪf/ *n* (*of fresh air*) sopro *m*, lufada *f*; (*smell*) baforada *f*
while /waɪl/ *n* (espaço de) tempo *m*, momento *m*. once in a ~ de vez em quando □ *conj* (*when*) enquanto; (*although*) embora; (*whereas*) enquanto que □ *vt* ~ away (*time*) passar
whim /wɪm/ *n* capricho *m*
whimper /'wɪmpə(r)/ *vi* gemer; (*baby*) choramingar □ *n* gemido *m*; (*baby*) choro *m*
whimsical /'wɪmzɪkl/ *a* (*person*) caprichoso; (*odd*) bizarro
whine /waɪn/ *vi* lamuriar-se, queixar-se; (*dog*) ganir □ *n* lamúria *f*, queixume *m*; (*dog*) ganido *m*
whip /wɪp/ *n* chicote *m* □ *vt* (*pt* whipped) chicotear; (*culin*) bater □ *vi* (*move*) ir a toda a pressa. ~-round *n* (*colloq*) coleta *f*, vaquinha *f*. ~ up excitar; (*cause*) provocar; (*colloq: meal*) preparar rapidamente. ~ped cream creme *m* chantilly
whirl /wɜ:l/ *vt/i* (fazer) rodopiar, girar □ *n* rodopio *m*
whirlpool /'wɜ:lpu:l/ *n* redemoinho *m*
whirlwind /'wɜ:lwɪnd/ *n* redemoinho *m* de vento, turbilhão *m*
whirr /wɜ:(r)/ *vi* zunir, zumbir
whisk /wɪsk/ *vt/i* (*snatch*) levar/tirar bruscamente; (*culin*) bater; (*flies*) sacudir □ *n* (*culin*) batedeira *f*. ~ away (*brush away*) sacudir
whisker /'wɪskə(r)/ *n* fio *m* de barba. ~s *npl* (*of animal*) bigode *m*; (*beard*) barba *f*; (*sideboards*) suiças *fpl*
whisky /'wɪskɪ/ *n* uísque *m*
whisper /'wɪspə(r)/ *vt/i* sussurrar, murmurar; (*of stream, leaves*) sussurrar □ *n* sussurro *m*, murmúrio *m*. in a ~ baixinho, em voz baixa
whist /wɪst/ *n* uíste *m*, (*P*) whist *m*
whistle /'wɪsl/ *n* assobio *m*; (*instrument*) apito *m* □ *vt/i* assobiar; (*with instrument*) apitar
Whit /wɪt/ *a* ~ Sunday domingo *m* de Pentecostes
white /waɪt/ *a* (-er, -est) branco, alvo; (*pale*) pálido □ *n* (*colour; of eyes; person*) branco *m*; (*of egg*) clara (de ovo) *f*. go ~ (*turn pale*) empalidecer; (*of hair*) branquear, embranquecer. ~ coffee café *m* com leite. ~-collar worker empregado *m* de escritório. ~ elephant (*fig*) trambolho *m*, elefante *m* branco. ~ lie mentirinha *f*. ~ness *n* brancura *f*, alvura *f*
whiten /'waɪtn/ *vt/i* branquear
whitewash /'waɪtwɒʃ/ *n* cal *f*; (*fig*) encobrimento *m* □ *vt* caiar; (*fig*) encobrir
Whitsun /'wɪtsn/ *n* Pentecostes *m*
whittle /wɪtl/ *vt* ~ down aparar, cortar aparas; (*fig*) reduzir gradualmente
whiz /wɪz/ *vi* (*pt* whizzed) (*through air*) zunir, sibilar; (*rush*) passar a toda a velocidade. ~-kid *n* (*colloq*) prodígio *m*
who /hu:/ *interr pron* quem □ *rel pron* que, o(a) qual, os(as) quais
whoever /hu:'evə(r)/ *pron* (*no matter who*) quem quer que, seja quem for; (*the one who*) aquele que
whole /həʊl/ *a* inteiro, todo; (*not broken*) intacto. the ~ house/*etc* toda a casa/*etc* □ *n* totalidade *f*; (*unit*) todo *m*. as a ~ no conjunto, como um todo. on the ~ de um modo geral. ~-hearted *a* de todo o coração; (*person*) dedicado. ~-heartedly *adv* sem reservas, sinceramente
wholefood /'həʊlfu:d/ *n* comida *f* integral
wholemeal /'həʊlmi:l/ *a* ~ bread pão *m* integral
wholesale /'həʊlseɪl/ *n* venda *f* por grosso *or* por atacado □ *a* (*firm*) por grosso, por atacado; (*fig*) sistemático, em massa □ *adv* (*in large quantities*) por atacado; (*fig*) em massa, em grande escala. ~r /-ə(r)/ *n* grossista *mf*, atacadista *mf*
wholesome /'həʊlsəm/ *a* sadio, saudável
wholewheat /'həʊlwi:t/ *a* = wholemeal
wholly /'həʊlɪ/ *adv* inteiramente, completamente
whom /hu:m/ *interr pron* quem □ *rel*

pron (*that*) que; (*after prep*) quem, que, o qual
whooping cough /'hu:pɪŋkɒf/ *n* coqueluche *f*
whore /hɔ:(r)/ *n* prostituta *f*
whose /hu:z/ *rel pron* & *a* cujo, de quem □ *interr pron* de quem. ~ **hat is this?**, ~ **is this hat?** de quem é este chapéu? ~ **son are you?** de quem é que o senhor é filho?
why /waɪ/ *adv* porque, por que motivo, por que razão, porquê. **she doesn't know** ~ **he's here** ela não sabe porque *or* por que motivo ele estáaqui. **she doesn't know** ~ ela não sabe porquê. **do you know** ~? você sabe porquê? □ *int* (*protest*) ora, ora essa; (*discovery*) oh. ~ **yes**/ *etc*
wick /wɪk/ *n* torcida *f*, mecha *f*, pavio *m*
wicked /'wɪkɪd/ *a* mau, malvado; (*mischievous, spiteful*) maldoso. ~**ly** *adv* maldosamente. ~**ness** *n* maldade *f*, malvadeza *f*
wicker /'wɪkə(r)/ *n* verga *f*, vime *m*. ~**-work** *n* trabalho *m* de verga *or* de vime
wicket /'wɪkɪt/ *n* (*cricket*) arco *m*
wide /waɪd/ *a* (-er, -est) largo; (*extensive*) vasto, grande, extenso. **two metres** ~ com dois metros de largura □ *adv* longe; (*fully*) completamente. **open** ~ (*door, window*) abrir(-se) de par em par, escancarar(-se); (*mouth*) abrir bem. ~ **awake** desperto, acordado. **far and** ~ por toda a parte. ~**ly** *adv* largamente; (*travel, spread*) muito; (*generally*) geralmente; (*extremely*) extremamente
widen /'waɪdn/ *vt/i* alargar(-se)
widespread /'waɪdspred/ *a* muito espalhado, difundido
widow /'wɪdəʊ/ *n* viúva *f*. ~**ed** *a* (*man*) viúvo; (*woman*) viúva. **be** ~**ed** enviuvar, ficar viúvo *or* viúva. ~**er** *n* viúvo *m*. ~**hood** *n* viuvez *f*
width /wɪdθ/ *n* largura *f*
wield /wi:ld/ *vt* (*axe etc*) manejar; (*fig: power*) exercer
wife /waɪf/ *n* (*pl* **wives**) mulher *f*, esposa *f*
wig /wɪg/ *n* cabeleira (postiça) *f*; (*judge's etc*) peruca *f*
wiggle /'wɪgl/ *vt/i* remexer(-se), retorcer(-se), mexer(-se) dum lado para outro
wild /waɪld/ *a* (-er, -est) selvagem; (*of plant*) silvestre; (*mad*) louco; (*enraged*) furioso, violento □ *adv* a esmo; (*without control*) à solta. ~**s** *npl* regiões *fpl* selvagens. ~**-goose chase** falsa pista *f*, tentativa *f* inútil. ~**ly** *adv* violentamente; (*madly*) loucamente
wildcat /'waɪldkæt/ *a* ~ **strike** greve *f* ilegal
wilderness /'wɪldənɪs/ *n* deserto *m*
wildlife /'waɪldlaɪf/ *n* animais *mpl* selvagens
wile /waɪl/ *n* artimanha *f*; (*cunning*) astúcia *f*, manha *f*
wilful /'wɪlfl/ *a* (*person*) voluntarioso; (*act*) intencional, propositado
will[1] /wɪl/ *v aux* **you** ~ **sing**/**he** ~ **do**/*etc* tu cantarás/ele fará/*etc*. (*1st person: future expressing will or intention*) **I** ~ **sing**/**we** ~ **do**/*etc* eu cantarei/nós faremos/*etc*. ~ **you have a cup of coffee?** quer tomar um cafézinho? ~ **you shut the door?** quer fazer o favor de fechar a porta?
will[2] /wɪl/ *n* vontade *f*; (*document*) testamento *m*. **at** ~ à vontade, quando *or* como se quiser □ *vt* (*wish*) querer; (*bequeath*) deixar em testamento. ~**-power** *n* força *f* de vontade
willing /'wɪlɪŋ/ *a* pronto, de boa vontade. ~ **to** disposto a. ~**ly** *adv* (*with pleasure*) de boa vontade, de bom grado; (*not forced*) voluntariamente. ~**ness** *n* boa vontade *f*, disposição *f* (to do em fazer)
willow /'wɪləʊ/ *n* salgueiro *m*
willy-nilly /wɪlɪ'nɪlɪ/ *adv* de bom ou de mau grado, quer queira ou não
wilt /wɪlt/ *vi* murchar, definhar
wily /'waɪlɪ/ *a* (-ier, -iest) manhoso, matreiro
win /wɪn/ *vt/i* (*pt* **won**, *pres p* **winning**) ganhar □ *n* vitória *f*. ~ **over** *vt* convencer, conquistar
winc|e /wɪns/ *vi* estremecer, contrair-se. **without** ~**ing** sem pestanejar
winch /wɪntʃ/ *n* guincho *m* □ *vt* içar com guincho
wind[1] /wɪnd/ *n* vento *m*; (*breath*) fôlego *m*; (*flatulence*) gases *mpl*. **get** ~ **of** (*fig*) ouvir rumor de. **put the** ~ **up** (*sl*) assustar. **in the** ~ no ar. ~ **instrument** (*mus*) instrumento *m* de sopro. ~**-swept** *a* varrido pelo vento
wind[2] /waɪnd/ *vt/i* (*pt* **wound**) enrolar(-se); (*wrap*) envolver, pôr em volta; (*of path, river*) serpentear. ~ (**up**) (*clock etc*) dar corda em. ~ **up** (*end*) terminar, acabar; (*fig: speech etc*) concluir; (*firm*) liquidar. **he'll** ~ **up in jail** (*colloq*) ele vai acabar na cadeia. ~**ing** *a* (*path*) sinuoso; (*staircase*) em caracol
windfall /'wɪndfɔ:l/ *n* fruta *f* caída; (*fig: money*) sorte *f* grande
windmill /'wɪndmɪl/ *n* moinho *m* de vento
window /'wɪndəʊ/ *n* janela *f*; (*of shop*) vitrine *f*, (*P*) montra *f*; (*counter*)

guichê *m*, (*P*) guichet *m*. **~-box** *n* jardineira *f*, (*P*) floreira *f*. **~-cleaner** *n* limpador *m* de janelas. **~-dressing** *n* decoração *f* de vitrines; (*fig*) apresentação *f* cuidadosa. **~-ledge** *n* peitoril *m*. **~-pane** *n* vidro *m*, vidraça *f*. **go ~-shopping** ir ver vitrines. **~-sill** *n* peitoril *m*

windpipe /'wɪndpaɪp/ *n* traquéia *f*, (*P*) traqueia *f*

windscreen /'wɪndskri:n/ *n* pára-brisa *m*, (*P*) pára-brisas *m invar*. **~-wiper** /-waɪpə(r)/ *n* limpador *m* de pára-brisa

windshield /'wɪndʃi:ld/ *n* (*Amer*) = windscreen

windsurf|er /'wɪndsɜ:fə(r)/ *n* surfista *mf*. **~ing** *n* surfe *m*

windy /'wɪndɪ/ *a* (-ier, -iest) ventoso. **it is very ~** está ventando muito

wine /waɪn/ *n* vinho *m*. **~ bar** bar *m* para degustação de vinhos. **~-cellar** *n* adega *f*, cave *f*. **~-grower** *n* vinicultor *m*. **~-growing** *n* vinicultura *f*. **~-list** *n* lista *f* de vinhos. **~-tasting** *n* prova *f or* degustação *f* de vinhos. **~ waiter** garçon *m*

wineglass /'waɪnglɑ:s/ *n* copo *m* de vinho; (*with stem*) cálice *m*

wing /wɪŋ/ *n* asa *f*; (*mil*) flanco *m*; (*archit*) ala *f*; (*auto*) pára-lamas *m invar*, (*P*) guarda-lamas *m invar*. **~s** (*theat*) bastidores *mpl*. **under sb's ~** debaixo das asas de alguém. **~ed** *a* alado

wink /wɪŋk/ *vi* piscar o olho; (*light, star*) cintilar, piscar □ *n* piscadela *f*. **not sleep a ~** não pregar olho

winner /'wɪnə(r)/ *n* vencedor *m*

winning /'wɪnɪŋ/ *see* **win** □ *a* vencedor, vitorioso; (*number*) premiado; (*smile*) encantador, atraente. **~-post** *n* meta *f*, poste de chegada *f*. **~s** *npl* ganhos *mpl*

wint|er /'wɪntə(r)/ *n* inverno *m* □ *vi* hibernar. **~ry** *a* de inverno, invernoso; (*smile*) glacial

wipe /waɪp/ *vt* limpar; (*dry*) enxugar, limpar □ *n* limpadela *f*. **~ off** limpar. **~ out** (*destroy*) aniquilar, limpar (*colloq*); (*cancel*) cancelar. **~ up** enxugar

wir|e /'waɪə(r)/ *n* arame *m*; (*colloq: telegram*) telegrama *m*. (**electric**) **~e** fio elétrico *m*, (*P*) eléctrico □ *vt* (*a house*) montar a instalação elétrica em; (*colloq: telegraph*) telegrafar. **~e netting** rede *f* de arame. **~ing** *n* (*electr*) instalação *f* elétrica, (*P*) eléctrica

wireless /'waɪəlɪs/ *n* rádio *f*; (*set*) rádio *m*

wiry /'waɪərɪ/ *a* (-ier, -iest) magro e rijo

wisdom /'wɪzdəm/ *n* sagacidade *f*, sabedoria *f*; (*common sense*) bom senso *m*, sensatez *f*. **~ tooth** dente *m* (do) sizo

wise /waɪz/ *a* (-er, -est) (*person*) sábio, avisado, sensato; (*look*) entendedor. **~ guy** (*colloq*) sabichão *m* (*colloq*), sabe-tudo *m* (*colloq*). **none the ~r** sem entender nada. **~ly** *adv* sensatamente

wisecrack /'waɪzkræk/ *n* (*colloq*) (boa) piada *f*

wish /wɪʃ/ *n* (*desire, aspiration*) desejo *m*, vontade *f*; (*request*) pedido *m*; (*greeting*) desejo *m*, voto *m*. **I have no ~ to go** não tenho nenhum desejo *or* nenhuma vontade de ir □ *vt* (*desire, bid*) desejar; (*want*) apetecer, ter vontade de, desejar (**to do** fazer) □ *vi* **~ for** desejar. **~ sb well** desejar felicidades a alguém. **I don't ~ to go** não me apetece ir, não tenho vontade de ir, não desejo ir. **I ~ he'd leave** eu gostaria que ele partisse. **with best ~es** (*formal: in letter*) com os melhores cumprimentos, com saudações cordiais; (*on greeting card*) com desejos *or* votos (**for** de)

wishful /'wɪʃfl/ *a* **~ thinking** sonhar acordado

wishy-washy /'wɪʃɪwɒʃɪ/ *a* sem expressão, fraco, inexpressivo

wisp /wɪsp/ *n* (*of hair*) pequena mecha *f*; (*of smoke*) fio *m*

wistful /'wɪstfl/ *a* melancólico, saudoso

wit /wɪt/ *n* inteligência *f*; (*humour*) presença *f* de espírito, humor *m*; (*person*) senso *m* de humor. **be at one's ~'s** *or* **~s' end** não saber o que fazer. **keep one's ~s about one** estar alerta. **live by one's ~s** ganhar a vida de maneira suspeita. **scared out of one's ~s** apavorado

witch /wɪtʃ/ *n* feiticeira *f*, bruxa *f*. **~craft** *n* feitiçaria *f*, bruxaria *f*, magia *f*

with /wɪð/ *prep* com; (*having*) de; (*because of*) de; (*at the house of*) em casa de. **the man ~ the beard** o homem de barbas. **fill/*etc* ~** encher/*etc* de. **laughing/shaking/*etc* ~** a rir/a tremer/*etc* de. **I'm not ~ you** (*colloq*) não estou compreendendo-o

withdraw /wɪð'drɔ:/ *vt/i* (*pt* **withdrew**, *pp* **withdrawn**) retirar (-se); (*money*) tirar. **~al** *n* retirada *f*; (*med*) estado *m* de privação. **~n** *a* (*person*) retraído, fechado

wither /'wɪðə(r)/ *vt/i* murchar, secar. **~ed** *a* (*person*) mirrado. **~ing** *a* (*fig: scornful*) desdenhoso

withhold /wɪð'həʊld/ *vt* (*pt* **withheld**) negar, recusar; (*retain*) reter; (*conceal, not tell*) esconder (**from** de)

within /wɪ'ðɪn/ *prep* & *adv* dentro (de), por dentro (de); (*in distances*) a

menos de. ~ **a month** (*before*) dentro de um mês. ~ **sight** à vista
without /wɪ'ðaʊt/ *prep* sem. ~ **fail** sem falta. **go** ~ **saying** não ser preciso dizer
withstand /wɪð'stænd/ *vt* (*pt* **withstood**) resistir a, opor-se a
witness /'wɪtnɪs/ *n* testemunha *f*; (*evidence*) testemunho *m* □ *vt* testemunhar, presenciar; (*document*) assinar como testemunha. **bear** ~ **to** testemunhar, dar testemunho de. ~**-box** *n* banco *m* das testemunhas
witticism /'wɪtɪsɪzəm/ *n* dito *m* espirituoso
witty /'wɪtɪ/ *a* (**-ier, -iest**) espirituoso
wives /waɪvz/ *see* **wife**
wizard /'wɪzəd/ *n* feiticeiro *m*; (*fig: genius*) gênio *m*, (*P*) génio *m*
wizened /'wɪznd/ *a* encarquilhado
wobbl|e /'wɒbl/ *vi* (*of jelly, voice, hand*) tremer; (*stagger*) cambalear, vacilar; (*of table, chair*) balançar. ~**y** *a* (*trembling*) trêmulo; (*staggering*) cambaleante, vacilante; (*table, chair*) pouco firme
woe /wəʊ/ *n* dor *f*, infortúnio *m*
woke, woken /wəʊk, 'wəʊkən/ *see* **wake**[1]
wolf /wʊlf/ *n* (*pl* **wolves** /wʊlvz/) lobo *m* □ *vt* (*food*) devorar. **cry** ~ dar alarme falso. ~**-whistle** *n* assobio *m* de admiração
woman /'wʊmən/ *n* (*pl* **women**) mulher *f*. ~**hood** *n* as mulheres, o sexo feminino; (*maturity*) maturidade *f*. ~**ly** *a* feminino
womb /wu:m/ *n* seio *m*, ventre *m*; (*med*) útero *m*; (*fig*) seio *m*
women /'wɪmɪn/ *see* **woman**. ~**'s movement** movimento *m* feminista
won /wʌn/ *see* **win**
wonder /'wʌndə(r)/ *n* admiração *f*; (*thing*) maravilha *f* □ *vt* perguntar-se a si mesmo (if se) □ *vi* admirar-se (**at** de, com), ficar admirado, espantar-se (**at** com); (*reflect*) pensar (**about** em). **it is no** ~ não admira (**that** que)
wonderful /'wʌndəfl/ *a* maravilhoso. ~**ly** *adv* maravilhosamente. **it works** ~**ly** funciona às mil maravilhas
won't /wəʊnt/ = **will not**
wood /wʊd/ *n* madeira *f*, pau *m*; (*for burning*) lenha *f*. ~**(s)** *n* (*pl*) (*area*) bosque *m*, mata *f*, floresta *f*. ~**ed** *a* arborizado. ~**en** *a* de *or* em madeira, de pau; (*fig: stiff*) rígido; (*fig: inexpressive*) inexpressivo, de pau
woodcut /'wʊdkʌt/ *n* gravura *f* em madeira
woodland /'wʊdlənd/ *n* região *f* arborizada, bosque *m*, mata *f*
woodlouse /'wʊdlaʊs/ *n* (*pl* **-lice** /laɪs/) baratinha *f*, tatuzinho *m*
woodpecker /'wʊdpekə(r)/ *n* (*bird*) pica-pau *m*
woodwind /'wʊdwɪnd/ *n* (*mus*) instrumentos *mpl* de sopro de madeira
woodwork /'wʊdwɜ:k/ *n* (*of building*) madeiramento *m*; (*carpentry*) carpintaria *f*
woodworm /'wʊdwɜ:m/ *n* caruncho *m*
woody /'wʊdɪ/ *a* (*wooded*) arborizado; (*like wood*) lenhoso
wool /wʊl/ *n* lã *f*. ~**len** *a* de lã. ~**lens** *npl* roupas *fpl* de lã. ~**ly** *a* de lã; (*vague*) confuso □ *n* (*colloq: garment*) roupa *f* de lã
word /wɜ:d/ *n* palavra *f*; (*news*) notícia(s) *f*(*pl*); (*promise*) palavra *f* □ *vt* exprimir, formular. **by** ~ **of mouth** de viva voz. **have a** ~ **with** dizer duas palavras a. **in other** ~**s** em outras palavras. ~**-perfect** *a* que sabe de cor seu papel, a lição etc. ~ **processor** processador *m* de textos. ~**ing** *n* termos *mpl*, redação *f*, (*P*) redacção *f*. ~**y** *a* prolixo
wore /wɔ:(r)/ *see* **wear**
work /wɜ:k/ *n* trabalho *m*; (*product, book etc*) obra *f*; (*building etc*) obras *fpl*. **at** ~ no trabalho. **out of** ~ desempregado. ~**s** *npl* (*techn*) mecanismo *m*; (*factory*) fábrica *f* □ *vt/i* (*of person*) trabalhar; (*techn*) (fazer) funcionar, (fazer) andar; (*of drug etc*) agir, fazer efeito; (*farm, mine*) explorar; (*land*) lavrar. ~ **sb** (*make work*) fazer alguém trabalhar. ~ **in** introduzir, inserir. ~ **loose** soltar-se. ~ **off** (*get rid of*) descarregar. ~ **out** *vt* (*solve*) resolver; (*calculate*) calcular; (*devise*) planejar □ *vi* (*succeed*) resultar; (*sport*) treinar-se. ~**-station** *n* estação *f* de trabalho. ~**-to-rule** *n* greve *f* de zelo. ~ **up** *vt* criar □ *vi* (*to climax*) ir num crescendo. ~**ed up** (*person*) enervado, transtornado, agitado
workable /'wɜ:kəbl/ *a* viável, praticável
workaholic /wɜ:kə'hɒlɪk/ *n* **be a** ~ (*colloq*) trabalhar como um possesso (*colloq*)
worker /'wɜ:kə(r)/ *n* trabalhador *m*, trabalhadora *f*; (*factory*) operário *m*
working /'wɜ:kɪŋ/ *a* (*day, clothes, hypothesis, lunch etc*) de trabalho. **the** ~ **class(es)** a classe operária, a(s) class(es) trabalhadora(s), o proletariado. ~**-class** *a* operário, trabalhador. ~ **mother** mãe *f* que trabalha. ~ **party** comissão *f* consultiva, de estudo *etc*. ~**s** *npl* mecanismo *m*. **in** ~ **order** em condições de funcionamento
workman /'wɜ:kmən/ *n* (*pl* **-men**)

trabalhador *m*; (*factory*) operário *m*. ~**ship** *n* trabalho *m*, execução *f*, mão-de-obra *f*; (*skill*) arte *f*, habilidade *f*

workshop /'wɜ:kʃɒp/ *n* oficina *f*

world /wɜ:ld/ *n* mundo *m* □ *a* mundial. **a ~ of** muito(s), grande quantidade de, um mundo de. ~**-wide** *a* mundial, universal

worldly /'wɜ:ldlɪ/ *a* terreno; (*devoted to the affairs of life*) mundano. ~ **goods** bens *mpl* materiais. ~**-wise** *a* com experiência do mundo

worm /wɜ:m/ *n* verme *m*; (*earthworm*) minhoca *f* □ *vt* ~ **one's way into** insinuar-se, introduzir-se, enfiar-se. ~**-eaten** *a* (*wood*) carunchoso; (*fruit*) bichado, bichoso

worn /wɔ:n/ *see* **wear** □ *a* usado. ~**-out** *a* (*thing*) completamente gasto; (*person*) esgotado

worr|y /'wʌrɪ/ *vt/i* preocupar(-se) □ *n* preocupação *f*. **don't ~y** fique descansado, não se preocupe. ~**ied** *a* preocupado. ~**ying** *a* preocupante, inquietante

worse /wɜ:s/ *a* & *adv* pior □ *n* pior *m*. **get ~** piorar. **from bad to ~** de mal a pior. ~ **luck** pouca sorte, pena

worsen /'wɜ:sn/ *vt/i* piorar

worship /'wɜ:ʃɪp/ *n* (*reverence*) reverência *f*, veneração *f*; (*religious*) culto *m* □ *vt* (*pt* **worshipped**) adorar, venerar □ *vi* fazer as suas devoções, praticar o culto. ~**per** *n* (*in church*) fiel *m*. **Your/His W~** Vossa/Sua Excelência *f*

worst /wɜ:st/ *a* & *n* **(the)** ~ (o/a) pior (*mf*) □ *adv* pior. **if the ~ comes to the ~** se o pior acontecer, na pior das hipóteses. **do one's ~** fazer todo o mal que se quiser. **get the ~ of it** ficar a perder. **the ~ (thing) that** o pior que

worth /wɜ:θ/ *a* **be ~** valer; (*deserving*) merecer □ *n* valor *m*, mérito *m*. **ten pounds ~ of** dez libras de. **it's ~ it, it's ~ while** vale a pena. **it's not ~ my while** não vale a pena. **it's ~ waiting**/*etc* vale a pena esperar/*etc*. **for all one's ~** (*colloq*) dando tudo por tudo. ~**less** *a* sem valor

worthwhile /'wɜ:θwaɪl/ *a* que vale a pena; (*cause*) louvável, meritório

worthy /'wɜ:ðɪ/ *a* (-ier, -iest) (*deserving*) digno, merecedor (**of** de); (*laudable*) meritório, louvável □ *n* (*person*) pessoa *f* ilustre

would /wʊd/; *unstressed* /wəd/ *v aux* **he ~ do/you ~ sing**/*etc* (*conditional tense*) ele faria/você cantaria/*etc*. **he ~ have done** ele teria feito. **she ~ come every day** (*used to*) ela vinha *or* costumava vir aqui todos os dias. ~ **you please come here?** chegue aqui por favor. ~ **you like some tea?** você quer um chazinho? **he ~n't go** (*refused to*) ele não queria ir. ~**-be author/ doctor/***etc* aspirante a autor/médico/*etc*

wound[1] /wu:nd/ *n* ferida *f* □ *vt* ferir. **the ~ed** os feridos *mpl*

wound[2] /waʊnd/ *see* **wind**[2]

wove, woven /wəʊv, 'wəʊvn/ *see* **weave**

wrangle /'ræŋgl/ *vi* disputar, discutir, brigar □ *n* disputa *f*, discussão *f*, briga *f*

wrap /ræp/ *vt* (*pt* **wrapped**) ~ **(up)** embrulhar (**in** em); (*in cotton wool, mystery etc*) envolver (**in** em) □ *vi* ~ **up** (*dress warmly*) abrigar-se bem, agasalhar-se bem □ *n* xale *m*. ~**ped up in** (*engrossed*) absorto em, mergulhado em. ~**per** *n* (*of sweet*) papel *m*; (*of book*) capa *f* de papel. ~**ing** *n* embalagem *f*

wrath /rɒθ/ *n* ira *f*. ~**ful** *a* irado

wreak /ri:k/ *vt* ~ **havoc** (*of storm etc*) fazer estragos

wreath /ri:θ/ *n* (*pl* -s /-ðz/) (*of flowers, leaves*) coroa *f*, grinalda *f*

wreck /rek/ *n* (*sinking*) naufrágio *m*; (*ship*) navio *m* naufragado; restos *mpl* de navio; (*remains*) destroços *mpl*; (*vehicle*) veículo *m* destroçado □ *vt* destruir; (*ship*) fazer naufragar, afundar; (*fig: hope*) acabar. **be a nervous ~** estar com os nervos arrasados. ~**age** *n* (*pieces*) destroços *mpl*

wren /ren/ *n* (*bird*) carriça *f*

wrench /rentʃ/ *vt* (*pull*) puxar; (*twist*) torcer; (*snatch*) arrancar (**from** a) □ *n* (*pull*) puxão *m*; (*of ankle, wrist*) torcedura *f*; (*tool*) chave *f* inglesa; (*fig*) dor *f* de separação

wrest /rest/ *vt* arrancar (**from** a)

wrestl|e /'resl/ *vi* lutar, debater-se (**with** com *or* contra). ~**er** *n* lutador *m*. ~**ing** *n* luta *f*

wretch /retʃ/ *n* desgraçado *m*, miserável *mf*; (*rascal*) miserável *mf*

wretched /'retʃɪd/ *a* (*pitiful, poor*) miserável; (*bad*) horrível, desgraçado

wriggle /'rɪgl/ *vt/i* remexer(-se), contorcer-se

wring /rɪŋ/ *vt* (*pt* **wrung**) (*twist; clothes*) torcer. ~ **out of** (*obtain from*) arrancar a. ~**ing wet** encharcado; (*of person*) encharcado até os ossos

wrinkle /'rɪŋkl/ *n* (*on skin*) ruga *f*; (*crease*) prega *f* □ *vt/i* enrugar(-se)

wrist /rɪst/ *n* pulso *m*. ~**-watch** *n* relógio *m* de pulso

writ /rɪt/ *n* (*jur*) mandado *m* judicial

write /raɪt/ *vt/i* (*pt* **wrote**, *pp* **written**) escrever. ~ **back** responder. ~ **down** escrever, tomar nota de. ~ **off** (*debt*) dar por liquidado; (*vehicle*) destinar à sucata. ~-off *n* perda *f* total. ~ out (*in full*) escrever por extenso. ~ up (*from notes*) redigir. ~-up *n* relato *m*; (*review*) crítica *f*

writer /'raɪtə(r)/ *n* escritor *m*, autor *m*

writhe /raɪð/ *vi* contorcer(-se)

writing /'raɪtɪŋ/ *n* escrita *f*. ~(s) (*works*) escritos *mpl*, obras *fpl*. in ~ por escrito. ~-paper *n* papel *m* de carta

written /'rɪtn/ *see* write

wrong /rɒŋ/ *a* (*incorrect, mistaken*) mal, errado; (*unfair*) injusto; (*wicked*) mau; (*amiss*) que não está bem; (*mus: note*) falso; (*clock*) que não está certo □ *adv* mal □ *n* mal *m*; (*injustice*) injustiça *f* □ *vt* (*be unfair to*) ser injusto com; (*do a wrong to*) fazer mal a. what's ~? qual é o problema? what's ~ with it? (*amiss*) o que é que não vai bem?; (*morally*) que mal há nisso?, que mal tem? he's in the ~ (*his fault*) ele não tem razão. go ~ (*err*) desencaminhar-se; (*fail*) ir mal; (*vehicle*) quebrar. ~ly *adv* mal; (*blame etc*) sem razão, injustamente

wrongful /'rɒŋfl/ *a* injusto, ilegal

wrote /rəʊt/ *see* write

wrought /rɔ:t/ *a* ~ iron ferro *m* forjado. ~-up *a* excitado

wrung /rʌŋ/ *see* wring

wry /raɪ/ *a* (wryer, wryest) torto; (*smile*) forçado. ~ face careta *f*

X

Xerox /'zɪərɒks/ *n* fotocópia *f*, xerox *m* □ *vt* fotocopiar, xerocar, tirar um xerox de

Xmas /'krɪsməs/ *n* Christmas

X-ray /'eksreɪ/ *n* raio X *m*; (*photograph*) radiografia *f* □ *vt* radiografar. have an ~ tirar uma radiografia

xylophone /'zaɪləfəʊn/ *n* xilofone *m*

Y

yacht /jɒt/ *n* iate *m*. ~ing *n* iatismo *m*, andar *m* de iate; (*racing*) regata *f* de iate

yank /jæŋk/ *vt* (*colloq*) puxar bruscamente □ *n* (*colloq*) puxão *m*

Yank /jæŋk/ *n* (*colloq*) ianque *mf*

yap /jæp/ *vi* (*pt* yapped) latir

yard[1] /ja:d/ *n* (*measure*) jarda *f* (= 0,9144 *m*). ~age *n* medida *f* em jardas

yard[2] /ja:d/ *n* (*of house*) pátio *m*; (*Amer: garden*) jardim *m*; (*for storage*) depósito *m*

yardstick /'ja:dstɪk/ *n* jarda *f*; (*fig*) bitola *f*, craveira *f*

yarn /ja:n/ *n* (*thread*) fio *m*; (*colloq: tale*) longa história *f*

yawn /jɔ:n/ *vi* bocejar; (*be wide open*) abrir-se, escancarar-se □ *n* bocejo *m*. ~ing *a* escancarado

year /jɪə(r)/ *n* ano *m*. school/tax ~ ano *m* escolar/fiscal. be ten/ *etc* ~s old ter dez/*etc* anos de idade. ~-book *n* anuário *m*. ~ly *a* anual □ *adv* anualmente

yearn /jɜ:n/ *vi* ~ for, to desejar, ansiar por, suspirar por. ~ing *n* desejo *m*, anseio *m* (for de)

yeast /ji:st/ *n* levedura *f*

yell /jel/ *vt/i* gritar, berrar □ *n* grito *m*, berro *m*

yellow /'jeləʊ/ *a* amarelo; (*colloq: cowardly*) covarde, poltrão □ *n* amarelo *m*

yelp /jelp/ *n* (*of dog etc*) ganido *m* □ *vi* ganir

yen /jen/ *n* (*colloq: yearning*) grande vontade *f* (for de)

yes /jes/ *n* & *adv* sim (*m*). ~-man *n* (*colloq*) lambe-botas *m invar*, puxa-saco *m*

yesterday /'jestədɪ/ *n* & *adv* ontem (*m*). ~ morning/afternoon/evening ontem de manhã/à tarde/à noite. the day before ~ anteontem. ~ week há oito dias, há uma semana

yet /jet/ *adv* ainda; (*already*) já □ *conj* contudo, no entanto. as ~ até agora, por enquanto. his best book ~ o seu melhor livro até agora

yew /ju:/ *n* teixo *m*

Yiddish /'jɪdɪʃ/ *n* ídiche *m*

yield /ji:ld/ *vt* (*produce*) produzir, dar; (*profit*) render; (*surrender*) entregar □ *vi* (*give way*) ceder □ *n* produção *f*; (*comm*) rendimento *m*

yoga /'jəʊgə/ *n* ioga *f*

yoghurt /'jɒgət/ *n* iogurte *m*

yoke /jəʊk/ *n* jugo *m*, canga *f*; (*of garment*) pala *f* □ *vt* jungir; (*unite*) unir, ligar

yokel /'jəʊkl/ *n* caipira *m*, labrego *m*

yolk /jəʊk/ *n* gema (de ovo) *f*

yonder /'jɒndə(r)/ *adv* acolá, além

you /ju:/ *pron* (*familiar*) tu, você (*pl* vocês); (*polite*) vós, o(s) senhor(es), a(s) senhora(s); (*object: familiar*) te, lhe (*pl* vocês); (*polite*) o(s), a(s), lhes, vós, o(s) senhor(es), a(s) senhora(s); (*after prep*) ti, si, você (*pl* vocês); (*polite*) vós, o senhor, a senhora (*pl* os senhores, as senhoras); (*indefinite*) se; (*after prep*) si, você. with ~ (*familiar*) contigo, consigo, com você (*pl* com vocês); (*polite*) com o senhor/a senhora (*pl* convosco, com os senhores/as senhoras). I know ~ (*familiar*) eu te conheço, eu o/a conheço (*pl* eu os/as conheço); (*polite*) eu vos conheço, conheço o senhor/a senhora (*pl* conheço os senhores/as senhoras). ~ **can see the sea** você pode ver o mar

young /jʌŋ/ *a* (-er, -est) jovem, novo, moço □ *n* (*people*) jovens *mpl*, a juventude *f*, a mocidade *f*; (*of animals*) crias *fpl*, filhotes *mpl*

youngster /'jʌŋstə(r)/ *n* jovem *mf*, moço *m*, rapaz *m*

your /jɔ:(r)/ *a* (*familiar*) teu, tua, seu, sua (*pl* teus, tuas, seus, suas); (*polite*) vosso, vossa, do senhor, da senhora (*pl* vossos, vossas, dos senhores, das senhoras)

yours /jɔ:z/ *poss pron* (*familiar*) o teu, a tua, o seu, a sua (*pl* os teus, as tuas, os seus, as suas); (*polite*) o vosso, a vossa, o/a do senhor, o/a da senhora (*pl* os vossos, as vossas; os/as do(s) senhor(es), os/as da(s) senhora(s)). **a book of** ~ um livro seu. ~ **sincerely/faithfully** atenciosamente, com os cumprimentos de

yourself /jɔ:'self/ (*pl* **-selves** /-'selvz/) *pron* (*familiar*) tu mesmo/a, você mesmo/a (*pl* vocês mesmos/as); (*polite*) vós mesmo/a, o senhor mesmo, a senhora mesma (*pl* vós mesmos/as, os senhores mesmos, as senhoras mesmas); (*reflexive: familiar*) te, a ti mesmo/a, se, a si mesmo/a (*pl* a vocês mesmos/as); (*polite*) ao senhor mesmo, à senhora mesma (*pl* aos senhores mesmos, às senhoras mesmas); (*after prep: familiar*) ti mesmo/a, si mesmo/a, você mesmo/a (*pl* vocês mesmos/as); (*after prep: polite*) vós mesmo/a, o senhor mesmo, a senhora mesma (*pl* vós mesmos/as, os senhores mesmos, as senhoras mesmas). **with** ~ (*familiar*) contigo mesmo/a, consigo mesmo/a, com você (*pl* com vocês); (*polite*) convosco, com o senhor, com a senhora (*pl* com os senhores, com as senhoras). **by** ~ sozinho

youth /ju:θ/ *n* (*pl* -s /-ðz/) mocidade *f*, juventude *f*; (*young man*) jovem *m*, moço *m*. ~ **club** centro *m* de jovens. ~ **hostel** albergue *m* da juventude. ~**ful** *a* juvenil, jovem

yo-yo /'jəʊjəʊ/ *n* (*pl* -os) ioiô *m*

Yugoslav /'ju:gəsla:v/ *a* & *n* iogoslavo (*m*), (*P*) jugoslavo (*m*). ~**ia** /-'sla:vɪə/ *n* Iogoslávia *f*, (*P*) Jugoslávia *f*

Z

zany /'zeɪnɪ/ *a* (-ier, -iest) tolo, bobo

zeal /zi:l/ *n* zelo *m*

zealous /'zeləs/ *a* zeloso. ~**ly** *adv* zelosamente

zebra /'zebrə, 'zi:brə/ *n* zebra *f*. ~ **crossing** faixa *f* para pedestres, (*P*) passagem *f* para peões

zenith /'zenɪθ/ *n* zênite *m*, (*P*) zénite *m*, auge *m*

zero /'zɪərəʊ/ *n* (*pl* -os) zero *m*. ~ **hour** a hora H. **below** ~ abaixo de zero

zest /zest/ *n* (*gusto*) entusiasmo *m*; (*fig: spice*) sabor *m* especial; (*lemon or orange peel*) casca *f* de limão/laranja ralada

zigzag /'zɪgzæg/ *n* ziguezague *m* □ *a* & *adv* em ziguezague □ *vi* (*pt* **zigzagged**) ziguezaguear

zinc /zɪŋk/ *n* zinco *m*

zip /zɪp/ *n* (*vigour*) energia *f*, alma *f*. ~**(-fastener)** fecho *m* ecler □ *vt* (*pt* **zipped**) fechar o fecho eclerde □ *vi* ir a toda a velocidade. **Z**~ **code** (*Amer*) CEP de endereçamento postal *m*, (*P*) código *m* postal

zipper /'zɪpə(r)/ *n* = **zip(-fastener)**

zodiac /'zəʊdɪæk/ *n* zodíaco *m*

zombie /'zɒmbɪ/ *n* zumbi *m*; (*colloq*) zumbi *m*, (*P*) autómato *m*

zone /zəʊn/ *n* zona *f*

zoo /zu:/ *n* jardim *m* zoológico

zoolog|y /zəʊ'ɒlədʒɪ/ *n* zoologia *f*. ~**ical** /-ə'lɒdʒɪkl/ *a* zoológico. ~**ist** *n* zoólogo *m*

zoom /zu:m/ *vi* (*rush*) sair roando ~ **lens** zum *m*, zoom *m*. ~ **off** *or* **past** passar zunindo

zucchini /zu:'ki:nɪ/ *n* (*pl* *invar*) (*Amer*) courgette *f*

Portuguese Verbs · Verbos portugueses

Introduction

Portuguese verbs can be divided into three categories: regular verbs, those with spelling peculiarities determined by their sound and irregular verbs.

Regular verbs

in -ar (*e.g.* comprar)

Present: compr|o, ~as, ~a, ~amos, ~ais, ~am

Future: comprar|ei, ~ás, ~á, ~emos, ~eis, ~ão

Imperfect: compr|ava, ~avas, ~ava, ~ávamos, ~áveis, ~avam

Preterite: compr|ei, ~aste, ~ou, ~amos (*P*: ~ámos), ~astes, ~aram

Pluperfect: compr|ara, ~aras, ~ara, ~áramos, ~áreis, ~aram

Present subjunctive: compr|e, ~es, ~e, ~emos, ~eis, ~em

Imperfect subjunctive: compr|asse, ~asses, ~asse, ~ássemos, ~ásseis, ~assem

Future subjunctive: compr|ar, ~ares, ~ar, ~armos, ~ardes, ~arem

Conditional: comprar|ia, ~ias, ~ia, ~íamos, ~íeis, ~iam

Personal infinitive: comprar, ~es, ~, ~mos, ~des, ~em

Present participle: comprando

Past participle: comprado

Imperative: compra, comprai

in ~er (*e.g.* bater)

Present: bat|o, ~es, ~e, ~emos, ~eis, ~em

Future: bater|ei, ~ás, ~á, ~emos, ~eis, ~ão

Imperfect: bat|ia, ~ias, ~ia, ~íamos, ~íeis, ~iam

Preterite: bat|i, ~este, ~eu, ~emos, ~estes, ~eram

Pluperfect: bat|era, ~eras, ~era, ~êramos, ~êreis, ~eram

Present subjunctive: bat|a, ~as, ~a, ~amos ~ais, ~am

Imperfect subjunctive: bat|esse, ~esses, ~esse, ~êssemos, ~êsseis, ~essem

Future subjunctive: bat|er, ~eres, ~er, ~ermos, ~erdes, ~erem

Conditional: bater|ia, ~ias, ~ia, ~íamos, ~íeis, ~iam

Personal infinitive: bater, ~es, ~, ~mos, ~des, ~em

Present participle: batendo

Past participle: batido

Imperative: bate, batei

in ~ir (*e.g.* admitir)

Present: admit|o, ~es, ~e, ~imos, ~is ~em

Future: admitir|ei, ~ás, ~á, ~emos, ~eis, ~ão

Imperfect: admit|ia, ~ias, ~ia, ~íamos, ~íeis, ~iam

Preterite: admit|i, ~iste, ~iu, ~imos, ~istes, ~iram

Pluperfect: admit|ira, ~iras, ~ira, ~íramos, ~íreis, ~iram

Present subjunctive: admit|a, ~as, ~a, ~amos, ~ais, ~am

Imperfect subjunctive: admit|isse, ~isses, ~isse, ~íssemos, ~ísseis, ~issem

Future subjunctive: admit|ir, ~ires, ~ir, ~irmos, ~irdes, ~irem

Conditional: admitir|ia, ~ias, ~ia, ~íamos, ~íeis, ~iam

Personal infinitive: admitir, ~es, ~, ~mos, ~des, ~em

Present participle: admitindo

Past participle: admitido

Imperative: admite, admiti

Regular verbs with spelling changes:

-ar verbs:

in -car (*e.g.* ficar)

Preterite: fiquei, ficaste, ficou, ficamos (*P*: ficámos), ficais, ficam

Present subjunctive: fique, fiques, fique, fiquemos, fiqueis, fiquem

in -çar (*e.g.* abraçar)

Preterite: abracei, abraçaste, abraçou, abraçamos (*P*: abraçámos), abraçastes, abraçaram

Present subjunctive: abrace, abraces, abrace, abracemos, abraceis, abracem

in -ear (*e.g.* passear)

Present: passeio, passeias, passeia, passeamos, passeais, passeiam

Present subjunctive: passeie, passeies, passeie, passeemos, passeeis, passeiem

Imperative: passeia, passeai

in -gar (*e.g.* apagar)

Preterite: apaguei, apagaste, apagou, apagamos (*P*: apagámos), apagastes, apagaram

Present subjunctive: apague, apagues, apague, apaguemos, apagueis, apaguem

in -oar (*e.g.* voar)

Present: vôo (*P*: voo), voas, voa, voamos, voais, voam

averiguar
Preterite: averigüei (*P*: averiguei), averiguaste, averiguou, averiguamos (*P*: averiguámos), averiguastes, averiguaram
Present subjunctive: averigúe, averigúes, averigúe, averigüemos (*P*: averiguemos), averigüeis (*P*: averigueis), averigúem

enxaguar
Present: enxáguo, enxáguas, enxágua, enxaguamos, enxaguais, enxáguam
Preterite: enxagüei (*P*: enxaguei), enxaguaste, enxaguou, enxaguamos (*P*: enxaguámos), enxaguastes, enxaguaram
Present subjunctive: enxágüe, enxágües, enxágüe, enxagüemos, enxagüeis, enxágüem (*P*: enxágue, enxágues, enxágue, enxaguemos, enxagueis, enxáguem)
Similarly: aguar, desaguar

saudar
Present: saúdo, saúdas, saúda, saudamos, saudais, saúdam
Present subjunctive: saúde, saúdes, saúde, saudemos, saudeis, saúdem
Imperative: saúda, saudai

-er verbs:
in -cer (*e.g.* tecer)
Present: teço, teces, tece, tecemos, teceis, tecem
Present subjunctive: teça, teças, teça, teçamos, teçais, teçam

in -ger (*e.g.* proteger)
Present: protejo, proteges, protege, protegemos, protegeis, protegem
Present subjunctive: proteja, protejas, proteja, protejamos, protejais, protejam

in -guer (*e.g.* erguer)
Present: ergo, ergues, ergue, erguemos, ergueis, erguem
Present subjunctive: erga, ergas, erga, ergamos, ergais, ergam

in -oer (*e.g.* roer)
Present: rôo (*P*: roo), róis, rói, roemos, roeis, roem
Imperfect: roía, roías, roía, roíamos, roíeis, roíam
Preterite: roí, roeste, roeu, roemos, roestes, roeram
Past participle: roído
Imperative: rói, roei

-ir verbs:
in -ir with -e- in stem (*e.g.* vestir)
Present: visto, vestes, veste, vestimos, vestis, vestem
Present subjunctive: vista, vistas, vista, vistamos, vistais, vistam
Similarly: mentir, preferir, refletir, repetir, seguir, sentir, servir

in -ir with -o- in stem (*e.g.* dormir)
Present: durmo, dormes, dorme, dormimos, dormis, dormem
Present subjunctive: durma, durmas, durma, durmamos, durmais, durmam
Similarly: cobrir, descobrir, tossir

in -ir with -u- in the stem (*e.g.* subir)
Present: subo, sobes, sobe, subimos, subis, sobem
Similarly: consumir, cuspir, fugir, sacudir, sumir

in -air (*e.g.* sair)
Present: saio, sais, sai, saímos, saís, saem
Imperfect: saía, saías, saía, saíamos, saíeis, saíam
Preterite: saí, saíste, saiu, saímos, saístes, saíram
Pluperfect: saíra, saíras, saíra, saíramos, saíreis, saíram
Present subjunctive: saia, saias, saia, saiamos, saiais, saiam
Imperfect subjunctive: saísse, saísses, saísse, saíssemos, saísseis, saíssem
Future subjunctive: sair, saíres, sair, sairmos, sairdes, saírem
Personal infinitive: sair, saíres, sair, sairmos, sairdes, saírem
Present participle: saindo
Past participle: saído
Imperative: sai, saí

in -gir (*e.g.* dirigir)
Present: dirijo, diriges, dirige, dirigimos, dirigis, dirigem
Present subjunctive: dirija, dirijas, dirija, dirijamos, dirijais, dirijam

in -guir (*e.g.* distinguir)
Present: distingo, distingues, distingue, distinguimos, distinguis, distinguem
Present subjunctive: distinga, distingas, distinga, distingamos, distingais, distingam

in -uir (*e.g.* atribuir)
Present: atribuo, atribuis, atribui, atribuímos, atribuís, atribuem
Imperfect: atribuía, atribuías, atribuía, atribuíamos, atribuíeis, atribuíam
Preterite: atribuí, atribuíste, atribuiu, atribuímos, atribuístes, atribuíram
Pluperfect: atribuíra, atribuíras, atribuíra, atribuíramos, atribuíreis, atribuíram

Present subjunctive: atribua, atribuas, atribua, atribuamos, atribuais, atribuam
Imperfect subjunctive: atribuísse, atribuísses, atribuísse, atribuíssemos, atribuísseis, atribuíssem
Future subjunctive: atribuir, atribuíres, atribuir, atribuirmos, atribuirdes, atribuírem
Personal infinitive: atribuir, atribuíres, atribuir, atribuirmos, atribuirdes, atribuírem
Present participle: atribuindo
Past participle: atribuído
Imperative: atribui, atribuí

proibir
Present: proíbo, proíbes, proíbe, proibimos, proibis, proíbem
Present subjunctive: proíba, proíbas, proíba, proibamos, proibais, proíbam
Imperative: proíbe, proibi
Similarly: coibir

reunir
Present: reúno, reúnes, reúne, reunimos, reunis, reúnem
Present subjunctive: reúna, reúnas, reúna, reunamos, reunais, reúnam
Imperative: reúne, reuni

in **-struir** (*e.g.* **construir**) - like atribuir except:
Present: construo, constróis/construis, constrói/construi, construímos, construís, constroem/construem
Imperative: constrói/construi, construí

in **-duzir** (*e.g.* **produzir**)
Present: produzo, produzes, produz, produzimos, produzis, produzem
Imperative: produz(e), produzi
Similarly: luzir, reluzir

Irregular verbs

caber
Present: caibo, cabes, cabe, cabemos, cabeis, cabem
Preterite: coube, coubeste, coube, coubemos, coubestes, couberam
Pluperfect: coubera, couberas, coubera, coubéramos, coubéreis, couberam
Present subjunctive: caiba, caibas, caiba, caibamos, caibais, caibam
Imperfect subjunctive: coubesse, coubesses, coubesse, coubéssemos, coubésseis, coubessem
Future subjunctive: couber, couberes, couber, coubermos, couberdes, couberem

dar
Present: dou, dás, dá, damos, dais, dão
Preterite: dei, deste, deu, demos, destes, deram
Pluperfect: dera, deras, dera, déramos, déreis, deram
Present subjunctive: dê, dês, dê, demos, deis, dêem
Imperfect subjunctive: desse, desses, desse, déssemos, désseis, dessem
Future subjunctive: der, deres, der, dermos, derdes, derem
Imperative: dá, dai

dizer
Present: digo, dizes, diz, dizemos, dizeis, dizem
Future: direi, dirás, dirá, diremos, direis, dirão
Preterite: disse, disseste, disse, dissemos, dissestes, disseram
Pluperfect: dissera, disseras, dissera, disséramos, disséreis, disseram
Present subjunctive: diga, digas, diga, digamos, digais, digam
Imperfect subjunctive: dissesse, dissesses, dissesse, disséssemos, dissésseis, dissessem
Future subjunctive: disser, disseres, disser, dissermos, disserdes, disserem
Conditional: diria, dirias, diria, diríamos, diríeis, diriam
Present participle: dizendo
Past participle: dito
Imperative: diz, dizei

estar
Present: estou, estás, está, estamos, estais, estão
Preterite: estive, estiveste, esteve, estivemos, estivestes, estiveram
Pluperfect: estivera, estiveras, estivera, estivéramos, estivéreis, estiveram
Present subjunctive: esteja, estejas, esteja, estejamos, estejais, estejam
Imperfect subjunctive: estivesse, estivesses, estivesse, estivéssemos, estivésseis, estivessem
Future subjunctive: estiver, estiveres, estiver, estivermos, estiverdes, estiverem
Imperative: está, estai

fazer
Present: faço, fazes, faz, fazemos, fazeis, fazem
Future: farei, farás, fará, faremos, fareis, farão
Preterite: fiz, fizeste, fez, fizemos, fizestes, fizeram
Pluperfect: fizera, fizeras, fizera, fizéramos, fizéreis, fizeram

Present subjunctive: faça, faças, faça, façamos, façais, façam
Imperfect subjunctive: fizesse, fizesses, fizesse, fizéssemos, fizésseis, fizessem
Future subjunctive: fizer, fizeres, fizer, fizermos, fizerdes, fizerem
Conditional: faria, farias, faria, faríamos, faríeis, fariam
Present participle: fazendo
Past participle: feito
Imperative: faz(e), fazei

frigir
Present: frijo, freges, frege, frigimos, frigis, fregem
Present subjunctive: frija, frijas, frija, frijamos, frijais, frijam
Imperative: frege, frigi

ir
Present: vou, vais, vai, vamos, ides, vão
Imperfect: ia, ias, ia, íamos, íeis, iam
Preterite: fui, foste, foi, fomos, fostes, foram
Pluperfect: fora, foras, fora, fôramos, fôreis, foram
Present subjunctive: vá, vás, vá, vamos, vades, vão
Imperfect subjunctive: fosse, fosses, fosse, fôssemos, fôsseis, fossem
Future subjunctive: for, fores, for, formos, fordes, forem
Present participle: indo
Past participle: ido
Imperative: vai, ide

haver
Present: hei, hás, há, hemos/havemos, haveis/heis, hão
Preterite: houve, houveste, houve, houvemos, houvestes, houveram
Pluperfect: houvera, houveras, houvera, houvéramos, houvéreis, houveram
Present subjunctive: haja, hajas, haja, hajamos, hajais, hajam
Imperfect subjunctive: houvesse, houvesses, houvesse, houvéssemos, houvésseis, houvessem
Future subjunctive: houver, houveres, houver, houvermos, houverdes, houverem
Imperative: há, havei

ler
Present: leio, lês, lê, lemos, ledes, lêem
Imperfect: lia, lias, lia, líamos, líeis, liam
Preterite: li, leste, leu, lemos, lestes, leram
Pluperfect: lera, leras, lera, lêramos, lêreis, leram
Present subjunctive: leia, leias, leia, leiamos, leiais, leiam
Imperfect subjunctive: lesse, lesses, lesse, lêssemos, lêsseis, lessem
Future subjunctive: ler, leres, ler, lermos, lerdes, lerem
Present participle: lendo
Past participle: lido
Imperative: lê, lede
Similarly: crer

odiar
Present: odeio, odeias, odeia, odiamos, odiais, odeiam
Present subjunctive: odeie, odeies, odeie, odiemos, odieis, odeiem
Imperative: odeia, odiai
Similarly: incendiar

ouvir
Present: ouço (*P also*: oiça), ouves, ouve, ouvimos, ouvis, ouvem
Present subjunctive: ouça, ouças, ouça, ouçamos, ouçais, ouçam (*P also*: oiça, oiças, oiça, oiçamos, oiçais, oiçam)

pedir
Present: peço, pedes, pede, pedimos, pedis, pedem
Present subjunctive: peça, peças, peça, peçamos, peçais, peçam
Similarly: despedir, impedir, medir

perder
Present: perco, perdes, perde, perdemos, perdeis, perdem
Present subjunctive: perca, percas, perca, percamos, percais, percam

poder
Present: posso, podes, pode, podemos, podeis, podem
Preterite: pude, pudeste, pôde, pudemos, pudestes, puderam
Pluperfect: pudera, puderas, pudera, pudéramos, pudéreis, puderam
Present subjunctive: possa, possas, possa, possamos, possais, possam
Imperfect subjunctive: pudesse, pudesses, pudesse, pudéssemos, pudésseis, pudessem
Future subjunctive: puder, puderes, puder, pudermos, puderdes, puderem

polir
Present: pulo, pules, pule, polimos, polis, pulem
Present subjunctive: pula, pulas, pula, pulamos, pulais, pulam
Imperative: pule, poli

pôr
Present: ponho, pões, põe, pomos, pondes, põem

Future: porei, porás, porá, poremos, poreis, porão
Imperfect: punha, punhas, punha, púnhamos, púnheis, punham
Preterite: pus, puseste, pôs, pusemos, pusestes, puseram
Pluperfect: pusera, puseras, pusera, puséramos, puséreis, puseram
Present subjunctive: ponha, ponhas, ponha, ponhamos, ponhais, ponham
Imperfect subjunctive: pusesse, pusesses, pusesse, puséssemos, pusésseis, pusessem
Future subjunctive: puser, puseres, puser, pusermos, puserdes, puserem
Conditional: poria, porias, poria, poríamos, poríeis, poriam
Present participle: pondo
Past participle: posto
Imperative: põe, ponde
Similarly: compor, depor, dispor, opor, supor etc

prover
Present: provejo, provês, provê, provemos, provedes, provêem
Present subjunctive: proveja, provejas, proveja, provejamos, provejais, provejam
Imperative: provê, provede

querer
Present: quero, queres, quer, queremos, quereis, querem
Preterite: quis, quiseste, quis, quisemos, quisestes, quiseram
Pluperfect: quisera, quiseras, quisera, quiséramos, quiséreis, quiseram
Present subjunctive: queira, queiras, queira, queiramos, queirais, queiram
Imperfect subjunctive: quisesse, quisesses, quisesse, quiséssemos, quisésseis, quisessem
Future subjunctive: quiser, quiseres, quiser, quisermos, quiserdes, quiserem
Imperative: quer, querei

requerer
Present: requeiro, requeres, requer, requeremos, requereis, requerem
Present subjunctive: requeira, requeiras, requeira, requeiramos, requeirais, requeiram
Imperative: requer, requerei

rir
Present: rio, ris, ri, rimos, rides, riem
Present subjunctive: ria, rias, ria, riamos, riais, riam
Imperative: ri, ride
Similarly: sorrir

saber
Present: sei, sabes, sabe, sabemos, sabeis, sabem
Preterite: soube, soubeste, soube, soubemos, soubestes, souberam
Pluperfect: soubera, souberas, soubera, soubéramos, soubéreis, souberam
Present subjunctive: saiba, saibas, saiba, saibamos, saibais, saibam
Imperfect subjunctive: soubesse, soubesses, soubesse, soubéssemos, soubésseis, soubessem
Future subjunctive: souber, souberes, souber, soubermos, souberdes, souberem
Imperative: sabe, sabei

ser
Present: sou, és, é, somos, sois, são
Imperfect: era, eras, era, éramos, éreis, eram
Preterite: fui, foste, foi, fomos, fostes, foram
Pluperfect: fora, foras, fora, fôramos, fôreis, foram
Present subjunctive: seja, sejas, seja, sejamos, sejais, sejam
Imperfect subjunctive: fosse, fosses, fosse, fôssemos, fôsseis, fossem
Future subjunctive: for, fores, for, formos, fordes, forem
Present participle: sendo
Past participle: sido
Imperative: sê, sede

ter
Present: tenho, tens, tem, temos, tendes, têm
Imperfect: tinha, tinhas, tinha, tínhamos, tínheis, tinham
Preterite: tive, tiveste, teve, tivemos, tivestes, tiveram
Pluperfect: tivera, tiveras, tivera, tivéramos, tivéreis, tiveram
Present subjunctive: tenha, tenhas, tenha, tenhamos, tenhais, tenham
Imperfect subjunctive: tivesse, tivesses, tivesse, tivéssemos, tivésseis, tivessem
Future subjunctive: tiver, tiveres, tiver, tivermos, tiverdes, tiverem
Present participle: tendo
Past participle: tido
Imperative: tem, tende

trazer
Present: trago, trazes, traz, trazemos, trazeis, trazem
Future: trarei, trarás, trará, traremos, trareis, trarão
Preterite: trouxe, trouxeste, trouxe, trouxemos, trouxestes, trouxeram

Pluperfect: trouxera, trouxeras, trouxera, trouxéramos, trouxéreis, trouxeram
Present subjunctive: traga, tragas, traga, tragamos, tragais, tragam
Imperfect subjunctive: trouxesse, trouxesses, trouxesse, trouxéssemos, trouxésseis, trouxessem
Future subjunctive: trouxer, trouxeres, trouxer, trouxermos, trouxerdes, trouxerem
Conditional: traria, trarias, traria, traríamos, traríeis, trariam
Imperative: traze, trazei

valer
Present: valho, vales, vale, valemos, valeis, valem
Present subjunctive: valha, valhas, valha, valhamos, valhais, valham

ver
Present: vejo, vês, vê, vemos, vedes, vêem
Imperfect: via, vias, via, víamos, víeis, viam
Preterite: vi, viste, viu, vimos, vistes, viram
Pluperfect: vira, viras, vira, víramos, víreis, viram
Present subjunctive: veja, vejas, veja, vejamos, vejais, vejam
Imperfect subjunctive: visse, visses, visse, víssemos, vísseis, vissem
Future subjunctive: vir, vires, vir, virmos, virdes, virem
Present participle: vendo
Past participle: visto
Imperative: vê, vede

vir
Present: venho, vens, vem, vimos, vindes, vêm
Imperfect: vinha, vinhas, vinha, vínhamos, vínheis, vinham
Preterite: vim, vieste, veio, viemos, viestes, vieram
Pluperfect: viera, vieras, viera, viéramos, viéreis, vieram
Present subjunctive: venha, venhas, venha, venhamos, venhais, venham
Imperfect subjunctive: viesse, viesses, viesse, viéssemos, viésseis, viessem
Future subjunctive: vier, vieres, vier, viermos, vierdes, vierem
Present participle: vindo
Past participle: vindo
Imperative: vem, vinde